In the Balance

Themes in Global History

Candice L. Goucher
Portland State University

Charles A. Le Guin
Portland State University

Linda A. Walton
Portland State University

Boston, Massachusetts   Burr Ridge, Illinois   Dubuque, Iowa
Madison, Wisconsin   New York, New York   San Francisco, California   St. Louis, Missouri

McGraw-Hill

A Division of The **McGraw·Hill** *Companies*

IN THE BALANCE: THEMES IN GLOBAL HISTORY

This book is printed on acid-free paper.

1 2 3 4 5 6 7 8 9 0   DOC/DOC   9 0 9 8 7

ISBN 0-07-024179-1

Editorial director: *Jane Vaicunas*
Sponsoring editor: *Leslye Jackson*
Developmental editor: *Roberta Fishman*
Editorial coordinator: *Amy Mack*
Marketing manager: *Annie Mitchell*
Senior project manager: *Mary Conzachi*
Production supervisor: *Scott Hamilton*
Design manager: *Kiera Cunningham*
Senior photo research coordinator: *Keri Johnson*
Compositor: *York Graphic Services, Inc.*
Cartographer: *Mapping Specialists Limited*
Typeface: *10/12 Garamond*
Printer: *R. R. Donnelley & Sons Company*

Library of Congress Cataloging-in-Publication Data

Goucher, Candice Lee
      In the balance: a thematic global history/Candice L. Goucher,
    Charles A. Le Guin, Linda A. Walton.
          p. cm.
      Includes index.
      ISBN 0-07-024180-5 (v. 1: acid-free paper). –ISBN 0-07-024181-3
    (v. 2: acid-free paper)
        1. World history.   I. Le Guin, Charles A.   II. Walton, Linda A.
    III. Title.
    D22.G68 1998
    909–DC21   97-31292

http://www.mhhe.com

About the Authors

Candice L. Goucher (B.A. Visual Arts and Chemistry, University of California, San Diego; M.A. African Art History & Archaeology, Columbia University; Ph.D. African History, University of California, Los Angeles) is Professor of Black Studies and International Studies, Coordinator for African Studies, and Chair of the Black Studies Department at Portland State University. She has conducted historical, archaeological, and ethnographic field research on gender and technology in West Africa and the Caribbean, and is the author of numerous articles and reviews in African and Caribbean studies.

Charles A. Le Guin (A.B. Mercer University; M.A. Northwestern University; Ph.D. Emory University) is Professor of History Emeritus at Portland State University. He has been a Fulbright scholar in France, a fellow at the Center for Advanced Study in the Behavioural Sciences at Stanford University, and has taught at several universities. He is the author of articles, reviews, and two books, *Roland de la Platière* (Philadelphia: American Philosophical Society, 1966) and *A Home-Concealed Woman* (Athens, Georgia: University of Georgia Press, 1990).

Linda A. Walton (B.A. *cum laude* Wellesley College; Ph.D. University of Pennsylvania) is Professor of History and International Studies and Director of Asian Studies at Portland State University. She has conducted research in Japan, Taiwan, and the People's Republic of China and is the author of several articles and book chapters on medieval Chinese social and intellectual history as well as a forthcoming book, *Academies and Society in Southern Sung China* (University of Hawaii Press).

These labors are dedicated to our children and their worlds:
Kosa, Miranda, Elisabeth, Caroline, and Theodore.

Brief Contents

Table of Contents

List of Maps

List of Daily Lives Boxes

List of Engaging the Past Boxes

Preface

This text had its genesis in a team-taught world history course developed at Portland State University more than a decade ago. The course aimed to supplement the perspectives available from either the required Western Civilization courses or the courses that represented individual regional history and culture fields, such as East Asian History or Africa since 1800. We began this project as a result of our failed attempt to find a suitable book with a global and thematic approach designed for university, college, and community college world history courses similar to ours. In developing both the course, and eventually our book, we also addressed the general education goals of our university's curriculum, including critical thinking, communication, the diverse human experience, and exploration of issues of ethical judgment and responsibility. Our principal aim remains: to expose readers to the rich diversity and complexity of human historical experience by selectively and thematically introducing the histories of societies and cultures in major world regions from early times to the present. Central themes are used to organize comparatively the vast array of events, peoples, and places, highlighting the diversity of human experience against the backdrop of common human concerns and endeavors.

We are convinced, on the basis of extensive reviews by our students and other university teachers, that our book is both timely and controversial in its embrace of a thematic and selective approach that departs from familiar textbook territory and charts a new course. Our approach is selective out of practical necessity, since we cannot cover everything in world history without sacrificing a reasoned structure for understanding the past. Second, we believe a thematic approach is essential for creating a truly global history that is meaningful from a variety of cultural perspectives.

The approach used by most world histories remains linear, narrative, and chronological, despite recent attempts by some authors to add topical essays that address themes such as women and the family. As one world historian has pointed out, "the traditional civilization course, western or world, is not working because it is based on nineteenth-century positivist epistemological and pedagogical assumptions which are untenable." We share the conviction that the endless recital of "facts" bombarding the hapless reader is not the way to approach the study of any history; such an approach is particularly inadequate as an organizational framework for the global past. A linear chronology recounting facts misrepresents the profound changes in the ways we in the late twentieth century think about and understand the construction of knowledge, its acquisition, and its meanings. An ancillary aim of our book, therefore, is to make readers aware of how historical knowledge has been constructed and to encourage critical thinking about the meaning of given "facts" and the relevance of accepted historical models, which may be rooted in the European, Asian, African, or other experience. We ask readers to consider the meaning of many distinct pasts for the world community in contemporary times.

Our attention to Africa, Asia, and Latin America as integrated parts of any meaningful world history is reflective of our determination to approach history with a balanced perspective, constructing a view of human historical experience free of Eurocentric (or other) biases.

Our themes here are broadly organized in a flexible chronology. These themes have been developed from what we believe to be a balanced approach that is equally inclusive of all human historical experience. This text tackles the new territory of making comprehensible the global reality we face at the end of the twentieth century.

■

THEMATIC STRUCTURE

The degree to which this book is different from the majority of world histories currently on the market has already been suggested and will be reflected below in the summary of each section. The book explores key comparative themes in the human experience, ranging from the intimate ordering of family and daily life to cultural memory systems to the global politics of power and resistance. Our book is organized into four parts. Part One, "Emergence," presents the earliest human beginnings in various regions of the world, including migrations from one region to another, and explores the use of various kinds of sources for reconstructing the early human past. The origins of agriculture are presented as part of a discussion of human adaptation to the environment, which also includes gathering–hunting and other strategies of human survival. The question of origins is a universal human concern that we explore from the perspective of various early cultures. Finally, a discussion of the emerging complexity of human communities provides the context for examining the rise of urbanism in various regional and chronological settings.

Part Two, "Order," treats the ordering of the world in religious and philosophical systems by human communities around the globe from earliest times through about 1500. It suggests that bringing order to the world through the construction of belief systems is common to all human historical experience. This section also presents various levels of human interaction in both social and political structures, from the most private and intimate—family and household—to larger communities: extended kinship units, patron-client relations such as those institutionalized in "feudalism," small-scale political communities such as city-states, and empires. This part considers the social and political aspects of historical experience, embracing both private and public spheres of action. It concludes with two chapters that suggest profoundly different ways of looking at history: one on cultural memory systems, and one on connections among world cultures before 1500.

Part Three, "Transformation," begins with a discussion of commercial revolutions in Europe and China, suggesting that European domination of the world after 1500 represented a shift of the world system core from east to west. The construction of an Atlantic world through European expansion and interaction explores the theme of continuity and discontinuity, as we look at how Europe influenced other parts of the world and was itself transformed by that experience. Finally, we discuss the realms of cultural and social change as they reveal continuity and discontinuity in the age of transition.

Part Four, "Balance," begins with the theme of European global dominance, focusing on the eighteenth through the twentieth centuries. Included in this section are discussions of nationalism, the industrial revolution, imperialism, and colonialism. The impact of Europe on Asia, Africa and the Americas is treated as part of larger themes that integrate the colonial and noncolonial experiences of peoples throughout the world. Concerns prominent in the late twentieth century, such as ecology and family, bring us back to some of the central themes of earlier parts, such as human adaptation to the environment and historical views and voices of those sometimes silenced or neglected by traditional history. We thus consider the nature of historical change as it constructs patterns of similarity and difference, resistance, revolution, crisis, uncertainty, and, potentially, the restoration of balance.

We believe that our book has a relevance beyond classroom walls. We hope that readers who may have never taken a world history course will be moved beyond a generally accepted Eurocentric view of history to construct a new vision of the human past based on multiple perspectives that integrate many world historical experiences into a common framework. This is the power and potential of historical construction in a global society embarking on a new millennium.

■

DISTINCTIVE FEATURES

In the Balance, while narrative in style, provides students with several features intended to help them keep their focus on the key concepts presented, and to enhance their interest in what they are studying.

THREE HEADING LEVELS

By including three levels of text headings, we provide students with more pedagogical guidance while keeping the advantages of a compelling narrative. The third level of headings runs alongside the paragraphs of the chapters keeping students focused on key terms and concepts.

PART OPENER WITH COMPARATIVE TIME LINE

Key themes in world history are organized under the titles of "Emergence," "Order," "Transformation," and "Balance." Part openers provide vivid, sweeping introductions to these concepts as they are explored in individual chapters. Because of the flexible nature of a thematic and comparative text, it may be more difficult for students to orient themselves with regard to when events happen comparatively in different cultures. Part-Opener time lines will provide an easy, conceptual way for students to look at key events in different world regions at a glance.

CHAPTER-OPENER NARRATIVES AND PRIMARY SOURCE EXCERPTS

We use narratives—often first-hand accounts—to draw students into the theme of a given chapter. In Chapter 8, for instance, we see the differences in family structure across cultures through the eyes of two Venetian fishermen stranded on the coast of Norway in 1432. In Chapter 10, we are immersed in the smells and tastes of a thirteenth-century fast-food hangout in the great Chinese city of Hangzhou. These accounts give voice to the theme of the chapter in a truly compelling way. The opening narratives, combined with liberal doses of primary sources interspersed throughout the text, give students an up-close look at the societies about which they learn. We also believe that by making primary sources a vital part of the narrative, we encourage students to become engaged with the material, think critically, and to develop their own impressions and conclusions about the world's cultures.

BOX FEATURE: DAILY LIVES

Where appropriate in every chapter, we include one or more Daily Lives boxes to more fully explore some aspect of the cultures and societies we write about. These boxes are denoted by a symbol of an abstract spider web, suggesting the Akan (Ghana, West Africa) story of Ananse, the trickster spiderman who learned the hard way that knowledge is shared equally around the world. No single person knows everything and wisdom is to be found in the simplest experience. Often the Daily Lives boxes are substantial primary source excerpts that help to illuminate how ordinary people lived from day to day. Examples of this kind of box include the ancient Egyptian scribe Ramose in the Valley of the Kings (Chapter 3), fourteenth-century Muslim female scholar Umm Hani (Chapter 9) and the Zulu resistance fighter Matobana Mjara in 1929 South Africa (Chapter 19).

BOX FEATURE: ENGAGING THE PAST

History is seldom "cut and dried," but in the course of reading textbooks often students do not get to see what historians do. Nor do they see the problems of interpretation that historians sometimes confront in plying their craft, or the evolution in ways of thinking historically. In keeping with our goal to help students to think critically about history and evidence, we include an Engaging the Past box at the end of each chapter. These boxes are denoted by the symbol of a bird looking backwards, suggesting the Akan (Ghana, West Africa) proverb meaning *sankofa,* literally to reach back and use the past. They provide students with a thought-provoking exposition of some of the problems and issues that confront historians. In Chapter 7, we discuss the problems inherent to historical generalization through a discussion of the concept of feudalism as it is applied to both European and non-European historical experience. Chapter 9 looks at how new evidence can radically alter received historical understanding by looking at changes in the way the Inca *quipu* system of knotted strings has been interpreted. In Chapter 19, we explore humor and history in political cartoons.

EXTENSIVE MAP AND ILLUSTRATION PROGRAM

This text includes a wide selection of two-color maps that visually demonstrate the global and comparative nature of historical themes and relationships explored, and over 300 illustrations depicting art, archaeology, people, and places. Each photo carries a caption that ties it in with the text and provides students with another visual source for learning about the global past.

FULL COLOR PHOTO ESSAYS

Each volume contains an illustrated essay highlighting universal themes in the history of world art. In Volume I, we discuss views of death expressed in world art before 1500. In Volume II, we explore the meaning of borrowing in the cultural crossroads of world art since 1500. These essays provide another way of visually examining the themes of the book: the thematic and comparative nature of human experience as seen through the eyes of individual artists. The essays are accompanied by full color photographs representing the important artistic achievements and compelling images of key world regions.

OTHER PEDAGOGY

Concise chapter summaries recapitulate the most important comparative thematic aspects of the chapter, and also provide a transition to the theme for the next chapter. Finally, a list of suggested readings provide students with further resources for learning about world history.

■
ACKNOWLEDGEMENTS

We find our debts during the making of this book are also global: the gentle, but enthusiastic guidance from our sponsoring editor, Leslye Jackson, and her assistant, Amy Mack, inspired our confidence and directed our labors. Bobbie Fishman, our development editor, became soulmate and inner voice, seeing us through the seemingly endless process of revision. Expert handling of permissions, production, copyediting, and art and map manuscripts was provided us by the McGraw-Hill team and we are grateful for their careful work and patience. We particularly thank Deborah Bull of Photosearch for her contributions to the project. Students and colleagues in history, anthropology, archaeology, and black studies endured our enthusiasm and entered into countless fruitful discussions, sharing their knowledge and ideas as well as resources; among these Kofi Agorsah and Katherine Sadler deserve special note. Thanks also to Jon Mandaville and Joseph Scholten, who taught world history with us in the early years and helped to develop the concepts that shaped this book. Gary Leiser's contributions on West Asia provided essential support at a critical stage. Thanks to Ursula for sharing her beach house on the Oregon coast for memorable writing retreats. We also want to thank the many reviewers who contributed to the development of this manuscript.

Karl F. Bahm
University of Mississippi

Robert Blackey
California State University, San Bernardino

Edward Davies
The University of Utah

Lane Earns
University of Wisconsin, Oshkosh

Jerry Gershenhorn
North Carolina Central University

W. Travis Hanes, III
University of North Carolina, Wilmington

Gerald Herman
Northeastern University

Catherine M. Jones
North Georgia College

Thomas K. Keefe
Appalachian State University

Richard D. Lewis
St. Cloud State University

John J. Little
St. Augustine's College

Noel-Joseph Ku-Ntima Makidi
Paine College

Art Marmorstein
Northern State University

John A. Mears
Southern Methodist University

Wayne S. Osborn
Iowa State University

James L. Owens
Lynchburg College

Melvin E. Page
East Tennessee State University

Dennis Reinhartz
The University of Texas at Arlington

Lynda Shaffer
Tufts University

Douglas P. Sjoquist
Lansing Community College

Juanita Smart
Washington State University

David R. Smith
California Polytechnic University

Kimberly Welch
St. John's University

Robert H. Welborn
Clayton State College

Ken Wolf
Murray State University

Our special thanks go to two reviewers who were particularly helpful, insightful, and critical in shaping the final manuscript: Nancy Fitch at California State University, Fullerton, and Michael Galgano at James Madison University.

■

SUPPLEMENTS

We are especially proud of the package of ancillary materials we have assembled to accompany this text. These supplements include a *Study Guide, Instructor's Manual and Test Bank* (which is available in either paper or computerized versions). Overhead *Map Transparencies,* including all the maps in the text, our unique *Presentation Manager CDROM* for instructors, and our *World History Web Page* are specifically designed to complement the text and provide an integrated program of learning and teaching global history from a thematic point of view.

The *Study Guide,* authored by Robert H. Welborn of Clayton State College, nicely complements the narrative text, providing excellent assistance to students. It contains learning objectives, chapter summaries, identification of significant individuals, map exercises, objective multiple-choice questions (with correct answers and page references provided), analytical essay questions, evaluation of documentary evidence, and chapter glossaries. The *Study Guide* will also include distinctive timelines, which will help students organize the culturally specific information discussed in each chapter. The *Study Guide* is available in a two-volume format.

The *Instructor's Manual and Test Bank,* prepared by Edward Davies at The University of Utah, provides a useful teaching tool, especially for professors who are new to teaching from a thematically organized textbook. Each chapter of the *Instructor's Manual* will contain a Test Bank, which will include multiple-choice questions (with answers and page references provided), matching exercises, sentence completion exercises, identification questions (terms and concepts, people and places, and map questions), and factual and interpretive essay questions. Computerized versions of the Test Bank are also available, in Macintosh, Windows, and DOS formats, which allows instructors to alter, replace, or add questions as they wish.

Introduction

■

THE CHALLENGE OF WORLD HISTORY

What is world history? History can be briefly described as the study of peoples and their experiences and achievements in time. World history considers the experiences of all peoples of the globe, rather than the history of one group. The task of the historian is to attempt to reconstruct, recreate, and explain past human experiences by using suitable evidence, critical thinking, and informed imagination. Historians are aided in their job by the knowledge and insights of other social and behavioral sciences, such as anthropology, psychology, sociology, political science, and economics.

Historical evidence takes many forms, including oral traditions and archaeology as well as written texts. Study of the very distant past necessarily relies primarily on oral traditions and archaeology; these two kinds of evidence offer different perspectives on the past and answer different historical questions. Oral tradition is the means by which knowledge—both fact and myth—was passed on until it was written down. Even in literate societies, which preserved the past in written form, oral traditions also existed. Archaeology, in contrast, is the scientific study of the material remains of past human life and activities; fossil relics, artifacts, monuments. Archaeology supplies physical evidence of material culture, while oral sources provide insight into the nonmaterial world of ideas, values, and beliefs. Archaeological investigation may present evidence from millions of years before the present or from the most recent historical past. Oral traditions, some of which are ultimately written down, are more ephemeral, extending across a single lifetime or as far back as the past 10,000 years or so of remembered human experience.

The collection of evidence is clearly the first basic step in reconstructing the past. Since evidence does not speak for itself—objects can be faked and documents can be forged—the historian must act as interpreter. Establishing the validity and authenticity of the evidence is therefore the first task of the researcher. For example, not all archaeologists agree on the meaning, or even the dating, of stones and bones. There may be disagreement as to how objects came to be associated with one another and whether or how an archaeological site has been disturbed. Similarly, not all scholars respond to or interpret oral and written sources in the same way. Attempts to synthesize evidence into a composed story of the origins of human history adds yet another level of explanation. The many planes of subjective interpretation that make up historical reconstruction of the past result in continued scholarly investigation and debate. Such retelling of the past gives life to it, and used critically, each version contributes to a fuller historical understanding.

The challenges of evidence, interpretation, and recreation that all historians meet are intensified in the study of world history, where concern with a variety of pasts complicates fundamental historical tasks and introduces new ones. World history is the study of the pasts of all peoples who live on this earth. Since there are many pasts everywhere and they are perceived in so many different ways, writing global history is a complex and challenging task, though it is by no means a new one. Historians in other times and places have tried to re-count and explain the past they knew, often presenting culturally specific accounts as representing all human history. In a world where there are numerous and varied pasts, few historians have been able to recognize the limitations of their perspectives and acknowledge the validity of other views of the past that challenged their own.

Since it is apparent that the human experience is various, what do we understand of our shared past? Since all societies have their own discrete views of their pasts, the construction of a global version of human achievements in time is a complicated and difficult process. Late twentieth-century global awareness—shaped by the information superhighway, satellite communications, and common environmental issues such as global warming and nuclear energy—has created an imperative for reordering our collective knowledge of the past within a global framework in order to comprehend the present and plan for the future. Basic to the integration of separate histories into global historical understanding are challenges to accepted assumptions, such as the use of the European historical experience as the measure and model for understanding the totality of the human past. The process of weaving a global history includes decisions about what constitutes significant human experience and which events and ideas are worthy of inclusion. The practice of world history requires new processes of interpretation and integration so that a global past may be known, shared, and debated.

PART 1

Emergence

	Geological	Biological	Historical
20 myr	Tertiary Cenozoic	Paleocene: early mammals, first primates	
5 myr	Quaternary Cenozoic	Hominids Pleistocene: present-day animals and humans	Hominid migrations
1 myr			Paleolithic (Old Stone Age)
10,000 B.C.E			Neolithic (New Stone Age)
5,000 B.C.E			Age of Metals

In the hit comedy film *The Gods Must Be Crazy,* a Coke bottle falls from the sky and disrupts the predictable world of a young African man. As he attempts to return the bottle to the gods he holds responsible, he tries

Scene from the film *The Gods Must Be Crazy*

SOURCE: Photofest.

Cultural Characteristics	Features	Structures
	Earliest Stone Tools	Unknown (cooperative subsistence)
Gathering-Hunting Migrations: *Africa, Asia, Europe, W. Hemisphere*	Fire, Stone Tools, Language, Rock Art	Family Groups Social Organizations (lineage)
Animal & plant domestications/Agriculture: *Africa, Asia, Europe, W. Hemisphere*	Architecture	Settled Communities
Early Metallurgy: *Africa. Asia, Europe, W. Hemisphere*	Writing Systems and Trade: *Africa, Asia, W. Hemisphere*	Urban Societies: *S. Asia, China, N. Africa, Meso-America, N. America*

to make order of the chaos. The character's foibles in a now-strange land set off a hilarious sequence of events.

It strikes us that the role of the historian is not unlike that of the young man in the film. "Coke bottles" in the form of changing historical evidence are constantly falling from the sky, adding new perspectives and creating the need for reconciliation, reconsideration, and reconstruction of the past as it was once understood. At the same time, new questions arise that alter our understanding of the past by framing old evidence in new ways. The process of making sense out of a disparate and various past is the seemingly hopeless—and always unfinished—task of the historian. Each new "Coke bottle" alters one's individual understanding of the present as well as the collective view of the past. Finding integrating themes to explain the discontinuity, similarity, and variety of pasts is the challenge of global history. Part I introduces three major themes of world history: the human origins and population of the globe; environment, technology, and the shaping of human cultures; and the increasing social complexity associated with the "urban revolution." Although the first three chapters of this book consider these themes sequentially in time, covering earliest prehistory up to as recently as 1500 C.E., they represent inseparable, intertwined aspects of the human experience.

1

World History and Human Origins

S cene 1. The First Hadar Field Season: The Knee Joint. Location: National Science Foundation research tents camped in the center of the Afar desert overlooking the dry beds of the Awash River, Ethiopia, 1975. Action: A young paleoanthropologist, Donald Johanson, on his first expedition wonders what will happen if he fails to find the fossils he had written about in his grant application.

I did my share of sweating, and hoping, and dogged surveying. I kept wondering how I was going to explain that start-up costs had been big. I had had to buy all those tents. I had had to put up $10,000 for a Land-Rover. . . . Out in the deposits, I realized every day that all my money would be gone by the end of the year, whisked away on one spin of the wheel. Would I ever have a chance at another? Would it have been prudent to have started smaller, to have planned on a field force of four or five scientists instead of eleven?

Those thoughts so preoccupied me that when I was out surveying late one afternoon I idly kicked at what looked like a hippo rib sticking up in the sand. It came loose and revealed itself, not as a hippo rib but as a proximal tibia—the upper end of the shinbone—of a small primate.

A monkey, I thought, and decided to collect it. I marked the spot in my notebook and gave it a locality number. As I was writing that down, I noticed another piece of bone a few yards away. This was a distal femur—the lower end of a thighbone—also very small. It was split up the middle so that only one of its condyles, or bony bumps that fitted into the shinbone to make a knee joint, was attached. Lying in the sand next to it was the other condyle. I fitted the two together and then tried to join them to the shinbone. They were the same size and the same color. All three fitted perfectly. A rare find.

As I studied it, I realized that I had joined the femur and the tibia at an angle. I had not done it deliberately. They had gone together that way naturally; that was the way they *had* to go. Then I remembered that a monkey's tibia and femur joined in a straight line. Almost against my will I began to picture in my mind the skeleton of a human being, and recall the outward slant from knee to thigh that was peculiar to upright walkers.

I tried to refit the bones together to bring them into line. They would not go. It dawned on me that this was a hominid fossil.

The team went on to find nearly forty percent of the skeleton, the remains of a single female individual of a new species, *Australopithecus afarensis*. The camp rocked with excitement as its members began to realize how significant the finds of an upright walking three-million-year-old female hominid were. As they celebrated, a Beatles tape played on a cassette recorder: "Lucy in the Sky with Diamonds." In their exuberance, they affectionately called the fossil "Lucy."

FIGURE 1.0 Reconstructed Hominid Skeleton of *Australopithecus afarensis* ("Lucy")

SOURCE: National Museum of Ethiopia. © 1985 David L. Brill/Atlanta.

   This and other discoveries like it have provided evidence of human origins, evidence that has required a reconstruction of our understanding of the most distant human past. In this chapter, we consider the various versions of this past and the sources of evidence upon which they rely, from oral traditions thousands of years old to ongoing scientific expeditions.

■ INTRODUCTION

History can be briefly described as the study of peoples and their experiences and achievements in time. The task of the historian is to attempt to reconstruct, re-create, and explain past human experiences by using suitable evidence, critical thinking, and informed imagination. Historians are aided in their job by the knowledge and insights of other social and behavioral sciences, such as anthropology, psychology, sociology, political science, and economics.

Types of Historical Evidence: Oral Traditions and Archaeology

Historians rely primarily on two sources of knowledge about the very distant past: oral tradition and archaeology. Each type of historical evidence provides different knowledge of the past, and each answers different historical questions. Oral tradition is the means by which knowledge—fact and myth—was passed on until it was written down. Even in literate societies, in which history was in written form, oral traditions also existed. Archaeology, in contrast, is the scientific study of the material remains of past human life and activities: fossil relics, artifacts, monuments. Archaeology provides physical evidence of material culture, while oral sources provide insight into the nonmaterial world of ideas, values, and beliefs. Archaeological and oral sources generally provide evidence from different periods of time, although in some instances the two kinds of historical sources may provide different perspectives on the same past. Archaeological investigation may present evidence from millions of years before the present or from the most recent historical past. Oral traditions, some of which ultimately come to be written down, are more ephemeral, extending across a single lifetime or as far back as no more than the past 10,000 years or so of remembered human experience.

Both archaeological and oral sources have been regarded as legitimate historical sources for centuries. Archaeologists and historians who use the techniques of archaeology provide evidence that is often essential for the reconstruction of past societies and their peoples in many parts of the globe. Indeed, much written history, particularly that dealing with the beginnings of the human story, is based on archaeology and oral tradition. The Bible provides an unusual example of an integrated relationship among archaeological, oral, and written accounts. The written text of the Bible is a compilation of oral evidence: remembrances and accounts collected over a considerable period of time. This fundamental document of the Judeo-Christian tradition and modern interpretations of it are the documentary bases against which biblical archaeologists measure, arrange, and date the artifacts they excavate. Historians of this period have used both archaeology and oral tradition, subjecting the two kinds of evidence to methods of verification, analysis, and interpretation.

Historical Interpretation Collection of evidence is clearly only the first basic step in reconstructing the past. Since evidence does not speak for itself, the historian must act as interpreter, a task that interferes with absolute objectivity. Even the evidence itself may not be entirely objective. For example, objects can be faked and documents can be forged. Establishing the validity and authenticity of the evidence is the first task of the researcher. Next, not all archaeologists agree on the meaning, or even the dating, of stones and bones. There may be disagreement as to how objects came to be associated with one another and whether or how an archaeological site has been disturbed. Similarly, not all scholars respond to or interpret oral and written sources in the same way. Attempts to synthesize evidence into a composed story of the origins of human history interpose yet another level of explanation. The many planes of subjective interpretation that make up historical reconstruction of the past result in continued scholarly investigation and debate. Such retelling of the past gives life to that past, and, used critically, each version contributes to a fuller historical understanding. Historians have another function as well: their versions of the past have played a role in influencing subsequent human events. History has, accordingly, a mythic quality, shaping accounts of the past that can have an impact on the future.

The challenges of evidence, interpretation, and re-creation to which all historians must rise are intensified in the study of world history, where concern with a variety of pasts complicates fundamental historical tasks and introduces new ones. World history is the study of the pasts of all peoples who live on this earth. Since there are many pasts everywhere and they are perceived in so many different ways, writing global history is a complex and challenging task, though by no means a new one. Historians in other times and places have tried to recount and explain the past they knew, often presenting culturally specific accounts as representing all human history. In a world in which there are numerous and varied pasts, few historians have been able to recognize the limitations of their perspectives and to acknowledge the validity of other views of the past that have challenged their own.

CULTURAL PERSPECTIVES ON WORLD HISTORY

History Writing in Ancient Greece

Even historians from the same culture can produce accounts of the past that are very different. The Greek historians Herodotus (484?–425 B.C.E.) and Thucydides (ca. 471–400 B.C.E.), who were born about fifteen years apart, are examples of different historical approaches to a common world. Herodotus used a variety of oral, physical (artistic), and written evidence in writing his history, including accounts that came from peoples living in cultures and times other than his own. His evidence was wide-ranging, and he used it uncritically to create a historical account of the world as he knew it. Despite the somewhat anecdotal character of his *History,* Herodotus did have a purpose. Everything led to the great Persian War, the clash between the Greeks and the "barbarians." Herodotus traced the history of Greece and Persia before the great war between them, narrating accounts of North African and West Asian peoples known to him. Though well traveled and learned, Herodotus ignored the histories of parts of the world such as Phoenicia, Carthage, and Etruria, about which he could not have been totally ignorant, and of vast areas of the world about which he knew nothing. Within the limitations of his *History,* Herodotus nonetheless set the standard for the writing of history by dealing with the geography, climate, and peoples of the world he examined, along with their manners, customs, modes of production, political systems, and antiquities.

In contrast, Thucydides, in his *History of the Peloponnesian War,* wrote about an event he had personally experienced and could recount from direct observation, the conflict between the Greek city-states of Athens and Sparta. Thucydides' specific and direct account gives the impression of painstaking research and balanced judgment while, at the same time, it grapples with such concerns as "cause" in history and the interrelationship of economic and personal factors in human events. The works of these two Greek historians are different, resulting from different evidence and subjective concerns. They represent two possible approaches to reconstructing the past and have had such great influence on the way Europeans went on to write history that their authors are generally regarded as the "fathers" of European historiography (history writing).

Sima Qian and Chinese Historiography

Only a few centuries later than Herodotus, in around 100 B.C.E., a Chinese historian named Sima Qian (ca. 145–90 B.C.E.) similarly undertook the writing of a history of the world as he knew it. His world, of course, was different. Thus, his record began with a crucial event in the life of the philosopher Confucius (551–479 B.C.E.), who lived two generations before Herodotus and Thucydides, and it encompassed the world of China and the people on its periphery. Just as the Greeks contrasted "civilized people"—those who belonged culturally to their world—to "barbarians" (from the Greek word *barbaroi,* meaning "those who do not speak Greek"), so the Chinese believed that the world of China was equivalent to civilization. All peoples living outside the sphere of Chinese culture, often characterized as *hu* (the sound of a language that is unintelligible), were considered to be uncivilized "barbarians," much as the Greeks regarded those who did not speak Greek.

Orosius and Christian   History written in Europe during the first thousand years of the Chris-
Historiography   tian era was intended as world history in that it was not limited geo-
▬▬▬▬▬▬▬▬▬▬▬   graphically to the European world. Like the works of the early Greek
and Chinese historians, however, early European history was viewed through its own particular cultural prism: that of Christianity. For Christian Europeans, the ultimate end and purpose of history was to illustrate the unfolding of a divine plan for God's children. The work of
the fifth-century Spaniard Orosius became a basis on which subsequent Christian historians
expanded. Orosius's history of God guiding humanity was a chronicle of the calamities that
had befallen humans from Adam to the author's own time. Subsequent medieval historians
also attempted to show that the history of the world provided evidence of the perfectibility of
humankind through the influence of Christianity.

Ibn Khaldun, a   In the fourteenth century, the Muslim historian Ibn Khaldun
Muslim Historian (1332–1406), wrote a monumental global history entitled *Ibar*. The Is-
▬▬▬▬▬▬▬▬▬   lamic world, created by Muslim expansion into Europe, Africa, and Asia,
provided Ibn Khaldun with access to more geographical knowledge and cultural experience
than other historians had ever known. His historical writings were informed by this diverse
knowledge, and by collating it, Ibn Khaldun sought an understanding of human social behavior in the world he knew. According to Ibn Khaldun, the desire to write history had little
to do with social need but rather emerged when people were forced to acknowledge their own
place in history, when their collective existence was threatened. In recording historical
thought, he considered the nature of change and continuity.

European Historiography During the centuries of the European Renaissance, ca. 1300–1600,
▬▬▬▬▬▬▬▬▬▬▬▬▬ European historians abandoned the sort of history that had been
written by their medieval predecessors. The histories of Niccolò Machiavelli (1469–1527)
and Francesco Guicciardini (1483–1540), who wrote about their native Italy, tended to define
the scope of history in a more limited and secular (worldly, rather than religious) way. During
the eighteenth century, however, interest in global history was revived. A new global view of
history that reflected secular and rational ideals was produced by Voltaire (1694–1778), a
major historian of the European Enlightenment. His *Essay on Customs and Manners* is a short
history of civilization and a representative example of Enlightenment historiography. Another
French historian of this period, Abbé Raynal (1713–1796), adhered to similar ideals and applied them beyond Europe. Raynal's *Philosophical and Political History of European Settlements
and Commerce in the Two Indies* chronicled the crimes and follies of European civilization inflicted on native and colonial populations in both the Eastern and Western Hemispheres.
Though this history did deal with non-European lands, the principal historical actors were
still Europeans.

    As Raynal's work indicates, European interest in constructing world history was renewed
following Columbus's voyages, after which Europe began to define itself in relation to "the
Other," the rest of the world it sought to colonize. By the nineteenth century, Europeans conceptualized history as a ladder that represented the continuous and progressive sequence of
ancestors and descendants. At the base of the ladder was the distant past, where "barbarians"
and "savages" dwelled. These people survived in the "distant corners" of the world, in societies without histories. Their communities might be studied by anthropologists but generally

attracted little attention from historians. At the top of the ladder were Europeans, who had reached the pinnacle of human achievement—civilization as Europeans themselves defined it.

ETHNOCENTRISM AND HISTORY

The European "Ladder" Model of History The historical "ladder" model formed the basis of nineteenth-century European intellectual life, from which the modern academic discipline of history emerged. Yet European historians were not unique in their engagement in ethnocentric reconstruction of the past. All societies have held both explicit and implicit assumptions about the scope of the past that govern their representations of human history. None, however, has been as influential as the nineteenth-century European assumptions that shaped a view of the whole of human history. When the Europeans applied their concept of the evolutionary ladder to other communities, each with its different values, beliefs, cultures, and institutions, the result was the placement of "others" on one or another lower rung, since non-European societies were considered to be somehow inferior if they differed from their European counterparts.

Written and Oral Pasts For the European historian, the story of the past invariably began with European ancestors, just as human history in southwestern Nigeria began with Yoruba gods and Yoruba ancestors. Both the European and the Yoruba views of history are shaped by their respective views of their past. European history is informed by a sense of European global dominance that, as it emerged following the voyages of Columbus, indicated to Europeans their inevitable superiority. Yoruba history is centered at Ife, a sacred city, where the gods descended to create the world and human life, including the royal dynasty. It was transmitted orally through stories and traditions until the 1890s, when a version of it was written down. The fact that European history is written history was for generations taken to indicate its superiority to the histories that were spoken and not written down.

Global History Contemporary efforts to include African, Asian, and Native American histories, among them unwritten and often silenced pasts, has required a revision of world history. Once again historians are asking the basic questions: What is history? Since it is apparent that the human experience is various, what do we understand of our shared past? The European version is only one of many, and since each society has its own discrete views of its past, the construction of a global version of human achievements in time is a complicated and difficult process. Historians today question the European ladder theory of history. Late-twentieth-century global awareness—shaped by the information superhighway, satellite communications, and common environmental issues such as global warming and nuclear energy—has created an imperative for reordering, within a global framework, our collective knowledge of the past if we are to be able to comprehend the present and plan for the future. Basic to the integration of separate histories into global historical understanding are challenges to accepted assumptions such as the Eurocentric version of history. The process of weaving a global history includes decisions about what constitutes significant human experience and which events and ideas are worthy of inclusion. The practice of world history requires new processes of interpretation and integration so that a global past may be known, shared, and debated.

■
THE MEASUREMENT OF TIME

Time is the arena in which historical events happen. The variety of global history is in part the consequence of the ways in which historical time is constructed by different cultures, how they place events in time, how different people answer the question of *when.* A society's notion of time is a socially constructed category that expresses the concept of time that is common to the group. All cultural clocks are systems of reckoning time, which arise through human interaction with the natural world. Regardless of what the "clock" is—whether reigns of kings, human generations, planting seasons, plagues of locusts, or the movements of planets—practical and ritual events are perceived to have meaning because of their placement in time.

LINEAR CHRONOLOGY

Since well before the European Renaissance, Western historians have understood historical time in a linear fashion: human events are seen as beads strung on a string. The linear pattern of human history stems from the Judeo-Christian belief that human events tend purposefully toward a final conclusion, the coming of a Messiah. According to this tradition, the history of the past is an orderly, progressive narrative of events. In the Christian tradition, historical time became the preserve of the Church and was consequently shaped to conform to the calendar established by Pope Gregory VII in the sixteenth century, the basis of the one used today in the West. Islam, which shares common cultural roots with the Judeo-Christian tradition, measures time in a similar linear fashion, starting with its own beginning, the flight of Muhammed from Mecca to Medina known as the *hejira.* This took place in 622 C.E., according to the Christian Gregorian calendar, or the first year A.H. (after *hejira*), according to the Muslim calendar.

NONLINEAR CHRONOLOGY

Early Calendars Before the emergence of the linear European and Muslim calendars, astronomical calculations were carried out in North Africa. The ancient Egyptians devised a solar calendar which divided the calendar year into three seasons of four months. Each month had thirty days, and five days were added at the end of each year to create the 365-day calendar. Egyptians also used a religious, lunar calendar. A dual chronology was developed by other cultures, including the Maya (ca. 300–900 C.E.) in the Americas. The Mayan calendar was based on two recurring cycles of different length and with different purposes. The ritual, or sacred, calendar of 260 days was used together with a solar calendar of 365 days, resulting in a dual name for each day; the same combination of names, however, occurred only once every 52 years and was recognized in special ceremonies. In addition, Mayans reckoned time according to a lengthy linear pattern, beginning with a point in the distant past identified with the creation of the world.

Cyclical Time Other nonlinear chronological traditions have been based on the notion of circular or cyclical time. Early South Asian astronomers measured world cycles (*kalpa*) in terms of billions of human years. These cycles repeated the creation and dissolution of the universe. Some sub-Saharan African societies also reject the emphasis on a strictly linear progression. Time, they feel, is process-linked and abstract. For example, historical time may be measured by remembered plagues of locusts or by generations, established by those coming of age or initiated at about the same time. Longer durations are understood in terms of the rebirth of ancestors and ritually structured. These systems of reckoning and recording time provide culturally constructed chronological categories that do not conform to a linear, measurable pattern. For some peoples and places, the task of assigning dates to events recorded in oral tradition remains impossible and unwarranted, even culturally inappropriate.

Chinese Chronology   The early Chinese understanding of time was derived from an organic
and Cosmology   theory of the universe in which human and cosmic events were part of a
                      seamless whole. Perception of the rhythmic cycles of nature, knowledge
of which was vital to agricultural societies, led the Chinese to recognize the regularities of celestial events. A calendar adopted more than 2000 years ago was based on the movements of both the moon and the sun. One of the ruler's crucial responsibilities was to establish the official calendar. For this purpose, court astronomers recorded the movements of celestial bodies. The role of astronomer evolved into that of historian as the record of celestial events was correlated with that of human events.

Dynastic Cycles   The Chinese defined the beginning of time as the moment when the sun,
                   moon, and all the planets were perfectly aligned in the heavens. The longest
cycle of cosmic time was the period that elapsed between these recurring perfect alignments. Within these cosmic cycles, human events were recorded in the framework of political time: the spans of dynasties.

Dynasties corresponded to reigns of families, within which era names were chose to reflect moral or auspicious symbolism, such as the symbol for "rectified government." Each era within a dynasty progressed in linear fashion: "rectified government" 1, 2, and so on. But the dynasty itself had a "life cycle" of birth, maturity, and decline, a cycle that would be repeated with the next dynasty. The Chinese conception of time thus encompassed both the enormous, astronomically based cycles of cosmic time and the much smaller units of repetitive dynastic cycles, in which the linear time of era names measured political events on a still narrower scale. The Chinese were not troubled by the apparent ambivalence of a history that incorporated both cyclical and linear senses of time.

WORLD HISTORICAL TIME

Maps of time are constructed to negotiate a common understanding of the individual in the human and natural worlds. In this way, calendars and power are intertwined. Ancient Chinese bureaucrats said that when they had incorporated some new region into the empire, its inhabitants had "received the calendar" (meaning the emperor's time map). When Europeans colonized parts of the globe in the nineteenth century, they also imposed their calendars and clocks on other cultures. Multiple notions of time sometimes converged, as they still do in ritual performances based on the cyclical repetition of events that contrasts with linear time; linear time, while recognized, is not acknowledged in the context of the repetitive, cyclical time of ritual. Since each system of reckoning time constitutes a way of knowing as it organizes and contextualizes knowledge, cultural clocks are an essential aspect of understanding the human experience, and they are significant to a people's understanding of the past. In this book, we have chosen the conventional system of representing historical time along a linear timeline.

The terms B.C.E. (Before the Common Era) and C.E. (Common Era) are used to distinguish between the two directions to the left (before) and right (after) of the timeline's zero mark, replacing the Christian terms B.C. (before Christ) and A.D. (*Anno Domini,* "in the year of our Lord") with less culturally specific ones. This system has gained currency through its avoidance of explicit cultural references, but it, too, contains an arbitrary beginning point.

World history is also constructed temporally, within a conceptualized experience of time. Events have meaning through their being told as narrative; in turn, narration is construction in time. History, by definition, implies a distanced relationship—between the historian and the event, between the present and the past, between the "here and now" and the "then." The historian's concern with the chronology of the distant past has been greatly refined by scientific improvements in dating techniques. From Chinese water clocks to microprocessor clocks, technological tools for measuring time have also altered the human perception of temporal events.

Radiocarbon Dating One of the most important discoveries of the twentieth century for historians was the invention of radiometric (radiocarbon) dating, by which dates are assigned to objects through the use of measurements of the radioactive decay of such substances as carbon 14, potassium 40, and other radioactive elements. Conceived around the time of World War II by the Nobel Prize–winning chemist Willard Libby (1908–1980) and his coworkers, radiocarbon (carbon-14) dating has been refined to produce increasingly more accurate measures and calibrations. The application of this and other scientific techniques to dating physical evidence of the past has permitted historians more confidently to compare the time and place of the material remains of the human experience in one part of the globe with that of another part, independent of historical assumptions. Once excavated objects or remembered events have dates associated with them, they can be placed into a time perspective that permits comparison or allows relational links to be established.

Prehistory Since chronological reckoning clearly varies, there is no common agreement on the beginning of time or the beginning point of history. Reliance on written documentation of the past has tended to limit the subject of historical inquiry to what has been recorded in written texts. Since, by definition, such evidence is largely the record of those who were literate and held power, it excludes much of humanity and ignores what came before written records, that majority of the human story termed "prehistory."

Most historians now regard prehistory as a legitimate part of the reconstruction of the past. Evidence for the systematic study of world prehistory relies on stones and bones, changing environments, the scientific record of human fossils, archaeology, myth, and legends. The earliest evidence for the human experience is material and oral rather than written.

■

ORIGIN MYTHS: THE CREATION OF THE WORLD

Once the standards for historical reconstruction were set in the nineteenth century, oral history and legend—a source of the earliest remembered or imagined beginnings of human life—were customarily excluded from historical writing. Professional historians considered such sources to be dubious and unscientific, to belong to literature or folklore, much as they assigned "stones and bones" to archaeologists. It was not until the twentieth century that historians generally began to accept oral tradition and myth as attempts to explain and comment on, rather than merely remember, the past. Accepted as explanation and commentary, oral accounts, like archaeological evidence, became useful in reconstructing the distant past. Incorporating into history oral evidence that has been written down or recorded on tape or disc is especially important to the global understanding of human origins.

CREATION MYTHS

Creation legends or myths explain how people believed the world began, and origin myths tell how human beings came to be a part of the world. There are varying versions of what people believed or imagined about what happened at the beginning of the human story. They reveal much that is common, as well as much that is unique, about how the past is perceived. By doing so, they are powerful sources of cultural identity, not only telling us how early people understood the world but also giving some sense of important aspects of their cultures and experience, such as social and political organization, family life, gender and ecological relationships, spiritual life and values. Oral history, like other kinds of history, frames events, lives, and processes through culturally specific points of view.

Australian Versions of their origins unique to Australian aboriginals reflect archaeologically proven migrations that took place perhaps 50,000 years ago. The legends refer to the era of creation as the "Dreamtime," and they explain the migration of their ancestors to Australia in terms of beliefs about superhuman spirit ancestors who lived during the Dreamtime. The Kakadu people of Australia believe that the arrival of Imberombera, the Great Earth Mother ancestress, was by canoe, a mythical version of an event which archaeologists

FIGURE 1.1 Western Australian Rock Art

SOURCE: Josephine Flood, *The Archaeology of the Dreamtime* (Honolulu: University of Hawaii Press, 1983). Photo G. Walsh. Courtesy of General Research Division, New York Public Library, Astor, Lenox and Tilden Foundations.

and prehistorians accept, even though no canoes—since they are perishable artifacts—have survived. Kakadu legend further explains the populating of Australia by the fact that when Imberombera came to Australia, she was pregnant, her womb filled with children. Once on the continent, she created the natural landscape—hills, creeks, plants, and animals—and peopled it with her children.

South Asian The people of the Indus Valley civilization of South Asia (ca. 3000–1600 B.C.E.) left little indication of their beliefs about their origins other than some archaeological evidence of a fertility cult, which, like many others, centered on a mother or Earth goddess. The earliest South Asian creation texts date from the period of the Indo-European invasions (ca. 1500–500 B.C.E.) and represent ideas introduced by the invaders. The texts are collectively known as the Vedas (literally, "knowledge") and include hymns, ritual texts, and philosophical works. The central narrative in the oldest of these texts, the Rig-Veda, concerns the deity Indra, who slew a serpent demon and by this act created cosmic order:

> Indra's heroic deeds, indeed, will I proclaim, the first ones which the wielder of the thunderbolt accomplished. He killed the dragon, released the waters, and split open the sides of the mountains.
> When you, O Indra, killed the first-born among the dragons and further overpowered the wily tricks of the tricksters, bringing forth, at that very moment, the sun, the heavens, and the dawn—since then, indeed, have you not come across another enemy.
> Indra, who wields the thunderbolt in his hand, is the lord of what moves and what remains rested, of what is peaceful and what is horned [aggressive]. He alone rules over their tribes as their king; he encloses them as does a rim the spokes.

Other scriptures in the Vedic tradition present the idea that the creation of the universe was the product of the sacrifice of the primeval man, Purusha, who was sacrificed by his children and from whose body the universe was created. One of the later scriptures in the Rig-Veda, the "Hymn of Creation," displays a questioning attitude toward the idea of creation, implicitly expressing doubt about various theories that existed, such as the suggestion that creation was the result of a sexual act or the product of a "cosmic egg." This text exhibits a high level of abstract thinking and is one of the earliest examples of philosophic doubt:

> Then even nothingness was not, nor existence.
> There was no air then, nor the heavens beyond it.
> What covered it? Where was it? In whose keeping?
> Was there then cosmic water, in depths unfathomed?
>
> Then there were neither death nor immortality,
> nor was there then the torch of night and day.
> The One breathed windlessly and self-sustaining.
> There was that One then, and there was no other.
>
> But, after all, who knows, and who can say
> whence it all came, and how creation happened?
> The gods themselves are later than creation,
> so who knows truly whence it has arisen?
>
> Whence all creation had its origin,
> he, whether he fashioned it or whether he did not,
> he, who surveys it all from highest heaven,
> he knows—or maybe even he does not know.

West Asian: Judeo-Christian The role of a creator god is present in the Judeo-Christian tradition as reflected in the story of creation in the Book of Genesis,
found in the Bible. This story attributes the act of creation to one god, who forms human beings in his own image:

> In the beginning God created the heaven and the earth. . . .
> And God said, Let there be light: and there was light. . . .
> And God made the firmament, and divided the waters. . . .
> And God called the dry land Earth; and the gathering together of the waters called he Seas. . . .
> And God said, Let the earth bring forth grass, the herb yielding seeds, and the fruit tree yielding
>   fruit. . . .
> So God created man in his own image. . . .

Chinese In contrast to this, an early Chinese account (second century B.C.E.) offers an account
of creation without a creator:

> When heaven and earth were joined in emptiness and all was unwrought simplicity, then *without
> having been created,* things came into being. This was the Great Oneness. All things issued from this
> oneness but all became different, being divided into the various species of fish, birds, and beasts.
> (author's italics)

The creation of the world is often seen as a process of separating the heavens from the
earth or the waters from the heavens, either by a creative force or without an agent.

Cherokee A Cherokee myth from North America described the primal environment as a wa-
tery one. An image of primeval water covering a not-yet-created earth was found
among all American peoples with the exception of the Inuit in the farthest North.

Yoruba In the Yoruba myth from Nigeria in West Africa, the earth was created from the beginning of heavens and primeval waters. The creator deities are humanized to the extent that one of them even falls asleep, having drunk too much palm wine, and misses his
chance to create land.

Sumerian In the region of Sumer in ancient West Asia, the earth sat upon a vast primordial
sea of sweet water, and creation was a matter of differentiating the raw matter of
earth, heaven, and air into specific things. There was an assumed prior existence of a god and
goddess, from which sprang the gods of the Sumerian pantheon:

> When on high the heaven had not been named,
> Firm ground below had not yet been called by name,
> Naught but primordial Apsu, their begetter,
> And Mummu Tiamat, she who bore them all,
> Their waters commingling as a single body:
> No reed hut had been matted, no marsh land had appeared,
> When no gods whatever had been brought into being,
> Uncalled by name, their destinies undetermined—
> Then it was that the gods were formed within them.

The god Apsu was killed by his offspring because they feared he would kill them. The sea was then made from the body of the father; the sky was made from the body of the mother, Tiamat, who tried to destroy the children who had murdered her husband but was herself killed by them. There is a sequence of the acts of creation carried out by the gods—light, day and night, earth and sky, sun, moon, and stars, and with them the ordering of time. Then humanity was created, with its obligations and duties to the gods.

Greek There are striking parallels between the Sumerian and Greek traditions, since those of Sumer influenced those of Greece. The anthropomorphic gods of the Greek tradition showed a similar pattern of human and superhuman behavior as they created the world. Heaven and Earth gave birth to numerous gods and goddesses. The youngest, who attacked and castrated his father, married his sister and devoured their children, with the exception of Zeus. When Zeus grew up, he was able to disgorge his brothers and sisters alive from his father's body. Zeus thus became the leader of the Olympian gods, deities held in common by all Greeks, and had the capacity to mate with humans. The Olympian gods exhibited human passions and failings, just like the mortals over whom they ruled.

Nordic The gods of northern Europe were divided into two families of deities, one connected with war, one with peace. There was a struggle between the two groups of gods that was resolved in favor of the warlike deities, chief of whom was Odin. Odin presided over Valhalla, where human heroes are received after death. Odin gave his name to the English day, Wednesday ("Odin's day"), as other gods and goddesses did to other days, for example, Thor to Thursday ("Thor's day").

Japanese Gods also play a central role in the creation of the world described in the *Kojiki,* the earliest textual source of native Japanese beliefs, compiled in 712 C.E. Like Apsu and Tiamat in West Asia, a pair of gods, Izanami and Izanagi, gave birth to the Japanese islands and a host of deities:

> When the primeval matter had congealed but breath and form had not yet appeared, there were no names and no action. Who can know its form? However, when heaven and earth were first divided, the three deities became the first of all creation. The Male and Female here began, and the two spirits (Izanagi and Izanami) were the ancestors of all creation.

The progeny of these two gods included Amaterasu, the Sun Goddess, who became the central deity of Shinto (literally, "Way of the Gods"), the native belief system of Japan. The Sun Goddess of Shinto is only one example of a solar deity.

SOLAR DEITIES

Solar deities were present in many early societies that were dependent on agriculture, since the sun was vital to their welfare. The Egyptians worshiped Ra, a solar deity. The Aztecs of Mesoamerica, the area between the United States and South America, believed that the sun ordered and structured the universe. For them, the sun and moon were dualities of masculine and feminine, darkness and light, life and death. An eclipse was viewed as an upsetting of the necessary equilibrium between the two, leading to a collapse of the world order. Eclipses were depicted in drawings as mythical animals "eating" or "biting" the sun. In early China, an eclipse was explained as an archer shooting the sun. The Incas of South America believed that the sun created the first Incas, a brother and sister, who set out on a journey to be tested and founded the Incan empire.

ORIGINS OF HUMAN CULTURE

Chinese records, which are thought to reflect a historical memory of community leaders in the fifth or sixth millennium B.C.E., portray the rulers of antiquity as wise rulers who bequeathed to their subjects the knowledge of agriculture, writing, and medicine. Although ideas about the creation of the world can be identified in early Chinese thought, there was no dominant creation myth. It was the origins of human culture and society, not the creation of the world, that concerned early thinkers in China. The recorded bequests of agriculture and writing illustrate definitive elements of Chinese culture: an agrarian economy with an elabo-

FIGURE 1.2 Wu Liang Tomb Shrine Relief Showing Chinese Culture Heroes with the Symbols of Order and Construction (China, second century C.E.)

SOURCE: Joseph Needham, *Science and Civilization in China,* vol. 1 (Cambridge, England: Cambridge University Press, 1954). General Research Division, New York Public Library, Astor, Lenox and Tilden Foundations.

rate textual tradition in which the farmer and the scholar are both idealized. The importance of agriculture, and grain in particular, was reinforced in the account of the birth of the progenitor of the Zhou (pronounced "Joe") people, "Lord Millet," in the *Book of Songs,* the earliest poetic anthology in China (sixth century B.C.E.):

> She who in the beginning gave birth to the people,
> This was Jiang Yuan.
> How did she give birth to the people?
> Well she sacrificed and prayed
> That she might no longer be childless.
> She trod on the big toe of God's footprint,
> Was accepted and got what she desired. . . .
> She gave birth, she nurtured;
> And this was Houji [Lord Millet]. . . .
> He planted large beans;
> His beans grew fat and tall.
> His paddy lines were close set,
> His hemp and wheat grew thick,
> His young gourds teemed.
> Truly Houji's husbandry followed the way that had been shown.

Certain commonalities are apparent in the creation stories discussed here: the creative act by which earth was separated from sea and air; the anthropomorphic struggle among deities; the tangible connection between gods and humans; and the role of gods in originating cultural knowledge, including knowledge of the past. These various versions of the distant human past suggest that all myths, despite unique cultural features, reflect common human experiences and concerns.

■

WORLD PREHISTORY

Most of the human past belongs to the time period traditionally labeled prehistoric, literally "before written history." Ninety-nine percent of the shared story of our evolving humanity has happened outside the framework of written, or even remembered, history. The study of prehistory was shaped by attempts to identify centers, or "cradles," of humanity as beginning points of a linear evolutionary story. From prehistoric beginnings physical and technological adaptations were perceived to lead toward the happy ending of the human story: human survival and civilization.

Processes of Human Development in Prehistory — Recent prehistorians, working from a global rather than a Eurocentric view of human origins, have begun to shift from a preoccupation with the linear, progressive narrative of *what* happened to the questions of *how* and *why* changes came about at different times and in different places. It is the processes rather than the results of human development that concern prehistorians today. There are two processes involved in the biological evolution of the species into anatomically modern humans: adaptation and exaptation. Adaptation involves intentional adjustment to new circumstances. For example, individuals with physical equipment such as strong, well-controlled hands and psychological abilities that enable them to understand the making and use of tools external to their bodies intentionally adjust to new situations and are thus better able to survive and pass on their skills. Exaptation is the result of chance occurrences and unintentional change. Exaptations may be co-opted for long-term use, though they were not designed for that purpose. For example, essential human characteristics such as a large brain or bipedalism (walking upright on two feet) did not necessarily come about as conscious or intentional reactions to changing environments; they may have been accidental occurrences that unexpectedly proved to be useful. At some turning points in evolutionary history, humans made the best of exaptive, or chance, features that then became sources of future development. The concept of exaptation—human development as a result of chance—provides an alternative to the conventional adaptive view, which suggests that successful intentional adjustment to change results in a superior, progressive, linear pattern of human evolution. Taking the role of chance in shaping human behavior in all its landscapes into consideration helps avoid ranking or judging evolving human history and is particularly suitable to the study of world history.

Human Ancestors The picture of human ancestors drawn in the early twentieth century by those who deal with life in past geological periods (paleontologists) looked very different from how it looks today (see Table 1.1). Based largely on undated circumstantial evidence, the focus of prehistory was on European ancestors, some of whom, it turns out, emerged late in the evolution of the species. The popular prehistoric person was imagined as

TABLE 1.1 A Guide to the Prehistory of World Colonization. Four Major Migrations Are Identified (B.P. = Before Present)

Time Period	Migration
5 million–1 million B.P.	**Early hominids:** Apiths (Australopithecines), early *Homo* (sub-Saharan Africa)
1 million–200,000 B.P.	**Early migrants:** *Homo erectus,* "archaic" *Homo sapiens*
200,000–60,000 B.P.	Early Neanderthals, anatomically modern humans (Africa, mid-latitude Asia, and Europe)
60,000–40,000 B.P.	**Transition Phase/later migrants:** Classic Neanderthals, "archaic" *Homo sapiens* Anatomically modern humans (continental Eurasia)
40,000–10,000 B.P.	**Moderns:** Anatomically modern humans (Australia, Eastern Siberia, Pacific margins, Japan, Americas. unglaciated mountain chains)
12,000 B.C.E.–C.E. 1500	(Arctic, Indian Ocean, deep Pacific, tropical rain forests, great sand deserts)
C.E. 1500–present	(Central and southern Atlantic Ocean)
Unoccupied	(Antarctica)

SOURCE: Clive Gamble, *Timewalkers* (Cambridge, Mass.: Harvard University Press, 1993), p. 8.

FIGURE 1.3   Cave Painting of Bison (Lascaux, France)

SOURCE: Giraudon/Art Resource, New York.

brutish and male. Such a view of prehistoric ancestors reveals more about the society that produced and accepted them than about prehistory. Nineteenth-century European history was as
gender-bound as it was culture-bound; thus the prevailing image was one of prehistoric males
making stone tools and fire, prehistoric women being dragged to caves by the men and reproducing the (evolving) species.

Cave Paintings Some of the most popular notions about prehistoric communities were rein-
                       forced by the discovery in 1940 of the Lascaux Caves in France, on whose
walls were found the conscious artistic achievement of prehistoric artists, remarkable images
of bison, deer, and horses, animals important to the fully erect *Homo sapiens* who painted
them. To Europeans who wanted to think of themselves as the descendants of these artists,
the paintings discovered at Lascaux revealed an expressive, sensitive prehistoric inner life. Europeans romanticized what they saw: the animal images at Lascaux have been interpreted as
aiding prehistoric hunters in the efforts to secure food. More recently, cave paintings discovered at Apollo Cave in South Africa, Jinmium in Australia, and Vallon-Pont-d'Arc in France
have provided deeper insights into the lives of our human ancestors. Some of these images

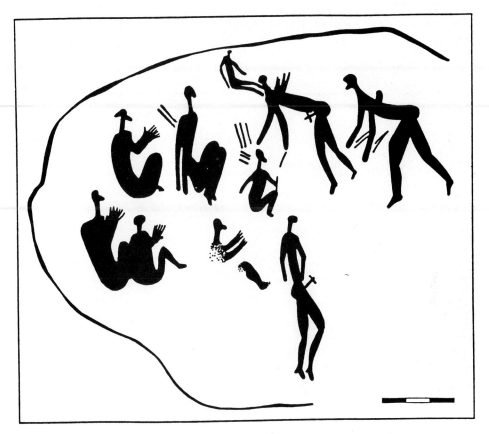

FIGURE 1.4 Rock Art of Ceremony (San, Southern Africa)

SOURCE: San Heritage Center, University of Witwatersand.

may be associated with the most basic of human experiences: life and death. Around the world, prehistoric artists depicted childbirth, hunting, and ritual experience. The common subject matter and variety of artistic styles remind the historian of the universal themes of continuity and change reaching back to the most distant human past.

AFRICAN ORIGINS

Archaeological discoveries on the African continent were central to transforming European assumptions about prehistoric beginnings. Scientists had been searching the African continent for fossils since 1871, when Charles Darwin first proposed that people and apes had a common ancestor. Early European prehistory tended to focus on European evidence, although in the 1920s, the view that the earliest human ancestors (hominids) had arisen in Asia was accepted. After the 1960s, research in eastern and southern Africa began to alter the priority given to European and Asian prehistory.

Location of Early Hominid Sites in Africa

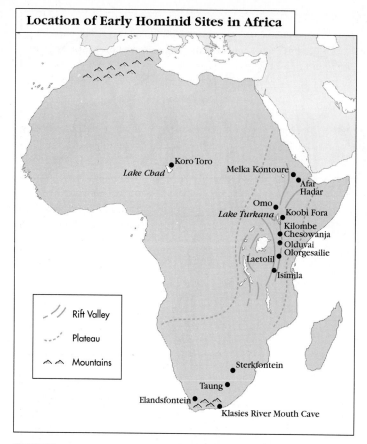

Koro Toro
Lake Chad
Melka Kontoure
Afar
Hadar
Omo
Lake Turkana
Koobi Fora
Kilombe
Chesowanja
Olduvai
Olorgesailie
Laetoli
Isimila

⟋⟋ Rift Valley

⌐⌐ Plateau

ᴧ ᴧ Mountains

Sterkfontein
Taung
Elandsfontein
Klasies River Mouth Cave

MAP 1.1

"Lucy"   At Hadar, Ethiopia, archaeologists identified what may have been a new branch on
▩▩▩▩ the evolutionary tree, a species called *Australopithecus afarensis,* who lived more than
3 million years ago and more than a million years before any other hominid lineage. This
classification was used to develop a model for the possible descent of the species *Homo* (humans or their ancestors) from some form of *Australopithecus.* It pushed back human origins
and human history to 4.6 million years ago. The evidence points clearly to the fact that the
early *Australopithecus* hominids were descended from African mammals. The genetically nearest ancestors of hominids were those of the chimpanzees and gorillas.

Reconstruction of   Today the reconstruction of human evolution is selected from many and
Human Evolution   extraordinary sets of evidence. At the Rift Valley site near Lake Turkana in
▩▩▩▩▩▩▩▩   Tanzania, a team of paleontologists found complete upper and lower jaws,
teeth, skull fragments, arm bones and a leg bone that pushed the emergence of bipedalism
back to at least 4 million years ago. The species has been named *Australopithecus anamensis*
(*anam* is the Turkana word for "lake"). At another archaeological site in Tanzania known as
Laetoli, a set of hominid footprints was preserved in a cement of volcanic dust and rain nearly

3.5 million years ago. These footprints are evidence of the movements of hominids walking upright on two legs on a rainy day. Paleontology records only selected chapters in our biological evolution, such as the major adaptation of bipedalism. Other important chapters in prehistory, such as the development of omnivorous behavior (consuming both animals and plants) or the emergence of culture (distinct patterns or styles of behavior), are less well documented because such evidence is less tangible and permanent.

Olduvai Gorge   One major site of hominid research in Africa has been the Great Rift Valley, including Olduvai Gorge in Tanzania, investigated over two generations by a family of scientists: Louis Leakey (1903–1972), Mary Leakey (1913–1996), his British wife, their son, Richard, and their daughter-in-law, Maeve. In the sand, gravel, and other detrital material deposited by running water in the Olduvai Gorge, the Leakeys discovered stone tools and other evidence relating to human activity that date from about 3 million years ago. Numerous significant paleontological finds have subsequently been revealed at Olduvai and in Ethiopia and Kenya, including the skull of *Homo habilis,* one of the oldest and reasonably complete skulls attributed to this species (dating to about 1.8 million years ago) and only

FIGURE 1.5   Suggested Uses of Oldowan Stone Tools

SOURCE: Clive Gamble, *Timewalkers* (Alan Sutton Ltd, 1993). General Research Division, New York Public Library, Astor, Lenox and Tilden Foundations.

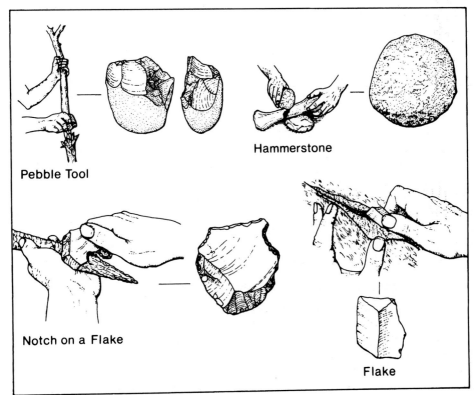

Pebble Tool

Hammerstone

Notch on a Flake

Flake

slightly older than the earliest *Homo erectus* species in East Africa. The stone tools excavated at Olduvai Gorge by the Leakeys and others provide the longest chain of evidence of tool use, beginning about 2 million years ago and continuing to several thousand years before the present. Australopithecines have also been found recently in Chad in Central Africa, and they may have roamed across West Africa, too.

Africa: Birthplace of the Human Species Evidence strongly indicates, then, that the African continent was the birthplace of the human species. Africa is rich with evidence of the oldest genetic human relatives: paleontological evidence for early human ancestors (hominids); the oldest footprints of upright, two-legged hominids; remains of a variety of scientifically dated fossil species; and the oldest evidence of human behavior—the first use of fire and the first stone tools—are all found in Africa. By contrast, evidence of human ancestors elsewhere dates from much later. For example, the earliest fossils and stone tools in China date to 1.78 million to 1.96 million years old; the teeth look like those of early *Homo* members found in Africa. Evidence of *Homo erectus,* the first human ancestor that walked

FIGURE 1.6 Acheulean Stone Tools (Africa, 1.6 Million Years Ago)

SOURCE: Clive Gamble, *Timewalkers* (Alan Sutton, Ltd, 1993). General Research Division, New York Public Library, Astor, Lenox and Tilden Foundations.

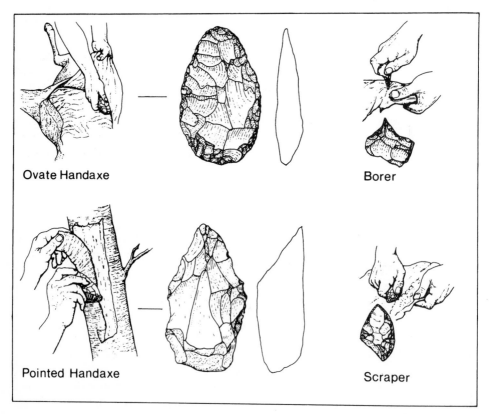

Ovate Handaxe

Borer

Pointed Handaxe

Scraper

upright, dates from more than a million years later in Europe than in Africa. Our species, the anatomically modern *Homo sapiens,* seems to have appeared first in Africa and subsequently in other parts of the world, though this is not as clearly delineated as the story of the *Homo erectus* migration out of Africa. It is thought by some that *Homo sapiens* may have appeared as recently as 100,000 years ago; and, to date, many archaeological sites in Africa have revealed evidence of human cultural evolution from living sites, tool manufacture and use, and ritual and artistic expression, including the oldest evidence yet discovered in the world. These findings reveal much about the process by which patterns of distinctly human behavior emerged.

The Environment's Impact on Evolution
───────────────────
Why Africa? Why does the earliest evidence of human ancestors appear to have emerged in Africa? Some theories take into account the importance of the changing environment. In Africa and elsewhere, the period before the emergence of hominids saw glaciers moving to cover lower latitudes. The consequent destruction and fragmentation of the forest had important consequences for African environments. Another theory suggests that about 10 million years ago, toward the end of the geological age known as the Miocene, the environment between the African, West Asian, and European landmasses deteriorated as a result of the rapid formation of huge salt deposits. Following this change, between 5 and 6 million years ago the massive East African savannas were formed. Today these savanna grasslands comprise about 65 percent of all African vegetation. They extend over the continent for 13,000 kilometers (8080 miles) from Senegal in West Africa toward southern Africa.

Isolated by oceans and deserts, the African savanna provided an ideal environment for the appearance of many animal species, including humans, and for about 3 million years Africa was apparently the breeding ground for the evolution of large mammals, just as Southeast Asia, where tectonic instability (earthquakes) threatened animal populations, was the site of the evolution of large numbers of plant species. In Africa, characteristic fauna (animal life), such as chimpanzees and gorillas, moved out of the savanna grasslands into forests. It now appears that the earliest hominids learned to walk upright in the relative safety of the forests. While their cousins were able to maintain themselves in the African forest, hominids were not, and their development was the result of adaptation to the changing conditions in the savanna.

GLOBAL COLONIZATION

The most significant event of world prehistory is the colonization of the planet: humans are the only animals to have achieved near-global distribution. According to one prehistorian, "humans went everywhere in prehistory, because humans have purpose." Understanding the process of global colonization raises the questions of how and where humans emerged as a species and how and why humans moved across the earth's landscapes to eventually occupy all environments found on this planet.

Human Migration
───────────────────
Between about 1 and 2 million years ago, the first global migration of hominids is believed to have taken place. This migration carried African hominids to other continents: to Europe, parts of Asia, and beyond. Why these earliest migrants left Africa to colonize the world is a complex, important question. The answer is likely to be

Global Migrations Out of Africa

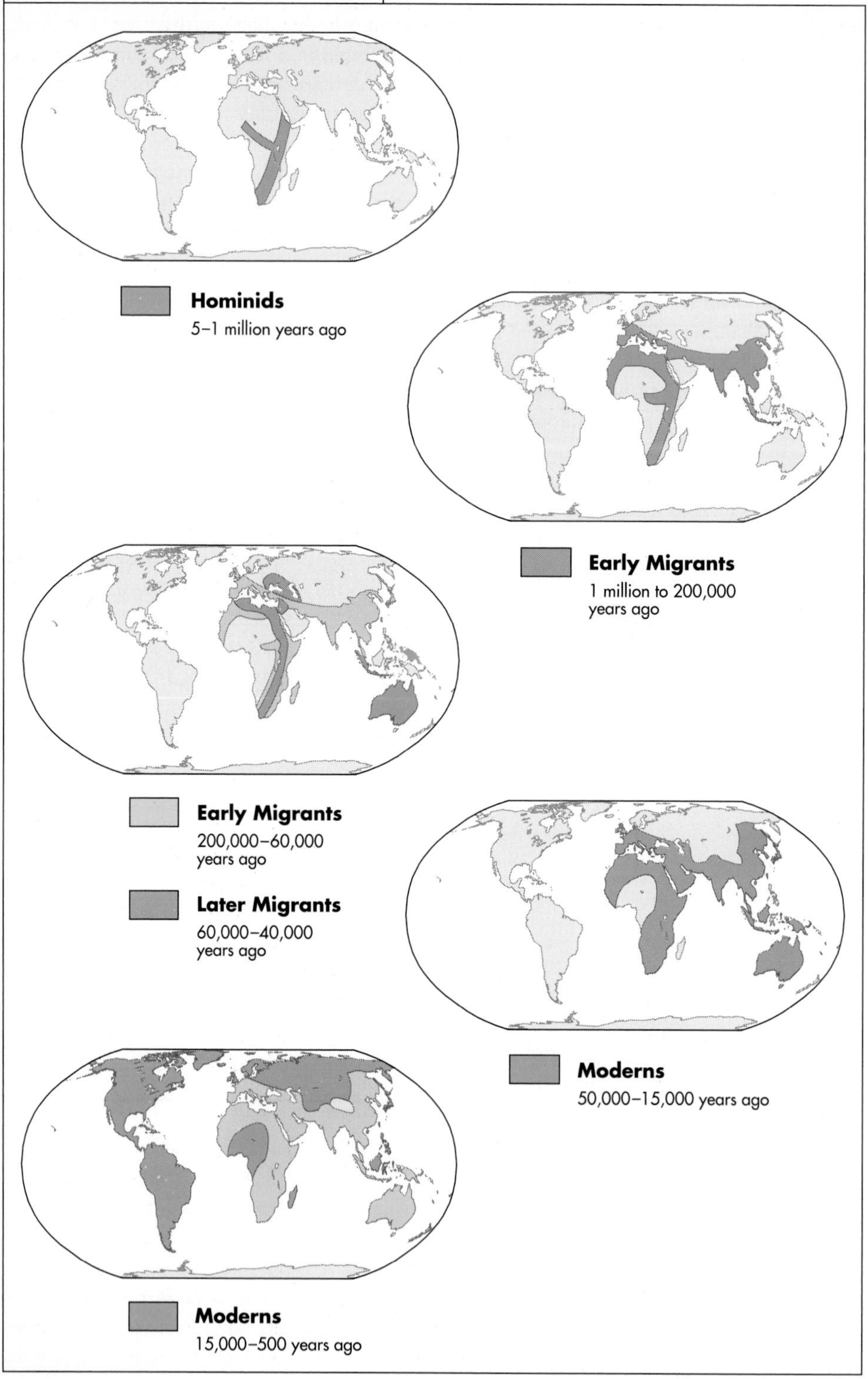

Hominids
5–1 million years ago

Early Migrants
1 million to 200,000
years ago

Early Migrants
200,000–60,000
years ago

Later Migrants
60,000–40,000
years ago

Moderns
50,000–15,000 years ago

Moderns
15,000–500 years ago

MAP 1.2

found in a web of interrelated factors centered around human behavior, specifically behavior selected to reduce risk and increase the individuals' fitness for survival. Calculated migration must have resulted from information sharing, alliance building, memory, and the ability to negotiate—all skills that necessarily accompanied increasingly complex social and cultural groups. The increasing complexity of existence inevitably led hominids out of Africa, resulting in a global distribution of diverse human groups. Increasing population may have prodded the migration of some groups. Armed with the attributes of culture, the distinctive, complex patterns of behavior shared by human groups, humans eventually adapted to and conquered virtually all global environments.

Whatever the nature of human origins, whenever or wherever human societies and cultures first appeared, the peopling of our globe has been a product of migration from place to place. Given the small numbers of people and the vast distances they traversed, and considering their technologically limited modes of transportation, the movement of people around the globe seems miraculous. It was undertaken entirely by people who walked, and who gathered and hunted food, across and between increasingly diverse and difficult environments.

Interaction Between People and Environments The examples of global colonization described below depended on interactions between people and between people and their environments. Gradually, sometime during the Middle Stone Age (perhaps 100,000 to 200,000 years ago), distinct patterns of interaction among humans and between them and the landscapes in which they lived emerged. Because the distinctive physical and social environments to which humans adapted were themselves constantly changing, cultures too continually changed. That early humans acquired technological and social skills can be inferred from widespread evidence of their material culture—stone tools and utensils, carved figurines, rock and cave art, and the like, dating from about 40,000 years ago—which has been found in most parts of the globe.

Language and Communication Humans also developed language, the highest level of communication skill and one still regarded as unique to humans. As they spread around the globe, our human ancestors developed efficient and various languages as the means of remembering and transmitting information within shared social contexts. Exactly how or when languages emerged remains obscure, but when they did, language and the ability to reason and abstract separated humans from their hominid ancestors, and both reinforced the uniqueness of the species and confirmed its humanity. All human languages, no matter how diverse or singular, are similar in being capable of expressing the needs, desires, and history of their speakers. Few would disagree that the ability to communicate verbally is at the core of the behaviors and increasingly complex social structures of human beings.

Linguistic, fossil, and paleontological evidence, along with oral tradition, have all helped create a broader and more accurate view of world prehistory, one freed of the traditional European perception of history as a ladder of progress. Archaeological evidence has been particularly useful both in establishing a firm basis for human origins and in measuring the ongoing story of our evolving humanity, the extent of prehistoric group behavior, and the origins of both cooperation and conflict. The development of language unquestionably furthered the social and technological evolution of humans and facilitated systems of reciprocity and social exchange. For example, the division of labor in food production and the exchange and transportation of goods and products were greatly expedited by speech. Being able to assign different tasks to different individuals furthered cooperation and fueled the processes of social and cultural evolution.

■ HUMAN ORIGINS: OUT OF AFRICA

The path out of East Africa leads across North Africa, through the Nile corridor, and across the Red Sea, or across the Indian Ocean and the strait of Bab el Mandeb to the Arabian peninsula and beyond to Eurasia. Most of this interconnected landmass of the so-called Old World, the continental area encompassing Africa, Europe, and Asia, received migrants from East Africa by about 1.5 million years ago. Very early Stone Age sites in Algeria, Morocco, and Israel are inconclusively dated, but two Eurasian *Homo erectus* sites, one in Israel and one in the Caucasus Mountains of Central Asia, are accurately dated to about 1.6 million years ago. Elsewhere, on the Deccan Plateau of the Indian subcontinent, locally produced stone hand axes dating to about the same time have been found, while in Central Asia, locally manufactured pebble tools attest to human occupation after 750,000 years ago. Although archaeological evidence of early human habitation in tropical parts of Asia has not been discovered, it is possible that hominids there would have used perishable material such as bamboo rather than stone for their tools, thus making it much more difficult for archaeologists to locate sites.

DAILY LIVES

THE SOUNDS OF PREHISTORY

The daily sounds of the prehistoric world are difficult to imagine. Some scientists argue that before about 100,000 years ago, actual languages did not exist and the only communications were much like the utterances and cries of primates. Monkeys vocalize to express emotion, but only chimpanzees approach the most human of characteristics: speech. Although chimps have about twenty or so vocalizations and gestures for expressing themselves, even they are unable to connect multiple concepts into a single phrase, let alone sequence the thousands of words contained in modern human languages.

The study of hominid fossil skulls suggests a slow evolution of speech among our ancestors. In modern humans, the enlarged front brain and the distinct organizational divisions between the two sides of the brain, called "lateralization," seem essential for the enhancement of human speech, motor skills, and perception. This lateralization appears more than 2 million years ago in Pleistocene ancestors, for whom some form of communication became increasingly necessary for cooperative hunting, seasonal activities, and survival.

After about 100,000 years ago, a cacophony of sounds existed in the prehistoric world. The oldest musical instrument yet discovered dates to between 43,000 and 82,000 years ago. It is a flute made from the hollow leg bone of a young bear. It was found in a Neanderthal cave in Slovenia. Four regularly spaced holes on the instrument attest to its intentional artistry. Even earlier forms of drums and ideophones, single-sounding instruments struck for rhythmic purposes, are likely to have been played by prehistoric individuals and maybe even groups. Whether these sounds would have seemed like music to our ears is another matter. That they celebrated the arrival and orchestration of increasingly human behavior is certainly the case.

Migrations of Early Modern Humans

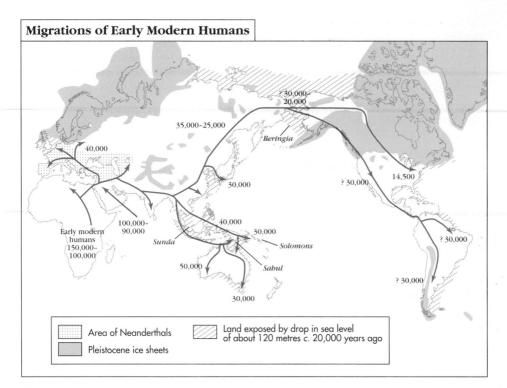

MAP 1.3

EAST AND SOUTHEAST ASIA

The most prominent hominid remains found in East Asia are those of the *Homo erectus* "Peking Man," discovered in the cave complex at Zhoukoudian near Beijing in north China around 1920 and dated to as early as half a million years ago. Associated archaeological

FIGURE 1.7 Skull of *Pithecanthropus pekinensis* Man

SOURCE: American Museum of Natural History, New York, New York. © 1996 David L. Brill/Atlanta.

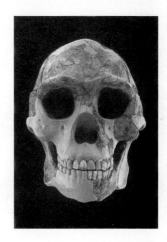

remains indicates that Peking Man (and Woman) ate the meat of wild animals, knew how to make fire to cook food and provide heat, and used stone tools. More recently discovered and still controversial evidence from another north China site has been claimed by some to be as old as 1.7 million years. If this date is correct, it would support an East Asian transition to anatomically modern human species chronologically parallel to that in Africa. However, even more recent finds from south-central China appear to come from a toolmaking member of *Homo* similar to those found in Africa. These finds are dated to about 2 million years ago.

In Southeast Asia, skulls that have been found around the Solo River and at Sangiran in Java are roughly no older than 730,000 years. Their relation to other Asian and African hominids remains obscure, in part due to geographical distance and limited evidence. Though the dating of East and Southeast Asian discoveries is subject to adjustment—recently many have been redated at half the age initially claimed—they indicate the possibility of other evolutionary models than the African route to *Homo erectus.*

EUROPE

The pattern of migration to Europe probably began with the spread of *Homo erectus* from Africa a half-million years ago, considerably later than the migration to Asia. Thanks to the slow retreat of the glaciers, the environment of Europe 1.5 million years ago was less inviting to the African migrants than that of Asia. The settlement of Europe by African migrants is supported by fossil evidence found in Africa, West Asia, and Europe. As the glaciers retreated around 500,000 years ago, Europe became more attractive to emigrants. As the climate improved, so did the food supplies: animal life underwent significant changes, and new species of deer, bovid, rhino, and horse appeared as more favorable foraging conditions emerged. The earliest, most widely distributed European hominid remains are not those of *Homo erectus* but those of the more recent Neanderthal, a name derived from discoveries made at a site in the Neanderthal Valley in modern Germany. Other Late Stone Age peoples, including the anatomically modern *Homo sapiens,* appear to have moved into Europe from West Asia during the earliest retreat of what is called the Wurm glaciation, about 35,000 years ago. These migrants, called Cro-Magnon after a site in the Dordogne Valley in France, eventually displaced earlier ones. However, for more than 15,000 years after modern *Homo sapiens* appeared in Europe, the northern parts of the continent remained unoccupied because of its uncertain climate and unpredictable food resources. At present there is no definite evidence to prove that speciation, the creation of modern *Homo sapiens* from the stock of *Homo erectus,* took place in many different sites in Europe or Asia as well as Africa, or whether a second wave of migration out of Africa accounts for the appearance of anatomically modern humans elsewhere.

Stone Tools   Even the evidence of stone tools fails to solve the mystery of human origins. If one had examined the evidence of stone technology worldwide about 500,000 years ago, tool types would have appeared very similar. By about 50,000 years ago, distinctive differences had appeared: regional specialization in toolmaking reflected cultural evolution and the occupation of different environments requiring different tools. On the basis of available evidence and its chronological pattern, the soundest judgment seems to be that continuous migration from the African continent peopled the adjacent landmass of West Asia and there created an ancient crossroads of cultural interaction. Scattered temporary settlements of

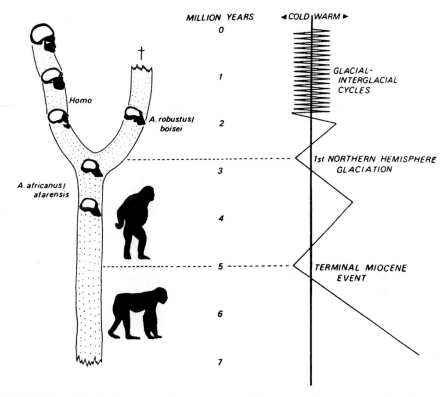

FIGURE 1.8 Possible Links between Environment and Evolution (Speciation and Ice Age)

SOURCE: Clive Gamble, *Timewalkers* (Alan Sutton, Ltd, 1993). General Research Division, New York Public Library, Astor, Lenox and Tilden Foundations.

Stone Age hominid culture appeared in West Asia as they did in most of the habitable world. Evidence of human societies in West Asia dating to about 35,000 B.C.E. is well established. Since there is no evidence of a significant migration of new peoples into West Asia between 1.5 million years ago and 35,000 B.C.E., the people who settled there were probably descendants of the early migrants from Africa. After about 10,000 years ago, their descendants gathered, and later planted, wild grain and were soon building the first West Asian cities.

Long after the first global migration of hominids from Africa to West Asia, beginning about 5000 years ago, the continuity of cultural style suggests the endurance of a population made up of only two or three language groups related to African languages. The development of West Asian culture and social structures was a product of slow change from within rather than an influx of new people coming from without.

Demographic Changes As prehistoric cultures evolved, peoples moved into previously uninhabited areas. It is likely that human population increases were largely responsible for these migrations. The influence of demographic changes, increases or decreases in population size or characteristics, interacted with other aspects of ecology, including cultural and environmental changes, to encourage people to move. Population pressures on scarce or limited resources forced people into ever more restrictive environments that in turn required adaptive strategies. Deserts and arid lands could be colonized by early humans with effective tools, food storage, and social cooperation.

We have already seen that the earliest African migrations extended the achievements of human evolution to other parts of the globe. Since these migrations, more than a million years ago, Africa has never been isolated. Not all migration was permanent, and descendants of early migrants sometimes returned to Africa, resulting in an interchange of peoples, products, and ideas between Africa, West Asia, and the lands bordering the Mediterranean. The Indian Ocean coast of East Africa was another entry point for peoples and their cultures, creatures, and crops. East Africans themselves also ventured on voyages across the Indian Ocean to the Indian subcontinent and ultimately beyond, to China.

Bantu Migration   Among the most historically significant of intra-African migrations was the so-called Bantu expansion, actually a series of population movements from the eastern Nigeria-Cameroon region of West Africa and spreading southward. Possibly beginning more than 7000 years ago, the Bantu expansion involved speakers of related languages that now make up the populations of the southern half of the African continent. This largest and longest of recent African migrations also accounts for the shared cultural and political patterns that have helped to mitigate that continent's environmental and cultural diversity. The movement of Bantu speakers, like the spread of Asian peoples into the Pacific, may initially have been the result of dramatic climatic fluctuation. Both the Bantu and Asian migrations have been documented by archaeological and linguistic evidence, including the similar styles of and decoration on excavated pottery and the shared vocabulary of distant peoples.

Celtic Migration   The Late Stone Age migration of the Celtic people who inhabited the trans-Alpine area north of the Mediterranean basin and west of the Urals was one of the most widespread movements of peoples in Europe. Better conditions and the lure of other cultures drew the Celts south to the Mediterranean and West Asia and west toward the Atlantic and the British Isles, where they settled during the first millennium B.C.E.

The End of the Ice Age   The recession of glaciation permitted migration and settlement from West Asia to Europe, and by the time the ice age ended (ca. 10,000 B.C.E.) distinctive societies and cultures had evolved there. The end of the ice age was of similar significance in East Asia, where it allowed early humans to develop a more complex array of subsistence strategies that included hunting, fishing, gathering, and the use of diversified and specialized tools. For these and other early migrations, historians have only the most general chronological outlines for thousands of people over generations.

Human Ancestors in China   The direct ancestors of the modern Chinese were probably the descendants of the Upper Cave populations at Zhoukoudian, whose remains can be dated to between 12,000 and 20,000 years ago. Although the Upper Cave site appears to have been used for burial purposes rather than habitation, remains found in the Upper Cave indicate that Zhoukoudian people were *Homo sapiens* who hunted in the woods, fished the lakes, and made abundant bone and shell artifacts. Marine shells found in this site

FIGURE 1.9   History of the Zhoukoudian Cave, China

SOURCE: K. C. Chang, *The Archaeology of
Ancient China*, 4th ed. (New Haven,
Conn.: Yale University Press, 1986). Gen-
eral Research Division, New York Public
Library, Astor, Lenox and Tilden Founda-
tions.

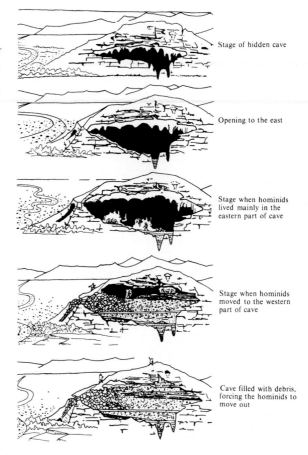

Stage of hidden cave

Opening to the east

Stage when hominids
lived mainly in the
eastern part of cave

Stage when hominids
moved to the western
part of cave

Cave filled with debris,
forcing the hominids to
move out

suggest either extensive trade connections or long-distance seasonal migrations. Human
skeletal remains in the caves include an adult male over sixty, a relatively young male adult,
two young adult females, one adolescent, and two children. One view holds that these were
members of a single family who may have died violently (according to skullcap injuries) and
were buried in the Upper Cave, where the surrounding earth was covered with red hematite,
suggesting that a funeral rite took place. The physical similarities between these people and
the Koreans and Japanese connect them with populations who migrated into the Korean
peninsula and the Japanese archipelago much later. The original settlement of Japan, however, might not have involved a sea crossing. Stone tools discovered in Japanese settlements
may date from around 40,000 B.C.E., when the Japanese islands of Hokkaido, Honshu, and
Kyushu were fused and joined to Sakhalin Island and the Asian mainland.

What all these migrations have in common is the evidence each provides for the extraordinary success story of early human populations. From East Africa to other continents, human
populations steadily increased in number and human groups increased in size and complexity.
Expanding populations sent new migrants into the next valley or across the sea to the next
port, to occupy virtually every conceivable environmental niche on this planet. Population increase has been the single most critical factor shaping the human story.

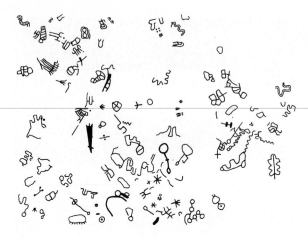

FIGURE 1.10 North American Rock Art Possibly Recording Sleep Visions (Lewis Canyon, Texas)

SOURCE: Courtesy of the Texas Memorial Museum, Austin, Texas. Acc. 2261–57.

MIGRATION BY SEA AND LAND BRIDGES

The peopling of the landmasses we now call Africa and Eurasia was largely accomplished on foot across land, over hundreds of centuries, and by hundreds of generations. Some migrations to other parts of Asia, the Pacific, and the Americas required long-distance travel across water, either by boats or across the temporary land bridges that appeared in various parts of the world during the glacial lowering of the world's sea levels, approximately 50,000 years ago. For some parts of the world—Australia and New Guinea, for example—both land bridges *and* boats would have been necessary for successful human migrations.

The Americas It is generally recognized that the earliest inhabitants of the Americas were immigrants from Asia, though the picture of migration to the Americas is less clear than elsewhere. Biological evidence from blood types and dental patterns indicates that the nearest relatives of the earliest Americans are found in northeast Asia. Disagreement over dating has resulted in debate about who exactly the immigrants were and how and when they arrived. It has long been hypothesized that people came from Eurasia (Siberia) to the northernmost reaches of North America. Pebble tools discovered at a Siberian site only tentatively dated to between 1.5 and 2 million years ago suggest hominid inhabitants in Asia at that date, far earlier than the appearance of humans in Beringia, the area of the connecting bridge between Asia and North America. There is also a lack of evidence south of the ice sheet in the Americas. Consequently, informed opinion places migration from Eurasia across Beringia to the Americas during the period between 12,000 and 35,000 years ago.

The most noncontroversial dates for the peopling of the Americas, 11,000 to 11,500 years ago, are based on evidence of human habitation far to the south of Beringia, at a Clovis, New Mexico, site. There are possibly earlier sites of human habitation which may date back as far as 19,000 years ago in North America and to 33,000 years ago in South America. Though all the dates are controversial, widely accepted evidence indicates that the Americas

FIGURE 1.11 North American Rock Art of Childbirth (Kane Creek, Utah)

PHOTO: Ursula K. LeGuin.

were most likely inhabited by humans around 12,000 years ago. This dating is supported by the widespread evidence in the eastern Arctic regions of Greenland, Canada, and the former Soviet Union. Colonization of the Arctic took place as ice sheets retreated at the end of what is known as the Wisconsin glaciation about 10,000 years ago.

Theories of Settlement The Beringian theory of the arrival of Eurasians in the Americas holds that at the time of the migration to the Americas, Siberia, and central Alaska were connected by a land bridge across what is now the Bering Sea. Having crossed this bridge into the Americas, people found that there were two great fluctuating ice sheets, one covering the area around and south from Hudson Bay, another flowing down the Rockies. Between the two was an ice-free corridor, a route south roughly from the Yukon down through Montana, which humans and animals took as they occupied what had been a land without people.

Another theory of settlement of the Americas is that the Eurasian migrants might have sailed south along an ice-free Pacific Coast. The close connection of the culture of Pacific Coast peoples with marine resources might lend credence to the idea that migration to the Americas was by sea. Important adaptive strategies were developed by Pacific Coast peoples to utilize marine resources: specialized harpoons have been discovered that, with seaworthy canoes, allowed Pacific Coast peoples to kill sea mammals. Some historians have gone as far as suggesting that migration from Asia to the Americas was entirely by boat, across the Pacific Ocean. Similar theories of migration to the Americas across the Atlantic from Africa have also been proposed. None has found general acceptance.

Pacific Island Settlement Human settlement of the Pacific island world, Australia, and New Guinea may have begun as early as 50,000 years ago, although recently excavated Australian rock-shelter sites may testify to human presence there earlier than 60,000 years ago. This was a period of fluctuating glaciation when the sea level was temporarily low. Even so, as much as 50 kilometers (31 miles) of open sea would have had to be crossed to reach Australia, since at no time in the last 3 million years was there a complete land bridge between the Asian and Australian continents. Whether humans arrived as castaways, adrift on logs or other vegetation, or on boats or canoes deliberately constructed for intended voyages, they would have found themselves isolated once the glaciers retreated and the sea returned to its former levels. Along with the human inhabitants of Australia, the fauna and flora were also isolated, each to evolve in ways unique to its isolated environment: kangaroos, for example, are one product of the separation and isolated evolution of species. Recent dating of discoveries of rock engravings, red ochre, and stone artifacts at a site called Jinmium in northwestern Australia may push back the dates of the earliest migrations to between 75,000 and 116,000 years ago, suggesting to some researchers that the first artists were not modern humans at all but rather an earlier, archaic species of *Homo sapiens.* Perhaps art may not be a defining characteristic of human behavior.

Though scattered Early Stone Age sites have been found across much of Australia and New Guinea, full-scale and continuous occupation of these difficult environments began as a result of later migrations during the last glacial age, around 12,000 B.C.E., when Indonesia, Malaya, and Borneo were once again attached to one another and to the Asian mainland. Bands of gathering and hunting people moved steadily eastward and southward. From Indonesia, some crossed by canoe or raft to the continent of New Guinea–Australia–Tasmania. The presence of these new migrants can be documented by linguists, who have studied the distribution and relatedness of Australian Aboriginal languages. Both the expansion of land created by the lowering sea levels and the eventual restriction of lands as the sea rose again effected demographic changes and the movement of peoples.

Southeast Asia A more recent migration of people culturally related to the Southeast Asian mainland has been dated to 7000 years ago. This Late Stone Age migration is divided into four distinct groups, and it is clear that people from both the islands and the mainland of Southeast Asia participated. Were they pushed south by the cold of the extended glaciers or by other northern peoples fleeing harsh environmental changes? Were they propelled by the pressures of expanding populations? The evidence is insufficient to provide an answer. As was the case for most coastal and island settlements, early sites dating to the period of actual migration have been destroyed by the changing sea level.

The Melting of Glaciers By about 3500 B.C.E., the glaciers melted for the last time, and the ▬▬▬▬▬▬▬▬▬▬▬ oceans rose to their present level. The previous land bridges were submerged, and today's archipelagos and islands were created. Until recently it was thought that not long afterward, another wave of migrants, mainland Malays, moved by canoe into Indonesia, the Philippines, Melanesia, and finally Micronesia. There only the easternmost Pacific island world of Polynesia remained unpeopled, to be settled between 1000 B.C.E. and 1300 C.E. These late dates have recently been questioned by archaeological finds dated to about 30,000 B.C.E. in Melanesia, on the islands of New Britain and New Ireland, and in the East China Sea on Okinawa.

The crossing and settling of the Pacific were no more extraordinary than crossing the ice and drifting snow of Beringia to reach the Americas. Both movements are impressive evidence of the wide range of potential human response to environmental change. The final settlement of Polynesia testifies to this flexibility: Polynesians moved from an equatorial tropical zone that had no winter to the cool, seasonal world of New Zealand and eventually to the semitropics of the Hawaiian Islands. Thousands of miles separated these colonies, and a thousand years or more separated their initial settlements. Each colony developed different material cultures in response to different environments. Yet today, as a result of continuous migration, all the Polynesian settlements share related languages and systems of belief.

■

ORIGIN MYTHS: THE FLOOD

One important means of reckoning time has been based on the geologic ages identified through scientific understanding of the changing physical features of the earth. The period between about 12,000 and 7000 B.C.E. was a period of worldwide warming, when the glaciers of the last ice age melted. Like the changing environmental conditions that prehistorians believe initiated human speciation, this period witnessed dramatic ecological responses: rainfall increased and ocean levels rose some 300 feet. Memories of the melting of the glaciers are reflected in flood legends, which are common throughout the world. Some flood legends are integral parts of origin myths, while others reflect punishment on humans who have displeased their creator. In either case they provide compelling arguments for the comparability of early human experience.

For 3000 years following the glacial retreat that marked the end of the ice age, the climates of West Asia and the rest of the world oscillated relatively widely between wet and dry, finally settling around 4000 B.C.E. into the pattern we see today. In lower Iraq, where Sumer was located, by 5000 B.C.E. heavy rains and raised oceans pushed the Persian Gulf coastline up as far north as the vicinity of Baghdad. By 3500 B.C.E., the climate dried, opening up huge expanses of land to settlement. For Sumerians, this "postflood" period was the beginning of their world.

West Asia The West Asian flood story most widely known is the story of Noah and the ark ▬▬▬▬▬▬▬ written into the sacred literatures of Judaism, Christianity, and Islam. In this version, Noah's god, Yahweh, angry at the corruption of humanity, sends a flood to destroy it. But he is merciful to Noah and his family, who do not share in the corruption of the rest of humanity, and allows them to survive. This story dates back to 2800 B.C.E. in the long

Sumerian epic of *Gilgamesh*. The Sumerian epic was picked up and altered by the Assyrians, and it was incorporated into Hebrew creation literature by the seventh century B.C.E.

South Asia Memories of the melting of the glaciers are reflected in other flood legends around the world. In South Asia, early Hindu Vedic hymns (ca. 900 B.C.E.) describe the gods' gift of fire for sacrifices to Manu (Sanskrit for "man"). Manu plays a key role in a South Asian version of the flood story, which is also a creation myth. Manu, warned by a large fish, whom he had earlier befriended, of the coming of a great, destructive flood, builds a boat, hooks it to the fish, and is pulled to a mountaintop, where he remains until the waters recede. He pours a libation of butter and sour milk onto the waters, and from this a woman is created who becomes his wife. Their children are the beginning of a new humanity.

Ancient West Asian cities all had trade links with early urban centers in the Indus basin, and it seems likely that versions of the flood story in all these areas were related. Later versions of the flood story in South Asia are knit more closely to the Hindu sense of the nature of the world. By the sixth century B.C.E., the Hindu time cycle was elaborated, and the flood story acquired a cyclical character, with a new Manu repeatedly producing a new humanity through a new flood.

China Although there is no integrated, systematic origin myth in China, there is a flood legend that provides the background for the rise of a culture hero, Yü, founder of the first dynasty, who ordered the empire out of chaos:

> Yü divided the land. Following the course of the hills, he cut down trees. He determined the highest hills and largest rivers in the several regions. . . .
> Thus throughout the nine provinces order was effected: lands along the waters were everywhere made habitable; hills were cleared of their superfluous wood and sacrificed to; sources of rivers were cleared; marshes were well banked; access to the capital was secured for all within the four seas.

The flood legend in China provides the basis of dynastic rule. It is concerned with the ordering of the physical world, especially the control of flooding, a major problem in the agricultural zone of the north China plain along the Yellow River, and the preparation of the land for farming by a human figure who then rules the people who inhabit the land. The flood is seen as a condition of nature that is altered by human effort, and the human being capable of doing this has proven his ability to rule by channeling and controlling the floodwaters. The West Asian flood tradition identifies the unleashed waters as the gods' (or God's) punishment for humanity's corruption. Purified humanity begins with the survivors of this disaster. The South Asian flood tradition carries something of the same message but adds the unique qualifier that it will be a cyclical, repeating process.

SUMMARY

History begins with the attempts of humans to understand their beginnings. The earliest attempts at history were origin stories, and they were produced in the language of metaphor and myth, a language that has its own historical truth. We know about them because they have been passed down orally from generation to generation and, in modern times, collected and recorded. Initially, professional historians were skeptical of such sources, but in recent years they have become accepted evidence for understanding and reconstructing the distant past. Historians have also accepted the evidence of such sciences as archaeology and paleontology. By broadening their sources, historians have come closer to understanding both the variety and the commonality of world prehistory. This chapter is based on the assumption that the earliest record of our shared human past is global and that evidence of it existed long before writing. Nonwritten sources of evidence—both oral testimony and "bones and stones"—along with methods from other disciplinary fields such as archaeology and literature have been increasingly and effectively used by historians to reconstruct a past that existed before writing. To suggest that history begins with written records denies that oral cultures and preliterate peoples have any history at all. Every society has its own way of presenting its unique historical vision, the shape of which may vary from generation to generation and which can be known through a variety of historical evidence: archaeological, oral, and written.

The questions of who our ancestors were and where they originated may never be answered with absolute finality, but the understanding of what happened as humans evolved from hominid ancestors and how they spread out around the world becomes clearer and clearer as more material evidence is discovered. The reaction of humans to one another and to the places in which they lived produced a variety of distinctive cultures around the world, and the remains of these cultures provide increasingly solid evidence of early human experiences. The origins and development of human culture in various societies will be discussed in subsequent chapters, in which the historical processes that carried human societies from their most distantly remembered past to the present will be addressed. The themes of shared humanity and human purpose will guide our journey through world history just as surely as they did the journeys of our ancestors when they moved out from the prehistoric East African forests and savannas to create new worlds.

FIGURE 1.12 Caricature of Charles Darwin (Ca. 1880)

SOURCE: *Punch* Magazine, 1881.

MAN IS BVT A WORM

ENGAGING THE PAST

EVOLUTION AND CREATIONISM

The biologist Charles Darwin had been dead for forty-three years when he was placed on trial in the small, sleepy town of Dayton, Tennessee. The Scopes trial captured international attention in July 1925. The "Monkey Trial," as it came to be known, pitted the theory of evolution associated with Darwin against the traditional views of Christian fundamentalists, who held that divine creation alone was responsible for the beginnings of humankind. The trial pitted the urbane Clarence Darrow, a famous criminal lawyer and avowed agnostic, against the folk hero of rural America, William Jennings Bryan. The high school biology teacher John Thomas Scopes, on trial for violating the State of Tennessee's antievolution laws, was convicted and fined. Outside the courtroom, the monkey motif was everywhere: from children with monkey toys to circus men displaying chimpanzees. Booksellers hawked Bibles and biological treatises. In the end publicity exposed the antievolutionary beliefs of fundamentalists to national ridicule and helped prevent similar "monkey laws" from enactment in other states. For decades following, the fear of controversy had an impact on textbook production.

The Scopes trial debated a controversy between new and old orders or paradigms, of which evolution was the pivot. Few persons failed to have an opinion, and few changed their minds as they watched and read about the trial. Behind the farce and comedy lay disturbing issues of change for the generation of the 1920s. Darwin was held responsible for everything from destructive nationalism to socialist Germany. Remarkably different worldviews embraced science and academic freedom, seeking to demonstrate the compatibility of science and religion, on the one side, while others eyed the same ideas with suspicion from the other side. In Darwin's view, evolution was purposeless, nonprogressive, and materialistic. Evolutionary theory dramatically altered our view of the past and our place in the natural world. The history of the material world shows little if any of the unilinear progress once imagined but rather shares with natural history the story of balance, seemingly punctuated by singular, if dramatic or even catastrophic, events. The patterns and lessons of history remain the creation of the historian, whose reconstructions reflect the constraints and opportunities, the values and politics of particular historical and social contexts.

Few debates in world history before or since Darwin have presented such clear and contending positions about meaning, politics, and nature. Charles Darwin is buried in Westminster Abbey, London. Despite the accumulated facts of evolution, the debate about history and meaning is still alive.

SUGGESTIONS FOR FURTHER READING

Kwang-chih Chang, *The Archaeology of Ancient China* (New Haven, Conn.: Yale University Press, 1986 [1963]). Revised fourth edition of a classic work by a leading anthropologist-archaeologist. Detailed illustrations and account of human beginnings in China.

Steve Jones, Robert Martin, and David Pilbeam, eds., *The Cambridge Encyclopedia of Human Evolution* (Cambridge, England: Cambridge University Press, 1992). Comprehensive presentations of the major issues in human evolution. Excellent bibliography and supplemental materials.

Richard G. Klein, *The Human Career: Human Biological and Cultural Origins* (Chicago: University of Chicago Press, 1989). Summarizes issues, emphasizing the African evidence; already a bit outdated.

Changing Environments, Changing Societies

W hat follows is an account by the Roman writer Pliny the Younger of the eruption of Mount Vesuvius on the Italian peninsula on August 24, 79 C.E., that destroyed and buried the towns of Pompeii and Herculaneum. After describing his uncle's heroic efforts to rescue people with ships of the fleet he commanded off the coast, Pliny records his own escape:

> By now it was dawn, but the light was still dim and faint. The buildings round us were already tottering, and the open space we were in was too small for us not to be in real and imminent danger if the house collapsed. This finally decided us to leave the town. We were followed by a panic-stricken mob of people wanting to act on someone else's decision in preference to their own (a point in which fear looks like prudence), who hurried us on our way by pressing hard behind in a dense crowd. Once beyond the buildings we stopped, and there we had some extraordinary experiences which thoroughly alarmed us. The carriages we had ordered to be brought out began to run in different directions though the ground was quite level, and would not remain stationary even when wedged with stones. We also saw the sea sucked away and apparently forced by the earthquake: at any rate it receded from the shore so that quantities of sea creatures were left stranded on dry sand. On the landward side a fearful black cloud was rent by forked and quivering bursts of flame, and parted to reveal great tongues of fire, like flashes of lightning magnified in size. . . .
>
> Soon afterwards the cloud sank down to earth and covered the sea; it had already blotted out Capri and hidden the promontory of Misenum from sight. Then my mother implored, entreated and commanded me to escape as best I could—a youth might escape, whereas she was old and slow and could die in peace as long as she had not been the cause of my death too. I refused to save myself without her, and grasping her hand forced her to quicken her pace. She gave in reluctantly, blaming herself for delaying me. Ashes were already falling, not as yet very thickly. I looked round: a dense black cloud was coming up behind us, spreading over the earth like a flood. "Let us leave the road while we can still see," I said, "or we shall be knocked down and trampled underfoot in the dark by the crowd behind." We had scarcely sat down to rest when darkness fell, not the dark of a moonless or cloudy night, but as if the lamp been put out in a closed room. You could hear the shrieks of women, the wailing of infants, and the shouting of men; some were calling their parents, others their children or their wives, trying to recognize them by their voices. People bewailed their own fate or that of their relatives, and there were some who prayed for death in their terror of dying. Many besought the aid of the gods, but still more imagined there were no gods left, and that the universe was plunged into eternal darkness for evermore. There were people, too, who added to the real perils by inventing fictitious dangers: some reported that part of Misenum had collapsed or another part was on fire, and though

FIGURE 2.0 *Vesuvius in Eruption,* by
J. M. W. Turner, 1827.
Watercolor.

SOURCE: Yale Center for British Art,
Paul Mellon Collection. Photo by Richard
Caspole. B1975.4.1857.

their tales were false they found others to believe them. A gleam of light returned, but we took this to be a warning of the approaching flames rather than daylight. However, the flames remained some distance off; then darkness came on once more and ashes began to fall again, this time in heavy showers. We rose from time to time and shook them off, otherwise we should have been buried and crushed beneath their weight. I could boast that not a groan or cry of fear escaped me in these perils, but I admit that I derived some poor consolation in my mortal lot from the belief that the whole world was dying with me and I with it.

At last the darkness thinned and dispersed like smoke or cloud; then there was genuine daylight, and the sun actually shone out, but yellowish as it is during an eclipse. We were terrified to see everything changed, buried deep in ashes like snowdrifts. We returned to Misenum where we attended to our physical needs as best we could and then spent an anxious night alternating between hope and fear. Fear predominated, for the earthquakes went on, and several hysterical individuals made their own and other people's calamities seem ludicrous in comparison with their frightful predictions.

43

■

INTRODUCTION: NATURE AND CULTURE

Not all interactions between humans and their landscapes were as dramatic as the devastating volcanic eruption of Mount Vesuvius described by Pliny the Younger, but all were characteristic of the essence of history: change and continuity. Global migration and colonization by early humans presented a sequence of changing landscapes and eventually brought people into intimate contact with every natural environment the globe offers. People's very movements brought about changes, too. The connections between people and the landscapes they inhabit, each affecting the other, constitute a central theme in world history. In this chapter, we examine the different ways in which humans have been part of ecosystems, the patterns by which environmental and human histories are intricately woven together.

Culture is the patterned behaviors which a social group develops to understand, use, and survive its environment. Culture is shaped by human and natural forces; it encompasses both ideas and artifacts and includes such things as technology, language, beliefs, and values. Transmitted both consciously and unintentionally, culture perpetuates itself as learned behavior, molding the ways societies behave across generations. Though individuals make use of inherited cultural knowledge to guide their actions and interpret their experiences, cultures are not permanently fixed. They undergo change as members of a society learn new things and encounter and respond to new experiences, ideas, and peoples. In this way cultures reconstruct themselves. Early cultures, the subject of this chapter, have been identified by studying archaeological finds; patterned cultural variations called style can be observed in the evidence of material culture, such as 2-million-year-old stone tools or the rock art that began to appear about 40,000 years ago. Style helped ensure continuity of peoples and their groups, and it enabled groups to retain the memory of valuable information, such as the manufacturing process of a hand ax, beyond a single lifetime. As groups spread out across the globe, this communication and its historical memory became critical to the community's survival.

■

TECHNOLOGY AND HUMAN CULTURE

No aspect of culture had a greater impact on human history than did technology, the totality of means used to create objects necessary for human survival and comfort. The earliest axmakers shaped pebbles into tools and changed the course of history. The manufacturing process required manual dexterity and the development of a means of remembering the sequential steps of production. It has been estimated that more than 100 separate, precise blows were needed to shape an individual stone into a useful flint tool. Technology includes ideas as well as tools because it relies on human memory. The continuity of technological styles required the communication of complex processes from one generation to the next. Technological change became the cutting edge, so to speak, of human history, as tools replaced biological evolution as the main source of change.

Knowledge and Specialization The acquisition of tools also necessitated the control of knowledge. By about 20,000 years ago, some of the earliest human artifacts appear to be associated with the control of specialized information. These magical objects of carved antler or bone are called batons by archaeologists, who interpret their use as devices for extending human memory. Engraved markings on many of these objects refer to observed patterns of nature, such as lunar phases or seasonal migrations of animals. Possession of batons would have enabled those skilled in their translation to predict changes in the landscape. Such tools also created and altered people's inner landscapes, how humans perceived the world around themselves. Symbols that could be used and reused to manipulate the world constituted a source of power. The power was accumulated by those specialists, who recognized the imagined possibilities of technology and who could express them successfully in the physical world, whether in the identification of seasons or the shaping of stone tools. No further biological adaptations were necessary for human expansion into new environments. Rather, cultural innovations, especially the invention of clothing and shelter, enabled the successful human career. Using tools, human communities began to thrive in the new environments into which they expanded, and they altered the physical landscape as they conquered the globe.

■

TECHNOLOGY, ENVIRONMENT, AND CULTURE

Another important determinant of culture is environment, the landscapes in which people live. Throughout history, cultures have been influenced by the natural worlds in which they are rooted. Although humans moved from place to place—collectively, an average of about 200 miles per year in their earliest migrations—they also became attached to specific landscapes. Environment thus plays a major role in the construction of culture and in cultural variation. For example, Inuit culture, shaped by its Arctic environment, necessarily differs from that of the East African peoples of the Serengeti plains or the Rift Valley. Inuit technology allowed adaptation to the extremely cold temperatures of a world of ice and snow and provided specialized tools of bone and stone for fishing and hunting seals. The stable freshwater lakes of East Africa, on the other hand, provided vastly different conditions for establishing scavenging, hunting, and fishing technologies in its warm, prehistoric wooded savanna and grassland environment.

Just as contacts with other ethnic groups resulted in cultural readjustment and change (as, for instance, the recent Euro-American impact has destroyed the nomadic Inuit culture), so too did ancient environmental change contribute to cultural change. For example, Saharan dessication occurred after about 15,000 years ago, drying up the region's great lakes and rivers and creating a vast desert in which hippopotamus and elephant could no longer survive. The dramatic environmental shift caused major changes in early African cultures and required equally dramatic shifts in lifestyles and technologies, even the forced migration of populations. Archaeologists have identified tool kits among the artifacts carried by the early emigrants in their global colonization, suggesting the importance of retaining technological information in times of changing environments.

ECOLOGY AND CULTURE

The cultural relationship between humans and their environment varied according to people's perceptions of the landscape. In this way, technology and culture altered both the inner landscape of the individual and the physical landscape of the natural world. Though in the modern world, influenced by the powerful impact of industrialization, we tend to see nature as some-

Global Environmental Zones

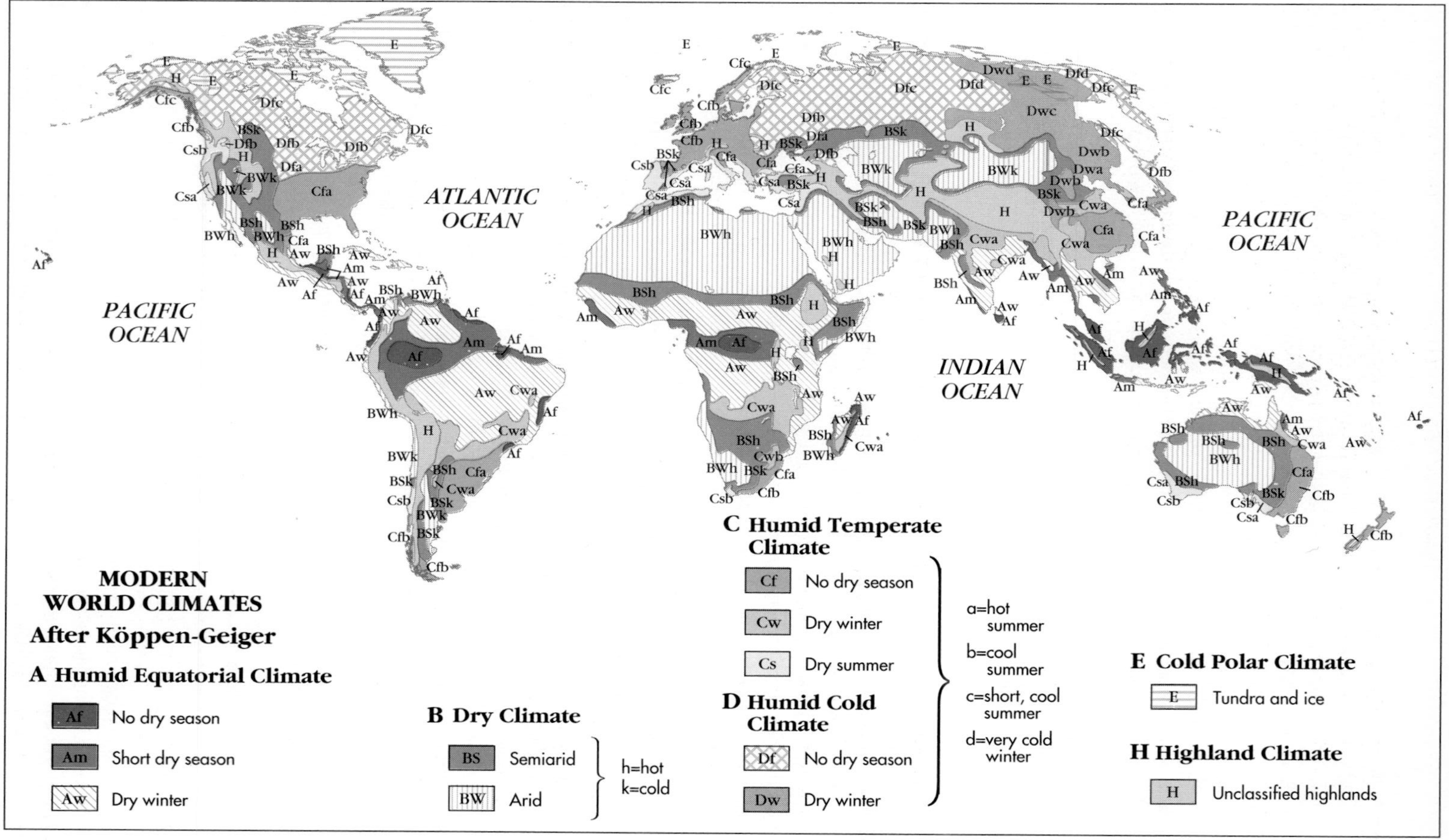

PACIFIC OCEAN

ATLANTIC OCEAN

PACIFIC OCEAN

INDIAN OCEAN

**MODERN
WORLD CLIMATES
After Köppen-Geiger**

A Humid Equatorial Climate

Af	No dry season
Am	Short dry season
Aw	Dry winter

B Dry Climate

BS	Semiarid
BW	Arid

h=hot
k=cold

C Humid Temperate Climate

Cf	No dry season
Cw	Dry winter
Cs	Dry summer

a=hot summer
b=cool summer
c=short, cool summer
d=very cold winter

D Humid Cold Climate

Df	No dry season
Dw	Dry winter

E Cold Polar Climate

E	Tundra and ice

H Highland Climate

H	Unclassified highlands

MAP 2.1 SOURCE: Original.

FIGURE 2.1 Headdress (*chi wara kun*) (Female) (Bambara peoples, Bamako region, Mali)

SOURCE: National Museum of African Art, Eliot Elisofon Photographic Archives, Smithsonian Institution Washington, DC. Gift of Dr. Ernst Anspach and Museum purchase. Photo by Franko Khoury.

thing to be dominated and controlled by human effort, early human cultures were shaped and informed by an awareness of the power of nature. Even in modern times, many peoples, such as the Fang in Africa and Native Americans, believe that humans must seek a balance between themselves and the natural world, not try to dominate or control it. The human-built order of the Fang village and its dependence on the surrounding Central African rain forest was a balancing act shaping the Fang culture. Modern ecology similarly derives its core notion of the essential relationship between human society and nature from this kind of thinking.

The Bambara of Mali believed that a being known as Chi Wara guided humans in their dealings with the environment. The superhuman Chi Wara was envisioned as an antelope who introduced agriculture and selflessly taught humans how to manipulate the plant world. Chi Wara was the connecting link between humans and the earth, animals, and plants. Like the sage-kings of Chinese antiquity, who taught people the arts of agriculture and medicine (which required extensive knowledge of horticulture) as well as animal husbandry, Chi Wara was a powerful figure who mediated between human society and the natural world. Although concern with the order of human society and the arts of human culture became predominant characteristics of Chinese thought, the school of thought in early China known as Daoism displayed a sharp sensitivity to the need for humans to live in harmony with nature, to acknowledge and appreciate the patterns of human birth, life, and death as part of the constant transformation of nature.

Based on a belief in the oneness of all things—humans, stones, trees, water, animals—Native American cultures were shaped by the environments in which they took form. Native Americans of the Northwest Coast regulated their activities around the natural life patterns of the salmon; the pattern of Inuit life was determined by the seasons: caribou hunts and fishing in the summer, seal hunts and ice fishing in the winter. Even their homes were seasonally determined: tentlike structures in the summer, ice structures in the winter. Such societies minimized their demands on their ecosystems by moving their settlements in accordance with natural patterns. For these societies, cultural activity and the cycle of environmental change were interdependent.

What these differing views have in common is an acknowledgment that the relationship between human society and the environment, whatever it is, is fundamental. The influence of nature on human societies and the ways different cultures have responded to their places in the natural world are crucial elements of historical understanding and basic to the ways in which cultures explain their pasts. Studying these relationships also increases our understanding of the past as process. Seeing human historical events in the context of long-term ecological or geological time produces a perspective on human history and a set of historical concerns very different from one based on single historical events or the accomplishments of individuals. The work of the French historian Fernand Braudel has had a profound influence on contemporary historians, encouraging them to set the study of historical events into the context of slow geological time and stressing the relationship between human history and the environment.

Awareness of the relationship between environment and historical cultures has also been heightened and intensified by current ecological concerns. How the Romans polluted their water sources, the extent to which West African iron smelters deforested their environment, the relationship between population and resources in Chinese history—these historical problems echo familiarly in the late twentieth century. The continuum between past and present gives shape to historical inquiry. In the sections that follow, we will deal with some of the aspects of ecology that were affected by a variety of technologies and methods of subsistence employed by early human communities.

■ WORLD DEMOGRAPHY

The major feature of world populations through time has been their increasing numbers. Historical demography is the study of changes in population in history. The natural biological increase of early human populations reflected the initial success of the species in adapting to a variety of changing environments. It is likely that many early human migrations resulted

DAILY LIVES

CROWDED DAILY LIVES

From a global perspective, the biggest consequence of the sedentary and farming communities appearing between about 4,000 and 10,000 years ago was the increased rates of population growth. Communities became crowded. Larger, denser settlements were common to every continent. Agricultural peoples experienced more than the annoyances of crowded, daily lives. They had less balanced diets, tooth decay for probably the first time in human history (if adult burials are the indicator), and occasionally longer lifespans despite more susceptibility to contagious diseases, possibly as a result of their closer association with animals and animal viruses. They also had higher fertility rates.

Did these early settled populations enjoy more sex? Probably not. Most of the demographic increases common to prehistory were not the result of migrations or shifts in mortality rates but rather appear to have been associated with higher

fertility rates. Why settled agriculturalists gave birth to more children is a matter of speculation. Demographic studies of contemporary gathering and hunting peoples provide a possible clue. Although many factors can affect the number of births each female has during her lifetime, birth spacing as a result of breast-feeding has been observed in many populations. Nursing a child stimulates hormones that suppress ovulation and menstruation (called lactational amenorrhea) with the consequence of producing a birth-spacing pattern that reduces fertility rates. Because infant formulas (high-carbohydrate, easy-to-digest cereals, and animal milk) were more readily available in the diets of agriculturalists than those of gatherers and hunters, infants were weaned from mother's milk at an earlier age, and the space between births became considerably shorter. The result was a trend in population growth that has characterized a more crowded human history ever since.

from the pressure of such demographic increases on limited food resources. Although the long-term, cumulative trend of human populations has been in the direction of a regular increase over time, increases were not always possible or desirable in the shorter-term historical experience of individual groups and societies. Disease, drought, famine, war, and natural disasters figure among the causes of temporary declines of populations in parts of the world. As we will see, the success of ever-larger human groups was dependent on cultural innovations, especially technology. The relationship between demographic change and technical innovation has led some scholars to suggest that constant population increase should be considered one defining characteristic of human achievement. While neither demography nor any other single factor can explain human history, the increasing size of human communities has challenged their members throughout world history by providing both an impetus for change and a reminder that humans live within the context and limits of a natural world.

GATHERING-HUNTING SOCIETIES AND ETHNOARCHAEOLOGY

For most of human history, people lived in relatively small groups, gathering and hunting what they needed from their immediate environments. Success was ultimately measured by the group's survival.

Subsistence Strategies Sometimes effective subsistence strategies depended on people's seasonal movements, sometimes on their cooperation, and sometimes on the occasional sharing, storage, and exchange of foods. For tens of thousands of years and, in some parts of the world throughout the twentieth century, such subsistence patterns survived. Gathering and hunting were essential activities of the earliest cultures, as they provided the

FIGURE 2.2 Rock Art of Women Gathering Food (Sahara, 4500 B.C.E.)

SOURCE: Photo by P. Colombel.

basic food supplies. The continuing search for food sources was a motivating force for human migration that resulted in global colonization.

From 30,000 years ago to the present day, gatherers and hunters have occupied many different environments, from the Arctic to the tropics. Much of what we surmise of life in the Late Stone Age has been extrapolated from studies of very recent gathering and hunting peoples. Though the study of modern hunters and gatherers may provide useful information, it cannot be viewed as a mirror of Stone Age cultures. Today gatherers and hunters live in barely sustaining environments that are far different from the prehistoric landscapes of even a few thousand years ago, which were richer in resources. Today's gatherer-hunter life systems are, however, sufficiently comparable to those of the Late Stone Age that they offer some important examples for interpreting the archaeological record.

Ethnoarchaeology is the methodology of studying living peoples in order to understand past cultures known only through archaeology. Ethnoarchaeological observations of recent gathering and hunting societies have revealed the complementary importance of the gathering of plant foods by women and the hunting activities of men.

Gender Gender describes the socially constructed roles and meaning ascribed to being female or male. If the gender divisions of labor in early gathering and hunting societies were comparable to ethnoarchaeological examples, women's subsistence efforts contributed the bulk of the prehistoric diet. In a modern study of the San people of the central Kalahari desert in southern Africa, gathering by women produced more than 95 percent of the diet by weight. The wealth of women's detailed knowledge of plants and the environment appears to have ensured their special powers in prehistoric societies. Women gatherers likely played a pivotal role in the gradual intensification of plant-collecting activities. The focus on gathering specific foods to satisfy the needs of ever-larger social groupings is thought to have led many human societies to the doorstep of agriculture. Of course, the gender divisions of known gathering and hunting societies may not have existed uniformly and unambiguously in the past. The early rock art associated with the San, for example, occasionally depicts women holding bows and arrows and suggests that women may have hunted as well.

The traditional view of prehistoric cultures has been that they became complex as a result of the development of agriculture and human settlement in permanent communities that were hierarchical and patriarchical and in which labor, duties, and responsibilities were gender-specific. Knowledge gained by the methods of ethnoarchaeology challenges the view that sedentary agrarian societies were a prerequisite for such cultural complexity. Ample evidence indicates that gathering and hunting peoples did not wander aimlessly across prehistoric landscapes but engaged in systematic and ordered activities. Their cultures included not only stone technologies and temporary, simple shelters but body art and rock engravings, religious practices, and artistic expression as well. Gathering-hunting peoples enjoyed a rich ritual life, their social relations were relatively egalitarian with respect to labor and gender, and they appear to have had more leisure time and greater flexibility of lifestyle than later cultivators of plants or domesticators of animals.

One of the causes of many migrations, and also of the formation of sedentary cultures, is believed to have been climatic changes, which made adjustments in the relationship between humans and their environments necessary. The climatic changes were often slow, natural processes: for example, the African Sahara became a vast, dry desert in the course of fluctuations between 10,000 B.C.E. and 1000 C.E. Change may also have been the result of human intervention, sustained manipulation of the natural world, and overexploitation of natural resources: such environmental abuse is not confined to the present day. Extensive alteration of the environment, whether of natural or human origin, made it essential that humans change their subsistence patterns. It was not, however, necessary for change to be as extensive as the shift from gathering-hunting to sedentary agarian cultures. Detailed scholarly regional studies, such as have been undertaken by archaeologists in southern Africa, indicate how prehistoric cultures there reflect their environmental conditions and how humans have adjusted to these conditions over time. Patterned movements of early populations, resulting from changes in environment and population size, as well as from conscious scheduling of seasonal activities, have been revealed by early tool kits discovered in South Africa. Though these artifacts are imperfect and incomplete (their stone components were preserved while wood, bone, plant fibers, and shells did not survive), they have made it possible to identify the patterned, seasonal movements of early populations. Such evidence indicates that prehistoric peoples in the Western Cape region of southern Africa exploited marine resources part of the year and then moved inland, where they followed territorial herds of small mammals and intensively collected plants and tubers in other seasons. Beginning 20,000 years ago, the culture of these peoples was based on a complex, interactive pattern of land use and technology adapted to their region.

It is important to understand that many of the traditions of earlier gathering-hunting peoples were retained by succeeding agriculturalists. The knowledge of flora and fauna that were not normally a part of agricultural diets (such as edible insects, grubs, and wild plants) was used by farmers during famines and droughts. Although they can seem to be archaeologically "invisible" next to the splendor of later villages, towns, and monumental architecture, the gathering-hunting populations and their unique patterns of relationships between environment and society remained important to the herders, sedentary farmers, and townsfolk who succeeded them.

■

EARLY ECOLOGIES

The earliest gathering-hunting societies had a profound effect on their environments. Even though early humans had no more than stone or bone tools at their disposal, they altered the environment more significantly than other species with whom they shared this planet. Early gathering-hunting societies, which might be expected to have been less destructive of their environments than later agricultural and sedentary societies with their greater potential for ecological abuse, did not enjoy an idyllic relationship with nature.

The simplest levels of technology were capable of altering the environment and adversely affecting users' health. Smoke from fires in small, closed, poorly ventilated houses would have caused chronic pulmonary disease in Stone Age humans. Human-built fires, especially the burning of forests and fields, left a residue of pollutants that can be found in the last 100,000 years of polar ice strata. Pollutants such as lead aerosols, produced by ancient metallurgical technologies, have been detected in polar strata dating to periods as early as 800 B.C.E.

The botanical evidence available in lake-bottom sediments in Asia and East Africa suggests that significant modifications in plant and animal communities took place there as a result of prehistoric human activities such as the manufacture and use of substances that turned out to be poisonous to plants and fish. Intensive resource collecting, overhunting, and overgrazing also created disequilibrium and change in early ecologies. The loss of primary forest cover and destruction of the world's rain forests, currently a major global ecological concern, first began as a result of the systematic application of fire as an aid to hunting and food preparation. Agricultural change is only one way in which increasingly populated societies adapted their cultural lifestyles to the changing landscape.

Agriculture   Agriculture is the domestication of plants and animals to make them more pro-
▭▭▭▭▭▭   ductive. The processes of deforestation accelerated with the introduction of agricultural practices, the intensified use and genetic manipulation of plants and animals to make them more productive, and new technologies, such as pottery making and metallurgy, that utilized fire. Pollution and deforestation have been the seemingly inevitable artifacts of human technological history from ancient to contemporary times.

The pulse model describes the interaction of environmental and cultural changes. This model imagines environmental change as creating a pulselike response in societies: a wave of reactions in the form of specialization, further adaptation to microenvironments, and an increase in economic and social opportunities. This model does not see environmental change as deterministic, that is, as necessarily bringing about a certain kind of response or adaptation by humans. However, by stressing the impact of environment as the primary agency of change, the model offers an explanation of the diversity of human societies and the discontinuity of their varying development. In order to survive in the face of critical environmental change, societies often must construct new identities through redefinition of the relationship between nature and human culture.

Archaeological evidence has tended to suggest that the populations of agricultural communities were greater than those of smaller-scale gathering-hunting societies. In many parts of the world, farms and fields used primarily for herding and grazing did supplant the diverse resources on which the foraging and hunting peoples depended. Yet remarkably, agriculture was not universally exclusive or desirable, and gathering-hunting lifestyles persisted in many cultures where knowledge of cultivation was present. The process of replacement, overlap, and interaction between agricultural societies and gathering, hunting, fishing, or herding ways of life contributed to the emerging complexity of world cultures.

■

TRANSITIONAL SOCIETIES

Skara Brae, a Preagricultural   Complex, settled human communities that existed before the
Community   emergence of sedentary agriculture are known as transitional so-
▭▭▭▭▭▭▭▭▭▭▭▭▭▭▭▭▭▭   cieties.

Skara Brae, in the Orkney Islands off the northwest coast of Scotland, is a splendidly preserved example of such a community. Around 2500 B.C.E., various populations that practiced agriculture were migrating to Britain from the European continent. They brought with them livestock and seed and destroyed Britain's forests to clear the land for cultivation and herding, beginning a change that would permanently alter the landscape of the British Isles. While this process was under way, the gathering-hunting-fishing-pastoral community of Skara Brae flourished, isolated from and resistant to the new people who had moved onto the mainland to the south and the practices they had brought with them.

When the sands of the shore that had covered Skara Brae three millennia before shifted, an unmatched picture of the life of a transitional British community that existed without agriculture was revealed. The inhabitants of Skara Brae were isolated from all intercourse with the outside world and forced to rely on what their limited and rather bleak environment provided them. Lacking metals and having almost no imported objects, they exclusively used locally manufactured implements of stone and bone. The community was supported by an abundant supply of shellfish, seabirds, fish, and venison, which apparently were so plentiful that specialized fishing and hunting equipment was not required. Crops were not planted, but, in addition to hunting, the community kept herds of sheep and cattle. Life in this isolated, self-supporting, and independent hunting-herding community may have been hard, but it was relatively peaceful: no armaments were found.

The hamlet of Skara Brae consisted of a communal workshop and about a half-dozen houses, several times rebuilt, some of which were about 1.4 square meters (15 square feet) in size. Each had a central hearth, on either side of which were fixed beds. There were dressers and cupboards and an efficient sewage system of slate-slab drains. The dwellings and the furniture, as well as the implements, were all manufactured of stone. All the structures were huddled together and connected by narrow, roofed alleyways, for mutual warmth and shelter. The indications are that life was not neat and orderly. Shells and bones were scattered haphazardly over floors, beds, and cupboards. The pendants, pins, and beads made in the community, together with its equipment and tools, exhibit a certain aesthetic sense as well as providing an impressive example of environmental accommodation.

Sedentism (settling down in one place) was easier in environments rich in resources not easily depleted than it was at Skara Brae. In other transitional societies, the environment for hunting and gathering was lusher and more bountiful and could sustain ever-higher population levels without the group's having to resort to agriculture and its labor-intensive practices. The Pacific Northwest of the North American continent and the "aquatic" civilizations of west-central Africa are two such examples. In both, marine resources and fishing were abundant enough to support sizable villages. Preagrarian settled communities had their own individual technologies, some of which were also used by sedentary agricultural societies. Grinding slabs and stones in West Asia dating from about 15,000 years ago were used to process gathered seeds, nuts, and berries. The sickles of Ethiopian harvesters cut wild, not domesticated, grains. Pottery, once principally associated with agriculture, has been widely found in transitional villages without domesticated crops. Sedentism itself required both cultural continuity and change. Disease control was a new requirement of larger populations aggregated in permanent settlements, whose complexity included management of water resources, parasites, and infectious diseases previously unknown to more mobile populations. The use of gathering-hunting tools such as stone hammers and scrapers was continued by much later agricultural communities. Given this continuity, agriculture appears not to have been technologically revolutionary; it was, however, a successful response to the growing needs of increasing populations around the world.

■

EARLY AGRICULTURAL MODELS

Since sedentary agriculture entails more consistent effort and less flexible labor requirements and patterns of settlement than hunting and gathering, why did early peoples take up this more demanding way of life? Among the possible explanations are stress or crisis, the effect of a demographic change, such as overpopulation, or an environmental change, such as an alteration in climate. By endangering previously successful subsistence strategies or creating op-

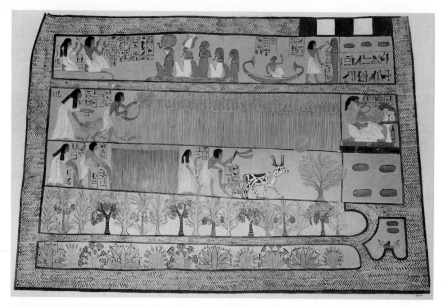

FIGURE 2.3 Deceased and Wife in Fields of Iaru, Adoring Deities. Tomb of Sennedjem, Egyptian Wall Painting (Thebes. Dynasty IX). (Detail), Copyist: Charles T. Wilkinson.

The intensification of agriculture in the Nile Valley was recorded in Egyptian art and beliefs about rebirth.

SOURCE: The Metropolitan Museum of Art, New York.

portunities for new, more productive ones, both could act as catalysts to induce modifications in ways of life. Agricultural practices might require greater effort, but they had the potential to sustain larger populations on smaller areas than gathering-hunting practices did.

Scenarios for the Beginnings of Agriculture   The emergence of various agricultural systems and sedentary societies occurred quite independently and followed different scenarios in many different parts of the world. Until quite recently, it had been assumed that agricultural origins were limited to several centers: the river valleys of Africa and Asia (the Nile, Tigris-Euphrates, Indus, and Yellow Rivers). From these centers, it was supposed that the "idea" of agriculture diffused to other regions of the world. But the pattern of agricultural origins as now understood is far more complicated than this fairly simplistic model would suggest. There were also other agricultural centers, indicating multiple agrarian origins: for example, some West Asian sites, exceptionally well suited to preserving botanical and archaeological evidence of early cultivation, were not in river valleys but in dry, temperate, upland areas.

WEST ASIAN AGRICULTURAL BEGINNINGS

Sometime between 9000 and 6000 B.C.E., gathering and hunting peoples in West Asia gradually became both sedentary and reliant on domesticated plants and animals that they had previously collected wild. The emergence of agriculture in West Asia followed the creation of permanent settlements. The earliest such settlements found thus far are in Iran, Iraq, Syria, and Turkey, located in hill country between mountains and plains, near but not on rivers and streams. These are regions of complex ecology that offer a changing variety of wild food sources throughout the year. The people of these early settlements are called "Natufian," after the name of the earliest identified site. They lived on collected wild foods: grains such as emmer, einkorn, barley, and rye. They also exploited gazelle, cattle, sheep, goats, birds, fish, and molluscs.

A few of the early Natufian sites show some indication of small round wood and clay huts. At one such site, Ain Mellaha, people lived in about fifty houses, one or two of them painted with red ochre. At all the sites, polished stones were used to grind the collected grains. The grain was stored in pits lined with clay that had been hardened by fire. Such storage techniques, which allowed the preservation and the gradual biological evolution of more productive grains, are thought to be a necessary first step to grain domestication.

Staying in one place through the seasons year after year allowed for the effect of accidents; a spillage of gathered barley germinating near the settlement, for example, might have been the inspiration for habitual "spillage," or sowing, of seed in a nearby field. In this fashion, the development of agriculture took generations of trial and error. The evidence from West Asia suggests that it could have taken 1500 years before settled generations produced, around 7500 B.C.E., an unmistakable pattern of deliberate planting of wheat and barley around settlements wherein there also lived domesticated dogs, sheep, and goats.

Domestication of Animals   The beginnings of agriculture included both the domestication of animals (pastoralism) and the cultivation of plants (arable agriculture). Pastoralism is even more difficult to identify in the prehistoric archaeological record than is the cultivation of plants, largely because it was not dependent on either sedentism or the use of pottery. Consequently, far less has been understood about the historical importance of pastoralists. Many early pastoralist societies were nomadic. The seasonal movements of peoples with their herds precluded the kind of material accumulation reflected in the historical records of cultivators and even sedentary, nonagricultural fishing populations. Domesticated animals varied widely from one part of the world to another: from dogs to llamas to camels to chickens, cattle, sheep, and goats. A number of farming communities also had significant pastoral components, which provided a productive mosaic of subsistence strategies that would ultimately ensure the community's survival. Animal products, including milk, fur, and skins, also provided essential trade and subsistence items around the world and reduced the reliance on hunting.

Domestication of Plants   It has been suggested that the preliminary period of habitat management, or experimentation and selection, that evolved out of gathering activities marked the transition to arable agriculture. If this scenario is correct, then women, who were the primary gatherers, played a critical role in the transformation of early societies from gathering-hunting to agriculture. In the Late Stone Age, tools associated with the domestic activities of women, such as grindstones and grinding hollows, indicate the intensive use of plant foods and suggest that supplies may have come from domesticated as well as gathered plants. Domestication of both plants and animals was a slow process involving both human skills and long-term genetic changes in wild species.

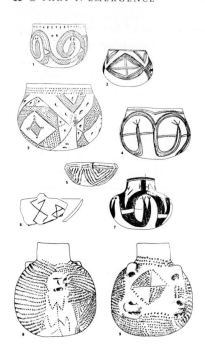

FIGURE 2.4 Early Balkan Neolithic Pottery

Archaeologists have used the elaboration of pottery in the Neolithic period as an indication of the intensification of plant use and increased food storage needs of preagricultural societies. LBK vases incised with symbols: snakes, crosses, V's, lozenges, chevrons, double triangles (hourglass shapes), and a frog. (1,3,5) Early; (2,4,6–9) Middle and Late; (1,3,5) Elsloo, Holland; (2,4,8,9) Königsaue; (6) Halle-Trotha; and (7) Seehausen, E Germany. Scale (1,3,5): 1/2: (2,4,6,7): 1/3; (8,9): 2/3.

SOURCE: Marija Gimbutas, *The Civilization of the Goddess,* HarperCollins San Francisco, 1991. General Research Division, New York Public Library, Astor, Lenox and Tilden Foundations.

Crop domestication occurred in regions in which cultigens (wild varieties) of the crop were native. Cultivated rice could and did appear everywhere from East Asia to West Africa that varieties of wild rice were available to be exploited, while *ensete,* a bananalike plant whose cultigens were unique to Ethiopia, was first domesticated there. The search for agricultural origins has required the cooperative efforts of botanists and archaeologists, who examine the current and past patterns of plant distribution and the potential patterns of agricultural origins.

THE TRANSPORT MODEL

It is possible that agriculture emerged in some places without conscious human intent. Another model for the emergence of agriculture, the transport model, has supposed that systematically harvested and stored wild plants will evolve biologically over time. In this model, the ease by which grain could be transported served as a selective factor in domestication. That is, plants with desirable characteristics, such as grains that stay longer on the stalk (and thus can survive the journey from field to village), those that thrive under disturbed circumstances, and those that reproduce more effectively after storage will be the majority genetic sample planted and reproduced. The transport model has particularly been used for evidence of early agriculture in West Asia.

THE HYDRAULIC MODEL

Another historical explanation for the beginnings of agriculture was a theory associated with the belief that the earliest agricultural societies occurred in river valleys. The theory of "hydraulic civilization" connects water-related technology—dams, canals, waterwheels, wells—with successful cultivation and surplus agricultural production. The linkage of technology to the transition to agriculture and the growth of complex organization in sedentary societies was based on examples from the Nile and Indus Valleys, Mesopotamia, China, and the Valley of Mexico. Though river valleys are no longer considered the original sites of sedentary agrarian cultures or "cradles of civilizations" (as they were once called), domestication did, of course, occur in river valleys scattered around the world. The earliest widely accepted evidence of Nile agriculture, carbonized grain found at village sites, dates from between 6000 and 5000 B.C.E. This evidence suggests that the transition to agriculture in the Nile Valley occurred at approximately the same time that it did in other river valleys and somewhat later than the 7500 B.C.E. dates for the upland areas of West Asia.

EARLY AGRICULTURAL SOCIETIES

What characterized the earliest societies based on agriculture? Although the crops varied around the globe and across vastly different environmental regions, agricultural societies provided early peoples with the opportunity to settle in one place, be committed to a single geographic location, and intensively exploit local resources in order to support their expanding populations. Without exception, early agricultural societies became socially and materially complex communities.

CHINA

By at least the sixth millennium B.C.E., people who inhabited various regions of what we now know as China practiced sedentary agriculture, ceramic technology, social stratification observable in burial forms, human and animal sacrifices, and systems of notation or protowriting, including oracle bones. The traditional Chinese view of the origins of agriculture attributed it to a sage-king called the "Heavenly Husbandman," who taught the people how to cultivate the land: "In the time of the Heavenly Husbandman, millet fell as rain from the heavens. The Heavenly Husbandman then tilled the land and planted the millet . . . he fashioned plows and hoes with which he opened up the wasteland."

At least two, and perhaps three, major culture complexes dominated the sixth and fifth millennia B.C.E. in China. One was centered in northwest China, represented by a reconstructed village site, Banpo, of the Yellow River Valley Yangshao pottery culture. The other was located along the east coast, at the Qinglian'gang site of the Longshan pottery culture in the Yangtze River delta. Some scholars believe that yet another culture complex, located along the southeastern coast and Taiwan, called Dapenkeng, was roughly contemporaneous. To a large extent the cultures of the south and east represented adaptations to an environment that was substantially different from that of the north. The cultivation of rice began in the wet, marshy lowlands of the Yangtze Valley, an area dramatically unlike the arid northern plains, where millet was the primary crop. The cultivation of rice required well-irrigated fields and intensive labor, which encouraged cooperative efforts among the members of a settled community.

Rather than seeing the Yellow River Valley as the East Asian "cradle of civilization" like the Nile in North Africa, the Tigris-Euphrates in West Asia, and the Indus in South Asia,

FIGURE 2.5 Chinese Neolithic Pottery

Pottery types of the Yangshao Culture. Chinese Neolithic, 3000–2000 B.C.E.

SOURCE: K. C. Chang, *The Archaeology of Ancient China* (Yale University Press, 1986, 4th ed.). General Research Division, New York Public Library, Astor, Lenox, Tilden Foundations.

where the practice of agriculture developed and from which it radiated outward, it seems now, given the explosion of archaeological discoveries over the past few decades, that there were multiple centers of agriculture that flourished before 5000 B.C.E. There were certainly two distinct ways of farming that developed in north and south, and they remain characteristic today of a basic ecological division in China: between the steamed bread–and noodle-eating north and the rice-eating south. Similarly, early sites for both horticulture, the cultivation of plants without systematically planting them, and agriculture have been identified in Southeast Asia, evidence of a contemporary and independent evolution of agriculture there. The earliest human cultures identified in the Japanese archipelago (dating to 10,000 years ago) did not practice agriculture until it was diffused there from Southeast or East Asia late in the first millennium B.C.E. However, there is evidence of horticulture as well as extensive tool

FIGURE 2.6 Chinese Neolithic Bone Tools and Implements

Bone Weaving Shuttles. ca. 5000–4000 B.C.E.

SOURCE: K. C. Chang, *The Archaeology of Ancient China* (Yale University Press, 1986, 4th ed.). General Research Division, New York Public Library, Astor, Lenox, Tilden Foundations.

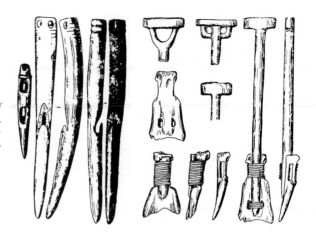

kits associated with sophisticated gathering and hunting cultures. As in West Asia and Africa, it seems likely that there were several East and Southeast Asian paths to the substitution of sedentary agriculture for hunting and gathering. Agriculture should be seen as one ecosystem manipulation strategy among many, including horticulture, gathering and hunting, and pastoralism.

AFRICA

Elsewhere, subsistence patterns of early sedentary peoples altered with shifts in ecological systems. An African site of environmental disequilibrium and crisis, Dhar Tichitt in Mauritania, witnessed the successful transition from the use of wild to domesticated cereals. There, between about 1100 and 1000 B.C.E., the use of millet and sorghum was incorporated into pre-agricultural subsistence strategies when the lakes around which large, settled populations lived began to dry up. Solid, direct evidence of the domestication of plants has been established by the dating of carbonized grains and seeds, but there is also much indirect and speculative evidence of the slow transition to agriculture that reveals much about the process. Such things as seed impressions on the bottoms of storage pots or "sickle sheen," the gloss produced on stone tools by the polishing effect of the silica contained in plant stalks as they were cut and harvested in fields, are indicators of agricultural beginnings. Such evidence has been found in archaeological sites from West Asia and Africa that date back to thousands of years before the earliest domesticated plants. For some types of early domesticates, such as yams, there is also the fact that direct physical evidence is unlikely to have been preserved, since the tuber itself becomes the "seed" that propagates a new generation. There is early African evidence of the cultivation of rice along the Niger River in West Africa, and at the site of Jenne-Jeno in Mali, evidence of domesticated rice (by about 500 B.C.E.) exists alongside that of exploitation of other resources in the inland Niger delta, an area of periodic flooding. People fished and hunted, using their abundant resources to support increasingly complex societies. Their mud-walled houses multiplied, and the increase in population led to greater social complexity over time.

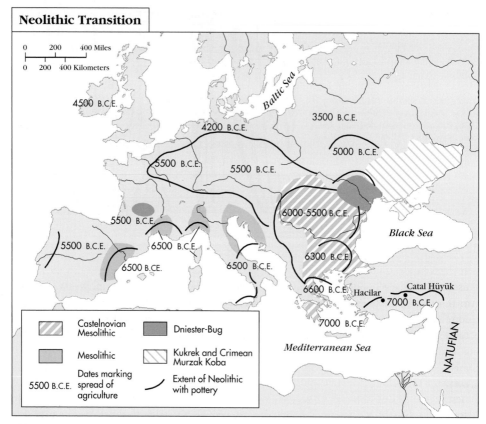

Neolithic Transition

0   200   400 Miles

0   200   400 Kilometers

Baltic Sea

4500 B.C.E.

3500 B.C.E.

4200 B.C.E.

5000 B.C.E.

5500 B.C.E.

5500 B.C.E.

6000-5500 B.C.E.

Black Sea

5500 B.C.E.

5500 B.C.E.

6500 B.C.E.

6500 B.C.E.

6300 B.C.E.

6500 B.CE.

6600 B.C.E. Hacilar Catal Hüyük

7000 B.C.E.

7000 B.C.E.

Mediterranean Sea

NATUFIAN

Castelnovian Mesolithic	Dniester-Bug
Mesolithic	Kukrek and Crimean Murzak Koba
5500 B.C.E. Dates marking spread of agriculture	Extent of Neolithic with pottery

MAP 2.2

SOURCE: Gimbutas, p. 6.

EUROPE

The study of the emergence of agriculture in Europe has centered on the historical issue of diffusion: the transfer from one society to another of complex or small traits associated with a technology, in this case sedentary agriculture. The pattern of the spread of agriculture in Europe suggests diffusion. Despite the evidence of an indigenous Neolithic transition (a period of gradual settling down, intensive plant exploitation, and widespread use of pottery), for many years historians believed that the Neolithic agricultural revolution came to the European continent from West Asia, spreading first to neighboring Greece and then in a series of waves to the rest of Europe. However, as archaeologists and historians working in other parts of the world began to examine the role played by topographical, climatic, and ecological conditions in the emergence of agriculture, their perspectives suggested that diffusion was a questionable and too-simple explanation for the European transition to agriculture. Ecological conditions—climate, soil quality, rainfall—varied as widely in Europe as elsewhere, and the areas in which agriculture developed were widely separated: the Mediterranean basin was separated by the Alps from the Danube and Rhine River basins, each of which was distinct, and they were all unlike the rocky fringe lands of Scandinavia and the northern British Isles. Despite the effect of such variety on the development of European agriculture, a common European transformation from gathering-hunting to sedentary agrarian culture has been identified. Evidence of scattered and divergent transitions to agriculture dates from the mid- to late Neolithic era (after 5000 B.C.E.) and is derived from pottery and the indigenous grains and fruits which Europeans domesticated. These remains suggest that the European transition to agriculture appeared independently and was not necessarily the result of diffusion.

Though European agrarian societies emerged somewhat later than those in West Asia and elsewhere, Europe was endowed with good resources and conditions for animal and plant domestication: there were widely scattered but large areas of arable land, and the climatic conditions—temperature and rainfall—in most of them are suitable for agriculture. The European model suggests that generic agricultural concepts, such as cultivation, and certain specific fruits and grains emerged independently in various European regions while particular agrarian practices and products, such as tools and seeds not indigenous to the continent, appeared in parts of Europe as a result of diffusion from elsewhere.

The process of the European transition to a sedentary agrarian culture has been connected with the pottery that accompanied it. An early ceramic ware, known as Linear Pottery I, was in use between 4700 and 3700 B.C.E., in central and eastern Europe, in an area stretching from the North Sea coast and the Rhine Valley to the western portions of the former Soviet Union. Evidence found at Linear Pottery sites indicates that a number of varieties of grains, including wheat, barley, millet, flax, and peas were cultivated during this period.

Domestication of Animals Among the earliest innovations suggesting the emergence of agrarian life in Europe is the domestication of animals. Europeans domesticated the dog, probably as an aid to hunting, between 8000 and 5000 B.C.E. Evidence of domestic dogs has been found in western European coastal regions, where people lived as hunters and shellfish gatherers, as well as in sites in northern and central Europe. Many of

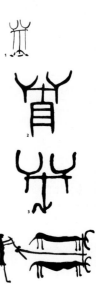

FIGURE 2.7 Yoked Oxen Depicted in Rock Art, Balkans

Rock engravings of yoked oxen pulling a vehicle and a plow, c. 3500–3000 B.C. from the North Pontic area and central Germany. (1) Züschen, C Germany. (3,4) Valcamonica, N Italy. Scale: various sizes. (2) Kamennaya Mogila, north of the Sea of Azov.

SOURCE: Marija Gimbutas, *The Civilization of the Goddess, HarperCollins, 1991.* General Research Division, New York Public Library, Astor, Lenox, Tilden Foundations.

these sites are contemporary with Neolithic communities whose culture extended over a long period. Domestication of animals may have spread across Europe before the cultivation of plants, and the advent of cultivation contributed to the sorts of animals domesticated. Sheep, which were domesticated in Asia as early as 9000 B.C.E., along with cattle, goats, and pigs, were a part of the European transition to agriculture as early as the fourth millennium B.C.E. By 2500 B.C.E., the horse was domesticated in the southwestern portion of the Eurasian steppes, when it spread to the rest of Europe. The domestication of the dog and horse suggests that not all Europeans were sedentary agrarians and that early populations continued to be mobile.

While northern Europeans were domesticating dogs, peoples in the Balkan area of southeastern Europe were beginning to plant and cultivate seeds. There, evidence of plant cultivation, domestication of animals other than dogs, and pottery date from as early as 6000 to 5000 B.C.E. The spread northward and westward was apparently rapid: by 4000 B.C.E., similar evidence exists for trans-Alpine Europe.

Early Agricultural Techniques Domestication of grains and other plants depended on the use of the hoe and the digging stick, a tool also used around the world by gatherers. In some areas, particularly the heavily wooded parts of northwestern trans-Alpine Europe such as modern Germany, it was necessary to use slash-and-burn techniques in order to make the transition to agriculture. Dense forests were cleared and burned,

MAP 2.3 **Different Regions of the World Give Rise to Main Food Crops**

Different regions of the world gave rise to the main food crops: A1, Near East (barley, wheat, peas, lentils and chickpeas); A2, Africa (millets, sorghum, groundnuts, yams, dates, coffee and melons); B1, North China (millets and rice); B2, Southeast Asia (rice, bananas, sugar cane, citrus fruits, coconuts, taro and yams); C1, Mesoamerica (maize, squash, beans and pumpkins); C2, South America (lima beans, potatoes, sweet potatoes, manioc and peanuts).

SOURCE: *Cambridge Encyclopedia of Human Evolution.*

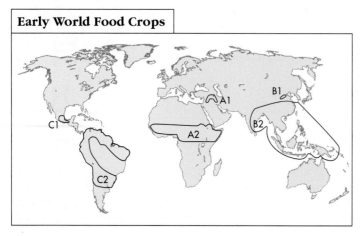

Early World Food Crops

and the cleared area was cultivated until the soil was exhausted. Without properly spaced fallow periods or fertilizer, cultivation caused soil to lose its fertility rapidly. This resulted in frequent relocation, which meant, in essence, repeating the slash-and-burn techniques in a new area.

The transition to sedentary agrarian cultures in Europe and elsewhere was accompanied by continuing gathering, hunting, and fishing activities, though they were adjusted to life in permanent settlements of sturdy dwellings fixed to a single site. The earliest European evidence of such communities, dating from about 6000 years ago, has been found in the Balkans. Elsewhere, in northern and western Europe, temporary settlements and horticulture, combined with gathering and hunting, continued for a millennium or so. The establishment of permanent agrarian communities, in which wheat, millet, and other grains were cultivated in combination with stock breeding and herding, was the final stage of the European agricultural transition. It was, however, only the beginning of technological changes in European agriculture, which would benefit greatly from the application of horsepower to the plowing of fields after about 800 C.E., the introduction of the harness from the nomadic peoples of Asia, or the even earlier (ca. 100 B.C.E.) use of water and wind power for grinding grain.

THE AMERICAS

The emergence of agriculture in the Americas follows patterns similar to those elsewhere and raises similar questions of diffusion and variation. The Americas encompass a variety of climates and ecologies, ranging from frigid to tropical, wet to arid. Despite some claims that certain plants domesticated in the Americas suggest African origins for Western Hemisphere agriculture, it is accepted that the transition to agriculture there was a separate process, not a product of diffusion from Africa, Asia, or Europe.

The Long Drought The separate origin of agriculture in the Americas has an ecological consideration: desiccation or extended drought. A dramatic crisis, often referred to as the Long Drought, affected the region of the southwest of the present United States and northern Mexico; it began around 8000 B.C.E., reached a peak about 5500 B.C.E., and lasted until around 2000 B.C.E. The Long Drought was very likely the major impetus for the emergence of agriculture in North America and suggests that the transition to agriculture in parts of the Western Hemisphere is chronologically comparable to the development of agrarian practices in other parts of the world. Both the maize culture of Mesoamerica and the root culture of northwestern South America were well established by the mid–sixth millennium B.C.E. A corollary to drought, maize culture emerged as an alternative or supplement to poor gathering-hunting conditions. At the time of this transition to plant cultivation, animals were also being domesticated, but not for food; it appears that the essential American diet as agriculture emerged was largely vegetarian, supplemented by hunting and fishing.

Mesoamerican Maize Culture Even given the emphasis on plant foods in the Americas, the development of agrarian societies, as elsewhere, was gradual. Following the initial ventures into planting and domestication, cultivation improved and became more structured. The earliest model of such development occurred in the Valley of Mexico. The climate of this area alternated between wet and dry spells, with the rains being brought by west winds from the Gulf of Mexico to modify the effects of drought. Early grain

FIGURE 2.8 Mesoamerican Maize: 5000 Years of Evolution

Left to Right. 5000 years of maize evolution from tiny wild corn to a modern example ca. 1500 C.E.

SOURCE: © Robert S. Peabody Museum of Archaeology, Phillips Academy, Andover, Massachusetts. All Rights Reserved.

cultivation included a large variety of plants with edible seeds; how long it took for maize to develop as the primary crop is currently being debated by archaeologists. Until recently, it was thought that maize, supplemented by beans and squash, was established as the pattern for agriculture between 5000 and 4000 B.C.E., but recent excavations have pushed the dates back, without, however, altering the factors that caused the shift to agriculture. One thing is obvious: it took a long time to transform the indigenous plant ancestors of corn (maize) and squash into productive food sources and even longer to spread their cultivation across sharply differing climates.

South American Root Culture Other American centers developed both root and grain crops. The potato, an Andean domesticate, was developed from wild varieties that grew on mountain slopes from modern Colombia south to Bolivia. Here, too, desiccation had pushed peoples into the valleys fed by the annual Andes snow melts. Andean grain agriculture may possibly be an example of diffusion within the Americas; it is uncertain whether the cultivation of corn and cassava (both among the world's most difficult plants to domesticate) in Peru was learned from Mesoamerican peoples or was indigenous to South America. Incan cultural explanations exist but do not resolve the issue of diffusion as a source of agricultural practices. Corn and cassava, a tuberous root from which bread flour is made, were believed by the Incas of Peru to have their origins in a dramatic time of crisis:

> Pachacamac, who was a son of the sun, made a man and a woman in the dunes of Lurin. There was nothing to eat, and the man died of hunger. When the women was bent over searching for roots, the sun entered her and made a child. Jealous, Pachacamac caught the newborn baby and chopped it to pieces. But suddenly he repented, or was scared of the anger of his father, the sun, and scattered about the world the pieces of his murdered brother. From the teeth of the dead baby, corn grew; from the ribs and bones, cassava. The blood made the land fertile, and fruit trees and shade trees rose from the sown flesh. Thus the women and men born on these shores, where it never rains, find food.

The question of the diffusion of maize agriculture is not limited to South America; it is also considered a possible explanation of the origins of North American agriculture, where the oldest corn found (in New Mexico's Bat Cave) dates from about 5500 years ago. In the manner of the Incan cultural explanation of the origins of corn and cassava, the following legend of the Hopi people of the American Southwest offers an explanation of agriculture in North America:

> Moing'iima makes corn. Everything grows on his body. Every summer he becomes heavy, his body full of vegetables: watermelon, corn, squash. They grow in his body. When the Hopi plant, they invariably ask him to make the crop flourish; then their things come up, whether vegetables or fruit. When he shaves his body, the seeds come out, and afterwards his body is thin. He used to live on this earth and go with the Hopi. When things grow ripe, he becomes thin and is unhappy. He stays in the west.

In some parts of North America, agriculture emerged tentatively or made no headway at all. In the Pacific Northwest, an abundance of nourishing plants and fish allowed gathering-hunting lifestyles to persist long after agriculture emerged elsewhere. The Mississippian culture, which reached from Appalachia to the Great Plains and from the Great Lakes to the Gulf of Mexico, turned to sedentary agriculture only gradually, between 2000 B.C.E. and 800 B.C.E.; the Mississippians retained their gathering-hunting patterns alongside part-time farming, in which domesticates were exploited but not necessarily relied upon.

What is perhaps noteworthy is that diverse peoples scattered throughout the Americas all turned to agriculture at about the same time. Whether directly or indirectly resulting from factors such as environmental change or population growth, agricultural development was never a designed, sudden process but a slow and uncertain drift.

■

THE EMERGENCE OF COMPLEX TECHNOLOGIES

Even the earliest human communities were dependent on tools that enabled them to sustain themselves by exploiting their environments more efficiently. Appropriate technology was basic to the ways humans organized themselves to utilize the natural resources available to them.

Early Stone Tools Gathering-hunting communities relied on stone tools ranging from crude stone grain, seed, and nut pounders to intricate, refined small stone instruments, or microliths, such as scrapers and knives, in addition to wooden digging sticks and implements fashioned from bone and other organic materials. The technology involved in tool production became increasingly proficient with experience and need. It is clear, for example, that a well-fashioned Late Stone Age tool involves greater technological expertise than a stone whose intrinsic size and shape enabled it to be used as a tool without much modification. Technology continually developed as it kept up with the changing environments and changing demands of various cultures around the world, and, as both accompaniment and cause, its impact reached revolutionary proportions during the global transitions from hunting-gathering to sedentary agrarian lifestyles.

FIRE, TECHNOLOGY, AND MOBILITY

Many agricultural and preagricultural sedentary societies were supported by technologies that relied on the control and use of fire. Fire enabled human groups to survive in the climatically least inhabitable environments around the world, beginning more than a million years ago. When used in cooking, fire expanded the range of food resources and significantly changed the menu of early populations. Firing pottery at high temperatures produced more durable utensils for purposes of food and water storage. These uses of pyrotechnology, the systematic application of fire, enabled early toolmakers to conquer their environments. The impact was visible even in the earliest communities: the cutting down of trees for firewood contributed to the early evidence of deforestation that has continued until today. Wood fueled the firing of pottery and the working of metals. The depletion of sources encouraged mobility.

Gatherers and hunters were not the only populations to spread across the landscape. Migrant farmers and herders also moved in response to changing environments and other reasons. The domestication of animals further increased human mobility. On foot, mobility was estimated to be about 72 kilometers (45 miles) per century. The harnessing of the Asian camel, the South American llama, and the European horse expanded the migratory activity of early groups. Their use was costly but speeded up journeys and made contacts between regions of the world more frequent.

METALLURGY

No pyrotechnology changed the world as dramatically as that associated with metalworking. About the time fired pottery generally came into use (ca. 6000 B.C.E.), technologies for working metal into objects were developed. Metals occur naturally in surface rocks but usually must be removed from the other elements with which they were combined by applying heat to them. The technology by which metal is extracted from ore, refined, and prepared for use is known as metallurgy. Perhaps the earliest form of metallurgy was hammering, by which ore was extracted from the rocks in which it was found and then shaped for use. Using high-temperature fire to melt ores converted them into a liquid, which could be poured into molds to achieve a rough shape that, when cool, could be hammered or chiseled into a finished tool or object. Both of these metallurgical technologies were in use in West Asia by 4000 B.C.E. Both were used to produce tools that had a great effect on agriculture—and commerce and war as well—at the time the transition to sedentary societies was occurring.

The Age of Metals   The "Age of Metals" varied from place to place and came earlier to some places than others. Not all societies developed technologies for the same metals. In West Asia, the Balkans, Spain, and the Aegean, for instance, copper metallurgy was the first to develop (between 6000 B.C.E. and 2500 B.C.E.). After iron metallurgy was developed (ca. 2500 B.C.E.) it began to supersede all others in areas where iron ore was available because iron, being a harder, stronger metal able to retain sharp edges, could be used to create more durable and useful tools. As the demand for metal tools increased, the uneven distribution of ores around the globe endowed some societies with riches and others with the need to trade. For example, by 1500 B.C.E., the demand for bronze, a mixture of copper and tin (or lead or antimony) that was harder than copper (though not as hard as iron), resulted in the importation of tin to West Asia for use in bronze metallurgy. What the ancient sources of tin used in bronze metallurgy will remain a puzzle, although archaeological evidence and scientific examination of excavated objects to determine the source of metals, together with written sources available after 2000 B.C.E., have provided abundant evidence of long-distance trade in metals, especially tin. Such evidence provides a valuable addition to the story of both

Early Metal Sources

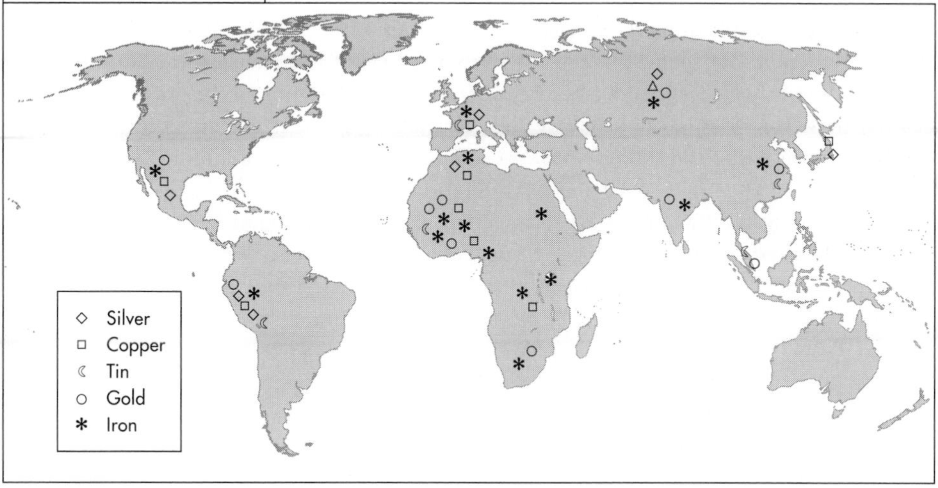

◇ Silver
□ Copper
◖ Tin
○ Gold
＊ Iron

MAP 2.4 Sources of Metals before 1500 C.E.

SOURCE: Original

metals and trade in the ancient world. Because of the relative scarcity of certain metals (copper, tin, and gold), societies in search of metals and the specialists whose skills were their passports were encouraged to increase international contacts and trade.

Everywhere the use of metals signaled an important achievement in technological and human history, and gold, silver, copper, and iron played a role in the definition of various cultural identities. As societies grew more complex, technology increasingly became an essential component of historical change. Unlike the working of stone, a material that remained essentially unchanged except in shape, metalworking represented a fundamental alchemy: the very nature of matter was changed by human skill and technology.

TECHNOLOGY, SOCIETY, AND CULTURE

Technological, social, and cultural change are inseparably linked. Societies with iron technology produced objects useful for peaceful pursuits (agriculture, commerce) and invaluable for success in war. Other societies commanded advantages based on different technologies. Silver, gold, and copper metallurgy served the needs of pre-Columbian inhabitants of the Americas, and copper and bronze metallurgy were sufficient for the needs of the Chinese, who were familiar with iron metallurgy but did not use it for tools until long after iron was in general use in Africa, West Asia, and Europe. Even such a tool as the plow, which had an enormous impact on the social organization, labor practices, and expansion of production in sedentary agrarian societies in Europe and Asia, was not used in many parts of Africa and the Americas, where it was useless because of the kind of agriculture practiced. The interrelationship of technology and society is undeniably global in its historical significance, but the impact of even the same technologies on specific cultures varies widely.

Metallurgy had a devastating impact on the environment everywhere it was employed. Mining activities themselves were destructive, as neolithic miners of silex (chalk), flint, and obsidian demonstrated around the world. The first use of native copper required no underground extraction, but soon afterward the copper and tin of most ancient workings began to be found in veins or lodes in older, harder rock. Its extraction required the use of fire and specialized stone hammers, and ultimately the construction of shafts and support and drainage systems. Deforestation and soil erosion were common consequences of mining and working of metals.

Both mining and metallurgy were dangerous activities that required skill and hard labor. The use of forced labor, especially the labor of captured slaves, was common in mining. Diodorus of Sicily, who wrote between 60 and 20 B.C.E., describes the dangers of hard labor by child, female, and male slaves in the North African gold mines of Nubia:

> . . . here the overseers of the labor in the mines recover the gold with the aid of a multitude of workers . . . and all are bound in chains—work at their task unceasingly both by day and throughout the entire night, enjoying no respite and being carefully cut off from any means of escape . . . working in darkness as they do because of the bending and winding of passages, carry lamps on their foreheads.

Many chapters in the history of technology illustrate the often critical relationship between technology and ideology. How aspects of technology came to dominate society and economies, gender and world views can be seen in examples of the complex metallurgies that developed in Africa.

West African Metallurgy In West Africa, the production of iron and steel (probably after 2000 B.C.E.) was perceived to harness both technical and spiritual forces. Adepts in changing the very nature of matter, metallurgy specialists emerged as powerful members of the community. Their powers depended on the most powerful deities: those controlling the manufacture of iron tools and weapons. The site of Meroe (ca. 400 B.C.E.) in the middle Nile is an example of the intensive exploitation of pyrotechnological knowledge. Substantial quantities of slag, the waste product of iron smelting, together with surviving tools, including spears, tweezers, adzes, axes, hoe blades, and shears, suggest an impressive industry. The fuel consumption of major African metallurgical centers such as that at Meroe created serious problems of deforestation, and industries eventually declined as forests disappeared. The specialists—workers in iron, copper, gold, and glass—who altered the environment with such devastating impact were held in awe, both revered and feared. Control over technology, in Africa as elsewhere, served as a vehicle for the expression of social and political dominance and subordination. Metals acquired symbolic importance as expressions of power and social distinctions.

The Impact of Technology on Society These and other examples of complex technologies indicate that social inequalities appear to have increased as technology became more complex. Technologies increasingly relied on complex systems of organizing labor and resources. Control over technology became a powerful engine for the expression of political office and elevated a person's social and economic status. For example, the Luba ceremonial hand ax, a symbol of royal prerogative in Central Africa, has not only been found in excavated burials (ca. 600 C.E.) but more than a thousand years later was associated with rituals involved in kingship and the exercise of power. Wherever specialists

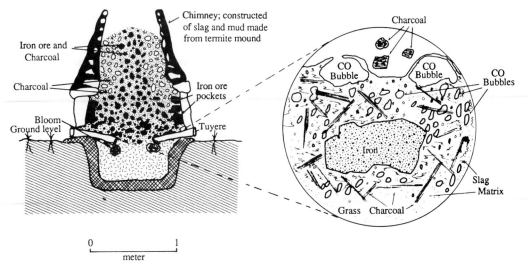

FIGURE 2.9 Reconstruction of Haya Iron-smelting Furnace, East Africa

A schematic profile of a Haya iron-smelting furnace; this elaborates on the profile published in the 1978 *Science* article. It adds an inset that shows a summary of the reduction process inside the furnace, in particularly illustrating the explosion of CO bubbles—a carbon boil—on the top of the slag mass. Note that the tuyeres are inside the furnace and therefore are conduits that preheat the air passing through them. Iron ore pockets are added inside the foundation blocks to prepare and partially sinter iron ore for the next smelt.

SOURCE: *The Culture and Technology of African Iron Production* (University of Florida Press, 1996). Photo courtesy Schomburg Center for Research in Black Culture, New York Public Library, Astor, Lenox and Tilden Foundations.

appeared, they extended control over human labor and natural resources. Essential to cities and empires, technology tended both to increase the complexity of society and to express its growing inequalities.

■

THE IRON AGE IN AFRICA

Archaeological investigation of African iron smelting indicates that it originated in the second millennium B.C.E., as early as anywhere else. Moreover, early iron-smelting sites in East and West Africa appear to represent regional centers of production that differ technologically from systems known elsewhere in the world. Such evidence strengthens the case for an independent development of metallurgy in Africa.

Metallurgy and Society   African metallurgical systems for the production and working of iron expressed and were intricately interrelated with fundamental political and spiritual aspects of African life. Even in its earliest forms, technical knowledge in much of Africa was proprietary, that is, it belonged to those who possessed it and were empowered by their possession. The dissemination of technology was carefully managed, and it was not fully shared since its use was subject to spiritual and political control. Some technological spheres were the exclusive domains of men; others were controlled by women. Technology was subject to the intervention of gods, deities, spirits, and ancestors. For example, the West African god of iron, Ogun, was a key Yoruba deity who even survived the Atlantic journey during the slave trade of the second millennium C.E. and endured as the central religious figure in African-derived societies in Brazil, Cuba, Trinidad, and Haiti. The powers of Ogun exemplified the practical powers of technology and its ability to order and control society, while empowering its users to create change—in both the natural world and the human sphere.

Iron was common on the African continent. Iron and its alloys were ultimately shaped by smiths into tools that played a revolutionary role in the early cultivation of fields, in warfare, in commercial and urban life, and in belief systems.

Technology and Spiritual Power Early blacksmiths wielded technological and spiritual power that they frequently translated into political authority. If surviving technological practices provide any indication, the boundaries between the natural and supernatural worlds did not exist for early African metallurgists. Even today Yoruba smelters and smiths call on the participation of Ogun and his unseen forces when making iron and carefully guard their technical expertise. Successful metallurgy requires a knowledge of high temperatures, how to make specialized charcoal from hardwood trees, and how to refine ores to produce tons of high-quality iron and steel annually. From the beginning of iron smelting, the toll on local forests was devastating, and the impact of early deforestation and pollution by furnace dust and fumes did permanent ecological damage in Africa.

Metallurgy and Gender The transformational powers of early iron smelting were often expressed in human terms: the metaphor of a female furnace, which gave birth to iron. These associations between female sexuality and the production of iron are documented in the excavation of ancient furnaces decorated with female breasts and genitalia, and they are recorded in much more recent observations by travelers, historians, and anthro-

FIGURE 2.10 Luba Ceremonial Axe, Zaire (Central Africa)

A Luba ceremonial axe.

PHOTOGRAPH: Collection of the Linden Museum, Stuttgart.

pologists. Iron technology was a symbolic opportunity to usurp the ultimate metaphor of creativity: the female reproductive power. Accordingly, smelting was from the beginning conducted exclusively by men, and widespread prohibitions controlling women's roles in metallurgy were commonly used to reaffirm men's control over economic production and reproductive relationships. The exclusion of women served to protect valuable proprietary knowledge of a complex technology from being transferred to other societies via marriage, and served to confirm gender inequality in a technologically complex society.

In much of sub-Saharan Africa, the use of iron preceded the use of bronze. When copper-based metallurgies appeared (after 2000 B.C.E.), they were also linked to aspects of power, in part the result of copper's relative scarcity and its luminosity, durability, and bloodlike coloring. For example, jewelry fashioned from copper and its alloys has been found in the burial sites of elites across West Africa. Whether copper was hammered or cast as an alloy, its practical and artistic uses (in ceremonial objects, sculpture, and jewelry) contrasted with the everyday, fundamental utility of iron, which was used primarily for weapons and tools. Perhaps because of the relative scarcity of copper and the abundance of iron in Africa, the technologies developed independently, in vastly different places and periods. This pattern of metallurgical development in sub-Saharan Africa stands in contrast to the European and West Asian models, which present linear and seemingly progressive sequences of Copper Age followed by Bronze Age and, finally, by Iron Age. The technology that dominated in each of these new eras was defined by the inevitable replacement of the older metal by the newer one.

EARLY TECHNOLOGICAL CHANGE IN CHINA AND EUROPE

As Late Stone Age Eurasians became primarily farmers rather than gatherers, the nature of their labors changed. Agricultural labor was diversified, both by its nature and by the seasons: some members of agricultural communities were required for sowing, cultivation, and harvesting; some were charged with pastoral duties—herding and the care of animals; others were primarily responsible for preserving, preparing, and trading both plant and animal products. As the populations of sedentary agrarian societies increased and technologies grew more complex to keep up with common needs, complex relationships and labor systems within and between communities developed. Social organization became more elaborate: hierarchies were established and became fixed, and gender divisions became sharper and less egalitarian. The organization and structure of agrarian societies became institutionalized by the politics of the community and sanctioned by its ideology and beliefs.

By the third millennium B.C.E., such communities in China, the Indus Valley, and the western Mediterranean basin constituted examples of Bronze Age culture as a result of their significant advances in metallurgical expertise. Bronze (an alloy combining copper and tin) was an elaboration of the earliest copper metallurgy, which had developed in areas adjacent to abundant ancient copper sources such as those near the Balkans, in the Sinai, and in East and Southeast Asia. In Thailand, where the earliest evidence of a tin and copper alloy was once thought to predate the third millennium, development of bronze is not thought to have begun before 2000 B.C.E. The Egyptians had previously added arsenic to copper (probably around 3000 B.C.E.) to produce silvered bronze mirrors with reflective surfaces; they did not alloy copper with tin before about 2000 B.C.E.

FIGURE 2.11 Chinese Bronze Ritual
Vessel, Shang Dynasty

Bronze tripod, with "monster mask" design.
Height 240 mm, 15th–12th century B.C.E.

SOURCE: Courtesy of the Freer Gallery of Art,
Smithsonian Institution, Washington, DC.

THE BRONZE AGE IN CHINA

In China, bronze weapons were used by the founders of the first historic dynasty, the Shang
(ca. 1600–1027 B.C.E.), which emerged on the north China plain in the early part of the second millennium B.C.E. In addition to weapons, bronze ritual vessels were cast for use in ceremonies sanctioning the political legitimacy of the Shang kings. Although the introduction of
bronze technology was closely tied to the new social, political, and economic conditions that
characterized the Shang, the precise relationship between bronze technology and the social
stratification of the Shang period cannot be neatly drawn. It is unclear whether the production of bronze was a response to, or the cause of, the rise of a social elite that favored its use
for ceremonial and ritual purposes. Bronze weaponry, however, played a substantial role in the
ability of this elite and its supporters to gain and keep political control.

Skilled artisans in service to the Shang kings and their nobles labored in workshops
where they produced bronze vessels, weapons, and other artifacts for the use of the aristocracy.
Elegant bronze ritual vessels were fashioned by what is known as the piece-mold process. A
clay model of the object was made and another layer of clay was placed over the model to produce a mold. The outer clay mold was then cut into pieces or segments and removed. A thin
layer of clay was scraped from the surface of the inner model, and the outer pieces of the mold
were reassembled to leave a cavity between the model ("core") and the mold. Molten metal
was then poured into the cavity to cast the vessel. When the metal had cooled, the clay molds
and model were broken away from the bronze. Much of what we know about this early period
of history in China comes from inscriptions on bronze vessels, many of which were cast to
commemorate a military victory, marriage, or similar event.

Although bronze was used in a limited way for agricultural implements, it was neither
plentiful nor substantial enough to be widely used for farming tools and plows. Commoners

in Chinese society remained reliant on stone technology and materials such as bone, wood, and bamboo until the advent of iron technology during the first millennium B.C.E. With the coming of iron, widespread use of tools and weapons made of this metal indicated that China had finally entered an age of metals.

FROM THE BRONZE AGE TO THE IRON AGE IN EUROPE

The transition from bronze to iron in the Mediterranean basin and Europe was late and sporadic. Bronze metallurgy there dates variously from the second millennium B.C.E.; it was accompanied by the rise of increasingly hierarchical communities with growing populations. Bronze fulfilled Europeans' needs for perhaps a thousand years before it was superseded by iron. From the sixth century B.C.E., Greek and Roman societies relied on iron for tools and weapons, but as early as the eighth century B.C.E. the Greek poet Hesiod (fl. ca. 776 B.C.E.) had lamented the new Iron Age: "I wish that I were not any part of the fifth generation of men. . . . For here now is the age of iron." Hesiod's doubts about the effects of iron weapons on Greek culture were hardly an enthusiastic endorsement of inevitable or progressive change. Indeed, technological innovations have produced mixed responses throughout history.

Certainly, an important factor in the adoption of iron for use in weapons was its relatively widespread availability. Though iron ore was difficult to extract and purify, once successful metallurgical techniques could produce useful amounts, iron superseded all previous metals for weapons and tools. The iron product most often worked by blacksmiths was wrought iron—slag-producing, malleable iron containing so little carbon that it will not harden well when cooled suddenly. It was produced by variations in and improvements on

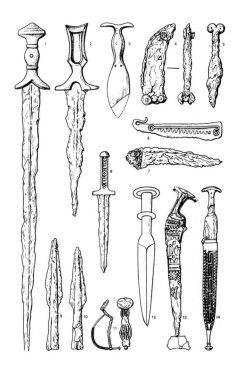

FIGURE 2.12 Early Iron in Europe

Examples of some of the most ancient iron objects in Europe. 1, Forte di Rivoli; Hag, 2, Souš near Most, Bohemia; 3, Cumae, Campania (after Randall MacIver); 4, Gánovce, North Slovakia (dagger hilt); 5, Norbjär, Sweden (miniature iron sword); 6, Arnitlund, Jutland (bronze razor with inlays of iron); 7, Tarquinia-Impiccata, Etruria gr.74; 8,Kotouč-Štramberk, Moravia; 9, 10, Hostomice, Bohemia; 11, Tarquinia-Impiccata gr. 74 (brooch with bronze pin); 12, Vetulonia-Sagrona, Etruria; 13, Servici, Picenum; and 14, Torre Galli gr. 99 (bronze sheath). Dating: 4 about 1500 B.C., 6 about 1000 B.C., the rest about 800 B.C., 1 after Barfield, 2, 9, 10 after Pleiner, 3, 12–14 after Randall MacIver, 5,6 after Stjernquist, 7–11 after Randall MacIver, 8 after Podborsky.

SOURCE: Pleiner in Theodore Wertime & James D. Muhly, *The Coming of the Age of Iron* (Yale University Press, 1980). General Research Division, New York Public Library, Astor, Lenox, Tilden Foundations.

early forms of metallurgy. It was the principal form of iron produced in Europe until the nineteenth century, when new techniques revolutionized iron metallurgy there.

THE IRON AGE IN CHINA

In China, the preferred iron product was cast iron—iron containing so much carbon that it is usefully malleable at any temperature—and steel—iron containing enough carbon to become extremely hard when cooled suddenly. Chinese artisans were producing cast iron and steel by the fourth century B.C.E. Both were widely used in the era known as the Warring States (481–221 B.C.E.). As the name suggests, this was a time of frequent warfare. The introduction and widespread use of iron were related to the dramatic social and economic changes that resulted from conflict and frequent shifts of power during this period. Iron was used for weapons, and warfare created conditions in which those with access to iron technology were at an advantage. A third-century B.C.E. text refers to "spearheads of steel . . . sharp as a bee's sting." Iron was also used by the time of the Warring States for the share, or blade, of the ox-drawn plow, probably based on simpler plows used earlier by Chinese farmers.

Despite the chaotic conditions in China resulting from war, or perhaps in part because of them, iron acquired great value and even commercial exchange utilized iron currency. Merchants grew rich on its profits and agriculture prospered, aided by the use of iron tools. By the first millennium C.E., cast-iron technology was commonly used to manufacture household items such as scissors and to build temples, pagodas, and bridges. By the second millennium, the technological and production levels of the iron industry in north China equaled that of the early stages of the industrial revolution in England over five hundred years later.

■

TECHNOLOGY IN THE AMERICAS

In North America, yet another pattern of metallurgical systems prevailed. Before the arrival of Europeans, copper was worked in limited quantities and traded widely, and unsmelted, hammered iron was produced from meteorite sources in North America for tools and weapons. In the pre-Columbian (before the arrival of Christopher Columbus in 1492 C.E.) technology of South America, an Iron Age was bypassed and, in accordance with the metals available to the region's early artisans, complex gold-, silver-, and copper-working techniques were developed. As in Africa, Native American metallurgy was integrated into American cultures and its technologies were reflected in social and political behavior and value systems. Copper, which was rare, was highly valued and traded widely among people unfamiliar with its sources. Copper native to the Great Lakes region was, for example, much sought after and prized in the Pacific Northwest as a prized, but unaltered, exchange good.

ANDEAN METALLURGY

The technology developed in the Andean zone of western South America (modern Peru, Bolivia, Ecuador, and Colombia) could not have been more different from that developed in Eurasia and Africa. Metals played only a minor role in warfare: there were no Andean bronze- or steel-tipped weapons, and cloth and worked fibers provided weaponry (slings for projectiles) and protective armor. Obsidian, a naturally formed volcanic glass, was highly prized and widely traded in its raw form, which was shaped into arrowheads and spear points. The role of metals was relegated to nonutilitarian realms. In the Andean region, copper, gold, and silver were used decoratively and artistically to convey both secular and religious status and power. The Andean craftworker was interested in a metal's color and appearance, not in its strength or durability. Sophisticated techniques of alloying, gilding, and silvering that used electrochemical methods of surface alteration dominated the repertoire of metalsmiths in Andean societies during the first millennium C.E.

Copper Metallurgy Complex copper metallurgies helped to shape South American societies. As early as 500 B.C.E., peoples on the northern Peruvian coast worked copper and gold. They were followed by artisans who emphasized alloys of copper that produced metals easier to mold and harden. These artisans also produced a copper-gold alloy well suited to sheet-metal working. At a reconstructed Peruvian site dating to between 900 and 1500 C.E., archaeologists have excavated the earliest evidence in the world of intensive smelting of copper-arsenic alloys. The furnace openings revealed elaborate sacrificial offerings of llamas and food. Ceramic-tipped cane blowing tubes were used to raise the furnace temperatures, and additives were used to help remove impurities so that nearly pure copper could be produced. Each smelting would have produced only about 0.3 to 0.6 kilogram (.66 to 1.32 pounds) of metallic copper. Accordingly, the burial of a leader with about 500 kilograms (1100 pounds) of copper objects was an ostentatious statement of power and wealth.

Copper-silver and copper-gold alloys were hammered and shaped into highly valued objects. These objects expressed significant cultural aspects of Andean value systems. For example, when copper encased or was alloyed with pure gold, the hidden or disguised gold was thought to represent the divine quality of a seemingly human ruler. The object was a tangible

FIGURE 2.13 Chimu Mask in Gold and Turquoise, Peru, South America

SOURCE: Girandon/Art Resource, New York.

expression of political ideology in which the nobility's inherent but not always apparent golden or celestial essence was affirmed. In South America as elsewhere, technology reflected cultural preoccupations and provides critical evidence for understanding early societies and cultures.

SUMMARY

From the times of the earliest stone-ax makers to those of the powerful specialists of iron and copper metallurgy, the ways in which humans organized themselves in relation to their environments became increasingly diverse and complex. While it is clear that there was no common pattern or pace in cultural change throughout the world, the direction of change has been overwhelmingly toward increasing complexity. There may appear to have been a "progression" from early gathering-hunting strategies to sedentary agrarian ones and then on to larger urban societies, which have traditionally been considered to mark the beginnings of "civilization," but close examination indicates that there was no orderly, inevitable pattern of change.

On most continents, the transition to agriculture eventually occurred, signaling more complex social systems that manipulated their environments in different ways than gathering-hunting societies had. The chronologies of transitions to sedentary agricultural societies are very diverse, but in most areas with high population densities, sedentary communities de-

FIGURE 2.14 Chinese Farming, Han Dynasty (207 B.C.E.–220 C.E.)

Intensive hoeing and row cultivation of crops originated in China in or before the sixth century B.C.E. Here we see the technique in operation during the Han Dynasty (207 B.C.E.–220 C.E.).

SOURCE: Robert Temple, *The Genius of China* (NY: Simon and Schuster, 1986).

veloped increasingly specialized and complex technologies (including metallurgy) to exploit their environments. The possibility of unintentional or accidental developments and the role played by chance in transitions to new technological and subsistence strategies cannot be ignored. Environments changed as a result of shifts in both climate and human use. Some scholars have characterized the patterned process of ecological and cultural change in systematic maps of change and continuity, such as the pulse model.

As agricultural and other settled societies became more permanent, they became materially more complex. Certain technological changes appear to have accompanied, if not resulted from, the increased material complexity of sedentary society. As the scale and complexity of societies increased, so did the range of inequalities and the means by which some group members established and maintained an advantage, especially in eras of scarcity. Metallurgy in particular became a vehicle for the expression of male power and dominance in early societies, and control over metal technology was used by men to exclude women from the accumulation of wealth and political office. Technological development, which provided new means of exploiting resources to support larger numbers of people, influenced the organization of societies as they adjusted to the constant pulse of change. Technologies for the production and distribution of goods also contributed to the hierarchical structure of societies, to gender relationships, and to the social and economic controls by which communities ordered themselves.

Given the limitations of current knowledge, it is not always possible to determine the exact relationship between changes in technology and changes in society. Undoubtedly, social changes took place that made technology useful, and in turn technology helped to bring about social changes. It is important to remember that the discovery of a new technology alone was never sufficient to ensure its inevitable and widespread use. From Eurasian to African societies, from the Americas to the Mediterranean, technological change was the result of selectivity based on cultural and other factors. Both independent development and borrowing of technology were interconnected with social, political, and economic conditions that encouraged its use and created the contexts in which its users might enable or inhibit historical change. The web of interlocking relationships resulting from increasingly larger settled communities is examined in the following chapter.

FIGURE 2.15 Egyptian Tomb Model of Baking and Brewing, XIIth Dynasty

SOURCE: Reproduction by permission of the Syndies of the Fitzwilliam Museum, Cambridge, from Beni Hasan, Tomb of Khety (366); Gift of Beni Hasan Excavation Committee.

ENGAGING THE PAST

THE DREGS OF HISTORY

The relative merits and pitfalls of the products of technology have been debated throughout history. Greek legend claims that the god Dionysus left Mesopotamia in disgust because its people were so addicted to the local barley beer or ale. About 40 percent of the grain produced locally went for the production of Sumerian beer. In ancient Egypt, both emmer and barley were used for brewing a popular beverage drunk through tubes from ceramic cups. As early as 1400 B.C.E., the beer of pharaohs and workers alike was consumed in taverns, where one risked the dangers of loose talk while drinking a beverage called "Joy Bringer." Early rice beers in India, palm wines in West Africa, and the fermented juice of cactus in Mesoamerica intoxicated peoples throughout history.

Scientists have examined beer residues in vessels found in Egyptian tombs and workers' villages to determine the technology and reproduce the beer-making recipe. They found that ancient brewers used a complex two-part process: first sprouting and heating a batch of grains to increase their susceptibility to attack by enzymes that increase the sugar content; then mixing this batch with sprouted and unheated grains in water. Yeast was added to the combination of sugar and starch, and this concoction was fermented to make beer.

Fire was one of the earliest tools, and one that produced some of the most dramatic changes in the lives of early humans. The application of fire transformed the physical landscape. Its application to the sciences of cooking and fermentation altered mental landscapes, as the examples of these early drinks attest. Technology can transform our understanding of the past, just as modern scientific study of the dregs of ancient Egyptian beer has made it possible to identify the sophisticated technology of brewing used by the Egyptians. As the role of technology in transforming society continues to be studied and debated, there is little doubt that the technology of brewing helped fuel the lively social interactions of ancient peoples.

SUGGESTIONS FOR FURTHER READING

Francesca Bray, "Origins of Chinese Agriculture," in Joseph Needham, *Science and Civilization in China,* vol. 4, no. 2 (1988), 27–47. An overview and summary of controversies over origins of Chinese agriculture, balanced treatment with attention to trends in general archaeological theory that have affected interpretation of Chinese material.

Alfred Crosby, *Ecological Imperialism: The Biological Expansion of Europe, 600–1900* (New York: Cambridge University Press, 1986). Examines the ecological implications of population movements.

Marija Gimbutas, *The Civilization of the Goddess: The World of Old Europe* (San Francisco: Harper, 1991). Provocative and controversial reexamination of West Asian and European evidence, especially from a gender perspective.

Steve Jones, Robert Martin, and David Pilbeam, eds., *The Cambridge Encyclopedia of Human Evolution* (Cambridge, England: Cambridge University Press, 1992). Excellent world coverage of issues in cultural evolution; see useful excellent.

Journal of World History. This journal presents current articles and book reviews in the field of world history.

David N. Keightley, ed., *The Origins of Chinese Civilization* (University of California Press, 1983). Articles by specialists on such topics as environment and agriculture, Neolithic cultures and peoples, metallurgy, writing, and early political organization.

William H. McNeill, *Plagues and People* (Garden City, N.Y.: Doubleday, 1977). A provocative study of the relationship of disease to demography and its effect on global history.

Joseph Needham, "The Evolution of Iron and Steel Technology in East and Southeast Asia," in Theodore A. Werthime and James D. Muhly, eds., *The Coming of the Age of Iron* (New Haven, Conn.: Yale University Press, 1980), pp. 507–41. Explanation of technology of iron and steel making as it developed in East and Southeast Asia.

Peter R. Schmidt, ed., *The Culture and Technology of African Iron Production* (Gainesville: University of Florida Press, 1996). Good introduction to current issues in African Iron Age studies.

Technology and Culture. This journal covers issues in the history of technology and society.

Theodore A. Wertime and James E. Muhly, *The Coming of the Age of Iron* (New Haven, Conn.: Yale University Press, 1980). Although somewhat outdated, presents a look at the age of iron in various cultural settings.

Donald Worster, *Nature's Economy: A History of Ecological Ideas* (New York: Cambridge University Press 1977). An essential history of human relationship with the natural world and how this has been expressed in human thought.

3

Settled Societies: The Emergence of Cities

I n the third century C.E., a southern Indian poet recounted his visit to the city of Madurai, vividly portraying the social, economic, and religious life of this city on the southern tip of the South Asian subcontinent:

> The poet enters the city by its great gate, the posts of which are carved with the images of the goddess Lakshmi. It is a festival day, and the city is gay with flags; some, presented by the king to commemorate brave deeds, fly over the houses of captains; others wave over the shops which sell toddy [a fermented drink made from blossoms of the palm tree]. The streets are broad rivers of people of every race, buying and selling in the market place or singing to the music of wandering minstrels.
>
> The drum beats and a royal procession passes down the street, with elephants leading and the sound of conches [shell trumpets]. An unruly elephant breaks his chain and tosses like a ship in an angry sea until he is brought under control. Chariots follow, with prancing horses and fierce footmen. Stall keepers ply their trade, selling sweet cakes, garlands of flowers, scented powder, and rolls of betel nut [to chew]. Old women go from house to house selling nosegays and trinkets. Noblemen drive through the streets in their chariots, their gold-sheathed swords flashing, wearing brightly dyed garments and wreaths of flowers. The jewels of the perfumed women watching from balconies and turrets flash in the sun.
>
> People flock to the temples to worship to the sound of music, laying flowers before the images. Craftsmen work in their shops, bangle-makers, goldsmiths, cloth weavers, coppersmiths, flower sellers, wood carvers, and painters. Food shops are busily selling mangoes, sugar candy, cooked rice, and chunks of cooked meat. In the evening, the city's prostitutes entertain their patrons with dancing and singing to the accompaniment of the lute. The streets are filled with music. Drunken villagers, in town for the festival, reel about in the streets. Respectable women visit the temples in the evening with their children and friends, carrying lighted lamps as offerings. They dance in the temple courts, which resound with their singing and chatter.
>
> At last the city sleeps . . . all but the ghosts and goblins who haunt the dark and the housebreakers, armed with rope ladders, swords, and chisels. But the watchmen are also vigilant, and the city passes the night in peace. Morning comes with the sounds of brahmins intoning their sacred verses. The wandering bands renew their singing, and the shopkeepers open their booths. The toddy-sellers ply their trade for thirsty early morning travelers. The drunkards stagger to their feet. All over the city the sound is heard of doors opening. Women sweep the faded flowers of the festival from their courtyards. The busy everyday life of the city is resumed.

In many ways this strikes us as being much like any modern city. Food and goods in dizzying amounts and varieties can be bought, day and night. Craftsmen, noblemen, prostitutes, shopkeepers, minstrels, captains,

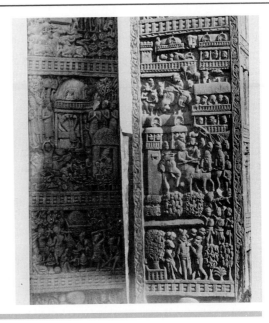

royalty—all are thrust together in the fabric of city life. At night, a different world emerges, that of "ghosts and goblins" but also of well-provisioned thieves and the watchmen who safeguard the city while it sleeps. Because it is a festival day, there is a vibrant religious atmosphere. But religion is also more deeply and permanently present, from the images of the goddess carved into the posts of the city gate to the temples that dot the urban landscape.

Many aspects of this portrait of city life in early India could be found in almost any city, ancient or modern. What is striking, and characteristic even of modern Indian cities, is the atmosphere of a festival day. We might say that this is something culturally distinctive to Indian society. But what is common to the origins of cities throughout the world, and what is distinctive about cities as they evolve in different cultural settings? Why do people congregate in cities, and what benefits and drawbacks are there to urban life?

INTRODUCTION

Human population increase on a global scale has been a constant factor in changing community forms and evolving relationships between humans and their environments, despite dramatic, though usually short-term and regionally limited, decreases due to war or disease. The previous chapter examined relationships between the increasing number and size of human communities and their ecosystems, between culture and environment in early societies. This chapter is concerned with one particular form of human organization: the emergence of early cities, where growing populations of sedentary peoples were concentrated in increasingly complex settlements. Complexity was both a necessary condition for and a consequence of larger communities. Complexity appeared in the form of bureaucracies that registered populations, taxed them, and maintained order, as well as in the form of systems of trade, communication, and defense. No less important were rituals of public order, both religious and secular, and aspects of everyday life such as going to the market to buy food or taking part in an annual festival. In this chapter we explore a wide array of forces and circumstances that encouraged human settlement in early urban forms. We examine relationships between urban communities and their environments, as well as the structures of the communities themselves. Finally, we look at the human experience of city life, its benefits and its challenges.

Gathering-hunting Societies Small social groupings were characteristic of gathering-hunting societies. These units usually consisted of persons related by bloodlines and organized into groups that we might today term family structures, either nuclear (parents and children) or extended (nuclear plus siblings, their offspring, and grandparents). As groups increased in number, greater social complexity was apparently required by the demands of decision making and organization. Groups formed clans or tribes, as well as larger social and family units, based on shared cultures and blood relationships. Often members shared a fictive identity, an invented or socially constructed history that served to create a shared sense of belonging and promote social cohesion. What forces brought these people together in large communities? What encouraged the particular form of complex social and economic organization characteristic of the city?

Urban Societies Early cities were the result of multiple factors of growth and change. Urbanism was most often due to combinations of factors, though selected examples from around the globe suggest the primacy of some causes at the expense of others. Whatever immediate causes and conditions led to the rise of cities throughout the world, the emergence of urban societies was an intensification of earlier social dynamics, not a revolutionary process. Even as cities emerged, the majority of people remained in rural communities, linked through trade and systematic contact with urban centers. In this chapter we survey early cities in various regions of the globe, identifying characteristic features of each in order to illustrate the complex nature of both the process of urbanization and the phenomenon of urbanism as experienced by peoples in widely varying cultural contexts throughout the world.

CAUSES OF URBANIZATION

The earth's increased human populations were fed by successful economic systems that integrated regular food supplies and other connections between communities. The emergence of the city as a form of human community required the creation of such systems to connect urban and rural activities and resources. Agriculture was only one reason that people settled down and populations began to be concentrated in urban clusters. Successful agricultural systems supported larger populations, including nonfarming peoples, in towns and villages. As gatherers and hunters began to cultivate crops and domesticate animals, they became less mobile and began to settle in more fixed communities. In time, most of these communities grew in size.

Other reasons that people settled together in large communities included the advantages gained from increased access to trading opportunities, the desire to be near religious shrines or other sacred sites, and, finally, the safety and defense afforded by large numbers of cooperating community members. Social structures in large communities became more varied and complex, and kinship ties were replaced by other bonds, such as ties based on loyalty, economic gain, or protection. Social stratification is characteristic of most cities. Whether the most basic social structures were invented or the natural consequence of familial or blood relationships, they were perceived essentially as kinship-based units with a common identity and culture. They served a primarily economic function. In the increasingly ambiguous and complex social settings created by the challenges of larger communities, a strong group identity and sense of belonging became essential to successful social interaction.

Groups eventually developed culturally distinct governing rules, hierarchies, gender roles, beliefs, and values. Management of this complexity encouraged the concentration of power, which in turn required large bureaucracies to administer the populations brought under the control of powerful individuals or groups. Large sedentary communities multiplied around the globe after the ninth millennium B.C.E., when a variety of circumstances accounted for their growth in size and scale. These settlements became increasingly diversified according to function, necessitating ever more interdependent economic and social structures. The more densely populous and complex settled societies became the first cities.

CITIES, COMPLEXITY, AND CIVILIZATION

The formation of cities was accompanied by increasing economic, social, and political complexity. This complexity meant that many peoples, occupations, goods, and ideas came together into a single settlement that satisfied the diverse needs of that community. Though cities appear around the world, they were not a universal state in the development of civilization, a term derived from the Latin word for "city," *civitas,* nor were they the logical and necessary culmination of earlier forms of community. The most common definitions of "civilization" include the presence of some or all of the traits commonly found in the large-scale, complex communities we call cities: monumental architecture, usually religious in nature; writing or other formal systems of record keeping and communication; trade, government, social stratification, and representational art.

Agriculture and Cities The development of agriculture was important to the rise of cities, since agriculture supported the population growth that cities housed. Surplus food produced as a result of technological innovations in cultivation and other forms of subsistence or specialization allowed people to settle in communities that grew in size and density and became cities. Reliable food supplies were essential to the emergence and survival of cities. The resources needed for expanding and densely settled populations could be obtained by trade or by other means, such as war, as well as by integrating agricultural hinterlands with the concentration of population in an urban center. In addition to the production of surplus food as a condition conducive to urban development, the concentration of people in cities was also caused by population pressure on limited resources (causing people to flee farms and villages looking for work and food), drastic environmental change, the need for protection, the need for periodic markets for trade and exchange, the concentration of political power, and the institutionalization of religion.

Cities as Ceremonial Centers Once material needs were provided, one characteristic (though not the only) urban form that emerged was the ceremonial complex. As symbols of cosmic, social, and moral order, public ceremonial structures such as pyramids, mounds, and temples were centers of political, social, and sacred space. Staffed by priests in service to rulers, these monuments represented the redistribution of resources essential to the economic relationship that existed between the urban center and its agricultural hinterland. In other words, religious practices often served as a symbolic means of redistributing resources.

■

WEST ASIA: THE EARLY GROWTH OF AGRICULTURAL AND URBAN SYSTEMS

Urbanism has been more extensively studied in West Asia than in almost any other part of the world. This is partly due to the abundant and well-preserved evidence and partly the result of scholarly interest in studying what were thought to have been the world's first cities. The earliest West Asian cities were based on gathering and hunting as well as on the cultivation of domesticated crops by sedentary farmers. Hunting and gathering continued to supply needs after groups became sedentary and the products of farming were among many resources in a broad-based lifestyle.

EARLY WEST ASIAN CITIES

By around 6500 B.C.E. in West Asia, settlements such as Tepe Guran in the western Zagros Mountains of Iran or Jericho in Palestine were large enough to be considered small cities. They initially served their hinterlands, the surrounding rural areas, as exchange centers for goods and services, culture, and ideology. Tepe Guran was a seasonal town, serving as winter quarters for nomadic people who, following their herds, moved twice a year, once from summer pasture and once for winter pasture.

Jericho Jericho was an older, year-round settlement, dating back to as early as 9000 B.C.E., when the site was established as a sanctuary beside a spring for hunter-gatherers. Over the next millennium, their descendants made the transition from a wandering to a settled existence. By the eighth millennium B.C.E., Jericho had a population of about 2000. The community was surrounded by defensive and protective walls to which were attached such monumental architectural features as a heavy stone tower. Jericho seems to have been only incidentally a farming community. It perhaps drew its wealth from trade, the exchange of goods that traveled from the Red Sea to Anatolia. Around 7000 B.C.E., Jericho was abandoned and replaced by a more modest and straightforward farming community with houses and walls built of sundried mud brick, a material widely used throughout West Asia at this time.

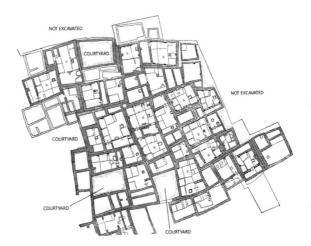

FIGURE 3.1 Plan and Reconstruction of a Section of Çatal Hüyük

Plan (a) and schematic reconstruction (b) of a section of Çatal Hüyük town with mud brick houses rising in terraces. Houses had flat roofs and entry was by roof. Mid-7th millennium. B.C.E.

SOURCE: Marija Gimbutas, *The Civilization of the Goddess* (San Francisco: HarperCollins, 1991). General Research Division, New York Public Library, Astor, Lenox and Tilden Foundations.

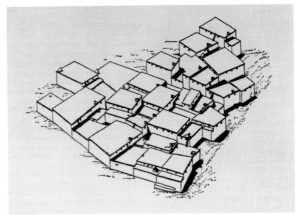

The decline and replacement of Jericho seem indicative of a pattern in West Asia. Like Jericho, there were many other settlements that appeared and declined, expanded and contracted, as cities eventually became more closely connected with the agricultural development of their hinterlands.

Çatal Hüyük The size of later West Asian cities reflected, in most cases, the agricultural potential of the immediately surrounding region. One of these cities, Çatal Hüyük in central Turkey, is an example of a complex urban society that eventually came to be based on agriculture but which also relied on game hunting and the gathering of undomesticated plants. By 5800 B.C.E., the city had a population of some 5000 people settled in about a thousand densely built houses surrounded by a well-watered plain. Çatal Hüyük's economy centered on large herds of domestic cattle, though grain farming dependent on irrigation was also practiced. Built on the side of a hill, the town was a solid block of interlocking one- and two-story adobe buildings, each sharing walls with its neighbors. Although a labyrinth of alleys wandered through the town, access to many of the residences was across the roofs of their neighbors. This sort of town planning may have been dictated by concern for defense of the city against outside marauders or interlopers in trade.

From evidence excavated so far at Çatal Hüyük, it is clear that the city served as a cultural as well as economic center. Excavations have indicated the existence of a complex, ranked society, whose priesteshood and shrines suggest a possible matriarchy, or female rule. In fact, the presence of ritual or ceremonial functions at Çatal Hüyük may have been as significant for the center's existence as any economic or military reasons. Early civic leaders may have been spiritual as well as political rulers. Their powers are depicted in wall paintings as male deities who were partners of female goddesses, and necessary to the fertility of the community.

Specialists in Cities The role of religious specialists was only one activity common to cities. Other specialists were skilled laborers or artisans, some of whom passed on the valuable secrets of their trade through family or household relationships. At Çatal Hüyük, for example, there was a specialized labor force producing ground and chipped stone implements and excellent woolen textiles. Both copper and lead smelting were done, and both metals were worked into ornaments. Pottery was also produced, though none of it was more than basic utility ware. Specialists were important to cities, because they relied on unique skills and knowledge unavailable to the ordinary field laborer; their diverse activities flourished because urban centers provided for the centralized collection of resources needed by their craft and for the sale and distribution of their products in urban markets. Like other city dwellers, specialists were dependent on their rural counterparts, who remained full-time food producers.

Çatal Hüyük's society and culture, taken together with that of the earlier and smaller Jericho, underlines the difficulty of making a unilinear connection between agriculture and the emergence of cities. The process of urbanization was a slow one of trial and error, complicated by environmental and other accidental factors. The interplay of environment, food supply, and urban formation was a dynamic social process. No "first city" emerged in West Asia during this earliest period, only many towns, each in its own way seeking to sustain a society that became more dense and complex. Some were successful and some were not; success, in some cases, meant building larger, even more complex urban systems and political orders. Elsewhere, success meant survival of populations in smaller human communities and the disappearance of urban centers.

Environmental Factors Environmental factors also offer clues to the process by which peoples
and Urban Growth settled down and cities appeared. Between the seventh and fourth millennia B.C.E., when the agricultural world of West Asia was being consolidated, the climate remained fairly constant, but around 3500 B.C.E. it began to change. Glaciers ceased their rapid melting and rains diminished. By 3500 B.C.E., the oceans were as high as they would be. For example, the upper limits of the Persian Gulf coast lay well north of Basrah, and the heavy runoff of the Tigris-Euphrates watershed flooded the area with lakes and marshlands. Over several hundred years, when the oceans began to drop, the Persian Gulf slowly receded and the water table dropped. Following 3500 B.C.E., in Sumer, as the area at the head of the Persian Gulf came to be known, the extent of arable land was greatly enlarged due to an ample supply of water from the Tigris and Euphrates Rivers. As fast as land became available for cultivation, people moved in from nearby regions, from the

northern Iraqi plains, and even from the southern coastal regions of Arabia, where steadily in-creasing desiccation (drying up) was making vast tracts of land uninhabitable.

THE SETTLEMENT OF SUMER AND THE CITY OF URUK

Within this context of environmental change, Sumer was an attractive area for settlement in the late fourth millennium B.C.E. Those who moved into the area from other parts of West Asia carried with them the heritage of more than 2000 years of experimentation in agricul-ture and settled communities. In Sumer they joined an already established population which had cultivated the marshes for a thousand years and developed small town settlements scat-tered along the gulf coast. Together, the new and old settlers used the latest farming tech-niques, including irrigation, and equipment on fertile soil as it dried out. The result was a greatly increased agricultural production, which in turn attracted more people and created denser settlements.

Uruk was one of several cities that emerged in Sumer following the climatic changes that occurred after 3500 B.C.E. Growing out of two smaller farming communities, Uruk eventu-ally encompassed 9 square kilometers (3.5 square miles), but it served a much wider hinter-land as a focus of economic, social, and cultural interchange. Uruk differed from smaller farm communities in the diversity of its economic production and the fact that its large labor force was paid wages in the form of surplus grain, as meticulously recorded by scribes.

Uruk as a Ceremonial Center   The conversion of the small village or domestic shrine into a temple occurred by the first half of the fourth millennium B.C.E.. The White Temple at Uruk, dated to about 3100 B.C.E., is built of mud brick with whitewashed walls and decorated with elaborate buttresses and recesses. Built on a raised platform or ziggurat, this temple incorporates the remains of earlier sanctuaries, which were bricked over to form the successive foundations of new temples; because the god of the tem-ple was believed to be the landowner in perpetuity of the ground that had been consecrated to him, his shrine could not easily be transported to a new site. Both temples and their support-ing ziggurats were "mountains" where the natural potency of the earth and therefore all of life was thought to be concentrated. A city's shrine served its inhabitants and attracted wor-shipers and traders from the hinterland. Priests first appeared at some time prior to 3000 B.C.E., when they are depicted on seals and stone carvings. They were perhaps the first social group to be released from direct subsistence labor, since their role in religious ritual and as spokesmen for gods was related to the exercise of power by kings (see Chapter 4). The term for "king" appears in Sumerian inscriptions by the beginning of the third millennium B.C.E., and the rise of kingship is further attested to by the presence of monumental palaces and royal tombs from this period.

Urbanization and the Invention   It is likely that the complexity of business transactions and of Writing in Sumer   administrative and legal needs presented by the challenge of organizing larger urban communities stimulated the writing system developed by the Sumerians around 3000 B.C.E. The centralization of the economy through the integration of urban center and hinterland required the systematic collection and allocation of goods, aided by a means of recording such transactions. The redistribution of re-sources administered by the newly centralized Sumerian kingdoms was documented in the earliest written records: lists of the contents of storehouses. Though the earliest script appeared in Sumer and, like the origins of scripts elsewhere in the ancient world, was pictographic in nature, cuneiform, or "wedge-shaped," script, developed by the Sumerians to write on clay tablets, eventually spread throughout West Asia among peoples whose languages were unrelated.

The Urban Diet Grains supplanted livestock as the local diet of city folk. Barley, wheat, and ▬▬▬▬▬▬ millet were served with lentils, beans, turnips, onion, garlic, leeks, cucumbers, lettuce, cress, and mustard. The daily diet of barley paste or bread was accompanied by onions or a handful of beans and washed down with beer. More than fifty varieties of fish are mentioned in texts before about 2300 B.C.E. Along the city streets of Uruk, vendors of cooked foods offered customers fried fish and grilled meats. Mutton was common (the Sumerian language contained more than 200 words describing the types and varieties of sheep), along with goat, beef, and pork.

The business of agriculture and food supply was only one of the enterprises on which Uruk was based. The ubiquity of mosaic decoration in the area has led many to believe that a considerable number of the inhabitants did nothing but turn out colored clay tiles. As the lower Iraqi area of ancient Uruk had no source of strong, workable stone at hand, hundreds of people were engaged in importing stone and cutting it for use in building. Ensuring a water supply was another major activity in Uruk. As the years of drying continued, major projects were undertaken to straighten and clean river courses and canals, which were cut away from the rivers to the fields in ever more complex patterns.

Uruk provides an example of the relationship of environment to the emergence of cities. By 2800 B.C.E., the plains of Sumer were no longer profusely dotted with small settlements. Instead, there were lines of cities—Uruk, Lagash, Nippur, Kish—each with its hinterland of associated settlements that followed the lines of the rivers and main canals. Because they had developed considerable organizational experience during the earlier centuries of plenty, they were able to use complex irrigation methods to adapt to the increasingly dry conditions and scarcity of food.

■

NORTH AFRICA: EGYPTIAN CITIES OF THE LIVING AND DEAD

Egypt was settled rather slowly, probably at first by peoples who moved in from areas in east-central Africa, perhaps as early as 13,000 B.C.E. These peoples domesticated and raised barley and wheat in communities scattered along the Nile Valley. Other peoples moved into Egypt from the Persian Gulf region several thousand years later and are thought to have brought with them sheep, which grazed in the upland country of the Nile Valley. Arable land was found only along the narrow confines of the river banks; thus early Egyptian communities were constrained by the limited amount of useful land available and by the vagaries of the Nile's water flow. With the climatic changes brought on by the end of the last glaciation, desiccation and changes in the Nile Delta intensified the land problem in the Nile Valley. People were forced to live in dense settlements, which survived only by intensively exploiting resources and controlling their distribution. By the end of the fourth millennium B.C.E., cities developed, sustained by the relationships between those situated on the river and those in the

MAP 3.1

Early Cities of the Nile

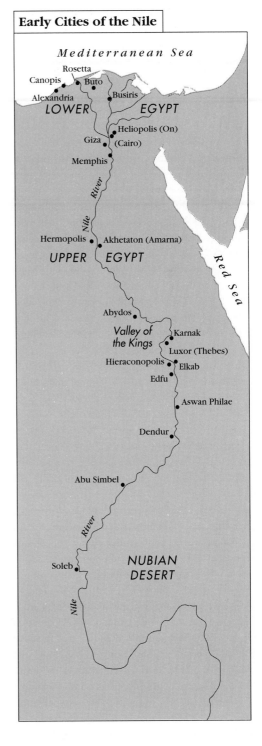

hinterland of earlier agricultural-herding communities. Two Nile Valley cities became paramount: Thebes in Upper Egypt (the Nile Valley proper) and Memphis in Lower Egypt, which made up most of the Nile Delta. The upper and lower regions of Egypt were united around 3200 B.C.E.

THE ECOLOGY OF THE NILE

Both cities were the consequence of religious and political developments that centered around the remarkable environmental conditions of the Nile itself. By the end of the fourth millennium B.C.E., environmental factors had helped shape a stable agricultural society in the Nile Valley, based on irrigated farming in the natural floodplains and delta of the Nile. Regional rainfall and the short- and long-term trends of Nile flooding required systematic responses, and these responses were made by community efforts and interests. The needs of the peoples in the Nile Valley helped determine the growing complexity of activity in Egyptian cities. Supported by their agricultural hinterlands, they became centers of both exchange and culture.

Known mostly by their monumental temples and royal structures of stone, such as the Great Pyramid of Cheops at Giza (2600 B.C.E.), Egyptian cities were actually built mostly of mud brick. The pyramids, tombs of the pharaohs (divine kings), were built at sites outside the cities. The pharaoh resided near the place where his tomb was to be built; during his lifetime, work on the pyramid continued, while government was carried out in the nearby city. Specialization was a feature of the economic and social organization of these settlements, which supported bakers, potters, watchmen, scribes, goldsmiths, and dog keepers, to name a few of the many specialists. The laborers who built the pyramids lived in workers' quarters close to the site of the pharaoh's tomb.

Irrigation and Water Control The most important concern of Egyptian society was control of the waters of the Nile. Artificial irrigation methods, including the cutting of canals and basins, were under way by the time of the Old Kingdom (ca. 3200–2700 B.C.E.), the earliest period of unified Egypt. A technique for lifting water by means of the *shaduf,* or pole-and-bucket lever, came later, around 1350 B.C.E. The organization of irrigation systems took place on the local level and did not in itself generate the social stratification, bureaucracy, and concentration of power usually connected with the rise of cities. However, establishing successful agricultural systems and being able to predict Nile flooding were associated with effective religious and political leadership. One of the pharaoh's most important tasks was feeding his people.

Ecology and Society Famine and plenty were seen as indicative of a cosmic order, from the flooding of the Nile to the growth of vegetation and the increase of flocks. Egyptians responded to times of famine and abundance in a variety of ways. For example, the period of "Lamentations" (2250–1950 B.C.E.) recorded in the Hebrew Bible was a time of low Nile floods, desiccation of delta marshlands, dust storms, and sand dune activity. This ecological crisis produced famine, mass dislocation of starving people, plundering, and civil war, resulting in political anarchy. Though such social disintegration was not an uncommon result of environmental stress in the long history of Egypt, environmental and economic stress also provided opportunity for the concentration of power in the hands of the ruling pharaohs and their bureaucracies, those whose essential task was to ensure the continuity of the Nile ecological system and thus the cosmic order.

MEMPHIS AND THEBES

The ancient Egyptian city of Memphis became a political center and dominated the country-side until the rise of Thebes around 2050 B.C.E. Located on the west bank of the Nile near the apex of its delta (near modern Cairo), Memphis lay on the border between Upper and Lower Egypt and was thus a fitting site for the capital of unified Egypt. Memphis was also an ancient religious center, the chief seat of the cult of Ptah, the artisan deity. The necropolis— "city of the dead"—at Memphis was as impressive as its palaces, temples, and markets. It contained funerary monuments and tombs of early pharaohs and was also a residence of the city's principal deity, Ptah. Though subsequent dynasties established their seats elsewhere up and down the Nile Valley, Memphis remained the largest city and seat of government until Thebes replaced it.

Monumental Architecture One of the characteristic features of a city was monumental architecture. In Thebes, which succeeded Memphis as the capital of Egypt in about 2200 B.C.E., following the disintegration of the Old Kingdom, inscriptions, funerary monuments, and great buildings record the achievements of Theban rulers of the

FIGURE 3.2 The Theban Necropolis (across the Nile) as Seen from Luxor

Columns of the great Luxor temple built by Amenhotep III and enlarged by Tutankhamen, whose work was usurped by his successor Haremhab. Across the Nile can be seen the Theban necropolis, with its temples and tombs.

SOURCE: Foto Marburg/Art Resource, NY.

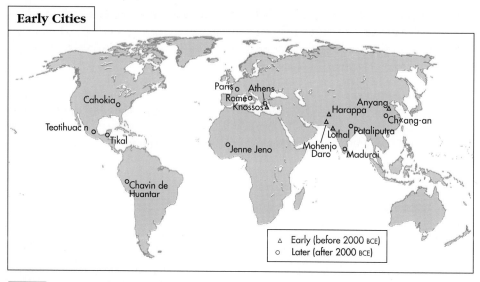

Early Cities

Paris
Rome
Knossos
Athens

Cahokia

Teotihuacán
Tikal

Jenne Jeno

Harappa
Anyang
Ch'ang-an
Lothal
Pataliputra
Mohenjo Daro
Madurai

Chavin de Huantar

△ Early (before 2000 BCE)
○ Later (after 2000 BCE)

MAP 3.2 Cities Mentioned in the Text

New Kingdom (ca. 1575–1085 B.C.E.). These inscriptions, monuments, and buildings were also physical reminders to city residents of the spiritual or divine realms. As at Memphis, among the most impressive architectural achievements are those found in the necropolis. One mortuary temple consisted of a long, unroofed causeway leading to a court with a platform on which was a giant altar. To the rear of this was the temple proper; the burial chamber was hewn out of the rock of the cliff against which the temple abutted and was entered from a concealed place in the pavement of the temple floor.

The principal deity of Thebes was Amon-Ra, chief of the gods, and Egyptians sometimes referred to Thebes as "No-Amon," or "City of Amon." Sections of the city were devoted to lesser local gods. Initially, the necropolis, a vast city of temples and tombs along with the dwellings of priests, was on the west bank and the living city on the east bank of the Nile. As the city grew in size, eventually covering an area of three square miles, royal palaces and their accompaniments were added to the necropolis as individual rulers died and were reborn into the afterlife. The city of the dead stretched back from the western shore of the river as far as the desert hills. Each of the city's many temples collected its own community of living members, too; one of the oldest of these communities was around the temple of Karnak. New temples were constantly being built, and a long series of royal tombs and funerary monuments extended far into the desert in the Valley of the Kings.

EL-AMARNA AND URBAN LIFE

Many resources were dedicated to the building of the great pyramids that were the tombs of pharaohs and to the temples of the gods of Egypt, and these stand today as monuments to the power of the pharaohs. In contrast, the remains of urban settlements, which were simpler and less permanent constructions of mud brick, are relatively few. One exception to this is the recently excavated site of El-Amarna, located midway between Cairo and Luxor. Built by the pharaoh Akhenaten (d. 1358 B.C.E.) to escape the power of the priests of the god Amon at Thebes and to proclaim his belief in the sun god Aten as the only god, El-Amarna was occupied for only about forty years. It was abandoned in 1356 B.C.E., when Akhenaten's successor returned to Thebes and to the worship of Amon. At El-Amarna, in addition to temples to Aten and Akhenaten's palace in the city, as well as police and military barracks, the wealthy people of the city built their residences along the main thoroughfares of the grid pattern of the urban plan, while the poor squeezed their dwellings into whatever spaces remained. About 4 kilometers (2.5 miles) to the east lay the workers' village for those who labored on the pharaoh's tomb.

 DAILY LIVES

IN THE VALLEY OF THE KINGS

The building of monumental architecture associated with urban centers such as the ancient Egyptian capital city of Thebes required the skilled and intensive labor of many. Often these workers who built the temples and citadels of great cities received little reward for their labors and benefited little from access to goods and services that were part of the advantages of urban life. One of the most ambitious and impressive construction projects, the necropolis known as the Valley of the Kings, was built outside the city of Thebes to house the royal dead in their afterlife. The workers whose lives were dedicated to building this city of the dead were themselves housed in a village close to the building site. The village was home to quarrymen, stonemasons, and artisans, including the scribe Ramose, whose job it was to keep records of the work on the pharaoh's tomb and rations of food and supplies sent to the village.

More privileged than a common laborer, Ramose had earned his position through the hard work and discipline necessary to learn the art of writing. But no less than a stonemason or a quarryman, Ramose served the pharaoh in his capacity as a scribe, since writing was an essential component in the smooth operation of the well-oiled machinery of the state. Though Ramose's profession differed from that of his father, a court messenger, his father's contacts with court officials likely brought him to the attention of scribes, who then enlisted Ramose as one of their own and saw that he received the proper training.

Life in the village community differed dramatically from that of Thebes; it was quieter and more serious, dedicated to the task at hand: building the eternal resting place of the pharaoh. Yet village residents must also have had their relaxation and pleasures, living even as they did amid the constant awareness of death, the journey into the afterlife. Near the village lay a cemetery where Ramose and other inhabitants of the village built their own much more modest tombs.

Ramose was around thirty years old when he began his work as a scribe in the Valley of the Kings in 1275 B.C.E. He married a woman of the village, whom he affectionately called by the nickname of "Wia," and became the head of quite a large household, which included members of his wife's family and several female servants. His grain rations—emmer (a species of wheat) for bread and barley for beer—were sufficient to support a household of twelve to fourteen people. Ramose served as unofficial scribe for his village, an extension of his professional role, writing petitions and pleas to the gods for the unlettered villagers. His most precious possession remained his scribal kit, consisting of slates for grinding ink, dishes for mixing the ink, stones to smooth the papyrus for writing, brushes, and a palette to hold the implements.

SOURCE: Based on Lynn H. Nelson and Steven K. Drummond, *The Human Perspective: Readings in World Civilization,* vol. #1 (New York: Harcourt Brace, 1977 [1987]), pp. 52–60; citing John Romer, *Ancient Lives: Daily Life in the Egypt of the Pharaohs* (New York: Holt, Rinehart, and Winston, 1984), pp. 6–7; 13–15; 19–26.

FIGURE 3.3 Egyptian Tomb Wall Painting Depicting Specialists (From Top to Bottom: Shoemakers, Carpenters, Metalworkers)

This magnificent wall painting is in the tomb of the vizier Rekhmire, in Thebes. It shows shoemakers at work (top row) and carpenters (middle row) using bow drills, saws, adzes and chisels. Note how, in the absence of a plane, three men are smoothing a beam with rubbing stones. Bottom right, a metal-worker uses a blowpipe to raise the temperature of his fire.

SOURCE: Brian Brake/Photo Researchers.

The agricultural wealth of the Nile supported the city folk with food. At the same time, their labor (used by the elites to construct the temples and tombs and fill them with artistic treasures) was also thought to support the working of the cosmos: the material and spiritual worlds were inseparable. Whether artisan or farmer, deified king or enslaved foreigner, everyone contributed to the maturing barley fields and estates.

The Egyptian Diet Among the remains of tombs dated to about 3000 B.C.E. were meals left to feed the deceased until she or he reached the other world. These included dishes of barley porridge, cooked quail, kidneys, pigeon stew, fish, beef ribs, bread, cakes, figs, berries, cheese, wine, and beer. Most likely they were comparable to the meals enjoyed by wealthy living Egyptians. The poor ate mainly the commonest kind of flatbread, called *ta,* and a variety of less desirable marsh and canal creatures, including eel, mullet, carp, perch, and, according to a Greek observer in about 200 B.C.E., "slimy magpies." Tombs contained not only food but also jewelry, clothes, wigs, and furniture. Their artwork, especially wall paintings, describes visually and in hieroglyphic (sacred picture writing) forms much about the daily lives of rural and urban Egyptians, from the royal family to their slaves.

Urban Crowding As settlements became more crowded, living space was expanded upward to city rooftops and sometimes to second stories. Many specialized activi-

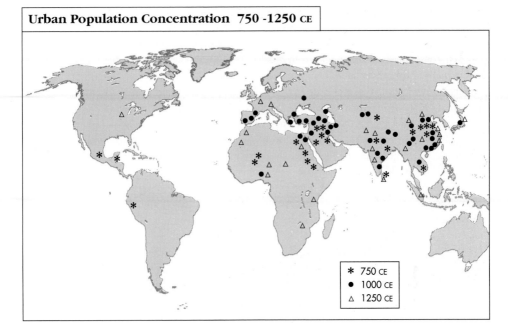

MAP 3.3 Emerging Centers of Population, ca. 750–1250 C.E.

ties, including baking and brewing, weaving, and other craft production, took place within household compounds. Traders traveled up and down the Nile carrying on their transactions from boats, so that Nile cities were, in many ways, floating cities. Never far from the Nile waters, ancient Egyptians lived in cities and smaller villages as part of an elaborate system that linked land and labor to a world of belief.

CITIES IN SOUTH ASIA: THE LIMITS OF ARCHAEOLOGICAL EVIDENCE

The earliest south Asian cities, like those of Sumer and the Nile, appeared in a river valley, the valley of the Indus, in the area of northwest India that is now Pakistan. The Harappan culture of the Indus Valley flourished from around 2300 to around 1500 B.C.E. The origins and development of urbanism at the sites of Harappa and Mohenjo-Daro, both of which were revealed to the modern world only by excavations made in the second decade of the twentieth century, are linked to the rise of Indus culture. They remain partially buried with no fewer than seventy unearthed sites covering more than half a million square miles.

HARAPPAN CULTURE: HARAPPA AND MOHENJO-DARO

The area of northwestern India where Harappan culture, the earliest known culture on the Indian subcontinent, emerged seems to have been a region of communities based on herding and the limited practice of grain cultivation, not unlike the Tigris-Euphrates region. Sites in-

dicate numerous village communities of mud brick scattered along the Indus and its tribu-
taries and along the shores of the Arabian Sea. The eventual appearance of large cities, some of
which housed populations estimated at more than 35,000, suggests that the sort of desiccation that contributed to urbanization in Sumer and Egypt may also have been a factor in the
development of urban settlements in the Indus Valley.

Like other cities, those of Harappa and Mohenjo-Daro were centers of an agricultural
hinterland. Mohenjo-Daro, the best-documented site, was located midway along the Indus
River, and Harappa lay about 6500 kilometers (4000 miles) to the northeast on a tributary of
the Indus. The annual natural inundation of the Indus Valley, along with simple irrigation
techniques, made possible the settling of relatively large communities in the Indus Valley by
the third millennium B.C.E. Harappan cities were part of systems of local trade and economy
linking rural producers to urban centers of specialists. They also became centers of long-
distance trade, establishing contacts with the Persian Gulf and Mesopotamia, Persia,
Afghanistan, and areas to the south of the Indus.

Lothal Lothal was an important trading center on the coast southeast from the Indus delta,
approximately 725 kilometers (450 miles) from Mohenjo-Daro. Excavations at Lothal
have yielded evidence of a docklike structure and a locking mechanism to control the inflow
of tidal water; both of these suggest the existence of sea vessels and seaborne trade. Trading
connections provided such raw materials as gold, tin, copper, and jade that were used by
craftspeople. By 2000 B.C.E., the Indus people had begun to spin cotton into yarn and weave
it into cloth for trade.

Urban Planning The Indus cities were also ceremonial or religious centers, as remarkable for
their monumental structures as for the technology of city planning employed by the people who built them. Temple sites are found in each urban center, where
worshipers gathered to conduct rituals. Water purification rites, still found in modern Indian
culture, were an important part of ancient rituals, and evidence of public baths has been excavated. Their streets of shops and brick houses, in orderly rows, were arranged in a grid pattern. There were such amenities as effective drainage systems and public wells, as well as
baths. Objects of gold, silver, copper, stone, and pottery attest to the presence of specialist
craftspeople. To the west of each city was the citadel, a group of public buildings raised up
above the level of the rest and surrounded by fortifications. The regularity of construction
down to the size of each brick suggests uniformity and control over the production processes,
probably by the city's government.

The urban societies of the Indus were literate. Their script, dated to about 2500 B.C.E., is
unlike any early West Asian script and remains undeciphered. Evidence of this script is confined to about 2000 carved seals, usually made of soft stone, delicately engraved and hardened
by heating. Examples of these seals, which include engraved images of religious figures, have
been found as far away as Sumer, attesting to the role that literacy played in the trade and
communication links required by successful urban centers and their systems. Once they are
translated, we may have a better idea of the culture and daily reality of life in South Asian
cities. Until then, historians must rely on the archaeological evidence—selective examples of
what has physically survived at the early sites of urban occupation—and make inferences
based on its interpretation.

FIGURE 3.4 The Great Bath at Mohenjo-Daro

SOURCE: Borromeo/Art Resource, NY.

Environmental Change Shortly after 1750 B.C.E., the character of this civilization was disrupted by a series of floods caused by earthquakes and by other environmental changes such as the depletion of resources due to human and animal population increase. The Indus River changed its course, and the patterning of irrigation, food surplus, and commercial activity was destroyed. Squatters from neighboring villages and nomadic communities replaced the urban population, and crumbling walls replaced the glorious citadels. Chariot-riding peoples from south-central Asia laid claim to the remains of Harappan culture, bringing their seminomadic way of life, new languages, and vastly different ideas about food, social organization, and religion. These newcomers gradually settled the region surrounding the other great river system of northern India, the Ganges, and by the sixth century B.C.E. the Ganges Valley was the primary center of population, productivity, cities, and commerce.

LATER INDIAN CITIES

A fourth-century B.C.E. account by the Greek Megasthenes (ca. 350–290 B.C.E.) describes the city of Pataliputra, a political and economic center strategically located along the Ganges River trade route. Pataliputra was the capital of the Mauryan empire founded by Chandragupta Maurya in 322 B.C.E. (see Chapter 4). At the time this account was written and for perhaps two centuries afterward, Pataliputra was probably the largest, most sophisticated city in the world. Surrounded by large wooden walls with 570 towers and 64 gates, Pataliputra was the center of a wealthy, highly organized economic system that included farms, granaries, textile industries, and shipyards that built ships for seaborne trade. Pataliputra was also the seat of a famous university and library, along with palaces, temples, gardens, and parks.

Several centuries later, in the third century C.E., the city of Madurai, capital of a southern Indian state, flourished as a cultural, economic, religious, and political center. Like other south Indian cities of the time, Madurai was enriched by maritime trade, largely with Southeast Asia, and dominated by a temple complex. As described in the introduction to this chapter, Madurai displayed the social, economic, and cultural complexity characteristic of other cities found throughout the world in the first centuries C.E.

■
URBANISM IN EAST ASIA

Occurring later than in West and South Asia, the rise of urbanism in China was directly related to the formation of early political orders, in particular the first dynastic state, the Shang (ca. 1600–1027 B.C.E.). Shang kings based their political authority on their claim of descent from ancestors who were able to intercede with the central deity of Shang religion. Because political authority was legitimized by religion, the royal capital where the ruler lived was a sacred ceremonial center that embodied the close relationship between kingship and urbanism in early China. Shang rulers moved their capitals several times during the course of the dynasty, possibly in response to shifting defense needs or access to resources.

ANYANG: CEREMONIAL CENTER AND STRATIFIED SOCIETY

Near the modern city of Anyang on the north China plain lie the ruins of the late Shang capital, which was excavated in the early twentieth century. Like earlier Shang capitals, Anyang was a ceremonial center, including royal tombs containing evidence of human sacrifices as well as a rich material culture, such as bronze vessels, chariots, and jade. The "palace" itself, like other buildings at the Anyang complex, was made of daub-and-wattle (mud-and-thatch) construction on a pounded-earth foundation, creating a dirt floor that over time would become polished by use. Storage pits and drainage ditches fulfilled the practical needs of the concentrated population, many of whom lived in subterranean "pit" dwellings built into the ground. Social stratification was evident in the distinction between the nobility's ground-level dwellings with their pounded-earth floors and the 4-meter-deep (13-foot-deep) pit dwellings of urban commoners, which resembled those of their social status who lived in the countryside.

The ability of a relative few—the Shang king and nobility—to claim the right to the fruits of labor of the many—farmers and producers—made possible the settlement of urban sites by allowing ruling elites to be fed and supported by the labor of those subject to their political control. Not only the evidence of rich material culture displayed in tomb artifacts, but also articles and foodstuffs that supported daily life, were produced by artisans and farmers whose labor was controlled by a small elite.

Religious Specialists Within the Shang capital, specialization was evident in the groups of religious specialists who served the rulers and in the organization of artisans—especially bronzeworkers—into common workshops and living quarters. The crafting of bronze ritual vessels was carried out by hereditary artisans who marked their wares with symbols of their clan. Their work was as vital to the legitimacy of the state as that of the religious specialists, since bronze vessels were an essential part of ritual sacrifices to the ancestors of the Shang kings as well as to the central deity, Di (see Chapter 4).

CITY AND COUNTRYSIDE

Outside the capital, the landscape of Shang China was dotted with earth-walled towns, the residences of families descended from mythological ancestors subordinate to the ancestor of the royal family. The Shang king exercised his authority primarily by ceremonial visits to these towns, by which he demonstrated his power and confirmed the ties between the town and the capital city. Shang walled cities stood as islands in a sea of unfriendly or even hostile "barbarians," peoples ethnically distinct from the cultural heritage claimed by the Shang. In fact, some scholars have argued that the impetus for the organization of the Shang state lay in the need for defense against ethnically different groups that also inhabited the north China plain.

The distinction between town and countryside was seen as the line between what was civilized (the city) and what was suburban: farmland, pasturage, forest, or even borderland. Areas occupied by hostile ethnic groups not related to the Shang were, by definition, "uncivilized." As elsewhere, however, the relationship between the city and its hinterland was crucial: farmers produced food and other goods that were necessary for the provision of urban dwellers and for the support of the ruling elite. The protection of access to such vital resources was an essential function of the Shang military.

CITIES, COMMERCE, AND COMPLEXITY

In the succeeding Zhou period (ca. 1027–250 B.C.E.), towns were organized into *guo*, states whose leaders were ranked and titled according to a hierarchy based on the intimacy of their relationship to the Zhou king. The hierarchical link between each of these territories and the Zhou capital was confirmed by the ceremonial placement of a mound of earth that came from the king's own altar of earth in the capital city. A network of kinship ties bound clans identified by common surname and lineages sharing common descent in the towns with the Zhou king in the capital city.

By about 700 B.C.E., a second stage of urban development took place. As the power of the Zhou king waned because of the weakening of kinship links with each new generation, cities evolved from fortified ceremonial enclaves dependent on periodic expeditions to acquire resources to centralized facilities serving a spatially integrated hinterland. In addition to structural change, cities grew in size and number. Less a weblike organization based on kinship ties and more an aggregation of dwellings, markets, and public buildings, a city of the late Zhou period housed otherwise diverse and unrelated people based on their common goals. These developments were related both to the breakdown of the kin-based social structure and to the rise of the bureaucratic centralized state, as well as to the development of commerce. They reflected the increasing complexity of purpose and participation of many different segments of population common to city life everywhere.

FIGURE 3.5 Han Dynasty Tile Showing the Symbolic Orientation of a Chinese City, with Four Cardinal Directions Symbolized by a Black Turtle-snake (North—Bottom); a Red Bird (South—Top); a Green Dragon (East—Left); and a White Tiger (West—Right)

SOURCE: K. C. Chang, *Art, Myth, and Ritual* (Harvard University Press, 1983). General Research Division, New York Public Library, Astor, Lenox and Tilden Foundations.

Chinese Cities as Ceremonial Centers

After the unification of the empire in the third century B.C.E., the Chinese capital cities retained the ceremonial function of the Shang and Zhou capitals. Like the cities of the Shang and early Zhou periods, the imperial capitals and other urban sites were administrative and political centers rather than primarily centers of population, production, and trade. Sites were chosen using principles of geomancy: selection of landscapes with topographical properties that were believed to confer benefits on the residents of the city. In the imperial capital, the ruler's palace and other important buildings were built in a south-facing direction, to take advantage of the benevolent southern winds. The city itself was laid out in a regular square, with thoroughfares running north–south and east–west, embodying symmetry and order as the imperial capital manifested the patterned order of the empire.

CHANG'AN: IMPERIAL CAPITAL

Chang'an, the imperial capital during the Han (206 B.C.E.–220 C.E.) and Tang (618–907 C.E.) dynasties, located in northwest China, is a superb example of the representation of order and symmetry in the building of an imperial capital. Extending to 25 kilometers (15.5 miles) around the city, the walls of Chang'an were built of pounded earth and some bricks by large forces of both men and women conscript laborers. Twelve gates in the walls each measured 6 meters (20 feet) across. The gates had watchtowers for watchmen to monitor the comings and goings of people into and out of the city and to call for the closing of the gates if danger threatened. The city was probably crisscrossed by major thoroughfares that ran both east–west and north–south, with earthenware gullies at the sides to drain away waste water. There existed perhaps as many as 160 wards, divisions of the city set up for residences, temples, palaces, or markets. A Han poet described the dwellings in some of the wards as being packed together "as closely as the teeth of a comb." Marketplaces, of which there were several in Han Chang'an, were more than sites of commercial exchange where urban residents purchased food, textiles, pottery, lamp oil, and other necessities; they were also public places where such things as executions took place to warn people of the punishment for disloyalty or other crimes, where entertainers such as jugglers or acrobats could be found, and where imperial announcements would be made to the population at large.

The imperial palace faced southward to receive the benefits of the direction associated with the sun. In addition, there were religious shrines such as the "Hall of Light," where the emperor performed rituals designed to ensure cosmic order. Other shrines and ceremonial buildings provided places for the populace to demonstrate their loyalty to the emperor or for members of the upper classes to venerate their ancestors and otherwise show their status.

Life in Imperial Chang'an Already in the first century C.E., the affluent lifestyle of urban residents who belonged to the nobility was coming under criticism, revealing something of the luxurious lives lived by some people in the city. They lived in splendid, multistoried houses and kept richly ornamented horse-drawn carriages to ride about the city in. Wealthy people wore fine silks, ate exotic foods such as quails, baby goat, pickles, and oranges, and drank imported wine in inlaid silver goblets. They were entertained by private orchestras, dancers, acrobats, and trained animals. The lives of the majority of the urban population contrasted sharply with the world of the nobility. The city housed a large population of families who lived in poor dwellings, wore rough clothing, and ate inadequate amounts of even the simplest food. Occasionally crime became rampant in the city, and possibly the poorer residents of Chang'an saw robbery as a means of improving their lot in life. Gangs, distinguished by particular clothing, weapons, and armor, sometimes roamed the streets. The inequality characteristic of the society as a whole was intensified in urban settings, where rich and poor were thrust up against each other with greater intimacy and frequency than in rural life, sometimes resulting in violence.

COMMERCIAL AND CAPITAL CITIES

In the mid–eighth century C.E., Chang'an was probably the largest city in the world, with a population of more than 1 million enclosed within the city walls and immediate suburban surroundings. It was the terminus of the Silk Road, the great caravan route across Central Asia, that brought goods to China and carried Chinese silks and spices to other parts of the Eurasian continent. Thus Chang'an was both an imperial capital—a ceremonial political center—and a center of international trade.

Beginning in the late Tang, towns and cities increasingly grew up as centers of commerce, but these commercial cities existed side by side with administrative towns that were walled enclaves of political authority. As early as the ninth century, the southern port city of Canton was a center of international trade. Despite the growth of Canton and other commercial cities, the urban legacy of early China remained throughout its history in the walled towns that dotted the rural landscape, and in the planned imperial capitals of later dynasties. The city of Beijing was built as a capital by the Mongol rulers of China in the thirteenth century and today remains the capital of China.

■

CITIES IN MEDITERRANEAN EUROPE

Cities rose in Europe conspicuously later than they did elsewhere in the world. Because urbanization was late in appearing, the rise of cities in Europe is perhaps more directly related to the development of agriculture there, though no single model holds sway. Despite the di-

THE CITY AS A COSMO-MAGICAL SYMBOL

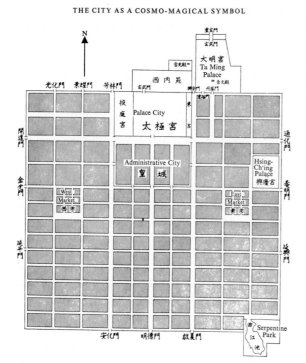

FIGURE 3.6 Plan of Chang'an, Tang Dynasty, China

SOURCE: Paul Wheatley, *The Pivot of the Four Quarters* (Chicago: Aldine, 1971). General Research Division, New York Public Library, Astor, Lenox and Tilden Foundations.

versity of the European continent—the Mediterranean basin is as different from the Danube and Rhine River basins as they are different from the rocky fringelands of Scandinavia and the northern British Isles—a common relationship existed between agricultural developments and urbanization. As elsewhere, in the process of settling down, Europeans practiced agriculture and pastoralism in combination with gathering and hunting. This pattern of subsistence was subsequently replaced by developments that were considerably affected by environment. It was in fertile Balkan valleys that some of the earliest permanent agricultural settlements took root. Such settlements did not mean the abandonment of a mixed economy, and farming continued to be combined with collecting, fishing, and hunting. Many Balkan communities specialized in metalworking, providing some of the earliest evidence of copper and bronze technology.

Permanent settlements supported by agriculture appeared throughout Europe, though in a variety of patterns and at differing times. They were at once the final stage of the European agricultural revolution and the first stage in the emergence of European cities. European agricultural village societies were in time replaced by densely populated, complex organized urban centers based on expanding technologies and economies.

KNOSSOS

Something of the pace and character of early urban development in Mediterranean Europe can be seen in the examples of Knossos, Athens, and Rome. By around 1800 B.C.E., the complex of Knossos on the island of Crete displayed characteristics associated with the rise of urban centers throughout the world. Our knowledge of Knossos, the center of Minoan civilization, is derived from myth, archaeology, and written inscriptions. According to Greek legend, the Minotaur—the mythical half man, half bull—was confined in a labyrinth in the palace of the founder of Knossos, King Minos. Archaeological excavations have confirmed the existence of the labyrinth by revealing vast complexes beneath the palaces in Knossos. In addition to the palaces, Knossos included working people's residences, as well as, businesses and warehouses that supplied the trading networks of Cretan merchants throughout the Aegean Sea. The chief building was the Great Palace, the "House of Minos," consisting of numerous rooms around a central paved courtyard. Among the rooms was a throne room, residential chambers, and bathrooms. Much of the palace was made up of private rooms connected by halls. Walls in some of the rooms were decorated with beautiful murals, and the palace also included practical facilities such as a remarkable drainage system and water supply. When excavation was completed, the palace complex was found to cover 874 square meters (9400 square feet).

ATHENS

The early history of Athens is obscure, but there are traces—remains of walls, early fortifications, pieces of a tower, and tombs—that suggest a settlement as early as around 1500 B.C.E. These remains indicate a small place of minor significance, a settlement primarily of local importance. The Greek poet Homer (ca. 800 B.C.E.) made scant mention of Attica, the area where Athens was located; indeed, at the time he described, Athens was no more important than other communities found there. Athens did enjoy an ongoing and unbroken course of development, in part because of the favorable situation of the abrupt hill—the Acropolis—on which Athenians erected their earliest settlement. The Acropolis dominated the surrounding plain and possessed easy communication with the sea. Soon dwellings spread around the base of the Acropolis. Relying on its agricultural hinterland, Athens absorbed the other communities of the Attic plain as it grew. Public buildings were built, and those who lived in the town were interconnected with those who dwelt in the countryside around it by political and religious activities, by commerce and society, by their interdependency. Those in the rural areas benefited from the trading connections made possible by political and economic links overseas. In turn, they fed their city neighbors.

Athena, the Patron Goddess of Athens It was also the city's role as the reserved precinct of the goddesses and gods of Attica that distinguished Athens as the urban center for the farmland and villages that made up its hinterland. Ancient Greek religion focused neither on sacred texts nor on abstract dogmas but was rooted in community practices: rituals, festivals, processions, athletic contests, oracles, gift giving, and animal sacrifices. Fully one-third of the calendar year was devoted to festivals, opportunities for public communal assemblies in which people could honor the gods and goddesses and enjoy feasting and entertainment. The most important festival in ancient Athens was the Panathenaia, the annual state festival honoring the city's patron deity, the goddess Athena Polias ("of the city"). Every four years the festival was celebrated on a much grander scale, including musical competitions, recitations of Homer's epic poetry, gymnastic and equestrian contests, and a long, colorful procession through the city to the goddess Athena's shrine on the Acropolis. The culmination of this spectacle was the presentation of a *peplos,* a richly woven robe, to the cult statue of Athena. Spinning and weaving occupied most of women's time, even elite

Athenian women's. In Homer's *Odyssey,* while the hero Odysseus is on his long voyage home from the Trojan Wars, his patient and faithful wife, Penelope, has spent her time weaving and then unraveling her father-in-law's burial shroud, thus fending off unwelcome suitors whom she could not marry until the shroud was completed. Athena's *peplos* was traditionally woven by young women selected from upper-class Athenian families.

The Agora, Focus of City Life   Almost as important a priority to residents of Athens as religion was the *agora,* or market, the focus of commercial life, where everyone had a right to trade agricultural surplus or manufactured articles. No elites controlled the access to or distribution of valuable goods. The *agora* was a civic forum too, where, after worship and marketing, property owners might discuss common community issues—such as customs duties or the issues of government or war—in a sort of open-air town council. It was accepted in Athens that decisions made in common were preferable to any made by a single person.

Small farmers were always of decisive importance to Athens, as they provided the connection between independent agrarian village life and urban society. As infantrymen they protected the city. They preferred to live in small communities and to go out to their fields each day, but they went to the urban center on market days, for religious occasions, or to attend the town council. The first Athenians to abandon this pattern and become permanent residents in the city were artisans and craftspeople, blacksmiths, potters, weavers, and tanners. These small-business concerns made up of skilled workers held both rural laborers and the urban poor in contempt. Between 750 and 550 B.C.E., the number of city dwellers swelled as the result of a population explosion which lessened the already sparse amount of arable land in Attica. Increasing urbanization lead to expanding trade beyond the city as well as increasing complexity within it.

Commerce and the City   Athenians looked to the sea, and trade and entrepreneurship resulted in overseas connections and expansion. Commerce and values associated with commerce became triumphant. Great fortunes were made by merchants who traded across the Mediterranean, and by the fifth century B.C.E. numerous commercial middlemen had begun to share in the profits of that trade. Athens began to develop specialties and, as it did so, to import much of its raw materials and food: two-thirds of the grain consumed by Athenians was imported. But it was trade and industry that became basic to the city's future greatness.

Life in Athens took place largely outdoors. Meals were eaten outside, and talking and drinking lasted into the night. After about 500 B.C.E., the gap between rich and poor began to be felt in city life. As the city became a magnificent intellectual and trade center, Athenians' tastes became more exotic. Peacock eggs or pigs which had died of overeating were considered delicacies. Wine and olives were plentiful on the tables of the wealthy elite. The period of classical Athenian "greatness," was also a time of impoverishment for many city dwellers: the poor might have to make a meal of a few beans, greens, turnips, wild fruit, seeds, or grasshoppers swallowed with a mouthful of barley paste.

Urban Life and Epidemics One major problem that appeared wherever there was a concentration of population in urban environments was the spread of disease. Although documentation of epidemics in early history is sparse, the famous Greek historian Thucydides recorded an epidemic of an unknown disease that swept through Athens in 430–429 B.C.E. The introduction of this disease into the Athenian population was probably related to its reliance on Mediterranean trade, since the disease began in the Athenian port city of Piraeus before it attacked Athens. The expansion of population in the Mediterranean, China, and India that made urban growth possible attests to the balance achieved in these regions between parasitic infectious disease organisms and the inherited resistance found in the gene pools of inhabitants of these regions. Nevertheless, sudden outbreaks of new diseases were intensified by the crowded conditions of urban life.

ROME

The story of the other great Mediterranean city, Rome, follows a pattern similar to that of Athens. Evidence suggests that the hills along the banks of the Tiber River in central Italy were inhabited at an early period: flint as well as Bronze Age implements have been found. There is a continuous archaeological record from the early Iron Age, and graves indicate that the hills were inhabited from as early as the ninth century B.C.E. The agricultural communities that came together to form Rome were clustered around seven hills; the valleys between the hills were drained by ditches or sewers, known as cloacae, which are among the most ancient Roman remains. The hills, naturally adaptable for defense, were crowned by separate fortifications, their object being to render their communities inaccessible to outsiders. The task of uniting these separate agricultural communities into one city was as much a matter of architecture and engineering as of politics.

It seems likely that the earliest settlement bearing the name "Rome" was on the Palatine Hill, which was among the more defensible ones. It had the added advantage of being close to the Tiber River, thus possessing easy communication with the sea, 27 kilometers (17 miles) away. Tradition has it that the first king of the community on the Palatine Hill was Romulus; his successors brought the other six hill communities under their sway, thus forming the city of Rome. The traditional date for the founding of the city is 753 B.C.E.

Growth in the size, wealth, and power of the city was accompanied by social and political tension. Divisions between the privileged patricians—the "fathers" of the Roman state—

FIGURE 3.8 The Roman Forum Viewed from the Palatine Hill

The Roman Forum, view from the Palatine Hill. In foreground, columns of the temple to Castor and Pollux; on left, remains of Caesar's basilica; above left, the arch of Septimius Severus; above right, the curia or Senatehouse.

SOURCE: Art Resource, NY.

and the plebeians, the ordinary Romans, transformed the separate communities on the seven hills beside the Tiber into a city that became the focus of a vast political empire. Urban processes were both the result of and the impetus for political centralization, which exploited growing inequalities.

Poverty and Inequality as Conditions of Urban Life One of the measures of those inequalities was the documented presence of poverty and hunger in Rome. *Annona* was the term for the distribution of free grain by the city's authorities, a drastic measure to address the persistent poverty that had begun to plague the urban center as early as the second century C.E. From as early as the sixth century B.C.E., serious shortages and famines had occurred; by the time of Julius Caesar's successor, Augustus, in the first century C.E., about 320,000 persons (just under one-third of the population of Rome) were receiving public assistance in the form of *annona,* reckoned to be about 14 million bushels of wheat.

The Roman Diet The poor citizens of Rome were crowded into tenements: tall, narrow *insulae.* Fuel was expensive and cooking fires were dangerous, so many people avoided cooking themselves, instead relying on "grimy cookshops" on the streets below that

FIGURE 3.9 Roman Tile
Mosaic Depicts
Pressing Olives

SOURCE: Lauros-Giraudon/Art
Resource, NY.

served questionable meats grilled beyond recognition and dry bread. By contrast, the food of the rich was remarkably diverse and ostentatious. Foods were decorated and elaborately presented in feasts: a cooked rabbit given bird wings might be arranged to look like Pegasus. The tables of wealthy Romans held pickles from Spain, pomegranates from North Africa, oysters from Britain, and spices from as far away as Indonesia. But even for the wealthy, foods had to be imported from long distances and stored in warehouses. Disguising the taste of rancid foods was a necessity. Heavily spiced foods were a necessary, if ineffective, antidote to spoiled food. Many Romans also suffered from lead poisoning, a condition brought about by the use of lead in the manufacture of lead-lined water pipes and wine storage vessels.

■ CITIES IN TRANS-ALPINE EUROPE

Cities were much later appearing in Europe north of the Alps than Athens or Rome. For a thousand years after the "fall of Rome" (476 C.E.), only small, frontierlike towns were found north of the Mediterranean basin. The history of Paris is typical of Trans-Alpine (the area north of the Alps) urbanization. Little in the early history of Paris suggested its future importance. Yet, like Athens and Rome, it had certain environmental and geographical advantages that account for its ultimate rise to prominence as one of the earliest important north European urban centers. Paris occupies the center of the Paris basin, a fertile and naturally endowed area in north-central France. It owes its development to several factors: its proximity to fertile agricultural country, particularly grain-growing areas, such as Brie and the Beauce; the existence of quarries, with good building material lying bare in several areas; and its position as the meeting place of great natural highways such as the Rhône and Seine Rivers from the Mediterranean and the Atlantic, and from Spain over the western French lowlands.

PARIS

Paris began on an island in the Seine much smaller than the present Ile de la Cité, both a central and a defensible location. From this location, its people navigated the lower course of the Seine and perhaps reached the coast of Britain. They were so few in number that in time they placed themselves under the protection of other powerful neighbors. In 53 B.C.E., Paris was subjugated by Julius Caesar, who made it the meeting place of political deputies from all over the Roman province of Gaul. As Paris expanded its river commerce and grew in wealth, it also became a religious center. Romans built a temple to Jupiter there, and subsequently Christians located one of their earliest north European bishops there, probably in the third century C.E. By becoming the seat of a bishop, Paris, as Christian Europeans reckoned it, became a city. It took another thousand years for it to become a major urban center—of secular government, commerce, industry, and culture.

Early Paris suffered the growing pains of many expanding population centers. The divisions between countryside and urban life were often blurred. Streets were muddy pastureland where sheep and pigs grazed on grass and garbage. A twelfth-century C.E. Parisian "traffic jam" caused a pig to run between the legs of a horse, upsetting his rider, the heir to the royal throne. Individual households sometimes had gardens and vineyards (on the other side of town walls) to supplement the availability and offset the high cost of foods. Still, there were many poor and many hungry. Even the wealthy Parisian could not escape the unpleasantness and pollution that was the consequence of an increasing urban population. The concentration of specialists who flocked to cities to produce and sell their wares in the great city markets contributed to a significant decline in the quality of water and hygiene, even as it helped develop the city's trade and economy. The city government faced enormous problems and complaints about activities it tried to regulate and control. Blood and carcasses from slaughter-

FIGURE 3.10 Farming Outside the Walls of the City of Paris, ca. Fifteenth Century C.E.

SOURCE: Musée Condé/Giraudon/Art Resource, NY.

houses and chemicals from tanneries, waste products from smelting and smithing, choking smoke from the burning of coal and other fuels, noisy industrial activities—all created undesirable living conditions for city residents. Disease and vermin, such as rats, were rampant. Filth was everywhere a condition of urban existence. Public baths—there were only thirty-two in Paris in 1268 C.E.—were eventually banned by the Church because of their noted contribution to rampant promiscuity, no doubt to the regret of many except the *parfumeurs.*

■
WEST AFRICA: EARLY CITIES OF TRADE

Urban development occurred in parts of Africa other than the Nile Valley at later dates and was perhaps less environmentally determined than was urbanization in ancient Egypt. In the present-day West African nation of Mali, oral traditions indicate that the city of Jenne-Jeno dates from about the eighth century C.E. Written historical records mention Jenne (or Jenne-Jeno, "old Jenne") only in 1447 C.E., when an Italian merchant wrote about "Geni," located at the southwestern edge of the navigable inland Niger Delta. Arab chroniclers writing after 1300 C.E. described the city as flourishing and prosperous. Before archaeological investigation, these historical sources had led historians to conclude that the city had developed only 500 years ago in response to the stimulus of Arab trade in North Africa.

JENNE-JENO

Evidence from excavations of Jenne-Jeno made in 1977, however, confirmed a much earlier and entirely indigenous growth of urbanism in the western Sudan. Radiocarbon dates document the continuous settlement of Jenne-Jeno from before 250 B.C.E. In the early phases of the site, its inhabitants fished, hunted, used pottery, and had domesticated the cow. By the first century C.E., they were cultivating African rice. About the same time, people began to build more permanent mud structures and the size of the settlement increased to an area of more than 10 hectares (approximately 25 acres); at the height of the settlement (400–900 C.E.), Jenne-Jeno had spread to more than three times that size. Its population may have reached between 7000 and 10,000 inhabitants. Finds of pottery and terra-cotta sculpture, copper, iron slag, and gold indicate a rich material culture, craft specialization, and the involvement of the city in long-distance trade.

Jenne-Jeno was a city without a citadel. A large wall, however, that measured about 3 meters (10 feet) across was built around the city. As was characteristic of West African urban wall-building traditions, the Jenne-Jeno wall was probably not built for defensive purposes. Walls served to define the settlement's identity and allow the city's elite to protect and tax the flow of goods, caravans, and people.

Like a number of other West African urban centers, Jenne-Jeno was located on trade routes. The city was an important collecting point for gold and other goods and was critical to the development of West African commercial relations. Like other centers of social, economic, and political complexity, Jenne-Jeno enjoyed a stable agricultural base. The rich flood-plains of the inland Niger Delta produced a considerable surplus in rice, sorghum, and millet and supported trade in these and other foodstuffs, such as smoked and dried fish. Well placed on the axis between the savanna and the edge of the desert, called the Sahel, and situated at the highest point for reliable transport by canoe along the Niger River, Jenne played an important role in the pre-Arab trade network. Both copper and iron were unavailable locally and were brought in from more than 50 kilometers (31 miles) away. By the first millennium C.E., Jenne-Jeno was also participating in long-distance trade in African gold. These early African trade networks appear to have made possible the rapid expansion of trade with Arabs in later centuries.

Regional Systems The example of Jenne-Jeno suggests that a city should not be thought of as an economic breach with the countryside. The origins of West African trade have long been attributed to the external stimulus of North African and Mediterranean contacts, and these contacts, in turn, were believed to have led to the emergence of West African urbanism and political centralization. The evidence from Jenne-Jeno contradicts this view and suggests indigenous trade and independent urban development effectively related to the city's relationship with its own hinterland in an integrated regional system. Archaeologists have surveyed a 100-kilometer-square (62-mile-square) area of Jenne-Jeno's rural hinterland and sampled some forty-two contemporary sites. On the basis of their size and diversity, it is clear that these sites functioned in a hierarchical relationship to Jenne-Jeno with Jenne-Jeno as their center and increasingly smaller settlements spaced at further distances as though along spokes on a wheel. Their patterning further supports the presence of a high degree of urbanism and an intraregional economy with Jenne-Jeno as its center point. Jenne-Jeno flourished not in isolation but within a rich and ancient urban system. The failure of written historical sources prior to the mid–fifteenth century to mention Jenne-Jeno by name may be taken as silent testimony to the independent emergence of the city in West Africa.

■

THE AMERICAS: ANDEAN SOUTH AMERICA AND MESOAMERICA

The complex relationship between agricultural development and urbanization processes in the Americas corresponds to the evidence in Asia and Africa. Village life based on subsistence agriculture was replaced by systematic cultivation and sedentary urban society at about the same time in both South and North America. Population increase made possible by agricultural success was one pathway to the formation of cities. More commonly, urban processes revolved around sacred sites that attracted large populations.

CHAVIN DE HUANTAR

One of the earliest cities in South America was Chavin de Huantar, located in the northern highlands of modern Peru from about 1000 to 100 B.C.E. Substantial stone buildings, probably for ceremonial or religious purposes, were erected on temple platforms. Outside the city center and surrounding its religious core were the dwellings of its inhabitants, which were made of perishable materials. Here is where people traded and practiced their crafts. The specialists of Chavin produced a distinctive pottery: "Chavin" has become the name attached to a particular style of pottery as well as to a general culture. Evidence indicates that there were contact and trade between the people of Chavin and the Olmecs of Mesoamerica, where a transition to urban culture was also taking place.

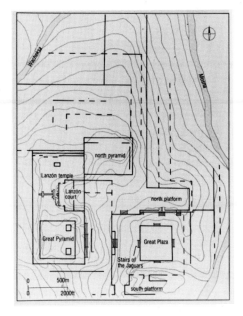

FIGURE 3.11 **Plan of the Andean City of Chavin de Huantar**

Pyramids and plazas occupied the higher elevations in this early South American city.

SOURCE: Michael Coe, Dean Snow, and Elizabeth Benson, *Atlas of Ancient America.* © Andromeda Oxford Ltd.

After about 200 B.C.E., Chavin's primacy gave way to regionalism and smaller, dispersed settlements. A number of cities appear to have existed in northwestern South America, and urban enterprises such as stonemasonry and metalworking had reached a high degree of complexity before the Incas established their dominance many centuries later. How and why these centers of complexity and population formed is still unknown, but they did rely on the domesticated plants and animals familiar to later periods: potato, bean, maize, pepper, dog.

OLMEC URBAN CULTURE

Accompanying the gradual transition from food gathering to food raising in Mesoamerica, a number of sedentary village communities merged into larger urban cultures. Again, why and how this happened is difficult to "read" from the archaeological record. One complex society that developed along the coasts of and inland from the Gulf of Mexico is the Olmec culture. Important archaeological remains—monumental stone architecture and sculpture—indicate that the urban society of the Olmec people flourished between 1200 and 900 B.C.E. As elsewhere in the Americas, buildings were primarily ceremonial in nature—temple-crowned pyramids facing vast plazas—and they were generally set outside the city sites. Evidence of irrigation systems that suggest reliance on an agricultural hinterland have been found, and both artifacts and the widespread influence of Olmec artistic style and motifs suggest that the Olmecs engaged in long-distance trade in raw materials such as stone and obsidian. Following the decline of the Olmec center, the city of El Pital developed as a sprawling seaport between 100 and 600 C.E. The core of this city and its suburbs extended over 103 square kilometers (40 square miles), and it is estimated to have had more than 20,000 inhabitants. When systematic excavations are eventually conducted, historians may know more about the relationship between urban growth here and elsewhere in Mesoamerica.

FIGURE 3.12 Pyramid of the Sun at Teotihuacán, Valley of Mexico

SOURCE: Foto Marburg/Art Resource, NY.

TEOTIHUACÁN: "PLACE OF THE GODS"

In the Valley of Mexico, the powerful urban center of Teotihuacán ranks as one of the great cities of the ancient world. It was founded about 100 B.C.E. and lasted until about 750 C.E. Approximately 2600 buildings have been excavated at its site not far from present-day Mexico City. The palaces, temples, apartment compounds, ceremonial plazas, and markets of Teotihuacán were laid out in an orderly grid pattern, which was occupied by at least 100,000 city dwellers. The uniform large apartment compounds organized around patios, each with its own drainage system, may have been inhabited by clans or guilds. The Pyramid of the Sun, measuring 220 by 232 meters (720 by 760 feet) at its base, is twenty stories high; it is linked to the smaller Pyramid of the Moon by a stately avenue. Quarters for priests and storehouses flank the larger pyramid.

The most important inhabitants of the city were the goddesses and gods of Teotihuacán. These included the Sun and Moon, the Feathered Serpent known as Quetzalcoatl (god of the wind), the Fire Serpent (who each day caries the sun across the sky), and the Rain Spirit Tlaloc. Life in the city of Teotihuacán was crowded and animated by the constant arrival of daily visitors. Brightly colored parrot and quetzal feathers, foods from rural fields, prisoners of war to be sacrificed in the urban capital—all manner of ordinary and exotic goods and peoples entered the city. The inner city's residents were mainly the wealthy elite and their servants, who lived in luxurious dwellings that consisted of rooms around a common courtyard. Laborers and specialists lived on the outskirts of the city, but daily markets must have brought many to the city center for trade and exchange. Life inside the city probably also included many masked performances in splendid costumes. The mural art of these and other activities shows a rich vocabulary of images, masked figures, and deities. The laws of the city were embodiments of the natural order of the universe, as harsh and demanding as it was a lush and bountiful paradise. Mortality rates were high; overcrowding, problems of sanitation, and poverty were ever present.

Mesoamerican Connections Teotihuacán was involved in the trading network that linked Mesoamerican cultures together and ultimately connected with those of North and South America. One of the most prominent Mesoamerican cultures was that of the Maya (classic Maya fl. ca. 250–900 C.E.) Tikal, one of the main Mayan cities, boasted a population of nearly 50,000. This and other cities controlled outlying territories and extracted the resources of these areas to support the rich material life of the urban centers. The economy of the Maya was based on the cultivation of maize, and most of the population were farmers who depended on agriculture and trade for their livelihood. In the lowlands of the Yucatán peninsula, where the Maya were concentrated, there were around fifty cities, ceremonial centers for the practice of religious ritual on graduated-platform mounds.

Many artifacts of other cultures and traditions have been found at Teotihuacán. Objects crafted from the shiny black volcanic rock called obsidian, one of the specialties of the more than 500 workshops there, has been found widely distributed. Teotihuacán attracted outside invaders as well as merchants, and around 750 C.E. it was sacked and burned by the Toltec people, who were expanding southward. The great houses and temples were abandoned, but the city's site was not. Despite fluctuations in their fortunes, urban centers have continued in the Valley of Mexico since Teotihuacán's heyday: modern Mexico City, not far distant from the site of the ancient city, is proof of that continuity.

NORTH AMERICA

In the period before the arrival of Europeans, many of the peoples who lived north of the Rio Grande in North America remained gatherer-hunters, thanks to the bounty of their environment, and perhaps most of those who did practice some form of agriculture did so only to supplement other activities. Complex agricultural systems comparable to those that developed in Mesoamerica did in time appear in an area that is now the southeastern United States, between the Atlantic and the Great Plains, the Mississippi and Ohio Valleys, and the Gulf of Mexico. This is the area of the Mississippian culture.

MISSISSIPPIAN URBANISM: CAHOKIA

Mississippian culture began developing before 700 C.E. and spanned the next 700 years. A pattern of cultivation of beans, corn, and squash similar to that of Mesoamerica made it possible for full-time agriculture to sustain an increasing population. The Mississippians—a general name for many different peoples and cultures scattered over thousands of square miles—lived on farms and in villages, towns, and cities. None can compare, however, with Cahokia, clearly the principal center of Mississippian culture, which was located in present-day southern Illinois just across the river from the modern city of Saint Louis, Missouri. About 25,000 people lived in Cahokia at its peak around 1100 C.E., and it was the focus of a much larger group of people who lived in the hamlets and villages that constituted its hinterland. With the increasing complexity of the urban center at Cahokia, these smaller hinterland settlements adapted to meet the demands of increasingly structured obligations and opportunities by altering their production of goods, provision of services, and participation in ceremonies that linked them ritually to the urban center. Urban development thus affected not only the people living in cities but also people outside the cities.

Monumental Architecture Built of Soil   Cahokia, like other Mississippian towns, was part of a trading network that stretched from Hudson Bay to the Gulf of Mexico and probably on into Mesoamerica, and from the Atlantic to the Rocky Mountains. Graves at Cahokia reveal the extent of the trade that centered there. In them, copper from Lake Superior, flints from the areas of Oklahoma and North Carolina, and many art objects from afar have been found. Cahokia covered almost 16 square kilometers (6 square miles) and was protected by a series of stockades and bastions. It contained more than 100 human-made earthen mounds, dominated by the largest earthen mound in North America, Monk's Mound, the base of which covers 37 hectares (15 acres). Standing a hundred feet high, Monk's Mound was one of the largest human-made structures in the Americas before the European conquest. Mounds, which were common to Mississippian towns, account for the description of the Mississippians as "Mound Builders." As in Mesoamerica and South America, the mounds were used for ritual and ceremonial purposes, as temple or burial mounds. They were built with great effort of the most readily available local material: dirt, every grain of which was carried and put into place by humans. The Mississippian culture reached its peak sometime between 1200 and 1300 C.E., after which its populations began to decline and cities to be abandoned.

FIGURE 3.13 **The Mississippian Urban Center of Cahokia**

Moundville Reconstruction of Cahokia from the west, ca. 1200

SOURCE: Michael Coe, Dean Snow, and Elizabeth Benson, *Atlas of Ancient America.* © Andromeda Oxford Ltd.

SUMMARY

This chapter has provided examples of the transition from early settled communities to urban centers beginning as early as the sixth millennium B.C.E. These early cities were concentrations of increasingly diverse and highly stratified populations. Many originated as or became ceremonial centers, drawing large numbers of people to participate in rituals that were believed to propitiate deities, to encourage good agricultural harvests, or to request the support of the gods in war against their enemies. The great Pyramid of the Sun at Teotihuacán was the site of sacrificial rites that were believed to ensure the constancy of the sun's daily movement across the sky. The exercise of political power, including the symbolic representation of that power in monumental architecture, played a key role in the rise of cities. Cities as ceremonial centers were established at sites that were both economically and strategically advantageous. The Shang capital of Anyang was located on the boundary between the north China plain and the mountainous regions to the west, a good defensive site in close proximity to resources needed to provision the ruling elite, the priests who were responsible for overseeing the ritual divination essential to the sanctioning of the king's authority, and the urban workers who crafted ritual bronzes.

Cities gradually transcended their original primary functions. They were the centers from which ideology, institutions, material goods, and other urban "products" were transmitted to their hinterlands, on which they in turn depended. Such systems were also recipients of goods, peoples, and ideas from areas beyond their radii. The degree of urbanism in any part of the world was dependent on the ability of each large community to maintain an integrative system between itself and its hinterland. Though cities flourished around the world, most people still did not live in cities; most did, however, live in intricate relationship with them, visiting them, trading with them, and supporting them with food and other necessary and valued goods and services.

Wherever urban systems appeared, they had common characteristics. Urban society became more complex than that of earlier gathering-hunting-agrarian communities. It involved larger numbers of people and greater management and control of resources and environments, resulting in a wider variety of economic activity and a more rigid structuring and organization of the city's inhabitants. In addition to more opportunities and the availability of more goods and services, urban life often meant the intensification of inequality and rigid divisions along lines of class, status, and gender. The systems of authority and relationships of inequality found in urban settings grew out of earlier patterns of larger social groupings and evolved to suit the conditions of urban life: complex and large communities of varied, interdependent parts required the mechanisms of control and centralized decision making to negotiate these differences. For example, gender differences and relations became more clearly defined. Even in early agricultural communities, male dominance was more accentuated than it had been in gathering-hunting societies, an accentuation that was powerfully confirmed and perpetuated in urban societies. Some male gods were even credited with the growth of cities, and male warriors and rulers protected the trade routes that connected cities with their supporting hinterlands.

The growth of cities was neither quick nor regular. It was a slow, varied, and disjointed process by which prior social dynamics were merged into developing urban systems; but once under way, the process of accumulating levels of complexity and diversity continued without cessation or reversal. Complexity inevitably resulted from the successful integration and exploitation of differences—whether of gender, status, family group, or occupation—which in turn characterized successful urban life. Cities everywhere thus shared another common feature: they became hierarchical enclaves in which inhabitants were increasingly subject to the experience and expectation of inequality and injustice. Privilege and power were further defined by the accumulation of wealth made possible by the centralizing momentum of urban life.

Cities became centers of complex social space. Some urban residents were stratified, dominated, and exploited by others. The tools of authority and control necessary for territorial and material expansion were also directed toward the control of diverse urban populations. Well-organized, exploitative systems enabled cities and their elites to accommodate their expanding populations and maintain growth and order. City dwellers built buildings and produced art; they engaged in abstract intellectual expression, producing artifacts that historians have used to define urban cultures. But urban processes resulted not only in the benefits enjoyed by complex societies and cultures; homelessness, exploitation, and injustice have also been characteristic of the urban experience throughout world history. People residing in the hinter-

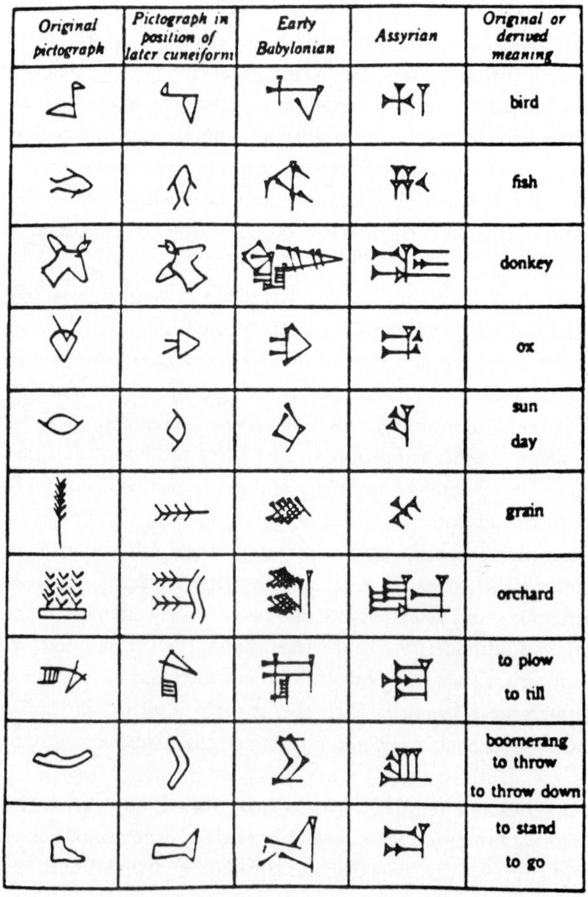

Original pictograph	Pictograph in position of later cuneiform	Early Babylonian	Assyrian	Original or derived meaning
				bird
				fish
				donkey
				ox
				sun / day
				grain
				orchard
				to plow / to till
				boomerang / to throw / to throw down
				to stand / to go

FIGURE 3.14 Cuneiform Characters from West Asian Writing Systems Have Been Used as One Measure of "Civilization"

SOURCE: William McNeill, *A History of the Human Community,* vol. 1 (Prentice-Hall, 1990, 3rd edition).

lands were drawn to emerging cities by the promise of opportunity for economic gain or material benefits. But often this proved elusive and led only to the exchange of rural hardships for misery and exploitation in an urban setting.

It is difficult to find one all-embracing reason that explains the origins of all cities, but it is impossible to understand the historical rise of urbanism without taking into account the functional relationship between the urban center and its surrounding area. The process of successful integration of city and countryside, of constructing a larger political or community identity from increasingly diverse and divergent parts, is common to all the urban societies described in this chapter. Cities remain a constant throughout history after their appearance in the sixth millennium B.C.E., and both cultural and historical circumstances determine the changing nature of cities and their variety. In the following chapters we will discuss cities such as Baghdad, an Islamic city, and Constantinople, the capital of the Byzantine empire, as they reflect changing ideologies and political structures, the subject of Part II.

ENGAGING THE PAST

THE MEANING OF HISTORICAL MODELS

In the nineteenth century, the German sociologist Max Weber listed five criteria as the defining characteristics of a city, including such things as having a marketplace and the use of writing. Weber's definition of a city can be seen as one example of an ideal type, a model that helps to organize disparate facts into a coherent whole. In the 1950s, the British archaeologist V. Gordon Childe proposed the following ten criteria of urbanism: concentration of population; craft specialization; a redistributive mode of economic integration; monumental public architecture; social stratification; the use of writing; the emergence of exact and predictive sciences; naturalistic art; foreign trade; and group membership based on residence rather than kinship. Clearly, many of the cities discussed in this chapter would not fit the prescriptive definitions of either Weber or Childe, yet their ideas have been profoundly influential in the study of cities. Both Weber's and Childe's definitions of a city should be seen as ideal types that help us to compare, interpret, and analyze information, not as evaluative models against which to measure what should be considered a city and what should not.

As pointed out in this chapter, the English word "civilization" is derived from the Latin *civitas,* which is also the root of the term "civic," relating to a city. Until quite recently, cities were viewed as an evolutionary stage in the development of human society, a stage identified with "civilization."

Both Weber's and Childe's definitions of a city were drawn from a European historical perspective, even in the case of Childe, whose work on ancient west Asia formed the background of his approach to cities. Like the traditional approach to the origins of agriculture critiqued in Chapter 2, which focused on river valleys as the centers of agriculture and settled societies and therefore as the origin of "civilization," cities have been seen as the next stage on the evolutionary model of human history. This model follows a unilinear, Eurocentric pattern, assuming that all human history follows a similar path to the same place. But just as recent archaeological findings have challenged the view of river valleys as the only sites of the origins of agriculture and thus "civilization," so cities can no longer been seen as a necessary next "stage" on the road of human history.

Cities—concentrations of population dependent on access to resources provided by an agricultural hinterland, enhanced by overland or maritime trade—are found throughout the world. But it is important to remember, too, that throughout history, the vast majority of people have not lived in cities, though their lives have been profoundly influenced by the relationships between cities and their hinterlands. No single definition or list of criteria is adequate, apart from the recognition that cities represent a level of complexity distinct from other forms of community.

SUGGESTIONS FOR FURTHER READING

F. R. Allchin, *The Archaeology of Early South Asia: The Emergence of Cities and States* (Cambridge, England: Cambridge University Press, 1995). Up-to-date and useful source on south Asian urbanism.

Carlo M. Cipolla, *The Economic History of World Population* (Harmondsworth, England: Penguin, 1967). Brief, stimulating view of demographic and economic development tracing the history of the great trends in population and wealth that have affected global societies as a whole.

Colin McEvedy and Richard Jones, *Atlas of World Population* (London: Allan Lane/Penguin, 1978). Fully illustrated (with graphs, maps, and diagrams) history of world demography.

Roderick J. and Susan Keech McIntosh, "The Inland Niger Delta before the Empire of Mali: Evidence from Jenne-Jeno," *Journal of African History* 22 (1981): 1–22. Summarizes key research on early west African urbanism at one site and introduces concepts of settlement hierarchy.

A. E. J. Morris, *History of Urban Form: Before the Industrial Revolutions* (New York: Longman Scientific and Technical, 1994). Third edition of the classic introduction to the historical evolution of cities.

Gene S. Stuart, *America's Ancient Cities* (Washington, D.C.: National Geographic Society, 1988). Emphasizes connections and continuity between Mesoamerican and North America.

Reay Tannahill, *Food in History* (New York: Stein and Day, 1973). Classic look at food history in many world cultures.

Paul Wheatley, *The Pivot of the Four Quarters* (Chicago: Aldine, 1971). History of ancient Chinese urbanism in comparative context.

The Deadly Arts: Expressions of Death in World Arts before 1500

Death is perhaps the only truly universal experience in world history. According to the Akan (Ghana, West Africa) proverb, "It is the destiny of every man to descend the ladder of death." This proverb is represented by the symbol of a ladder on Akan funerary pottery from the Late Iron Age. A survey of world art before 1500 C.E. leaves no doubt that death was a universal and serious concern of early artists. Artistic expression became the universal medium for communicating beliefs, fears, questions, and longings about the mysteries of human life and death.

Because life was short (the average lifespan was an estimated 28 years), and perhaps because relatively little could be done to prevent most deaths, one important artistic focus was the continuity of an afterlife. The promise of an eternal life after death has very ancient roots, dating from the earliest human burials in which traces of red ochre

FIGURE CI-1.1 Funerary Terracotta Pottery (Adanse area, Ghana)
SOURCE: National Museum of African Art, Eliot Elisofon Photographic Archives, Smithsonian Institution. Museum purchase, 86-12-4. Photograph by Frank Khoury.

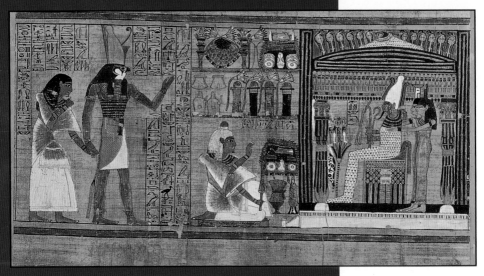

FIGURE CI-1.2 Illustration from the Book of the Dead (Egypt, New Kingdom ca. 1310 B.C.E.), Showing the Deceased Scribe Hu-Nefer, being led to his Hour of Judgment with Osiris, God of the Dead (seated right)
SOURCE: The British Museum/Bridgeman Art Library, London, Bridgeman Art library, Encarta 96, "Illuminated Art Manuscripts"

pigment (connoting blood and life force) have been found. Most societies held beliefs that suggested a spiritual existence after death. This afterlife was portrayed by artists as a site of liminality (between the two realms of the living and dead), or punishment (such as the Buddhist or Judaeo-Christian hells), or promise (images of heaven).

DEATH AS DEPARTURE TO THE AFTERLIFE
Ancient Egyptians envisioned the journey to the afterlife, a liminal state, as a boat trip down the Nile. Egyptian stone inscriptions, wall and coffin paintings, and illustrated manuscripts on papyrus depict the transition as a rather frightful trip to the underworld; others portray preparations for the deceased's travels. Commissioned by private individuals, Egyptian coffin paintings often were personal, autobiographical laments, such as "The Dialogue of a Man with his Soul" (2255–2035 B.C.E.), a debate on suicide. Egyptian funerary beliefs were collected in the Book of the Dead, dating to the time of the

New Kingdom (ca. 1570–1070 B.C.E.) and containing an illustrated set of hymns, prayers, and magic formulas to guide and protect the soul in its journey.

Like Egyptians, Vikings in northern Europe around 1000 C.E. believed the dead journeyed by boat across the sea. Because they were a seafaring people, some Viking chieftains were actually buried in wooden ships, which were sometimes set adrift. While the prows of their ships were decorated with fearsome creatures such as dragons to terrify their enemies, frightening demons believed to protect the Viking dead from evil spirits were carved on the prows of funeral ships. If they died a heroic death in battle, Viking warriors were led to Valhalla, the "hall of the slain," which was ruled by the chief god, Odin. Brought to Valhalla by warrior maidens called *Valkyrie*, the souls of heroic warriors slain in battle nightly feasted with the god Odin.

Funerary arts from around the world share the common concern that the deceased person's life after death be materially comfortable if not better than their lifetime had been. Furniture, food, and sometimes people accompanied the deceased person, as in Aztec, Egyptian, or Chinese society. In Shang China (ca. 1600–1050 B.C.E.), slaves and prisoners of war were executed to accompany a ruler in his afterlife. After Confucius (ca. 500 B.C.E.) criticized this practice, clay figures of servants and entertainers were placed in tombs to accompany the deceased in the afterlife.

FIGURE CI-1.3 Head of elaborately carved post from ship burial at Oseberg in Norway. Probably to protect dead from malignant spirits
SOURCE: Werner Forman/Art Resource, NY.

In both ancient Egypt and China, tombs were filled with elaborate grave goods for use after death. At the site of Mawangdui in south central China a mid-second-century tomb has yielded such items of daily use as red and black lacquer dishes, ladles, and food containers along with the mummified body of a woman known as Lady Dai, who was entombed there with her husband and son. Among the artifacts retrieved from this tomb is a painted silk funerary banner that was draped over Lady Dai's coffin. The figures and symbols depicted on this banner attest to the practice of a ritual described in literary texts as the "summons of the soul." Chinese of the Han period (206 B.C.E. –220 C.E.) believed that the soul had a dual aspect: one part was earthly and returned to the earth at death, and one part was spirit, which left the body at death. The "summons of the soul" ceremony was held to call back the departing spirit. The ritual was performed by waving a banner similar to the one found on Lady Dai's coffin on the rooftop to plead with the spirit to return and thus to bring back the deceased.

PROTECTION OF THE DEAD

Protection of the dead was a paramount concern in many societies' beliefs about the afterlife. Jade was believed by the Chinese to endow its wearer with power. In the Han dynasty a few nobles were buried in elaborately crafted jade suits, made by linking small jade

FIGURE CI-1.4 Han Dynasty Chinese Jade Funerary Suit
SOURCE: Erich Lessing/Art Resource, NY.

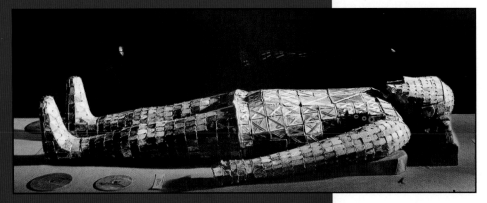

FIGURE CI-1.5 Women Mourners Dance at a Roman Funeral

SOURCE: Scala/Art Resource, NY.

squares with fine gold wire drawn through holes in each corner of the squares. The jade was believed to protect the spirit of the deceased and not allow it to escape, much in the same way that all body orifices of the deceased were stopped up with jade plugs. Other common protective materials used elsewhere for the same purpose were copper and precious stones.

DEATH AND REBIRTH

By the fifth century B.C.E. in the Mediterranean, temples were dedicated to Ceres, a Roman goddess of birth and death associated with the agricultural seasons and the transformations of nature. The link between fertility and returning the dead to the earth was basic to the concept of death as part of the life cycle. Roman women were responsible for preparing and mourning the corpse and thus played an important role in funerary rites.

Central to Christian theology is the death and resurrection of Jesus of Nazareth. In the Flemish painting *The Deposition* by Rogier van der Weyden (ca. 1438), the crucifixion is portrayed as a mournful, human event. Grieving onlookers droop and sag under the profound emotional weight of the death scene. In contrast, the death of Buddha portrayed a state of entering enlightenment, since the Buddha had attained an enlightened state that would allow him to escape the endless cycle of birth-death-rebirth on the Wheel of Life.

FIGURE CI-1.6 "The Deposition"
By Rogier van der Weyden, Flemish, ca. 1438, Prado,
Madrid
SOURCE: Giraudon/Art Resource, NY.

Unenlightened persons would have to face being reborn in a new incarnation according to their karmic record. In popular Buddhism, people looked to a savior deity to help them reach the Western Paradise, where they could be reborn and achieve enlightenment.

DEATH AND JUDGMENT

The counterpart to the Western Paradise was a Buddhist Hell, where the deceased would be judged and their fates determined according to whether or not they had followed the Buddhist prohibitions against such things as taking life or eating meat. At the cave temple site of Dunhuang in northwestern China, a well-preserved series of illustrations in ink and colors on paper from the late ninth or early tenth century depict the Ten Kings of Hell and the Six Ways of Rebirth. Souls are judged and again sent off along one of six paths,

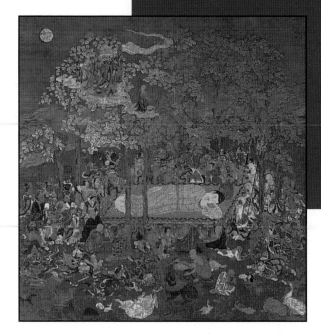

FIGURE CI-1.7 The Death of Buddha
Mid-14th-century Japanese painting showing followers mourning the death of Buddah
SOURCE: Courtesy of the Freer Gallery of Art, Smithsonian Institution, Washington, D.C.

FIGURE CI-1.8 Illustration to the Ten Kings Sutra (Cave 17, Dunhuang, China)
SOURCE: British Museum.

FIGURE CI-1.9 A Muslim vision of heaven where the blessed are seen in a beautiful garden, visiting one another and exchanging nosegays of flowers. Illustrated manuscript of the *Miraj Namah*, the Miraculous Journey of Muhammad, painted at Herat in the 15th century.
SOURCE: Bibliothèque Nationale de France.

shown by the artist as clouds trailing away from the place of judgment. On the lowest, the Way of Demons is represented by a horned beast stirring a cauldron. Next a distraught figure stands for the Way of Hungry Ghosts. A camel and horse represent rebirth in the Way of Animals, followed by the Way of Men. Above the illustration of rebirth in human form is the Way of Demons and finally, the highest path, the Way of Divine Beings.

Heaven, hell, and judgment were equally part of Islamic beliefs about death and the afterlife. Muslims believed that the trumpet would sound the day of judgment when the dead would be raised and called to account. Much as the beliefs of popular Buddhism pictured a place of judgment and entry either into the Western Paradise or a hell of torment, Muslims who had followed God's laws would be summoned to enter paradise, where they would live eternally in the most luxurious conditions imagined in their earthly existence. As the Christian Biblical paradise, the Garden of Eden, Muslims pictured paradise as a garden of earthly delights.

In early Mesoamerica, the ballgame known as *tlachtli* by the Aztecs, was associated with death, judgment, and ritual sacrifice. Well before the Aztecs, the game was played with solid rubber balls as early as 1000 B.C.E. according to various rules. In one version, the ball had to be kept in motion and could not be hit with hands or feet. The ballgame was more than simply sport; *tlachtli* involved a public ritual reenactment of judgment. Stone reliefs graphically

FIGURE CI-1.10 Ballplayers in the Underworld, from 7th-century Vase
Peter Region, Maya. Undeciphered glyphs probably contain names and titles of deceased.
SOURCE: Justin Kerr.

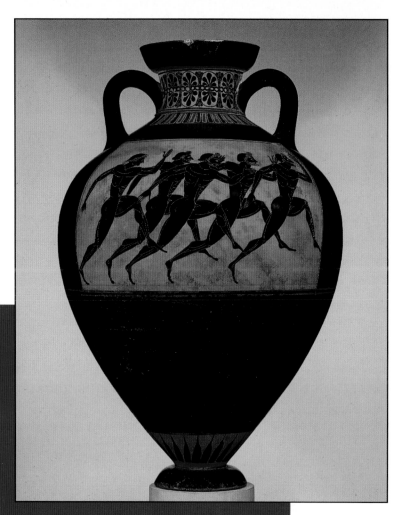

FIGURE CI-1.11 Painting of a footrace on an Athenian vase, ca. 530 B.C.E. Athletics were an important part of Greek culture. The gods were honored with athletic games, and physical training was part of the essential education of young men. SOURCE: The Metropolitan Museum of Art, Rogers Fund, 1914 (Acc. # 14.130.12) Photograph © 1977 The Metropolitan Museum of Art.

show defeated players being sacrificed and ball courts at the Maya site of Chichen Itza and the Aztec city of Tenochtitlan, where the ball courts were next to the skull rack. A Mayan painted vase shows a ritual ball game being played in the Mayan underworld, Xibalba.

Unlike the Mesoamerican game of *tachtli*, a ritual reenactment of judgment, funeral games in ancient Greece honored the dead. In the Homeric poem, the *Iliad*, funeral games are held for Patroclus, the slain companion of the hero Achilles. Chariot races and footraces that took place as part of funeral games were an important part of Greek culture, as physical training was considered essential. The bloody gladiatorial contests of Rome originated as funeral games. For example, in 65 B.C.E. Julius Caesar gave elaborate funeral games for his long dead father. Writing at the end of the second century C.E., the Roman Christian critic Tertullian offered an explanation for the connection between funeral rites and gladiator shows: "Once upon a time, men believed that the souls of the dead were propitiated by human blood, and so at funerals they sacrificed prisoners of war or slaves of poor quality bought for the purpose."[1] As the practice became more popular and more elaborate, gladiator games began to simulate human sacrifice in commemoration of the dead. These games continued to have a religious element: slaves who dragged dead bodies from the gladiatorial arena were dressed as the god of the underworld, Pluto. While the public aspect of these performances magnified the respect paid to the dead and the honor of the family, the games were a kind of cruel judgment for prisoners of war, rebels, Christians, and slaves.

For medieval Europeans, death was "an unavoidable occurrence, an uncertain journey, the tears of the living, the confirmation of the testament, the thief of man." The appearance of the Black Death, a plague that decimated Europe in the fourteenth century, only intensified these feelings and fears. The cruel fantasies of hell became a powerful theme during the following centuries of Christian art. In the ca. 1510 triptych (three-part painting) by the Dutch painter Hieronymus Bosch (ca. 1450–1516), the animal world appears to take revenge amidst human anguish and confusion. The rats symbolize the force of evil, thought to be responsible for diabolical suffering.

---

[1] Tertullian, *On the Public Shows* 12, cited in Keith Hopkins, *Death and Renewal* (Cambridge: Cambridge University Press, 1995), p. 3.

Bosch was one of the first European painters to use a style of painting known as realism to represent something the human eye had not actually seen.

THE CRYPT AND CEMETERY AS ACTIVITY CENTERS

In medieval Christian Europe, the cemetery was like a public square, the center of social life. The bones of ordinary people were periodically removed from their graves and stored, the rich and the poor jumbled together indiscriminately to make room for new burials. Monastery churches were almost always built over a funerary monument that included the sacred relics of important figures in the past of the living church, such as a patron saint, bishop, or martyr.

The crypt was not only the burial place, but also a treasure chamber. Chief among the treasures was the relic, the entire body or a single body part

FIGURE CI-1.12 "Hell," Dutch Painting by Hieronymous Bosch (Right Wing of Triptych, Escorial, Madrid)
SOURCE: Scala/Art Resource, NY.

of the deceased, believed to have spiritual powers. Its container or shrine would be shaped like the body part itself, as in the case of the hammered gold foot-shaped container commissioned by Archbishop Egbert of Trier in the tenth century, presumably containing a foot. In times of famine or plague, people might compel the priests to bring out the relics and parade them around in order to stave off disaster. Relics were sometimes used to swear oaths or validate feudal contracts; they were often buried under the altar or chapel floor.

Islamic painting, especially after the twelfth century, adorned scholarly manuscripts; their illustrations reveal much about the daily aspects of life and death thought to be memorable. Muslim cemeteries were popular places where people socialized, for pilgrimage, picnics, public meetings, or family gatherings. The cemetery is the

FIGURE CI-1.13   Foot Shrine of St. Andreas; Cathedral Treasure of Trier
SOURCE: Dom St. Peter, Trier/Hirmer Verlag, Munich.

site of piety in a Muslim burial scene from a thirteenth-century Arab manuscript. Distress and emotion are partially hidden in the half-covered faces of onlookers.

Cemeteries also figured in Hindu and Muslim traditions of India. Tombs could become sites for the evolution of cults organized around the memory of the deceased. The tomb coverings or flags associated with such memorialized tomb sites were also referred to as a tablecloth (kanduri) because offerings of food and drink were made to it.

ANCESTOR IMAGES: THE CONTINUITY OF LIFE
The images of departed family members and other personages were recorded in many media. Their representation ranged from nonspecific, as in Yoruba society where masqueraders could become vari-

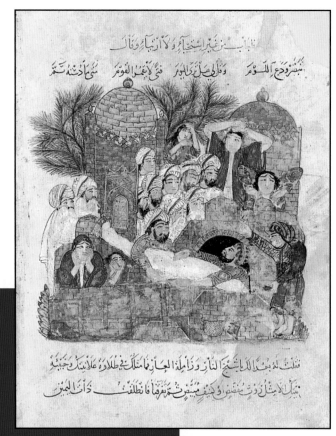

FIGURE CI-1.14
Muslim Burial in Cemetery, 13th-Century Arab Manuscript, Arabe 5847 fol 29v
SOURCE: Bibliothèque Nationale de France.

FIGURE CI-1.15 Obalufon Mask, 12th-century Portrait of the Oni (king), Ife (Nigeria)
SOURCE: National Museum, Lagos. Photo © Dirk Bakker, 1978.

ous ancestors through spirit possession, to actual portraits, such as the twelfth-century image of the Oni of Ife cast in almost pure copper, or the effigy of an English crusader carved in stone. Both images likely originated as death masks actually moulded over the face of the deceased (while living or after death). Terracotta figures, some in the same style as the modern *akuaba* (see Chapter 8), are taken to Akan (Ghana, West Africa) gravesites, where they are believed to hold the invoked spirits of ancestors who will be reborn in future generations.

The tradition of portraiture was widespread, perhaps representing the human desire for immortality. In contrast, the arts of Islam demanded geometric and abstract representation (the Quran is only illustrated with ornamental designs), since representation of the human form in religious manuscript illumination was forbidden by Islamic law. Whether primarily verbal or visual, remembrance was a common and comforting human attempt at immortality.

FIGURE CI-1.16 Stone Effigy of William Longspee the Younger (d. 1250 c.e.), Salisbury Cathedral, England; By his head is the figure of a bishop, probably the spot where the heart of Bishop Richard Poore, the cathedral's founder, was buried.
SOURCE: Salisbury Cathedral.

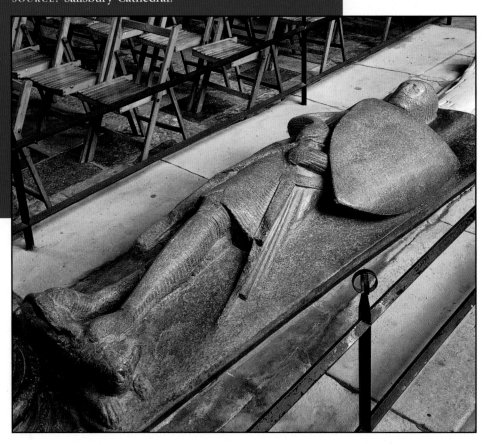

PART II

Order

	East Asia		Southeast Asia	South Asia
	China	Japan		
4000 B.C.E.		Jomon culture		Indus Valley Civilization
2500 B.C.E.				
1500 B.C.E.	Shang Writing		Dongson Bronze Culture	Indo-European Invasions (ca.1500) Hinduism Vedas (ca.1500-500)
1000 B.C.E.	Zhou (ca.1050-250)			Buddha (ca. 566-486) / Mahavira (ca. 540-468) BUDDHISM / JAINIS
500 B.C.E.	Warring States Confucius (551-479)			Mauryan Empire Ashoka
B.C.E.	Qin Han Silk Road / Xiongnu (Central)			
C.E.	Chinese Buddhism	Shinto	Funan	Gupta Empire
		Yamato State		
500 C.E.	Tang	Introduction of Buddhism	Srivijaya Borobudur	
1000 C.E.	Song Mongol Conquest (1200s) Marco Polo Yuan (1271-1295) (1260-1368)	Tale of Genji Rise of Samurai	Khmer Angkor Wat Majapahit	Mongol Conquest
1500 C.E.				

T he young boy was growing up. He had reached the moment when he would join the society of the uninitiated. Camara Laye's entry into manhood and the secrets of the community of Kouroussa, in mid-twentieth-century colonial French Guinea:

> But what were those long white threads which hung from, or, rather, waved from the top of the bombax tree* and which appeared to write on the sky the direction in which the town lay? . . . all the principal huts had these threads on the very tops of their roofs.
> "Do you see the white threads?" I asked Kouyate.
> "I can see them. They are always there after the ceremony in the clearing."
> "Who puts them there?"

*A tree as high as sixty feet and usually found in the sacred clearing of a village.

...ner Cuneiform (ca. 3000)	Crete/Mycenae	Egypt Hieroglyphics	
...ttite Empire			
...ylonian Kingdom Hammurabi's Code (1792-1750)		Continuous Bantu Expansion	
			Lapita Culture
...DAISM			Polynesian Settlement
	Homeric Age		Olmec
			Chavin de Huantar
...yrian Empire Zoroastrianism (ca. 600)	Athens	Kush	
...haemenid Persian ...mpire		Origins of West African Urbanism: Jenne Jeno	
	Emergence of City-States Rome founded (753) Roman Republic (509)		Plains Indians
	Aristotle Alexander the Great	Saharan Trade Regularized	
	Expansion of Rome	Roman Occupation of North Africa	Hopewell
...HRISTIANITY ...anichaeism (3rd c.) ...sanid Persian Empire		African-Indian Ocean Routes	Teotihuacan
	Byzantine Empire	Axum	Maya Hieroglyphics
		Bantu Speakers Reach Southern Africa	
Mohammad (ca.570-632)	Frankish Empire		Eastern Woodland Indians
Umayyad Caliphate Abbasid Caliphate	Viking Expansion	Spread of Islam	
	Feudal Era	West African Forest States	Toltec Cahokia
	Crusades	East African City States	Aztec
Ibn Battuta (1325-1353)	Mongol Invasions	Swahili Culture Great Zimbabwe	
	Black Death		Inca
	Mali Empire		

Kouyate shrugged his shoulders.

"That's where they come from," I said, pointing to the distant bombax tree.

"Someone must have climbed up."

"Who could possibly climb a bombax tree?"

"Could anyone possibly get his arms around such a huge trunk?" I said. "And even if he could, how could he hoist himself on bark all covered with those thorns? You're talking nonsense. Can't you imagine what a job it would be just to reach the first branches?"

"Why do you expect me to know more about this than you do?" asked Kouyate.

"Because this is the first time I have taken part in the ceremony, while you—"

I didn't finish my sentence. We had reached the main square of the town. I stared in amazement at the bombax trees in the market place. They too were ornamented with the same white threads. All but the humblest huts, indeed, and all the big trees were tied to one another by these white threads whose focal point was the enormous bombax tree in the clearing, the sacred place marked by the bombax tree.

"The swallows tie them on," said Kouyate suddenly.

"Swallows? Are you crazy?" I said. "Swallows don't fly by night."

I questioned one of the older boys who was walking beside me.

"It is our great chief who does it," he said. "Our chief turns himself into a swallow during the night. He flies from tree to tree and from hut to hut, and all these threads are tied on in less time than it takes to tell."

"He flies from tree to tree like a swallow?"

"Yes. He's a real swallow and as swift. Everyone knows that."

"Isn't that what I told you?" asked Kouyate.

I did not say another word. The night of Konden Diara was a strange night, a terrible and miraculous night, a night that passed all understanding.

Like the white threads in Camara Laye's village, the threads of beliefs, values, and ideas helped interconnect people and create community ties throughout human history. Not all such threads, nor even the manner of their spinning, were made manifest to the eyes of ordinary individuals. Shamans, priests, and kings were often called upon to confirm their existence and interpret their essence and meaning. Explaining the visible and invisible ties that bind people together and order them into community is what concerns us as we explore the many ways of ordering and interpreting the world in Part II.

Every culture inevitably seeks to satisfy the human psychological need to bring order to chaos and to provide reassurance in confronting the unknown, leading to the construction of belief systems that explain the world and the place of humans in it. Equally important are human efforts to construct their world in accordance with notions of justice and morality. In their efforts to understand and interpret the world, human beings have made use of a wide variety of concepts and beliefs. In the chapters that follow, the variety of links constructed between human and sacred realms is explored. Varying degrees of emphasis are placed on human and nonhuman elements, combined in complex belief systems that give meaning to individual human life, provide ethical guidance for human action, and assure the continuity of the human community. The spiritual and ethical dimensions of human existence—whether in the form of beliefs in anthropomorphic gods, ancestors, and nonhuman spirits, or the human experiences of trance or contemplation—have histories, chronicled sometimes as myths that give meaning to human social and historical reality. Myth and history are closely interrelated, not only in societies at early stages of development but in all societies.

In the beginning was the word, sometimes written, mostly just spoken, words transmitted from mouth to ear. The Bambara tradition of the Komo (Mali, West Africa) teaches that spoken words reflect the vibrations of forces behind all material life. The creator's (Maa Ngala's) divine speech animated the cosmic forces of the universe, just as human speech empowers an idea with words. The Dogon people of Mali visualize this in sung and spoken stories of a divine spider spinning the threads of life. Similarly, the more than one thousand hymns, chants, incantations, and rituals known collectively as the *Vedas* (wisdom or knowledge) and probably compiled and committed to memory in South Asia between 900 and 1200 B.C.E., were believed to be the eternal words of the gods. The Vedic hymn "To Indra" celebrates the slaying of the dragon (drought) and the creation of the "king of all that moves and moves not, of creatures tame and horned, the thunder-wielder." Indra rules over all living men, "containing all as spokes within a rim." Whether written or spoken, ideas such as these are the spun threads that link together the invisible realm of beliefs and values with both the human desire for community and the exercise of power in institutionalized religions and systems of belief and in social, political, and economic orders. Part II explores the ways in which ideas and power are linked to create order. Chapters 4 and 5 describe the ordering that occurs through religions, belief systems, and ideas that interpret the world. Chapters 7 and 8 look at the ordering of societies by the ties of kinship, family, and shared residence. Chapter 9 suggests the importance of ordering the past through systems of culture memory. Finally, Chapters 6 and 10 consider the powerful connections created by economic relationships. Part II examines these links as they formed from earliest human history up to 1500.

4

Ideas and Power: Goddesses, God-Kings, and Sages

Though seldom acknowledged, historical imagination is essential to the historian's task. Bringing the past to life demands a firm grasp of evidence, along with an ability to evoke from artifacts, texts, and other potential sources the information they may yield reluctantly or even deliberately suppress. In this way, the past is not made up but imaginatively re-created, as authors Linda Schele and David Friedel have done for the people of Cerros, an early Mayan settlement (ca. 100 B.C.E.–300 C.E.), in *A Forest of Kings: The Untold Story of the Ancient Maya:*

> Let us imagine a day in the lives of the Cerros people at the time they had decided to adopt the institution of kingship. It is late afternoon and the heat of the day has begun to yield its brilliance to the shadows cast by the tall thatched roofs of the white one-roomed houses. Each dwelling is grouped around an open paved patio space filled with the cacophony of playing children. . . . The women toil over large red and brown coarsely made bowls, full of maize soaking in lime, which they will grind into dough. . . . Engrossed in quiet conversation, people are working in the shade of the house walls, weaving cotton cloth on backstrap looms, repairing nets for the fishermen, and fashioning tools. . . .
>
> Suddenly, from farther up the coast, comes the sound of the conch-shell trumpets and wooden drums of the lookouts announcing the arrival of a trading party. Some of the elder men, who have been expecting this event by their day counts, move with dignity to the white stone and lime plaster docking area. . . . The elders in their painted and dyed cotton cloaks, colorful hip cloths and turbans, jade earrings, and strings of bright orange shell beads, are unspoken testimony to the wealth and power of the community. . . .
>
> The visiting traders are themselves patriarchs, wise in the ways of the neighboring Maya cities and the foreign peoples beyond. They are knowledgeable in magical power and its instruments, which they have brought to trade or give as gifts, and they are warriors capable of defending themselves both at home and abroad. Amid loud music, noise, excitement, and confusion, the group moves slowly across the plaza to a low red platform which has been built to look like a stone model of a house. . . . Instead of a doorway leading inside, however, there is a stairway leading up to an unobstructed summit. In solemn dignity, the leaders ascend the platform and spatter strips of paper with blood drawn from their ears and arms. They then burn these papers with pellets of tree-gum incense in open bowls resting upon clay, drumshaped stands bearing the masks of the Ancestral Twins. This ritual is an act of thanksgiving to the gods and the ancestral dead for a safe and successful trip. Several curers and sorcerers of the village pray over the patriarchs and bless them on behalf of the spirits of this place. . . .
>
> Through the night the firelight flickers on the angular, bright-eyed faces of the leaders, who have painted images over their features to encourage the

Maya Supreme God Itzamna Receiving a Sacrificial Offering. Painted Pottery Figure (Tikal, Maya)

SOURCE: University of Pennsylvania Museum, Philadelphia.

illusion of their resemblance to the gods. . . . Finally, deep into the night, the gray-haired leader of the visitors broaches the subject everyone has been waiting for. He pulls a
small, soft deerskin bundle from within the folds of his cloak and opens it carefully onto his palm, revealing five stones of glowing green jade carved in the images of gods. Four of these stones are sewn onto a band of the finest cotton, ready to be tied around the head of an ahau [king or lord]. The fifth, a larger image that looks like the head of a frowning child, will ride on the king's chest suspended from a leather band around his neck. The trader has brought the jewels of an ahau to the patriarchs of Cerros.

The dark eyes of the principal patriarch glitter in the light of the fire. He sees before him the tools he needs to sanctify his rank among his own people. These kingly jewels assert the inherent superiority of their wearer within the community of human beings, transforming a person of merely noble rank into a being who can test and control the divine forces of the world. To have ahauob [plural of ahau] and an ahau of the ahauob will establish the Cerros community as a presence among the kingdoms of the mighty and the wealthy who rule the wetlands of the interior. Now that the people of Cerros have the means to declare themselves a place of kings, they will be able to deal with the new and changing world of kingdoms and divine power. . . .

The Cerros patriarch is in his prime. He has already proved himself in battle and he knows the rituals which call forth the gods and the ancestors from Xibalba [the underworld]. His family is ancient and respected in the community, and wealthy in land and water-going vessels. . . . The people of the community also need the resolution that kingship will bring to their own ambiguous feelings toward the wealthy and powerful among them.

The assertion of kingship sanctioned by ritual and ideas of divine power seen in this description of Cerros is the subject of this chapter. How were ideas about gods and goddesses translated into power in the realm of human affairs and how were ideas about divinity and the cosmos themselves reflections of power relations, social hierarchies, and the experiences of daily life in the human world?

■

INTRODUCTION

The expansion of human communities both by growth in numbers and by the concentration of population in cities brought about changes in the scale and complexity of society. As human communities grew in size and complexity, the relations among their members changed. The reciprocal obligations, benefits, and conditions of belonging to small gathering-hunting societies differed greatly from those of the earliest sedentary agricultural communities, and agrarian village communities were no less different from urban societies. Changing forms of community were accompanied by new notions of status, power structures, and forms of authority. The main theme of this and the two chapters that follow is the relationship between changing forms of community and structures of power—how people ordered their worlds—and changing cosmologies—how they understood and interpreted their worlds.

Cosmology A cosmology is the systematic expression of a people's understanding of the universe, or cosmos. It is the means by which people interpret the universal relationship between human society and the natural world and make sense of their unique social and political worlds. Cosmologies are grounded in material conditions; ideas do not spring pristine from the minds of human beings but are related to the physical, economic, social, and political environments in which they develop. At the same time, ideas affect the way human beings interact with one another and thus can bring about alterations in human social and political organization as well as in the physical landscape. A cosmology provides a framework for the values of a society and justification for a particular ethics or morality and for hierarchical and power relationships, as individual and social life is placed in a context that imparts meaning to existence.

Religion A religion is a particular system of beliefs and practices rooted in and addressed to either the individual or the community. Religion may be viewed as having to do with the spiritual dimension of human existence as it concerns the individual or as a means of expressing community identity through practices that validate the community in relation to the natural or spiritual world. Religion can also reinforce power relations by lending sanction or legitimacy to social hierarchies or political orders.

Ideology Ideology refers to a set of ideas or framework of values that imparts meaning to the social and political order, establishes acceptable limits to behavior within that order, and rationalizes the often unequal distribution of power and allocation of material resources in a society. The authority of a ruler, whose power may have been gained by force, needs ideological validation and legitimation or it cannot be sustained for more than a short period of time. The legitimation of political authority can be accomplished through more than one means: for example, religious sanctions derived from deities and exercised through a priesthood or historical sanctions based on sacred or secular texts.

Animism and Shamanism Nature was perceived by early human communities as a source of spiritual power to which human beings must conform by recognizing natural forces and their ability to affect human lives. This type of belief system is referred to as animism. Animistic beliefs endow the natural and animal worlds with spiritual power. Many cosmologies have been constructed around the actions of anthropomorphic (in the form of humans) deities—benevolent ones, whose good will is to be solicited through prayer and ritual; or malevolent ones, whose ill will is to be propitiated, often through ceremonial sacrifice. Gods are sometimes thought to be able to interact directly with humans; they can cavort and converse. Both kinds of deities were often manipulated by the ritual intercession of individuals who displayed special abilities that enabled them to communicate with the spiritual world on behalf of the community. These spiritual specialists were known as shamans, and they practiced shamanism. Shamans, who could be either male or female, were thought to communicate with anthropomorphic or other spiritual beings through ceremonial trances. We have seen (in Chapter 1) that rock art around the world recorded these earliest belief systems many tens of thousands of years ago.

As human communities became larger and power relations more complex, early community-centered religions evolved or gave way to new ideas that sanctioned the exercise of power by those who had physical control of people and territory, usually through military force. Tensions often arose between these different uses of religion: community-based religious beliefs and practices provided a source of identity distinct from that associated with the exercise of power over the community, as by a king or an emperor. Unless a ruler could subsume or absorb a community's religious beliefs and practices into a new ideology that validated and legitimized his or her rule, such religious ideas could threaten or challenge the power to rule.

In this and succeeding chapters, we will examine the dynamic interaction between ideas and power, showing how religious beliefs and political ideologies sanctioned the exercise of power and validated the increasingly unequal distribution of material and cultural resources through a variety of social and political hierarchies. In considering changing community forms and power structures, the second aspect of our main theme, we will use the general term polity to refer to ways of organizing and institutionalizing power relations among individuals and groups in society.

Polities Polities such as city-states, kingdoms, and empires were products of the centralization of power. City-states were independent urban centers that either controlled an agricultural hinterland or depended on trade. Kingdoms were larger in scale than city-states and directly controlled a territory that included more than one urban center. Empires were the largest-scale polities and often resulted from the expansion of one polity, such as a kingdom or city-state, at the expense of others. Empires were also characterized by a combination of several factors: the control and manipulation of human and material resources over a wide area; the development and utilization of technology; the creation and maintenance of effective political and social organization over a sizable territory; and the successful promotion of an ideology that sanctioned and legitimized the exercise of power.

While the complex belief systems that sustained city-states, kingdoms, and empires were widespread after about 2000 B.C.E., they were not the only forms of spiritual expression. Reconstructing the history and impact of ideas for peoples and periods for which there is little or no written evidence is a complex task. Alongside the textual evidence (stone and metal inscriptions and sacred manuscripts) and material evidence (such as monuments or temples) of official religions, we can find evidence of the persistence of popular beliefs, including shamanism, household shrines, and widespread goddess worship. Sometimes older beliefs were incorporated into or subsumed by new religions; sometimes they provided a basis for underground or open resistance to state power.

■

EARLY BELIEF SYSTEMS: THE GODDESS

Religions often provide lenses through which the ideas that order human societies can be observed. For example, based on evidence from religion, historians have considered how views of gender may have influenced and been influenced by transformations in social and political organization. Soon after the rise of sedentary societies, the reliance on agriculture promoted gynocentric (female-centered) societies because of the importance of women in the reproduction and sustenance of society through their contributions to agricultural labor. In gynocentric societies, women played key roles in social and political life. Their knowledge about the realms of fertility and childbirth were regarded as vital to the community. The position of women was reflected in belief systems that focused on a goddess, who often symbolized the earth or mother.

The beginnings of religion can be recognized in some of the earliest evidence of complex symbolic systems (interpretation of the world through the use of symbols) in Eurasia, which center around worship of a goddess in various forms. Beginning about 25,000 B.C.E., female images representing procreative powers are recorded in cave paintings, rock carvings, and sculptures. These rounded female figures are depicted with exaggerated breasts, vulvae, and

FIGURE 4.1 Clay Goddess Figure from the Cernavoda Graveyard, ca. 4800 B.C.E.

Hamangian Stiff Nude, clay figurine from the Cernavoda graveyard, c. 4800 b.c.

SOURCE: National Museum of History of Romania, Bucharest.

buttocks. By Neolithic times (ca. 6500 B.C.E.), examples of these images in religious artifacts increase. In many parts of the world, goddess beliefs, which both reflected and shaped social organization in early agricultural societies, were eventually, when protection of resources became paramount, supplanted by belief in male god-kings.

Goddess Beliefs Evidence of early goddess beliefs derives from the excavation and interpretation of archaeological sites. Artifacts such as female masks and anthropomorphic vases from the early-sixth-millennium B.C.E. Sesklo (Greece) and Starveco (Bulgaria) cultures display chevrons and triangles that are recognized as signs of the goddess. Slightly later arts of the Vinca culture (ca. 5300 B.C.E.) in the Balkans commonly have images of the Bird Goddess: a characteristic mask with a large nose or beak with no mouth, exaggerated buttocks and thighs, a specialized costume, and incised or painted symbols.

By contrast, quite different sculptural themes are associated with the horse and ox cults of invading pastoralists from the south Russian and eastern Ukraine regions after the fifth millennium B.C.E. Examples of powerful female deities in the pantheons of early dynastic states after 3500 B.C.E., reminiscent of the Neolithic mother goddesses, suggest the persistence of elements of earlier belief systems even as religious ideas were transformed under the influence of new political and social orders.

GODDESSES, GODS, AND GOD-KINGS: ASIA, AFRICA, AND THE AMERICAS

Goddesses and gods could create the earth, generate the cosmos, and even give birth to human rulers. Their actions might be responsible for the fertility of fields or success at war, so their cooperation was sought through ritual practices specific to particular belief systems. Gods and goddesses were also believed to be able to empower individuals, both rulers and ruled. A pattern that emerged early in human history was recognition of a human ruler as a representative of gods or spirits, thus linking religious and political power. The term theocracy is used to describe this linkage.

Population and Resources As human populations increased in numbers and diversity, competition for scarce and valuable resources more frequently determined the concerns of spiritual life as well as the nature of social and political interactions. The development of agricultural systems supported population growth, which in turn placed demands on scarce resources (see Chapter 2). The protection of resources, including at times the seizure of other people's land and labor, was increasingly undertaken by powerful warrior groups.

Military Power The control and organization of warriors by a ruling power constituted early military forces, whose primary role was to defend the community's resources. Coordination of resources, usually by means of controlling trade between ruling centers and their hinterland suppliers, depended on territorial control and sometimes relied on military force. Dependence on warriors to ensure the safe movement of goods and people led to the elevation of warrior status and the promotion of military values and interests.

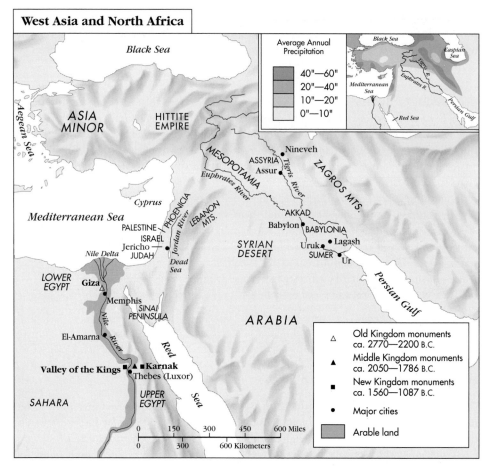

West Asia and North Africa

MAP 4.1 Early Polities and Urban Centers in West Asia (Mesopotamia) and North Africa (Egypt)

Military might alone, however, was rarely sufficient to cement ties between diverse communities and maintain control over them. As military leaders strengthened their hold over expanding territories, they began to claim to have powers that were conferred on them by gods, and in some cases to become god-kings. This process was characteristic of early dynastic states (in which rulers inherited succession to the throne) not only in West Asia (Mesopotamia) but also in North Africa (Egypt) and East Asia (China). In South Asia (India) and Mesoamerica, ideals of the universal god-king also shaped the exercise of power over expanding territories.

WEST ASIA: MESOPOTAMIA

In West Asia during the mid–fourth through the mid–third millennia B.C.E., the concentration and expansion of military power in the region of Mesopotamia ("between the two rivers") led to the formation of a series of dynastic states in the watershed of the Tigris and Euphrates

Rivers in modern Iraq. The foundation of these lay in the region of Sumer, where city-states provided the earliest forms of political organization enabling the exploitation of economic resources through military control.

Urban Gods and Goddesses The transition from urban center to territorial (or dynastic) state was closely tied to religious ideas and practices. In the early urban centers of West Asia, residents chose one of their members to become the consort of the city god or goddess. This position, known as *en,* was temporary, and either a man or a woman could be selected depending on whether the deity was a god or a goddess. In addition to their religious role, sometimes the *en* would also assume some administrative functions for the city.

Each city had its own particular deity, but some were also worshiped throughout the region of Sumer, such as the goddess Ishtar (the Sumerian Inanna) who was the city deity of Kish but worshiped elsewhere as well. In cases where the city deity was a god and required a female consort, a second person, a male, would also be appointed by the residents to act as a military leader, known as the *lugal,* to protect and defend the city. Both of these positions were limited in term and were not inherited. In the third millennium B.C.E., the Sumerian city of Nippur seems to have acquired a uniquely sacred status, thus elevating its city deity, the warrior god Enlil, to a position of dominance over other gods; later conquerors were careful to associate their rule with the sanction of Enlil.

FIGURE 4.2 Ziggurat at Ur, a stepped pyramid for worship of the city god, ca. 2100–2000 B.C.E.

SOURCE: Hirmer Verlag.

The Akkadian Empire Although both Sumerian and Akkadian settlements coexisted in the
watershed of the Tigris and Euphrates during the third millennium
B.C.E., it was the Akkadians who began the centralization of political authority that resulted
in the first unified empire in this region. In the early third millennium B.C.E., the Akkadian
ruler Sargon I (ca. 2334–2279 B.C.E.) brought the region of Sumer under his control and
claimed power over a territory that stretched from the Mediterranean to the Persian Gulf.
The Akkadians depended on military force to control and redistribute resources and on writing as an essential tool in the accounting and record keeping necessary to the administration
of their state. Religious inscriptions from the time of Sargon I, written in both Sumerian and
Akkadian, promoted the notion that he had been appointed to rule by the Sumerian god
Enlil.

The Invention of Writing One of the most important developments in human history, useful
to commerce, the exercise of political authority, and the transmis-
sion of both sacred and secular knowledge, was the invention of writing. The earliest record
of using symbols to extend human memory and to record or communicate ideas appears as incised or painted markings on prehistoric bone batons and rock art. These markings may have
emerged in the context of early belief systems, as has been speculated for the sixth-millen-
nium B.C.E. signs inscribed on Eurasian archaeological finds associated with goddess worship
and for the markings on Neolithic pottery found in China. The earliest known and identified
script, however, was created in Sumer before 3000 B.C.E. Although the writing system in
Sumer began, as elsewhere, with pictographs that associated symbols with meanings, it gradually evolved into a conceptually more sophisticated system of representation that identified
symbols with sounds, a syllabary. By this means, a relatively limited number of symbols
could easily be manipulated to express a variety of meanings, including abstractions not
suited to pictographic representation.

The cuneiform (from the Latin *cuneus,* meaning "wedge") script, formed with a wedge-
shaped reed stylus on unbaked clay tablets, was adopted by the Sumerians and Akkadians, as
well as by later peoples in West Asia, including the Babylonians, the Assyrians, and the Hittites. Initially, its primary use was for keeping accounts; later it was used for transcribing law
codes as well as government archives. While many societies continued to rely on the oral
skills and memory devices of specialists, others became increasingly dependent on written
systems to record the vast amount of information that had begun to accumulate in settled societies.

Babylonia The collapse of the Akkadian Empire came about through the invasions of Semitic
peoples from Syria on the eastern end of the Mediterranean. These invaders established in succession two dynastic states, Babylonia and Assyria. Though there were earlier
laws used by Sumerians and Akkadians, the written law code of the Babylonian ruler Hammurabi (ca. 1792–1750 B.C.E.) is the earliest extant codification of legal and administrative
regulations.

The Code of Hammurabi The Code of Hammurabi is a collection of case law, consisting of
decisions handed down by Hammurabi that could be used as prece-
dents for other cases. These cases reveal much about Babylonian life, such as a belief in sorcery, ideas of female chastity, contractual obligations, the principle of reciprocity in punish-

ment, and fair repayment for services and restitution for property (including family members, servants, and slaves, as well as material property). As other kings before him, Hammurabi ruled through a theocracy. In the case of his laws, Hammurabi claimed that the god Marduk had commanded him to use them "to give justice to the people of the land."

Ishtar In a Babylonian version of the Sumerian creation myth, the warrior-king Marduk defeated the goddess Tiamat, bringing order to the world under his rule. The deity Tiamat, who at first represented the feminine power to give birth to the world, was later identified with the forces of chaos, which were tamed by the organizing powers of male gods. A legacy of earlier views of Tiamat, and still earlier Neolithic goddesses, may be seen in the cult of the goddess Ishtar, which dates to the third millennium B.C.E.

Representations of Ishtar show similarities to Neolithic fertility images, including bulbous hips and prominent breasts. The cult of Ishtar reveals some of the complexities and ambiguities in the transition from Neolithic goddess cults to warrior cults associated with early dynastic states. Depending on whether she was considered the daughter of the moon god or the sky god, she was a goddess of either love or war, a dichotomy that suggests the shift in power and influence from mother to warrior.

The Hittite Invasions The development of dynastic states in early West Asia was a complex process that involved the interaction of various cultures and ethnic groups native to the region, as well as invasions by peoples from sometimes distant places, such as the Hittites, who sacked Babylon, the dominant city of southern Mesopotamia, in 1595 B.C.E. The Hittites were invaders from central Eurasia who had established domination over Anatolia (modern Turkey) in the early second millennium B.C.E. The Hittites had a distinctive urban culture, including the use of the cuneiform script, and until the thirteenth century B.C.E., they maintained a kingdom bordering northern Syria.

Assyria Movements of peoples such as the Hittites and shifts in centers of power throughout the Mesopotamian region of West Asia were related to ongoing migrations of semi-nomadic peoples from the steppes. In the fourteenth century B.C.E., a new kingdom rose in the northern part of Mesopotamia to carry on regional political and cultural traditions and eventually to challenge Babylonia in the south: Assyria. The sacred city of the Assyrians was Assur, located on the banks of the Tigris, and the Assyrian ruler was also the chief priest of the cult of the god Assur. Assyrian priests replaced the Babylonian deity Marduk with Assur as king of the gods. A revived Assyrian Empire (911–612 B.C.E.) defeated rival powers of the day, including Babylonia and Egypt, creating the most expansive empire yet seen in the region.

The distinction between a city-state order, such as that exhibited in Sumer, and an empire, exemplified by Assyria, lay in the ability of the imperial center to exercise direct administrative control over a large territory. This contrasted with the shifting dominance among city-states that was characteristic of the Sumerian political order. By the mid–second millennium B.C.E., both the military force needed to create an empire and the ideological base needed to sustain it, including religion, law, and writing, were present among the expanding states of West Asia.

Religion supported the rule of kings by showing their close link with gods, such as Enlil with the Akkadian ruler Sargon or Marduk with the Babylonian ruler Hammurabi. Laws, such as the Code of Hammurabi, provided rules to order society that were sanctioned by religion, in the manner of Hammurabi's claim that Marduk had commanded him to bring justice to the people he ruled. Writing was an important corollary to both religion and law, as it enabled the recording of myths and laws, subjecting both to the permanence of clay or even stone and conferring status on those who commanded scribal skills.

NORTH AFRICA: EGYPT

At approximately the same time as West Asian dynastic states were expanding (fourth and third millennia B.C.E.), religion and government were becoming closely tied in the emergence of Egypt in North Africa. Terra-cotta female figurines fashioned of Nile mud suggest the existence of fertility beliefs and possibly goddess worship in this region of North Africa during Neolithic times, but by the third millennium B.C.E., there was a multitude of Egyptian gods and goddesses with anthropomorphic qualities. The Egyptian pantheon as it existed by this time suggests a shift to stronger forms of male authority in tandem with the clear preference for male rulers.

Pharaohs as Living Gods The Egyptian ruler, *pharaoh,* was worshiped as a living god who was the point of contact between the human and divine realms. It was the pharaoh's responsibility to preserve and maintain *maat,* the order of the universe and the harmony of human society. Pharaohs claimed to be sons of Amon-Ra, the sun god. Immediately below Amon-Ra were three principal deities who reflected the ecological conditions of the Nile Valley that were essential to the survival of humans in that region: Osiris represented the fertilizing power of the annual Nile floods; Isis, the fertility of the earth; and Horus, the vital force of vegetation resulting from the union of Isis and Osiris. Osiris was also associated with the dead and the afterlife, an important component of Egyptian religion that led to the building of elaborate pyramids filled with treasures for the use of pharaohs in the afterlife.

Female Deities Hathor, the daughter of Amon-Ra, was the sky goddess who was represented as a cow or a cow-headed deity nourishing the living with her milk. She is sometimes depicted as a cow suckling the pharaoh. Such images suggest a continuity between the maternal symbolism characteristic of Neolithic fertility figures and later goddesses who were conceived as part of a male-dominated pantheon but who also retained significant powers of their own. The potential power of women was also reflected in the worship of goddesses such as Isis, the daughter of the sky goddess and the earth god. She wed Osiris, god of the dead and the most important deity in the Egyptian pantheon after the sun god. By the end of the first millennium B.C.E., the cult of Isis had spread throughout the Mediterranean world from Spain to Asia Minor (modern Turkey) and from North Africa to Europe (as far as modern Germany).

Egyptian Popular Beliefs Ordinary Egyptians were largely excluded from the temple rituals integral to state control, except at the times of the great festivals. Nonetheless, they popularized official beliefs in a variety of ways by naming their children after major gods and seeking oracles from gods in public processions. On their behalf, scribes inscribed amulets and wrote letters to the dead as well as directly to the gods to seek their assistance. At village sites such as Deir el-Medina (ca. 2000 B.C.E.), houses contained shrines of lesser, popular divinities.

Far from the watchful eyes of the state, in time of misfortune workers consulted local "wise women," who explained the death of a child or identified divinely manifested illness in a community. A plea to the god Khons, who by the period of the New Kingdom (ca. 1560–1087 B.C.E.) was regarded as an exorcist and healer, was recorded on a stone whose carving had been commissioned by the son of a woman who was ill: "How sweet is your mercy, Khons, to the poor women of your city."

Hieroglyphics Egypt, which was sharply stratified by class and gender, was administered by an all-male bureaucracy composed of trained and literate scribes. A written script known as hieroglyphics ("sacred carvings") emerged from priestly functions and was, as the name suggests, used for inscriptions on stone. Some of the earliest writing was used by the state as the "words of the god": to record its possessions, note its administrative power, and display its royal prerogative. Cursive script was a shorthand, simplified version of hieroglyphic used in daily life.

Scribes kept financial accounts as well as historical and religious records. As in earlier Sumer and Babylonia, the invention of a writing system was a powerful supplement to military control over the redistribution of resources centralized under the administrative authority of the state. Writing was used to preserve kingship records; it also supported the religious sanctions employed by rulers to sustain their authority by preserving sacred texts that described the link between kings and gods.

Writing was a skill taught to men who aspired to status and power within the framework of Egyptian society, and probably no more than 1 percent of all Egyptians were literate. In addition to the value of writing as a tool in the administration of political authority, writing introduced new social divisions between those who could write (and read) and those who could not. Often this division was based on gender, as literacy was restricted to male scribes or priests.

Egyptian Women Although Egyptian women could hold property and had certain other economic and legal rights, they were barred from formal education and thus were excluded from holding positions of power and influence in Egyptian society. Individual women could rise in political positions as queen, queen mother, and queen wife or daughter, although they acquired their influence by reference to the king, either father or husband. Queens had their own insignia of office that was considered to be of divine origin, and they occasionally used their position as the god-king's consort to become rulers.

Hatshepsut (r. ca. 1473–1458 B.C.E.) married her brother Thutmose II and after his death manipulated her position as coregent with her stepson to become pharaoh herself. Hatshepsut is portrayed holding a man's weapon and wearing a beard and man's dress. In inscriptions she commissioned for her mortuary temple, she is referred to by the male pronoun. During her twenty-two-year reign, she sent out military expeditions to Nubia, where Egyptian soldiers laid claim to the wealth of Nubian gold mines, and naval expeditions to open up new trade routes.

Though she did not become ruler in her own right, another example of a powerful woman was the famous queen Nefertiti. She was the wife of the pharaoh Amenhotep IV (r. ca. 1353–1335 B.C.E.), who attempted to transform the polytheistic (having many gods) Egyp-

FIGURE 4.3 Stela from a Household Altar at Amarna Showing Akhenaten, Nefertiti, and Their Children beneath the Rays of the Aten

SOURCE: FotoMarburg/Art Resource, NY.

tian religion to a monotheistic focus on one god, Aten, represented as a solar disk. To accomplish this radical transformation, Amenhotep moved the capital from Thebes to Amarna in order to escape the power of the Theban priesthood who served Amon-Ra; he renamed himself Akhenaten, "beneficial to Aten." Akhenaten's new religion was not strictly monotheistic, since the pharaoh assumed a position equal to that of Aten; nor did the new religion survive Akhenaten's reign. His son-in-law Tutankhamen (r. ca. 1347–1337 B.C.E.) returned to Thebes and restored the Theban priests of Amon-Ra to power.

EAST ASIA: SHANG CHINA

Slightly later than states in West Asia and North Africa, the Shang dynastic state in the Yellow River Valley of East Asia emerged in the early second millennium B.C.E. Its rise from Neolithic centers in the north China plain was linked to the introduction of bronze technology and the appearance of a religious cult that validated the rule of the Shang kings through the power of their ancestors to intercede with the supreme deity, Di. Elaborate bronze vessels held sacrifices of food and wine offered to the ancestors of the Shang kings.

Oracle Bones Oracle bones, the shoulder blades of oxen or sheep or turtle plastrons (the flat underside of turtle shells), were inscribed with questions to the gods in archaic

East and South Asia

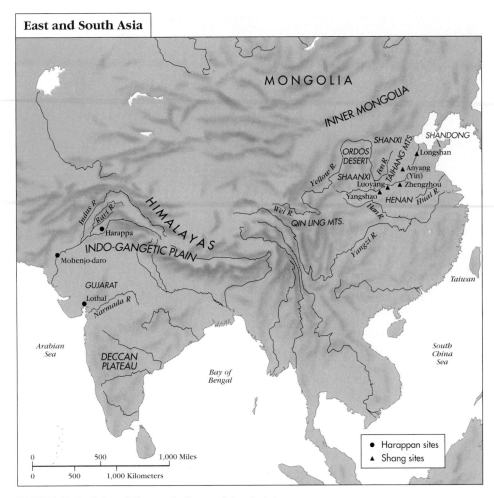

MAP 4.2 Early Cultural Centers in East and South Asia

Chinese script. Questions such as "Will there be a good harvest?" or "Will we [the Shang] be successful in battle against our enemies?" were addressed to Di, and the answers were read by interpreting cracks made in the bones when heated over a fire.

Divination and Writing These divination, or fortune-telling, practices were under the control ▬▬▬▬▬▬ of priestly scribes, and the ritual value of writing in early China foreshadowed the sacred character of written texts and the power associated with literacy in later Chinese history. As in early West Asia, the invention of writing in China played an important role in the establishment of political authority and in the maintenance of administrative control over expanding resources and territory by enabling the keeping of records: for the commemoration of events, the documentation of state policies, and the redistribution of goods.

The Shang state was a series of walled communities, and the capital was a shifting center that periodically moved to a new urban site. The power exercised by Shang kings was not

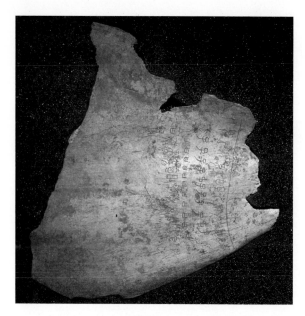

FIGURE 4.4 Oracle Bone with Archaic Chinese Script

SOURCE: Werner Forman/Art Resource, NY.

that of a central ruler governing a clearly defined territory but rather that of a ruler who was compelled to confirm his role by periodic visits to outlying walled communities, where he displayed his authority by the number of followers in his retinue, the splendor of his armaments, and his own personal charisma.

Shang society was dominated by chariot-riding warriors organized according to lineages identified with totemistic figures, such as the black bird that was the ancestor of the Shang ruling family. Hunting and warfare were the primary occupations of the noble families who served the king, but farmers made up the majority of the population.

Women in Early China We know little of women in this early period of history in China, but ▬▬▬▬▬▬▬▬▬▬ evidence from a royal tomb suggests that women could hold military power virtually on a par with men. The tomb of Fu Hao, consort of a king who ruled about 1400 B.C.E., has yielded evidence that she controlled a large army in her own right. Apart from this, the limits of current knowledge make it difficult to say much about the position of women in Shang society and attitudes toward women or to trace the shift from earlier matristic (womb-based) social orders to the clearly patriarchal order that was in place by Shang times. Though female fertility figures, which may represent a goddess, have been found in Neolithic sites in China, these do not appear in Shang and later sites.

SOUTH ASIA: INDUS VALLEY AND VEDIC CULTURE

The Indus Valley civilization (ca. 2500–1500 B.C.E.) in South Asia shared beliefs, such as goddess worship, with other parts of the world. Terra-cotta figurines of female fertility deities have been found in sites at the Indus Valley centers of Harappa and Mohenjo-Daro. Animal figures molded in clay indicate that, like the ancient Egyptians and Shang Chinese, the Indus Valley peoples attributed special powers to animals, and animal imagery was a prominent artistic motif. The cow held a position of special importance, like the cat in Egypt and the bull in the Mediterranean world.

Indo-Europeans Beginning in the mid–second millennium B.C.E., nomadic cattle herders and warriors from Southwest Asia introduced their belief in male sky gods to the peoples of the Indus Valley civilization. Migrations of peoples from Southwest Asia, Indo-Europeans, had earlier been responsible for the Hittite invasion of Anatolia (ca. 1900 B.C.E.) and the Hyksos invasion of Egypt (ca. 1700 B.C.E.). Technologically well equipped with horse-drawn chariots, the culture of the Indo-European invaders, like that of the Hittites in Anatolia and the Hyksos in Egypt, glorified war. They rode war chariots into battle, led by their warrior god, Indra. As they conquered the remnants of the Indus Valley civilization and settled in India, the invaders assimilated indigenous ideas and gradually integrated the early Indus Valley goddess beliefs with their own, culminating over centuries in the rich Hindu ("belonging to the Indus") pantheon of gods and goddesses.

Vedic Culture The dominant culture of the Indo-European invaders, who are also often identified by the linguistic term Aryan ("noble" or "pure"), is represented in the tradition of the Vedas (knowledge), a collection of ritual hymns which had been orally transmitted and were compiled as written texts between around 1200 and 600 B.C.E. These were transcribed in the classical Indian language, Sanskrit, which uses a phonetic script and belongs to the Indo-European linguistic group, which includes such diverse modern languages as Persian, Greek, Hindi, Latin, French, German, and English. The Vedas, along with later epics (long poems about heroes) such as the *Mahabharata* and the *Ramayana,* portray the Indo-Europeans as heroes who triumphed over the inferior "alien" peoples who had inhabited the Indian subcontinent before them.

The social and political order that emerged in South Asia during the Vedic period (ca. 1000–500 B.C.E.) was a product of the interweaving of ideas introduced by the Indo-European newcomers with indigenous beliefs and practices, and the process of assimilation of Indus peoples into a new social and political order shaped by the Indo-European invaders. This new social and political order was sanctioned by a pantheon of deities and by texts, the Vedas, that laid out the cosmological foundations of human society.

The Origin of Caste Unlike the archaeological evidence we have for Indus Valley civilization, exemplified by the sites of Harappa and Mohenjo-Daro, for the Vedic period there are few archaeological remains and so we are forced to reconstruct Vedic society and culture from largely textual sources. We know little about the origin of caste, the division of society into rigid hierarchical ranks assigned by birth. The caste system may have been produced by the imposition of rule by Indo-European invaders over the indigenous population of the Indian subcontinent. Distinctions among castes were perhaps initially drawn according to skin color, since the Sanskrit term *varna* ("color") is the term first used to classify social groups.

A hymn in the Rig-Veda, one of the earliest texts, describes the creation of four social groups from the ritual sacrifice of a cosmic being, Purusha, who is a composite of deities. Purusha's body is cut into different parts, each of which represents a caste: *brahman* (priest), *kshatriya* (warrior), *vaishya* (merchant), and *shudra* (slave). In this way the idea of caste was given a cosmic sanction, at least according to the Rig-Veda. For modern Indians, however, the concept of caste is much more narrowly defined as an endogamous group related by birth (*jati*) or by occupational groupings that can be traced back as far as the remnants of the Indus Valley civilization. Those beyond or outside the caste system were "untouchables" whose occupations (grave digging, hide tanning) made them too impure or unclean to associate with others.

Brahmanism The concept of caste was developed and transmitted as part of Brahmanism, the ▓▓▓▓▓▓▓▓ name given to the belief system and ritual practices of early India associated with the priestly tradition of the Brahmanas (sacred utterances), Vedic texts dating from the ninth to seventh centuries B.C.E. These texts emphasize the importance of ritual in regulating social relationships, including ranking by caste, and in preserving *dharma,* the divine order and sacred law of the cosmos reflected in the notion of human duty to fulfill one's obligations according to caste. *Brahman*s ("those who chant sacred utterances," or priests) who carried out the rituals were in a position of superiority to even warrior rulers because they controlled the ritual link between the cosmic order, personified in the numerous deities of the Vedic pantheon, and the human social order.

The Hindu Pantheon By the late Vedic period (ca. 600 B.C.E.) the Hindu pantheon included ▓▓▓▓▓▓▓▓▓▓▓ the creator god, Shiva, and the solar deity, Vishnu, along with their consorts, Parvati and Lakshmi. Kali, or Durga, is the demonic version of Shiva's consort, a

FIGURE 4.5 Vishnu Reclines on the Body of a Serpent Demon He Has Slain in His Role as Protector of the World

Sandstone, 59 × 46″. Gupta period, sixth century C.E. Vishnu Temple at Deogarh, Central India.

SOURCE: Courtesy of the Trustees of the British Library.

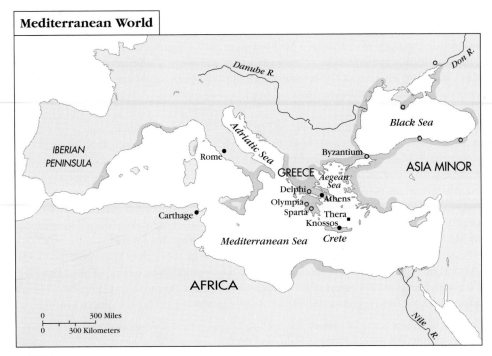

Mediterranean World

MAP 4.3 Greek Cities and Colonies in the Mediterranean World, ca. 7th c. B.C.E.

grim goddess associated with death and destruction, as Shiva himself is portrayed as both creator and destroyer. Goddesses figure in the Vedic pantheon in relatively minor ways until much later (ca. 400–800 C.E.), when female divine power *(shakti)* was recognized and the image of the mother goddess as a supreme being became an important part of the Hindu tradition, thus reconnecting with the beliefs of the earlier Indus Valley culture. As in the Indus Valley culture, animals continued to be important in the Hindu pantheon. For example, Ganesh is the benevolent elephant-headed son of Shiva, and Hanuman, the monkey god, symbolizes loyalty and strength.

THE MEDITERRANEAN WORLD

Early Greece was a composite of both Indo-European and Mediterranean influences. Between 1200 and 900 B.C.E., contemporary with invasions of the Indus Valley civilization in South Asia, various Indo-European peoples invaded the Aegean basic, where they conquered and co-opted centers of earlier Mediterranean culture such as Knossos (see Chapter 3) on the island of Crete and Mycenae on the Greek mainland. The Minoan (Cretan) and Mycenaean cultures had much in common with those of early West Asia and North Africa, such as a belief in the great goddess or universal mother. Like the Neolithic female images, this anthropomorphic conception of divinity symbolized fertility, controlled the heavens, and also ruled the underworld and afterlife.

Minoan Goddess Belief Figurines from the palace at Knossos wearing dresses that expose and ▨▨▨▨▨▨▨▨▨▨▨▨▨ emphasize the breasts represent priestesses of the great earth mother and fertility goddess of the eastern Mediterranean. The Minoan goddess was paired with a male god, usually thought to be subordinate to her, and she was believed to be the mother of Zeus, the most powerful of the subsequent Olympians, twelve gods and goddesses dwelling on Mount Olympus and presided over by Zeus.

Homeric Greece Such cultural conflation had taken shape by the Homeric Age, a period that ▨▨▨▨▨▨▨▨▨▨▨ takes its name from the blind poet Homer (ca. ninth century B.C.E.), to whom the epic poems the *Iliad* and the *Odyssey* are attributed. Though probably the work of oral bards and storytellers rather than a single poet, these poems record many aspects of eastern Mediterranean culture from around 2000 B.C.E. to the invasion of the Aegean basin by Indo-Europeans in the twelfth century B.C.E. After the Indo-European invasions, Greece entered a "Dark Age" between about 1150 and 800 B.C.E., when technology shifted from bronze to iron, rural villages replaced urban centers, and even writing disappeared.

Although the Homeric poems are supposedly set in the earlier Mycenaean times (ca. 2000–1500 B.C.E.), they more likely reflect the ways of life characteristic of the Dark Age. The poems recount the exploits of heroes and the role played by the Olympian gods in human affairs, as in the description of the warrior Achilles preparing to slay the Trojan hero Hector:

> The beam came down on Hector's side, spelling his doom. He was a dead man. Phoebus Apollo deserted him; and Athene, Goddess of the Flashing Eyes, went up to Achilles and spoke momentous words. "Illustrious Achilles, darling of Zeus," she said, "our chance has come to go back to the ships with a glorious victory for Achaean arms. Hector will fight to the bitter end, but you and I are going to kill him. There is no escape for him now, however much the Archer-King Apollo may exert himself and grovel at the feet of his Father, aegis-bearing Zeus.

The Olympic Pantheon A post-Homeric introduction to the Olympic pantheon is found in ▨▨▨▨▨▨▨▨▨▨▨▨▨▨▨ the *Theogony* of Hesiod (fl. ca. 700 B.C.E.). The Olympic deities were portrayed in concrete anthropomorphic terms. They may originally have been nature gods and goddesses, but by the time of Homer and Hesiod they were nature deities only in the sense that they were thought to have control of certain natural forces: Zeus, for example, sent rain and lightning, and Poseidon stirred up the sea and the earth. Hesiod added ethical notions such as justice to the Greek pantheon and worldview, and Zeus became someone who interfered in the lives of humans, meting out punishment to those who transgressed and rewarding those who were just.

The Cult of Isis Contemporary with the Olympic pantheon, popular mystery cults centering ▨▨▨▨▨▨▨▨▨▨ around rebirth and regeneration flourished. The worship of Isis and other divinities imported from West Asia and Egypt blended austerity with eroticism; the Isis cult in particular attracted women, many of whom took vows of virginity in the goddess's service. Cults, open to anyone and appealing to the individual, were rooted in the mysterious powers of nature and veneration of ancestors and taught rebirth, regeneration, and immortality. They contrasted strongly with the Olympic beliefs and practices, which were communal and public, concerned with community rituals honoring one or another of the twelve immortal Olympians. Olympic worship, based on community rather than personal bonds with the gods, was for the benefit of society, which it helped to define and unify.

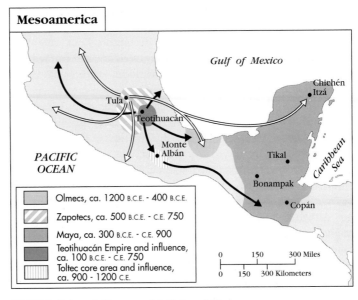

MAP 4.4 Selected Mesoamerica Cultural Sites

MESOAMERICA: TEOTIHUACÁN AND THE MAYAN WORLD

On the opposite side of the globe from the Mediterranean, the Mesoamerican cultural world included the area of modern central and southern Mexico, Guatemala, Belize, El Salvador, and much of Honduras. The relatively late Mayan culture (ca. 300–900 C.E.) in the Mesoamerican lowland rain forests of the tropical Yucatán Peninsula was heir to traditions transmitted from much earlier cultures in the region, such as the Olmecs (ca. 1200–400 B.C.E.).

Olmec Culture While many aspects of the Olmecs' culture remain a mystery, we know that they irrigated their farmlands, produced monumental sculpture in basalt, introduced both calendrical and writing systems, and, like the Shang Chinese, practiced totemism—belief in clan descent from an animal or natural object—as part of a complex set of religious beliefs. The Olmecs have been referred to as the "mother civilization" of Mesoamerica, since their legacy provided the foundation for later cultures in that region. Their calendar, in particular, became the basis of all later Mesoamerican calendar systems, one of the most highly developed aspects of Mesoamerican cultures.

Teotihuacán Heirs to the Olmecs, the rulers of the city-state of Teotihuacán (see Chapter 3) by around 100 C.E. controlled the largest urban site in the Valley of Mexico and probably in all of Mesoamerica. By 500 C.E., it had reached a peak population of 200,000, but it was gradually eclipsed by other cultural centers in Mesoamerica and in decline by the mid–eighth century. For the more than seven centuries of its existence, Teotihuacán unified the population and culture of the Valley of Mexico through its religion.

Religion and Power in Teotihuacán Central to Teotihuacán's religion was the powerful goddess, usually depicted in mural paintings as giving gifts, especially the bounty of nature. While no written documents exist, complex notational signs—sometimes appearing in sequence—on pottery, rock art, and painted murals provide much of the evidence of the goddess. Military and sacrificial elements are also common: the goddess has claws and wears a headdress adorned with human hearts. Overall, her imagery appears to be associated with the unity or integration of the community with the cosmos. In contrast, the storm god, a male deity perhaps worshiped in the Pyramid of the Moon, is associated with warfare, external relations, and the political values of the rulers of Teotihuacán.

Performance art played a prominent role in religious and political culture of Teotihuacán. Masked dancers who impersonated deities wore elaborate, feathered headdresses, necklaces, and mirrorlike back ornaments; the high-ranking elite were identified by a special tassel headdress.

Although the power of Teotihuacán extended over a fairly wide territory and its military might was formidable, it remained primarily a city-state, as did other Mesoamerican cultural centers. In this way, Teotihuacán may be seen as similar to the Sumerian city-states in West Asia. No single empire unified Mesoamerica before the coming of Europeans in the sixteenth century. One reason for this may have been the difficulty of traversing the terrain, which was dominated by rain-forest jungles and highland plateaus.

Mayan Culture and State Religion The Maya were also heirs to the Olmecs and their successors in Mesoamerica, such as the rulers of Teotihuacán, with whom the Maya had contact. Warfare was one activity of the elite in Mayan society, along with trade and religious ritual, as shown in the description of Cerros at the beginning of this chapter. Mayan culture was characterized by a sophisticated state religion represented in hieroglyphic inscriptions on stone stelae erected in urban centers and at sacred sites. As in Shang China and pharaonic Egypt, knowledge of the written script conferred power on scribes who served the Mayan rulers.

The Mayan Writing System The Mayan writing system was used to record lists of kings, their achievements, and chronology. Accurate historical record keeping, however, was not the object of these efforts; rather, these records were to be used to commemorate kings and, to an extent, to maintain their legitimacy as monarchs. The interweaving of fact and myth in such record keeping is characteristic of early dynastic states elsewhere in the world, such as Egypt and China. The Maya were preoccupied with the measurement of time, and much of their intellectual and religious life centered on a complex calendrical system, a tradition that can be traced to the Olmecs.

The Mayan Pantheon The Mayan pantheon included at least 166 deities; many of the male deities in the pantheon were paired with females, reflecting the notion of dualism (the unity of opposites) at the core of the Mayan belief system. The supreme deity was probably Itzamna ("Lizard House"), who was pictured as an old man, the inventor of writing. Mayan religious beliefs also intersected with political authority. Unlike god-kings such as the Egyptian pharaohs, Mesoamerican rulers, including Maya, were believed to rule for the gods but were not themselves gods. Kukulcán, depicted as a feathered serpent, was god of the ruling class.

A series of remarkable murals (ca. 800 C.E.) in Bonampak, Mexico, relates a single narrative of a battle and its aftermath. Magnificently adorned Mayan warriors are accompanied by musicians blowing long war trumpets of wood or bark. At a stepped platform, the prisoners of war have been stripped and are having their nails torn from their fingers. A captive rests on the steps; nearby a severed head lies on a cluster of leaves. A great lord in jaguar-skin battle dress is accompanied by other noble spectators, including women in white robes. In the final ceremonies, sacrificial dancers wear towering headdresses of quetzal plumes and performers disguised as water gods are accompanied by an orchestra of trumpets, rattles, drums, and turtle shells struck with antlers. The Mayan social hierarchy, based on beliefs in the primacy and sacredness of warfare, is above all recorded in the colorful and dramatic wall paintings.

Mayan Popular Beliefs Outside the cycle of elite warfare, ordinary people had their own deities. There were patron deities of beekeepers, hunters, fishers, dancers, tattoo artists, lovers, and suicides. Agricultural rites and ceremonies filled the Mayan calendar with a constant cycle of activities. Some events—such as the annual reconstruction of a new road outside the town limits—were of particular importance and reassured the community of its common, auspicious direction at the beginning of the New Year.

In early Mesoamerica, as in ancient Asia and North Africa, belief systems focused on gods who sanctioned the power of kings to rule. In Egypt, the pharaohs were considered to be "living gods," while elsewhere kings ruled with the divine sanction of gods, as in Sumer or in Shang China. Shamans and scribes played important roles in confirming the authority of rulers by claiming to communicate with gods and ensuring the legitimacy of rulers.

■
WEST ASIAN MONOTHEISM: JUDAISM

During the first millennium B.C.E., new religious ideas arose that did not focus on god-kings or on the sanction of gods to sustain political power. New belief systems challenged the power of shamans, priests, and god-kings and focused instead on ethical questions of right and wrong or good and evil, on the meaning of human existence and suffering, and on the order of human society. One such belief system was west Asian monotheism.

From its beginnings among the Hebrew peoples of ancient West Asia, Judaism (from the Israelite kingdom of Judah) was to make a major contribution to the shaping of Mediterranean and European societies. The origins of the Hebrew peoples and the rise of Judaism, like other early histories, must be reconstructed from a variety of different sources, including both archaeology and written documents, which provide uneven coverage and often have huge gaps. Though composed of layers of materials written by different authors for different purposes, the Hebrew Bible, or Torah (the first five books of the Christian Old Testament), remains one of the richest sources for the early history of Judaism.

THE HEBREW PEOPLE

The roots of Judaism can be traced among the semipastoral peoples of Iraq as early as the second millennium B.C.E. The Hebrews, one group among these peoples, moved westward early in the second millennium under the leadership of the patriarch Abraham. According to the

Bible, Abraham abhorred the idol worship found in his birthplace, Ur, in Mesopotamia, and moved his family and herds through the Syrian desert to a new home in Palestine at the eastern end of the Mediterranean, where they continued to worship their ancestral clan divinity. This area was a crossroads between Egypt, Anatolia, Arabia, and Mesopotamia, and the fate of the Hebrew people was closely tied to the rise and fall of kingdoms and empires that shaped the history of the entire region.

Around the middle of the second millennium B.C.E., the Hebrews moved to Egypt, probably as part of the Hyksos ("rulers of foreign lands") army that invaded Egypt at that time. After the Hyksos were forced out of Egypt, the Hebrews were enslaved. About 1250 B.C.E., following a leader named Moses, the Hebrews fled Egypt and resettled in Palestine. Under the guidance of Moses, Yahweh, originally the most powerful of numerous gods, emerged as the favored god of the Hebrew tribes. Moses claimed that God (Yahweh) had transmitted to him the sacred laws by which the community should live. These were the Ten Commandments, and they were sealed up in a box called the "Ark of the Covenant," reflecting the covenant, or pact, with God made by the Hebrew people.

THE KINGDOM OF ISRAEL

Under Moses' successor, Joshua, the twelve Hebrew tribes that traced their descent from Abraham and his sons staked out territory in Palestine, and in the eleventh century B.C.E., Saul became the first king of Israel. Under the rule of his son David (r. ca. 1000–960 B.C.E.), the transition from a tribal confederacy to a unified monarchy was completed. The Ark of the Covenant was brought to David's new capital of Jerusalem, which became the political and religious center of the kingdom of Israel. The First Temple was built by David's son and successor, Solomon (r. ca. 960–920 B.C.E.), after which the kingdom split into two, divided between Israel in the north and Judah in the south.

The Assyrians destroyed Israel in 721 B.C.E. and deported many Israelites to the east. It was during this time of tribulation that the teachings of a series of great social and moral critics and reformers—the prophets Ezekiel, Amos, and Isaiah, among others—confirmed Abraham's tribal god, Yahweh, as not just the most powerful god but the only god. In 587 B.C.E., the Babylonians captured Jerusalem, destroyed the Temple, and deported many leading Jewish families to Babylon, along with skilled workers such as blacksmiths and scribes.

Diaspora This was the origin of the diaspora (Greek for "scattering" or "dispersal") in which ▬▬▬▬▬ Jews were forcibly deported or fled their homelands to settle elsewhere and establish communities. One of the most important steps in setting up a new community was the establishment of a synagogue (Greek for "bringing together"), a communal meeting place that served educational and social, as well as religious, functions.

In addition to religious ritual focused on the Temple in Jerusalem or on a synagogue elsewhere, a central issue of Hebrew belief became just and moral behavior among human beings. Such behavior was the result of obeying Yahweh's laws, while transgression of his laws led to punishment. The eighth-century conquest of Israel by Assyria and the sixth-century captivity of Hebrews in Babylon were interpreted as examples of Yahweh's punishment for the Hebrews' misbehavior. In the fifth century B.C.E., the Temple was rebuilt and the Deuteronomic Code was introduced, embodying the laws to be followed by the Hebrew people so that they would not err again. By this time, Judaism was a cosmology based on one god, who was the creator and lawgiver, and on humans, who ideally ruled the earth justly, guided by God's laws.

SOUTH AND WEST ASIA: HINDUISM, JAINISM, BUDDHISM, ZOROASTRIANISM

During the sixth century B.C.E. as the Israelites were claiming their god, Yahweh, to be the only God and his laws to be the only laws, new ideas rose in India to challenge both the domination of the Brahman priests and the emphasis on rituals characteristic of Vedic religion. Though some secular rulers resisted priestly power and in this way challenged the Brahman priests, newer texts expressed critical reflection on Vedic ideas and practices from within the tradition itself.

THE UPANISHADS

The internal critical tradition is represented by the Upanishads ("sessions"), which refer to esoteric knowledge gained from sitting at the feet of a master. Chronologically the last of the Vedic tests, the Upanishads were compiled between the seventh and third centuries B.C.E. and represent a speculative and ascetic (contemplation and self-denial for religious purposes) tradition. The Upanishads focus on the meaning of ritual rather than ritual itself, demythologize the Vedic pantheon, and raise questions concerning the meaning of human existence.

Concepts such as *karma,* meaning "law of causality," and *samsara,* "wheel of life," were used differently in the Upanishads than in previous Vedic texts. *Karma,* for example, in earlier contexts had meant "ritually prescribed behavior," as emphasized in the priestly tradition; in the Upanishads its meaning was transformed to "cumulative causality determined by human actions." The goal of human existence, according to the Upanishads, should be to escape the endless cause–effect sequence of the continuous cycles of existence and achieve individual identification with a unified cosmic essence. Because of their focus on metaphysical (beyond physical reality) or abstract questions concerning human existence rather than rigid adherence to religious practices, in these texts the importance of ritual and the role of priests was greatly reduced.

HINDUISM

The assimilation of new ideas and the reformulation of traditional Vedic ideas and practices between the second century B.C.E. and the second century C.E. led to the emergence of the religious tradition later known as Hinduism. The Book of Manu, composed during this era, represents the reassertion of the priestly tradition. It contains the instructions of the creator of the universe to the first man and king, Manu, and it explains the caste system as a consequence of *karma* (actions) accumulated in earlier incarnations. The book's injunction to humans is to achieve a state of being without longings or desires in order to realize the cosmic essence or the eternal truth.

Ideas about both social and spiritual life were further developed in other religious and philosophical literature, including the Sanskrit epics, the *Mahabharata* and *Ramayana,* both completed in their final written form in the first centuries C.E. The latter work, the *Ramayana*, tells of the heroic exploits of Prince Rama, while the *Mahabharata* focuses on a great battle fought among descendants of Rama's brother, King Bharata. Although not an integral part of the epic, the most influential Hindu scripture, the sacred poem Bhagavad Gita ("Song of God"), composed in the second century C.E., was inserted into the *Mahabharata* and became part of this great epic.

The Bhagavad Gita In the Bhagavad Gita, the god Krishna, an incarnation of the Hindu solar deity Vishnu, takes human form as a charioteer who befriends and counsels Arjuna the warrior. Arjuna, a representative of the warrior caste, faces a battle in which he must slay his own relatives. As Arjuna wrestles with the moral dilemma this presents, Krishna recites the Bhagavad Gita.

Krishna counsels Arjuna that he must fulfill his duty as a warrior and that he is not to worry about his role in the deaths of his friends and relatives because their deaths in battle will allow their souls to move on to the next life. Arjuna, he says, is merely an agent of a cosmic process, and his own salvation depends on his carrying out his duty. He must act, without attachment and without personal ambition, to fulfill his role in society, as must every individual according to his caste. The moving and eloquent injunction on how to live one's life expressed here says that, like Arjuna, one must live and act according to what is expected of one's place and role in the world, without the interference of personal ambition or even human emotional attachments to kin and friends.

Often characterized as a way of life as much as a religion, Hinduism drew from beliefs of the Indus Valley civilization, including worship of the god Shiva, as well as from the culture and religion of the Indo-Europeans, such as worship of the warrior god, Indra, or the fire god, Agni. Southern Indian contributions to the Hindu pantheon probably included the god Krishna. The Vedic scriptures portray the gods of the Hindu pantheon and prescribe the ritual practices to be followed by priests, and the Upanishads provide a metaphysical context for ethical questions having to do with good and evil, morality, and human duty. The Bhagavad Gita, however, can be regarded as the main ethical text of Hinduism, showing how carrying out the faithful execution of one's duty *(dharma)* results in good *karma*.

JAINISM AND BUDDHISM

By the sixth century B.C.E., an era of commercial expansion, social conflict, and religious turmoil on the Indian subcontinent, the rich Ganges River plain of northern India was dotted with more than a dozen kingdoms, one of which was the birthplace of Buddha. In this setting, Jainism and Buddhism rose as challenges to the Vedic establishment. Both were rooted in a "wandering ascetic" movement that opposed the power of Vedic priests; both also rejected caste ideology and the sacrificial rituals of the Vedic religion, drawing on the critical intellectual tradition associated with the Upanishads.

Mahavira Mahavira (ca. 540–468 B.C.E.), whose name means "Great Conqueror," was the founder of Jainism (followers of *jina,* the "conqueror"). He abandoned his comfortable life as the son of a tribal chief to become a wandering ascetic at about the age of thirty. He reacted to priestly ritualism by promoting ascetic practices for his followers and taught the annihilation of *karma* by penance and disciplined conduct.

FIGURE 4.6 Sandstone Buddha in Teaching Posture. Sārnāth Fifth Century C.E.

Jains believe that everything in nature is alive and endowed with a form of spiritual essence; they also believe in the doctrine of nonviolence, which has had a profound influence on Indian culture and society into modern times. Jainism never gained a wide following, either in India or elsewhere, although the founder of the Mauryan Empire, Chandragupta Maurya (r. ca. 324–301 B.C.E.) was said to have abdicated his throne to become a Jain monk in south India.

Buddha Like Mahavira, the man later known as Buddha was born in the sixth century B.C.E. to the ruler of a kingdom in the Himalayan foothills and grew up amid the luxurious surroundings of palace life. As he became an adult he began to recognize the existence of suffering, sickness, and death. He sought an understanding of the causes of human suffering by following the teachings of various ascetics and holy men. Dissatisfied with their teachings, Buddha eventually achieved *nirvana* (the extinction of forces that cause rebirth), "enlightenment," or the realization of the true nature of existence through a combination of meditation and ascetic practices.

The Four Noble Truths of Buddhism The Four Noble Truths, taught by Buddha in a famous sermon at the Deer Park in Benares, contain the basic precepts of Buddhist belief: that life is suffering; that the cause of suffering is desire; that in order to stop suffering, one must stop desire; and that the way to accomplish this is through the Eightfold Path, which includes ascetic practices and mental disciplines followed by monks, holy men who live apart from society and have committed their lives to religious practice.

The debt of Buddhism to earlier Indian cosmology and thought, particularly that of the Up-anishads, is evident in fundamental concepts such as *samsara,* the cycle and bondage of re-birth, and *karma,* the cumulative causality of actions that propels humans through life after life.

In contrast to Jainism, which remained confined to India, Buddhism was later transmit-ted to East and Southeast Asia to become one of the great world religions. By the sixth cen-tury B.C.E., when both Buddhism and Jainism took shape in South Asia as reformist chal-lenges to the dominant Vedic tradition, a new system of religious belief that challenged prevailing ideas and was similarly concerned with ethical questions began to form in the set-ting of the Persian Empire in West Asia: Zoroastrianism.

INDO-IRANIAN RELIGION: ZOROASTRIANISM

South Asia was linked to West Asia in the first millennium B.C.E. through a common Indo-European language and culture. The Medes and Persians, who ruled Iran in the seventh cen-tury B.C.E., spoke an Indo-European language, and their culture derived from Hinduism. They used Sanskrit texts and believed in a pantheon of Hindu gods and goddesses. They saw existence, the world, and themselves as moving through eternal cycles on the Hindu "Wheel of Life." Their place on that wheel was defined by birth into a rigid caste system.

Zoroaster Though we cannot be certain when he lived, by the early sixth century B.C.E., an Indo-Iranian priest known to us by his Greek name of Zoroaster began preaching to farmers and semisedentary herders who lived south of the Aral Sea in eastern Iran. This tra-ditional borderland between settled Iran and the wide-ranging nomads of the Central Asian steppe was subject to frequent border raids and wars. The sixth century was no exception to this perennial instability, and Zoroaster's ideas gained a receptive audience because they called for change.

Ahura Mazda In place of the numerous Indo-Iranian gods and goddesses, Zoroaster proposed a dualistic pairing of gods: Ahura Mazda, the "Wise Lord," who represented the ethical good, and Ahriman, the embodiment of darkness and falsehood. Life was a con-stant moral war between two forces, and human beings had to choose between lies and truth, darkness and light. Unlike the eternal turning of the Hindu Wheel of Life, there was in Zoroaster's preaching a certain end to the war, when all humans would be called to account for their actions here on earth and rewarded with either eternal paradise or hell.

The teachings and principles of Zoroaster are found in the Avesta, a collection of hymns and sayings made sometime after his death. Zoroaster's ideas attracted the support of Iran's ruling aristocracy, and for the next 1,200 years, some variation of Zoroastrianism continued to find followers in Persia and the territories it controlled. Zoroastrian ideas were also influen-tial in shaping later Judaism, particularly the dualism of God and Satan and of Heaven and Hell.

THE PERSIAN ACHAEMENID EMPIRE

The Persian Empire (550–334 B.C.E.) was the largest of the successors to the ancient West Asian dynastic states. The founder of the Persian Achaemenid (named for a common ancestor,

Eurasian Empires

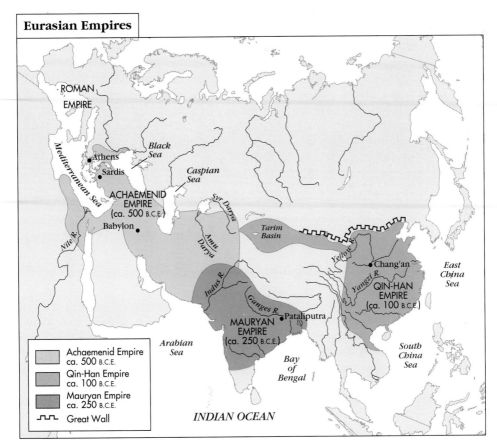

☐	Achaemenid Empire ca. 500 B.C.E.
☐	Qin-Han Empire ca. 100 B.C.E.
☐	Mauryan Empire ca. 250 B.C.E.
⊓⊔⊓	Great Wall

MAP 4.5 Early Empires in West, South, and East Asia

Achaemenes) dynasty, Cyrus the Great (r. ca. 550–530 B.C.E.), conquered the Mesopotamian kingdom of Babylon in 539 B.C.E.; under one of his successors, Darius I (r. 521–486 B.C.E.), the frontiers of the Persian Empire were expanded from Egypt in the west to Central Asia and the Indus River in the east.

The strength of the Persian Empire grew from the incorporation of the agricultural heartland of Mesopotamia under the military control of nomadic, tribal troops, thus securing a rich resource base, expanding the boundaries under their control, and opening up opportunities for trade. The Persian army, according to the account of its later invasion of Greece in 480 B.C.E. by the Greek historian Herodotus, was composed of representatives of many different cultural and ethnic groups, including Assyrians, Indians, Arabians, and Ethiopians, among others.

In addition to reliance on its powerful army, the Persian Empire was administered by a complex government bureaucracy and used a common legal system, common coinage, and standardized weights and measures. A well-maintained imperial highway system linked its provinces together, and its people shared a common religious ideology focused on an emperor. The Achaemenid ruler claimed sovereignty based on rights granted them by the principal

FIGURE 4.7 A Stone Relief Showing Darius I Receiving His Son, Xerxes. The Two Fire Altars in Front of the King Show the Importance of Zoroastrian Fire Worship at the Persian Court.

SOURCE: Oriental Institute Museum, The University of Chicago.

Zoroastrian deity, Ahura Mazda. Kingship was thus both semidivine and universal. Darius commemorated his conquests with an inscription in three languages carved on a cliff face over a highway leading out of Babylon, beginning "I am Darius the Great King, King of Kings, King in Persia, King of Countries." Darius apparently regarded himself both as an ethnic Iranian ruler and as a universal monarch.

Focus on the emperor as semidivine was only one aspect of religious belief, though the one that is perhaps best known. There is some evidence of deities other than Ahura Mazda also being worshiped in the Persian Empire; these include Mithra, a solar deity. As elsewhere, a process of assimilation and coexistence took place as Persian power expanded. The interests of rulers such as Darius in legitimizing their power led them to claim divine rights from Ahura Mazda but also to tolerate other forms of local religious belief and practice. The Magians, for example, were Iranian priests whose precise role in Persian society is not clear, though we do know that they performed a variety of religious rituals, including animal sacrifice, and acted in ways reminiscent of shamans in other cultures.

■

THE SAGE AND SOCIETY: PHILOSOPHY AND POLITICS IN EARLY CHINA AND GREECE

In the sixth century B.C.E., as Judaism's cosmology took shape in West Asia, Buddha searched for the meaning of life in India, and Zoroastrianism began to flourish in the Persian Empire, in both China and Greece philosophers (those who love knowledge or wisdom) began to construct visions of society and politics that would shape their worlds for the next two millennia. In contrast to the monotheism of the Hebrews and the metaphysical orientation of early Buddhist cosmology, both of which sought to explain the purpose of human existence and the meaning of human suffering, philosophers in Greece and China were more concerned with the nature of reality, human knowledge, and the ordering of society.

The concerns of early Greek and Chinese thinkers were also distinct from animism, shamanism, or theocracy, which viewed nature with a sense of mystery and awe and deities as powerful forces to be feared and propitiated. In contrast to these, the systems of thought that developed in sixth-century Greece and China were human-centered and built on rationalistic explanations of the cosmos not dependent on the intervention or favor of gods.

Rationalism and Humanism These approaches to ordering and interpreting the world can be described by the terms rationalism, the notion that by reason humans can understand the patterns that govern both the human and the natural worlds, and humanism, which emphasizes the human mind rather than deities or superhuman spiritual powers as the source of understanding and interpreting the world. In contrast to the integrative relationship between humans and cosmic or spiritual forces found in theocratic states, such as those of Shang China and early West Asia, the humanistic and rationalistic ways of thinking developed in early China and Greece were based on an oppositional relationship between humans and the cosmos. In other words, unlike the integration of the human and natural worlds in theocracies, whose rulers were identified with a deity or some cosmic force, in classical China and Greece philosophers saw the human world and the cosmos as two distinct realms. It was not that gods and spirits did not exist, but they existed in a separate realm which was unknowable and thus was not the subject of philosophical speculation.

CHINA: CONFUCIANISM, LEGALISM, AND DAOISM

As we have seen above, the religion of the Shang people in early China was shamanistic, dependent on the ability of shamans to communicate with the world of gods. Shang China can also be characterized as a theocracy, since the ancestors of the Shang kings were believed to be deities who served the principal god, Di. When the Shang dynastic state was replaced by the Zhou people, who invaded their territory and conquered them in the mid–eleventh century B.C.E., there was a corresponding transformation of concepts that sanctioned kingship.

Religion and Rulership The Shang anthropomorphic supreme deity, Di, was gradually replaced by a far more abstract concept of Heaven, which represented an idea of order imposed on the human world through the person of the ruler, the "Son of Heaven." In Zhou texts such as the *Book of History,* written down in the sixth century B.C.E., Heaven at times displayed an anthropomorphic quality, but this gradually disappeared and Heaven came to signify a more abstract moral order that the ruler must achieve and maintain.

The Zhou king exercised power by appointing his kin to rule over territories within the Zhou realm. The king's relatives were conferred with titles and ranks that gave them status as an aristocracy with the right to rule in the name of the Zhou king. The relationship between this titled nobility and the Zhou king was symbolized and confirmed by the transfer of a mound of earth from the central altar of the Zhou king to altars in each of the territories. The rulers of these territories owed the king allegiance, as well as military support if called upon to provide it. This decentralized form of government worked well for about two centuries.

By the eighth century, the authority of the Zhou king began to erode as the blood ties that had been the basis of bonds between the king and the territorial lords in his domain grew thinner with each generation. As the bonds that held Zhou society together were strained and weakened by the passing of time, military struggles broke out among the lords

FIGURE 4.8 Qing Period (1644–1910) Rubbing of the Chinese Sage Confucius

Qing dynasty rubbing, made over 2,000 years after the death of the sage, of whom there are no contemporary portraits.

SOURCE: Corbis-Bettmann.

of the territories that made up the Zhou state. By the sixth century B.C.E., there was warfare among independent states that had formerly been part of the Zhou realm.

Confucius During this chaotic time, a man we know by his Latinized name, Confucius ▬▬▬▬ (551–479 B.C.E.), was born in the small state of Lu in the modern province of Shandong in northeastern China. Confucius sought a post as adviser to rulers of states; though he was unsuccessful in this, the power of his ideas and personality eventually gained him a following of devoted disciples who later recorded his teachings in a work called the *Analects*.

Like many of his contemporaries, Confucius was greatly troubled by the disorder of his time and sought answers to the question of how to restore order to society. Confucius looked to the early days of the Zhou as a golden age; he idealized the institutions of the sage-kings of antiquity as models for his own society because he saw them as the source of political and social order in that earlier time. Confucius believed that the founders of the Zhou dynasty, who had displaced the Shang in the late eleventh century, had been ideal rulers or sage-kings and provided models to be emulated by rulers of his own time.

Confucius challenged the social order of his time by redefining the basis of elite status. He transformed the meaning of the term *junzi* ("son of a prince or ruler") to "gentleman," a person of exemplary conduct who can serve as a model to others. Confucius also made learning, rather than administrative or military skill, the basis of elite status and the defining characteristic of the elite; thus the scholar should be at the pinnacle of the social hierarchy. The aristocratic code of ceremonial behavior, *li* ("ritual"), became in Confucius's thinking the social forms that structured human relationships, including everything from proper etiquette to the performance of ancestral sacrifices.

Mencius Though dramatic social and political changes associated with the breakdown of the ▬▬▬▬ Zhou system of rule were already well under way during Confucius's lifetime, warfare intensified in the generation after his death, ushering in a period known as the "Warring States" (ca. 480–250 B.C.E.). Approximately a century after Confucius's death, the philosopher Mencius (ca. 372–289 B.C.E.) was born into a world of even more brutality and chaos. Unlike Confucius, however, Mencius succeeded in gaining the ear of rulers, who sought his advice on how to rule their states. The collection of his writings, known as the *Mencius,* is composed of short accounts of his discussions with rulers, whom he frequently scolded for their selfish and single-minded pursuit of power and wealth.

In his conversation with King Hui of the state of Liang, for example, Mencius was asked by the king how he could benefit his state. Mencius replied, "Why must Your Majesty use the word 'benefit'? All I am concerned with are the benevolent and the right." Like his predecessor, Mencius held a highly moralistic view of politics; the concept of *yi* ("right") was central to Mencius's political ideology and meant doing what was morally right in given circumstances. For him, the ideal ruler was one who looked after the welfare of his people and ruled only so long as he kept the covenant with them to act in the best interests of society, not in the interest of increasing his own power.

The Mandate of Heaven Mencius expounded the theory of the Mandate of Heaven, the major contribution to political theory of the Confucian school. According to this theory, Heaven confers the right to rule on the person who is morally qualified; the sanction for rule thus depends on moral character, not on military strength or on the power of gods. The concept of the Mandate of Heaven provided the principal sanction for rule in China for more than two millennia and was used in later times, for example, to explain the Zhou conquest of the Shang, which, according to this theory, had lost its moral right to rule.

In his discussion of the Mandate of Heaven, Mencius added the corollary that the people could express the will of Heaven by rising up against an unjust ruler, unseating him, and thereby transferring the mandate to a new ruler. This doctrine, known as the "righteous uprising of the people," was later used to justify popular rebellions in imperial China when their success brought a new ruling family to the throne.

Xunzi Xunzi (312–235 B.C.), the third major figure in the Confucian school, differed from Mencius in a number of important ways. For example, whereas Mencius stated that human nature was originally good, Xunzi believed that human nature was bad and must be guided by education to ensure social order. All Confucian thinkers, including Xunzi, believed in the necessity of a social hierarchy determined by one's demonstrated ability or merit, not birth.

For Xunzi a hierarchical social order was essential to the inequitable allocation of limited resources among a growing population with increasing demands and limitless desires. The more pragmatic and practical aspects of Xunzi's views, as well as his relatively pessimistic view of human nature, were much influenced by the intensification of warfare and the increasing concentration of power in the hands of a few states during his lifetime.

Legalism An alternative to Confucian ideas that rose in the ferment of the Warring States period, Legalism (stressing law) presented a profoundly practical and utilitarian set of ideas designed to ensure the unchallenged power of the state and the ruler. Like Confucian thinkers, those associated with Legalism were also searching for solutions to disorder of the times, but their answers were profoundly different.

One of the early Legalist thinkers was Shang Yang (fl. ca. 356–338 B.C.E.), whose views were articulated in the *Book of Lord Shang,* a manual on how to administer a state, and who served as adviser to the ruler of the Qin state in northwestern China. Shang Yang was concerned with how to maintain the ruler's power and authority in a setting of competing states. According to the *Book of Lord Shang,* the primary functions of the state are agriculture and war, emphasizing the necessity of both an economic base and the maintenance and extension of the power of the state through military means.

The Confucian thinker Xunzi was the teacher of Han Feizi (d. 233 B.C.E.), the principal philosopher of the Legalist school. In accord with his teacher's view that human nature was bad, Han Feizi argued that it was necessary to control people by the use of "strict laws and harsh punishments" and thus to manipulate individual self-interest to serve state power.

Daoism In contrast to Confucian concerns with human nature and social order, and Legalist concerns with the state and political order, Daoist thinkers of the Warring States period argued that people should aspire to live in harmony with nature and take nature as the model for human behavior. The term *dao* ("path") was also used by Confucian thinkers to refer to the "path of humanity," meaning ethical social behavior. In Daoism, the path is one of nature, in distinction to human society and culture.

The two classic texts of early Daoism are the Daodejing ("The Classic of the Way and Its Power"), compiled in the third century, and the Zhuangzi ("Master Zhuang"), the writings of the philosopher Zhuang Zhou (369–286 B.C.E.). Both the Daodejing and the Zhuangzi emphasize the relativity of intellectual categories, such as big and small or beautiful and ugly, and the concept of transformation as a fundamental cosmic principle. Human life and death are placed into the context of the creative transformations of nature, where death is part of a natural process that begins with birth and at death returns to a new beginning. As Zhuangzi put it, "How do I know that enjoying life is not a delusion? How do I know that in hating death we are not like people who got lost in early childhood and do not know the way home?"

Mysticism and Language Both the Daodejing and the Zhuangzi also emphasize mystical approaches to knowledge of the cosmos and the human condition. Mysticism is a way of knowing ultimate truth through direct apprehension rather than through rational intellectual processes. The opening lines of the Daodejing, "The Way that can be spoken is not the eternal Way," suggest the critique of language that runs throughout much of the work. Language, it says, is a trap that inhibits understanding rather than enabling it. Paradoxes are used in the Daodejing to jolt the reader out of normal intellectual patterns into a new way of apprehending the cosmos.

Although attributed to the pseudohistorical Laozi (literally, "old master"), the Daodejing seems to have been compiled by different people at different times because of inconsistencies in both the text itself and the ideas it contains. A poetic work concerned with the cosmic rather than with the secular and mundane, the Daodejing does not ignore politics. Some even consider it primarily a political text. One of the central concepts articulated in this work is that of *wuwei* ("nonaction"), used to describe the nature of the ideal ruler: "In doing nothing, everything is done." The meaning here is that the ideal ruler does not do anything that is contrary to cosmic patterns of harmony.

The Era of the "Hundred Schools of Thought"
The ideas that are labeled "Confucian," "Legalist," and "Daoist" took root in a common cultural background known as the era of the "Hundred Schools of Thought" in the sixth through third centuries B.C.E. This was a period of great intellectual ferment, as old social and political structures were crumbling. As people began to question the received tradition, new concepts were generated in a flood of "schools of thought" related to power struggles among the states that controlled parts of what would later be known as China.

Although we know relatively little about the popular beliefs of the time, from later evidence it is possible to speculate that there were probably numerous localized cults to deities of nature, as well as deified figures from both the human and animal worlds, including mythological people and creatures. One glimpse of this world comes from a passage in the writings of the philosopher Xunzi: "Why does it rain after a prayer for rain? I say, for no reason. It is the same as raining when you had not prayed." Though Xunzi rejected belief in rain deities, this passage suggests that it must have been a common practice for people to pray to such deities of nature.

GREECE: PHILOSOPHERS OF THE *POLIS*

The dualism of mystery cults and the Olympic pantheon in the early Mediterranean world indicates that there was a variety of ritual practices and beliefs held by those who inhabited the Greek mainland and the surrounding islands by the beginning of the Dark Age (ca. 1200 B.C.E.). By the end of this period (ca. 800 B.C.E.), a people known by their Greek name of Phoenicians appeared and helped to reconnect the inhabitants of Greece to the rest of the Mediterranean.

The Phoenicians
The Phoenicians were a maritime trading people who originally lived along the Lebanese coast of the eastern Mediterranean. Thriving commerce supported Phoenician city-states such as Tyre and Sidon, which were eventually overshadowed by the power of the North African port of Carthage, one of the largest cities in the world in the mid–first millennium B.C.E. Carthaginian ships plied the Mediterranean and found ports of call all around the shores of that sea.

The Development of an Alphabet
In addition to their role in maritime commerce, the Phoenicians introduced a writing system based on alphabetic characters throughout the Mediterranean. The advantages of an alphabetic script over earlier systems such as cuneiform and hieroglyphics are great: there are relatively few symbols to learn, and they are easily adaptable to different languages. The relative simplicity of an alphabetic script made literacy a possibility for more and more people.

The development of an alphabetic script for writing Greek contributed to the cultural flourishing of the Greek world over the next three centuries. Between about 800 and 500 B.C.E., both Greek society and Greek beliefs were transformed by the emergence of city-states, the expansion of the Greek world resulting from colonization and trade, and the introduction of influences from West Asia and North Africa. By the fifth century B.C.E., Greek thought and society were closely intertwined with the development of the *polis,* the city-state.

Athens Athens, based on its hinterland, Attica, was one of the independent city-states that
▨▨▨▨▨▨ flourished on the Greek mainland by the fifth century B.C.E. The Olympian deity
Athena, goddess of wisdom, was the focus of the public cult that gave unity and harmony to
the city-state, and mystery cults continued to flourish as well. However, the fame of the
Athenian city-state has less to do with its religious practices, whether the Olympian civic or
mystery cults, than with two developments that grew out of changing patterns of Greek life
after the eighth century B.C.E.: democracy (power held by the people) and the emergence of
rational and humanistic thought.

Democracy The development of democracy is closely linked to the evolution of the Athenian
▨▨▨▨▨▨ city-state. As Athens developed in the turmoil of Greek politics, it was essential
that order and balance between individual interests and those of the community be found.
The Olympic cult of Athena was one means of inspiring civic unity; another was the development of democracy.

Through the seventh century, like other Greek city-states, Athens was ruled by aristocratic clans, whose power was probably rooted in petty kingships of the Dark Age era. These
aristocratic clans provided the membership of the *areopagus,* the council, which they joined after being elected one of nine *archon*s, or magistrates. During the seventh century, Athens began to experience social and economic conflict among aristocrats, wealthy merchants, and
farmers. In 621 B.C.E., a judge named Draco was granted powers to deal with the violence
that plagued Athens; his laws and punishments were so severe that the word "draconian" is
now used to describe particularly harsh rules or punishments.

In 594 B.C.E., an aristocratic merchant named Solon (ca. 630–560 B.C.E.) was elected chief
archon with authority to restructure the government of the city-state. He broke the aristocracy's monopoly on power by opening up membership in the governing council to those with
wealth as well as aristocratic ancestry, and by forbidding the enslavement of free citizens for
the repayment of debts, he secured the basis of a free peasantry. Though his reforms helped to
restore order and reduce conflict, they did not entirely resolve the problems that plagued the
city-state.

A further step toward democracy took place under the leadership of Kleisthenes (fl. ca.
507 B.C.E.), whose reforms changed the basis of selection to the governing council in such a
way as to further undermine aristocratic power. He reorganized the units, or "tribes," from
which council members were selected using the *deme,* or place of residence, to determine
membership in a territorial unit rather than the previous criterion of ancestry. To the general
assembly of citizens, the basic arena of political activity, Kleisthenes added new institutions,
including popular courts. Athenian justice, like Athenian politics, became a matter of popular participation; citizens made the laws and pronounced the judgments as well. Each person
appearing before the court argued his own case, and decisions were made on the basis of the
will of the majority of citizens.

Periclean Athens Athenian democracy reached its peak under the leadership of Pericles
▨▨▨▨▨▨▨▨▨▨ (495?–429 B.C.E.), a skilled orator and military commander. But even at
this period of its fullest development, participation in the politics of the Athenian city-state
was limited to a minority. Periclean Athens (including Attica, its hinterland) had a population of more than 300,000, of whom less than 14 percent qualified as legal citizens. Other
Athenians—slaves, resident aliens (*metic* s), and women—were denied participation in the po-

litical process. Native-born Athenian males between eighteen and fifty-nine (about 43,000 in number) alone had the right to vote and serve in public office. The chief executives of the city-state were ten generals, elected annually, who then selected their own chairman, such as Pericles.

The Persian Wars During the Persian Wars (494–445 B.C.E.), Athens, along with Sparta, a city-state on the Peloponnesian peninsula, thwarted the designs of the Achaemenid Persian emperors Darius and Xerxes to drive the Greeks out of Anatolia and to invade the Greek homeland. The Delian League (named for the island of Delos, where the League met) had been formed by Greek city-states during the Persian Wars but came under Athenian control in 478 B.C.E. After the wars, using the Delian League as a base, Athens expanded its power throughout the Aegean and created an empire based on the strength of its fleet and its armies. The creation of the Athenian Empire, which extended political, economic, religious, and judicial control over a wide region, alarmed other Greek city-states, especially Sparta.

The Peloponnesian War Sparta, unlike Athens, was a city-state based on war, and its social and political organization reflected this. Male citizens were reared and trained by the state to serve in the military. Having made important contributions to the defeat of the Persians and dominating the Peloponnesus, Sparta assumed the leading role in challenging Athens in the fifth-century B.C.E. Peloponnesian War. This conflict, begun when

DAILY LIVES

WOMEN WARRIORS

In the vast and open landscape of the Ural steppes of southern Russia, at a place called Pokrovka, archaeologists have found the final resting place of the bones of a young thirteen- or fourteen-year-old girl. She lived more than 2,500 years ago in a nomadic society of people who grazed their sheep and horses across the steppes, moving seasonally from pasture to pasture. The Greeks called such people "Sauromatians;" their contemporaries were best known from the description by the Greek historian Herodotus of the female warriors he called "Amazons" (those who are not breast-fed). These daughters of nomads rode horses, used bows and arrows, and were required to have killed an enemy before they married.

From the bowed leg bones of the young girl's skeleton excavated at Pokrovka, it can be determined that she had spent her brief lifetime on horseback. Buried with her was an array of weapons, including a dagger and dozens of arrowheads in a wood and leather container. Around her neck she wore a bronze arrowhead amulet in a leather pouch. A great boar's tusk once probably suspended from her belt now lay at her feet. It is likely that the amulet and tusk had been worn to enhance her warrior abilities and ensure success.

Other excavations in the Russian steppes have shown that some Early Iron Age women held a unique position in society. They controlled wealth, performed family rituals, rode horseback, hunted, and fought. Such Amazons have been identified in other parts of the world, from West Africa to the Americas and Australia. These and other data from early societies suggest that women were not inherently more peaceful than men. However, there is also evidence that the militarism that accompanied the formation of complex societies also contributed to the subordination of women, who increasingly were excluded from warrior training and the high status it conferred.

Pericles was still in power and Athenian democracy was at its height, lasted nearly three decades (431–404 B.C.E.) and resulted in widespread destruction and loss of life. It ended with the defeat of Athens and the end of the golden age of Athenian democracy.

Politics and Philosophy The evolution of Athenian political democracy was accompanied by an explosion of creativity in ideas. By the time of Pericles, questions about the natural world and the origin and essence of things led some to reject both civic and cult religious beliefs to seek understanding of the world in *philosophia,* or wisdom.

A variety of thinkers sought the permanent or essential nature of things in a world of continuing change. The idea that all things consisted of four primordial, contrasting elements—wet/dry; hot/cold—emerged by the early sixth century B.C.E., but by the fifth century B.C.E. it was proposed that all things were made of fundamental particles called atoms (from the Greek word for "indivisible"). While some thinkers sought immutable truths of nature, others, like Daoist thinkers in early China, believed that change was the essence of things.

Sophists The fundamental question that exercised Greek thinkers of the fifth and sixth centuries was: How do we know what we know? Skepticism and relativism were introduced into Athenian thought between 450 and 350 B.C.E. by a group of professional teachers of rhetoric known as Sophists. Sophists were given to arguing both sides of a given idea or thesis, an exercise that fostered a relativistic view of things.

The intellectual differences and cosmic debates among the Greeks were a reflection of the conflicts that went on within and between the Greek city-states during what may be considered their "warring states" period (fifth to fourth centuries B.C.E.), roughly concurrent with the Warring States period in China and the flourishing of various schools of thought there. During this uncertain time, the Sophists' skepticism led them to reject the traditional religious and political guidelines for society. For them it was not the community, with its religious and political sanctions, but the rational individual that was the source of truth and knowledge.

Socrates Socrates (469?–399 B.C.E.), one of the most influential Athenian thinkers, sought to go beyond skepticism and to establish acceptable moral and ethical codes, much as Confucius had some years earlier in China. Unlike Confucius, however, Socrates sought an intellectual rather than a traditional historical basis for his views.

According to Socrates, all ideas are preconceptions and true knowledge is to be arrived at by questioning them. Examination and reexamination are the means by which we know what can be known. As a result of his suggestion that all knowledge is relative and final truths are unattainable, Athenian judges imposed the death sentence on him, and Socrates was put to death in 399 B.C.E. His ideas were viewed as particularly dangerous because he espoused them during the collapse of Athens in the war against Sparta, a time when certain truth and final answers were wanted.

Plato Socrates' most famous pupil, Plato (427–347 B.C.E.), undertook to create a system of thought that united the natural and the theoretical and to provide a worldview that was both ordered and beautiful. In his *Timaeus,* Plato returned to the traditions of ancient Greek beliefs and postulated a creator god who designs an orderly world that is maintained

FIGURE 4.9 *The Death of Socrates,* Painting by French artist Jacques-Louis David (1748–1825)

SOURCE: The Metropolitan Museum of Art, Wolfe Fund, 1931. Catharine Lorillard Wolfe Collection. (31.45)

by the actions of gods. The duty of humans is to carry on with the gods' efforts through the performance of religious sacrifices, which ensures harmony and order. Plato's emphasis on religious ceremony suggests a comparison with Confucius' emphasis on ritual; but Confucius' concern was with maintaining social harmony, not harmony between gods and men as in the *Timaeus.*

The *Republic* In his *Republic,* Plato described the ideal state as a commonwealth ruled by a ▬▬▬▬▬▬ philosopher-king. The world of phenomena, Plato believed, is a shadow world dimly reflecting the real world of ideas. It is this world of ideas that philosopher-kings understand and what qualifies them to govern. Beyond the world of things and experiences, apprehended by the senses, there is another, more fundamental world of eternal forms and types. In everything we experience through the senses there is an essence of this unchanging reality, independent of the material "accidents" that surround it. The "accidents" of everyday life are transcended by eternal essences and forms, which are the goals of knowledge. The philosopher-king is by education, if not by desire, able to guide the state out of the chaos and illusions of the external world of sense phenomena to eternal patterns and order.

On the basis of his observation of Athenian democracy, which had brought about the death of his mentor, Socrates, Plato believed that the people *(demos)* were an unruly lot, incapable of governing properly: "Whenever the populace crowds together at any public gathering, in the Assembly, the law-courts, the theatre, or the camp, it expresses its approval or disapproval, both alike excessive, of whatever is being said or done; booing and clapping till the rocks ring and the whole place redoubles the noise of their applause and outcries."

Following the death of his teacher and travels in Sicily and Italy, Plato returned to Athens around 387 B.C.E. and began teaching at the academy he opened there. He used the dialogue method to teach his students, working out his own ideas in discussions with his students as he had with his teacher, Socrates. Plato's most famous student was Aristotle (384–322 B.C.E.), who studied at Plato's academy for nearly twenty years but ultimately rejected his teacher's idealistic view of knowledge in favor of the systematic study and investigation of nature as the source of knowledge. Aristotle also had a more successful career than his teacher; he was hired as tutor to Philip of Macedon's young son Alexander who was to become Alexander the Great, "Conqueror of the World."

PHILOSOPHY AND POLITICAL THOUGHT IN EARLY CHINA AND GREECE

The flowering of ideas in China during the fifth century B.C.E. was paralleled by the development of philosophy in the Greek city-states at about the same time. In both the Chinese world and the Greek world, the growth of new ideas and debates among thinkers took place in an unstable political and social environment that provided fertile ground for conceiving new ways of achieving and maintaining social and political order. In China, the "Hundred Schools of Thought" flourished in an arena of competing states that rose against the background of the breakdown of the central authority of the Zhou kings; in Greece, the ferment of ideas was associated with the political form of the city-state and the practice of democracy.

It was the imperial model, however, such as that embodied in the Athenian Empire, that emerged in the following centuries to dominate a wide region from the Mediterranean to East Asia. Sanctions for empire drew on earlier god-king ideologies of theocracy, not on rationalism or humanism. As we will see below, the Hellenistic Empire of Alexander the Great, along with the Mauryan (India), Han (China), and Roman Empires, were heirs of early Chinese and Greek intellectual traditions and integrated aspects of earlier thought into their legitimizing ideologies.

■

THE HELLENISTIC EMPIRE: FROM THE MEDITERRANEAN TO THE HIMALAYAS

Both a weakened Athens and its competitor city-state, Sparta, were among the many Greek city-states that were overcome in the fourth century B.C.E. by the rising power of Macedon, a region in the northernmost part of Greece. Under Philip (r. 359–336 B.C.E.) and his son Alexander the Great (356–323 B.C.E.) Macedon was unified and gained control of the Greek world along with much of West Asia and North Africa.

ALEXANDER THE GREAT

The Persian Achaemenid Empire was conquered by Alexander the Great, whose Hellenistic (Greek-like) empire built directly on the experience of its Persian predecessor. After his first victory over the Persians, he advanced along the eastern Mediterranean seacoast and south-

FIGURE 4.10 Alexander the Great Charges into Battle (Fragment of Wall Painting from Pompeii)

SOURCE: Alinari/Art Resource, NY.

ward into North Africa, where he was welcomed as pharaoh by the Egyptians, who were resentful of Persian rule.

Alexandria In 331 B.C.E., Alexander founded the city of Alexandria at a strategic location with a good harbor that served both military and commercial purposes. City temples were dedicated both to Greek gods and to the Egyptian goddess Isis, reflecting Alexander's policy of accommodating local religious beliefs along with Greek ones. The population of the city likewise was mixed, consisting of Greeks, Macedonians, and local people; in later times, as Alexandria grew to be an important Mediterranean port, it attracted people from all over the Mediterranean. Alexandria served as a model for other cities founded by Alexander during the course of his conquests.

The Oracle of Amon During his stay in Egypt, Alexander also visited the oracle of the Egyptian god Amon at Siwah, along the Libyan border. This oracle was known and respected in the Greek world as a place of pilgrimage and homage to a god regarded by the Greeks as a manifestation of the Greek Zeus. Alexander consulted the oracle about his ancestry: Was he the son of a god, Zeus Amon? The oracle supposedly confirmed Alexander's belief that he was indeed the son of Zeus Amon. Though the Greeks believed that the offspring of mortals and divinities were human heroes, not gods, the Egyptians believed in the divinity of their rulers, a notion to which Alexander easily adapted.

After completing his conquest of Persia and acquiring the riches of cities such as Babylon and Persepolis, Alexander turned his armies toward India. In 326 B.C.E., he crossed the Indus River and pressed on until his army refused to go farther. Following his return, in order to reconcile the Macedonians and Persians under his rule, Alexander held a mass wedding for himself and other high-ranking Macedonians. He had previously wed the daughter of the defeated ruler of Bactria; now, according to the Macedonian tradition of royal polygamy, he married both the daughter of the Persian king Darius and the daughter of Darius's predecessor.

THE POST-ALEXANDRINE HELLENISTIC WORLD

After Alexander's premature death, such centralized authority as he had been able to maintain was replaced by a loose confederation of Greco-Asian states administered by his generals and their successor dynasties. The post-Alexandrine Hellenistic world was an empire only in the sense that it was united by a common culture with varied political centers. By 301 B.C.E., a relatively stable system had emerged: the Macedonian general Seleucus and his successors gained control of Persia and its Central, South, and West Asian (Iraqi and Syrian) possessions. After the Seleucids were overthrown around 250 B.C.E. by the Parthians, who in turn were replaced by the Sasanids (224 C.E.–651 C.E.), the Iranian plateau and much of Mesopotamia were ruled for almost 900 years by these heirs of the Persian Achaemenid Empire.

Ptolemy, another Macedonian general, and his successors took Egypt, Palestine, and Phoenicia. Others controlled Anatolia, Thrace, and the "home" territories of Macedonia and Greece. These successor states dominated West Asia for more than two centuries. They constituted a variant of Alexander's empire and illustrate a recurrent theme: the continuity of imperial ideals and achievements following the disintegration of imperial power. While a centralized imperial polity did not survive Alexander, many of his political and cultural traditions did, giving rise to what has come to be called Hellenistic civilization.

Following his death, the remnants of Alexander's empire shared a common law, language, trade, and cosmology; and Alexander's successors shared a distinctive approach to the world. In all cases, rulers such as the Ptolemies in Egypt or the Seleucids in Persia presented themselves as gods, just as Alexander had in Egypt and elsewhere. As religion continued to be used to support political authority and could be manipulated to sanction new rulers, there was a rich blending of religious traditions; some cults, such as that of Isis, spread throughout the Hellenistic world.

■

SOUTH ASIA: THE MAURYAN AND GUPTA EMPIRES

Influenced by, and almost precisely contemporary with, the Hellenistic Empire created by Alexander, the Mauryan Empire was founded in South Asia by Chandragupta Maurya (r. 324–301 B.C.E.). Reflecting the conditions of the times, a statecraft manual called the *Arthashastra,* commonly attributed to Kautilya, an adviser of the Mauryan founder, described a system of small states and prescribed how the rulers of these states should act. The author of the *Arthashastra* also provided a philosophical basis for the practice of politics. Like his Chinese contemporary, Shang Yang, Kautilya emphasized both the science of politics or state-craft, especially strategies designed to expand and strengthen the king's power, and the ex-ploitation of material resources necessary to support the consolidation of his rule.

ASHOKA'S EMPIRE AND BUDDHISM

The Mauryan Empire reached its height during the reign of Ashoka (ca. 272–232 B.C.E.), when Buddhism was adopted as the official religion. Although the empire fragmented shortly after the death of Ashoka, an essential element that contributed to the sustenance of imperial unity under the Mauryans was the use of Buddhism as a universal religion joining disparate ethnic and linguistic groups. Inscriptions of edicts issued by Ashoka during his reign are the oldest extant written records of Indian history, and they illustrate the use of Buddhism as a sanction for rule. They also show the influence of the Hellenistic states and the contact between northern India and the Mediterranean that was established by the successors of Alexander.

Ashoka as a   In these inscriptions, Ashoka is called "Beloved of the Gods"; he is de-
Chakravartin Ruler   scribed as regretting the death and destruction that accompanied his conquests and looking on to the next life rather than taking pleasure in the power and luxury of his role as king. Unlike his grandfather, Chandragupta Maurya, who had renounced his throne to become a Jain monk, Ashoka established legitimacy for his rule over many different peoples on the Indian subcontinent by claiming to be the first true *chakravartin* ("he for whom the wheel of the law turns"), or universal monarch.

THE GUPTAS AND HINDUISM

Waves of Greek and other Indo-European invaders into northwestern India brought about the fragmentation of the Mauryan Empire, but the model of the Hellenistic Empire continued to exercise an influence on the Indian subcontinent for later rulers, such as the Kushana, a no-madic people commanding a large steppe empire in southwestern Asia and northwestern In-dia during the first centuries C.E. After the disintegration of the Kushan Empire, the Guptas (ca. 320–500 C.E.) succeeded in uniting northern India. The Ganges city of Pataliputra (see Chapter 3) was the Gupta capital, serving as a center of the monumental architecture and lit-erary culture that flourished under the Guptas. The Mauryan and Gupta Empires were brief intervals of unity on the Indian subcontinent, which tended to fragment into smaller states that were then periodically fused together in a fragile, temporary union.

RELIGIOUS SANCTIONS FOR RULE

In India, Buddhism was sometimes used to support the rule of kings such as Ashoka, but Hinduism provided a much more powerful and common sanction for both the rule of kings and the order of society through its justification of the caste system. Under the Guptas, al-though they were Hindus and therefore supporters of the Brahman establishment, religious tolerance was practiced and Buddhists were allowed their own religious beliefs.

    Within the Hindu tradition, it was only toward the end of the Gupta period that the ideal of *shakti,* the female power that pervades the universe, began to be expressed in the form of goddesses who served as powerful consorts to gods and eventually of an independent goddess with supreme cosmic power. This change had a profound influence on the nature of Hinduism and on its expression in art, though not on the position of women in Hindu society, where they remained subordinate to men.

■
EAST ASIA: THE CHINESE EMPIRE

Contemporary with the Mauryan Empire in South Asia and the Hellenistic Empire of Alexander the Great in West Asia, the Chinese Empire was created in East Asia. In the mid–third century B.C.E., the northwest state of Qin (pronounced "chin") established its dominance over other states and molded these previously independent political units into a centralized administrative structure under the rule of an emperor *(huangdi)*.

THE QIN STATE AND THE UNIFICATION OF CHINA

Qin Shihuangdi (r. 221–210 B.C.E.), the "first emperor of Qin," took the title of emperor for the first time and ruled through a central government that included civil, military, and censorial branches. The function of the censorial branch, a distinctive characteristic of the Chinese bureaucracy, was ensuring the compliance of government officials in carrying out imperial

FIGURE 4.11 Terra-cotta Chinese Warrior Figure Wearing Armor (Qin dynasty, 221 B.C.E.–207 B.C.E.)

SOURCE: An Keren PPS/Photo Researchers.

commands by acting as an intelligence network that reported to the emperor. The censorate, along with the other two branches of the tripartite structure of imperial administration, was adopted by succeeding dynasties. Similarly, the administrative system that divided the empire into military commands, each of which in turn was subdivided into counties, was used as the basic structure of imperial rule well into the twentieth century.

The Qin state acquired power over other states by gaining control of agricultural resources in the Wei River Valley, west of the sharp bend in the Yellow River as it flows eastward out of the loess (loam or clay) highlands in the northwest on its way to the sea. This economic base, along with the creation of a powerful military and a tightly organized state structure, led Qin to conquer other states contending for power in the Warring States era (ca. 480–250 B.C.E.).

LEGALISM AND THE QIN STATE

The Qin state's triumph over its adversaries was directly related to the political philosophy known as Legalism. Legalism was adopted by the Qin state as the ideological apparatus of rule, and other ideas, most significantly Confucian ones, were banned as their proponents were executed or banished and their works were condemned and destroyed. In the states brought under Qin control, imperial officials imposed centralized controls such as standardization of weights, measures, and currencies. The adoption of a formal legal code and the unification of various written scripts into one made possible the relatively uniform implementation of government legislation over a wide geographical area that included vastly different cultural and linguistic regions.

The Qin unification also marks the birth of a distinct Chinese cultural zone that began to exert an influence over East Asia. The Western term "China" is derived from "Qin," and the geographical definition of China was symbolized by the incorporation of various defensive barriers built by earlier states into the Great Wall during the Qin. The Great Wall divided the area of Chinese culture—ideological, material, and political—from that of the largely nomadic or pastoral peoples to the north, who were regarded as "barbarians" beyond the bounds of civilization.

THE HAN DYNASTY

The Han dynasty (206 B.C.E.–220 C.E.) followed the fall of the short-lived Qin. In contrast to "Qin," which is identified with the geographical territory of China, "Han" is used to refer to the Chinese people and their culture. The Han Empire was built on the foundations laid by the Qin, but the Han founders rode to power on a tide of rebellion against the tyranny of the Qin. The formal rejection by the Han founder of the Legalist ideas associated with Qin rule and the adoption of Confucian ones as the legitimizing ideology of the Han state during the reign of Emperor Wu (r. 141–87 B.C.E.) obscured the reality of the Legalism-inspired institutions that formed the basis of imperial rule.

In the manner of the Qin, the Han emperors ruled through a tripartite structure of authority at the center and sometimes selected and appointed officials on the basis of merit or ability, rather than aristocratic privilege. The Mandate of Heaven, in Han Confucian thinking, related the authority of the ruler to his ability to carry out the fundamental responsibility to maintain harmony and order in human society.

Han Confucianism Han Confucianism blended elements of Daoism and other cosmological
▬▬▬▬▬▬▬▬▬ ideas together with the classical Confucian concepts of hierarchy and harmony in the human social order. Human society and the natural world were understood to be
part of an organic whole, intimately interrelated in such a way that changes in and patterns of
human society resonated in nature and vice versa. Correspondences and correlations between
the human and natural worlds were systematically detailed in intellectual patterns we can call
"correlative thinking," such as correlating colors with dynasties or the four cardinal directions
with animals. Imperial misrule, it was believed, would be manifested in nature by negative
signs, such as solar eclipses or earthquakes. In contrast, benevolent and correct government
could resonate in nature as a supernova or a comet.

Popular Beliefs in Han China Apart from the imperial religion of Han Confucianism, many
▬▬▬▬▬▬▬▬▬ deity cults flourished. Prominent among such deities was the
Queen Mother of the West, a Daoist deity who was part of the emerging Daoist pantheon.
Distant from the philosophical precepts of early Daoist texts such as the Daodejing, practitioners of popular or religious Daoism performed rituals to seek good fortune from deities,
practiced alchemy (attempts to turn one element into another), and sought ways of achieving
immortality through potions or physical practices.

Rebellion against Han Rule Ironically, the ideology of the Mandate of Heaven that legit-
▬▬▬▬▬▬▬▬▬ imized and helped to sustain Han imperial rule also provided
sanction to rebel leaders calling for the overthrow of the dynasty. Even in the early Han, the
Confucian philosopher Dong Zhongshu (ca. 179–104 B.C.E.) pointed out to Emperor Wu the
hardships of the peasantry in the face of wealth and extravagance among the aristocracy. According to Dong, because the rich had such large estates, the poor were "left without enough
land to stick an awl into" and "reduced to eating the food of dogs and swine."

By the latter Han, such conditions led many peasants to join a messianic (promising deliverance or salvation) religion called the "Way of Great Peace," a combination of popular beliefs and religious Daoism. Donning yellow scarves and calling themselves "Yellow Turbans,"
the members of this group adopted the color yellow as a symbol of their overthrowing the
color white, associated with the Han. Such ideas were part of the correlative thinking of Han
Confucianism, in which five elements (wood, fire, earth, metal, water) replaced one another in
a cyclical pattern. Each element was correlated with a color, such as earth with yellow.

The Han dynasty fell in the mid–third century C.E., prey to foreign invasions from beyond the Great Wall but also undermined from within by social, political, and economic dis-
cord. The pressure of domestic unrest coupled with the challenge of foreign invasion became
a theme in the undulations of the dynastic cycle that was used to explain the transfer of the
Mandate of Heaven, which would be restored three centuries later.

THE MEDITERRANEAN AND EUROPE: THE ROMAN EMPIRE

A century before the Qin state created the first Chinese empire (221 B.C.E.), the vast Hellenistic Empire of Alexander the Great broke apart into a number of successor states ruled by
some of his generals and supporters, such as the Parthian Empire in Iran (ca. 250 B.C.E.–

250 C.E.). By the second century B.C.E., these successor states found themselves faced with a challenge from the West. That challenge was Rome.

THE FOUNDING AND EXPANSION OF ROME

The legendary founding data for the city-state of Rome is 753 B.C.E. Early on, the Latin peoples who settled on the banks of the Tiber River in central Italy began an expansion which would create, by the first century C.E., a vast empire encompassing large parts of Europe, West Asia, and North Africa. Already by the sixth century B.C.E., their expansion brought them into contact with neighboring peoples on the Italian peninsula such as the Etruscans and the Greeks. The Romans were quick to acculturate, to accept new influences and ideas from peoples with whom they came into contact. For example, Roman religion was greatly modified by Greek influences.

Roman Religion Early Roman religion was an animistic cult of personified spirits or *numina,* ranged in a hierarchy of good and evil. Religious rites were connected with the family, with attempts to secure protection from *numina* for domestic life and livelihood, and each family had its protective spirit, or *genius,* who inhabited the home. In each home there were sacred spots: for example, in the hearth dwelt Vesta, the spirit of fire; in the storeroom dwelt a guardian spirit. Rites to keep good spirits in the home and evil ones away were plentiful. The practice of throwing spilled salt over the left shoulder, for example, which many people still do today to ward off bad luck, originated in such early Roman rites.

Roman Gods and Greek Influence By the third century B.C.E., even before they expanded eastward into Greece and West Asia, the Romans incorporated into their practical agricultural animism many anthropomorphic deities they appropriated from the Greeks. The process was to continue as Rome became an empire. The newer gods were generally communal rather than familial, worshiped publicly rather than privately in the home, and their organization and ritual practices were controlled by the state.

By the time Rome expanded beyond Italy, cults centering around Apollo and Hercules and the great mother goddess, Cybele, had taken root in Rome. Great temples were built to public deities such as Jupiter and Juno, the Roman name for the Greek Zeus and Hera, his wife; to Mars (the Greek Aries), god of war; and to Neptune (the Greek Poseidon), god of the sea. Along with the newer deities, the early Roman *numina* remained important but took anthropomorphic form: Vesta, the spirit of fire, became identified with Rome itself, and priestesses known as vestal virgins were responsible for maintaining and protecting her sacred flame.

The Hellenistic influences on Rome were accelerated as the Romans expanded eastward to impose their control over the post-Alexandrine eastern Mediterranean and North African coastline; at the same time, Rome extended its sway into northern and western Europe. Roman expansion beyond the Italian peninsula began with three Punic Wars (between 264 and 146 B.C.E.) with the North African state of Carthage, Rome's major competitor for power in the western Mediterranean. Carthage was defeated, and its territories became the Roman province of Africa.

At the beginning of the second century B.C.E., the Romans turned to Greece and then to the successor states of Alexander's empire in West Asia and Egypt. By the middle of the first century B.C.E., Roman armies had also conquered much of western Europe south of the Rhine and Danube Rivers, along with England. Military campaigns under the leaderships of generals such as Julius Caesar (100–44 B.C.E.) and his nephew Augustus (63 B.C.E.–14 C.E.) created a Roman empire that stretched from Spain to Syria and from Britain to North Africa.

THE TRANSFORMATION OF ROME: FROM REPUBLIC TO EMPIRE

The expansion of Roman territory created political and social tensions. Having expelled its last king in 509 B.C.E., Rome became a republic in which decisions were nominally made by assemblies of citizens. But the Roman republic was, like Athens, neither egalitarian nor democratic. Property ownership and gender were both criteria for participation in government. During the Punic Wars, the freedom of even upper-class Roman women, who had previously been allowed to attend public ceremonies and to move about openly in the city, was curtailed. The divisions between the poor and the well-to-do became increasingly aggravated rather than ameliorated by Roman expansion, and by the first century B.C.E. conflict between rich and poor was a major problem in Rome, as it had been in Han China.

Rule by Oligarchy   The dominant authority of the Roman republic was the Senate, the male members of which came from wealthy and powerful families. As long as the power of the Senate was unchallenged, Roman rule may be described as an oligarchy, a group of leaders, much as Athens and other Greek city-states were at one time. From the late second century B.C.E., oligarchical control in Rome was challenged by popular discontent. Power eventually fell into the hands of a succession of military leaders, culminating in the dictatorship of Julius Caesar (r. 49–44 B.C.E.) and the transformation of the Roman republic into the Roman Empire by his nephew Octavian, who ruled as Emperor Augustus Caesar (r. 31 B.C.E.–14 C.E.).

Augustus Caesar   Augustus based the bureaucratic structures of his empire on the models of the Roman Republic and the Hellenistic states that succeeded the empire of Alexander the Great. For the European portions of the Roman Empire, Augustus shaped to his purposes institutions such as the Senate. Similarly, he modified and used the administrative personnel and practices of the Hellenistic successor states, such as Ptolemaic Egypt, in the eastern portions of the empire, at least until he found it necessary to annex and rule these areas directly. By employing a common language (Latin), common law, and common ideology, Augustus created a loyal and efficient bureaucracy throughout the vast reaches of the Roman Empire and thereby "Romanized" the empire.

The Roman Imperial Cult in   Asia Minor (modern Turkey), previously under the domination
Asia Minor   of Persia, Athens, and the Hellenistic Empire of Alexander and
his successors, provides an example of how Augustus used ideology to support imperial control. Under Roman rule, this network of Greek-speaking city-states and Hellenistic kingdoms was divided into several provinces, each administered by a governor who was appointed by Rome. But Roman rule was necessarily superficial, and the peoples of Asia Minor continued to identify primarily with their cities.

FIGURE 4.12 Augustus Caesar with Cupid, Symbolizing Descent from the Goddess Venus

SOURCE: Alinari/Art Resource, NY.

Emperor-venerating rituals formed the basis of an imperial cult, which took shape during the reign of Augustus. The imperial cult became an important means of establishing Roman authority in a region long familiar with such ritual practices. Residents of cities in Asia Minor had little difficulty accommodating the Roman imperial cult to local traditions venerating other deities. The imperial cult coexisted with other earlier, indigenous religious cults, such as that of the great mother goddess Cybele, who was possessed of the same sort of life-giving, creative powers associated with the Neolithic fertility goddesses.

Roman Law   The imperial cult was but one of the things that held the government of the early empire together. The Roman Empire rested equally on the military power that had enabled the Romans to conquer vast territories; on an imperial bureaucracy concerned with the collection of taxes and application of laws; and on a common system of courts and laws. Roman law reached a high stage of development during the first through third centuries C.E. Augustus extended its jurisdiction beyond Rome and beyond Italy by means of judicial opinions that took on legal authority. These opinions were of three sorts, which together made up the body of imperial law: (1) *jus civile,* the law of Rome and its citizens; (2) *jus gentium,* the law of peoples other than Romans, regardless of nationality; and (3) *jus naturale,* natural law, the sense of justice and right embodied in the order of nature. This system, a composite of Roman legal ideas and practices, those of other peoples in the empire, and abstract legal principles, transformed the legal tradition of the republican city-state of Rome to serve the needs of the Roman Empire.

DIOCLETIAN AND THE DOMINATE

Beginning about 180 C.E. and lasting a century, Rome was gripped by a period of internal dissent and external pressures resulting from economic instability, continuing social tension between the wealthy and the poor, and problems with imperial succession resulting in a series of emperors who were incompetent to cope with pressing problems. When Diocletian (r. 285–305 C.E.) came to the throne, he attempted to restore and reinvigorate the empire by creating what is known as the Dominate.

Diocletian ended the Senate, whose role had become nominal only, and ruled with the support of the army that had placed him in power. By such means he succeeded in establishing hierarchical control over both military and civil administrations. He split the administration of the empire into eastern and western halves with the dividing line at the Adriatic Sea. Each half of the empire was further subdivided into prefectures, dioceses, and provinces. At the bottom of the structure were the *municipia,* or local units. The governing officials were civilian and were mainly responsible for judicial and administrative functions. This political structure was part of the lasting heritage of the Roman Empire.

Roman Emperor-Gods An intensified association of the rituals of the imperial cult with imperial power was characteristic of Diocletian's rule. Augustus had allowed temples to be built to "Rome and the emperor" and sacrifices to be made to the *genius,* or spirit, of the emperor; some emperors, such as the possibly insane Caligula (r. 41–37 B.C.E.), had insisted on being worshiped in their own right. But it was customary for emperors to be deified only after their deaths until Diocletian assumed the role of emperor-god during his lifetime and thus brought Roman practices into conformity with those of the West Asian theocracies conquered by Rome.

Neither Diocletian's innovations nor the vigorous efforts of his successor, Constantine (see Chapter 5), were able to defer the fate of the Roman Empire. In the year 476, the Visigoths, a Germanic people, invaded Italy and sacked Rome, an event that is generally taken to signal the end of the Roman Empire in western Europe.

SUMMARY

Early dynastic states in West Asia, North Africa, East Asia, and Mesoamerica expanded their territorial control through military means and used religious ideas to sanction the exercise of power by central rulers. The rise of dynastic states suggests a shift to warrior societies from matristic societies, which had been characterized by emphasis on the creative power of women and veneration of women as symbols of fertility. Archaeological and other evidence hints at this transition, but it is difficult to describe with precision exactly what kinds of societies are reflected in Neolithic fertility figures, let alone how such a transformation in social and political organization may have taken place. Even for later times, when we have evidence of images of Ishtar or other goddesses that suggest parallels with or continuity from the Neolithic fertility goddess cults, we cannot directly infer attitudes toward women or their roles in these societies from religious symbols. In the case of Asia Minor under the Roman Empire, the cult of the mother goddess Cybele coexisted with that of the cult of the Roman emperor.

Though it is difficult to know just how the relationship between ideas and power took shape in remote antiquity, we can say that, from earliest times, ideas have been used to explain and justify the unequal distribution of power among individuals and groups in society or to sanction and legitimize the power of rulers and states. Politics and religion are both ways of systematically constructing power, and the expression of symbolic systems through religious ritual has been as effective and important a means of imposing order on the world as administrative systems or military force.

In early dynastic states political authority was associated with religious beliefs and practices. In East Asia, Shang kings asserted their right to rule through claiming that their ancestors held the power to mediate with the supreme deity worshipped by the Shang people. The ability to transmit knowledge through writing was also an important aspect of power related to religion. Priests with the ability to read and write the archaic script commanded status and authority in Shang society because they held the key to interpreting the will of the supreme deity. This was equally true for Egyptian pharaohs and their priests, who had knowledge of hieroglyphics; for the kings of Sumer and Akkad, whose priests and administrators used cuneiform script for both sacred and secular purposes; and for Mayan rulers in Mesoamerica, where scribes employed hieroglyphics in the service of the state cult.

In contrast to the use of ideas to further power, as in early theocracies, religious ideas could also be used to contest the established order of things and to challenge the power of rulers and states. Both Buddhism and Jainism, for example, emerged from but also challenged the Vedic tradition and its priesthood. Rejecting the Vedic priests' emphasis on ritual, Buddhism posed questions having to do with the meaning of human existence and suffering; its answers drew on Indian cosmology.

The Hebrew prophets sought an explanation of human existence and suffering in the special relationship of the Hebrew people with a transcendent God, and Judaism drew on other West Asian cosmologies, including Zoroastrianism. Zoroastrianism grew out of ancient Indo-Iranian religious traditions in West Asia and taught a doctrine of ethical reform rooted in the cosmological dualisms of good and evil, light and dark. Zoroaster refined the polytheistic Indo-Iranian religious tradition to a starkly dualistic war between good and evil, which in turn influenced Judaism's conception of Heaven and Hell, God and Satan.

As Buddha, Abraham, and Zoroaster challenged the dominant religious traditions of their times, thinkers in Greece and China envisioned new social and political orders. In the decentralized, competitive political environment of the Greek city-states and the Warring States in late Zhou China, new visions of political community were created by thinkers compelled by circumstances—the absence of either centralized rule or community structures that ensured some degree of order—to consider how best to achieve social and political order.

The political form of democracy was worked out in the institutions of the Athenian city-state, and the philosophical underpinnings of this and other ideals were expressed by thinkers such as Socrates and Plato. In China during the same period, Confucius and his followers envisioned an ideal society rooted in the institutions of the past, the rule of the sage-kings of antiquity, much like the philosopher-king idealized by Plato. This society was not democratic in any sense of the word but rather was founded on the notion of hierarchy. Those who debated the Confucian school, particularly the thinkers known as Legalists, ridiculed the Confucian emphasis on ethical values and ritual as the means of achieving a harmonious society, arguing that only "strict laws and harsh punishments" could ensure social order and the stability of the state.

These pragmatic strategists, the Legalists, provided the ideological underpinnings for the first unified empire in China, the Qin, and for its successor, the Han, which rejected the harshest ideas of Legalism in favor of the ideals of Confucianism but adopted the form of the Legalist state with central authority vested in the emperor. Han emperors then made use of cosmological notions related to early Daoism to support their right to rule. Unlike Roman emperors, Han rulers were not deified; rather, they were seen as standing at the pinnacle of human society, a crucial link between the cosmos and humanity, and as being responsible for the proper ordering of society as a reflection of the perfect cosmic order, Dao.

After the demise of Alexander and his empire in West Asia, the imperial tradition was extended by his successors in various forms throughout West, Central, and South Asia, as well as North Africa. While they drew on the legacy of Alexander to sanction their rule, they also made use of local beliefs to reinforce their power, just as Roman emperors did in the imperial cult. In South Asia, Hellenistic influence provided a powerful model for the Mauryan and Gupta Empires, whose rulers were also god-kings, manifestations of cosmic order associated with either Buddhism or Hinduism. No less than Egyptian pharaohs, whose role was to maintain cosmic order, or *maat,* and Chinese emperors, who claimed the Mandate of Heaven to order the world, the Mauryan ruler Ashoka relied on a Buddhist sanction to rule, taking the title of *chakravartin,* "he for whom the wheel of the [Buddhist] law turns," to reflect his central role in promoting *dharma,* the law of the universe.

Alongside, and sometimes subsumed by, the official belief systems of dynastic states and empires were popular beliefs that celebrated the spiritual values of the individual within the larger community. These spiritual and ethical values almost certainly existed on a widespread and popular scale, preserved only through private and household ritual practice, often in the shadow of the magnificent displays associated with state cults. In the next chapter we treat the development of universalistic religions and their interaction with established political structures, showing how the dynamic relationship between religion and power was sometimes expressed in the rise of empires. Even within empires, spiritual and ethical values distinct from state religion continued to find expression in individual and group beliefs and practices.

ENGAGING THE PAST

BLACK ATHENA?

Were Cleopatra and Athena black? Was the legacy of ancient Egypt stolen from Africa and appropriated by the civilizations of the Mediterranean? Did Aristotle rip off the library of Alexandria? These are some of the emotionally charged questions that have fueled the debate between traditional classicists—those who study the classical world of Greece and Rome—and Afrocentrists—those who assert that African people and their descendants must interpret the world from their own perspective.

The debate around the ideas of Afrocentrism dates from earlier in this century, when Carter G. Woodson, the scholar who established Negro His-

tory Week (later Black History Month), called for an African-based view of world history to foster African-American self-identity and pan-African political unity. Adherents to the concept of Afrocentrism claim that white racists conspired over the centuries to deny the rich cultural legacy of Africans, including the ancient Egyptians, asserting that what the Greeks "stole" from Egypt has formed the foundation of the greatness of Western heritage. The work of Martin Bernal, a white historian at Cornell University, has been used in support of these claims, especially his 1988 book *Black Athena.*

SUGGESTIONS FOR FURTHER READING

A. L. Basham, *The Wonder That Was India* (New York: Grove Press, 1954). Classic detailed survey of India up to about 1200 C.E.

John Boardman, Jasper Griffin, and Oswyn Murray, eds., *The Roman World.* (New York: Oxford University Press 1988). Collected essays on various aspects of life in the Roman Empire.

Nancy Demand, *A History of Ancient Greece* (New York: McGraw-Hill, 1996). A recent textbook survey of ancient Greece through Alexander stressing analysis of different kinds of sources.

David Hall and Rogers Ames, *Thinking through Confucius* (Albany, N.Y.: State University of New York Press, 1987). Comparative examination of key concepts in Confucius's thought by one specialist in Chinese philosophy and one in Greek philosophy.

A. L. Herman, *A Brief Introduction to Hinduism: Religion, Philosophy, and Ways of Liberation* (Boulder, Colo.: Westview Press, 1991). Historical foundations and key texts of Hinduism related to modern religious leaders and movements.

Chang Kwang-chih, *Art, Myth, and Ritual: The Path to Political Authority in Ancient China* (Cambridge, Mass.: Harvard University Press, 1983). A provocative and stimulating thematic approach to political culture in Shang and Zhou China.

Frederick Mote, *Intellectual Foundations of China.* Brief but interesting and accessible overview of early development of key intellectual traditions in China.

S. R. F. Price, *Rituals and Power: The Roman Imperial Cult in Asia Minor* (New York: Cambridge University Press, 1984 [1982]). A scholarly monograph on the theme of religion and empire in Asia Minor under the Romans.

Gay Robins, *Women in Ancient Egypt* (London: British Museum Press, 1993). An illustrated survey of women in ancient Egyptian society.

Linda Schele and David Friedel, *A Forest of Kings: The Untold Story of the Ancient Maya* (New York: William Morrow, 1990). An imaginative recreation of the world of the Maya.

Karl J. Schmidt, *An Atlas and Survey of South Asian History* (Armonk, N.Y.: M. E. Sharpe, 1995). Part of the *Sources and Studies in World History* series by this publisher, this atlas survey is a useful guide to the basic outline of Indian history.

Benjamin Schwartz, *The World of Thought in Ancient China.* (Cambridge, Mass.: Harvard University Press, 1985). Thoughtful and provocative survey of classical period of Chinese philosophy by an eminent China scholar.

According to historian Mary Lefkowitz, author of *Not Out of Africa*, the most influential intellectual exploration of Egypt by Europeans occurred in the eighteenth century with the publication of the three-volume French novel *Sethos* by the Abbé Jean Terrasson in 1713. This novel was also the source of the story line of Mozart's opera *The Magic Flute*. Terrasson believed that hieroglyphics were mystic symbols, not writing. These views were widespread until the deciphering of the ancient Egyptian script in the last century. It soon became apparent that those who read the ancients in translation or out of context frequently missed major truths about their world. One of these "truths," claims Lefkowitz, is that race had little significance to ancient peoples and that ancient Egyptians came in all colors.

In most ancient societies truth was not independently determined by the individual; rather, truth was what a person was told by the oracle, the priest, or the ruler, thus placing accepted knowledge in the domain of politics. The debate between those who believed the "truth" of tradition and those who questioned authority was current in ancient Greece, and it continues in the context of today's political agendas and the debate about "black Athena."

5   *Religion and State: Buddhism, Christianity, and Islam*

T he relationship between sacred and secular authority is a key theme in human history. Three texts from the history of Buddhism in China illustrate both ongoing tensions and shared interests in the dynamic relationship between church and state. In 403 C.E., the prominent Buddhist monk Huiyuan (334–417 C.E.) was asked to present his opinion on whether monks should follow the customary etiquette in showing respect to their sovereign. Monks were holy men who lived apart from the rest of society. The issue was whether they, like laypeople, were obligated to demonstrate their loyalty to the ruler or whether their status as religious figures exempted them from such expressions of allegiance. In his response, entitled "A Monk Does Not Bow Down before a King," Huiyuan argued that "he who has left the household life [a monk] is a lodger beyond the earthly [secular] world, and his ways are cut off from those of other beings." According to Huiyuan, unlike lay believers, monks were not bound by the conventions of customary etiquette in showing respect for the sovereign.

The sovereign himself could, however, appropriate the sanction of Buddhism. The founder of the Sui dynasty (589–617 C.E.), which reunited China in the sixth century, used Buddhist terms and drew on Buddhist ideology to legitimize his claims to rule:

> With the armed might of a *chakravartin* [universal king], We spread the ideals of the ultimately enlightened one [Buddha]. With a hundred victories in a hundred battles, We promote the practice of the ten Buddhist virtues. Therefore, We regard the weapons of war as having become like the offerings of incense and flowers presented to Buddha, and the fields of this world as becoming forever identical with the Buddhaland.

Like the Mauryan ruler Ashoka in the third century B.C.E., who converted to Buddhism after the death and destruction of his enemies, the Sui founder claimed the loyalty of his Buddhist subjects using the language and ideas of the Buddhist faith and likening the weapons of war to offerings of Buddhist believers.

From an entirely different stance, in the latter part of the Tang dynasty (618–907 C.E.), a Confucian scholar named Han Yu (768–824 C.E.) attacked the veneration of a relic of the Buddha by the reigning emperor in a famous essay entitled "Memorial on the Bone of Buddha":

> Your servant begs leave to say that Buddhism is no more than a cult of the barbarian peoples which spread to China in the time of the Latter Han [25–220 C.E.]. . . . Now Buddha was a man of the barbarians who did not speak the language of China and wore clothes of a different fashion. His say-

FIGURE 5.0 Buddhist Monk Seated in Meditation

Ink drawing from Dunhuang caves in northwestern China, late ninth–early tenth century C.E. The monk's hands are placed in the gesture of meditation and he is shown with the gear of a traveling monk: Stoppered vase for water, leather bag and rosary (hanging from the thorn tree), the mat on which he sits, and his shoes.

SOURCE: © British Museum.

ings did not concern the ways of our ancient kings, nor did his manner of dress conform to their laws. He understood neither the duties that bind sovereign and subject, nor the affections of father and son. . . . How then, when he has long been dead, could his rotten bones, the foul and unlucky remains of his body, be rightly admitted to the palace?

These three statements—by a Buddhist monk, a Chinese ruler, and a Confucian scholar—suggest basic issues in the relationship between religion and the state, mirrored in various ways in the histories of Christianity and Islam as they interacted with political forces from Asia to Europe and Africa: What position should the clergy occupy in society, and how is it distinguished from the rest of the population? What is the proper relationship between the state and religious institutions, between state authority and religious clerics? In other words, how is power to be shared between sacred and secular authorities, and what conflicts emerge from the competition for allegiance between church and state? How do sacred and secular authority reinforce each other?

INTRODUCTION

In the previous chapter we stressed the interaction between ideas and power, both the use of religion in Asia, Africa, and the Americas to sanction political authority and the development of ideas that provided models of community life and social order in early Greece and China. We approached the relationship between ideas and power as a dynamic and interactive one: politics and religion are both ways of structuring power relations, and each influences the other. In this chapter, we focus on the development of Buddhism, Christianity, and Islam as institutionalized religions, their relationships with rulers of states and empires, and their influence on societies in Asia, Europe, and Africa. Buddhism, Christianity, and Islam are sometimes referred to as universal religions, belief systems that transcended the particular cultures and societies where they began and spread across vast regions of the globe. As universal religions, Buddhism, Christianity, and Islam crossed geographic, political, and cultural boundaries; over time, each developed a power structure that interacted with secular states in Asia, Europe, and Africa, sometimes dominating them. We do not deny or ignore the reality and validity—the "power"—of religion in the lives of individuals, something that is separable from structures of power relations and institutions; we simply do not focus on it here.

Christianity and Islam Christianity and Islam arose in the same geographic and cultural setting: West Asia. Both drew from the ancient traditions of that region, particularly that of the Jewish people and Judaism (see Chapter 4). Despite the dispersal of the Jewish people, their religion survived both in its own right and as a profound influence on the development of Christianity and Islam. Christianity came first, inspired by the life and death of its founder, the Jewish prophet Jesus of Nazareth (d. ca. 35 C.E.). His death and resurrection (restoration to life), according to Christian belief, became the mythic center of the Christian religion as it symbolized to Christians the eternal life of those who followed the Christian faith. The name of the religion is drawn from the appellation Christ, Greek for the Hebrew "Messiah," which means "anointed." Five hundred years later, Islam, which means "submission to the will of God," was founded by the prophet Muhammad (ca. 570–632 C.E.). Believers in Islam also regarded Jesus as a prophet, though Muhammad was believed to be the ultimate prophet of God, known in Islam as Allah.

Buddhism Buddhism originated in India during the sixth century B.C.E., and its founding figure, Buddha, was a contemporary of Confucius in China and the early Greek philosophers, antedating Jesus by 500 years and Muhammad by a millennium. Buddhism was rooted in early Indian cosmology and adapted concepts such as *dharma,* "duty" in the Upanishads and the "fundamental law of the universe" in Buddhism, to its own ends. By the beginning of the first millennium C.E., however, the influence of Buddhism waned in its South Asian homeland as it began to spread from India to East and Southeast Asia, where it gained many followers and became a potent cultural, social, and even political force.

Religion and State Like Christianity and Islam, Buddhism was a proselytizing religion: Buddhists, Christians, and Muslims all tried to convert others to their beliefs. Also like Christianity and Islam, Buddhism was at times patronized by rulers and became entangled in the politics of states in South, East, and Southeast Asia. But Buddhism did not become the kind of political force that both Christianity and Islam did, inspiring conquest and empire. Chinese emperors, for example, patronized Buddhism as a means of strengthening their rule by gaining the favor of the Buddhist clergy and lay believers, but the fundamental structure of the Chinese state was sanctioned by the political ideology of Confucianism rather than Buddhism. In contrast, Christianity and Islam both shaped the governments that supported and propagated them. In the case of Christianity, it was the heirs of the Roman Empire, such as the Byzantine and Carolingian Empires, that both promoted and were influenced by Christianity. The papacy (government of the Roman Catholic church led by the pope) became a political force in its own right. In the Islamic world, Islam provided the laws by which empires were governed, as well as the justification for conquest.

As they spread through West Asia, Africa, and Europe, Christianity and Islam encountered other belief systems and cultures, which were variously absorbed and adapted by Christian and Islamic rulers. Buddhism similarly engaged the religious beliefs and cultural ideals of the societies its missionaries penetrated. In contrast to the monotheistic background of Christianity and Islam, Buddhism grew in a cultural and philosophical environment that recognized the coexistence of many deities, even many different pantheons. As it spread from India to China, Korea, Japan, and Southeast Asia, it encountered and adapted to many different cultures, changing them as Buddhism itself was transformed by exposure to these cultures. In this chapter, we trace Buddhism's expansion into East Asia and its relationship to political forces in that region of the world. We then follow the rise of Christianity and Islam from a common background, along with the political expression of Christianity and Islam in the form of empires.

BUDDHISM, STATE, AND SOCIETY IN EAST ASIA

By the beginning of the first century C.E., Buddhist missionaries were carrying Buddhist beliefs and practices beyond India to East and Southeast Asia. Before its transmission beyond the frontiers of India, Buddhism had divided into Mahayana ("Greater Vehicle") and Theravada ("Doctrine of the Elders") traditions. Mahayana Buddhists emphasized universal salvation through devotional practices accessible to lay believers. This contrasted with the Theravada (also known pejoratively as Hinayana, or "Lesser Vehicle") concentration on the discipline of renunciation, spiritual self-cultivation, and meditation characteristic of monastic life, and the belief that only those who devoted their lives to Buddhist practice could attain enlightenment. As the goal shifted from enlightenment, at the heart of early Buddhism, to salvation in Mahayana Buddhism, there was a profound change in the fundamental orientation of Buddhist believers.

The central religious goal of Mahayana belief was that of the *bodhisattva,* one who seeks enlightenment for the purpose of aiding other beings in the pursuit of awakening, in contrast to the Theravada *arhat,* who was concerned only with individual spiritual liberation. The *bodhisattva* ideal was rooted in the altruism of Buddha in his former lives, when he sought to help other living beings, and it was represented in Mahayana Buddhism by the Buddhas and *bodhisattvas* who became the focus of worship by Mahayana believers, such as the *bodhisattva* Avalokiteshvara or the Buddha Amitabha, both of whom became the center of sectarian Buddhist beliefs and practice in Central and East Asia. As Buddhism was transmitted from India across Asia, the Mahayana tradition came to dominate Central and East Asia, while Theravada became dominant in Southeast Asia, and these differences continue to the present day.

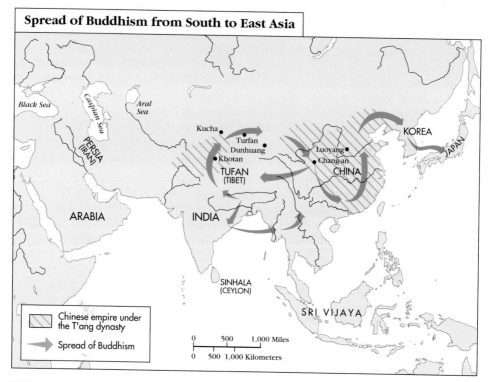

Spread of Buddhism from South to East Asia

MAP 5.1 Spread of Buddhism from India to Japan

BUDDHISM IN CHINA

When the Han dynasty fell in 220 C.E., China entered a long period of political turmoil and social disorder. The Buddhist belief that life is suffering and that the world of the senses is impermanent and illusory held great appeal for people living in chaotic conditions of frequent warfare and political, social, and economic instability, making them easily susceptible to conversion. Central Asian monks translated the sutras, the sacred scriptures of Buddhism, from Sanskrit and Pali (the classical languages of South Asia) into Chinese and transmitted Indian Buddhism to an elite Chinese audience. These monks were transcultural heroes who dedicated their lives and talents to the propagation of Buddhism; their translation projects produced thousands of pages of sacred texts in Chinese. Often these monks were patronized by the non-Chinese rulers of the nomadic peoples who invaded and conquered north China during the three centuries following the fall of the Han dynasty.

Chinese Buddhist Sects Though all sutras (Buddhist sacred texts) were supposed to be the teachings of Buddha, in fact they were highly inconsistent in the doctrines they taught, and this gave rise to differing sectarian traditions within Chinese Buddhism. One of the most important sectarian developments was the Pure Land school, said to have originated with a devotional cult to the Buddha Amitabha established by the learned cleric Huiyuan. Although the Pure Land school is drawn from a sutra of the same name, the sutra that became the principal doctrinal source for Pure Land believers was the Lotus Sutra. The Pure Land school preaches the efficacy of complete faith in the precepts of Buddhism to attain salvation and practices worship of the Buddha Amitabha and the *bodhisattva* Avalo-kiteshvara, or Guanyin in Chinese. These two deities preside over the Western Paradise, the "Pure Land," where believers seek to go to attain enlightenment with the aid of Amitabha and Avalokiteshvara. The Pure Land school reached a far wider audience than did more text-based, scholastic doctrines, such as that of the Heavenly Platform school.

The Heavenly Platform school, dating from the latter sixth century, attempted to recon-cile and synthesize the earlier Buddhist traditions into one by arguing that each represented a different level of truth. The ultimate truth, of course, was the Heavenly Platform. Another distinctively Chinese sect was Chan ("Meditation"), which originated during this early period from the teachings of a monk who stressed the potential of even nonbelievers to attain salva-tion and the possibility of instantaneous enlightenment. The development of the Chan sect in China was heavily influenced by Daoism and better known in the modern West by its Japan-ese name, Zen. Practitioners of Chan sought individual enlightenment through a variety of methods, principally by lengthy meditation or by means of intellectual techniques such as a riddle or puzzle designed to break down normal rational intellectual processes in order to achieve enlightenment.

Buddhism and the Confucian State in China By the sixth century C.E., Buddhism was thoroughly integrated into Chinese culture, and believers could be found at all levels of society. When China was reunified in the latter sixth century by the founder of the Sui dynasty (589–617 C.E.), he made use of both Buddhist and Confu-cian sources of legitimacy for claiming the right to rule. He declared that he had received the Confucian Mandate of Heaven, but he also laid claim to the Buddhist ideal of the *chakravartin* ruler, as shown at the beginning of this chapter. The Sui was swiftly displaced by a new dy-nasty, the Tang (618–907 C.E.), which inaugurated an era of great cultural flourishing and imperial expansion in east Asia. Like their predecessors, the founding emperors of Tang laid claim to the Mandate of Heaven, but they also made use of Buddhism to support their rule. One of the most famous ruler patrons of Buddhism was the Empress Wu (r. 690–705 C.E.), who claimed power after the death of her husband and who used Buddhism to promote her interests. Called "Imperial Bodhisattva" by those who sought to win her favor, she had Bud-dhist images carved into mountains in north China to demonstrate her devotion to the faith and thus to gain the goodwill of both powerful Buddhist clergy and aristocratic lay believers.

Both the imperial house and wealthy aristocratic families made donations to Buddhist monasteries and temples, and devout individuals took vows as monks or nuns. The Buddhist Church acquired great wealth and power as both the size and number of monastic estates and the population of monks and nuns soared during the seventh and eighth centuries. Later em-perors attacked the wealth of monastic Buddhism, reclaiming lands and forcing monks and nuns to return to lay life. The suppression of Buddhism in 845 C.E. caused thousands of tem-ples and monasteries to be razed and restored hundreds of thousands of monks and nuns to lay status.

THE SPREAD OF BUDDHISM IN EAST ASIA

At the height of its power in the seventh and eighth centuries, when Tang China influenced all of East Asia, Buddhism became an important conduit of Chinese cultural influence. As Buddhism lost ground in China, its fortunes began to rise elsewhere in East Asia. Buddhist missionaries went out from China to other parts of East Asia, especially Korea and, later, Japan. In the mid–sixth century C.E., the Korean peninsula was divided among three kingdoms concentrated in the northeast, northwest, and south. Korea had earlier come under the influence of Buddhism, and the Buddhist ruler of one of these kingdoms sent an image of Buddha to Japan. Gradually the scriptures of Buddhism were introduced into Japan, initially by Korean scribes and missionaries, and later by Chinese as well.

Shinto in Japan Sixth-century Japan was in the process of transforming a confederation of clans into a centrally organized dynastic state. Buddhism played a role in this process by presenting an alternative to indigenous religious beliefs, later known as Shinto, or "Way of the Gods." Both animism and shamanism were part of early Shinto, as were totemistic clan ancestors who were venerated as progenitor deities. The "Way of the Gods" was that of both the deities and spirits found in nature and the anthropomorphic deities that populated the Japanese creation myths.

Shinto beliefs in early Japan before the advent of Buddhism and the influence of Chinese culture were closely integrated with political authority. Chinese records of Japan in the second century C.E. describe a shaman-queen, Himiko or Pimiko, who was said to rule more than a hundred communities. Her power apparently derived from her ability to communicate with the gods. Sculptures from the early Jomon culture (ca. 8000–300 B.C.E.) in Japan suggest the existence of a fertility cult similar to those found elsewhere in the world.

Matriarchy in Early Japan Himiko's power may reflect not only earlier cults but possibly also the existence of a matriarchal order in early Japan. The chief deity of Shinto belief as it evolved by the formation of the state in the early fifth century C.E. was a female solar deity, Amaterasu, who remained the central Shinto deity after the establishment of patriarchal authority through the rule of the Sun line. Empresses as well as emperors ruled in the first centuries of the early Japanese state, but after the eighth century, empresses were barred from political power. The last empress to hold power was associated with a powerful Buddhist monk, who was said to have made a play for the throne. This reason was used as a justification for preventing women from ruling. We can acknowledge here, perhaps more clearly than elsewhere, a transition from women's sometimes holding political power to the exclusion of women from ruling. Evidence of a powerful female ruler and the persistence of this in the person of the solar deity at the center of Shinto, even after the rise of the Japanese state and the male authority of the Sun line, confirms this.

Shinto and Buddhism Like Hinduism, which acquired the name only centuries after the ideas and practices associated with it were formed, the term "Shinto" was created to refer to indigenous beliefs and practices associated with the clan-based society of early Japan only after the advent of Buddhism. The new religion of Buddhism was championed by one of these clans, the Soga, as a means of promoting its own interests in power struggles at the "court" of the Sun line, the imperial family who claimed descent from the central Shinto deity, the sun goddess.

The son of a Soga mother and imperial father, Prince Shotoku (574–622 C.E.) served as regent for his young empress aunt at the Japanese court during the late sixth and early seventh centuries and was a devout patron of Buddhism. He encouraged the copying of Buddhist scriptures in classical Chinese and supported the building of temples. Patronage by the imperial court through the actions of Prince Shotoku helped the Buddhist faith gain adherents among the aristocracy.

Buddhism and Chinese Influence in Japan The transmission of Buddhism to Japan from China and Korea also served as a means of transmitting aspects of Chinese civilization other than religion, such as political institutions, literature (poetry and history), and Confucian thought. In 604 C.E., Prince Shotoku issued a series of moral injunctions designed to promote loyalty to the sovereign; these injunctions reflect Confucian influence as well as Shinto and Buddhist ideas, woven together to provide sanction for imperial authority over powerful clans. The era of the Taika reforms, beginning in 645 C.E., saw the adoption of administrative rules and institutions directly modeled on those of Tang China and designed to further centralize power in the imperial court. The formal literary language of classical Chinese was used for government documents, historical records, and poetry and other writings.

By the beginning of the Nara period (712–784 C.E.), named for the imperial Japanese city modeled on the Chinese capital, Chang'an, Buddhist sects established monasteries and temples in the new city, resplendent with Buddhist images produced by Korean and Japanese artisans. Buddhist priests became powerful figures in the society of the new state, which was modeled on the imperial government of Tang China. In the 770s, one of these priests even made an unsuccessful play for the throne, relying on the favor of a reigning empress.

FIGURE 5.1 *Bodhisattva* Avalokitesvara Attended by a Nun and a Young Man

Inscription reads: "Praise to the great merciful, great compassionate savior from hardship Avalokitesvara *Bodhisattva*, in perpetual offering. Offered in the hope that the empire may be peaceful and that the Wheel of the Law may continually turn therein. Secondly, on behalf of my elder sister and teacher, on behalf of the souls of my deceased parents, that they may be born again in the Pure Land. I reverently made this great Holy One and with whole heart dedicated it." Translated in Roderick Whitfield and Anne Farrer, *Caves of the Thousand Buddhas: Chinese Art from the Silk Route* (New York: George Braziller, 1990): 37–38.

SOURCE: © British Museum.

East Asian Buddhism By around 1000 C.E., Buddhism was deeply rooted in East Asia and ▬▬▬▬▬▬▬▬▬▬ had undergone profound changes with the development of sectarian traditions distinctive to East Asia, such as the Chan, Heavenly Platform, and Pure Land schools. Focused on belief in salvation by faith in a savior deity, the Pure Land sects gained large followings in both China and Japan. With the development of popular sects, Buddhism penetrated all levels of society in East Asia, from the elite ruling aristocracies to the unlettered common people. The Buddhist Church played a role of economic, social, and political importance, and Buddhist priests were members of the educated establishment in China, Korea, and Japan. Buddhist monks in China engaged in welfare activities, providing charity for the poor, while the large estates that belonged to some temples and monasteries made them among the wealthiest landholders in the empire. But the Buddhist Church never challenged the state in either China or Japan, nor did Buddhist priests assume roles of political leadership, unlike Christian Church leaders in the West.

■

THE ORIGINS OF CHRISTIANITY

At the beginning of the first millennium C.E. in Palestine, then a province of the Roman Empire, a Jew named Jesus was born in the town of Bethlehem. Palestine had come under Roman control about 65 B.C.E., but some Jewish groups continued to resist the Roman occupation. Jewish political activists, called "Zealots," a small minority of the Jewish population, carried out guerrilla attacks against the Roman government.

THE RELIGIOUS CONTEXT OF EARLY CHRISTIANITY

The Essenes Another group of Jews, the Essenes, chose to withdraw from the tensions of ▬▬▬▬▬▬▬ everyday life under Roman occupation and settle in communities to await the imminent end of the world that would usher in a new age. The Essenes held baptisms in their communities to commemorate the repentance of sins and entry into the Army of God. In 1947, the first of several caches of Essene writings, known as the "Dead Sea Scrolls," was discovered in hills near the Dead Sea. Since these writings are militant in style, it seems possible that the Essenes were more than figurative soldiers in the Army of God.

Mithraism Mystery cults, based on secret rites or doctrines known only to the initiated, flour-▬▬▬▬▬▬▬ ished in Palestine as they did throughout the Roman Empire. The dominant mystery cult was that of Mithra, a Hindu variant of the sun god. Mithra was a savior god who, by slaughtering a mythical bull, fertilized the earth. The sacred day of Mithraism was December 25, the winter solstice. Mithraism was a militant cult that was especially popular with the Roman military. It preached the virtues of courage and fraternity. In its standardized chapels, *mithraea,* the ritual of baptism to cleanse away previous sins was carried out before a large mural that portrayed Mithra slaying the bull. The celebrants ate a sacred meal of bread and wine and were confirmed in the Army of Righteousness.

EARLY CHRISTIANITY

The Life of Jesus When he was about thirty years old, Jesus set out to preach reform in this ▬▬▬▬▬▬▬ Palestinian milieu of many religious beliefs and practices. He spoke against narrow reliance on ritual, attacked the legalistic and too-worldly character of community religious leaders, and again and again warned of the imminent end of the world, the resurrection of the dead, judgment, and the establishment of the Kingdom of God. After three years of preaching to increasingly receptive audiences, the Romans tried Jesus on two counts: for blasphemy and for claims of being "king of the Jews." Jesus did not deny the claim of kingship, although he had never asserted it. Given the combination of armed Jewish Zealots hostile to Rome and the popular belief that the "Kingdom of God" would result from the apocalyptic struggle between good and evil, Jesus seemed very much a political danger to Roman authority in Palestine. He was convicted of the charges and executed by crucifixion around 35 C.E.

The Early Christian Community The small community Jesus left behind could easily have collapsed or become just another separatist community like the Essenes. The issue that tested it was the question of the acceptability of Gentile (non-Jewish) membership in the community of Jesus's followers. A number of Jesus's early followers in Jerusalem refused to accept Gentiles into their community, feeling that a Gentile presence would defile what they considered Jewish worship. As a result, a division developed among the followers of Jesus, and those who would not accept the Gentiles into common worship as they believed that Jesus's message had been meant primarily or exclusively for the Jews, withdrew to worship separately from those who admitted Gentiles to worship. Following the Roman occupation of Jerusalem in 70 C.E., the separate Jewish Christian community disappeared. Under the leadership of Paul, the strongest supporter of joint worship, Christianity became increasingly Gentile and expanded rapidly.

Christian Sacred Texts Between 70 and 100 C.E., the sacred texts of Christianity were established. There were four Gospels, or "Good Stories," written in Greek by four of Jesus's apostles. These described the sayings and deeds of Jesus and spell out collectively how these sayings and deeds were to be understood. To these Gospels was added the Epistles of Paul, couched in the form of advisory letters and sermons written by him to early Christian communities in need of advice. In contrast to the more formal biographical approach of the Gospels, Paul's Epistles described his experience with Jesus and were a highly personalized and spiritual account. These texts (the "New Testament") were attached to the Judaic sacred scriptures (the "Old Testament"). While early Christians believed that the practice of Jewish law and ritual was not necessary for salvation, they clearly felt that the Old Testament was God's word and a key source of guidance.

Christian Cosmology Christian cosmology, following the teaching of these texts and early spokesmen, was a direct descendant of West Asia's Sumerian and Judaic traditions, modified since the beginning of the fourth century B.C.E. by Hellenistic and Zoroastrian concepts. According to Zoroastrianism, a single god, transcendent and beyond material experience, created the universe and rules it. A righteous god, he was contrasted to Satan, the source of evil. War was constantly being waged between Good and Evil, with humanity choosing one side or the other. The war would end in a final apocalyptic battle, led on the side of good by a savior, the Messiah. At this apocalyptic end, all of the dead of generations past would arise to be judged by God for the good and evil of their lives. Depending on the outcome, they would dwell forever in Paradise or Hell. The result would be the establishment of the perfect Kingdom of God throughout the universe.

The role of Jesus as the Messiah in this scheme was to warn of the imminence of the day of reckoning and to encourage the leading of a moral life. This vision of the imminent apocalypse dominated the world of the first Christian communities. As time passed and the end of the world seemed less imminent, other aspects of Jesus came to the foreground. His appearance in the world, it was believed, was witness to his compassion for humanity, and Christians believed that if Jesus were "accepted into one's own heart," he would ease the sorrows of this painful world because, as the son of God who had appeared on earth and ascended to sit at the right hand of his father following his crucifixion, Jesus, Christians believed, could mediate between them and God. This approach to knowledge of God was accompanied by the emergence of a Christian sacred priesthood, an anointed elite who maintained a special affiliation with the Divine through rituals over which they exercised the monopoly.

Christianity in the
Roman Empire

At the time of its inception and early development, Christianity was not embraced by those in power to sustain and justify their social and political systems. Indeed, the Romans initially perceived Christianity as a challenge to the legitimacy of the political and social order of their empire rather than as a support for

FIGURE 5.2 Horyuji Temple, Nara, Japan.

First built in the 7th century, this Buddhist temple complex was modeled on Chinese precedents.

SOURCE: Japan Information Center, Consulate General of Japan, New York.

it. Later, by the fourth century C.E., as Christianity grew in strength despite official hostility and as the Roman Empire began to weaken, a powerful, mutually beneficial alliance of the Christian Church and the Roman state was formed. This became a model for subsequent European history.

THE GROWTH AND SPREAD OF CHRISTIANITY

Within a century after the death of Jesus in about 35 C.E., there were small communities of Christians strewn across Eurasia and North Africa. These communities developed from the efforts of Jesus's disciples and their followers. As Christian believers spread geographically, Christianity began to adapt to and absorb both the ideas and the practices of different cul-

 DAILY LIVES

THE LIFE OF A CHRISTIAN MARTYR

Many faithful believers were persecuted in the first few centuries of Christianity, including both during the Roman Empire and after its disintegration. The victims of emperors, these heroines refused to worship the gods of the Roman state and they preached pacifism. The third century C.E. Christian woman known as Saint Perpetua of Carthage stands out especially as a model of the pious believer, to whom later generations of Christian women would aspire. Like many spiritual warriors, Perpetua was imprisoned, and she left her own account of the days and hours leading to her martyrdom. Still nursing her baby in prison, she began to have dreams of herself as a man fighting as a gladiator in the arena:

> My clothes were stripped off, and suddenly I was a man. My seconds began to rub me down with oil, as they are wont to do before a contest. . . . We drew close to one another and began to let our fists fly. My opponent tried to get hold of my feet, but I kept striking him in the face with the heels of my feet. . . . He fell flat on his face and I stepped on his head. . . . I began to walk in triumph towards the Gate of Life. Then I awoke.[1]

When Perpetua was about to die, she remained rebellious and calm. Led to the arena, she refused to dress in the robes of a priestess and when knocked down by a charging cow, she merely straightened her clothes, repinned her hair, and walked steadfastly across to the other side. Even-

tually she guided the hand of the soldier ordered to execute her.

While Perpetua was exceptional in her bravery and faith, she was apparently not unusual in her crossing of the gender lines of her culture and time. Christian women commonly assumed duties outside those typically associated with women. They converted their families and strangers. Sometimes they refused to marry and give birth to children, eventually establishing ascetic orders in which people lived in isolated communities that denied the body's needs for food, water, sex, cleanliness, and sleep.

By 800 C.E., monasteries, convents, and abbeys founded by both men and women spread across the European landscape, where the faithful practiced and taught the beliefs of Christianity. Eventually the traditional beliefs in women as weak, inferior, and polluting threats were emphasized and the Christianity that had empowered women like Saint Perpetua instead reinforced women's subordination by men.

[1]Bonnie S. Anderson and Judith P. Zinsser, *A History of Their Own: Women in Europe from Prehistory to the Present,* vol. I (New York: Harper and Row, 1988): 71; citing Mary R. Lefkowitz and Maureen B. Fant, *Women's Life in Greece and Rome: A source book in translation.* Baltimore: Johns Hopkins University Press, 1982: 269–70. The "Gate of Life" was the exit from the arena for those who were allowed to live.

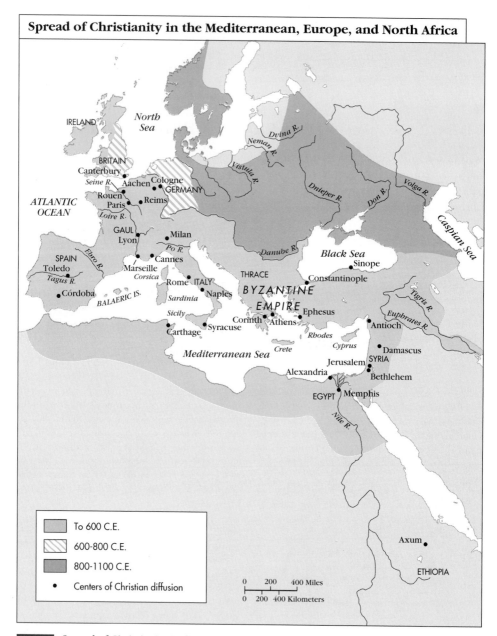

Spread of Christianity in the Mediterranean, Europe, and North Africa

MAP 5.2 Spread of Christianity Before 1100 C.E.

tures. The number of Christians expanded through the second and third centuries, and by the fourth century Christianity rivaled both Persian Zoroastrianism and its later manifestation, Manichaeism, in influence in West Asia.

MANICHAEISM

The familiar Zoroastrian concept of an ongoing war between Good and Evil, Light and Dark, (see Chapter 4) provided crucial background for the development of Manichaeism, named after its founder, Mani (ca. 216–277 C.E.), an itinerant preacher and physician from southern Iraq. Mani served at court in Iran in the early years of the Persian Sasanid dynasty (224–651 C.E.). Mani developed a fully detailed cosmology based on Zoroastrianism. The war between Good and Evil, Light and Dark, he said, would go on throughout eternity. According to Mani, humanity was created to be soldiers on the side of Light but through defeats and setbacks had become hopelessly entangled in the material Dark world. All humans had a spark of divine Light in them. Every child born took from that spark, however, diluting Light further in Dark matter. A series of messengers and prophets had been sent down to earth to offer salvation from the swamp of evil darkness that is earth; Buddha had been one of them, Zoroaster another, and Jesus had been one of the greatest of them. Following him, Mani came as the "seal of the prophet," the "apostle of Jesus Christ," to enlighten humanity on how to identify and venerate its spark of Light.

In this portrayal, Zoroastrian dualism has been blended with Gnosticism, a Hellenistic current of thought popular in the first and second centuries. According to Gnosticism, true *gnosis* (Greek for "knowledge") can be found only through intense meditation, leading the individual directly to Truth. Anything from the material world is at best imperfect and can only distract from the search. As Mani put it, senses and the material world are part of Darkness and Evil. Manichaean cosmology, though similar on the surface to that of Zoroastrianism, differed from it significantly enough that the chief Zoroastrian priest prevailed upon the Sasanid ruler of Persia to execute Mani as an archheretic.

Manichaeism offered, through its learned priesthood, a path to salvation from the difficulties of the world. During the third and fourth centuries C.E., Manichaeism gained many adherents in West and Central Asia, North Africa, and Europe, eventually spreading as far as China. Some Manichaean ideas influenced the early Christian church during the fourth century, when it was shaping its doctrines. Augustine (351–430 C.E.), one of the great Christian thinkers and a "Church Father," professed Manichaean beliefs between 373 and 382 C.E. He considered Manicheans to be simply radical Christians.

CHRISTIANITY, COMMUNITY, AND STATE

Despite rivals such as Manichaeism and official opposition and persecution by Roman rulers, Christianity continued to spread. In the early fourth century C.E., the movement was given enormous encouragement by the ruler of the eastern half of the Roman empire. In 312, on the eve of a major battle, the Emperor Constantine (r. 306–337) promised to declare for the Christian god in the event he won. The victorious Constantine was true to his pledge, sanctioning Christianity by giving it legal status and favoring Christians the rest of his life. In 380 Christianity became the imperial state religion, a recognition granted it by the Emperor Theodosius. By the fifth century the secure position Christianity had achieved tended to supplement and increase imperial authority, as emperors, now resident in Constantinople, were supported by an increasingly institutionalized and powerful Christianity.

Causes of Christian Success The social values of early Christianity also contributed to its success. Although from the formative years of the Christian move-
ment women were regarded as inferior members of Christian society—denied the right to become priests, for example—they were accepted as members of the church. This was not the
case among other contemporary religions. And, whereas membership in some of the Gnostic
cults was socially exclusive, confined to elite males, Christians came from all segments of society. Because Christianity was neither elitist nor socially exclusive, many of its adherents were
poor laborers. Christian communities practiced mutual support, providing both practical and
spiritual help for each other. This communal reinforcement, the sense of membership in a
group with a clear purpose, was very attractive in the politically and economically difficult
times of the period between 200 and 400.

Moreover, Christians quickly showed exceptional organizational skills. During the second century the distinction between clergy and laity was made clear and as the movement
expanded, the clergy increased in numbers and developed hierarchical structures. A centralized and carefully organized priestly administration emerged, one unmatched by any other
cult. This administrative organization enabled the church to recruit new members efficiently
and to support and integrate them into the community. In the fourth century, as Christianity
became the imperial religion of Rome, its organization became a mirror image of Roman
imperial structures, and state and church became dependent upon each other, partners in
power.

Orthodoxy and Heresy Once Christianity became an imperial ideology, the state encouraged
it to define its ritual and doctrine in detail. Up to 300, disagreements
on the nature of Jesus were of no interest to the Roman state; after the acceptance of Christianity, agreement on the nature of Jesus was important to the Roman state. It became essential to establish orthodox doctrine so that criteria for loyalty to the state religion could be
clearly determined. Beginning in 325, the first of a series of church conferences under imperial auspices met at Nicaea in Asia Minor to define doctrine. An "orthodox" position was
reached in the Nicene Creed, acceptance of which defined both Christian belief and imperial
loyalty. Those "heretics" who disagreed were alienated and when opposition movements appeared they were subject to state persecution in the name of orthodoxy.

The integration of "state and church" was not new to the Christian community. Christian cosmology, drawn in part from Hellenized Judaism, incorporated the image of a state led
by priest-kings and guided by Yahweh's laws. But Christianity, despite its official imperial
status after 380, had grown up as a persecuted minority movement cautiously concentrating
on spiritual matters and leaving government to Caesar (Latin for "emperor"). The contradiction implied in these two attitudes would vex the history of the Christian world for centuries,
just as it has done the world of Judaism.

By the seventh century, the cosmologies of the majority of the peoples of West Asia,
North Africa, and Europe were dominated by two systems, Zoroastrianism and Christianity,
both of which included splinter groups of heterodox believers, or heretics. Both were state
ideologies, and the priesthoods of both were in some fashion integrated into their respective
political structures, the Sasanid and Roman Empires, through appointments, salaries, and
other devices.

CHRISTIANITY AND EMPIRE: WEST ASIA, NORTHEAST AFRICA, AND EUROPE

The unity of the Roman world was split in two within a century of the recognition of Christianity as the official religion of the empire in 380 C.E. The political capital of the Roman Empire had already been moved east to Constantinople, the new imperial city built by the Emperor Constantine at the site of Byzantium, an ancient Greek settlement on the Bosporus, which connects the Black Sea and the Mediterranean and links Europe to West Asia. The vast bureaucratic apparatus of imperial Rome reconstituted itself at Constantinople, the "Second Rome," where highly trained cadres of clerks, inspectors, and spies kept close scrutiny over the lives and possessions of the city's inhabitants. In the fourth century, as emperors became Christian, the bureaucracy served as both a support and a model for Christianity. The Christian emperors were no less divinely sanctioned theocrats then their pre-Christian predecessors, such as Diocletian (r. 284–305), but their sanction came from the Christian God. After 380, emperors ruled as "vicars of God" with religious authority equal to that of the Apostles. Cae-

FIGURE 5.3 The Sixth-century Christian Church, Hagia Sophia in Istanbul (formerly Constantinople, capital of the Byzantine Empire)

SOURCE: Foto Marburg/Art Resource, NY.

FIGURE 5.4 Mosaic in the Church of Hagia Sophia, Istanbul, Turkey, ca. 1000 C.E.

The Madonna is shown with the Byzantine Emperor Constantine and Roman Emperor Justinian.

SOURCE: Vanni/Art Resource, NY.

saropapism, the absolute control of all aspects of society—religious as well as social, economic, and political—characterized the "Second Rome" for a millennium.

Though it failed in attempts (between 630 and 655) to reconquer Italy permanently and reestablish imperial control in the western Mediterranean, the eastern Roman, or Byzantine, empire produced a rich synthesis of Greek culture, Roman institutions, and Christianity. Its Christian character was perhaps most brilliantly expressed in the great sixth-century church of Hagia Sophia ("Holy Wisdom") with its splendid mosaics; its political sophistication was shown in the revision and codification of Roman law. A commission appointed by the Emperor Justinian (r. 527–565) undertook the task of legal codification between 529 and 565. They produced the Corpus Juris Civilis, or "Body of Civil Law," the means by which Roman law would influence later European law.

ETHIOPIAN AND COPTIC CHRISTIANITY IN NORTHEAST AFRICA

In northeast Africa, Christianity reached the Nile Valley during Roman times and the region of the middle Nile, Nubia, early in the first millennium, probably through trade and missionary connections. Evidence along the Nile suggests that Christian communities may have survived there in secrecy for many of their early years. Murals painted on walls reflect local interpretations of Monophysite doctrine, that held that Christ had only one (divine) nature, rather than two (both human and divine).

Christianity in Egypt Monophysite Christianity in Egypt became known as the Coptic Church. The Coptic language, rather than the Greek of the elites, had been used to preach to the masses. There was another aspect of resistance in Egyptian Christianity. The history of Christianity in Egypt was bound up with the relations between Alexandria and Constantinople. Egypt officially became Christian under the Emperor Theodosius in the fifth century C.E. After the Council of Chalcedon (450 C.E.), which declared the two natures of Christ as an article of faith, a crisis was instigated in Alexandria. Bloody feuds occurred between fervent believers in the single nature of Christ (followers of the Monophysite Patriarch) and those in the Byzantine camp (led by the Constantinople-appointed Melchite Patriarch). Large numbers of believers retreated to a monastic life in communities that ultimately would have to withstand both the end of Byzantine rule and the Arab conquest in 642 C.E.

Christianity in the Middle Nile In the middle Nile, Christianity encountered the kingdom of Kush (ca. 900 B.C.E.–400 C.E.). Pharaonic gods continued to dominate Kushite ideology until the demise of the kingdom, surviving in Kush much longer than they did in Egypt itself. Isis and Amon-Ra were most prominent of these pharaonic gods; the rulers of Napata and Meroe, the centers of Nubia's Kushite kingdom, even took the name of Amon-Ra as an element of their throne names. Rulers were personifications of gods and thus expressions of divine and secular authority.

With the advent of Christianity, the ruler was no longer divine, but it was likely that his conversion gave him trading advantages. Archaeological remains from this time no longer include royal tombs, a change suggesting that rulers' access to material wealth and spiritual power had been reduced. Instead, the Christian states of Nubia were ruled by both the local political authority and the Church, which was represented by its links to the larger, international Christian community. The Christian cross appears on buildings and coinage from this era. Replacing the early signs of divine kingship, the cross was considered an emblem of hu-

FIGURE 5.5 Gold Coin Showing Ruler, Crescent, and Cross, Pre-Christian Axum

SOURCE: From *General History of Africa. UNESCO* and Heineman Educational Books. General Research Division, New York Public Library, Astor, Lenox and Tilden Foundations.

FIGURE 5.6 Christian Rock-hewn Church at Lalibela, Ethiopia

SOURCE: Chester Higgins, Jr./Photo Researchers, Inc.

man authority and sanctioned the ruler's control over people. This control did not necessarily extend to their beliefs. The continuing use of pre-Christian cities as ceremonial and political centers in Christian times suggested how tenuous the foreign religion was and how necessary traditional links were for gaining local acceptance by later political rulers.

The early Christian period in Nubia was shaped by the decline of Meroe and Kush by the third century B.C.E. and the rise of Roman North Africa and Christian Egypt to the north. By the end of the sixth century C.E., a substantial Christian community existed in the middle Nile as three distinct kingdoms: Nobadia, Makuria, and Alodia. Excavations at the sites of Dongola and Faras have revealed multiple churches and cathedrals, as well as a Christian royal palace. Most of the sacred buildings were built of unbaked brick. Both paintings and written documents survive from this period. By 711 C.E., however, the spread of Islam would surround and isolate these Christian lands. Invasions of Egypt (641 C.E.) and north Africa (660 C.E.) by Muslim forces led to the presence of Islam that has continued to today. It would take several more centuries for the cultural impact to be felt across this vast region.

Axum Further east, toward the Ethiopian highlands, the state of Axum was also reached by the dispersion of eastern Orthodox Christianity, this time through the Red Sea port cities. The official introduction of Christianity has been attributed to the first consecrated bishop of Axum, Frumentius of Constantinople, in 315 C.E. Frumentius received the support of the two brother kings, Abraha (Ezana in the only surviving inscription of the time) and Atsbaha. One of the primary motivations for the fourth-century conversion to Christianity by

FIGURE 5.7 Painting of the Apostles from the Church of Guh, Ethiopia, ca. 1400 C.E.

SOURCE: © David Beatty/Robert Harding Picture Library.

Axum's King Ezana was the trading advantage offered to Axum as a result of religious connections with the Byzantine world; status as a Christian polity conferred certain guarantees of prices and trading partners. Axum was renowned as a center of gold and other luxury-good production. Some notice of the Axumite kingdom's wealth and power was taken by classical authors such as Pliny the Elder, who mentioned the trade port of Adulis on the Red Sea around 60 C.E. The *Periplus of the Erythraean Sea,* a sailing guide to the Mediterranean, Red Sea, and Indian Ocean, also from the first century C.E., mentions both Adulis and the city of Axum. From the time of Ezana, pilgrimages of Ethiopians to holy places in Jerusalem and Rome became common and continuous.

By the sixth century C.E., Axum stood at the axis of a giant web of trade routes reaching from the interior of the African continent to Asia and the Mediterranean. Pre-Axumite and early Axumite religions included the moon god, of south Arabian origin, and Mahrem, a god of war. Their associated symbols, the crescent moon and disc, eventually gave way to the cross, which appeared exclusively on stone stelae and coins minted from the time of Ezana. Like the inscriptions from the time of the Mauryan ruler Ashoka in the third century B.C.E., who claimed the support of Buddha for his kingship, inscriptions carved into stone monuments and appearing on coins during King Ezana's reign proclaimed his reliance on the new Christian religion: "I will rule the people with righteousness and justice, and will not oppress them, and may they preserve this Throne which I have set up for the Lord of Heaven." From its beginnings at Axum, the Christian state of Ethiopia survived throughout much of the second millennium C.E., in part because the mountainous terrain permitted the isolation of the Christian communities and their defense against hostile neighbors.

THE CHURCH IN WESTERN EUROPE: PAPAL CAESARISM

In contrast to Byzantine Caesaropapism (the control of both the sacred and secular worlds by the ruler), the pattern in western Europe was papal Caesarism, the primacy of the institutional church and its head, the pope, in all economic, social, and political affairs, as well as religion. In 476, the western half of the Roman Empire, including the old imperial capital of

Rome, was occupied by successive waves of Germanic invaders, some of whom were directed westward by emperors at Constantinople anxious to rid the eastern portions of the empire of the Germanic threat. As the Germans settled into the western portions of the empire, they replaced the imperial political control with their own, such as the Visigothic and Ostrogothic kingdoms on the Iberian peninsula and in Italy. But Roman Christianity was not displaced, even though the Germans were either non-Christians or heretical Christians. The Roman Church quickly and effectively stepped into the vacuum left in western Europe by the removal of imperial control there. In the absence of Roman imperial authority, the organization and ideology of Christianity provided western Europe with its major unifying force, and once the Germans were converted, the alliance of the Christian Church with Germanic states made it a major force in western Europe.

Only one of the Germanic successor kingdoms persisted: that of the Franks, whose territories occupied the area from the Rhine River south toward the Pyrenees and the Mediterranean, the area that today is known as France. The Frankish state was the crucible in which western European culture would be formed, and it was there that its basic elements—the Greco-Roman (Mediterranean), Germanic, and Christian cultures—mingled and fused.

The Expansion of the Franks The Frankish kingdom resulted from the Frankish leaders' success in defeating and controlling other Germanic peoples with whom they came into contact as they spread out, filling the vacuum that resulted from the decay of Roman authority in western Europe. The Frankish chieftain Clovis (r. 481–511 C.E.) succeeded in establishing dominance over other Germanic peoples in Gaul by means that confirmed two fundamental elements of Frankish power: its reliance on force and its alliance with Roman Christianity.

Following the typical German practice, Frankish chieftains shared the fruits of victory with the warriors over whom they exercised control, a practice that provided the Frankish kings with a structure of government. The land they conquered was parceled out by the king (the chieftain) to his principal subjects (warriors) on the basis of reciprocal obligations and obedience. The subjects owed the king military service and certain other duties in exchange for the land assigned to them; the grant of land enabled them to fulfill their obligations. In turn, the fact that the king was the source of land increased his importance. The king's authority was further enhanced by the sanction of the Roman Church, a relationship which was of inestimable value to both.

Clovis's successors were less able than he, a situation that particularly imperiled the Frankish state following the Islamic invasion of the Iberian peninsula in 711 (see below). Muslims crossed the Pyrenees and pressed northward into the heartland of the Frankish kingdom. In 732, at the Battle of Poitiers, Charles Martel, a palace official, halted the Muslim raids and confined the invaders to the northern slopes of the Pyrenees. Charles Martel's success assured that Europe north of the Mediterranean basin would continue to develop along Latin-Christian-German, rather than Islamic, lines. It also led to placement of the Frankish kingdom into his own family's hands.

The new dynasty resulted from the actions of Pépin, the son of Charles Martel. Furthering the Frankish tradition of close relations with the Roman Church, Pépin entered into an alliance with the head of the church, Pope Stephen, against the Lombards, an aggressive, ambitious Germanic people who settled in the upper Po River Valley in north Italy and began expanding southward from there. In 751, the pope appealed to Pépin for protection against the Lombards and the Frank indicated he was willing to help—for a price: if the pope would approve of his usurpation of the Frankish crown from Clovis's Merovingian dynasty, Pépin would rescue the pope from the Lombards. The pope approved the plan and in 754 went to France to crown Pépin. Pépin kept his part of the bargain and restored papal authority in central Italy. In 756, he made the Donation of Pépin, assigning a girdle of lands stretching across central Italy to the papacy. The Papal States remained the temporal possession of popes until 1870, and today's 32-hectare (13-acre) Vatican City is the last vestige of Pépin's donation.

Charlemagne and the Revival of the Western Empire Pépin's successor, Charles (r. 786–814), came to overshadow his predecessors, on whose achievements he built his empire. By following the patterns and precedents that went back to Clovis, Charles vastly expanded Frankish power. Like his vigorous ancestors, Charles spent most of his life fighting—conquering in the name of his dynasty and the Roman Church. In 800, as his father before him, Charles invaded Italy, to rescue Pope Leo III from a rebellious Rome and restore his authority over the city. In return, the pope crowned Charles emperor, adding the final touch to Frankish aggrandizement. This revival of the imperial title by Charles the Great, or Charlemagne, raised for the future the question of the source of sovereignty in western Europe: Was it the gift of the pope and thus by the authority of the Church, or was it an inherent right of the prince and therefore by the authority of the state? The dilemma Charlemagne's coronation posed was one that was to plague subsequent European rulers, both emperors and popes.

THE IMPERIAL PAPACY

Following the disintegration of the Carolingian Empire, the Roman Church provided the only organization for pan-European unity. Closely allied with imperial polities since Constantine, the Church had learned much from the secular state. As the Church prospered, it developed hierarchically ascending structures assigned to geographical units, many of which corresponded to the Roman patterns. The basic unit of ecclesiastical organization was the congregation, the parish, which was under the authority of a priest. A number of priests and their congregations constituted a diocese (a late-Roman administrative unit) under the authority of a bishop. Dioceses were gathered into provinces headed by archbishops. Though this pyramidal structure describes the chain of command affecting the "secular" clergy, that is, those closely involved with daily, mundane affairs, the "regular" or monastic clergy, those who withdrew from the world and lived lives of contemplation, were also hierarchically organized. At the peak of the ecclesiastical (Church-related) organization was the bishop of Rome, the Holy Father, or pope, the vicar of Christ on earth.

Doctrine of Apostolic Succession The pope's special spiritual authority derived from his succession to the position held by the first bishop of Rome, Saint Peter, the prince of the Apostles. Peter's designation by Christ as the "rock" on which His Church would be founded gave his successors at Rome special significance, thanks to the doctrine of Apostolic succession, by which Peter's spiritual authority was passed on to his successors. Practically, the authority of the bishop of Rome rested on the fact that the Roman congregation of which he was head was the oldest in western Europe. It was also located at the center of secular, imperial power. Subsequent congregations in western Europe were "children of Rome" and were subject to papal (paternal) control. Though popes were elected by the Roman clergy, elections were subject to secular manipulation until the eleventh century, when they became secret and sequestered. By that time, the dominance of the bishop of Rome over western European Christians was secured as a result of doctrine and the practical support of a vast and highly efficient bureaucracy, the practices of which were influenced by the close relationship of the Church with the Empire.

Exercise of Imperial Power by the Papacy The Roman Church's exercise of power between the tenth and early thirteenth centuries was truly imperial. During these centuries, the papacy undertook to emancipate itself from its earlier partnership with the Germanic secular sovereigns and to assert its claims to superiority over them. The process was by no means smooth, but in the long run the papacy emerged as a major force in Europe. The peak of papal power came during the reign of Pope Innocent III (r. 1198–1216). Innocent exercised the prodigious power he had inherited to extend the papal authority to a degree previously unrealized. The question raised by Innocent's exercise of power is how papal imperial power differed from a lay emperor's power. The answer lies in Innocent's extension of his authority far beyond the limits of the Papal States of central Italy. Innocent's authority extended all over western Europe, from Muslim lands in the south to Scandinavia in the north and from the British Isles in the west to the Slavic lands in the east. During Innocent's reign, this was the realm of Roman Christendom, and the pope was its sovereign.

The Church was the largest individual landholder at a time when land was synonymous with wealth and power, and Innocent III exercised unrivaled power over a vast area that contained many diverse peoples. The orderly hierarchical organization which the Church had evolved from Roman imperial models provided a functioning network for this control. Innocent, who was trained in law, was able to organize the "City of God" in the world of man, and his "city" had the most efficient administrative system of his time.

The Papal Administrative System The keystone of the papal administration was the Curia, the papal court, composed of the chief or cardinal clergy and lay and clerical officers of the papal household. The Curia was divided into four major bureaus: one handled correspondence and documents; another handled such religious means of control as absolutions and dispensations; a third dealt with judicial appeals and legal matters; and a fourth was in charge of finances and taxation. These bodies maintained the central authority of the papacy.

The power of papal government beyond Rome rested on the hierarchical structure of the Church: a network of officials representing papal authority who scattered out from Rome to the corners of Roman Christendom, attending to the mundane as well as the spiritual needs of the Church. Extensive use was made of legates, special agents who handled Church business; some were residents in a assigned community; others acted as special representatives assigned to an area by the pope. Some, against whose decisions there was no appeal, possessed the full authority of the papacy. This efficient administrative machinery had no equal in Europe.

The Papal Legal System The papal judicial system was equally extensive and hierarchical. Church courts were everywhere, with elaborate appeals procedures through diocesan courts on to Rome itself. Church courts functioned under their own code of canon law, which was based on the Bible, on the writings of the Church Fathers, on decrees of Church councils, and on the civil law of the Roman Empire. Canon law had a twofold authority: over cases that affected the clergy in any way and over cases that dealt with the organization and property of the Church, sacraments, civil personal matters (such as divorce), heresy, usury, and the like. It touched, in fact, on all aspects of social life in western Christian Europe. Canon law achieved final codification in the twelfth century, and bishops used it to tighten their authority by reclaiming a monopoly on jurisprudence in their dioceses. Cases were appealed from bishops' (episcopal) courts to archbishops' (archepiscopal) courts, and on to the Curia in Rome, with the pope himself as final judge. The ecclesiastical legal system was one of the major sources of papal revenues and kept the road to Rome busy. Other sources of the church's wealth were its lands and its tithes, gifts, donations, and special levies such as "Peter's pence," which were directed toward such uses as the Crusades.

Although papal authority began to decline after the reign of Innocent III, it lasted in the west as long as the Byzantine Empire lasted in the east. The Byzantine capital, the cosmopolitan and populous city of Constantinople, was conquered by the rising Turks in 1453. By that time the Roman Church's power, which for nearly three centuries had maintained the attributes and traditions of imperial authority in western Europe, had already begun to erode.

■

THE RISE OF ISLAM

Islam, the third universal religion, provides an even more powerful example of the interaction between religion and empire. Islam appeared in the seventh century C.E. in Mecca, a flourishing trade city located halfway up the Red Sea coast between Egypt and the Indian Ocean. The people of Mecca traded heavily in Indian spices, Chinese silks, and Yemeni incenses with both the Byzantine and Sasanid Persian Empires in the north. They were well aware of world politics. They were also aware of the main belief systems of West Asia. They knew Zoroastrianism through trading contacts in Iraq and the Persian Gulf, and Christianity through trading trips north to Syria and Egypt or across to Christian Ethiopia. They knew something of Judaism, not only because of business but also because large numbers of Jews lived in Yemen and even closer in the agricultural town that would later be known as Medina. The Meccans were themselves believers in a south Arabian pantheon of gods and goddesses. Little is known of these early beliefs other than that they centered on the sun and moon; there were also local sacred places that were pilgrimage sites.

MUHAMMAD AND THE ORIGINS OF ISLAM

In the year 610, one of the businessmen of Mecca, Muhammad, experienced what he later described as a vision on an evening walk in the hills outside the city. In it he was enjoined by the angel Gabriel to speak God's word, to warn humanity of the imminent coming of the day of judgment and the need to correct greedy and immoral ways. Persuaded that he had been chosen to be a messenger of God, he dedicated the rest of his life to exhortation and action: exhortation to lead a just and moral life, action to establish a godly community in which all members accepted, or submitted to, God's plan and laws. *Islam* is the Arabic word for "acceptance" or "submission." A Muslim is one who follows Islam. The community of Muslims was to include all of humanity, not just Arabs.

FIGURE 5.8 Dome of the Rock in Jerusalem where Muhammad is believed to have ascended into heaven.

SOURCE: Israel Ministry of Tourism.

In the first years, Muhammad's street-corner preaching of the coming apocalypse was ignored by most of the citizens of Mecca. His attacks, however, on the morals of the wealthy and powerful and on the false gods of Mecca and the evils of polytheism led to his persecution. Ultimately, in 622, persecution led to the migration (*hejira*) of Muhammad and his now fairly sizable group of followers to the town of Medina, 300 miles north of Mecca. There the first Muslim community was formally established. To commemorate this event, the Muslim calendar, one calculated in lunar months, begins in 622.

Establishment of Islam Within two years, Muhammad had begun a vigorous policy of bringing the people of Mecca to God's path. Since Medina was on the caravan routes to Mecca, Muslims could interfere with trade, which was a serious threat to the primacy of Mecca in the Arab world. The leading families of Mecca gathered armies to destroy Medina and the Muslims, but their attacks failed. In 629, during the pilgrimage season, the victorious Muslims of Medina moved toward Mecca as a group, ostensibly on a pilgrimage to perform the religious rite of making a circuit around the sacred stone, the Ka'aba, which had become part of Muslim worship. The Meccan leadership came halfway out to meet them, and a postponement of the pilgrimage until the next year was negotiated "to ready the city for the large crowd." In 630, Muhammad and his supporters returned to Mecca unchallenged, and the city rapidly became Muslim. Muhammad lived only two more years, but during those years the community expanded to include the whole of the Arabian peninsula and part of southern Syria as well. After Muhammad's death in 632, the expansion of Islam continued even more rapidly.

ISLAMIC COSMOLOGY

Like Christianity, the cosmology of Islam bears much resemblance to those of the earlier Sumerian and Judaic traditions. As preached by Muhammad, it conceived of a universe unfolding, with a beginning, God's creation, and an end, a cataclysmic war between Good and Evil and a day of judgment. Like them, it also has a sacred book. This similarity is openly recognized: Islam is called by Muslims "the religion of Abraham." This is because it is believed that the same laws of God were previously revealed by prophets to both Jews and Christians and that Muhammad was the last of a long line of prophets. Jews and Christians, along with Zoroastrians, are considered by Muslims to be "People of the Book" and are held in higher regard than those of other beliefs. As in Judaism, all the prophets, including Muhammad, were human and mortal. The divinity of Jesus is not recognized in Islamic theology, though the ideas of his conception by the Virgin Mary and his resurrection are.

Muslim Sacred Text The Qur'an is the sacred book of the Muslims. This book, a collection made in 651 of Muhammad's revelations written down by followers as he uttered them, contains all the principles and precepts necessary to live life according to

FIGURE 5.9 Illustrated Page from the Qur'an in Kufic (square) script.

SOURCE: Courtesy of the Freer Gallery of Art, Smithsonian Institution, Washington, D.C.

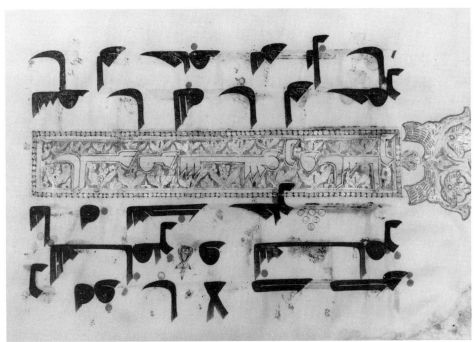

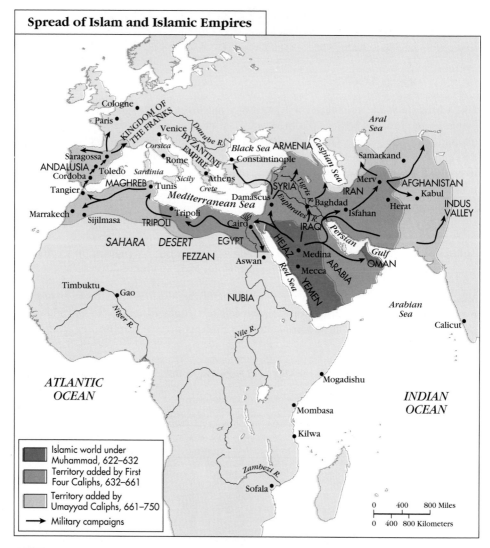

Spread of Islam and Islamic Empires

Islamic world under
Muhammad, 622–632

Territory added by First
Four Caliphs, 632–661

Territory added by
Umayyad Caliphs, 661–750

➤ Military campaigns

0   400   800 Miles

0   400 800 Kilometers

MAP 5.3   Spread of Islam and Early Islamic Empires

God's plan. Considered to be God's word and eternal, the Qur'an was revealed and copied down in Arabic. The effect has been to make Arabic the official, if not sacred, language of Islam, learned to some degree by all Muslims.

Islamic Law   In addition to the Qur'an and its language, Islamic law and daily ritual held the Islamic community together in faith as it rapidly expanded to include many diverse cultures. *Shari'a*, or Islamic law, took its final shape in the ninth century. Like the Jewish Talmud, it is comprehensive, dealing with dietary laws and prayer ritual as well as with building codes and punishment for murder. The *shari'a* is based on the Qur'an, which functions in effect as the constitution of God. For cases not clearly addressed by the Qur'an, local customs, *hadith* (stories about the sayings and actions of Muhammad), general consensus, and analogy were used to modify and extend the *shari'a,* which became the law of the land wherever Muslim governments held sway.

Muslim Prayer and Pilgrimage While the *shari'a* defined legal relations in the Islamic world, the "Five Pillars of Islam" guided everyday individual practice of Islam. To be a Muslim, one must follow the five primary rules spelled out in the Qur'an. The first is that Muslims must bear witness or testify that they believe in the one and only God and that Muhammad was his last prophet. The second is that they must pray daily. Five times per day is specified in the Qur'an, and they must pray especially on Friday, when the whole community gathers to hear a sermon. Third, Muslims must voluntarily give a tenth of their annual income to provide for the poor of the community. Fourth, during one month of the year, Ramadan, all Muslims must fast during daylight hours. Finally, at least once in their lives, they should go to Mecca on pilgrimage. Today, about 2 million pilgrims from all over the world visit Mecca each year.

THE EXPANSION AND DIVISION OF ISLAM

These factors—the Qur'an and its Arabic language, the Five Pillars of Islam, and the *shari'a*—together provided a cosmology that would be the basis for a multicultural community reaching from West Africa to China. From the beginning of Islamic expansion, efforts were made to hold this multicultural community together under a single imperial government. These attempts proved unsuccessful, even though Islam remained the official state ideology of component parts of the Muslim world just as Judaism had been in the Jewish Palestinian state and Christianity was in the Roman Empire after 380. As with Judaism and Christianity, there was pressure from rulers to create and maintain an orthodoxy, an "official" Islamic credo and ritual.

Political and Religious Authority in Islam Because Islam, like later Judaism, has no ordained priesthood, religious authority was invoked by scholars and judges. Informal councils, and conferences of scholars and judges produced over time the standard positions on free will, revelation, and the role of reason in law and theology. The close association of political and religious authority made opposition to established government an issue that had to be justified on theological grounds. Similarly, theological differences became political issues. Both theological and political differences caused long-standing and profound divisions in Islam.

THEOLOGICAL AND POLITICAL DIVISIONS IN ISLAM

One such division is the split between Sunni and Shi'i Islam. This originated as a political dispute over government succession following the death of Muhammad. Some felt that a member of his family should succeed him, while others thought it should be someone elected by and from the general council of community leaders. The latter was the *sunni,* or "traditional" way, and it won out. The other was the way of the *shi'is,* or "partisans" of the Prophet's family and their descendants. Initially, there was little theology involved in this. After 200 years of underground resistance, however, the majority *shi'i* position evolved into a messianic doctrine by the ninth century, a time of political turmoil in the Islamic Empire. According to this doctrine, the seventh (some say the twelfth) descendant of Muhammad through his son-in-law Ali did not die but rather was lifted up by God as the Mahdi, or Messiah, and waits in heaven for judgment day. While waiting, he guides the *shi'i* leaders on earth below, making those leaders in turn very powerful figures in the *shi'i* community. Other political disagreements produced theological differences, but only the *sunni/shi'i* split resulted in significant divisions.

■

EARLY ISLAMIC EMPIRES AND THE SPREAD OF ISLAM

The Islamic state that expanded out of Arabia in the mid–seventh century looked at first to be nothing more than a series of raids by the rural farming and nomadic Arabs of the peninsula. It was anything but that. Rapidly seizing Palestine, Syria, and Iraq by 640, the armies moved steadily west through Egypt and across north Africa into Spain, east through Iran, and south into India. By 730 an Arab Islamic empire stretched across west Asia into continents beyond, well established and functioning much as other empires did to provide order to the world. The functions were the same; the ideology behind them was, however, different.

THE NATURE OF ISLAMIC GOVERNMENT

The Islamic government established by Muhammad in Mecca in 630 began as an expression of the revealed word of God. Islamic ideology called on all people, including government leaders, to return to God's path for humanity. This path spelled out how individuals were to relate to God and to others in society. Its political dimension focused on the ordering of the community according to God's plan. The Muslim community rested on the assumed universality of membership in Islam. Membership was determined not by birth but rather by an individual's professed faith in God and ethical behavior according to God's laws. Accordingly, the expansion of the Muslim community was potentially limitless. The role of Islamic government was to maintain God's law and order as described in God's book, the Qur'an, which functioned as a constitution for Muslim society. Islamic rulers, and their laws and decrees, were as subject to the Qur'an as were ordinary citizens.

The role of the Muslim ruler and the principles of succession to rule were established in the first decades of the Islamic state's history. As long as Muhammad was alive (up to 632), his power as ruler was unchallenged, though he claimed no divinity. Upon Muhammad's death, however, the choice of his successor, or caliph, triggered controversy. Despite the problems of succession, the early Islamic state was well served by experienced leaders supported by the sophisticated merchant aristocracy of Mecca, who were well aware of the political and economic systems of West Asia. With the rapid conversion and recruitment of large numbers of nomadic lineage groups throughout Arabia into its army, Islam expanded by conquering Roman Syria, Egypt, and parts of the Persian Empire.

THE UMAYYAD CALIPHATE

In 656, the caliphate was assumed by Muawiyyah, son of the aristocratic Bani Umayah family of Mecca. Muawiyyah moved the Islamic Empire's capital to Damascus, where it remained until 750, when the dynasty he founded, the Umayyads, was overthrown. In Damascus, which was the old Roman capital of the province of Syria, the institutional foundations of Islamic imperial administration were established as further expansion of the state took place.

The Umayyad Expansion The success of this expansion was astonishing. By 650, Syria, Iraq, and Egypt had fallen to Muslim armies, and much of Persia as well. North Africa was brought under Islamic governmental control in the following decades. Spain was invaded in 711; by 730, nearly all of it was governed by Muslim administration and would remain so for another 700 years. By the end of the eighth century, the city of Córdoba on the Iberian peninsula was the leading city west of Constantinople. Though dwarfed by contemporary Asian cities such as the Chinese capital of Chang'an, Córdoba housed a population of perhaps half a million Muslims, Christians, and Jews.

Muslim Invasions of India The same course of rapid conquest was followed in the east. By 715, Muslim armies had crossed the Indus River and moved north to occupy much of its huge river basin in northwestern India. The Muslim invaders of India encountered fragmented political authority in the form of regional kingdoms that had unsuccessfully attempted to unite north India. In the mid–seventh century, the ruler of one of these

FIGURE 5.10 Umayyad Great Mosque at Damascus, 714–715 A.D.

SOURCE: Giraudon/Art Resource, NY.

kingdoms had established control over the Ganges plain, but this political unity had not survived his death. The Muslim invaders also encountered Hinduism and Buddhism among the populations they conquered in north India, as well as the strict social hierarchy shaped by the caste system. Previous invaders had been absorbed by the ancient civilization of the subcontinent, but the Muslims were bearers of a proselytizing religious faith with a powerful social and political ideology that sharply challenged the cultural and social, as well as political, orders of India. After the Muslim invasions that began in the eighth century, India became a land where Muslim mosques (places of worship) and Hindu temples stood side by side.

Afghanistan and Central Asia were integrated into the caliphate through a series of campaigns between 699 and 740. When Kashgar fell to an Arab general in 738, the Islamic Empire had reached the Chinese border. Chinese forces were defeated near Lake Balkhash in 751, and Tashkent fell in the same year. China itself, however, was never invaded: the distance was too great and the terrain too difficult. By 750, manpower to administer the enormous empire, let alone to expand its boundaries, had grown very scarce. There would be more conquests after 750 under the Abbasid dynasty, which followed the Umayyad, but nothing comparable to those carried out by the Umayyads.

The Umayyad caliphate in Damascus (656–750) was a time of empire building, in administration as well as conquest. The centuries of Roman and other imperial administrative experience in Syria contributed to the transformation of provincial West Asian rule. To many of the original Muslims of Mecca and Medina, the caliphate centered in Damascus looked like a secular Syrian kingdom. Though Muawiyyah, the first Umayyad caliph, and most of his court were from Mecca or Medina, by 700 their successors had been away long enough and were so engrossed in empire building that they and their government had grown away from their west Arabian beginnings.

Lineage and Empire Implicit in many of the conflicts that divided the Islamic Empire—those between Arabic peninsular and Mediterranean societies, between rural and urban cultures, and between nomadic and sedentary lifestyles—lies the major problem facing Islamic rulers: the difficulty of creating an empire in a society based on lineage (line of descent) as a source of identity. Throughout history, the source of power for many states, some of them very large, has been an alliance of lineage groups. Very few of these states, however, have succeeded in developing institutions that last beyond one or two generations since shifting personal, familial loyalties of lineages to distant or abstract central authority have proved difficult and transitory.

Under the Umayyads, the process of aligning the dynasty with powerful lineage groups was achieved by borrowing heavily from the Roman administrative practices with which they came into contact in Syria and on the basis of which they succeeded in extending Islamic and Arab influences throughout the lands they conquered and ruled. As had been true of Roman law in the Roman empire, Islamic law was an additional source of the unity and control the Umayyads sought, although it took a century after they came to power before sufficient precedent and scholarship had built a full legal structure.

The Use of the By 700, all Umayyad coinage was standardized with Arabic letters and the
Arabic Language declaration "In the Name of God." By that time also, Arabic was the language of administration throughout the empire, from Spain to India. The

use of Arabic was greatly reinforced throughout the empire by the conversion of large numbers of its population to Islam and hence their need of Arabic to read the Qur'an. By the end of Umayyad rule, even certain aspects of Islamic architecture had become standardized throughout the empire as well, most obviously the mosque with its attached minaret (tower) for calling the community to prayers.

Umayyad Government The accomplishment of the Umayyad government was to sketch out the basic outline of imperial administration while keeping the armies occupied and paid. That they were able to do the latter was a triumph, when one considers that at any given time there were several hundred thousand troops on campaign somewhere between Europe and central Asia. It was the persistent inability of the Umayyads to meet their budgetary demands and the inequitable tax policies they consequently instituted that ultimately led to their downfall.

According to Islamic policy, in addition to normal taxes non-Muslim subjects were obliged to pay a special poll, or head, tax, as well as higher land taxes than Muslims. Avoidance of these taxes—along with the natural inclination to become part of the group in power—had a great deal to do with the rapid conversion of the conquered populations. Few if any forced conversions took place during the Islamic expansion. Converts expected their tax liabilities to be lifted immediately upon conversion, but they found the government to be very slow to do so.

By 700, the government could not at once maintain its armies of conquest and cut taxes. There were a few efforts at tax reform over the next several decades. The Umayyad court clearly favored Arabs and Arab culture, particularly Arabs of the peninsula, over other peoples and cultures for official governmental and military positions within their state. Arab historians today speak of this period as one of "Arabism." This ethnic bias reinforced the growing feeling that the Umayyads were using Islam only as a tool for power, and this view increasingly undermined them. In 750, the Umayyads were overthrown by a well-organized popular uprising mobilized under the ideological banner of shi'ism.

THE ABBASID CALIPHATE

The army that marched successfully against the Umayyads came mostly from Persia, but there were many Arabs who fought along with them. The Abbasid revolution, so called after the dynasty that took over from the Umayyads, represented a shift from Arabism and the resurgence of a key element in Islam, the equality of all in the faith.

Baghdad The Abbasid capital was almost immediately moved east to Iraq, where a city called Baghdad, or "City of Peace," was planned and built in the following decades. By 800, Baghdad's population was close to 1 million, comparable to that of the Tang Chinese capital at Chang'an in 750. This shift to the east was paralleled by the full integration of Persian and other new Muslim subjects into the state administration. While the Umayyad state had claimed to be Islamic in ideology, it had in fact functioned as an Arab empire; the empire created by the Abbasids was in practice, as well as in theory, Islamic. This equalization of ethnic status among subjects greatly accelerated the process of Islamization of West Asia and increased the incentive for conversion.

FIGURE 5.11 Abbasid Capital at Bagdad Besieged by Mongols in 1258

SOURCE: The Granger Collection, New York.

For a little more than 100 years after it replaced the Umayyad dynasty, there was no significant opposition to the Abbasid government, nor was there any significant new expansion of the empire. These were years of relative peace, used to develop the institutions of Islamic government further.

Persian Influence on the Abbasids Just as the Umayyads had utilized the Roman institutions they found in Syria, the Abbasid caliphate incorporated many of the institutions and rituals of the Persian Empire, the center of its territory. The position of caliph grew to share many of the trappings of the old Persian emperor. Though not divine, the Abbasid caliph's title became "Prince of the Believers" and even "Shadow of God on Earth."

Harun al-Rashid The best-known Abbasid caliph was Harun al-Rashid (r. 786–809), who was hardworking, well educated, and competent. A contemporary of Charlemagne, Harun al-Rashid plied him with exotic gifts, including an elephant, and succeeded in getting the Frankish king to cross the Pyrenees and raid the Muslim government in Spain, which had resisted Abbasid leadership. But Harun al-Rashid was also a good example of the new mystique that had grown up around the caliph as he withdrew within the steadily expanding walls of imperial bureaucracy. Caliphs had become more and more a symbol of the Islamic state, while the vizier (prime minister) was left to wield the actual power through the bureaucracy.

Abbasid Government By 800, the Abbasid bureaucracy had been fully developed to serve the needs of the empire. There was a Department of Finance; an Audit Office to check the Department of Finance's accounts; a Correspondence Office for both internal and foreign affairs; an Administrative Appeals Board to review salaries, dismissals, and other civil service matters; and a Police Department, separate from the army. One of the most important government offices was that of the postal service. Carrying primarily government correspondence, a pony express system with well-rested animals and inns at regular intervals along the imperial highways moved news and correspondence throughout the empire with great speed. All these offices were supported by scribes, thousands of clerks at all levels of government service who kept information flowing through the system. These civil servants held an elite status in Abbasid society. They were literate members of a largely illiterate society and had access to inside government information.

The Abbasid Army Parallel to the institutional development of the civil bureaucracy under the Abassids, the army changed as well. The early Abbasid army was based on volunteers drawn heavily from Persia's province of Khorasan, many of whom wished to stay on after the revolution succeeded. Wishing to emphasize the equality of all Muslims and to balance the Persian divisions with other elements of their empire, the Abbasids recruited Arabs, largely in Syria and ostensibly to be used against Byzantium. In the ninth century, the Abbasid effort to balance the army broke down during a dispute over succession between two of Harun al-Rashid's brothers. One was supported by the western, largely Arab, army, the other by the eastern, largely Persian army, and a civil war between Arabs and Persians was the result.

The Abbasid power degenerated following the civil war, and the government began more and more to turn to foreign mercenaries, who could be trusted in that they were not allied to either Persian or Arab factions, and for so long as they were paid. Almost always, these Turkish mercenaries were brought in from their homeland in Central Asia. Ironically, it would be the Seljuk Turks, invited in 1055 to protect the Abbasid dynasty, who would finally overthrow it.

Islamic Ideology under the Abbasids Just as the bureaucracy and army were reshaped into larger, more complex structures to fit the varying circumstances of a multicultural imperial government, so also was the ideology of Islam. The purpose of reshaping Islamic ideology was to establish an official orthodox position on all important matters of faith. In order to reinforce their power, the Abbasids endowed their caliphs with a greater degree of religious authority than had previously been the case. Scholars were called upon to clarify and establish an orthodox credo and ritual, and the Abbasids enforced it with threats of imprisonment or worse. Heresy was a violation of state policy. The authority of the caliphate was further increased by additions to Islamic law. Scholars under Abbasid patronage developed a legal theory that the caliph held absolute power. Thanks to this and other standardizations of both content and procedure, the *shari'a* took its final orthodox form in the eighth and ninth centuries.

In all of these developments of the Abbasid imperial government, there is a pattern common to other early empires: a common language, common systems of belief, and an empirewide legal system and bureaucracy. Arabic was the language of administration across the Abbasid Empire and also the language of sacred knowledge, the Qur'an. As many Persians as Arabs were bureaucrats in the Abbasid government, but they all used Arabic. The law itself, fully developed to cover every possible source of litigation whether in India or North Africa, was also a critical factor in holding the empire together in the eighth and ninth centuries. The weak point of the imperial structure was the legitimacy of the Abbasid caliphate. Having displaced the Umayyads, the Abbasids themselves were liable to being overturned. Abbasid legitimacy, like that of any Islamic government, was measured by its ability to provide ethically correct Islamic governance and equitable policies for the distribution of wealth. With its vast accumulation of capital, the Abbasid government was especially vulnerable on the charge of inequity of wealth. In 867, a slave revolt spread through southern Iraq, touching off a series of revolts throughout the empire from northeast Persia to Syria, Yemen, and North Africa. Within a hundred years, the Abbasid caliphate's power was confined to Iraq. Elsewhere, new governments had sprung up, Islamic to be sure but independent of the central imperial government.

Breakdown of Abbasid Empire Abbasid caliphs continued to exist as figureheads for the ▬▬▬▬▬▬▬▬▬▬▬▬▬▬▬▬▬▬ Seljuk Turks, who succeeded them in actual power in 1055 while continuing the dynasty in name. In 1258, a Mongol army sacked Baghdad and killed the last Abbasid caliph; so ended the first and largest Islamic Empire, culturally distinctive yet in function very much like other early empires of the world. Like them also, the first Islamic Empire was a blend of many cultural styles and governmental techniques. At the same time, the provincial peninsular Arab nature of its origins never wholly disappeared beneath the Roman and Persian administrative borrowings. Like early empires in other parts of the world, this first Islamic Empire established its own patterns, symbols, and structures, which have been used by Muslim governments since, both in West Asia and elsewhere in the world.

SUMMARY

This chapter has developed the theme of the relationship between ideas and power by examining the interaction between the universal religions of Buddhism, Christianity, and Islam and states in Asia, Africa, and Europe. Buddhism, Christianity, and Islam alike were proselytized by their followers, adapted to different cultural settings, and used to provide religious sanctions for rulers. Unlike Buddhism, however, both Christianity and Islam used military power to conquer and convert peoples and created their own governments.

From its origins in sixth-century B.C.E. India, Buddhism was transmitted through central to east Asia by the beginning of the first millennium C.E. to become one of the great proselytizing, universal religions of world history. Emerging from the Sumerian and Judaic traditions of early West Asia, both Christianity and Islam were, by the close of the first millennium C.E., institutionalized universal religions with large populations of adherents in lands that stretched from northern Europe to North Africa and from the Mediterranean to East Africa and the Himalayas. As all three of these religions were introduced into different cultures and societies, they underwent significant adaptations to indigenous belief systems at the same time that they dramatically altered the religious ideals and values of peoples around the globe.

All three early universal religions—Buddhism, Christianity, and Islam—were further expanded by those who held the reins of power in the areas where they took root. Although

Buddhism interacted with political authority in various cultural settings, lending its sanction to some rulers, it did not become the engine of empire that Christianity, and especially Islam, did. Just as political forces shaped the growth and spread of these religions, so Christianity and Islam both played powerful roles in legitimizing political authority.

Ideological systems, including religious beliefs, practices, and institutions, are a means of articulating and consolidating relations of power, as well as a source of personal, community, and state or larger political identities. As Buddhism expanded into Southeast Asia, it interacted with both Hinduism and indigenous belief systems in varying political contexts, from empires to city-states. Islam spread into Africa, where it flourished alongside African belief systems in the West African Mali Empire and in East African coastal port cities. In the following chapter, as we look at Southeast Asia, Africa, and the Americas, we turn from a focus on ideas and power to stress the material basis of power: how economic systems are shaped by ecological conditions and how economic forces such as trade influence structures of power—kingdoms, empires, city-states. Economic systems, such as political structures and ideological systems, are one of the frameworks within which power is negotiated. In the following chapter, we stress the economic dimensions of power as we continue to examine the role of religion in the construction of political orders: How do economies, along with religion and politics, order the world?

FIGURE 5.12 *Torii* (Entrance to a Shinto Shrine) at Itsukushima, Miyajima Island in Japan's Inland Sea.

A *torii* marked the entrance to a sacred sanctuary, a site which was often identified with an aspect of nature.

SOURCE: L. Rebmann/Exploreur/Photo Researchers, Inc.

RELIGION IN HISTORY: INDIVIDUAL, FAMILY, COMMUNITY, AND STATE

People who study the history of religion want to understand how religions have changed over time, how they have influenced people's lives, and how they have shaped societies and cultures in the past. From the perspective of world history, it is sometimes easy to focus on major institutionalized religions and to neglect what religion really meant in the daily lives of people. Even the question of what constitutes a religion is often unclear. For example, people have sometimes asked whether or not Confucianism was really a religion, because it did not appear to conform to traditional definitions of religion. Yet Confucius himself and some of his disciples were in fact deified and worshiped through rites performed in the state Confucian temple from as early as the Han dynasty (206 B.C.E.–220 C.E.). Families made ritual sacrifices to their ancestors at shrines in their homes, and Confucian values permeated many aspects of family and community life. What Confucianism did not directly address was the spiritual life of the individual; the individual was recognizable only as a part of the family unit, as the family was part of the community and society at large. From the Han dynasty on, Confucianism also had a political role; in the form of "imperial Confucianism," Confucian ideas were used to bolster the position of the emperor as the mediator between Heaven and human society, and to validate the role of officials in assisting the emperor to carry out the Mandate of Heaven to rule China.

Unlike Confucianism, which has a body of sacred texts and ethical doctrines, Shinto does not, and thus it does not conform to certain commonly accepted criteria for religion. Shinto beliefs were practiced in and for the community; they were ceremonies designed to ensure the welfare of the community, to protect its members from harm. The beliefs and practices we call "Shinto" did not distinguish its followers from followers of other religions. It was just the way the world worked. Only with the advent of Buddhism in the sixth century C.E. did it become necessary to coin a term to characterize those beliefs in distinction to Buddhism. Though Shinto, like Confucianism, became a political cult with the formation of the early Japanese state by around 500 C.E., it nonetheless retained its character as a set of community practices rooted in common descent, whether fictive or real. Like the Sun Goddess, whose descendants became the Sun line—the imperial family—others traced their descent to ancestors who were nature spirits or anthropomorphic Shinto deities.

SUGGESTIONS FOR FURTHER READING

Bonnie S. Anderson and Judith P. Zinsser, *A History of Their Own: Women in Europe from Prehistory to the Present*, vol. 1 (New York: Harper and Row, 1988). Rethinking European history from the perspective of women's lives.

Graham Connah, *African Civilizations* (Cambridge, England: Cambridge University Press, 1987). Survey of precolonial African civilizations.

Michael W. Doyle, *Empires* (Ithaca, N.Y.: Cornell University Press, 1986). A stimulating look at the way empires have imposed control and shaped political development.

Kenneth S. Latourette, *A History of Christianity* (New York: Harper and Row, 1975).

Religions have many dimensions and operate on many levels. They can be addressed to the spiritual concerns of the individual and to the maintenance of the family or community, as well as to legitimizing a ruler's authority or the state's power. The personal relationship of an individual with God and the communal character of religious practice were both part of early Christian belief and persisted through the rise of Christianity to become a powerful political force in the Papacy. In Islam, the "community of true believers" forms the basis of Muslim identity, reinforced by such practices as individual daily prayer and the once-in-a-lifetime pilgrimage to Mecca. In theory, this community transcends that of the secular state, directing the exercise of power by Islamic rulers to carry out the conversion of all to Islam.

As we have demonstrated in this chapter, religion can be a powerful political force, just as politics can shape religious experience, belief, and practice. Religion can just as effectively challenge structures of power as validate and reinforce them. As Confucianism was used to sanction the power of the emperor and the state, Daoism could be used to challenge that power. "Religious Daoism" is a term that has been used to describe popular religious beliefs and practices in China that drew on some early Daoist texts, such as the fourth-century B.C.E. Daodejing, but also incorporated worship of a pantheon of Daoist deities, beginning with the Jade Emperor at the pinnacle. In their search for the secrets of longevity and immortality, Daoist priests engaged in the study of alchemy, herbal lore, and physical exercises, which led them to discover many things that became part of the body of Chinese medical knowledge. People called on Daoist priests to cure their illnesses and to exorcise malignant spirits, and sometimes the power of Daoist priests competed with that of Confucian state officials. Led by Daoist priests, a popular movement known as the "Way of Great Peace" brought about a rebellion against Han rule in 184 C.E. At roughly the same time, the early Christian community challenged the basis of Roman rule. Early Christians were persecuted by the leaders of the Roman Empire because their vision of community through spiritual union with God was believed to threaten the legitimacy and authority of the Roman emperor. Like the Daoist Way of Great Peace, early Christians belonged to a group whose common identity was based on shared religious beliefs and the practices that reinforced them, independent of political authority.

Bernard Lewis, ed., *Islam and the Arabic World* (New York: Knopf, 1976). Essays on Islamic history and culture edited by a prominent authority.

G. Mokhtar, ed., *Unesco General History of Africa,* vol. 2 (Berkeley: University of California Press/Heinemann/UNESCO, 1981). A comprehensive history of early African civilizations.

Francis Robinson, *Cambridge Illustrated History of the Islamic World* (Cambridge, England: Cambridge University Press, 1995). Comprehensive, illustrated thematic survey of Islam and the Islamic world.

Arthur F. Wright, *Buddhism in Chinese History* (Stanford, Calif.: Stanford University Press, 1971). A brief and useful overview of Buddhism's development in the context of Chinese history.

Trade, Transport, Temples, and Tribute: The Economics of Power

N ot only religion and politics directed the flow of power across the globe, the lure of gold and other treasures prodded travelers through the ages to leave home and explore new horizons. Descriptions of gold glittered from one continent to the next. For example, the Mongol envoy and Chinese traveler Zhou Daguan observed the procession of the Cambodian (Khmer) monarch in the capital of Angkor Wat in 1296 c.e.:

> When the king rides forth, soldiers march at the head of the procession, followed by the banners and standards and the musicians. . . . Then come waiting-women bearing the king's gold and silver plates and insignia, all fashioned for his special use. . . . And after these come carriages drawn by goats or horses, all of them ornamented with gold. . . . Next come the wives and concubines of the king . . . assuredly their gold-spangled parasols number more than a hundred. Behind these comes at last the king, standing on an elephant, his precious sword on hand. . . . From this you may perceive that these people know full well what it is to be a king.

Maps of Africa before 1500 c.e. invariably included an image of the king of Mali seated on his throne, holding a gold nugget nearly the size of his head. It was the fourteenth-century Malian ruler and his entourage, who had given away so much gold while on *hajj,* or pilgrimage, to Mecca that the price of gold on the Cairo market had collapsed shortly thereafter. Egyptian chroniclers wrote about the event in the next century, and the traveler Ibn Battuta described the West African ruler around 1350: "[The sultan] has a lofty pavilion, of which the door is inside his house, where he sits for most of the time." His image of the gold-turbaned sultan under a silken dome stands in stark contrast to the vivid description of the desert caravans that actually carried goods such as highly prized salt and copper in exchange for gold. Ibn Battuta writes of the merchants of Sijilmasa that "they load their camels at late dawn, and march until the sun has risen, its light has become bright in the air, and the heat on the ground has become severe. . . . When the sun begins to decline and sink in the west, they set off [again]." Twenty-five days later, the caravans would reach Taghaza, a major salt-mining area. Describing the enormous amounts of gold traded in the grim and perilous mining town, Ibn Battuta says, "This is a village with nothing good about it. It is the most fly-ridden of places."

Although they relied on the trade, gold-bedecked rulers in city centers around the world had little concern for and probably little direct knowledge either of those who slaved in mines or those who traveled afar, providing goods to support their lavish lifestyles. One of the consequences

FIGURE 6.0 Mansa Musa of Mali Holds
a Gold Nugget as an Arab
Trader Rides in to Barter
with Him.

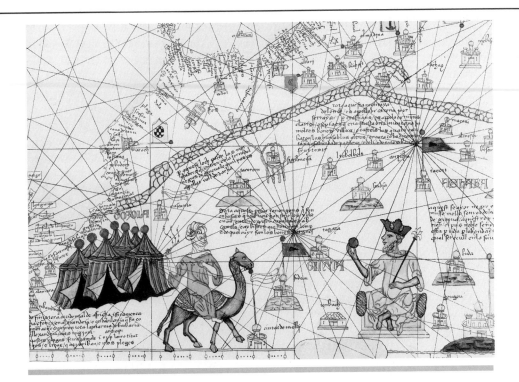

of the ordering of increasingly complex societies was the growing gaps between the lifestyles of the few rich and the many laborers who produced the wealth they controlled. While trade, transport, temples, and tribute contributed much to the material world, they did so at a high price for some.

INTRODUCTION

In Chapters 4 and 5, we emphasized the role of ideas in structuring and sanctioning relations of power. Chapter 4 showed how religion and politics interacted in the formation of early dynastic states and empires in West, East, and South Asia, North Africa, and the Americas; Chapter 4 also described the growth of humanistic and rationalistic ideas among communities of thinkers in early Greek city-states and preimperial China. Chapter 5 traced the evolution of three universal religions and their role in the creation of empires in Europe, Asia, and

215

Africa. In this chapter we shift away from a focus on the ideological or ideal in history, as expressed in ideas and power, to stress the material conditions that give rise to, or enable the development of, increasingly complex social organizations and concentrations of power. The connection between material conditions and the construction of political orders highlighted in this chapter's examples from Southeast Asia, West and East Africa, and the Americas also suggests ways of thinking about the polities discussed earlier, in examples ranging from the Greek city-states to the Islamic empires.

Political Economy In considering interrelated material conditions such as economic systems, ▬▬▬▬▬▬▬▬ physical environments, or technology, we make use of the concept of political economy, the relationship between material wealth or resources and power that shapes economic and political systems. Supply and demand are not simply objective conditions dependent on the amount of material resources in relation to population. Distribution systems that dictate the allocation of economic resources are directly tied to the structure of power relations. For example, tribute describes a system of economic exchange in which goods or services are provided according to the demands of a ruler or a state in return for protection or religious favors, or simply to avoid punishment. Trade can take place between equal partners but is always subject to the influence of political forces as well as conditions of production, markets, and transportation systems. Technologies of land and sea transport, such as the horse, llama, camel, bridge and ship, are vital determinants of the efficiency of exchange.

Although this chapter shifts the emphasis from ideological to material conditions, it continues to stress the role played by belief systems in making sense of the material world and explaining or justifying the inequitable distribution of both power and material goods. The role of temples, for example, in providing a network for the collection and redistribution of goods is one example of the economic role of religious institutions. As this chapter continues to demonstrate, religion can provide the ideological glue that makes an economic system as well as a political order work.

■

SOUTHEAST ASIAN RIVERINE AND ISLAND EMPIRES

The Monsoon Climate Southeast Asia is a world of northern mountains and southern seas, of ▬▬▬▬▬▬▬▬ broad mainland river-delta plains and a profusion of large and small islands. Watered by the monsoons, heavy rains brought by winds that also moved sailing ships over the seas with great seasonal regularity, Southeast Asia shares the climate of the Indian subcontinent. In the early centuries of the first millennium, Southeast Asia sat astride an ancient maritime trade highway between West Asia and Africa on the one hand, and East Asia on the other. It was also the meeting place of local, as well as Indian and Chinese, cultures and belief systems. This physical and cultural environment provided the setting for the political orders that emerged in Southeast Asia before 1500.

Views of early Southeast Asia have often been shaped by assumptions drawn from historical experience outside the region. Situated at the intersection of Indian and Chinese civilization, Southeast Asia has been seen either through an Indian lens stressing the Hindu influence on the formation of the first state, Funan, or through an equally distorting Chinese lens reflected in the Chinese accounts of Funan. In contrast to either of these perspectives, it seems better to conceptualize early Southeast Asian polities in terms of indigenous ideas and prac-

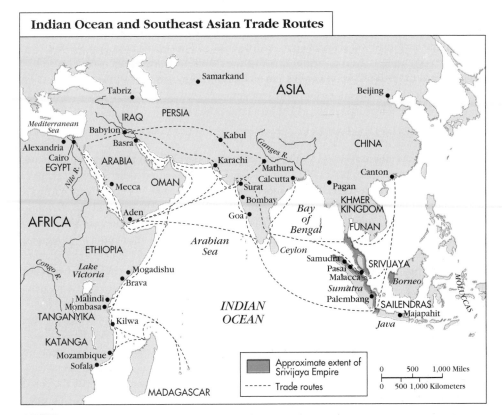

Indian Ocean and Southeast Asian Trade Routes

MAP 6.1 Trade Routes Connected Funan, Srivijaya, and Khmer Kingdom with India, and West Asian, Southeast Asian, and East African Port City-States

tices that emphasize a complex system of personal loyalties as the basis for power relations rather than to consider them as territories with defined boundaries administered by representatives of one or another ruler. The precise boundaries of the territory controlled by a ruler were not of primary concern; what mattered was the network of loyalties on which that ruler could depend. The mandala, a symbol drawn from early Indian cosmology, has been used to characterize the nature of political authority in early southeast Asia. The mandala image, a sacred diagram of the cosmos constructed of concentric circles or rectangles, represents the ruler's personal charismatic authority radiating out from a center, in contrast to the vertically organized hierarchy of power directly exercised through the ruler's representatives.

Riverine and Island Polities Many polities rose and fell in southeast Asia before 1500. The most impressive of these were empires that continued to influence regional traditions long after they had fallen. These empires were built on distinctive regional economic structures and created cultural and political foundations for their successors. The major polities of this period can be loosely categorized into two types: those of the mainland, based on intensive irrigated rice agriculture on river plains, and those of the islands, based on control of the river network and sea trade. Each economic system alone could sup-

port a strong regional polity. Only the two systems together, however, could provide sufficiently diversified material and human resources to maintain an empire. Here we will look at
two empires of this period that achieved such a linkage, Funan and Srivijaya. We will also
consider one example of a strong regional polity, the mainland Khmer state, which controlled
and organized the redistribution of resources produced by wet-rice agriculture on the Mekong
River delta through a network of Buddhist temples.

FUNAN: A RIVERINE EMPIRE

By the end of the first century C.E., the area of present-day Vietnam, Cambodia, Thailand,
and Burma, the great river plains of mainland Southeast Asia, was divided among a number
of regional polities. Made fertile by the silts of regular and relatively gentle monsoon flooding, these plains were very productive for rain-fed and increasingly irrigated rice farming.
They were, moreover, quite large and capable of supporting sizable and concentrated populations. The plains were also easy to dominate politically, in contrast to mountainous regions,
where communication and transportation were more difficult. One of the first states there to
undertake empire building successfully was Funan. Sometime around 50 C.E., what later Chinese sources would describe as the "Kingdom of Funan" emerged on the lower Mekong delta
and along the coastline of Thailand to the west.

Early Funan was composed of a number of communities, each with its own ruler, linked
loosely together by a common culture and by a shared economic pattern of rice farming supplemented with participation in the regional coastal trade. Funan's population was made up
primarily of farming people in the hinterland and maritime traders in the coastal towns, who
were economically interdependent. Surplus rice production found a ready market at the ports,
where ships passing along the coast supplied themselves. Ship traders in turn had no difficulty paying for the rice and other agricultural products with goods brought from foreign
ports. This nicely balanced exchange system, which may have been in place a hundred years
or more previously, underwent a significant change between about 50 and 150. The change
was brought about by external factors and reinforced internally by ambitious rulers, who
transformed Funan into an empire. The catalyst for this transformation was a boom in the
India–China maritime trade, which intensified the importance of exchange.

Funan in Myth and Symbol The mythical account of the founding of Funan reflects in symbolic terms the conditions that led to Funan's rise as a regional
power by around 150 C.E. According to this story, sometime in the early first century C.E. a
woman ruler of the lower Mekong delta region led an attack on a passing merchant ship. Successfully defending themselves, the merchants made their way ashore. Their leader, an Indian
upper-caste scholar named Kaundinya, "drank water from the land" and married the woman
ruler, who is described as the daughter of the ruler of the Realm of Water. Kaundinya then
became king of the region, which is described as a number of settlements, each with its own
ruler. Seven of the largest of these settlements were assigned to the children of this marriage,
while the remainder were held directly by the new king.

There are several layers of interpretation to this story, each related to the others. The imagery is common to Southeast Asian traditions. The arrival of foreign traders from India and
their "marriage" with local rulers to build a larger, more powerful state clearly relates to the
intensification of international trade in the area during this period. The strength of the new

capital afforded by the trade was controlled by merchants, Indian or Malay, experienced in the administration of large states such as India, the nearest great trade center.

The story suggests the social implications of this new political/economic structure. By all accounts, before Indian influences became prevalent in Southeast Asia women had considerable access to positions of public power. Matrilineage, tracing descent through the maternal line, appears to have been characteristic of social structure there. Indian society and ideology, on the other hand, was patrilineal, tracing descent through the male line, and strongly patriarchal. In the original story, a woman ruler represented the land of Funan; but after the marriage, the Indian husband took over as king. Although the regimented patriarchy and caste system seen in India did not overtake Funan's culture, it did affect the ruling class structures, and for the next several hundred years Funan's empire was ruled only by men.

Trade and Ideology in Funan Funan, which began as a group of autonomous agricultural communities on the lower Mekong and Tonle Sap Rivers, found that the growth of maritime shipping passing through the region brought enough profit through trade to support a larger population base. With an increased population, the leaders of Funan expanded their land's agricultural productivity by investing in more intensive irrigation, and they began to engage in the conquest of neighboring communities. They also sought to monopolize the region's maritime trade by conquering rival coastal emporiums, or trading centers. While doing so, they legitimized their expanding rule by blending the features of the increasingly accepted Hindu ideology with the local cosmology. Funan rulers of the early first century legitimized their rule on the basis of claimed descent from heroic ancestors. By the end of the second century C.E., those ancestors and the rulers themselves had become representatives on earth of the Hindu god Shiva, who ruled from the "Sacred Mountain," maintaining order throughout the universe. Shiva was also identified with fertility, a notion that blended well with the indigenous beliefs in fertility deities and allowed the grafting of Hindu ideas onto local traditions.

By the second century, Funan rulers had established control over the strategic coastline of the India–China maritime route, and expansion continued through the third century. Funan established trading relations with the Chinese, and, after the collapse of the Han dynasty in the early third century, they continued to exchange delegations with rulers of the successor states in southern China. Chinese reports of "tributary" missions from Funan provide us with the most comprehensive description of Funan's government and economy, though these accounts are colored by the Chinese people's view of themselves as the recipients of tribute, a recognition of their centrality and dominance over surrounding states.

Once a region was conquered and attached to Funan territories, the region's leaders continued to rule there, although they now owed allegiance and taxes to the rulers of Funan. In exchange for this, the entire region enjoyed relative peace and stability under a common ideology, a blend of indigenous and Indian themes, and a generally accepted regional legal system. Such stability, reinforced by regular investment in agricultural development throughout the region under Funan's control, ensured continued good external trade relations.

International Trade and Although Funan's income was relatively diversified through trade
the Decline of Funan and agricultural taxes and profits, a significant decline in one sector or the other could jeopardize the empire's stability. This may have been what happened in the fifth century. Just as international trade shifts had earlier led to

the emergence of Funan's empire, so also did such a shift fatally undermine its economic strength and contribute to its breakup. In this case the restructuring of trade developed out of worsening political conditions in Central Asia and north China. Constant warfare there in the fourth and fifth centuries all but cut off the overland east–west trade. Southern Chinese traders, frustrated by the closure of the overland routes, sought both a faster and less expensive maritime route than that offered by their traditional partner, Funan. That route was through the Strait of Malacca.

By the end of the fifth century, international trade through southeast Asia was almost entirely directed through the Strait of Malacca. Funan, from the point of view of this trade, had outlived its usefulness. Unable to affect the new direction of trade in any way, the Funan rulers turned back to the land in the hope that increased agricultural productivity would cover the country's trade losses. The fifth and sixth centuries saw the transformation of the agriculture of the Mekong delta and lower Cambodia and Thailand into intensive, irrigated rice production, with the addition of hundreds of new dikes, canals, and holding tanks built by the government.

Pressured by the constantly eroding economic base, struggles for power within the court weakened the dynasty and left it prey to attack from neighbors. In the second half of the sixth century, Funan's eastern regions were taken by the Hindu Champa rulers of southern Vietnam. The Khmer rulers of northern Cambodia and northeastern Thailand conquered the Mekong and Funan's western territories. Funan as an empire was destroyed, its place taken by two successor states which, each keeping largely to its own culturally and ecologically defined boundaries, survived well into early modern times. Both of these successor states built on Funan's experience in administration and political ideology, and both were ruled by dynasties claiming legitimacy based on their claims to descent from the rulers of Funan.

THE KHMER KINGDOM: A MAINLAND STATE

The Khmer state dominated the Mekong River Valley and delta for more than 400 years, from 802 to 1432, and at its height in the twelfth century controlled probably a million people in the area of modern Cambodia, Laos, Thailand, and parts of Burma, Vietnam, and the Malay peninsula. A network of canals used for both transportation and irrigation linked the Khmer state physically, and reservoirs helped control the uneven rainfall of a monsoon climate by storing monsoon rainwater for later use. Both Hinduism and Buddhism provided sanction for the authority of rulers and the common cultural and religious bonds among the Khmer people. As in Funan, the rulers initially blended Hinduism with indigenous beliefs to consolidate their power over their expanding territory, and the Sanskrit language was adopted by the Khmer court. Worship of the Hindu god Shiva, who was identified as the "Lord of the Mountain," was connected with indigenous beliefs in the sanctity of mountains, the home of ancestral spirits. Shiva was also associated with fertility, and similarly worship of Shiva was merged with local fertility beliefs in Shiva's representation by the stone or metal phallus, the *lingam,* inserted upright into the circular "vulva," or *yoni,* at shrines to him in the Khmer state.

The Devaraja Cult Worship of Shiva was formalized in the *devaraja* (god-king) cult of the ruler Jayavarman II (770–834), who built the Khmer state through a combination of conquest and the formation of a network of personal alliances. Jayavarman consolidated the worship of regional deities in the *devaraja* cult and built the principal temple at the center of the royal capital on a mountaintop. After Jayavarman, statues and *lingams* of gods were fused with the person of the ruler, symbolized by the merging of the monarch's personal title with the name of a god. For example, Jayavarman's successor was associated with the Hindu god Indra and thus became known as Indravarman I (r. 877–889). Rulers were believed to be the earthly incarnation of gods and responsible for maintaining order in the world.

Angkor Wat Massive public works projects carried out by the Khmer monarchy, such as the Hindu temple complex of Angkor Wat (*wat* means "temple") built by Suryavarman II (1113–1150) are testimony to the ability of the Khmer state to collect and redistrib-

FIGURE 6.1 Aerial View of Angkor Wat, Early Twelfth Century C.E.

SOURCE: Eliot Elisofon/*Life* Magazine, © Time Inc.

ute economic resources on a huge scale. This was accomplished through a network of temples, which served as centers of redistribution from villages to local temples and on up through a hierarchy to the central temple in the king's capital. In this way both the material wealth and the symbolic capital, the cultural and religious symbols used to integrate Khmer society, were distributed through a complex temple network spread throughout the realm.

The Buddharaja Cult After the twelfth century, at the capital city of Angkor Thom, Buddhist dominance was reflected in the Bayon temple complex façade, which showed the Buddhist deity Lokeshvara. This Buddhist deity was identified with the builder of Angkor Thom, Jayavarman VII, who was honored in the new Buddharaja cult.

Pagan Burma Other mainland states, such as Pagan in Burma along the Irrawaddy River (mid–eleventh to late thirteenth centuries), were similarly based on irrigated rice agriculture and built religious monuments that both reflected the use of Hinduism and Buddhism to consolidate control over local communities and testified to the ability of their rulers to commandeer sufficient resources to construct such monuments to their own power and glory, often identifying themselves with Hindu or Buddhist deities. Wealthy and powerful though their rulers were, mainland states such as the Khmer and Pagan Burma could not control the sea trade that would have allowed them to connect their agricultural hinterland with the maritime trade and expand into empires as both Funan and later Srivijaya did.

SRIVIJAYA: AN ISLAND EMPIRE

Funan's origins lay in agriculture-based communities transformed into an empire by wealth and power that came from control of the international coastal trading networks. In contrast, Srivijaya emerged from river-based coastal trading communities which were joined together to form a maritime empire. By developing good relations with the agricultural hinterland in order to gain a dependable supply of commodities for trade, the founders of Srivijaya were able to support a larger maritime trade zone and thus to establish an empire that dominated the region from about 670 to 1025.

Malay Merchant Mariners In the sixth century, when major international trading powers began to shift their routing southward from mainland Funan, several fleets operated by Malay seamen competed for the southern trade as it developed through the Strait of Malacca. Like their land-based cousins, these seamen—sometimes described as "sea nomads" by foreign observers—were organized into lineage groups. Power was measured by the number of boats one controlled. These boats were outrigger canoes—with floating timbers rigged out from the side to prevent tipping—up to 27 meters (90 feet) long with fore-and-aft sail rigging. Like all merchant mariners, Malay seamen spent much of their lives on water, but all had home ports upon which their lives and livelihoods depended. The ports provided food and boat equipment for the voyages; backing up the port was a hinterland trading system which delivered commodities for the maritime trade. The port government, headed by a *datu,* the common Malay term for "ruler," thus had one foot on land and one in the water. It was obliged to maintain good alliances with both farmer and seaman in order to maintain the equilibrium of this complicated economic and political system.

Srivijaya was such a port state. Its capital, Palembang, on the island of Sumatra in mod-ern-day Indonesia, was strategically situated near the southern entrance of the Strait of Malacca. With its fleets and armies, it gradually established dominance of the coastlines and built a major coastal emporium on the southeast coast of Sumatra. It eliminated piracy—which is another way of saying it eliminated competition from rival port states—and thus ensured safe passage for foreign shipping. In return for this, in the seventh century Srivijaya became by treaty the favored trading partner of the Chinese government, replacing Funan and gaining in effect a monopoly on the enormous China trade. Srivijayan ports cornered the lion's share of the India–China shipping business: ship repairs, outfitting, storage, supplies, and layovers between monsoons for thousands of ships and boats per year.

The large Srivijayan island empire was built on a combination of military force and the political acumen of the *datu*s of the capital, Plambang. Given the fluctuations in international trade and variations in human abilities, military power and political skill alone were insuffi-cient to ensure the survival of Srivijaya. It also needed a belief system that could unite con-quered regions with differing religious and ethnic groups under a common loyalty to Palem-bang. Srivijaya found such a unifying ideology in the universal religion of Buddhism.

Buddhism in Srivijaya Buddhism grew rapidly in the Southeast Asian archipelago during the seventh century. Early stone inscriptions at Palembang reveal a ruler there blending the local imagery of the sacred mountain and sea with the traditional venera-tion of ancestors into Buddhist symbols and ethics. Buddhist themes imposed upon indige-nous traditions provided a common set of ideas that transcended local communities. To rein-force this ideology and build regional prestige upon it, the Srivijayan rulers used some of the profits of their empire to become the major builders of Buddhist temples and patrons of Bud-

FIGURE 6.2 Meditating Buddha on Stupa Terrace at Borobudur, Java, Eighth Century C.E.

SOURCE: © Dominique Roger/Rapho Agence/Liaison Interna-tional.

dhist scholarship in their territories. By the tenth and eleventh centuries, the empire was dedicating temples as far away as Bengal and the southeast coast of India. At the same time, practices reflecting both the indigenous worship of the water realm and the recognition of the importance of maritime trade were maintained. For example, the greatness of a deceased monarch was measured by the number of gold bars retrieved from the harbor at Palembang, into which the living ruler threw a gold bar every day to propitiate the ocean, a testimony to the debt of Srivijaya to the sea for providing the wealth in trade on which the empire had been built and a sign of the continuity of traditional beliefs in the power of the sea.

The Srivijayan Political Order The structure of the Srivijayan political order in the eighth century reflects its Malay *datu* origins. The king, who was in theory an absolute monarch, ruled nearby provinces through his sons and other royal family members. In more distant territories, however—on the Malay peninsula, for example, or to the south on Java—conquered *datu*s were left in place to continue their family rule in the king's name. In one sense, the empire was an alliance system between one powerful *datu* and many others, among them the fleet captains who functioned in alliance with the king, under whom they worked. In this system, Srivijaya's kings maintained their central position by carefully building alliances of regional leaders against rebels. Many of these leaders had private armies, the commanders of which were responsible to both the king and the local leader. Palembang's own royal army, paid for with imperial taxes and trade receipts, was large but not large enough to undertake major wars on its own. When the army of Srivijaya went on large campaigns, it did so as an organization of regional armies. It seemed a shaky system, yet by the beginning of the eighth century Palembang's *datu* was unmistakably the ruler of an empire, whose carefully planned succession reflects a well-established central government.

A structured court bureaucracy helped to maintain this imperial monarchy. One division of the bureaucracy was made up of the king's judges, who administered a common court law throughout the provinces. Another group was made up of priests, advisers on Indian court ritual, which remained important in legitimizing the ruler's authority, at the same time as Buddhism was being used to unify the realm and consolidate the ruler's control of the Srivijayan state. Still another category of official was that of market supervisor. Appearing deceptively low in the court hierarchy, this post was of key importance in an empire in which much of the surplus wealth came from international trade. The market inspector was responsible for setting and enforcing throughout Srivijaya's territories standard measures for gold and silver, the currency of trade, along with standard market weights and measures, and to some extent even standard prices for the main trade commodities. Market stability was of critical importance in attracting and holding foreign trade.

Srivijaya's success in maintaining law and order on the seas of the strait and in its markets brought an increase of shipping to its ports, which encouraged the empire to expand still further. Many of the goods sought by international traders originated in the islands to the south and east; Srivijaya accordingly moved in that direction, taking over by force or agreement the main port towns of eastern Java.

Sailendra in Java For example, the marriage of a Srivijayan princess into the Sailendra dynasty, which controlled the strongest state on Java during the eighth and ninth centuries, integrated that state into the Srivijayan sphere. Although the Sailendra continued to rule their central Javanese realm independently, the union meant that the Srivijayan

Empire had little challenge to its dominance of southeast Asian trade over the next hundred years.

The Buddhist Monument at Borobudur in Java The wealth the empire gathered produced not only better standards of living for the region's peoples but also large temple complexes, such as the great eighth-century Buddhist monument at Borobudur on the island of Java, which helped knit the people of the region together under a common religious ideology. Yet, as in the case of Funan and its dependence on international trade, the Srivijayan Empire weakened and collapsed when trade shifted and its balanced system of alliances between land and maritime interests crumbled, as it did in the twelfth and thirteenth centuries.

Muslim Merchants and Srivijaya's Decline During the same period, new powers were also emerging on the Southeast Asian mainland, in Burma, Sri Lanka, Cambodia, and Thailand. At a time when its control of the Malacca Strait trade was threatened by Burma and the Thai monarchy, Srivijaya was challenged by the advent of a new religion, Islam, and by merchants who were Muslim. It was unable to meet the dual challenge. Malay shipping in the region was replaced by Arab and Persian boats, with owners and merchants who, given the opportunity, preferred to deal with Muslim harbormasters and ship chandlers. In some of the smaller ports of northern Sumatra, these Muslim port officers began

FIGURE 6.3 Terraces of the Buddhist Monument at Borobudur, Java, Eighth Century C.E.

SOURCE: © Frederic/Rapho Agence Photographique/Liaison International.

to appear in increasing numbers. The Srivijayan Empire broke up into a collection of smaller independent city-states and trading confederations such as Majapahit, the clearest successor to Srivijaya. Several of these polities found their legitimacy in claims of descent from Srivijaya's ruling family. All used the administrative and ideological legacy of the old empire, including the established patterns of standardized weights and measures and coinage. As Funan's legacy in mainland Southeast Asia survived in its successor states, so too did the tradition of the Srivijayan Empire live on in polities that claimed legitimacy through links to the era of Srivijayan power.

MAJAPAHIT

In Java during the declining years of the Srivijayan Empire, the east coast maritime trading region became unified under the government of Majapahit, a dynastic city-state and trading confederation whose ruler, according to Javanese Buddhist ideology, was divine. By the 1290s, Majapahit had developed its own extensive and tightly controlled trade network with the Malay peninsula and islands to the north, including Sumatra, Borneo, Sulawesi, and the Moluccas. With its highly centralized taxation and efficient administrative structures, four-teenth-century Majapahit has been described by some historians as the first state in the region

FIGURE 6.4 Indonesian Ship with Outrigger

Typical vessel from the reliefs of the temple complex of Borobodur in Java, ca. 800 C.E.

SOURCE: © Ralph Agence/Liaison International.

to move from an "ally-tribute" relationship with its hinterland—a system of economic exchange embedded in a framework of political alliance—to one more clearly defined as direct rule from the center. Throughout its territories, the state effectively standardized taxes, as well as the coinage, weights, and measures necessary to its economy. The rulers of Majapahit, beginning with Kertanagara (r. 1268–1292), cemented their political and economic control through splendid religious ceremonies and monuments, and through ritualized economic exchange.

THE MARVELS OF MAJAPAHIT

A contemporary description of Majapahit portrayed the wonders of that eastern Javanese center around 1300:

> The [Majapahit] Emperor was famous for his love of justice. The empire grew prosperous. People in vast numbers thronged the city. At this time every kind of food was in great abundance. There was a ceaseless coming and going of people from the territories overseas which had submitted to the king, to say nothing of places within Java itself. Of the districts on the coast, from the west came the whole of the west, from the east came the whole of the east. From places inland right down to the shores of the Southern Ocean the people all came for an audience with the Emperor, bringing tribute and offerings. . . . The land of Majapahit was supporting a large population. Everywhere one went there were gongs and drums being beaten, people dancing to the strains of all kinds of loud music, entertainments of many kinds like the living theater, the shadow play, masked-plays, step-dancing and musical dramas. These were the commonest sights and went on day and night in the land of Majapahit.[1]

Travelers who visited Majapahit first came to Bubat, a cosmopolitan market town with many quarters, including Chinese and Indian ones. Javanese traders brought their goods here to sell along with merchants from China, India, Cambodia, Vietnam, and Thailand. Bubat, as the port of entry to the ceremonial and royal center of Majapahit, acquired some of the attributes of a ritual center in its own right. Every spring it was the site of the Caitra festival dedicated to the rice goddess Sri and celebration of the first fruits of the season. The Majapahit ruler and his court came to Bubat for the first seven days of the festival to enjoy food and entertainments such as those described by the Samudra-Pasai chronicler.

The Caitra festival was an occasion for the political and economic power of Majapahit to be displayed, and ceremonies were held in which the exchange of goods was paramount. The king received goods such as rice, salt, sugar, cloth, oil, and bamboo as well as cash from his Javanese subjects. International traders also brought gifts to present to the king. But since the honor bestowed on the king through the presentation of tribute and gifts was in part measured by his generosity in sharing wealth, the king in turn bestowed gifts on the artisans, musicians, and poets whose skills provided the cultural underpinnings of this display. The king also redistributed part of the wealth he received among his allies to ensure their loyalty to him.

The festivities at Bubat were followed by seven more days of celebration at Majapahit, culminating in a great feast in which the relationship between the ruler at the center and his allies was reinforced by distinctions in eating utensils and the kind of food eaten. Those of highest status close to the royal line feasted on such delicacies as wild boar and bees served on gold plates, while those of lesser rank, including commoners, ate less relished cuisine on silver dishes. All indulged in drinking prodigious quantities of palm wine and other alcoholic beverages and were entertained by musical plays in which even the king himself acted and sang.

[1]A. H. Hill, "Hikayat Raja-Raja Pasai," *Journal of the Malay/Malaysian Branch of the Royal Asiatic Society* 33:2 (1960): 161; cited in Kenneth R. Hall, *Maritime Trade and State Development in Early Southeast Asia* (Honolulu: University of Hawaii Press, 1985): 340–1, n. 47.

SOUTHEAST ASIAN CITY-STATES

With a population scattered over a thousand or more islands, the geography of maritime Southeast Asia militated against strong central government on a large scale. When centralized rule, such as that of the Srivijayan Empire, was exercised, it was the result of particular historical conditions. With the decline of the Srivijayan Empire in the second half of the thirteenth century, political authority became decentralized and devolved onto local island leaders. In only a few cases did these smaller polities manage to reach beyond their own immediate cultural and economic systems. Those that did were the port city-states, and even they were rarely able to control significant portions of their rice-growing hinterlands. As a consequence, all of them were dependent on maritime trade for survival. These port city-states were intensely competitive. Efforts to corner oceanborne goods and prevent rival port city-states from gaining a piece of the market led to frequent raids and harassment of one another. Only a few of the many port city-states of the thirteenth through the fifteenth centuries have been studied in any detail. Among them are the paired port cities of Samudra-Pasai and Malacca.

SAMUDRA-PASAI

While Majapahit was the clearest successor to the Srivijayan Empire in terms of a state built on combined agricultural and commercial wealth, other smaller city-states, which lived primarily off the profits of trade, emerged in the northern territories of the empire. One of them, Samudra, was located on the far northeast coast of the island of Sumatra, which takes its current name from this state. Samudra, founded in the late thirteenth century, sought to capture the east-west trade moving through the Strait of Malacca. A river harbor city-state, it was plagued by poor relations with its hinterland neighbors; it did, however, succeed in extending its control somewhat along the Sumatran coastline and eventually shifted its capital south to another port city, Pasai.

Samudra-Pasai's importance derives from the fact that it was one of the first Southeast Asian Muslim city-states, basing the legitimacy of its rulers on Islam. In 1282, Samudra-Pasai opened trade relations with the Chinese government, using Muslim merchants as its spokesmen. According to inscriptions of the time, by 1296 the ruler himself was Muslim. No doubt the commercial success of the state was due in part to the lure of dealing with Muslim Persian or Arab officials and traders far from home.

MALACCA

Islamic influence grew steadily in the island world of Southeast Asia. Another port successor city-state there was Malacca, which, like Samudra-Pasai, became Muslim, though it was built upon the cultural and political traditions of Southeast Asia. Malacca established its legitimacy on the foundations of its old royal lineage and on both old and new ideologies, especially Islam.

Parameswara The founder of Malacca is known only by his title, Parameswara, meaning "prince-consort." This aristocrat, attempting to seize leadership, challenged

Majapahit and was defeated. Around 1390, he fled to an island near present-day Singapore, where he built a fleet. Ten years later, he established himself and his fleet at the river port town of Malacca, on the central coast of the Malay peninsula, and shortly thereafter he obtained a trade agreement with the Chinese government, which was seeking trade alternatives to the Majapahit monopoly. This agreement provided the Parameswara with protection against pressure from the expanding Thai kingdom on the Malay peninsula. In 1414, he married a princess of the ruling dynasty of Samudra-Pasai across the Strait of Malacca, converted to Islam, and changed his name to Iskendar Shah. By 1420, he had parleyed his marriage alliance into full control of both sides of the strait and all of the trade flowing through it.

By 1500, Malacca was the largest and most populous commercial emporium in the international trade world of Southeast Asia. As a maritime city-state, it maintained a large fleet to police the length of the strait, administering trade and standardizing weights and measures, as well as port charges. Harbormasters, now generally known by the title *shahbandar* (Persian for "port captain"), maintained hostels, warehouses, and local liaison offices for visiting merchants. The large revenues obtained by its monopoly of the strait allowed Malacca to conquer as well as hold its hinterland, which consisted of nearly all of the southern Malay peninsula. It defended that territory successfully against several major attacks by Thai armies in the second half of the fifteenth century.

The great success of Muslim Malacca did much to spread the new Islamic ideology through the islands, first to the main trading ports and from them to the people of the hinterlands. By 1500, nearly all of the port city-states of the island world from Java to the Philippines were ruled by Muslim sultans.

■

EAST AFRICAN CITY-STATES: PATE AND KILWA

At the other end of the Islamic world, autonomous East African city-states also functioned as political centers for the administration of maritime trade. Situated on islands off present-day Kenya and Tanzania on the East African coast, complex urban societies such as Kilwa, Pemba, Lamu, and Pate emerged (after the second century C.E.) from the background of early civilization on the African mainland. These coastal urban centers were the crucibles in which Swahili language (based on a local Bantu linguistic core with Arab elements added) and culture emerged by around 1100 C.E.

The wealth and political importance of the Swahili were based on their control of the extensive Indian Ocean trading networks. Trading gold, ivory, slaves, iron, rare woods, and other goods obtained from the African hinterland for Chinese porcelains, Islamic glazed wares, glass vessels, and beads, wealthy sultans built luxurious entrepôts, commercial centers for importing and exporting, with collection and distribution functions. Not only were the city-states the far-flung outposts of the Islamic world, they were equally the centers of the East African world in which they were situated. Archaeological excavations and critical analysis of Arabic and Swahili chronicles have increasingly stressed the East African social and economic underpinnings and the African political continuities of these island communities.

Both Pate and Kilwa are well documented by chronicles, later written versions of oral traditions, archaeology, and other sources. When the fourteenth-century North African traveler Ibn Battuta visited Kilwa, he described this important urban center as "one of the most beautiful and well-constructed towns in the world." Excavations have confirmed the written

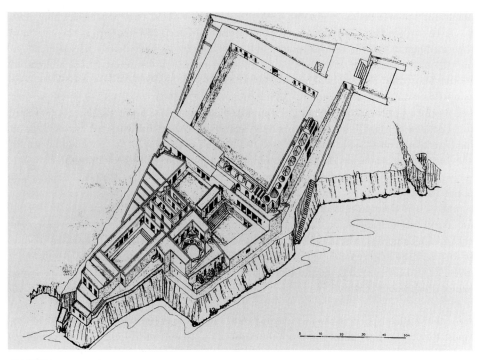

FIGURE 6.5 Palace of Husuni Kubwa, Kilwa (East Africa)

SOURCE: Connah, Graham, *African Civilizations.* (Cambridge University Press, 1987.)

descriptions of the palaces and other buildings of stone, the exotic goods that defined the material culture, and the ostentatious lifestyles of the elites of the East African coastal settlements. The origins of these communities are clearly indigenous. Cultural transformation came about gradually, as prestige and economic opportunity came to be associated with the descendants of foreign merchants, who often married into politically powerful indigenous families. Like their Southeast Asian counterparts, local African cultures experienced urban growth as a result of the expansion of maritime trade established after the ninth century. Elites sometimes converted to Islam; their descendants claimed connections to powerful and wealthy families in the Islamic world, while simultaneously utilizing their ties and connections to the African mainland's wealth.

Unlike the southeast Asian examples, Kilwa and the other African coastal communities did not emerge from the breakup of an empire. Rather, the particular characteristics of East African geography provided the setting that determined the relations between a hinterland rich in resources and difficult to access and a coast connected to other continents by trade winds. The interior sources of gold, ivory, and other goods were centralized by the inland states, some of which grew large and powerful. The excavation of one significant trade and urban center, Great Zimbabwe, has revealed Chinese porcelain, Persian pottery, cowrie shells, coastal coins, thousands of imported glass beads, and other goods amid its impressive stone palaces. The development of coastal "hubs" was a solution to the rapid rise of an urban, literate, mercantile Islamic society reliant on the administrative control of trade between the African hinterland and the Indian Ocean and Asian ports.

Some oral traditions and genealogies stress the lineage connections of those whose descendants would become identified as Swahili with Persian and other Islamic dynasties of the ninth century. Written documents also clearly reveal local means of legitimizing political office and power in the East African city-states. Powerful Islamic merchants married daughters of African kings, and these daughters retained their inherited titles, although their husbands exercised the authority of the office. Their male offspring claimed both. Power thus remained in local African hands, and the city-states continued as African political and trading entities.

■

TRADE, TECHNOLOGY, AND CULTURE: THE MALI EMPIRE IN WEST AFRICA

Of the numerous empires that developed and disappeared on the African continent, Mali was one of the first south of the Sahara to capture the attention of both the Islamic and European worlds. Mali also illustrates the range and diversity of historical sources, written and nonwritten, that may be brought to bear on the reconstruction of empires. Mali is an example of an empire that used culture, ideology, and language (Mande) to dominate an expanding territory. The grassland and semiarid region included virtually all of what was known as the savanna, or "Sudan," and the Sahel, from the Sahara's edge to the forest's edge in West Africa. The empire's manipulation of technology (iron and horses) and ecology (beneficial climatic shifts) emphasizes two of the possible means by which smaller polities may be integrated into the structure of a larger empire. At its height in the fourteenth century C.E. the Mali Empire covered an area greater than 24,000 square kilometers (9000 square miles), and it influenced, through trade connections, an even larger portion of West Africa for several centuries.

EARLY WEST AFRICAN STATES AND THE CARAVAN TRADE

Mali was not the first empire to occupy the large grasslands region of West Africa that straddled the Sahara, the semiarid edge of the desert known as the "Sahel" (literally the "shore" of the great ocean of sand, in Arabic) and the inland delta of the Niger River. According to oral traditions, the first state in that area was known as Ghana by the sixth century C.E. These traditions suggest that the political unity of ancient Ghana was based on its control of the very lucrative gold trade of the western Sudan and Sahara. Two of the three major sources of gold, Bambuk and Bure, were situated within reach of the Senegambia region, between the Senegal and Gambia Rivers and the inland Niger delta.

Caravans, small parties of merchants, carried goods from one town or settlement to the next, exchanging southern forest products such as kola nuts (chewed for their stimulant properties and everywhere offered as a symbol of hospitality), gold, ivory, wood, smoked and salted fish, cloth, and copper. These caravans had plied the desert sands for centuries before the rise of the West African states. The introduction of the camel in the second century C.E. allowed greater regularity of contact than the merchants traveling on foot in the earliest centuries of Saharan trade had achieved. By the twelfth century, West African gold and other products, such as so-called Moroccan leather, which actually came from the Hausa area of northern Nigeria, were supplied to Mediterranean markets and found their way to the fairs and markets of such places as Normandy and Britain. A prolonged series of droughts, diminishment of the alluvial sources of gold, and repeated attacks by North African peoples trying to control the lucrative caravan trade combined to bring about the disintegration of Ghana and the disruption of trade at the end of the eleventh century.

In the place of Ghana, the even greater empire of Mali developed from the conquest and union of several smaller states. It has been estimated that during the time of the Mali Empire, West Africa produced and supplied almost two-thirds of the world's gold. At its height, the Mali Empire covered much of West Africa and incorporated into one polity hunters, herders, nomads, merchants and farmers from many different language groups. Written historical sources, especially the writings of Arab scholars, have been too preoccupied with the wealth of Mali. The full historical understanding of the empire also relies on archaeological and oral sources.

SUNJATA AND MALI ORAL TRADITION

Oral traditions credit a single legendary and heroic figure with the final act of unification: Sunjata, the most powerful of the Mali rulers, finally subjected the Soso people to the authority of Mande languages and culture, with the ascendancy of the Keita clan. The praises of Sunjata today are sung by every *griot,* or Mande oral historian. The performance of the *griot* within Mande society and on behalf of the royal clan is an example of how history is used to legitimize the formation of an empire.

The epic of Sunjata devotes a major portion of its tale to sorcery and its relationship to political power. All great exploits, including the founding of empires, require control of the supernatural, or *nyama,* which the Mande view as both natural and mystical energy. Access to sorcery is a component of political leadership and as such is needed to wage successful military campaigns, to subdue enemies, and even to protect one's personal fortune. One of the central battles in the history of the Mali Empire is a sorcery war between Sunjata and a rival. Calling on great powers, Sunjata obtained the formula for a substance called *nasi,* "power of darkness, a thing used to harm someone." His *griot* poured it over the personal objects and sources of his rival's power, which were duly neutralized, and Sunjata triumphed.

Like many African divine rulers, Sunjata overcame obstacles, exile, and a physical handicap (the inability to walk from birth) in order to demonstrate his power (*nyama*). The *griot*s generally attribute most of the empire's administrative structures and innovations to the reign of Sunjata, who was probably responsible for the division of the empire into two military regions and for the codification of hereditary craft clans. During and after his reign, blacksmithing, leatherworking, and other specialist activities became associated with statecraft. The products of such activities supported the expansion of trade and empire.

Sunjata's Capital, Niani Sunjata rebuilt his capital at Niani, where he ruled for about twenty-five years, until his death. The location of Niani was forgotten for many generations. Archaeologists recently located the probable site of the Malian capital of Niani on the Sankarani River, an area rich in iron and gold. It was well situated on the forest edge to become the intersection of extensive trade routes that linked the different ecological zones of the empire. Excavations have revealed an Arab quarter and a royal villa, as well as stone house foundations and a mosque. Not unlike other well-known West African trading centers, such as Jenne on the Niger, Niani's royal quarter was surrounded by dispersed quarters or villages organized for various trades: smithing, weaving, fishing, leatherworking. Such concentration of specialist activities and the consequent exchange of goods and services controlled by the centralized authority are classic features of most world empires. Their formation having resulted from conquest, their continued control of material wealth not only cements the incorporation of new territories into a single unity but also pays the costs of government.

According to oral tradition, the unification of Mali occurred during the time of Sunjata. A popular epic poem records the struggles of Sunjata, the first Malian king, in a war between Sunjata's polity and several smaller states about 1220 and 1235 C.E. From the time of Sunjata's victory, the Mali Empire was cemented by the idea of Mande cultural superiority. While praise singers, oral historians who sang and performed the past, helped to spread the ideology, blacksmiths and others provided the tools of empire. Without iron weapons and leather and iron trappings for horses, military success would not have been possible.

CONTEMPORARY DESCRIPTIONS OF MALI

The travels of Mansa Musa (King Musa), a fourteenth-century ruler of Mali, however, brought attention to the golden wealth of the African empire. Like many of his predecessors, Mansa Musa had eagerly embraced Islam, in large part because of the international commercial world the religion opened up. As the Islamic faith gradually spread across North Africa and south across the Sahara (between about 750 and 1400 C.E.), it brought merchants and clerics, goods and ideas. Mali, with its capital at Niani not far from the Niger, became the trading partner of merchants with connections to West Asia and beyond. Like any devout Muslim, Mansa Musa was required to attempt the pilgrimage (*hajj*) to Mecca, which he did in 1325. According to contemporary accounts, Mansa Musa traveled with thousands of porters and servants bedecked with gold. In Cairo, his generosity and wealth were legendary. It was Mansa Musa who gave away so much gold that he caused the market to crash and depressed world prices. From this time forward, European and Arab cartographers depicted the Sudan with portraits of the African ruler holding a large gold nugget. Yet Mansa Musa is rarely mentioned in the oral tradition. He is remembered for having been unfaithful to Mande traditions and having wasted the imperial treasury.

The caravans of gold made the Mali Empire a celebrated name far beyond West Africa. The caravan routes met at Niani and other staging posts, and their protection was a major function of the empire. Gold, salt, copper, and kola nuts were central to Mali's economy. Following the reign of Sunjata, Mali became the world's largest producer of gold. Along with the movement of material goods went the dissemination of Mande language, technology, and culture. Even later, the empire would serve as the major promoter of Islamic ideology and culture across the West African savanna.

Ibn Battuta While the vast majority of written historical sources on the Mali Empire were compiled by non-Africans who rarely set foot in Africa and never ventured south of the Sahara, an important exception is the eyewitness account by the Arab traveler Ibn Battuta. Its wealth of detail and observation makes his memoirs, *Rihla,* an unprecedented portrait of life in fourteenth-century Mali. Ibn Battuta was born in Tangier, Morocco, in 1304.

Although he studied law, he began his celebrated travels as a young man in 1326 with the pilgrimage to Mecca. In the course of his lifetime he journeyed more than 70,000 miles to China, Southeast Asia, India, East Africa, the Niger, and the Byzantine Empire. Ibn Battuta considered himself a citizen of the Dar al-Islam, the entire "abode," or world, of Islamic civilization. It was through this lens that Ibn Battuta viewed Mali in 1352–1353.

After two months of traveling across the Sahara from Sijilmasa in Morocco, Ibn Battuta's caravan reached Walata. The oldest city of Mali, Walata was a trading center where Sudanese and Berber merchants and scholars interacted. It was here that Ibn Battuta had his first taste of the inroads Islam had made into the integrity of Mali's indigenous ceremonial and cultural life. A meeting with the provincial governor shocked the visitor, not only because of the meagerness of his host's offering to him of a calabash of millet, honey, and yogurt, but because the man, according to West African custom, never addressed his visitor directly but spoke only through an interpreter.

The route between Walata and Niani, the Mali ruler's capital, was safe and well secured by the administrative and military controls of the Mali Empire. But here, too, Ibn Battuta was shocked by the lack of adherence to orthodox Islamic custom and practice. He wrote of partially clothed women, subjects who prostrated themselves before the *mansa* (king), and royal poets who danced in feathers and masks, all of which were spectacles outlawed by the orthodox Islam Ibn Battuta knew. From Ibn Battuta's account we learn that although Mali officially belonged to the Islamic world and thereby had expanded the trading opportunities available to the empire and its ruling elite, it was clear that Islam was to be found only in the veneer of Mali's material life; the underlying substance of Mali's culture was a belief in Mande superiority.

GROWING INEQUALITIES IN THE MALI EMPIRE

Another important feature of the Mali Empire that we learn from Ibn Battuta is how much social inequality existed. One of the consequences of the expansion of empire through trade and military means was the capture of prisoners of war, who then became sources of male soldiers and female slaves. The Sahelian and Saharan towns of the Mali Empire were organized as both staging posts in the long-distance caravan trade and trading centers for the various West African products. At Taghaza, for example, salt was exchanged; at Takedda, copper. Ibn Battuta observed the employment of slave labor in both towns. During most of his journey, Ibn Battuta traveled with a retinue that included slaves, most of whom carried goods for trade but would also be traded as slaves. On the return from Takedda to Morocco, his caravan transported 600 female slaves, suggesting that slavery was a substantial part of the commercial activity of the empire's fringes.

Gender Divisions There were many more female slaves than male slaves traded in the empire, a fact that points out the inequality that existed between the genders. The variation in women's social positions increased with the growth of the empire's towns. Women, usually slaves, were valued porters in the trans-Saharan caravan trade. They sometimes served as concubines. Additionally, female labor produced salt, cloth for export, and most of the local foodstuffs essential to the provisions required by urban centers. Men were hunters, farmers, merchants, and specialists, in addition to frequently being conscripted as soldiers.

A general feature of empires is the increased exploitation of social inequality. Imperial growth everywhere depended in part on women, the appropriation of female labor as well as the mechanisms for the exclusion of women from the sources of political and economic power. An empire's expansion ultimately relied on its increasing the supplies of food for its armies and other sources of wealth for trade. In addition to their reproductive role, women produced goods. Not surprisingly, women had not played a prominent role in the preimperial male-dominated elite authority of West African society, either. Women are rarely mentioned in the oral historical record, which was controlled by male *griot*s and their male descendants. In the epic of Sunjata they do appear as potential power sources—mothers, sisters, and sorceresses—despite their unequal access to true political power.

ECOTONE, ECOLOGY, AND CHANGE

Management of the trans-Saharan trade was a central feature of the Mali Empire, as well as of its predecessor (Ghana) and successor (Songhai); our discussion of this management would be incomplete without an explanation of the ecological control required by the imperial expansion. The geographical boundaries of the empire straddled three distinct ecological zones. That is to say, Mali was situated on an ecotone, an area that straddled the borders of desert, Sahel, and savanna. The exchange between these regions, which supplied quite different products, also created a lucrative source of income. Internal trade and occasional tributary relations, with outlying regions being tapped for support, proved necessary to the functioning of the empire. Centers of trade such as Jenne, Gao, and Timbuktu were similarly situated on ecotones. However, this incorporation of the products of several different ecological zones was not the only way in which ecology played a role in the fortunes of the Mali Empire: much of

MAP 6.2 The Main Trans-Saharan Routes, Fourteenth Century, Enhanced the Mali Empire

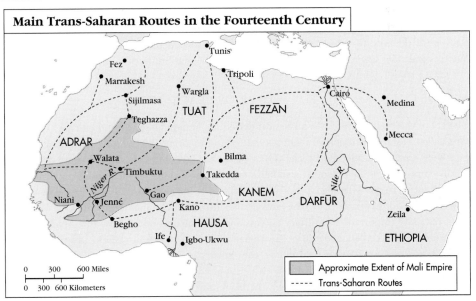

Main Trans-Saharan Routes in the Fourteenth Century

Tunis
Fez
Tripoli
Marrakesh
Wargla
Cairo
Sijilmasa
TUAT
FEZZĀN
Medina
Teghazza
Mecca
ADRAR
Walata
Bilma
Timbuktu
Takedda
Niani
Gao
KANEM
DARFŪR
Jenné
Kano
Zeila
Begho
HAUSA
Ife
Igbo-Ukwu
ETHIOPIA
Niger R.
Nile R.

0   300   600 Miles
0   300 600 Kilometers

Approximate Extent of Mali Empire
- - - - - Trans-Saharan Routes

the expansion of the Mali Empire was made possible by the Mande's military use of the horse, which made them dependent on certain ecological conditions for its breeding and survival, and these conditions existed in the savanna grasslands of Mali.

Horses and Ecological Change   Traders from Mali carefully controlled the breeding and use of horses in West Africa. Reportedly, they rarely traded mares south of the Sahara; therefore, despite their obvious value, horses remained rare items, connoting prestige and status outside the empire. The cavalry was extremely important in gaining a military advantage, particularly in the savanna grasslands. Although many towns in the Sahel had been walled before the introduction of the horse, probably to help control the influx of trade as early as the second-century C.E. introduction of camels, the number of settlements and villages surrounded by protective mud walls increased during the era of the Mali cavalry. The walls were necessary to stop sudden attacks by warriors on horseback. Here, as in other parts of the world where the horse was successfully exploited, the element of surprise was significant.

Ecological factors played a paramount role in defining and limiting the extent of the spread of Mande culture and society. In tropical Africa, the humidity and presence of the tsetse fly limited the use of the horse. The tsetse fly thrived in damp and swampy conditions and spread diseases that were deadly to horses. Thus, the occurrence of a particularly dry climatic period in West Africa between 1100 and 1500 takes on a certain significance. Horse breeders, warriors, and traders alike derived great advantage from that progressive dessication, which inhibited the spread of the tsetse fly. With the onset of a drier climate, expansion on horseback was favored over a much wider area. Sunjata's military success over his rival was closely associated with cavalry warfare. Also, the regions occupied by Sahelian and savanna vegetation pushed southward at the expense of the southern forests, increasing the territory in which horses could survive. The elliptical lines of the Mandes' expansion with the aid of their cavalry could then extend east and west. Only the rain-forest zone, where other ethnic groups lived, remained inhospitable to the empire's warriors and their horses. Conversely, changing ecological conditions during the wet period between about 1500 and 1630 also influenced the fortunes of the empire, which had begun to collapse toward the end of the fifteenth century. Wetter conditions limited the use of cavalry and put the Mali military at a disadvantage.

MANDE CULTURE AND THE POWER OF BLACKSMITHS

The era of the Mali Empire was a classical period for Mande language and culture. The military, economic, and commercial relations that bound together the far-flung reaches of the empire were crucially cemented by the power of Mande cultural imperialism. How notions of Mande superiority were extended also helps explain the fluidity of the empire's internal relations. Central to the effective spread of the Mande cultural system and its worldview were power associations controlled by the empire's blacksmiths. The metallurgical skills of smiths were critically important to military success and agricultural operations. But Mande metalworkers were more than essential occupational specialists who followed behind the warriors. They constituted a caste that held *nyama,* the "energy of action" and supernatural power. Together with *griots* and leatherworkers (who supplied saddles, bridles, sword sheaths, garments, pouches for amulets, and so on), the blacksmiths provided necessary services of both a practical and a spiritual nature.

FIGURE 6.6 Men's Meeting House, Ireli Village, Mali

Associations of men consolidated power and trade connections across much of West Africa.

SOURCE: National Museum of African Art, Eliot Elisofon Photographic Archives, Smithsonian Institution. Photo by Philip Ravenhill.

According to tradition, it was blacksmiths who were responsible for the founding of lodges, or centers for the transmission of Mande culture inside host communities, and they occupied the principal leadership roles within the lodges they established wherever they settled. The lodges were secret associations, that is, membership was limited to those initiated into the secrets of the craft. Like the later mosques of the Islamic era, they offered spiritual protection and moral leadership to the members of their community. They were where Mande speakers gathered. Lodges also maintained control over the physical roads and bridges that linked the empire's commercial realms, by repairing them and ensuring their safety. They protected trade and the trader, who enjoyed the professional affiliations and sense of common community provided to lodge members. While they were dependent on clients both inside the Mande associations and in the larger community, blacksmiths also maintained their separateness and control over the knowledge of smelting, metalworking, ritual, and healing powers that constituted the source of their power. Within the association and against the backdrop of host communities, the *griots* functioned as amplifiers of Mande superiority, articulating the claims of a heroic age.

The dessication of the first half of the millennium limited the extent of regions that could support iron-smelting activities. Both smelting and smithing required large quantities of wood to make charcoal for fuel. It is also likely, however, that the smiths helped extend the boundaries of their empire by moving further and further afield in search of wood to sustain their industry. The deforestation that resulted from extensive smelting and concentrated smithing opened up savanna woodland to their comrades on horseback. Thus, for many West African peoples the era of the Mali Empire meant their first encounter with the economic, cultural, and ecological forces of imperialism.

THE IMPACT OF MALI

The Mali Empire's fortuitous combination of technological skills, cultural control, and ecological circumstances came to an end in the late fifteenth century, but the legacy of the Mali Empire would be felt far and wide for centuries. Mande words that survive in the languages of forest regions are evidence of the empire's widespread linguistic influence and of the probable prestige associated with using the language of the elite trading culture. In Hausa, the language spoken in northern Nigeria, for example, the word for "Muslim" is *Imale,* which suggests that the Mali Empire may also be credited with the diffusion of Islam after the mid–fourteenth century. Through contact with Mande traders, items of technology were dispersed throughout the empire and southward into the West African forest towns and states. The evidence comes from the material culture of places distant from the empire: the use of the horizontal loom for weaving cloth spread from North Africa to the Niger and then southward, as evidenced by the spindle whorls excavated at sites along the Niger and south in the trading town of Begho in what is today modern Ghana; the introduction of the horse-mounted cavalry in the Yoruba state of Oyo, in Nigeria, spread from the savanna through a gap in the forest; Arabic-inscribed brass vessels appear in the towns of the Akan (Ghana) forest. Long after the fall of Mali, the institutions of lodges remained in societies from the west Atlantic to the Niger, albeit reduced in power and influence. There remained as well the voices of the *griot*s, whose ancestors had created the heroes of the Mande world and who continued to sing the praises of Sunjata, recalling the events of past centuries. In so doing, they breathed life into the history of the Mali Empire long after the walls of its palaces had crumbled.

■

NOMADS AND EMPIRE IN EURASIA

By the early first millennium C.E., a regular pattern of relationships developed in many places between nomadic or pastoral economies and agrarian ones. Different economic systems emerged from different environments and gave rise to various forms of social organization and political order. For example, the needs of water control on the north China plain contributed to the early creation of a highly centralized bureaucratic government, which taxed the agricultural economy. In contrast, the nomadic pastoralists who inhabited the lands beyond the Great Wall were highly mobile, dependent on herding and pasturage, conditions not conducive to the development of a centralized political order. Across the frontiers that divided these two different ways of life, trading relationships and warfare were both common. This frontier in East Asia was marked by the incorporation of defensive walls built by earlier northern states into the Great Wall during the third century B.C.E., at the time of the first unification of China and the creation of the first empire.

ACROSS THE GREAT WALL: NOMADIC STATES AND THE CHINESE EMPIRE

For nearly 2000 years, the Great Wall symbolized the barrier between the peoples, cultures, and ecologies of the steppe and those of the sown land. Beginning in the third century B.C.E., much of the history of China was dominated by its relations with the nomads and pastoral peoples beyond the Great Wall. The two major dynasties of the Han (206 B.C.E.–220 C.E.) and Tang (618–907 C.E.) were separated in time by four centuries of foreign invasion and conquest by northern nomads; during the Song dynasty (960–1279), pastoral peoples founded states on the northern frontiers of China; and in the thirteenth century, the full conquest of China was achieved by the Mongols.

The growth of states among China's neighbors to the north, northeast, and northwest was in part the result of the long-term evolution of Chinese-style political institutions among the non-Han peoples beyond the Great Wall. The assimilation of Chinese political ideas enabled their leaders to unite various groups into confederations and in some cases to create a centralized bureaucratic state.

Qidan Liao The Qidan Liao (990–1126) was the earliest such state, bringing other ethnic groups to the northeast of China together under its leadership. The Chinese-style dynastic name "Liao" was adopted by the Qidan, a Mongolic people, who laid claim to territory within the Great Wall and stabilized their relationship with Song China through diplomacy. The Liao was later destroyed by an alliance between the Chinese and the Jurchen people from Manchuria, former vassals of the Qidan Liao. The Jurchen established their own Chinese-style state, with the dynastic name of Jin, in 1115. They soon overcame their Chinese allies, and in 1127 all of north China fell under the control of the Jurchen Jin state.

Jin Rule in North China The Jin ruled north China through a combination of native Chinese and Jurchen institutions and personnel, unifying their tribal background in the forested river valleys of Manchuria with centralized bureaucratic rule modeled on the Chinese government. Both native Chinese and Jurchen, along with other non-Chinese peoples, served in the Jin government. The fusion of political orders representing two distinct ways of life rooted in different economies is vividly illustrated by the Jurchen rule of north China.

THE RISE OF THE MONGOLS

Sometime around the close of the eleventh and the beginning of the twelfth centuries, Mongol clans began to organize into tribal collectives under the leadership of chieftains whose power was based on personal loyalty. Dwelling in the steppes of Mongolia, they had a pastoral economy based on sheep, goats, and yaks for sustenance (food, clothing, and shelter), camels for trade-related transportation, and horses for hunting, herding, communication, and warfare. Because their economy was subject to the vagaries of drought and cold, as well as other potentially devastating problems such as animal diseases, the Mongols were dependent on trade in grain, textiles, tea, and other goods with their sedentary agricultural neighbors, particularly the Chinese. The Chinese likewise had need of goods from their nomadic neighbors, especially horses. The trade relations between the neighboring states periodically disintegrated into warfare, with Chinese raids on Mongol camps or Mongol raids on Chinese communities.

The Technology and Environment of Mongol Success The success of the Mongols in their expansion across Eurasia relied heavily on the adaptation of the traditional technology of horsebreeding to environment. Mongol horsebreeders

FIGURE 6.7 Training Horses. By Zhao Mengfu (1254–1322) of the Mongol Yuan Dynasty

SOURCE: National Palace Museum, Taipei, Taiwan, Republic of China.

had preserved an early form of domesticated horse, one that resembled the prehistoric horse depicted in Paleolithic cave art. Its stocky body and thick, coarse mane helped it to survive in the extremely cold and dry temperatures of Mongolia. Furthermore, Mongols did not shelter or feed their animals, instead breeding qualities of independent foraging in a semiwild state. The Mongol technology of warfare also differed from the rest of Asia's, forcing the abandonment of chariots and the use of well-armed warriors on horseback. Almost all men and women rode horseback with great agility and endurance, and the elite militarism of other cultures was unknown in nomadic Mongol society. Indeed, other cultures borrowed heavily from their Mongol enemies. From the Abbasids of West Asia to the Chinese Tang dynasty in East Asia, men began to wear trousers for horseback riding through their influence.

Chinggis Khan By 1200, the Mongol tribes had joined together in a large confederation. Under the leadership of Chinggis (ca. 1162–1227), who was elected *khan* (chief) in 1206 by an assembly of tribal chieftains, they began to bring other tribes, such as the Turkic Uighurs, under their control. With this step, the Mongol conquest of Asia began. Chinggis was a charismatic political leader who organized the Mongol tribes and a brilliant military strategist who led the Mongol armies to victory. Along with the military strength that made conquest possible, the Mongols were driven to conquest by the uncertain nature of their economic base, which depended in part on the fluctuating fortunes of trade and made more precarious by a climatic change that produced colder weather and consequently poorer pasturage for their animals.

Religion and Mongol Rule Religious sanction for the authority of Chinggis Khan and the conquest of the world came from the sky god, the principal deity of the steppe. Under Chinggis's leadership a written script, adapted from Uighur Turkic, was created for the Mongol language, and a law code was issued to provide guidance first for the administration of the Mongol tribes and later, as it was modified, for the governing of con-

FIGURE 6.8 Portrait of Chinggis Khan in His Sixties

SOURCE: National Palace Museum, Taipei, Taiwan, Republic of China.

quered lands and peoples. Succession to the position of *khan,* however, was not institutionalized, and at Chinggis's death, despite his stated will that he be succeeded by his third son, Ögödei (1186–1241), there was no clear successor. In 1229, two years after Chinggis's death, the territories under Mongol control were divided among Chinggis's grandson Batu (d. 1255),

MAP 6.3 The Extent of the Mongol Empire

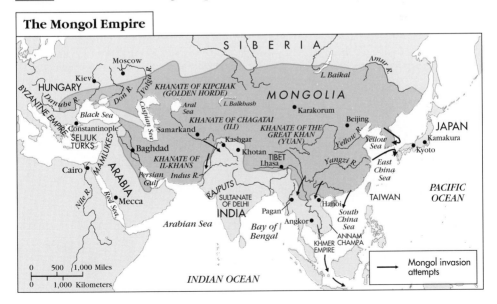

who became the *khan* of the Golden Hordes (the western lands, eventually including Russia); Chinggis's son Chaghadai (ca. 1185–1242), who assumed control of central Asia; and another son, who was assigned responsibility for the Mongolian homeland and north China. In a gesture of compliance with Chinggis's will, Ögödei became the *khaghan,* or Khan of Khans, ruler over all Mongol domains.

The Expansion of the Mongol Empire   During the next generation, the Mongol Empire expanded into China, Russia, and Islamic lands in West Asia, confronting vastly different political, religious, and social conditions in each region. Despite continuing conflicts among themselves over leadership, Mongol rulers in each khanate (territory ruled by a *khan*) of the empire were able to implement an efficient administrative system that integrated Chinese, Muslim, Turkic, and native elements. The Chinese empire under Chinggis's grandson Khubilai Khan (1215–1294) may be taken as one example of Mongol administration of a conquered territory. With a population sixty times that of the entire Mongol population of Asia, an agricultural economic base, a complex and sophisticated political and cultural tradition, and the rule of a highly educated elite, China presented a formidable challenge to its Mongol rulers.

FIGURE 6.9   Mongols Using Catapult in Battle. From Rashid al-Din's (d. 1318) *Collection of Histories.*

Rashid al-Din was a Persian historian, doctor and official at the court of the Mongol rulers of Persia, the Il-Khans. He wrote a universal history which remains an important source on the Mongols.

SOURCE: Edinburgh University Library.

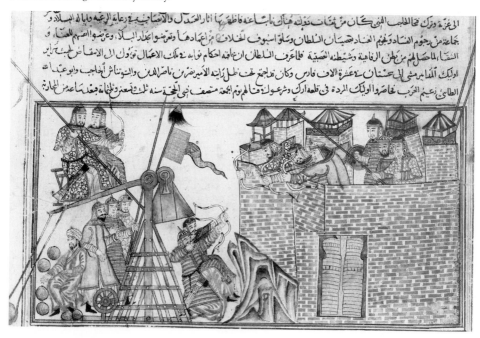

MONGOL RULE IN CHINA

Before the Mongol conquest of the Jurchen Jin state in north China, an official of the Jin government had convinced Ögödei (r. 1229–1241), against the advice of other Mongol leaders, not to turn north China into pasturage for the Mongols' herds but to utilize its agricultural productivity to enrich the Mongol rulers. When the Jin state was absorbed by the Mongols, the advanced iron technology and the skilled labor force of north Chinese ironworkers, developed during the Northern Song dynasty, also came under Mongol control. The Mongols' ability to make use of such resources, in addition to the agricultural output of north China and eventually that of the fertile Yangzi delta, was a crucial factor in the continued expansion of the Mongol Empire in the decades after Chinggis's death. With the conquest of Jin, the Mongols were also able to make use of Jin institutions that had been adapted from Chinese models. The Mongol experience made the transition to ruling over the entire population of China relatively smooth.

The Mongols and the Mandate of Heaven   Chinese political ideology favored the adaptation of Mongol rule, in that the Mandate of Heaven in theory could be conferred on any ruler, and non-Chinese peoples, including most recently the Jurchen rulers of the Jin state in north China, had a long history of establishing states and kingdoms within China's borders. But many Confucian scholars nevertheless scorned serving their Mongol lords, regarding them as "barbarian" conquerors. While some members of the Chinese scholar-official elite served the Mongols as administrators, others withdrew from public life and refused to become officials in Khubilai Khan's administration. Khubilai and his successors did adopt Chinese institutions and practices to a considerable degree, including the renewal of the civil service examination system in 1315, although the Mongols instituted ethnic quotas for examination degrees that seriously disadvantaged Chinese in favor of Mongols and other non-Chinese peoples, such as the Uighurs. Khubilai built a new capital, site of the modern capital of Beijing and imperial capital without interruption from 1421 until the twentieth century.

Beginning in the 1350s, rebellions led by the Chinese against their Mongol conquerors gradually brought an end to Mongol rule. The effects of these rebellions were exacerbated by power struggles among the Mongol leaders that seriously weakened their authority and control. When the Yuan (Mongol) dynasty fell in 1368 and the restoration of native Chinese rule under the Ming was declared, other khanates of the Mongol Empire similarly began to crumble. Chinggis and his successors in the thirteenth and early fourteenth centuries had succeeded in creating a huge empire by their military prowess, discipline, and strength, and by their strategic and logistical skill at maneuvering large numbers of troops over long distances. Their military abilities were grounded in their superior horsemanship, honed in the course of Mongol life as nomadic herders and hunters. Their efficient communication network in the form of a courier system operated by riders on horseback was an essential part of their military operations. But their expansion and conquest of the Eurasian world would have stopped short of creating an empire had they not been able to successfully make use of the human and material resources of the lands they conquered to fuel the machinery of expansion and to provide the tools of empire.

Mongol rule had to be adapted to vastly different circumstances across the Eurasian continent. China was only one khanate among four, and the Mongol penetration of Europe left a profound legacy in European history as well. The Mongols moved westward out of Asia into Europe in a series of invading waves followed by settlement among and control of the indigenous peoples among whom they appeared.

THE MONGOLS IN RUSSIA AND EUROPE

The earliest Europeans among whom the Mongols appeared were the peoples of the southern Russian steppe. As they advanced during the winter of 1237–1238, the conquerors were preceded by envoys demanding that the inhabitants of the steppe accept Mongol supremacy. Resistance led to the forceful taking of fortresses and occupation of territories, including the north Russian forest lands as well as the southern steppe. The invaders were determined to break the power of the Russian princes and to leave them no escape. By early 1238, the north Russian principalities had ceased to exist, and the Mongols turned south into the steppes to recuperate before undertaking new advances westward.

Their strategy was effective, their harsh policy deliberate, and they moved over great distances at incredible speeds unmatched by their European opponents. In their panic, thirteenth-century Europeans justified their failure to halt the Mongol invasion with legendary excuses, many of which have persisted. The Mongols' savagery was much commented upon, and their success was explained by their having made an alliance with Satan. They were accused of cutting an ear off every Christian they killed. Following the initial fury and success of their invasion, the Mongols settled down on the Hungarian plain in the Danube Valley, where they established a government administration. They appointed judges and officials, placed Mongols in charge of towns, and proclaimed amnesty for any who would recognize Mongol authority. Then, just as the Mongol leaders were making plans to resume their assault on western Europe, news came that Ögödei, the Khan of Khans, was dead. Mongol law required that, after the death of a ruler, all offspring of the dynasty, wherever they might be, must return to Mongolia for the election of a new *khan*. This law had greater weight than the opportunity of conquering the Western world, and accordingly Europe was saved.

Following the death of Ögödei Khan in 1241, the Mongols vanished from central Europe unexpectedly, as suddenly as they had come. They remained on the eastern edge of Europe, in Russia, until they were defeated by a Russian army in 1380, the beginning of a process that was to drive them back into Asia. The princes of Muscovy (the region of modern Moscow) assumed leadership of this effort and accordingly gained control of the emerging Russian state. One of them, Ivan the Great (r. 1462–1505), who proclaimed himself czar (ruler) of all the Russias, succeeded in pushing the Mongols out of north Russia and drove them eastward beyond the Ural mountains.

THE MONGOLS IN SOUTH ASIA

The Mongols also moved into South Asia, where they established themselves in India. An enormous peninsula jutting out from the Eurasian landmass, divided from other lands by sea and by the mighty Himalayan mountains along its northern border, India is penetrable by only two corridors. The northeast one, through Burma, is long and difficult and not easily used. There are also a number of usable passes in the northwest corridor that links India, through Afghanistan, with Central Asia. These geographical features are significant to the movement of peoples into the relatively isolated subcontinent. Several different Central Asian peoples, who had come under the sway of Chinggis Khan and his descendants, subsequently invaded India via the northwest corridor.

THE MONGOL EMPIRE IN WORLD HISTORY

In the early thirteenth century, the foundations were laid of what has been called "the largest contiguous land-based empire in human history." The Mongol Empire endured for only a century, but it had a profound impact on world history. Mongol armies linked vast areas of the Eurasian continent, bringing about an era known ironically as the *pax Mongolica,* the "Mongolian peace." What is remarkable about the Mongol Empire is not that it was relatively short-lived but that an empire of such scale and complexity existed at all at a time when communication and transportation were largely dependent on the horse and camel. The Mongol courier system was known for its speed and efficiency, and the effectiveness of this communication network, along with military skill and administrative ability, accounts in large part for the rise of the Mongols from a tribal confederation to one of the most powerful empires in world history.

■

TRADE AND TRIBUTE: EMPIRES IN THE AMERICAS

Earlier in this century, historians wrote of trade as "the great civilizer." Definitions of civilization aside, there is no doubt that trade has supported increasingly complex social and political orders throughout the world. As we have seen with the Southeast Asian empires of Funan and Srivijaya, maritime and riverine trade was the basis of the knotting of political ties that bound diverse communities together under centralized rule. Though based on overland rather than maritime or riverine trade, both the Aztec and Incan Empires of the fifteenth century were the culmination of empire building based on complex systems of trade and tribute in central Mexico and in the Andean highlands of South America. As Hinduism, Buddhism, and Islam in Southeast Asian empires, and both Islam and indigenous beliefs in Mali, provided sanctions for rulers, for both the Aztecs and the Incas, religion played a central role in legitimizing the power of ruling elites and in sanctioning warfare and the exaction of tribute from conquered territories.

THE AZTEC EMPIRE

The Toltecs and the Rise of the Aztecs With the demise of the great city of Teotihuacán in the Valley of Mexico (ca. 750 C.E.) and the abandonment of Mayan cities in the Yucatán peninsula by around 800 C.E., the Toltecs rose to power. The Toltec Empire grew to be extensive, stretching over much of central Mexico and the former Mayan territories. Evidence of trade between the Toltecs and their neighbors to the north suggests that the Toltecs' influence reached far beyond the limits of their political control, perhaps even to regions as distant as the Mississippian culture in North America.

Following the collapse of the Toltecs in about 1150, city-states in the Valley of Mexico competed with one another to become the Toltecs' heirs. Known for their skill as warriors, the Aztecs (or "Mexica," as they called themselves) gradually established dominance over rival groups in the Valley of Mexico, where in the aftermath of the Toltec collapse the population was concentrated around a string of life-sustaining lakes. Claiming Toltec ancestry to legitimize their conquests, the Aztecs continued the Toltec concerns with genealogy and militarism, along with religious rituals, including human sacrifice and ritual cannibalism.

The Aztec Religion The Aztec religion drew on common Mesoamerican traditions, including those of the Olmecs, the Mayas, and the Toltecs, providing an identity rooted in the past that could be adapted to the needs of a new political order. The most important ideological change associated with the Aztec transition from wandering warrior groups to empire was the elaboration of ancient Mesoamerican religious beliefs and practices relating warfare to human sacrifice. Combining the Aztec patron god Huizilopochtli (the sun) and their own military ambitions with an ancient vision of a constant struggle among the forces of the universe, Aztec belief made the regular appearance of the sun dependent on the continuation of military exploits and human sacrifice. The sacrifice of humans was tied to the sun god's demand for ritual offerings, and war was necessary to provide sacrificial victims. Warfare was imagined as the earthly reenactment of the titanic battle waged across the skies, the sacred war of the sun, which daily had to fight evil to make its way from east to west. Only human sacrifice could assist in the positive outcome of this sacred event and thus ensure the daily rising of the sun.

The Aztec ruler eventually became identified with both secular authority and divine power, a representative of the gods on earth. In Aztec theology, human sacrifice and wars of conquest were combined with the political authority of the ruler as aspects of a state cult. Aztec rulers believed that two things were necessary to maintain the empire: tribute in food and raw materials from conquered peoples in outlying provinces, and sacrificial victims. Warfare provided both. The tribute gained was a major consequence of the warfare waged on behalf of the empire, which included most of Mesoamerica. It has been estimated that millions of pounds of maize, beans, and chocolate, and millions of cotton cloaks, war costumes, feathers, shields, and precious stones, were drawn to the Aztec center at Tenochtitlán each year.

FIGURE 6.10 Coatlicue, or "Serpent Skirt," Mother of Aztec Ancestral Deity, Huitzilpochtli, Mexico

SOURCE: Werner Forman/Art Resource, NY.

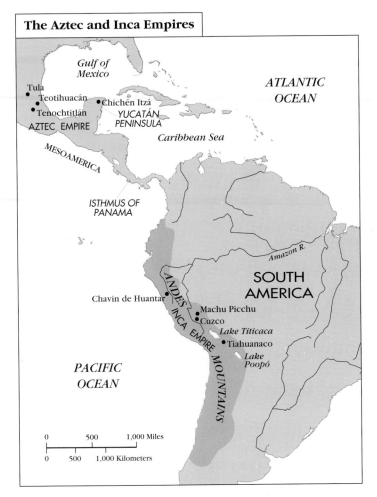

The Aztec and Inca Empires

MAP 6.4 The Empires of Mesoamerica and South America

Aztec Society Aztec society was profoundly urban. In the fifteenth century, approximately one-quarter of the population of the Valley of Mexico resided in cities and towns. The Aztec capital of Tenochtitlán, the site of modern Mexico City near the ancient center of Teotihuacán, was built on swampland in the Valley of Mexico. This and other urban centers were supported by the rural populations of the surrounding areas, who were required to pay tribute and engage in trade. A specialized class of long-distance traders functioned as "advance men," or merchant-spies, on behalf of the state. They would be followed by warriors whose military success ensured a steady flow of goods. The successful maintenance of the relationship between the urban center and the hinterland, compelled by military control exercised by Aztec warriors, was essential to the empire's survival. The administration of the Aztec Empire was carried out by an elaborate bureaucracy of officials, including tax collectors,

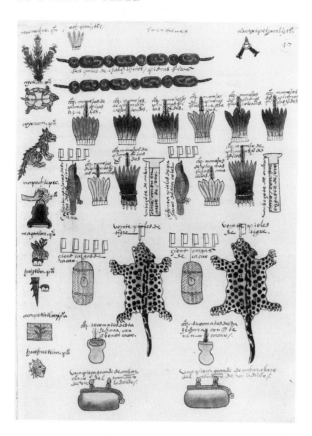

FIGURE 6.11 Tribute-Roll Section of Codex Mendoza Showing Extent and Complexity of Aztec Tributary Relationships.

Symbols at top and along left-hand margin indicate places that owed tribute to Tenochtitlan; other symbols depict amounts of tribute due, such as jade feathers or jaguar pelts.

SOURCE: The Bodleian Library, Oxford. MS Arch. Selden A.1, fol. 47.

judges, priests, ambassadors, treasurers, and a security force. Occupants of such positions were appointed by the Aztec ruler from either the nobility or warrior classes. Each status carried with its title well-defined privileges, duties, and powers. They were distinguished by observable differences in dress, accommodation, diet, and the respect accorded them.

A good way of assessing the distribution of power and the allocation of social status is by comparing the tribute commitments of various groups. In Aztec society, which may be visualized as a pyramidal sructure, tribute was based on class affiliations and economic specialization. The nobility, at the apex of the pyramid, provided military service, as did the class of professional warriors, who through bravery could achieve a higher status than the one into which they had been born. Further down the pyramid were commoners and farmers. Their labor and production supported those above. Merchants and craft specialists provided the goods that flowed through the arteries of the empire. In the more distant reaches of the empire, trade was conducted and tribute paid in regional specialties, such as feathers or obsidian. The much larger population at the pyramid's base was composed of persons with limited or almost no rights. Slavery existed as both a temporary condition, into which destitute individuals voluntarily sold themselves or their children to pay debts or were sent as punishment for crimes, and as the permanent status of prisoners of war. Prisoners of war often became the unfortunate victims of ritual torture and sacrifice by the state.

The Aztec Economy The Aztec economy was based on a system of highly intensive agriculture. Agricultural workers were attached to large rural estates, where
they labored in fields belonging to the nobility and warrior classes. Irrigation works, effectively controlled rural labor, and an elaborate series of canals, dams, and terraces helped to
feed the empire. While the grandeur of large monumental architecture and the rich, colorful
material culture of the upper classes have impressed and captured the attention of scholars,
the Aztec Empire was sustained by the agricultural labor of the masses, who received from
the empire little protection or spiritual sustenance in return.

The rulers of the Aztec Empire explained the need for wars as a means of obtaining slaves
for sacrifice, rather than as an economic enterprise. A kind of circular logic maintained that
sacrificial victims could be obtained through war, while war could be waged successfully only
by sacrificing victims. Equally important were the complex systems of roads and waterways
that brought goods and peoples to central markets. The complex tributary empire was a violent world in which war was deemed necessary and duly glorified.

THE INCAN EMPIRE

Like the Aztecs in Mesoamerica, the Incan Empire in South America rose to power in the fifteenth century by building on earlier cultures in the region between the Pacific Ocean and
the chain of Andes Mountains extending along the western flank of the continent. The Incan
Empire covered a highly diverse topographical area as it descended from mountains as high as
three or four miles, down upland basins and plains, and across a narrow desert strip transected
by small rivers to the ocean shore. In the uplands, terraces and spillways were necessary for
cultivation; in the desert, canals were essential. These differing environments required and
enabled a variety of human activities and gave rise to the organized exploitation of these activities through a centralized political order. Systematic authority was essential for managing
reciprocal production, and the movement and exchange of goods necessitated a hierarchical
political organization.

Efforts by other Andean people to control the area of the Incan Empire, six times the size
of modern France, were made as early as 800, but they were unsuccessful. The two centuries
before the establishment of Incan dominance in the fifteenth century were, in fact, a period
of political fragmentation. In 1400, the Incan state, one of several small states, was about
200 years old. During the reign of the Pachacuti ("he who remakes the world") Inca
(r. 1438–1471), the expansion that created the Incan Empire began after a vision in which
Pachacuti was told that he would conquer many peoples. The Incan Empire was vast but
short-lived; it is considered to have ended with the Spanish conquest in 1536.

Expanding from their center, Cuzco, the Incas created a vast state spread along the western coast of South America for more than 2500 miles (4300 km), from modern Colombia to
modern Chile. The area contained an estimated 9 to 13 million inhabitants who, prior to the
Incan conquest, had resided in agricultural communities under the leadership of local chieftains. The Incas' success in establishing control was only partially the result of their military
prowess.

Inca Conquest and Rule If the Incas' success at empire building cannot be wholly explained
by their military power, it can be understood in terms of their orga-

nizational skill and by the power of their religion. As they conquered, they co-opted, organized, and converted. They aimed to be beneficent, lenient conquerors, preferring peaceful incorporation of local communities to the destruction of those who resisted. Those who acquiesced to Incan control avoided being plundered. Chieftains of conquered areas who did not resist were adopted into the structure of the empire as it emerged. Some were co-opted by marriage into the royal family; blood and lineage ties were important. By contrast, those who resisted the Incas or rebelled were harshly dealt with and subject to severe penalties ranging from mass removal and redistribution to slaughter. The ideology of conquest claimed that Incan rule brought reason; that is, it saved people from themselves and lifted them out of savagery and war, out of the chaos that had existed before the conquest.

Those who accepted Incan conquest also adopted the cult connected with the Incan ruler, for the Incas propagated their religion as they conquered. The founders of the Incan Empire called their supreme god Viracocha ("Lord"), after an earlier ruler, and they considered him equivalent to the sun. According to the legends transmitted by the court historians, the first Inca was created to propagate and spread the cult of the sun. Pachacuti, who consolidated the empire, worked out a ceremonial order and theology that elevated Viracocha to a position of supremacy over other gods and that justified expansion in ways that appeared to serve the interests of both conqueror and conquered.

The Sapa Inca Like the Aztec rulers, who claimed descent from the god Huizilopochtli, the Sapa Inca, or "Sole Ruler," was believed to be a descendant of the sun god and his representative on earth. Incorporating the Andean traditions of ancestor worship, the mummified bodies of dead kings became the tangible link between the Incan people and their pantheon. To preserve this link and to ensure the continuity of their own political order, the Incas had to maintain the royal dead in fitting splendor for perpetuity; thus a constant income was necessary, and this could be supplied only by continual conquests. Upon every conquest, the Incas made a thorough inventory of the people, land, and resources they had conquered, all of which accrued to the Sapa Inca.

The cult of the sun was an integral part of the imperial apparatus; it had elaborate ritual, a large priesthood, and many shrines. The Temple of the Sun built by the Inca Pachacuti at Cuzco was the center of state religion and housed the mummified bodies of former rulers. As a basis of imperial control, the Incan religion worked together with the all-encompassing bureaucracy, which the cult sanctioned and sustained. For example, Incan law, which was orally transmitted, was in the hands of judges. Breaking an Incan law was sacrilege, punishable by death. Priests, as guardians of morals, confessors, and imposers of penance, maintained the close connection of religion and law, of cult and state.

The Incan Theocracy Such an empire was a theocracy, in which virtually everything belonged to the Sapa Inca, the personification of the state: all land, all gold and silver, all labor (a form of tax as well as a duty), all people. As in many other societies, women were considered a form of property. Adultery, therefore, was punished as a crime against property. Subjects of the Sapa Inca were all provided land, although they might be moved from place to place according to bureaucratic inventories of people and resources, as a guarantee against sedition and rebellion. The state did its best to keep people busy and well fed, storing large quantities of food and clothing against years of hardship and need. Administrative officials were held responsible if anyone went hungry.

Private property, with the possible exception of clothing and houses, did not exist. Taxes were levied in labor, and trade seems to have consisted largely of barter on the local level and a government monopoly over long distances. Indeed, for ordinary people, mobility was minimal; they were expected to stay at home and work. Guards controlled entry and exit to towns; crossing a bridge was allowed only when one was on official business.

The Sapa Inca's authority was maintained by an elaborate hierarchical administrative system, by blood lineage ties, and by his religious function. All his subjects were divided into groups, arranged in an orderly fashion of responsibility; for example, fathers were responsible for their children's actions. Another organizational pattern had to do with labor: all subjects had assigned tasks. The major labor obligation was cultivation of the land, which was divided into three types: what was necessary for the state, what was necessary for the cult of the sun, what was necessary for the people. Other general labor duties included keeping llama flocks, which were state-owned, and keeping up roads, bridges, and public monumental buildings.

Incan Highway System The vast Inca state was spread over a mountainous territory of more than 3,000 miles (4,830 kilometers), linked together by an elaborate system of roads and bridges. It is possible that some of these roads date from the time of earlier Andean civilizations, perhaps even Chavin de Huantar, but under the imperial structure of the Incas these and other highways became a lifeline for the political and economic integration of the state.

Roads ranged from narrow footpaths to terraced and fortified structures with pavements, walls, and canals. Bridges were woven and sometimes suspended structures spanning rivers and mountainous chasms. Government messengers, armies, and trading caravans traveled their length, stopping at one or more of the several thousand roadside lodges or rest stops that also served as local seats of government, spread along the imperial highway. Few Incas could have traveled all the roadways by foot in a single lifetime, but many journeys were no doubt facilitated by the use of the domesticated llama, which carried loads of 100 lbs (up to 45 kg) at high altitudes.

The Incan Government Controlling this highly organized society required an elaborate bureaucracy, one that continued to grow as the empire expanded. Closest to the person of the Sapa Inca, at the center of power, was a council, though its somewhat vague authority decreased as the empire grew. Also important was a corps of learned men and poets whose regular responsibility was putting together the official version of Incan history, an important task in maintaining authority. As there was no system of writing, these men memorized their political-historical accounts, which were modified when necessary to create versions effective for indoctrinating and controlling conquered peoples.

At its height, the Incan Empire was divided into four viceroyalties subdivided into provinces, each of which contained 40,000 families. Viceroys and provincial governors ranked with imperial court officials as the dominant aristocracy of the empire. These aristocrats had their own style of dress and their own language, but they were charged with imposing the ideology of Incan rule on their subjects. It was their duty to unite the remnants of earlier local cultures that functioned under the Incan imprint. Beneath the high aristocracy were intricate, hierarchically connected cadres of people, ending with family units. Fathers were responsible for their families and cadre leaders for their respective cadres. The empire remained an amalgam of different units, each contributing to the whole through tribute and trade.

SUMMARY

In this chapter we have presented examples of political orders ranging from city-states to empires in regions of the globe with widely differing cultural and historical traditions, as well as geographical and environmental conditions. The concept of political economy provides a useful perspective on the ordering of the world presented in Chapters 4 to 6, in which an emphasis on the relationship between ideas and power also informs the discussion of political orders in these chapters. While stressing the material conditions that led to the expansion of political orders and the concentration of power, in this chapter we have continued to show how religion was able to explain and sanction power and how ideologies were constructed from the joining of local community beliefs with either universal religions, as Buddhism in Southeast Asia and Islam in West Africa, or the absorption of local beliefs into a new complex structured by the beliefs of conquerors, as the Aztecs and Incas in the Americas.

At the beginning of the first millennium C.E., there were many different belief systems in Southeast Asia, all of which had some common elements: animism, ancestor worship, and a sacred role for mountains and the sea. Political leaders gradually adopted key features of Hinduism and Buddhism to sanction their rule and provide a unifying ideology for their states. Later, especially in the fourteenth and fifteenth centuries, Islam in turn was adopted by regional political leaders with much the same unifying results. In each case, foreign belief systems were grafted onto indigenous ones. Foreign religions initially penetrated along trade lines into parts of Southeast Asian society, and thus the demands of commerce and economic motives brought ideas that were then used to support the concentration of power. Nowhere was the role of religion as an aspect of political economy more sharply brought out than in the network of temples that provided the mechanism for the collection and redistribution of wealth in the Khmer state.

Empires such as Funan and Srivijaya were constructed in part on the foundation of hinterland–port relationships, and the city-states of Southeast Asia and East Africa similarly depended for their survival on mutual exploitation: the hinterland needed the ports for its markets, and the ports depended on the production of the hinterlands for their livelihood. Both were dependent on technology and on the maintenance of sea routes, just as the Mali Empire was dependent on the horse and on caravan routes. Technology was important in the concentration of power in Southeast Asian and West African states: maritime technology in Southeast Asia and the horse and the associated technologies of metalworking and leatherworking in West Africa and Central Asia. Technology is closely related to trade, and empires as well as port city-states in both Southeast Asia and Africa were dependent on trade not only for the resources that sustained them but also, in the case of the Southeast Asian riverine and island empires and the West African empire of Mali, for providing ties that connected distant peoples and places to political centers. Port city-states such as Pate and Kilwa in East Africa and Malacca in Southeast Asia depended on trade for their very existence.

In the cases from the Americas discussed in this chapter, the Aztecs and Incas, we encounter empires constructed on trade and tribute networks. The Aztec and Incan Empires relied on the supply of tribute goods from territories they conquered to support their ruling elites. Military expansion was dependent on both religious sanction and on the economic incentives provided by expanding population. As in Southeast Asian and West African examples, religious ideologies were crucial to the construction of the Aztec and Incan Empires.

However, religious ideologies that supported military expansion and economic exploitation in these Mesoamerican and Andean empires were based on shared traditions inherited from common predecessors, rather than from the integration of indigenous beliefs and practices with new ones imported from other cultures, such as Hinduism and Buddhism in Southeast Asia and Islam in West Africa.

In the Americas, Aztec expansionism was fueled by the desire for goods to feed the growing needs of an increasingly complex culture and society, as well as an expanding population. The relatively loose, far-flung empire of the Aztecs was well suited to their purpose of gaining captives for sacrificial purposes, since populations in outlying areas could be viewed as distinct and separate enough to fit the role of sacrificial victims. The Incas exacted tribute from territories they conquered not only to meet the demands of growing cultural complexity but also to sustain their religious ideology through the wealth necessary to support dead kings as links between the human and cosmic orders. The primary function of religious ideology in such highly stratified societies as those of the Aztecs and Incas was to justify the existing order, including the unequal distribution of both power and property.

The Mongol Empire was constructed on the basis of military conquest that enabled the expropriation of resources from a vast range of ecological and cultural zones. Military strength honed in the inhospitable environment of the steppe, where horse riding was a vital skill, was necessary for conquest; but military strength alone was insufficient to enable the Mongols to consolidate their hold over conquered territories. Sophisticated administrative ability was needed to govern and manage the human and material resources of peoples and lands in Central, East and West Asia, Russia, and eastern Europe, which included among their populations nomadic tribesmen, urban dwellers, and farmers. Territories conquered by the Mongols were the home of followers of virtually every major religion of the time, including Buddhism, Islam, Christianity, and Hinduism. Although Mongol religious beliefs originated in steppe shamanism and the Mongols eventually adopted a Tibetan form of Buddhism known as lamaism, the Mongol rulers were able to successfully integrate regions with vastly differing religious beliefs in part because they did not attempt to impose their own religion.

In the following chapter, we turn to consideration of the forms of social organization characteristic of the Mongols and other nomadic peoples of Asia, but found throughout the world: tribal, clan, lineage and kinship groups. We will also look at decentralized forms of political order, such as feudalism, exploring overlapping and alternative ways of ordering the world to those seen in Chapters 4 to 6.

THE INVISIBLE EXCHANGES OF THE ANCIENT WORLD

Far more than trade and tribute traveled along the economic roadways and sea-lanes of states and empires. Merchants carried with them not only ideas but also diseases that were invisible to the eyes of the world before 1500 C.E. The impact of both was great. It is believed that the plague that was known as the "Black Death," which devastated the population of Europe between 1347 and 1351 C.E., probably originated in India. It was transferred via the fleas carried by infected rats, which skillfully climbed the ropes of ships and sailed with merchants from India to Egypt and thus into the Mediterranean. Even earlier, epidemics (857 C.E.) in western Europe are thought to have been caused by poisoned grain, since the pathways of the disease followed established grain trade routes.

The links between the invisible realms of ideas and disease were sought both by ordinary people and by religious writers. In the Christian city of Carthage, the bishop Cyprian wrote a tract about the plague that raged during his time (251 C.E.): "Many of us are dying in this mortality, that is many of us are being freed from the world. This mortality is a bane to the Jews and pagans and enemies of Christ; to the servants of God it is a salutary departure. . . . How suitable, how necessary it is that this plague and pestilence, which seems horrible and deadly, searches out the justice of each and every one and examines the minds of the human race."

New patterns of contact among peoples created new epidemiological (distributions of disease in a population) frontiers. The creation of the

---

FIGURE 6.12 *The Plaguehouse at Jaffa,* Painting by A. J. Gros (1804)

SOURCE: Giraudon/Art Resource, NY.

Mongol Empire was particularly notable in shifting the boundaries of communities across a wide expanse, inevitably bringing together many peoples who shared trade routes and communications systems. Elsewhere, climatic and ecological conditions limited or increased the distribution of disease. Climatic changes in West Africa altered only slightly the territorial boundaries of insects such as mosquitoes and flies that were the carriers of certain diseases. The presence of tropical conditions near the equator provided an inescapable breeding ground suitable for the spread of malaria, which has infected human and animal populations in Africa, South America, and much of South and Southeast Asia, where high infant mortality rates represent the constant battle with infection from ancient times to today.

Historical research continues to identify ancient diseases on the basis of current medical knowledge. The plague of Athens, for example, wiped out one-fourth of the city's population between 430 and 427 B.C.E. The Greek historian Thucydides wrote that after the "abrupt onset, persons in good health were seized" with various symptoms, including "in most cases an empty heaving ensued . . . produced a strong spasm." Recently, the Greek word *lugx* ("heaving") was retranslated to mean "hiccup," and the symptoms Thucydides described were identified as the earliest known outbreak of the Ebola virus, which in the 1990s produced uncontrollable hiccuping in victims in the Congo (Zaire).

SUGGESTIONS FOR FURTHER READING

Thomas Allsen, *Mongol Imperialism: The Policies of the Grand Qan Mongke in China, Russia, and the Islamic Lands, 1251–9.* A scholarly monograph on Mongol imperialism from a Eurasian perspective.

Francis Berdan, *The Aztecs of Central Mexico: An Imperial Society* (New York: Holt, Rinehart, and Winston, 1982). A valuable synthesis of Aztec life and society.

George A. Collier, Renato Rosaldo, John D. Wirth, eds., *The Inca and Aztec States, 1400–1800* (New York: Academic Press, 1982). Collection of articles treating topics relevant to both the Aztec and Inca states.

Geoffrey W. Conrad and Arthur A. Demarest, *Religion and Empire: The Dynamics of Aztec and Inca Expansionism* (New York: Cambridge University Press, 1984). A comparative treatment of the theme of religion and its role in the Aztec and Inca states.

Kenneth Hall, *Maritime Trade and State Development in Early Southeast Asia* (Honolulu: University of Hawaii Press, 1985). Classic study of relationship between trade and development of early states in Southeast Asia.

John Hyslop, *The Inka Road System* (New York: Academic Press, 1984). A descriptive account of the Inca road network.

Adam T. Kessler, *Empires beyond the Great Wall: The Heritage of Genghis Khan* (Los Angeles, Calif.: Natural History Museum of Los Angeles County, 1993). Catalogue of an exhibit organized by the Los Angeles County Natural History Museum and the Inner Mongolia Museum of China focusing on the art and material culture of nomadic peoples in East Asia through the Mongols.

Lynda Shaffer, *Maritime Southeast Asia to 1500* (M. E. Sharpe, 1996). Survey of Southeast Asian history before the coming of Europeans.

7

Ties That Bind: Lineage, Clientage, and Caste

Belonging to a group is a universal human social need. Creating a sense of belonging is also key to the success of a community. As societies grew in size and complexity, the web of social relations holding individuals in place and determining their positions became increasingly important. One form this web frequently took was the lineage, or descent group. Providing a primary source of identity, lineage has endured as a vital building block of human communities and has had the power to shape large-scale political structures as well as individual destinies.

What it means to belong to a group was an issue of concern to the Muslim historian Ibn Khaldun (1332–1406). The Arabic word that Ibn Khaldun used to refer to group identity, *'asabiya,* has been variously translated as "public spirit," "social solidarity," "group cohesion," or "group feeling." The root of the word means "to bind." Ibn Khaldun believed that group feeling resulted from blood relationship or something corresponding to it and produced close contact that led to mutual help and affection. In the excerpt below, Ibn Khaldun described the cohesive community of the lineage-based society of the fourteenth-century Bedouins in North Africa and recognized the group defined by common descent, or lineage, as a key source of social support and identity:

> The hamlets of the Bedouins are defended against outside enemies by a tribal militia composed of the noble youths of the tribe who are known for their courage. Their defence and protection are only successful if they are a closely-knit group of common descent. This strengthens their stamina and makes them feared, since everybody's affection for his family and his group is more important than anything else. Compassion and affection for one's blood relations and relatives exist in human nature as something God puts into the hearts of men. It makes for mutual support and aid *('asabiya).*

Such observations led Ibn Khaldun to theorize that the rise and fall of states were dependent as much on the interplay of lineage and other internal social factors as on military prowess, great male leaders, or the power of gods. While the subordination of women was almost universal, the traditional view of power as equated with public authority has tended to marginalize women's power and influence. As noted by Ibn Khaldun, support and solidarity were frequently founded on kinship, lineage, and patronage networks.

FIGURE 7.0 Muslim Communal Celebration of
Ramadan Feast

A cavalcade comes together to celebrate the feast
at the end of Ramadan, the month of fasting.
Flags bear religious inscriptions.

SOURCE: Bibliothèque Nationale de France.

INTRODUCTION

The central theme of Part II is the ordering of human societies: by ideas; by political structures; by economic systems; and, finally, in this chapter, by forms of social organization such
as lineage. In Chapters 4 to 6 we discussed the relationship between ideas and power, between
belief and polity. In these chapters we stressed ideology, including religion, as an ordering
principle for both social and political organization. In the previous chapter, we focused on
trade relations and economic systems as means of distributing both wealth and power among
individuals and groups, showing again how ideology reflects and reinforces the distribution of
power in a society. Continuing the theme of the relationship between ideas and power treated
in Part II, this chapter emphasizes the shaping of political structures by ideologies based on
social organization such as lineage or caste, and their interaction with religious beliefs and
practices. Whether stress is laid on religion, political ideology, or trade as an integrating force

in the construction of both large- and small-scale polities, all relied on ideas about social organization and concepts of community to cement the ties between—and minimize the differences among—the diverse elements of complex societies.

Lineage refers to the perceived community of persons related by blood ties, by their belonging to a traced line of common descent from a real or fictive (imagined) ancestor. The nature of a particular lineage was frequently tied to both religious beliefs and political authority, such as the notion that the lineage ancestor was a deity and therefore that the lineage was endowed with political power. An example of this is the Japanese imperial family, the Sun line, who ruled with the divine sanction of claimed descent from the Sun Goddess. Other lineages that served the imperial family traced their descent from lesser gods in the Shinto pantheon or from deified spirits of nature. Descent also determined succession to rule within dynasties throughout Chinese history. Elsewhere, such as in the Roman and Byzantine Empires, the authority to rule was similarly inherited by lineal descendants.

It is as a form of social linkage, however, rather than as a source of political authority, that lineage organization has shown extraordinary strength and adaptability. In this chapter, we turn to societies in which kinship remains important to social and political organization and is not replaced by other sources of identity beyond the kinship group, such as community, state, or even empire. In the Mongol Empire, for example, kinship remained the major integrating principle throughout Mongol society, even within the structure of the largest land-based empire in human history. The empire Chinggis Khan built was divided among his four sons and their sons after them; when the empire crumbled, the Mongol clans (lineages sharing a common joint ancestor) returned to their homelands.

Basic forms of kinship organization, such as lineage, often served as a model for clientage and patronage. These terms describe patterns of power relations between and among individuals or groups in which someone, the patron, exercises power over someone else, the client. Within a lineage, for example, various kinds of power relations might appear, including patronage, in which the clients were the weaker, poorer, or more distantly related members of a large family group who served other family members who were wealthier or more powerful. "Patron-client" also describes the lord-vassal relationship of European feudalism discussed in this chapter. Another form of social organization, caste, refers to inherited group membership in a society composed of hierarchically ranked groups or castes. Caste has been associated largely, though not exclusively, with Indian society.

Lineage, clientage, and caste were patterns of social organization based on the understanding and acceptance of social differences and the resulting unequal relationships that existed between individuals. Relationships defined by lineage, clientage, and caste were inherited, yet personal, and they provided a basis for the construction of both individual and social identity. Such relationships were also a means of distributing power in society, and together with religion and other forms of ideology, political structures, and economic systems, patterns of social organization helped to weave the fabric of human communities throughout the world. Exploiting and extending familiar social bonds, communities created the organization necessary to cement small polities and at times large empires. Tension between the forces of centralization that led to the growth of large-scale polities such as empires, and the decentralized patterns of political life characteristic of societies ordered by lineage, clientage, or caste, both fueled historical change and highlighted the powerful continuities of lineage, clientage, and caste.

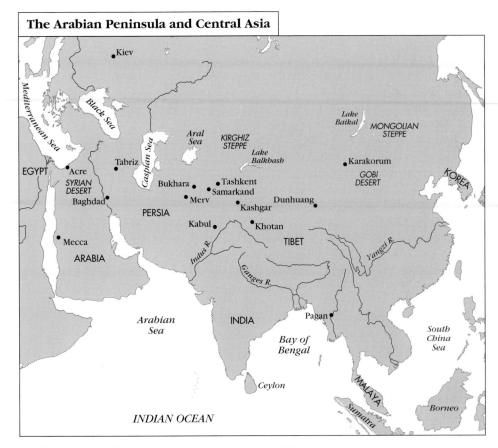

The Arabian Peninsula and Central Asia

MAP 7.1 Peoples of West and Central East Asia, ca. 1200

LINEAGE AND CLIENTAGE IN WEST ASIA

Among the most enduring lineage-based societies were those found on the Arabian peninsula, traceable through both written and oral evidence to at least prebiblical times. With striking continuity to the present, these lineage societies were composed of urban dwellers and farmers, as well as pastoral nomads.

Environmental Diversity Reaching southward from Syria and the Mediterranean more than 3000 kilometers (1875 miles) to the mountains of Yemen and the Indian Ocean, the Arab homeland included broad regions of flat dry desert in the north and high fertile lands in the south, where as much as a meter (40 inches) of rain fell per year. Because of its environmental diversity, many different economic systems and ways of life were found there. Nearly every individual, however, whether city trader, farmer, or nomad, lived either as a member (if related by birth) or as a client (if adopted) of a lineage. All these groups were patrilineal, that is, they traced descent through the father's line, and they all claimed descent from one or two ancestors, which all the groups had in common.

THE ORIGINS OF ARAB LINEAGES

The first of these common ancestors was Qahtan, the biblical Joktan, described in the Book of Genesis. The line he established was popularly believed to be the original genealogical line of the Arabs. Most of the hundreds of Qahtani lineages were found in southern Arabia, though some had scattered as far north as central Arabia and southern Iraq. The second genealogy was that of Adnan, son of Ishmael. His descendants were the hundreds of Arab lineage groups located in northern Arabia, Palestine, Syria, and northern Iraq.

Each of these two family trees was made up of eight or nine major branches, known as "tribes," and each of these branches in turn consisted of smaller lineage divisions. Further out on the branches were found hundreds of twigs, the family units. Although the Adnani-Qahtani division may indeed reflect real descent lines in the far-distant Arab past, it more likely reflects a myth built upon the cultural and economic differences between the well-watered southern and the dry northern Arab world. Whether or not the genealogical division was real, it functioned as if it were. In major crises, Adnanis supported Adnanis and Qahtanis, Qahtanis.

The Meaning of Lineage Identity   Political as well as economic and social loyalties were attached first and foremost to the individual's lineage group. In times of personal trouble, individuals expected and gained support from their relatives, however distant. Wealth and power were held by the group (family, lineage branch, tribe), not the individual. A successful leader from the smaller family level up to that of the largest lineage network was judged by his ability to mediate in disputes between members and ensure distribution of wealth among all members of that lineage. A leader was also judged by his ability to defend the lineage against the aggression of others. Though the welfare of the community took precedence over that of its individual members, this lineage-based system of governance was both relatively decentralized and highly competitive.

LINEAGE AND HIERARCHY IN ARAB SOCIETY

Among Arab societies in both north and south, hierarchies of status existed. Especially in the north and center, nomadic camel-herding lineages carried the highest status even though they were the poorest in natural resources and wealth and probably represented no more than 25 percent of the population. Their status reflected their military abilities and their mobility in the arid environment, an asset that allowed them greater independence. Raiding one another for animals was an ongoing part of the lives of these nomadic peoples, since ownership of animals meant life to those who subsisted in the parched environment. Beneath the camel herders were the nomadic and seminomadic sheep and goat herders, and lower still in the status line were the sedentary farmers and townspeople. Even within each economic group, some lineages were thought to have more honor than others, honor being measured in terms of regional power, reputation for hospitality, and the security provided members of the lineage. Within a lineage, certain families also had high status, and they usually provided perennial leadership to the lineage as a whole.

Religion and Political Power Honor and status could also be obtained in another way. Some
▬▬▬▬▬▬▬▬▬▬▬▬▬▬▬ towns, such as Mecca and Ta'if in western Arabia and San'a in
Yemen, were the sites of sanctuaries for gods and goddesses identified with springs, trees,
rocks, or other natural features. Certain families gained sacred status by maintaining those
sanctuaries. Since warfare was forbidden around these sanctuaries, the families who had the
maintenance rights held leverage in lineage politics and sometimes parlayed this into leadership.

Lineage and Clientage The vast majority of the peninsula's population was Arab and fit into
▬▬▬▬▬▬▬▬▬▬▬▬▬▬ some niche or another in the prevalent lineage patterns. Some, however, were immigrants into the area, having come as either individuals or groups, typically
from neighboring Africa or Iran. In any case, migrants could ill afford to be socially isolated
and without protection or support. These people negotiated a client relationship with as powerful an Arab lineage as possible, thereby to gain both a functional membership in the lineage
and the support of that lineage. Traditional laws within the lineages set out the respective responsibilities incumbent on both parties of the clientage relationship. Through marriage,
clientage often became full lineage membership within a generation or two. The overall lineage system thus swallowed up immigrant groups and individuals, making them Arabs by
declared kinship as well as by language and culture.

URBANIZATION, CENTRALIZATION, AND LINEAGE SOCIETY IN ARABIA

Two features of seventh-century life in Arabia created tension within its lineage society: urban
life and the centralized governments that were being formed in the region. The small farm
towns that dotted the landscape of central Arabia and the coastline presented no problem.
The economics of pastoralism and sedentary agriculture blended easily with the needs of the
neighboring non-Arab populations, who moved back and forth within the lineage system as
clients. However, larger cities, such as Mecca, San'a, and the coastal towns of the Persian
Gulf, based as they were on trade, industry, and the accompanying individual specialization
of work, required a different, individualistic ethic that clashed with the group ethic of a lineage society.

Arabian Lineage   In a period of change characterized by expanding, increasingly complex
Society and Empire communities, the lineage societies of the Arabian peninsula were at a dis-
▬▬▬▬▬▬▬▬▬▬▬▬▬ advantage. The Byzantine and Persian Empires caused particular tensions
for Arabian lineages as they sought to co-opt the manpower and resources of Arabia by setting up and maintaining client states. These appeared superficially to be monarchies, but in
fact they were lineage polities functioning as mercenary reserves or loosely organized buffer
states protecting the empire's economic control over its territory while preserving the political and cultural independence of the lineages contained within the territory. The largest of
such states were those of the Ghassanids of Syria (ca. 490–600), supported by the Byzantine
Empire, and the Lakmids (ca. 300–602) of southern Iraq, allies of the Persians. Rather than
conquering them, the Byzantine and Persian Empires dealt with their decentralized neighbors through a combination of co-option (threatening military force if cooperation was not
gained), annual payoffs masquerading as salary for the lineage leaders, and the building of for-
tification lines along frontiers. When nothing else worked to bring them into the fold of the

empire, intimidation by military campaigns was utilized in an attempt to secure political control.

Centralization versus These methods resulted in an unstable arrangement. The social, eco-
Decentralization nomic, and ideological systems of centralized empires and decentral-
ized lineage polities were too different. The ideology of lineage politics required the sharing out of resources, rather than their centralization. The web of reciprocity and patronage demanded constant negotiation and consensus, which was impractical at the level of political strategy and control in a polity the size of an empire. Even the Islamic empires, which stressed faith over kinship, were unable to break down the Arabian lineage system. Tension between successive Islamic empires and lineage societies of the Arabian peninsula was characteristic of the relations between empires elsewhere and the lineage societies that bordered and interacted with them. The histories of both the Chinese and the Roman Empires were marked by shifting relations between an imperial center and lineage societies on their fringes: the Xiongnu and other northern nomads for the Chinese and the Franks, Celts, and Picts for the Romans. Like the Great Wall of China, Hadrian's Wall, which divided Scotland from England, was built across the neck of Great Britain in order to demarcate territory and protect the Romans south of the wall from the Picts north of it.

■
LINEAGE SOCIETIES IN EAST AND CENTRAL ASIA

Though Chinese society from earliest recorded history in the Shang dynasty (1600–1050 B.C.E.) was ordered by lineage, with the first empires (Qin, 221–207 B.C.E., and Han, 206 B.C.E.–220 C.E.) a centralized bureaucratic state was imposed over the patterns of lineage organization. Lineal descent determined inheritance of the throne through each dynasty, but imperial lineage could not transcend dynastic changes: each new dynasty set up its own line of descent. In contrast, the largely nomadic, pastoral peoples of Central Asia were lineage-based societies that periodically united into centralized political orders under powerful leaders.

ARISTOCRATIC LINEAGES AND THE STATE IN CHINA

The noble lineages created by the Han founder to reward his supporters evolved into an aristocracy that competed with the emperor, considered themselves his social equals, and jealously guarded their claims to descent. Tang (618–907) society was dominated by great aristocratic lineages whose members inherited privileges, titles, and rank from generation to generation and whose status was largely independent of imperial authority. These aristocratic lineages belonged to a group of approximately 100 that practiced group endogamy (marriage within the group) and carefully preserved records of their descent lines to protect their social status. They excluded those who could not document, or in other ways substantiate, claims to aristocratic ancestry.

While lineage remained important as a fundamental organizing principle of Chinese society in later periods, the power of the state at least balanced that of the lineages so that political life was dominated by the bureaucratic state rather than by ties of descent. The domination of political life by the state and its power over lineage ties was expressed most vividly in the civil service examination system.

Lineage and the   The civil service examination system, which would come to play a role
Examination System of profound importance in the shaping of Chinese society and politics in
▬▬▬▬▬▬▬▬▬▬ the later imperial period, took root in the struggle between imperial authority and aristocratic privilege during the early Tang. As a means of reducing the power of
a hereditary elite while recruiting talented officials, a policy of soliciting recommendations of
good men for appointment to office in the imperial government began during the Han. Confucian ideology was used to sanction the adoption of an ostensibly meritocratic system of recruitment and selection of government officials. One of the hallmarks of Confucian thinking
is the ideal of a meritocracy as a ruling elite, and the examination system can be seen as a
means of implementing that ideal.

Beginning in the seventh century, the examination system gradually undermined the
claims of aristocratic birthright by awarding status to those who demonstrated their merit by
passing the examinations. In theory, and to a large extent in practice, talent or ability—defined by the state—mattered more than descent; in this way, the examination system subverted the claims of ancestry to power and status in Chinese society. Though lineage remained
important as a source of identity in Chinese society and lineages provided support for education so that individual members could pass the examinations and thus bring rewards to the
lineage as a whole, the power of the state to determine status was essentially unquestioned
until the twentieth century.

NOMADIC LIFE AND LINEAGE SOCIETY

The nomadic peoples who confronted the Chinese Empire across the Great Wall, traded with
the Chinese, warred with them, and at times adopted Chinese political institutions came
from societies organized by lineages into clans that extended into tribes.

FIGURE 7.1   Great Wall of China

SOURCE: Werner Forman/Art Resource, NY.

Xiongnu The great historian of the Han dynasty, Sima Qian (ca. 145–90 B.C.E.), recorded
▬▬▬▬ his observations of the social and political organization of nomadic life among the
Xiongnu, Turkic, and Mongolic peoples who formed a large confederation in the second century B.C.E. that periodically threatened the Chinese Empire:

> They move about in search of water and grass [for their herds], having no cities, permanent
> dwellings, or agriculture. . . . Their leaders have under them a few thousand to ten thousand
> horsemen. There are twenty-four chiefs altogether, each titled a "ten-thousand horsemen." All of
> the major offices are hereditary. The three clans of the Huyan, Lan, and later the Xubu are the no
> bility.

Many aspects of Xiongnu life offended, even horrified, the Chinese, whose adoption of Confucianism by the Han period made them obsessive about what they considered to be proper relations among kin. Chinese restrictions on marriage, for example, contrasted sharply with the
practices followed by the Xiongnu, such as the marriage of a son to his widowed stepmother.

The Tuoba Wei The Tuoba Wei, who ruled much of north China from the fifth to the early
▬▬▬▬▬▬ sixth centuries, were a proto-Mongolian people who adopted Buddhism and
extended their patronage of that faith over the northern Chinese population. They adapted
their nomadic way of life to rule the Chinese, as later nomadic peoples also learned to shift
from life on the steppes to ruling the sedentary agrarian population of China by adopting
Chinese-style political institutions that centralized power in the hands of a ruler who distributed administrative authority to his subordinates.

The Qidan Liao The Qidan Liao (916–1126) were a Mongolic people from the northeastern
▬▬▬▬▬▬ edges of China just beyond the Great Wall. They rose as a power in the early
tenth century, claiming authority over other non-Chinese peoples in the region, including the
Tungusic Jurchen people, who inhabited the forested river valleys of what is now Manchuria.
Like other pastoral nomads, Qidan economic life was based on herding animals, and the control of the herds was assigned to Qidan males since Qidan society was both patrilineal and patriarchal. Qidan clans traced their descent to a common ancestor for a span of perhaps nine
generations, after which they segmented into distinct lineages and marriages were possible
between members of these lineages. Women were relatively powerful in Qidan society because of their role in supervising the camps and herds during the frequent absence of males
for hunting and warfare. Even after the Qidan transition to a Chinese-style state, Qidan empresses were far more powerful co-rulers than their Chinese counterparts.

The Jurchen Jin The Jurchen people, who gradually gained power over their overlords, the
▬▬▬▬▬▬ Qidan, and established their own Chinese-style state in the early twelfth
century, were accustomed to life in an environmentally diverse region where hunting, fishing,
and agriculture were part of their subsistence, along with herding. Jurchen clans were patrilineal, with each clan consisting of several lineages. For example, the ruling clan that founded
the Jurchen Jin state (1115–1222), the Wanyan, consisted of twelve lineages. The lineage was
the basic organizational unit, and every lineage occupied a village or walled town under the
control of a chief whose authority lay in acting as a military leader in the event of war.

The Mongols The Mongols, who in turn defeated the Jurchen to control north China and fi
▬▬▬▬▬▬ nally conquered the Chinese Empire in the south in 1275, came from a gener-

Europe and the Mediterranean, ca. 1190

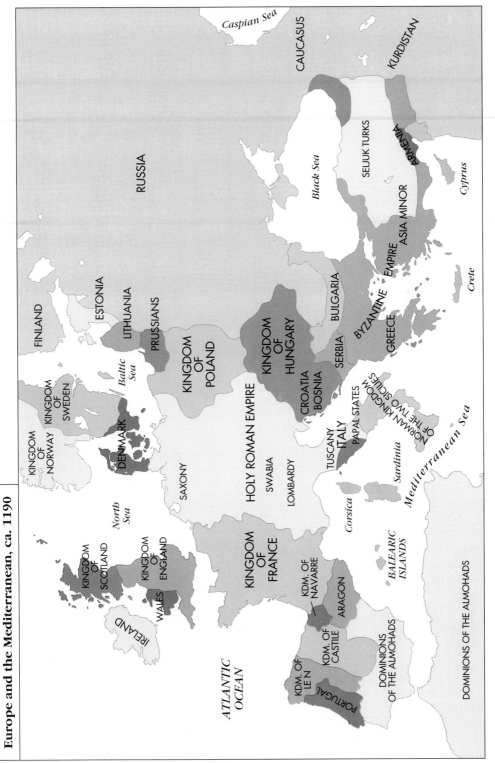

MAP 7.2 Early Kingdoms of Europe and the Mediterranean

ally arid environment that included grasslands, mountains, and desert. Theirs was a pastoral economy based on the sheep and horse, supplemented in the most arid regions by the camel. Herding and hunting were the primary occupations, and their social organization, like that of their predecessors, the Qidan and Jurchen, was based on common lineage, extending to clans and then to tribes. Loyalty to a leader was what held the tribes together, and personal bonds were the glue that cemented lineages, clans, and tribes. Common lineage operated even at the level of ruling the vast Eurasian empire created by the Mongols: the descendants of Chinggis

 DAILY LIVES

DAILY LIFE AMONG THE MONGOLS

The following observations of Mongol life were made by an envoy of the pope to the Mongols in the thirteenth century:

> The dwelling in which they sleep is based on a hoop of interlaced branches, and its supports are made of branches, converging at the top around a smaller hoop, from which projects a neck like a chimney. They cover it with white felt: quite often they also smear the felt with chalk or white clay and ground bones to make it gleam whiter, or sometimes they blacken it. And they decorate the felt around the neck at the top with various fine designs. Similarly they hang up in front of the entrance felt patchwork in various patterns; they sew onto one piece others of different colors to make vines, trees, birds and animals. These dwellings are constructed of such a size as to be on occasion thirty feet across: I myself once measured a breadth of twenty feet between the wheeltracks of a wagon, and when the dwelling was on the wagon it protruded beyond the wheels by at least five feet on either side. I have counted twenty-two oxen to one wagon, hauling along a dwelling, eleven in a row, corresponding to the width of the wagon, and another eleven in front of them. The wagon's axle was as large as a ship's mast, and one man stood at the entrance to the dwelling on top of the wagon, driving the oxen.
>
> In addition, they make thinly cut twigs into squares large enough to form a large box, and then they place on top of it from end to end a carapace fashioned of similar twigs, and make a small entrance at the front end. Next, this chest or miniature house is covered with black felt smeared with fat or ewe's milk, to render it rain-proof, and is again decorated with patchwork or embroidery. In these chests they put all their bedding and their valuables, lashing them tightly onto high wagons which are drawn by camels, to enable them to ford rivers. These chests are never removed from the wagons. When they unload their dwelling-houses, they always turn the doorway towards the south, and following that draw up the wagons with the chests half a stone's throw away from the dwelling on either side, so that the dwelling stands between two rows of wagons as if they were two walls. . . .
>
> It is the women's task to drive the wagons, to load the dwellings on them and to unload again, to milk the cows, to make butter and *grut* (cheese) and to dress the skins and stitch them together, which they do with a thread made from sinew. They divide the sinew into tiny strands, and then twist them into a single long thread. In addition, they stitch shoes, socks, and other garments. They never wash clothes, for they claim that this makes God angry and that if they were hung out to dry it would thunder: in fact, they thrash anyone doing laundry and confiscate it. . . . They never wash dishes either, but instead, when the meat is cooked, rinse the bowl in which they are to put it with boiling broth from the cauldron and then pour it back into the cauldron. In addition, the women make the felt and cover the dwellings.
>
> The men make bows and arrows, manufacture stirrups and bits, fashion saddles, construct the dwellings and the wagons, tend the horses and milk the mares, churn the *comos* (mare's milk), produce the skins in which it is stored, and tend and load the camels. Both sexes tend the sheep and goats, and they are milked on some occasions by the men, on others by the women. The skins are dressed with curdled ewe's milk, thickened and salted.

SOURCE: The Mission of *Friar William of Rubruck: His journey to the court of the Great Khan Möngke,* 1253–5, trans, Peter Jackson; introduction notes, and appendixes by Peter Jackson with David Morgan (London: The Hakluyt Society, 1990, pp. 90–91).

FIGURE 7.2 Nomad Encampment with Four Yurts, Showing Typical Dwelling and Activities of Camp Life

Painting by artist Mir Sayyid 'Ali from ca. 1540.

SOURCE: Courtesy of the Arthur M. Sackler Museum. Harvard University Art Museums. Gift of John Goelet.

Khan continued to rule after his death, though the great Khan was selected by a convocation of representatives of noble clans.

The Mongol Religion Like other nomadic and seminomadic peoples of Central and East Asia, the Mongols practiced shamanism as their principal religion. They worshiped a sky god and an earth goddess, who was associated with fertility. But much of their religious belief and practice centered around worship of ancestors and on maintaining contact with spirits of the dead, which they did through shamans. Images of ancestors were kept in the tents of their descendants and carried around in wagons as the camps moved. Divination by heating a sheep's shoulder blade until it cracked and split—reminiscent of the ancient Chinese oracle bones—was carried out by shamans to determine the best course of action for leaders as well as ordinary people. Shamanistic beliefs, however, did not necessarily exclude other religious ideas, including Christianity and Buddhism.

The Uighurs The Turkic Uighurs, who founded their own empire in Central Asia contemporary with the Chinese Tang dynasty, by the time of the Mongol rise to power in the thirteenth century had abandoned the economy of pastoral nomadism and settled in the oasis regions of the Tarim basin, where they practiced agriculture. Like the Uighurs, many Central Asian peoples relied on a mixed economy, practicing agriculture in oases that lay on the fringes of pasturelands and even establishing settlements in areas where metals could be mined and weapons produced.

The Tanguts The Tangut people, whose ruling clan claimed descent from the Tuoba Wei, ▨▨▨▨▨▨▨ dominated the Gansu corridor and surrounding areas from late Tang times and depended on a combination of pastoralism and agriculture for their economic base. For nearly two centuries, from 1038 to their conquest by the Mongols in 1227, the Tanguts ruled a region that encompassed parts of modern Tibet as well as northwestern China. They adopted Buddhism as the state religion and developed a rich cultural tradition that included translations of Chinese and Tibetan texts along with original works in the Tangut language.

Like other nomadic and seminomadic peoples who formed tribal confederations and conquered parts of Central and East Asia, the Tanguts relied on a mixed economy of pastoralism and agriculture, along with hunting and fishing, and adopted the trappings of Chinese imperial rule. The Tangut ruler, who took the Chinese dynastic name Xia for the Tangut state, announced his decision to assume the title of emperor to the Chinese ruler. In his declaration to the Chinese court, he claimed legitimacy in typical Chinese fashion, characterizing his rule as bringing order to the world. He thereby paid homage to the Chinese dominance of East Asia at the same time that he declared Tangut independence.

Centralization versus Decentralization The Qidans, Jurchens, Uighurs, and Tanguts were nomadic or seminomadic peoples of mixed Turkic-Mongolic-Tungusic (Manchurian) ethnic background who formed tribal confederations, Sinified (Chinese-style) centralized states, and even empires in the case of the Uighurs and Tanguts, from the late Tang (ca. 750) through the Mongol conquest in the thirteenth century. Although these societies' nomadic or seminomadic way of life and their basic tribal and clan organization worked against the concentration of power characteristic of centralized states, the rise of a charismatic leader whose base of support through ties of personal allegiance was strong enough, could unite tribal leaders into a large confederation.

Adopting some aspects of administration from the model of the Chinese state, which loomed large as an influence throughout the region, this confederation could be transformed into a powerful organization for rule of an extended territory as well as a highly skilled and mobile fighting force. Chinggis Khan and his unification of the Mongol tribes is only the best-known example of this process. The Mongols' rule was aided by the experiences of their predecessors, as Qidan, Uighur, Jurchen, and Tangut advisers counseled the Mongols on how to administer the territories they conquered in Central and East Asia.

As the Mongols constructed their Eurasian empire in the thirteenth century, beginning with China, they encountered vastly different peoples, cultures, religions, and patterns of social organization. Like China, the Indian subcontinent was the home of an ancient civilization with deeply entrenched ideas of how social and political life should be ordered, ideas that differed greatly from those of the Mongols and other Turkic peoples who invaded India in the thirteenth century.

■

CASTE AND SOCIETY IN SOUTH ASIA

The pattern of social organization encountered by Mongolian and Turkic conquerors as they invaded India in the thirteenth century was the caste system, a distinctive alternative to lineage and clientage as approaches to social organization and relations of power. The history of the caste system can be traced to the period of Indo-European migrations to the Indian subcontinent during the mid–second millennium B.C.E. By about 1000 B.C.E., the population of the Indus River Valley and the Ganges plain had been divided into four groups: warriors, priests, farmers, and servants or slaves. This division of society was justified and explained in the Vedic scriptures (the earliest surviving written literature of the region) as the result of the dismemberment of a cosmic being into four pieces. The system of castes, which became one of the key features of South Asian life, evolved from this four-part division of society.

THE CASTE SYSTEM AND INDIAN SOCIETY

Around the beginning of the first millennium C.E., ideas about caste were codified in the Book of Manu, which explained the caste system as a result of *karma* (actions) accumulated in earlier incarnations. Priests, or *brahman*s, were at the top of the caste hierarchy, followed by warriors, then peasants (including both farmers and traders), and finally servants or slaves. There was a wide gap between the third and fourth castes, and outside this hierarchy entirely were the "untouchables," the lowest caste, with whom contact was strictly avoided.

The concept and practice of caste involved corporate membership, common descent, and endogamy: members of castes shared a common identity because they belonged to the same cultural and social group; they were descended from common ancestors; and their relatedness continued across generations through marriage practices restricting liaisons to others within the group. Three of the four initial groups were defined by occupation, although the fourth appears to have been an ethnic category.

Caste became a hereditary distinction that was demonstrated by rules forbidding marriage to outsiders, requiring that members eat together, and restricting other kinds of activities between members of different castes. Members belonging to one caste were believed to be ritually impure by members of other castes; contact between different castes resulted in contamination. Although such notions as ritual purity and pollution limited the contact between different caste groups and provided an ideological justification for caste, it is also likely that these practices resulted from the early social distinctions, rather than having generated them, and so helped maintain members and nonmembers in an orderly social and political structure.

Subcaste Distinctions   The use of caste distinctions as a means of establishing social organization was neither rigid nor unchanging. Over time, caste divisions were further subdivided into increasingly complex occupational and ethnic groups, each with its own distinct rules of behavior. Breaking these rules would lead to social ostracism, while following them rigidly might allow one to be reborn into a higher caste. Thousands of subcaste distinctions based on geography and occupation, called *jatis,* were created as a result of inter-caste and inter-*jati* marriages, which, while defying the caste system, also constantly redefined it. The *jati* categories were intimately linked in complex economic relationships of interdependency, including exchange of services, goods, and land-use rights.

Caste and Religion   Caste intersected with kingship and religion, as the priests of Brahmanism served the rulers of the north Indian kingdoms and established themselves at the pinnacle of the caste hierarchy of Indian society. Like kinship ties and systems of clientage, caste was a means of ordering society that expressed religious ideas and interacted with systems of political authority to shape power relations in South Asia. Like the lineage

FIGURE 7.3 The Heroine Elopes

From a manuscript of the *Laur Chanda,* Mulla Da'ud, Uttar Pradesh, ca. 1450–75 [Bharat Kala Bhavan, Banaras Hindu University, Varanasi (5440)

Laur Chanda tells the story of two lovers who are married to others and plot to elope. Shown here (from lower right, clockwise) are: the obliging guard, the lover Laurik tossing up a rope ladder, and the beautiful Chanda encouraged by her maid.

SOURCE: Varanasi Hindu University, Varanasi. Photo by Dr. Stuart Cary Welch.

patterns of West Asia, caste has persisted through more than 2000 years as the fundamental organizing principle of Indian society. The patterns and order created by caste remained, despite the challenges to Hinduism presented by other religions (Buddhism and Jainism) and through the rise and fall of numerous kingdoms and empires, including invasions from outside. The complex intersection of kinship, clientage, and caste also found expression in African systems of social and political order.

LINEAGE, CLIENTAGE, AND CASTE IN AFRICA

The many forms of social organization found on the African continent have been better studied by anthropologists than by historians. With a few important exceptions, written historical documentation is recent. Yet until historians began to develop methodologies that utilized archaeological and oral or other ethnographic evidence (based on the study of living peoples), an understanding of the variety of African political experiences was incomplete. Discussion of lineage societies in Africa was confined to a substratum of anthropology, not history, with research demonstrating the political dimensions of contemporary kinship without reference to chronology or historical change. Kinship-based polities were significant in the past of many African societies, though the process of their historical reconstruction has differed markedly from that of the histories of literate societies.

THE IGBO-UKWU SITE: A LINEAGE-BASED POLITY

Archaeological Evidence at Igbo Ukwu

The archaeological complex called Igbo-Ukwu (ca. 900), situated in a forested region of roughly 10,000 square kilometers (3860 square miles), east of the Niger River in present-day southeastern Nigeria, provides evidence of an early lineage-based polity in West Africa. Despite the region's high population density, neither large cities nor centralized states or empires are known to have existed there. Evidence of the lineage-based society here is primarily archaeological. Excavations of three sites have produced an extraordinary array of technically complex bronze sculptures and objects, imported glass beads and textiles, and human remains. Among the objects excavated is a horseman's hilt, perhaps once attached to a staff of office and depicting a seated male astride a horse. The seated figure bears signs of deliberate facial scarring identical to face designs found among Ibo-speaking peoples in the same area in modern times. Ibo oral traditions similarly attest to a millennium of ethnic continuity in the region.

In more recent times, the Ibo have been studied by anthropologists as an example of a decentralized ("stateless") political system based on highly democratic, lineage-based connections. Unlike the hierarchical structure of highly centralized societies, the lineage-based society emphasized the common goals and achievements of the group. Membership in lineages was useful for settling disputes (since a member could be assured of the support and protection of other members) and redistributing wealth across generations.

The Ibo Religion Belonging to the same lineage also meant that members shared a common spiritual heritage, central to which was the belief that ancestors were reborn again within the same lineage. The Ibo religion included a creator deity, as well as a component that provided each reincarnated person with a personal *chi,* or deity guide, from the spirit world. Political power was thus a worldly reflection of individual spiritual achievement.

Community Politics The rule by a council of titled elders at Igbo-Ukwu provided members with opportunities to develop to their highest abilities and increasingly accumulate wealth and wield influence over others. Through their control over social relation-

FIGURE 7.4 Bronze Fly Whisk Handle, Igbo Ukwu (9th–10th Century) Horse and Rider with Local Scarification Marks

The pose of the rider astride a horse suggests leadership, power, and high status. Horses, metals, and other goods were traded across the Sahara to forest societies.

SOURCE: National Museum, Lagos, Nigeria.

FIGURE 7.5 Brass Figure of Oni, Ife Ruler (14th Century)
Wearing symbols of office, the Oni's authority extended beyond the palace walls and included the right to exact labor and services.

SOURCE: National Museum, Lagos, Nigeria.

ships, council members made group decisions and received support in return. Their power and influence were developed gradually and relied on group consensus and the fruits of patronage. Both spiritual and political power were recognized in the award of titles and ranks. The excavator of Igbo-Ukwu has interpreted one of the sites as a possible burial of a priest-king figure, the highest-ranking person within Ibo titled society. Evidence from the site of Igbo-Ukwu also confirms the existence of long-distance trade in which horses, metals, and other goods were imported across the Sahara in pre-Islamic times (before the tenth century). Involvement in such trade networks did not invariably lead to the establishment of a centralized authority. The society's organizational complexity should not be confused with its physical size. Many decentralized societies were large, involving hundreds or thousands of people in voluntary, cooperative endeavors.

CLIENTAGE IN AFRICAN SOCIETIES

In other African societies, reliance on clientage, a relationship of dependence not necessarily based on kinship, was the essential cement for political systems. It was commonly said in the oral traditions of West and Central Africa that a king was his people. For example, in Dahomey, the metaphor of a perforated pot was used to describe the state: the king was like the pot's water, which everyone had to help keep inside. In other words, authority figures were necessary and existed to serve the essential needs of members of the social group, including protection and the extraction of labor for large social enterprises. Membership in such societies was based not on blood ties or genealogy but on service to the king, a dependency relationship in which the king was the patron and the people his clients.

Clientage and Inequality The presence of clientage relationships in African societies reveals the social and political inequalities that brought them into being. Whereas in some parts of the world clientage involved landowners providing land to the landless, these relationships in Africa rarely involved land. They did sometimes involve the transfer of other forms of property, such as human beings and the value of their labor. For example, around 1000 the king at Ife (Yoruba, Nigeria) did not own the land surrounding the city, but he controlled the available labor and assigned persons to work the land surrounding the royal city. His counterpart to the north of Nigeria, the ruler of Kanem in the eleventh century, was celebrated in a song that commemorates his ability to capture and control labor:

> The best you took (and sent home) as the first fruits of battle,
> The children crying on their mothers you snatched away from their mothers,
> You took the slave wife from a slave, and set them in lands far removed from one another.

The Economic Dimensions of Clientage In sub-Saharan Africa, where the population density remained low and land was valued less than people, authority was frequently expressed in personal rather than territorial terms. This was especially true in herding societies. In Rwanda, clientage was initiated by a cattle transaction between the owner of the cattle and the client herder: "Give milk, make me rich, be my father." In the Sena society of Mozambique, a pre-European system of clientage was the result of economic motives often arising during times of drought and famine, when a desperate lineage group could temporarily pawn a member's labor to a larger, wealthier household. It also frequently indicated the need for protection and was initiated by the ritual act of "breaking the *mitate*," literally walking into the potential patron's household and smashing a clay pot, an act that created obligations and resulted in a period of servitude by the "offender."

The various means of establishing reciprocal relationships resulted in the accumulation of human resources by the larger and wealthier groups, which in turn derived greater political importance. The political and social order of the nearby fifteenth-century Mwenemutapa Empire in southern Africa was built on relationships of personal dependency that successfully expanded over a large territory. Individuals owed allegiance, service, and agricultural labor to the ruler, who in turn provided protection and other benefits.

Clientage and Political Systems As elsewhere around the globe, in Africa the presence of clientage resulted in ties of obedience on the part of the client and obligation on the part of the patron. Reliance on clientage relations appears to occur when states are emerging or disappearing. The clientage system could be part of either the devolution of power (as in the breakup of polities) or of the evolution of highly centralized states (such as empires). The African examples indicate a variety of flexible polities in which inequalities based on inherited positions with differing access to wealth and influence were integrated in such a way as to enable all parties—both the more powerful and the less powerful—to sustain their common social fabric in the face of external threats. These various systems were temporary and indigenous solutions to the central problem of holding hierarchical power relations together amid great social inequality.

CASTE IN AFRICAN SOCIETIES

Social forms called "castes" also existed in parts of West Africa. These were primarily artisan and musician groups that practiced endogamy, marriage rules that restricted unions to those born within the defined group. These rules protected the proprietary knowledge contained within the group. Many of these castes appeared before 1300 and can be documented in part on the basis of historical linguistics and oral historical studies. Historians have shown that the West African castes were initially migratory groups of blacksmiths or other specialists who were foreigners, initially isolated as social groups and eventually adopted by their new communities.

Caste Identity Caste characteristics could and did change over time. For example, the defin-
ing occupations might alter, as in the case of iron smelters exhausting their fuel or ore supplies, and even strict marriage rules did not necessarily ensure that the populations remained isolated. Outsiders could, for example, be adopted or captured. Among the Malinke, who founded the thirteenth-century empire of Mali, West Africa, the origin of some restrictions—exclusion from political office and prohibition of intermarriage—may have been to ensure the creation of politically subordinate groups out of conquered specialists, who otherwise might have threatened the Malinke leadership. This example indicates that the defining features of social forms not only were reconstructed in response to changing political contours, such as the emergence of an empire or state, but were purposefully altered to serve the political interests of those in power.

■

KINSHIP AND COMMUNITY IN NORTH AMERICA

The North American continent was home to a bewildering array of small-scale societies based on communities organized by lineage. In addition to the Mississippian culture exemplified in the North American urban site of Cahokia discussed in Chapter 3, examples include peoples from such diverse environments as the Eastern Woodlands, the Northwest Coast, and the Great Plains. Despite differing ecological habitats, these peoples shared certain common features of social organization, culture, and political life.

THE EASTERN WOODLANDS: IROQUOIS SOCIETY

Iroquois Religious Beliefs Iroquois, who dwelled on the northern fringes of the Mississippian
culture in the Eastern Woodlands, lived by a combination of hunting, gathering, fishing, and subsistence agriculture in semipermanent settlements dating from about 500. Women were almost certainly the traditional cultivators in Iroquois society and accordingly had importance in Iroquois religious beliefs as well. Animistic and shamanistic, Iroquois belief centered on both malevolent and guardian spirits. There were five principal deities, including an agricultural god, who brought rain and caused crops to grow, and an earth mother and her sisters, who represented the spirit of various crops. Traditionally, the Iroquois practiced swidden, or slash-and-burn agriculture, in which they abandoned old fields when they were depleted and created new ones from forest land, burning off the vegetation to enrich the soil and clear the land. Accordingly, communities were forced to move every twenty years or so, and large settlements, such as the Mississippian city of Cahokia, were not possible.

Agriculture and Changes By 1000, the Iroquois had adopted improved hardy strains of the
in Social Organization "three sisters" crops—beans, maize, and squash—which enabled
them to shift toward a greater dependence on agriculture. This resulted in important changes in the organization of their society. First, the increased food supply made rapid population growth possible, and this meant that individual households began

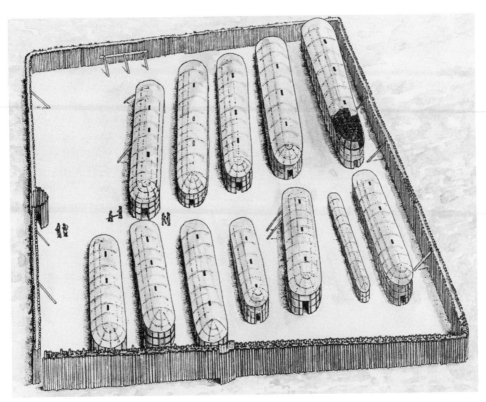

FIGURE 7.6 Iroquoian Longhouses, Mohawk Village, Caughuawaga
Family groups resided in wood-and-thatch structures that contained sweat baths, cooking hearths, pits, storage cubicles, and benches.

SOURCE: Coe, M., Snow, D., Benson, E., *Atlas of Ancient America.* Andromeda Oxford, Ltd. General Research Division, New York Public Library, Astor, Lenox and Tilden Foundations.

joining together and living in multifamily dwellings. Multifamily longhouses were probably occupied by matrilineal families, connected by kinship through women who traced their descent from a common ancestress. The new importance of agriculture reinforced the importance of women in subsistence and domestic affairs, and males had no authority in the household. The longhouse was dominated by a matron assisted by a council of women.

Lineage and Community A second level of community change was the formation of villages, which occurred when multifamily houses began to be built next to others of the same type. Archaeological evidence suggests that each multifamily house in a village came to hold a lineage or a segment of one and bore an animal name, such as Bear, Turtle, and so on. Kinship relations were used to facilitate cooperative efforts (such as land clearing) and to maintain order in a society of increasing size and complexity. Councils of lineage heads were formed to manage village affairs. Villages maintained networks of both overland and canoe trade routes.

Increasing Complexity After about 1300, villages that were stockaded and positioned on de- ▬▬▬▬▬▬▬▬▬▬▬▬▬▬▬ fensible hilltop locations began to be occupied on a more permanent basis. There are also indications of increased warfare that come from human burials, in which skeletal remains show a growing number of traumatic injuries. Archaeological excavations provide evidence of the increasing complexity. At the abandoned Iroquoian village site called the "Draper site," in southern Ontario, Canada, settlement pattern studies suggest that as the population increased between about 1450 and 1500, longhouses were added in clusters with a spatial orientation similar to preexisting structures. It is likely that each set of houses represented a distinct social unit, perhaps a lineage or clan. Each expansion also created new plazas, places for village ceremonies and social activities that helped to integrate the larger community. In this way, lineage became the means by which Iroquois society organized its settlements and adapted to the challenges of social and political change.

THE PEOPLES OF THE PACIFIC NORTHWEST

On the opposite side of the North American continent, inhabitants of the Northwest Coast displayed some similarities to the Eastern Woodland Iroquois but also differed in important ways. As a result of the mountain ranges that parallel it, the entire Pacific Northwest coastal area from the Alaska panhandle to northern California is a temperate rain forest. Ocean currents and relatively warm air masses encourage natural food production, and rivers that descend from the mountains are filled with migratory fish during spring and summer. This environmentally rich area was home to dense populations settled in scattered sites. Because of the plentiful natural food sources, these people lived relatively easy lives characterized by elaborate ceremonialism, with an emphasis on material wealth and distinct social ranks based on wealth.

Subsistence Patterns Subsistence patterns over the last two millennia depended on the ex- ▬▬▬▬▬▬▬▬▬▬▬▬▬▬▬ ploitation of fish runs, sea mammal hunting, shell gathering, and other forms of fishing, gathering, and hunting. Though agriculture was unnecessary and not practiced, intensive foraging for nature's bounty allowed for scattered, basically permanent settlements. Giant cedar trees in the region were used to create dugout boats and—with the aid of only wedges and mauls—were split into planks that became the principal building material for northwest coast homes. By about 1000, large, permanent settlements of several hundred people appeared, despite the absence of agriculture.

Wealth and Social Stratification Northwest Coast people's emphasis on wealth was well estab- ▬▬▬▬▬▬▬▬▬▬▬▬▬▬▬▬▬▬▬▬▬ lished by 500 B.C.E., as was social ranking and stratification, which were closely related to it. The wealth provided by nature resulted in huge surpluses, but the uniformity of the environment in virtually every locale was so great that trade and redistribution of subsistence goods were never developed much, except between the upstream (interior) and downstream (coastal) communities. Even here, exchange was not important enough to lead to the emergence of more centralized or complex political orders. Elaborate material articles made from the bounty of the region—blankets made of mountain-goat hair; shell, copper, and bone pipes and spoons; baskets and other woven artifacts; elaborately decorated boxes, masks, and totem poles—were indications of wealth, supplementing food and gathered products and acting as symbols and currency of rank and social mobility. The eventual end product of this material accumulation was the potlatch ceremony, which validated a person's rank in the community and featured extravagant gift giving or even deliberate destruction of hoarded surpluses for the purpose of displaying rank. Vast quantities of goods and even human slaves were sometimes ritually destroyed when giving them away failed to be a sufficiently convincing statement of rank gauged by wealth.

Language Differences The independence of the self-sufficient Northwest Coast communities led to each developing its own language. Linguistic contrasts from the Alaska panhandle to northern California indicate the divisions between the Northwest Coast peoples. In southern British Columbia, for example, the Coastal Salish were divided by language from the Inland Salish. Despite their differences, however, the northwest coast people had more in common than the bounty of resources which so shaped their lives.

Common Religious Beliefs Like the Iroquois of the Eastern Woodlands, they shared beliefs that were generally animistic and shamanistic but that admitted a chief divinity who lived under the bowllike earth. For many, the raven was the creator; for others, it was the trickster. Above was a sky god, who ruled over life and death. There was a myriad of supernatural beings to be appeased before one went hunting, fishing, or gathering. Shamans were important because they could summon spirits for aid, appease them, and treat disease. It was believed that certain women were seeresses who could prophesy.

Kinship and Social Organization The basic social unit among Northwest Coast peoples was similar: politically autonomous groups of relatives, their spouses and children, aligned according to one of three methods. Some of them were based on matrilineal descent, wherein membership and inheritance came from the mother and her side of the family; others were patrilineal (wherein kinship, membership, and inheritance were through the father); still others followed a bilateral (determined through both the mother's and the father's line) reckoning of descent and membership. When these various patterns are analyzed, it is apparent that all the methods derived from a few basic concepts and social forms common to the peoples of the Northwest Coast. There were two basic principles. First, the fundamental social unit of autonomous northwest coastal groups consisted of either a lineage, a group that could trace its descent to a common ancestor through either a male or female line, or an extended family, in which descent was treated less formally and rigidly. Second, social status, involving the system of rank, derived from neither heredity nor wealth alone, but from a combination of the two.

Longhouse Life Typically, Northwest Coast lineage or extended family groups lived in separate households, about thirty or so people living in a longhouse made of cedar logs. Longhouses were headed by a chief—any man who owned a house was a chief—and each had its totem, such as a bear, a whale, or a raven, often decorating a totem pole located at the residence.

Political Organization Chieftaincy was inherited both matrilineally and patrilineally, but chiefs were also dependent on wealth. The chief's wealth was the source of his independence and prestige and that of his lineage. The greater the collection of gifts accrued, the greater the potlatch (the manifestation of wealth) that could be created, and

FIGURE 7.7 Northwest Coast Indian Housepainting of Mythological Animals

Thunderbird (above), Killer Whale (below), Lightning Snake (Left), and Wolf (right) were used as totems by lineages at Nootka, Vancouver Island, British Columbia.

SOURCE: American Museum of Natural History, New York.

the more important the chief and his clan. Alliances were sometimes made with similar social groupings for purposes of common defense or for ceremonial ends, but groups never surrendered to one another certain highly individual and important rights, such as totems, crests, and dances.

PEOPLES OF THE PLAINS

The center of the North American continent was dominated by temperate grasslands, home to a number of grazing and burrowing animal species that provided bounty for hunting peoples. It was also home to a variety of seeds, fruits, and tubers, but the Great Plains were so marginal for farming that horticultural practices developed elsewhere had to be introduced along river valleys by communities already adept at farming. Accordingly, the earliest Plains peoples were nomadic hunter-fisher-gatherers.

Permanent Communities After about 900, during what is called the Plains Village period, influences and migrants from the east led to the development of substantial Plains Village communities that were comparatively permanent. Sometimes they were fortified by dry ditches and stockades, and they were usually equipped with underground storage pits. The houses within these villages were multifamily square or rectangular lodges, larger and more substantial than those seen earlier on the Plains. They carried a larger and more complex inventory of stone, bone, and wooden tools and a more varied pottery. Farming was restricted to the alluvial bottomlands of larger rivers, and the horticulture of the Plains Village sites indicates the use of advanced strains of maize and beans along with other domesticates. Groups such as the Blackfoot of the northwest Plains were probably occupying this region by the fifteenth century.

Community and Clan   The earliest (before 900) Plains peoples banded together in their joint search for sustenance, based primarily on hunting bison. Membership in the group was determined by residence. Later, by the Plains Village horticultural period, membership in the community was fixed by heredity, which was achieved by consistently ignoring one side of the family and stressing the other. All persons of either sex descended from the male ancestor, through the male line only, formed a patrilineage community, or clan; all those descended from a female ancestor, through the female line only, formed a matrilineage community, or clan. Such clans differed from earlier bands in absolutely fixing membership and differed from families in being unilaterally determined groups. Whereas the family unit recognized both parents, in determining membership clans ignored one parent in favor of the other. This sort of organization meant that one-half of one's ancestors, either maternal or paternal, counted for certain purposes (admission to a ceremony or feast or the sharing of an inheritance), while for other matters the other half might be equally important. Clans bore names, usually of animal origin, such as Wolf, Eagle, Elk, and Beaver, and some of them had distinctive ceremonial and political functions.

Nonkinship Associations   Apart from social ties to family and clan, most Plains peoples belonged to organizations whose membership did not rest on kinship. Societies—military, dancing, spiritual—were far more frequently male in membership than female, but neither from these nor from any other aspect of Plains life were women sharply excluded. For example, the Blackfoot considered women's nature to be more innately religious. Women auxiliaries figured even in the military societies. These associations served a great many purposes, some religious and some secular. Visions, dreams, and the quest for a guardian spirit played a large role in Plains religion, especially for men in their desire to increase their own spirituality. Rituals such as the Sun Dance provided key roles for women,

FIGURE 7.8 **Mobility of Proprietary Symbols on Plains Indian Tepee, Blackfoot**

Belonging to a group afforded access to and ownership of certain symbols. Even when highly mobile people moved across vast territories, they wore or displayed their appropriate insignia and designs.

SOURCE: C. Wissler drawing from *Ceremonial Bundles of the Blackfoot Indians*, 1911. From *Art and Aesthetics in Primitive Society*, by Carol E. Jopling. (E/P Dutton, 1971.) Photo courtesy Schomburg Center for Research in Black Culture, New York Public Library.

who had the sole power to move between the Holy People of the Above and the people below. Especially gifted visionaries became shamans and exercised an important role in Plains society.

ENVIRONMENTAL DIVERSITY AND COMMON CHARACTERISTICS

Environmental diversity accounts in part for variations in the social organization of the peoples who inhabited the North American continent before 1500. By around 1000, the eastern woodland Iroquois had become dependent on agriculture, resulting in the concentration of population in villages, which enabled cooperative efforts in the practice of agriculture. Because of the rich natural sources of food, the northwest coast peoples were able to live in settled communities and subsist by gathering, fishing, and hunting. In contrast, before the beginning of the Plains Village period around 900, inhabitants of the Great Plains were nomadic hunter-fisher-gatherers who needed to move frequently to find new sources of food. All three examples increased in population and used wealth to distinguish families, their status and rank.

By around 1000, peoples in all three environmental zones—Eastern Woodlands, Northwest Coast, and Great Plains—lived in settled village communities made up of multifamily dwellings, or longhouses. Despite great variations in methods of tracing descent—patrilineal, matrilineal, or bilateral—the lineage or clan was consistently the primary organizational unit, and lineage heads jointly managed the affairs of village life. Totemism was common to peoples in all three areas, as Iroquois, Northwest Coast Salish and others, and Plains peoples all traced their lineages to animal ancestors, such as the wolf, the eagle, or the raven. Commonalities can also be seen in religious beliefs and practices that promoted the welfare of the community.

Small-scale Communities Large-scale political structures characterized by the concentration of power at the center did not develop among the societies of North America before the coming of Europeans. Although trade was carried out among settled communities, it did not lead to large, centralized states. Social hierarchies and political influence derived from holding high rank or status within these hierarchies, such as those seen among Northwest Coast peoples, did not become manifestations of the large-scale institutionalization of power relations but remained aspects of relatively small-scale communities that were sometimes connected by a common language and culture. Even in larger-scale societies of Central and South America, lineage relationships helped cement the ties between diverse populations.

▪

LINEAGE IN THE AZTEC AND INCAN EMPIRES

The complex tribute society of the Aztecs centered around the city of Tenochtitlan, founded in 1325. From this center, the Mexica-Aztecs ruled through seven *calpulli*, or tribal-kinship units. Together the *calpulli* formed the *calpullec*, a council of elders who elected two chiefs. One was in charge of war and the other was in charge of religious functions. They were called "the father and mother of the people" and "the snake woman," suggesting that kinship and women were important in the organization of this large empire.

The Incas established their empire in the Andes on the eve of the Spanish conquest, integrating territory and peoples across a vast terrain. Similarly, the family or *ayllu* provided the basis of Inca social organization. It functioned to allocate land to its members and joined with others to form a council whose powers included the election of the emperor.

LINEAGE AND KINSHIP ALLIANCES

In both complex polities, the organization of state society relied on the familiar and local forms of kinship and lineage relations. Brute force was not enough to bring together conquered peoples. Marriages helped build some alliances. By strategically selecting women of certain families to become "wives of the sun," the secondary wives of the emperor available for marriage to political allies, the Sapay Inca and his sister, the Coya (or "queen of women"), helped cement political ties. Manipulating marriages was not the only way kinship was used to enhance political power.

Both areas were also characterized by highly stratified societies that increasingly were marked by differences in wealth and power. These distinctions were expressed in the clothes and ornaments people wore, the food they ate, and their material possessions and houses. Social distinctions were inherited. For example, Aztec lords dressed in fine cotton garments, ate venison, and resided in elaborate residences with servants, while commoners wore clothes made of coarse fibers, ate little meat, and lived in small adobe and stone structures. Keeping track of family lines was thus necessary for the organization of society. Over time, the importance of warriors increased, noble status could also be achieved, and the political roles of women were eliminated. The role of lineage faded in importance.

■

CELTIC SOCIETY IN EUROPE

Known to the Greek historian Herodotus as Keltoi and centuries later to the Roman general Julius Caesar as Galli, Celtic peoples inhabited parts of modern France and western Germany beginning around 1200 B.C.E. Two Iron Age archaeological sites, Halstatt in Austria (eighth to sixth centuries B.C.E.) and La Tene in Switzerland (fifth to first centuries B.C.E.), have told us much about the material culture of the Celts; and Greek and Roman accounts of the Celts, biased though they may be, have also enriched our understanding of Celtic social organization, political structure, and religious life. Celtic myths and legends transmitted orally by bards who composed and sang stories about heroes and their exploits have been preserved in written form since the medieval period, and though influenced by Christianity, these works still provide glimpses of the pre-Christian Celtic past. Celtic heroes described in these legends bear some resemblance to the Homeric heroes of the *Iliad* and *Odyssey* and to the Indian heroes in the epic poem, *Mahabharata*.

CELTIC LIFE

The economy of the early Celts was both agricultural and pastoral and they were organized into tribes. They lived in or close to hill forts which were enhanced with earthen fortifications. Each tribe was headed by a king, and Celtic society was divided into Druids (priests), warrior nobles, and commoners. Warriors owned flocks of cattle and sheep, and commoners labored on the land. Elaborate burial sites of the elite—women as well as men—have yielded rich collections of clothing, jewelry, and other objects for use in an afterlife.

Like their counterparts in Central Asian nomadic societies, similarly organized along kinship lines and economically dependent at least in part on tending herds, Celtic women appeared to be relatively equal to men, though their labor was primarily devoted to childrearing, food production, and some crafts. The rich graves of Celtic noblewomen suggest that, also like their counterparts elsewhere, elite women must have been able to hold a considerable amount of economic power in their own right. We do know that women both contributed property upon marriage and had the right to inherit it at the death of a spouse.

Celtic Religion   Druid priests played a very important role in Celtic society, a role that often transcended tribal ties. They presided over a set of religious beliefs and practices that included the worship of many gods and goddesses, most of which were associated with particular localities and kinship groups, much like the early Shinto deities in Japan. As in Japan, spirits of nature are prominent in the Celtic pantheon; and the early Celts worshipped at natural sites such as springs or groves of trees where they felt the presence of divinity rather than building elaborate temples to honor their gods and goddesses.

The Celts in European History   By around 500 B.C.E. the Celts were in contact with Mediterranean peoples, trading for wine and crafted goods such as wine jugs and drinking cups. In the fourth century B.C.E., the Celts invaded the Greco-Roman world and gained control of territory as far as sites in Anatolia. By this time groups of Celts had also migrated into the British Isles, where many were converted to Christianity. The Romans gradually subdued the Celts in western Europe and by the first century C.E. most of Britain also came under Roman rule. As hardy and fearsome as Celtic warriors were—according to contemporary accounts and later myths and legends as well as archaeological evidence of weaponry—their decentralized political organization made them no match for Roman imperial armies dispatched to fight them.

■

FEUDALISM IN EUROPE

Feudalism was an alternative to societies based primarily either on the personal ties of kinship or on the impersonal bureaucratic structures of centralized polities. Broadly defined, feudalism describes a hierarchy of power in which land constitutes the principal form of wealth and provides the basis for political and social orders as well as economic structures. Feudalism is a form of clientage that resulted in hereditary distinctions and may even have originated in them. The institutions and practices of European feudalism developed after the power of a strong centralized state (the Roman Empire) had shifted onto local political units. Central to feudalism was the personal, specifically military, relationship between lord (patron) and vassal (client). The relationship was often perpetuated through family structures and in some cases actually reflected blood ties.

Feudalism in some parts of Europe developed when central government broke down and public functions, obligations, and privileges were taken over by individuals operating under a variety of private hierarchical arrangements created by personal obligation. Feudalism in its various forms was prevalent in western Europe from the ninth to thirteenth centuries, when private administrative structures—law, ideology, economic functions, and social relationships—assumed many of the attributes of centralized states. In parts of eastern Europe, feudalism was imposed later and lasted longer.

ORIGINS AND CHARACTERISTICS OF EUROPEAN FEUDALISM

European feudalism is commonly considered to be two closely interdependent systems. Feudalism involved the relationship between landowners, in which the most powerful landowners provided aid and protection to less powerful landowners who had enough wealth to own horses and arms. The less powerful landowners, in turn, owed allegiance and military service to the most powerful. The vassal (or client) gradually became identified as a knight, a warrior around whom evolved a highly elaborate culture and lifestyle. The knight's prestige depended upon fighting, and knights justified their existence by waging wars. Many knights were descended from elites through the male line, and they maintained their power through kinship networks and alliances with other powerful lords. Because of the cultural and political significance of warfare among the elite, the status of women declined as they were culturally excluded from warfare in most cases.

The economic basis on which the feudal system rested, manorialism, was essentially a relationship of dominance and subordination between those who claimed authority over the land and those families who cultivated it. People and land, then, were the basic ingredients of feudalism. A fief, commonly a grant in the form of land, was presented by a lord to a vassal. The vassal accordingly became a landholder, the lord of the fief. The land was organized into a manor or manors, which were worked by serfs, laborers with limited rights, whose labor and produce sustained the landlord and indeed the whole feudal-manorial system. Serfs were obligated to remain on the land and sometimes to give a portion of the annual harvest to the lord. Their claims to the land were more or less permanent and could be inherited by their children.

Feudalism developed in the centuries during and after the disintegration of the Roman Empire, in a period of great turmoil and political instability, and there is no doubt that warfare was among its causes. In agricultural practices, Roman gang slaves were gradually replaced with laborers tied to the land. Germanic invaders sometimes modified the arrangements using their traditional notions of clan affiliations and loyalty to the chieftain or leader. What emerged under feudalism was the peasant family as the basic unit of production.

The specific arrangements of the contract that were basic to the feudal relationship varied widely across Europe, although they often involved military protection and service. The contractual relationship was a way of reconciling the tension between authority and liberty by way of contract. The individual gave up only enough freedom to ensure effective cooperation. When feudalism began to work on a local level to stabilize relations of power, kings and emperors also adopted it to strengthen monarchies. Feudalism flourished in the twelfth and thirteenth centuries as it spread across Europe from the areas between the Rhine and Loire Rivers.

Patron-Client Relationships The feudal characteristic of personal dependence also had Roman and Germanic origins. The Romans had instituted patronage, by which the wealthy and powerful took clients under their protection. Many clients acted as guards for their patrons, and in time German immigrants, not just Romans, became clients.

When they took over western Europe, the Germans continued to use the patron-client relationship. The system was, after all, not altogether different from the practices of the Germanic system, wherein chieftains shared the fruits of victory with their warriors. When the Germans shared out the Roman lands they conquered, the personal warrior-chief relationship was combined with tenant-landlord dependency, and the feudal-manorial relationship was eventually the result.

The practice of men without resources placing themselves under the protection of a wealthy, stronger patron dates from at least the eighth century. The following description from that time suggests both the voluntary and reciprocal nature of entering into the contractual relationship between patron and client:

> Inasmuch as it is known to all and sundry that I lack the wherewithal to feed and clothe myself, I have asked of your pity, and your goodwill has granted to me permission to deliver and commend myself into your authority and protection . . . in return you have undertaken to aid and sustain me in food and clothing, while I have undertaken to serve you and deserve well of you as far as lies in my power. And for as long as I shall live, I am bound to serve you and respect you as a free man ought, and during my lifetime I have not the right to withdraw from your authority and protection, but must, on the contrary, for the remainder of my days remain under it.
>
> And in virtue of this action, if one of us wishes to alter the terms of the agreement, he can do so after paying a fine of ten solidi to the other. But the agreement itself shall remain in force. Whence it has seemed good to us that we should both draw up and confirm two documents of the same tenor, and this they have done.

Immunity The granting of rights over land in return for military or òther services is the essence of the feudal system, but before this relationship could be firmly established, land had to be free or immune to possible intervention by the centralized authority. Immunity created a territory free from interference by the state, so that public functions, such as the administration of justice or protection, became the prerogative of private individuals. For example, the early Frankish kings granted churches and monasteries immunity for their lands and thus created a sort of religious state within their kingdom. Similarly, when fiefs—grants of land—were handed down by lords to vassals (and by inheritance to the vassal's heirs), local government functions, ranging from road building to administering justice, were assumed by the vassal to whom the fief had been given.

Fiefs were primarily pieces of land held on terms of personal obligation. There were three main varieties of such tenure (landholding): ecclesiastical (Church), military, and general. Ecclesiastical fiefs were those given to the Church, which provided spiritual benefits to the donor—and often nothing else—in return. There were two principal types of military tenure. Field service in the overlord's army, generally for up to forty days a year (though the service might be shorter), was one type. The other main form of military tenure involved guard service at the overlord's residence. According to one medieval view:

> It is seemly that men should plough and dig and work hard in order that the earth may yield the fruits from which the knight and his horse will live; and that the knight who rides and does a lord's work, should get his wealth from the things on which his men are to spend much toil and fatigue.

Other forms of tenure also existed, and these involved general, rather than spiritual or military, services. Fiefs were granted to vassals for supplying overlords with goods (horses, equipment, provisions) or personal services (hospitality or comfort in sickness, or even hold-

FIGURE 7.9 Land Rights in Feudal Europe Included Hunting

Detail of late 15th-century Flemish Tapestry illustrates the variety of interactions and activities that took place on a feudal estate. Hunting and gathering supplemented peasant households.

SOURCE: Victoria & Albert Museum, London/Art Resource, NY.

ing their heads when they grew seasick crossing the English Channel). Toward the end of the feudal age, with the return of a money economy, these services were commuted into payments into the overlord's treasury.

The Feudal Contract The basis of all feudal relationships was the contract, a powerful legal and cultural force for cohesion in a world that was effectively localized and decentralized. A contract took the form of an oath of fealty (loyalty), by which homage was sworn by the vassal to the overlord for the grant of a fief. Oaths of fealty were complicated by the fact that vassals commonly held fiefs from more than one overlord. Thus two

FIGURE 7.10 Knights in Battle Depicted in Scene from the Bayeux Tapestry, about 1095 CE {Musee de la Reine Mathilde, Bayeux}

SOURCE: Erich Lessing/Art Resource, NY.

forms of homage became necessary. Liege homage was that paid to the first lord from whom a fief was received. Simple homage, which recognized and accepted the priority of liege homage, signified a contract with other overlords. In exceptional cases, such as in Normandy and in England after the Norman Conquest (1066), liege homage was paid to the king as well as to the first lord, and the king took precedence.

The contract between overlord and vassal confirmed their obligations to each other and lasted so long as its terms were honored or enforced. In general, the overlord owed the vassal support in the form of administration of justice, defense against attack, and honorable treatment as an equal. Vassals owed their overlords services such as the military and general services described above, payments (inheritance, ransom, dowry, knighthood fees), and the acceptance of various other obligations. Since the feudal contract rarely involved an actual written document, dramatization and ceremony were used to emphasize and publicly record the agreement. Often the dramatization took the form of humiliating rituals that underscored the subordination of the vassal (or client). For example, the vassal might be forced to kneel down or kiss the lord. The hair of a would-be knight might be shorn to symbolize the new state into which he was entering. The serf belonging to a monastery might put the bell rope around his neck as a symbol of the perpetual servitude into which he had entered.

Subinfeudation Vassals who possessed extensive fiefs divided out portions of them in a ▬▬▬▬▬ process known as subinfeudation. The result of subinfeudation was that every landholder in the feudal system became both a vassal and an overlord, excepting (theoretically) the lord king and the lowliest vassal holding a single, indivisible fief. This arrangement grew unsystematically in western Europe in the tenth and eleventh centuries and so complicated tenure relationships that it carried with it the seeds of its own disintegration. In actuality, lords had little control over their lesser vassals. The descriptive phrase of the time, "The vassal of my vassal is not my vassal," describes the dissolution of the ability of the overlord to maintain effective authority over fiefs granted to vassals. Even kings "holding only from God"—who owed homage to no one and were purportedly above such fractionalizing involvements—became mere landlords bound by feudal contracts to vassals who were their equals and sometimes their superiors in military strength and political power. The power of feudal monarchs was so limited by contracts to a position that they were little more than first among equals. The limitation of royal power, a striking feature of feudal society, was a result of such practices as subinfeudation. Attempts to end the erosion of the power of monarchies and to reestablish centralized sovereignty were the process by which feudal society in western Europe was ultimately transformed.

GENDER AND FEUDAL SOCIETY

Feudal society in western Europe was crude and often violent, given the instability and constant competition inherent in feudal relationships. The Church sought to soften the harshness and brutality of feudal life by proclaiming the Truce of God, which prohibited fighting during certain times, and the Peace of God, which prohibited brutality to women, children, and the clergy. But male warriors were idolized, and social relationships revolved around them.

FIGURE 7.11 Elizabeth (or Isabeau) of Bavaria, Queen of France.

The marriage of Elizabeth of Bavaria to the French King Charles VI meant political alliances and new lands to increase the holdings of powerful families. Elizabeth (right) was instructed in the ways of the court by the Duchess of Brabant.

Late 14th century. Palais Ducal, Poitiers.

SOURCE: Palais de Justice, Poitiers/Collection Cap-Viollet

Indeed, the most representative example of feudal literature, the eleventh-century *Song of Roland,* an epic description of an event that occurred during the withdrawal of the Frankish armies from Spain, is a celebration of the belligerent, male "virtues" that were so basic to feudal relationships. Women are not mentioned in the poem, despite the fact that female labor and services made possible the feudal era.

While the basic purposes and interests of feudal contracts may not apparently have been served by women, circumstances at times lessened the male monopoly of power in the feudal system, particularly as the system began to disintegrate following the tenth century. Women did become vassals, were integrated into the system, and came to play decisive roles in it, particularly as feudalism began to be transformed. With the disintegration of centralized authority in the ninth century, claims to land by families became easier to assert.

Control and inheritance of land passed from the hands of kings to those of families, and this tended to enrich women as well as men. The system of lineage accepted in some parts of western Europe, in which the line of descent of the familial surname was followed and recognized through female as well as male ancestors, guaranteed family control of land and allowed females, in the absence of male heirs, to inherit property. They held land in their own right and fulfilled the family obligations, including military ones, for the holding of fiefs.

Probably the best-known example of this occurred in the twelfth century, when the vast fiefs of Duke William X in Aquitaine were bequeathed to his daughter Eleanor, who accordingly became the most important vassal of the king of France, possessing approximately one-third of that sovereign's territory. By the end of the thirteenth century, the rise of towns and the shift of economic and political forces away from the household toward the public sphere probably worked to undermine women's power.

MANORIALISM

The feudal era was initially a period of insecurity and uncertainty, an era in which trade declined. With that decline came a temporary decline in the importance of large towns and cities. From the ninth to eleventh centuries, large-scale, integrative regional commerce on an international level was sparse in western Europe, limited to exorbitantly expensive luxury goods. Even the petty, localized trade of peddlers was scant. Coinage became localized and nonconvertible. Accordingly, feudal Europe retreated to a self-sufficient, localized, domestic economy until the rise of city-states and empire beginning about the eleventh century. The characteristic unit of this early economic system was the rural manor or estate, and manorialism determined the way in which manors functioned.

Manor Life The inhabitants of the manor were the landlord, his family, and the people who maintained the manorial economy, the laboring peasants or serfs, who by virtue of their services had use of the land granted to the landlord. There would also most likely be a priest, who attended to the spiritual needs of all the people who lived on the manor, and perhaps a steward or overseer.

A manor was commonly made up of a manor house, where the landlord and his family lived, and a village, where the peasants lived. The land of the manor was divided between the lord's domain and that allotted to the peasants. The pattern of cultivation was traditional and fixed. All arable land was normally laid out into two types of fields, with rotation of crops based on seasonal planting and half the fields commonly left idle or fallow. Fields under cultivation were divided into long, narrow strips, some assigned to peasants, some to the landlord, and some that were called "God's acre" and set aside for the priest. Cultivation was labor-intensive. In many cases, the fields were cooperatively plowed and harvested, with produce being shared proportionately, but some peasants cultivated only their own strips and those of the landlord.

Serfs and Their Obligations To maintain tenure of the strips assigned to them, serfs owed more than labor service to the landlord. Along with the customary dues and rents, the peasants were obliged to give a percentage of all they harvested to the lord, a tithe to the priest, and perhaps a share to the steward. There were also extra obligations, such as gifts made to the landlord on certain holidays and other special occasions, and there was additional labor owed, boonwork, such as collecting the lord's firewood or doing other errands for him and maintaining the roads and bridges on the manor. If they wished, lords could arbitrarily impose additional charges on their serfs.

All these obligations were satisfied by labor or produce. The landlord had control of certain products of the manor, known as banalities. They included products of the manorial winepress, gristmill, and oven, which belonged to the lord and which the serfs had no choice but to use and for which use they shared their wine or flour with the lord. Common land was held collectively by the village community, whereas forests, meadows, and waterways were controlled by the lords. Lords held hunting privileges that were denied the peasants, including the right to ride roughshod through fields in pursuit of prey without responsibility for damages.

Landlord Obligations Landlords did have certain obligations to their serfs. They were obliged to make land or some other means of livelihood available to them, and once all obligations to the landlord were satisfied, peasants were granted what remained of their produce for their own needs. Sometimes landlords also offered peasants aid and support in times of dearth and, on special days, provided them with feasts and celebrations. Landlords were the source of livelihood, however circumscribed, for the servile population of the manor.

In the narrow world of the manor, landlords or their surrogates, the stewards, had the authority of a king or emperor, who was a distant and vague ruler beyond the ken of most peasants. Landlords fulfilled the basic functions of local government for their peasants. They offered protection from external harm and maintained internal peace on the manor when peasants revolted against abuses and unwarranted corruption.

Subordination was emphasized by the lord's control over local justice and by his manipulation of laws and justice in his favor, often at the expense of tenants. Beyond providing protection, landlords generally tried to get as much from their serfs as possible. In some cases, "protection" was afforded in response to threats exhorted by the landlord himself in order to frighten peasants into farming for him. In Central France, for example, even manorial priests were so closely identified with the landlords that they ceased to be agents of God in the eyes of the peasants.

The feudal period of western Europe was a time in which personal freedom was severely limited by unequal interdependency. Even so, at a time when there was a conspicuous absence of either political or economic choice, feudal-manorial structures primarily based on personal relationships of labor or military service provided a viable means of living that was independent of the centralized authority of a large state.

■

FEUDALISM IN JAPAN

The term "feudalism" has been used to describe Japanese political and social institutions from the twelfth to nineteenth centuries, and Japan represents possibly the closest parallel to the model of European feudalism. Both European and Japanese feudal institutions emerged from the crumbling of a centralized imperial government and its legal-administrative apparatus: the weakening of the Roman Empire and Roman law in the case of Europe and that of the Japanese state of the Nara and Heian periods (eighth to twelfth centuries), modeled on the imperial government of Tang China. The development of contractual relationships between patrons and clients in both cases rested on prior legal and administrative foundations.

ORIGINS OF JAPANESE FEUDALISM

Early Japan, before the advent of Buddhism and Chinese influence in the sixth century, was ruled by the descendants of the Sun Goddess, whose god-parents had created the Japanese islands. In the seventh and eighth centuries, Chinese influence inspired the creation of a centralized bureaucratic state through which the emperor ruled. But by the end of the eighth century, the centralized structures of this state were beginning to disintegrate. Though it took centuries for the institutions of central rule to disappear, new sources of power outside the emperor were increasingly responsible for maintaining order and for appropriating and redistributing wealth, defined primarily as land.

Heian Japan and the Fujiwara The influence of Tang China as a model for centralized government declined as contact between Japan and China was severely curtailed for a century following the end of the Nara period (784–884). During the Heian period (794–1185), the authority of the imperial line was undermined by the indirect rule of a powerful family at the Japanese court, the Fujiwara. By serving as regents to young-adult emperors, who were often married to their daughters, the Fujiwara built their power at court and successfully subverted the emperors' authority.

Dominating a court culture famed in later history for its aesthetic ideals and intricate social life, the Fujiwara never usurped the throne of the Sun line, but they did rule the country. Fujiwara no Michinaga (966–1027) took the title *kampaku* (civil dictator), moving a step beyond regent and consolidating his own personal rule as well as the domination of the Fujiwara family in Japanese court politics. Though imperial authority was renewed to some degree by the institution in 1086 of the *insei* (cloistered or retired emperor system), in which still-vigorous emperors abdicated the throne and exercised influence from retirement, government was carried out through a balancing of power among the Fujiwara, the symbolic authority of the reigning emperor, and the political influence of the retired emperor.

Landholding and Taxation By the end of the Nara period (712–784), the imperial army had dwindled to a force centered on the capital and was incapable of maintaining order in the provinces outside the capital. Tax collection had broken down as the imperial authority to back up officials responsible for collecting taxes weakened. Though in accord with the model of imperial authority derived from Tang China the Japanese emperor claimed all land as his own, to be distributed and utilized as he commanded, in fact privately held land existed from the foundation of the Japanese state in the pre-Nara period.

In addition to lands privately held by the imperial family, aristocratic families received grants of land from the emperor as rewards or as part of official ranks they held at court. The great Buddhist temples and Shinto shrines also received lands as a sign of court patronage. In the middle of the eighth century, in order to encourage the reclamation of uncultivated land, more or less permanent land rights were given to those who opened new fields to cultivation. Many of these landholdings enjoyed either temporary or permanent degrees of tax exemption.

By the tenth century, many large landholders sought and obtained immunity to tax payment as well as from interference by local government officials, who were then prohibited to enter an estate or interfere with its administration. There were thus two kinds of land: public domain, which was taxed by the imperial government to fund the state treasury, and private land, which was largely immune to tax collection or other responsibility to the state. Small landholders sometimes commended their lands to a more powerful landholder, where they became part of a large estate protected from tax collection. The commender would then obtain the right to till the land in perpetuity for himself and his heirs, with obligations such as paying rent to the estate owner rather than paying taxes to the imperial government.

Rights to Land Land rights, the key to the economic base of feudalism, were defined in Japan by the term *shiki,* which originally meant "office" and implied certain duties toward the land. It eventually came to mean the "right to profit from the land." The estate protector, the proprietor, the local manager, and the peasant cultivator all held rights to the land, called *shiki.* The cultivator would have the right to till the land in return for payment of rent; the protector, often a member of the Heian nobility resident in the capital, would derive income from the estate and protect its immunity to taxation or other interference; the estate manager would receive a share of the harvest for managing the peasantry and sending rents to the proprietor. The proprietor had the most power: to survey the land, to keep land records, and to exercise control over estate residents. Like the protector, the proprietor was likely to be an absentee landholder who lived in the capital.

JAPANESE AND EUROPEAN FEUDALISM

Though we might use the same English term, "manor," for the Japanese estate known as the *shoen,* the latter differed substantially from a European manor. *Shoen* lands, like manor lands, were not necessarily contiguous; the *shoen* was often made up of a group of scattered plots. Unlike their European counterparts, however, the Japanese estate did not center on a manor house, and it had no seigneurial demesne (lord's land) farmed by the boonwork of the peasantry, as on the European manor. The economic base of the Japanese estate was irrigated rice agriculture, which demanded cooperative labor from cultivators, in contrast to the rainfall-dependent agriculture of Europe, in which individual cultivators and their families worked the land. It was also probably more profitable. Though the Roman state existed only as a ghostly remnant through scattered practices that continued under the European monarchies and the Church, in Japan the edifice of imperial government created on the model of the centralized bureaucratic state of Tang China remained in formal structures and institutions, if not so much in practice.

Japanese feudalism evolved from the reassertion during the Heian period of a lineage-based aristocratic social tradition in which patron-client relations were the basis of political organization and the means of governing the state, exemplified by the rule of the Fujiwara family during the ninth to eleventh centuries. The culture of the Heian nobility was far more sophisticated than that of the courts of the Franks, Germans, and Anglo-Saxons in Europe. The Heian nobility lived a life of great luxury and refinement, supported by the income from landed estates that lay outside the capital, often in provinces far distant from the center of cultural and political life at the Heian court. They were absentee landholders, dependent on estate managers to supervise their landholdings and secure their income. Control of the manors gradually slipped out of the hands of the court aristocrats and into those of the local managers and military men, who in the absence of imperial authority protected the manors from assault.

As with European feudalism, Japanese feudalism was based on two institutions: the manor (*sho*), to which was connected the idea of rights to the land, and the military power of a warrior elite. With the decline of Fujiwara power in the late twelfth century and the subsequent weakening of central authority, a new warrior elite, known as *bushi* or *samurai,* developed outside the capital. *Samurai* replaced the court aristocracy as a social and political elite whose power was consolidated through personal ties of loyalty and military service. As the military dictator, or *shogun,* rose to a position of political dominance in the twelfth century, Japan entered a long era of "feudalism," in which political power and authority were directly linked to landholding and the rights to land were conferred by "lords" on their "vassals" in return for military service.

The wars that led to the final demise of the Heian originated with conflicts between two families, the Taira and the Minamoto, who were descended from ninth-century emperors and had been given aristocratic surnames and lucrative rewards in the form of lands or posts at the capital. In this way their lines had been removed from succession to the throne, but they became strong in their own right as they secured their positions: the Taira in the capital area and the Inland Sea, and the Minamoto in the Kanto region (the area surrounding modern Tokyo).

EVOLUTION OF THE SHOGUNATE

When the wars between the Taira and the Minamoto came to an end in 1185, Minamoto Yoritomo's *bakufu* (literally "tent government"), or shogunate, centered at his military base of power, Kamakura, became a military government that balanced and then dominated the civil government of the imperial court at Kyoto. In 1192, the title of *shogun* (military dictator) of all Japan was conferred by the emperor on Minamoto Yoritomo (1147–1199).

Allegiance to Yoritomo by his vassals was based on his military strength and on personal loyalty. But the latter was also cemented by material rewards, which were enabled by Yoritomo's position as military protector of the emperor. One of the most important rights (*shiki*) the Minamoto conferred on their vassals was appointment to positions as land stewards on private estates, where the vassal had essentially the same duties as an estate manager and was similarly entitled to income from the estate. Yoritomo also appointed his vassals to official posts as provincial constables, responsible for maintaining order and able to derive income from this position.

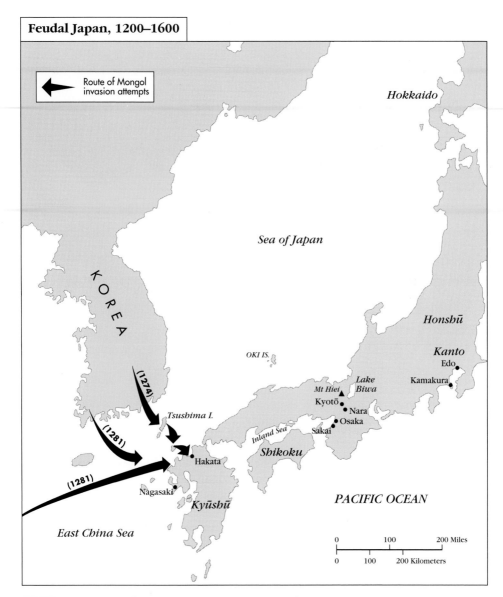

Feudal Japan, 1200–1600

Route of Mongol invasion attempts

Hokkaido

Sea of Japan

KOREA

OKI IS.

Honshū

Kanto

Edo

Lake *Biwa*

Mt Hiei   Kamakura

Kyotō •Nara

•Osaka

Sakai

Inland Sea

Shikoku

Tsushima I.

(1274)

(1281)

(1281)

•Hakata

Nagasaki

Kyūshū

PACIFIC OCEAN

East China Sea

| 0 | 100 | 200 Miles |
| 0 | 100 | 200 Kilometers |

MAP 7.3 Mongol Invaders Reach Japan in the Thirteenth Century

After Yoritomo's death, the Kamakura shogunate (1185–1333) was under the control of his wife, Hojo Masako (1157–1225), and her father, brothers, and their descendants, who ruled as the Hojo regency. Emperors continued to reign as symbolic figures of authority from the old imperial capital at Heian, though two attempts to reassert imperial authority over the Hojo regency failed, in 1221 and again in 1333–1336. The latter imperial rebellion brought about the collapse of the Kamakura shogunate and the founding of a new one (1338–1573)

FIGURE 7.12 Late Heian Warriors

Painted handscroll from the mid-13th c. depicting wars that brought *samurai* to power a century earlier.

SOURCE: Fenollosa-Weld Collection. Courtesy Museum of Fine Arts, Boston.

by the military leader Ashikaga Takauji (1305–1358) centered at Kyoto (the old imperial capital of Heian).

In the Ashikaga period, as the personal ties that had existed between Minamoto Yoritomo and his vassals weakened under the Hojo and vassals no longer felt the bonds of loyalty and obligation that bound them to the *shogun,* a fuller form of feudalism began to flower. The single-lord (*shogun*)–vassal relationship exemplified by Minamoto Yoritomo and his heirs in the Kamukura shogunate evolved into many-lord (*daimyo*)–vassal relationships, with the *shogun* the symbolic apex of the feudal hierarchy. The key relationships, though, were those between the provincially based *daimyo* and their vassals, which remained personal and strong. By 1300, the warriors were in control of Japan and the estate system had collapsed, as most land became integrated into the domains or fiefs of the *daimyo,* supervised by their vassals. In contrast to Europe, where by 1300 feudalism had all but disappeared, the full flowering of Japanese feudalism dates from the thirteenth century.

SUMMARY

Political and social orders based on either genealogical ties or patron-client relationships can be found in most regions of the world, including Africa, the Americas, Asia, and Europe. In the exceptional case of the Mongols, a lineage-based society composed of different tribes united according to either real or fictive kinship ties coalesced to create probably the largest empire in world history (see Chapter 6). This was a temporary phenomenon, however, that demonstrated the capacity for large-scale action of such lineage-based societies given particular circumstances, rather than the logical outcome of such societies over time. The social and political complexity of Aztec and Incan empires similarly was lineage-based. South Asia yields yet another, distinctive approach to the ordering of society in the evolution of the caste system. The West African examples illustrate that polities sometimes recognized the political utility of changing caste categories.

Societies organized on the principle of kinship ties, such as lineage societies in West Asia, did not show significant signs of disappearing until modern times. Lineage societies and neighboring centralized states developed strategies for dealing with one another based on the differing economic strengths and needs of both sides. Centralized states sometimes made insatiable demands on agrarian manpower and resources, and both nomadic and sedentary lineage societies worked out exchanges with empires that at least partially satisfied the needs of both, with less centralized groups receiving the protection of states when they needed it, while urban centers and large bureaucracies were supported by rural production. In this way, lineage-based polities played a major role in world history, though they were seldom understood and often attacked by their centralized neighbors.

Despite the tensions and hostility between them, centralized and decentralized polities have consistently enjoyed an interdependent coexistence, a fact that was a major theme in the writings of Ibn Khaldun, who discussed the connection between decentralized, lineage-based and centralized polities in his *Muqaddimah,* a five-hundred-page introduction to the methodology of history. Ibn Khaldun concluded that while all civilizations have risen and fallen because of socioeconomic factors, the immediate agents of this cycle were the lineage groups of rural areas, pulled together by a charismatic leader offering a powerful religious ideology. Only armies such as those tied by kinship, the tightest bond of loyalty in society, had the strength to overwhelm the defenses of the centralized state. Ibn Khaldun's hypothesis, developed in great detail in the *Muqaddimah,* sheds useful light on the workings of lineage politics not only in West Asia but also wherever lineage-based societies have been found.

In his discussion of the social, cultural, and economic bases of human behavior, Ibn Khaldun recognized the importance of forms of association based on both kinship and economic interest. But he considered the primary unit of human action to be the family, the subject of the next chapter. Building on examples of the social organization—lineage, clientage, and caste—that shaped relations of power, in the following chapter we will focus on the most intimate and basic historical and social experience of the individual: the life of the family and household.

FEUDALISM AS A HISTORICAL CONSTRUCT

As the Carolingian monarchy under Charlemagne had turned to Rome for sanction, illustrated by Charlemagne's crowning as Holy Roman emperor in 800, Minamoto Yoritomo in twelfth-century Japan looked to Kyoto to legitimize his power as "military protector" of the emperor. Both cases were a transition from centralized institutions (the Roman and Chinese Empires) to the accommodation of a rural warrior class: the *samurai* in Japan and the European knight. Despite the compatibility of the Japanese case with the European model, it is important to note that Japanese social and political institutions evolved independently, in their own specific historical and cultural context. The similarities between European and Japanese feudalism might be seen as an example of the fact that human beings have found only a relatively limited number of ways of organizing themselves socially and politically, rather than as an example of the diffusion of a political system. We should take notice of parallels of this nature and use them to help us organize our understanding of historical facts, but we should neither see one example as the model for another nor assume diffusion of political institutions and ideas across vast cultural, temporal, and geographical boundaries.

The concept of feudalism originated from generalization on the basis of specific facts derived from European history. Since the concept of feu-dalism is European in origin, use of this term to describe aspects of non-European societies, such as Japan, is problematic. Our use of the term feudalism provides a good illustration of the problems inherent in using an abstract concept developed by historians to classify and organize historical data. Although such concepts are necessary for understanding and interpreting the numerous specific facts that make up the historical record, we need to be aware of their limitations and to be cautious about their implications.

There is an inherent comparative element in all generalization, since historians are constantly involved in the process of comparison between data and the general terms used to describe those data. But when we label a particular social form in Central Africa or Japan feudalism, we are comparing complex social organizations from vastly different historical and cultural contexts to those of Europe, and we may then assume that their similarities are more important than their differences. Misunderstanding can arise from using an abstract model, such as feudalism, to shape historical facts rather than using facts to refine and alter the model. When used appropriately and carefully, however, concepts such as feudalism can illuminate common characteristics in widely divergent historical and cultural circumstances, such as those of Europe and Japan.

SUGGESTIONS FOR FURTHER READING

Thomas J. Barfield, *The Perilous Frontier: Nomadic Empires and China* (Cambridge, Mass.: Basil Blackwell, 1989). Overview with sustained argument showing how the rise and fall of nomadic empires was linked to their relationship with China.

Marc Bloch (L.A. Manyon, trans.), *Feudal Society* (Chicago: University of Chicago Press, 1961). A classic study of European feudal society.

Georges Duby, *The Three Orders: Feudal Society Imagined* (Chicago: University of Chicago Press, 1980). Stimulating examination of European feudalism by an imaginative French scholar.

Peter Duus, *Feudalism in Japan,* 3d ed. (New York: McGraw-Hill, 1993). Survey of evolution of feudal institutions in Japan from the sixth through the nineteenth centuries, with some comparative commentary.

Mary Erler and Maryanne Kowaleski, eds., *Women and Power in the Middle Ages* (Athens and London: The University of Georgia Press, 1988). Collected articles explore aspects of women and family in medieval society.

Joseph Fletcher, "The Mongols: Ecological and Social Perspectives," *Harvard Journal of Asiatic Studies* 46:1 (1986): 11–50. A very useful discussion of tribal organization and both religious and political aspects of Mongol life.

Miranda J. Green, ed., *The Celtic World* (London and New York: Routledge, 1995). Collected articles of the most recent scholarship on all aspects of Celtic material life and culture.

John Iliffe, *Africans: The History of a Continent* (Cambridge, England: Cambridge University Press, 1995). A comprehensive and thematic approach to the vast African past, including lineage-based societies.

Laura F. Klein and Lillian A. Ackerman, eds., *Women and Power in Native North America* (Norman, Okla. and London: University of Oklahoma Press, 1995). Collected articles on gender issues in Native North American societies.

Thurstan Shaw, *Igbo Ukwu: An account of archaeological discoveries in eastern Nigeria* (Evanston: Northwestern University Press, 1970). Account of the archaeological evidence.

Ordering the World: Family and Household

W orld travelers looked with keen interest on the domestic and intimate lives of the different peoples they encountered. That family life could vary greatly even between the Mediterranean and northern Europe is vividly demonstrated in the description of fisherfolk by a pair of Venetian sailors shipwrecked on the coast of Norway in 1432:

> In this Iland there are twelve little Houses, with about one hundred and twentie persons, for the most part Fishermen. . . .
>
> The Inhabitants of this place both young and old, are of so great simplicite of heart, and obedient to the Commandement of God, that they neither understand, know, nor imagine in any wise, what Fornication, or Adulterie may bee: but use Marriage according to Gods Commandement. And to give you a true proofe hereof I Christophoro [Cristoforo] say, that we were in the house of our foresaid Host, and slept in one and the same Cottage, where hee also and his Wife slept, and successively in one Bed neere adjoyning, were their Daughters and Sonnes of ripe age together, neere to the which Beds we also slept, almost close adjoyning to them: so that when they went to sleepe, or when they arose, or when they stripped themselves naked, and wee in like manner, we indifferently saw one another, and yet with this puritie, as if wee had beene little children. But I will tell you more, that for two dayes together, our said Host, with his elder Sonnes arose to goe a fishing, even at the time of the most delightfull houre of sleepe, leaving his Wife and Daughters in the Bed, with that securitie and puritie, as if he had properly left them in the armes and embracements of the Mother, not returning to his home in lesse time than the space of eight houres.

An individual's earliest and most profound experience of the world takes place at home. Whether positive or negative, the experience of family and home leaves a lasting and distinctive social imprint that forms cultural expectations of how the world outside the home works. As in the case of Cristoforo Fioravanti, this can make for strange bedfellows and challenge one's understanding of all other societies.

INTRODUCTION

Family and household comprise the most basic level of human social interaction and historical meaning. Only recently, however, have historians begun to study the history of families and households and to consider the do-

FIGURE 8.0 Man Sleeping and Women Preparing Food in Medieval Home

Medieval women were the first to rise and light the fire. Their household duties included heating the morning porridge and other food for breakfast, milking, feeding domestic animals, drawing water, gathering foods, egg, butter, and cheese production, sometimes baking brewing, and weaving, and caring for young children.

main of private, as well as public, life to be an important aspect of historical study. Sources for the study of family and household history may not be obvious, but they do exist: in oral testimony, mythology, genealogies, life histories, legal codes, archaeological excavations, language, and literature.

Families and households may be universal units of historical study, but they are not unchanging constants. The meaning and nature of family and household change and vary widely among cultures and over time in any given society's historical development. In Europe after 1500, households were defined as groups of related persons living under a common roof. In other parts of the world, kinship ties among mother, father, and children did not always result in shared residency. Family and household members were sometimes adopted from outside the kin group and were treated with little noticeable difference from those related by blood. In this book, we will use household to refer to shared residence and family to refer to shared (including adopted) kinship relations recognized by a particular society. Obviously, these definitions of residence and relationship may overlap in different cultural, linguistic, and social contexts. Those who share kinship relationships may or may not also share residence. Families and households can be units of economic production and socialization and may provide emotional as well as tangible support to members.

In some societies, the complete designation of family or household requires several linguistic terms rather than a single word. For instance, the modern Chinese word *jia*, usually translated as "family," refers more properly to what English speakers would call a *household*, a corporate unit with a common residence and shared economy. The term *zong* refers to the patriline (those who trace common descent through the father), a multigeneration group that links kin over time, while *zu* refers to the same-generation group of kin who share a common surname and descent, such as aunts, uncles, cousins, and so on. Usually, *zong* and *zu* are used together to mean both ancestral line and the extended kinship group, which is sometimes referred to as a lineage or clan. Thus the Chinese family can refer to both the corporate household unit and the broader connections of the extended kin group, both through common ancestry and through shared surname.

Elsewhere, linguistic designations distinguish between family groups that are natal, or nuclear (consisting of mother, father, and children), and extended (also including aunts, uncles, cousins, and grandparents)—that is, groups which are directly related by kinship ties and recognized by appropriate terminology—and larger-scale descent groups (lineages, clans, tribes, etc.) that may have political rather than familial bonds. These long-distance connections are found in the social and political orders of lineage-based societies (discussed in Chapter 7).

In the Akan language of West Africa, the word for "family" is *abusua*, a matriline, or matrilineal descent group or clan, that traces common descent through its female relatives. Within the *abusua*, the sense of shared belonging and the rights and protections afforded to members could be acquired only by men and women through birth ties to one's mother or aunt. In contrast, among the Sioux peoples of North America, the word for "family" or "relatives" included all living things, from ants to aunts.

These various familial units have been used by peoples around the world to construct the hierarchies of social and political life. Like the concepts of gender and community, families were socially and culturally constructed, not biologically determined and they changed over time. Unrelated persons could be adopted into family units based on kinship, or they could share common residence and belong to households. These constructed social units, whether or not recognized by the society at large or sanctioned by the state, functioned in similarly important ways to families composed of individuals related by blood ties or marriage.

More than an agency for biological reproduction and socialization, the family or household is frequently a unit of economic production. Often a microcosm of the social and political patterns of domination and submission, gender relations, and the exercise and control of power, the family in world history must be seen as a necessary key to the unlocking of major historical themes. Its study is essential to understanding the social fabric of human cultures. Both families and households interact with and relate to larger-scale institutions, both responding to and creating historical change. Like the family, the household was universal in its appearance and significance throughout world history. In this chapter, we explore how the most intimate and basic social order intersects and interacts with the ideas, institutions, and communities from ancient times to 1500 C.E.

FAMILY AND HOUSEHOLD IN ANCIENT EGYPT

Of the best-known states in Africa, ancient Egypt, from early dynastic times (ca. 3000 B.C.E.) to Alexander's conquest (332 B.C.E.), has received the most historical attention. Yet the numerous surviving examples of hieroglyphic inscriptions and archaeological excavations (until recently, more than the rest of the continent's research put together) provide virtually no information on the families and households of the majority of the population. Only limited evidence has been available to reconstruct the daily lives of even the elite classes. The one constantly important level of social organization among elite Egyptians throughout these centuries was the family group, which centered around a man, a woman, and their children. It is highly debatable whether there was a concept of "marriage"; the sole significant family-establishing act appears to have been cohabitation for reproduction. The concept of fertility was important to social and political orders that evolved along the Nile.

PATRIARCHY

Like many other societies, ancient Egyptian society was patriarchal: men and their male heirs controlled the majority of relationships. In the realm of the household, elite Egyptian women controlled property, business, ritual, and family matters. This is not always obvious from the surviving records, which are frequently biased and, in the case of documents composed by the all-male scribes, directed toward an all-male audience of readers.

Women were accorded theoretical equality under most laws relating to property and inheritance. However, the absence of women from government posts and the realities of patriarchy (including differences in the ability of women to inherit and own property) prevented

FIGURE 8.1 Limestone Figures Depicting Nefertiti and Ahkenaten, Wife and Husband (Egypt, ca. 14th century B.C.E.

The royal family provided an idealized model of relationships and roles. Most importantly, their fertility was the foundation for social and political rule.

SOURCE: Erich Lessing/Art Resource, NY.

equal access to influential positions and limited the independent accumulation of wealth. Subordination was linked to the concept of fertility, which ascribed to a woman the responsibility and duty of reproduction as service to her husband. This is revealed by Old Kingdom (third-millennium) authors, who advised men, "When you prosper, found your household. Take a hearty wife, a son will be born unto you" and "Gladden her [the wife's] heart as long as you live; she is a fertile field for her lord."

RECONSTRUCTING THE EGYPTIAN HOUSEHOLD AND FAMILY

Archaeological studies have provided us with the physical plans of Egyptian houses and some clues to spatial organization—how the space was used in social interactions—from two sites: the town of Kahun (ca. 1897–1878 B.C.E.) and El-Amarna, a city built by Akhenaten (r. ca. 1350 B.C.E.). From these sites, we have an idea of the room sizes, functions, and furnishings of households. Using the data to answer questions of family residence patterns and household size has proved much more difficult. We do know that many children were desirable and that families were often large. A man typically established a household with his wife, children, and any other unmarried female dependents for whom he was responsible, which might include his grandmother, mother, sisters, and aunts.

Women and Household Duties One of the most common female titles on monuments is that of "mistress of the house"; that women remained at home in charge of the running of household affairs is implied by passages from New Kingdom (ca. 1550–1050 B.C.E.) documents and supported by the idealized tomb scenes where women are shown engaged only in household duties of child rearing and food preparation, as opposed to men, who were engaged in activities outside the household (hunting, bureaucratic functions). Household activities such as beer brewing and baking are depicted on tombs as being overseen by the male tomb owner, but it was probably women or their servants who actually performed the tasks. Evidence also indicates that women engaged in weaving, grain storage, animal husbandry, and craft production within the household confines. For much of her life, the mistress of the house was pregnant; a woman often gave birth to twelve or more children, few of whom survived into adulthood.

Children and Family Ideals Children were desired, and the state of childlessness is noted with concern by Egyptian authors and on tomb inscriptions. Children were important because they were responsible for the domestic altar and for performing rituals in the cult of the ancestors. Children were given special cylindrical charm cases to wear around their necks for protection. In turn, they were expected to show affection and respect for both parents. In the document *Teaching of Duaf's son Khety* from the Middle Kingdom (ca. 2100–1785 B.C.E.), the author tells his son to "thank God for your mother and for your father, who put you on the path of life."

Household Economy The employment of wet nurses and nannies freed elite women from some of the burdens of child rearing. Households were not self-sufficient. Women were responsible for supplying household needs through the exchange and sale of garden provisions, cloth, and other goods. It is likely that in managing the household economy, they could also accumulate wealth. According to written documents, women could own houses, but men owned households; that is, they controlled the production and activities that took place inside. Because men were typically landholders (land being "owned" by the pharaoh and usually controlled by men), they controlled the grain rations. They were responsible for the support of the female members of the household. Even a small landholder in the Middle Kingdom might support as many as sixteen people from the grain grown on his fields.

Although the establishment of nuclear families was the desired norm, some Egyptian men and women found themselves without spouses. Homosexuality was acknowledged among all classes but advised against by the scribes. Since homosexual cohabitation did not result in children, it did not conform to the ideal of family life based on fertility and was even thought to hinder the cycle of rebirth.

Gender Roles and Ideology In contrast, motherhood and the related concept of fertility were greatly valued in ancient Egypt. The elaborate ritual and ceremony of kingship were based on fertility, and political controls exercised by the pharaoh rested on his kingdom's agricultural achievements. The ruler's ability to organize labor and perform proper rituals was believed to ensure agricultural success. When a pharaoh died, the concept of rebirth into an afterlife relied on female metaphors of childbirth and suckling. Gender distinctions existed as part of the formal structure of ancient Egyptian society. While men and women were complementary in concept and even in the roles they played, the subordinate status of women was epitomized on the great stone monuments by the secondary placement of women relative to their husbands and sons. Women were conceptually integral to both religious and political realms; in practice they were subordinated in both. Like the ideals described later for Chinese society, the dominant ideology of ancient Egypt demanded subservience of women to men, from the most basic social levels of family interaction to the public political realm.

FAMILY AND HOUSEHOLD IN WEST ASIA BEFORE ISLAM

Ancient Egypt in North Africa shared common historical, ecological, and social conditions with Mesopotamia and ancient Israel in West Asia, and, though their cultural traditions were distinct, they were linked in early times as well as after the coming of Islam. The Judeo-Christian Bible illustrates well the connections among the peoples and cultures of these regions; the history it tells moves from Egypt to the Sinai, from Syria to Babylon, and from pastoralism to urban life. The customs of marriage, disposition of household property, and kinship relations practiced by the peoples who inhabited West Asia before Islamic times did differ, mainly according to whether the people in question were nomadic and pastoral or sedentary and urban; at the same time, some common features can be noted throughout the region.

PROPERTY AND THE FAMILY

Since many of the surviving documents record the disposition of property, these documents are also excellent sources for determining the nature of power and relationships that made up families and households. However, they tell us little about the personal and private realms of family and household life. The position of women in ancient Egypt was in some ways favorable to elite women's accumulation of wealth, since land and household property could be inherited by women as well as men. Similarly, dowry inventories (the lists of property brought by the bride to her husband in order to finalize a marriage) from Mesopotamia include such things as ivory and furniture, and there is evidence to suggest that girls were entitled to inherit a share of their family's wealth unless they had received a dowry, in which case they were considered to have been provided for. In the absence of sons, however, a daughter might inherit her parents' entire property. The endowment of wives with property by their families sometimes allowed them to play important roles, even representing their ruler husbands during absences. Among the ancient Hebrews, the bride's receipt of property from her husband was part of the marriage document, which also specified his obligations to her. Women, on the other hand, were expected to produce children and run the household.

Women's Rights In ancient Sumer, there is some evidence of the gradual erosion of women's rights. This occurred as a result of chronic warfare (possibly reflecting scarcity of resources and an ecological crisis) and the growth of private property. Where kin-based control over resources existed, this control was centered in the household and dominated by women. The control over property by individuals rather than families tended to shift emphasis to the activities performed by men outside the household; this gave way to

FIGURE 8.2 The Code of Hammurabi, Found at Susa (18th century B.C.E.)

The relief at the top of the seven-foot-high stone stele depicts Hammurabi (standing) with the sun god. The law code outlining the limits of male authority in the household is inscribed below.

SOURCE: Louvre/© RMN.

male control and female dependence. The code of the Mesopotamian king Hammurabi (ca. 1792–1750 B.C.E.) is one of the earliest written documents that provides explicit regulations concerning the family. Among other things, the Code of Hammurabi (see Chapter 4) viewed the family as an economic unit and made definite gender relationships and parental authority, as shown in the following example:

> If a man has taken a wife, and she has borne him children and that woman has gone to her fate, and he has taken a second wife, and she also has borne children; after the father has gone to his fate, the sons shall not share according to mothers, but each family shall take the marriage-portion of its mother, and all shall share the goods of their father's estate equally.

PATTERNS OF MARRIAGE

Marriage practices in ancient Egyptian society permitted and encouraged brother-sister marriage among the upper classes and also among peasants. This practice can be documented in Egypt as early as the beginning of the second millennium B.C.E., and variations on brother-sister marriage were not unknown in other parts of the ancient Mediterranean world; Athenians permitted paternal half siblings to marry, and Spartans permitted the marriage of maternal half siblings. Even much later, after the Greek conquest of Egypt in the fourth century C.E., one of Alexander the Great's successors who ruled Egypt divorced his wife to marry his sister.

One explanation for the marriage of siblings, and in general for marriages of close kin, is that such marriages help to keep property within the family, since either the indirect dowry (what a prospective groom would give to his bride's family) or the direct dowry (property or wealth bestowed on a daughter at her marriage) remains within the family. Unlike women in ancient Mesopotamia and Egypt, women in ancient Israel received dowries from both sides of the family. When the biblical character Jacob worked to earn the hand of Laban's daughters Rachel and Leah, both women declared their right to the property endowed to Jacob through his labor as well as through their inheritance of a share of their father's property.

The laws of Moses, given by the Hebrew God to lead the children of Israel, specifically rejected the ways of Egyptian life, including the West Asian practice of brother-sister marriage. Although Moses himself was the product of a marriage between his father and his paternal aunt, **Mosaic law** prohibited such unions. The marriages of other close kin such as cousins, however, were allowed. Although ancient Israel distinguished its practices from those of Egypt—and perhaps also those of its surrounding neighbors—the motivation for close kin marriage remained powerful. Among the Israelites, both sororate (marriage of a man to two sisters, as Rachel and Leah to Jacob) and levirate (marriage of a widow to her dead husband's brother) were ways of keeping property within limited family circles.

■

FAMILY AND HOUSEHOLD IN WEST ASIA AND NORTH AFRICA AFTER ISLAM

It has been common for historians to note a sharp division between pre- and post-Islamic society in West Asia, that is, between the nomadic, tribal organizations characteristic of West Asia before the seventh century and the settled societies of West Asia after the time of the prophet Muhammad. This contrast has also been described as a transition between the male-based solidarity of desert lineage societies and the domestic household family units of settled farming communities in which women asserted more influence. The solidarity of desert lineages provided political opportunities for men, whereas the autonomy of domestic units in settled communities promoted greater female participation in household affairs and even some political influence.

Despite the great impact of Islam on West Asia, in terms of both codified religious law and social custom, there was a strong element of continuity in this region of the world. For example, the divisions into tribal or lineage-based society, village-based farmers and herders, and urban merchants both predated the coming of Islam and continued in post-Islamic West Asia; also, there is no evidence that women were excluded from property rights in pre-Islamic West Asia, as would be consistent with contemporary law codes of the region's Byzantine, Roman, Persian, and Jewish peoples. Therefore, the legal grant to Islamic women of the right to inherit parental property probably did not represent a significant change.

FAMILY AND LAW IN THE ISLAMIC WORLD

The critical change that accompanied the introduction of Islam to the region lay in the imposition of a written religious text, the Qur'an, as a guide to social and political order and the interpretation of this text into a law code, the *shari'a*. For example, the foundations of the *shari'a* were the unambiguous commands and prohibitions found in the Qur'an. This encapsulation of systematic codes of behavior began in the eighth and ninth centuries, with the work of several schools of legal scholars. The legal code regulated individual and family life within the community, which was defined as consisting of those who were "true believers" in Islam.

Written codes, by their very nature, changed social customs because they removed practices common to members of a society from their everyday context and transformed them into general principles to be applied across the Islamic world without regard to context. But there was another source of wisdom known as *hadith*s, or oral sayings. The intersection of these two authorities, written and fixed, oral and fluid, required varying degrees of personal reasoning and interpretation. The written laws in general tended to deal with the public level of the Islamic community, particularly stressing its patriarchal structure, rather than with the domestic world of the conjugal family unit, which was dominated by women.

THE FAMILY AS A MODEL FOR RELIGIOUS COMMUNITIES IN WEST ASIA

In early Islam, as in early Christianity, a new religious ideology demanded both a break from previous social customs and continuity with them. As they rejected pre-Islamic and pagan practices, both Muslim and Christian believers drew on the social symbolism of kinship relations and family life in creating their new religious communities. Beginning with the concept of Jesus as the "son of God" and the idea of "God the father," the symbolism of the family was a powerful model in Christian ideology, though in other ways Christianity undermined the roles played by elders and families in traditional Judaism.

The family had been a tribal unit held together by blood ties. But when the apostle Paul, a Hellenized Jew, called upon "elders" and "brothers" as leaders of the Christian community, he gave new meaning to these terms: they no longer identified status dependent on seniority and blood ties but leaders of a community of faith that cut across ethnic and kinship groups. Similarly, in Islam, the group would be defined as the community of true believers. Kinship models were likewise powerful concepts for understanding relationships within the faith. In Muslim brotherhoods, members addressed one another as "brother," suggesting the strength and permanence of the bonds of faith.

ISLAMIC LAW AND GENDER

There is little evidence that Islam brought any major change with regard to women's property rights. As before, under Islamic law women were entitled to a settlement by their husband or parents at the time of marriage. Although descent was reckoned patrilineally, authority within the family was patriarchal and residence was patrilocal, that is, the family would reside with the husband's family; women were entitled to a share of the parental property. Unlike in East and South Asia, where adoption was one strategy for passing on property within the family—that is, a male would be adopted into the family of his bride—in Islamic West Asia, adoption was prohibited, and close-kin marriage (which was not absent but often prohibited in East and South Asia) was a means of preserving family property.

Emerging out of the clan lineage society of Mecca, the Islamic family was portrayed in the Qur'an and in the *shari'a* as a highly valued institution and the primary social, economic, and political unit of the community. Women were described by some Islamic writers as inferior to men by nature and thus as owing men obedience. For others, like al-Ghazzali (1056–1111), the pivotal duties of Islam applied equally to men and women. In the urban settings of Mecca and Medina, as in Damascus and Byzantium, women could exercise some limited power in their own as well as their husbands' affairs. And like Judaism and Christianity, Islam offered equal access to heaven for both men and women.

Marriage in Islamic Law Marriage and its contract defined the primary relationship of the family unit. Muslim women could marry only Muslim men, a restriction that prevented the flow of property and population from the Muslim community to other groups. The legal contract of marriage, whether written or not, linked the resources of two families and was the single most important event in an individual's life. It required four witnesses, and if a court lay within a reasonable distance, it was recorded there. The contract might specify gifts of land or other family property.

Inheritance Laws The introduction of Islamic inheritance laws made custom one of the guiding principles of the law. Overall, the family was strengthened by these laws and the patriarchal authority of senior male family members was constrained, but social and economic practice in some regions and some periods found loopholes: the ideals of Islamic law could be and often were modified to allow individuals to benefit at the expense of family, for example, or to permit societies to ignore the rights of women to the advantage of patriarchy. Thus, the eventual codification of an Islamic concept of family and household relied on both the written ideal and the flexibility to deviate from that ideal in practice.

SLAVERY IN THE ISLAMIC WORLD

Early West Asian society also included significant numbers of slaves, who were largely integrated into free Muslim family units. Slaves, mostly captured in war, were used almost exclusively as domestic servants or, by some governments, as soldiers. By law, Muslims could not be enslaved; slaves were drawn from the surrounding non-Muslim populations. Under Islamic

FIGURE 8.3 Inner Courtyard of Islamic House
Only household members and invited guests intruded on the privacy of the family.

SOURCE: Bruno Barbey/Magnum Photos, Inc.

law, a slave was a person whose rights had been severely restricted but not totally lost by enslavement. Manumission, or release from the condition of slavery, was encouraged. Many female slaves became concubines, and their children were accorded the same rights as children born within marriage contracts. One of the purposes of *shari'a* law was to establish rules to integrate persons into the family unit and into Islam.

ISLAMIC HOUSEHOLDS

Housing varied throughout the Islamic world, depending on the pre-Islamic culture, climate, available building materials, and geography. However, two household concerns were widely shared: the right of the family to keep its affairs private and the impact of Islamic law and religious practice on women. Households looked inward for strength and satisfaction. Wealth, social interactions, and the intimate areas of family life remained hidden inside the household. Nothing of a house's façade revealed the inner workings or material comfort of the group. The family lived around a courtyard often ornamented with trees and fountains.

According to the Qur'an, believers should "not enter the dwellings of other men until [they] have asked their owners' permission and wished them peace." If visitors were entertained, they were admitted only as far as a men's reception area. Women remained secluded in their own separate area *(harem)* with apartments. The extent to which women might be permitted to leave the house varied across time and class. Strict Muslims in tenth-century Baghdad, for example, felt that women should never be seen on public streets.

ELEVENTH-CENTURY CAIRO: THE GENIZA DOCUMENTS

By the latter half of the first millennium, the Islamic world of West Asia had begun to encroach on the cultures of North and East Africa. The extent of this maritime trade is revealed in the business papers of a group of merchants who migrated from Tunisia to Cairo and then across the Indian Ocean. Called the Cairo Geniza documents, they have yielded rich material on marriage, family, and household within the Jewish community of medieval Cairo in the eleventh century and suggest something of the diversity and interconnection of Jewish, Muslim, and Christian life there. Among these documents, marriage contracts provide some of the most useful insights of the time into the social life centered on family and household.

According to the Cairo Geniza documents, marriages were conceived as partnerships, with mutual, if not equal, obligations between spouses; both partners had the right to terminate a marriage (although women's rights were more limited), with protection of property rights for women as well as men upon dissolution of the union. By the eleventh to thirteenth centuries, divorce was common—45 percent of all women married a second or third time—but not always amicable. The Islamic scholar Sakhawi (d. 1497) records the case of the woman Umm Kulthum's third husband taking another wife "so Umm Kulthum went mad and never remarried until her dying day."

Jews, Moslems, and Christians coexisted in medieval Cairo of the eleventh century, each group having a distinctive religious and ethnic heritage but also sharing some common regional and cultural identity with the others. For example, love was recognized as part of the marriage relationship, and conjugal sex was regulated according to different religious cus-

FIGURE 8.4 Divorcing Husband and Wife Accuse Each Other before a Qadi (Judge)

Here a scribe listens and records the complaints. Most divorces took place without the intervention of a judge.

SOURCE: Bibliothèque Nationale de France.

toms: on Thursday for Moslems, Friday for Jews, and Saturday for Christians. All such activity was to occur before bathing in preparation for attending the mosque, synagogue, or church. Mosques, synagogues, and churches all provided charity for indigents, and especially for widows and orphans, thus supplanting the family when necessary. Donations to such charitable enterprises by women from their dowry wealth have been documented. Wives were regarded as companions of their husbands, and they were independently involved in commercial business activities as well as able to go to court for the resolution of legal disputes.

The Jewish, Christian, and Muslim traditions of family and household spread as these religions expanded their territorial control into Africa and Europe. Adopting an urban, commercial way of life, West Asian merchants helped to transform notions of property, emphasizing other forms than lands and flocks. Medieval and later Jews placed great importance on learning and scholarship as necessary for marriage. In the Jewish communities of eastern Europe, the three main criteria of status were learning, family, and money. All three were linked in considerations for marriage, as the daughter of a wealthy merchant, for example, would preferably be married to a scholar or the son of a scholar. Each of these traditions—whether Christian, Jewish, or Muslim—would eventually exclude women from the activities deemed most important, from warfare to the study of sacred books.

■

CONFUCIANISM, FAMILY, AND STATE IN CHINA

Beginning in the Han period (206 B.C.E.–220 C.E.), Confucian textual tradition, beliefs, and practices dominated Chinese intellectual, cultural, and social life. Ideals of family life and familial relationships were the core of Confucianism. Ideals, however, do not describe reality: they *prescribe* the way things ought to be, and in doing so they often affect the ways in which things change. In considering the profound influence of Confucianism on the organization of the family in East Asia, we must be careful to distinguish between the ideals expressed in canonical texts and the realities of family life as it changed over time in response to varying historical conditions and regulation by the state.

As with most societies, we know little about family and household in early history and relatively more as we move closer in time to the present. Although a formidable body of historical records in China covering nearly two millennia is available, these formal documents usually exclude details of family life and household organization other than those pertaining to state concerns. In trying to reconstruct family and household in Chinese history, we must make use of a wide range of sources, including literature and material culture.

Rituals venerating ancestors were practiced in the Shang period (ca. 1600–1050 B.C.E.), at least ten centuries before the time of Confucius (551–479 B.C.E.). Society was organized into patrilineal (through the father's or male line) descent groups, or lineages. Lineages were the building blocks of social and political life in early China, as descent determined one's place in society. The king and aristocratic lineages performed sacrifices to their ancestors, who were believed to be powerful deities upon whose favor the welfare of the entire society depended.

CONFUCIANISM AND CHINESE SOCIETY

Confucius was born into an age of political and social disorder, the waning of the Zhou dynasty (ca. 1050–250 B.C.E.), when the power of the Zhou kings had weakened and the institutions of the early Zhou had begun to disintegrate. Along with other thinkers of his time, Confucius sought ways of bringing order to society. For Confucius, the performance of correct ritual behavior was the way of achieving social order, and he considered the family, not the individual, to be the fundamental unit of society. A legacy of earlier times, rites venerating ancestors were an important activity of the family, and each generation was obligated to produce heirs so that succeeding generations could continue ancestral rites.

Family and State State and society were an extension of the family. The ruler was to treat his subjects as a father treats his sons, and vice versa. Ideally, the virtue of filial piety characterized this relationship: the father had absolute authority within the family, and absolute obedience was required from the son. In addition to the relationship between ruler and subject, the father-son relationship, along with that between elder brother and younger brother and between husband and wife were among the five fundamental human relationships (the fifth was between friends). Certain aspects of these relationships as prescribed by Confucius are apparent: the dominance of age over youth and male over female. Age and gender determined hierarchy within the family. Women, no matter how old they became, could not escape the authority of men unless they became the widowed head of a household. As daughters they were dependents and subordinates of their fathers; as wives, of their husbands; and as widows, of their sons.

ARISTOCRATIC CLANS AND THE CHINESE STATE

Aristocratic clans dominated Chinese society throughout the Zhou dynasty. With the rise of a centralized, bureaucratic state through the Qin dynasty's (221–207 B.C.E.) unification of China, an attempt was made to reduce the power of extended kinship groups; they were broken up into smaller units, each of which was to have the direct relationship to the state of taxpaying household. This was only partly effective, however, and the tension between state authority and the interests of aristocratic clans—those sharing a common surname and tracing common descent—continued to be a prominent theme in Chinese social and political history.

Han Society During the succeeding Han period (206 B.C.E.–220 C.E.), aristocratic clans once again dominated Chinese social and political life. Descent was the basis of not only social status but also political power and economic standing. Emperor Wu (r. 141–87 B.C.E.) instituted a number of aggressive economic, political, and social reforms that somewhat reduced the power of the aristocratic clans. Despite state restrictions on their accumulation of landed wealth, however, the aristocratic clans continued to reside on large estates worked by tenant families in varying degrees of servitude. The aristocratic clans thus formed economic units, as did the households of the tenant families who worked their lands for them.

The Adoption of Confucianism The reign of Emperor Wu also saw the adoption of Confucianism as official orthodoxy. This meant that Confucian ideas about family were accepted as determining what was valued and how people should act, both within the family and in relation to the larger community and the state. Male authority was reinforced as gender roles were defined according to Confucian doctrines derived from early texts and reinterpreted in the Han period. One of the most influential interpreters of Confucian ideals with regard to the roles of women in the family was Ban Zhao (ca. 45–115 C.E.), the daughter of a famous scholarly family of the time and a noted scholar in her own right. She compiled *Admonitions for Women,* a treatise on the moral and ethical principles by which women should order their lives that also provided guidance for the practical concerns of everyday life for daughters, wives, and mothers. Some of the chapter titles of this work suggest Ban Zhao's themes: humility, respect and caution, devotion, obedience, harmony. She urged women to yield to others, respect others, and put others first.

SOURCES ON FAMILY LIFE AND HOUSEHOLDS

We know relatively little from standard sources about the intimate details of family life in early imperial China (ca. Han through Tang [618–907] dynasties). We do learn from these sources about the importance of lineage and ancestry, for example, and about practices that limited marriage partners in the aristocracy to those who came from a relatively small group of aristocratic clans. In addition to the genealogical records of great clans that have become available as a result of the remarkable finds made in the early twentieth century at Dunhuang in the arid northwest of China, we have some household registration records compiled around 750 for the purpose of taxation. These records tell us something about the family members, their ages, and the generations that comprised a household. One household included the head, whose age is given as 56; a widowed stepmother, 60; a wife, 58; two younger brothers (of the household head), 28 and 42; a son, 18; one younger brother's wife, 25; five daughters, ranging in age from 13 to 31; two sons of a deceased elder brother, 23 and 17; and a younger sister (of the household head), 43.

Literature from the Tang dynasty (618–907) and later eras can also be a valuable source documenting emotional and psychological dimensions of family relationships and suggesting how stated ideals were lived in practice. By around 1000, we begin to have much more documentation available to reconstruct the Chinese family and household, and literary sources, especially poetry, provide personal and private perspectives that greatly enhance what we can learn from official records. For example, Mei Yaochen (1002–1060) wrote the following poem in mourning for his wife:

> We came of age, and were made man and wife.
> Seventeen years have gone by since then.
> I still have not tired of gazing at her face
> but now she has left me forever.
> My hair has nearly turned white,
> Can this body hold out much longer?
> When the end comes I'll join her in the grave;
> until my death, the tears flow on and on.

CHANGES IN CHINESE SOCIETY AND FAMILY LIFE

During the five centuries between 750 and 1250, Chinese society underwent a series of dramatic changes that have led historians to see this long era as a divide between the early imperial and later imperial periods. During the Song dynasty (960–1275), society was no longer dominated by aristocratic clans whose claims to social status, economic privilege, and political power derived from their ancestry. A new elite had risen in part as a result of the civil service examination system. The status and power of these "new" families derived from producing examination degree holders who were appointed to government office, rather than from aristocratic birthright.

Marriage and Social Mobility Marriage ties were used by rising elite families in the Song as a ▬▬▬▬▬▬ means of enhancing their economic, political, and social status. For example, a wealthy family with no sons who had examination degrees might marry a daughter to a degree holder from a relatively poor family who had prospects of office. Adoption could also be used as a means to gain a son with the potential to achieve status through the examinations, particularly if a family had no male offspring. By the thirteenth century, the economic exchange involved in marriage shifted from bride-price (the transfer of wealth and property from the groom's family to the bride's) to dowry (wealth and property brought to the marriage by the bride), suggesting a relatively equal balance in terms of the exchange of property between the families of the bride and groom.

CONFUCIAN IDEOLOGY, MARRIAGE, AND CHILDREN

The extended household, consisting of multiple generations and branches, characterized earlier aristocratic clans as well as the new elite families of the Song. Confucian ideology, which had begun to be adopted as orthodoxy a millennium earlier in the Han, idealized the extended family. But for families with few economic resources, it was not financially feasible to maintain an extended family. Extended families may have been desirable according to Confucian dogma, but they were economically viable for only a relatively small portion of the population.

Children Bearing children to continue the ancestral line was a Confucian obligation, but for ▬▬▬▬ poor families it was often an economically disastrous burden. Infanticide, particularly female infanticide, was practiced out of economic desperation. We know about the practice of infanticide in the twelfth century, for example, from written sources that document state officials' efforts to establish orphanages to alleviate the problem of infanticide, which was viewed as a great social evil by Confucian authorities. Children of poor families were often sold as servants. In more desperate circumstances, children were abandoned—left to die or be cared for by others.

Gender Preference Confucian ideas contributed to the favoring of sons over daughters, so ▬▬▬▬▬▬ that female infants tended to suffer at least benign neglect, if not infanticide, far more than male ones. Daughters were considered less desirable than sons, since daughters would marry out while sons would remain in the family to care for their parents in old age. If it was possible to feed a daughter until she was old enough, she might be sold as a bride, a servant, or a concubine. The purchase of women through the practice of concubinage was condoned by Confucians as a means of producing male heirs who would continue the family line and the ancestral rites.

Footbinding Although its origins are veiled in legend, we do know that the practice of foot-▬▬▬▬ binding became established sometime around 1000. The binding of a female child's foot with the toes turned under so that the foot would be malformed and stunted, shaped into the desired tiny "lily foot," possibly began with a style of dancing with bound feet not unlike those of modern ballet dancers, who wear toe shoes. The practice of binding feet apparently spread from the court as a fashion; it was appealing to men because it caused women to walk with a mincing, dainty step and may have caused physical changes that heightened male sexual pleasure. The spread of the practice was also related to economic prosperity brought about by the commercial revolution of Song times, as only wealthier households could support women whose feet were bound and therefore were unable to perform physical labor. Bound feet also gave women a languid, passive appearance that contrasted with a masculine image of strength, virility, and activity. Gradually, footbinding came to be seen as essential to the marriageability of young girls, and literary appreciations of the "lily foot" enhanced the aesthetic appeal of this cultural practice.

Family and Emotional Life Marriage was more than simply a means to enhanced social or economic status, and families were more than units for the production of examination candidates or marriageable daughters. Marriage and family life reflected a complex of notions about the role and position of women and their relationships with men, and they created complex emotional ties that were often denied or thwarted by social custom and practice. Here literature provides a glimpse into the more private world of individual emotions as they were produced by ties of blood and marriage. A famous poet of the twelfth century, for example, wrote of his anguish over being forced to divorce his wife because she did not please his family. Lu You (1125–1210) lamented:

> Joys of love scarce,
> One heart full of sad thoughts,
> How many years of separation!
> Wrong, wrong, wrong!

FIGURE 8.5 A Woman Paying Respect to Her Husband

From a handscroll illustrating the *Classic of Filial Piety for Girls,* attributed to Ma Hezhi (twelfth century).

SOURCE: National Palace Museum, Taipei, Taiwan, Republic of China.

Genuine and tender feelings often grew between husband and wife, despite the view of marriage as primarily a social institution. Similarly, even though Confucian ideas decreed the importance of filial piety and the unquestioned obedience of children to their parents, parental affection and the emotional bond between parent and child were also expressed by poets, who wrote moving poems of grief at the death of a child, or humorous affectionate ones. For example, Huang Tingjian (1045–1105) wrote the following poem, entitled "Teasing Xiaode, My Son":

> This young boy on my hands at middle age,
> A prodigal offspring in the years of decline.
> Learning to speak—he trills like a spring bird!
> He smears the windows black—a bevy of dusky crows!
> He's never been scolded for Grandma dotes on him;
> Big sister glorifies his least show of wit.
> Perhaps he'll compose someday Treatises by a Hermit:
> Don't let low family status stand in your path.

A Guide for Family Life A guide for family life written in the twelfth century (see box) gave practical advice on how to deal with problems that affected family harmony, such as the treatment of women (as wives, concubines, servants, unmarried relatives, or widows) and how to maintain status. Rather than being the idealization of family life portrayed in Confucian texts, this guidebook was written from the perspective of the day-to-day concerns of family life and often showed a more flexible and tolerant attitude toward women and a more realistic view of human behavior.

Family genealogies of the later imperial period sometimes included instructions to family members on how to conduct themselves, what to wear, what to eat, and what kinds of occupations are acceptable and admonishing them to honor their ancestors with the proper rites.

Literature as a Source on the Chinese Family Short stories and anecdotes about remarkable events also reveal much about the realities of family life in the later imperial period (post-Song [960–1275]). One story from about 1300 tells of a woman who is talkative, strong-willed, and independent of mind. She eventually marries but after a short time is formally repudiated by her parents-in-law because of her sharp tongue. Her own family is deeply embarrassed by this, and she finally becomes a Buddhist nun, a traditional refuge for women who rejected society's demands or who could not live up to their families' expectations for marriage, bearing children, and generally compliant, submissive behavior.

CONFUCIAN IDEALS AND SOCIAL REALITY

Although Confucian piety demanded the strictest standards of moral behavior within the family and in society, prostitution, homosexuality, and other practices frowned upon by Confucianism flourished. Homosexuality, both male and female, was not widely acknowledged but was practiced at all levels of society. By the Tang and Song dynasties, there is anecdotal literature about Buddhist priests and their young male paramours, both male and female prostitutes, and other such practices that flaunted Confucian conventions but were to be found flourishing in the prosperous urban areas of Song China.

HOW TO MANAGE A FAMILY IN TWELFTH-CENTURY CHINA

An upper-class man in twelfth-century China, Yuan Cai (ca. 1140–1195), wrote a book of advice for managing a family and household that tells us much about how people viewed the role of women and their position in the household. In contrast to other works that prescribe ideals for women, such as the Confucian-inspired book by Ban Zhao (ca. 45–115), *Admonitions for Women,* which stresses the importance of humility and obedience for women in their relationships with husbands and in-laws, Yuan Cai's book is a practical guide for family heads, recognizing the realities of daily life that may make the realization of such ideals impractical. Yuan makes some of the same basic assumptions as more idealized works about a woman's place in the home, the "inner quarters," though he challenges other assumptions about daughters being outsiders (because they will marry out and leave their natal family) and about inheriting property. This work makes clear the corporate nature of the household as an economic unit.

Women Should Not Take Part in Affairs outside the Home

Women do not take part in extrafamilial affairs. The reason is that worthy husbands and sons take care of everything for them, while unworthy ones can always find ways to hide their deeds from the women.

Many men today indulge in pleasure and gambling; some end up mortgaging their lands, and even go so far as to mortgage their houses without their wives' knowledge. Therefore, when husbands are bad, even if wives try to handle outside matters, it is of no use. Sons must have their mothers' signatures to mortgage their family properties, but there are sons who falsify papers and forge signatures, sometimes borrowing money at high interest from people who would not hesitate to bring their claim to court. Other sons sell illicit tea and salt to get money, which, if discovered by the authorities, results in fines.

Mothers have no control in such matters. Therefore, when sons are bad, it is useless for mothers to try to handle matters relating to the outside world.

For women, these are grave misfortunes, but what can they do? If husbands and sons could only remember that their wives and mothers are helpless and suddenly repent, wouldn't that be best?

Women's Sympathies Should Be Indulged

Without going overboard, people should marry their daughters with dowries appropriate to their family's wealth. Rich families should not consider their daughters outsiders but should give them a share of the property. Sometimes people have incapable sons and so to have to entrust their affairs to their daughters' families; even after their deaths, their burials and sacrifices are performed by their daughters. So how can people say that daughters are not as good as sons?

Generally speaking, a woman's heart is very sympathetic. If her parents' family is wealthy and her husband's family is poor, then she wants to take her parents' wealth to help her husband's family prosper. . . .

It is Difficult for Widows to Entrust Their Financial Affairs to Others

Some wives with stupid husbands are able to manage the family's finances, calculating the outlays and receipts of money and grain, without being cheated by anyone. Of those with degenerate husbands, there are also some who are able to manage the finances with the help of their sons without ending in bankruptcy. Even among those whose husbands have died and whose sons are young, there are occasionally women able to raise and educate their sons, keep the affection of all their relatives, manage the family business, and even prosper. All of these are wise and worthy women. But the most remarkable are the women who manage a household after their husbands have died leaving them with young children. Such women could entrust their finances to their husbands' kinsmen or their own kinsmen, but not all relatives are honorable, and the honorable ones are not necessarily willing to look after other people's business.

When wives themselves can read and do arithmetic, and those they entrust with their affairs have some sense of fairness and duty with regard to food, clothing, and support, then things will usually work out all right. But in most of the rest of the cases, bankruptcy is what happens.

SOURCE: Patricia B. Ebrey, *Chinese Civilization: A Sourcebook* (NY: Macmillan Free Press, 1993) p. 166–8.

In China, as in other societies, ideals of family life and gender roles were often in conflict with the realities of daily life for much of the population. This is not to say that Confucian ideals were unimportant; to the contrary, Confucianism prescribed ideals of behavior to which many people aspired and which molded the actions of much of the Chinese population from Han times until very recently.

■
GENDER, FAMILY, AND STATE IN JAPAN

Matriarchy? There is considerable evidence to show that early Japan may have been a matriarchal society in which women exercised great power. Chinese records from the third century tell of a shaman-queen, Himiko or Pimiko, who ruled over 100 "countries" (*kuni*) in Japan. The indigenous religious beliefs that became the foundation of Shinto, as the native religion was known after the introduction of Buddhism in the sixth century, also reflect the power of women: the central solar deity, Amaterasu, is female, and priestesses continue to play an important role in rites at Shinto shrines even in the present.

Early Japanese Social Structure The earliest social unit was that known as the *uji,* often translated as "clan." The *uji,* however, unlike a clan, included people who were not related by blood ties. *Uji*s were associated with certain geographical locations, and *uji* chiefs served as religious leaders who represented the group to their common ancestral deity, often a spirit of a mountain or other natural site. Gradually, one of these *uji*s, whose progenitor deity was the Sun Goddess, became dominant over the others and established itself as the Sun line. Claiming the right to rule by divine descent from the Sun Goddess, this *uji* became the imperial family of Japan, reigning through the late twentieth century.

HEIAN SOCIETY AND MARRIAGE POLITICS

Even after successive waves of influence from China had introduced Buddhism, the structure of a bureaucratic, centralized state, and other new ideas and institutions, Japan continued to be a patrimonial state, in which the affairs of the country were the affairs of the imperial household or its representatives. Court families such as the Fujiwara in the Heian period (794–1185) entrenched themselves at court in part through marrying into the imperial family. Women were barred from succession to the throne after the eighth century, but they retained political importance as pawns in the practice of "marriage politics." By marrying his daughter to the heir to the throne, a Fujiwara male, for example, could become the father-in-law of the emperor. If his daughter gave birth to a son, he would become the grandfather of the new heir and hence a powerful and influential member of the court.

Women in Heian Court Life Women in the Heian period were more than daughters to be married and wives to bear children. They could hold and inherit property, and thus their legal position was relatively strong. The flowering of native Japanese literature, especially the novel and the poetic diary, in this era was largely a product of women writers. Denied the possibility to hold government office and conduct affairs in the weighty

FIGURE 8.6 *The Tale of Genji,* **Section of 12th c. Handscroll; Color on Paper**

The personal intrigues and romantic liaisons of Heian court life are depicted in scenes such as this illustrating Lady Murasaki's novel.

SOURCE: Tokugawa Art Museum, Nagoya/Laurie Platt Winfrey, Inc.

official language of classical Chinese, Heian women wrote in *kana,* the phonetic syllabary for Japanese developed in the ninth century.

Court ladies such as Murasaki Shikibu (ca. 978–1016), the author of the *Tale of Genji,* described their world, the Heian court, and the emotional and psychological background of the social relations that occupied their daily lives. It was a narrow world, perhaps, but one nevertheless real to its chroniclers. The greatest of these writers were capable of endowing their works with universal human meaning that makes their world accessible to modern readers. Although what we know of family and household in Heian Japan concerns only a miniscule proportion of the total population—perhaps 5000 out of a total of five million—the works of court writers, particularly women writers, of the Heian period have left a rich literary and cultural legacy

Heian Social Mores Heian social mores, while seeming in some ways to allow great sexual freedom, were precise and highly regulated. Prince Genji, the hero of Murasaki's famous novel, was married to Lady Aoi, the daughter of an important court minister and thus an appropriate spouse for the emperor's son. By Heian convention, Lady Aoi continued to reside with her parents, and her husband visited her there. It was acknowledged and expected that men such as Genji would have relations with other women. In Genji's case, tragedy was brought about by the spiteful jealousy of one of his lovers, whose malevolent bewitching caused the death of his wife in childbirth. Women did not have quite the same sexual freedom as men, but they did engage in amorous affairs and intrigues.

WOMEN IN SAMURAI SOCIETY

In subsequent centuries, the status of women changed dramatically as Japanese society came to be dominated by military values with the rise of the *samurai*. By the late twelfth century, the court-centered, elegant world of the Heian aristocracy had given way to a society ordered by warriors and animated by martial values. Although the family of Hojo Masako (1157–1225), the wife of the founder of the first shogunate, ruled after the *shogun*'s death, it was her father and brothers who ruled through her marriage to the *shogun*. Apart from the fragile and emasculated court nobility, who exercised less and less control over the country, military strength and skill were what determined political power and social status.

The family provided a mechanism to produce heirs to "fiefs," and the role of women was to bear the heirs. A woman was expected to exhibit loyalty to her husband's lord, even to the

DAILY LIVES

LADY MURASAKI

Like those of other high-born ladies of the time, the personal name of the author of the *Tale of Genji* was not recorded: "Shikibu," by which she is known, designates the office held by her father. Her family shared a common ancestor with the Fujiwara, the powerful family that dominated court politics in Japan during her lifetime. When her father was appointed governor of a province north of the capital on the Japan Sea coast in 996, she accompanied him. One of the few glimpses of her childhood given in her diary tells of her father, upon discovering her capacity for learning, expressing the wish that she had been born a boy. She was married in 998 or 999 to a distant kinsman, gave birth to a daughter in 999, and was widowed in 1001. Sometime later, she went to court to serve as a lady-in-waiting to the empress. Based on her observations of court life, Murasaki's great novel was written in the *kana* syllabary, a phonetic system for transcribing the Japanese language that had been developed in the ninth century. The *kana* script was also known as "women's hand," because it was viewed as a script to be used by those who dealt with less weighty affairs than those of the government, whose officials were male and used classical Chinese for official documents as well as for writing poetry. Women, however, excluded from such exalted positions, were able to exercise their imaginations and their creativity in responding to the society around them. Although Murasaki learned classical Chinese as a child and even instructed the empress in it, she

felt compelled to conceal her learning and even to carry out her teaching of the empress in secret. Murasaki's use of the *kana* script liberated her, in the words of one commentator, from the oppression of secondhand (Chinese) ideas. Her diary relates some of these feelings:

> When my elder brother Shikibu no Jo was a boy he was taught to read the Chinese classics. I listened, sitting beside him, and learned wonderfully fast, though he was sometimes slow and forgot. Father, who was devoted to study, regretted that I had not been a son, but I heard people saying that it is not beautiful, even for a man to be proud of his learning, and after that, I did not write so much as the figure one in Chinese. I grew clumsy with my writing brush. For a long time I did not care for the books I had already read. . . .
>
> Having no excellence within myself, I have passed my days without making any special impression on any one. Especially the fact that I have no man who will look out for my future makes me comfortless. I do not wish to bury myself in dreariness. Is it because of my worldly mind that I feel lonely? . . .
>
> When I am bored to death I take out one or two of [my books]; then my maids gather around me and say: "Your life will not be favored with old age if you do such a thing! Why do you read Chinese? Formerly, even the reading of the *sutras* was not encouraged for women."

SOURCE: Donald Keene, ed., *Anthology of Japanese Literature* (New York: Grove Press, 1955), p. 155.

extent of allowing her own offspring to die in place of the lord's heir. She was also expected to aid her husband in carrying out the final act of honor and loyalty to the *samurai* ethic: assisting her husband in ritual suicide and joining him in death by her own hand. Women widowed by warfare might take Buddhist vows and enter a nunnery. As in China, Buddhism provided a refuge for elite widows as well as for those who rejected society's expectations. Buddhism, by its very nature, provided an alternative to family in which individuals severed all ties to family and society outside the religious community.

One of the most striking aspects of the history of gender roles in Japan is their dramatic transformation after the Heian period, which idealized a kind of feminine aesthetic in its court culture. Beginning with the rise of warrior rule around 1200, women lost their right to inherit property and other rights they had enjoyed as members of the Heian aristocracy. Because of the limited sources that survive, however, we know little about family, household, and gender for the vast majority of the population until the sixteenth century.

FAMILY AND HOUSEHOLD IN CENTRAL ASIA

The relative lack of written sources for the ethnically diverse and complex societies of Central Asia makes it more difficult to trace historical change in the patterns and structures of family and household. Central Asian nomadic societies were patrilineal and patrilocal. Property—the herds—was normally divided among the sons of a family, with a share reserved for the parents. In contrast to many societies, where primogeniture (inheritance by the eldest son) prevailed, the youngest son ultimately inherited the paternal household's share along with his own. The household, measured in numbers of tents, was the basic social unit among steppe nomads. As in China, where patrilineal relatives might share common lands and residences, patrilineal kin in nomadic societies often shared common pastures and camps. The labor of an extended family was very useful in pastoral nomadism, which depended on the management of animal herds. Efficiency was increased by the combining of smaller herds, made possible by extended family ties; and women's work in milk processing or felt making was similarly improved by cooperation. The extended family, however, as in China, was a cultural ideal and had some economic advantages, as suggested; but it was also difficult to maintain, due to the inherent instability of large groups.

GENDER ROLES AND MARRIAGE TIES AMONG THE MONGOLS

Although the position of women was certainly lower than that of men, women were able to fraternize with men more freely and openly than in the more sedentary agricultural societies of Asia. Women could own, manage, and dispose of property. They managed the households, and often the camps while men herded, although women sometimes also managed the herds.

In the thirteenth century, the Pope's envoy to the Mongols, Johann de Plano Carpini, made the following observation about men's and women's work in the Mongol camps:

> The men do nothing but occupy themselves with their arrows and to a small extent look after their herds; for the rest they go hunting and practice archery. . . . Both men and women stay in the saddle for a long time. . . . All the work rests on the shoulders of the women; they make the fur coats, clothes, shoes, bootlegs, and everything else made from leather. They also drive the carts and mend them, load the camels, and are very quick and efficient in all their work. All the women wear trousers, and some of them shoot with the bow as accurately as the men.

The man would bring to a marriage his share of his family's herd, and the woman would bring a tent. But it was often not economically feasible for a newly married couple to form an independent household, and so they would remain with the husband's family, participating in the cooperative management of the herds. Marriage bonded two kin groups or even two tribal groups together, and thus daughters could be an important political asset. For example, the clan of Chinggis Khan's wife claimed that their marriage alliances, not their military strength, were the source of their political power: "They are our daughters and daughters of our daughters, who become princesses by their marriage, serve as shields against our enemies and by the petitions they present to their husbands obtain favors for us." Though **polygyny** (many wives) was practiced, each wife had her own **yurt,** or tent.

As in many other societies, marriage could be an important political strategy for families seeking power and status. After the death of her husband, a woman might retain considerable power through her sons and sometimes even in her own right. When a crisis in the succession of political leadership occurred, the wife of a former chief could wield power as a regent until a new successor was chosen. One example of this was the selection of the senior wife of the "Great Khan" as regent during the interregnum in the early Mongol Empire. In such instances, the strategies of elite Mongol women differed little from those of thirteenth-century elite women in other cultures.

■
FAMILY AND HOUSEHOLD IN INDIA

Critical to understanding family and household in India is the caste system, the inherited divisions of society based on corporate membership, common descent, and endogamy. The origins of the caste system are not clear but are related to religious beliefs formed in the wake of Indo-European migrations in the mid–second millennium B.C.E. These religious beliefs evolved into Hinduism, which provided the ideological foundations of family and household practices. With the development of Buddhism and Jainism in the latter half of the first millennium B.C.E., new ideas emerged to challenge Hinduism. But Hinduism remained the dominant religious ideology of the subcontinent and caste the essential organizing principle of Indian society.

CASTE, FAMILY, AND MARRIAGE

Ideas about caste were codified in the Book of Manu around the beginning of the first millennium C.E. Caste determined what Indians should do with their lives, whom they should marry, with whom they should eat and work, and where they should live. While greatly restricting individual choice, caste provided a kind of security in that individuals knew what place they were to occupy in life and what was expected of them.

Caste helped to shape families since it determined the boundaries of group membership and placed restrictions on marriage, though families were shaped by other factors as well. The patriarchal and patrilineal extended joint family—sons or brothers, their wives and children, grandsons, and their wives and children—was the basic structure of family life. Unlike in China, where there was an elaborate and highly specific terminology of kinship relations, relationships within the Indian family were much less clear-cut, so that a son might acknowledge all his father's wives, for example, as mothers. An individual's ancestry, especially in the upper castes, was important in both religious ritual and marriage practices, and ancestral rites helped to consolidate the family.

Marriages were arranged by families, and sons brought their wives into the parental home and reared their children there. The three purposes of marriage were religious (the performance of ancestral rites), continuation of the family line, and sexual pleasure. Marriage practices varied greatly according to region as well as caste. For example, in south India cross-cousin marriage (marriage of a son to his father's brother's daughter) was not only permitted but encouraged. For Hindus in north India, such marriages were generally prohibited, while Muslims in the north often chose spouses from within the patrilineal clan or lineage and thus married a cross-cousin.

As in many other societies, marriage was often a means of establishing alliances between families and of balancing economic against political or social status; for example, a wealthy family might form an alliance with a politically powerful family by contracting a marriage for their daughter with a son of that family. These goals in marrying, however, were always tempered in the case of India by the caste system. In most castes, inheritance was through the male line, but in some castes family property was inherited through the female line. In both north and south India, however, and for Muslims as well as Hindus, marriage as economic exchange involved both bride-price and dowry.

GENDER IN INDIAN SOCIETY

The position of women varied across region and over time but was generally inferior to that of men. For example, the Book of Manu states: "In childhood a female must be subject to her father, in youth to her husband, when her lord is dead, to her sons; a woman must never be independent." Women were subordinated and isolated by their change of residence and family

FIGURE 8.7 Woman Holding Child, Sandstone Sculpture from North India, 11th c. C.E.

The fluid, sensuous form of this figure is typical of Hindu sculpture, but portrays the intimacy and warmth of the maternal bond, rather than the erotic coupling of woman and man.

SOURCE: Borromeo/Art Resource, NY.

affiliation at the time of marriage. However, in terms of the three worldly ends of the Hindus, one of which was pleasure, especially sexual pleasure, women were regarded as equal partners of men. The *Kama Sutra,* a manual written in the fourth century, laid out the textual foundations of this principle, and its artistic expression is reflected in the many Hindu temple sculptures that depict voluptuous female forms locked in erotic embraces with male partners.

Muslim Influences   Muslim influences appear to have contributed to a decline in the position of women in India. The custom of *purdah,* the rigorous seclusion of women and the requirement that they cover their faces in all company except that of the immediate family, came to India with the Muslim invasions beginning in the eighth century. Although this practice may have primarily affected elite women and lower-class women may have never observed complete *purdah,* women did tend to keep out of sight when men were present.

Polygamy and Widowhood   Women were usually married at a very early age—before puberty—in theory to protect them from engaging in sexual activity before marriage and humiliating both themselves and their families. Polygamy (having multiple spouses, especially wives) was customary, although there were many variations, even **polyandry** (having multiple husbands). Widows were expected to follow a harsh regimen of daily life to honor their dead husbands, and in some upper classes, widows even threw themselves onto their husbands' funeral pyres to demonstrate their fidelity to their husbands.

Gender Ambiguity Another category of person existed in Indian society from at least the
▬▬▬▬▬▬▬▬ thirteenth century and probably well before. This was the *hijra,* literally
"neither male nor female," individuals who were castrated males (eunuchs) and crossdressed as
females. According to the late thirteenth-century Venetian traveler Marco Polo, Bengal
province was the center of a trade in slaves who were castrated prisoners of war. As early as
the second century, castration was also a punishment for adultery or for certain other crimes
of the lower castes. Homosexuality was acknowledged in the *Kama Sutra,* which devoted a
chapter to eunuch courtesans. There is some evidence that such gender ambiguity provided
individuals with the opportunity to cross other boundaries of acceptable behavior and
protocol.

■

FAMILY AND HOUSEHOLD IN EUROPE

When the French historian Marc Bloch observed that things do not exist until they have a
name, he might well have had in mind terms such as "family" and "household." Before 1500,
the basic social structures in Europe were household units of persons sharing residence and
making up an economic unit. European households maintained a hierarchical division of labor and rewards, and patterns of dominance and submission were commonly determined by
gender. Household groups in the societies of the Mediterranean basin were different from
those in the warrior societies of trans-Alpine Europe, but both were firmly patriarchal.

FAMILY AND HOUSEHOLD IN ANCIENT GREECE

Family groups in the Mediterranean basin became subject to the laws of city-states or other
political orders as they were formed. The relationship of the Athenian family to the city-state
and the roles assigned to family members by law were in place by the mid–fifth century B.C.E.
The social interactions within male-dominated families were not essentially altered by the
laws of the Athenian city-state, but the relationship of families to the larger patriarchal state
was. The family unit was expected to subordinate itself to the community in the same manner as women in the family were subordinated to men.

Patriarchy in Athenian Society Greek tradition held men to be logical and reasonable, in con-
▬▬▬▬▬▬▬▬▬▬▬▬▬ trol of emotion and instinct; women were considered to be im-
pulsive and selfish. Men were associated with order and civilization; women with emotion
and chaos. The premise of women's innate inferiority was not questioned, even by the Greek
philosopher Aristotle, who wrote in the fourth century B.C.E. that "the male is by nature superior, and the female inferior; the one rules and the other is ruled." Citizenship was reserved
for men. Few women received formal education, although many were taught to read and
write. The duty of the wives of the exclusively male citizenry was bearing the next generation
of citizens, warriors, workers, wives, and mothers.

Patriarchy within the Family Within the family, a woman was subject to the authority of the
▬▬▬▬▬▬▬▬▬▬▬▬▬ nearest male relative, although wives were their husbands' partners in family enterprises and in supporting the *polis* by upholding religion and morality. In
the household, the woman was mistress or manager, a position that required her being eco-

nomic and thrifty in order to keep the family financially independent. Poorer women did go out to work, were able to engage in retail trade, and were allowed certain privileges in the marketplace.

Otherwise, the only independent public roles for Athenian women were generally those of courtesan and priestess. The most eminent public women were priestesses of cults having strong female participation, such as that of Athena, the city's chief deity. Yet Athena was also a mother, and her motherhood added to her powers, which derived from her warrior status. Many other goddess cults required priestesses, and in these roles Greek women achieved great spiritual power and positions of religious and, occasionally, secular leadership.

Sexuality and Intimacy The social and sexual freedom of Greek women of the citizen class ▬▬▬▬▬▬▬▬▬▬▬▬▬▬▬ was restricted, while Greek male citizens held to at least a double standard. Patriarchal ideals enforced female virginity until marriage and sexual intercourse for wives only for the purpose of breeding children. While citizen males were free to seek sexual and social gratification wherever they could find it, their wives were legally restrained. Female adultery was dealt with severely by law, and wives were denied the social influence and position allowed courtesans.

Gender Ambiguity The highly gendered order based on male and female principles was not ▬▬▬▬▬▬▬▬▬▬▬▬▬▬▬ without its recognized ambiguity. Some deities in the Greek pantheon combined traits considered to be masculine and feminine. It is generally noted that classical Greeks were fully bisexual, participating in both heterosexual and homosexual intercourse. There were men, who were primarily men and sought men, women, who were primarily women, and sought women, and men/women who needed each other. While Greeks had a deep admiration of male beauty (the female body was thought to be a distortion of male perfection), in Athens the practice of sodomy was strictly circumscribed. Homosocial, if not homosexual, desire was believed to be critical to the educational process during which time students desired their teachers. Boys at school were protected against sexual assault by law, and adult males who engaged in sexual intercourse with boys suffered legal punishment, including diminution of their civil rights. Athenian citizens probably practiced homosexual inter-

FIGURE 8.9 Black-Figure, ca. 540 B.C.E. Terracotta. Amphora with Birth of Athena

Because she was not born from a woman, but from Zeus's head, Athena had a masculine character.

SOURCE: Virginia Museum of Fine Arts, Richmond, The Arthur and Margaret Glascow Fund. Photo: Ann Hutchinson. © Virginia Museum of Fine Arts.

course for a short period of their lives, from about age sixteen, when they began body strengthening in anticipation of military training, through the period of their military service.

Sappho In apparent violation of the patriarchal ideals that projected the importance of men, ▓▓▓▓▓▓ some women also participated in same-sex liaisons. For example, the Greek poetess Sappho of Lesbos (b. ca. 630 B.C.E.) only partly acquired family and household through the socially sanctioned means of marriage. She married (although her husband's identity is unknown) and had a daughter. Outside marriage, Sappho also constructed family groups and households from her homosexual relationships. Something of their nature is recorded in her poetry, of which many fragments but only one complete poem, a plea to Aphrodite, the goddess of love, remain.

Like humans, the anthropomorphic gods and goddesses of ancient Greece were not immune to the full range of human desires and romantic love, bisexuality, and even incest. The intimate relationship between the god Zeus and his daughter the goddess Athena appears in the chorus of the *Eumenides,* a play by the Greek playwright Aeschylus (525–456/5 B.C.E.): "Zeus, beloved by the maiden he loves, civilized as years go by, sheltered under Athena's wings, grand even in her father's sight."

Polis, Family, and Gender The economic demands of the independent city-state, the *polis,* also ▓▓▓▓▓▓▓▓▓▓▓▓▓▓▓▓▓▓▓▓▓ affected Athenian families by prescribing strict limits to the family's independence and size. For example, the interrelated economic considerations of *polis* and family dictated the number of children that parents could rear (usually at least several). Surplus children were "exposed"—abandoned in a public place rather than killed outright—and girls were at greater risk for this treatment than boys. This practice continued for centuries throughout the Mediterranean.

Legal documents provide many insights into Athenian family life. The wife of an Athenian citizen was legally guaranteed some property rights. If she left her matrimonial home, her husband had to return her property to her or pay interest on it. If her husband abandoned the household, he was required to pay support. Few respectable women left home; public opinion supported the seclusion of women, except for prostitutes and servants in taverns. Houses were designed to further separate men and women in separate sleeping and living quarters, sometimes on different stories. In contrast to the public buildings, private residences were dark, squalid, and unsanitary.

Just as the Athenian family was defined by the *polis,* women were defined by their roles within the family, and within the family by their relationship to men. A complete system of values and institutions protected and supported women so long as they functioned in their socially approved roles of daughter, wife, mother, and widow. In this way women's dependence and subordination were institutionalized.

THE ROMAN FAMILY AND HOUSEHOLD

The Latin word *familia* is the origin of the modern English word "family," and the Latin *domus,* often translated as "household," is the root of such modern English terms as domestic and domicile. Since Roman laws and legal institutions, which became the foundation of later

European family law and customs, addressed issues related to the family as defined by these two terms, it is important to gain some understanding of how the Roman family was organized and how it functioned. Though people have begun to look at archaeological and other sources to put together a picture of family life outside the Roman elite and to make use of Egyptian sources, for example, to see how family life differed in the far reaches of the Roman Empire, most studies of the Roman family have focused on elite families in Rome.

Familia and Domus The Roman *familia* was a conjugal unit, consisting of parents and children, plus their non-kin dependents, including slaves, freedmen servants, and foster children. Roman society had three basic legal categories of status: freeborn citizens, freedmen (ex-slaves), and slaves. Though slaves were not legally free to marry, they often did form unions within the *familia;* freed slaves also tended to marry within the *familia* and took the family name *(nomen)* of their former owners. Since the basis of economic production was the family—usually specialist slaves who provided labor—*familia* was also used to designate a business.

In the widest sense, *familia* referred to all persons and property under the control *(patria potestas)* of the head of the family *(paterfamilias),* so it meant the household itself rather than a line of descent or a kin group. In fact, *familia* was rarely used by Romans in the sense of kin. *Domus* could refer to everything from the physical dwelling to its residents, the entire kin group (whether resident or not), and its patrimony (property and other financial holdings).

Low Birth and Survival Rates The primary purpose of marriage and the family unit was to produce heirs, since continuation of the family name was of great importance. At the same time, Romans had a low birth rate, which may have been due to lead poisoning from the lining of the aqueducts, among other possible causes. Other factors contributing to a low birth rate among Romans were contraception practices, which were widely known, and high infant mortality, which included the abandonment of children. Evidence of the routine exposure of female infants is found in the Law of the Twelve Tables (451/450 B.C.E.), legal codes of the early Roman Republic wherein it is written that a father is required to raise all of his sons but only one daughter.

The Encouragement of Childbearing In response to these conditions, which threatened to reduce the population of Roman citizens, the Roman state undertook to encourage the bearing and rearing of children and to discourage celibacy or childless marriages. For example, Julius Casear's law of 59 B.C.E. made land available to fathers of three or more children. In the first century B.C.E., Sulla divorced his third wife, Cloelia, for infertility; she left his house honorably and Sulla suffered no criticism for the divorce.

Among the many new policies instituted by Emperor Augustus (r. 31 B.C.E.–14 C.E.), social engineering focused primarily on matters of the family and household: marriage, child-rearing, and slavery. In 18 B.C.E. and again in 9 C.E., Emperor Augustus issued legislation to promote childbearing. Political preference was given to fathers of three or more children and both political and financial liabilities were imposed on childless couples as well as unmarried persons over the age of 20 for women and 25 for men. In later Roman times, male children were guaranteed state support, a program aimed at ensuring an available population for recruitment as soldiers.

We have few historical sources on children and know relatively little about childhood, other than the participation of young girls and boys in festivals and games. Adolescent boys lived at home with their parents, while their female siblings married, left home, and began to bear children. Despite the paucity of sources that tell the intimate details of family life, epitaphs and other more personal sources such as letters bear witness to the emotional ties that bound wife to husband and parents to children. In the year 58 C.E., the politically troubled Roman orator Cicero wrote to his wife, Terentia, "My dear, I truly desire to see you as soon as possible, and to die in your arms, since neither the gods whom you have piously worshiped nor the men whom I have always served, have shown us any thanks."

The encouragement of childbearing continued throughout the later Roman Empire. Roman coinage of the second century C.E. was used to advertise ideals of Roman motherhood, often in association with women of the imperial family. The violation of family bonds was linked to social breakdown, and laments of moral decay within the family echoed throughout the later Roman Empire, to be exploited by early Christian communities who criticized the decadence of Roman life.

FAMILY AND HOUSEHOLD IN TRANS-ALPINE EUROPE

Celtic Society Elsewhere in Europe, families and households were less subject to the interference of the state. Much of what we know about the social structures and habits of northern peoples such as the Celts and the Germans has been derived from and shaped by observations written down by male Roman observers. As in Mediterranean Europe, women in northern Europe were subject to male dominance and were primarily valued as mothers and household managers. In Celtic society, described by Julius Caesar (100–44 B.C.E.) as belligerent, lives bordered on extreme forms of domination and submission, and people were afraid to act independently, living in utter dependence on the few dominant male warriors.

Women were excluded from society's most important roles. They could not be warriors, **druids** (priests), or poets, though a few women became priestesses. They were excluded from public roles that gave men access to political power and influence. Their roles were categorized basically by their sexual relationship to men. Celtic societies made distinct judgments about women based on virginity and performance as wives and mothers; good mothers produced sons and good wives managed households efficiently, but all were denied equal justice by Celtic law.

Tacitus on German Family Life The Roman historian Tacitus (ca. 55–118 C.E.) presented an admiring portrait of Germanic family life as a moral lesson to the Romans, whom he felt were growing decadent. Though Tacitus seems to imply that women's position in Germanic society was higher than in the classical patriarchies of the Mediterranean world, what he described was a vigorous, decidedly male-dominated society. According to the Roman historian, when not engaged in warfare men spent little time in hunting, more in "idling, abandoned to sleep and gluttony."

Germanic males were reportedly monogamous warriors, and the wife was the warrior's partner in all things, though it would appear that it was an unequal partnership, since care of the household and cultivation of the fields was left to women, who in turn were expected to live in "impregnable" chastity. Cases of women committing adultery were rarely reported, according to Tacitus, and were punished in summary fashion by the husband. From birth, care of her children was also the woman's responsibility. Young men were slow to mate, nor were girls hurried into marriage. Blood ties were close and perhaps sacred, and large, extended families were esteemed. The greater number of a man's offspring and relations, the greater his influence and security when he was old. Old women were highly regarded, apparently being considered to have prophetic or spiritual powers.

FAMILY AND HOUSEHOLD IN MEDIEVAL EUROPE

Later centuries saw little deviation from the pattern of male domination in European society. By the ninth century, European families, shaped by classical Greek, Roman, Celtic, and Germanic traditions, were groups of people with a shared sense of belonging, subject to institutional controls. Families in feudal society consisted of two sorts: those who possessed property and those who labored to make the property productive. Landlord and peasant families were mutually responsible for each other's actions and were contractually bound to each other by elaborate duties and responsibilities.

Women and Family   The basics of feudal contracts were apparently not served by women. Be-
in Feudal Society   cause women could not be warriors, they could not fulfill the military
                     obligation basic to feudal relationships, in which land was exchanged for
military service. However, between the ninth and twelfth centuries there are some rare examples of women subverting the ideal feudal relationship. Women might only occasionally fight as soldiers and inherit titles and responsibilities, but because their labors supported the warrior knights and nobles, they were necessary to the functioning of the feudal system. Elite women were overseers of estates and supervisors of households. They bore children, who assured the creation and continuity of the lineage.

Landlords were warriors and had warrior status—the highest status in feudal society— by virtue of possessing land, and both landholding and warfare confirmed and consolidated patriarchy. The dominance of a class of warrior males supported by possession of land could be maintained only if marriage produced heirs, preferably male. Women had further importance to landed families since through marriage they could be the means of acquiring additional land and prestige. Accordingly, feudal custom gave the heads of landowning families the right to arrange marriages, which was commonly done in the interest of maintaining the integrity of family property or increasing it.

By the tenth century, whenever royal power lessened, control and inheritance of land passed from the hands of kings to those of vassals, subvassals, and their families. As a result, women were able to inherit, and land could be kept in the family. A woman who held land in her own right also had to fulfill the obligations of holding it, including military service. Though women landholders were not warriors themselves, they were responsible for providing warriors in fulfillment of the feudal contract.

Eleanor of Aquitaine   The most familiar example of a woman landholder is that of Eleanor of
                        Aquitaine (1122–1204). Duke William X of Aquitaine, a vassal of
King Louis VI of France, bequeathed his lands to his daughter Eleanor, who accordingly possessed approximately one-third of the territory nominally belonging to the French king. Louis VI, wishing to secure her lands for the French dynasty, arranged for Eleanor to marry his son Louis. When the marriage was annulled, Eleanor regained control of the land be-

queathed her by her father. In the face of the French designs, even so powerful an heiress could not hope to keep her inheritance without a husband to control and direct the power needed to guarantee it. The dominance of the male in feudal society was reiterated by Eleanor's marriage to the future Henry II of England, who, like their son and her French husband before him, controlled her territories through his military power.

Powerful and privileged women such as Eleanor of Aquitaine could only circumvent the patriarchal system; they could not reconfigure it. By the thirteenth century, the feudal wars between families resulted in the consolidation of family domains into ever-larger holdings. Since women could transmit to their heirs key positions in a lineage, they occasionally found themselves in pivotal political alliances between families since their rights to property would eventually be inherited by heirs produced through strategic marriages. Women protected the property of their families and lineages, even though they passed it on to males to whom they were subordinate.

The Peasant Family and Household In medieval Europe, peasant family groups, whose labor sustained the feudal warrior landlords, were first and foremost economic units. As such, they were controlled by landlords and by the requirements of agricultural production. Since the labor of all members of a peasant family was vital to productivity and wealth, landlords commonly would allow neither male nor female members of peasant families on their land to marry off their property (since this would result in a loss of labor), though they welcomed marriage onto their estates. Peasant women on feudal manors were valued as producers of laborers, as well as for their own labor. Labor duties were family responsibilities, equally burdensome and confining to men and women, though peasant women shouldered household tasks along with those of the field.

Before 1500, even prosperous European peasant households were still, by most standards, unpleasant. An extended-generation peasant family lived in a single room above a stable containing their chickens, cows, straw, and hay, where, according to the Dutch scholar Desiderius Erasmus (1466?–1536), "almost all the floors are of clay and rushes from the marshes, so carelessly renewed that the foundation sometimes remains for twenty years, harboring, there below, spittle and vomit and wine of dogs and men, beer . . . remnants of fishes and other filth unnameable." The standard centerpiece of the family's room was a huge bed in which all, regardless of age and gender, slept. Privacy was unknown, as was noted by the fifteenth-century traveler Cristoforo Fioravanti at the beginning of this chapter. Alcoholic beverages were commonly consumed in huge quantities, as much as a gallon per person each day. Household members experienced both feast and famine, depending on weather, crop failures, diseases, and the scarcity or availability of labor. In contrast to the gluttony and excesses of the noble manor, an average of about one in four years of a peasant's life was spent in miserable hunger.

Christianity, the Church, and the Family in Europe Whether in foraging societies, hierarchical authoritarian states, or decentralized feudal societies, the European household persisted as a basic social and economic unit. However, the forms of family changed continuously in response to changing social conditions, despite the efforts of institutional Christianity to define the family and regulate it in permanent and immutable ways, including, after the eighth century, written legal systems. The influence of the Church on the family was perhaps most clearly summed up by the inclusion of marriage among the

FIGURE 8.10 Giovanni Arnolfini and His Wife by Jan van Eyck, Dated 1434

This detail from *Arnolfini Marriage* celebrates the pride and acquisitions of a successful European merchant: wife, mirror, chandelier, bed-hangings, and pet. While the woman's figure and features are idealized, the face of the man may be an actual portrait.

SOURCE: Foto Marburg/Art Resource, NY.

Church's sacraments and by the Church's assignment of celibacy to the clergy. Both were in place by the end of the first millennium of the Christian era, and both indicate that organized religion joined economic considerations and male dominance to help shape and define the European family.

The Church's intrusion into family life went beyond its control of the marriage sacrament. It prescribed the roles of men and women, excluding women from the priesthood and justifying this subordination by reference to Jesus's life without women. The practice of regular confession to a priest who prescribed penance meant that the Church, through its clergy, exercised control over family behavior. As the Church gained wealth and came to influence almost all social groups, it exercised even more influence on European families.

Through its role in the economic activity that accompanied the revival of urban society around 1200, the Church had an impact on the material lives of families of all classes. Guilds, which provided relief from some family stress by providing economic support in times of illness or death, were sanctioned by the Church through their identification with patron saints. The Church helped shape economic life in towns by insisting on the just price for goods (defined as the cost of raw materials and labor) and prohibiting usury (exorbitant interest).

Religious festivities provided enjoyment and relief for the lower classes and even, sometimes, an occasion for revolt. The revival of town life and trade may have improved opportunities for women somewhat, but male dominance remained unquestioned. After 1500, changes in the customs and roles of European families and households would accelerate, but the patriarchal pattern of society that relegated women to the household remained unshaken and constant.

■

FAMILY AND HOUSEHOLD IN NORTH AMERICA

Concepts of family and household vary as widely as do the kinds of historical evidence describing them. The recovery of family history in the pre-Columbian Americas depends on written, nonwritten, archaeological, and orally transmitted sources. Households in North America before 1500 were cooperative kinship groups varying in size from fairly small (several hundred) to large (5000). As we have seen previously in examining kinship and community in North America, the size of cooperative household units adjusted to economic and ecological conditions.

LONGHOUSES AND LINEAGE

Multifamily dwellings, or longhouses, were common to communities in the Pacific Northwest Coast region, the Great Plains, and among the Eastern Woodland Iroquois. At the beginning of the sixteenth century, one of the earliest European observers of native peoples in the Americas, Amerigo Vespucci, wrote of hundreds of persons sleeping in shared households. In some cases, multifamily dwellings were associated with the development of agriculture, since joint residency encouraged the cooperative labor required by intensive food production, though they were also characteristic of the nonagricultural Pacific Northwest. More commonly, shared kinship was the basis for establishing multifamily dwellings, with membership in a lineage determining joint residence.

Matrilineal and patrilineal descent were recognized in different societies, and in some cases, as in some Northwest Coast groups, bilateral descent (acknowledgment of both sides of one's ancestry) was recognized. Matrilineal families, in which descent and property were transmitted through females, were common among groups such as the Iroquois of the Eastern

FIGURE 8.11 Mogollon Bowl, Mimbres style

Its ritual hole is necessary for the woman to be allowed into the Hopi underworld (thus marriage is necessary for a proper afterlife).

SOURCE: Maxwell Museum of Anthropology, Albuquerque/Werner Forman Archive/Art Resource, NY.

Woodlands. The Zuni of the American Southwest were matrilocal, as well: when a woman married, her husband left his mother's house and came to live in her house, where he remained forever an outsider. The house and its possessions, the sacred objects and wealth, principally in the form of stored corn and access to the fields, belonged to the women who lived there. The family related by blood through the women was the central and permanent social group.

GENDER IN ZUNI FAMILY AND HOUSEHOLD

Religious ceremony and ritual, which permeated Zuni life, as well as economic production were centered in the family household. The working life of a Zuni man was spent in the household into which he married. As a farmer, he was an essential household member, though to the Zuni, a person's importance was not economic. Wealth was important only insofar as it made it possible for a man to undertake and pay for the responsibilities and ritual obligations that would make him truly respected.

Lhamana   Within the context of meanings and roles structured by gender, women were considered responsible for the family and community; men were responsible for the universe. Their roles were distinct and complementary. The Zuni believed that gender was acquired through a gradual awareness of the individual, usually in childhood. The most striking illustration of Zuni gender construction is the identity known as *lhamana* (referred to as *berdache* by anthropologists), who combined the cultural traits and roles of both male and female. The decision to become *lhamana* was made by a boy in childhood and finalized at puberty, when the youth adopted female dress. Rather than assimilating the ritual knowledge of men, the boy destined to become *lhamana* hung around the house and learned women's skills, mostly those of weaving and potting.

Archaeological evidence supports the antiquity of the *lhamana* identity. Burials are recorded in which women wear both a dress and a man's kilt and in which men are buried with implements associated with women, such as a clay ball and baskets. In Zuni **kivas** (the clan's ceremonial houses) at the archaeological site called Pottery Mound (1300–1425 C.E.), some 100 miles north of the Zuni pueblo, paintings of masked dancers wear the distinctive *lhamana* hairstyle: half the hair is plaited in a characteristic female whorl and the other half is allowed to hang straight in the male manner. Other figures carry both bow and arrows and a basketry plaque.

GENDER AND WOMEN'S POWER AMONG THE BLACKFOOT

The Blackfoot of the northwestern Plains provide an example of the difficulty of documenting women's power before the fifteenth century. Male roles were more visible, flamboyant, and assertive, while women's behavior was properly docile and quiet. Yet several aspects of gender roles intersect and even crosscut this portrait of male dominance, and upon closer examination the boundaries of gender roles that seem at first glance clear can easily become blurred. For example, one way to explain the fact that men, not women, were involved in spirit quests to increase their spirituality is to assume that only men had the potential to achieve spiritual power. An equally valid interpretation would be to attribute the exclusion of women from spirit quests to their innate spirituality: they had no need to engage in spirit quests.

Evidence from traditional myths and ritual practices suggests that women were innately more spiritual. Women's power was manifested in rituals such as the Sun Dance Ceremony, in which women played a prominent role. In the Sun Dance, the Holy Woman carries a medicine bundle as a sign of the power of women to move between the Holy People of the Above World and ordinary people below.

Age was also an important factor that intersected gender. A large number of elderly women could become "manly-hearted" over the course of their lives. Such powerful women were able to control social situations as well as property. Although both men and women were believed to be necessarily paired, it was primarily women who brought blessings and powers from spiritual realms to be enjoyed by all.

CULTURAL REPRODUCTION, FAMILY, AND COMMUNITY

Family life maintained and expressed the Native American culture, not only through its reproductive functions but also because it functioned as a vehicle for sharing language, beliefs, and behavior. The family adapted and transmitted cultural knowledge across generations. The expression of group belonging reflected the economic and political context in which families resided. For example, among other matrilineal and matrilocal groups in the Pacific Northwest, such as the Tlingit, Haida, and Tsimshian, what was inherited was often intangible: the right to wear certain crest designs and to perform particular ceremonial dances and songs.

The sense of belonging to a group resulted from this intangible inheritance, but in the Pacific Northwest environment of abundant and renewable resources, the indication of belonging to the community was not limited to the plentiful economic or material possessions, which all shared. The most egregious crime in such communities was often theft, since anything that injured one member of the group was felt by all. The sense of a shared family or group identity was frequently reiterated by moral imperatives that emphasized commitment to community and enduring relationships to the landscape that transcended a single lifetime.

■

FAMILY AND STATE IN ANDEAN SOUTH AMERICA AND MESOAMERICA

Not all native American peoples were hunter-gatherers or subsistence farmers living in small communities. Families also persisted in large corporate groups, such as the Incan state (1438–1536) in the Andean highlands of South America. Families were patriarchal and regulated and controlled not only by the male head of household but also by the state, through laws issued by rulers and supported by the sanctions of religion. In this way, the family was incorporated into the hierarchical and absolutist state, the largest unit with which people identified.

THE FAMILY IN INCAN SOCIETY

As Incan society expanded after about 1000, the family was regarded as a unit of economic production. Men paid their tribute to the state through laboring on public works or in agriculture, or through military service; women spent much of their time weaving. Woven cloths had extraordinary ritual and ceremonial value. A special public building served as a convent for Chosen Women, brought to the Incan capital to weave cloth and participate in rituals. Male dominance was maintained in the patriarchal Incan society by treating women as property. Adultery was considered theft of the female involved, and the male was punished for having committed a crime against property. Boys and girls were educated in separate schools.

Families were provided with land by the state, which claimed everything produced and had the power to move family members and households to anywhere their labor was needed. This strategy also reduced resistance among conquered peoples. In turn, the Incas, aware of the benefits of keeping their basic economic units in functioning order, took the care and maintenance of family groups seriously.

Ideological changes accompanied territorial expansion and led to the establishment of the empire in the mid-fifteenth century. Men came to symbolize the conqueror and women, the conquered. As a result of the pervasive warfare, in which female enemies were incorporated into households as slaves and wives and male enemies were killed, the status of Incan women was devalued and the power they had once held because of their economic and reproductive roles was diminished. Warfare became as important as childbirth in increasing populations. Although some elite women could gain political influence through their relationship with the Sapa-Inca, both slavery and warfare reduced women's power. Family groups, modified by the authority of the Incan state, would be further transformed following the establishment of European control in the sixteenth century.

FAMILY AND HOUSEHOLD IN MESOAMERICA

Less is known of family and household in Aztec society, centered in the Valley of Mexico and reaching its peak in the fifteenth century, just before the European conquest. The cult of the warrior that dominated Aztec culture and society was reflected in the beliefs and practices associated with childbirth and child rearing. The metaphor of battle was used for childbirth, and the infant was described as a "captive," won in battle. Women giving birth were possessed by the spirit of the Earth Mother. If a woman died in childbirth, the Earth Mother would have to be appeased. From birth, female infants were carefully distinguished from their male counterparts by differences in care and feeding, according to the roles that each would fulfill in society. The social duty of the male was to be a warrior; that of the female was to be a wife. Marriage was a secular rite that symbolized the transfer of a young male from the care of his mother to that of his bride.

Although women were restricted to the domestic sphere, some did have public roles— healers and physicians, and especially midwives. These occupations had spiritual dimensions. Whereas the constant marking of sexual differences and consideration of gender were central to the ordering of the world in Aztec thought and culture, in the sacred realm sexual differences were often blurred. Many deities, in fact, had androgynous forms, and the gender of healers could be strategically ignored.

Sources that reveal the nature of family and household in both Aztec and Incan society are restricted for the most part to accounts recorded by Spanish scribes after the conquest. Neither the largely male informants nor the Spanish conquerors took great interest in the affairs of the domestic sphere, which was regarded as the domain of women.

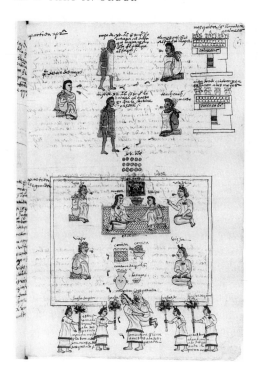

FIGURE 8.12 **Aztec Marriage Ceremony**
The bride is carried to the groom's house (bottom) and their garments are ritually knotted (above) to signify the union.

SOURCE: The Bodleian Library, Oxford. MS Arch. Seld. A. 1, fol. 61.

FAMILY AND HOUSEHOLD IN WEST AFRICA

In many African societies, there is no term equivalent to the word "family." Links created by descent and marriage did not always exist between persons sharing a residence. A household, which consisted of people sharing a residence, was as often defined by significant relations of production as it was by functions of reproduction. In other words, the household as an economic unit was often as important as the family as a social unit.

THE FAMILY AND SPIRITUALITY

As elsewhere throughout the world, a pervasive concern of African societies throughout history was continuity, the ability of the family and group to reproduce itself. An adult's sense of social completeness was dependent on his or her ability to sire or bear children. Motherhood was an essential aspect of female identity in most societies. Children guaranteed the well-being of an individual in old age and ensured the transition of the parent's spirit to the community of the ancestors, who would be honored by their descendants. The prevalent belief in reincarnation of ancestors as newborn members of the lineage meant that children were highly valued as visible symbols of the continuity of life. The pragmatic concern of many African women and men over fertility ensured a large and productive household labor force.

The Human Household In many West African societies before 1500, there existed more than a figurative association between humans and their households.

Houses were often quite literally human in shape and concept. The human body, household, and family were physical manifestations of the ideology that wove people into a single social fabric. Like the actual white threads observed by author Camare Laye (in the opening to Part II) after his initiation into the social group, the human body (as individual and group) and the built world of society were interconnected.

The Batammaliba For example, among the Batammaliba of northern Togo and Benin, who lived in dispersed, stateless settlements in the fifteenth century, the same word designated both the extended family and the house in which its members lived. The meaning of household (those sharing physical space) and family (those sharing social space) was a conceptual continuity. Lacking a household, an individual would be without social and spiritual support. The house was dressed in human clothes, and its parts were identified with parts of the human body as well as with specific human ancestors in its lineage.

The Batammaliba house also reflected the importance of historical ancestors in the identity of the family's compound. Every house served to symbolize a tomb; without the death of an elder, there was believed to be no new life. The arrangement of a settlement's cemetery was identical to the placement of family houses within the village, reinforcing the complementarity of house and tomb, present and past. In the house, family history was evoked and manipulated through daily contact between living family members and their ancestors.

KINSHIP AND POWER

Almost everywhere in pre-1500 Africa, kinship played a critical role in both the formation and the transmission of property, power, and prestige. "Family" mirrored the concepts of gender in society at large. "Household" represented a zone of social activity as often as it did an actual physical residence. The notion of extended family, the belonging of multiple generations and their siblings (grandparents, aunts, uncles, cousins) to a single family group, is common in African historical contexts. Family connections had political currency whether they were remembered as shared genealogy legitimizing the right to rule or as proof of descent from the first settlers.

Sunjata The reciting of the epic of Sunjata, the thirteenth-century founder of the West African empire of Mali, almost always began with a legitimizing list of ancestors that connected the singer (even centuries removed) with the chronological and political context of the historical hero. In the epic, Sunjata of the Keita clan overcomes a physical affliction and a questionable right to the throne and establishes himself as ruler. Sunjata's defeat of his opponent was a political and spiritual victory, but his right to rule as *mansa* (guardian of the ancestors or chief) was claimed through kinship ties. The continuity of the family line reinforced the continuity of male dominance in the social and political spheres of a patriarchy such as that of Mali.

Matrilineal Society in Ghana The Akan people of Ghana created some of west Africa's most powerful forest states and empires, beginning around the fourteenth century and culminating in the Asante Empire in the late seventeenth century. Central to Akan identity was the matrilineal structure of society centered on the *abusua* (which referred to family or matrilineage, as well as clan). Matrilineal descent in Akan society refers to

the pattern by which Akan men and women marked their place in the continuum of ancestors, by reference to the female side of the family. It had no special connotations for the distribution of political power, which as elsewhere in large-scale states worked in favor of men.

The Akan concern with fertility and bearing children was a recognition of the importance of the *abusua* in acquiring individual and community identity. Individuals had recognized rights only through their positions within an *abusua*. Without the protection afforded
to members, they were considered without ancestors and without sexual identity. The uncertainty and ambiguity inherent in the lack of ancestry and status are best exemplified by the
fact that enemies captured by the expanding Akan state became permanent slaves unless they
were integrated into an *abusua* through adoption. During the expansion of the Akan state
during and after the fourteenth and fifteenth centuries, neither women nor children gained
position or power. The emphasis on warfare resulted in men gaining status, and the increased
numbers of slaves available to perform household tasks generally devalued women's labor and
diminished their influence even further.

THE AKUABA: MOTHERHOOD AND FAMILY

One of the best-known sculptural traditions from the Akan region is the small, abstracted
carving of a human figure known as *akuaba,* literally "Akua's child." Oral traditions claim
that a woman named Akua, desperate to produce children, once approached a local priest. He
consulted the spirit world and then instructed Akua to commission the carving of a small
wooden child. She was told to carry the child on her back, feed it, and care for it as if it were
real. The whole village laughed at her until she succeeded in her quest to become pregnant
and gave birth to a beautiful daughter. The tradition illustrates the high status and importance associated with motherhood in matrilineal societies, even ones in which women are politically subordinated.

The *akuaba* images remain in use today. While images of children and infants are rare in
African art history, motherhood is frequently depicted as a source of empowerment. Children
had relatively few rights, since knowledge and power, considered to be the basis of rights,
were thought to accumulate with age. Still, children were accorded respect because they were
believed to be the reincarnation of ancestors. The *akuaba* fertility figures suggest the impor-

FIGURE 8.13 Akua'ba Fertility Figure (Akan, Ghana)

The idealized image reflects the desirability of children believed to be the
reincarnation of ancestors.

SOURCE: © British Museum.

tant role of children in reflecting spiritual harmony, ideals of individual beauty, and the well-being of the family order. In Akan society, an early proverb was symbolized by the image of two crossed crocodiles sharing the same belly. The associated proverb reminded members of a household that no matter who tasted the food, it would end up in the same place. That is, that which benefited one member of the group benefited all.

The extent to which such a unit as the household-family was mediated by the Akan state or local political authority varied according to the status of its members. Typically, interference in the creation of marriage alliances allowed a patriarchy to control the labor of women and their children and thus the accumulation of any household surplus. Even when wealth was inherited through the female line, most women were excluded from most political offices. Exceptions were made for elite Akan women who were beyond their childbearing years. The female office of queen mother was secondary to that of the king, but she was omnipresent and consulted in the ascension of the head of state. Women acted as priestesses and even diplomats who could find themselves making significant contributions to statecraft and foreign policy.

SUMMARY

The examples of families and households presented in this chapter have suggested something of their variety of forms and functions in world history. Investigation of family and household requires a reevaluation of historical evidence and of the questions that historians deem relevant and significant. Too often, the private, daily realm of human activity has been subsumed by the historical preoccupation with large-scale political affairs and the actions of "great men." The intimate and common human experiences of families and households have remained elusive. The historical record as represented by official documents such as law codes merely reports the prescribed and dictated ideal behavior. As seen by careful examination of other kinds of historical sources, such as literary and non-written evidence, historical practice often differed greatly from the ideals.

Within the limits of the historical record, it has been possible to reconstruct the differing character of families and households in many world societies. Family and household interacted with and were influenced by larger political and social orders; we have examined a variety of the historical contexts in which families served as vehicles for the accumulation and transfer of property, knowledge, and power. In the relatively few matrilineal societies, women held power within the family. In most of our examples, the structures of family and household and their relationships to larger social and political orders were shaped by a patriarchy. In ancient Egypt and in the Akan society of West Africa, where an ideological basis for sociopolitical ordering was the concept of fertility, women were an essential, complementary force, though subordinated to men in status and opportunity. In some cases, marriage itself was largely an economic transaction, marking the transfer of wealth and creating political alliances between families. Women were sometimes owned by lineages and subordinated within family and political orders.

Ideology had as much impact on families and households as material conditions did. Religion, ranging from family veneration of ancestors to hierarchical institutions, defined and determined the meaning and functions of families everywhere. In China, Confucianism provided the cementing ideology for patriarchy; in the Muslim world, Islam did. Laws sanctioned by religion, such as the Islamic *shari'a,* reinforced state controls over family, marriage, and inheritance. Similarly, European families after about the ninth century were strongly influenced by the Christian Church. The paternalistic and economic aspects of family groups in early West Asian and European societies and the Incan state were both modified and confirmed by what happened in the political realm. Warrior conquests or the appearance and disappearance of dynastic states were closely connected with both the operation of institutionalized religions and forms of family and household. The connection between family-household units and larger political orders gave ideological sanction to the family as an economic unit and, within the family, to the dominance of the male.

Households reflected widely varying patterns of economic organization. Where a number of families resided together in larger common households, the household became a unit of production, as well as reproduction. In the case of small societies, such as the Zuni, labor was divided according to individual choice and socially constructed gender roles, including the ambiguous *lhamana* status. The state did not interfere with decisions and relationships. Elsewhere, in male-dominated societies, men controlled most of the household's wealth and held greater access to political power than women did. Individual women of privilege, by virtue of circumstance, cunning, or their spiritual role, could and did circumvent the male-dominated hierarchies of ancient Egypt, Greece, feudal Europe, Andean South America, and Japan, and they often acquired economic wealth alongside political power.

Families were equally shaped by economic considerations. They were commonly governed by a desire to possess, expand, and perpetuate wealth (whether in land, trade, or office). The economic needs of the larger social groups also shaped the size and structure of families. Shifting patterns of economic activity and changing modes of production had profound effects on family groups. For example, the development of agriculture had an inevitable impact on foraging families, and agricultural families were transformed when they moved into towns and cities. The pastoral economy of Central Asian nomadic peoples similarly shaped the structures of family life and gender roles.

Families constitute the most basic threads in the social fabric; they are the most common units of society in world history. As spheres of human interaction, families are arenas in which culture and values are reproduced. Their differences suggest the staggering range of significant variation in the human past. Indeed, though states and empires rise or fall, the family and household remain central to understanding world societies. The features of various forms of family and household around the world—as basic social units, units of shared residence, or units of economic production—were in place by about 1500. The same forces that shaped family and household before 1500 continued to influence and change them after that date. Only the dominant position of males in society, family, or state would remain relatively unchanged.

The cultural imprint of intimate and daily family life can be seen at other levels of group and community politics as well. Families did not exist in a timeless void; they interacted and negotiated with factors of ecology and economy. The ways in which private and public spheres have interrelated historically have helped create order in world communities. Understanding oneself as a simultaneous member of various groups, from family to polity, is essential to creating identity. Identity is also the product of cultural memory, the transmission and reproduction of cultural knowledge across generations. Cultural memory from the shifting perspectives of individual and community will be the subject of Chapter 9.

Historians haven't always agreed on food as a suitable object of historical inquiry. Because food was associated with the household, Western historians often trivialized its importance. This was not so in ancient China. Food production and ceremonial feasts were included in ritual texts dating from at least the Han period (206 B.C.E.–220 C.E.). Suggesting the continuity of the historical concern about food into contemporary times, modern Chinese often greet each other by asking, "Have you eaten?"

ENGAGING THE PAST

MY DINNER WITH ATTILA THE HUN

Sharing food inside the home is one of the most necessary and intimate of human social acts. Human children are born incapable of sustaining themselves independently, so eating food within a family context has served to ensure both the survival of individual offspring and the creation and maintenance of the group system in which children are socialized. In many societies, the choice and preparation of food and the organization of its consumption occur according to strict cultural rules, based on gender and place or rank within the family or household order.

The customs of dinner etiquette (table manners) are more than the fussy rules of modern matrons. They reveal much about the order of social groups. Since ancient times, societies have followed strict and meaningful cultural rules when it came time for dinner, as the following excerpt from an account of Priscus (from about 450 C.E.), describing his experience of a meal with the king of the Huns, suggests:

> Attila invited both parties of us to dine with him about three o'clock that afternoon. We waited for the time of the invitation, and then all of us, envoys from the Western Romans as well, presented ourselves in the doorway facing Attila. In accordance with the national custom the cupbearers gave us a cup for us to make our libations before we took our seats. When that had been done and we had sipped the wine, we went to the chairs where we would sit to have dinner. All the seats were ranged down either side of the room, up against the walls. In the middle Attila was sitting on a couch with a second couch behind him. Behind that a few steps led up to his bed. . . . I

think that the more distinguished guests were on Attila's right, and the second rank on his left. . . .

> When all were sitting properly in order, a cupbearer came to offer Attila an ivy-wood bowl of wine, which he took and drank a toast to the man first in order of precedence. . . .

> After everyone had been toasted, the cupbearers left, and a table was put in front of Attila and other tables for groups of three or four men each. This enabled each guest to help himself to the things put on the table without leaving his proper seat. Attila's servant entered first with plates full of meat, and those waiting on all the others put bread and cooked food on the tables. A lavish meal, served on silver trenchers, was prepared for us and the other barbarians, but Attila just had some meat on a wooden platter, for this was one aspect of his self-discipline. . . . When the food in the first plates was finished we all got up, and no one, once on his feet, returned to his seat until he had, in the same order as before, drunk the full cup of wine he was handed, with a toast for Attila's health. After this honour had been paid him, we sat down again and second plates were put on each table with other food on them. This also finished, everyone rose once more, drank another toast and resumed his seat.

Whether or not we find king and subjects, husband and wife, or father and children eating together varies greatly across times and cultures. Whatever the nature and pattern of social interaction occurring during mealtimes, food sharing was and is a basic—perhaps the earliest—of human cultural experiences and profoundly shapes social encounters of all kinds throughout a lifetime.

FIGURE 8.14 Banquet Scene, ca. 1416. Royal banquets in the French court were served with great ceremony and lasted from ten o'clock in the morning to midday.

SOURCE: Musée Condé/Giraudon Art Resource. NY.

SUGGESTIONS FOR FURTHER READING

Suzanne Dixon, *The Roman Family* (Baltimore and London: The Johns Hopkins University Press, 1992). Recent study of the Roman family, dealing with marriage, children, law, and the life cycle.

Patricia B. Ebrey, *The Inner Quarters: Marriage and the Lives of Women in Sung China* (Berkeley: University of California Press, 1993). An intimate and thorough exploration of women's lives in Song China, including marriage, family life, and economic roles.

Mary Erler and Maryanne Kowaleski, eds., *Women and Power in the Middle Ages* (Athens and London: University of Georgia Press, 1988). Collected articles dealing with gender issues in medieval European history.

S. D. Goitein, *A Mediterranean Society: The Jewish Communities of the Arab World as Portrayed in the Documents of the Cairo Geniza.* (Berkeley: University of California Press, 1967, 3 vols.) Careful study of the Cairo Geniza documents, including much about women, marriage, and family life among the urban mercantile elite of Cairo during the eleventh through the thirteenth centuries.

Jack Goody, *The Oriental, the Ancient, and the Primitive: Systems of Marriage and the Family in the Pre-Industrial Societies of Eurasia* (Cambridge, England: Cambridge University Press, 1990). Comparative treatment of kinship and marriage practices in West, East, and South Asia, concluding with comparison with ancient and modern Mediterranean societies.

David Herlihy, *Medieval Households* (Cambridge, Mass: Harvard University Press, 1985). Provides a broad picture of medieval family life and structure.

Michael Mitterauer and Reinhard Sieder, *The European Family: Patriarchy to Partnership from the Middle Ages to the Present* (Oxford: Basil Blackwell, 1982). Traces the theme of family in relation to patriarchy.

Jennifer Neils, *Goddess and Polis* (Hood Museum of Art, Dartmouth, and Princeton University Press, 1992). Emphasizes the social context of festivals and arts of the Athens community.

Sarah B. Pomeroy, *Goddesses, Whores, Wives, and Slaves: Women in Classical Antiquity* (New York: Schocken Books, 1975). Explores family life and the roles of women in Greek and Roman society.

Gay Robins, *Women in Ancient Egypt* (London: British Museum Press, 1993) Comprehensive look at women and families in ancient Egyptian society.

Doran Ross and Herbert Cole, *Arts of Ghana* (Berkeley: University of California Press, 1978) Explores material culture's record of life and beliefs in Ghana's past, especially Akan art.

Culture and Memory

The colossal stone monument known as the Sphinx stands guard to the Giza plateau's greatest pyramids of ancient Egypt. Towering more than ten times the height of humans, the Sphinx—a sculpture that is part man, part god, and part animal—was built about 2600 B.C.E. It serves as a powerful reminder of Egypt's past. Although we tend to think of such monumental treasures as unchanging cultural memories, such is not the case. By the time of the Pharaoh Thutmose IV, living in 1401 B.C.E., the Sphinx was already ancient, already altered, and in need of major restoration. According to the inscriptions on a red granite slab erected in front of the statue, Thutmose cleared away the desert sand and restored the damaged lion body with large limestone blocks for protection against wind erosion.

After another thousand years, the Greeks and Romans visited and again restored the Sphinx. The Greek historian Herodotus (fifth century B.C.E.) toured the valley and wrote the definitive tourist guide before the nineteenth century. Beginning with the Romans, visitors have also stolen smaller, more portable monuments, in attempts to appropriate their power as historical icons. The appropriation of history, it seems, is as enduring as the monuments. In the fifteenth century, Islamic leaders defaced the great sculpture, fearing that local Egyptians were still paying homage to its grandeur and durability. An Arab proverb claims that "man fears time, but time fears the pyramids." Perhaps the most blatant example of plunder was that of the French Emperor Napoleon, whose troops invaded the Nile in the nineteenth century C.E., and uncovered the Sphinx again, followed by European explorers who began digging up hundreds of ancient treasures that eventually found their way into the museums and collections of the world.

Today, if the Great Sphinx could look backwards, it would gaze on a transformed landscape marred by fast-food restaurants, polluted air, and tourists. The view ahead remains the desert sands of the Sahara; like the sands of time they are constantly shifting. That the Sphinx and other Nile Valley monuments have survived the millennia was precisely the intent of the Egyptians, who built and painted them bright colors in antiquity. However, their intent was also that they not be entered ever again. While later generations have treated the great structures as human monuments, for the ancient Egyptians these were monuments to something cosmic and eternal. Yet, the deterioration of the stone surfaces of the Great Sphinx continues at an alarming rate. Perhaps it is fitting that the symbol of the Internet service America On-Line is a pyramid, since the hundreds of Web sites dedicated to ancient Egypt soon may be the only way to visit such monuments as the Great Sphinx.

Many historical memories are neither as durable nor as monumental as a pyramid. Ideas about the past can be embedded in the tall tales historians tell or in the songs children sing. They can be reflected in objects or in the technologies that create the material world. Their shape is the subject of this chapter.

■

INTRODUCTION

In previous chapters, we developed key themes in human history, themes that give meaning to accounts of major events, institutions, people, and ideas. History is concerned not only with the products of the past but also with its processes: how we know what we know of the past, what the processes of remembering the past are, how they influence what is passed on, and how and by whom the processes of historical memory are controlled. What is passed on as history, what people remember and think it important to tell about the past, are the products of many complex human processes. These processes involve not only collecting evidence about the past but also how and to what end that evidence is selected, arranged, and ordered so as to create a coherent and meaningful cultural memory.

Memory is not passive. In Chapters 1 and 2, culture was defined as patterns of expression and behavior by which a community understands, uses, and survives in its environment. It was noted that culture was learned and that it was malleable, changing over time. Changes in cultures are responses to material conditions—either natural or human in origin—such as environmental and climatic shifts or war and conquest, and the memory of change is preserved in cultural memory systems. Memory is a dynamic social process. Memory systems do not preserve or reproduce cultural knowledge without sometimes altering, shaping, or even inventing it, either consciously or unconsciously. Agents of the changes they record and preserve, memory systems exert powerful influence over the communities whose cultural experiences they record.

History is but one of the memory systems by which community is defined and cultural knowledge is transmitted. Among other systems of cultural memory dealt with in this chapter are visual and performing arts, literature, theology and philosophy, and scientific and technical knowledge. These memory systems share with history the processes of shaping, defining, and perpetuating community cultural memory. Transmitters of community cultural knowledge, such as teachers and preachers, historians and dramatists, entrepreneurs and artists, help define the identity of the community whose cultural memory they shape. Historians, artists, scientists, religious leaders, and philosophers all share responsibility for the cultural memory systems of their communities, creating, propagating, and perpetuating communal culture over time and across spatial boundaries. Their role in transmitting and transforming cultural memory can either sustain and support or challenge institutions of power and the authority of rulers and elites.

Though culture is shaped by all members of a community, most humans individually have neither the power nor the ability to create cultural memory systems, which are often controlled by an institution or a group. Official forms of historical memory, such as that produced by governments or churches, can impose a selective forgetting as well as a selective remembering. Popular cultural memory, however, manifested in a variety of forms such as performance art or literature, often provides a means of expressing resistance to official cultural memory and thus can function as an agency of cultural change, following its own principles of selective remembering and forgetting.

This chapter offers evidence of a variety of cultural memory systems as they evolved around the globe up to about 1500 C.E. We begin with consideration of the basic tools of cultural memory, the spoken and written word, and the institutions by which the word is perpetuated. This is followed by a discussion of other kinds of memory systems, among them technology and visual and performance art, which rely primarily on image and practice. Examination of cultural memory systems in Asia, Africa, Europe, and the Americas leads to a consideration of resistance to politically sanctioned cultural memory and its effect on changing historical consciousness: the process that transforms historical identity along the bridge between past and present.

■

CULTURAL MEMORY SYSTEMS: ORAL TRADITIONS

The oldest system of cultural memory may be the spoken word. Written systems of cultural transmission are less than 6000 years old, but oral traditions, orally transmitted cultural knowledge, date from the time the human species became capable of speech and communication. Since that time, human communities have transmitted their shared cultures orally. Even in the age of the computer, oral tradition remains an important means of preserving and transmitting cultural memory.

Oral tradition is a formal and highly ritualized system of cultural transmission, but it can also reflect change. As human agencies, oral memory systems are subject to revision. Some aspects of oral narratives conform with and support current political and social realities of their communities, while others resist revision and remain historically valid, fixed features of orally transmitted memory. The revised and fixed aspects of oral histories are not as oppositional as they might at first appear. They reflect the tendency of oral evidence to provide both immutable and historically dynamic cultural memory.

ORAL TRADITIONS IN WEST AFRICA

Many oral cultures relied on specialists, who, like the scribes, priests, or scholars in literate societies, either were themselves elites (by virtue of the cultural information they controlled) or were connected intimately to elites through relations of patronage. Across much of West Africa, the oral historian known popularly as the *griot* held a position of power and importance as the individual responsible for preserving and transmitting the records of the past in oral form.

The *Griot* in Mande Society The historical role of the *griot* is described in the version of the
Mande epic *Sundiata,* attributed to the *griot* Mamadou Kounyaté.
He sums up the importance of oral memory, explaining his role as the agent of cultural transmission:

> [W]e are vessels of speech, we are the repositories which harbour secrets many centuries old. The
> art of eloquence has no secrets for us; without us the names of kings would vanish into oblivion,
> we are the memory of mankind; by the spoken word we bring to life the deeds and exploits of
> kings for younger generations.

In Mande society in the Mali Empire, the *griot* played a key role in political continuity.
He was judge and counselor to kings as well as court historian, who, by knowing the past,
was able to shape and control it. According to Mamadou Kounyate', "history holds no mystery" and knowledge itself is a form of power. The influence and power of the *griot* was such as
to make any modern-day historian envious. Their words not only brought to life the past but
also profoundly affected the present course of events. Because they possessed and could shape
knowledge of past events, *griots* could enhance the power of the king and his court and influence the cultural traditions they preserved.

Yoruba Cultural In another West African society, that of the ancestors of the Yoruba in
Memory Systems southwestern Nigeria, those who preserved cultural memory were known as
arokin. They were court functionaries, official historians who performed as
bards and drummers. The Yoruba people also reenacted founding myths of lineages, quarters,
towns, and kingdoms in annual festivals and installation ceremonies associated with chiefs
and kings. The *arokin* performed royal and religious rituals that helped preserve myths.
Yoruba cultural memory categorized the past in several different ways. Their view of the past
consisted of immutable views of their world which were publicly accepted and of myths and
rituals that were constantly subject to review and revision by contesting political and social
forces in their community. There were also "deep truths," the knowledge of spiritual realms,
that might subvert shifting myths and rituals and thus were dangerous to the status quo because they undermined it and provided subversive resistance and opposition to those in authority, including those who controlled official Yoruba cultural memory.

CENTRAL AFRICA: LUBA CULTURAL MEMORY SYSTEMS

For the Luba of Central Africa (called "Kamilambian" and "Kisalian" from about 600 C.E.), a
rich vocabulary of images and words exists to describe ideas about historical memory and connectedness, about remembering and forgetting as interdependent sides of memory. Luba officials still stage oral recitations of local history. Traditionally, state historians were rigorously
trained men called *bana balute* ("men of memory"). They recited genealogies and king lists
and recounted the founding charter of kingship. They traveled with kings and, like the *griots,*
spread propaganda about the prestige and power of their patrons' culture. They used
mnemonics, visual devices or objects that aid in and order remembering.

Luba Memory Boards The Luba world is quite literally strewn with mnemonic devices, images, and objects that are used to remember and reconfigure the past.
These include royal emblems, shrines and grave markers, staffs, thrones, bead necklaces, and

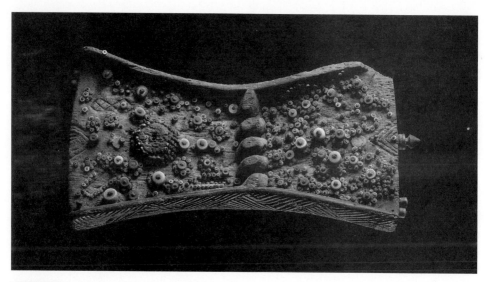

FIGURE 9.0 Luba Memory Board *(lukasa),* Zaire
Felix Collection

SOURCE: Felix Collection. Photo by Dick Beauxlieax. Courtesy of the Museum of African Art, New York.

the object known as a *lukasa* (memory board). The *lukasa* is a handheld wooden board covered with colored pins and beads; sometimes painted or incised geometric markings are added to evoke particular events, places, or names from the past. Such objects represent visually the vocabulary of memory, to be "read" only by those skilled and trained to convey the complexity of meaning encoded therein. The *lukasa* is used in initiation ceremonies to teach initiates the stories of culture heroes, clan migrations, and sacred lore. It also provides a visual mapping of the complicated political and social ordering of society, the natural world, and the world of the spirits.

INCAN ORAL TRADITIONS

Like the traditional memory systems of the Luba, Mande, or Yoruba in Africa, that of the Incas in the central Andes of South America was oral. Incan oral traditions were organized in ways specific to their culture and transmitted with the help of mnemonic devices unique to it. Though their cultural memory system was fundamentally oral, Incan communities also used a knotted cord, called a *quipu,* the colors and lengths of which recorded important numbers such as census figures, chronological data, and everyday transactions. Like the Luba's *lukasa,* the *quipu* seems to have functioned as a mnemonic device, a shorthand tool to aid in the memorization of large bodies of information.

The general history of the Inca Empire was secret and transmitted by specialists known by the term *amauta* and which were similar to the Yoruba *arokin.* The *amauta* taught in schools reserved for members of the elite who were given room and board by the state. Like Mali *griots,* Luba memory men, and Yoruba *arokin,* the Incan *amauta* ensured state control of cultural memory.

By preserving those aspects of a ruler's exploits that he wished to be remembered and thus censoring the past, the *amauta* selectively reordered the past to serve present needs.

■

CULTURAL MEMORY SYSTEMS: WRITING

Like all memory systems, from its beginnings writing, wherever it emerged, has served a variety of different purposes in shaping and transmitting culture. Writing coexisted with other memory systems, which either supported or sometimes subverted written cultural memory. The interplay of written and nonwritten memory systems at times created significant political and social change.

The development of cuneiform script among the peoples of Mesopotamia in West Asia during the third millennium B.C.E., and the later evolution of an alphabetic script which was transmitted by Phoenician traders around the eastern shores of the Mediterranean, were related to the needs of commerce. Merchants needed a way of keeping inventories and financial records of transactions.

WRITING AND POWER

The development of writing was also associated with the exercise of power in early West Asian states, enabling scribes in service to rulers to record events, keep population records for taxation, and propagate and preserve law. Written law codes, such as that of the Babylonian ruler Hammurabi, are examples of the lasting importance of written systems of cultural memory. The writing down of myths that supported royal power, such as those surrounding the god Marduk in Babylonia, contributed to the establishment of states and rulers and their continuity with earlier cultural traditions.

Sacred Scripts In early North Africa, Egyptian hieroglyphics ("priestly pictographs") were a sacred script under the control of a priesthood who served the pharaohs after about 2900 B.C.E. Later scripts include those developed during the second millennium B.C.E. in the kingdom of Kush and at Axum, where sacred and secular powers were recorded on stone engravings and inscriptions.

Mayan Script In the Americas, the Mayans created a script in the first millennium C.E. that was used in the keeping of historical and astronomical records. The Mayan script was a mixture of ideographic and phonetic elements, using graphic symbols or pictures to represent both objects and sounds. It included a complete syllabary, so theoretically everything could be written phonetically, as it sounded when spoken; however, the Mayan script was never used entirely to communicate phonetically since ideographs were considered to be religiously symbolic and thus to have great prestige. This probably reflects the desire of literate elites—priests and scribes—to maintain their monopoly of writing, knowledge of which gave them power. Scribes, who controlled astronomical, historical, and religious information, had their own patron deities, such as Itzamna, considered the creator and inventor of writing. Mayan hieroglyphics appeared on a variety of materials, including stone and bark paper, although relatively few manuscripts on paper have survived.

Sanskrit and Indo-European
Cultural Memory

Sanskrit, the language of the Indo-Europeans who migrated into India in the mid–second millennium B.C.E., was transcribed in an alphabetic script and used to record religious texts of the Vedic tradition in early South Asia. The writing down of hymns to Indo-European gods, for example, helped to maintain Indo-Europeans' cultural memory and consolidate their power as they moved into the Indian subcontinent. Much later, in the third century B.C.E., inscriptions carved to proclaim the Indian ruler Ashoka's belief in Buddhism and to assert his claim to secular power further illustrate the utility of writing to preserve and transmit a politically useful message.

Chinese Writing and Religion

While writing systems may be found in virtually every region of the world, nowhere was the written word endowed with greater power than in China. In Shang China (ca. 1600–1050 B.C.E.) the development of the archaic script found on oracle bones was linked to divination practices. It was believed that the ancestors of the Shang kings, deities who could communicate with the supreme god, Di, would make their wishes known through the bones of animals used for sacrifice. To contact the spirits of these royal ancestors, a diviner would engrave a bone or turtle shell with written characters and then apply a heated bronze pin to them. Various lengths and patterns of cracks would appear on the shell or bone, and their relationship to the written characters would be interpreted by the diviner as oracles and kept as records. The characters on oracle bones are archaic forms of the modern written script and thus provide evidence of the foundation of Chinese writing.

The practice of using oracle bones for prophecy and guidance, known as **scapulimancy,** also illustrates the role of a priestly elite in the creation and preservation of cultural memory. As in Egypt and among the Mayas, a scribal priesthood controlled a memory system and im-

FIGURE 9.1 Indian Woman Writing with a Stylus
Sandstone sculpture, north India, 11th c. C.E.

SOURCE: Courtesy of the Trustees of the British Library.

bued it with a sacred quality and ritual character. The close association of the Chinese scribal elite with those who exercised political power provided the early Chinese state with religious underpinnings. Even the earliest oracle bone inscriptions, which recorded events such as battles, harvests, and royal marriages and births, can be seen as historical records, and the keeping of written accounts of the past became a central concern of those who held power in imperial China.

The Transmission of Culture through Writing Systems
More than 2000 years later, the Chinese writing system spread to other parts of East Asia, primarily as a means of transmitting Chinese culture and Buddhism to Korea and Japan. Adapted by Koreans and Japanese to transcribe their own cultural memory, Chinese script was used by the emerging centralized states in Korea and Japan for the same purposes it served in China: the preservation of cultural memory to serve the interests of those in power. For example, the *Kojiki,* a record of myths and chronicles of the founding of Japan compiled under imperial sponsorship in 712 C.E., was written using Chinese script in different ways, for both sound and meaning, an example of the process of adaptation. The writing down of myths that supported the claims of the imperial family to divine descent are a clear indication of the power of the written text as a cultural memory system.

■

CULTURAL MEMORY SYSTEMS: HISTORY

History began as an oral memory system which became transformed into a written one wherever and whenever scripts were developed. For example, the Book of Deuteronomy in the Judeo-Christian Bible is history containing a law code embellished with legends and court records that validate the worship of Yahweh and explain the sacred role of the children of Israel. In early Judaism, Deuteronomy, learned by heart as a central act of religious faith, is an example of oral history that was eventually written down as a chapter of the Old Testament of the Bible.

HISTORY IN ANCIENT GREECE

The relationship between oral and written transmission of the past was close and complex, even in societies such as Greece, where written history developed early. By the late fifth century B.C.E., when the Greek "father of history," Herodotus, wrote his *Histories,* those who used writing to record their histories were designated chroniclers. But Herodotus himself gave oral performances of his works, either from memory as a recitation or reading from a written text. Herodotus sought a wider audience for his work by giving public readings, and his oral performances were the most effective way of gaining public recognition. Thus, even though writing was employed as a cultural memory system in fifth-century Greece, public and oral performances remained an important continuation from earlier traditions of the memorialist, a person who transmitted the past through memory and recitation.

While Herodotus was in West Asia and North Africa collecting information, he acquired long king lists and myths and legends from oral memory systems. Lengthy sections of his *Histories* existed in oral form before being written down by him. Herodotus's credo—"to say

[in his writing] what is said"—reflects his use of oral sources, which he would introduce in his text with a phrase such as "The Athenians say . . ." Herodotus heard different traditions recalled by different groups, and he saw his task as one of trying to verify and reconcile differing accounts. Herodotus's work is indicative of the transition from oral to written culture that was taking place during his lifetime. His *Histories* were written down and distinguished from other oral history because it came to be believed that the written word was less subject to alteration than the spoken one.

HISTORY IN EARLY CHINA

In China, where the written script early acquired a sacred character through the preservation of records of the past on oracle bones or bronze inscriptions, after the sixth century B.C.E. written historical texts attributed to Confucius (551–479 B.C.E.) became the foundation of the Confucian canon (sacred or basic works). Confucius used the past to support his views of the ideal society. The Book of Documents (or History) is supposed to be a collection of documents from the first three dynasties (Xia, Shang, and Zhou), compiled and edited by Confucius to reveal his understanding of antiquity, which provided the model for rulers and for the ordering of society.

The *Spring and Autumn Annals,* also part of the written canon attributed to Confucius, is a chronicle of events in his home state of Lu, one of the states of the Warring States period (ca. 500–250 B.C.E.). The terse entries in this chronicle, such as "The duke of Chao died," have been interpreted in later times as commentaries by Confucius on events and people through his careful use of particular terms such as "died" or "passed away" to reveal his judgment. Later embellishments, such as the "Traditions" *(zhuan),* date to the third century B.C.E. and added accounts of intrigue, passion, and heroism to the terse recounting of events in the

Spring and Autumn Annals. Like the written history of Herodotus's time, these works were probably meant to be read aloud, to be appreciated in a group setting through oral performance.

According to Confucian views, the historical record was thought to be the repository of "truth," the Confucian Way *(dao)* of humanity manifested in the pattern of the past. History was a mirror in which to reflect the present age against the exemplary model of antiquity. The historical record was thus a guide to political action and ethical behavior in the present. From earliest times in China, the writing of history was a moral obligation of those who ruled, and the historical record itself acquired a sacred quality.

Sima Qian (fl. ca. 100 B.C.E.), who held the post of Grand Historian at the court of Emperor Wu of the Han dynasty (206 B.C.E.–220 C.E.), wrote a history of the Chinese world up to his own time. He introduced a major innovation in the writing of history, as he shifted from an annalistic form exemplified by the *Spring and Autumn Annals* to a more sophisticated and complex thematic organization that included biographical accounts and topical treatises as well as court annals and imperial genealogies.

Although court historians who came after Sima Qian, such as Ban Gu (fl. ca. 100 C.E.), the author of the history of the Han dynasty, followed Sima Qian's model, their chronological coverage was limited to single dynasties. The dynastic histories, compiled by each dynasty in succession, reinforced the notion of the Mandate of Heaven as the principal agent of historical change, since each dynasty rose and fell according to the moral character of its rulers. The writing of history, dynasty by dynasty, also reinforced the cyclical model of historical change.

■
CULTURAL CATEGORIES OF KNOWLEDGE: HISTORY, THEOLOGY, PHILOSOPHY

The way in which cultures categorize knowledge structures the transmission of cultural memory and determines the culturally specific roles of memory systems such as history, theology, and philosophy. In early China and Greece, history and philosophy were the primary categories of cultural knowledge, transmitted in both oral and written forms, though the written text gained currency as the dominant mode of transmission. In this book we privilege history as a category of knowledge, as people in other times or other cultures privileged theology, philosophy, literature, or technology. Such categories of knowledge are primary, though intangible, means of control over cultural meaning.

Since the time of the Greeks, two distinct and parallel categories of knowledge had emerged: one, based on experience, was more inclusive; the other, based on representation, privileged the world of writing and scholarship. The world of books was like a photograph of knowledge, rather than a world lived. These two kinds of knowledge—represented and experienced—were not unique to the European world. There and elsewhere, the two were sometimes viewed as complementary systems; other times, they were perceived as sources of tension in relation to the institutional ordering of society.

Whatever categories of knowledge are privileged, the transmission of cultural memory seldom takes place without conflict. The debate between Christian faith and human reason in the medieval European world, between Islamic theology and Greek philosophy in medieval West Asia, or between Buddhism and Confucianism in medieval China are prime examples of conflicts between categories of knowledge that shape the transmission of cultural memory.

CHRISTIANITY, HISTORY, AND THEOLOGY IN MEDIEVAL EUROPE

European historical writing during the thousand years following the establishment of Christianity as the official religion of the Roman Empire in 380 C.E. demonstrates the role of Christianity in the writing of history and thus in the shaping of cultural memory. For example, the English chronicler The Venerable Bede (673–735) wrote the *Ecclesiastical History of the English People,* which relates the story of the conversion of the Saxons to Christianity. Later Christian historians, such as Bishop Otto of Freising (ca. 1114–1158), adopted a framework for writing history that was designed to reveal the ultimate end of mankind according to Christian beliefs. A linear narrative carried human history from the creation to the end of the world and the second coming of Christ, followed by a day of judgment that would inaugurate a new age. Biographical works of this millennium recorded lives of exemplary Christians. One such work is Einhard's *Life of Charlemagne* (ca. 829–836), which sought to preserve the memory of a king who championed the Church, while the *Life of Saint Louis,* by Sieur de Joinville (ca. 1224–1317) celebrated the noble deeds and character of the only French king to be canonized as a saint by the Church.

As Christianity shaped the writing of history in medieval Europe, theology, the methodically formulated understanding of the divine, was the characteristic intellectual activity of twelfth-century European scholars and represented a peak of Christian influence on European thought, as Islamic theology dominated West Asia. In Europe, theology was the "Queen of the Sciences," and its development was largely the work of university professors who were all Christian clergymen. The works of these men, known as scholastics or schoolmen, were based on the close study of sources such as the Bible and the writings of earlier theologians. Their primary concern was the reconciliation of conflicting authorities, essential to securing the foundations of their faith. A fundamental problem of belief was the resolution of potential conflict between human reason and divine revelation. This was closely connected to a third scholarly problem, that of the universals: whether absolute reality was to be found in individual things or in general or universal concepts.

The Reconciliation of Theology and Philosophy   In thirteenth-century Europe, the struggle between theology and philosophy, the product of human reason inherited from the Greeks, was reflected in attempts to reconcile Christian faith with reason. This struggle was resolved in a compromise satisfactory to the Church by Thomas Aquinas (1225–1274), whose *Summa Theologica* was a synthesis of medieval learning that reconciled Christian theology and rational philosophy. By arguing for the acceptance of human reason while demonstrating its limits, Aquinas' work had a profound impact on the relationship between religion and philosophy in medieval European thought and contributed to the undermining of Christianity's monopoly on knowledge.

ISLAM AND CULTURAL CATEGORIES OF KNOWLEDGE IN WEST ASIA

In West Asia after the Arab conquest, knowledge was divided into discrete subjects, each of which was regarded as a separate field of knowledge (*ilm,* or "science"). The most important distinction was between the Muslim religious sciences—Qur'anic exegesis, the study of the Traditions of the Prophet, jurisprudence, speculative theology, and mysticism—and everything else, that is, the profane sciences. Though theology was the most important category of knowledge in Islamic societies, Islam shaped the writing of history much as Christianity did in Europe.

According to Islam, knowledge was believed to have several sources. The first and most important was the word of God as revealed to the Prophet Muhammad; this knowledge was recorded in the Qur'an and interpreted in seven traditions of recitation. The second source of knowledge was the collective memory of the sayings and doings of the Prophet known as the *sunna* (literally, the "beaten path" or "custom" of the Prophet). Individual statements of the *sunna* were known as *hadith*s, traditions attributed to particular individuals. One of the most esteemed early collections of *hadith*s was that of Bukhari (d. 870 C.E.), valued because of the careful manner in which Bukhari had culled through the thousands of *hadith*s to determine the reliability of each.

Muslim scholars were called *ulama,* or those with knowledge *(ilm),* and their scholarship was subject to the consensus of community. An important *hadith* said, "My community will never agree upon an error," suggesting the extent to which consensus was perceived to be a guide to truth. *Ulama* were found in almost every reach of the Islamic cultural world. In most communities, their main task was the transmission of formal legal knowledge or law *(shari'a).*

While Islamic culture placed a high value on the book and on written works, the emphasis remained on oral transmission. Muslims were fundamentally skeptical of the written word and questioned its reliability. According to the historian Ibn Khaldun, "When a student has to rely on the study of books and written material . . . he is confronted by . . . [a] veil . . . that separates handwriting and the form of the letter found in writing from the spoken words found in the imagination." The search for true meaning was to be conducted by reading a text

FIGURE 9.3 Islamic Scholars Listen to a Recitation before a Library Wall of Books

The oral transmission of textural knowledge ensured personal relationships between students and their teachers.

SOURCE: Bibliothèque Nationale de France.

out loud if it was written; students gained authority by oral transmission of a text to the satisfaction of the teacher who himself had gained authority from his teacher.

Theological disputes in Islam occupied many thinkers in medieval West Asia as they had in medieval Europe. The schism in Islam between Sunnism and Shi'ism began after the death of the Prophet Muhammad as the result of a dispute among the Arabs over his succession and hence the political leadership of Islam. From Egypt to Central Asia, the region was divided by both political and religious rivalries. Sunni (orthodox) Muslims, who tended to be in the majority, were often alarmed by the growth of political power in the hands of Shi'ite heretics.

ISLAMIC THEOLOGY AND SUFI MYSTICISM

Over the centuries, the orthodox Sunnis faced not only the political and religious challenge of Shi'ism but also the task of coming to terms with popular mysticism, or Sufism. Sufism coexisted uneasily with Sunni orthodoxy for several centuries after the rise of Islam. It developed out of an ascetic movement that appeared in the first Muslim century in reaction to the great material wealth generated by the Arab conquests.

Sufi mysticism emphasized a special spiritual love of God and, above all, provided the means for direct personal religious experience of the divine, which held great appeal for the common believer. Not surprisingly, orthodox Sunni theologians regarded Sufism with suspi-

DAILY LIVES

THE BRILLIANT LIGHT OF UMM HANI (1376–1466)

The Islamic tradition of compiling biographical dictionaries, somewhat like the lives of the Christian saints, forms the basis for understanding the history of the Islamic community as the cumulative contributions of individual men and women who created and transmitted Islamic culture. One such individual life is that of the female scholar Umm Hani, who appears in the twelve-volume dictionary by Sakhawi (d. 1497) as a "brilliant light."

According to Sakhawi, Umm Hani was born and died in Cairo. First taught by her grandfather, she studied with about twenty different masters of learning. Umm Hani eventually married twice, and her sons were educated in law. She became a teacher of other scholars, including Sakhawi himself, who wrote that she knew more than he was able to learn. As a young woman, Umm Hani memorized the Qur'an and could recite lengthy passages of *hadith*s (traditions). She was an accomplished poet and would make up verses instantly

on the spot. When her second husband died, she inherited his fortune and his business, a textile workshop that she managed. Sakhawi also tells us that Umm Hani performed the *hajj* (pilgrimage) to Mecca thirteen times, often staying on for months in Medina and Mecca to teach.

The dictionary entry for Umm Hani is one out of a total of 11,691 entries, one of 1,075 women for whom citations were written. In the fourteenth and fifteenth centuries, women figured prominently among the biographical listings of Islamic scholars, probably encouraged by the assertive promotion of women's religious learning by the Syrian and Egyptian *ulama* (clerics) of Aisha, wife of the Prophet and daughter of the first caliph, Abu Bakr. In later centuries, however, women practically disappeared from the dictionaries; by the end of the nineteenth century, al-Baytar (d. 1918) found room for only two women out of the 777 persons remembered in his biographies.

FIGURE 9.4 Sufi Khwaja Khidr, who first appeared in the Mesopotamian *Epic of Gilgamesh*

Here in a Bengali incarnation, he reflects the incorporation of local fertility beliefs

SOURCE: Courtesy of the Trustees of the British Library.

cion, for they feared that popular mysticism would deprive them of their religious leadership and authority. Their attempts to suppress it, however, were futile.

Al-Ghazzali, Muslim Scholar Finally, one of the most remarkable religious personalities in Islam, al-Ghazzali (1058–1111), succeeded in reconciling orthodoxy with mysticism. Although al-Ghazzali was a master of both Sunni and Shi'ite theology and philosophy, his greatest work, *The Revival of the Religious Sciences,* succeeded in bringing emotion back to religious life and in breaking the yoke of scholasticism that had stifled the feeling of personal relationship with God. He did this by reintroducing the fear of Hell to religious practice and by showing that mysticism was not only compatible with orthodox religious experience but could also amplify it. Al-Ghazzali's great work had a profound effect on the course of Islam and Islamic thought. Not only did Sufism become orthodox, but philosophy lost much of its glow.

Averroes After al-Ghazzali's death, the few lights that shone in the Muslim world came chiefly from Spain and North Africa. Most noteworthy was Ibn Rushd (1126–1198), known in Europe as Averroes. Trained in the Greek sciences and medicine, he believed that philosophy and religion were both true, and he wrote an important book to show that they were in harmony. Ibn Rushd even attempted to refute what al-Ghazzali had said about philosophy, but he did not convince the mainstream of Muslim opinion that there was a place for philosophy alongside theology. He was perhaps more successful in his serious commentaries on Aristotelian thought, which were translated into Latin and Hebrew and became the foundation of an important school of thought in medieval Europe. Though Ibn Rushd's works achieved harmony between unreasoned belief and human rationalism, Sufi mysticism became the preoccupation of devout Muslims and spread beyond the confines of West Asia.

RELIGION AND PHILOSOPHY IN SOUTH ASIA

By the twelfth century, several Sufi orders had migrated from West Asia into the Indian subcontinent following the Turko-Afghan invasions that had begun in the eleventh century. Although Islam never overwhelmed Hindu culture the way it had other cultures it conquered elsewhere, the Muslim invasions of India had a great impact on the subsequent cultural and political history of the Indian subcontinent. The Muslim Sultanate of Delhi in north India flourished in the early thirteenth century and became a center of Islamic learning and culture to which scholars, artists, and theologians went in great numbers.

Sufism found many parallels in Hindu *bhakti,* which was focused on devotion to a personal god, through common language, imagery, and motifs. Sufism in India provided a means of establishing contact between Muslims and Hindus, was responsible for many conversions to Islam, and contributed to Hindu-Islam syncretic movements. In Hindu *bhakti,* God was seen as having three forms: Vishnu (generally in the incarnation of either Rama or Krishna); Shiva; and *shakti,* a female form. No caste or social distinctions were made among people in *bhakti,* although the movement was typically led by *brahman*s. *Bhakti* can be seen as a reaction against the highly ritualized, exclusive Brahmanism of the period.

Vedanta By the late classical period (ca. 800–1300 C.E.) in India, the Vedanta ("end of the Vedas") school, which derived its inspiration from Upanishadic speculation rather than Vedic sacrifice and the extreme attention to ritual characteristic of rigid Brahmanism, eclipsed most others as the dominant school of Indian philosophy. Expounding the monistic belief that reality is a unitary, organic whole with no independent parts, Vedanta philosophy sought to reconcile all seeming differences and conflicts in the Hindu scriptures. Vedanta became Hinduism's most influential philosophic system. Ramanuja (ca. 1017–1137 C.E.) was a *brahman* who emphasized rituals in the expression of devotion to Vishnu. Ramanuja founded a popular school of Vedanta in the twelfth century, blending the intense devotionalism of *bhakti* with the modified monism of Vedanta.

■

SCIENCE AS A CATEGORY OF KNOWLEDGE

Like history, theology, or philosophy, science systematized knowledge of nature and the physical world and is a memory system that transmits cultural knowledge. As a category of knowledge, science is not independent of other cultural categories but interacts with them in a dynamic process. For example, Christian theology shaped the way people in medieval Europe thought about the natural world, but so did systematic observation of nature. For Muslims, Islam provided the framework within which the natural world could be understood and gave them reasons for understanding it. For people everywhere, despite culturally distinctive emphases on different categories of knowledge, the practice of medicine was of obvious utility, circumscribed though it may have been by Christianity, Islam, or other powerful institutionalized theologies.

SCIENCE IN THE ISLAMIC WORLD

According to Islam, science was a category of profane learning; it included such areas as astronomy and medicine, which were accepted and even encouraged because they could be considered to have practical value. One center of "practical" learning at the time of the Arab conquest of the heartlands of West Asia in the late seventh century was Antioch in Syria. Pre-Islamic Antioch had a tradition of Hellenistic learning, especially in medicine, and it was from Antioch that much of the Hellenistic heritage reached the Islamic world. This heritage was epitomized by the Hellenistic physician Galen (ca. 129–199), whose works were to dominate medicine in both the Islamic and Christian worlds. Galen's ideas influenced the renowned Arab philosopher-physician Ibn Sina (d. 1037), known as Avicenna in the West, who composed an enormous medical work entitled *Canon of Medicine.* A magnificent systematization of medicine, its five books covered physiology, symptomology, the principles of therapy, pathology, and pharmacology.

In addition to medicine, mathematics received considerable attention following the Muslim conquest of India. In the eighth century, an Indian form of calculation using ten figures, including one for an empty space (*sifr* in Arabic, hence the English words "cipher" and "zero") was introduced. The introduction of the empty space was nothing short of revolutionary for the history of mathematics and such related sciences as astronomy and physics. Arabic writers referred to these figures as "Indian" numerals. In the twelfth century, when they were introduced to Europe by the Muslims, they were called "Arabic" numerals.

In West Asia, higher mathematics was primarily used for astronomical calculations, such as those carried out at the observatory constructed in the thirteenth century at the Iranian city of Maragha. The facility at Maragha had a professional staff of some twenty scientists from throughout West Asia and at least one Chinese mathematician. It had a large library, and the staff constructed a number of sophisticated instruments for making precise measurements. The study of astronomy was especially easy to justify in the Islamic world because it measured time. For Muslims it was critical for fixing the hours of prayer, determining the direction of Mecca, and ascertaining the beginning and end of each lunar month, the most important of which was Ramadan, the month of fasting.

THE SCIENTIFIC TRADITION IN CHINA

Mathematics, astronomy, and medicine all developed to sophisticated levels in China during the centuries between the Han (206 B.C.E.–220 C.E.) and Song (960–1275 C.E.) dynasties. Daoism, with its interest in nature, provided a strong stimulus to the accumulation of knowledge about the natural world. Ultimately, however, the impetus to understand nature came not from the urge to control it or the belief that it could be completely and rationally comprehended, as in Europe. It came instead from the desire—in the case of Neo-Confucians—to learn the underlying principles of nature as part of a process of moral cultivation leading to Confucian sagehood. For Daoists, knowledge of nature provided understanding of the *dao,* the "Way," in order to live in accord with it, not to gain control over it.

Mathematics had a largely practical function in computing numerical problems, as well as in enabling court astronomers to predict regularities in the movements of celestial bodies. Astronomy and astrology were closely linked, and both were servants of the state. Astronomers used mathematics to prepare the calendar, one of the sacred responsibilities of the emperor. In addition to predicting regularities, they also observed unpredictable phenomena, and their duties included interpreting them as omens of significance in the governing of the empire. These methods were well developed by the Han period, and the link between astronomy/astrology and history was reflected in the title of the historian Sima Qian, "Grand Astrologer," which identified his position with responsibility for recording celestial events together with human ones, both the territory of the historian.

The theoretical foundations of Chinese medicine also lay in the Han period. The concepts of *yin* and *yang* and the Five Phases, recognizable as integral parts of Han Confucianism, were fundamental underpinnings of the system of Chinese medicine. Much as Han Confucians envisioned the cosmos as an organic whole together with human society, so the human body was seen as an organic whole. Treatment by acupuncture, for example, was based on an understanding of the systemic circulation of vital fluids found in the human body.

Shen Gua, A Song Scientist One of the most remarkable figures in the history of science and technology in China is the famous Song polymath, Shen Gua (1031–1095). After a very successful political career, Shen was disgraced and forced into retirement. His reputation in later times as a brilliant scientific thinker rests in large part on what he wrote in the *Dreampool Essays,* compiled during his retirement. In the *Dreampool Essays,* Shen Gua recorded his observations concerning the magnetic compass, printing technology, optics, geology, medicine, and other scientific matters.

THE VEDIC TRADITION AND SCIENCE IN EARLY INDIA

Early Indian science was reflected in complex astronomical and astrological systems, derived in part from the ancient Vedas. Astronomers' concern with the motion and magnitude of heavenly bodies was closely connected to an astrological interest in the influences of the stars on human affairs. Like astronomy and astrology, medicine began in Vedic times as a magic art. The classical Indian medical texts were the *Ayur Veda,* the earliest of which is possibly traceable to the sixth century B.C.E. These form the basis of modern Ayurvedic medicine.

Mathematics—geometry, algebra, and trigonometry—was developed to aid in laying out sacrificial sites and making astrological calculations. The numerical system of nine digits plus zero, in use in India as early as the sixth century C.E., was borrowed by the Arabs, who introduced it to Europe. Medieval Indian mathematicians understood positive and negative quantities; they could find square and cube roots and could also solve quadratic equations. This knowledge was also adopted by the Arabs and transmitted by them to Europe.

SCIENCE IN EUROPE

Greek, Indian, and Chinese knowledge of astronomy, physics, mathematics, and other sciences were brought to Europe in the works of Arab scientists and philosophers, which were then translated into Latin. Thirteenth-century European thinkers displayed an intense interest in works of science and philosophy. Though the primary concern of medieval European thinkers was dictated by the Church and its preoccupation with the reconciliation of theology with reason, one European thinker approached the achievement of the great Muslim philosophers and scientists who greatly influenced him.

Roger Bacon Roger Bacon (ca. 1214–1292) was an Oxford clergyman who, because of his clear understanding that experimental methods gave certainty in science, stands out from all the other Christian philosophers of his time. He does not appear to have done much experimenting himself, except in optics, but his reading of all the Arabic and

Greek authors he could find convinced him that natural knowledge could not be verified by authorities, such as the Bible, the Church, or even Aristotle, but only by observation and experiment. Bacon insisted on the importance of mathematics both as an educational exercise and as a basis for other sciences and experimentation. At a time when mathematics had a bad name in Christian Europe because it was chiefly studied by Muslims and Jews, Bacon insisted that mathematics must underlie all other studies and way the key to truth.

LITERATURE AS A CULTURAL MEMORY SYSTEM

Both oral and written literature, like oral traditions and written history, provided ways of transmitting culture from generation to generation and were thus important cultural memory systems. Literature, whether prose, poetry, or drama, whether oral or written, not only transmitted and preserved culture but also altered and sometimes even created it. Like other cultural memory systems such as history, the very act of transmission—the reproduction of cultural knowledge—transforms cultural memory. Literature and history may have overtly different purposes, be subject to different standards of "truth," and have different audiences, but both tell stories about the past and the telling of those stories influences the present.

GREEK DRAMA AS CULTURAL MEMORY

Greek drama is a good example of the way a literary and performance art shapes and gives expression to cultural memory. Among the many creative developments taking place in fifth-century B.C.E. Greece, drama was one of the most lively. Greek drama, which incorporated mythic and historical elements, made use of a chorus to provide commentary on events and characters. Aeschylus' (525–456 B.C.E.) trilogy, *The Oresteia,* is the story of the young man Orestes, who slays his own mother for the murder of his father. His matricide is punished by avenging goddesses until Athena, goddess of wisdom and patron goddess of Athens, intercedes on his behalf. Sophocles' (ca. 496–406 B.C.E.) best-known play, *Oedipus Rex,* tells of the hero, Oedipus, learning that he has unknowingly murdered his father and married his mother. In the works of both these playwrights, individuals resist the dictates of divine will or fate and suffer, but they ultimately achieve a resolution or reconciliation with the forces that brought about the suffering.

Euripides Increasingly, the nature of man, not gods, became the focus of Greek drama. The work of Euripides (ca. 480–406 B.C.E.) exemplifies this shift, as his plays used natural dialogue from everyday life and focused on the experience of the ordinary individual rather than gods. Euripides lived at a time of great intellectual ferment at the end of the fifth century B.C.E., when many new ideas were being expressed by philosophers and there was a growing consciousness of human will playing a role in the fate of individuals. Still, Euripides, like his predecessors, drew on characters and plot from traditional myth and legend, elaborating on them as he needed to create dramatic works with humans at the center. Thus both continuity and change in cultural memory were reflected in the evolution of Greek tragedy.

Comedy Comedy was also a means by which playwrights contributed to shaping the cultural memory of their times. The comedies of Aristophanes (ca. 445–386 B.C.E.) mercilessly attacked the hypocrisy of powerful people, institutions, and public policy by satirizing them. At the height of the Peloponnesian War between Athens and Sparta, his *Lysistrata* proclaimed peace preferable to war by portraying women who withheld sex from their husbands as a protest against war. Political commentary thus took the form of comedy that entertained while conveying a message.

POETRY AS CULTURAL MEMORY IN CHINA

The Tradition in China Whether orally transmitted or written, poetry, like drama, is a cultural memory system. In China, the basis of a written poetic tradition emerged early as a major form of cultural memory. Beginning with the sixth-century B.C.E. compilation of the *Book of Odes,* an anthology of poetry later included in the Confucian canon, an art form developed that preserved, in written form, poetry that had been transmitted orally over many generations. The very act of writing down this poetic tradition also transformed it, as a literate elite appropriated it and gave the poems its own meanings. Although the *Book of Odes* contains a rich assortment of poems, including love songs, complaints about taxes, and so on, over time it acquired a thick veneer of Confucian interpretation, which moralized even the mildly erotic love poems contained in the collection, much as some of the Psalms in the Bible were love songs that were given moral or ethical meanings by later interpreters.

Poetry as Alternative By late Han (206 B.C.E.–220 C.E.) times, China already had a rich po-
Cultural Memory etic tradition that included The *Songs of the South* by the fourth-century B.C.E. minister of the southern state of Chu, Qu Yuan, who drowned himself after being wrongly accused of treachery by his sovereign.

> Oftentimes I grew dejected and sobbed,
> Bewailing that I had fallen foul of the times . . .
> Kneeling down, I adjusted my clothes and stated my case—
> How splendid that I had kept my integrity!
> I rode the phoenix carriage, drawn by a team of jade dragons,
> And before long, on a gust of wind, I ascended the Heavens.

This collection of poetry includes rich material that attests to the persistence of shamanic traditions even as the forces of centralization were altering the political world, culminating in the third-century B.C.E. Qin and Han Empires. The continued appeal of The *Songs of the South* to readers in later centuries is testimony not only to the skill of the poet, Qu Yuan, but also to the alternative cultural memory these poems preserved as the imposition of a centralized, bureaucratic state attempted to homogenize distinctive regional cultural traditions into one.

Poetry as Communication Poetry in imperial China continued to be written not only as a form of literary expression but also as a means of communication, and it was an important vehicle for the transmission of elite—requiring literacy and erudition—cultural memory. Poets demonstrated their erudition and poetic ability by a rich display of allusions to earlier poetry, linking themselves to great poets of earlier times and claiming the role of guardians and preservers of that poetic tradition in their own day. Poems were written to bid farewell to a friend departing to a new official posting, to lament death and war, to describe the hardships of peasant life, to express longing for the life of the recluse, and to praise the beauty of nature.

The Chinese poetic tradition reached a high point in the Tang with poets such as Li Bai (701–762), Du Fu (712–770), and Bai Zhuyi (772–846). All three poets lived during a period when Chinese power was beginning to ebb, and they displayed this in different ways in their poetry. Li Bai, for example, is perhaps most famed for his famous poem about drinking with his companion the moon because that way he doesn't drink alone. But Du Fu and Bai Zhuyi both took a more serious tone in their poetry, lamenting the loss of power in the capital and the moral failures of the rulers. A poem by Du Fu expresses sorrow over warfare and the political and social disorder that accompanies it:

> I have heard the affairs in Chang'an are like a game of chess;
> For a hundred years, the business of the state has caused sorrows unbearable.
> Over there, the mansions of great nobles and princes all have new owners,
> And the court dresses of officials and generals have changed from former times.
> Straight north, on the mountain pass, gongs and drums shake the earth;
> To horses and chariots in the westward expedition, war dispatches race.
> Here the fish-dragon is solitary and the autumn stream cold
> To live peacefully in the old country is all I cherish.

EPIC POETRY AND CULTURAL MEMORY

Although applied to both written and oral literary forms throughout much of the world, the term epic comes from Greek and refers to a long narrative poem about the deeds of a hero or heroes. Unlike other forms of poetry that may express emotion, make commentaries in society; or describe nature, epic poems by their very nature—recounting the feats of heroes—represent and transmit ideals that people were expected to admire, if not emulate. In Greece, the *Iliad* and the *Odyssey,* conventionally attributed to the blind Greek poet Homer (fl. ca. 800 B.C.E.), are epic poems that became core works in the European literary canon. The wrath of the warrior Achilles in the Trojan Wars is the subject of the *Iliad,* in which gods play a role, but humans are responsible for their own fate. The adventures of Odysseus making his way home after the Trojan Wars are the subject of the *Odyssey.* Both preserve the cultural memory of early Greece, and have shaped European literary and cultural ideals.

Epic Poems in India In India, the *Mahabharata,* the longest single epic poem in world literature with 90,000 stanzas in eighteen books, was a product of continuous accretion over the centuries between about 400 B.C.E. and 400 C.E. The central story of this epic concerns a great battle fought by the descendants of a king. The *Mahabharata* was constructed from hero songs of ancient India and genealogical histories sung by bards who transmitted the oral traditions of the past. The *Ramayana,* an epic written down in the first century C.E., concerns the exploits of Rama, an incarnation of Vishnu, one of the three principal Hindu deities. Both the *Mahabharata* and the *Ramayana* were originally secular, martial epics that became Hindu sacred texts when religious interpolations were added, an illustration of how cultural memory can be transformed in the process of transmission.

The Epic in Iran In Iran after its integration into the Islamic Empire, the epic became a means of preserving Persian culture despite the dominance of Arabic language and culture, a demonstration of how poetry as a memory system can preserve cultural identity against challenges that would transform it. Of all the countries that were conquered and held by Arabs in the seventh century, only Iran succeeded in preserving its own national language. By the ninth century, Persian reemerged to challenge Arabic as a great language of the Muslim world. Persian was the language of the *Shahname* ("Book of Kings") composed by Firdawsi (d. ca. 1020) in the early eleventh century. A history of Persia from the creation of the world to the Islamic conquest, this Iranian national epic preserved the cultural memory of pre-Islamic Iran by using collections of heroic tales and other documents and traditions. Dealing with battles, intrigues, and illicit love affairs, Firdawsi's *Shahname,* like many other epics, was read aloud to musical accompaniment.

The Epic in Northern and Western Europe Like the use of the Persian language to preserve Persian culture within the Arab-dominated Islamic Empire, vernacular (spoken rather than literary) languages elsewhere were used to express the emergence of cultural differences. In northern Europe, the Latin epic of Roman times was replaced by epic literature in native dialects and languages such as Norse, German, Anglo-Saxon, and Old French vernaculars. Scandinavian epics wove together stories of gods and heroes to record Norse expansion, the chief cultural memory of which are the Icelandic (Old Norse) epics, the *Poetic Edda* and the *Prose Edda.* Originally orally transmitted, Norse epics were written down in the thirteenth century. The best-known Anglo-Saxon epic is *Beowulf,* a fantastic story full of exceptionally valorous deeds against natural and supernatural foes. The tale of the struggle of the hero, Beowulf, with an evil monster, Grendel, *Beowulf* is based on popular stories that accumulated over centuries and suggests in epic form the memory of the triumph of Christianity over paganism.

In France, vernacular *chansons de geste* ("songs of mighty deeds") also preserved the memory of real events, generously embroidered with legend. The best known is the *Song of Roland* (ca. 1100), which tells a heroic story of warfare between Christians and Muslims in Europe. It is the tale of the Battle of Roncesvalles in 778, actually a minor episode in one of Charlemagne's campaigns, but it also displays the military values of the feudal age, such as knightly loyalty and treason, death and honor, symbolized by the heroism of Roland, a knight of Charlemagne's court. Preserving the cultural memory of its time, the *Song of Roland* elevates a minor historical event into great literature. Epic poetry was a cultural memory system particularly suited to the deeds and legends of what has been remembered as a heroic age in European history. By preserving heroic deeds, epics helped to shape cultural memory of them.

LYRIC POETRY AND ROMANCES IN MEDIEVAL EUROPE

By the end of the twelfth century, there was a shift in the tone and forms of European poetry that reflects changes in cultural values. Heroic epics gave way to romantic and emotional poetry, the lyric, and prose as well, that reflected chivalric ideals and practices and concepts of courtly love characteristic of late medieval Europe. The Arthurian cycle of romances, which deals with the magic and adventures of King Arthur and the knights of his Round Table, is an example or oral literature that was written down and transmitted through many European lands. Originating in Celtic legend and written down in Latin by Geoffrey of Monmouth (ca. 1100–1154), the cycle was translated into French and transformed for a French audience by Chrétien de Troyes (ca. 1160–1180) and passed into Germany in the form of *Parzival* by Wolfram von Eschenbach (ca. 1170–1220) and *Tristan* by his contemporary Gottfried von Strasbourg.

Women, who were a principal subject of lyric poetry, were also accomplished authors of courtly and chivalric lyrics. As early as the eleventh century, Provençal noblewomen were composing songs and narrative poetry. For example, the works of Marie de France (fl. twelfth century) are skillful, though sometimes mocking, portrayals of courtly behavior and values.

Troubadours The subject of late medieval European lyric poetry was primarily love. Lyric poetry expressed unusually intense personal emotions and was initially spoken or set to music and sung. The popular songs of their time, lyric poems appeared in a multitude of forms composed and written by specialists, who were known as troubadours, and sung by professional entertainers called minstrels. Though the Provence region of France was the center of troubadour literature, the practice of lyric poetry was easily spread by the wandering minstrels to England, Germany, Italy, Spain, and elsewhere.

TRANSFORMATIONS OF ELITE LITERARY CULTURE IN JAPAN

As in China, poetry was a major medium for elite communication and transmission of culture in early Japan. The *Manyoshu,* an anthology of early poetry somewhat comparable to The *Book of Odes* in China, was compiled under imperial patronage in 760. Although the *Manyoshu* represented a native poetic tradition, during the Nara (712–784) and Heian (794–1185) periods poetry written in classical Chinese reflected the persistent influence of Chinese culture in Japan since the sixth century.

FIGURE 9.5 A Muslim and Christian Perform the Lute, 13th Century

SOURCE: Escorial. Monastery Library/Oronoz.

Heian Literary Culture By the ninth century, however, contact between China and Japan was ▬▬▬▬▬▬▬▬▬▬▬ greatly reduced, and in the tenth and eleventh centuries, both court life in the new capital of Heian and the culture associated with it manifested a brilliant native tradition quite unlike anything found in China. Much of the new literary culture associated with Heian court society was produced by women. Like Marie de France, Sei Shonagon (fl. ca. 1000), the author of the *Pillow Book,* an anecdotal account of court society, was a skilled observer of her social world and entertained her audience with humorous and sarcastic portrayals of court life.

> Someone comes, with whom one has decided not to have further dealings. One pretends to be fast asleep, but some servant or person connected with one comes to wake one up, and pulls one about, with a face as much as to say "What a sleep-hog!" This is always exceedingly irritating.

The best-known writer of eleventh-century Japan is Murasaki Shikibu (ca. 978–1016), a resident of the Heian court and the author of the *Tale of Genji,* a rich, complex, and ultimately tragic depiction of courtly life that is resonant with Buddhist themes. Prince Genji is a charming and elegant hero who pursues the pleasures his position affords him, but ultimately an awareness of the impermanence of beauty and pleasure intrudes on his life as his sense of loss and suffering overwhelms his transient happiness.

One important factor that explains the role played by Japanese women in the rich literary culture of Heian Japan was the development of *kana,* the phonetic syllabary for the transcription of the native language. The invention of *kana* made it possible for women to exercise their powers of social observation and literary creativity in their native language and culture, while men of the time were still engrossed in Chinese learning and the classical Chinese language, which was used in politics and official life, the domain of men. The relatively high status of elite women is related to their right to inherit property from their fathers or husbands, thus giving them some degree of economic independence.

Warrior Culture In Japan, both the imperial court tradition dating from the eleventh and ▬▬▬▬▬▬▬▬▬▬▬ twelfth centuries and the warrior tradition associated with the rise of the government of the *shogun* (military dictator) influenced literary arts. After 1200, the domination of Japanese society by a new warrior elite brought about substantial changes in the status of women and in the values that had dominated elite society and culture focused on the Heian court. Court and warrior patronage of artisans of various kinds contributed to the development of skilled professionals, such as the itinerant musicians who entertained audiences by chanting the *Tale of the Heike,* a warrior romance of the thirteenth century, to the accompaniment of the stringed lute, or *biwa.*

Like the minstrels of medieval Europe, *biwa* players, who were often blind, traveled through medieval Japan performing the *Tale of the Heike* and singing of the exploits and heroism of warriors as well as the loyalty and nobility of women. The *Tale of the Heike* chronicled the rise and fall of the Taira family, who battled the founders of the military government, the Minamoto family, in a series of wars at the end of the twelfth century. Although the chronicle focused on wars, battle, and warrior heroism, like the courtly *Tale of Genji* in the Heian period, it was suffused with a powerful Buddhist theme of impermanence and the futility of human suffering in such conflicts.

In fourteenth- and fifteenth-century Japan, the Ashikaga shogunate (government of the *shogun*) continued military rule at the old imperial capital of Kyoto, and the culture of this period reflects the fusion of warrior and courtier, as Ashikaga *shogun*s became patrons of the arts. Zen Buddhism, which had been transmitted from China in the twelfth century, became a major influence on cultural forms. Zen monks and priests served the military rulers of Japan as educated cultural and literary advisers, and Zen monasteries preserved and transmitted learning, much as Christian monasteries had in medieval Europe.

Noh Drama Zen was also influential in the development of Noh drama. Although the Noh drama evolved from religious dances associated with Shinto, plays in the Noh repertory were based on themes that drew heavily from Buddhist sources. Zeami (1363–1443), who was responsible for writing most of the plays in the Noh repertory, was inspired by Zen ideas in his approach to this dramatic form. The idea of the "mystery behind appearances" derives from the Zen emphasis on intuitive understanding. No plays are retellings of events that took place in the past, and there is usually a resolution, often religious, of some painful conflict that occurred. There is a chorus, somewhat like that in Greek tragedy, that chants background and commentary on the actors and the events.

The Noh play *Atsumori* is based on an episode in the *Tale of the Heike,* in which the young Taira warrior Atsumori is slain by his enemy Kumagai, although the latter wanted to spare Atsumori because of his youth and beauty. In the Noh play, Kumagai has become a priest and encounters the ghost of Atsumori, who forgives him in a demonstration of Buddhist compassion. The Noh play transmitted the cultural memory of the Atsumori episode from the *Tale of the Heike,* preserving the values of the aristocratic warrior in the setting of the Ashikaga shogunate (1336–1568), which in its own time fused the culture of the warrior and the courtier.

FIGURE 9.6 Scene from Noh Drama

The scene shows elaborately dressed main actor wearing a mask, waited upon by an attendant. The chorus and musicians are at the side of the stage.

SOURCE: Robert Isaacs/Photo Researchers, Inc.

POPULAR LITERATURE AS CULTURAL MEMORY

In Europe after about 1000 C.E., the rise of a secular literature written in the vernacular reflects the growing importance of the bourgeoisie (inhabitants of cities, or *bourgs*) and the weakening of the cultural dominance of the Church, whose clergy wrote treatises on Christian theology or lives of Christian saints in Latin. The popular literature of townspeople continued to reflect Christian influence and outlook, but it also revealed the changes that were taking place in European society with the growth of cities and commerce (see Chapter 11) and indicates a shift to less spiritual and more earthly concerns.

Fabliaux and Goliardic Verse The earthy, humorous, satirical, and realistic qualities of this popular literature are found in two literary forms characteristic of the period: *fabliaux* and Goliardic verse. Fabliaux are allegorical satires and fables, seldom more than four hundred lines in length, that delighted medieval European townsfolk from the twelfth to fifteenth centuries. A typical *fabliau* tells of a nobleman who has taken a poor old woman's cow. Told that she can get it back by "greasing the paw" of the nobleman's agent, she goes to the castle armed with a piece of lard, finds the agent strolling with his hands behind his back and literally carries out the advice given her by stealing up and applying the lard to the agent's hands. Such coarse and humorous *fabliaux* reflect cultural change by their ridiculing of chivalric ideals, courtly love, and even the Church. As a cultural memory system, this kind of literature transmitted new values through entertaining its audience.

Though written in the Latin of the European university rather than a vernacular, the pagan drinking songs of the Goliardi, students organized into a sort of international fraternity under the patronage of Saint Golias (Goliath), were similar in intent to the *fabliaux*. Delighting in sacrilege, the Goliardi were wandering scholars, moving from one center of learning to another, sworn to vows of poverty (for others), chastity (for none), and obedience (to no one). Goliardic verse pilloried the Church in the same way that *fabliaux* satirized the elite, by parodying religious hymns and condemning the clerical hierarchy.

Popular Fiction and Storytelling in China The beginnings of popular fiction in China can be traced to the plot books of storytellers who gathered audiences on the street corners of cities such as Hangzhou, the Chinese capital that so impressed the Venetian traveler Marco Polo in the late thirteenth century. These stories detail episodes from the lives of common people as well as cultural heroes, such as Guanyu, the god of war, who was modeled on the historical figure of a hero of a thousand years before.

The Novel in China The piecing together of these episodic stories led to the development of the novel in China during the fourteenth century. The *Romance of the Three Kingdoms* portrays conflicts among the leaders of the Three Kingdoms, states that ruled China after the breakup of the Han dynasty in the third century C.E. The writer depicts the two main opposing sides, the heir of the Han and his challenger, as representative of good and evil, right and wrong. The drama of the competition for the Mandate of Heaven animates this rich tapestry of historical romance. *Water Margin,* a historical romance, also written down in the fourteenth century, is an episodic novel based on accounts of the twelfth-century exploits of a band of outlaws. The novel reflects a popular tradition—often likened to that of the Robin Hood legends of medieval England—in which the outlaws were popular heroes fighting for the common people against oppressive government officials. Both this work and the *Romance of the Three Kingdoms* were constructed as episodic historical fiction, and both reflect the influence of a popular audience and oral tradition.

Chinese Drama under the Mongols During the period of Mongol rule in China, the Yuan dynasty (1279–1367), drama developed as a formal literary genre. Themes from Yuan plays dramatize social and political concerns of the time: how to get an heir to continue the family line and to inherit property; making a good match in marriage; succeeding in the examinations. Yuan drama also drew on themes and dramatic devices from folk opera, another means of giving shape to and preserving popular historical memory.

The rise of drama in this period of Mongol rule has often been explained as a response to the need to express opposition to foreign rule through subtle means such as veiled criticism in the portrayal of an evil character popularly understood to represent Mongol authorities. Sources such as Yuan drama tell us something of the cultural memory of people outside the educated elite who wrote official histories of the state or composed poetry based on complex historical and literary allusions. Such nonelite, alternative versions of the past, sometimes secular, at other times imbued with religious meaning, were transmitted orally or through visual and performing arts.

Religion and Secular Literature in India The *jataka*s ("birth stories") were the tales of Buddha's former births, written in Pali, the ancient language of Sri Lanka, between the third century B.C.E. and the third century C.E. Although the purpose of the tales is a didactic one—to illustrate Buddhist ethical ideals—they provide a wealth of information about the daily life of people in ancient India, including secular tales and fables that feature the future Buddha in one of his previous incarnations.

Although Buddhism provided the source for the *jataka* tales, the great works of Indian literature are those related directly to Hinduism, such as the *Mahabharata* or *Ramayana*. The beloved poet and dramatist Kalidasa (fl. ca. 400 C.E.) is best known for the drama *Sakuntala*, based on a story in the first book of the *Mahabharata* about the birth of King Bharata.

By the seventh century C.E., Vishnu, one of the principal Hindu deities, had gained great importance in Indian religion because he appeared as a god of love and kindness for humanity, one who could be approached by individuals without the mediation of Brahman priests. Popular cults emphasizing personal devotion (*bhakti*) to Vishnu in his earth-dwelling form of Krishna spread, and Hindu devotionalism came to be expressed in terms of reciprocal love between the worshipper and god.

In the tenth-century *Bhagavad Purana,* the most popular of the eighteen Sanskrit *purana*s ("ancient stories"), Krishna appears as a cowherder, enshrining the sanctity of the cow in Hindu cultural memory. In the later twelfth century, Jayadeva, a court poet from Bengal in India who followed a *bhakti* movement focused on Krishna, created one of the most beloved works of Indian literature, the *Gitagovinda* ("Song of Krishna, the Cowherd"). Jayadeva portrays in the *Gitagovinda* the physical love between Krishna, in the form of a cowherder (*govinda*), and a maiden. This work has an openly erotic character, but it is eroticism in the service of devotion to Krishna.

The *bhakti* movement encouraged the flourishing of vernacular literature by promoting translations of Sanskrit religious works into popular local languages. Even the *Ramayana* was translated into the south Indian language Tamil during the twelfth century. Between about

1000 and 1300 C.E., other vernacular Indian languages, such as Marathi and Bengali, were used to recount stories of Hindu deities, in contrast to the classical sacred languages of Sanskrit and Pali, much as European vernacular languages by medieval times (ca. 1000–1300) became the means of expression for popular European literature in place of Latin.

Arabic and Persian Literature in West Asia ▬▬▬▬▬▬▬▬▬ Despite the fact that non-Arabic peoples, such as Seljuk Turks and Mongols, invaded and conquered Islamic West Asia between the eleventh and fifteenth centuries, Arabic literature continued to flourish there almost as it had at the height of the early Umayyad and Abbasid Islamic Empires. While much of this literature was historical and theological epic, nonofficial cultural memory was preserved in a flourishing popular literature recorded in a variety of forms. The poet al-Hariri (1054–1122) composed a series of dramatic anecdotes in rhymed prose called maqamat. The purpose of his *Maqamat,* which was rooted in the popular life of the Islamic city, was to amuse and entertain by realistically portraying the manners and humor of the people. Al-Hariri's *Maqamat* became esteemed after the Qur'an as one of the chief treasures of the Arabic language.

Following the conquest of Iran by Central Asian Seljuk Turks, pastoralists who had converted to Islam, Persian literature reached its zenith. During this time, roughly 1055–1243, there appeared a host of Persian poets, the best known in the West being Umar Khayyam (?–1123?), whose *Rubaiyat* ("Quatrains") became well known to Europeans as a result of Edward FitzGerald's nineteenth-century English rendition, however unfaithful to the original it is. This song of wine drinking and love, part of a medieval Persian "hunting poem" tradition, is actually more famous today in the Anglo-American world than in Iran, where the author's fame rests mainly on his mathematical and astronomical achievements. Yet the *Rubaiyat* represents in many respects the epitome of Persian lyric poetry that celebrated the wine cult, a major poetic focus in the Seljuk period. This developed in reaction to the intense religious fanaticism of the period. For the poet, the tavern rather than the mosque became the place in which to gain wisdom.

For other poets, mysticism provided literary inspiration, and their works reflect life experience viewed through the lens of religious feeling. The Persian Sufi mystic poet Jalal ad-Din ar-Rumi (1207–1273), better known outside the Islamic world as Rumi, wrote the *Mathnawi,* a passionate song of love for God and the universe that became a masterpiece of Persian literature and for many Muslims the most sacred Islamic text after the Qur'an and the Traditions of the Prophet.

Another well-known example of West Asian literary cultural memory is the famed *Thousand and One Nights,* which took its final form in Egypt between the thirteenth and sixteenth centuries. Many of the stories found in the *Thousand and One Nights* originated in India and came west in a Persian translation to which different material from diverse sources was added over the years. Unlike the censored translations that have delighted the West, the original Arabic is "earthy," full of coarse jokes and explicit sex, in addition to the mockery of institutions and fantastic flights of imagination.

■

THE REPRESENTATION OF CULTURAL MEMORY

Themes of the connection between the world of gods and the world of humans can be seen in such culturally diverse sources as Greek drama and the *Mahabharata.* As a cultural memory system, literature portrays the complex relationships between gods and humans, between individuals, families, or communities, and between different cultures. Literature can preserve cultural memory in the face of challenges that would erase it, such as the Arab conquest of Iran, or reflect emerging cultural differences, as in the vernacular epics of northern and western Europe or the court literature of Heian Japan. Literature inspired by individual experience, such as that of Rumi, can also be the agent of cultural memory for a community, as his *Mathnawi* became a classic of Persian literature.

We have seen how written and oral memory systems utilize both word and image to convey and remember the past. Equally important as a cultural memory system are the more material monuments of past cultures as well as the plastic and other representative arts such as painting. Buildings and monuments, sculpture and painting are tangible and visible means of maintaining cultural continuity across the centuries and also of engineering change. Like historians and poets, artists and artisans create works that reflect and help shape the culture of their times. And like the written (and orally transmitted) word, works in stone or paint—pottery and pictures, buildings and statues—are records of culture.

THE ARCHITECTURE OF CULTURAL MEMORY IN AFRICA

Large buildings of permanent materials such as stone are among the oldest examples of cultural memory. By constructing buildings that reflect the needs and ideals of their times, architects and artisans embed the memory of those times in their work. For example, no record preserves the culture of ancient Egypt more clearly than the pyramid, a monumental stone form that represented the sun, a power nearly as important to the Egyptians as the Nile itself. Pyramids also intentionally commemorated the power of the pharaoh who ordered them built and, as one element of the royal burial complex, signified the survival of the ruler's power beyond his individual reign.

The pyramid of Khufu at Giza is the largest single building ever known to have been constructed. It is recognized as an extraordinary achievement in workmanship, accuracy, and proportional beauty. The architects and artisans who built the temples and pyramids of ancient Egypt created monuments to their technical skill and artistic vision that are important repositories of cultural and historical information about Egyptian social and political practices and religious ideals.

Elsewhere on the African continent, monumental architecture appeared not only in stone but also in mud or other perishable materials where stone was not available. The mud walls surrounding West African urban centers such as Jenne-Jeno (before ca. 900 C.E.) or Benin (after ca. 900 C.E.) required an impressive organization of labor and indicate the defensive needs and commercial purposes of those cities. Their maintenance was visible and ongoing, representative of the process of a centralized authority conscripting labor and thereby defining the limits of community.

ART AND KINGSHIP IN WEST AFRICAN FOREST STATES

Much of the visual art of the West African forest states was associated with divine kingship. Because the succession of kings relied in theory at least on genealogical claims, the knowledge and control of history were used to validate power and authority. Within the palace of the *oba*, or king, of Benin, shrines and altars were built to remember past kings and their exploits. Linked by ritual and containing visual reminders such as ivory tusks carved with his-

FIGURE 9.7 Benin Plaque Depicting an Acrobatic Festival Dance *Amufi,* which Recalls a Legendary War Against the Sky

SOURCE: Nigerian National Museum, Lagos.

torical scenes of battles and cast bronze and brass memorial heads portraying specific kings and queen mothers, the shrines formed an important part of the extensive calendar of ritual life at the palace.

Another source of historical information in Benin was the collection of rectangular plaques cast in various copper alloys. The plaques were thought to have been attached to the pillars of the royal palace structure. Scenes on the plaques depicted events in the kingdom's history. They could be read like a history book of costume, technology, politics, and culture over time. The plaques were kept inside the palace, and their production was limited to members of the *oba*'s guild of brass casters. Within an oral culture, they also served as mnemonic devices enabling the recovery of past knowledge for the purpose of recitation and ritual.

ARCHITECTURE AND COMMUNITY AT GREAT ZIMBABWE

To the south was the urban community of Great Zimbabwe, the center of a state whose wealth rested on gold, with an estimated population in about 1250 C.E. of perhaps 20,000. At the site of Great Zimbabwe among and around the boulders on a hillside are buildings, including a stone tower about 9 meters (30 feet) high and 5.5 meters (18 feet) in diameter and protective walls 10 meters (32 feet) tall, all of drystone construction using no mortar. These stone buildings are believed to have served political and economic and ceremonial and possibly religious purposes. Similar smaller stone structures, or *zimbabwes,* served as cattle enclosures and are found over the highland plateau occupied by Shona speakers and south into what today is the Transvaal of South Africa. It is believed that small stone sculptures once surmounted the stone walls and defined the boundaries associated with individual clans or family groups.

Buildings such as the Egyptian pyramids and the monumental stone architecture of ancient Zimbabwe preserve religious cultural memory. Both architecture and visual arts around the world also strongly express the role of religions such as Buddhism, Hinduism, and Christianity while making their ideas concrete and culturally relevant.

BUDDHIST ART AND ARCHITECTURE IN ASIA

In India, the homeland of Buddhism, religion inspired monumental art, which was also influenced by invading foreign peoples. Following the death of the devout Buddhist ruler Ashoka and the collapse of his empire in the third century B.C.E., waves of migrating peoples—Greeks, Scythians, Central Asian Kushans—brought new and foreign influences into the subcontinent. By the first and second centuries C.E., elaborations of Buddhist thought and doctrinal disputes led to the division of Buddhism into Mahayana and Theravada (see Chapter 5).

FIGURE 9.8 Great Zimbabwe: Aerial View of the Great Enclosure (built c. 12th century)

SOURCE: Robert Aberman/Heller/Art Resource, NY.

Indian Buddhist Art and Architecture   Mahayana doctrine, with its elaboration of Buddhas and *bodhisattva*s (enlightened beings) as deities, had a profound influence on Indian art. The Buddha Amitabha, who presides over the Western Paradise, his attendant *bodhisattva* Avalokitesvara, the compassionate "lord who looks down," and the historical Buddha, Sakyamuni, are widely represented in both sculpture and wall painting. Early Buddhist art, reflected in the Bamiyan caves (fourth to fifth centuries C.E.) in Afghanistan, shows the influence of Greek and Roman sculpture transmitted by the Kushans from Central Asia. The Ajanta caves on the Deccan plateau in south-central India contain extensive remains of Mahayana Buddhist wall paintings, dating from the fifth through the seventh centuries, many of which illustrate the *jataka* tales of Buddha's previous incarnations.

Indian Buddhist temples, or *stupa*s, which took their characteristic form between the third century B.C.E. and the third century C.E., were formal arrangements of gateways and stone railings that enclosed a burial shrine, or tumulus, of Buddhist relics, such as a bone or other physical remains of the historical Buddha. The dome of the *stupa* that covered the tumulus was a symbol of the dome of heaven, enclosing a world mountain. Worshipers walked around the circular terrace within the railings, which was a sacred space showing scenes from the life of Buddha as well as symbols of death and rebirth. Tactile sculptured frescoes adorn *stupa*s in a continuous flow of images, somewhat like a narrative fresco painting. Many *stupa*s are large, with domes raised on elaborate platforms.

Chinese Buddhist Art   The cave temples of Yun'gang and Longmen in north China are testimony to the powerful influence of Buddhism as it spread from India through Central and East Asia. Buddhist sculpture in China during the period when Buddhism spread (ca. third to sixth centuries) reflected both Indian and Central Asian influences. Giant images of Buddha and numerous smaller carvings at Yun'gang and Longmen display the devotion of wealthy and powerful believers, such as the Empress Wu (r. 690–705) in China, who commissioned the Longmen complex as an act of devotion. Religious art was produced under the patronage of Buddhist temples and monasteries as well as rulers throughout East Asia. Wall paintings from the excavations at Dunhuang in northwestern China dating to the sixth through eighth centuries illustrate Buddhist themes designed to appeal to a Chinese audience, but they are clearly influenced by Central Asian styles.

Buddhism spread from China through Korea and Japan, influencing architecture and plastic arts as well as religious beliefs. The tradition of Buddhist sculpture characteristic of eighth-century Japan, the era of intensive continental influence, shows close parallels with Chinese and Korean models. Korean artisans trained the Japanese in the sculptural styles they had adapted from China. Images of Buddhist deities became objects of worship in the Buddhist temples and monasteries that proliferated throughout Japan, symbolized by the erection of the statue of the Great Buddha at Nara in 752.

HINDUISM AND INDIAN ART AND ARCHITECTURE

Under the Gupta (ca. 320–540) rulers of India, who were Hindu patrons of the cult of Vishnu, Buddhism declined as an independent faith and was reabsorbed into Hinduism. The great age of Indian Buddhist art ended, and Hinduism became the primary source of inspiration for South Asian artists, though Buddhist images by no means disappeared. With the rise in the seventh century of Hindu devotional (*bhakti*) cults, centered either on Shiva, the De-

FIGURE 9.9 Image of Vairocana (Universal) Buddha, Surrounded by Attendant *bodhisattvas,* at Longmen in North China, ca. 672–675.

Carved into stone cliffs near the modern city of Luoyang, this Buddhist cave temple was built with the support of rulers who patronized such projects as an act of faith.

SOURCE: Photo Linda Walton.

stroyer, or on Vishnu, the Preserver, and his incarnations Rama and Krishna, their images, both in round and in relief, joined figures of Buddhas and *bodhisattvas* as decorative art.

Hindu temple architecture and sculpture illustrate the unitary quality of Indian art, in which the erotic and the demonic are mutual expressions of cosmic unity. Sensuous sculptures showing such deities as Shiva and his wife, Parvati, locked in erotic embrace manifest the erotic aspect of divinity, while portrayals of Parvati as a fierce female brandishing weapons in preparation for battle illustrate its demonic side. By the ninth century, Hindu temples were covered with such relief carvings and sculptured patterns. There was a preference for human figures, though they usually represented gods or mythical beings, sometimes hybrid half human half animal, such as Ganesha, the son of Shiva, portrayed as a human body with the head of an elephant. Epic stories were also represented, and female figures, graceful nymphs and goddesses, were common.

BUDDHISM AND HINDUISM IN SOUTHEAST ASIAN ARCHITECTURE

The spread of Buddhism and Hinduism to Southeast Asia is exemplified by two impressive temple complexes, Borobudur in Java and Angkor Wat in Cambodia. Created in the eighth century, Borobudur is an artificial mountain that combines the concept of a Buddhist *stupa* with that of Mount Meru, the world mountain in early Indian cosmology. The entire complex represents a huge magic diagram of the cosmos. As pilgrims mounted the terraced sanctuary, they were believed to reenact symbolically the ascent of a soul from the world of desire to the world of spiritual perfection and ultimate union with the cosmic Buddha.

Angkor Wat, built by the Khmer rulers of Cambodia in the twelfth century, shows the powerful influence of Hinduism in Southeast Asia. Angkor Wat is a vast architectural complex serving simultaneously as a temple for Vishnu and a sanctuary for the *devaraja,* or "divine king," Khmer rulers who were believed to be earthly incarnations of Vishnu. The main sanctuary at Angkor Wat is 40 meters (130 feet) high and stands on a stone-encased platform 12 meters (40 feet) high and 46 meters (150 feet) square. Although it was abandoned as an active temple site in the fifteenth century, it remains an impressive record documenting the flow of Hinduism to Southeast Asia and the ability of Khmer rulers to mobilize artisans and workers sufficient to build a monument of such scale.

CHRISTIAN ARCHITECTURE IN EUROPE

Religious themes similarly dominated European art in the medieval period (ca. 1000–1300), when the Church was the dominant force in European society and the principal patron of the arts. Although religious themes dictated the subjects of painting and sculpture, such as figures of the Virgin Mary, Christ, and saints, religion inspired artistic genius most visibly in the architectural monument of the cathedral. As cities grew and flourished, their residents built handsome and impressive churches which were as much monuments to urban wealth and pride as they were dwellings of the Christian divinity.

FIGURE 9.10 Cathedral of Beauvais: Aerial View (begun 1247)

European cathedrals were monumented statements of wealth, labor, and creativity.

SOURCE: Scibilia/Art Resource, NY.

One of the most celebrated of these monuments was the French cathedral of Saint Pierre in Beauvais, the vaulting of which exceeded 46 meters (150 feet), making it the highest of all Gothic churches. Having collapsed twice, this cathedral was never completed. It remains an impressive example of the civic pride and religious fervor that produced such art. Cathedrals represent the unity of sacred and secular functions in other ways as well. They served their communities as refuges for the homeless and destitute, thus embodying the ethical virtues expected of the wider cultural community.

ISLAMIC ART AND ARCHITECTURE AS CULTURAL MEMORY

In West Asia, the counterpart of the Buddhist and Hindu temples in South and East Asia and the cathedral in Europe was the Islamic mosque, characteristically a domed structure. Although the dome was in use in West Asia before the Arab conquest, the Muslims subsequently raised this architectural form to monumental proportions; mosque domes are evidence of the unequaled skills of West Asian engineers and architects. Hundreds of domed structures, above all mosques, were constructed throughout West Asia and beyond when Islam spread. There were several shapes: small or vast, squat or bulbous. Some were made of large blocks of stone, and others were made of bricks covered with dazzling colored tiles. As domes were introduced to parts of West Africa by the spread of Islam, they were constructed of indigenous materials following local traditions, which dictated their construction out of mud, requiring a constant cycle of devotional upkeep and repair.

The coming of the Turks to West Asia, symbolized by the eleventh-century conquest of Baghdad, inaugurated a cultural revolution in the Islamic world. Their arrival meant changes in artistic style and decoration; it also led to the introduction of architecture with entirely new functions. One such structure that rapidly spread under the Turks was the *turbe,* or "tower tomb," a tall building that was a popular burial place for Muslim rulers and religious mystics and often became an object of pilgrimage. Its shape may have originated in that of the Central Asian Buddhist *stupa*s or in the circular tent houses, called yurts, of nomadic Turks.

NORTH AMERICAN ARCHITECTURE AS CULTURAL MEMORY

The tangible remains of North American communities suggest a spiritual basis for culture that was as pervasive as Christianity was in Europe. Many North Americans led nomadic lives requiring little in the way of permanent structures. Some, such as the peoples of the Pacific Northwest and the Inuit, lived in sedentary communities but built structures of perishable materials. There are, however, monumental remains from North American communities that were dependent on agriculture and trade. Such peoples inhabited much of the Mississippi and Ohio River valleys and the southeastern part of the United States. North American cultures known as Hopewell and Mississipian centered on towns and cities characterized by mounds and other urban features.

Earthworks, such as the Great Serpent Mound in Ohio, appear to have been designed to function as sacred effigies. There are others in the form of panthers, bears, birds, and humans, found at a variety of sites. The most impressive visual evidence of these pre-European North American cultures is found at Cahokia, the largest of these towns, located in southern Illinois across the Mississippi River from Saint Louis. Monumental mounds at Cahokia served political and religious purposes. Some were burial mounds, log tombs covered with earth piled up in various shapes (square, circular, rectangular, octagonal), often exceeding 500 meters (1650 feet) in diameter or length.

The contents of these burial mounds provide evidence of the considerable artistic skill of Cahokia's inhabitants and reflect their religious practices and their conspicuous consumption of luxury goods (metals, shells, teeth) traded from noncontiguous areas. Public structures and residences were built on some of the mounds and reflect the ranked political and social structures of the community. Generally, the largest mounds are temple mounds. "Monk's Mound," at Cahokia was 360 by 241 meters (1181 by 73 feet) and contained 600,000 cubic meters (21 million cubic feet) of earth, all carried to the site in baskets filled with 18-kilogram (40-pound) loads. This, the largest earthen structure built in the Americas before the arrival of Europeans, was an engineering feat comparable to the stone pyramids of Egypt.

ART AND ARCHITECTURE IN MESOAMERICA

It is possible that the monumental traditions of North America were imported by immigrants from the south or at least inspired by earlier Mesoamerican architecture. There is general agreement that the Olmec culture (ca. 1200–400 B.C.E.) provided a common foundation for the Mesoamerican cultures that came after it. Olmec art had a strong ritual aspect, focusing on a wide variety of supernatural combinations of animal and human features in bewildering complexity. Formidable animals predominate in Olmec art, and cave paintings, like sculpture, combine human-animal motifs. Especially common was the combination of snarling jaguar and bawling human infant.

Olmec art objects and the influence of their style stretched by trade and conquest from Central America to Costa Rica. Later Mesoamerican cultures, such as that of the Maya, were once believed to descend directly from the Olmecs. Recent discoveries in the tropical forests of Guatemala and Belize now suggest local origins beginning around 300 B.C.E. Classic Mayan culture flourished in the Yucatán Peninsula of modern Mexico between about 300 and 900 C.E., and one of its best-known sites is Tikal. The monumental Mayan art reflects an environment in which stone was plentiful. Characteristic of Mayan remains are temple-pyramids made of stuccoed limestone, multiroomed "palaces," causeways connecting groups of structures in cities, and cities themselves, including stone monuments often inscribed with Mayan hieroglyphics. At Tikal, the buildings of a central acropolis were built over earlier tombs of elites cut into bedrock. The acropolis was for ceremonial purposes and was surrounded by substantial suburbs. Stone was the primary medium of Mesoamerican art and Tikal's monuments provide significant evidence of political complexity and cultural connections across the southern lowlands.

ART AND ARCHITECTURE IN ANDEAN SOUTH AMERICA

The earliest commonly occurring artistic and architectural remains in Andean South America are designated "Chavin," after the style of art centered at Chavin de Huantar, located in the highlands of modern Peru. The style of Chavin pottery art was uniform across northern Peru during the period 1000 to 200 B.C.E., suggesting the possibility of intensive exchange, communication, and military competition between highland and coastal communities. Substantial stone buildings were erected for ritual and ceremonial purposes. As with Olmec culture in Mesoamerica, pre-Incan ceremonial centers were located in rural areas rather than being part of urban centers, with two important exceptions: Tihuanaco and Huari. The people of Chavin probably never numbered more than 2000, but they built intricately terraced fields to make the steep slopes and hilly regions of the area more productive. They had highly developed weaving techniques and had sufficient metallurgical knowledge to be able to produce refined ornaments of copper and copper-gold alloys.

Most of the Chavin visual art can be explained in terms of religion, royal power, agriculture, or warfare. In general, the Chavin style, like that of the Olmecs in Mesoamerica, emphasized composite creatures, especially serpents and felines such as the jaguar, and Chavin sculpture portrayed the attributes of creatures in nature that suggest their supernatural qualities. Figures from the Chavin pantheon are depicted in Chavin pottery, painted cloth, worked metal, and small stone and bone objects, as well as in sculpture and temple carvings. Chavin styles and forms were later integrated into other Central Andean cultures. As was the case with the widespread Olmec style, adopting stylistic elements from Chavin de Huantar may have enhanced the cultural legitimacy of competing elites in other communities.

In the centuries between Chavin and the rise of the Incan culture in the fifteenth century, regional centers of culture, such as Chimu (ca. 750–1450 C.E.), dominated the central Andean area. On Peru's north coast, the giant pyramids at Moche (ca. 200 B.C.E.–600 C.E.) provide even earlier evidence of political and artistic complexity. The pyramids were built of hundreds of millions of adobe bricks, each brick marked with a symbol pressed on its top surface. The symbols may represent their makers, thus recording the tribute provided as labor. A variety of styles, suggesting some influences inherited from Chavin, emerged during this period. More than a millennium later, the Inca ruled the Andean highlands using a tribute-based empire. Incan culture was particularly noted for its fine stonework. Buildings in large cities, such as the Incan capital of Cuzco, showed impressive architectural skill. Public structures for religious or political use were constructed of mortarless masonry. Large, irregular stones were fitted so closely that a knife blade could not pass between them. Equally amazing stonework went into elaborately engineered irrigation systems and agricultural terraces and the network of roads and bridges that bound the Incan Empire together. Machu Picchu, a complex of remarkable stone structures high in the Andes, is perhaps the best-known Incan remain. Machu Picchu was one of several royal estates built by Pachacuti (ca. 1440) to commemorate specific military exploits. Its temples and terraces bear dramatic witness to the power of the Incan Empire and its religious underpinnings.

DECORATIVE ARTS AS CULTURAL MEMORY

Public architecture, particularly if monumental, represents community culture in its largest and most public sense. Other art forms were more exclusive representations of cultural memory directed at individual or personal, and sometimes elite, experience. Decorative arts around the world illustrate the culture of the private sector of society and also of the patterns appreciated in the objects of daily life. Artists applied distinctive and varied patterns and skills to the most mundane and functional objects. For example, silver ear picks in Ethiopia from the fourth century C.E. were cast in elaborate cross shapes, reflecting a Christian influence; laborious attention was given to style and ornament in the design of hair combs and cooking vessels.

By virtue of patronage by the religious, political, and commercial elite, both sacred and secular works of European decorative artists generally reflect elite rather than popular culture.

Miniature portrait painting captured the essence of their subjects, whether secular or religious, while the delicate skills of manuscript decoration were principally applied to religious documents. Frescoes, the wall paintings done on fresh plaster, were another characteristic form of medieval religious art, but by the thirteenth century Italian artists increasingly began to paint on wood and canvas. As they did so, the subjects of their painting became more diverse. The works of the Florentine painter Giotto (ca. 1267–1337) signaled a new direction in European art by treating traditional religious subjects in a more fully human and naturalistic style. The adoption of the one-point perspective in drawing and painting began to change the ways in which people saw the world around them, and its use increased the accuracy of represented sizes and distances.

WORD AND IMAGE IN EAST AND WEST ASIAN ART

In China, painting was perceived to be an art form related to poetry, and both painting and poetry were profoundly influenced by Buddhism and Daoism during the period of division between the fall of the Han dynasty in the third century and the reunification of the empire in the sixth century. By the Song period (960–1275), landscape ("mountain-water") painting and "bird and flower" genre painting flourished among court academy painters and among amateur literati painters. The power and beauty of nature that dominate Chinese landscape paintings are not achieved by infinite detail. Instead, Chinese artists relied on space to suggest the vastness of the cosmos. Humanity's place as a part of the cosmos was shown by the miniscule portrayal of individual human beings in the landscape. Poems were often written in elegant calligraphy—another art form—on the paintings, describing and expanding on what was suggested in them.

In Japan, works such as the eleventh-century *Tale of Genji* were illustrated on horizontal scrolls on which portions of the text were interspersed with painted images. Later "water-and-ink" painting flourished in Japan during the fourteenth to sixteenth centuries. This style of painting was adapted from China and was inspired in part by Chan (Japanese Zen) aesthetics. The spare lines and allusive, suggestive quality of these paintings were related to Zen notions of the impossibility of rendering reality by painting the detail of human portraits, landscapes, or other objects.

In contrast to the Zen distrust of representation—either word or image—as an aid to understanding, a West Asian counterpart to the adornment of paintings with texts in China or illustrated scrolls in Japan was the painting of miniature pictures to illustrate various literary texts, an art form that reached perfection after the eleventh century. The Arabs, Persians, and Turks all excelled at this art. With the Arabs, the art of the book flowered in the twelfth and thirteenth centuries, primarily in Baghdad. A wide variety of texts was illustrated, including astronomical, botanical, medical, and pharmacological works.

The tradition of Persian miniatures began in the late thirteenth century, following the Mongol conquest, and reached its perfection in the fifteenth and sixteenth centuries. Persian miniatures were often highly detailed—brushes with a single hair were used—and were ablaze with color. An artist could spend years on a single painting that was about the size of this page. In addition to delighting the eye, the spectacular depictions of the court and everyday life, as well as animated hunting and awesome battle scenes, give us a unique glimpse of contemporary fashions, tools and implements, art and architecture, and customs and activities.

■
TECHNOLOGY AND CULTURAL MEMORY

Technology is a category of cultural knowledge and, along with memory systems such as history, literature, and architecture, transmits essential cultural knowledge from generation to generation. Technology includes both tools and practices, the ways in which tools are used by people to manipulate their environment and to construct the physical world around them. Technology is a memory system, a cultural link that is as revealing of historical experience as art or literature.

Technological advancements were rarely documented before late medieval times. Even then, they were usually mentioned by accident, perceived to be merely incidental to historical narratives of great men and dramatic events. How and when a particular tool, device, or process came into being in a given region was almost never stated in historical sources. Moreover, societies tended to adopt rather quickly anything that appeared to be to their immediate benefit or advantage, without showing much interest in its origin. By trade, war, and other means, many technologies were therefore diffused, perhaps from more than one source, over vast areas, while their origins were actually unknown or forgotten. For the most part, historians, archaeologists, and others must infer the origins and uses of technology from the physical remains of a culture or region.

PRINT TECHNOLOGY AND THE TRANSMISSION OF CULTURAL MEMORY

Paper, which is essential to printing, was invented in China early in the Han dynasty (202 B.C.E.–220 C.E.). The earliest extant printed texts on paper were made in eighth-century Korea and Japan by carving text onto wooden blocks, which were then smeared with ink and covered with paper, producing an impression of the text. The earliest surviving Chinese text made by wood-block printing is a Buddhist sutra from the mid–ninth century. Wood-block printing became the favored method of reproducing texts throughout East Asia, in contrast to copying by hand using brush and ink. This method allowed fewer errors and omissions or other changes to creep into texts because the carved woodblock, though subject to deterioration over time, was a relatively permanent and unchanging means of reproducing texts. In addition to propagating religion and spreading culture through literature, printing was used to spread new technologies for agriculture and silk production and in this way contributed substantially to the economic revolution of Song times.

The Invention of Movable Type In the eleventh century, movable type—in clay, wood, and metal—was invented in China, 400 years before its appearance in Europe. Ultimately, because of the use of an ideographic script with thousands of characters as opposed to an alphabetic one with fewer than a hundred letters, movable type did not dominate printing in China because it was relatively more efficient to carve a woodblock page than to keep available the thousands of pieces of type necessary to set a page of text. Still, the development of a commercial printing industry in the Song period and the proliferation of printed books made learning and written culture more accessible to a wider population, aiding in the transmission of popular literature as well as the historical and philosophical texts used in studying for the civil service examinations.

Printing in Europe In contrast to China, where wood-block printing remained important despite the invention of movable type, the introduction of movable type in Europe in the fifteenth century brought about changes in the way cultural memory was shaped, transcribed, and transmitted, changes comparable to those resulting from the invention of writing in the third millennium B.C.E. or the introduction of the word processor and computer in the late twentieth century. Although initially most works printed in Europe were in Latin, the language of the Church and state, increasing numbers of works in European vernacular languages were printed. By contributing to the expansion of vernacular and secular literatures, printing in Europe, as in China, made knowledge more widely and easily available to an increasingly literate audience.

Papermaking The spread of papermaking technologies increased the impact of printing technologies in Europe, Asia, and Africa. Papermaking technologies made their way from China, where paper was invented in the first century C.E., westward over the routes of commerce and conquest by the ninth century. In the twelfth century, papermaking spread from North Africa to Muslim Spain and Sicily, then beyond to the European continent. Much cheaper than the Egyptian papyrus or the vellum (calf- or kidskin) used in Europe, paper made possible the development and widespread distribution of books, stimulating literacy and the expansion of an educated elite, while more generally spreading knowledge in Africa, Europe, and West Asia.

FIGURE 9.11 Reproduction of Movable Type Based on Description in the Song Polymath Shen Gua's *Dreampool Essays,* ca. 1045

SOURCE: Ontario Science Center, Toronto.

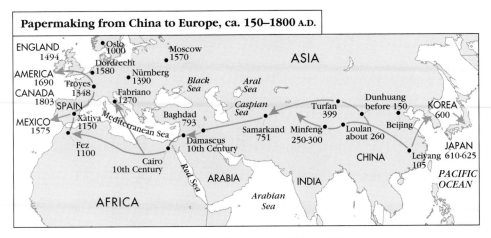

MAP 9.1 The Technology of Papermaking Spread from China to Europe

SOURCE: *China: 7000 Years of Discovery* (Ontario Science Centre, Toronto, 1982): 14

CERAMICS AND CULTURAL MEMORY

The technologies of material culture were also subject to cultural imitation and borrowing. For example, in West Asia excellent pottery for both utilitarian and artistic purposes was produced by experimentation with different kinds of clay and glazes. But potters were also influenced by the foreign pottery technologies introduced to West Asia as a result of commerce and conquest. Beginning in the tenth century, Turkish invasions brought many changes to pottery making in West Asia. A new white composite clay material was introduced throughout the region, and there was a gradual evolution in the methods of decorating this material. It could be carved, stained with glaze, painted and then covered with glaze, or painted in luster, monochrome or polychrome over the glaze.

Chinese ceramics reached a high point by the twelfth century with the development of specialized kilns in which artisans produced highly refined varieties of milky white, oxblood red, celadon green, and blue-and-white porcelain. Chinese styles and methods increasingly influenced West Asian pottery following the initial Turkish invasion in the eleventh century, reaching a height in the thirteenth century as the Mongol Empire enhanced Eurasian connections. Major attempts were made to imitate Chinese porcelain, though they were never quite successful. West Asians, however, perfected a major ceramics technology, perhaps as early as the eighth century, with the invention of lusterware. This process, in turn, was widely adopted and influenced pottery making around the world.

TEXTILE TECHNOLOGY AND CULTURAL MEMORY

Silk Manufacturing The technology of silk manufacturing, from silkworm to fabric, is rooted in the cultural memories of Asia, Africa, and Europe and provides a clear example of the interconnections among them. Silk was being produced in China already during the Shang dynasty (ca. 1600–1050 B.C.E.), and by the time of the first emperor (third century B.C.E.) silk production was being officially promoted by the state. By the second century C.E., Chinese merchants and adventurers who had made their way to West Asia noted

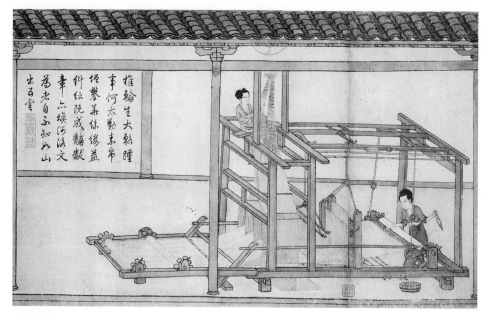

FIGURE 9.12 Chinese Women Weaving Silk

Detail from 13th c. handscroll depicting steps involved in making silk

SOURCE: Courtesy of the Freer Gallery of Art, Smithsonian Institution, Washington, DC.

there only tussah silk, a primitive form of silk made from filaments shredded from destroyed cocoons of the wild moth.

The Chinese considered their silk technology, which relied on cultivated cocoons from which continuous filaments were extracted, to be superior to that of the West Asians. The introduction of Chinese-cultivated cocoon silk technology to West Asia and ultimately the Mediterranean basin, and the organization of trade in silk between China and the West, which was under way by the early Han (second century B.C.E.), provided West Asia, Europe, and Africa with a basic fabric which also appeared in a variety of elegant forms, such as brocades, satins, and velvets. These luxury fabrics came to be in great demand and helped establish and affirm the elite social position and cultural identity of those who could afford them.

Cotton Production Among other textile technologies, that for producing cotton goods provides an enigmatic and unique example of cultural interconnection. Cotton is the only common cultivated plant found in both Asia and the Americas before the sixteenth century, and the technologies for converting cotton into yarn and cloth were almost identical. Yet cotton could have played no part in the arctic Bering Strait region, which is the only point of cultural contact between ancient Asia and America. The answer to the enigma lies in the fact that the types of cotton produced in Asia and in South America do not belong to the same species. As far as the technology of spinning and weaving is concerned, humans are endlessly inventive: Peruvians in South America and Indians in the Asian subcontinent solved the problems of spinning and weaving in similar ways without borrowing from each other.

Cotton textile production and trade were as important to India as silk was to China. Indian production and technology expanded with the demand for cotton cloth, often aided by innovations made by others. For example, Indian looms were improved by ingenious devices for mechanical pattern weaving that were perfected in Persia; and during the Tang period (618–907) China made the great, if unconscious, contribution of block printing to Indian cotton textile arts. The process, an adaptation of early printing technology, replaced the earlier Indian method of painting designs on fabric; it confirmed India's supremacy in the manufacturing of cotton textiles. The technology spread across many regions, including West Africa.

Textile technology illustrates both the individuality and the interconnectedness of technology as a cultural memory system. Achievements in textile technology in different parts of the world made it possible for fabric and clothing, ranging from diaphanous gowns to thick felt cloaks, to became major items of international trade. The products of that technology carried distinct cultural messages. Textile patterns were equated with particular ethnic groups and sometimes illustrated ethnic identities, social categories, or even specific historical or cultural events.

Conquest as well as trade had effects on textile technology. One of the results of the tenth-century Turkish invasion of West Asia was the introduction and spread of carpet weaving there. Persians rapidly adopted the art of carpet making from the Turks and then made their own innovations, producing fine carpets that were in great demand. Since West Asian peoples sat on stools or sofas covered with textiles and ate and slept on the floor, making themselves comfortable with carpets, cushions, and mattresses, textile production provided important products for daily life. Carpets were as much functional as decorative art. They also became a significant trade item, as attested by their appearance in European paintings from the fifteenth and sixteenth centuries.

IRON TECHNOLOGY AS CULTURAL MEMORY

Technology can reveal cultural memory in profound and explicit ways. The technology of sub-Saharan African societies before 1500 suggests that technology was not necessarily distinct from spirituality and material power. In sub-Saharan Africa, iron smelting was a cultural performance choreographed by the master smelter and smelting furnaces had both technological and spiritual functions. The smelter was typically a man with great knowledge and considerable political power who, in some societies, was also a spiritual leader. Among the MaShona in southern Africa, knowledge of iron making was claimed through contact with spirits and spirit-inspired dreams in which ancestors provided master craftsmen with the power to create. Such technological and spiritual skills were passed from one generation to the next through exclusive systems of apprenticeship and training.

Ironworking was linked to other activities that were also believed to be controlled by ancestors, such as human reproduction. By the thirteenth century, the Bassari of Togo in West Africa smelted iron in what they considered to be gendered furnaces. The furnace was believed to be a woman who was impregnated by the smelter to "give birth" to red, glowing iron. Each furnace was constructed from pieces of an old furnace once used by the smelter's grandfather, thus supplying a physical genealogical link between past and present. According to the smelter, "It is not I who build this furnace, it is you [the ancestors and spirits] who build it."

While the repeated performance of past cultural traditions was not always so conscious, the reliance of cultural memory on practice was commonly a means of preserving information about the past. Through apprenticeship systems, patterned motor skills and the complex bodies of knowledge utilized in activities such as pottery making, metalworking, textile manufacturing, and other crafts became essential and familiar parts of cultural memory transferred from one generation to the next.

■

INSTITUTIONS AND THE TRANSMISSION OF CULTURAL MEMORY

The various systems of cultural memory we have discussed—history and science, technology and literature, architecture and theology—may be private products of individual creation or the results of public, community design and effort. Whatever the forms of cultural memory or the means by which they are created, the maintenance and transmission of cultural memory are often associated with institutions such as churches, schools, guilds, brotherhoods, libraries, and universities. In the process of preserving and transmitting cultural knowledge, institutions are agents of cultural memory, adding a distinctly social dimension to cultural knowledge. Such institutions can consolidate the authority of social and cultural elites, but they can also act as agents of change by expressing resistance to prevailing cultural norms and ideals.

MONASTICISM

Monasticism, the way of life of those who have taken religious vows to live apart from society, fostered religious communities throughout the world. These religious communities, known as monasteries, were predominantly, though not exclusively, Christian or Buddhist; as institutions of cultural memory, they transmitted religious ideas through practice and sometimes became powerful agents in the political and social world outside the monastery. Monasteries adopted rules for living, encouraged the practice of religious vows, provided temporary refuges for laypeople, and often served the secular community through charitable activities in times of need.

Christian Monasticism Christian monasticism originated at the end of the fourth century in West Asia, where the first rules for governing a community, stressing prayer, work, and obedience, were written by Saint Basil (d. 379 C.E.). Monasticism was introduced to western Europe by the end of the fourth century and quickly spread from the Mediterranean northward and westward as far as Ireland, to which Saint Patrick (ca. 389–461) introduced an early form. Irish monasticism was responsible for extensive missionary efforts in northern Germany, and some Irish monasteries became prominent centers of learning and culture.

The rules established by Saint Benedict (ca. 480–543) for the monastery he founded on the heights of Monte Cassino, midway between Rome and Naples, became common to most religious communities in Europe. Benedict's rule swore monks to poverty, chastity, and obedience; they could possess no individual property and submitted their individual wills to that of the abbot, who headed the monastery. The individual lost his identity and became part of

FIGURE 9.13 Palkhorchoede Monastery in Gyantse, Tibet

Built in the 15th century, this monastery was a center of the "Yellow Hat" sect of Tibetan Buddhism, founded by the monk Tsongkhapa (1357–1419).

SOURCE: Erich Lessing/Art Resource, NY.

the whole, which was a strictly regulated community with a regimented routine of prayer, meditation, and works.

Women and Monasticism Religious communities for women appeared at the same time as those for men and were aided and encouraged by Church leaders. By the sixth century, major French cities had religious communities for women, and in the eighth century, Saint Boniface (680–754), an English missionary to the Germans, founded communities there for women as well as men.

Religious communities in medieval Europe attracted and supported women because they offered them opportunities not otherwise available. For example, Eleanor of Aquitaine (1122–1204), variously queen of France and England, gave money to and otherwise patronized monasteries. Other noblewomen founded convents, monasteries, and charitable institutions such as orphanages and hospitals. Women also continued to enter the cloistered life, which enabled them—no longer wives, mothers, daughters—to dedicate themselves, like men, to study, good works, and spiritual growth.

In late medieval Europe, foundresses and abbesses were able to acquire religious and secular knowledge usually reserved for men. Hildegard of Bingen (1098–1179), founder and abbess of a convent in Germany, was widely known for her learning. The breadth and scope of her knowledge were extensive, ranging from music to theology to science. Popes and emperors, who believed her to be a prophetess, took her scientific and theological treatises seriously.

Though monks and nuns were removed from secular life, they also served lay society by providing hospices for the ill and hostels for travelers. But their main contribution lay in copying manuscripts and maintaining libraries, and monasteries thus served as a principal institution for the transmission of European cultural memory. Christian monasteries in Europe controlled the preservation and reproduction of cultural knowledge, much as Confucian institutions and ideas dominated this process in China, Buddhist and Hindu ones did in India, and Islamic ones did in West Asia.

Buddhist Monasticism Buddhist monasticism reached across Asia from India to China, Southeast Asia, and Japan. In China, independent Buddhist sects established networks of monasteries that housed hundreds of thousands of monks and nuns. By the Tang period (618–907), Buddhist monasteries were wealthy landowners and Buddhist abbots and priests socialized with the court aristocracy and were highly educated members of the literati elite. Buddhist monasteries and temples also served as schools, providing primary education in Confucian texts as well as Buddhist ones. Buddhist monasteries, like their counterparts in Europe, often served as repositories of learning and also functioned as educational institutions that preserved and transmitted knowledge, including secular ideas such as Confucianism in East Asia.

In Heian Japan, an emperor might enter a cloistered life as a monk in order to avoid public ceremonial functions and thereby be able to operate more effectively as a political influence from behind the scene. Noblewomen in Heian Japan similarly entered nunneries to

DAILY LIVES

VISIONS AND VOICES: Hildegard of Bingen

The cloistered life of the convent provided a refuge for women who sought to flee worldly troubles or to devote themselves to a religious life. For the abbesses who supervised convent life, the convent was a source of power. Abbesses assumed responsibility both for the religious life of the nuns of their order and for the laity living on convent lands. Since convent lands were part of the feudal system, abbesses were responsible for fulfilling the feudal obligations of a vassal and for administering the manors and fields on which the convent depended.

In addition to their spiritual and material duties, a number of churchwomen devoted themselves to learning. Hildegard of Bingen, for example, took her vows as a nun at age 14 or 15, became abbess of her convent at 38, and founded a new convent near Bingen in Germany. A mystic and visionary, Hildegard distinguished herself in science, music, literature, and theology, and her counsel was sought by kings, emperors, and popes. From the age of 3, Hildegard had experi-

enced visions in which she saw or heard images and their meanings. At 40, she began to write a remarkable series of works, including the visionary *Scivias Via Domini* ("Know the Ways of the Lord"), which established her authority as an interpreter of divine mysteries.

Her revelations included an analysis of the function of the body, so she also wrote on medicine. The *Physica* ("Book of Simple Medicine") lists some 300 herbs and their medicinal uses, and the *Causae et Curae* ("Book of Medicine Carefully Arranged") lists 47 separate diseases, their causes, and possible cures. Hildegard was also a gifted author and composer. Her *Book of Life's Rewards* and her devotional allegories and poems were freer in form and image than most of the poetry and prose of her time. She wrote a "Symphony of the Harmony of the Heavenly Revelation," a cycle of seventy-seven devotional songs for performance on feast days of the Virgin and saints, as well as what has been called the first European opera.

preserve and protect their honor if their husbands were killed in battle or somehow dishonored, or to grieve. Buddhist monastic institutions in medieval Japan were centers of learning patronized by the military leaders of the time, much like monasteries in medieval Europe. Buddhist monasteries in both China and Japan served as sources of refuge for women who wanted to escape from miserable lives in the world because of marriage, politics, or both.

BROTHERHOODS AND GUILDS

Like the community of monks and nuns in Buddhist and Christian monasteries throughout Asia and Europe, in the Islamic world Sufi brotherhoods, called *tariqa*s (paths to union with God), sprang up in the twelfth and thirteenth centuries and established networks of lodges throughout West Asia. These lodges were typically organized around an outstanding mystic, whose tomb was usually incorporated into the main lodge. Branch lodges were subsequently founded wherever groups of his disciples and adherents might meet. Each lodge had its own rituals and costume, and some were restricted to particular professions or strata of society. The brotherhoods in the cities, especially those associated with the professions, often adopted their own code of ethics, generally referred to as the *futuwwa*.

*Tariqa*s played a major role in the spread of Islam. Each was in fact a popular movement that appealed to emotion rather than to rigid dogmatism. The emotional and syncretic nature of *tariqa* rituals and practices was something anyone could respond to. One of the most famous brotherhoods was inspired by Jalal ad-Din ar-Rumi (1207–1273), a Sufi mystic and poet whose tomb at Konya in Anatolia became a site of pilgrimage for his disciples and their followers. Jalal ad-Din had used music and dance to help induce a mystical state, and dancing became the outstanding feature of religious rituals associated with Sufi brotherhoods.

The early Turkish brotherhoods had strong overtones of shamanism. The pagan Turks from Central Asia saw the leader (*shaik*) of a brotherhood as a shaman and his attempts to induce a mystical state by chanting, music, and dance as consistent with their traditional shamanistic ceremonies. By making conversion easier, the brotherhoods played an important role in the spread of Islam. Eventually *tariqa*s of every description emerged, from the scholarly and contemplative to those whose followers babbled incoherently and handled poisonous snakes. Some brotherhoods exhibited a fanatical devotion to Islam, and their militancy was put to good use by the Turks in wars against Christian Byzantium. *Tariqa*s were a critical factor in the Islamization of Anatolia (modern Turkey) by both peaceful and aggressive means.

Muslim Brotherhoods in West Africa *Tariqa*s appeared in West Africa with the spread of Islam that accompanied the expansion of the Mali Empire (ca. thirteenth and fourteenth centuries). Muslim brotherhoods proved compatible with indigenous West African cultural institutions and made conversion to Islam easier. Among linguistically related West African peoples, secret men's and women's societies centering on commerce and its regulation existed among the merchant classes. Such urban lodges, scattered throughout the Mali Empire, increased cultural solidarity within the merchant community, defrayed the costs of individuals' trade and travel, and further enhanced the success of West African commercial and cultural connections within the Islamic world.

Medieval European Guilds Counterparts to these Islamic lodges can be seen in the medieval European guild system. With the expansion of trade in Europe from about 1200 to 1500, associations for mutual aid and protection developed among town dwellers engaged in common pursuits. Known as "guilds," these societies were the urban counterparts of agrarian manorialism, the means by which manufacturing, trade, labor, and even government in towns and cities were regulated and protected. Like the urban lodges of West Africa, guilds provided a basis for the retention and transmission of specialist knowledge, offered community solidarity, and were among the agencies of political and cultural change in late medieval Europe. Guilds were among the most important institutions in medieval Europe.

There were almost as many guilds as there were different activities: there were guilds for bellringers, minstrels, candlemakers, masons, roadmenders, and weavers, to name but a few. Guilds assisted destitute or ill members and paid for the funeral Mass after death. Many guilds assumed judiciary roles, settled quarrels, and even investigated crimes. They also participated in public rituals and ceremonies, such as the celebration of the Doge (ruler) of Venice in 1268, a parade in which each of the city's guilds marched in bands, sumptuously dressed, carrying banners and flags, and heralded by musicians.

EDUCATION, UNIVERSITIES, AND SCHOOLS

Many societies systematically developed means of acquiring and transmitting vital cultural knowledge through a variety of educational institutions, both religious and secular. Cathedral schools, along with the traditional monastic centers of learning, were the centers of education in Europe until the appearance of universities in the twelfth century. Students were considered clerks (clerics, clergy), even though they might never become priests. The earliest universities may be thought of as urbanized, expanded cathedral schools. The first appeared in Italy at Bologna in the early twelfth century, and the first north of the Alps was at Paris (1200). The University of Paris became the foremost center for theological and philosophical studies in Europe, an indication of its origins and the dominant role of the Church in education.

Buddhist and Hindu Education in India In India, the great Buddhist university at Nalanda in Bihar was founded in the sixth century C.E. and had an enrollment of around 5,000 students, including many foreign scholars and distinguished lecturers. Buddhist texts and the Vedas and Hindu philosophy were taught at this and other Buddhist universities. Caste divisions were reflected in other educational institutions, as brahman boys (and occasionally girls) were educated in the Vedic tradition; members of the warrior caste were educated largely by household tutors, who taught them reading, writing, military arts, dancing, painting, and music.

In contrast to China, where the written word was endowed with sacred power, there was far more regard for oral tradition in early India. Rote memorization of the Vedas was emphasized, although writing was eventually used as an aid to memorization. As in medieval Europe, libraries were found in monasteries and palaces. Manuscript copying was an industry involving professional scribes and was often considered a pious activity, also centered in monasteries and palaces.

Education and the Examination System in China In China, the Confucian notion that schools were a responsibility of the state persisted from antiquity. By the second century B.C.E., there was an "Imperial University" in the capital that taught the Confucian classics. Educational institutions were closely linked to the operation of the examination system. Based on the use of systematic recommendations of those judged suitable for government service as early as the Han dynasty (206 B.C.E.–220 C.E.), the examination system instituted in the Tang period (618–907) was designed to recruit and select men for office in the imperial government. Over time, it became the single most powerful mechanism for the reproduction of the cultural, social, and political elite in imperial China.

To acquire the vast learning necessary to pass the examinations, students would have to begin at an early age and work long hours for many years to master the entire corpus of the Confucian classics, the commentaries written on those classics, and historical works documenting the transmission of the scholarly tradition of Confucianism over time. Literary works, both poetry and essays, were included in this curriculum. Some early education took place in Buddhist monasteries, where Confucian texts were often transmitted along with Buddhist ones. The civil service examinations not only tested knowledge of the classics, their commentaries, and histories but also required candidates to propose policies to deal with problems of government administration, such as fiscal matters. In addition, candidates were asked to write poems of a certain form on specified themes in order to demonstrate their abilities as men of culture.

Prospective candidates from families deeply entrenched in this cultural tradition or from those that aspired to status and power were educated by private tutors in their homes if they were wealthy, or through an extensive network of schools that radiated out from the capital to nearly every region of the empire by the twelfth century. These schools were not "public," in the sense of being open to everyone, but they were an important source of learning for the elite, whose sons filled these schools. Families sometimes endowed lands to provide income for a family school, and sometimes community leaders would promote joint efforts to establish a school to serve the sons of elite families. Private academies also began to proliferate by the twelfth century, and these academies were the seat of the new synthesis of classical learning called "Neo-Confucianism."

The Islamic *Madrasa* In Islamic West Asia, educational institutions (*madrasa*s) arose mainly ▬▬▬▬▬▬▬ to provide religious and legal instruction according to the Qur'an and its interpreters. Arabic was the language of instruction in the *madrasa*s, which were established to train orthodox Sunni theologians. One or more of these colleges were built in most of the major cities of the empire, where they eventually became an element in the Muslim definition of a town or city as a place where there was a mosque, a *madrasa*, a public bath, and a bazaar. Generally, a *madrasa* was a square building with one to four arched halls (classrooms) that opened onto a central arcaded courtyard and that had residential rooms for students and teachers.

Islamic Libraries Magnificent libraries were also established throughout West Asia in the ▬▬▬▬▬▬▬ ninth and tenth centuries. Although all kinds of books were collected, among the most important were those on the Greek sciences. The libraries served as academies where scholars of all faiths and origins came to study, discuss, and debate the hard sciences as well as other subjects. Libraries had a major influence on the transmission of ancient learning throughout the Islamic world and from there to Christendom. Among the most famous Muslim libraries were one founded in Baghdad in 833 and another founded in Cairo in 1005.

Islamic Education in West Africa — Like its European, West Asian, and North African counterparts, the University of Timbuktu, on the banks of the great Niger River, witnessed the intellectual awakening across the Islamic societies of fifteenth-century West Africa. The university actually consisted of a constellation of nearly 200 small schools, mosques, and libraries, which together acquired and disseminated knowledge from the Arab world and various African oral traditions. Two famous *tarikh*s, or written histories, date from this period and were actually transcriptions in Arabic of local Sundanese traditions. For the most part, the university curriculum was controlled by the clerics, and it represented a privileged culture of elites that was reproduced through family ties. The curriculum included Muslim theology, jurisprudence, astronomy, geography, and history, subjects of interest to only a small minority of the urban elite.

■

CULTURAL HEGEMONY AND RESISTANCE

By controlling the transmission and dissemination of cultural knowledge, institutions of cultural memory, such as monasteries, churches, universities and brotherhoods, tend to reproduce the prevailing patterns of power relations and reinforce cultural hegemony, power or control exercised from above. Such institutions generate ideological authority that can sustain a social and political order as well as reinforce elite cultural ideals. At the same time, these institutions can be sources of dissent and contribute to the revision of cultural memory through challenging or resisting inherited cultural knowledge. In the process of transmission and reproduction, transformation can take place that fundamentally realigns power relationships or rejects the power of dominant elites by challenging the underpinnings of their authority.

The rise of the individual, secular scholar in western Europe served to extend the control of knowledge to a more diverse population—even to include exceptional women, such as the author Christine de Pisan (ca. 1364–1430)—thus also becoming part of the dialogue between experienced and represented knowledge. Finding herself without husband or father, Christine turned to her studies. In Christine de Pisan's *La Cité des Dames* ("City of Women"), written in 1407, women are portrayed as actively constructing the ideal community and being essential contributors to the construction of knowledge. Christine criticized male authority and challenged the widely held views of male writers, who claimed that women were by nature weak and feeble-minded.

Tensions were resident in cultural settings in which both writing and experience served memory systems. They constituted an important source of resistance and transformation. For example, in Christianity and Islam the experience of the divine or sacred was the means by which individuals might challenge or oppose the elite controls over written religious law and its interpretation. Mysticism, the direct experience of a spiritual dimension, was popular in Christian Europe and the Islamic world, but it was also looked upon with some fear by authorities simply because mystical experience evaded their controls. Mysticism generated movements in different religions, including Islam, Christianity, and Hinduism. Sufism in West Asia was a reaction to the rigidity of Islamic orthodoxy, which was protected by the legal scholars (*ulama*) who interpreted Islamic law based on the teachings of the Qur'an. In the same way, in South Asia the *bhakti* movement was a reaction to the rigid ritualism of the *brahman*s in Hinduism. In both Islam and Christianity, the notions of orthodoxy, officially approved religious doctrine, and heterodoxy, doctrines regarded as incorrect or dangerous,

FIGURE 9.14 Christine de Pisan Constructs the Ideal City

Illumination from *La Cité des Dames* (c. 1407) portrays women alone engaged in the tasks of building a community.

SOURCE: Bibliothèque Nationale de France.

caused deep divisions that often led to social, political, and even military conflict before they were resolved. At the most fundamental level, Judeo-Christianity and Islam can be seen as divisions that evolved out of the same West Asian monotheistic tradition, but each in turn developed its own deep divisions.

ORTHODOXY AND HETERODOXY IN EAST ASIA

In China notions of heterodoxy were used to describe religious practices and associations that were distinct from Confucian, Buddhist, or even Daoist ones. Cults to local deities, for example, often became the focus of religious groups that were seen to pose a potential threat or challenge to the power of the state. These were criticized and suppressed to varying degrees, depending on the amount of official disfavor they drew. Religious movements viewed as heterodox from the viewpoint of the state were often described in official documents by such phrases as "demon worshipers," not unlike the conventional phrases used to characterize Christian heretics.

Such divergent religious beliefs and practices drew on Buddhist, Daoist, and other sources and created new images of faith and devotion that expressed resistance to the Confucian order of society as well as to Buddhist and Daoist institutions. Examples of such practices include worship of the Queen Mother of the West, a female deity known since at least the Han (206 B.C.E.–220 C.E.) who empowered believers to achieve spiritual transcendence, and the White Lotus movement, founded by a Buddhist monk in the twelfth century. This became the center of a folk Buddhist religion that emphasized congregational worship and the fellowship of believers in the saving grace of the compassionate Buddha, Amitabha, the "Lord of the Western Paradise."

Popular Buddhism in Japan Popular Buddhism in Japan, which developed in the late Heian period (794–1185) and flourished in the Kamakura period (1185–1333), brought an awakening of faith to the broad masses of the people. The Pure Land sect, focused on belief in salvation through faith in the compassion of Amitabha Buddha and his female attendant, the *bodhisattva* Avalokitesvara, took root in eleventh-century Japan. In contrast to the ideals of enlightenment that animated more orthodox Buddhist sects, Pure Land followers believed that the saving grace of Amida would bring them to the Western Paradise, the "Pure Land." Like its counterpart and predecessor in China, Amidism in Japan reached out to a mass audience which was excluded from the complex and often esoteric doctrinal teachings of established orthodox scholastic sects, such as the Heavenly Platform (in China, *Tiantai*; in Japan, *Tendai*).

ORTHODOXY AND HERESY IN EUROPE

Christianity in Europe produced its own sectarian traditions and encountered resistance movements, some of which it suppressed and some of which it managed to incorporate, as it had done with pre-Christian beliefs and practices. Popular religious festivals frequently had pagan origins which were masked behind Christian meanings. Aspects of popular belief in pre-Christian magic were transformed by the Church into belief in Christian miracles, and the veneration of pre-Christian deities was incorporated into the cults of saints. During the twelfth century, while scholastics were debating the boundaries of faith and reason, the miracles central to Christianity, including the birth of Jesus of Nazareth to a chaste mother, Mary, also were scrutinized. The veneration of the Virgin Mary (a cult promoted mostly by male clerics) became such a popular movement that it had to be incorporated into traditional ritual and practice.

Witchcraft The magical aspects of religious ritual and practice became a part of Christian dogma. Such "good" magic was orthodox, but there was other "black magic," such as sorcery, which the Church condemned and rejected as belonging to the realm of the Devil. The Church viewed witchcraft as a danger to orthodox standards and doctrines and considered those guilty of practicing heresy to be punished. In times of social or economic crisis, the perception and perhaps the reality of unorthodox practices such as witchcraft increased. It was no coincidence that a witch craze swept Europe in the fourteenth century at the same time as the great plague known as the Black Death devastated the European population. Heretical religious sects, a more present danger to orthodox Christianity than witches, were also accused of satanic practices and suffered the same condemnation and persecution as individuals accused of sorcery.

From the thirteenth to fifteenth centuries, persecutions of witches and heretics were conducted under the auspices of the Church's Inquisition, a process which sought to identify and destroy heresy within the Church. In 1235, Stephen of Bourbon, inquisitor in southern France, recorded an account of a witches' Sabbath rite drawn from a confession. This account describes elements that become familiar in many later records: meeting in an underground place, the presence of Satan, the extinction of lights, and indiscriminate sexual intercourse. Accusations of similar activities were hurled at Christian reformist sects, such as the Waldensians, in the fourteenth and fifteenth centuries. At the time of the Inquisition, Jews were frequent targets of persecution for crimes such as suspected poisonings of wells during the plague.

Assuming that these descriptions of ritual orgies do have some basis in reality because of their frequency and widespread nature (including parallels in other cultures), it is possible to see such orgiastic rites as expressions of the dormant magicoreligious properties of sexuality. Ritual orgies may also express a nostalgia for pristine human beginnings, before the fall from grace according to Christian dogma. The Adamites, sectarians of the fourteenth and fifteenth centuries, went naked and practiced free love in an attempt to re-create the innocence of Paradise before Adam's fall. The expression of sexual power was a threat to the authority of the Church because such power could transform ordinary Christian believers into heretics. These practices could endanger social order and theological institutions by expressing the possibility of an alternative mode of being. They expressed protest against the way things were and the potential of rebellion against Christian institutions, which had failed to protect believers from disease, poverty, and suffering.

RITUAL AND RESISTANCE

Even in memory systems where tensions between experience and written knowledge were absent, resistance could threaten the elite's control over knowledge. Popular and elite cultures sometimes served different populations and represented conflicting versions of cultural memory, just as family histories and court histories might differ vastly in their interest in and interpretation of the past. For example, the Yoruba conceive of rituals as both actual and virtual journeys. Transformation of cultural memory can take place whether rituals are performed as a procession or public parade, pilgrimage, masquerade, or possession trance.

Ritual performance can as easily subvert the mundane order as it can reinforce it. What may be more difficult to capture in this written description of ritual and other experienced performance is its simultaneous links to tradition or cultural memory and to impermanency and change. The religion of the ancient Greeks was similarly focused on action: rituals, festivals, processions, athletic contests, oracles, sacrifices. The cult of Athena, goddess of wisdom, centered around splendid festivals rather than any fixed or written representation.

SUMMARY

The Japanese drama form Noh can serve as a convenient metaphor for the theme of this chapter: the production and reproduction of culture and its transmission as cultural memory through distinctive memory systems. In the case of Noh, the retelling of a past event functions as a means of dramatic catharsis, a way of not only explaining the event but also commemorating and controlling it by re-creating it. The point is not the objective recounting of the story but the assignment of meaning to it. In a similar way, as human cultures reproduce themselves over generations, they do so in part with intent. That is, people construct memories of the past embedded in cultural forms and practices through which they transmit that past in a purposeful way.

Some cultures stressed the keeping of formal historical records and transmitted the past in an explicit, conscious fashion through written texts, as the Chinese, or through oral traditions, as the Mande in West Africa. Other cultures paid greater attention to the transmission of religious ideas or cosmological conceptions, as those influenced by Hinduism and Buddhism in India and Southeast Asia. But all cultures, whether explicitly or implicitly, found ways to impart a particular understanding of their past through formal and informal means, through institutions and organizations, community rituals and distinctive structures. In this way, they negotiated, produced, and reproduced culture in the very process of expressing and transmitting it. It is no accident that the words "memory" and "commemorate" are related. The institutionalization of memory through commemorative rituals of the past is an essential means of cultural reproduction and transmission.

In this chapter, we have emphasized the transmission of cultural memory through memory systems largely, though not exclusively, within cultures. We have also highlighted the transmission of ideas and practices across cultures as well as across time, such as the Arab transmission of Greek science and philosophy to medieval Europe. In the following chapter, we turn to a focus on connections among cultures throughout the world before 1500.

ENGAGING THE PAST

THE INCA *QUIPU*

Knotted strings called *quipu*s were used by the Incas as a systematic method of recording the contents of warehouses, the number of taxpayers in a given province, and census figures. We know that the complexity and number of knots indicated numbers, but until recently it was assumed that the *quipu* system was limited to accounting. The recent discovery of a seventeenth-century Jesuit manuscript in Italy has raised the possibility not only of deciphering these string documents but also that *quipu*s were used to record information other than accounting, such as calendars, astronomical observations, accounts of battles, and dynastic successions, as well as literature:

> Quechua [the Incan language] . . . is a language similar to music and has several keys: a language for everyone; a holy language, [which] was handed [down] only by knots; [and] another language that was handed [down] by means of woven textiles and by pictures on monuments and in jewels and small objects. I will tell you . . . about the quipu, which is a complicated device composed of colored knots. . . . There is a general quipu used by everyone for numbering and daily communication and another quipu for keeping all religious and caste secrets. . . .
>
> I visited . . . archives for those quipus that tell the true story of the Inka people and that are hidden from commoners. These quipus differ

from those used for calculations as they have elaborate symbols . . . which hang down from the main string. . . .

> The scarceness of the words and the possibility of changing the same term using particles and suffixed to obtain different meanings allow them to realize a spelling book with neither paper, nor ink, nor pens. . . . This quipu is based by its nature on the scarceness of words, and its composition key and its reading lie in its syllabic division. . . . [It was] explained, "If you divide the word *Pachacamac* [the Inka deity of earth and time] into syllables Pa-cha-ca-mac, you have four syllables. If you . . . want to indicate the word 'time,' *pacha* in Quechua, it will be necessary to make two symbols [in the quipu] representing *Pachacamac*—one of them with a little knot to indicate the first syllable, the other with two knots to indicate the second syllable."

If this newly discovered manuscript is shown to be authentic, it should be possible to understand even Incan poetry, which was recorded using the *quipu*. However the scholarly debate about the authenticity of this manuscript is resolved, its discovery highlights the complexity of *quipu*s as a cultural memory system and reminds us that even the knotted strings used for accounting purposes can be a rich and enduring repository of cultural memory.

FIGURE 9.15   *Quipu* Reader and an Official

SOURCE: From *Los Retratos de los Incas en la Cronica de Fray Martin de Murua.* Oficina de Asuntos Culturales de la Corporacion Financiera de Desarrollo S. A. COFIDE. (Lima, 1985) Photo courtesy Dr. Gary Urton.

SUGGESTIONS FOR FURTHER READING

Andrew Apter, *Black Critics and Kings: The Hermeneutics of Power in Yoruba Society* (Chicago and London: University of Chicago Press, 1992. Examines how Yoruba forms of ritual and knowledge shape history and resistance.

A. L. Basham, *The Wonder That Was India* (New York: Grove Press, 1954). See earlier citation.

Yves Lacoste, *Ibn Khaldun: The Birth of History and the Past of the Third World* (London: Verso, 1984). Develops the historiographical importance of the Islamic scholar Ibn Khaldun.

Ivan Morris, *The World of the Shining Prince* (Oxford: Oxford University Press, 1964). A classic reconstruction of the world of the *Tale of Genji,* using literary sources to illuminate court life, culture, and society in eleventh-century Japan.

Hugo Munsterberg, *The Art of India and Southeast Asia* (New York: Harry N. Abrams, 1970). Richly illustrated overview of Indian and Southeast Asian art.

Mary Nooter Roberts and Allen F. Roberts, *Luba Art and the Making of History* (New York: The Museum for African Art, 1996). Brilliant consideration of art as cultural memory in Zaire.

Francis Robinson, *The Cambridge Illustrated History of the Islamic World* (Cambridge, England: Cambridge University Press, 1996). Comprehensive overview of Islamic history.

R. W. Southern, *Western Society and the Church in the Middle Ages* (New York: Penguin, 1990). A useful survey of the Church's role in European society in the medieval period.

Lynn White, Jr. *Medieval Technology and Social Change* (New York: Oxford University Press, 1966). Classic view of technology as a memory system.

10   *Connections*

People living in the early centers of world trade found variety to be the spice of life, especially when it came to food. In the city of Hangzhou, China, in the thirteenth century, at a hangout called the Cat Bridge, the chef known as Wei-the-Big-Knife was famous for his cooked pork. Hungry and harried cityfolk might purchase food from Wei or from one of many short-order restaurants that served the popular *jiaozi,* a type of spring roll—little fast-food packages of thin dough filled with vegetables and flavored with soy sauce.

The cosmopolitan city dweller enjoyed fresh local and imported food, exotic foods, and delicately balanced flavors in restaurants, hotels, taverns, and teahouses. Ships brought spices such as ginger or black pepper from the Indian Ocean routes. The local fish market provided ocean fish daily from a distance of about 40 kilometers (25 miles). Iced delicacies, honey fritters, fish soups, silkworms, and shrimps made into pies were favorites.

While Hangzhou's poor ate bean curd or rice and snakes, rats (called "household deer"), grasshoppers, oysters, and frogs, a wealthy city merchant might take friends to dine at a grand banquet offering more than a hundred elaborately prepared dishes. Even in the earlier Tang (618–907) dynasty, wines from the western end of the Silk road, pistachio nuts from Persia, and kohlrabi, a favorite vegetable, from Europe were brought to the capital city of Chang'an.

While it seems that many different foods in these and other early cities were available in greater variety than in rural areas, they were not always in certain supply. Scarcity and famine were the risk of those who lived far from field and stream. The life of the poor in urban centers was especially hard, and contrasted sharply with that of the upper classes. Sei Shonagon, an eleventh-century Japanese court lady, expressed amazement at the manner in which poor carpenters fell on their soup bowls and gulped down the contents of their rice bowls, leaving not a single grain. The English nursery rhyme "Pease porridge hot, pease porridge cold, pease porridge in the pot, nine days old" probably describes the monotony of poverty to be found worldwide. We know the poor in Rome avoided cooking whenever possible, eating raw beans, figs, or cheese with their bread. There is no doubt that the expanding connections between world peoples altered the variety of cuisines across the globe. The study of world markets before 1500 C.E. provides ample evidence that people through the ages

FIGURE 10.0 "Spring Festival Along the River," Detail from
1736 copy of Painted Handscroll by Zhang Zeduan
(fl. late twelfth century)

Peddlars and shops selling food and other goods are lined up along
the bridge of the Chinese city portrayed in this scroll.

SOURCE: National Palace Museum, Taipei, Taiwan, Republic of China.

were willing to travel far and pay dearly for the spice of life—more than enough food for
thought.

INTRODUCTION

The creation of empires and the spread of religion were, along with trade, the most important
ways in which connections were established among peoples of the world both before and after
1500. Expanding networks of military, political, economic, and religious ties created connections among cultures and societies in Europe, Asia, and Africa at least as early as the time of
the Roman (31 B.C.E.–476 C.E.) and Han (206 B.C.E.–220 C.E.) Empires. In some cases, cultural influences survived the demise of an empire, as in post-Alexandrian West Asia, where
Hellenism extended Greek influence into North Africa and South Asia.

Similarly, the Chinese Empire expanded the influence of Chinese culture throughout East
Asia, initially through the establishment of military control and political domination of areas
such as Vietnam and Korea. Though the empire's political control waned, Chinese cultural

influences remained to interact with and shape the historical development of both Vietnam and Korea. In Southeast Asia, Vietnam was the southernmost point of Chinese cultural and political penetration, where Chinese influence encountered the Hindu religion and Indian culture that dominated the rest of the Southeast Asian region. Korea, on the other hand, served as a conduit for Chinese culture to be transmitted to Japan, which was greatly influenced by China in its early history, even though it was never subjected to Chinese political domination.

In building their empire, the Mongols extended military and political control from Central and East Asia over widely differing cultures, bringing into contact regions of the world that had been previously unconnected and strengthening commercial and other ties among regions that had. Islamic empires in West Asia, inspired by religious fervor, similarly built links among disparate cultures as they propagated Islam throughout West, South, and Southeast Asia, North Africa, and even Spain.

In contrast to Islam, which was proselytized by Muslim armies as well as merchants, Buddhism was carried by both merchants and missionaries from its roots in India across the Central Asian caravan routes to China and along maritime routes to Southeast Asia. By the first century C.E., Buddhism had been introduced to China; by the fourth century, to Korea; and by the sixth century, to Southeast Asia and Japan.

Empires built on trade, such as Mali and Zimbabwe in Africa and Funan and Srivijaya in Southeast Asia, relied on either continental trade, which was dependent on the horse or camel, or maritime trade, which was dependent on ships and navigational technology. In South America, llamas and alpacas played similar roles. The expansion of empires often resulted in contacts that facilitated trade, such as that between the Roman and Han Empires across the Central Asian caravan route that became known as the Silk Road. Numerous such highways over both land and sea connected most regions of the world by the first century C.E. Trade led to other connections as religious ideas flowed along trade routes and as economic dependency created political ties. Travelers, all of whom had their own purposes for being under way, moved year after year along routes connecting people and transmitting knowledge from culture to culture. In this chapter, we will explore the varieties of connections among peoples of the world before 1500.

■

MAPPING THE WORLD

The development of scientific cartography (mapping) was crucial to navigation across long distances for purposes of trade, exploration, and the spread of religion. Cartography was related to the sciences of the heavens, and the most famous astronomer-cartographer of the ancient Mediterranean world was Ptolemy (fl. 127–151), the librarian of Alexandria, the center of the Egyptian and Greek community. Ptolemy devised maps of the world that provided a general picture of the relationships of the known oceans and landmasses. Ptolemy was the first to use parallels (of latitude) and meridians (of longitude) in his mapping, and his maps of the world were the best transmitted to medieval Europe from antiquity. Ptolemy was aware that the world was round, but errors, such as his underestimate of the circumference of the globe, hindered the practical use of his geography. However, Ptolemy's miscalculations did have one practical effect: they encouraged Columbus, who, based on information from Ptolemy, greatly underestimated the distance westward to the Indies. Geographers elsewhere,

Islamic Map of the World from *Kitab al-Rujari*

Al-Idrisi's circular world map with curved parallels has a south orientation.

SOURCE: The Bodleian Library, Oxford. MS Pococke 375 fol. 3v-4r.

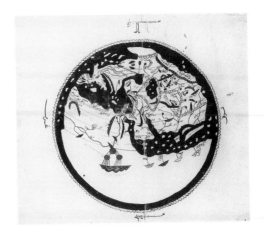

from Africa to China, produced far more accurate descriptions in both narrative and cartographic forms.

Around the time of Ptolemy, the rise of religious cosmography (representations of the cosmos) in Europe retarded the development of scientific cartography. According to Christian cosmology, the world was represented as a disk symbolizing the relationship of man to heaven, and the grid system of coordinates mapping the world in parallels and meridians was abandoned. Just as this was occurring in Europe, a cartographer-astronomer and seismologist named Zhang Heng (78–139) made use of a grid system to map the world. Although religious cosmography in East Asia also played a role in the creation of maps constructed on the basis of religious ideas, Zhang Heng's grid provided an independent, standardized framework for Chinese maps from his time forward to the present day.

Religious cosmography dominated Arab cartography until the world map of the North African scholar al-Idrisi (1099–1166). This sophisticated world map was made in the mid–twelfth century for the Norman ruler of Sicily, Roger II (r. 1132–1154), who was known for his interest in foreign ideas and institutions, particularly the Chinese civil service examination system. Al-Idrisi's map was drawn in the Ptolemaic tradition, based on a grid system that resembled Chinese grid maps, extant examples of which can be dated to the mid–twelfth century. It is not clear how the Ptolemaic tradition was transmitted or to what extent Chinese influence played a role in the revival of scientific cartography in Europe, but by around 1300 sea charts were in use in the Mediterranean, testimony to the reintroduction of scientific cartography based on the use of the mariner's compass, which became known in Europe just before 1200.

■ COMMERCIAL CONNECTIONS

Traders made up the largest number of world travelers. By the second century, travel by ship and caravan was adequate for both regional and long-distance commerce. Trade moved steadily through a series of regional exchanges between West Africa and East Asia and culminated in large markets where both ordinary and exotic goods were traded. Along the lines of

FIGURE 10.2 Travellers Arriving at a Small Town in the 12th Century

These Arab travellers are welcomed while the activities of the urban world go on around them.

SOURCE: Bibliothèque Nationale de France.

communication connecting Asia and Africa with the Mediterranean coast, basic types of ship and sail construction, as well as navigation and caravaning routes and practices, were commonly known and used, regions borrowing from one another and each using what suited it best.

Between 100 and 500 C.E., the camel, the "ship of the desert," was introduced to the Sahara from West Asia via Egypt. The use of the camel was an innovation in African overland trade equivalent to improvements in maritime technology. The camel led to faster, more frequent, and more regular commerce. Bred in different sizes and structures for different terrains, the standard one-hump camel could carry loads of up to 250 kilograms (550 pounds) while traveling more than a week without water. Sometimes described as a difficult and disagreeable pack animal, those who used camels paid homage to them in poems and essays by extolling their beauty, gentleness, speed, and patience or by comparing the human experience to that of the animals, as in this northeast African love poem by the Somali poet Maxamed Good:

> Unless I see you I never get nourishment from sleep
> Like a young camel I bellow out to you
> I am to you as a she-camel is to her adopted calf when her own has been killed.

Other poetry, such as this excerpt from a poem by the Somali poet Axmed Ismaaciil Diiriye, reveals the realities of desert journeys:

> The camels are packed and ready for the weary trek
> And men's thoughts dwell on distant destinations.

By both land and sea, merchants moved luxury goods and commodities between towns, regions, and continents, delaying or changing their shipments according to shifting markets, wars, rumors, and weather. Driven by hopes of profit, they sought out trade items that might increase their wealth. Commodities in general demand, such as salt, which is essential to both humans and animals but is not readily available everywhere, were commonly traded in both regional and international commerce.

TRADE COMMODITIES

Salt Until major improvements in production in the eighteenth century, governments commonly maintained monopolies on the production and trade of salt. As a major source of governments' finances, salt was politically and economically important. In some parts of the world, government monopolization of major salt deposits and the trade lines associated with them provided the basis for large regional empires. As early as the second century B.C.E., the Chinese government instituted a controversial domestic salt monopoly to direct profits from the production and sale of salt into state coffers. Centuries later, a revival of the salt monopoly contributed substantially to the fiscal health of the Tang imperial house and thus to prolonging its rule after domestic rebellion and foreign losses in the mid–eighth century. The prosperity and vigor of the fifteenth-century sub-Saharan empire of Borno was closely tied to its monopoly of the salt trade, which provided much of North Africa with its salt.

Horses Everywhere, heavy and bulky items were generally confined to regional trade; only a few offered a large or certain enough profit to be moved regularly in long-distance trade. Governments' interest in trading such bulky items as horses, essential to effective cavalry in time of war, resulted in horse trading over both middle and long distances. For example, India was a major importer of horses from Central and West Asia and by the third century was regularly transshipping them to Indonesia. In the regions of West Africa where horses could survive, horse-mounted cavalry transformed states politically and economically. West African states were able to control and monopolize interregional trade by controlling the breeding of horses (they sold only stallions).

Grain Throughout the first millennium C.E., grain was a common middle-distance trading commodity. Because it was needed to feed the inhabitants of great cities such as second-century Rome, eighth-century Chang'an, and eleventh-century Cairo, each with a population of more than a million and without sufficient local access to grain supplies, the perishable food staple was intensively produced and traded from hinterlands of usually no more than one week's journey. The southern Mediterranean shores of North Africa were the initial granary for imperial Rome, while the Nile and Yangzi Valleys supplied Cairo and Chang'an.

THE LUXURY TRADE

While many traders dealt in bulk goods, traversing the continents in long caravans or sailing along their coasts in lumbering ships, others dealt in smaller quantities of more profitable luxury goods. Of these the most common were fine ceramics, jewelry, woven and embroidered silks, incense, and spices. Manufactured goods originating in East, South, and Southeast Asia were traded into West Asia, Africa, and Europe in exchange for gold and silver. Caravan routes across the Sahara were established by African traders in salt, metals, and other com-

modities and across Central Asia by traders in silk. Around the seas, from the first centuries
C.E., a string of ports of call marked routes from southern China down through the islands of
Southeast Asia across the Indian Ocean and up the Red Sea to Africa and West Asia.

The Spice Trade　Spices, arguably the most lucrative of the global luxury trade in the period
between 100 and 1450, moved for the most part by sea. A world without
refrigeration had powerful reasons to pay high prices for pepper, cloves, cumin, cinnamon,
and nutmeg, all sources of strong flavors that masked the taste of overage meat and other per-
ishables. Nearly all these items originated in India and the islands of Southeast Asia. Some
were traded east and north to China for ceramics, silks, and other finished goods. Much of the
spice trade throughout this period went as far west as the Mediterranean basin.

MERCHANTS AND INTERNATIONAL TRADE

International traders and travelers, appearing to local people as foreigners with strange languages, customs, and goods, nearly always lived apart when they were in foreign lands. Cities
around the world where trading took place had neighborhoods occupied exclusively by foreign traders and their businesses. Arab merchants occupied special quarters in the medieval
Chinese capital of Chang'an and in the southern port of Canton. Often the establishment of
separate quarters was the result of a policy of the host government that was intended both to
control the import and export of wealth and goods for its own benefit and to isolate new cultural ideas which might undermine the local belief system that legitimized government
power. In western sub-Saharan Africa in the eleventh and twelfth centuries, cities such as Gao
on the Niger River were constructed as double cities, one-half being for foreign traders. In
fourteenth- and fifteenth-century Christian Ethiopia, Muslims engaged in international trade
were forced by the government to live in entirely separate market towns, while Muslim governments across North Africa enforced foreign merchant quarters in every large city from Fez
in Morocco to Cairo in Egypt.

Merchant Associations　Merchant associations were another feature of world trade before 1500
that maintained connections and encouraged commerce in the centers
and along the routes of exchange. Based sometimes on common kinship ties or ethnic background and sometimes on a commonly held legal system or shared religious outlook, these associations provided financial, legal, and logistical support that facilitated the enterprise and
helped protect the commercial monopolies of their members.

Even before the voyages of exploration that were to shift the center of commercial activity and power to the Atlantic, world trade had become so large-scale and risky that individual
mercantile enterprise had given way to complicated multiparty arrangements. The most common of these arrangements were partnerships. Nearly all these partnership arrangements,
whether in Africa, East Asia, or Europe, began as arrangements between family and lineage
members. They continued up through the fifteenth century as a common form of business organization all along world trade routes.

Partnerships　The terms of partnerships, which proportionally strengthened the wealth, responsibilities, and liabilities of enterprises, were also shaped by regional legal

systems or customs and enforced by government authorities or by merchants themselves through their professional associations. In West Asia, North Africa, northern India, and Spain, where *mudarabah* partnerships emerged, Islamic law was applied by state governments after the eighth century. The *mudarabah* and its variations provided a contractual means by which unrelated individuals could pool large amounts of capital to outfit and supply long-term, long-distance caravans and fleets and share out the risk. Whether influenced by Islamic practice or emerging out of indigenous practices, *commenda* and *compagnia* partnerships, which offered similar advantages, emerged in Europe by the twelfth century. Similar economically based power associations in West Africa helped unify the Mande-speaking peoples of Mali and contributed to the expansion of the Mali Empire in West Africa in the fourteenth century.

Lodges and Brotherhoods In thirteenth- through fifteenth-century West Asia, the Muslim *futuwwa* lodge functioned like a modern businessmen's fraternal organization, complete with charitable activities. These organizations evolved from brotherhoods of men that sprang up in urban settings to provide protection for the interests of its members, who were often young and poor. By the thirteenth century, *futuwwa* lodges served the needs of the merchant class, especially in the Turkish and Persian territories of the Muslim world. A member merchant from western Anatolia could visit Aleppo or Baghdad and find a hostel there maintained by the lodge for its members; he would also find ready-made business connections among the local membership.

Similar lodges functioned in the same fashion in North and West Africa, where the *karimi* merchant society, headquartered in Cairo, flourished as early as the eleventh to thirteenth centuries. Its membership was made up mostly of Jewish, but also of Muslim, long-distance traders who worked a commercial network that stretched from Spain to India. Arabic language and culture plus common business interests held this society together. Jewish members wrote their contracts in Arabic using Hebrew characters; among themselves they used Talmudic contract law, but with Muslim colleagues commonly accepted legal variations were practiced.

MONEY AND INTERNATIONAL EXCHANGE

International merchants—Malayan, African, Chinese, Arab, or European—were all knowledgeable in world monies and their exchange rates. Most trade was carried out through the bartering of one good for another. Even so, internationally understood units of money were needed. One of the earliest international currencies was gold-based. We know that African gold was traded to Europe and beyond as early as the fifth century, as evidenced by the gold coinages struck by Vandals and later Byzantines.

For international exchange, cowrie shells were the commonest form of currency as late as the twelfth century. Cowrie shells, actually several species including the *Cypraea moneta*, mined from the sea near the Maldives and with a limited distribution, were used in China for commercial purposes as early as the seventh century B.C.E. Cowries had the advantage of being durable, portable, and nearly impossible to counterfeit. Eighth-century Arabs, trading for gold in the western Sudan and ancient Ghana, found that African merchants demanded cowries in payment.

FIGURE 10.3 Eshu Staff, Yoruba Peoples, Nigeria. Wood Fiber.

Eshu is the Yoruba god of the crossroads, perceived as both meeting place and site of transformation. This dance staff has faces pointing in opposite directions, referring to Eshu's role as mediator/messenger.

SOURCE: University of Iowa Museum of Art, The Stanley Collection, X1986.284.

Government and Currency By 1000 C.E., gold and silver coins became more common as international currency than cowries. In some parts of the world, other metals, such as lead, tin, or copper, were rarer, and their scarcity permitted their use as forms of currency. By assuming monopolies over both the mining and the production of valuable metals and by establishing the weight, degree of adulteration, and value of metal coins, large and small states throughout the world began to mint and control currency. This intrusion of government into commerce served as proof and publicity of political legitimacy and power as well as a convenient means for governments to accumulate capital and simplify tax collection. Some state currencies quickly became accepted as units of exchange thousands of miles distant from their origins. At the height of Abbasid power in Baghdad (ninth to eleventh centuries), their dinars (minted from African gold) and dirhems were commonly accepted throughout the Mediterranean, as well as in Central and South Asia and eastern Europe. By the fifteenth century, Florentine ducats had become the basic international currency in Europe.

DIPLOMATIC CONNECTIONS

Seeking to expand their bases of material and human resources, both large empires and smaller states sponsored missions to neighboring regions, sometimes to form military or trade alliances, sometimes to exchange gifts, but always to gather information about potential resources. Trade and diplomacy tended to go hand in hand.

Diplomatic communications were made difficult by each government's view of its own importance and by fundamental ideological as well as linguistic differences. To prevent the collapse of negotiations over misunderstandings, commonly accepted rules in matters of precedence and etiquette, and formalities in the recording and documentation of transactions with foreigners, developed. Every government developed its own protocol, the mastery of which was a prerequisite for any who wished to deal with it successfully. In the absence of a bureaucracy specializing in foreign affairs, the business of diplomatic missions, which might nominally be headed by a highly placed government official or an aristocrat, was typically carried out by those involved in trade or in government postal, road, and harbor systems or by

FIGURE 10.4 Venetian Diplomats are Received in Damascus (Mamluk Syria)

Trade in spices and silks connected Venice and Genoa with the Mamluk lands in the late fifteenth century. The governor of Damascus (seated next to the gate) prepares to receive the diplomats.

SOURCE: Louvre, Paris/Réunion des Musées Nationaux.

the military, those most likely to be familiar with foreign places and governments through experience.

Han Chinese Diplomacy and Exploration Zhang Qian, a Han ambassador, traveling on missions which began in 139 B.C.E., not only developed military and political intelligence of great use to Han policy but also had an eye for commercial opportunities. While in Bactria about 128 B.C.E., Zhang Qian noticed for sale Chinese bamboo and textiles which came from southwest China by way of Bengal. This suggested to him the possibility of establishing safe roads from China to Bactria through India, thus protecting trade from the unfriendly peoples in Central Asia. His report on the famous horses of Ferghana inspired Han Wudi to send an expedition of 30,000 soldiers on a campaign to obtain them. Zhang Qian not only served Han diplomatic interests, he alerted Central Asian people to the possibilities of Chinese trade, and the resulting commercial relationships served to carry Chinese products west. The subsequent Western demand for Chinese silk and other products, and the Chinese interest in Western horses, had a powerful commercial and cultural impact on Eurasia.

Diplomatic Accounts as Historical Sources Accounts by envoys to foreign lands provide some of the most important historical sources we have today. Megasthenes (fourth century B.C.E.) was posted by a successor of Alexander the Great, Seleucus Nicator, as an envoy to the court of the Mauryan ruler, Chandragupta, at Pataliputra. The book he wrote detailing his observations of Mauryan India has been lost, but later Greek and Latin

FIGURE 10.5 Foreign Envoys in China

Detail from a painting "Barbarians worshipping Buddha," ca. 13th century, showing diversity of peoples and cultures. Note differences in clothing, headgear, hairstyle, and facial features. Attributed to Zhao Guavfu. Northern Song Dynasty, ca. 970.

SOURCE: © Cleveland Museum of Art, 1997. Gift of Severance and Greta Milliken, 1957.358.

writers drew on it and it remains the earliest description of India by an outsider. The Chinese official Zhou Daguan was appointed by the Mongol ruler of China in the late thirteenth century to represent him in Cambodia, and Zhou's accounts of Cambodian society are a valuable historical source. The mission of Friar William of Rubruck to the Mongols in the fourteenth century provides a unique perspective on Mongol life at that time.

Diplomacy and Culture   Diplomatic delegations linked one government to another. Their stays in a foreign land were normally brief; they traveled to initiate or confirm specific trade and political agreements between governments, although permanent embassies began to appear in the fifteenth century. For example, during the entire span of the Song dynasty (960–1275) in China, various diplomatic delegations were sent to negotiate with the rulers of border states that threatened the Song. The accounts of some of these delegations reveal much about how the Chinese viewed peoples they regarded culturally as "barbarians" but whose military strength seriously compromised the Song state. In Africa, the delegation of Mansa Musa, ruler of Mali (1312–1337), served multiple purposes: it was a religious pilgrimage, a trading venture, and a diplomatic mission to lands beyond Mali's borders, namely Mecca and Cairo.

RELIGIOUS CONNECTIONS

Traders and diplomats were by no means the only travelers maintaining international connections and cultural interchange in the centuries before European routes through the Americas to Asia were established. Pilgrims were far more numerous than diplomats as long-distance travelers on the world's highways. They were drawn from all walks of life; everyone participated. To go on pilgrimage was to visit sacred places where the spiritual and material worlds touched. In such places, distinctions of social status disappeared. Kings and commoners, slaves and slave owners, the poor and the rich were as one on pilgrimage. To emphasize this sense of commonality, many of the long-distance pilgrimages required standardized clothing.

Every culture in the world had its shrines, recognized and visited by its people as centers of power. Some were in sacred groves of trees, as in the case of Celtic Europe, or caves, as at Zimbabwe in Africa. Others were on mountaintops, on seashores, or in towns. And as some religions stretched far beyond their original cultural boundaries, spread by political or economic pressures and sometimes by persuasion, pilgrims became world travelers.

CHRISTIAN AND ISLAMIC PILGRIMAGE

By the fourth century, Christian pilgrims were visiting Palestine from Africa, Europe, and West Asia. At shrines in Bethlehem, Nazareth, and Jerusalem they sought their god's intervention for healing, children, and wealth. Some sought their god's forgiveness for past sinful acts, and later, after the eleventh century, many came from Europe to fulfill a vow. In part because of the large numbers of homeless wanderers and pilgrims on the road, it was customary Christian practice to open one's door to strangers and provide them with food and drink. Any poor or homeless person had the right and privilege to find shelter in churches. In the tenth century, Christians also traveled to shrines in Europe, most of which were either tombs of saints or churches holding the bones or other relics of saints. By this time towns had sprung up around the holy sites to provide services to the pilgrims. Guides knowing several languages, as well as restaurants and lodgings, were available in these towns. Downpatrick in Ireland, the site of a shrine to Saint Patrick, the patron saint of Ireland, was one such tenth-century resort town; similar towns could be found all over Europe. In eastern Europe, Christian pilgrims more often visited monasteries, seeking mediation with God by the holy men within.

Pilgrimage was more formally structured into Islam. By the tenets of the faith, all Muslims were expected to go on pilgrimage (*hajj*) to Mecca at least once in their lifetime. By the eighth century, that city was receiving thousands of pilgrims from all over West Asia during the month of pilgrimage each year. By the tenth century, still more arrived and from much farther afield: India, West and North Africa, and Spain. Mecca became the largest pilgrimage town site in the world. Muslim pilgrims also visited the tombs of prophets in Palestine and the tombs of saints elsewhere, but in smaller numbers.

THE CRUSADES

The crusading expeditions by which western European Christians sought to recapture Palestine were in part an outgrowth of contacts between Muslims and Christian pilgrims visiting

FIGURE 10.6 Pilgrimage Caravan Arriving at Mecca from the *Maqamat* by al-Hariri (12th century)

SOURCE: Bibliothèque Nationale de France.

their "Holy Land." Beginning in 1095, European Christian monarchs launched a series of eight crusades that were carried out over the next two centuries to restore Palestine to Christian control. They were initially successful and established Christian kingdoms in Palestine, but by the end of the thirteenth century their kingdoms had been lost to the Muslims.

The long-term effects of the Crusades were undoubtedly greater on Europe than on the Muslim world. Through their experiences and contacts in the eastern Mediterranean, European Crusaders were able to regain from the Arabs much knowledge that had been lost after the fall of Rome. In addition to making much Greek knowledge available to western Europe, Arab mathematics, science, and medicine were more advanced than either knowledge or practice in western Europe, and European trade and agriculture had much to learn from Arab business practices and horticulture. Common words such as algebra, alfalfa, and alcohol, and agricultural products such as oranges, nectarines, and eggplants, are examples of what Arab contact provided western Europe.

PILGRIMAGE IN ASIA: HINDUISM AND BUDDHISM

Pilgrimage was also an important religious practice throughout Asia. For Hindus, in addition to visits to temple shrines to Shiva, Vishnu, and other gods and goddesses, bathing in the seven main rivers of India, especially in the Ganges, was considered a means of sacred purification. Pilgrimage tours to several temples in succession, each of them located in different parts of India, were popular as well. Hindu pilgrimage, however, except for a few instances in Southeast Asia, was primarily limited to India proper.

Buddhists, on the other hand, took part in long-distance pilgrimages. By the first century C.E., Buddhist pilgrims from Central and Southeast Asia, as well as from all over India, regularly visited places in northern India where the Buddha had lived. By the seventh century, the Buddhist pilgrimage network had been expanded to include China, Japan, and much of Southeast Asia. Pilgrims traveled not only to India but also to temples holding relics of the Buddha in such places as Sri Lanka and Burma.

All these long-distance pilgrims returned to their societies different people than when they had left. Having completed their pilgrimage brought them a higher status and more leverage in business and social affairs; they had a greater knowledge of other peoples and cultures, their ideas and practices. Like returning modern tourists, they passed such knowledge on to their neighbors.

Chinese and Japanese Buddhist Pilgrims Faxian, a Chinese Buddhist pilgrim, left for India in 399 by land and returned fifteen years later by sea. His account of this journey, the *Record of the Buddhist Kingdoms,* is the oldest known travel book in Chinese literature and a valuable source of information on the political, social, and religious life of Central Asia, India, and the Indian Ocean lands Faxian visited. Another famous Chinese Buddhist pilgrim, Xuan Zang (600–664), journeyed to India via Central Asia in the mid–seventh century in search of Buddhist scriptures and left an account of his travels that reveals much about Indian life at that time. *Journey to the West,* the chronicle of his trip, later became the basis of one of the most popular novels of Chinese literature.

Xuan Zang served as an important conduit between Indian and Chinese cultures, translating not only Buddhist scriptures into Chinese but also, on the order of the Chinese emperor, Chinese works such as the Daoist classic, the Daodejing, into Sanskrit. During the eighth century, a Chinese Buddhist monk known best by his Japanese name, Ganjin, traveled to Japan and taught Buddhism to many disciples there. In the ninth century, the Japanese monk Ennin, like his Chinese predecessors who had journeyed to India in search of the true doctrines of Buddhism, traveled to China on a pilgrimage. The account he wrote of his travels in China provides a rich source of information on China during the waning days of the Tang dynasty.

PILGRIMAGE, GOVERNMENT, AND ECONOMY

Pilgrimage as a vehicle for connecting the world also had its effect on governments and economies. Major pilgrimages such as the Muslim *hajj* were big business. Ferrying Christian pilgrims from Europe to Palestine was important to the economies of Venice, Genoa, and other southern European port towns, especially after the crusading wars of the eleventh and twelfth centuries. Governments along the routes took special interest in protecting—and taxing—the pilgrimage trade and services industry. They also identified themselves with the shrines within their territories and maintained old temples, churches, and mosques on the sites and built new ones. In the fifteenth century, Egypt's Mamluk government and the expanding Ottoman state in Anatolia fought over the right to claim primacy in defending Mecca and its pilgrimage. With that claim, it was felt, came ideological supremacy in the Muslim world.

Pilgrims commonly brought along small goods and traded them to pay their way on the lengthy journey. At established international shrines, annual markets developed which sometimes became more important for the region's economy than the pilgrimage business itself. Long-distance pilgrimages, finally, meant increased traffic along established highways and, in a few instances, the building of new roads. For example, before Islam, Mecca was a way station on the Red Sea trade line. After Islam, it became a terminus of world pilgrimage and new transregional roads were built to it. Caravanserais, overnight stopping stations, were built at regular intervals on roads in the Arabian Peninsula leading to Mecca.

Pilgrimage, trade, and diplomacy accounted for nearly all of the long-distance world travelers before the fifteenth century. Missionaries such as Buddhist monks and Muslim sufis were added to these travelers. Both Buddhist and Muslim missionaries carried with them more than their faith: new technologies, different social and cultural customs, and a broader knowledge of the world were products of missionary activities. For example, the distribution of cotton and the horizontal weaving loom in West Africa follows the spread of Muslim merchant-clerics after the eighth century.

■

TRADE AND TRAVEL ROUTES

From the first century C.E., people, goods, and ideas moved over several well-known and long-established routes: the Indian Ocean route by sea and the Central Asian Silk Road by land, as well as the two established African connections, the trans-Saharan roads and the East African coastal system. In Europe, middle-distance systems, including the Viking route into Russia, were well established by the tenth century. Along such major systems of communication and exchange and at their ends were regional and local distribution networks.

 **DAILY LIVES**

ENNIN'S TRAVELS IN TANG CHINA

Ennin's diary tells not only of the practice of Buddhism in Tang China and life in Chinese society but also of the official procedures and complexities involved in undertaking pilgrimage in a foreign land. Following is the documentation received by Ennin from Chinese officials to serve as credentials for the next stage in his pilgrimage:

Wendeng county of the Government General of Deng prefecture notifies the Japanese traveling monks Ennin and three others.

The monk Ennin, his disciples, Isho and Igyo, his servant Tei Yuman, and the clothing, alms bowls, etc., which they have with them.

Notice: On examination of the dossier, we find the statement of the said monk, [saying that] in the sixth moon of the recent fourth year of Kaicheng, they came on a Japanese tributary ship to the Korean Cloister of Mt. Chih in Chingming township in Wendeng county and stayed there and that they are now free to travel and wish to go to various places on a pilgrimage, but that they fear that everywhere in the prefectures and counties, the barriers and fords, the passes and market places, and along the road, their reasons for travel will not be honored, and so they humbly seek to be granted official credentials as evidence and ask for a decision.

In accordance with our examination of the aforementioned traveling monks, we find that they still have no written permit and that they ask for something to be done about granting them official credentials. In accordance with the said statement, they are given official credentials as evidence. Respectfully written.

Notice of the twenty-third day of the second moon of the fifth year of Kaicheng by the Intendant Wang Zuo.

Hu Chunzhi, the Superintendent of Registers and the Vice-Chief of Employees.

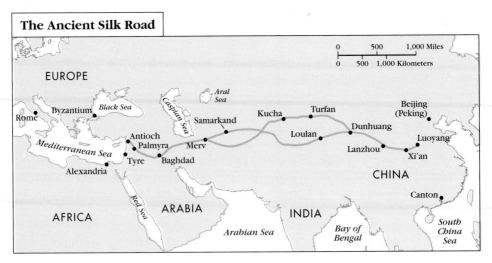

The Ancient Silk Road

MAP 10.1 The Silk Road across Central Asia

SOURCE: *China: 7000 Years of Discovery* (Ontario Science Centre, Toronto, 1982), p. 50

THE SILK ROAD

For a thousand years before the Mongol conquest of Eurasia in the early thirteenth century, one of the most important east–west interconnections was the Silk Road across Central Asia, created between the second century B.C.E. and the second century C.E. By the first century C.E., large and wealthy market zones lay at the eastern and western ends of Asia: Han China to the east and, to the west, the Parthian Empire in Persia with its connections to the Roman Empire in Europe. Routes through Central Asia linked trade between these markets, but there was little guaranteed security to reassure cautious merchants.

Before the Silk Road, goods moved sporadically and in small quantities. For 1500 years following its establishment, the Silk Road provided the main land connection over which people, technology, trade, and ideas moved between East and West Asia, Europe, and North Africa. As West Asian merchants and Roman soldiers reached eastward and Chinese merchants and Han armies stretched westward, Central Asian oasis states thrived along this caravan route. Gold was one of the most important items of trade, but spices and other luxury items were also traded. Han mirrors and coins found their way into Roman tombs as symbols of an era of rich contacts between East and West.

Origins of the Silk Road The beginning of the Silk Road can be dated from expeditions sent out by the Han government (206 B.C.E.–220 C.E.). In 139 B.C.E., the Chinese emperor commissioned an expedition into Central Asia to solicit support against the Turkic Huns who were pressing China's northwest borders. The Chinese government sought to bring Central Asian states into tributary relations, but it also wanted to establish trade relations to obtain commodities such as the famous horses of the Central Asian kingdom of Ferghana. Although the ten-year expedition failed to gain the support the Han sought, it brought to the Chinese knowledge of peoples and places as distant as Syria, and by the end of the first century C.E. China had succeeded in imposing sufficient political control to ensure security for trade across Central Asian regions.

Commerce and Culture Along the Silk Road Not only goods such as silk, for which the caravan route was named, but also ideas traveled the Silk Road. For example, Buddhism was initially brought to China via the Silk Road from India in the beginning of the first century C.E. Commerce along the Silk Road reflected the course of Chinese political history. During times of imperial vigor, trade was protected and goods moved expeditiously. When Chinese imperial power weakened and became ineffective, trade declined. With the fall of the Han Empire in the early third century, the Chinese presence in Central Asia waned. But with the rise of the Tang dynasty (618–907) and the restoration of Chang'an in the northwest as the capital of a powerful Chinese empire, the Silk Road once again flourished with its eastern terminus at the Chinese capital.

The Travels of Marco Polo The Mongol conquest of China in the thirteenth century led to the creation of a Eurasian empire that stretched from China to Europe. The imposition of a *pax Mongolica* enhanced the importance of the Silk Road as the principal thoroughfare linking the Mongol government in China with its counterparts westward across Eurasia to the eastern frontiers of Europe. European interest in and knowledge of Asia were spurred by the travels of Marco Polo in the thirteenth century.

Accompanying his father and uncle on a commercial expedition to China, Marco Polo left his native Venice in 1271. The Polos traveled overland through Mesopotamia, Persia, and

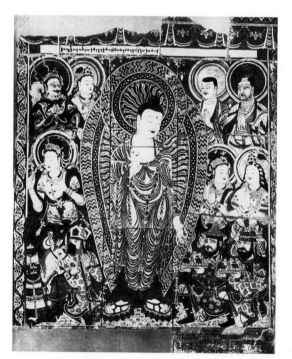

FIGURE 10.7 **The Vow of the Merchant**
Fresco detail from Turfan, Chinese Turkestan, ca. 8th c., showing relationship between commerce and religion along the Silk Road. Uighur merchants are shown at the bottom paying homage to Buddhist deities.

SOURCE: Courtesy of the Fine Arts Library, Harvard College Library.

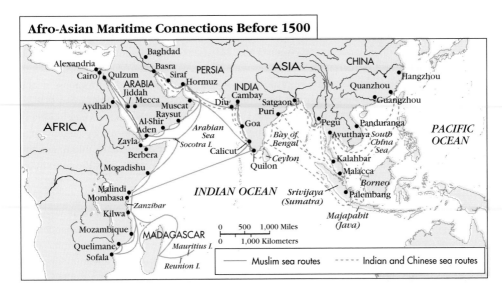

MAP 10.2 The Indian Ocean World: Maritime Connections from East Africa to Southeast Asia across the Indian Ocean

SOURCE: Janet Abu-Lughod, *Before European Hegemony* (Oxford, 1989): 202

Turkestan, reaching China in 1275. Attracting favor at the court of Khubilai Khan, Marco Polo was able to observe the commingling of cultures in the khan's empire that were the result of Mongol adoption of aspects of the traditions and cultures of the settled peoples over whom they ruled. He noted that indigenous Mongol customs and manners had degenerated and been abandoned as the practices of conquered people were taken up. For example, Marco Polo reported that Khubilai Khan was interested in Christianity and considered the possibility of mass conversion of his subjects. Polo remained in China until 1292, returning to Venice via Sumatra, Ceylon, India, and Arabia. By the time he arrived home in 1295, he had traveled both the overland and maritime routes connecting Europe and Asia.

THE INDIAN OCEAN

The maritime routes of the Indian Ocean were established about the same time as the overland Silk Road and were its primary competitor in east–west world trade. They were less subject to breakdowns of security and political disruptions than the overland routes were and consistently carried larger quantities of goods and people. Long-distance maritime trade in the western Indian Ocean existed from the third millennium B.C.E., and by the first century C.E. the number of ports had significantly expanded.

Shipping linked East Africa and Southwest Asia with India, Southeast Asia, and China. The earliest connections were made by ships that moved slowly, hugging the great northern loop of coastline between East and West. Early in the first century C.E., at both the eastern and western ends of this long, complex route, market conditions and political circumstances forced a change in the pattern of coastal trade: the Indian Ocean route became a maritime highway spanning the ocean between eastern and western ports.

Conflicts accompanying the Chinese expansion into Central Asia in the period 100 B.C.E. to 100 C.E. interrupted commerce along the Silk Road and access to the Siberian gold that had provided the main currency of Asian trade. Merchants moved south to the maritime routes as a safer means of increasing exchanges with West Asia and the Mediterranean, where the wealthy and stable Roman Empire could provide new supplies of gold. In response to the new demand for the rapid movement of larger amounts of goods through the Indian Ocean, the main shipyards of the Persian Gulf, the Red Sea, and the southern Arabian coastline built larger ships for heavier loads and refined sailing rigs to add speed. Supported by larger, faster ships and tempted by the larger market demand, Indian Ocean mariners were able to cut the four-month west–east coasting voyage to forty days by taking advantage of steady monsoon winds to sail directly from southwest Arabian ports to India.

Expansion of Indian Ocean Connections The effects of the first-century expansion of Indian Ocean trade were felt all along the route. From the west, the Roman government expanded its shipping down the Red Sea and into the Indian Ocean. To reinforce its new trading position, it signed international trade agreements with Indian governments, setting price ranges and guaranteeing protection for Roman shipping. Increased Roman trade along the Indian Ocean route meant a steady flow of gold to Asia, a fact commented on by Pliny the Elder (23–79), who in his *Natural History* speaks with disapproval of the drain on Roman gold reserves. According to Pliny, more than half of Rome's gold went to India, primarily for pepper and cotton textiles.

India and the Indian Ocean Route Following the withdrawal of Alexander the Great from India in 326 B.C.E., the centralized government of the Mauryan Empire (ca. 326–184 B.C.E.) developed administrative offices to cultivate and control the flow of wealth derived from increasing trade. The *Arthashastra,* a book of statecraft

FIGURE 10.8 Sailing from Oman to the Port of Basra

Note the Indian crew and Arab passengers from the *Maqamat* by al Hariri (12th century).

SOURCE: Bibliothèque Nationale de France.

begun by the first Mauryan prime minister and probably completed around 250 C.E., describes how certain ports for international trade were managed and controlled by a port commission headed by a director of trade, whose job it was to set fair prices on international goods based on costs of production, customs duties, shipping costs, warehouse rent, and other expenses. Even with the decline of Mauryan power and regulations, port towns, concentrated on the southern coasts of India, continued the trade with Southeast Asia and China as well as with West Asia and Africa, developing a demand for goods and services to support their activities and thereby maintaining southern India's population and economy with the east–west connections of the Indian Ocean trade routes.

China and the Indian Ocean Route China, too, was affected by the emerging Indian Ocean highway, especially in its southern coastal provinces. First-century Chinese sources document the trade facilities and goods available along the route, as far west as Persia and Roman Egypt. Even more than China, Southeast Asia was shaped by the burgeoning east–west long-distance maritime trade. Sustained by the wealth of such commerce, regional empires were established and became the standard pattern of large government in the area during the first 1500 years C.E.

To a large extent, Southeast Asian ports served as a conduit for Chinese trade with the Arabs and Africans. Arabian frankincense, one of the main ingredients in incense used in religious ceremonies and also in many medicines, and African ivory, along with Southeast Asian spices, were among the staples of Indian Ocean trade destined for Chinese markets that passed through the ports of Southeast Asia. Chinese products in demand by its trading partners included silk, tea, and manufactured goods such as ceramics. Technology, people, ideas, and institutions also diffused along the same trade routes used by merchants. The *Record of Foreign Countries* (1225), by Zhao Rugua, a Chinese maritime official probably based in the southern port of Quanzhou, provides detailed descriptions of such distant places as Baghdad, information gleaned from his contact with both Chinese and foreign traders.

Built on market demands and innovations in maritime technology, the economic power of the Indian Ocean trade network was impressive. By the second century, despite the efforts of some states to monopolize the ocean trade, the east–west maritime route helped create an interdependent Indian Ocean world. The Indian Ocean connection provided societies and cultures along its borders with a constant fertilization of new goods, people, and ideas.

AFRICAN ROUTES: TRANS-SAHARAN AND EAST AFRICAN CONNECTIONS

Africa, at the far western end of the Silk Road and Indian Ocean routes, in addition to participating in the east–west exchange, provided a south–north connection which added another dimension to established global commercial and cultural interaction. Across the huge continent, main highways were developed to link the inter-African markets and to connect them with Asia and Europe.

The Saharan Land Route There were two major historical frontiers of global interconnection in Africa: the Red Sea and Indian Ocean frontier of East Africa, and West Africa's Sahara frontier. Although the commerce of the Red Sea–Indian Ocean frontier was maritime and that of the Sahara frontier was land-based, both seemed to border on oceans: the Sahara, a formidable desert some 3 million square kilometers (3 million square miles), may be considered an ocean of sand. The Arabic word *sahel* translates as "coastline," and in the Sahel region that borders the desert's southern edge were situated many "ports" of entry. Like the oceans of the East African frontier, the desert sands were not a barrier but rather a space to be regularly traversed, which Africans did along well-established trade routes beginning at least as early as the second century.

Of the southbound caravans we know little. Mediterranean and North African goods certainly must have included foodstuffs such as wheat and honey, textiles, books and paper, perfumes, jewelry, and other luxury items. The remains of a twelfth-century caravan found near Majabat al-Koubra included 2000 brass rods, in all weighing a ton, tied to the backs of camels. Historians can only surmise that the caravan became lost in the desert between oases. Salt mined in the Sahara was also a significant part of the desert's commercial relations. Northbound caravans carried southern products: kola nuts and pepper from the forest, ostrich feathers, leather goods, and gold. Kola nuts were especially important in the Muslim world from Asia to Africa, where they were chewed as a stimulant and used socially in place of alcohol, which the teachings of Islam forbade.

In the centuries before 1500, trans-Saharan trade with Europe is documented by the regular appearance in European markets of such items as "Moroccan" leather, a product actually manufactured in the Sudanic region of present-day Nigeria. For the centuries of the Common Era, no African goods captured the attention of world trade so much as West African gold. Like Siberian gold, that of Africa supported many contemporary European currencies. It was the rumor of gold, as well as other wealth on the African continent, that inspired the Portuguese and later European sea voyages that were to change the established global connections and significantly affect the global balance.

Problems and Profits of the Saharan Trade Journeys across the Sahara were filled with danger, as the bones and debris of lost caravans show; they could last for months, and oases could be as far as ten days apart. Even once tolls and duties were paid to local authorities to ensure safe passage, caravans were under constant danger of attack by thieves and bandits. Shifting dunes and blowing sands could confound even experienced guides. The hazards were great, but so were the potential fortunes to be made. Reliable estimates of Akan gold production, a major source of Saharan trade, suggest that during the 1400s, 5,000 to 22,000 ounces of gold were produced each year. This enormous wealth was supplemented by fortunes to be made in the trading of brass vessels, kola nuts, and salt. In addition, the Saharan commercial network served as a conduit for the transfer of technology and ideas. The great Saharan ports of Sijilmasa, Timbuktu, Gao, and others were the entry points for a lively exchange of peoples and cultures. Through these ports passed traders and travelers from Genoa, Venice, Ghana, Cairo, Morocco, and beyond. The area known as Ghana was reportedly ruled by the Kaya Maghan, or "Lord of Gold." In the eighth century, the Arab writer al-Bakri reported that the king had a thirty-pound nugget of gold to which he tethered his horse.

African Indian Ocean Routes The second African long-distance trade network focused along the East African coast and was linked to the Indian Ocean trade. The area's seasonal winds and the Indian Ocean's currents reverse their direction every six months, which enabled voyages to return to the East African coast from southern Arabia, the Persian Gulf, and the Indian subcontinent within a single year. Beginning at least as early as the first century, the East African coastal strip thrived on regularized seaborne trade, which proved as profitable as that along the West African trans-Saharan routes. Ports from Adulis on the Red Sea down to Mogadishu on the Somali coast of the Horn of Africa supplied products from the hinterland to the Indian Ocean world.

In East Africa, coastal settlements served as trading posts in a complex African commercial system; there, goods were produced both for Indian Ocean export and for trade with the interior of the continent and for local conspicuous consumption. Archaeological excavations of East African settlements dating from the ninth to fourteenth centuries confirm a wide array of exotic imports, such as glazed Arab, Persian, and Indian ceramic wares, Chinese porcelain, glass beads, and the like. Chinese coins and ceramics have also been excavated in inland sites such as the fourteenth-century city of Great Zimbabwe, located 300 miles inland from the Mozambican coast.

DAILY LIVES

THE TRAVELS OF IBN BATTUTA

Occasionally, adventuresome individuals attached themselves to caravans or voyages for distant parts simply to "discover," to satisfy their own curiosity or add to their culture's scholarly knowledge about the world. Ibn Battuta was one of these. This pious Muslim departed his home in Tangier in 1325 to make a pilgrimage to Mecca. His pilgrimage turned into a massive tour of his known world. He proceeded by land and sea to Mesopotamia, Persia, India, the Maldive Islands, Ceylon, and China. He was a keen observer of local customs and cultures and was particularly interested in the impact of Islam on the lands he visited. Sometimes he settled for periods, and he even assumed official roles, as he did in India (as envoy to China for Sultan Muhammad Tughluq of Delhi) and the Maldive Islands, using his position to confirm Islamic values and enforce Islamic law with zeal. He returned from Asia to Morocco in 1349, but his wanderlust continued. In 1350, he toured the Muslim kingdom of Granada in the Iberian peninsula; in 1351, he crossed the Sahara and spent two years in the empire of Mali.

The early-fourteenth-century visit to Mogadishu by Ibn Battuta provides a rare eyewitness account of an East African coastal city. Battuta describes the procession of the local ruler through the town. Richly dressed and protected by a silk parasol which was carried over him, he was accompanied by an entourage with trumpets, drums, and pipes. Ibn Battuta found the inhabitants of Mogadishu obese, and he himself feasted to excess on a seasoned stew of meats and vegetables, served with rice cooked in ghee (clarified butter) and side dishes of bananas cooked in ginger and milk, peppers, and mangoes. The cosmopolitan character of coastal East Africa is illustrated by the various foods served to Ibn Battuta that were not indigenous to Africa: rice and bananas, for example, had been introduced to East Africa from India and Southeast Asia. In return, increasing quantities of indigenous African grains were exported to the drier regions of southern Asia.

Recent calculations suggest that Battuta set an early record for global travel: he visited the equivalent of forty-four modern countries, traveling more than 73,000 miles—all before the age of the internal combustion engine! Like other tourist-scholars before and after, he played a role in linking the world together. Both Marco Polo's and Ibn Battuta's odysseys transcended their original purposes. Their journeys of discovery not only expanded geographical knowledge in their own cultural contexts but also stimulated cultural and commercial connections between Asia, Africa, and Europe. Ibn Battuta's written description of his travels from West Africa to China were circulated in numerous copies around West Asia. Similarly, although the Venetian traveler Marco Polo began his journey to China as a trading venture, it became a journey that linked Western Europe with East Asia and helped to cement the ties of that world system.

Afro-Eurasian Travelers

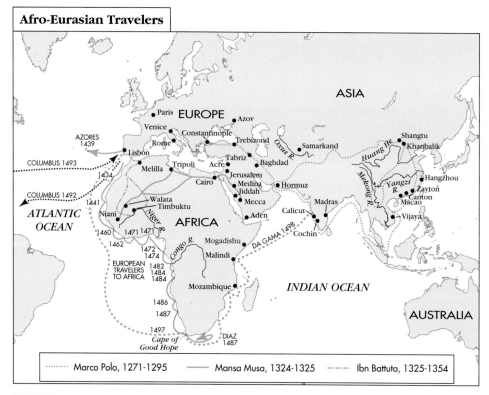

MAP 10.3 Routes of Selected Travelers in Africa and Eurasia before 1500

Great Zimbabwe was the capital of a twelfth-century state which controlled large gold-fields that made it very important to Indian Ocean trade. Cloth was also of special significance along the East African trade frontier. Locally woven cotton textiles were exported, and silks and other exotic fabrics, in locally unavailable patterns, were imported. In exchange for imports, Africans exported products they manufactured, natural resources, and their labor: iron and steel, stone vessels, gold, ivory, tortoiseshell, rhinoceros horn, frankincense, myrrh, ebony and other hardwoods, and slaves, who were prisoners of war or victims of famine and debt.

The Social and Cultural Impact of Trade

As in West Africa, the development of long-distance commercial relations added to the prosperity of the East African coastal settlements. Such prosperity rested on preexisting African mercantile interests, a well-established, stable indigenous foundation that could welcome the arrival of foreign merchants and support the increasing complexity of coastal society. A distinctive culture that was influenced by other Indian Ocean trading peoples, particularly the Arabs, developed along the East African coastal strip. It was urban, literate, and cosmopolitan, and its large and impressive centers were cities along the coast and on islands such as Lamu, Zanzibar, and Kilwa. From the mix of Arabic and Bantu-speaking residents developed the uniquely African language and culture known as "Swahili." In turn, that culture spilled back along the trade routes to influence, among other things, the architectural style of coastal and southern Arabia.

While historians once viewed the East African coast as being on the periphery of an international maritime commercial network and subject to external influence or even colonization, the participation of coastal cities and settlements in trans-African and Indian Ocean commerce has now come to be viewed in a different light. No massive immigration seems ever to have taken place. Rather, local coastal economies and cultures increasingly became centers of a remarkable process of urbanization and state formation. Here, as elsewhere, the selectivity of Africans resulted in the adoption of some ideas and items of material culture brought there by Indian Ocean voyages and the rejection of others. Like the cities, states, and empires connected with the West African and trans-Saharan trade routes, East African coastal cities were products of indigenous peoples and cultural traditions enriched by foreign contact.

EUROPEAN CONNECTIONS: THE VIKINGS

Even in imperial Roman times, northern and western Europe were only partially connected with the rest of the world. Although they benefited from the flow of peoples and goods along the secure road systems the Romans constructed, the western European markets were too small to draw much business. After the fifth-century collapse of Roman imperial government in western Europe, old connections were maintained along the Mediterranean coast through Venice and Constantinople, while in trans-Alpine regions the dominance of a self-sufficient agriculture-based manorial system meant that the demand for imported goods nearly vanished. In the ninth and tenth centuries, Vikings from northern Europe built a sea-based empire on conquest and trade.

Early steps in this direction were undertaken by the Norse—or Viking—peoples of Scandinavia. During the ninth century, the harshness of the Scandinavian environment and the pressure of an increased population on lands of limited productivity, along with the lure of profit and adventure, stimulated ambitious Viking rulers to set their people into motion. As immigrants, conquerors, and traders, Vikings left their northern homelands in open boats of 21 to 24 meters (70 to 80 feet) in length. Long and narrow, elegant and efficient, these were primarily rowed ships with a supplementary square sail, with high sides but a shallow draft. They could carry as many as sixty or seventy people across the open sea as well as down the quieter waters of inland rivers.

THE VARANGIANS: THE EASTERN ROUTE

The eastern route taken by the Scandinavians was followed largely by Swedes. Crossing the Baltic, sailing down the Gulf of Finland, they used south-to-north-flowing rivers as aquatic highways for penetrating the plains of Russia. Indigenous people there called these Norse in-

FIGURE 10.9 Viking Ship from the Bayeux Tapestry

The nuns of Normandy embroidered this tapestry to commemorate the Norman conquest of England in 1066. Multicolored horses and men on Viking ships are among the scenes depicted.

SOURCE: Scala/Art Resource, NY.

vaders "Varangians" or "Rus" (from which was derived the name "Russia"). The Varangians first appeared as plunderers and adventurers; they stayed as traders and mercenaries. In their remarkable boats, they followed river routes further south to the Black Sea and imposed their control over the various disunited Slavic peoples among whom they appeared. By 850, they had gained control of Novogorod and soon thereafter Kiev.

Varangian Kiev   The traditional history of the origins of the Kievan state begins with its capture by the Rus in 882, but almost everything connected with Varangian Kiev is subject to historiographical controversy. A Kievan state predated the arrival of the Rus, and there appears to be little basis for asserting a fundamental Scandinavian influence on Kievan culture. This does not negate a ninth-century Varangian presence there; indeed, archaeological, philological, and other evidence substantiates it. For example, the names of the ninth-century princes and the diplomats who negotiated treaties with Byzantium confirm a Varangian dynasty in Kiev.

From their base at Kiev, the Varangians maintained trade routes north to Scandinavia and south to Constantinople; indeed, Kiev was successful because of its position on the road "from the Varangians to the Greeks." Various Byzantine products found in Swedish tombs and grafitti that can still be seen on the columns of the great mosque of Hagia Sophia in Istanbul offer testimony to Varangian-Byzantine connection through Kiev. In addition, Kiev also traded with Central and West Asia, establishing commercial relations with the Islamic Empire, supplying slaves from Russia and Central Asia to the Abbassid caliphate in Baghdad.

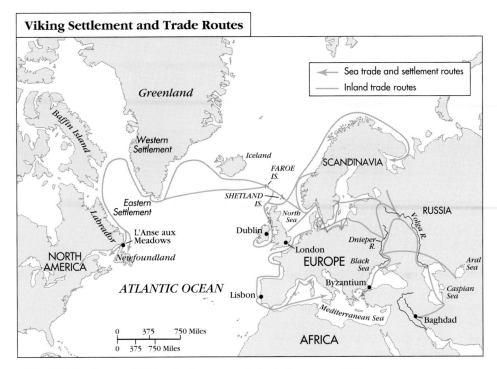

Viking Settlement and Trade Routes

Sea trade and settlement routes
Inland trade routes

Greenland

Baffin Island

Western
Settlement

Iceland

FAROE
IS.

SCANDINAVIA

SHETLAND
IS.

Eastern
Settlement

North
Sea

RUSSIA

Volga R.

Labrador

L'Anse aux
Meadows

Dublin

London

Dnieper
R.

NORTH
AMERICA

Newfoundland

EUROPE

Black
Sea

Aral
Sea

ATLANTIC OCEAN

Lisbon

Byzantium

Caspian
Sea

Mediterranean Sea

Baghdad

0   375   750 Miles

0   375 750 Miles

AFRICA

MAP 10.4 The Extent of Viking Settlements and Trade Routes, ca. 1000

The Vikings: Western Routes Other Vikings, principally from Norway and Denmark, went west and south. Before the end of the eighth century, they were skirting and raiding Scotland and Ireland. By 830, they were establishing villages there and on the offshore islands; they used these small colonies as bases from which to raid and plunder the rich monastic establishments on the fringes of Christian Europe. From their stations in Ireland and the North Sea islands, the Vikings sailed westward across the open North Atlantic.

Shortly after the middle of the ninth century, they reached Iceland and settled there permanently; from Iceland they were lured on to Greenland, where Erik the Red set up a colony in 981. From there, Erik's son, Thorvald Eriksson, who had been told about a place called "Vinland" (an Old Norse term for "grassland" or "pasture") by his brother Leif, who had reached this land (actually thought to be Nova Scotia) about the year 1000, pushed westward to Labrador and southward to Newfoundland, on whose northernmost point, at L'Anse aux Meadows, the first known European colony in North America was established. Vikings may also have sailed further south to Massachusetts and Martha's Vineyard, but their colony at L'Anse aux Meadows lasted scarcely a year and their connection with North America was not permanent.

The Vikings: Southern Routes Westward-moving Norse also turned south, to both Carolingian and Islamic Europe and North Africa, where they conquered lands and were successfully integrated into existing political systems in Spain and

North Africa. By 1100, they had taken over southern Italy and all of Sicily. From this base, they became active, if ephemeral, participants and competitors in the political economy of the Mediterranean, the western terminus of the ancient east–west world trade routes.

As the Vikings moved into the Mediterranean, they came up against competition from Venice and the Byzantine Empire. These two experienced trading powers had achieved a successful relationship with the Africans and West Asians who controlled the east–west avenues of the world trade system before the Vikings appeared, and they concentrated their maritime energies on achieving a naval domination of the Mediterranean that would enable them to control the extraordinarily profitable trade connections between European and eastern and southern markets. From the twelfth century, the Mediterranean was increasingly a Venetian monopoly.

■

THE MONGOL EMPIRE AND THE THIRTEENTH-CENTURY WORLD SYSTEM

The Mongol Empire, which rose in the thirteenth century, created connections across Eurasia that brought a new world system into being. By the eleventh and twelfth centuries, following centuries of localized economies and manorial self-sufficiency in western Europe, cities with market economies based on large-scale production and long-distance trade began to revive. Driven by population growth, the increasing importance and wealth of merchant-manufacturers, and the growing power of ambitious princes, European roads were rebuilt and connections were established with global routes of exchange and intercommunication.

Before the Mongol conquest of China in the mid–thirteenth century, the Chinese economy had developed to a high level as the core of the East Asian world. Increases in agricultural productivity, commercialization, the establishment of a money economy, expansion of the iron and steel industry, and urbanization characterized the Chinese economy as it grew in the centuries between about 750 and 1250. Although the wars preceding the Mongol conquest contributed to the demise of this spectacular economic growth, the Mongol conquest brought the East Asian world into sustained contact with the Islamic and European worlds.

For about a century, the *pax Mongolica* provided a steady means of contact across the broad reaches of Eurasia and strengthened earlier links across the Silk Road, while forging new routes farther to the north. European regions and port cities around the Mediterranean were linked to West Asia (Persia and Iraq), South Asia, and East Asia, and indirectly North Africa and as far east as Japan. Textiles, ceramics, and other goods were transported in both directions, bringing Chinese silks to European markets and Iranian pottery to influence Chinese ceramic design.

As the Crusades had brought renewed knowledge of Arabic science and philosophy to Europe on a much larger scale, the vast empire created by the Mongol conquest facilitated the exchange of ideas as well as goods across vast distances and wide cultural gulfs. At the same time, the military advances of the Mongol armies wrought devastation and, less obviously and far more destructively, contributed to the spread of disease across Eurasia. The "Black Death" that decimated European populations in the fourteenth century was probably a consequence of movements of Mongol troops into areas such as southwestern China, where bubonic plague was endemic, and the transmission of the disease over the Central Asian caravan routes.

CONNECTIONS: THE SPREAD OF DISEASE

Although it is difficult to know precisely how the disease was spread, the appearance of bubonic plague in fourteenth-century Europe must have been a consequence of disease-carrying rodents infecting Mongol troops and of fleas infesting goods that were carried across the caravan routes. In areas where the disease was endemic, local populations developed ways of dealing with the disease and resisting its spread. Outsiders—soldiers, traders, and so on—who entered these areas were ignorant of these practices and either died from the disease or became carriers of the infection.

The Black Death in Europe The distribution of bubonic plague across Eurasia and North Africa coincided in time with new patterns of movement of human populations that were inaugurated by the Mongol conquest. Between 1346, when the Black Death first made its appearance in Europe, and 1350, one-third of the population of Europe died. Recurrences in the next two decades further reduced the European population. The devastation of the population produced severe labor shortages and resulted in dramatic social and economic transformations. The value of labor rose as population declined, and as laborers became more independent and demanding, governments determined to curb them by imposing new regulations and controls.

All over Europe, peasant revolts, such as the *jacqueries* (popular uprisings named for the common man, or "Jacques") in France and Wat Tyler's Rebellion (1381) in England were common. The Black Death also resulted in a revival of religious fervor and enthusiasm in Europe. Interpreting the disease as punishment for sinful nonbelief, many, including kings, became zealous Christians. By the time the plague reached England and Scotland, it was expected and preparations were made by religious authorities to deal with the great numbers of dead and dying. Henry Knighton, writing in 1348, described the arrival of the plague:

> The dreadful pestilence penetrated the sea coast by Southampton and came to Bristol, and there almost the whole population of the town perished, as if it had been seized by sudden death; for few kept their beds more than two or three days, or even half a day. Then this cruel death spread everywhere around, following the course of the sun. And there died at Leicester in the small parish of St. Leonard more than 380 persons; in the parish of Holy Cross, 400; in the parish of St Margaret's, Leicester, 700; and so in every parish, a great multitude. Then the Bishop of London sent word throughout his whole diocese giving general power to each and every priest, regular as well as secular, to hear confessions and to give absolution to all persons with full episcopal authority, except only in case of debt. . . . Likewise the Pope granted full remission of all sins to anyone receiving absolution when in danger of death, and granted that this power should last until Easter next following, and that everyone might choose whatever confessor he pleased.

Spread of the Black Death The Black Death was not limited to Europe. There is evidence that the bubonic plague also reached the Islamic world. Both Egypt and Syria experienced epidemics of the plague, probably carried through the Mediterranean ports with which they had constant contact. Approximately one-third of Egypt's population died in the first onslaught of plague in the late 1340s. By the end of the next century, the plague had reached across the Sahara, where its path was slowed by the tropical tsetse fly, which killed the rats that were the carriers of the plague. Tracing the spread of this devastating plague has allowed historians to perceive the interconnections between Europe, Asia, and Africa and between the social and natural environments.

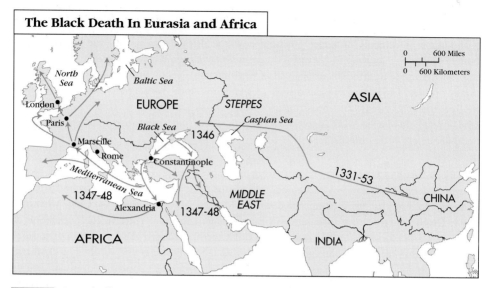

The Black Death In Eurasia and Africa

MAP 10.5 Spread of the Black Death in Eurasia and Africa during the mid-fourteenth century

The thirteenth-century Afro-Eurasian world system, three continents bound by economic and political connections, can be seen as a successor to a pre-Mongol Asian (perhaps even China-based) system, the center of which moved from east to west. The Mediterranean and the Indian Ocean, the major maritime centers of the thirteenth-century world system, were further connected through the land-based Mongol empire. The Afro-Eurasian world was a precursor of the fifteenth- and sixteenth-century world system focused on the Atlantic and inaugurated by Europeans. The world system core once again shifted, this time to the Atlantic. As Europeans crossed this sea route, they brought with them diseases that were new and devastating to the inhabitants of the Americas.

PRE-COLUMBIAN CONNECTIONS IN THE AMERICAS

Until the fifteenth century, the Americas remained isolated from the land and sea highways that had established commercial and cultural connections among Asia, Africa, and Europe, just as the Europeans were equally isolated from the societies and the trade and cultural connections of the Americas. The Viking foray into Greenland, Labrador, and Newfoundland did not alter this mutual isolation, though it may be seen as a prelude to its end. As with the European, Asian, and African connections, those indigenous to the Americas were both regional and intercontinental. The American routes differed in nature and scope from the Asian-African-European connections, but they nonetheless enabled contacts to be made between the peoples of the Americas long before they were bound together by European conquest.

MESOAMERICA

Mesoamerica serves as a model and a sort of keystone of inter-American connections. Several Mesoamerican societies had connections that led to the exchange of goods and cultures. Jade deposits in territory controlled by the Olmecs (fl. ca. 1000 B.C.E.) contributed to far-flung trade, from Costa Rica and Guatemala in the south to the Mexico Valley in the north. Teotihuacán (ca. 100 B.C.E.–750 C.E.) was involved in a wide trading network that probably linked all major contemporary Mesoamerican cultures. Teotihuacán obsidian, one of the most common materials used for weapons, has been found widely distributed.

Evidence suggests that the cultural brilliance of Teotihuacán was known to the early Maya (ca. 300–900 C.E.) as a result of trade conducted between these two cultures. The Maya's regional trade in salt, hard stone, and pottery brought together outlying districts and may have been a major basis for the integration of Mayan society. The Aztecs (ca. 1300–1521) controlled a trading empire that spanned Mexico and incorporated larger and larger adjacent territories. By the time the Aztec state fell to the Spanish in the early sixteenth century, its connections bound the Gulf of Mexico to the east with Oaxaca in the south and extended even to the Yucatán Peninsula.

Mesoamerican and South American Connections Mesoamericans also had intercontinental connections with South and North America. The appearance of maize in agriculture along the Peruvian coast about 1500 B.C.E. suggests early connections with Mesoamerica, where maize was first domesticated. Little is known about the nature of that contact or how it came about, but the appearance of maize and of a distinctly Mesoamerican style of figurine in Peru confirms an ancient connection. It is likely that the connections between Mesoamerica and South America were neither close nor continuous before Columbus, though there is evidence of Incan maritime contact with Mesoamerica.

SOUTH AMERICA

Regional connections in South America existed early, flourished, and were continuous. As early as the time of Chavin de Huantar (ca. 1000–200 B.C.E.), when the llama and alpaca were domesticated for transportation as well as wool, exchange routes were established along the west coast of South America. These were expanded by other cultures, such as the Chimu (ca. 800–1400), and were ultimately brought under the sway of the Incas (1438–1536), who organized control over some 2300 miles of territory stretching along the western coast of South America from mid-Ecuador in the north to the upper half of Chile in the south.

The interweaving of the incredible range of ecological zones and altitudinal levels in Inca territories produced complex patterns of exchange and required concentrated authority to maintain routes and supervise trade. This may account for the special character of exchange during the period of Inca dominance. There was no private or open exchange; rather, goods, cultural influences, and the routes along which they moved were controlled by the hierarchically organized state. Highland basins traded produce and textiles to lowlands for the gold needed for ritual and conspicuous consumption. Connections were even established east of the Andes. Andean precious metals, copper, and produce passed east as far as the upper Paraguay River, and cotton cloth, feathers, jaguar skins, coca, fish poisons, and medicines returned from the trans-Andean lowlands.

Ecuadoran Voyages Sedentary villages along the coast of present-day Ecuador date from about 4000 B.C.E., and archaeologists have documented that the villagers relied heavily on marine resources for food. It appears that their Pacific connections also brought them wealth in the form of the *Spondylus* seashell. The shell, which is found only in the warmer waters of the Pacific near Mexico, was excavated in ritual contexts dating to around 3000 B.C.E. After about 700 B.C.E., its use was more common; the shell had become an exchange currency. Ecuadoran voyagers used large, balsa wood sailing rafts with movable centerboards and rigged sails for their Pacific travels. The same sailing routes may also have permitted the diffusion of early metalworking technology from South America to Mesoamerica.

MESOAMERICAN AND NORTH AMERICAN CONNECTIONS

The connections between Mesoamerica and North America are somewhat more clearly understood than those between Mesoamerica and South America. As early as Teotihuacán, there were northern routes that extended westward into Arizona and New Mexico to the Anasazi of the Colorado plateau, where Mesoamerican feathers, gold, and cacao beans (then the major medium of monetary exchange) were traded for turquoise. Other routes of trade and sociocultural influence extended eastward toward Oklahoma and Arkansas. Later Toltec (ca. 750–1150) traders and explorers in search of such things as alum, salt, incense, and raw copper also reached as far as the present-day southwestern United States, where they seem to have influenced the Anasazi. Much of the characteristic southwestern ceremonial art derives from the end of the Toltec period and may reflect a fusion of Mesoamerican rain god cults with local religious traditions.

Mesoamerican influence also spread north and eastward, to the area of the warm and wet woodlands around the confluence of the Mississippi, Missouri, and Ohio Rivers, the center of Mississippian culture. The routes of the Mississippian prototypes remain unknown, but the Mississippians' architectural styles, including temple-topped pyramids built around a central plaza, and their ceremonial art styles all show a generic relationship to Mesoamerican features. As in the case of the peoples of Andean highland South America, the heavy reliance of the Mississippians on maize, along with squash and beans, suggests early connections between North and South America, while copper seems to have been carried to South America from the eastern woodlands.

FIGURE 10.10 Teotihuacan Mask Carved from Serpentine (stone)

Eyes were inlaid with white shell, black obsidian or golden iron pyrite (Probably Tlamimilolpa-Metepec, 200–750 C.E.).

SOURCE: Dumbarton Oaks Research Library and Collections, Washington, DC.

NORTH AMERICA: MISSISSIPPIAN CONNECTIONS

Mississippian regional connections are better known. They focused on the great center at Cahokia (fl. ca. 900–1300), a city built by native North Americans. Through extensive trading connections, Cahokia was in constant contact with other communities scattered across nearly a third of the North American continent. The ruling elite at Cahokia controlled trade in raw materials, such as seashells, coppers, flint, and mica, which were drawn from a wide radius extending from north of Lake Superior to the Gulf Coast shoals of Florida and from the Appalachians as far west as the plains of North and South Dakota and Nebraska. In addition, the Cahokians manufactured a variety of goods for export: salt, tools, jewelry, and ceremonial goods.

The exports and imports—it took a steady flow of some 25,000 to 30,000 pounds of food a day to feed the people of Cahokia—traveled mainly by water, since domesticated draft animals (other than dogs) were not in use. Much of the produce was transported on streams and lakes, perhaps linked by canals; indeed the city may have been so interlaced with waterways that it would have resembled European Venice. Tons of goods carried in canoes up to 15 meters (50 feet) in length moved along water routes to satellite centers and outposts. Cahokia must have maintained a small fleet of such vessels, together with auxiliary vessels, docks, and boatyards.

Similar in kind to those of Asia, Africa, and Europe, connections in the Americas bound two continents together and served as avenues for trade and cultural interchange. Extending over distances comparable to the east–west and north–south connections between Asia, Africa, and Europe, they had unique features: for example, the lack of horses and camels as draft animals on overland routes and the differences in ships used for maritime and riverine routes. They served the needs and purposes of Americans before the European conquest and were integrated into the shifting pattern of connections that underlay the establishment of European global dominance following 1500.

■

PACIFIC CONNECTIONS BEFORE 1500

Like the Americas, the thousands of islands that lay scattered over the face of Pacific Oceania remained isolated from the connections that had been established between Africans, Asians, and Europeans before 1500. Pacific Oceania is divided into Melanesia, Polynesia, and Micronesia. The peoples who inhabited these islands established their own regional connections across the Pacific as early as the first and second millennia B.C.E. when maritime traders identified with the Lapita cultural tradition began to settle in Melanesia, the islands south of the equator from Papua New Guinea to the west to Fiji to the east.

Lapita Culture The Lapita culture was probably an extension of much earlier migrations to Pacific Islands from Southeast Asia. Sedentary agriculturalists, the Lapita brought with them domesticated plants and animals along with a distinctive pottery style. They cultivated crops such as taro, yams, bananas, breadfruit, and coconuts, which were spread by occasional voyages among the islands. By 1300 B.C.E. these people had reached the outer boundary of Fiji and soon after made their way to Polynesia by way of Tonga and Samoa.

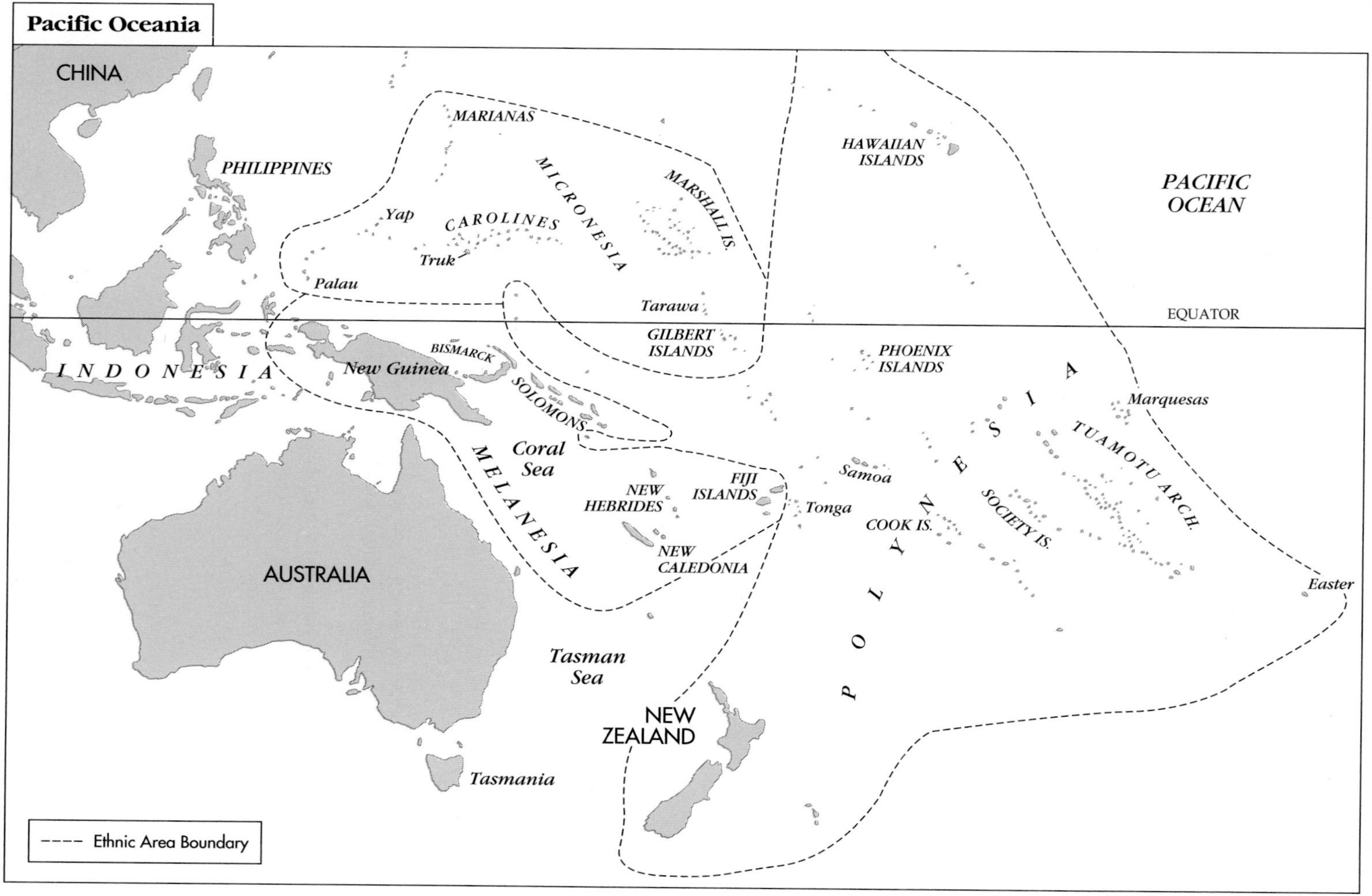

Pacific Oceania

PACIFIC OCEAN

EQUATOR

Easter

Marquesas

TUAMOTU ARCH.

SOCIETY IS.

P O L Y N E S I A

HAWAIIAN ISLANDS

PHOENIX ISLANDS

Samoa

COOK IS.

Tonga

MARSHALL IS.

Tarawa

GILBERT ISLANDS

FIJI ISLANDS

NEW CALEDONIA

NEW ZEALAND

MARIANAS

M I C R O N E S I A

CAROLINES

Yap

Truk

NEW HEBRIDES

SOLOMONS

Coral Sea

M E L A N E S I A

Tasman Sea

Palau

BISMARCK

New Guinea

AUSTRALIA

Tasmania

PHILIPPINES

CHINA

I N D O N E S I A

- - - - - Ethnic Area Boundary

MAP 10.6 Pacific Oceania

MELANESIA: VANUATU

One of the major island groups in central Melanesia, Vanuatu is a string of verdant volcanic islands. The archipelago of Vanuatu lies outside an ecological boundary at the Solomon Islands to the northwest; beyond this boundary there are no native land mammals, and the vegetation and bird life on the islands is distinct from that on the other side of the boundary. The earliest evidence of human habitation dates to about 3000 years ago and is consistent with the spread of Lapita culture from an early center northwest of the Solomons. In addition to pottery style, the spread of Lapita culture to Vanuatu is associated with the introduction of the pig, dog, and chicken, as well as evidence of stone tools and shell ornaments.

We can identify the spread of Lapita culture to Vanuatu with the expansion of regional exchange networks, and archaeological evidence of change about 2000 years ago can be seen as the product of a process of diversification that took place in Lapita culture because of difficulties in maintaining regular contact among relatively distant island groups. This change indicates the constriction of regional exchange networks.

A third major change in Vanuatu's connections with other South Pacific islands is suggested by archaeological sites dating from about 750 years ago. Archaeologists who have excavated the grave of an individual known as Roy Mata, an important chief from "the south," suggest that he was a Polynesian immigrant and that his and other graves from this period and later show a wave of Polynesian migration to the Vanuatu chain. Whatever new discoveries yield about the past of Vanuatu and whatever new interpretations are shaped by them, it is clear that Vanuatu, like other islands in the Pacific was part of a complex and dynamic system of regional exchange networks and subject to changes brought about by fluctuations in contact as well as by migration of peoples across extensive sea routes.

POLYNESIA

Polynesians inhabited the group of islands within a triangle in the central Pacific bounded by Hawaii, New Zealand, and Easter Island. This area, along with Micronesia to the west of it, was among the latest to be occupied by humans, probably around 3000 years ago. During the first millennium C.E., trading relations established by the dispersal of peoples led to the transfer of crops, technology, and some aspects of a common culture. Around 300 C.E. Samoans made their way by canoe eastward to the distant Marquesas Islands. Between 400 and 850 the Marquesas served as a primary center for the diffusion of a common culture—people, animals, plants, technology, and arts—across Polynesia, including the most distant corners of the Polynesian "triangle:" the Hawaiian Islands; the Society Islands, and Easter Island; the Southern Cooks and New Zealand.

Maori Polynesians who settled in New Zealand, the Maori, provide a well-documented example of how Polynesians explored and settled the Pacific in decked vessels capable of carrying 100 to 200 persons, with water and stores sufficient for voyages of some weeks. They had knowledge of the stars and were able to determine favorable seasons for voyages. They were keen navigators, setting their courses from familiar landmarks and steering by the sun and stars and the direction of winds and waves.

Polynesian settlement of New Zealand presented an enormous ecological challenge, since most of the domesticated plants and animals from the Marquesas either failed to survive the long voyage or died out soon after in the different climate. Polynesian settlers adapted to the new environment by becoming hunter-farmers, which led to environmental changes and in turn to the necessity to adopt new strategies for survival that were no longer linked to Marquesan origins.

Megaliths of Easter Island Formed of three extinct volcanoes, Easter Island, also known as Rapa Nui, lies about 3700 kilometers (about 2300 miles) off the west coast of modern Chile, at the outer edge of Polynesia. The fertile volcanic soil and year-round warm climate allow the cultivation of potatoes, sugar cane, taro, and tropical fruits. The earliest settlement of the island probably took place about 1800 years ago, though some believe it was more recent; the original inhabitants are thought to have been of South American origin. Strong trade winds brought early Polynesians to Easter Island. It is believed that people from the Marquesas Islands traveled in canoes and invaded Rapu Nui, taking over the island from its original inhabitants.

Since the arrival of a Dutch explorer on Easter Day in the early eighteenth century and later Chilean occupation of the island, archaeologists have puzzled over the large stone monuments (megaliths) found on the island. Ranging in height from three to twelve meters (ten to forty feet), about 100 of these statues—huge heads with elongated ears and noses—remain standing today. Large stone burial platforms called *ahus* support rows of statues; within the *ahus* are burial chambers for individuals or groups.

The burial platforms are located on bluffs overlooking the sea, and it is thought that there were perhaps as many as 600 statues at the time of the Polynesian invasion, many of which were destroyed as Polynesians wrested control of the island from its original inhabitants. Smaller sculptures of wood and wooden tablets have also been found on Easter Island. The tablets are inscribed with what appears to be a form of picture writing, providing the only evidence of a writing system in Polynesia, though it remains undeciphered.

MICRONESIA

To the west of Polynesia and the north of Melanesia lie the hundreds of islands of Micronesia, scattered over an ocean larger than the United States but containing a total of only 3260 square kilometers (1,260 square miles) of land area. The most southerly and westerly Micronesian islands are the Marianas, the largest of which is Guam; the most southerly are the Carolines; and the most westerly, the Marshalls. Despite the great distances between the island groups and the fact that each inhabited island or the waters around it produced only the bare essentials for the peoples living on it, connections among the islands were maintained.

Overseas trade was a prominent feature of Micronesian life. Nearly every place produced a specialty—flat mats or baskets, unique dyes or special shell ornaments—which it exchanged for something unusual from another place. For example, Yap islanders sailed to Palau to quarry and carry back home the large disks of stone they used for a special kind of money. Fleets of atoll dwellers from the islands between Yap and Truk regularly sailed to Guam, and similar enterprises went on throughout Micronesia. Exploits over such distances produced daring sailors and skilled navigators. To maintain the connections among their islands, Micronesians mastered the intricacies of seasons, currents, and winds and even developed charts to guide them on their long voyages.

SUMMARY

Most of the world was linked by land and sea routes before the fifteenth century. Traders, pilgrims, missionaries, and other travelers traversed these routes, carrying goods and ideas over long distances and creating interconnections among regions, cultures, and even continents. Although the Americas were not connected with the Afro-Eurasian linkages, within the Americas there was a complex array of interregional contacts, facilitated by the organization and power of the large states that appeared in Mesoamerica and Andean South America.

In Asia, Africa, and Europe, the rise of empires such as that of the Mongols brought previously isolated cultures and societies into contact. From Asia to Europe to Africa, interregional systems of trade and political connections also resulted in cultural exchange. For example, the Chinese Empire during the Han (206 B.C.E.–220 C.E.) and Tang (618–907 C.E.) dynasties, like the Islamic empires from about 800 to 1100, had similar cultural impacts on Asia and Africa, respectively. The expansion of China facilitated the spread of Buddhism to Korea (and later Japan), and thus the transmission of religion was a by-product of imperial expansion. In South and Southeast Asia, both religion and trade were conduits of cultural influence, as first Buddhism and Hinduism, and then Islam, spread through the Indian subcontinent and subsequently into Southeast Asia. In the case of the Islamic empires, their influence spread a new faith worldwide, across Africa and, with the eighth-century conquest of Spain, into Europe. Religion was one of the most important, but certainly not the only, motive for the expansion of the Islamic empires. Subsequently, Mongol conquests changed the face of the Afro-Eurasian experience and cemented interregional connections into a world system, its core shifting westward toward Europe, whose hegemony would dramatically alter the nature of African, Asian, American, and European connections in the centuries after 1500.

ENGAGING THE PAST

CARTOGRAPHY AND CULTURAL MEMORY

Cartography is the study of maps, which vary in the nature of artistic and scientific presentation according to their purpose and place within the larger context of cultural memory systems. Maps were convenient devices for the storage of geographical and spatial information. Typically, maps reflect a combination of written, visual, scientific, and cognitive processes. Historical linguists have pointed out that intimate environmental and geographical knowledge and names constitute an area of language that is highly resistant to change. For example, few invasions in world history have completely eradicated the indigenous names of mountains, streams, and other natural features of the landscape.

Cartography, like art, preceded writing. In an early map from ancient Egypt, the theoretical route to the afterlife was depicted in a painting on the side of a sarcophagus. Other Egyptian examples describe the relationship (distance and direction) between sites in relation to shifting geographical boundaries (such as the flooding of the Nile). An early Mesopotamian map on a clay tablet from about 2500 B.C.E. found at Nuzi is oriented with east at the top and provides a plan view of natural features and built settlements. Another Mesopotamian clay tablet documents a world map, round and flat with Babylon at its center.

Early Chinese maps painted on silk have survived from the third century B.C.E. Han dynasty officials used maps extensively for administrative and military purposes. Dated to before 1137 C.E., an early Chinese stone map utilized the grid familiar to more modern cartographers around the world. The culmination of Chinese cartography is found in the work of Zhu Siben (1273–1337 C.E.), whose grid map of China was refined for generations after his death. Away from the center of Chinese culture, the maps became increasingly inaccurate and vague.

Visual, performance, oral and writing systems that were utilized by societies for the transmission of cultural memory usually contained a specialized sphere that related geographical information. Some cultures relied more heavily on visual mapping of phenomena. For example, mapmaker-navigators in the Marshall Islands constructed charts from narrow strips of palm leaves lashed together with fiber cords. These stick charts represented the patterns of waves and swells caused by winds. Cowrie shells marked the position of islands. Such charts communicated the knowledge and experience gained by generations of canoers on multiple scales and for multiple purposes, both instructional information to be transmitted and utilized as navigational guides.

Different kinds of maps and approaches to cartography highlight differences among cultural memory systems. Maps made possible connections among the world's peoples, but the encounters were shaped by the cultures that produced the maps.

SUGGESTIONS FOR FURTHER READING

Geoffrey Barraclough, ed., *The Times Atlas of World History* (London: Times Books, Ltd., 1979). Richly informative maps accompanied by concise summaries of key themes and events in world history.

Jerry H. Bentley, *Old World Encounters: Cross-Cultural Contacts in Pre-Modern Times* (New York: Oxford University Press, 1993). Excellent survey of world commercial, cultural, and political connections before Columbus.

Kathleen Berrin and Esther Pasztory, eds., *Teotihuacan: Art from the City of the Gods* (New York: Thames and Hudson, 1993).

Joel Bonnemaison, Kirk Huffman, Christian Kaufmann, and Darrell Tryon, eds., *Arts of Vanuatu* (Honolulu: University of Hawaii Press, 1996). A beautifully illustrated collection of articles on the most recent archaeological and anthropological studies of this archipelago in the South Pacific.

Philip D. Curtin, *Cross-Cultural Trade in World History* (Cambridge, England: Cambridge University Press, 1984). Comparative approach to commercial links in world history.

Ross E. Dunn, *The Adventures of Ibn Battuta* (Berkeley and Los Angeles: University of California Press, 1989). Account of the fifteenth-century Muslim traveler's adventures.

William H. McNeill, *Plagues and Peoples* (New York: Anchor Doubleday, 1976). Pathbreaking survey of epidemiological connections in world history, especially the spread of the Black Death.

Transformation

	East Asia		Southeast Asia	South Asia
	China	*Japan*		
750 C.E.	Tang (618-907) Examination System An Lushan Rebellion (755-763)	Chinese Influence in Japan	Srivijaya (602-1025) Khmer State (802-1432)	Muslim Invasions
	Song (960-1272)	Heian (794-1185)		
1000	Printing Gunpowder Compass Commercial Revolution Foreign Trade			
		Rise of Samurai Japanese Feudalism		Chola (11th-13th c.) Tamil Traders Delhi Sultanate (1206-1526)
1250	Marco Polo in China Mongol Conquest Yuan (1260-1368)	Kamakura Shogunate (1185-1333)	Majapahit	
	Ming (1368-1644) Zheng Ho Expeditions (1405-1433)		Malacca (1401) Spread of Islam 15th-18th c. Age of Commerce 15th-18th c.	Vijayanagar (1336-1530) Sikhism
1500	Portuguese Macao (1557) Manchu Conquest Qing (1644-1912)	Tokugawa (1603-1867)	Portuguese Malacca and Spanish Trade Dutch East Indies Co. Islamic States	Portuguese Goa 1510 Mughal Empire (1525-1707)
		Merchant Wealth Kabuki Urban Culture		
1750				

I n the Chinese language, the idea of critical juncture is represented by the combination of the characters for danger *(wei)* and opportunity *(ji)*. History is filled with critical junctures, moments of crisis that can appear to determine the flow of events for centuries afterward. That crisis or danger is also opportunity is clear from the unfolding of world historical events around 1500. Continuity as well as change is characteristic of history, but it truly seems that change has intensified in the last 500 years. Each generation, however, may feel that it is facing the most profound crises that humanity has ever confronted, so change is also a matter of perception.

The world faced a critical juncture in the sixteenth century with the expansion of Europe. It was a defining moment in global history, a critical juncture of danger and opportunity whose long-term impact would be

West Asia	Europe	Africa	Americas/Pacific
Fall of Umayyad Caliphate (750)	Holy Roman Empire	Spread of Islam	Decline of Mayan Civilization
	Feudalism	Trans-Saharan Trade	
	Rise of Towns and Cities		
		West African Forest States	Cahokia (ca. 1050-1250)
	Crusades (1095-13th c.)	Benin	
		Great Zimbabwe (12th c.)	
		Swahili Culture	Cuzco (ca. 1200) (Inca Capital)
Seljuk Turks	COMMERCIAL CAPITALISM	Mali	
Mamluk Egypt	Black Death Italian Renaissance	Zanzibar Kilwa	Tenochtitlan (1325) (Aztec Capital)
	Merchant Princes	Ibn Battuta (1325-1353)	
Ottoman Turks			
	European Renaissance	Songrei	Eastern Woodland Iroquois League (ca. 1400)
	Portuguese Capture of Ceuta (1415)		
	MERCANTILISM	Kongo	
Ottoman Empire		Portuguese Elmina	Columbus (1492-1494) Treaty of Tordesillas (1494)
Safavid Empire (c. 1500-1722)	Portuguese at the Cape of Good Hope (1488)		Magellan (1519-1521)
	Printing Press	Atlantic Slave Trade (1518-1860)	Atlantic Slave Trade (1518-1860)
	Protestant Reformation		Spanish Conquest of Aztecs and Incas
	Society of Jesus (1540)	Moroccan Invasion (1591)	European Colonies in North America
	SCIENTIFIC REVOLUTION	Dutch East Indies Co. (1602)	Sugar Cane to West Indies (1640)
	British Royal African Co. (1672)	Era of Merchant Princes	
Qajar Empire (1722-1922)	French Enlightenment		Horses Expand into Plains
	INDUSTRIAL REVOLUTION		
			Cook Voyages (1768-1779)

profound and enduring. The forces of economic or economic change that propelled cultures and societies across the globe into collision with each other. Older conduits of both commercial and cultural exchange such as the Silk Road were overtaken by newer and more wide-ranging sea routes that marbled the world's oceans. The divergence of individual cultures linked by periodic trade or warfare shifted into a pattern of convergence shaped by intensified global connections. The potentially fruitful outcome and advantage for some involved in such encounters was balanced by the dangers of domination, struggle, and misunderstanding for others.

As the Part III title, "Transformation", suggests, Chapters 11 through 15 take up these processes of change, beginning with commercial revolutions in Europe and China that took place against the backdrop of the thirteenth-century world system. In Chapter 12 we trace the shift of that world system increasingly to Europe as the core, and in subsequent chapters we describe the impact of the new world system on the entire globe in the form of economic, cultural, social, and political change.

Commerce and Change in Asia, Europe, and Africa, 750–1500

When the famous Venetian traveler Marco Polo visited China in the late thirteenth century, he was awed by what he saw. He called the former capital Hangzhou "the greatest city . . . in the world, where so many pleasures may be found that one fancies himself to be in Paradise." Though his European contemporaries were skeptical of the wonders Marco Polo described in China, he was not far off in his assessment of Hangzhou, probably the largest city in the world at the time, with a population estimated at close to 2 million by the early part of the thirteenth century. Both Marco Polo's account and contemporary Chinese sources describe Hangzhou as a crowded city with multistoried buildings, divided by major thoroughfares and crisscrossed with smaller roads and canals. Sophisticated methods of garbage disposal, fire fighting, and policing of the population were used by the local government to maintain order.

Ten principal markets and numerous smaller ones dotted the city, testimony to Hangzhou's place as a central market for the empire. Residents could buy fruit, meat, medicine, wine, and cloth shipped into the city along the Grand Canal, which connected the fertile Yangzi delta with the Yellow River and the north China plain, medicine and cloth sent via the Yangzi River from Sichuan, and fruit, rice, and medicine brought from southern China. The wealthy could satisfy their tastes for luxury in clothing, food, furnishings, and entertainments, while the poor worked to provide these things through agricultural labor, craft production, and employment as servants or workers in restaurants, bars, and brothels.

Parks and gardens provided respite from the hectic pace of urban life. Especially famed was West Lake on the outskirts of the city, a place praised by poets for the beauty of its landscape. Villages in the surrounding countryside geared their economies to provide for the needs and desires of city residents, though villagers in mountainous areas far removed from Hangzhou and its environs remained largely self-contained, relatively untouched by the commercial activity and cultural dynamics associated with urban life.

Had Marco Polo described his native Venice as well as Hangzhou, he would have noted that the European city in the thirteenth century was smaller, with a population of less than 150,000, but no less devoted to trade and no less remarkable than the Chinese metropolis. Situated at the head of the Adriatic Sea, Venice grew up on mudflat islands located in brackish lagoons between the mainland and the banks formed by the de-

FIGURE 11.0 Venice, the Rialto.
Painting by Vittove
Carpaccio, 1494.

SOURCE: Alinari/Art Resource, NY.

bris of a number of rivers, notably the Po, that emptied into the sea there. Its location served two purposes: protection from the mainland and trade.

From its earliest days, Venice depended on the sea. Though Venetians had to collect rain for drinking water, the sea served them in almost every other way. The sea was the major source of food, since land on the islets was scarce and most of it was unsuitable for agriculture. It was maritime commerce that made Venice wealthy and powerful. From early trade with the mainland in fish and salt to the virtual monopoly of east-west trade that Venice achieved by the thirteenth century, commercial progress was steady.

Venetians cut channels, which became canals, into their mud islands both to drain them and to retain water for transportation at low tides. Canals determined the placement of houses and public structures, all of which were built on piles driven into the mud. Palisades along the canals helped make the ground solid and protect it from corrosion, creating quays. The whole was dominated by one great main canal, the Grand Canal, into which the smaller canals fed as arteries. The Grand Canal wound through the city in the shape of an "S," dividing it into half. Houses opened onto quays and thus onto the canals, and churches, facing plazas, were built on almost all the islets. The connections between this collection of isolated groups were water and bridges. By the thirteenth century, bridges were being built of stone and the quays and streets on the islets were being paved. By this time, thanks to the growing security and prosperity of the city, large public structures—guildhalls; palaces, both private and commercial—were being constructed in a uniquely Venetian style that was a mixture of Germanic and Byzantine styles. The Ducal Palace and the neighboring great Basilica of Saint Mark with its vast domes, soaring arches, and unparalleled richness of decoration, both of which still stand, represent the grandeur of Venetian architecture at this period. Given thirteenth-century Venice, Hangzhou must have been marvelous indeed to so impress Marco Polo.

A year after the death of Marco Polo, another great traveler left his home in Tangier, on the coast of Morocco. Ibn Battuta traveled to even more places than did Marco Polo and his narrative, the *Rihla* ("Book of Travels") offers details about almost every conceivable aspect of the Muslim cultural world and its frontiers, from Delhi to East Africa to China and Ceylon and back to Africa—an estimated 73,000 miles in almost thirty years. His experience of fourteenth-century Cairo suggests the richness and vitality of urban commercial and cultural life there. Cairo was situated at the commercial fulcrum of trade between Africa and West Asia. Within the city walls, living conditions were so crowded and the surge of people, camels, and donkeys on the city's main avenue so frantic that Ibn Battuta's stroll through its commercial district in April 1326 must have been nerve-racking. Thousands of shops and more than thirty markets beckoned. Hordes of vendors and peddlers jammed the noisy streets, offering foods and trinkets, all manner of services and wares, from gold and iron to slaves, silks, candles, and spices. There were centers of international trade, the caravansaries, where the desert caravans offloaded their goods. These were often huge and magnificently decorated multilevel structures built around a courtyard, with storage rooms on the ground floor and accommodation upstairs for up to 4,000 merchants and guests at a time.

■

INTRODUCTION

As suggested in the accounts of Marco Polo, Ibn Battuta, and others, the development of commerce transformed societies in Asia, Europe, and Africa both before and after 1500. This chapter begins by describing commercial revolutions in both China and Europe, and the impact of economic change on both European and Chinese societies. The European commercial revolution has customarily been viewed as the "takeoff" phase in the rapid rise of that continent to a position of worldwide dominance. By examining the earlier Chinese commercial revolution, as distinct from the later European one, we show that economic change has complex origins and results and cannot be explained by reference to any single cultural pattern or model.

Though the two commercial revolutions took place independently, neither the European nor the Chinese economies were isolated. Europe and China were situated at opposite ends of the thirteenth-century world system, a network of trading ties that extended across the Eurasian continent and linked the economic, political, social, and cultural lives of peoples in places as distant from each other as Hangzhou and Venice or Cairo and Palembang. Following the descriptions of commercial revolutions in China and Europe, this chapter will explore commerce and change in the thirteenth-century Afro-Asian world system extending from the overland caravan trade in West Africa and Central Asia to the great maritime highway of the Indian Ocean. The chapter will conclude with the breakdown of that system and the expansion of Europe as prelude to the creation of a new European-dominated world system beginning in the sixteenth century.

THE COMMERCIAL REVOLUTION IN CHINA, CA. 750–1250

The wealthy and sophisticated urban society observed by Marco Polo in thirteenth-century China was a product of changes that took place between about 750 and 1000, changes that fundamentally altered the Chinese economy. The first half of the Tang dynasty (618–907), up to about 750, was a time of imperial order, symbolized in the symmetry and regularity of the city plan of Chang'an, the Tang capital. Chang'an was the capital of a huge empire that dominated East Asia, extending the influence of Chinese culture eastward to Japan and westward to Central Asian oasis states such as Khotan. Chang'an was also the eastern terminus of the Silk Road and the destination of great Central Asian caravans that brought foreign goods and traders to China. Arab merchants and other foreigners, such as Central Asian Buddhist monks, resided in Chang'an.

COMMERCE IN TANG CHANG'AN

Commercial activity was subject to regulation by the government according to the Tang legal code, which stipulated punishments for such practices as the use of unofficial weights and measures, the sale of poor-quality goods, and the fixing of prices. Though such regulation applied in theory to markets throughout the empire, it was particularly apparent in the imperial capital. The gates in the walls of the city were closed at night, and the opening and closing of the two central marketplaces on the east and west sides of the city were controlled by the government.

Hang Merchants and craftsmen were organized by location according to the commodities they handled or produced into *hang*, literally "alleys." *Hang* have often been likened to medieval European guilds, associations of merchants or craftsmen, but the differences far outweigh the similarities. The only similarity between them is that they both were organizations of merchants and craftsmen. The important distinction is that the *hang* was an association organized by the state to oversee such things as the prices and quality of goods traded as well as the behavior of merchants, while the European guild was organized by merchants and craftsmen themselves to further common interests and protect their rights to trade (see below).

TANG CHINA AND THE EAST ASIAN WORLD

Tang China was the great power in East Asia through the first half of the eighth century, employing both political and cultural means to achieve this position. By exerting military force through the exploits of imperial armies and at times through diplomatic alliances, China exercised varying degrees of dominance over border regions in Central Asia, Southeast Asia (Vietnam), and Korea. Cultural influence was equally important in China's dominance of East Asia during the Tang. For example, the Korean state of Silla adopted aspects of Chinese governance and Buddhism from China. Silla was able to defeat competitor states and unify the peninsula under its control in 668 in part through its close ties with Tang China. Chinese cultural influence penetrated beyond the Korean peninsula to Japan, where both Chinese and Korean Buddhist missionaries carried Chinese ideas and institutions along with Buddhist religion.

Weakening of the Tang Imperial Order   In the mid–eighth century, however, two momentous events took place that substantially weakened the Tang central government and reduced Tang power in East Asia, setting the stage for the transformation of Chinese society over the next several centuries. In 751, Tang armies confronting the expanding Islamic Empire in Central Asia were defeated by a coalition of Arabs and Turks at the Talas River, significantly altering the balance of power in Central Asia, where China had previously been dominant. This defeat was followed in 755 by the rebellion of An Lushan, a court favorite and regional military commander who sought to topple the Tang ruling family and claim the throne for himself. Though Tang rule survived this challenge, the suppression of the An Lushan Rebellion in 763 had a high cost. Regional military commanders, whose support had been vital in suppressing the rebellion, gained greater independence from the court and from control by the central government. The weakening of the central government, coupled with commercial growth and change, helped to bring about the demise of the old economic and social order and thus to set the stage for the commercial revolution of Song (960–1279) times observed by Marco Polo.

CONFUCIANISM AND COMMERCE

Scholar-officials traditionally occupied the highest position on the Confucian social scale, while merchants were relegated to the lowest. In order to protect the status of scholar officials merchants were subject to sumptuary laws that regulated what kinds of clothes they could wear and what kinds of residences they could build. They were also not allowed to take the civil service examinations. Beginning in the mid–eighth century, concurrent with political changes that weakened the Tang state and Tang power in Central Asia, merchants grew in wealth and power as commerce began to expand beyond the neat boundaries set up by imperial government authority, reflected in the regulated marketplaces of Chang'an. An early-ninth-century poet provides us with a description of a wealthy merchant that contrasts sharply with Confucian dogma about the social position of merchants: "Wherever profit is to be made he goes. . . . His food and drink are sweet and well spiced. With interest and capital constantly breeding rich profit. . . . He frequents noblemen's houses, the residences of royal princesses. . . . Knowing that his riches make him powerful as a prince."

The negative view of merchants and commercial activities in much written documentation of this era reflected traditional Confucian attitudes, which viewed commerce as a vulgar occupation decidedly inferior to scholarship and government service, as well as agriculture. The comments of an early-ninth-century writer observing the lively economic activity taking place in a market on the outskirts of an administrative city suggest something of the tension between Confucian ideals that disparaged commerce and the vital reality of the marketplace: "Hearts intent on profit are excited. . . . At midday they throng together, ten thousand feet led by the single thought that they all fear somebody else will forestall them. . . . All desire only to act like scavenger dogs or carrion crows, delighted to get hold of some putrid leftovers." Antipathy toward commerce in Confucian thinking did not prevent merchants from being prosperous nor scholars from engaging in commerce indirectly by investment. Confucian hostility to commerce did mean that the official attitude toward merchants was negative, that the state sometimes attempted to control and regulate commerce, and that merchants never developed the kind of autonomy they acquired in Europe (see below).

THE COMMERCIAL REVOLUTION OF THE SONG (960–1279)

Though the political breakdown of the Tang Empire allowed commerce to expand beyond the confines of official markets and for merchants to grow wealthy by operating more freely, the conjunction of factors that produced the commercial revolution of the Song did not come together until around 1000, a generation after the reunification of China under the Song dynasty (960). The Song established its imperial government in the city of Kaifeng, along the Yellow River in north China, which became a lively center of population and commerce in addition to government. Kaifeng lay at the terminus of an extension of the Grand Canal that linked the Yellow and Yangzi Rivers and was thus strategically located as a transport depot for goods brought by boat from the rich Yangzi delta region. An efficient transportation network, by both water and land, along with increased agricultural production, population growth, and the expansion of markets were key factors in the commercial revolution of Song times.

Agriculture and Population By around 1000, the introduction of new strains of early-ripening and drought-resistant strains of rice from Southeast Asia began to increase the supply of food. These imported strains of rice either allowed planting and harvesting more than one crop a year, because the rice plants matured quickly, or enabled farmers to plant rice in places that were not well irrigated and where it had not been possible to plant before. At the same time, improvements in dam technology allowed the reclamation of lowland swampy areas to open up new land for farming.

The resulting increases in food production contributed to population expansion. From a rough estimate of 60 million in the Tang dynasty, China's population grew to around 100 million by the mid–thirteenth century. Population growth, in turn, contributed to the expansion of markets for products. An expanded marketplace, coupled with efficient transportation networks facilitated by stable political conditions under the Northern Song (960–1126) encouraged regional specialization of production for the market.

Market Economy In contrast to the localized economy of the Tang, in which villages produced what they used and trade was limited to local exchange (with the exception of long-distance trade in luxury goods and salt), the growing market economy of the Song encouraged the production of goods for the market which had expanded with the increase in population. Specialization in the production of certain goods for the market generally means more efficient use of labor and raw materials. Regional specialization was feasible because there were relatively rapid and efficient means of transporting goods to central markets—both roads and waterways—and a distribution network of merchants and warehouses to store goods and bring them to markets in a timely fashion. Regions began to specialize in the production of textiles, such as silk, which required the cultivation of mulberry bushes and the feeding of silkworms as well as the skill of weavers, or in agricultural products such as oranges. Tea, for example, was produced in the southeastern province of Fujian but was marketed to regions all over China.

Trade with China's nomadic neighbors, who were at times enemies, provided the Chinese both markets for their own products and a source of necessary or luxury goods. During the Northern Song, the Chinese imported silver, hemp cloth, sheep, horses, and slaves from the Khitan people in southern Manchuria. During the Southern Song (1127–1279), after the north had been conquered by the Jurchen Jin state, the Chinese exported tea, rice, porcelain, sugar, silk, and other goods to the Jurchen in exchange for medicines, horses, and other items.

MARITIME TRADE AND THE COMMERCIAL REVOLUTION

Maritime trade had begun to prosper under the Tang, when Indian and Arab merchants traveling Indian Ocean maritime routes established permanent communities at the southern port of Canton. With the commercial revolution of the Song, maritime trade was recognized as a vital part of the economy and received official patronage and supervision. By the mid–twelfth century, profits from maritime commerce were about one-fifth of the state's total cash revenues.

Shipbuilding and Navigational Technology Shipbuilding was highly developed during the Song, and inland shipping as well as oceangoing trade supplied regional needs and contributed to the economic prosperity of the Chinese empire by providing extensive markets for its products. Seagoing vessels had from one to four masts, with bamboo matting often used for sails. Relying on monsoon winds, these ships traveled south in the winter and north in the summer. With favorable winds, it was possible to go from Fujian along the southeast coast of China to Korea in as few as five days. Since oceangoing sailing ships could not navigate shallow coastal waters or rivers, goods were transferred to shallow-draft oared galleys for inland transport. In addition to the use of sails and oars, boats were pulled over dangerous rapids and through passages such as the Yangzi gorges by haulers who walked along the riverbanks dragging the boats by ropes. Navigation for ocean going vessels was aided by the magnetic compass, the origins of which go back to the Han (206 B.C.E.–220 C.E).

Trade Goods By the Song, the southward-pointing compass was regularly relied upon by Chinese navigators, who carried on trade with Japan, Southeast Asia, and lands as far as the east coast of Africa and the Arabian Sea. From Japan came gold, pearls, shells, copper vessels, and weapons, among other things. The Chinese exported to Southeast Asia precious metals, iron implements and utensils, ceramics, lacquerware, silks and other textiles, paper, books, grains, and other specialized items. From Southeast Asia came spices, cotton, and a number of luxury items such as ivory and rhinocerous horn.

Quanzhou Maritime trade focused on Southeast Asia and the Arab world was overseen by superintendents of trade appointed to serve at major port cities such as Quanzhou. Quanzhou, known as Zayton in Marco Polo's writings, was an important center of oceangoing trade during the Song and the home of foreign merchants who prospered on the profits of trade with the Chinese. One of these, an Arab merchant who took a Chinese name, Pu (for the Arabic "Abu") Shougeng, was appointed superintendent of trade at Quanzhou and commander of the provincial naval squadron during the thirteenth century. He was the most influential official on the southeast coast, and his power was reflected in the wealth of his son-in-law, who possessed eighty seagoing ships and warehouses filled with pearls and other valuable imported goods.

COMMERCE AND CURRENCY

In the Northern Song, state revenues from commercial taxes and state monopolies (principally iron and salt) equaled the yield from agrarian taxes; by the Southern Song, commercial revenues far exceeded the income from agrarian taxes. The increasing use of both metal and paper currency and the development of institutions of banking and credit that took place in the Song were both vital aspects of the commercial revolution of the period. Between the eighth and eleventh centuries, for example, the output of currency quadrupled, while the population grew much more slowly.

Growth of Money Economy The shift from localized economies based on barter or exchange of goods to an increasingly monetized economy of scale that integrated regional economies was aided by the use of paper currency and credit. The round copper coin with a square hole, called "cash," which was strung in units of 1,000, was the basic unit of currency minted by the Song state, but it was heavy and cumbersome to use and transport in any great quantity. Innovations such as the use of certificates of credit or bills of exchange (documents showing that money deposited in one place could be exchanged for a receipt that could be used to pay for goods in another) made it possible for merchants to carry on trade across regions with ease.

Paper Currency Paper had already come into use in the first and second centuries, and the use of paper currency began in the late Tang as groups of merchants made use of paper certificates in place of metal coinage. In the Tang these certificates were known as "flying cash"; by the Song, official paper currency was printed by the government. Merchants could deposit a large amount of metal currency with a reliable person, family, or institution, such as a Buddhist temple, in one location and receive a receipt redeemable for the same amount in another location with a similarly reliable agent.

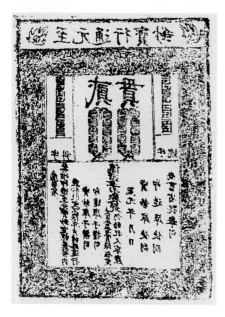

FIGURE 11.1 Printing Block for a Chinese Bank Note. Mongol Period (late 13th or early 14th century).

Both paper currency and metal coins facilitated the expansion of the economy in Song China. The printing of paper money was continued by the Mongol Yuan dynasty (1279–1368).

TECHNOLOGY AND THE COMMERCIAL REVOLUTION

In addition to shipbuilding and navigational technology, advances in printing, the textile industry, and ceramic production were part of the technological changes of this era. The earliest extant texts printed on paper with carved woodblocks, dating from the eighth century in Korea and Japan and from the ninth century in China, were Buddhist texts. The inspiration for printing in China, as in Europe, came from the desire to propagate religious ideas; printed books in China promoted Buddhism, and the European Johannes Gutenberg's first printed text was the Christian Bible.

Printing Technology Movable type—separate letters or characters made of clay, wood, or metal arranged to make a page of text—was invented in China 400 years before its appearance in Europe. However, because written Chinese uses a script with thousands of different characters, as opposed to an alphabetic one with fewer than a hundred letters as in European languages, movable type did not dominate printing in China as it eventually did in Europe. Carved woodblocks remained the favored method of printing because it was actually easier and more efficient to carve a page of text than to create the vast number of pieces of type necessary to typeset a page of Chinese characters.

Textile and Ceramics Industries The new technology of printing was used to spread knowledge of other new technologies used in agriculture and textile production, and in this way contributed substantially to the economic revolution of Song times. Advances in the textile industry improved production, the scale of which is suggested by an early-fourteenth-century account of a mechanical spinning wheel that could spin 130

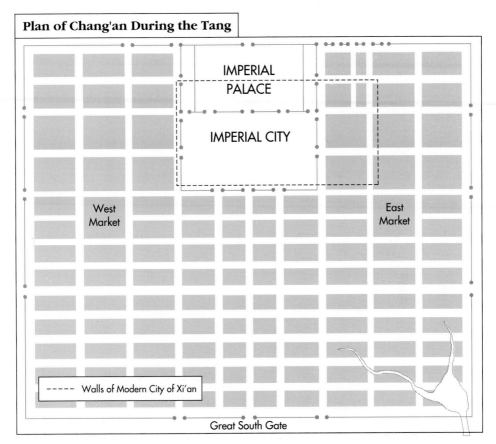

Plan of Chang'an During the Tang

IMPERIAL PALACE

IMPERIAL CITY

West Market

East Market

- - - - - Walls of Modern City of Xi'an

Great South Gate

MAP 11.1 Chang'an, the Capital of Tang China, was laid out according to a grid pattern and centered on the southward-facing imperial palace.

SOURCE: Fairbank, Reischauer, Craig, *East Asia: Tradition and Transformation* (Boston: Houghton Mifflin, 1978), p. 106.

pounds of thread in twenty-four hours. Along with cotton and silk textiles, the production of ceramics expanded, with both imperial and private commercial kilns scattered throughout the empire. The technique of making porcelain was perfected in the twelfth century, and a wide variety of ceramic art was produced, many examples of which are preserved in museums throughout the world today.

Iron and Industry For many centuries Chinese craftsmen had produced cast iron, and they also made steel, utilizing smelting techniques well in advance of Europe. The iron and steel produced were used for many purposes, but farm tools, currency, and armaments were by far the most important. By the early twelfth century, the production of crude iron concentrated in north China ranged between 35,000 and 125,000 tons, a level comparing favorably with that of England several centuries later. Since the north China plain was already deforested by the Tang and therefore access to charcoal was limited, growth in the production of iron during the Northern Song was dependent on the use of coal, an innovation that Europe did not employ until the eighteenth century.

The life of Wang Ge, an industrial entrepreneur of the twelfth century, illustrates something of the scale of enterprise and the conditions of production in the iron industry. With a modest capital investment Wang acquired a timber-covered mountain and began to produce charcoal, utilizing the slack-season labor of local farmers. He then set up two foundries to produce iron, making use of local iron ore deposits. He employed around 500 workers, all of whom were members of the "floating population," vagabonds who for some reason had lost or left their farms and homes. Wang himself managed one of the foundries, but the other was under the supervision of a manager. With the profits of the two foundries, he also acquired other enterprises, such as a wineshop, and a lake where he engaged several hundred families in fishing.

DAILY LIVES

THE ATTRACTIONS OF THE CAPITAL

Cities proliferated in Song China, and urban life was freer in movement and activities than in Tang China as well as socially more complex, as rural folk crowded into the Southern Song capital of Hangzhou and other cities seeking work in the entertainment quarters, businesses, or other establishments. In contrast to Tang Chang'an, the city boundaries of Hangzhou were irregular, shaped by the expansion of population as waves of immigrants flooded into the city fleeing war in the north. Textual descriptions of life in the city of Hangzhou, which Marco Polo praised so highly, provide evidence of the rich texture of urban life similar to that of the painting "Spring Festival Along the River." A Chinese account written in 1235 details the wide variety of goods available and the ceaseless activity of the populous city:

> In the evening, with the exception of the square in front of the palace, the markets are as busy as during the day . . . In the wine shops and inns business also thrives. Only after the fourth drum does the city gradually quiet down, but by the fifth drum court officials already start preparing for audiences and merchants are getting ready for the morning market again. This cycle goes on all year without respite . . .
>
> On the lot in front of the wall of the city building, there are always various acting troupes

performing, and this usually attracts a large crowd. The same kind of activity is seen in almost any vacant lot, including those at the meat market of the Great Common, the herb market at Charcoal Bridge, the book market at the Orange Grove, the vegetable market on the east side of the city, and the rice market on the north side . . .

. . . Some of the famous specialties of the capital are sweet-bean soup at the Miscellaneous Market, the pickled dates of the Ge family, the thick soup of the Guang family at Superior Lane, the fruit at the Great Commons marketplace, the cooked meats in front of Eternal Mercy Temple, Sister Song's fish broth at Penny Pond Gate, the juicy lungs at Flowing Gold Gate . . .

. . . Today, having been the "temporary capital for more than a hundred years, the city has over a million households. The suburbs extend to the south, west, and north; all are densely populated and prosperous in commerce as well as agriculture. The size of the suburbs is comparable to a small county or prefecture, and it takes several days to travel through them. This again reflects the prosperity of the capital.[1]

[1]Translated in Patricia B. Ebrey, *Chinese Civilization* (New York: Macmillan Free Press, 1991): 178–9; 184; "Duzheng jisheng," in *Dongjing menghua lu, wai si zhong* (Shanghai: Zhonghua Shuju, 1962:91–107.

FIGURE 11.2 Detail of *Spring Festival on the River,* 1736 copy of painted handscroll by Zhang Zeduan (fl. 12th c.).

The scene shown here depicts the busy commercial life along the river and on the streets of this idealized Chinese city during the commercial revolution of the Song.

SOURCE: National Palace Museum, Taiwan, Republic of China.

Technology Transfer: Iron, Gunpowder, and the Mongols   One Chinese invention, gunpowder, when combined with the production of iron, had dramatic consequences not only for the Chinese but also for the world. The first evidence of knowledge of gunpowder dates from the ninth century and is connected to Daoist alchemical experimentation, by which Daoists sought ways to transform one element into another. By the year 1000, the combination of charcoal, saltpeter (potassium nitrate), and sulfur that yields gunpowder was being used by the Chinese in small incendiary devices. Gradually more complex and sophisticated weapons were used in Song warfare against their northern nomadic neighbors, and both the discovery of gunpowder and the advanced state of the iron industry in north China would seem to have made the Chinese formidable foes. But in the early twelfth century, north China was conquered by the Jurchen people from Manchuria whose horsemanship and military skill enabled them to defeat the Chinese. With the Jurchen conquest of north China, an early form of technology transfer took place that eventually put both iron and gunpowder into the hands of the Mongols, who succeeded the Jurchen, and contributed significantly to the Mongol conquest of Eurasia in the thirteenth century.

CHINESE SOCIETY AND THE COMMERCIAL REVOLUTION

Even as a "commercial revolution" took place in Song China, the lives of the vast majority of the population were still tied to the land and to agricultural production. Many of those who farmed the land were also bound to landlords as tenants who owed rent and often labor service to their masters. Others were free and farmed plots of land independently. The continuities of life in rural villages, however, were also affected by the changes of the commercial revolution. For example, cities might offer better prospects of employment for landless laborers in the countryside who were otherwise dependent on being hired for seasonal agricultural work.

Gender Roles Material prosperity brought often contradictory changes to the lives of women. ▬▬▬▬▬▬▬▬ The commercialization of textile production, for example, meant that the traditional female work of spinning and weaving cloth took on greater economic value at least within the household. But this shift did not appear to produce any gains in the status of women in society as a whole. There is no evidence that their status was any less subordinate to men simply because the economic value of their labor had increased.

In other ways, there are clear signs that the status of women declined, but it is difficult to explain why this should be the case. The most notorious of Chinese customs with regard to women is without doubt the practice of footbinding. We know little about the origins of this custom other than that it began sometime in the late Tang (618–907)—commonly attributed to a technique used by a court dancer that appealed to the emperor—and by the early Song had spread beyond the court to at least the upper levels of society. The feet of young girls were tightly bound so that their toes were turned under to produce a tiny foot, which was considered beautiful. This painful procedure was carried out on daughters by their mothers so that they would meet standards of beauty and be good candidates for marriage.

The spread of footbinding, precisely during the era of the commercial revolution, suggests that increasing material prosperity made it possible for some women not to engage in physical labor, since the bound foot would at the very least make a woman's mobility limited. It may even have been regarded as a kind of status marker indicating wealth to have women in a household whose feet were bound and who were relatively inactive, though they could work at sedentary tasks. The spread of footbinding is a powerful example of the sometimes contradictory effects on society of economic changes and transformations in material life produced by the commercial revolution.

■

THE CRUSADES AND COMMERCE: EUROPE AND THE THIRTEENTH-CENTURY WORLD SYSTEM

Concurrent with the erosion of Chinese dominance in the East Asian world and the collapse of the Tang dynasty, the Roman Empire was revived in the West when Pope Leo III (r. 795–816) crowned Frankish King Charlemagne emperor in 800. It was, however, very different from the empire that had ended in 476, with the occupation of Rome by Germanic tribes. The new empire was more German than Roman and more connected to northern Europe than to the Mediterranean. Within half a century of Charlemagne's death in 814, the revived empire was split between his French and German descendants; a century later, in 962, the imperial title was once again revived, when German king Otto I was crowned emperor by the pope in Rome. Henceforth the western empire, known as the Holy Roman Empire, was a German empire, whose territories were somewhat loosely stretched across central Europe from the Baltic to the Mediterranean. To its east was Muslim West Asia and Slavic Europe; to its west, smaller kingdoms emerged in France, England, and Spain.

THE CRUSADES: POLITICS AND RELIGION

While the commercial revolution in China was underway, western Europe was being transformed by the effects of a series of holy wars, Crusades to West Asia, sponsored by the papacy from the late eleventh through the early thirteenth centuries. The Crusades were a result of many factors. In one sense, they were a transferral of the longstanding conflict between Christians and Muslims in Spain, where Christians had been engaged since the eighth century in trying to drive the Muslims from the Iberian peninsula. The Crusades to the Holy Land were also a result of recent religious developments. In 1054 a serious theological dispute split Byzantine (Eastern Orthodox) Christians from Roman Catholics in western Europe, where the pope believed that a Crusade might reunite the two halves of Christendom. There was also western European economic interest in a Crusade to West Asia, where Europeans had long been in competition with Byzantines and Arabs whose wealth they both admired and envied.

In 1071 Byzantine armies were soundly defeated by the Turks, who took over much of Asia Minor, and the Byzantine emperor appealed to Roman Catholic western Europe for help. It was to this appeal that Pope Urban II (r. 1088–1099) responded when he called for a holy war against the Muslims in 1095. Between 1095 and 1291, the Christian Crusaders expanded connections between Europe and the rest of the world in their attempt to recapture Palestine and other parts of the "Holy Land," sacred to both Muslims and Christians, from Muslim control.

Twelfth century European rulers such as Richard I (r. 1189–1199) of England, the Holy Roman Emperor Frederick Barbarossa (r. 1152–1190), the French King Philip II Augustus (r. 1180–1223), and the Spanish King Alfonso of Castile (r. 1126–1157), strove to enlarge their territories and powers, which remained limited by feudal privileges that these monarchs shared with clergy and nobility. Since they were Christians, such rulers saw Crusades as opportunities to gain religious benefits (remission of penalties for sin was granted to those who went), approval from the papacy, great prestige, as well as economic and political benefits (such as diverting troublesome nobles to the Holy Land).

THE CRUSADES AND THE REVIVAL OF TRADE

As a result of the collapse of the Roman Empire in the fifth century, trading relations between Europe, Asia, and Africa were severely curtailed. Between the ninth and twelfth centuries, when the imperial ideal was resurrected in western Europe in the form of the Holy Roman Empire and feudal monarchies began to take shape as well, European trade was principally a matter of local exchange and barter, though Venice continued to trade with the Byzantine Empire. Only certain necessities, such as salt, and limited luxury goods were traded over great distances. This began to change by the end of the eleventh century, when the First Crusade inaugurated a process of trade revival that reconnected European economies to those of Asia and Africa and opened Europe to the world.

In the long run the most important impact of the Crusades was economic, since they were the means by which Europe was reconnected to Asia and Africa, with the result that Italian cities became commercial centers of long-distance trade. The Italian peninsula, unlike the rest of Europe, had maintained contact with the Byzantine Empire: Ravenna remained

Byzantine until the eighth century and parts of Sicily until the eleventh. Italian merchants continued to carry on limited trade with the east, essentially in such luxury goods as spices, jewels, fabrics, and perfumes. By 1100 C.E., Venice commanded the routes to the eastern Mediterranean, could supply the necessary transport for and reap large profits from European Crusaders bent on recovering their Holy Land, and created a Venetian empire in the process.

Venice Venice came into its own during the first four Crusades, vanquishing its rivals, such ▬▬▬ as Genoa, dominating the eastern Mediterranean, reaping the riches of the trade routes between Constantinople and western Europe and between Asia Minor and western Europe, and elevating the city on the mudflats into the position of major European power. The effort to recapture the Holy Land proved a boon to trade, and Italian merchants reaped vast profits. Venice's success found expression in the rapid development of the city, its flamboyant architecture, and the strength and wealth of its commercial oligarchy.

It was the Fourth Crusade, in 1204, that marked Venice's triumph. In small ships, averaging about 500 tons of cargo, using sails and oars, the Venetians transported in one year 4,500 horses, 9,000 knights, 20,000 soldiers, and their supplies—but not to the Holy Land. Along the way, the Fourth Crusade was translated into an attack on Venice's competing cities along the Dalmatian coast, and finally on Constantinople, the capital of the Byzantine Empire. In 1204, Constantinople fell and was sacked; in the division of spoils Venice received "a half and a quarter" of the Byzantine Empire.

By 1300, the Italian peninsula was the center of a flourishing trade that extended from western Europe to the eastern end of the Mediterranean. Although this trade was costly and risky, the profits were enormous. The rebirth of agriculture, mining, and manufacturing in northwestern Europe, as well as commercial growth and innovations in commercial practices, can be attributed in part to the expansion of Europe's horizons and the heightened opportunities for trade generated by the Crusades.

■

THE COMMERCIAL REVOLUTION IN EUROPE, CA. 1200–1500

By the thirteenth century, changes that have commonly been labeled a "commercial revolution" can be documented in Europe. Expanding trade and industry brought about important innovations that would over time become the foundation of modern capitalism, the use of money or capital to increase wealth. The rate of change was slow and neither smooth nor uniform. Beginning in the twelfth century, the commercial revolution substantially altered European life by the thirteenth. But the mid-fourteenth-century "Black Death," the epidemic of bubonic plague that spread across Eurasia, severely disrupted the process of European economic transformation. After a century of crisis, however, the volume and variety of European trade once again began to grow.

MAP 11.2 *(Facing Page)* **Mediterranean Routes of Venice and Genoa, Crusader States at Eastern End of Mediterranean, and Overland Routes to Persian Gulf and Red Sea Ports.**

SOURCE: Janet Abu-Lughod, *Before European Hegemony: The World System, A.D. 1250–1350* (New York: Oxford University Press, 1989), p. 123, 187.

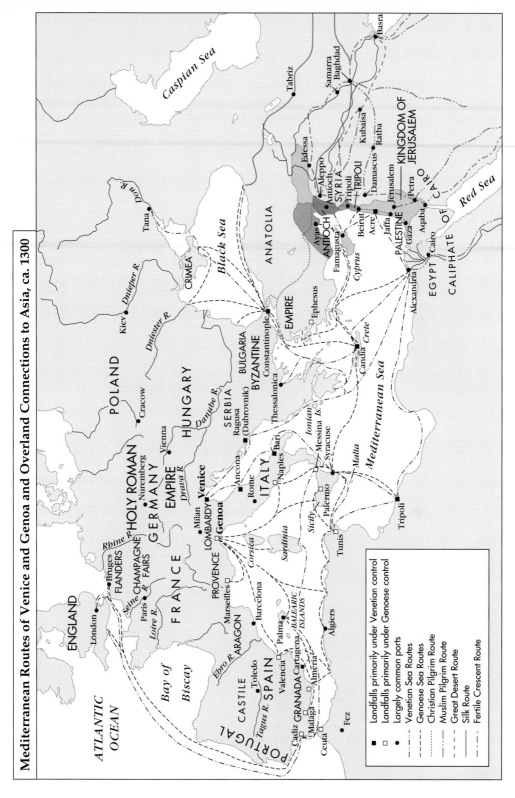

Mediterranean Routes of Venice and Genoa and Overland Connections to Asia, ca. 1300

ATLANTIC OCEAN

ENGLAND
London

Bay of Biscay

FRANCE
Paris
Loire R.
Seine R.
CHAMPAGNE & FAIRS
Bruges
FLANDERS
Rhine R.

HOLY ROMAN EMPIRE
GERMANY
Nuremberg
Milan
LOMBARDY
Venice
Genoa
PROVENCE
Marseilles

POLAND
Cracow
Kiev
Dnieper R.
Dniester R.

HUNGARY
Vienna
Drava R.
Danube R.
SERBIA
BULGARIA
Ragusa (Dubrovnik)
Thessalonica

Caspian Sea
Don R.

Black Sea
CRIMEA
Tana

BYZANTINE EMPIRE
Constantinople
Ephesus
ANATOLIA

Tabriz
Samarra
Baghdad
Basra
Edessa
Aleppo
Antioch
SYRIA
Tripoli
Damascus
Kubaisa
Ratba
KINGDOM OF JERUSALEM
Jerusalem
Petra
Beirut
Acre
Jaffa
PALESTINE
Gaza
Aqaba
ANTIOCH
Ayas
Famagusta
Cyprus
Crete
Candia

Red Sea
EGYPT
Cairo
Alexandria
CALIPHATE OF CAIRO

ITALY
Rome
Ancona
Bari
Naples
Mediterranean Sea
Ionian Is.
Messina
Syracuse
Malta
Sicily
Palermo
Sardinia
Corsica
Tunis
Tripoli

SPAIN
CASTILE
Toledo
Tagus R.
PORTUGAL
ARAGON
Barcelona
Ebro R.
Valencia
GRANADA
Cartagena
Almería
Palma
BALEARIC ISLANDS
Cadiz
Malaga
Ceuta
Fez
Algiers

Legend:
- ■ Landfalls primarily under Venetian control
- □ Landfalls primarily under Genoese control
- ● Largely common ports
- – – – Venetian Sea Routes
- — — Genoese Sea Routes
- ········· Christian Pilgrim Route
- –·–·– Muslim Pilgrim Route
- – – – Great Desert Route
- ——— Silk Route
- –··–··– Fertile Crescent Route

EUROPEAN DEMOGRAPHY AND ECONOMIC CHANGE

As in China, an important aspect of economic change beginning around 1200 was demographic. In 1000, Europe's population was approximately the same as it had been during the heyday of imperial Rome, a millennium earlier, approximately 36 million; during the twelfth and thirteenth centuries rose rapidly as a result of expanded cultivation to marginal lands, reaching about 80 million.

The Demographic Impact of the Black Death The Black Death devastatingly reduced populations across Europe for a decade or more, not only during the plague year of 1348. In many parts of Europe the plague continued, and population declined to an estimated 19 million in 1400. Its rebound in the fifteenth century was astounding, again reaching 80 million by 1500. In terms of density, by far the greatest increase was in northern Europe, though this was not necessarily a growth of large urban populations. In fact, cities, which were more affected by the plague than rural areas, may have declined in population. None of the European urban centers was large in comparison with contemporary Constantinople or Cairo. Reasonable estimates place the population of major Italian cities of the fourteenth and fifteenth centuries at 100,000, while north of the Alps, all except Paris were only half as large. Paris, which had had around 300,000 inhabitants in 1345, was reduced to 200,000 by 1500.

The changes taking place between 1200 and 1500 were full of conflict and by no means uniform, and the economic impact of the Black Death was complex and uneven. For example,

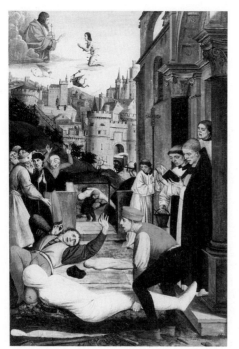

FIGURE 11.3 The Black Death, Showing Dead Wrapped in Shrouds as Others Fall Ill and Saint Sebastian Pleads for Mercy (above).

Despite the prayers of priests on earth and St. Sebastian (stuck with arrows) in heaven, the bubonic plague, indicated by the symptomatic bulba on the neck of the man lying left center of this picture, spread catastrophically across Europe.

SOURCE: *St. Sebastian Interceding for the Plague-Stricken,* Josse Lieferinxe. The Walters Art Gallery, Baltimore.

while reducing the labor force in Europe and therefore allowing some workers at least to improve their working conditions because of high demand for labor, the Black Death had the negative impact of reducing market demand—because of population decline—for both agricultural goods and manufactured products, thus retarding economic development. But population decline also meant that production of industrial crops (flax, wool, hemp) could be increased because there was less demand for grain. Expansion of manufacturing, commerce, and agricultural production, however, remained limited by the scarcity and imbalance in the distribution of money.

City and Countryside   Though Europe remained overwhelmingly rural, the rapid rise of population following the worst of the Black Death eventually aided economic development; and large scale trade and urban production accordingly increased urban wealth and political influence. Ties between cities and their surrounding countryside remained close, especially where, as in Italy and the Netherlands, cities were numerous, and the balance of power and dominance slowly shifted from the countryside to the city, from the land to the market.

Production for the Market   As in China, self-sufficient agriculture gave way over time to production for the market, usually of one crop such as wool or grain; as peasants no longer produced the variety of foods and other goods their living required, they traded at the market. This process of production-trade-purchase led to money replacing barter as the means of exchange. Those who produced for the market—both on the land and in workshops—and those who traded came to depend on money. In this setting, capitalism was born, and both the techniques and the tools necessary for its continued growth were created. From its earliest practice in Italy to its successful adaptation north of the Alps, capitalism began to transform European society.

THE ORIGINS OF CAPITALISM

The gradual shift from limited production for local markets that characterized manorial agriculture and guild production in towns failed to satisfy the expanding needs of general European markets, the expansion of which had been encouraged following the Crusades by continued and growing trade with West Asia and the Byzantine Empire. Italian cities such as Venice, which had profited from the Crusades, and other Mediterranean cities, such as Marseilles, which continued contact between the markets of northern and western Europe and the eastern Mediterranean region, stimulated the expansion of European markets and production.

A class of entrepreneurs, who organized, managed, and assumed the risks of production and trade by providing raw materials and marketing finished products, emerged as alternatives to the traditional production and marketing of craft and merchant guilds. Entrepreneurs succeeded by taking particular advantage of European markets as they expanded. Both expanding demand and new methods of production and marketing slowly reshaped limited production for local or regional markets into production driven by larger national and international market demands, which could only be satisfied by increased production and which resulted in increased profits. Associated with the transition from localized economies that relied on payments in kind, a European economy based on money and profit was a change in the ideals that governed both production and marketing.

Signs of change included the gradual abandonment of concepts such as the just price (the idea that the price of an object should be determined by the cost of the material and labor used to produce it), the sanctity of labor (that work well done was its own reward), and prohibitions against usury (the lending of money with an interest charge for its use). The success of entrepreneurialism changed traditional relationships between workers who produced and those who controlled production. Together with larger markets, new methods of increasing production, and increased profits, new economic attitudes and means of production were the ingredients of early capitalist development, which produced increasingly larger economic organizations that provided profit for those who belonged to them.

CHANGES IN IRON TECHNOLOGY

As in China, one of the important indications of an expanding European economy in the early centuries of the second millennium CE was progress in iron technology and production. Advances in iron metallurgy were a response to growing military needs, the result of the replacement of traditional feudal weapons (bows and arrows, spears, swords) with iron cannon and guns, and to the increasing demands of agriculture, where iron tools, especially plows, were important to the colonizing and exploitation of marginal lands of heavy soils such as those settled in Central and Northern Europe.

The increased production of iron began as early as the eighth century Muslim conquest of Spain. When Spanish mines fell into Muslim hands, new iron mines were opened in northern Europe. The increased supply of iron ore made the metal more available for ordinary as well as military uses, and peasants and knights used an amount of iron that would have been inconceivable earlier. Smiths, so skillful that even the Muslims in Spain imported them from Christian Europe, were central to every village. Their use of traditional methods of producing wrought iron was sufficient to meet demands until perhaps the eleventh century, after which technological innovations increased both the amounts and types of iron produced.

Wrought and Cast Iron In wrought iron production a bloom, or thick bar, of iron was formed by roasting (heating to red-hot condition) rather than melting the ore; the bloom was then purified by further heating and hammering. To make the bloom purer and larger, high temperatures and blasts of air were needed. Major steps in this direction were taken with the application of waterpower to metallurgical processes. There are instances of the use of waterpower at English forges as early as the eleventh century. Waterpower was used to stamp or crush the ore, to work bellows that provided the blast of air needed by furnaces, and to drive hammers used for working wrought iron. By the early twelfth century, each waterpowered blast furnace was smelting 200 tons of iron each year, a large quantity in relation to earlier times. Other significant technological change in the production of iron after 1000 centered on improved furnaces.

Innovations increased the levels of iron production and use. The casting of iron (as opposed to traditional wrought iron), which took place between the thirteenth and fifteenth centuries, was perhaps the most decisive innovation. It was made possible by higher furnace temperatures that produced the high-carbon-content iron necessary for casting. Cast iron was a new commodity and even though the process was initially inefficient, with only about half the iron recovered from the ore, increasing amounts of iron mined produced increased quantities of the metal.

The *Stückofen* In Germany, the *Stückofen*, an innovative furnace, further increased iron production. This furnace was ten feet or so high; strong blasts of circulating air made it possible to liquefy iron within it continuously. Molten iron could be topped off, molten slag tapped, and the process continued ceaselessly as long as charcoal was continuously supplied and the furnace walls withstood the heat. Increased production had a cost, however. One of the major consequences of advances in metal technology was the increased consumption of fuel. European forests were devastated by the cutting of trees for industrial activities between 1100 and 1500. Profound changes in the landscape and a shortage of fuel were problems with which later generations would have to deal.

Metallurgy and Military Technology Iron production grew very rapidly following late medieval advances in technology. By 1500, about 60,000 tons of iron were being produced in Europe annually. The impetus for improved iron technology was a result of the military use of the metal. Although many iron tools and implements used on farms and in crafts continued to be made in traditional ways in traditional places, the invention of the cannon indicates the end of traditional medieval metallurgy. Cannons were originally small and light, cast of copper and its alloys, and lacked firepower; the first iron cannons were larger and heavier, made of iron bars welded together longitudinally and bound by iron hoops, and they had increased firepower.

Artillery appears to have been in use in Europe by the beginning of the fourteenth century, and the first mention of the bronze cannon dates from 1326. By the second half of the fourteenth century, the use of the cannon was well established. In the mid–fourteenth century, forged iron cannons weighed as much as 600 pounds. Within a century's time, they were cast in a mold, a process made possible by the rise in blast furnace temperatures. Such artillery had a significant impact on warfare, for example, making obsolete traditional medieval fortified towns and castles.

CHANGES IN AGRICULTURAL TECHNOLOGY: THE HORSE, THE PLOW, AND THE THREE-FIELD SYSTEM

Several significant technological changes also contributed to increased agricultural productivity across Europe. These changes were irregularly adopted and by no means uniform in their impact; however, taken together they served to instigate widespread increases in levels of field cultivation and crop production. Both domesticated horses and the plow had been known from Roman times; their combined use greatly altered agricultural methods. Using the increasingly available supplies of iron, horseshoes were employed to protect the hoofs and thus to make the horse more useful. The horse-drawn plow was nearly twice as fast and could work for more hours than that drawn by oxen or humans. Horse-drawn plows were employed to dig more deeply in the heavy soils of much of Europe and enabled the traditional long narrow strips of arable land characteristic of manorial production to be combined into larger fields producing greater yields. The account books of some estates recorded yields that doubled or tripled during selected years of the fourteenth century.

The growth of trade in textiles, resulting in part from entrepreneurial production, also encouraged changes in the management of agricultural systems. Sheep raised for their wool were wise investments. For example, the farmer Thierry d'Hireçon at Roquetoire, France, in 1320 purchased 160 sheep and fleeced and sold them and their wool the following year. His

FIGURE 11.4 Ploughing, from the Heures de la Bienheureuse Vierge Marie, fourteenth-century Miniature.

The harnessing of animals (horses in northern Europe; oxen and mules in southern Europe) to plows greatly facilitated expansion of arable acreage and increased the yields of grain.

SOURCE: Bulloz.

total profit was about 100 percent of his investment. From field to city market stall, the capitalist revolution was under way.

CITIES AND COMMERCE IN WESTERN EUROPE

The commercial revolution made its most powerful impact in cities. Between 1200 and 1400, many of the towns and cities of central and western Europe were established. As early as the eleventh century in France and Flanders, townspeople were called bourgeoisie or burghers and noted as different from other medieval ranks such as nobles, peasants, or clergy. Personal freedom from the restraints and obligations of feudal and manorial society was fundamental to burghers. To engage in trade, they had to be free to come and go as they pleased. As was true of peasants, many of the earliest townspeople were bound by contractual ties to aristocratic landlords (including kings). Their occupations, however, connected with trade and travel, made freedom essential: no individual whose status was defined by personal bondage could succeed as a merchant. Gradually, as trade prospered and towns grew, the bourgeoisie were able to gain varying degrees of freedom and independence from their overlords in return for sharing their commercial profits and prosperity with them.

Guilds in City Life As they gained control of their own affairs, townspeople protected their independence by developing and relying on their own institutions. Merchant associations, or guilds, played an important role in town life. Initially, they served as a shadow government to the rule of a bishop or a landlord, but in time they gained independent control of municipal affairs. Central to the urban economy, merchant guilds persistently took over the management of town affairs. As the fundamental urban institution, they could ensure that all who lived in the town, artisan or merchant, master craftsman or apprentice, were free: any person became free who could prove residence in a town for a year and a day. The officers of the merchant guilds constituted the de facto city officials; they made up the courts of law, carried out police functions, and regulated urban economic activities. Wealth began to reflect a person's occupation, though social distinctions dependent on birth were not abolished.

THE HANSEATIC LEAGUE

As early as the fourteenth century, north German trading towns formed the Hanseatic League to improve their trading position in the Baltic and North Seas and to increase their profits. At its peak, nearly 100 cities belonged to the Hansa (as the league was known), which enjoyed a monopoly on Baltic and North Sea trade comparable to the Italian control of trade with the eastern Mediterranean. Hanseatic ships supplied the rest of Europe with Baltic fish, furs, timber, and metals; they also controlled the lucrative transport of wool from England to the manufactories of Flanders. The Hansa had outposts in Russia, Scandinavia, England, and Italy. The League, like the Italian cities, suffered from the sixteenth-century shift of trade routes westward, which opened opportunities that Atlantic-facing Holland and England rapidly took advantage of.

THE PRICE REVOLUTION: CRISIS AND EQUILIBRIUM

Currency based on the value of gold and silver began to link together the trading partners of European cities and countryside in new ways, but in the fourteenth and fifteenth centuries it also made Europeans vulnerable to the effects of price fluctuations. The mid-fourteenth century began a troubled period in Europe, the result of such things as the Black Death and the Hundred Years War (ca. 1327–1453), a conflict fought between the French and the British over control of French territory. With populations in some areas decimated and large areas of France reduced to anarchy by uncontrolled mercenaries and bands of vagabonds, political stability and economic productivity were in disarray.

The economic stability of Europe was further troubled by an unfavorable balance of trade with the Byzantine Empire and West Asia. The demand for Asian products remained such that European precious metals were drained eastward and, during a time when imports of African gold declined and central European silver production was disrupted, a severe shortage of money occurred. The progress of economic development was slowed and by the late fourteenth century, a crisis had been reached: poverty, hunger, and misery aggravated material and social inequities in Europe and revolts of peasants and urban workers became widespread.

At the conclusion of this dark era after the mid-fifteenth century, when order was restored, industry and trade revived and towns continued to grow in size and importance. Craftsmanship and merchandising supported a way of life that was rich in variety and grew increasingly independent of both religious and secular authority. By the fifteenth and sixteenth centuries, positive changes were visible in the towns of Europe. Planners rebuilt parts of them, replacing crooked streets and irregular plazas with straight streets and open squares. In new or renovated parts of cities, medieval complexity gave way to openness and regularity.

CHANGES IN PRODUCTION AND LABOR PRACTICES

The commercial revolution was accompanied by changes in the technology and methods of industrial production. Advances in industrial development were largely confined to a few crafts and on the whole were not dependent on power-driven machinery. Manufacturing continued to be done by hand, although hand tools became more efficient and ingenious. Power-driven machines operated by water, wind, or draft animals remained primarily in an experimental stage. Development tended to be confined to improved methods of production. There was increased standardization of production to increase the output of some articles and a division and specialization of labor. This led to an ordering and ranking of the labor force: supervisors, the aristocracy of labor, who maintained discipline and saw to productivity, exercised dominance over ordinary workers, who were expected only to submit to direction and produce proficiently in return for wages.

These changes were common to the entrepreneurial domestic system of production, but medieval guild master craftsmen also began to use their profits to finance economic ventures, providing the capital investment for merchant fleets, industrial machinery, and processes necessary for expanding production. Economic growth and the ambitions of enterprising individuals had inaugurated the process of transformation in Italy; and Italian cities set the pattern for satisfying Europe's market demand by undertaking production of their own luxury products as well as importing those of the east. North of the Alps, too, expansion of trade stimulated industry, especially textiles, metallurgy, and shipbuilding. International business connections were made: for example, by 1300, towns in Flanders, relying increasingly on imported wool, had developed weaving into big business that employed many workers and made large profits.

EUROPEAN ENTREPRENEURS: MERCHANT PRINCES

The role of individual entrepreneurs in the creation of urban capitalism can be seen in the careers of the Medici family of Florence, the French trader Jacques Coeur, and the German Fuggers. In northern Europe, as in Italy, the lives of entrepreneurs illustrate the opportunities that arose during the commercial revolution. These opportunities enriched both individuals and their families for generations.

The Medicis   The Medici name appears earliest in the chronicles of Florence in the twelfth century, but the first distinctive Medici was Salvestro, who, though newly ennobled, gained popular favor by taking an active role in support of the Florentine wool carders during their 1378 revolt to improve working conditions. Though the revolt was stillborn, Salvestro's participation established a pattern for his family, who continued to champion workers' causes, with the ultimate result of greatly increasing the Medicis' importance and power. The family also concentrated on making a fortune, which was equally basic to Medici power. From wool carding they turned to trade, and from trade to money lending. Giovanni de' Medici (1360–1429) established banks in Italy and abroad. In the hands of his successors these became efficient generators of the wealth on which Medici political power was founded.

As they grew rich, the Medici did not abandon their support for the less fortunate. Political demagoguery and the policy of making liberal loans to anyone who needed them were two foundations of Medici prominence. Giovanni's son Cosimo (1389–1464) first gained the absolute sway over Florence that the family was to hold for several generations. By grateful Florentines he was termed *pater patriae,* "father of his country," and he established the family habit of patronizing arts and artists. Cosimo's immediate descendants, notably his grandson

FIGURE 11.5 Benozzo Gozzoli, Detail from the *Procession of the Magi* Showing Members of the Medici Family.

Renaissance artists frequently placed secular patrons in religious paintings.

SOURCE: Alinari/Art Resource, NY.

Lorenzo the Magnificent (1449–1492), carried this policy to an unrivaled peak as both patron and participant. Two of Cosimo's later descendants became popes, and descendants of his younger brother, Lorenzo, became sixteenth-century grand dukes of Tuscany and, at two different times, queens of France. The widely influential Medici family was a particularly successful example of the merchant plutocracy that rose to economic and political prominence during the commercial revolution.

Jacques Coeur In France, Jacques Coeur, born about 1395 into the family of a local merchant in Bourges, became the founder of lucrative trade in the Levant. In a few years' time, he had personally amassed a tremendous fortune by many different means and placed his country in a position to contend successfully with the prosperous and powerful trading republics of Italy. Coeur—broker, banker, trader, farmer—dealt in everything. By initiative and speculation, he took advantage of an expanding market to become the wealthiest man in France, owning fleets and mines there and abroad, factories in many cities, vast amounts of land, and a house in Bourges that was of exceptional magnificence and remains one of the finest monuments of its time. In 1436, King Charles VII (r. 1422–1461) summoned him to Paris in 1436, from whence he operated mines and minted money that helped finance the reconquest of Normandy. He was too rich and successful to escape envy and jealousy, and in the end his career took on the quality of a cautionary tale. Charles VII coveted Coeur's wealth, condemned him to prison and then banished him, taking over all his goods and possessions.

The Fuggers The fortune of the house of Fugger, the most famous merchant princes of western Europe, originated in Augsburg and was based on weaving and trade in
spices. Fugger wealth was enhanced by marriage and by their growing political importance in
Augsburg. By the end of the fifteenth century, the family had built a business that was famous around the world. Jakob Fugger (1454–1525) and his three sons, men of great resource
and industry, added conspicuously to Fugger wealth. The Fuggers began to act as bankers for
the imperial house of Hapsburg, developed silver mines in the Tyrol and copper mines in
Hungary, and traded in spices, woolens, and silks all over Europe. They made large loans to
the Hapsburgs, who rewarded them with titles, lands, and privileges. One of them built a
castle in the Tyrol, and in Augsburg they built the Fuggerei, a settlement of 106 low-rent
dwellings for poor Catholics. They were also collectors and patrons of art and literature.

BUSINESS AND COMMERCIAL TECHNOLOGY

The extent and complexity of business and finance as they evolved during the early period of
capitalism required a variety of technological and institutional innovations to aid the new
economic activities. The invention of new writing materials connected with business needs
were among these innovations.

**Paper Technology
and Production** Although the techniques for producing paper from soaked, pressed, and
polished plant fibers had already been invented in China more than a millennium earlier, the most common everyday writing surfaces for business

FIGURE 11.6 Jakob Fugger and His Accountant,
German Engraving of the Sixteenth
Century.

Names on the dossiers are those of the great trading
centers of Europe when the Augsburg Firm was the
biggest in the world.

SOURCE: Photo © Armand Colin, Paris.

or government were cloth (in East and South Asia) and flattened, glued, and scrolled papyrus (in West Asia, Africa, and Europe). The old Greek and Roman preference for cumbersome wood planks covered with wax still continued, and the wealthy used vellum, thinly stretched lambskin. By the seventh century, paper was common in China, and from there it spread to other parts of East Asia at about the same time Arab armies encountered it in Central Asia. Under Arab patronage, Samarkand became a major producer of paper made of flax and hemp. Within a hundred years, this kind of paper had become the standard medium in West Asia and Africa, and by the eleventh century Muslin Spain and Sicily had become major paper manufacturers. A reviving western European economy picked it up at this point, and by 1300 there were several paper producers in France and Italy.

Commercial Paper By the fifteenth century, paper was in general use, and it was of particular importance to the commercial world. Paper was a major component of the creation of business arrangements and practices associated with growth and profit that came into use about the time that paper became commonly available. The term "commercial paper," which remains in use today as a business term, was applied to contracts and legal arrangements and documents of financial exchange. "Commercial paper" took the form of bills of exchange and included bookkeeping and inventories.

The Development of Financial Institutions The expansion of trading and manufacturing enterprises not only led to increased profits but also required steady supplies of money. Accordingly, the growth of financial institutions paralleled those of industry and trade. For example, the Medicis, by using the profits of their woolen trade and industry, became first moneylenders and then, by taking advantage of an expanding economy, its needs, and its profits, major international bankers. Those who profited were those who were willing and able to invest, which meant taking the risk of loss as well as increased profit. The management of the financial transition to capitalism became the task of bankers, who became large-scale moneylenders, money changers, and money transferers of international scope. Money made money: interest rates were high, thanks to both demand and the risks of lending, rising so high (to 266 percent) in Florence that in 1420 the city government sought to impose a limit of 20 percent. Businessmen needed money to finance expansion; kings and popes needed money to wage wars and to maintain their power and prestige. The risks involved in moneylending provided an excuse for forgetting the medieval Church's injunctions against usury. Indeed, the Church itself was willing to pay interest.

Banking Banking required expertise. It was necessary but not easy to agree upon the relative values of the unbridled proliferation of coins in circulation in Europe; minted by every form of polity, they varied widely in reliability. Bankers were also necessary to facilitate the transfer of money for both domestic and international trade. Medieval money changers in time became bankers who developed the skill and knowledge to create international credit networks. Among the earliest bankers were the crusading Knights Templars, who abandoned the crusades for banking, following the end of the "Lombard bankers" of Italy. Indeed, by 1300 Florence became the banking capital of Europe and the florin, the coinage of that city, became an international currency of the day. Successful banks and wealthy bankers appeared elsewhere as well; by the beginning of the fifteenth century, they were to be found from Spain to England.

SOURCE: © by British Museum. Add ms. 27695, f.8.

FIGURE 11.7 An Italian Bank in the Late Fourteenth Century.

In Italy banks, expediting business and trade, arose out of the services that merchant companies performed for one another. The top frame of this illustration shows the strong room of a banking house where coins are counted out on a desk; the bottom frame illustrates depositing and transfering money.

Business Organizations Ways of pooling resources for mutual economic benefit were devised. Partnerships were formed for specific ventures, in which capital would be furnished for a given enterprise in return for a specific share of profits. Eventually, permanent companies were formed, in which investors made deposits and from which they received regular dividends.

Joint-Stock Companies Probably the most efficient kind of business organization was the widely used joint-stock company, the members of which pooled their resources, selected managers, and shared profits in proportion to the amount of the stock owned. The joint-stock company had the advantage of remaining intact even though the stock of any member could be bought or sold. Equally important was the development of credit services and systems specifically provided by banks. Bills of exchange became available, much like the paper money and credit institutions and practices that were developed in China as part of the commercial revolution of the Song. These innovations, all of which were in use in Europe by the sixteenth century, were essential stimulants to economic growth there and aided the expansion of Europe beyond the continent.

■

THE THIRTEENTH-CENTURY AFRO-ASIAN WORLD SYSTEM

As the Crusades had begun the process of integrating Europe into the thirteenth-century world system, the Mongol conquest of Eurasia brought changes in trading routes and commercial relations that profoundly transformed the structures of economic exchange throughout the Afro-Asian world and affected both the European and Chinese economies at the most

The Eight Circuits of the Thirteenth–Century World System

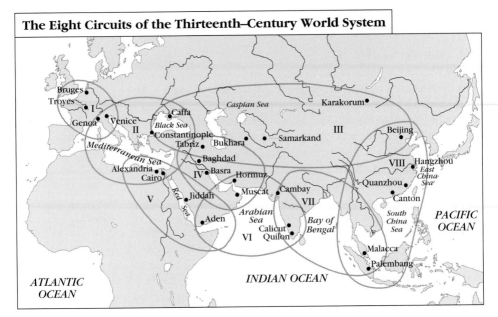

MAP 11.3 The Thirteenth-Century World System, from Europe, the Mediterranean, and Africa to China and Southeast Asia.

SOURCE: Janet Abu-Lughod, *Before European Hegemony: The World System*, A.D. *1250–1350* (New York: Oxford University Press, 1989), p. 34.

distant western and eastern frontiers of the thirteenth-century world system. The center of this world system was the land bridge at the eastern end of the Mediterranean that commanded three routes of access to Asia.

The northernmost route led from the Byzantine capital of Constantinople, which controlled access between the Mediterranean and the Black Sea, to the overland caravan route across Central Asia. The other two more southerly routes connecting the Mediterranean with the Indian Ocean were overland from the eastern Mediterranean coastline of Palestine through the Muslim city of Baghdad to the port of Basra on the Persian Gulf into the Arabian Sea and thence the Indian Ocean; and from the Muslim city of Cairo and its Mediterranean port, Alexandria, through the Red Sea to the Arabian Sea and the Indian Ocean.

The Red Sea was more difficult to navigate than the Persian Gulf, so the easier route was through Baghdad and Basra; but political changes in Persia and Iraq due to the Mongol conquest made the route through Cairo the favored one. The overland caravan route across Central Asia, which incorporated the ancient Silk Road, was also subject to fluctuation in its importance as a conduit of trade between Europe and Asia because of changes brought about by political and military conflicts in the region. Although the *pax Mongolica,* the "Mongolian peace," inaugurated by the creation of the Mongol Empire in the thirteenth century, stabilized conditions along the Silk Road and brought a degree of security for merchants transporting goods across Central Asia, conflicts generated by the collapse of the Mongol Empire in the fourteenth century resulted in a greatly reduced role of the Silk Road as a viable conduit for trade.

THIRTEENTH-CENTURY POLITICAL CHANGES IN THE AFRO-ASIAN WORLD

In the thirteenth century, the heartland through which all three routes from Europe to Asia had to pass was the center of conflicts between European Christian Crusaders and Muslims; at the same time, this region was coming under attack from Mongol forces as they moved westward. Chinggis Khan's empire was subsequently divided among his heirs: his grandson Batu was left in charge of the Russian and eastern European region; his son Chaghatai took Iraq and Persia, plus other areas of the Muslim world; and Ogodei succeeded Chinggis as the great khan. After Ogodei's death and the election of a new khan, Mongke in 1251, the Mongols concentrated their attacks on the Muslim world. By 1260, all of Central Asia and parts of West Asia were under Mongol control.

The Decline of Baghdad Mongke's brother Hulegu conquered the city of Baghdad in 1258 and established the Il-Khan Empire in Persia and Iraq with its new capital at Tabriz in Persia. Baghdad, which had been established in 750 as the capital of the Islamic Abbasid Empire and the home of the *caliph* (regent of the Prophet on earth) was reduced to a secondary city in the Il-Khan Mongol empire. Baghdad's role as the leading city of the Muslim world was overtaken by Cairo, where the caliphate was restored and through which most trade now passed from the Mediterranean to the Indian Ocean.

Mamluk Egypt and the Rise of Cairo The dual threat of the Crusaders and the Mongols led to the creation of the Mamluk (slave-soldier) state that controlled Egypt and Syria, including Palestine, by the 1250s. As their name implies, the Mamluks depended on slaves (generally Turks or Central Asians) they purchased and converted to Islam to staff their army, since free Muslims could not be conscripted into the army. This meant that the Mamluks were also dependent on the Mediterranean slave trade. The Mamluks rose to power as a result of the need to defend Egypt against attacks from the Crusaders. The Mamluks' success in repelling the Crusaders, coupled with the Mongols' conquest of Baghdad, led to the replacement of Baghdad by Cairo as the central city for Eurasian commerce. The less attractive route via Cairo through the Red Sea now became the most important trade link between Europe and Asia. After the Mamluk recapture of the Syrian coastline from the Crusaders in 1291, European merchants operating from the Holy Land were forced northward, and the crucial role in connecting European markets with Egyptian access to the Red Sea and Indian Ocean was taken over by the Italian merchant mariners of Venice and Genoa.

CAIRO: A CENTER OF INTERNATIONAL TRADE

As noted by Ibn Battuta in the fourteenth century, Cairo was a lively, prosperous city. Called by some the "mother [city] of the world," Cairo flourished in the thirteenth, fourteenth, and even early fifteenth centuries, though its population peaked at a half million in the first half of the fourteenth century.

Cairo Geniza Documents Based on information from documents contained in the Cairo Geniza, a repository where Jews placed all papers with writing in them to preserve them in case the name of God was in them and might be destroyed, we know that well before Cairo's elevation to its key role in east-west trade during the thirteenth

FIGURE 11.8 View of the Old Quarter of Cairo, Showing Hospital, Madrasa and Mosque, along with the Mausoleum of a Thirteenth-Century Mamluk Ruler.

SOURCE: Culver.

century, prosperous merchants were part of a vital commercial life in the city. The Cairo Geniza documents record daily transactions that allow modern historians to reconstruct daily life in eleventh- and twelfth-century Cairo, including trade with Spain, North Africa, the Levant (modern Turkey), and India. Although the Geniza was a Jewish repository, the records include information about Muslim and Christian inhabitants of the city as well.

Karimi Merchants *Karim* (meaning "great") was an Arabic term used to distinguish large-scale wholesale merchants from petty entrepreneurs. The Karimi merchants were a very important group in the late thirteenth and early fourteenth centuries, just as Cairo came into its prime in international trade. Karimi merchants monopolized the Indian Ocean spice trade, which by that time was a key element in the Egyptian economy. Although spices were the primary commodities traded by Karimi merchants, cloth, porcelain, precious stones, silk, and slaves (non-Muslims) were among other goods traded. Some Karimi merchants were bankers or shipowners. At their peak in the fourteenth century, there were 200 Karimi merchants in Cairo, nearly all of whom were Muslims, with perhaps a few Jews. Although we cannot be certain, the Karimi may have been organized into an association somewhat like a European guild.

Commenda Partnership Like their counterparts in Italian city-states such as Venice and Genoa, Karimi merchants formed partnerships for one overseas venture at a time in which one partner put up two-thirds of the capital and the other contributed the remaining one-third, plus the labor to accompany the goods abroad. Profits were equally shared, once the transport and other costs of the venture were subtracted. This kind of partnership was known in Venice and Genoa as a *commenda* and was widely used by merchants there, but its origins lay among the Karimi merchants in Egypt and the *commenda* drew upon Islamic law and custom for its structuring of commercial relations. Unlike Christianity in Europe and Confucianism in East Asia, Islam erected no barriers to commerce and placed no negative ideological restraints on the prosperity of merchant enterprise.

THE SAHARAN CARAVAN TRADE

The trans-Saharan gold trade predated the North African expansion of Islam in the seventh century C.E. More than seven centuries later, gold was still being loaded and carried on the backs of camels along the centuries-old routes that crossed the great desert. Once the camel and wheeled vehicles were adopted along the trans-Saharan caravan routes in Roman times, the patterns of commercial growth remained technologically stable until the introduction of firearms and horseback cavalries in the sixteenth century. The desert routes rarely changed course since they relied on the navigational abilities of African merchant families familiar

DAILY LIVES

MERCHANTS AND THEIR FAMILIES IN MEDIEVAL CAIRO

Merchants who resided in Cairo often had to leave on long journeys to buy or sell goods throughout the Mediterranean and North Africa. What of their families who were left behind? Since the journeys were dangerous and unpredictable in length due to the vagaries of both weather and politics, merchants had to make some attempt to provide for their families in their absence. Numerous letters in the Geniza records attest to the problems that could arise when the return of a merchant head of household was delayed, when friends reneged on promises to look after the needs of the merchant's family, or simply when business was bad and there was no profit forthcoming. The following letter describing dire circumstances at home was written by a boy, proficient (as were most sons of merchants) in both Hebrew and Arabic scripts, and was probably dictated by his mother. Though the letter was obviously not sent (since it ended up in the Geniza), it undoubtedly served as the draft of a letter that was sent to the father, who was in North Africa:

In Your name, oh All Merciful!
The letters of the Presence of my illustrious lord, my father, have arrived—May God make me his ransom from all evil and give him success and unite me with him in His kindness and mercy, if God will.

As to what you wish to know my lord: We [meaning, "I, your wife," plural of modesty, still used in Arabic speech] are in great distress, owing to bad health and loneliness. We have weaned the baby—do not ask me what we suffer from him: trouble, crying, sleepless nights, so much so that the neighbors—God is my witness—are complaining. We incur great expenses for him: the doctor, medicaments, and two chickens every day. We have sold the levers, the "swords," and the cupboard, and have let the upper floor; the proceeds, however, are really not sufficient for the baby's expenses; and for what we also need. After all this, I hope [here the wife becomes informal], he will remain alive—God is my witness, you would be happy to look at him. By God, do not tarry any longer. My eyes are lifted upon God, the exalted, and upon your return.

The dinars, sent by you from the West, have arrived, but nothing was given to us. Do not forget the beads for Zayn al-Dahr [the "Ornament of the House," the writer of the letter], do not forget the maidservant. I [the boy speaks] kiss your hands, and so does my mother, my grandmother, my maternal aunts, the wife of my paternal uncle, and everyone in the house. It happened that both you and the "elder" [grandfather] departed simultaneously, so that we remained like orphans without a man.

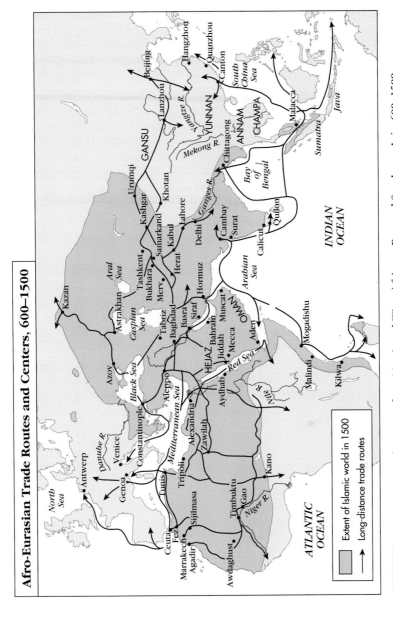

Afro-Eurasian Trade Routes and Centers, 600–1500

Extent of Islamic world in 1500
Long-distance trade routes

MAP 11.4 Trade Routes and Centers, from North and West Africa to East and Southeast Asia, 600–1500.

SOURCE: Robinson, *Cambridge Illustrated History of the Islamic World*, p. 126.

with the location of oases. The incorporation of early trade routes into the larger Islamic world commercial network occurred gradually and mostly peacefully as Muslim merchant-clerics traveled afar engaged in trade and pilgrimage. There is no doubt that the increasing Islamization of West African societies furthered their participation in the land-based commercial world that stretched from the Atlantic to the Indian Ocean and beyond.

As essential as the trans-Saharan caravans were in the trading system of North and West Africa, caravans organized for the profit of North African merchants were only temporary associations of firms that happened to be bringing goods across the desert at the same time. Individual firms, not the caravans themselves, were the organizational core of the trans-Saharan caravan trade and these firms were joined together in the caravan enterprise by both formal and informal bonds. Islamic law provided the basis for drawing up written agreements of partnership in trading ventures or credit advances between independent merchants.

The trans-Saharan caravan trade was protected from European oceanic competition by the natural barrier of the West African forest which had to be penetrated by seafaring traders to reach the inland sources of gold. Wherever caravans competed directly with European shipping, they lost out and found their trading position considerably diminished. But in trade between North Africa and the Sudan, caravan enterprise benefited from the fact that the alternative was not maritime transport but rather overland carriage through the West African forest, where disease affected pack animals and made transport costs too high.

Begho and the Gold Trade The trading city of Begho on the edge of the West African forest was strategically situated as an entrepôt for the Akan goldfields, shipping gold north to the Mande world and beyond through the trans-Saharan caravan routes interconnecting the Mediterranean and Islamic worlds. At its height (thirteenth-sixteenth centuries), Begho probably included some 15,000 people, including merchants from a vast number of cultural regions. Different language groups resided in distinct quarters of the town. Artisans lived and worked in a separate quarter, where they cast brass and bronze in crucibles, worked iron, steel, and ivory, and wove and dyed cotton cloth prized as far away as the Atlantic coast.

At Begho and other gold-trading cities, gold merchants used clay and brass gold weights, weight placed on counterbalance scales and in varying shapes and sizes were used to weigh gold dust and nuggets. These weights conformed to an Islamic ounce system used in North Africa and across the western Sudan as early as the ninth century. The heaviest of the Islamic standards, the ounce of 31.5 grams, became known as the troy ounce in Europe. Gold traders traveled under the charge of a chief trader and often in large groups as a protection against thieves. As the African-European coastal trade got under way, customary practices included rituals such as the giving of a _dash,_ or gift, as a sign of goodwill prior to trading, as well as precautions to avoid cheating, counterfeiting, and fraud. At the height of the trade in the seventeenth century, about 42,000 ounces of gold were exported annually from the Akan goldfields alone. It is little wonder that such wealth attracted the attention of traders as well as thieves around the world.

Commodities of Trade Gold was not all that was mined and traded in West and North Africa. Salt was mined at Taghaza and other towns that became trading entrepôts in the Sahara. Silver, copper, and copper alloys found their way from the Harz Mountains of eastern Europe to the foundries of West Africa. So-called Moroccan leather, actually manufactured in Nigeria, was regularly traded to the markets and fairs of Britain and

FIGURE 11.9 Gold Merchants of Timbuktu.

Gold was weighed on balance scales using counterweights of known value.

SOURCE: *Timbuktu the Mysterious,* by Felix Dubois, 1897. General Research Division, New York Public Library, Astor, Lenox, and Tilden Foundations.

Normandy. Foodstuffs and animal products also traversed the ecological boundaries from forest to grassland to desert.

CARAVANS AND COMMERCE IN CENTRAL ASIA

On the Asian continent, the Central Asian caravan trade linked Europe and Asia from as early as the second century B.C.E. and flourished from then until around the year 1000. The growth of nomadic empires on the northern borders of China in the tenth and eleventh centuries disrupted the Central Asian caravan trade because of warfare between these rising empires and established Central Asian kingdoms as well as China. Caravan trade was restored with the unification of the Eurasian world under the Mongols in the thirteenth century. The collapse of the Mongol Empire brought changes to Central Asia as it had to West Asia and North Africa.

Tamerlane Claiming descent from Chinggis Khan through his son Chaghatai, Timur the Lame (known as Tamerlane in Europe) was born near the Central Asian oasis city of Samarkand. As disorder grew throughout the Mongol Empire in the 1350s, Tamerlane rose as a leader in uprisings in 1357, and by 1370 he was powerful enough to proclaim himself sovereign and restorer of the Mongol Empire. Though his exploits fell far short of his goal of restoring the Mongol Empire, he succeeded in acquiring a reputation for terror among his adversaries and did conquer a vast amount of territory stretching from Central to West and South Asia, where he sacked the capital of the Delhi sultanate in 1398.

Samarkand and the Central Asian Caravan Trade

Under Tamerlane, who made it his capital, the city of Samarkand became the most important economic and cultural center of Central Asia. Tamerlane assembled artists and craftsmen who produced goods for a luxurious court life. Situated at the crossroads between an east-west lateral route and a north-south highway between India and Russia, Samarkand was one of the most ancient cities of Central Asia and had played a major role in the caravan trade that traversed this region for more than a thousand years. Conquered by Alexander the Great in 329 B.C.E., Samarkand had been ruled successively by Turks, Arabs, and Persians and was conquered again by Chinggis Khan in 1220.

A description of Samarkand by a disciple of the Chinese Daoist Changchun, who was summoned in 1219 by Chinggis Khan to give him religious instruction, has been recorded as part of a work called *Xiyouji* ("Record of a Journey to the West"), written in 1228. This account portrays Samarkand as a garden-filled city surrounded by three concentric walls: an outer wall with twelve wooden gates, enclosing a second wall around the city itself, and an inner walled area that enclosed the main mosque and the walled citadel containing the ruler's palace.

Samarkand, like other oasis cities such as Bukhara, Tabriz, or Turfan to the northwest of China, were essential to the caravan trade across Central Asia that connected China to West Asia and Europe. They provided necessary stopping places for water and provisions for the great caravans that traversed the deserts and steppes of Central Asia. But after the collapse of Mongol rule and the stability the Mongol Empire had restored to the Central Asian caravan routes, notwithstanding Tamerlane's efforts to rebuild the empire, the Central Asian caravan trade gradually declined. A fundamental link in the Afro-Asian world system was lost as China's position linking overland trade to the Indian Ocean routes was eliminated.

THE INDIAN OCEAN WORLD

There were three interlocking circuits of trade in the Indian Ocean: the Arabian Sea; the Indian Ocean; and the South China Sea. The first was dominated by Muslims, the second included Muslim merchants from East Africa and Hindus from South and Southeast Asia, and the third was dominated by Chinese. No single state, culture, or ethnic group dominated Indian Ocean trade as a whole; rather, it was a multiethnic world where Arab merchants resided in Chinese ports, East African merchants in Indian ports, and Indian merchants in East African and Chinese ports. Both goods and ideas were exchanged in these encounters among merchants, and the monsoon winds determined when trade took place and how it was configured.

The Indian Subcontinent

Three key areas on the subcontinent engaged in Indian Ocean trade: the Gujarat peninsula, the Malabar coast on the west, and the Coromandel coast on the east. Ibn Battuta praised the beautiful architecture of the city of Cambay, the major port of Gujarat, constructed by foreign merchants, who made up the majority of its inhabitants. Gujarati merchants played an important role in international shipping and commerce and were prominent in East African port cities as well. Far south of Cambay, along the Malabar coast, the city of Calicut was a commercial complex where Gujarati and Jewish merchants engaged in trade. Calicut rose in the mid–thirteenth century, when

Baghdad fell and the Persian Gulf was eclipsed in importance as a trade route when the Karimi of Cairo took over the spice trade from the Indian Ocean.

From the eleventh through thirteenth centuries, the Chola state at the southern tip of the subcontinent, including the island of Ceylon (modern Sri Lanka), supported commercial organizations of Tamil traders, the dominant ethnic group in that region of the subcontinent. Even in pre-Chola times, trading towns called *nagarams* were established in each administrative district of the region; this term was later used to refer to assemblies of merchants. Traders were given relative freedom to engage in commerce as long as they transmitted taxes to political authorities. By the late twelfth century, international traders were visiting ports on the Coromandel coast, trading in goods such as pearls, betel nuts, spices, and cotton products. The city of Kanchipuram along the Coromandel coast was a center of cotton production and weaving and attracted traders from all over the Indian Ocean world.

Political Changes in the 1350s In both north and south, political events in the mid–fourteenth century brought about changes that reduced the importance of trade and the roles both regions played in the world system. The Muslim Delhi sultanate, which had unified the north in the thirteenth century, began to decline in the mid–fourteenth century, and its capital, Delhi, was sacked by Tamerlane in 1398. In the south, the new Hindu state of Vijayanagar ("abode of victory") conquered small Muslim sultanates along the Coromandel coast and inaugurated a new system of military feudalism in which soldiers gained the right to extract surpluses from both land and trade. Unlike either their Chola predecessors, who supported commercial associations, or the small Muslim sultanates, which encouraged trade, the rulers of Vijayanagar concentrated on the consolidation of their power through control of a network of Hindu temples, leaving trade in the hands of Muslim merchants from the Malabar coast.

SOUTHEAST ASIA: THE "LAND BELOW THE WINDS"

Islam spread from South into Southeast Asia beginning in the fifteenth century, and there it blended with the earlier dominant Hindu and Buddhist influences. The most important common element uniting the diverse cultures, societies, and polities of Southeast Asia was not religion, however, but maritime commerce. Although Islam was carried by Arab sea traders to southeast Asia, they were traders, not missionaries, and commercial activities clearly took precedence over proselytizing religion. Prior to the Islamization of Southeast Asia, both Chinese and Indian influences had also reached this region by maritime trade, not by conquest or colonization. This part of the world was known to its inhabitants—and to outsiders who plied the waters of the Indian Ocean for trade—as the "Land below the Winds" because of the seasonal monsoons that carried shipping to it across the Indian Ocean. Both mainland and island Southeast Asia were dependent on this oceanborne trade, and certain port cities, such as Malacca on the Malaysian peninsula, existed solely as a result of maritime commerce in the Indian Ocean.

Founded in 1401, Malacca developed during the fifteenth century into a wealthy entrepôt (point of exchange or distribution), with a rapidly expanding volume of trade flowing through its strategically located port from north to south and south to north, through the narrow Strait of Malacca. Indian, Arab, and Persian traders set up their trading headquarters at Malacca, and the Malay language became the principal language of trade throughout Southeast Asia. Indian cotton was one of the main goods that passed through the port of Malacca, where it was traded for East Indian spices destined for the European market. Malacca flourished for a century before being overtaken by the intrusion of Europeans. Before its demise as an independent city-state and its incorporation into European trading networks after 1500, Malacca represented the importance of the maritime trading links that shaped the history of this region of the world to such an extent that the fifteenth century began in Southeast Asia what can be called the "age of commerce."

THE TRADING WORLD OF EAST AFRICA

From the perspective of Asian traders, East Africa was situated on the periphery of the Indian Ocean world. From the vastly different vantage point of East African merchants, the East African coast was the commercial center of an international network connecting the interior African producers of iron, charcoal, textiles, gold, ivory and slaves with their counterpart Asian maritime markets in India and beyond to China. Trading from coastal cities and island city-states, East African merchants developed far-flung cultural and economic ties. For example, archaeological finds at the twelfth-century site of Great Zimbabwe reveal commercial activities connected gold producers in the lower Zambezi with Chinese manufacturers of porcelain.

Since Greek and Roman times, East African dhows, or sailing ships, had plied coastal waters, taking advantage of the seasonal trade winds. Arab interlopers from Oman on the Arabian peninsula and the Shiraz in the Persian Gulf had increasingly been attracted to the East African coastal trade. Their presence and eventual absorption after the spread of Islam in

FIGURE 11.10 **Dhows, East African Sailing Vessel**

Maritime trade in the Red Sea and Indian Ocean has relied on seasonal winds for the past two millennia.

SOURCE: George Holton, Photo Researchers.

the late first millennium is witnessed by the large number of Arabic borrowings found in the Bantu language of Swahili by the mid–twelfth century. Swahili became the language and culture of the coastal towns and offshore islands, from Mogadishu in Somalia to Sofala in Mozambique. Swahili culture developed out of the cosmopolitan character of urban, coastal life.

Zanzibar The island town of Zanzibar was one of the oldest and most enduring city-states that flourished on the East African coast. Its coastal contact with East Asia may have dated from as early as the ninth to twelfth centuries. Chinese sources of that period describe pastoralists with sheep and cattle. By the fifteenth century, Zanzibar's orientation was toward its marine resources. The city-state was minting its own coinage and trading with the Persian Gulf and beyond. Other sites such as Gedi, with its coral palaces and marketplaces, quickly emerged as trading centers and then were abandoned when inland markets shifted.

Kilwa In 1331, Ibn Battuta, having traveled from the Mediterranean to West Africa and from Cairo to China, described the port of Kilwa on the East African coast as "elegantly built." For him, the great stone-built city was one of the most beautiful and well-constructed urban centers of the fourteenth-century Afro-Asian world. It was a place of great opulence, with a class-structured society and intensive commercialization. Its inhabitants enjoyed indoor plumbing, wore garments of silk and cotton and jewelry of gold and silver; they entertained their guests in sunken courtyards and served them sumptuous meals off imported Chinese porcelain. The Husuni Kubwa palace at Kilwa, with its massive conical, fluted vaults and domes of coral, was the largest single building in Africa at the time of its erection in 1245, containing more than a hundred rooms, as well as courtyards, terraces, and a sunken pool.

The demise of Kilwa was the consequence of its capture and destruction by the Portuguese in 1502. Although the Portuguese arrived in East African waters in the early sixteenth century, hoping to siphon off some of the lucrative gold trade from Zimbabwe east to Sofala on the coast, they never succeeded in doing much more than destroying existing Afro-Arab entrepôts and preventing European competitors from gaining a foothold. Instead, their attention was drawn to the wealth and riches farther to the east.

■

TECHNOLOGY, COMMERCE, AND THE EXPANSION OF EUROPE

Maritime and military technology played major roles in the development and expansion of European power both before and after the fifteenth century. Mediterranean maritime powers, such as Venice, did not adopt navigational innovations such as the compass until around 1000, in part because such innovations were of lesser importance to traffic on an inland sea such as the Mediterranean. From the twelfth century on, however, Venice actively pursued innovations in maritime technology as a means of maintaining dominance of trade in the Mediterranean between Europe and West Asia and enhancing profits. For example, the Venetians developed assembly-line techniques of shipbuilding based on the standardization of ship parts, which were warehoused in strategic ports around the Mediterranean. In this way and others, Venice became a sort of midwife to the transformation of European maritime technology that would enable the opening of the Atlantic frontier.

MARITIME TECHNOLOGY

Progress in improved ship design and construction was irregular and slow, but by the end of the fifteenth century European ships, particularly those used in the Atlantic, attained the essential form they were to keep until the nineteenth century. The basic innovation was in ship construction, which enabled sails, essential for transoceanic commerce, to replace the oars that were suitable to travel on the inland Mediterranean. Improvements included such things as the construction of skeletons that were then covered with wood and pitch and the adoption of the square-rigged mainmast (after 1300); the use of several sails per mast; the transition from one-masted to three-masted ships; and the introduction of the sternpost rudder. Such innovations increased speed, stability, and maneuverability.

By the fifteenth century, improvements in construction resulted in ships of multiple decks and of noticeably increased tonnage. For example, the average tonnage of Portuguese ships doubled between 1450 and 1550. Innovations were not systematically adopted. Mediterranean shippers, for example, were reluctant to abandon old traditions, refusing to recognize the disadvantage of galleys dependent on oarsmen compared to sailing ships, and accordingly they lagged behind. Placing cannons on ships aided Europeans in opening the Atlantic frontier and extending their seapower around the world. Shipbuilders set about improving firepower as well as maneuverability. One innovation, introduced in 1501 and attributed to the French, was cutting portholes on decks below the upper deck so that cannons could be placed on them. This greatly increased ships' firepower.

Navigational Aids Equally important to European maritime progress was the adoption and general use of navigational aids. The magnetic compass, coming from China by way of the Arabs, reached Europe shortly after 1000 and was in general use by Europeans within a matter of decades. The Arabic astrolabe, an instrument used to observe and calculate the position of stars and planets, followed soon after the compass. Navigational charts, the "roadmaps" of maritime travel, facilitated and emboldened open-sea navigation. The first recorded use of a navigational chart by European sailors is in 1270, but it was not until the fifteenth century that the use of such charts was common.

EUROPEAN VOYAGES OF EXPLORATION

Voyages by western and northern European states were inspired by Italian commercial success and made possible by developments in maritime and business technology: the high prices and high profits that accrued to Italians as a result of their Mediterranean monopoly lured ambitious transalpine Europeans to undertake voyages of exploration that sought alternative ways to trade and profit. These voyages were inaugurated by the small Atlantic-facing kingdom of Portugal on the Iberian peninsula.

Prince Henry the Navigator Prince Henry the Navigator (1394–1460), who was in fact no navigator, is nonetheless credited with being the inspiration and enthusiastic patron and organizer of the Portuguese voyages, which were responses to the

FIGURE 11.11 **Prince Henry the Navigator.**
Seventeenth-century English print, showing
navigational instruments, books, troops, and
the fortress of Ceuta on the North African coast.

SOURCE: Corbis-Bettmann.

kingdom's poverty and exclusion from Mediterranean trade. The maritime voyages began, at
least, as a latter-day "crusade." The Portuguese, together with the Spanish, had for centuries
engaged in wars (legitimized as "crusades") to expel Muslims and Jews from the Iberian
peninsula and to reduce the power and influence of both groups in surrounding areas. That
task, during which centralized kingdoms were created in both Portugal and Spain, had been
for all purposes achieved by the fifteenth century.

In 1415, Prince Henry extended the Iberian "crusade" to North Africa, ordering an attack on the city of Ceuta, a Muslim strategic and commercial center. The acquisition of Ceuta
gave the Portuguese access to African trade and became a base for further Portuguese expeditions southward, down the western coast of Africa to the area of the Kongo, a major Central
African kingdom, and on to the Cape of Good Hope, the southernmost point on the African
continent, reached by the Portuguese in 1488. There local groups of Khoikhoi pastoralists,
using indigenous military techniques including having bulls charge into battle, expelled
their Portuguese guests.

From the cape, subsequent expeditions moved northward, attempting to replace centuries-old African and Arab merchant enterprises in port cities along the eastern coast of
Africa. From East Africa, the Portuguese sailed across the Indian Ocean, reaching India in
1498. In their attempt to control the movement of goods, Portugal then built large fleets,
which were used to conquer Aden, Hormuz, Diu, and Malacca, key strategic ports on the established east-west Indian Ocean trade route. Here, as elsewhere, they were successful interlopers in vast and ancient international commercial networks.

In this way, Portugal built a sixteenth-century commercial empire on the seas that, although it fell far short of global monopoly, was enormously profitable. By proving that
Mediterranean trade was not the only way to commercial success, the Portuguese experience

stimulated the eventual shift of European trade and wealth northward and westward to the Atlantic. The Portuguese success showed how profitable a seaborne empire could be, and later fifteenth- and sixteenth-century European explorations sought alternative routes to Asia. Within the half century following the death of Prince Henry, the world had been circumnavigated.

■

COMMERCE AND CHANGE IN THE WEST AFRICAN GOLD TRADE

Even before the maritime expansion of Europe, the international transfer of metals dominated world trade systems. Hungarian silver, West African gold, East African iron, and Asian copper all played a role in the establishment and growth of world commerce. From the time of Charlemagne (ca. 800 C.E.), a standardized European currency or money of account (a system for calculating value for trading purposes) prevailed, based initially on the value of silver and later, by the fifteenth century, on gold.

International Gold Trade Gold was the staple export item of the trans-Saharan caravan networks. Its supply supported the system of international currencies that linked Cairo, West Africa, and Europe. Gold sources attracted the attention of North Africans and Europeans alike. When Leo Africanus, a North African Arab traveler, visited Timbuktu on the Niger River in 1513, he was impressed by the number of shops belonging to merchants and artisans. At the Niger city of Jenne, he found gold and local cloth traded for imported textiles, copper and brass vessels, iron, weapons, spices, and other exotic goods. Many of these goods were sold by weight. Throughout the fifteenth century, Europeans attempted to extend their trading ventures to reach the sources of gold directly. They established fortified bases on islands and coastal locations from which they might continue their search for gold and luxury items. At the island of Arguim off the northwest coast of Africa, a Venetian, Alvise da Cadamosto, witnessed the tight Portuguese control of trade in 1454:

> You should know that the said King of Portugal has leased this island to Christians for ten years, so that no one can enter the bay to trade with the Arabs save those who hold the license. These have dwellings on the island and factories where they buy and sell with said Arabs who come to the coast to trade for merchandise of various kinds, such as woollen cloths, cotton, silver, and "alchezeli" [coarse cloth], that is, cloaks, carpets, and similar articles and above all, corn, for they are always short of food. They give in exchange slaves whom the Arabs bring from the land of the Blacks, and gold dust.

By the 1450s, Portuguese ships exploring the West African coast were trading with Mande-speaking peoples for gold in the regions beyond the Senegambia. In 1471, vessels reached the Gold Coast, where Castilian mariners found Africans willing to trade gold nuggets for European goods. The gold supply was eventually so plentiful on the coast that the Portuguese named the place El Mina, "the Mine," and built a fort on land rented from the local African community.

Merchant Communities The gold traded directly to the early European sailors had been intended for different and more distant destinations accessible by land.

Merchant communities engaged in the trans-Saharan trade were well organized. Among the most successful merchant organizations was that of the Mande speakers, whose system of lodges housed merchants across a vast territory and formed the basis of the political order that resulted in the Mali state in the thirteenth and fourteenth centuries. Mali's successor state, Songrei, was more precarious. Weakened by shifting trade routes and civil unrest, Songrei faced an invasion by Moroccan armies in 1591 that disrupted the security of commercial networks. Songrei controlled salt from Taghaza to Awdaghast, gold from Bambuk, Bure and the Akan goldfields, and Saharan copper mines. Professional traders traveled thousands of miles from one end of the western Sudan to the other and crisscrossed the desert sands that led to other African societies, North Africa, the Mediterranean, and Asia.

Europeans and the Gold Trade The Portuguese capture of Ceuta in the first quarter of the fifteenth century brought one of the terminal points in the trans-Saharan gold trade into European hands. Yet Europeans were still thousands of miles away from the Senegambian gold sources of Bambuk and Bure and the Akan goldfields south of the Sahara that provided the foundation of their currencies, fully two-thirds of the world's gold supply. Although European merchants desired expansion across land to the mines and markets of Africa and Asia, they were effectively blocked by Islamic empires in West Asia and in West and North Africa. This massive Afro-Asian world system deflected European expansion toward the sea routes around the African continent and eventually westward across the Atlantic.

SUMMARY

Economic changes in both China and Europe were on such a large scale that they have been called "revolutionary." As commerce grew in importance, Europeans and Chinese experienced significant changes in the social order, particularly the growth of merchants as a social and economic class. The daily material lives of people were transformed by the expansion of commerce, which brought new goods and products to eat, wear, and use, and by developments in technology, such as printing and metalworking. These changes, however, took shape in different social and cultural settings and produced very different results in Europe and China. After the commercial revolution, which was followed by the Mongol conquest, China turned inward, rejecting the exploration of the rest of the world. In contrast, the combination of commercial growth and technological developments produced in Europe an outward expansion that sought to support and expand commerce through contacts with the rest of the world.

Earlier commercial developments in Europe, the desire for profit and power, and competition among emerging nation-states inspired the voyages of exploration that led to the shift of world trade and wealth—eventually to the Atlantic Ocean. Advances in maritime and commercial technology in Europe were essential to the development of capitalism and the expansion of Europe. Coupled with domestic political, economic, and social conditions that prompted expansion outward, improvements in navigation and shipping enabled western and northern Europeans to establish their preeminence over the world's seas, from the Indian to the Atlantic Oceans. Commerce in South and Southeast Asia, as well as coastal East Africa, was soon dominated by maritime Europe, and the great inland trans-Saharan and Central

Asian caravan routes declined. In East Asia, the effects of Europe's expansion in the fifteenth and sixteenth centuries were felt primarily through the indirect impact of the formation of a world economy that would eventually transform China from an East Asian core to a European periphery. By 1500, Europe was poised to reap, accumulate, and invest the profits of the developing capitalist economy of the new Atlantic frontier as the vital periphery to the expansion of the European core economy.

ENGAGING THE PAST

EUROPE, CHINA, AND SHIFTING WORLD SYSTEMS

The dramatic technological advances and economic growth that took place in China from the eighth through thirteenth centuries, including the "commercial revolution" described in this chapter, may lead one to question why China did not experience an industrial revolution well in advance of Europe. Most of the factors that have been identified as crucial to the industrial revolution in Europe were present in China by the eleventh and twelfth centuries: technological innovation, the expansion of markets, specialization of production, widespread use of money and institutions of credit, and efficient transportation. All of this was interrupted by the Mongol conquest in the mid–thirteenth century, and China's economic and technological development slowed, perhaps even halted, temporarily. Certainly this event had a major impact on the Chinese economy, disrupting not only domestic trade and production but foreign trade as well. The Mongol conquest may have also had more subtle long-term cultural and intellectual influences that were manifested in a xenophobic attitude toward the outside world that contrasted sharply with previous eras of intense engagement with the non-Chinese world, such as the Tang.

In the early fifteenth century, well before the steps were taken that led to the European circumnavigation of the globe, the Chinese government sponsored seven large maritime expeditions with hundreds of ships and tens of thousands of men that reached the distant coastlines of East Africa and the Arabian peninsula. After the last of these expeditions in 1433, no more were sent out, although clearly the Chinese had the navigational technology to undertake voyages of global exploration. Why the Chinese withdrew from such ventures at this point is related to their view of China's centrality and self-sufficiency. China's withdrawal from global exploration on the very eve of European voyages and China's "failure" to experience an industrial revolution before Europe, however, are arguably not the right focus of inquiry. What requires explanation is not why China "failed" to dominate the world through maritime power and an industrial revolution, despite its early commercial and technological advances, but *how* and *why* Europe "succeeded."

Commercial revolutions in both Europe and China need to be understood in the framework of shifting world systems. When the Chinese commercial revolution peaked in the thirteenth century, China was a core economy at the Asian end of the thirteenth-century Afro-Asian world system, one of several cores that stretched from Central to West Asia and North Africa, connected by both overland and maritime trade. Europe was on the periphery of that system, linked by trade through the Mediterranean. By 1500, as a new world system was being created by the expansion of Europe, China was increasingly on the periphery of a world system under the domination of Europe. The new world system that took shape in the sixteenth century was not the end product of a linear progression that culminated in the knitting together of the world through European global expansion but the product of complex historical changes; it should be understood as the most recent in a series of transformations that continually reshaped both the structures of regional economies around the globe and their mutual interactions.

FIGURE 11.12 Terrestrial Globe Made by Martin Behaim, 1492, a Commercial Undertaking for a Consortium of Nuremberg Merchants.

The globe was copiously annotated with inscriptions detailing the commodities and the nature of the business opportunities at various key commercial locations in the world.

SOURCE: Historisches Museum, Berlin/Bildarchiv Preussischer Kulturbesitz.

SUGGESTIONS FOR FURTHER READING

Janet D. Abu-Lughod, *Before European Hegemony: The World System, A.D. 1250–1350* (New York: Oxford University Press, 1989). An ambitious study of the world system that predated the rise of Europe in the sixteenth century.

Fernand Braudel, *Civilization and Capitalism, 15th–18th Century,* vol. 1, *The Structures of Everyday Life;* vol. 2, *The Wheels of Commerce;* vol. 3, *The Perspective of the World* (New York: Harper and Row, 1981–1984). The culminating works of a distinguished historian.

K. N. Chaudhuri, *Asia before Europe: Economy and Civilisation of the Indian Ocean from the Rise of Islam to 1750* (Cambridge: Cambridge University Press, 1990). An economic and cultural survey of the Indian Ocean world in the manner of Braudel's treatment of the Mediterranean.

Mark Elvin, *The Pattern of the Chinese Past:* (Stanford CA: Stanford University, 1973). A provocative argument concerning the commercial revolution of the Song period in China and subsequent developments.

David Hackett Fischer, *The Great Wave: Price Revolutions and the Rhythm of History* (New York, Oxford: Oxford University Press, 1996). A sweeping economic history of capitalism, proposing cycles of change, disequilibrium, and balance between the thirteenth and twentieth centuries.

Shiba Yoshinobu, *Commerce and Society in Sung China.* (Ann Arbor, MI: The University of Michigan Center for Chinese Studies, 1970). A detailed study of both social and economic changes in Sung China based on the close examination of multiple sources, including poetry.

Commerce and Change: The Creation of a Global Economy and the Expansion of Europe

hristopher Columbus, an Italian merchant from Genoa sailing under the aegis of the Spanish court, reached the Caribbean in 1492, some 500 years ago. Columbus wrote in a journal most evenings of that first voyage; although both the original version in the admiral's own hand and a copy were lost, a summary by the Spanish historian Bartolomé de Las Casas (1474–1566), who read the original, did survive. The following entry from Las Casas' journal is dated "Monday 17 December [1492]," a couple of months after Columbus's crew first sighted land, and shows the collaboration of culture and commerce in this early encounter:

> That night the wind blew strongly from the east-north-east. The sea did not get very rough because the island of Tortuga, which is opposite and forms a shelter, protected and guarded it. So he remained there that day. He sent the sailors to fish with nets; the Indians relaxed with the Christians and brought them arrows of the kind from *caniba* or of the *canibales;* and they are made from spikes of cane, and they insert into them little sticks, fired and sharp, and they are very long. Two men showed them [the Christians] that pieces of flesh were missing from their bodies, and gave them to understand that the *canibales* had taken mouthfuls from them. The admiral did not believe it. He again sent some Christians to the town, and in exchange for small glass beads they secured some pieces of gold worked into thin leaf. They saw one man whom the admiral took for governor of that land or a province of it, called *cacique,* with a piece as large as a hand of that sheet of gold, and it seems that he wanted to trade it. He went off to his house and the others remained in the square; and he had small pieces of that sheet made and, bringing one piece at a time, traded for it. When none was left, he said by signs that he had sent for more and that the next day they would bring it. All these things, and the manner of them, and their customs and mildness and behavior show them to be people more alert and intelligent than others they had found up to that time, the admiral says. . . . The admiral said that he did not believe that there were gold mines on Espanola or Tortuga, but that they brought it from *Baneque,* and that they brought little because the people had nothing to give for it. And that land is so rich that there is no need to work hard to get sustenance or clothing, since they go around naked. And the admiral believed that he was very near the source and that Our Lord would show him where the gold comes from. He had information that from there to *Baneque* would take four days, which would be thirty or forty leagues, so that they could get there in one day of good weather.

The "one day of good weather" was not to be: storms resulted in the shipwreck of one of the vessels, the *Santa María,* though the loss did not dampen the Europeans' desires or end their search for wealth across the Atlantic.

FIGURE 12.0 *America the Rich.*

Engraving by G. B. Goetz (c. 1750)\ depicts the arrival of
Columbus (on the left) while indigenous peoples from Africa,
Asia, and the Americas guard the globe in the foreground.

SOURCE: Courtesy of the John Carter Brown Library at Brown University.

■
INTRODUCTION

The effect of Columbus's first and subsequent voyages was to lay the foundations of a new Atlantic economy. For many of the peoples who became part of the new Atlantic connections,
however, the legacy of Columbus has been mourned, not celebrated. Columbus's first voyage
produced little for Europe. He returned to Europe with several indigenous Caribbean inhabitants (Arawaks from the island of San Salvador), cotton samples, an alligator, parrots, woven
hammocks, a wooden canoe, a bundle of tobacco, and a few gold nuggets and trinkets. One of
his ships sank, and its thirty-nine seamen remained behind in the misnamed West Indies, un-
willingly becoming the first European residents of the "New World" since the Vikings. The
Caribbean world in which the sailors found themselves was "new" and "undiscovered" only to
the Europeans however, and their presence was largely destructive to the indigenous inhabitants of the Americas. What was "new" subsequently emerged: a world system interconnecting peoples along the many shores of the Atlantic, from the west coasts of Africa and Europe

to the coasts of North and South America. Despite the meager rewards reaped by the first Europeans, there followed more voyages and many subsequent migrants who forged transatlantic commercial, cultural, and political connections.

The waves of change did not stop in the Atlantic. Following the first circumnavigation of the globe by European mariners in 1519–1522, new constellations of trade and politics were made possible across the Pacific. The new ways of knowing the world acquired through maritime travel interconnected peoples and places in revolutionary ways, though the impact of these connections varied from continent to continent.

■

MERCANTILISM AND THE ATLANTIC WORLD, CA. 1500–1750

The commercial revolution of the thirteenth through the fifteenth centuries and its accompanying technological changes enabled Europe to exploit the resources of the Atlantic world. After 1250, the growth of global commerce enabled those who lived in Europe's cities to acquire wealth and power.

THE IMPACT OF A MONEY ECONOMY

The progress of trade on an international scale, and the expanding use of money that was both necessary to it and a result of it, was a lengthy and inconsistent process which was greatly expedited by the opening up of Atlantic trade in the sixteenth century. The European economy began to be transformed when the self-sufficient feudal-manorial system of services and duties gave way to an urban economy based on money and trade and controlled by merchant-manufacturers. Because these merchant-manufacturers became very wealthy, rulers of city-states and monarchies—and even the pope—would turn to them and to their financiers for the cash wealth they needed to maintain and extend their power. In proportion to the princes' reliance on the wealthy merchant class, the political influence of this urban elite began to replace that of landholding feudal vassals. As their influence grew, the urban wealthy increasingly influenced state politics. What merchant-manufacturers needed and wanted most was freedom from the petty restrictions of a static medieval economy that was communal and largely self-sufficient, and in which production and trade for profit were hampered by such regulations and restraints as tariffs, road duties, and the concepts of a just price and the prohibition of interest (usury). The demands of merchant-manufacturers and bankers to expand their enterprises and increase profits brought them into conflict with the norms of the medieval agrarian and feudal society.

Rulers and Merchants In order to tap the growing wealth of the commercial elite, ambitious rulers increasingly supported their demands for changes in the economy. Use of political power to promote and protect trade was necessary to increase commercial wealth, which would benefit both prince and merchant alike. In his partnership with the urban elite, the ruler could increase his power independent of the constraints of feudal contracts that limited his power and establish a basis for new and unlimited power. In return,

FIGURE 12.1 *The Ambassadors.*

Portrait of Jean de Dinteville, ambassador of the king of France, and Georges de Selve, on a secret ambassadorial mission to London; by Hans Holbein (1533).

SOURCE: *Jean de Dinteville and Georges de Selve "The Ambasadors,"* Hans Holbein the Younger. Reproduced courtesy of the Trustees, The National Gallery, London.

merchant-manufacturers could expect the ruler to protect their interests and to allow them a greater voice in shaping government policy, especially in matters affecting production and trade. This relationship was the means by which the limited authority of feudal monarchy (based on contractual obligations and duties) was replaced over the course of several centuries by the potentially unlimited authority of dynastic monarchy, government in which power was based less on contractual relationships and more on the new aristocracy of commerce, manufacturing, and finance.

Kings sought to ally themselves with the highest levels of urban society, and after 1250 the urban world quickly developed its own hierarchy. The emerging elite were identified by everyday vocabulary that indicated distinctions between those who sold goods wholesale and on commission, shopkeepers, and artisans who worked with their hands. Top-ranked wholesale merchants were the aristocrats of trade, and those who understood the workings of finance became important allies of rulers in a period when the economy was increasingly based on money.

MERCANTILISM

The partnership that evolved between rulers and merchant-manufacturers enhanced the wealth and power of both. It also produced a set of doctrines and practices known as mercantilism, which aimed to enhance state power by increasing wealth. Mercantilism was based on the use of government intervention to promote the accumulation of profits, which, it was believed, would secure the prosperity and self-sufficiency of the state while benefiting those who contributed most to it, the urban commercial elite. Thomas Mun (1571–1641) described the essence of mercantilism in his *England's Treasure by Foreign Trade:*

> Although a kingdom may be enriched by gifts received [services], or by purchase taken from some other nations, yet these are things uncertain and of small consideration when they happen. The ordinary means therefore to increase our [private] wealth and [public] treasure is by foreign trade, wherein we must ever observe this rule; to sell more to strangers yearly than we consume of theirs in value.

The purposes of mercantilism were as much political as economic, and both princes and merchants gained from it during the sixteenth and seventeenth centuries, the emergent period of dynastic states and capitalism.

Mercantilism and   Mercantilism accompanied the evolution of absolutist dynastic states,
European Exploration in which absolute and total power are concentrated in the ruler, and
▬▬▬▬▬▬▬▬▬▬▬   their exploitation of the Atlantic world between the mid–sixteenth and mid–eighteenth centuries. Mercantilism depended on princely authority and support for expanding commercial enterprise, though princes neither created it nor benefited from it alone. The voyages of Christopher Columbus illustrate the role of the prince in mercantilism and the mutual benefits to be derived by both prince and merchant. Although Columbus was a native of Genoa, he sought financial backing for his voyages first from the king of Portugal and then from Isabella of Castile and Ferdinand of Aragon in Spain. The Spanish monarchs retained Columbus in their service, but it took about five years to convince them to provide the 2,500 ducats for the voyage. The person who finally persuaded Ferdinand and Isabella of the financial potential of the venture was a banker and papal tax gatherer from Valencia, who had successfully raised a number of loans for them and who had himself amassed a fortune as a shrewd businessman. Merchants, whose power rested on their wealth, were as necessary to mercantilist enterprises as kings, and they derived great advantage from them, at least until the mid–eighteenth century, when their need for government support and protection was felt to be unnecessary.

One of the components of the theory and practice of European mercantilism was bullionism. For ambitious rulers, bullionism, the acquisition of surplus bullion (precious metals, specifically gold and silver ingots), meant that more ships could be built, larger fleets and armies equipped, and territorial expansion financed. One strong reason for the decision to back Columbus's voyage was the Spanish monarchy's acute lack of currency (especially gold); the possibility of enormous profits from an entirely new set of trading networks loomed large enough to overshadow the risks of Columbus's venture. Another component of mercantilism was the fervent hope that European voyages of exploration would lead to the establishment of colonies, the extension of European activities overseas.

MERCANTILISM AND COLONIES

The extension of European control overseas in the form of colonies was supported by the state and merchants, both of whom expected to extend their wealth and power as a result. It took just about a century after the successful voyages of Portugal around Africa and Spain westward across the Atlantic for other European states to join in the Atlantic venture. They did so by establishing colonies that represented their interests.

Spanish Colonies The Spanish-American Empire grew upon two foundations: the initiative of
in the Americas private colonial entrepreneurs and the strategic support and direction of the
▬▬▬▬▬▬▬ Spanish state, whose unification had been completed only in 1492, the
same year as Columbus's first voyage. National and private urges were responsible for Spanish
colonization, and from their inception Spanish colonies were designed to serve the needs of
the Spanish state and the entrepreneurs who supported it. The state, having borne the early
risks of expansion and directed it, had the crucial role to play in the perceived role of Spanish
colonies. The wealth of the colonies existed solely to increase the power of Spain. Centralization was characteristic of Spanish-American colonization.

The experience in curbing powerful nobles and independent cities in Spain provided the
monarchy with the organizational basis for imperial expansion, the close control of resources
in the colonies, and trade between America and Spain. From the base in Hispaniola, conquest
of Puerto Rico, Jamaica, Cuba, and the mainland followed. The colonies, especially the gold
and silver some of them provided, gave the monarchy a seemingly endless supply of bullion,
and stimulated a price revolution in sixteenth-century Europe. Exploitation continued to be
essential for supporting the interests of both monarchy and entrepreneurs.

English, French and Dutch Another outgrowth of the Atlantic expansion was the establish-
in North America ment of European settlements in North America, where the
▬▬▬▬▬▬▬▬▬▬▬ more temperate climate was comparable to that of Europe.
Though it took place over a longer period of time, the effects of the arrival and settlement
of northern Europeans (especially the English, Dutch, and French) on the indigenous peoples of North America were as devastating as the impact of the Spanish on the inhabitants of
South America.

In 1497, John Cabot, sailing from Bristol and under the English flag, made the important recognition that he had not reached Cipangu, or Japan, by sailing westward, but a
"Newfoundland." Ships from the time of Cabot exploited the valuable fishing area off the
shores of this land, but continued to seek a more northerly route to the East Indies and many
entered the continent of North America through the Saint Lawrence River in this search. The
first voyage to what became Canada was made by Jacques Cartier in the service of the king of
France in 1534. The Dutch sent an English navigator, Henry Hudson, to find a northwest
passage to Asia in 1609. His claims gave the Dutch a foothold in North America, where settlements were created on Manhattan and Long Island (New York). Two years later, Hudson
sailed for the British and reached the broad landlocked bay now called Hudson's Bay. Both
Dutch and English efforts along the eastern seaboard were government-sponsored, but their
success relied heavily on the efforts of private companies and merchants and on the continued
presence of settlers who were able to reap profits from the lands and economies of the original
inhabitants.

British North American colonies, founded between 1607 and 1733, were part of the vast
English mercantilist empire. The thirteen Atlantic seaboard colonies varied widely in origin
and in nature. The earliest, Virginia, was founded by a joint stock company in 1607; the last,
Georgia, was founded as a penal colony in 1733; several—Maryland, Pennsylvania, Massachusetts—were begun as refuges of religious freedom. All were integrated into the British mercantilist imperial system, as is most clearly seen in the case of Virginia.

In 1606, King James I of England granted a charter to a group of English merchants and
aristocrats, incorporating them as the Virginia Company. With proceeds from the sale of

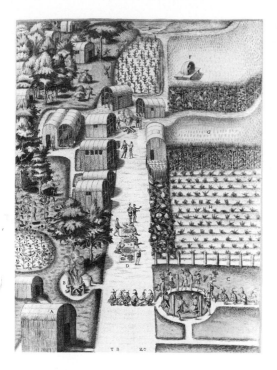

FIGURE 12.2 Sixteenth-Century Indian Maize Plantation at the Indian Camp of Secota, Virginia (1590).

SOURCE: Lauros-Giraudon/Art Resource, NY.

stock in this joint-stock venture, the officers of the Virginia Company planned to send poor and unskilled workers, along with skilled craftsmen, to settle in Virginia. In 1607, the first expedition sailed into Chesapeake Bay and founded the settlement of Jamestown, named for the king. Despite desperate conditions in the first years and the decimation of the colony by disease and starvation, the colony survived, and by the 1620s European demand for the tobacco it produced soared. The tobacco boom brought a wave of immigrant laborers fleeing unemployment and desperate circumstances in England. When the tobacco boom broke in the 1630s and 1640s, local planters diversified their crops, branching into cotton and corn.

Colonies and Marginalization The Spanish colonies in Latin America differed from those established in North America in terms of divergent governing structures and involvement, experiences, and inheritances. It has been customary to describe English colonies in the Americas as "settler colonies," where large numbers of Englishmen came to live, and Spanish colonies as "exploited colonies," where fewer Iberians under careful control from Madrid were basically concerned with what they could take away from the colonies. In the context of mercantilism, these distinctions are matters of degree rather than kind. Historian Fernand Braudel has described exploitation as marginalization, the condition within the world system of being condemned to serve others, of being told what to do by and for the benefit of the colonizing power. The way in which this was done in Spanish America was distinct from that in British America, where (until the late eighteenth century) colonists tended to serve their own as well as British interests. Whatever its methods, marginalization was a distinguishing feature of mercantilist imperialism.

Balance of Trade One of the by-products expected of the establishment of colonies was yet
▬▬▬▬▬▬▬▬▬▬ another component of mercantilism: a favorable balance of trade. Colonies,
it was believed, could provide raw materials for manufacture in the home country and markets for the finished products transported back to them. This exchange guaranteed that both
unfinished and finished products would be under the control of the state, whose independence
from other states would be matched by increased profits. Colonialism was an important component of mercantilist practice for two reasons: it would lead to a favorable balance of trade
(by which a state sells more than it buys) and thus to autarky (establishment of a self-sufficient and independent economy).

These mercantilist ideals were believed to enable the accumulation of surplus capital
(bullion). The mercantilist desire for a favorable balance of trade guided commercial relations
between states as well as the quest for colonies. Foreign imports were subject to high tariffs,
while bounties were paid for exports, and favors (including subsidization) were given to domestic manufactures. These devices to keep out foreign competition were expected to increase
the production of exports while keeping wealth at home.

MERCANTILISM AND CAPITALISM

Many other general, long-range effects on European societies became obvious as the aims of
the urban merchant-manufacturing and financial elite to make, increase, and protect wealth
became the aims of the state. Mercantilism was the implementation of some of these goals by
the state, and an important result of the partnership of rulers and merchants was the increased
use of money. If capitalism can be defined as the use of money to make money, then it had developed, at least in an early and prototypical form, by the mercantilist era.

Rapid changes in social relationships were a part of transformations taking place in this
early capitalist period. As the ideals and practices of capitalism spread, social divisions became more pronounced and aggravated. Gaps between classes and genders, between the dominant and the subordinated, between the privileged and less fortunate, became increasingly
difficult to bridge. The competition for profit that was inherent in capitalist practices proved
harmful to a sense of community and led to social tension, hostility, and even, on occasion,
revolution. These changes became obvious in the period after 1492, during what may be
called the "Atlantic era," when a new economy in Europe lead to the creation of a European
global hegemony. But the dramatic waves of change during the Atlantic era were not limited
to European shores.

■

EUROPEAN ARMS AND SAILS: MARITIME HEGEMONY

The success of European princes and merchants as they turned their efforts to the Atlantic
frontier rested in part on military and naval technologies. Technology enabled Europeans to
expand around and eventually dominate the globe, first on sea and then, after the sixteenth
century, on land. As we saw in the last chapter, much of the technology used in securing
global dominance was not European in origin. Europeans borrowed, adapted, and put to new
use technologies such as gunpowder and navigational aids such as the astrolabe that had been
developed by non-European peoples.

MILITARY TECHNOLOGY

Naval technology was essential to European success on the Atlantic frontiers. By the second half of the fourteenth century, the use of cannons was well established in Europe, where their effective use in field battles dates to the early 1500s. Despite early European use of cannon, the slow rate and unreliability of field artillery's firepower limited its effectiveness in battles involving large numbers of mobile troops. Because of this, cannon was more useful against fixed targets such as fortifications or anchored ships than against armies, and this made resistance to European encroachment possible. In Africa, for example, the European's cannon in fortified settlements were primarily directed toward the sea and other European competitors.

Beginning in the fifteenth century, Europeans built forts and castles along the West African coast, with permission from local rulers, on land rented from the local African community. Such fortresses as El Mina on the Gold Coast, built by the Portugese but captured by the Dutch, had mounted cannons that pointed seaward, toward possible European competitors in the slave trade.

MARITIME TECHNOLOGY

A peak of maritime technology was reached in the sixteenth century with the galleon, deadly as a warship and efficient as a merchantship. Galleons were probably of Spanish origin but were quickly adopted by the English and Dutch, who made efficient use of them to gain control of the Atlantic frontier and achieved a relative advantage on the oceans of the world. Navigational aids such as the sextant, a device that could determine a ship's location by measuring altitudes of celestial bodies and that superseded the earlier astrolabe, were as necessary to European expansion as improved ships were.

FIGURE 12.3 Depiction of a Portuguese Vessel inscribed on a Rock at the Entrance to a Chinese Temple in the Portuguese outpost of Macao.

This ship is typical of the vessels that carried Portuguese mariners to far-flung parts of the globe such as that of Macao, on the southern coast of the Asian mainland, founded as a Portuguese colony in 1557.

SOURCE: Roger-Viollet.

Sailing in West African waters helped train crews for ships that crossed the Atlantic and Pacific, including the navigator Christopher Columbus, who gained seafaring experience on West African voyages before he crossed the Atlantic. In addition, early Portuguese and Spanish voyagers relied on local navigators and guides, including West Africans and Amerindians in the circum-Caribbean region. In his Caribbean exploration, Columbus took Arawak guides on board. From the initial circumnavigation of the African continent by Vasco da Gama, which was achieved with the help of an Arab pilot from the East African port of Malindi in 1497, to the circumnavigation of the globe by Ferdinand Magellan, who sailed out into the Pacific in 1520, both technological advances and the navigational expertise of local inhabitants made possible the forging of new worlds.

■

THE CREATION OF AN ATLANTIC ECONOMY: SUGAR AND SLAVES

The European entry into the world of the Americas had catastrophic effects on the indigenous peoples, who succumbed to diseases and genocidal policies of the Europeans; and in the wake of Amerindian population decreases, other forms of coercive labor, including slavery, were exploited in the construction of the "new world." Central to the growth of Atlantic commerce were two commodities: sugar and slaves. The history of Atlantic commerce is inseparable

MAP 12.1 The Atlantic Trade Triangle, 16th–19th Century

SOURCE: Peter Ashdown, *Caribbean History in Maps* (Trinidad and Jamaica: Longman Caribbean, 1979), p. 16 top

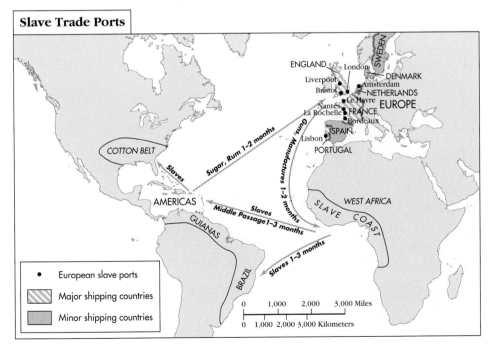

Slave Trade Ports

from the history of slavery, and the transfer of both labor and capital across the Atlantic is closely connected with the production of sugar. Technology and culture were intertwined in the development of the sugar industry, one of the mainstays of the new Atlantic economy.

EXPANSION OF SUGAR DEMAND AND PRODUCTION

Before the sixteenth century, northern Europe's only local source of sugar was bees. By the fourteenth century, the growing demand for sugar led first to cane sugar plantations on the Mediterranean coast and the islands of Cyprus and Sicily and then, by the fifteenth century, to Spanish and Portuguese plantations on Atlantic islands such as the Madeiras and São Tomé and Principe off the west-central African coast, where African slave labor was exploited, and finally in the Americas. Sugar sold for high prices as a rare spice or medicine. Its production and trade soon became enormously profitable.

With the increase in prices, expansion of sugar cultivation dominated the list of profitable Portuguese investments in Brazil and the Caribbean. The demand for sugar grew, and as supplies also expanded, new uses for sugar were found. French and Dutch merchants vied for power. Europeans came to crave the taste of sugar, especially as a sweetener for two other

---

FIGURE 12.4 Slaves Planting the Sugar Cane in Trinidad (Caribbean).

SOURCE: Bridgens, R., *Sketches of West Indian Scenery* (London, 1836). General Research Division, New York Public Library, Astor, Lenox, and Tilden Foundations.

products from the Afro-Asian world, coffee and tea. These became popular additions to the European diet, especially valued as stimulants and comforts by workers in European factories, the products of which in turn fed the markets of the Atlantic world with cheaply manufactured goods, such as hoes and cast iron pots.

The Dutch Sugar Industry The Dutch were pioneers in the technology and trade of the Atlantic. The Dutch West India Company seized and controlled the richest sugar-producing area in Brazil (around Recife) from 1630 to 1654. Dutch sugar enterprises in Brazil served as models for other large-scale Caribbean ventures. Dutch merchants controlled the copper trade that supplied plantation boiling houses with pots. These entrepreneurs relied on the systems of credit, insurance, and finance that Dutch trading companies experimented with and that were necessary to risky overseas enterprise. Corporate financing and state support jointly promoted the development of sugar plantations and, along with them, slavery. Creditors in Amsterdam, London, and other cities, who accumulated capital from the sale of both goods and people, financed shipping concerns involved in the transfer of these goods and people and invested their profits in manufacturing.

EXPLOITATION AND THE PROBLEM OF LABOR

Sugar cultivation in the Americas required both large investments of capital and a steady supply of labor, and investors were needed who could guarantee both. In order for sugar production to return a profit, expensive plantations, large-scale plots of land at least 80 to 100 hectares (33 to 41 acres) in size, were essential. Many of the largest plantations were run as businesses by absentee landlords across the ocean. Their successful operation required both skilled and unskilled labor, as well as a supply of industrial equipment to support the processing of crops and products for export.

Indigenous Laborers Providing labor for Caribbean plantations was a constant problem. Initially, Amerindians (mostly Arawaks and Caribs) had been enslaved and ordered placed in *encomiendas* (land grants) by the Spanish. Europeans demanded labor in exchange for their "protection" and "civilization," almost completely destroying indigenous populations and cultures. Many indigenous peoples resisted and were killed, and others fled into the most inaccessible regions of the interior of large islands and the mainland. Those who were not as fortunate succumbed to European diseases. In Mesoamerica, the population declined from 25.2 million in 1519 to 16.8 million in 1532 and 0.75 million in 1622. As entire villages of Amerindians disappeared, Europeans turned to other available sources of labor, including Europeans.

European Migrant Laborers Few European migrants were attracted to the Caribbean, and those who came were attracted only by the lure of gold and silver. Efforts were made by plantation owners to contract European bond servants, people who were offered meager land grants (that often did not materialize) in return for providing labor on plantations, and European convicts and prisoners of war also were shipped by the hundreds and even thousands. In this way Scots and Irish prisoners, for example, were brought to Jamaica.

African Slave Labor Since neither Amerindians nor Europeans adequately answered the labor ▬▬▬▬▬▬▬▬▬ needs of the plantations of the Americas, Africans became the solution. African slaves were brought across the Atlantic within a decade of Columbus's voyages. First in small numbers and later in astounding ones, regular supplies of slaves were provided by traders who had bought them in Africa, where most originated as war captives from conflicts between Africans. Even under appalling conditions, though, African slaves fared better than Amerindian slaves had. The African slave populations had come from often tropical environments, similar in many ways to the Caribbean; they were accustomed to heat and humidity. If they survived infancy and childhood, they already had, unlike adult Amerindians, developed resistance to the most deadly Old World (Afro-European) epidemics, including smallpox, and many tropical diseases.

In the end, costs favored the use of African slaves. The lower death rate of the Africans and their agricultural and technological skills, weighed against the hostility of European free and indentured laborers who knew the master's language, culture, and weaknesses, made African labor preferable. The reliance on slavery was so complete that by the eighteenth century Africans significantly outnumbered those of European descent in the circum-Caribbean region (by ratios typically as high as eleven or thirteen to one). Their darker skin colors also made them more easily identifiable as slaves, not free men; as "black" came to be synonymous with "slave," racism was born. Out of the European justification of the enslavement and trade of Africans emerged an ideology of superiority based on skin color. This ideology came to assert the superiority of white Europeans and their cultural values over the rest of the world's peoples.

THE PLANTATION AS A SOCIAL AND ECONOMIC UNIT

The system of plantation slavery that developed across the Caribbean was unprecedented as an economic, political, and social institution. The sugar plantation was a landed estate that specialized in export production. It combined large-scale tropical agriculture, African labor, European and African technology, European animal husbandry, Asian and American plants, and the climate and soils of the Americas. The typical sugar plantation was a big-business establishment, both farm and factory. Sugarcane was grown, raw sugar manufactured, and molasses distilled into rum.

Managing a Plantation Plantation owners were often absentee proprietors, who used attorneys ▬▬▬▬▬▬▬▬▬ or other Europeans as overseers. Managers, bookkeepers, carpenters, blacksmiths, masons, coopers, and doctors provided essential services. The breaking in or "seasoning" of slaves involved great brutality and coercion that imposed processes of cultural transformation and extracted gang labor from the workforce that survived. The "Great House" on the hilltop of the sugar plantation housed Europeans and their staff, while slave villages were usually situated down below at some distance from the master's house.

Life on a Plantation Plantation slave villages tended to replicate African social and spatial ▬▬▬▬▬▬▬▬▬ patterns, with small houses clustered around a common courtyard. Houses were built using lashed poles and lathes that were covered with mud; thatched roofs resembled those typical of West Africa. Because the food supplies provided by the plantations were insufficient to maintain the slave population, slaves grew their own provisions to supplement their diets. In about 1740, Charles Leslie described the slaves of Jamaica:

> Their owners set aside for each a small Parcel of Ground, and allow them the Sundays to manure it: In it they generally plant Maiz, Guiney Corn, Plantanes, Yams, Cocoes, Potatoes, &c. This is the Food which supports them, unless some of them who are more industrious than others, happen to raise a Stock of Fowls, which they carry to Markets on the Sundays (which is the only Market-day in Jamaica) and sell for a little Money, with which they purchase Salt-Beef or Pork to make their Oglios or Pepper-Pot.

The slaves developed an informal economy, based on West and Central African practices of bargaining and exchange, that often relied on specialized women traders called higglers. Higglers became critical agents of interplantation communication and slave resistance.

THE BUSINESS OF SLAVERY

The effects of the slave trade on Europe are perhaps not quite so obvious but nevertheless profound. Europeans benefited not only from the profitable use of cheap labor in the Caribbean but also from their control of the Atlantic trade that connected Europe to Africa, Africa to the Americas and the Caribbean, and the Caribbean and the Americas to Europe. European merchants and business interests were involved as suppliers of goods traded for slaves, as shippers of those goods and of slaves, and as dealers of goods produced by slave labor. The organizational experience and demands of the Atlantic system produced unrivaled entrepreneurial expertise and capital. Europe's control of the Atlantic world provided the means for its later world dominance.

Trade with Africa and between Africa and the Americas resulted in the expansion of seaport towns such as Bristol, Liverpool, Nantes, Bordeaux, and Seville. Profits from slavery and the slave trade directly financed such diverse enterprises as Barclays Bank, founded by David and Alexander Barclay, who engaged in the mid-eighteenth-century slave trade; Lloyds of London, which evolved from a small London coffeehouse to one of the world's largest banking and insurance houses; and the steam engine invented by James Watt, who was backed by West Indian slave owners.

Slavery as Mercantilism Many European states profited from involvement with the Atlantic slave trade. In 1602, the Dutch formed an East Indies Company to protect and encourage government control over commercial activities that were the result of their conquests in the East Indies. Two decades later, in 1621, by establishing a West India Company, the Dutch showed others how to spread the costs and profits of the slave trade among many investors. Shortly thereafter, the British and other European governments followed their example by founding companies that were granted monopolies for the sale of slaves in their colonies, thus bringing mercantilist practices to bear on the slave trade. In 1672, the British Royal African Company found backers among rich British merchants and aristocratic landowners, as well as members of the royal family.

Both private companies and companies enjoying government monopolies set up operations in African coastal towns, where they built forts and castles on land rented from African communities. Tropical diseases against which European adults had no immunity and a climate and environment considered harsh and difficult by Europeans prevented them from moving inland from the coast much before the nineteenth century. Moreover, their coastal trading stations satisfied the purposes for which they had come to Africa: they became the entrepôts for amassing wealth.

The Slave Trade Captains of slaving ships acquired their cargoes either by sailing along the ▬▬▬▬▬ West or Central African coast and purchasing slaves from several independent African dealers or by buying slaves directly from a European agent, called a factor, at one of the large coastal trading stations, called factories. These slaves were provided to the dealers mostly by African states. Slaves usually originated as war captives; they were victims of a period of numerous wars and a general atmosphere of political instability and personal insecurity that was common to many inland regions of the African continent during the era of the Atlantic slave trade. African hostilities, fueled by the possession of firearms acquired from European traders, became increasingly violent.

Slaves and Guns A vicious cycle of slaves and guns developed gradually. Europeans supplied ▬▬▬▬▬ guns selectively to African states that became trading partners. The use of guns altered the patterns of rivalries between Africans and made warfare increasingly violent. Originating as war prisoners, African slaves were sold to European traders in exchange for guns and other manufactured goods. Guns created slaves which were traded for more guns,

FIGURE 12.5 The Arrival of African Slaves on a Trading Vessel.

SOURCE: Hulton Getty/TonyStone Images.

which would be used to "make" more slaves. This exchange sometimes made independent African states dependent appendages to European capitalist expansion. Slaves were exchanged for such imported goods as cloth, metal, and guns, which were prestige goods used by African elites to enhance status. African elites also kept slaves, especially females, who contributed to productivity and furthered prestige. African slavery, conceived in social and political terms, eventually gave way to economic slavery, states relying on a slave mode of production, in which the production of wealth was dependent on slave labor. The Atlantic era resulted in the transformation of many Africans into dependent consumers of cheap European products living in increasingly violent slave societies.

SLAVERY AND THE AFRICAN DIASPORA

Slaves supplied by the Atlantic system represented the largest known transfer of people prior to the nineteenth century. Between 1518 and 1860, an estimated 15 to 25 million Africans were transported to the Americas. The impact of the Atlantic slave trade on the circum-Caribbean region is most obvious in the patterns of plantation production and profits, the legacy of Caribbean economic dependency on Europe, and the region's ethnic diversity.

The Middle Passage The journey of the slave ships across the Atlantic was known as the Middle Passage. Survival was by no means certain. Slaves were placed in iron shackles below deck, and ships were inhumanly packed with bodies. Foods of the Americas, which had been grown by slave labor, were fed to cargoes of slaves out of animal troughs. Provisions were minimal, and the trip could last from six to ten weeks. Only about half of those enslaved in Africa and traded by European merchants reached destinations in the Americas. Africans who arrived in Brazilian, Caribbean, or North American ports had left their homeland without material possessions, but their languages, skills, memories, beliefs, and cultures could not be left behind or easily forgotten.

The creation of an African diaspora (literally, "dispersal") across the Atlantic world relied on the survival of individuals and their ability to piece together a life in the Caribbean or Americas that owed much to their African heritage. There were obstacles to African cultural continuity. For example, slave masters outlawed drumming and separated persons speaking the same language in order to discourage communication and solidarity among slaves. Such conditions made African family life difficult and sometimes impossible. Yet the vitality of the hundreds of distinct African languages and cultures, together with the courage and resistance of African peoples in the Americas, ensured their continuity in the face of slavery and oppression even as they negotiated a new identity.

African Resistance Resistance to the conditions brought about by merchant capitalism was immediate and continuous. The success of resistance helped keep alive African cultures, while providing an ongoing source of African identity that promoted survival against great odds. Within both the societies of escaped freedom fighters and those of the plantations from which they came, African continuities in dance, language, food, informal economic systems, technology, music, dress, pottery, family organization, religion, and other areas are well documented in Caribbean and American life. They attest to the processes of transformation, in which both continuities and discontinuities create the patterns of historical change and determine its direction and scope.

AFRICAN TRANSFORMATIONS: AFRICAN SOCIETIES, EUROPEANS, AND THE SLAVE TRADE

No better example of the transforming effects of transatlantic slavery on African society can be found than the west-central African kingdom of the Kongo. The Kongo was already a centralized state when the Portuguese arrived there in the mid–fifteenth century. In the kingdom of the Kongo, early European traders found an elaborate court life, richly enhanced by locally manufactured textiles and other material culture. Portuguese traders brought with them Jesuit priests, who successfully converted the king to Christianity, a conversion that permitted the kingdom to maintain diplomatic ties with the Vatican and other seats of European power. When the Kongo king and his court converted to Christianity after 1482, it was for perceived trade and diplomatic advantages rather than merely religious beliefs.

In the wake of traders, priests, and artisans who accompanied the process of conversion, there was a fusion of European and Kongo cultures that resulted in the creation of a new Kongolese elite culture. The early trade with European merchants was monopolized by the

FIGURE 12.6 Procession of Kongo Nobleman with Attendants. Depicted in Johann Theodor de Bry's *India Orientalis* (Frankfurt, 1598), an edition of Duarte Lopes's earlier *Congo.*

SOURCE: By permission of the Folger Shakespeare Library, Washington, D.C.

kingdom's rulers, who then circulated imported prestige goods, especially fine textiles, to their dependents in exchange for tribute in the form of labor and goods, which traditionally gave status to powerful rulers. The availability of European trade goods after the fifteenth century provided a new set of status markers for Kongolese royalty and their dependents. Local velvets made of palm fibers were replaced by foreign brocades and silks.

By the time of King Afonso I in the early sixteenth century, members of the ruling elite were forced to buy imports in increasing amounts to exchange for the traditional tribute that was the basis of their domestic power. They adopted Portuguese dress, titles, technology, and language. To pay for imports, Kongo traders had to acquire goods desirable to their European counterparts. Increasingly, their payment to the Europeans took the form of slaves; dependents and captives were traded to the Portuguese, who transported them across the Atlantic to supply labor-hungry markets in the Americas. In 1526, Afonso complained to the Portuguese:

> Many of our subjects eagerly covet Portuguese merchandise, which your people bring into our kingdoms. To satisfy this disordered appetite, they seize numbers of our free or freed subjects, and even nobles, sons of nobles, even the members of our own family. They sell them to the white people. . . . This corruption and depravity is so widespread that our land is entirely depopulated by it. . . . It is in fact our wish that this kingdom should be a place neither of trade nor of transit for slaves.

Despite some African objections, trade expanded.

THE IMPACT OF THE SLAVE TRADE ON AFRICAN SOCIETIES

The expanding frontiers of enslavement in Africa produced violence and uncertainty and had devastating effects on African societies. To protect members of their lineages, Africans required arms, and to pay for guns, more Africans had to be captured for the slave trade. Thus the possession of guns produced increasing numbers of slaves while destabilizing traditional African society. The escalation of violence can be seen in estimates that in the eighteenth century 60,000 guns were imported along Central Africa's Angolan coast, producing about half that many slaves for export.

Other African states also became the targets of European commercial interests. As trade expanded, competition for African markets increased. European states relied heavily on their investments in slavery and the slave trade as the primary source of capital accumulation. Inter-African competition for access to European goods also intensified. The violence and insecurity of those made vulnerable by slaving activities undermined and destroyed some societies; and larger, more trade-dependent polities were created as people came together for purposes of defense. Trade routes in West Africa had for centuries linked environments and peoples across the Sahara. In the Atlantic era, the coast became a magnet, attracting trade and people to the opportunities of its seaport towns, while redirecting interior trade routes.

Independent African Societies Still other African societies maintained their independence despite centuries of involvement with Europe and the slave trade. For example, the kingdom of Benin was in continuous contact with European merchants from at least 1471. The king's palace established a special guild to trade with European merchants. The guild's language, based on Portuguese, was a state-guarded secret.

The forest state of Asante in the region of the Gold Coast emerged through the consolidation of political interests and military expansion beginning in the late seventeenth century. Although the existence of its capital at Kumase was well known, it was never visited by European traders, who were limited in their access to the interior until the nineteenth century.

Traditions from Oyo, a state on the edge of the forest, claim that hundreds of messengers sent by one early ruler to greet the Europeans never came back; thus Oyo avoided contact with Europeans for generations. Oyo's involvement in the slave trade was avoidable, in part due to Oyo's reliance on cavalry and more northward rather than seaward commercial and political orientation before the late eighteenth century.

Oral traditions record Africans' suspicions about greedy European trading partners. In Angola, the widespread death and dying caused by the slaving activities surrounding European trading ventures convinced some Africans that the Europeans were cannibals. Observing the Portuguese taste for red wine, Angolans claimed to have seen Europeans drinking the blood of slaves from the large barrel casks stored on board their ships. Cauldrons in which food was cooked were also watched with fear and suspicion by the slaves boarding the Atlantic's "floating tombs."

The Demographic Effects of the Slave Trade The widespread slaving activities altered much of African life. More men than women were traded to the foreigners, who found that African societies valued female slaves and preferred to keep them for their productive (not reproductive) capacities. The loss of population was dramatic and left African demographic change stagnant for centuries. The loss of potential sources of labor affected agricultural productivity, though this was somewhat offset by the introduction of new food crops from the Americas such as cassava and maize that could be grown in marginal agricultural environments. It has been argued that the lack of natural levels of population increase was responsible for Africa's technological stagnation and developmental lags during the time that slavery's profits were being reaped and reinvested by Europeans. Thus, Africans involved in the Atlantic world, both as consumers of European manufactured goods and as laborers exploited in European enterprises, provided the basis of the growth of the new global economy.

The Social Impact of Europeans Ideological and social changes resulted from the complex cultural and economic negotiation with European traders. Elite classes of merchants were created in some places—the *compradores* or merchant princes of West Africa, for example,—and culturally and materially impoverished groups were the results elsewhere, such as the South African Hottentots, a derogatory term given by the Dutch to Khoisan servants, who adopted Dutch language and dress in a desperate attempt to buy back their land and cattle and who eventually were decimated or absorbed by their contact with Europeans. Especially in coastal regions, the impact of merchant capitalism was deepened by the transformations of slavery and the accompanying political and social violence. The acceptance of human labor as a commodity after the sixteenth century was reflected in the increased reliance within African states on slavery and labor coercion, and in the rise of prostitution in urban areas. Alongside cheap European wares, both women's bodies and the titled ranks of gentlemen could be purchased without reference to traditional, ritually sanctioned, and inherited cultural categories of identity and access to power. These and other contradictions would be recalled to form the basis of resistance to European colonialism in later centuries.

AFRICAN MERCHANTS IN THE ATLANTIC WORLD

During the centuries of the Atlantic era, African women and men became great traders in the Atlantic economy. Many were known as "merchant princes." The most successful were able to circumvent the conventional pathways to political office. In the early eighteenth century, for instance, John Konny of the Gold Coast (Ghana) was one of a number of powerful coastal Africans who gained political influence through their accumulation of economic wealth. Konny's fortune was based on trade in foodstuffs, slaves, and other goods and on his ability to manipulate prices because the forces of supply and demand were in his favor. Konny maintained an army and controlled territory in the manner of an African state. Merchants such as Konny and his West African contemporary John Kabes used their wealth, rather than a traditionally inherited right, to claim political authority. Such independent African political economies resulted in their opposition by European alliances, such as in the Anglo-Dutch attempt "to repel the insolences of the Negro [Konny]" in the Konny War of 1711.

Some of the activities of the African merchant princes need to be understood against the background of competition and rivalries between Europeans. Wars between European trading partners were fueled by manipulative and clever African traders and these wars furthered the mercantile interests of both African and European merchants, while undermining traditional African chiefs and kings. A new African elite was born of the encounter with Europeans, an elite whose power was based on wealth derived from the Atlantic economy. Written descriptions of John Kabes describe him as everything from "famous" and "faithful" to "ungrateful defrauder" and "dishonorable knave." In the Senegambia and the Kongo, women traders sometimes used marriage to European merchants, whom they tended to outlive, to ensure their positions of wealth and power.

As links in the coastal access to inland producers, African traders were essential to the success of European ventures. In their turn, African merchant princes were dependent on their European counterparts for the guns and trade goods consumed by Africans who supplied captives for the slave trade. It seems that many of these traders launched their enterprises from the personal position of being caught between two cultural worlds, sometimes as the descendants of liaisons between African women and European men or as the inheritors of positions of providing service to European companies and/or African rulers.

European Dependence and Acculturation Like John Kabes, who had a penchant for wearing a fine, lace-embellished hat and carrying a silver-headed cane, African merchants often adopted European lifestyles at least partially. If they were well versed in the commercial diplomacy of the time, which they might use to create political power, their own dependents, and even armies, merchant princes who remained independent of European companies could amass enormous wealth. As individuals whose wealth was achieved at the expense of the collective good (since their presence undermined traditional states), merchant princes were evidence of the overall pattern of political and economic transformations that took place in Africa following the establishment of transatlantic connections.

While some eighteenth-century freed slaves, such as Olaudah Equiano and Ignatius Sancho, wrote passionate treatises against slavery from new homes in England, other former slaves, notably Afro-Brazilians, participated in the shipping and sale of slaves between the Atlantic ports of Ouidah and Luanda in Africa and Bahia in Brazil and grew rich in the trade. As Africa became a part of the Atlantic system, the economic and political fortunes of Africans were inextricably tied to the European-dominated economy.

FIGURE 12.7 West African Coastal Merchant-Prince in European and Turkish Fancy Dress, c. 1708.

Changing patterns of dress constituted one highly visible aspect of the transformation of elite culture along the African coast. This engraving depicted the King of Dahomey.

SOURCE: Pierre Duflos, *Recueil des Estampes,* Volume 1, 1780. Courtesy of the Trustees of the British Library.

Among the longest-lasting consequences of Africa's participation in the Atlantic trade system was the loss of independence by indigenous African economies that had become integrated into and dependent on the needs and demands of the triangular trade among Europe, Africa, and the Americas. As African merchant princes amassed great wealth and acquired political power, their status became dangerously vulnerable to outside manipulation, since it was based on the successful cultivation of the Atlantic trade rather than on the traditional, inherited patterns of African political systems. African merchant princes replaced traditional political authority and economic practices with socially upsetting relationships and personal profit dependent on Europeans, thus fulfilling the African proverb warning that "the river's mudfish grows fat to the crocodile's delight." Ultimately it would be the European capitalist crocodiles who would consume their African counterparts of the Atlantic world.

■

THE ATLANTIC WORLD AND THE AMERICAS

European exploration in the circum-Caribbean region was quickly followed by conquests in Mesoamerica and South America. The European desire for riches was satisfied by contact with complex trading societies such as the Aztecs and Incas. The conquest of the Aztecs and Incas by Europeans relied on a complex set of interactions.

CONQUEST AND COLONIZATION

Soon after the Spanish colonization of Cuba in 1519, a small army led by Hernán Cortés (1485–1547) conquered Mexico from the Aztecs. Cortés first attacked and then made allies of towns. Particularly strategic were communities which had been subject to the Aztecs, who had heavily taxed the people and practiced human sacrifice.

Aztec Conquest Many within the Aztec Empire came to believe that Cortés was Quetzacoatl, the god who would return to overthrow the god Tezcatlipoca, who demanded human sacrifice. Cortés was aided by an Indian woman La Malinche or Malintzin, who became an invaluable interpreter for and mistress and confidante of Cortés. What happened next is unclear. The Spanish claimed that the Aztec king Moctezuma was stoned to death by his own people and the Aztecs claimed that Cortés's second in command attacked priests, chiefs, and warriors during a celebration and strangled Moctezuma. After heavy losses, Cortés was forced to flee. He returned with thousands of Indian allies, who opposed the Aztecs. After a four month seige, during which time Aztec defenders succumbed as much to disease and starvation as to the force of arms, the new Aztec king Cuautemoc surrendered. By 1535, most of central Mexico was integrated under Spanish control in the kingdom of New Spain.

Inca Conquest Expeditions armed with guns and led by conquistadors on horseback swept outward from the Spanish base in Panama in search of Bolivian silver and the gold of the Amazon basin. In 1535, the Spanish conquistador Francisco Pizarro (ca.

FIGURE 12.8 Nahua Woman Translating the Negotiations between Spanish Conquistadors and the Otomi community of Atleucian.

This scene of the Aztec conquest by Cortés (on horseback, far right) was a version that emphasized the role of local allies.

SOURCE: Courtesy of the Department of Library Services. American Museum of Natural History. Neg. No. 329237.

1475–1541) brought down the once mighty Inca Empire. As in Mesoamerica, divisions among the Inca and their subjects aided the Spanish in their conquest. The Inca ruler Huayna Capac (r. 1493–1525) had moved the Inca capital north from Cuzco to Ecuador, angering many in his empire and dividing the vast territory into two. Civil war eventually broke out after his death. One of the rival successors was his son Atahualpa, who surrendered to Pizarro. In exchange for his life, Atahualpa offered Pizarro a room full of gold. Pizarro claimed the gold and killed Atahualpa. With the help of Indians loyal to Atahualpa's rival Huascar, Pizarro occupied and sacked Cuzco in 1533. The Spanish built a new capital at Lima, but Spanish rule continued to meet resistance until 1572, when "the last Inca," known as Tupac Amaru was captured and beheaded by the Spanish in a ceremony at Cuzco. His name lives on as the inspiration of Peruvian rebels today.

Religion and Resistance Conversion to Christianity, which accompanied Spanish conquest, sometimes led to resistance amongst the South American populations rooted in traditional Incan religious beliefs. In the 1560s, a millenarian (projecting the coming of a new age) movement known as the *taqui uncu* (the ritual song of the festival dress) became active. The followers of this movement held to traditional Incan belief in thousand-year cycles, and the present age for them had begun in the Christian year 565, so they anticipated the end of the thousand-year cycle in 1565. The arrival of the Spaniards was seen by this group as the last act in the passing away of the old Incan age and was believed to herald the coming of a new age that would bring about the overthrow of the Spaniards and their God and the restoration of the power of Inca gods.

Silver Mining and the Mita System One of the attractions of the Americas was legendary wealth, which was discovered in the form of rich silver mines. The most important source of silver was the mine at Potosí (in modern Bolivia). Spaniards mined the silver ore there by utilizing *mita,* the system of coerced labor which had roots in Incan tribute practices of enforced labor quotas that supported state power. This system was expanded by the Spanish and became the source of much misery for the Indian laborers who produced the wealth in silver that fueled the Spanish Empire and much world trade from the sixteenth century on.

The *mita* system and the abuse of Indian laborers was described in rich detail in the seventeenth century by Guamán Poma de Ayala, a Peruvian Indian who spoke both Quechua and Spanish and traced his ancestry to Incan nobility. As a loyal subject of Spain as well as a Christian, Guamán Poma had hopes that his report on conditions in New Spain would lead to improvements, but his writings were not published until the twentieth century.

Agrarian Change While the earliest Europeans sought gold and silver, later immigrants were satisfied with cattle raising and other lucrative agricultural enterprises. *Mestizos,* people of mixed Spanish and Indian ancestry, joined together with indigenous survivors in communal projects, producing foodstuffs for local needs. The complex hierarchy of racial identities would provide a lasting legacy of rulers and ruled. Alongside this rural production a market economy also emerged based on larger estates governed by Spaniards and *creoles* (Europeans born in the new land), which produced crops for export. The new societies forged by Spanish and Portuguese settlers were politically linked to monarchies in Spain and Portugal. European-born men ruled over two provinces known as viceroyalties, one based in

FIGURE 12.9 Painting of Spanish Colonial
Mixed Marriage by Castas
(Private Collection).

This eighteenth-century portrait of a richly dressed
Spanish colonial, along with his Amerindian wife,
and *mestiza* (mixed) daughter, both in European
dress, illustrates the mixing of ethnic groups and
the desire of Spaniards in the Americas to portray
themselves and their families in European style.

SOURCE: Photographer Camilo Garza/Fotocam, Monter-
rey, Mexico.

Mexico and another in Peru; in time, Argentina and Columbia were added to the highly centralized and bureaucratic system that emerged. In actuality, the territories were too large and
spread too far from their centers to remain entirely under control. Geographical barriers, such
as mountains and rainforests, also protected those who resisted the Europeans.

Spanish conquest resulted in the imposition of European urban patterns that transformed
the lives of indigenous peoples of Central and South America and in the Caribbean. From the
time of their arrival, the Spanish replaced pre-Columbian towns and cities with new ones organized and functioning on the Spanish model; the elites embraced Catholicism and European culture. For example, Cuzco, capital of the Incan Empire high in the Andes, gave way to
the Spanish imperial city of Lima, which was built in closer proximity to the Peruvian coast
and thus more easily accessible by ship.

TRANSFORMATIONS IN THE AMERICAS: EUROPEAN IMPACT AND RESISTANCE

The forging of the Atlantic world based on European dominance transformed the peoples and
places of the Americas. Undoubtedly, the most immediate and dramatic impact on the
transatlantic world was epidemiological. The effect of diseases brought by the earliest Europeans and Africans was both horrendous and prophetic. Disease resulted in the obliteration of
whole indigenous peoples, from the Caribes of the Caribbean basin to the Beothuks of Newfoundland, and the general decimation of most populations was common. For example, the
indigenous population of central Mexico in 1519 was estimated at 25 million; by 1580, after
Spanish conquest, it was less than 2 million. Within approximately one decade after contact
with Europeans, an estimated 90 percent of indigenous American peoples had disappeared.
The Amerindian populations had no immunity to diseases common in Europe and Africa,

such as swine flu and smallpox. Introduced by animal and human carriers, these virulent diseases brought from Europe and Africa killed most Amerindian adults upon contact.

European dominance was also expedited by a process described by historian Alfred Crosby and others as ecological imperialism. European cattle, swine, and goats multiplied rapidly in the favorable American environment and overgrazed and destroyed lands. European seeds, both wild and cultivated, were introduced and had an almost immediate impact on indigenous patterns of cultivation and nutrition. Native Americans were no better prepared to deal with European crops, weeds, and animals than they were to deal with European diseases, and the benefits of new crops and animals were counterbalanced by the new pests, weeds, and insects that came with them. The success of Europeans, backed by guns, greed, and genocidal policies, in gaining control over both American continents resulted in the disarray of Amerindian populations and their cultures.

RESISTANCE TO THE EUROPEAN PRESENCE

From the earliest period of contact on, native American peoples resisted European conquest. Abuses in the lands claimed by the Spanish following Columbus's voyages provoked revolts and established a pattern of resistance. The earliest encounters were fraught with misunderstanding and brutality. Sailing along the north coast of Haiti in early 1493, Columbus recorded in his journal the following:

> When the boat reached shore, behind the trees there were a good fifty-five naked men with very long hair, just like the women wear it in Castile. On the backs of their heads they wore plumes of parrot feathers and of other birds, and each one was carrying his bow. . . . Later they came to the boat and the men in the boat went ashore and began to buy from them the bows and arrows and other arms, because the admiral had so ordered. . . . Seeing them come running toward them, the Christians, being prepared (because the admiral was always warning them about this) attacked them, and they gave one Indian a great slash across the buttocks and another they wounded in the chest with a crossbow [gun] shot. Having seen by this that they could achieve little . . . they took flight. . . . Because they would fear the Christians, since without a doubt (he says) the people there are evildoers and he [the admiral] believed they were those of Carib and that they would eat men.

Maroon Society Within the same generation of the Columbus encounter, here were communities of runaway Amerindians and escaped slaves living in the mountainous interiors and most inaccessible reaches of the Caribbean and Americas. Called maroons (a term derived from the Spanish word *cimarrón* and used originally to refer to domestic cattle that had taken to the hills), these runaways were considered "fierce" and "unbroken." In communities that ranged from small temporary bands to large, powerful states, maroons maintained and protected their legacy. When joined by runaway African slaves, they shared their intimate knowledge of their environment and, in turn, adapted the cultures, skills, and beliefs of their African-Caribbean counterparts. The result was a lasting survival strategy that enabled maroon communities to pose a constant threat to European plantations and colonial life from Florida to Jamaica to Peru.

Under European cultural domination, other cultural elements were added. While indigenous peoples were decimated and assimilated, the centuries-long importation of slaves originating in Africa provided a steady influx of population and provided a more or less continuous cultural thread to the fabric of life in the Americas, one that added strength to the

FIGURE 12.10 Don Francisco and His Sons, Maroon Leaders at Esmeralda (Ecuador) Wear the Rich Attire of Spanish Noblemen and Ear and Nose Ornaments from Native American Tradition.

SOURCE: Museo de America, Madrid/Oronoz/Photo by Galque Sanchez.

resistance to Europeans. In Jamaica, maroons developed independent communities that preserved an African identity and maintained control of territory through treaty settlements first with the Spanish and later with the British.

The vast territory of Brazil was dotted with maroon settlements. The most famous of these, Palmares, was the largest of a number of *quilombos,* palisaded fortresses based on the war camps developed by Central African refugees from slaving. The Palmares community, a source of revolution throughout the seventeenth century, was essentially an African state within Brazilian territory. In the maroon community of Esmeraldas (Ecuador), a successful republic of runaways existed until their submission to the Spanish Crown by treaty in 1599. Portraits of their leaders reflect the mixture of African, native American, and European traditions and attire. Similar independent maroon territories have existed by treaty in Jamaica up to the present day.

Métis Society In Canadian North America, communities of people called Métis were in many ways similar to the southern maroon societies, though they rarely posed a threat to European colonists. Métis communities were principally French and, to a much lesser extent, English fur traders who abandoned European settlements and assumed lifestyles of the indigenous people of the region. They tended to avoid European settlements along the Atlantic seaboard and in the Saint Lawrence Valley and remain in the interior regions of North America, such as Saint Boniface (across the river from modern Winnipeg). They intermarried with the indigenous populations among whom they lived and upon whose intimate geographical knowledge they were dependent. The Métis, like the *mestizos* of South America, created a distinctive culture that was neither European nor Native American but a fusion and transformation of both.

Cultural Resistance and Revolt There were other more subtle forms of resistance to the oppressive Caribbean and American systems of plantation slavery. These included daily strategies of "go-slow" work-stoppage tactics designed to sabotage the productivity of slave masters. Poisonings of plantation masters and overseers were common. Although aspects of African culture were submerged, they were retained. African religious practices, for example, were disguised in the practice of Christianity. In Cuba, Brazil, and Haiti, Yoruba and Kongolese deities were given the names of Catholic saints; renaming did not alter the African-derived spiritual basis of understanding the world, one of the ways in which African communities were empowered. Dynamic and syncretic (blended) forms of political organizing were also masked, as performance art.

Areas where African religious and cultural identities were maintained became centers of revolt and resistance. At the Guyanese village of Winkle, blacksmiths and other slave artisans went on strike for better wages and finally demanded emancipation, which was granted years before the rest of the colony was emancipated by the British in 1834. In Jamaica, the Kumina people, who shared an African-derived religion, formed an underground training center for spiritual and political power, whose efforts helped inspire nineteenth-century rebellions that led to the abolition of slavery on the island.

The training and indoctrination of European and mixed-race children who were cared for by slave household servants and the elaborate systems of spying and covert communication used by African slave higglers (female traders) for plotting between plantations and organizing revolts are some of the forms of resistance that were largely handled by slave women. Maintaining and reproducing the African values of family, community, and culture was a persistent form of resistance and the one feared most by those who oppressed and exploited the Africans who had been transported across the Atlantic.

THE IMPACT OF EXPLOITATION

The European conquest created patterns of exploitation that characterized the history of Atlantic capitalism over the next three centuries. From their base in Hispaniola, the Spanish (and later other Europeans on other islands and on the mainland) systematically explored and exploited. Amerindians were forced, despite their resistance, to provide food and labor for the Europeans. When the decimated Amerindian populations proved insufficient or unsuitable for the labor demands of European mining, ranching, and farming activities, they were replaced by other oppressed peoples—European convicts, prisoners of war, and bond servants, African slaves, and laborers brought from Asia under contract. In time, the struggle of the indigenous populations to maintain cultural and political autonomy was taken up by African slaves.

Social distinctions and racial prejudices were characteristic of colonial Spanish America and the other territories claimed by European invaders. Racial hierarchies determined access to power and wealth. The racial structure was somewhat mitigated by the interracial mixing of peoples, as Spanish soldiers cohabited with indigenous peoples and slaves. In the end, these early encounters resulted in richly multicultural societies in which no individual or group remained unaltered.

DISTINCTIONS AMONG COLONIES

There were distinctions among the colonies established by Europeans in North and South America. Unlike the Spanish colonies in South America, the English colonies in North America lacked ready and obvious supplies of precious metals or labor to exploit the environment, at least until African slaves were introduced. Accordingly, English North American colonies were essentially rural, developing economies that were primarily farm-based. Towns were small communities of wooden houses, strongly cooperative in spirit, rural in outlook, and predominantly Christian in religion.

Because there were multiple European claimants to territory in North America—Dutch, French, English, and Spanish—there were lengthy struggles before any one of them could establish the political and cultural dominance and unity that the Spanish achieved in Central and South America. Despite this, in the North American colonies an effective transplantation of dominant European mercantilist principles and cultural values flourished because the barriers of disease and climate that hindered settlement in tropical parts of the Atlantic world were absent. The outcome was no less destructive to indigenous ways of life, however.

■
EUROPEAN EXPANSION IN THE INDIAN OCEAN

Christopher Columbus had mistakenly thought himself to be in Asia when he reached the Americas, and other Europeans after him were soon to realize his error and his goal. While the creation of an Atlantic economy drew European attention westward from European and West Central African shores, other Europeans ventured further eastward beyond the Cape of Good Hope in Southern Africa into the Afro-Asian networks of the established Indian Ocean world. The earliest penetration of European seaborne powers into Asia came in the region that was most accessible to and dependent on maritime trade: Southeast Asia.

Several factors account for the attraction of Southeast Asia to early European traders. The Asian spice trade originated there: the Moluccas were known as the "Spice Islands." Spices were profitable to overland and maritime long-distance trade because of their desirability, light weight, and relatively high value. Island Southeast Asia (in contrast to the vast Asian mainland) was more accessible and the indigenous political regimes there were smaller and weaker than the early modern empires of mainland Asia. The insular fragmentation of the terrain made the islands easier prey to expanding European maritime powers.

Portuguese Expansion The Portuguese were the first of the European powers to attempt to control the trade of Asia. They came from the direction of East Africa across the Indian Ocean in the late fifteenth century. From the establishment of their outpost at Goa on the southwestern Malabar coast of India (1510), the Portuguese followed with the conquest of Malacca (1511) on the Malay peninsula and Macao in southern China (1557). These conquests provided access to important sea routes, while inland sources of trade remained elusive. While they had reached the riches of the Indies sought by Columbus and others, the Portuguese faced hardship and competition in their attempts to wrest control of the centuries-old land-based Asian networks of commerce and culture. In 1594, the commander of a Portuguese fort on the Persian mainland complained to his king that the fort was made of mud and had to be repaired annually. According to a letter captured by English ene-

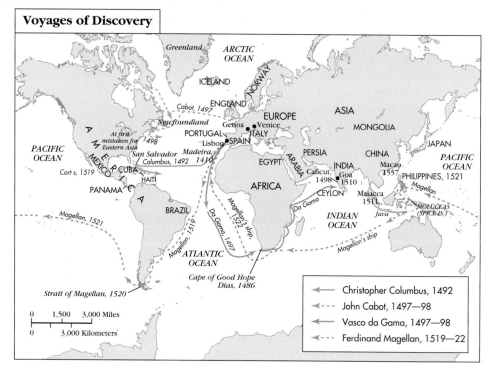

MAP 12.2 Early European Voyages of Discovery.

SOURCE: William Manchester, *A World Lit Only by Fire: The Medieval Mind and the Renaissance* (Boston: Little, Brown, 1992), p. 241.

mies, there was a continual shortage of weapons and ammunition and low morale among the European community. The Portuguese presence, however tenacious, was based on far-flung outposts in limited contact with the European core.

COMMERCE AND SOCIETY IN MUGHAL INDIA

When the Portuguese established their outpost of Goa on the southern coast of the Indian subcontinent in 1510 by wresting it from the Muslims, they acquired a foothold on the fringes of Mughal India. Shaped by successive waves of Muslim invaders, in the fifteenth century Mughal India was a cultural, political, and social hybrid of Islamic and Hindu influences. Tamurlane's descendant, Babur (1494–1530) laid the foundations of the Mughal Empire in India. With an army of only 12,000, in 1526 he gained control of the sultanate of Delhi, which had a population of 10 million. Division and contention between indigenous Indians made his task relatively easy. By the time of his death in 1530, Babur had created a state that stretched across most of north India, while southern India remained under the shifting control of Hindu states bordered by Muslim port enclaves along the coastline.

Commerce and Currency During the sixteenth century, the Indian subcontinent was home to between 125 and 150 million people, whose commercial needs were met by skilled merchants operating in rural villages and urban centers. A money economy flourished, and goods were produced for both local and distant markets. India was the world's major producer of cotton textiles. Cotton and other commodities, such as silk and pepper, were traded over long-distance routes by both land and sea in exchange for silver. The coinage of Mughal India was issued from mints throughout the country and functioned as an empirewide currency. Currency from all of Eurasia passed through the state coffers to pay for the highly prized cotton textiles. The wealth supported military and protective cavalries. Long-distance transporters, known as Banjaras, acted as carriers of goods among agricultural communities. Using herds of bullocks and camels, Banjaras moved goods slowly but cheaply, traveling in large groups for safety and united by strong clan ties.

The Merchant Caste Indian merchants belonged to a separate caste, a closed community that practiced intermarriage and defined social status. Banyas was the name given to the mercantile caste, which included many subgroups. They were primarily Hindus, though large numbers of Banyas in Gujarat and Rajasthan professed Jainism, following the teachings of the sixth-century B.C.E. religious leader Mahavira, a contemporary of Buddha.

Thrifty and restrained in the display of their wealth, Banyas were careful in maintaining their religious rituals and, like the upper-caste Brahmans, they were one of the pillars of or-

FIGURE 12.11 Banya Merchant and His Wife from Cambaya.

Watercolor by a sixteenth-century Portuguese resident in Goa and the Indies.

SOURCE: Biblioteca Casanatense, Rome/INDEX, s.a.s.

thodox Hinduism. Banyas were village and town merchants, and among them were peddlers, shopkeepers, brokers, and bankers. Brokers performed all kinds of services for merchants, including arranging the sale and purchase of goods and securing financing. Banyas were also money changers who tested and weighed currency to ensure its value. They functioned as bankers, who traded bills of exchange for currency or goods and thereby extended short-term credit, which allowed funds to be transferred from one location to another.

Belonging to a mercantile caste from birth, Banyas were taught arithmetic, accounting, and other business skills as children. Although Banyas usually acted individually as mer-

---

 DAILY LIVES

TOMÉ PIRES, *THE SUMA ORIENTAL* (ACCOUNT OF THE EAST), CIRCA 1517

Tomé Pires, a Portuguese adventurer, arrived in Goa in 1511, one year after its conquest by his countrymen. Apothecary to a member of Portugal's royal family, Pires was a health advisor and dispenser of medicines. Pires served his king in a similar capacity in Asia, in addition to acting as secretary and accountant. Before leaving for a post at Malacca, Pires collected data about India for a report to the Portuguese ruler. When he was stationed at Malacca from 1513 to 1517, he compiled *The Suma Oriental*. In 1517, shortly after completing *The Suma Oriental*, Pires was appointed as the first Portuguese envoy to China, where he died.

Pires's experience in Malacca, the hub of Indian Ocean commerce, provided the basis for his account of Indian and Southeast Asian trade. Gujerati (or Cambay) merchants brought Indian textiles to Malacca, where they were exchanged for finished goods or spices channeled through Malacca. Slaves from various parts of the archipelago were also traded at Malacca, especially destined for Siam. Raw materials such as wax, honey, and gold came from Sumatra.

I now come to the trade of Cambay. These [people] are [like] Italians in their knowledge of and dealing in merchandise. All the trade in Cambay is in the hands of the heathen. Their general designation is Gujaratees, and then they are divided into various races—Banians, Brahmans, and Pattars. There is no doubt that these people have the cream of the trade. They are men who understand merchandise; they are so properly steeped in the sound and harmony of it, that the Gujaratees say that any offense connected with merchandise is

pardonable. There are Gujaratees settled everywhere. They work some for some and others for others. They are diligent, quick men in trade. They do their accounts with figures like ours and with our very writing. They are men who do not give away anything that belongs to them, nor do they want anything that belongs to anyone else; wherefore they have been esteemed in Cambay up to the present, practicing their idolatry, because they enrich the kingdom directly with the said trade. There are also some Cairo merchants settled in Cambay, and many Khorasans and Guilans from Aden and Hormuz, all of whom do a great trade in the seaport towns of Cambay; but none of these count in comparison with the heathens, especially in knowledge. Those of our people who want to be clerks and factors ought to go there and learn, because the business of trade is a science in itself which does not hinder any other noble exercise, but helps a great deal. . . .

They trade with the kingdom of the Deccan and Goa and with Malabar, and they have factors everywhere, who live and set up business—as the Genoese do in our part [of the world]—in places like Bengal, Pegu, Siam, Pedir, Pase, Kedah, taking back to their own country the kind of merchandise which is valued there. And there is no trading place where you do not see Gujarat merchants, Gujarat ships come to these kingdoms every year, one ship straight to each place. The Gujaratees used to have large factories in Calicut.

The Cambay merchants make Malacca their chief trading center. There used to be a thousand Gujarat merchants in Malacca, because four or five thousand Gujarat seamen, who came and went. Malacca cannot live without Cambay, nor Cambay without Malacca, if they are to be very rich and very prosperous.

chants, brokers, or bankers, Banya families often functioned as firms, with joint investments and profits. Another form of business organization was the pure partnership firm, where kinship was not involved and partnership in an economic operation was established on the basis of contractual or other nonkinship ties.

Banya communities spread throughout northern India and the Deccan plateau, where they dominated the commercial world after the fifteenth century and worked closely with the Europeans. Other merchant communities based on ethnic and religious ties, such as the Khatris of Punjab and the Muslim Bohras of Gujarat, were powerful elsewhere. Foreign merchants, usually Persians or Armenians, also played a prominent role in the commercial life of the subcontinent before the European arrival. Arabs were the principal carriers of maritime trade to India, the center of east-west Indian Ocean routes, and the southern and western coasts of India were the site of Muslim port enclaves such as Goa.

▪
EUROPEAN EXPANSION IN THE PACIFIC

Official voyages of exploration and discovery beginning in the sixteenth century also took Europeans into the Pacific Ocean, and private traders followed in their wake. Together they established ties among societies that bordered the Pacific or lay within it to the links forged among societies in Africa, Europe, Asia, and the Americas by the creation of the Atlantic world economic system. As Europeans created economic and political ties across the Atlantic, incorporating Africans and native Americans into a system of economic dependencies, so the forging of links that extended into the Pacific created a maritime Pacific highway. This extension of the Atlantic economy was to a large extent the product of trade competition between European states that began in the late sixteenth century. While they profited from linking the economies of Pacific islands to those of the Asian and American mainland, European mercantile interests only gradually created new connections that eventually transformed the lives of peoples throughout the Pacific.

EUROPEANS AND TRADE IN THE ASIAN PACIFIC

The first documented link between the Americas and the islands of the Pacific was established by a Spanish expedition led by the Portuguese adventurer Ferdinand Magellan. Magellan's fleet sailed from Spain in the fall of 1519, wintered at Patagonia at the southern tip of South America, and then crossed into the Pacific through what is now known as the Strait of Magellan. After a hundred days at sea, Magellan's fleet reached a group of islands that they claimed under the terms of the Treaty of Tordesillas in 1494. This treaty, arbitrated by the Spanish Pope Alexander VI (r. 1492–1503), was a response to the Spanish challenge to the Portuguese monopoly on exploration and colonization. Following Columbus's voyage to the Caribbean, Spain was assigned all lands beyond a line 370 leagues west of the Azores, Portugal the lands east (Brazil and Africa), and there the matter rested until Magellan sailed into the Pacific.

For the Spanish, the Pacific islands Magellan reached (and where he died in 1521) were the "Western Isles" because they formed the westernmost boundary of Spanish claims under the Treaty of Tordesillas; for the Portuguese, they were the "Eastern Isles," marking the easternmost claims of Portugal. The dispute concluded in 1542, when the Spanish secured their

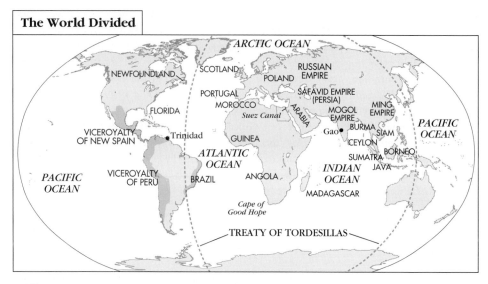

MAP 12.3 The Lines of the Treaty of Tordesillas (1494) Divided the World between Portugal and Spain.

claim to the islands, renaming them "Islas Filipinas" (the Philippines). Spanish occupation of the Philippines was confirmed in 1571, when a third expedition took control of Manila, an important trading center that became the principal Spanish entrepôt in Asia.

The Manila Connection By the second half of the sixteenth century, following the Spanish conquest of the Philippines, complicated patterns of both legitimate and contraband trade grew up around routes connecting the Spanish settlement of Acapulco in Mexico with Manila, from whence it reached China, principally through the Portuguese entrepôt of Macao. By the 1560s, Spanish "pieces of eight" had become the currency of expanding world trade, and Spanish galleons bearing goods, including silver bullion, became the object of piracy, either private or sponsored by Spain's European rivals and enemies. In 1573, the first galleon sailing eastward from Manila across the Pacific to Spanish America carried Chinese silks, satins, porcelains, and spices to Acapulco, from whence it returned to Manila with silver from Spanish-American mines.

By the end of the sixteenth century, the amount of bullion flowing from Acapulco to Manila surpassed the sum that was involved in transatlantic shipments. Between 1570 and 1780, an estimated 4,000 to 5,000 tons of silver flowed to East Asia along the Acapulco-Manila route. As Spanish-American bullion flowed westward as well as eastward, both Asians and Europeans were enriched. This trade lasted until the first half of the nineteenth century, when Spanish rule in the Americas came to an end.

Chinese Merchants The Spanish were aided in their quest for a trading empire in the Pacific by communities of Chinese merchants who had ventured out from their homes along China's southeastern coast to establish commercial settlements in places all over Southeast Asia. Unlike the Portuguese, who hoped to gain access to rich hinterlands and technically advanced indigenous populations through their conquest of port cities such as Goa and Malacca, the only Spanish claim in Asia, the Philippines, was an undeveloped chain of islands on the frontier of land-based Asian civilizations. The heart of this Spanish outpost in Asia was Manila, a fulcrum of Spanish trade between Asia and Spanish America. The luxury goods the Chinese provided in exchange for Spanish bullion passed through Manila, and by the end of the sixteenth century, as this trade flourished, the Chinese population of Manila, housed in a separate quarter of the city, swelled to approximately 10,000. The Chinese presence provided the Spanish with more than Chinese luxury items: they benefited from Chinese commercial and mercantile expertise and superior navigational technology.

The Dutch in Asia By the 1590s, the Dutch had obtained their independence from the Spanish Hapsburg Empire and had acquired the knowledge of navigation necessary to enter into world trade competition. Their initial target was the Portuguese-dominated spice trade in Southeast Asia. In 1602, the Dutch East India Company, a unified trading monopoly formed under state charter, began the administration of the Indonesian archipelago economy under Dutch control. By the 1640s, they had displaced the Portuguese and had consolidated their holdings across a vast sweep of islands from Ceylon in the west, through Malacca and Java (where they had an important administrative center at Batavia), to the Moluccas in the east. The Dutch had superior ships, arms, and organization, as well as more skilled merchants. They mixed piracy and missionary activities with trade.

Like the Spanish, the Dutch acknowledged the value of Chinese merchant communities and made use of them in their largest settlement, at Batavia on the island of Java, which was home to a large Chinese merchant community in the seventeenth century. The East India Company controlled all Dutch trade with Asia and maintained its monopoly by utilizing Chinese trading networks already in place in East and Southeast Asia. After the Portuguese were displaced in Asia and finally confined to Macao, both the Dutch in Batavia and the Spanish in Manila made use of the Chinese merchant communities in these two cities, the largest in Southeast Asia, in the service of their own maritime empires. Unlike their European counterparts, Chinese merchants were not organized into trading companies chartered by government, such as the Dutch and British East India Companies, nor were they in the service of rulers of states, such as Portuguese and Spanish entrepreneurs were. Chinese merchants were isolated entrepreneurs whose skills were recognized and utilized by Europeans when they were brought into contact in Asia.

The English in Asia The English were late entrants to the trade competition in Asia. Under Queen Elizabeth I (r. 1588–1603), rivalry with Spain prompted the growth of a strong English navy and culminated in the defeat of the Spanish Armada in 1588. By 1600, the British East India Company was formed and granted a royal charter by Elizabeth. Because of Dutch strength in Southeast Asia, British trade interests were diverted to South Asia, which became the base from which the British East India Company made inroads into Southeast and East Asia during the eighteenth century. In contrast to Spain, which reaped its wealth from the Americas, and Holland, which exploited the Indonesian archipelago, Britain concentrated, through its East India Company, on India and China, the heartlands of the two major Asian civilizations; the British government did not establish its ascendancy there until the nineteenth century, however. What all the seaborne European empires in Asia had in common by the eighteenth century was their starting point on the shores of the Atlantic.

Tea and Bullion Like the growing taste for sugar in Europe that fueled the plantation system of the Caribbean and contributed to the growth of the Atlantic economy, the introduction of products from Asia created new tastes among Europeans that drove trade in the Pacific and had global impact. Chinese tea was in great demand in European markets, to which it was introduced by Dutch merchants; by 1664 tea reached England and quickly became the national beverage. Tea importing became a major enterprise under the monopoly of the British East India Company and an important source of government tax revenue. China demanded payment in silver for its tea, and most of the silver flowing to China from European trade originated in the Americas.

Once the British acquired Jamaica in 1655, they were in a good position to carry on trade with Spanish possessions and effectively tap the flow of Spanish silver through the Caribbean. By the end of the seventeenth century, the amount of Spanish silver gained each year by the British through Jamaican trade is estimated to have been about half the amount

FIGURE 12.12 Japanese Depiction of Dutchmen Drinking Tea with the Chinese at Deshima, Eighteenth Century.

SOURCE: Bibliothèque Nationale de France, Cabinet des Estampes.

of bullion that the British East India Company exported annually to East Asia to pay for products such as tea. Together with the Spanish bullion that reached China through Manila, the amount of Mexican silver that ended up in China between 1719 and 1833 is estimated to have been one-fifth of all the silver produced in Spanish America during this period, an amount that represented perhaps 20 percent of all European stocks of silver.

■

THE EAST ASIAN CORE AND PERIPHERY: CHINA, JAPAN, AND THE WORLD ECONOMY

As Europeans sailed into East Asian waters in the sixteenth century, they encountered a world dominated by China, a civilization as ancient, complex, and sophisticated as any in Europe. European expansion in East Asia was limited during the sixteenth century to peripheral missionary and mercantile contacts; not until the nineteenth century would European power erode the dominance of China and shatter the stability of the East Asian world order. Nonetheless, the expansion of Europe and the creation of a global economy through the opening of the Atlantic frontier had an impact on China, the core economy of the East Asian world.

CHINESE PROSPERITY DURING THE ERA OF EUROPEAN EXPANSION

With the growth of the Chinese economy following the end of Mongol rule and the restoration of a native Chinese dynasty, the Ming (1368–1644), merchants once again became prosperous, and even powerful, members of society. The growth of domestic commerce, however, was not matched by that of foreign trade. Ming rulers generally followed policies designed to control foreign trade and bring it into the framework of the tributary system.

Tribute and Trade Though the tributary system was conceived as a means of conducting diplomatic relations, trade was an important aspect of tribute relations. Tribute was paid in the form of gifts to the Chinese emperor from rulers of states surrounding China to express their homage to the Son of Heaven, the ruler of the center of the world. Return gifts from the Chinese court made tribute relations a kind of commodity exchange. Tribute missions in China from foreign countries were allowed to engage in trade as well. Merchants traveling with the tribute missions also conducted their own private trade. Despite the hostility of the Ming government to foreign trade, a substantial amount of such trade took place within the framework of the tributary system.

Because of increasing pressures to open the Chinese market to foreign merchants, in the early sixteenth century the Ming government opened the port of Canton to foreign traders not accompanying tribute missions. By the mid–sixteenth century, a port on the Fujian coast was opened for trade with Southeast Asia, and Chinese also began emigrating to Asian ports in a merchant diaspora that shaped trading relations with Europeans throughout Southeast Asia. At approximately the same time, the Portuguese gained permission to reside on the small peninsula south of Canton called Macao and conducted trade with China from their outpost there. The Spanish, Dutch, and British soon followed in the wake of the

Portuguese. Because of China's size and self-sufficiency, however, foreign trade was peripheral to the economy, and the balance of trade was overwhelmingly in China's favor until the nineteenth century.

Agriculture and Population Ming prosperity was fueled by an agricultural revolution begin-
ning around 1500 that saw the introduction of new crops from the Americas—corn, peanuts, and sweet potatoes—indirectly transmitted to Asia by Europeans through their voyages of exploration. These crops contributed significantly to an increase in the food supply since they could be cultivated in marginal soils unsuitable for other crops and provided substantial nutrition. Partly as a result of increased food supply, population swelled from between 60 and 80 million (to which it had dropped as a result of the Mongol conquest) to at least 150 million by 1600.

CHINA AND THE EUROPEAN WORLD ECONOMY

The importation of new food crops was only one dimension of China's growing participation in a world economic system that would eventually be dominated by Europe. Though by the mid–fifteenth century, in contrast to European states' mercantilist policies, the Ming government had withdrawn its support from voyages of exploration, China could no longer remain entirely isolated from the world system being constructed through the expansion of Europe. By 1500, China was becoming part of a global monetary system through indirect links established by its Asian trading partners. East Asia in the age of European exploration and empire formed its own sector of the world economy, with silver flowing into Chinese coffers from Japan, Europe, and the Americas, often through intermediaries who used silver to pay for Chinese products, such as silks, spices, and porcelains, that were extremely profitable on the world market. The monetization of the Chinese economy that accompanied commercial growth during the Ming made China susceptible to shifts in the global economy and made even the poorest peasants in the most remote villages victims of inflation that pushed prices of goods beyond their reach, costing them more copper cash in taxes to make up the equivalent value of silver, which had appreciated on the international market.

The monetization of the economy and the rising price of grain from the early fifteenth through the early seventeenth centuries also dramatically affected the imperial and officeholding elite, whose stipends had been converted from grain to a fixed amount of silver in the early fifteenth century. This meant that as grain prices periodically rose, the real value of their stipends decreased. One of the primary reasons for government graft and corruption—officials' low salaries—was consequently enhanced, and this contributed to an overall decline in morale and confidence in the government. Corruption and extravagance in the highest reaches of government, the imperial court, contributed to a fiscal and political breakdown in the sixteenth century.

The Manchu Conquest Like their predecessors, the Mongols, the Manchus, a seminomadic
people from beyond the northeastern borders of China, were able to conquer and rule the Chinese Empire through their superior military skill and their adoption and adaptation of Chinese government. The wars that accompanied the Manchu conquest and their consolidation of power further contributed to population decline. Ironically, the Manchu

conquest, which took advantage of the weakened conditions of the Ming central government, helped to stabilize the political and economic order by providing a long period of peace.

The Chinese population began to grow again in the late seventeenth century, continuing through the eighteenth and into the early nineteenth centuries. During this period, China's population rose from 150 to 200 million in 1700 to more than 400 million in 1800, a doubling of the population in one century. The reasons for this dramatic population growth lay not only in economic conditions that allowed for the support of growing numbers of people and relatively peaceful social and political conditions, but also in cultural values that encouraged having as many children as possible, both for the continuity of the ancestral line and to ensure support in old age, given the relatively high mortality rate of a premodern society.

COMMERCE AND CHANGE IN JAPAN

The military rulers of Tokugawa (1600–1850) Japan, who came to power in the late sixteenth century, closely regulated foreign trade in order to prevent regional lords from becoming wealthy on the profits of foreign trade and possibly challenging their authority to rule. Following contact with Portuguese and Spanish traders and priests in the sixteenth century, the Tokugawa government began to fear encroachment on its sovereignty by European monarchies and social disruption by Christian converts. By around 1640, the Tokugawa government restricted foreign trade to Dutch and Chinese merchants based at the southwestern port city of Nagasaki.

Merchants and Domestic Trade Domestic trade was also profoundly altered by the reunification of Japan under the Tokugawa at the beginning of the seventeenth century. Previously, during the sixteenth century, merchants had prospered by providing goods needed by powerful territorial lords who waged war against one another for control of the country. Markets in castle towns and the countryside were centers of commercial exchange that were relatively free from regulation or control by a central authority. Merchant houses that dominated commerce during the wars of the sixteenth century were replaced in the seventeenth century by a new group of Osaka merchants who could handle the warehousing and sale of tax rice collected by regional lords (daimyo) in the Tokugawa political system. Despite the prosperity of these new merchant houses based in the commercial port of Osaka, the adoption and promotion of Confucian ideas by the Tokugawa government meant that merchants were relegated to a low social status relative not only to that of warriors (samurai) but also to that of peasants.

By the late seventeenth century a new group of wholesalers and shippers concentrated in Osaka and Kyoto invested in the production of textiles and other goods for the market, placing themselves in a favorable position to purchase the finished products and to distribute these goods to retail stores. Such groups of wholesalers were granted monopoly privileges in the mid–eighteenth century, and they retained this privileged position until the fall of the Tokugawa in the mid–nineteenth century.

The Social Impact of Though within the strict legal class system of the Tokugawa, merchants could not aspire to political power or to higher social status, Commercial Growth they did acquire considerable economic wealth and power. But when loans outstanding to a merchant became politically sensitive, such as when an important *daimyo* was deeply in debt to a merchant lender, the government could—and sometimes did—intervene and confiscate the property of the merchant. Both *samurai* and peasants were exhorted by the Tokugawa authorities to live frugal lives, but this did not prevent *samurai* from indulging in the consumption of goods and services far beyond their means. This inevitably led to borrowing from merchants and to the growing indebtedness of the *samurai* class as a whole.

Agriculture and Commerce Agricultural production in Japan increased during the seventeenth and eighteenth centuries, aided by the use of new fertilizers and technology. A new group of wealthy farmers emerged who increased their income through specializing in crops produced for the market and through the expansion of domestic interregional trade. Although population leveled off to about 30 million by 1725, the monetization of the economy, the commercialization of agriculture, and the expansion and regional specialization of the market generated economic growth and social change. Merchants benefited from the general growth of the economy as they became wealthy investors, lenders, consumers of goods and services, and patrons of the arts.

Konoikeya Zen'emon: The history of one important merchant family from the founding
A Tokugawa Entrepreneur of the Tokugawa shogunate through the seventeenth century
gives some idea of how merchants acquired financial power in the Tokugawa political system and how they participated in Tokugawa society despite the low official status imposed on them by Confucian ideology and the harsh dictates of the rigid Tokugawa social order. Konoikeya Zen'emon's family originated as *sake* (rice wine) brewers in the village of Konoike; hence the family name. Because they were among the wealthiest members of rural communities, *sake* brewers were also moneylenders and pawnbrokers. A technical innovation in the brewing process that made better *sake* caused the Konoikeya family to expand its production and to extend its activities into shipping to deliver its product to meet increased demands, including those of the residents of Edo, the capital city.

Zen'emon also acted as an agent in Osaka for the *daimyo* of western Japan, handling the transport, warehousing, and sale of tax rice for them. He advanced money to these *daimyo,* opening an "exchange shop," which functioned much like a bank, in 1656. When a banking consortium of Osaka merchants was set up in 1670 to handle the financial transactions of the shogunate and to supervise the Osaka money market, Zen'emon was in a strong position to be part of that group. This consortium functioned much like a central bank, regulating the market value of gold and silver, as well as the credit system of Osaka and other commercial centers in Japan, and acting as the financial agents of the Tokugawa government.

Economic and *Daimyo* often needed credit for the demands of the "alternate atten-
Demographic Change dance" mandated by the Tokugawa government. *Daimyo* were required
to maintain residences in the capital, Edo, and to spend periods ranging from six months to a year there in attendance on the military ruler *(shogun)*. The maintenance of residences and the periodic processions journeying to the capital in a manner appropriate to their status to meet the demands of "alternate attendance" required substantial outlays of funds, often provided by advances from Osaka bankers such as Konoikeya.

The "alternate attendance" system also had a significant economic impact in fostering interregional trade based on Edo as a central hub, with transportation routes converging there as spokes on a wheel. Goods brought from *daimyo* domains as gifts to the *shogun* encouraged regional specialization of production for an expanding market as the growing urban center of Edo created demands for these goods. The population of Edo attained a peak of about 1 million by the first quarter of the eighteenth century, at the same time that the population of Japan as a whole began to level off. Other urban centers, such as Osaka and Kyoto, reached at least a half million, and towns that grew up around the castles of major *daimyo* increased in size and population.

While it is difficult to provide a clear causal explanation for economic growth in Tokugawa Japan, we can isolate certain factors as having been important and identify unintended effects of policies adopted to achieve ends other than economic ones. For example, an indirect effect of the "alternate attendance" system, the purpose of which was to control *daimyo* and forcibly ensure their loyalty, was the knitting together of the country's many regional economies through the exchange of goods in Edo. Similarly, though Confucian ideology was adopted by the Tokugawa regime to provide a basis for social order and was reflected in the low social standing of merchants, that same ideology also influenced the Tokugawa government to pay little attention to regulating domestic commerce, with some exceptions. In the absence of direct controls over domestic commerce, merchants were able to build strong financial bases that served their economic interests.

Perhaps the most striking quality of the history of Japan during the seventeenth and eighteenth centuries was the high degree of economic change within the confines of the rigid Tokugawa social and political order and without significant external influences. This is not to say that Japan was "isolated" and unconnected with the outside world but to suggest that it was undergoing relatively rapid and substantial commercial development despite ideological and political conditions that were not conducive to commerce and were largely independent of externally generated stimuli.

SUMMARY

Between about 1500 and 1800, following Columbus's voyages, the economic relationships and societies of the Americas, Europe, parts of Africa, Asia, and the Pacific were transformed through the creation of an Atlantic world economy that provided the means for subsequent European expansion into Asia and the Pacific. Establishment of Atlantic connections had a profound impact on the lives and cultures of African peoples, particularly those of West and Central Africa. The new global connections upset the balance of the long-established relations among Asia, Africa, and Europe, replacing and redirecting their world systems of land-based and maritime, inter- and intraregional commerce.

Triangular connections among societies in Africa, Europe, and the Americas revolved primarily around an expanding Atlantic trade, with its foundations mired in slavery and merchant capitalism. Soon after its forging, the interconnected world of Atlantic commercial development was no longer a set of balanced relationships. European expansion into the Pacific added new global connections and constituted a westward shift of power away from earlier

Afro-Eurasian centers such as the Indian Ocean trading world and the East Asian core economy of China. Unlike the Americas, parts of Africa, and Southeast Asia, before 1800 East Asia remained a world economy on its own only indirectly affected by European expansion. Changes such as the commercialization of the economy in late Ming China and Tokugawa Japan were generated by internal, domestic developments.

In contrast, during the three centuries following the opening of the Atlantic frontier, Europeans tended to perceive its shores as the entry to areas they could dominate and commodities they could exploit. For example, they tended to view sub-Saharan Africa as a uniform, undifferentiated continent of peoples without a past. In part this was the consequence of ethnocentrism, a prevailing racism and ignorance that led Europeans to view African societies as homogeneous and interchangeable. For several centuries after 1500, Europeans saw Africans and other non-Europeans as they wished to see them and as their economic and political connections with them forced them to be. In parts of Africa and across the Americas and into Southeast Asia, the European worldview dominated and, although it was altered by its cultural encounters, endured as a fundamental component of understanding global relations in later centuries.

ENGAGING THE PAST

WEALTH IN PEOPLE, THINGS, AND KNOWLEDGE

The study of wealth—the things people infuse with value—and the associated meanings that they ascribe to them are among the most contested arenas of historical understanding. As the shift in world systems suggests, the period from about 1500 on witnessed dramatic changes in the availability and movements of goods, their ascribed meanings and value, and in the conversions and myriad uses of wealth, including as instruments of power.

During and after the Atlantic era, material life was undeniably enriched and diversified, but also contested. European systems of value, having just undergone a shift to a market economy, came into contact with other systems around the world. Some goods, valued almost universally, moved easily between cultural categories of valuation; ivory, art, gold, and silver, for example, could be shipped between any of the world's continents as "riches."

In Africa, where historians have debated the impact of the new money economy on the valuation of people, some scholars argue that the African-European encounters transformed indigenous systems from systems of valuing people in

terms of kinship, labor, or clientage into systems where humans became simply goods to be counted, bought, and sold. In actuality, the accumulation of people in precolonial equatorial Africa was considered a means by which rulers could acquire and mobilize *bodies* of knowledge, primary resources that could be elaborated, cultivated, and composed. During the same period, Europeans accumulated goods as conspicuous consumption, or what one historian has termed an "embarrassment of riches," their display constituted the display of personal power, their growth was based upon processes of accumulation, transaction, and revaluation.

The Atlantic exchange was a meeting place for European and African ways of structuring relationships between people and things. For many Africans, the Atlantic world was a spiritually empowered and interactive universe of living persons, spirits, and ancestors, who functioned as critical links to the past, that is, to human memory that served to help guide persons across a sea of cruelty and deprivation. These worlds of the living, spirits, and ancestors were coexistent and interactive; and those interactions denied and

FIGURE 12.13 Merchant Banker Negotiating in a Foreign Land.

SOURCE: Bibliothèque Nationale de France.

transcended the day-to-day reality and order/chaos imposed by slavery. Far from the historical stereotype of slave as passive victim, each person was essentially a spiritual being. As such, humans were active participants in a universe of familiar spirits and ancestors; whether free or slave, each human was ultimately empowered by unseen spiritual forces.

Things, or *boci*, provided one means of personal empowerment. *Boci*, as described by art historian Suzanne Blier, were "empowerment objects," best known from the regions of the Guinea Coast, the Slave Coast, and the Bight of Benin. Peoples there shared a belief in *vodun*, mysterious forces or powers that govern the world and the lives of people. *Boci* (the Fon words literally mean "empowered [*bo*] cadaver [*ce*]") functioned in conjunction with these *vodun* energies both in protecting humans and in offering avenues of individual empowerment and change. These beliefs and even these objects were carried to the New World, where they were employed by slaves to alter and subvert their conditions of enslavement.

Writing about Haiti in 1797, Moreau de Saint-Méry described the following example: "The Negroes believe in magic and that the power of their fetiches has followed them across the sea. Little rude figures of wood or stone, representing men or animals, are for them things of supernatural power and they call them *garde-corps* (body guards). There are a great number of Negroes who acquire absolute power over the others by this means."[1]

People were wealth, whether understood in European, African, or other cultural terms. The association of both people and things with knowledge helped to make them both substances of value. For example, Lakshmi, the Indian goddess of abundance, was also called "Sri," meaning wealth as measured in both material terms and spiritual knowledge. Unequal exchanges characterized the Atlantic era, as Columbus found when he was able to trade glass beads for gold in 1492. Ultimately, the pursuit of fundamental inequalities impoverished both those who were possessed and those who attempted to control the wealth of people and things around the world.

[1] Melville J. Herskovits, *Life in a Haitian Valley* (New York: Octagon Press, [1937] 1964), p. 221.

SUGGESTIONS FOR FURTHER READING

Alfred Crosby, *The Columbian Exchange: Biological and Cultural Consequences of 1492* (Westport, CT: Greenwood Press, 1972). A powerful examination of the impact of Atlantic world connections.

Alfred Crosby, *Ecological Imperialism: The Biological Expansion of Europe* (Cambridge: Cambridge University Press, 1986). An overview of the unseen connections across the Atlantic.

John Iliffe, *Africans: The History of a Continent* (Cambridge: Cambridge University Press, 1995). A comprehensive and thematic approach to the vast African past.

Sidney Mintz, *Sweetness and Power: The Place of Sugar in Modern History* (New York: Viking, 1985). A cultural and economic history of a major Atlantic link.

James D. Tracy, ed., *The Rise of Merchant Empires: Long-Distance Trade in the Early Modern World* (Cambridge: Cambridge University Press, 1990). A rich collection of articles on topics ranging from trans-Saharan and Central Asian caravan trade to merchant communities in India and Southeast Asia.

Richard von Glahn, *Fountain of Fortune: A History of Chinese Monetary Policy, ca. 1000–1700* (Berkeley: University of California Press, 1996). A new study that challenges the view that the seventeenth-century global economic crisis had a significant impact on China.

Traditions and Their Transformations

ollowing the Portuguese conquest of Goa in 1510 and their establishment of a key outpost there for trade between Europe and Southeast
Asia, Catholic missionaries traveled inland and began to establish contacts
with their learned counterparts in Indian society. Father Antonio Montserrate was a Catholic missionary to the court of the Mughal ruler Akbar
(r. 1556–1605) from 1580 to 1583. Father Montserrate kept notes of his
experiences and wrote them up as an extended commentary in Latin on
Akbar's realm. Noted for his policies of religious toleration, Akbar was also
the founder of his own eclectic religion. Something of the flavor of Akbar's
interest in a wide range of different religions, including (in addition to Islam), Hinduism, Zoroastrianism, Jainism, and even Catholicism, can be
seen in Montserrate's account. Despite Montserrate's biases due to his own
faith, he cannot help but recognize and admire the intellectual fervor with
which Akbar, though illiterate, engaged in discussions with representatives of all faiths:

> He is a great patron of learning, and always keeps around him erudite men,
> who are directed to discuss before him philosophy, theology, and religion, and
> to recount to him the history of great kings and glorious deeds of the past. He
> has an excellent judgment and a good memory, and has attained to a consider-
> able knowledge of many subjects by means of constant and patient listening
> to many discussions. Thus he not only makes up for his ignorance of letters
> (for he is unable either to read or write), but he has also become able clearly
> and lucidly to expound difficult matters. He can give his opinion on any ques-
> tion so shrewdly and keenly, that no one who did not know that he is illiter-
> ate would suppose him to be anything but very learned and erudite. And so
> indeed he is, for in addition to his keen intellect, of which I have already spo-
> ken, he excels many of his most learned subjects in eloquence, as well as in
> that authority and dignity which befits a King. The wise men are wont every
> day to hold disputations on literary subjects before him.

Through his avid interest in different religious viewpoints, Akbar sought
to reconcile the many religious beliefs represented among his subjects. Few
rulers or leaders of religious traditions themselves were as open-minded
and tolerant, showing genuine interest in diverse ideas. Yet traditions of
all kinds—ideas and practices inherited from the past—change constantly,
sometimes slowly and sometimes explosively, and the sources of change are
many and complex, including those from within the tradition as well as
influences from other traditions and from changing material conditions.

Mughal Emperor Akbar Presides at a Debate with Two European Catholic Missionaries Who Attack Islam.

Akbar's openness to all religions was opposed by orthodox Muslim clergy, but it was a wise policy for a ruler whose subjects were largely non-Muslim.

INTRODUCTION

As the commercial revolutions that took place in Europe and China before 1500 brought about significant changes in the ways people lived, ideas about the way the world worked began to change, too. The European Renaissance and the rise of Neo-Confucianism in China were both in part products of changing material conditions created by commercial expansion and urban growth in Europe and East Asia in the centuries before 1500. Beginning in the fifteenth century, the creation of the Atlantic world system wrought transformations not only in societies of the Americas, Africa, and Europe, but also in the mutual perceptions of peoples on both sides of the Atlantic frontier. The development of the Atlantic world system gradually brought changes to Asia, too, as the global expansion of Europe reached eastward over Indian Ocean maritime routes and into South, East, and Southeast Asia.

One of the most complex questions dealt with by historians is the relationship between changes in the material world, such as those made by commerce and technology, and changes in ideas. In this chapter, we explore the relationship between material conditions and ideas,

527

between economic, social, and political changes and transformations in religious, cultural, and intellectual traditions. How were ideas transformed in response to changing material circumstances, and how did new ideas reconstruct the world?

We begin by examining the notion of cultural rebirth, the revival of past tradition as a means of reinterpreting and reconstructing the present. We look at transformations generated by conflict as inherited traditions fracture and divide under the pressures of social, economic, or political changes. In contrast to rupture and division of inherited traditions as a response to changing conditions, we also consider other means of adaptation, such as syncretism, the selective integration of concepts, symbols, and practices drawn from different traditions. Finally, we examine the impact of new ideas drawn from exposure to peoples and cultures of the Americas, Africa, and Asia on European thought and culture, showing how the global expansion of Europe and the creation of a new world economy began to shape new world cultures across the globe.

■

EUROPEAN TRADITIONS, TRANSFORMATIONS, AND GLOBAL ENCOUNTERS

Late medieval European culture and society (ca. 1000–1200) had been dominated by the traditions of Christianity and the institution of the Catholic Church. After 1200, both were eroded by changes brought about in part by the expansion of commerce, the breakdown of feudal political structures, and, beginning in the fifteenth century, by the opening of the Atlantic frontier and influences from Asia, Africa, and the Americas.

THE EUROPEAN RENAISSANCE

The European Renaissance took place from the fourteenth through sixteenth centuries and meant to contemporaries, who coined the term, a rebirth of European culture as they turned to Greece and Rome for a source of inspiration and cultural ideals distinct from those of medieval Christianity. These cultural ideals can be described by the term secular humanism, emphasizing secular or worldly concerns over those of religious faith and humanistic concerns over those of God. Rejecting medieval preoccupations with Christian belief and the sense of community provided by the unity of medieval Christianity, Renaissance thinkers were attracted to the individualism they found in the works of Greek and Roman authors. The ideal of individualism was encouraged and supported by the social and economic realities of commercial capitalism and the process of urbanization that took place in the centuries between 1200 and 1500 (see Chapter 11).

The interests of Renaissance humanists in Greek and Latin texts led them to become linguists and to emulate in their own writings the language and style of classical literature. This was problematic, since many new ideas, experiences, and emotions could not be expressed in the language, grammar, and syntax of Roman orators such as Cicero or Athenian philosophers such as Plato. Accordingly, literary humanists had to find other ways of expressing their ideas. They could express the ideas and values of their time in their own "corrupt" Latin, a language that had evolved over the centuries, or they could write in a vernacular (common spoken form) language, such as Italian or French.

Literary Humanism The heart of the Italian Renaissance and the center of literary humanism was the city of Florence, located in Tuscany in central Italy. From that city and the surrounding Tuscan hills came a number of writers who wrote in the vernacular and whose works defined literary humanism in the fourteenth century. The most prominent were Dante Aligheri (1265–1321), Francesco Petrarch (1304–1374), and Giovanni Boccaccio (1313–1375). All made use of the Tuscan dialect in their writings to express humanistic values. Though he wrote other works in Latin, Dante used the dialect of his native Tuscany to compose *The Divine Comedy*. Based on Christian religious themes, *The Divine Comedy* tells the story of Dante's imagined journey to paradise through Hell and Purgatory, guided by the Roman poet Virgil. His entrance into Paradise is aided by the woman Dante loved in real life, Beatrice. As Dante's verse expressed the experience of real people even in the context of religious themes, his friend and fellow Florentine, the artist Giotto (ca. 1270–1317), painted frescoes (paintings in wet plaster) that showed new realism and vitality even as they portrayed religious subjects. Renaissance art, like literature, increasingly focused on a humanistic perspective, with humans at the center, the viewers of medieval religious subjects.

Petrarch took literature in a more secular direction. He was a passionate collector of Greek and Latin manuscripts, mastered classical Latin, and tried his hand with Greek. Like Dante, Petrarch wrote works in Latin modeled on masters such as Virgil, but his fame rests on his sonnets, love poems written in the Tuscan vernacular to an imaginary woman named Laura. Boccaccio also wrote his major work, *The Decameron*, in the Tuscan dialect. The hundred tales of this collection are bawdy and earthy, promoting the individualistic values of Renaissance Italy and showing little respect for Christian values. Though the work of literary

FIGURE 13.1 Piero della Francesca, *The Resurrection*, ca. 1460. Fresco.

Piero della Francesca (1420–1492) exemplified in his painting the new vision of humans at the center of the cosmos that characterized the Italian Renaissance in both literature and art. A master of geometry, he brought mathematical rigor to the new technique of perspective, making the viewer's eye the center point. This painting depicts one of the most sacred subjects in Christianity, but both Christ and the attendants are portrayed as deeply humanized figures.

SOURCE: Alinari/Art Resource, NY.

humanists was aimed at an elite educated audience, Boccaccio began a course of public readings of *The Divine Comedy* at a church in Florence in 1373. He accompanied the readings with his own commentaries to explain the meaning of what Dante had written to his largely illiterate audience. His efforts were met with condemnation by learned men of the time, suggesting the potency of the spread of new ideas beyond the guarded realm of scholarly circles and the apparent threat this presented to the monopoly of knowledge held by scholars of the time.

Transformation of Textual Tradition The radical potential of humanistic scholarship can also be seen in the work of Lorenzo Valla (1406–1457), considered the father of historical criticism in the West. Valla applied his method of historical linguistic analysis to major documents of Christian history. By careful scrutiny of literary style and expert examination of the internal evidence of documents, he was able to question their validity and raise doubts about the institutions and beliefs supported by them. In this way, Valla proved the Donation of Constantine, the purported fourth-century gift of western Europe by Emperor Constantine to the pope, to be a forgery of the eighth century and showed how subversive of tradition the study of ancient texts could be.

The Renaissance Humanist The work of Renaissance literary humanists focused on the revival of classical authors, placing humans at the center, and shifted from writing in Latin to expressions of contemporary ideas in emerging national vernaculars. As the interests of literary humanists broadened into other realms of knowledge, the ideal of the Renaissance scholar, one who knows much about many things, not the specialist

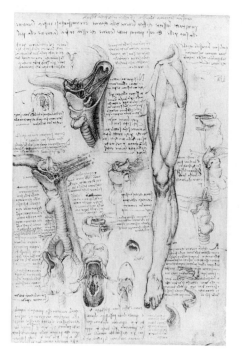

FIGURE 13.2 Leonardo da Vinci, *Anatomical Studies* (Leg and Larynx), 1510–11.

SOURCE: Leonardo da Vinci, *Anatomical Studies,* "Leg and Larynx," 1510–11. The Royal Collection. © Her Majesty Queen Elizabeth II.

or expert in a single area of knowledge, emerged. This concept is exemplified by Leonardo da Vinci (1452–1519). Born the illegitimate son of a wealthy Florentine, Leonardo was apprenticed to painters and accepted into the Florentine painters' guild as a young man. Like his contemporary, Michelangelo Buonaratti (1475–1564), Leonardo's depiction of religious subjects expressed humanistic qualities. Though known for his fresco *The Last Supper*, which portrays the religious subject of Christ and his disciples in a humanistic fashion, and his painting of the woman with the mysterious smile, *La Giaconda* (also known as *Mona Lisa*), his interests and talents were wide-ranging and included architecture, anatomy, engineering, and even the plan for a flying machine.

Patronage and Politics The cultural flowering in art, literature, and scholarship known as the Renaissance could not have taken place without the patronage of wealthy merchants and bankers such as the Medici family (see Chapter 11). Cosimo de' Medici (1389–1464) spent lavishly on paintings, sculptures, and public buildings, as well as scholarly enterprises such as the Platonic Academy, a research institute devoted to the study of Plato's philosophy. Under Cosimo's grandson Lorenzo "the Magnificent" (1449–1492) Medici, patronage of scholarship and the arts continued, and the influence of the Medici family in politics, commerce, and culture reached its peak, although the family continued to dominate Florentine politics until the eighteenth century.

The Florentine historian and politician Niccolò Machiavelli (1469–1527) depicted the power of the Medici family as well as other aspects of Florentine history in his *History of Florence to the Death of Lorenzo the Magnificent* (1492). Reflecting the rejection of the medieval Christian worldview shared by humanist scholars of his time, Machiavelli's history does not relate the unfolding of a divine plan for humankind, nor does it have a religious message or theological interpretation. It is based on the critical use of evidence to explain historical events, with analysis rooted in the realism of human and secular motives. Like most Florentine humanists, Machiavelli was deeply involved in the rough-and-tumble of politics, and he brilliantly showed his grasp of the political world in his manual of advice to rulers, *The Prince*.

International Rivalries The European Renaissance took place in the context of international political, cultural, and religious rivalries, dominated until the mid–fifteenth century by the Roman Catholic Papacy, Eastern Orthodox Christianity centered at Constantinople, and the rising power of the Ottoman Turks, who had begun to expand from Anatolia in West Asia into Europe in the mid–fourteenth century. The strategic importance of Constantinople, which controlled access to the Mediterranean, made the city the focus of struggles involving the Roman Catholic West, the Orthodox Byzantine Empire, and the Islamic Ottoman Empire. Though the Orthodox Byzantine Empire and the Roman Catholic Papacy shared a common Christian opposition to Islam, the West did not come to the aid of the Byzantine Empire in its final struggle with the Ottoman Empire, which ended in 1453 with the Ottoman capture of Constantinople. The importance of money in the diplomatic and military rivalries of the time is seen in the failure of the Byzantine emperor to raise the necessary funds for a huge cannon to defend Constantinople against the Ottomans that a Hungarian engineer proposed to build in 1452. The Hungarian went directly from the Byzantine capital to the Ottoman capital, where the sultan was able to supply the funds and technical assistance to build the cannon, which was then used by the Ottomans in the conquest of Constantinople the following year.

Commerce and Culture Once Constantinople had fallen to the Ottomans, who renamed the city Istanbul, commercial relations between Constantinople and the Roman West were quickly resumed by Venetian and Genoese merchants. The loss of Orthodox Christian control of Constantinople also had cultural benefits for Western Europe that were as important as commercial continuity. Following the Ottoman seizure of the city, there was an increased transfer of Greek learning to the Latin West as Byzantine scholars fled to Florence, other cities of the Italian Renaissance, and northern Europe. In this way, the scholarly riches of the Byzantine Empire moved westward. Greek knowledge, which had virtually been lost in the Latin West, was recovered and revived as part of the Renaissance. Both Byzantine and Islamic scholars, as well as Jewish ones who translated both Greek and Arabic texts, played a key role in transmitting the learning of antiquity to the West.

Technology and the Transmission of Ideas New understanding of the world among Renaissance humanists was initially inspired by the rediscovery of Greek thinkers such as Plato, whose works were translated from Greek and Arabic manuscripts into Latin. Until the introduction of the printing press in the mid–fifteenth century, manuscripts of texts were laboriously hand-copied, often in single editions available only to learned men in scholarly settings. Johannes Gutenberg (ca. 1394–1468), a goldsmith from the German city of Mainz, was responsible for a series of inventions that revolutionized the transmission of knowledge. Gutenberg's experimentation with print technology resulted in the development of stamping molds for casting type, which was made of a new alloy of lead, tin and antimony; the printing press; and ink with an oil base that would produce finely printed, multiple copies of texts. Gutenberg's efforts were financed by loans from another goldsmith, Johann Faust, but when after five years no book had appeared from his printing press, Faust sued for his money and bankrupted Gutenberg. Faust then brought out the first printed book in 1456 with another type designer, Peter Schöffer; ironically, it became known as the "Gutenberg Bible."

The Business of Books The Gutenberg Bible was the first book printed in Europe using movable type, but Gutenberg's process was soon used to print books of many kinds. Greek and Roman classics were made available to a much wider audience, and printing became a commercial enterprise in which profit often mattered more than scholarship. Consumer demands, production costs, and marketing strategies all played a role in determining which books were published and who could afford them. At the end of the fifteenth century, the complete works of Aristotle in Greek were published in five volumes by the printer Aldus Manutius at the price of 11 ducats, a costly investment for a prospective buyer such as a humanities professor, whose salary might be 150 ducats a year.

Like many of his humanist scholar contemporaries, the Dutch scholar Erasmus of Rotterdam (1464–1536) worked closely with printing houses throughout Europe to disseminate his works. Commercial and scholarly values went hand in hand. When Erasmus published his own edition of Aristotle in 1531, he pointed out to potential buyers that the price was competitive with that of the earlier Aldine edition, which had not dropped in price since its publication a generation earlier.

Latin Texts Representative of northern European Renaissance humanist scholarship, Erasmus was learned in both Greek and Latin. He applied this training to a new Latin

FIGURE 13.3 Bookmaking—Illustrating Type-Founding and Papermaking, Printing and Binding. From the Woodcuts of Jost Amman, 1562.

SOURCE: AKG London.

translation of the Greek New Testament published in 1516, a translation that supplanted the fourth-century Latin text. In other works, Erasmus satirized the church and society of his times. In 1516 Erasmus's English friend Thomas More (1477–1535) published his *Utopia,* another attack on early sixteenth-century society, written in Latin. More depicted a utopia, or ideal society. In More's book, a traveler arrives on the island where the utopia is located laden with Greek and Latin texts that would become the classical heritage of the people in the utopian society. More's utopia was a republic of scrupulous equality located somewhere in the Americas, and his work is one of the earliest English literary reactions to reports from the Americas. More's knowledge of the new world was gained from popular published works such as the letters of the Italian explorer Amerigo Vespucci (1451–1512) (from whom the name "America" derives).

Vernacular Texts Gradually, works in vernacular languages, the languages of everyday speech, made Renaissance literature available to a wider reading audience. Between 1450 and 1500, most printed books were in Greek and Latin; after 1500, most were in the new national vernacular languages of French, Italian, Spanish, English, and German. As the Renaissance spread through Europe from Italy to France, England, Spain, and Germany, both poetry and prose in the vernacular flowered. One of the most vivid expressions of Renaissance humanism was the work of the French writer François Rabelais (ca. 1493–1553). His *Gargantua and Pantagruel,* the story of a father and son whose appetite for life is prodigious, captured the sense of worldly joy and optimism characteristic of the times. In a letter to his son, Gargantua wrote, "The times when I was a student were not as fit and favorable to learning as they are today. . . . Indeed, the times were still dark. . . . But thanks be to God, learning has been restored in my age to its former dignity and enlightenment. Why, the very women and girls aspire to the glory and reach out to the celestial manna of sound learning."

Renaissance Women Rabelais's ironic observation on women and learning may reflect the fact
and Learning that many elite women, such as Christine de Pisan (1364–ca. 1430), had been educated in the new learning of secular humanism and become skilled along with their male counterparts in translating and making critical studies of classical texts. Educated by an Italian humanist father and brought up at the court of the French king, Christine de Pisan is the first known woman in Europe to have earned a living through scholarship and even great honor through her writings. Widowed at the age of twenty-five, she supported her family through her writing. She exchanged letters with famous humanists of the time and wrote autobiographical fiction in which she expressed her anger, her self-justification, and her dreams for women.

Rabelais's contemporary Anne of Burgundy, who was wife to two kings of France, had her own library and embraced humanistic studies with enthusiasm. Thomas More had his daughters tutored in Latin, Greek, philosophy, theology, mathematics, and astronomy by the most learned tutors available. More's belief in the education of women was shared at the court of the king he served, Henry VIII, whose first wife, Catherine of Aragon, wrote fluent Latin and provided their daughter, Mary Tudor, with an education similar to her own. Elizabeth I (r. 1558–1603), who succeeded Mary Tudor as queen of England, commanded both Latin and Greek, could engage in the intellectual dialogues of her day, and had a reputation as a poet.

Late Renaissance Literature During the late Renaissance in Elizabethan England, named for the long reign of the Tudor queen, the plays of William Shakespeare (1564–1616) helped to establish modern standard English. Shakespeare's dramas range far beyond the world of sixteenth-century England both in setting and in his portrayal of universal human themes. *Romeo and Juliet,* for example, touches upon universal human emotions—love, loyalty, and family honor—that transcend the Renaissance Italian setting of the play. Shakespeare's contemporary in late Renaissance Spain, Miguel de Cervantes (1547–1616), in his novel *Don Quixote,* made use of his background as a soldier to shape the satirical tale of a knight mesmerized by medieval chivalric ideals. Such literature, made available in printed texts or performances, provided commentary on changing values in a changing world.

THE IMPACT OF THE WORLD ON RENAISSANCE EUROPE

Exploration, trade, and conquest had a profound impact on European thought and culture in the Renaissance. The fifteenth-century Portuguese voyages around Africa to India and on to the East Indies, followed in short order by the Dutch and others, sparked the interest of Europeans in the wider world. Reports about foreign lands and their peoples and societies fed that interest. Technological changes in the creation and transmission of knowledge, especially the invention of the printing press, shaped popular European images of the rest of the world. Illustrated books about voyages and peoples in Africa, Asia, and the Americas became increasingly popular after the fifteenth century. Many of the illustrators and even some of the authors had never traveled to the parts of the world they portrayed, resulting, for example, in African kings and their palaces resembling European monarchs and castles. Though it may have been difficult to sort fact from myth and fancy in the sixteenth century, Europeans nonetheless had access to and were affected by the ever-increasing body of information from Africa and other parts of the world. Images of other peoples and other places became common in late Renaissance literature.

Images of Africans Ben Jonson's play *Masque of Blackness* (1605) made reference to the sixteenth-century travel accounts by the North African Moor Leo Africanus; Jonson made his principal characters the "twelve nymphs, Negroes, and the daughters of Niger." There is evidence that Shakespeare also knew of Leo's work, which was in translation by 1600, and used it for background material for at least two of his plays, *Othello* and *Antony and Cleopatra*. Shakespeare humanized Othello, the dark-skinned Moor, by providing him with a multifaceted character and complex psychology. Elizabethans in court life and on city streets knew Africans both as free men—even diplomats and rulers—and as slaves. They

FIGURE 13.4 Costume Design for African Nymph in Ben Jonson's *Masque of Blackness* (1605).

SOURCE: Devonshire Collection, Chatsworth. Reproduced by permission of the Chatsworth Settlement Trustees. Photo courtesy Courtauld Institute of Art.

were portrayed in the theater as "black," with European actors and mummers darkening their faces with paints and masks and wearing long black gloves for the performance of characters more frequently stereotyped than humanized as individuals.

Images of the Americas Following the voyages of Columbus, reports by explorers and travelers, soldiers, colonists, and missionaries stirred European interest in the peoples of the Americas. Hundreds of descriptions of American society flooded Europe, including such works as the *Brief Relations of the Destruction of the West Indies* by the Catholic missionary and later bishop Bartolomé de Las Casas, who had actually read the letters and journals of Columbus. Whereas earlier accounts of the Chinese, the Turks, and other Asians that attracted European attention did not mention liberty, freedom, or equality, telling more of kings and slaves, reports from the Americas portrayed "natural societies," where individuals lived in freedom and equality because they were masterless and propertyless.

Shakespeare and *The Tempest* Among others, Shakespeare was influenced by what he heard of the Americas. *The Tempest* (1611) is a play that serves both as a metaphor for English expansion into America and as a masquerade for a new society there. The play's title was inspired by a contemporary historical incident, the 1609 shipwreck in Bermuda of a vessel taking colonists to Virginia. It is almost as if Shakespeare had lifted material from contemporary accounts: the scene of the play is near the "Bermoothes," an innocent land depicted as an ideal commonwealth where everything is as yet unformed and unbound. One of the characters, Gonzalo, describes it as a place where there was "no use of service, of riches, or of poverty. . . . No use of metal . . . all men idle, all; and women too . . . nor sovereignty." This idyllic land was inhabited by people such as Caliban, one of the principal characters, whose name is an anagram of "cannibal" and derived from "Carib," a term for West Indians that had come to mean an American savage. Such characters signified the ambivalence about the inhabitants of the "brave new world" that persisted in many European minds.

THE IMPACT OF BOOKS AND LITERACY ON EUROPEAN ENCOUNTERS

The fifteenth-century revolution of printed books brought changes both to European society and to other societies in the orbit of European commercial expansion. In the course of maritime expansion, Europeans encountered a bewildering variety of cultural traditions, many of which were oral cultures, in which verbal arts were highly developed and virtually all intellectual traditions were transmitted through oral poetry, ritual, and recitation. Encounters with European traditions of literacy wrought transformations in the structures of knowledge and ideas and the paths of their transmission.

The International Book Trade The printing revolution made books available to wider audiences, both in Europe and on other continents, at economical prices. Books, especially reference works and guidebooks, were carried on board ships from the late fifteenth century. The first century of printing produced an estimated 42,000 works, most of which were printed in limited editions averaging 300 copies each. Limited supply and high demand in Europe constrained their distribution overseas. However, during the course of the next two centuries, book production exploded. Between 1550 and 1750, an estimated 1.9 million works were published. Whereas in medieval Europe, books had been so scarce that they had been chained to library or church shelves, printing allowed for the rise of literacy and books for unprecedented mobility.

In the seventeenth century, printing spread across the Atlantic. In Cambridge, Massachusetts, Stephen Daye, a locksmith by trade, acquired a printing press brought by Reverend Jose Glover, who had died. In 1640, Daye printed 1,700 copies of *The Whole Booke of Psalms Faithfully Translated into English Metre,* the first book printed in North America. Religious works and travel books were by far the most popular titles. Throughout the course of maritime expansion, literate European ship captains kept journals, hoping to later capitalize on the information collected by publishing their accounts. Books and manuscripts (correspondence) also constituted part of the cargoes intended for overseas markets as literacy in European languages spread. In Europe, the expansion of literacy and the spread of books and other printed materials also played an important role in the religious upheavals of the sixteenth century known as the Protestant Reformation.

THE PROTESTANT REFORMATION

Revisions of the medieval worldview that occurred during the European Renaissance were continued during the sixteenth-century Protestant Reformation, when religious divisions and conflict continued and furthered profound social, economic, and political change. A characteristic feature of medieval and Renaissance Europe was the great influence of the Roman Catholic Church on all aspects of European life, thought, and culture. The role of the Catholic Church as an institution and of Christian doctrine as a social and political ideology, though not as powerful, was somewhat comparable to that of Islam and the Muslim clergy in West Asia and North Africa.

Like the schism in Islam between Sunni and Shia, fractures in the Christian community were nothing new, but those in the sixteenth century that led to permanent division among western European Christians were due not only to controversies over religious issues but also to social, economic, and political changes taking place in European society. Well before the mid–sixteenth century, both the Papacy and the Holy Roman Empire, previously the two most powerful institutions in Europe, had been weakened by the growth of independent monarchies and by the spread of knowledge outside the Church and rulers' courts as a result of the influence of Renaissance secular humanism, which was increasingly disseminated by printed texts.

Martin Luther and the Reformation in Germany Martin Luther (1483–1546), a theologian and teacher at the University of Wittenberg, inaugurated a religious reform movement that gained acceptance in part because his teachings converged with changes taking place in sixteenth-century German society. Germans supported Luther because his challenge to Rome corresponded with rising German resentment against the power of feudal princes and against the interference and abuse of a "foreign" Italian papacy. Luther and his followers also exploited the relatively new technology of the printing press to rally support, relying heavily on the value and power of the printed word.

Luther challenged the position of the Catholic Church by arguing that the individual did not need the intervention of the clergy or the Church to reach God. He claimed that salvation was instead a matter of individual faith. When Luther refused to recant this belief, he was condemned and excommunicated; he escaped execution only by being taken into protection by one of his princely supporters. Luther subsequently translated the Bible into German, an

FIGURE 13.5 *Peasants Dancing,* **Attributed to Christopher Murer. Woodcut, Early Sixteenth Century.**

Early 16th-century German prints such as these satirized the peasants by showing them imitating the manners and customs of the nobility. Here peasants are shown clumsily dancing. The wealthy and privileged held peasants in contempt and Luther was no exception.

SOURCE: General Research Division, New York Public Library, Astor, Lenox, and Tilden Foundations.

event as important to German cultural identity as it was to the spreading popularity of Lutheranism. As Luther put it in 1518, "I thank God that I hear and find my God in the German language in a way which I have not found Him up to now in the Latin, Greek, or Hebrew tongues."

By writing and speaking in German, and by disseminating his ideas through print, Luther rallied many Germans to his cause. In 1529, when princes who supported him protested the emperor's refusal to allow them to determine the religion of their states, Lutheranism ceased to be a reform movement and became a religious and political revolution. The term Protestant comes from this princely "protest."

Lutheranism also had broad appeal for ordinary Germans and inspired them to take action on their own behalf. Lutheran beliefs in the equality of Christians before God and the "priesthood" of individual believers took on special meaning to people at the lower rungs of society, especially those involved in the widespread Peasants' War (1524–1525), when peasants rose up against their masters and landowners. Many historians have pointed to the link between the social unrest highlighted by the Peasants' War and the increasing economic stress of the time caused by both population growth and rising prices. While higher grain prices might have improved the economic conditions of the peasantry, rising interest rates and inflation greatly outpaced the price of grain, thus further impoverishing them. Disaffected peasants were inspired by Luther's theology of individual autonomy and equality and by the example of his challenge to authority, but the rebels received little support from Luther. Instead, Luther rallied the German princes to suppress the rebels, urging his followers to accept their rank and place in life.

Calvinism John Calvin (1509–1564), a Frenchman who underwent a sudden religious conversion, published his *Institutes of the Christian Religion* in Switzerland in 1536, where the Protestant reformer Ulrich Zwingli (1484–1531) had previously gained a following. Though Calvin wrote this work in Latin, it was quickly translated into vernaculars throughout Europe and gained him a place in the front ranks of Protestant theologians. According to Calvin, God alone decides who shall be elected for salvation, and who shall be damned because of Adam's original sin. Worldly success, Calvin suggested, would be among the signs of election, though it would not guarantee it.

Calvin assumed leadership in the city of Geneva, which had recently converted to Protestantism. He remained a guiding force in Geneva and in the Protestant Reformation until his death in 1564. Geneva became a Protestant Rome, the capital of the first international Protestant movement. Like both Luther and Zwingli, Calvin envisaged close relations between Church and state; unlike them, his model was of a society in which all matters, civil and religious, public and private, were subject to ecclesiastical governance.

In 1559, Calvin founded the Genevan Academy, dedicated to sound learning and the propagation of Protestant doctrine as he defined it. The academy was the springboard of an international Calvinist Protestantism. Lutheranism was essentially confined to Germany (and later Scandinavia), and other Protestant movements were equally localized. But Calvinism spread widely through France, the Rhine Valley, the Netherlands, Scotland, and parts of central Europe. Calvinistic views of the world quickly stretched from North America, especially New England, to southern Africa. Because worldly success might indicate an individual's election to salvation, Calvinism was compatible with the expansion of European commercial capitalism in the age of mercantilism.

The English Reformation The English revolt against Rome differed from those on the continent in that it was not inaugurated by a religious reformer, was theologically conservative, and had little in common with more radical Protestant sects. In England it was the ruler who took the initiative in the revolt against Rome. The desire of Tudor King Henry VIII (r. 1509–1547) to divorce his first wife provided him the excuse to sever bonds with the Roman Church and assume supreme authority over institutional religion in England. Long before the accession of the Tudor dynasty in 1485, there had been struggles between the Papacy and English kings for control of the English Church. English nationalism and the example of religious revolution on the Continent both played their part in the resolution of the conflict between the Papacy and the English monarchy. As England moved rapidly into an era of commercial capitalism, English people were impatient to claim some of the enormous wealth tied up in Church lands and properties. Henry VIII's Act of Supremacy (1534), which declared the king's authority over the Church, resulted in the final establishment of the independent Church of England by Henry's daughter, Elizabeth I.

Puritans and Pilgrims After the religious settlement that established the Church of England, Elizabeth's successor, James I, wanted to rid England of radical Protestant elements known as "Puritans." Puritans generally followed Calvinist ideas and objected to excessive ritualism in the Church of England as well as to such worldly activities as theatergoing, gambling, and extravagance in dress. One group of Puritans, the Separatists, were so alienated from the Church of England that they sought refuge in Holland. When they became disenchanted with religious life there, some of them decided to move to Virginia, where earlier settlers from England had established themselves in the tobacco-growing economy there. Their ship, the *Mayflower*, was blown off course and in 1620 landed instead at a place they called Plymouth on the coast of present-day Massachusetts. There the Pilgrims, as they were later known, established the first of the New England colonies in North America. In addition to the Puritans, other religious dissidents—Roman Catholics and Quakers among them—from many parts of Europe sought refuge in the Americas in the wake of the Reformation and established colonies there.

THE CATHOLIC COUNTER-REFORMATION

Reform movements within the Catholic Church were not new, but none had resulted in permanent schism within Roman Catholicism. Faced with the Lutheran and other Protestant revolts, Roman Catholic reform in the sixteenth century took on aspects of a counter-revolutionary movement and is known as the Counter-Reformation. The major direction of the Counter-Reformation was set by the Council of Trent (1545–1563), convened by the Church to deal with issues raised by the Protestant Reformation. The Council reconfirmed a number of basic Roman Catholic beliefs and practices and reiterated that the pope was supreme head of the Church, the guarantor of salvation. At the same time, in the mid–sixteenth century, reforming popes took several important steps to address and resist Protestantism including publication of the *Index of Forbidden Books* (1542), a list of books censored because they were considered heretical, doctrinally unsound, or subversive; revival of the Inquisition, the formal inquiry or investigation of heresy and subversion, used in medieval times against heretics and people accused of witchcraft; and chartering of the Society of Jesus, a Catholic religious order founded in 1534, whose members (known as Jesuits) helped to check the spread of Protestantism by preaching and teaching.

The Spanish Inquisition During the Counter-Reformation, the Inquisition was carried out in various European states. The Spanish Inquisition, for example, began in 1478 under Ferdinand and Isabella, who later supported Columbus's voyages to the New World. In the same year that Columbus undertook his voyage to the Indies, the Moors, descendants of the eighth-century Muslim conquerors of Spain, were expelled when Granada, the last Moorish stronghold on the Iberian peninsula, fell to the combined forces of Aragon and Castile, the kingdoms of Ferdinand and Isabella. The reconquista (reconquest of Spain from the Moors), as it was known, took ten years to accomplish, but it united the Christian population of Spain. Again non-Christians, such as Spanish Jews, were persecuted by the Inquisition and forced to flee the country. Since the Moorish conquest of Spain in 711, Jews had lived peaceably with Muslims on the Iberian peninsula, and many had become prosperous and powerful. The expulsion of Jews from Spain added another page to the continuing saga of the Jewish diaspora (dispersal), which had periodically claimed victims since the end of the Roman Empire.

Menocchio the Miller Victims of the Inquisition were often ordinary people who otherwise would have been unknown to later historians. One such Italian victim was a miller named Domenico Scandella, called "Menocchio," who was born in 1532 and executed for his heretical beliefs around 1600. According to accounts of his questioning by a representative of the Holy Office, as the institution of the Inquisition was known, Menocchio expressed such beliefs as the idea that since Christ had not prevented his crucifixion, he must not be God, who would be powerful enough to stop it, but simply a prophet. He also explained his view of the creation of the world by use of a homely analogy: rather than the world being created by the acts of an all-knowing and all-powerful God, as Church doctrine held, Menocchio believed that living things were produced naturally from chaos, just as maggots or worms appear in a decomposed cheese.

Menocchio's ideas were a product of his daily experience and familiarity with oral traditions and popular culture of his time, including utopian peasant traditions that envisioned a

FIGURE 13.6 St. Dominic and the Inquisition. St. Dominic presides over the Inquisition court trial of Count Raymond of Toulouse, a supporter of the French Albigensian heresy derived from an ancient West Asian religion. Smoke in the background is a visual warning of the fate of heretics (Count Raymond repented and was saved).

SOURCE: Prado/Oronoz. Photo by Pedro Berruguete.

world replete with food and other comforts. But he was also acquainted with written texts, since he could read and write and had a collection of books and writings of his own. Since his books and writings were confiscated and destroyed, we cannot know exactly what he read; however, enough is known to speculate on the breadth of his reading matter, which included imaginary accounts of other lands as well as references to the Qur'an and other non-Christian texts. The fate of poor Menocchio coincided with an intensification of social tensions that took place as a result of such things as a price revolution that fed the revolts known as the Peasants' War in Germany. Menocchio's story also reflects the impact of the spread of written culture to a wide audience through the technology of the printing press.

THE SOCIETY OF JESUS: TRANSMISSION AND TRANSFORMATION OF TRADITIONS

Though the activities of Jesuits can be seen as one part of the Counter-Reformation—the Society of Jesus was approved by the Church in 1540—their mission of teaching and preaching contrasted sharply with the goals of the Inquisition to suppress and punish heresy. Because they received intensive religious and academic training, in addition to their activities in Europe, Jesuits were major participants in the transmission of knowledge across cultures through the medium of the printed word: they wrote and read accounts of other cultures, spreading information as they attempted to spread their faith. In contrast to other Catholic orders, the Jesuits wore no particular dress, established no missions, and observed no rule of hourly prayer. Their goal was simply "to glorify God." Jesuits as preachers attracted multitudes; as confessors and chaplains, they gained the confidence of princes and influenced governments; as teachers, they developed educational institutions that inculcated orthodoxy; and as missionaries, they were to be found in every European country and beyond, in Asia, Africa, and the Americas. As transcultural agents, Jesuits helped shape the transfer of knowledge between Europe and the world.

Sacred Encounters in Africa Probably the best-known African society the Jesuits tackled was the Kongo, a powerful Central African state. Its notoriety and status derived largely from the successful efforts of Portuguese missionaries; Kongolese royalty had converted to Catholicism and made it the state religion. The Kongolese King Afonso (r. 1506–1545) not only remained a staunch Christian but in his lifetime saw his son Henrique ordained a bishop by Rome, which sent Jesuit missionaries at Afonso's request. Status as a Christian nation provided diplomatic and trading privileges to the Kongolese royalty, but the benefits soon gave way to political and economic dependency as Portuguese increasingly became involved in elite culture and local politics. In 1556, when local Portuguese tried to install their own choice as successor after the death of the king, the African commoners rebelled against the Kongolese aristocrats, killing the Europeans and gaining a reputation for xenophobia, resistance to outsiders.

The religious conversion of the kings wrought great cultural transformations that seeped down from elite culture and eventually embraced much of Kongolese society. Through the efforts of the Jesuits, elites (including kings) and others became literate in European languages. The Jesuits produced a dictionary of written Kongolese and the correspondence between the kings of Portugal and the Kongo are valuable historical documents.

The transfer of European ideas was not a matter of superimposing them on a pristine canvas in the Kongo. The new beliefs were, rather, incorporated into the matrix of politics and traditional beliefs in ancestors and spirits. This syncretism is especially apparent in the local expression of Catholic rituals. Descriptions of the Jesuits' 1620 canonization feast of Saint Francis Xavier at Luanda in the Kongo suggest something of the interplay and even tensions between African and European beliefs. Luandan bards competed to write praise songs for the new saint. The Portuguese governor, a slave trader from one of the great Jewish finance houses, ordered naval salutes of musketry and night illuminations throughout the city.

The carnival procession associated with the Catholic feast in Luanda was a blend of Mbundu and Kongolese rituals and symbols together with inventive European pagan and Christian rituals satirically portraying three African states ("Angola," "Ethiopia," and "Kongo") as three white giants dressed in formal wear accompanied by their "father," the European conqueror portrayed by a black dwarf captured in war. Such occasions permitted unprecedented criticism and role reversals, no doubt serving to relieve tensions and conflicts brought by the social and religious transformations that were under way.

Even the earliest Catholic movements exhibited tensions that came from the depths of the ideological and emotional impact of European thought and culture on African society. The adoption of Christianity was both pragmatic and eclectic, weaving together strands from Christianity and African traditions. In addition to attempting to Africanize the Catholic religion, Jesuits and Kongolese priests used local dress and language to help bridge the gaps between two distinct worldviews.

Millenarian movements that projected the hope of a new age—the coming of the Millennium that would usher in a new world—presented more abrupt breaks with the sources of European influence. One such movement originated with the claims of a young Kongolese girl to be Saint Anthony. She announced that she had come to teach the true religion: priests were imposters, God and his angels were black, and the kingdom of Heaven was near the Kongo country, where Christ had really lived and died. Suggesting such a radical alternative amidst the clash of cultures was a dangerous thing and the founder of the movement was executed. However, the movement itself survived and became the first Zionist African Church; the name "Zion" referred to the Biblical city that was a symbol of hope. The rise of the Zionist African Church was paralleled by the decline of traditional Christian influence in the Atlantic world as Christian elements became bits of religious belief embedded in the older Kongolese religion that had established itself in a series of African communities from the African continent to Brazil and Cuba.

The visionary role of women was not uncommon. Other transformations of power and identity appeared in the deep divisions and contradictions of the African-Atlantic world, which gave as many opportunities for change as it took away. One of the most successful transformations emerged in the small kingdom of Ndongo during a series of disputes over royal succession in 1623. Authority was ultimately grabbed by Ana Nzinga (r. 1624–1663), the deceased king's sister. She ruled over Ndongo and even expanded its territory to include Matamba, legitimizing her claim to rule by altering her gender. Queen Nzinga dressed like a man, married multiple "wives" (actually men dressed as women), and carried and used weapons in war and ceremony. Despite the fact that she found it necessary to undergo the transformation of her own gender, the success of her actions wrought lasting change since the majority of her successors were women, not men.

Sacred Encounters in Asia Jesuits also made their way to Asia. Mid-sixteenth-century Goa had as many as eighty churches and convents. Following missionary work elsewhere in Asia, Francis Xavier (1506–1552), one of the founding members of the Society of Jesus, landed on the southernmost Japanese island of Kyushu in 1549 and there began making converts to Christianity. Calling them "the best people that have yet been discovered," Xavier, like other Jesuits, was favorably impressed by the Japanese and their seemingly well-ordered society.

To the Japanese, Catholicism was the religion of the "southern barbarians," as the Portuguese and Spanish were known, and at first Christianity was assumed to be just another sect of Buddhism, like others that had reached the shores of Japan from the mainland of Asia. Some of the *daimyo* (lords) of southern Japan believed that conversion to Christianity would bring wealth and power, and so they adopted at least the superficial aspects of the new faith. One of the most powerful *daimyo* in the late sixteenth century, Oda Nobunaga, enjoyed dressing up in Portuguese clothes and wearing a rosary. Jesuits and other missionaries initially gained a substantial number of converts; the sixteenth century is sometimes known as Japan's "Christian century."

By the early 1600s, Japan was newly unified under the Tokugawa shogunate (1600–1867), and there were indications that all was not well for European missionaries. By then the Protestant English and Dutch had arrived in Japan, and, in order to promote their own interests, they spread fears among the Japanese about the motives of the Catholic missionaries. The connection between Christian missionaries and the expansion of European power was evident with the Spanish conquest of the Philippines in 1571, and when the Japanese heard about the Treaty of Tordesillas (1494), which divided the world between Spain and Portugal, their suspicions about European motives seemed to have been justified. In 1606, Christianity was declared illegal, and in 1614 the Tokugawa government began a campaign to eradicate it. There were already 300,000 converts, and by the end of the campaign, which included torture and the execution of more than 3,000 martyrs, the few remaining Christians went underground. The final blow came with a Christian-influenced rebellion in 1637–1638 near the southern port of Nagasaki. The rebellion was suppressed and some 37,000 Christian converts lost their lives. Once seen as a political weapon by the independent *daimyo* of a decentralized Japan, Christianity was viewed by a newly unified government, the Tokugawa shogunate, as a potentially dangerous threat.

Francis Xavier died in 1552, while waiting to gain permission to enter China. But others soon took his place. The most famous was Matteo Ricci (1551–1610), an Italian student of law, mathematics, and science, as well as cartography and mechanics. Ricci carefully prepared the way for Jesuits to be accepted by the Chinese by adopting the style of a Confucian scholar and impressing his Chinese hosts with both European knowledge and his understanding of Chinese culture. Unlike the experience of the Jesuits in Japan, however, where their efforts at conversion were relatively successful, few Chinese converts were made. Chinese toleration of the Jesuits, and even imperial patronage of them, was largely due to interest in the European scientific and technological knowledge they transmitted. A German Jesuit, Adam Schall von Bell (1591–1666) was appointed court astronomer by the Manchu Qing dynasty, the Belgian Ferdinand Verbiest (1633–1688) was similarly appointed court astronomer and became a favorite of the Emperor Kangxi (r. 1662–1722).

Jesuit accommodation to Chinese culture through the acceptance of such practices as Confucian ancestral rites, however, was denounced by competing religious orders in Europe.

FIGURE 13.7 Matteo Ricci and His Chinese Convert, Paul Xu (left); Adam Schall von Bell with His Astronomical Instruments, Wearing Garb of a Chinese Official as Director of the Imperial Board of Astronomy.

SOURCE: Rare Books and Manuscripts Division, New York Public Library, Astor, Lenox, and Tilden Foundation.

In the eighteenth century, the pope declared such rituals unacceptable for Chinese Christians to practice, and the influence of Catholic missionaries faded. In neither China nor Japan did Jesuits have more than a peripheral impact, and in both they were eventually expelled.

Sacred Encounters in the Americas Other Jesuit activities extended to the Americas, where they helped ensure Europeans' interest in the newly established colonies. Their annual written reports encouraged settlement, and they actively participated in exploration. In 1549, the Jesuits launched what would become one of their largest missionary undertakings among the Guaraní Indians in South America. The missions became known as the Paraguayan Reductions (from the Latin *reducere,* meaning "to lead back" or "to bring into the fold"), and they encompassed thirty towns and more than 80,000 Indians. During the course of their missions, the Jesuits instructed the Guaranís in European language and skills. Embracing European technology and culture, Guaranís became magistrates, sculptors, calligraphers, and builders of Baroque cathedrals.

Perhaps the best-known Jesuit explorer was Father Jacques Marquette (1637–1675), who was posted to the permanent central mission at Sault Sainte Marie in what is now the upper peninsula of Michigan, a territory inhabited by Huron Indians. Marquette accompanied voyages from Green Bay on Lake Michigan to the upper Mississippi and down the Arkansas River. Jesuit "missions" were scarcely more than outposts accommodated by Huron agricultural villages. In their dealings with the Iroquois, the Jesuits found themselves identified with the Huron-French alliance, and they met with fierce resistance from the Iroquois. In 1773, the Jesuits were expelled as an order from North America. However, their legacy was mixed, and its memory migrated to westward frontiers. Catholic Iroquois fur hunters such as Ignace Saxa (ca. 1811) moved from near Montreal to the northern Rockies, bringing an Indianized form of Catholicism woven from their recollections and experiences with Jesuits earlier in their lives.

The bloody violence of the initial encounters between the Spanish and Portuguese and the native populations of Mexico, the Caribbean, and South America (see Chapter 12) soon gave way to settlement and attempts at acculturation. Again, the Church played an important role in both settlement and acculturation; indeed, they were inextricably linked. A small number of Franciscan, Dominican, Augustinian, and later Jesuit orders came to the new territories to convert native peoples to Christianity. They did so with mixed success, though enough that their protection of converts angered settlers and led in one case to the death of several priests at the hands of Portuguese.

The most famous Spanish priest was friar Bartolomé de Las Casas, who defended Indians against the diatribes of his contemporaries and even succeeded in prohibiting Indian slavery. He is also credited with learning and recording native cultures, religions, and languages in order to teach people the tenets of Christianity. Where Las Casas and others succeeded was in the cities; in villages and among mixed-blood (*mestizo*) peoples, syncretic blends of local traditions and Catholicism persisted.

GENDER, RELIGION, AND DISSENT

Though in its persecution of heresy the Catholic Church condemned some women as witches, religious communities often provided a means for women to escape social and cultural restraints on their lives and to acquire education. Education made it possible for women to express their ideas in often powerful literary forms as a means of resistance to society, if not the Church itself. In Spain, Teresa of Avila (1515–1582) led the Carmelite order and encouraged women to withdraw from the world to realize true devotion. Her writings and the example of her life inspired other women to become educated and to use their learning to promote the interests of women.

Gender and Dissent in the Catholic Church: Sor Juana   One such woman was Juana Inés de la Cruz (1651–1695), a brilliant poet and early feminist. After a promising career at the court of the viceroy of New Spain, she spent the last thirty years of her life as the nun Sor Juana in a convent on the outskirts of Mexico City. Born in Mexico, she represents the first stirrings of resentment there against control by Catholic Spain. She became a nun because that was the only way to be allowed to read, study, and write. The hundreds of poems she wrote are an important contribution to Spanish literature and a manifesto of early feminist ideology. "Stubborn men, who accuse women without reason" is the opening line of one of her most famous poems, written in the late seventeenth century while she was living in the convent.

Sor Juana made use of the Bible and classical mythology in her writings, showing how subversive readings could be made of canonical texts. Some authorities of the Catholic Church in Mexico disapproved of her studies and sought to curtail them. In 1691, in response to a reprimand from a superior, she wrote a letter defending her secular interests and pleading for equal educational opportunities for women.

Gender and Dissent in The Protestant Reformation in Europe began as a heresy within the
Puritan New England Catholic Church, but eventually generated heresies of its own. Some
Europeans fled to the New World to escape persecution for their religious beliefs, but dissenters there also suffered persecution for their beliefs. Though Sor Juana's ideas were attacked by Catholic authorities in Mexico her sisters in the New England colonies along the Atlantic seaboard of North America fared even less well. One of the more radical Protestant religious groups in England was the Quakers. The Quakers believed that every man and woman had access to God without the intervention of clergy or the sacraments of the Church. According to Quaker beliefs, both men and women could know the will of God through an internal state of grace, the "Light Within," which enabled them to attain spiritual perfection. Two women, Ann Austin and Mary Fisher, were sent as the first Quaker missionaries to the Puritan Massachusetts Bay Colony in 1620. Because of the radical nature of their beliefs, one of the early Quaker converts, Mary Dyer, was hanged in 1656, along with three men. The independence and assertiveness of women as part of Quaker beliefs threatened the Puritan social and religious order of New England communities.

The suppression of ideas and behavior perceived as a threat to gender hierarchy and community order took a violent turn in the infamous Salem witchcraft trials in 1692, which resulted in the executions of twenty people, most of them women. Accusations of witchcraft because of heretical beliefs or alleged sexual improprieties in New England were reflections of the witchcraft mania that swept England in the seventeenth century. In both cases, social and economic tensions within communities often exacerbated fears of the supernatural and led to accusations that certain individuals were agents of the Devil and threatened the welfare of the communities.

Witchcraft and Magic The perception and role of witchcraft in Christian societies differed
markedly from its presence elsewhere. For example, in the Trobriand Islands of Melanesia and among the Zande of Central Africa, magic was part of the inherited culture, a tangible cultural weapon deriving from the knowledge of tradition. In contrast, in seventeenth-century Europe witchcraft had become countercultural, a dangerous expression of heresy and disbelief. It also came to house the traditions excluded by both religious and secular views of the world, such as alchemy and midwifery. Good magic used by the Church, such as the ritual of communion or miracles, came to be distinguished from bad magic, the realm of witchcraft. Though witchcraft was harshly rejected and suppressed by some seventeenth-century Europeans and Americans alike, aspects of witchcraft such as alchemy helped to lay the foundations of challenges to the prevailing worldview that emerged in the "scientific revolution."

THE SCIENTIFIC REVOLUTION

Following the challenge to the dominant medieval European Christian worldview by the rise of secular humanism in the Renaissance, the power of the Catholic Church was undermined by the Protestant Reformation. The effects of these two attacks on inherited ideas and institutions, along with influences from Europe's global encounters from the fifteenth through seventeenth centuries, paved the way for the conceptual transformation known as the "scientific revolution." Though many continuities remained and the processes of change were often slow, new understandings of the natural world and human relationships to it profoundly transformed the European worldview and ultimately had a global impact.

The Copernican Revolution The earliest important discoveries that paved the way for the scientific revolution were in astronomy. In the early sixteenth century, the Polish astronomer Nicolaus Copernicus (1472–1543) challenged the prevailing Ptolemaic theory, in which the sun revolved around the earth, asserting as had some ancient Greeks, that the earth revolved around the sun. Dissatisfied with the discrepancies between Ptolemy's geocentric (earth-centered) system and what he observed, Copernicus decided that the heliocentric (sun-centered) view offered the soundest explanation for the movements of the planets.

According to Ptolemy, heavenly bodies such as the sun or stars, enclosed within transparent spheres, rotated in perfect, circular motion around the solid, immovable earth. Copernicus did not reject the idea of revolving spheres and fixed orbits for heavenly bodies; he simply exchanged the positions of the sun and the earth. Nevertheless, the removal of the earth from the center of the universe made Copernicus's revival of the heliocentric theory unacceptable to religious authorities, since it contradicted the Ptolemaic view of Christian cosmology. His *Concerning the Revolutions of the Celestial Bodies*, published in the year of his death (1543), was condemned by both Catholic and Protestant religious leaders and even rejected by many other astronomers.

Galileo It was more than a century before Copernicus's theory gained any real acceptance, and it was the result of continued work in astronomy by a number of European scientists such as the Dane Tycho Brahe (1564–1601) and his student the German Johannes Kepler (1571–1630), whose studies established the laws of planetary motion. The work of the Italian astronomer and physicist Galileo Galilei (1564–1642) significantly enhanced understanding of the Copernican theory. In 1609 he constructed a telescope through which he could carefully examine the heavens. Using the telescope, Galileo could see that planets were

FIGURE 13.8 The Application of Measuring Instruments, Woodcut Showing Scientists Wielding a Range of Astronomical Instruments, 1553.

SOURCE: AKG London.

more than points of light and that they had dimensions like the earth and phases like the earth's moon that corresponded to their position with respect to the sun and earth. Galileo's discoveries gave additional support for the heliocentric theory and went further to suggest that there could be more than one center—more than one sun—for heavenly orbits.

Though he sought to reconcile religious belief and the new cosmology by arguing that Biblical references and scientific theories need not be incompatible, he was condemned by the Catholic Church for his views. His work, *The Starry Messenger*, was placed on the Index of Forbidden Books in 1616 by the Catholic Church, but the new cosmology this work represented could not be suppressed in a world where the printing press made knowledge accessible to a growing audience. In the end, the Copernican revolution radically altered European conceptions of the universe and the individual's place in it. No longer were humans at the center of the world, and the earth at the center of the universe. The humanistic world envisioned by Renaissance thinkers was profoundly undermined by Copernicus' revelation, just as Renaissance humanists had challenged and undermined the medieval Christian worldview.

Newton Sir Isaac Newton (1642–1727), a mathematician who discovered calculus (at the same time as the German Gottfried Leibnitz [1646–1716]), formulated a universal law of gravitation, which was the culmination of a revolution in celestial physics that began with Copernicus. Newton's discovery of calculus provided him with a shorthand system of calculation and annotation that enabled him to determine accurately physical phenomena such as varying speeds and curves of movement. To verify his hypotheses, Newton translated all elements into mathematical terms. He was successful in formulating a universal law of gravitation in precise terms, and by establishing empirical and mathematical proof of the existence of a universal law (*Principia*, 1687), Newton was hailed as a scientific genius. Other thinkers, both before and after Newton, provided the conceptual framework for understanding and integrating scientific knowledge into a new worldview. Newton's work, and that of other scientists, was expedited by the development of forms of higher mathematics, such as logarithms (1614), geometry (1637), and calculus (1665–1675). Inventions such as the pendulum clock (1656), the barometer (1645), and the telescope (between 1590 and 1621 in Holland) were crucial for the accurate observation that furthered scientific knowledge.

Science and Knowledge The Latin word *scientia*, which can be translated as "knowledge," is the source for the modern English word *science*, which has come to mean the practices and methods of highly specialized expertise in a particular realm of knowledge about the physical world. In contrast, the Renaissance ideal of knowledge was comprehensive, and humanistic learning encompassed all aspects of knowledge, from architecture to poetry. Reflecting this Renaissance ideal, Francis Bacon (1561–1626), who is often associated with the first stirrings of the European scientific revolution, is said to have boasted, "I take all knowledge for my province." However much this boast reflects the Aristotelian notion of having a respectable familiarity with all knowledge of his time, Bacon rejected Aristotle's method of scientific reasoning, known as the deductive method. Rather than deducing from a basic assumption conclusions about the real world (the deductive method), Bacon argued for the superiority of the inductive method, in which observations of the real world lead to general conclusions or principles. Though both methods are used in modern scientific reasoning, Bacon's ideas provided grounding for the conceptual transformation associated with the European scientific revolution.

Science and Human The ideas of the French thinker Rene Descartes (1596–1650) also influ-
Understanding   enced the development of scientific thinking. Despite having a deeply
▬▬▬▬▬▬▬▬▬ Catholic faith and a Jesuit education, Descartes' ideas contributed to undermining the authority of the Church. He rigidly rejected authority of all kinds, including
books, tradition, experimentation, even experience, as unworthy guides to truth and proclaimed a new method for arriving at knowledge: pure mathematical deduction. The process
begins with simple, self-evident truths or axioms, as in geometry, from which particular conclusions are reasoned. For Descartes, the source of truth and knowledge was human reason.

Toward the end of the seventeenth century, the English philosopher John Locke
(1632–1704) proposed a contrasting view in his *Essay on Human Understanding*. Locke predicated that all knowledge originated from the observation of external objects known through
the senses rather than being the product of reason and intuition, as Descartes had insisted.
For Locke, the mind at birth was a "white paper, void of all characters, without any ideas."
Ideas that came to be written on this paper came from immediate sense perceptions (sensa-
tions) and the operations of this mind in sorting and arranging perceptions (reflection).
Knowledge was thus the product of the application of reason to sensory observation.

Institutions and the The ideas of Bacon, Descartes, and Locke provided intellectual ground-
Scientific Revolution ing for the observations, theories, and inventions of astronomers and
▬▬▬▬▬▬▬▬▬ other scientists who contributed to the scientific revolution. Changes in
the institutional environment that encouraged research and the transmission of new knowledge were also important to the scientific revolution. Dominated by Christian theological
doctrines, the medieval university was ill suited to the new ideas that emerged and flowered
during the Renaissance. Accordingly, new institutions of learning were established between
the sixteenth and eighteenth centuries to better serve secular purposes and interests. Academies, institutions that encouraged scholarship outside the setting of universities and were
patronized by municipalities and wealthy or powerful individuals, first appeared in fifteenth-
century Italy and then proliferated throughout Europe. Learned societies, by-products of the
growth of monarchical power, appeared in the seventeenth and eighteenth centuries. The earliest was the Royal Society of London, a private organization chartered by English King
Charles II in 1662; the French Academy of Sciences was founded in 1666 as a state institution by French King Louis XIV. Thereafter societies were founded in other countries, particularly in the eighteenth century.

European academies and learned societies were secular institutions, the advance guard of
the investigation and exchange of new ideas and theories beginning with the Renaissance.
They were also quick to use technology such as the printing press to advance learning.
Though universities continued to expand throughout Europe until 1500, by the seventeenth
century academies and learned societies, which maintained laboratories and libraries, and
published, exchanged, and circulated their proceedings, had displaced universities as centers of
innovation in European thought and culture.

Gender and Science The men of science who contributed to profound changes in the under-
▬▬▬▬▬▬▬▬▬ standing of the natural world and in humans' ability to measure and
control that world were also products of their times. They did not see the world in the purely
rational terms of scientific models and laws. Their intellectual world was shaped by European

cultural and social ideals as well as scientific hypotheses. The central imagery and conceptual basis of the new science was rooted in notions of human domination over nature, which paralleled men's domination over women in human society.

European women's realms of knowledge, such as midwifery, were relegated to spheres labeled heretical or nonscientific, and a large increase in accusations of and executions for witchcraft paralleled the growth of the scientific establishment. Knowledge associated with women and practices regarded as nonscientific, such as alchemy, went underground as mechanistic rationalism assumed control over intellectual, and even spiritual, domains. In seventeenth-century England, witch mania reflected the growing power of male scientific nationalism to dominate both nature and woman.

Francis Bacon, who made important contributions to the development of scientific methodology, was Lord Chancellor to King James I, author of a book on witchcraft entitled *Daemonologie.* Bacon was involved in the king's persecution of heresy and witchcraft and displayed misogynistic attitudes in his writings. The utopian society that Bacon described in his *The New Atlantis* (1624) was a masculine scientific community dedicated to possessing power and control over nature. Ideals of celibacy were upheld in universities and monastic life was portrayed as the only way to avoid contamination by women. Bacon, though married, characterized wives and children as "impediments to great enterprises." Galileo, who never married his mistress or allowed her to live with him, though she bore him three children, must have felt the same way. Galileo, in fact, went to great lengths to ensure that the two daughters born of this union would never trouble him for dowries or intrude on his scientific work, forcing them, at the ages of eleven and twelve (before the age of legal consent), to enter a convent. Galileo's son, however, was made legitimate through the good offices of his benefactor Cosimo de' Medici.

Women were systematically excluded from education that would enable them to contribute to the scientific revolution as part of the social and intellectual world of male scientists. The few women who did engage in scientific work were kept outside the emerging scientific establishment. Despite this, some made lasting contributions, often aided by high social position or some degree of political power through their husbands. For example, the wife of a viceroy of Peru who had been cured of malaria by quinine bark, introduced this practice to Spain. As naturalists and herbalists, women found medical uses for many of the plants they studied. María Merian (1647–1717) trained as an artist and used her artistic skills to complement her interest in nature. She produced six collections of engravings that depict European plants and insects with rare accuracy and completeness.

Women and the Practice of Medicine   Though women were barred from the formal study of medicine, as they were from the study of the abstract or pure sciences, they were practitioners who delivered essential medical care. Prohibitions on women entering medical school or working as surgeons (surgery, generally practiced by barbers, was separated from the practice of medicine) suggest that there were enough women training and practicing in medical care that male professionals felt it necessary to seek legislation against them. Midwifery, in particular, provided an opportunity for women to circumvent the male monopoly on surgery. The midwife's role in assisting childbirth was based on experience transmitted over generations. A Swiss midwife in the sixteenth century perfected new techniques of cesarean section birth, a procedure in which male professionals had made virtually no changes since the birth of Julius Caesar, for whom it had been named. Male doctors were

FIGURE 13.9 Aztec Healer with Medicinal Plants.

Detail from Mexican muralist Diego Rivera's *History of Medicine*. Despite their exclusion from the formal study and practice of medicine like their male counterparts, European women transmitted knowledge of healing and medicine. This idealized Aztec healer on the opposite side of the Atlantic likewise had a rich working knowledge of medicinal plants.

SOURCE: Schalkwijk/Art Resource, N.Y.

rarely present at births, and even elite women, who might engage the services of male doctors, generally had the help of a midwife at childbirth.

Not until the end of the eighteenth century, when obstetrics became a separate branch of medicine, did male doctors begin to specialize in the care of pregnant and birthing women, and then it was mainly elite women who relied on the services of "male midwives," as they were known. This expansion to include men in all aspects of medical practice was not countered by the inclusion of women practitioners; indeed, after the eighteenth century, women were systematically excluded.

THE EUROPEAN ENLIGHTENMENT

As the scientific revolution brought new understanding to the natural world and the universe, some thinkers began to apply the notions of rational inquiry and scientific methodology to the understanding of human societies. They believed that if it were possible to discover the secrets of the universe through the exercise of human reason, then it should also be possible by the same method to discover rational laws governing human conduct and the affairs of this world. Mostly French, the *philosophes* (philosophers) who asked this question promoted a new rational and scientific cosmology and were committed to discovering a scientific understanding of human society. The *philosophes* believed that science was making possible a new age of "light." It is from this notion that the term "Enlightenment" comes; it is applied to the century from the publication of Newton's *Principia* (1687) to the outbreak of the French Revolution (1789) [See Chapter 16].

Montesquieu (1689–1755), a French jurist and man of letters, made one of the earliest attempts to create a science of society. He read, traveled, and observed extensively, studying political systems as they had operated in the past and in his own time, summarizing his studies in *The Spirit of the Laws* (1748). In this work Montesquieu argued that each form of government had its own particular 'spirit' and that laws must be used to moderate the tendency toward the abusive exercise of power by the state, no matter what the form of government. His *Persian Letters* (1725) made use of a non-European society to satirize and criticize his own.

Deism Religion as well as society was subject to the scrutiny of the philosophes. Science and Newtonian cosmology cast doubts on traditional religious belief, and some eighteenth-century thinkers sought to replace their doubts with a religion of reason, the principal expression of which was Deism. Deism originated in England, but it was popularized by *philosophes* such as Voltaire (1694–1778). Deists aimed to replace traditional religion with a rational faith that would conform to the Newtonian scheme of things. Deists portrayed the deity as a Creator who had made a rational, orderly universe and set it into motion according to natural laws that were discoverable by proper reasoning.

Voltaire and Rousseau Poet, playwright, essayist, historian, and voluminous letter writer, Voltaire was an artistic propagator of the ideas and trends of his time and a vocal critic of European society. He found an ideal of rulership in what he believed to be the "enlightened despotism" of the Chinese and wrote a play, *The Orphan of China,* to promote this ideal. In contrast, Voltaire's response to reports from America about the free and egalitarian society there was ambivalent, if not hostile. The article on "Savages" in the *Encyclopédie,* a compendium of eighteenth-century knowledge to which Voltaire contributed, contended that most of North America was inhabited by ferocious cannibals.

Tales of noble Indians found in reports from French North America had a significant impact on French thought, especially in the eighteenth century. Jean-Jacques Rousseau (1712–1778) burst upon the intellectual scene of the French Enlightenment in 1755 with his *Discourse on Inequality.* In some ways this work was the climax of more than two centuries of reports and discussion of American societies in which "noble savages lived in conditions of freedom and equality." Rousseau credits reports of North Americans as the basis for his assumption—the premise of his *Discourse on Inequality*—that humans are naturally good when they exist in a world of freedom, equality, and happiness. Rousseau's most influential work, *The Social Contract,* offered his view of how a society could be governed so that freedom, equality, and happiness would result. He concluded that these conditions would result only when a government's authority was derived from the consent of the governed, the "social contract."

Raynal Another important eighteenth century work in the theme of liberty and equality was based on tales of noble Indians was the *Histoire philosophique et politique des établissements des Européens dans les deux Indes* (1770), attributed to the French historian and philosopher Abbé Guillaume Raynal (1713–1796). According to Raynal, no event in history had been as important as the discovery of the route to the East Indies (via the Cape of Good Hope) and the Americas, where he believed the ideals of freedom and equality embraced by the *philosophes* were exemplified.

Gender and Society in Enlightenment Europe Aristocratic women were prominent in the intellectual salons of Enlightenment France, influencing language reform and changes in social sensibilities, though the more abstract sciences—mathematics and physics—were very much male preserves. Émilie du Châtelet (1706–1749), perhaps because of her connection with Voltaire, whose mistress she was, managed to intrude into the bastions of male science. Barred as a woman from admission to the coffeehouses where Parisian scientists, mathematicians, and philosophers met, Madame du Châtelet reappeared dressed as a man and was welcomed. During the last two decades of her life, Voltaire's support made it possible for her to devote herself to study and writing. Voltaire paid for the ren-

DAILY LIVES

OLAUDAH EQUIANO: AFRICAN CONSCIENCE IN THE EIGHTEENTH CENTURY

The life of the African Olaudah Equiano traces the outlines of the Atlantic world in the eighteenth century. Kidnapped in southeastern Nigeria as an eleven-year-old in 1756, he spent the next ten years as a slave in the Caribbean, America, and the British navy. After gaining his freedom, Equiano also experienced the Atlantic world as a free man: he felt earthquakes in the Caribbean, and he fought in the battle of Louisbourg during the Seven Years' War between England and France. He saw Mount Vesuvius erupt in Italy and Greek slaves dance in Turkey; he saw the coal mines of Newcastle and the ice of the Arctic.

In his travels, Equiano encountered religions on three continents: the Ibo religion of his childhood, which intersected with both Islam and Christianity, as well as the religions of Ottoman Turks, Quakers, and Anglicans that he met with after he left Nigeria. In 1788, he wrote *The Interesting Narrative of the Life of Olaudah Equiano,* an antislavery tract and spiritual autobiography. While Equiano's *Narrative* contains the decidedly Christian theme of struggle for salvation in the sinful world of slavery, Equiano's personal journey was also a material one. After accumulating capital from small trading transactions, he not only purchased his own freedom but married an Englishwoman, Susan Cullen, and succeeded in mastering the commercial world that had enslaved him. His book argued for the end of slavery on the basis of both economic and humanitarian reasons. By the time of Equiano's death in 1797, the book had become a best-seller, with multiple editions in four languages. In the following passage from his *Narrative,* Olaudah Equiano explores the racial biases of the Atlantic era:

These instances, and a great many more which might be adduced, while they show how the complexions of the same persons vary in different climates, it is hoped may tend also to remove the prejudice that some conceive against the natives of Africa on account of their color. Surely the minds of the Spaniards did not change their complexions! Are there not causes enough to which the apparent inferiority of an African may be ascribed, without limiting the goodness of God, and supposing he forebore to stamp understanding on certainly his own image, because "carved in ebony." Might it not naturally be ascribed to their situation? When they come among Europeans, they are ignorant of their language, religion, manners, and customs. Are any pains taken to teach them these? Are they treated as men? Does not slavery itself depress the mind, and extinguish all its fire and every noble sentiment? But, above all, what advantages do not a refined people possess, over those who are rude and uncultivated? Let the polished and haughty European recollect that his ancestors were once, like the Africans, uncivilized, and even barbarous. Did Nature make *them* inferior to their sons? and should *they too* have been made slaves? Every rational mind answers, No. Let such reflections as these melt the pride of their superiority into sympathy for the wants and miseries of their sable brethren, and compel them to acknowledge that understanding is not confined to feature or color. If, when they look round the world, they feel exultation, let it be tempered with benevolence to others, and gratitude to God, "who hath made of one blood all nations of men for to dwell on all the face of the earth;" "and whose wisdom is not our wisdom, neither are our ways his ways."

ovation of her husband's château so that she could conduct her experiments, and together they accumulated a library of 10,000 volumes there. Her knowledge earned her a reputation as a physicist capable of understanding and interpreting the theories of Newton and Leibniz, and her energy resulted in a three-volume work on Leibniz, a treatise on Newton (in collaboration with Voltaire), a translation of Newton's *Principia,* and a book on algebra.

Women also raised new questions about equality, one of the major concerns of the Enlightenment. Some women made themselves known by their harsh criticism of forced marriage and forced childbearing, by opting for singlehood and celibacy in preference to such unions, by their denunciation of male tyranny over women in all domains, and by their demand for equal education for women. One woman who attacked the oppression of women and argued for their education was Mary Wollstonecraft (1759–1797), who published *A Vindication of the Rights of Woman* in 1792. Through their writings, women such as Wollstonecraft challenged the division of space into a private sphere for women and a public one for men, a notion that had been fortified by the impact of the scientific revolution and the Enlightenment.

Despite the iconoclastic role played by women such as Emilie du Chatelet and the participation of women in literary salons where Enlightenment ideas of equality were discussed, male domination was sometimes actually reinforced by Enlightenment scientific thinking. The argument was advanced in Enlightenment Europe that women should not dedicate themselves to serious intellectual pursuits because their weak brains could not withstand such pressure. For example, a medical treatise published in France in 1769 argued that intellectual pursuits might facilitate the development of nymphomania in women, as their weak brains became hot during such pursuits and deranged their organism. The earlier ethical or religious idea that knowledge in women was tantamount to vice, returned in the "age of reason" under the guise of medical knowledge, in which the vice of knowledge was transformed into disease (nymphomania). In this way the idea was reinforced that the gender arrangement of society was a result of essential biological differences between men and women.

■

TRADITIONS AND THEIR TRANSFORMATIONS IN EAST ASIA

The European Renaissance signaled a "rebirth" of European culture against the background of medieval Christianity. European thinkers were inspired by Greek and Roman society, by values and ideals that were secular, not sacred, humanistic, not god-centered, and based on reason rather than on Christian faith. Similarly, a "rebirth" of Confucianism took place in China after the eighth century and culminated around 1200 in what is known in the West as Neo-Confucianism.

NEO-CONFUCIANISM: THE "REBIRTH" OF TRADITION

Like the rediscovery of classical Greek and Latin texts and the rejection of medieval Christianity that characterized the European Renaissance, the revival of Confucianism and the reworking of its fundamental ideas was linked to a rejection of Buddhist spiritual ideals as well as a response to the Buddhist challenge to Confucian social and political ideals. Neo-Confucian thinkers sought to provide Confucian answers to Buddhist metaphysical questions—about the nature of being and the universe—and to create Confucian institutions and practices that addressed the needs of society. In the realm of metaphysics, Neo-Confucians explained the purpose of existence in terms of Confucian sagehood: people should aspire to realize their true human nature, which was essentially good, and to utilize that in the service of the community.

Buddhism in Society In contrast, Buddhism called for people to reject their attachment to the world and to seek "enlightenment" in realization of their Buddha nature: the extinction *(nirvana)* of individual self in the oneness with all being. At the same time, Buddhist institutions provided not only refuge from society in monasteries and nunneries but also social welfare services, such as charitable granaries and orphanages. The Buddhist clergy also provided important functions for people by performing funeral rites, long a central concern of Confucians, beginning with the elaborate prescriptions for proper funeral rites described in the ritual texts of antiquity. The Neo-Confucian thinker Zhu Xi (1130–1200) authored a new set of Confucian-based practices for family life and needs, such as funeral rites and marriage ceremonies, that was intended to replace Buddhist practice and to eliminate dependence on Buddhist clergy and temples.

The Neo-Confucian In Confucian thinking, identity had always been defined in terms of fundamental human relationships, such as that of father and son or husband
Self and Identity and wife. The self was defined primarily in relation to others, especially to the family but also to the larger community. Neo-Confucianism laid new emphasis on the self as the source of order and harmony in the community, as thinkers such as Zhu Xi argued that self-cultivation of one's Heaven-endowed human nature was the key to social and political order. Neo-Confucian thinkers of the Song (960–1279) and after based this notion on ideas drawn from the *Great Learning,* a portion of one of the five Confucian classics, the *Record of Rites.* In this text, individual moral rectitude is linked to the regulation of the family, the order of the state, and harmony in the world.

The Context of Change These ideas focused on the self can be seen as related to the economic and social transformations of the Song described in Chapter 11. Expansion of the market, specialization of production, urbanization, commercialization, growth of the iron and steel industries, and other changes encouraged people of all social levels to engage in individual entrepreneurial activities. Among the cultural elite—those who studied for the imperial civil service examinations and aimed for careers as government officials—intense competition for a limited number of the highest-level degrees meant that the goal of self-cultivation encouraged by Neo-Confucian ideals of sagehood justified the expenditure of time and resources in acquiring the education necessary even to compete for success in the examination system. Economic competition in the marketplace was mirrored by cultural competition among the elite for the highest offices in the government.

SELF, SOCIETY, AND SAGEHOOD IN LATE IMPERIAL CHINA

During the Ming dynasty (1368–1644), Neo-Confucian thinkers carried the idea of self-cultivation further. External—largely textual—sources of doctrinal authority, including the Confucian classics and the words of the sages, became less important than the internal mind.

Wang Yangming and Wang Yangming (1472–1529) emphasized inner moral cultivation
His Followers through understanding the "innate knowledge" already present in the
▬▬▬▬▬▬▬ human mind as a natural endowment of Heaven. "Learning to be a
sage" meant self-cultivation, but it was for the purpose of the community, not simply for the
benefit of the individual. Wang also stressed the importance of action in the world as an essential component of knowledge: the "unity of knowledge and action," according to Wang,
meant that, for example, one could not claim to truly understand the key Confucian concept
of filial piety if one could not carry it out in one's actions.

Some followers of Wang Yangming carried the implications of his ideas about self-
cultivation further, arguing that even an ordinary person, not just scholars who belonged to the
cultural elite, could become a sage. Wang Gen (1483–1541) came from a family of salt merchants and was not highly educated. He was a follower of Wang Yangming who taught personal spirituality as opposed to scholarly study, was egalitarian in his approach to others, and
showed concern for the practical needs of the common man. Wang Gen was less interested in
the problems of society than in the individual; for him, self-cultivation could be an end in itself. Wang Gen's espousal of such ideas and his social background illustrate the tensions created by commercial expansion and prosperity that allowed people outside the cultural elite to
gain wealth and to challenge the dominance of that elite. In other words, commercial prosperity could create conditions that would allow an individual to challenge the status hierarchy by using wealth to gain access to status or power. Confucian sagehood no longer belonged
to the scholarly elite, steeped in the Confucian classics and commentaries; for Wang Gen and
his followers, sagehood was a goal available to everyone.

POLITICS AND HISTORY IN LATE IMPERIAL CHINA

The reformulation and "rebirth" of Confucianism known as Neo-Confucianism became the
dominant ideology of late imperial China (Ming and Qing [1644–1911] dynasties). But by
the latter part of the Ming, concerns about moral self-cultivation and sagehood were moved
to the background as political conditions deteriorated in the Ming government. During the
late sixteenth century, the Ming government was dominated by the rule of eunuch (castrated
male) imperial advisers, whose proximity to the emperor (because they were the only males
allowed within the imperial household with access to the imperial women) gave them exceptional influence. Confucian scholar-officials who dared to criticize them or their policies were
often publicly humiliated, exiled, imprisoned, and even executed. The Donglin Academy, an
association of Confucian scholars who criticized the eunuchs' power and sought to mobilize
advocates of political reform, was active in the early seventeenth century (1604–1620). The
subsequent collapse of the Ming dynasty and the conquest of China by Manchu peoples in the
mid–seventeenth century produced a crisis among Ming intellectuals that was manifested in a
reaction not only against political corruption and eunuch rule, but also against the excessive
idealism and subjectivism of Ming Neo-Confucianism, particularly the school of Wang Yangming and his followers.

Statecraft and Society In contrast to the Neo-Confucians' absorption with self-cultivation,
▬▬▬▬▬▬▬ many seventeenth-century thinkers focused on the study of "statecraft,"
the ordering of society by government, and tried to understand what had gone wrong in
China's political culture to bring about the collapse of the Ming dynasty and the Manchu

conquest. Huang Zongxi (1610–1695) lived at the time of the transition between the end of the Ming and the establishment of Manchu rule in China. He looked to history for an understanding of the Ming demise and the Manchu conquest. Huang, saw the growth of despotic rule and illegitimate power, such as eunuchs, in the imperial court as a cause of the political and moral collapse of the Ming. His father had been a high official under the Ming who had died in prison at the hands of eunuchs because of his association with the Donglin Academy movement. Huang refused, however, to serve the Manchu Qing dynasty (1644–1911) and saw history as the source for understanding the present as well as providing a model to follow.

PHILOSOPHY AND POLITICS IN LATE IMPERIAL CHINA

By the end of the seventeenth century, the political and social order stabilized and Manchu rulers began to patronize learning. Eighteenth-century emperors were well versed in Chinese culture, acquiring skills in calligraphy, painting, and poetry. A great compendium of traditional scholarship, the *Complete Library of the Four Treasuries,* was compiled under imperial direction in the late eighteenth century. The "Four Treasuries" referred to the classification system used to organize knowledge into four categories: classics, philosophy, history, and literature (literary essays and poetry, not fiction). Scholars employed by the state collected all the literary works considered valuable enough to be preserved, edited them, and had them copied. The process of editing also included weeding out materials that were regarded as unfavorable to the Manchus or other foreign predecessors, and this goal was as important as the collection and preservation of knowledge.

Han Learning In philosophy and scholarship there was a continuation of the seventeenth-century reaction against Ming Neo-Confucianism in a new emphasis on classical scholarship as opposed to metaphysical speculation. Known as the school of "Han Learning," these scholars identified the classical tradition with the careful scholarship of the Han (206 B.C.E.–220 C.E.) and Tang (618–907), not with the metaphysical speculation of the Song and Ming, under which Neo-Confucianism had developed. Since they could not pursue independent, critical study of the past as Huang Zongxi had done, because it would jeopardize their position as Chinese scholars in the Manchu state, they concentrated on textual criticism of the classics and on the retrieval of the past through the critical examination of sources and evidence. In this way, they resembled Lorenzo Valla and Erasmus, the greatest Latin philologists of the Renaissance, whose efforts led them to expose inconsistencies and inaccuracies in inherited tradition by careful study of texts.

SYNCRETISM AND SOCIETY IN LATE IMPERIAL CHINA

Syncretism, the selective combining of different inherited traditions, was a powerful force in the thought and religion of East Asia, where a movement comparable in its impact on religious thought to the Protestant Reformation in Europe may be found. The contrast is telling: whereas the Protestant Reformation created a definitive split in religious ideas, institutions, and practices within Christianity, beginning in the late fourteenth century, the syncretic movement known as the "Three Teachings" (Confucianism, Daoism, Buddhism) advocated the combining of the three dominant secular and religious ideologies of China. Similar processes may be found in Japan integrating native Shinto beliefs with imported Buddhism and Confucianism.

The Three Teachings Though Neo-Confucian thinkers from Zhu Xi to Wang Yangming sought ways to distinguish Confucianism from Buddhism, others searched for ways to integrate Confucianism with both Buddhism and Daoism. The founder of the Ming dynasty (1368–1643) proclaimed the "unity of the Three Teachings" and during the fifteenth and sixteenth centuries attempts to reconcile the three traditions continued and expanded. Confucian, Buddhist, and Daoist thinkers all contributed to a trend toward syncretism, seeing common truths reflected in the three different traditions. A Buddhist thinker, Jiao Hong (ca. 1548–1620), for example, saw the Three Teachings as forming a single teaching in which each could help to explain the others. All three teachings showed different aspects of the Way and had different applications in the lives of individuals—family life, ancestral rites, literary practices—but there was a unified and common Way for humanity.

Lay Buddhism In addition to the Three Teachings movement, the growth and spread of lay (non-clerical or popular) Buddhism was related to the general trend toward syncretism and was one of the most important developments in thought and religion during the late Ming. Much as Martin Luther's idea that faith, not the doctrines and practices mandated by the Church, was what mattered, Buddhist leaders such as the monk Zhuhong (1532–1612) appealed to lay believers by attempting to reconcile Buddhism and Confucianism, incorporating Confucian values such as filial piety into exhortations on the practice of the Buddhist faith in the moral living of daily life.

Commerce and Culture A contemporary of Zhuhong, Yuan Huang (1533–1606), made a contribution to the trend toward syncretism and to the development of practices to be followed in daily life through "morality books," guides to ethical behavior that began to circulate widely during the sixteenth century. Yuan Huang's forebears were Daoists, and after a Daoist fortune-teller predicted that Yuan would never take an examination degree or have a male heir, he first despaired and then roused himself to action. When he subsequently took a degree and fathered a son, he took up the personal mission to preach the value of moral effort as the means to success in life. Reflecting influence from the increasingly commercialized society of Ming China, as well as Buddhism, Daoism, and Confucianism, in his *Ledgers of Merit and Demerit,* Yuan Huang showed people how to calculate their good and bad deeds so that they would know how to accumulate sufficient merit to be rewarded in their afterlife. He applied a model of accounting, drawn from the world of commerce, to people's spiritual lives.

Despite the Manchu conquest in the mid-seventeenth century and the ambivalence of the imperial government—whether Chinese or Manchu—toward commerce and merchants, commerce continued to expand in Manchu China, especially during the stable and prosperous eighteenth century. Chinese merchants could invest their profits in education for their sons, since opportunity for social advancement was available to them through the civil service examinations. The merchants, however, were often criticized by political authorities and Confucian-minded ideologues for their extravagant consumption.

Merchants in eighteenth-century China were great patrons of the arts, and they cultivated amateur pursuits as bibliophiles (book-lovers) and art collectors. They patronized poets and scholars, providing funds to support the completion of writing projects. They purchased books to make great libraries, and collected paintings, calligraphy, and rubbings. In this way, merchant families acquired access to the social world of the literati, and literati received material support. It was a mutually advantageous relationship and mirrored somewhat the patronage by Italian merchant princes of scholars and artists in Renaissance Italy.

LITERATURE AND SOCIETY IN LATE IMPERIAL CHINA

As merchants patronized art and scholarship, the lives of merchants drew the interest of writers, and commercial presses that used wood-block printing expanded the availability of such writers' works to a large audience. *Golden Lotus,* a novel written during the heyday of merchant enterprise in the sixteenth century, reveals the intimate details of life in a rich merchant's household. Social relations within the household, a complex web of hierarchies and intrigues, are dominated by a clever concubine. Eroticism flavors the domestic realism of this episodic narrative, culminating in the death from sexual exhaustion of the merchant himself. Though fiction was still regarded by Confucian ideologues as a worthless pastime, *Golden Lotus* is only one example of fiction that portrayed the society of the time with lively realism and was read by highly educated members of the scholarly elite as well as by literate merchants.

Scholarly Satire Undoubtedly the audience of the satire *Scholars,* a novel written in the eighteenth century by an unsuccessful examination candidate, included merchants, who would enjoy making fun of the very social aspirations they shared. *The Scholars* satirizes the obsession people had with passing the examinations and critiques the corruption of the system. The position of women in Qing society is more subtly criticized, as the author portrays intelligent women who are themselves restricted by their gender from taking the examinations but are married to incompetent men who can.

Dream of the Red Chamber One of the most notable characteristics of the eighteenth-century novel *Dream of the Red Chamber* is the important role played by women, both family members and servants. Written by a descendant of a wealthy and privileged family whose grandfather was a protégé of the Kangxi emperor (r. 1662–1722), this novel portrays the intimate details of household and family life in late imperial China. At the same time that it is a rich tapestry of social life of the era, like *The Scholars* it is a stinging critique of the corruption and decadence produced by an increasingly hypocrisy-ridden and moribund elite social culture. The young hero, who enjoys more the company of his girl cousins and maidservants than that of other young men, resists the expectations of his father and family to prepare for the civil service examinations; when he finally does pass, he rejects the world and withdraws to a monastery.

GENDER AND SOCIETY IN LATE IMPERIAL CHINA

Social changes produced by the commercialization and urbanization of Chinese society created complex and sometimes contradictory new attitudes toward women. Both the practice of foot binding and the origin of the ideal of widow chastity, as opposed to remarriage, coincided with the increasing prosperity of the commercial revolution during the Song (960–1270), when women had the potential to gain mobility and some degree of independence because of the expansion of the market (see Chapter 11).

Women and Literacy Despite the emphasis placed on widow chastity and the widespread custom of foot binding, by the sixteenth century the spread of literacy began to erode traditional notions of gender, and the idea of the comparability of men and women became commonplace among male literati. A sixteenth-century author, Lu Kun (1536–1618), wrote a work entitled *Illustrated Biographical Sketches of Exemplary Women* based on a widely read text of the Han dynasty (206 B.C.E.–220 C.E.). In this work, in contrast to the original Han text, Lu revealed a far more complex and realistic attitude toward women than the extreme idealism of Confucian morality, and he promoted the idea of women's literacy.

Some male literati saw women's literacy only as an aid to moral instruction. Yuan Mei (1716–1797), one of the chief poets of the eighteenth century, however, rejected this notion along with the idea that the purpose of poetry was to convey moral instruction. Yuan Mei was criticized by contemporaries for encouraging the writing of poetry by women, since poetry that was not didactic, according to his critics, promoted emotional feelings rather than moral behavior. In addition to his support of female poetry students, Yuan Mei was also known for his opposition to the prohibition against widows' remarriage.

Though widow chastity had been encouraged since the Song period revival of Confucian values, it reached a peak in the Qing. Stone arches were erected by villages to honor chaste widows and other virtuous women, those who fulfilled in their behavior the highest ideals of Confucian virtue. Biographies of such exemplary women were included in local histories, alongside those of honorable officials. But works such as these tell us more about how educated men thought women should behave than about what women actually did. The very fact that an arch would be erected to honor a chaste widow suggests that such a woman was exemplary precisely because her behavior was a rarity.

One of the most memorable satires on the treatment of women took the form of an allegorical fantasy entitled *Flowers in the Mirror,* written by Li Ruzhen (1763–1830). One chapter of this novel, called "In the Country of Women," finds the principal character a hostage to the female ruler of the place, who treats him as her concubine, binding his feet, powdering and rouging his face, piercing his ears, and so on, in unbearable discomfort.

SYNCRETISM AND SOCIETY IN JAPAN

Religious syncretism in China was created from the dominant social ideology of Confucianism in combination with the two major religions, Buddhism and Daoism. In Japan, however, religious and philosophical syncretism arose from the merging of imported Confucianism and Buddhism with native Shinto beliefs. Yamazaki Ansai (1618–1682) studied the works of the Chinese Neo-Confucian philosopher Zhu Xi and taught the doctrines of moral self-cultivation and ethical behavior to his students. In his later years, Yamazaki became interested in the Japanese native religion of Shinto. He eventually found a way to blend Shinto with Confucianism, combining the traditions of the former with the ethical maxims of the latter. For example, he linked Shinto creation myths with Chinese cosmology and the pantheon of Shinto deities with Neo-Confucian metaphysical principles. Yamazaki's syncretism exemplifies one approach to the transformation of traditions in Tokugawa Japan.

A different use was made of Confucian ideas in seventeenth century Japan by Yamaga Soko (1622–1695), who adapted Confucian scholarly values to redefine the role of the warrior (*samurai* or *bushi*) in Tokugawa society. The consolidation of Tokugawa rule in the early sixteenth century ushered in an era of peace and prosperity when there were no wars for *samurai* to fight. Yamaga's doctrine of *bushido* (Way of the Warrior) urged *samurai* to master the skills of the scholar while disciplining themselves to retain their martial abilities.

Commerce and Culture   As in China, thinkers in Japan responded to the commercialization of ▨▨▨▨▨▨▨▨▨▨▨▨▨ society with new, syncretic ideas that reflected changes associated with the growth of commerce in Tokugawa Japan. In eighteenth-century Japan, the ideas of the Kyoto merchant-philosopher Ishida Baigan (1685–1744) represented a fusion of merchant-*samurai* culture and blended Confucian, Shinto, and Buddhist beliefs into a new religion. This new religion known as *Shingaku* (literally, heart learning) stressed the need for the spiritual development of each individual to fulfill his or her lot in life. Though society was hierarchically structured according to the Confucian four-tiered social order (samurai, farmer, craftsman, merchant) adopted by the Tokugawa, each part of the organic social body was equally important to its functioning.

> Although the *samurai,* farmers, artisans, and merchants differ in occupation, since they all appreciate the same principle . . . if we speak of the Way of the *samurai* . . . it goes for the farmers, artisans, and merchants, and if we speak of the Way of the farmers, artisans and merchants, it goes for the *samurai.*

The Confucian value of loyalty to one's superiors fit well with Tokugawa ideals of *samurai* loyalty to the lord, and compassion toward others flowed from Buddhist ideals, along with self-discipline from Zen Buddhism. Ishida Baigan promoted the worship of Amaterasu, the Sun Goddess, identifying her not only as the ancestress of Japan, but also with the Confucian cosmological concepts of heaven and earth as well as nature.

Merchants' wealth in Tokugawa Japan subsidized new literary and artistic forms that emerged from the urban culture of Tokugawa cities such as Osaka, Edo, and Kyoto, such as wood-block prints and the *kabuki* and puppet theaters. The famous chronicler of Tokugawa urban life Ihara Saikaku (1642–1693), who was himself of merchant background, criticized excessive consumption on the part of merchants, not from a Confucian stance but because it limited their capacity to make more money. Profits, he argued, should be saved and invested in further moneymaking enterprises, not wasted in profligate consumption. By the eighteenth century, Japanese merchants had begun to develop a sense of self-esteem in their identity as merchants. This was reflected in the Kaitokudo, an academy founded by Osaka merchant philosophers to encourage education and to foster a positive ideal of the place of merchants in Tokugawa society.

■

TRADITIONS AND THEIR TRANSFORMATIONS IN THE ISLAMIC WORLD

Despite significant cultural distinctions among China, Japan, and Korea, the East Asian world shared a common core because of the influence of China, including Confucianism, and Buddhism. Islam provided a similar link across the cultures it penetrated. The cohesion of the Islamic world in 1500 was reflected in the claim of the Egyptian scholar Jalal al-Din al-Suyuti (1445–1505) that his works had reached not only North Africa beyond Egypt but also West Asia and India. Islamic institutions of learning, *madrasa*s (colleges of Islamic law) flourished in al-Suyuti's Egypt, especially in Cairo, but also in more distant Islamic centers such as Timbuktu. Like European universities, which taught Christian theology and canon (Church) law, *madrasa*s were centers for the teaching of Islamic law and theology.

ISLAM IN WEST AFRICA

The Muslim traveler known as Leo Africanus observed about 1510 that Timbuktu on the Niger River was more than an African commercial center. From its origins as an oasis market town for trans-Saharan trade at the beginning of the twelfth century, from the fourteenth through eighteenth centuries Timbuktu was a center for the transmission of Islam in West Africa and had its own *madrasa*. Leo Africanus wrote that "here are great stores of doctors, judges, priests, and other learned men, that are bountifully maintained at the king's costs and charges." Furthermore, he described a center of learning and scholarship, where "hither are brought diverse manuscripts or written books out of Barbary, which are sold for more money than other merchandise." The book trade's high value reflected the importance placed on

FIGURE 13.10 The Shir Dar (Lion Bearer) *Madrasa* at the Central Asian Oasis City of Samarkand. Built between 1619 and 1636.

SOURCE: A. F. Kersting, London.

knowledge. The libraries of Timbuktu contained practically the whole of Arabic literature. A list of required readings for students in higher studies at Timbuktu in the second half of the sixteenth century includes twenty-five titles, all of them classics in Islamic studies.

Islam flourished in West Africa, though indigenous religious reliefs continued to dominate the lives of people outside the scholarly and commercial elites of urban centers such as Timbuktu. Syncretism characterized the early spread of Islam in West Africa. Whether in the Sudanic states of West Africa such as Songhay, the royal palaces of Central African states, or the East African cities, by the sixteenth century an urban elite culture invariably included scholars and writers, geographers, and mathematicians, all representative of the amalgam of Islamic or Christian learning alongside indigenous beliefs.

In Muslim West Africa, the written word was considered the word of God and as such provided power and protection. The important Sudanic book by Muhammad bin Muhammad al-Fulani al-Kashinawi, *A Treatise on the Magical Use of the Letters of the Alphabet,* describes the use of amulets containing small pieces of paper on which were written portions of the Qur'an. But the word was also a magical charm that conferred power to nonbelievers; Arabic script or an imitation thereof appeared on inscribed brass vessels and painted cloth used by non-Islamic peoples at great distances from the faith's strongholds. At times the magical properties and protective power believed by some to be conferred by Islam conflicted with the ideas of the *ulama,* the Islamic clergy. For example, the Muslim ruler of Songhay, Sunni Ali (1464/5–1492) persecuted the *ulama* of Timbuktu for criticizing his claim that he could turn himself into a vulture and make his armies invisible.

Islamic *Jihad*s in Africa   Beginning in the sixteenth century, a wave of *jihad*s (holy wars) swept over parts of West and West-Central Africa. Africans who studied in Mecca and Medina during their *hajj* (pilgrimage) absorbed ideas about *jihad* and conversion to Islam. When they returned to Africa, they took these ideas with them and helped to transform local political and social protests into Islamic reform movements. The *jihad* in the Senegambian region that established the Muslim-dominated state of Bundu in the 1690s is one example. Agricultural reforms accompanied the replacement of traditional elite by Muslim rulers. In contrast, the eighteenth-century victories at Fuuta Jaalo, south of the Gambia, installed Muslim rulers but did little else than convert their slaves to Islam. Reform movements continued into the nineteenth century and became increasingly representative of civil unrest in the wake of the Atlantic era.

CHRISTIANITY AND ISLAM MEET IN AFRICA: ETHIOPIA

Rumors of the presence of a Christian stronghold in North Africa had long inspired European voyagers to seek the fabled "Kingdom of Prester John" as a possible ally in their wars with Ottoman Muslims. Portuguese merchants finally reached the long-sought goal with their sixteenth-century capture of East African coastal trading towns that eventually led them north to the highlands of Ethiopia, where Christianity had thrived as a state religion since the fifth century.

The Islamic State   However, by the time the Europeans arrived in Ethiopia it had already of Ahmad Gran   fallen under Muslim control. Beginning in 1531, through a powerful and successful *jihad,* an Islamic religious reformer, Ahmad ibn Ibrahim or Ahmad Gran (1506–1543), had consolidated territory across the Ethiopian plateau with the aid of Ottoman weaponry. The Portuguese fleet, commanded by Vasco da Gama's grandson and carrying several hundred Portuguese soldiers, encountered fleeing Christians, joined the battle, and helped turn the tide against Ahmad Gran, who was killed in battle in 1543. For almost a century afterward, the Portuguese maintained a presence in Ethiopia, building an impressive stone castle at Gondar and dispatching Jesuits to Ethiopia. The Jesuits were eventually expelled in 1634, and Omani Arabs in Upper Egypt captured Nubia and entrenched themselves in the Sudan until the late eighteenth century.

ISLAMIC EMPIRES AND THE TRANSFORMATION OF TRADITION

At the same time that Portuguese merchants and missionaries were expanding into Africa, three powerful Islamic empires dominated a zone stretching from North Africa across West to South Asia. Though Islamic civilization flourished under all three, cultural and ideological differences distinguished the transmission of Islamic tradition under the Ottomans, the Safavids, and the Mughals and brought about transformations in that tradition. Cultural syncretism characterized both the Mughal Empire, including Persian and Hindi language and literature, along with Islam and Hinduism, and the Ottoman Empire, combining the Arabic and Persian languages, literatures, and peoples with Turkish peoples, language, and literature into an Islamic state. Under the Safavids, however, tensions among different divisions of Islam resulted in religious persecution, much as the hostilities between Catholics and Protestants drove conflicts in Europe during the Reformation and its aftermath.

The Ottoman Empire During the reign of Sultan Suleyman the Magnificent (r. 1520–1566), the expansion of Ottoman power reached its peak, with conquests in North Africa and the Balkans. Although initially the role of sultan was identified as both a religious and a political authority, by the time of Suleyman, the sultan had become a secular ruler and the *ulama,* a state bureaucracy. Suleyman's predecessor, Mehmet the Conqueror (r. 1444–1446 and 1451–1481), established eight *madrasa*s to train religious scholars as teachers, judges, and scribes; these then became the civil officials of the empire and staffed the state bureaucracy.

Ottoman writers and thinkers were also trained in these institutions. They included the encyclopedist Taskoprulu Zade Ahmet Husamuddin Effendi (d. 1553), who wrote biographies of *ulama,* scientists, mathematicians, and Sufis (Islamic mystics), along with compendia of religious and secular sciences. But by the late sixteenth century, the influence of religious authorities discouraged interest in the practical sciences. In 1580, for example, because of disapproval voiced by the chief Ottoman religious official, the Shaykh al-Islam, construction was halted on a new observatory in Istanbul modeled on that of Ulugh Beg in fifteenth-century Samarkand, and the partially finished building was torn down.

Nearly all the Arabic-speaking lands were part of the Ottoman Empire, which also included Anatolia and southeastern Europe. Turkish, however, was the language of the ruling family and the military and administrative elite, somewhat like Persian at the Mughal court. Western Turkish literature took root and expanded with the Ottomans in the fifteenth century, mainly after the capture of Constantinople and the transformation of that city into the great Turkish imperial capital, Istanbul ("Islam abounds"). Baqi (d. 1600) was one of a number of outstanding poets to appear at the Ottoman court. A great lyric poet, he flourished

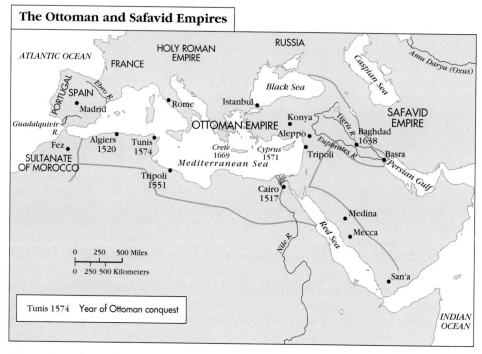

The Ottoman and Safavid Empires

MAP 13.1 The Expansion of Islamic Empires.

SOURCE: Albert Hourani, *A History of the Arab Peoples* (New York: Warner Books, 1991): 473.

during the reign of Suleyman the Magnificent, and his literary masterpiece was an elegy written upon Suleyman's death. His poems vividly reflect the happy life of the upper classes in sixteenth-century Istanbul, the colorful landscape and the picturesque scenes of the pleasure resorts in and about the capital. Like all Turkish court poets, he also wrote about the transitory nature of the world, advising that one should love, drink, and be merry, for all the beauties of life were doomed to perish.

Ottoman writers produced a vast number of prose works, though most were devoted to religion, history, and government correspondence. Two works that deserve special attention because they were outside these categories of prose were *Dede Korkut* ("Grandfather Korkut") and Evliya Chelebi's *Seyahatname* ("Book of Travels"). *Dede Korkut* was a collection of twelve tales taken from oral literature and written down in the fifteenth century. Grandfather Korkut, the minstrel who recites the tales, strongly resembles a pagan shaman. These stories were based on the reminiscences of the nomadic Turks concerning their life in their original home in Central Asia. They composed much of it as they migrated across West Asia. *Dede Korkut* is thus one of the oldest surviving examples of Turkish literature. The text that we possess today relates the life of the Turkish lineage groups in Anatolia, the deeds of their leaders, and their battles among themselves and against the Georgians and Greeks living along the Black Sea. It is now considered the national epic of Turkey.

Evliya Chelebi (1611–ca. 1680) came from a completely different world, the Ottoman court and the cosmopolitan city of Istanbul. After receiving a good traditional Ottoman education, he was smitten by wanderlust and embarked upon an amazing life of travel. For forty years he roamed the Ottoman Empire in West Asia, Europe, and Africa, officially and unofficially, on military campaigns, business, diplomatic, and financial missions. This peripatetic life provided the basis of his renowned ten-part *Book of Travels.* As a result of an insatiable curiosity, Evliya was able to give a remarkably comprehensive description of every place he visited, often city by city, from Hungary to the Caucasus and from the Crimea to Ethiopia. His work is packed with extensive material on religious, economic, political and social history, anthropology, folklore, and linguistics. Mixing fact, fiction, and humor, it is a monumental compilation that is a veritable treasure of information on seventeenth-century West Asia and neighboring regions.

The Safavid Empire   The Ottoman state was suspicious of the most radical forms of Sufism, devotional sects of Islamic mystics, and suppressed them, while sanctioning more acceptable, moderate forms of sufism. Sufism was also suspect to the Ottomans because of its association with its political and religious rivals, the Safavids (1501–1722), who traced their beginnings as leaders of a small Sufi sect in Iran under the Mongols. By the fifteenth century, however, the Safavids were becoming increasingly attracted to Shi'ite beliefs, the Islamic tradition that had originated among followers of the prophet Ali as the legitimate successor to Muhammad. The struggle between the Ottomans and the Persian Safavids over control of Anatolia and Iraq acquired religious overtones, as the Safavids were Shi'ites and the Ottomans became more Sunni (orthodox) as their empire expanded to include the main centers of Islamic urban culture.

Safavid *shaik*s (religious leaders) appealed to their followers with a combination of Sufi and Shi'ite ideology. By 1500, the Safavids had a strong military force, which, combined with the leadership of a charismatic figure, Shah Ismail I (r. 1501–1514), allowed them to capture the Iranian city of Tabriz, which they made their new capital, and to begin their dynasty. Under Shah Ismail, Shi'ism was imposed on the predominantly Sunni population of Iran. Sunnis were persecuted, along with Sufi orders that differed from that of the Safavids. Shi'ite shrines and other institutions were built under state patronage, and Shi'ite scholars were imported from Syria and Iraq. The best Sunni scholars and literary figures, including Sufi poets, moved to Mughal India, where the court language was Persian and the ideology Sunni.

The Ottomans defeated Shah Ismail in 1514 and weakened the Safavids, but in the late sixteenth century Shah Abbas (r. 1587–1629) successfully revived the Safavid state through mercantilist policies, such as support of the silk industry. Shah Abbas was also able to expand the Safavid territories. Isfahan was reconstructed in the seventeenth century as his new capital, and its beauty reflects the accomplishments of Shah Abbas. But his reign also witnessed the resurgence of the religious leadership of the Shi'ite *ulama,* who claimed that only an *imam,* a descendant of Ali, could understand the teachings of the Qur'an and be the legitimate leader of the Islamic community. By the early eighteenth century, they usurped the religious authority of the Safavid state and helped to bring about its collapse.

The Mughal Empire   A powerful and vibrant example of syncretism emerged in the encounters between Hinduism and Islam in India, where the imported faith of Islam collided with indigenous Hindu traditions, sometimes violently and sometimes as part of a dynamic relationship of cultural creativity. Mughal culture and religion in India joined Hindu and Muslim influences in a shifting balance of power that produced a rich material culture and led to equally complex syncretism in the world of ideas.

Babur (1483–1530), the founder of the Mughal (Turkish for "Mongol") empire, was a descendant of the Turkish conqueror Timur on his father's side, and the Mongol conqueror Chinggis Khan on his mother's. Unlike his ancestors, however, Babur was known for his poetry in both Persian and Turkish as well as for his military exploits and, like the Ottoman scholar Evliya Chelebi, represents the ideal of the "Renaissance man," one who is broadly skilled in many areas of knowledge and competence. His prose memoir, the *Baburnama* ("Book of Babur"), written in Persian, provides both a context for understanding his poetry and rich observations on Islamic culture and society in Central and Southwest Asia (Afghanistan) as well as Mughal India. Babur also composed versified works on Islamic law and the mystical Islamic beliefs and practices known as Sufism.

In 1556, Babur's grandson Akbar (r. 1556–1605) took up his grandfather's legacy and became a patron of Persian cultural influence at the Mughal court, though he married a Hindu woman and desired to bring about reconciliation between Hindus and Muslims. During Akbar's reign, Persian was made the official language of administration and law, but Akbar also encouraged Hindi literature, even naming a Hindi poet laureate. The first poet to hold this title was Raja Birbal (1528–1583), who helped popularize the northern vernacular now known as "Hindi" through poetry and through translations of Persian classics into Hindi. The most famous and popular of Hindi works in this era was a translation of the Sanskrit epic *Ramayana* into Hindi by Tulsi Das (1532–1623). In addition to Persian and Hindi, Akbar also patronized Urdu language and literature. *Urdu* is Turkish for "camp" and is applied to the mixed language that developed from the blending of the invading Muslims' Persian and indigenous languages in India. Akbar himself was a Sufi, and in time Sufi poets began using Urdu as well as Persian as a major vehicle of expression. Sufis incorporated music, local shrines, and local legends into their worship.

Sufism and Sikhism By Akbar's time, the second half of the sixteenth century, India was divided politically and spiritually into many religious and philosophical camps. Like Sufism in Islam, the devotional movement in Hinduism known as *bhakti* continued under the Mughals, whose rulers for the most part displayed tolerance of religious faiths. *Bhakti* movements borrowed little of significance from Islam and can be seen as reassertions of Hindu identity in the context of Mughal power.

In the early sixteenth century, medieval *bhakti* figures influenced the development of the Sikh religion, which was founded by the *guru* (master or teacher) Nanak (1469–1533). The sacred sayings of Nanak were recorded in a special script. This popular new community of faith flourished in the Punjab, drawing recruits of both Hindu and Muslim birth from the peasantry. However, Sikh customs and beliefs were drawn mainly from Hinduism, with little from Islam. The third *guru*, Amar Das, was patronized by Akbar, further inducing converts to the faith, which stressed community eating as well as prayer and abolished female *purdah* (seclusion) along with caste separation and the concept of untouchability. The seclusion of high-caste women was a practice adopted by Hindus from Islam, and its rejection by Sikhs can be seen as a symbol of the emphasis on Hindu identity characteristic of Sikh religion.

Ram Das, the fourth *guru*, served at Akbar's court and was granted land in the Punjab, which became the site of the sacred Sikh capital. Ram Das's son and successor, Arjun

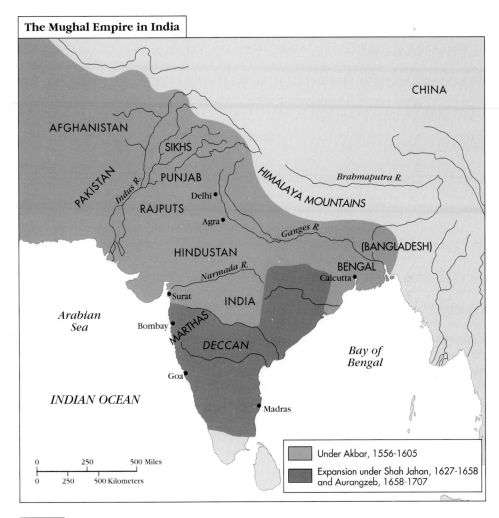

The Mughal Empire in India

CHINA

AFGHANISTAN

SIKHS

PAKISTAN

Indus R.

PUNJAB

HIMALAYA MOUNTAINS

Brahmaputra R.

Delhi •

RAJPUTS

Agra •

HINDUSTAN

Ganges R.

(BANGLADESH)

BENGAL

Calcutta •

Narmada R.

• Surat

INDIA

*Arabian
Sea*

Bombay •

MARTHAS

DECCAN

*Bay of
Bengal*

Goa •

INDIAN OCEAN

Madras •

| 0   250   500 Miles |
| 0   250   500 Kilometers |

Under Akbar, 1556-1605

Expansion under Shah Jahan, 1627-1658
and Aurangzeb, 1658-1707

MAP 13.2 The Expansion of the Mughal Empire in South and Southwest Asia.

(1563–1606), completed a great Sikh temple at this spot, naming the city Amritsar ("Pool of Immortal Nectar") for its tank filled with sacred well water. Under Arjun's guidance, the Sikh scripture, Granth Sahib, was compiled and deposited in Amritsar's temple. Arjun was said to have proclaimed that "in this vessel [Granth Sahib] you will find three things: truth, peace, and contemplation." Court support for the Sikh faith had waned since the time of Akbar. Akbar's successor, Jahangir ("World Seizer," r. 1605–1627) charged Arjun with treason and had him executed.

The Mughals' tolerance for other religious faiths waned by the end of the seventeenth century. Aurangzeb, who ascended the Mughal throne as Alamgir ("World Conqueror") in 1658 and reigned until his death in 1707, abandoned religious tolerance and the policy of equal treatment of Hindus and Muslims. Ultimately, despite earlier Mughal rulers' religious tolerance and movements that united Hindus and Muslims, such as the Sikh religion, by the eighteenth century, sharp divisions between Hindus and Muslims were evident in Indian society. Aurangzeb prohibited Hindus from holding positions of power, instead elevating Muslims. Hindu movements such as that in the state of Maharashtra led by Shivaji Bhonsle (1627–1680) challenged Mughal rule and threatened the stability of the Mughal Empire.

REFORM AND REVIVAL IN THE ISLAMIC WORLD

Eventually, the Safavid Empire fell in a single battle and Mughal power declined as Hindu powers reasserted themselves, while the Ottomans were forced to ally themselves with infidel states to stay the European advance. The political decline in the eighteenth-century Muslim world provided a context for religious reform and the revival of Islam. The disruptions and decay wrought by weak political rulers created opportunities for expansion, which were seized by the *ulama* and Sufis, guardians of the traditions of Islam. A purer vision of Islamic life and society was promoted through their teachings and through holy wars when necessary.

Reformist Movements Reformist ideas had been gathering steam even before the demise of the Islamic Empires. In the seventeenth century, leading scholars in Medina had debated political decisions together with doctrinal stances. In Syria, the scholar Abd al-Ghani of Nablus (1641–1731) strove to create a revitalized theology of reformed Sufism but with relatively little immediate consequence. Probably the most influential reformer was Muhammad Abd al-Wahhab (1703–1792), who moved the scholarly debate to the field of action. Though a Sufi, in his youth Wahhab traveled widely and began to preach Orthodox teachings and anti-Sufism as a result of the religious corruption he saw. Wahhab's puritanism suggested the overthrow of the medieval superstructure of Islam and a return to the "pure" authority of the Qur'an and *hadith*s, or teachings. His followers, known as the Wahhabis, continued into the nineteenth century, by which time they had extended their fundamentalist views throughout most of Saudi Arabia.

ISLAM AND THE TRANSFORMATION OF SOUTHEAST ASIAN SOCIETIES

Between 1500 and 1800, beginning from coastal fringes on the Malay peninsula and around the island of Sumatra, Islam made substantial inroads into Southeast Asia, acquiring a political role as well as a religious one. Islam interacted with indigenous beliefs, as well as with Hinduism and Buddhism, in reshaping Southeast Asian societies during the period of European expansion into this area of the world. European influences formed yet another stratum in the complex, multilayered societies of Southeast Asia. Unlike the expansion of Islam through the military conquest of the Ottoman, Safavid, and Mughal Empires, in Southeast Asia Islam was carried by Arab and other Muslim merchants who plied the waters surrounding the Malay peninsula and the Indonesia archipelago. Its gradual and relatively peaceful spread was much like the course of Islam in West or East Africa.

In the sixteenth century, increasing numbers of merchants from the southern part of the Arabian peninsula followed Indian Ocean trade routes and settled in port cities from East Africa to Southeast Asia. Many of these merchants held a special religious position in their homeland through the claim of descent from a descendant of Ali who had emigrated to the southern Arabian peninsula, and in the Indian Ocean ports where they settled they were often given special standing as religious authorities, which in turn conferred economic and political opportunities.

Islam and Southeast Asian Rulers Rulers of states that rose and fell in the region often made use of Islam to sanction their rule, as their predecessors had relied on Buddhism, Hinduism, and indigenous beliefs in earlier times. For example, Islam was adopted in the central Javanese state of Mataram, whose ruler, Agung (1613–1645), assumed the title of sultan and established the Islamic calendrical system in Java. But the rulers of Mataram often had difficulties controlling the *ulama*s and Sufis, and eventually they came to rely on Dutch support to uphold their control of the state and the Islamic clergy. This strategy proved fatal, however, leading to its defeat by the Dutch East India Company in 1629. In the case of Mataram, the dominance of Islam weakened rather than strengthened the state by forcing it to be dependent on the Dutch, who then took advantage of their position.

In contrast to Mataram, the Muslim state of Aceh worked together with the Islamic clergy and successfully resisted Portuguese and other European powers in the sixteenth and early seventeenth centuries. The most powerful Acehnese ruler, Iskandar Muda (1607–1636), was described as "the ruler who enforced the Islamic religion and required his people to pray five times a day, and to fast during Ramadan and the optional extra fast, and forbade them all to drink *arak* or to gamble." Both Mataram and Aceh, along with other Southeast Asian Muslim states, lost their independence in the eighteenth century, but the influence of Islam re-

MAP 13.3 Sacred Merchants Spread Religion from West Asia to Africa and Southeast Asia.

SOURCE: Cambridge Illustrated History of the Islamic World, 85

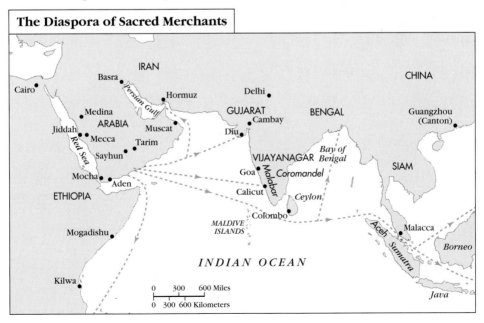

The Diaspora of Sacred Merchants

mained powerful throughout peninsular and island Southeast Asia, though not on the Southeast Asian mainland, where Buddhism and Hinduism continued as the dominant cultural and religious influences along with indigenous beliefs.

The Impact of Islamic Law Islamic law was incorporated along with traditional legal practices into the administrative structures of new Muslim states beginning in the sixteenth century. The degree to which Islamic law was imposed varied widely, but in the state of Aceh under Sultan Iskandar Muda in the early seventeenth century it was strictly applied through harsh punishments for gambling, drunkenness, and stealing. Throughout the seventeenth century the Islamic court of Aceh sentenced thieves to amputation. Deeply rooted local customs such as gambling associated with cockfighting and drinking the local liquor, *arak,* persisted, however despite Muslim injunctions forbidding them.

Islamic commercial law provided a necessary common ground for commercial transactions between Muslim merchants and their Southeast Asian counterparts. In non-Muslim

MAP 13.4 States and Port Cities of Southeast Asia.

SOURCE: John F. Cady, *Southeast Asia: Its Historical Development* (McGraw-Hill, 1964): 185

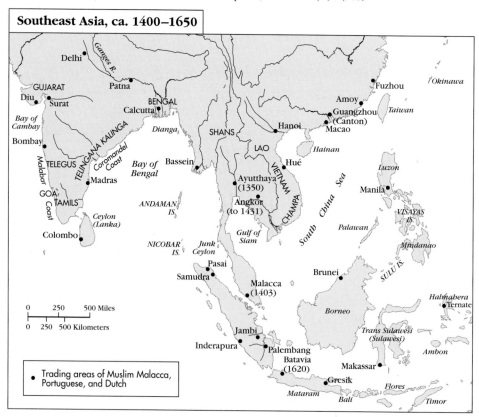

Southeast Asia, ca. 1400–1650

Trading areas of Muslim Malacca, Portuguese, and Dutch

ports, Muslim traders who resided there were often allowed to be subject to Islamic law carried out by the *ulama* of the urban mosque. Malay law codes of the sixteenth and later centuries followed Arabic law in matters of the sale of property, investment, and bankruptcy.

In matters of personal law, such as marriage and divorce, traditional local ideas and practices tended to shape the application of Islamic law and to moderate its harsher aspects. By traditional custom, monogamy prevailed, in part because divorce was easily obtained by either partner, and divorce was frequent. Both property and children were divided on a more or less equal basis. The court diary of the seventeenth-century state of Makassar details an elite woman's marital history that helps to illustrate this pattern of divorce rooted in local custom in contrast to Islamic law, which would not allow such freedom for a woman to divorce as she does. Karaeng Balla-Jawaya (b. 1634), daughter of one of the highest Makassar lineages, was married at the age of thirteen to Karaeng Bonto-marannu, who eventually became one of the greatest Makassar warriors. At twenty-five, she separated from him and soon married his rival, Karaeng Karunrung, the prime minister. In 1666, at the age of thirty-one, she separated from him, and she later married Arung Palakka, who was in the process of conquering her country with the aid of the Dutch. At thirty-six she separated from him, and she lived another fifty years.

Women in Southeast Asian Society
The relative freedom of sexual relations and marital practices in Southeast Asia conflicted sharply with both Islamic and Christian beliefs, which were increasingly influential after the fifteenth century. Both Islam and Christianity forbade premarital sexual relations, and Islam, in particular, imposed harsh punishments for transgressions. Islamic beliefs gradually imposed restraints on indigenous ways of life and influenced Southeast Asian societies on the Malay peninsula and throughout the Indonesian archipelago. This is particularly clear with regard to the position of Southeast Asian women, who had been independent and active participants in commerce and public social life and equal partners with men in matters of love and domestic life before the imposition of Islam.

Both Chinese and European traders, for example, often found themselves—to their surprise—dealing with women. As one European noted, "The money-changers are here [Aceh], as at Tonkin [Vietnam], most women." Some women even succeeded in joining the upper circle of large-scale merchants and shipowners, most of whom were male. Nyai Gede Pinateh was a female harbormaster (*shahbandar*) at Gresik around 1500 and sent her ships to trade in Bali, Maluku, and Cambodia. A woman of Mon a mainland Southeast Asian ethnic group descent, Soet Pegu, used her position as sexual and commercial partner of successive Dutch factors in Ayutthaya to virtually monopolize Dutch-Thai trade in the 1640s.

Although, with few exceptions, female rulers were virtually unknown in Hindu, Buddhist, Islamic, and Chinese political traditions, women occupied the thrones of Aceh, Jambi, and Inderagiri in the seventeenth century and exercised control over trade much as their male counterparts did. Women rulers seem to have been favored in some cases because their rule was likely to encourage trade. Though the four queens of Aceh (1641–1699) ruled at a time of political and military decline after Iskandar Muda, their reigns were associated with the maintenance of Aceh as the most important independent port in island Southeast Asia. The just rule of the first of these queens was noted by an Aceh chronicler as the reason for the primacy of Aceh in international trade at the time. Women also engaged in diplomacy as an accompaniment to their trade and political roles. These women were necessarily fluent in several languages, including European ones such as Portuguese or Dutch as well as Malay and other Southeast Asian languages.

Literacy in Southeast Asian Society   Europeans in the sixteenth and seventeenth centuries were sometimes astonished by the high rates of literacy they found among both women and men in Southeast Asia. A Dutch trading official at the court of Mataram in the mid–seventeenth century noted that the majority of Javanese could read and write. A Spanish observer in the Philippines stated, "So accustomed are all these islanders to writing and reading that there is scarcely a man, still less a woman, who cannot read and write in letters proper to the island of Manila."

Throughout Southeast Asia there was a strong tradition of poetry contests as part of courtship. Love letters and poems were written on easily available local materials such as palm leaves. Women as well as men had to be able to read and write the local scripts in order to participate in these basic social rituals. After Islamic influence became pervasive, Islamic authorities attempted to suppress such practices, and women were actively discouraged from learning to read and write for fear that they would use those skills to send love letters and engage in traditional courting rituals that were seen as improper and immoral according to Islam. As both Islam and Christianity introduced new scripts along with their religious beliefs and social values, the earlier scripts tended to disappear and a more restricted male literacy was the result.

Scripts, Schooling, and the Spread of Islam   Although the alphabetic writing scripts employed throughout Southeast Asia were probably derived from Indian script and thus used initially for the sacred literature of Hinduism and later Buddhism, the spread of these scripts served different purposes: those of commerce and daily life. The transmission of these scripts, which used a limited number of symbols, such as the Indonesian *ka-ga-nga* script, probably took place primarily within the home, taught by mothers to their children. Since women played an important role in commerce, they necessarily knew how to

FIGURE 13.11 Burmese Scribe.

SOURCE: Hiram Cox, *Journal of a Residence in the Burmhan Empire, and More Particularly at the Court of Amarapoorah* (London: John Warren, 1821. General Research Division, New York Public Library, Astor, Lenox and Tilden Foundations.

read and write, and their domestic responsibilities included teaching their children these skills.

Hindu and Buddhist monastic traditions, like those of Christian monasteries in Europe, taught literacy for sacred purposes to a largely male student population, and this tradition was strong in mainland Southeast Asia, though less so elsewhere in Southeast Asia. The teaching of Arabic for religious purposes by Islamic clergy similarly focused on men, so male literacy was associated with religious authority, which excluded women. In the absence of formal schooling outside these religious establishments, the preservation of local Southeast Asian scripts and literature, as well as female literacy, was associated not only with the needs of commerce but also with indigenous practices such as the writing of love poems used in elaborate courtship rituals that predated Islamic and Christian influence.

The spread of Islam in Southeast Asia was aided by the use of an Arabic script already modified for Persian to transcribe Malay. As Malay written in this script became the common language of Islam and of trade in the region, it served as an important conduit of Islam on the Malaysian peninsula and throughout much of the Indonesian archipelago. Another important means for the spread of Islam were the schools in which boys were taught to read and recite the Qur'an in Arabic. By around 1600, for example, there were many of these schools in Aceh, one of which had a reportedly brilliant student of the age of thirteen who later became the powerful Sultan Iskandar Muda. Such schools provided the foundation of a written culture in Malay dominated by Muslim literati. In the Philippines, within a century of Christianization, knowledge of the earlier Indonesian scripts had disappeared.

SUMMARY

The revival or rebirth of earlier traditions, such as that of Greco-Roman antiquity during the European Renaissance or Confucianism in late imperial China, is one type of response to dilemmas presented by changes in the material world that undermine prevailing worldviews, a condition characteristic of both Europe and China following the commercial revolutions that took place before 1500. Syncretism is another response to transformations in the material world that call for the reconstruction or renewal of inherited cultural, religious, ethnic, or intellectual traditions. The syncretism of Confucianism, Buddhism, and Daoism in Ming China, known as the "Three Teachings," was an attempt to adapt these diverse systems of thought to changing economic and social conditions of the fifteenth and sixteenth centuries. Syncretism is also characteristic of Southeast Asia after 1500 as both Islam and Christianity penetrated the societies and cultures there and reshaped people's lives and worldviews.

A contrasting response to that of syncretism is the division of inherited tradition. In the case of Europe, a powerful challenge to the inherited tradition of the Catholic Church took shape in the Protestant Reformation, which resulted in a profound split in Christianity between Catholicism and Protestantism. Similarly, doctrinal differences in Islam shaped the interaction of the Sunni Ottomans with the Shi'ite Safavids, as well as between both the Ottoman and Safavid states and Sufism. The notion of reformation, however, may also be used to describe more inclusive, rather than divisive, approaches to inherited traditions. Reformation used in this sense does not imply the weaving together of traditions, as in syncretism; rather, it describes a renewal of inherited tradition that is enriched by the incorporation of new ideas, new influences, and new adherents. Reformation understood in this way can be used to describe the development of the Sikh religion in Mughal India and the reform and revival of the Wahhabis in West Asia.

Ideas in Enlightenment Europe that elevated the role of the individual and reason, as opposed to the Reformation's stress on the individual and faith, had their counterparts in differing traditions and changing notions of the relationship between individual and community elsewhere. In China, for example, the evolution of the Neo-Confucian tradition brought forth ideas that placed great emphasis on self-cultivation and the inner capacity of each individual to realize Confucian sagehood. Tensions in Neo-Confucian thought between intuitive understanding and knowledge gained through study and experience mirrored differences in views of the human mind and its capacity for understanding in sixteenth- and seventeenth-century Europe, views that provided context for the scientific revolution. The scientific revolution produced a new understanding of the relationship between humans, the natural world, and the cosmos; these developments had a profound impact not only in Europe, but also on Africa, the Americas, and Asia through European economic and political domination after 1500.

When Europeans encountered cultural difference, they were forced to reconstruct their own identity, as views of the "natives" of the Americas, for example, raised new questions about ideal societies and governments. Similarly, when peoples in Asia, Africa, and the Americas encountered Europeans they also experienced transformations in the ways they understood themselves—their identities—as both ideological and material conditions of their lives were altered and their world changed. The processes of change could be divisive and disruptive, or they could bring about the successful integration and adaptive blending of difference. In the following chapter, we will explore the boundaries, encounters, and frontiers of European engagement with the world and of Asians, Africans, and peoples of the Americas with one another.

ENGAGING THE PAST

PROTESTANTISM AND CAPITALISM

One of the most influential works seeking to relate the effect of Protestantism to economic changes in Europe after 1500 was a small book published in 1904 by the German sociologist Max Weber and known by its English title of *The Protestant Ethic and the Spirit of Capitalism.* Observing that there was a correlation between countries where Protestantism had taken root and the successful development of first merchant and then industrial capitalism in those countries, Weber examined the possibility that this was more than just a coincidence. Was it not possible that capitalism was encouraged by the values and ideas associated with Protestantism?

Weber suggests that Protestantism, especially Calvinism, replaced the cultural values of medieval Europe with a specific Protestant ethic

that was ideal for the development of capitalism. By stressing the sanctity of labor, the idea that we should not waste a moment of our brief time on earth, that reward lies in doing our best in the place and position in which God has placed us, Protestantism undoubtedly supported a work ethic that might well result in material success in worldly activities. The Calvinist idea of preelection, the doctrine that God knows in advance who is to be saved and who is damned, further suggests a connection between Protestantism and the development of capitalism. Success in one's calling may be taken as a sign that one is among the elect. This idea enabled merchants and manufacturers who made fortunes to see their success as proof of election to salvation and encouraged pursuit of success as a guarantee of election. In such ways, Weber argued, the ideals and ethics of Protestantism were consistent with the spirit of capitalism and deserved as much credit as material factors for its success.

Weber's work has been subject to considerable attack and revision since he published his book. It has been pointed out that Catholic capitalists were just as successful as Protestants, that work was considered sacred by the medieval Church, and that Calvinism taught that there was no certainty that success was a sign of God's favor and that the use of wealth for luxurious living was a sure path to damnation. Weber was aware of some of the contradictions of his thesis, pointing out that the Protestant ethic had resulted in an ascetic form of capitalism that piously strove to suppress the spirit of wealth, while avidly seeking profit maximization.

Slightly more than fifty years after the publication of Weber's book, an American sociologist, Robert Bellah, published a study of a Japanese religious reformer, Ishida Baigan (1685–1744), called *Tokugawa Religion*. Applying some of the same general principles used by Weber to examine the links between Protestantism and capitalism, Bellah explored how the ideas of the merchant-philosopher Ishida Baigan expressed values that had contributed to Japan's commercial growth during the Tokugawa period. The position of merchants in Tokugawa society was low, and Ishida Baigan addressed his message to them. He urged his followers to do their duty, to live out their lives with honor and diligence, no matter what their station in life. Bellah made a convincing argument for the fit between the Tokugawa values reflected in Ishida Baigan's teachings and the Protestant ethic outlined by Weber. Though the content and context of the two were very different, both Bellah and Weber suggested the possibilities of rooting historical explanation of economic growth in religious values as well as in material conditions.

SUGGESTIONS FOR FURTHER READING

Elizabeth L. Eisenstein, *The Printing Press as an Agent of Change* (Cambridge: Cambridge University Press, 1979). A path-breaking study of the influence of the printing press on the transformation of the world beginning in the sixteenth century.

Benjamin A. Elman, *From Philosophy to Philology: Intellectual and Social Aspects of Change in Late Imperial China* (Cambridge, MA: Harvard University Press, 1984). The social context of intellectual change in late imperial China.

J. R. Hale, *The Civilization of Europe during the Renaissance* (New York: Atheneum, 1994). A comprehensive recent survey of aspects of European culture during the Renaissance.

Lisa Jardine, *Worldly Goods: A New History of the Renaissance* (New York: Doubleday, 1996). An engaging account of current perspectives on the European Renaissance, stressing the interdependency of economic and cultural factors.

Dorothy Ko, *Teachers of the Inner Chambers: Women and Culture in Seventeenth-Century China* (Stanford, CA: Stanford University Press, 1994). Richly textured study of gender in late imperial Chinese society.

Francis Robinson, *Cambridge Illustrated History of the Islamic World* (Cambridge: Cambridge University Press, 1996). Comprehensive coverage of the Islamic world.

14

Boundaries, Encounters, and Frontiers

Among the peoples who lived in provincial Spanish America in postconquest times were the Nahua, who, between 1550 and about 1800, produced numerous documents in their own language (Nahuatl) that were written in the European script. The Nahuatl sources show how the indigenous structures and patterns of Nahua culture survived the conquest on a larger scale and for a far longer period of time than if judged on the basis of Spaniards' reports alone. For example, although the Spanish "claimed" and "possessed" the land and determined its boundaries, land was granted to others, often reverting back to the indigenous inhabitants. The excerpt from the document below describes a 1583 land grant in the town of San Miguel de Tocuillán, Mexico. Its recipient and the family spokeswoman is Ana:

Ana spoke and said to her older brother Juan Miguel, "My dear older brother, let us be under your roof for a few days—only a few days. I don't have many children, only my little Juan, the only child. There are only three of us with your brother-in-law Juan."

Then her older brother said, "Very well, my younger sister. Move what you have, let all your things be brought up." . . .

Then Ana said, "Don't let us give you so much trouble; let us take a bit of the precious land of our precious father the saint San Miguel, and there we will build a little house." . . .

Then Juan Francisco said, "Who is going to measure it out?"

Then the lords said, "Who indeed? Other times, wasn't it good old Juan? He'll measure it out."

Then they said to him, "Come, take the cattle prod in your hands and measure it out. Measure out six lengths on all four sides."

And when he had measured it, then they said, "That's how much land we're giving you."

Then Ana said, "Thank you very much; we appreciate your generosity."

Then the rulers said, "Let it begin right away; don't let the stone concern you, but let it quickly be prepared to begin the foundation."

Then Ana said, "Let's go back and you enjoy a bit more pulque [an alcoholic drink made of the agave plant]."

Then the rulers said, "What more do we wish? We've already had (enough)."

And Ana wept, and her husband wept, when they were given the land.

Then Ana said, "Candles will be burnt, and I will go along providing incense for my precious father the saint San Miguel, because it is on his land that I am building my house." . . .

When all five lords had spoken, everyone embraced.

Only Aztec women past childbearing age were traditionally allowed to drink this ceremonial liquid.

SOURCE: The Bodleian Library, University of Oxford. Ms. Arch.
Seldan. A.I. fol. 71r.

This and other indigenous documents provide illustrations of the autonomy of peoples
living on the periphery of European hegemony, their retention of local culture (such as the
ritual sharing of food and drink signifying agreement), and their humanity. Native accounts
suggest that intensive interactions negotiated power and place. Finally, they remind us that
change and continuity can often be the same thing, depending on the emphasis and perspective from which the event is viewed.

INTRODUCTION

The establishment of the Atlantic world system and European hegemony, or dominance, from
the Atlantic to the Pacific after 1500, shaped the nature of political and economic change
over the course of the next 500 years. Beginning around 1500 until nearly the end of the
twentieth century, Europe dominated and directed the flow of global power through its hegemony over the Atlantic world system. The boundaries of social interaction and cultural exchange were altered accordingly, from Amsterdam to Zanzibar. Social relationships at the levels of individual through community were redefined by the changing boundaries of global
trade and politics. These were not the only forces of change; both religious and cultural identities also helped shape the contours of social interaction.

In many parts of the world, the movement of immigrant Europeans into indigenous
communities created zones of intensive intergroup interaction, called frontiers, in which social, cultural, and economic changes took place. On frontiers, no single authority dominated,

intense competition existed, and interaction often took place between two or more groups that had previously had distinct ethnic identities. The boundaries of frontiers often changed and then remained fluid, permitting great social and economic mobility. The outcomes of frontier interactions were equally variable, ranging from assimilation and alliance building to extermination, expulsion, or subjugation.

The concept of frontiers also suggests the drawing of boundaries, physical and mental lines of separation between political and social groups and the territories they claimed and inhabited. Though frontiers were not new—Roman colonists in Germanic territories, for example, lived on the frontiers of the Roman Empire, with shifting boundaries—increasingly after 1500, the fervent mapping of new worlds altered both identities and action. In the science of metallurgy, boundaries function as more than lines of separation. A boundary is also defined as the site where two particles or crystals, each made up of orderly patterns of atoms, meet. Where two particles or crystals intersect, there is a boundary. Boundary sites are subject to chemical instability and activity—in short, transformation. Not unlike the boundary sites in metals, boundary sites in human history produced opportunities for interaction, and the creation and crossing of boundaries in history also produced transformation. Even as the science of cartography, or mapmaking, advanced, the complexities of real and imagined boundaries remained formidable. By viewing the expansion of Europe's hegemony from the position of its outer boundaries and frontiers rather than from its European center we gain a considerably different perspective on Europe's impact.

The mapping of European global hegemony reconfigured the course of centuries-old interactions and encounters, both on land and sea. Not all lines recorded on early maps were the consequence of the identification of geographical features. The competition between Spain and Portugal for newly discovered lands in the fifteenth century led to conflicts that were eventually settled by a series of papal pronouncements, resulting in the Treaty of Tordesillas in 1494. The treaty's purpose was to draw an imaginary line between Spanish claims to the west and those of Portugal to the east, a dividing line roughly 370 leagues (960 nautical miles) west of the Cape Verde Islands, later moved further west to incorporate the Portuguese claims in Brazil. The treaty's line also appeared on maps of the early sixteenth century, and the consequences of drawing such boundaries were increasingly contentious, both reflecting and leading to political, economic, and cultural conflicts. In this chapter, we examine examples of changing boundaries and frontiers in world history beginning in the fifteenth century, exploring motivations for and consequences of their crossings.

■

CARTOGRAPHY AND EXPLORATION

Refugees fleeing to Italy from Turkish attacks on Constantinople in the fourteenth and fifteenth centuries had carried with them precious manuscripts from the city. Among them were Greek texts of Ptolemy's *Geography,* a second-century work known to Arab cartographers since at least the ninth century C.E. During the fifteenth century, Ptolemy's guide to making maps was translated into Latin, and later maps were added and updated. They had an enormous impact on the models and meanings attached to geographical discovery during the next century. The *Geography* included instructions for making map projections—maps that included meridians and parallels, longitudinal and latitudinal lines based on astronomical reckoning.

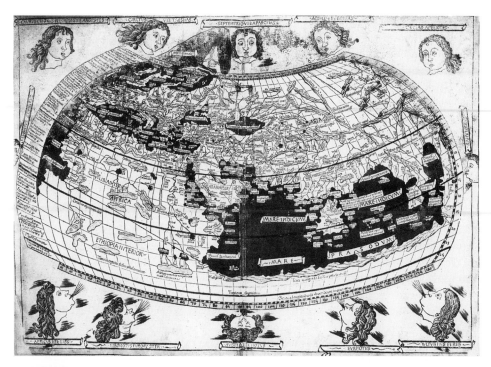

FIGURE 14.1 World Map from the Latin Edition of Ptolemy's *Geographia,* Printed in Ulmin in 1486.

SOURCE: Rare Books and Manuscripts Division, New York Public Library. Astor, Lenox, and Tilden Foundations.

An important consequence of the invention of printing during the European Renaissance was the creation and distribution of printed maps including Ptolemy's world map (first printed in Ulm in 1486). The ability to reproduce identical copies permitted multiple copies to circulate and increased the quantity of cartographic information that could be added to or refined on drawn maps. Centers of Renaissance learning, such as Florence and other Italian cities, attracted scholars as well as master craftsmen who constructed maps and model globes during the years of European exploration, a time when the understanding of land and water relationships altered drastically.

BOUNDARIES ON LAND AND SEA

The first maps to show the Atlantic world were the manuscript, portolan-style charts used by ship pilots. They were typically drawn on sheepskin. Used to guide ships, portolans were largely concerned with providing detailed, accurate information on shorelines and compass points for navigation, but they lacked the projection system of Ptolemaic maps, an orderly system of meridians and parallels. Juan de La Cosa's portolan-style map of 1500 shows the discoveries of Columbus's voyages and later explorations in South America, together with the voyages of the Englishman John Cabot (1497) along Newfoundland.

The first printed map showing the discoveries in the Western Hemisphere appeared in Florence in 1506. Unlike de La Cosa's map, the map by Giovanni Contarini and his engraver, Francesco Rosselli, has a regular projection. This map and an engraved 1507 map by Johannes Ruysch, a Dutchman living in Germany, provided the means for the gradual recognition that a new world had been discovered (not the Indies or Cathay, as Columbus had wrongly imagined) and that another continent therefore needed to be added to the cartographic representation of the world. This recognition was dramatically illustrated on Martin Waldeseemüller's 1507 map; his printed map is also the first dated map on which the name "America" appears.

Mercator Map The many advances in knowledge resulting from the geographical exploration of the sixteenth century culminated in the great 1569 world map by Gerardus Mercator of Flanders. Mercator's projection bore lines of constant compass bearing that made it readable by navigators. Finally, a true world navigational chart had been achieved. The Mercator world map included European discoveries that permitted delineation of the Americas, the Strait of Magellan, and other discoveries. It placed Asia, the Americas, Europe, and Africa into a single, systematic global vision corresponding to the incorporation of much of the world into a new world system dominated by Europe.

■

BOUNDARIES, ENCOUNTERS, AND FRONTIERS IN NORTH AMERICA

Advances in cartography corresponded with the opening of the Atlantic frontier and the colonization of North America by Europeans seeking both economic gain and religious freedom. During the seventeenth century, the new colonies of the North American seaboard (Chapter 12) constituted a frontier. Economic survival in an expanding global economy forced settlers to look back across the Atlantic. Expansion on land defined the colonies as the moving frontier of European culture, commerce, and Christianity, a zone of intensive interactions with indigenous peoples.

CULTURAL ENCOUNTERS IN NEW ENGLAND AND VIRGINIA

Most American schoolchildren know one version of the story of the Indian Squanto, who brought food to the starving Pilgrims of the Plymouth colony in their first dreadful winter and taught them how to cultivate maize. This version established the mythology of the American Thanksgiving festival, celebrated annually to commemorate the sharing of food and the cooperative relationship between the Pilgrims and the indigenous inhabitants of the land where these refugees from England settled. Similarly, the story of Pocahontas, who pleaded with her father, the chief Powhatan, to spare the life of John Smith and ultimately to ensure the survival of the Virginia colony of Jamestown, has become part of the mythology of the European settlement of the Americas. Rarely, however, is the end of the story for the two Native Americans remembered. Both Squanto and Pocahontas met unhappy fates: Squanto died in exile in his own land because of conflicts with his own people brought about by his relationship with Europeans, and Pocahontas died in England before she could return home.

Even less well known is the fact that both were at one time captives of Europeans. Rather, the image of captivity that dominated the imagination of early settlers in the Americas and their descendants was that of Europeans being kidnapped and held by Native Americans.

Images of Captivity The prominent New England Puritan religious leader and master of oratory, Cotton Mather, evoked powerful images of the captivity of women and children in a sermon delivered in 1698:

> How many Women have been made a prey to those Brutish men, that are Skilful to Destroy? How many a Fearful Thing has been suffered by the Fearful Sex, from those men, that one would Fear as Devils rather than men? Let the Daughters of our Zion think with themselves, what it would be, for fierce Indians to break into their Houses, and brain their husbands and their Children before their Eyes. . . . Our Little Boys and Girls, even these Little Chickens, have been seized by the Indian Vultures. Our little birds have been Spirited away by the Indian Devourers, and brought up, in a vile Slavery, till some of them have quite forgotten their English tongue, and their Christian Name, and their whole Relation.

Mather's rendering of captivity is a powerful one that must have moved his audience. The counterpart to Mather's vision, even to the extent of using bird imagery, is a legend of the Wampanoags, Algonquian-speaking inhabitants of southeastern Massachusetts. They saw the European invaders riding a giant bird on a river, snatching and holding several Wampanoags captive on the bird. Despite having to brave thunder and lightning (gunfire),

FIGURE 14.2 King Powhatan Commands Captain Smith to be Slain, While His Daughter Pocahontas Begs for His Life (1624).

Engraving from John Smith, *The Generalle Historie of Virginia, New England, and the Summer Isles.*

SOURCE: Courtesy of the Newberry Library, Chicago.

the Wampanoags succeeded in rescuing the captives of the English. Such images of captivity, generated in both European and Native American societies by their encounters, structured the relationship between the immigrants and the indigenous inhabitants. Ideas about the "Other" in turn emerged from these images of foreign peoples and guided policies pursued both by the immigrants and by the native inhabitants whose lands were being invaded. Despite the implications of Cotton Mather's vivid portrayal of the fate of English captives, far fewer Europeans were captured by Native Americans than Europeans were captured by Native Americans.

Squanto's Story   Squanto, for example, was one of about two dozen Wampanoags captured in 1614 by the English and sent to Spain, where some were sold into slavery and others were claimed by the Church. Squanto ended up spending time in England and Newfoundland before returning to his native land, where his newly acquired linguistic ability enabled him to act as an intermediary between Europeans and his own people. Eventually Squanto, whose Algonquian name was Tisquantum, returned to find his native village deserted because of an epidemic of a European disease that had claimed the lives of 75 to 90 percent of coastal Algonquians from southern Maine to Cape Cod. Squanto subsequently became an interpreter and intermediary for Massasoit, a Wampanoag *sachem* (headman), whom he served by negotiating a treaty with the Pilgrims. He was recaptured by Wampanoags who opposed his actions, rescued by Plymouth's Captain Miles Standish, and died in exile from his native Wampanoags, alienated even from Massasoit, who ordered his execution as a traitor. Under the protection of his English friends, who considered Squanto a "special instrument of God," Squanto reportedly requested conversion to Christianity on his deathbed.

Native American Warfare and Captivity   Before their encounters with Europeans, Native American peoples engaged in complicated practices of warfare, captivity, and diplomacy. The Iroquoian peoples of the northeastern woodlands, for example, carried out a complex ritual related to warfare known as a "mourning war," in which they would take a captive from a hostile group to assuage the grief or mourning over the loss of a member of their own group. The captive would then replace the lost member. In the mid–seventeenth century, in the midst of population decrease due to disease and emigration to mission villages in Canada, there was an intensification of warfare, aided by the introduction of firearms. Iroquois patterns of ritual warfare began to change under these pressures, leading to the assimilation not just of individuals, but of entire peoples, including the Tuscaroras, into the Five Nations of Iroquois (Mohawks, Oneidas, Onondagas, Cayugas, and Senecas). These changes altered the boundaries of subsequent interactions and all can be attributed to the European presence, which brought disease, missionaries, and guns. Thus, patterns of warfare, captivity, and diplomacy were transformed by the engagement of Native American peoples with European colonial powers.

Native American–European Interaction   Economics as well as religion and cultural practices such as ritualized warfare structured the interaction of Europeans and Native Americans along the boundaries of the Atlantic seaboard frontier. Like the story of Squanto introducing the Pilgrims to maize, Pocahontas was said to have demonstrated to Captain John Smith the benefits of tobacco as a commercial crop. From the perspective of Powhatan, Pocahontas's father and the leader of a confederation of tribes that numbered nearly 9,000 in 1607, when the settlers arrived, the English were just another tribe to be dealt with. They came in large boats, carried powerful weapons, dressed oddly, and built in Jamestown—in his territory—a fort they named for their king. But the English settlers were greatly outnumbered by Powhatan's people and unable to provide their own food, which they demanded from Powhatan.

Despite their miserable state, the English appeared to consider themselves superior, even boasting of the power of their God and denouncing the religious practices of their hosts. One of them, Captain John Smith, learned enough about their Native American hosts to gain some respect from Powhatan, who pursued a policy of toleration toward the English and made use of their weapons to strengthen his own forces against native rivals. In 1614, Powhatan married his daughter Pocahontas to John Rolfe, an Englishman, who brought a new kind of tobacco plant from South America that could be grown in Virginia and sold for profit across the sea. By the time of Powhatan's death in 1617, tobacco plantations were sprouting up throughout his land.

Crossing Boundaries: Marriage In the same year as her father's death, Pocahontas, known by her Anglicized Christian name as Rebecca, sat next to her husband, John Rolfe, and King James and Queen Anne at a performance in London of Ben Jonson's play *The Vision of Delight*. The first interracial marriage in American history was the product of an effort to ally the English and Powhatan's people, as well as to bridge the enormous gaps in culture and politics. After Pocahontas's death on board a ship destined for Virginia, her husband and their mixed-blood son returned to Virginia, where Rolfe died in an assault by Pocahontas's half uncle, who had taken her father's place. Though both Pocahontas and John Rolfe met unhappy fates and their union did not become the pattern for relations between Europeans and Native Americans, it demonstrated the unrealized possibilities for accommodation and reconciliation through intermarriage of two vastly different peoples on the North American frontier.

■

FRONTIERS IN NORTH AMERICA AND SOUTH AFRICA

North America was not the only site of European settlement during the Atlantic era. In southern Africa, frontiers existed as a result of similar processes of the expansion of European capitalism. Both North American and southern African frontiers had approximately the same chronology, and the expansion of both settlements met with resistance. In southern Africa, permanent settlement initiated by the Dutch East India Company began in the Cape during the 1650s; in North American seaboards, effective settlement appeared in the seventeenth century with the Virginia colony (in 1607) and New England (in 1620). In both cases, initial settlements quickly established European domination over indigenous inhabitants on the coast, with the consequence that new settlements turned inland towards an expanding frontier. In southern Africa, the frontier expanded northward from the strategic Cape peninsula; in North America, expansion was primarily westward.

The differing environments of the two regions promoted vastly different scales of migration. The temperate regions and rich forests of North America were strikingly similar to European forests across the Atlantic; in southern Africa, a temperate coast quickly gave way to harsher deserts, plateaus, river valleys, and mountainous terrain. By 1700, there were about 200,000 Europeans in English colonies in North America and only about 1,200 in the cape. A century later, the numbers of the intruders had increased twentyfold: more than 4 million in the United States and about 20,000 in southern Africa. Migrants in the English North American colonies had greater autonomy than the Dutch settlers in southern Africa, although both had to exist in an environment of international rivalry and resistance. Britain, France, and Spain entered into intense competition, including wars, over trade and lands in the Americas from the seventeenth century to the beginning of the nineteenth. And when westward expansion from the eastern seaboard occurred, it was further slowed by several wars of resistance in which Indian groups were defeated. Although historians can identify several distinct stages in the frontier process, it cannot be thought of as a singular, unitary advance of white domination.

THE NORTH AMERICAN FRONTIER: WAR, RELIGION, AND CULTURE

In North America, the strategic corridor of the northeastern frontier was the site of intense struggle between Native Americans, the British, and French colonials. Dozens of fort and battle sites are the scattered remains of the frontier era. The era's commercial rivalry culminated in the French and Indian War (1756–1763) which ended after the signing of the Treaty of Paris. Had the outcome been different, the United States might have been a French-speaking territory. Largely relying on tactics adopted from the Indians, groups of provincial "irregulars"—soldiers supported by commercial companies rather than governments—carried on forest warfare dressed in green outer coats, brown leggings, and moccasins. The most famous and daring of these warriors were Rogers' Rangers, based at Rogers Island north of Albany, New York. This island and the British Fort Edward on the banks of the Hudson River together became the third largest settlement in the North American colonies. Rogers' Rangers and the British forces combined to defeat Native American and French troops.

The links between Europe and North America were tentative and potentially hostile. Several of the thirteen North American colonies along the Atlantic frontier—Massachusetts, Pennsylvania, and Maryland—were established by nonconformist religious refugees from England. Similarly, early French settlements in New York and Canada were almost always accompanied by priests. Some of the communities founded by Europeans fleeing persecution for their religious beliefs quickly turned their backs on the Atlantic world and pushed westward. Migrants and their descendants crossed the Appalachians in 1760, following a hundred years behind the first French, and they kept expanding.

Religious groups contributed to moving the frontier westward. To the extent that there was never an official religion on the Anglo-American frontier, organized religion was not a formal partner of government as it moved westward across the continent. Much later, groups such as the Mormons moved westward to escape hostility, eventually settling in what would become the state of Utah. Refugees from European religious intolerance, such as Hutterites, Mennonites, and others, also escaped to the empty spaces provided as the American and Canadian frontiers moved westward.

Horses, Iron, and Guns The European introduction of the horse, iron, and the gun to North America brought significant technological additions to frontier life, but they were no less important than the knowledge of geography, locally adapted technology, and foods that indigenous peoples brought to bear on the fur trade and other economic pursuits on the frontier. The impact of European diseases (especially smallpox and including alcoholism, encouraged by the lucrative trade in brandy, whiskey, and other intoxicants) was devastating to indigenous lives and lifestyles.

Cultural conversion came about as a result of economic impoverishment, territorial marginalization, and even confinement. Changing patterns of landholding were critical factors in undermining Indian cultures, but European missionaries were also significant agents of change. They perceived their role in the frontier as critical for the conversion of Indians to the "proper" ways of thinking and acting. Europeans imposed their cultures, including ways of dress, hairstyles, names, and marriage and labor patterns, as well as Christian religious ideology and practice. The final closing of the frontier came about through the removal of culturally assimilated peoples from their ancestral lands, followed by their enforced placement on reservations.

CAPE COLONY: COMPETING CULTURES AND IDEOLOGIES

Across the Atlantic, the Cape colony of southern Africa, originally under Dutch and then British influence, was initially more tightly governed than the North American colonies. Its cultural identity was as diverse as that of North America, where immigrants were assimilated with Native Americans. The interior lands, interior to and beyond those just north of the coastal Cape colony, were arid and best suited to livestock raising. Accordingly, during the eighteenth and early nineteenth centuries many whites became *trekboers*, or pastoralist farmers. They became a part of the frontier zone, where they interacted with local Khoikhoi and San groups of herders and hunter-gatherers.

FIGURE 14.3 Dutch Colony on the Cape of Good Hope, 1762.

Drawing by J. Rach, *Atlas van Stolk,* 1762.

SOURCE: General Research Division, New York Public Library. Astor, Lenox, and Tilden Foundations.

Khoikhoi Assimilation The Khoikhoi who were not pushed aside into more marginal environments were relatively easily assimilated into the early European farming and mercantile communities through the Khoikhoi's traditional system of patron-client relations, by which they had also attached themselves as clients to other Bantu-speaking African farmers settled in large villages to their north and east. Whereas such attachments had usually been temporary and symbiotic, the Khoikhois' attachment to the capitalist Dutch community at the Cape wrought dramatic and lasting cultural and economic transformations. The loss of cattle through sale, warfare, and smallpox epidemics, together with the Khoikhois' abandonment of aspects of their culture (such as dress and language) and their conversion to wage-based employment, led to the ultimate loss of African control over Cape lands—and became the impetus for the Khoikhois' joining an expanding frontier of culturally mixed African and European pastoralists, a frontier that included slaves and impoverished lower-class immigrants.

Land, People, and Wealth Both the southern African and North American frontiers were sites where the preindustrial European theory of land-based wealth was tested and applied. Lands were perceived to be zones of potential development and enterprise, property to be invested in for future returns, vacant property to be trekked across and held or discarded as desired. Acquisition of land was essential to the politics of identity and status. This differed markedly from ideas of wealth in societies in Africa and the Americas before the Europeans arrived, where control over people constituted the measure of power and status. Obviously, the European concept, arising out of the land limitations in Europe, when applied to the vast reaches of the globe, accelerated the aggressive process of European capitalist expansion.

Afrikaans and Afrikaaners The eighteenth- and nineteenth-century frontiers in southern Africa and North America become zones dominated by European ideology and culture, but neither frontier was exclusively European. In southern Africa, where change was multidirectional, the dominant cultural identity of the frontier came to be called Afrikaaner and its language Afrikaans. Linguistically the descendant of seventeenth-century Dutch, Afrikaans was also heavily influenced by African and Asian languages, including Khoikhoi and Xhosa. Most of the earliest frontier peoples were bilingual, regardless of race or background.

Calvinism Culturally, the frontier movement drew from the Calvinist principles of European ancestors, and this ideology became increasingly racist and ethnocentric as Europeans turned to their Christian ancestry to claim privilege and advantage based on color. Calvinism, the Protestant religious movement of John Calvin common to both the North American and South African frontiers, emphasized the individual's role and responsibility in the practice of the faith, an ideological stance that was well suited to the independence of frontier life. Eventually, domination by the Afrikaaner culture in the closing southern African frontier would be seen as God's will, and the historical story of the frontier would become a crowning chapter in a sacred and mythic past. By the early nineteenth century in North America, the extermination of the Indians who refused to become subservient to white rule was predicted by French observer Alexis de Tocqueville, who traveled throughout America and recorded his observations in *Democracy in America* (1835).

Southern Africa: In southern Africa, the end of the eighteenth century is marked by the
The Era of Migrations onset of a devastating drought and famine known as the Madlethule,
the "time of suffering." Migrations caused by the drought triggered some changes and coincided with other changes in African trade and political organization, especially among the emergent and expanding Xhosa and Zulu states. The frontier era culminated with the period known as the Great Trek, the movement of Europeans inland beginning in 1834. The British acquisition of the cape colony furthered the aggression of European migration. The final expansion of the cape colony frontier was also an escape for the Dutch from the increasingly restrictive British control of the initial settlement both within and outside the cape.

Unlike the Europeans in North America, who expelled indigenous peoples in the wake of their expansion, the expansionist Europeans in the southern African frontier attempted to colonize the indigenous people there, but while the Khoikhoi were culturally assimilated by the Dutch, the Xhosa and Zulu peoples were not. Fierce resistance to the European presence took the shape of resurgent African kingdoms in the second half of the nineteenth century, and although the land was won by the Europeans, the people were not. After generations of resistance, the Xhosa and Zulu remained culturally distinct, albeit as subordinated, landless peasant farmers.

■

FRONTIERS OF THE RUSSIAN EMPIRE

On the other side of the world from North America and far distant from southern Africa, Russia itself was a frontier, both to western Europeans moving eastward and to Asians moving westward. From Charlemagne's ninth-century campaign, the Germanic peoples of Europe continued to push western Europe's frontiers east at the expense of the Slavic peoples who inhabited the area from the Danube basin to the Urals. In the late tenth century, the ruler of the principality of Kiev was converted to Eastern Orthodox (Greek as opposed to Latin) Christianity, an event that drew Slavic peoples into the cultural orbit of the Byzantine Empire and separated them from the Latin West.

The earliest Russian advance eastward across the Urals occurred during the eleventh century, when Novgorod was the most powerful Russian principality. Novgorod was made vigorous and prosperous by trade with western Europe and sought to exploit the great forests of northeastern Russia for timber, furs, wax, and honey for foreign export. In the thirteenth century, the Mongols under Chinggis Khan subdued and gained control over most of the people of Siberia and continued westward across the Urals, conquering Russia and moving on into the Danube basin. Russia remained the western frontier for subsequent Mongol khans until the sixteenth century. Ivan III (r. 1462–1505), who took the title of tsar (emperor), defeated the Tatars, the last of the Asian masters of Russia following the Mongol conquest. In the course of subduing the Tatars, Ivan III brought Novgorod under his control and Moscow became the center of power in Russia. In 1480, Moscow was declared the "Third Rome," claiming the lost legacy of the Byzantine Empire as the center of Eastern Orthodox Christianity.

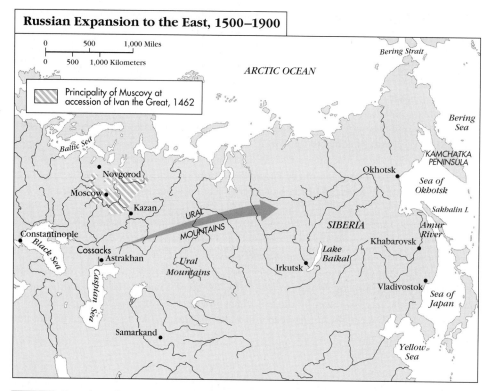

Russian Expansion to the East, 1500–1900

MAP 14.1 Frontiers of Muscovy and Russian Expansion into Siberia, 1500–1900.

SOURCE: Greaves et al. *Civilizations of the World* (New York: Harper & Row, 1990), Map 18.2, p. 451. *with* Martin Gilbert, *Atlas of Russian History* (New York: Dorset Press, 1972), p. 44.

Once the western frontier of Russia at the Urals was secured, Russians pushed their frontiers eastward toward the Urals and subsequently into Siberia.

THE SIBERIAN FRONTIER

Russians were lured eastward across Siberia to the Pacific for reasons similar to those that drew Europeans to cross the North American continent from the Atlantic to the Pacific coast. As in North America, one of the main attractions of Siberia was furs—sable, ermine, beaver—but in time exploitation of the land also became important.

The Stroganovs in Siberia By the middle of the sixteenth century, Russian entrepreneurs such as the Stroganov family used northern land and sea routes to gain access to Siberia. The Stroganovs, who had developed large-scale salt, fishing, and fur enterprises in northeastern European Russia, obtained large holdings in the trans-Ural Kama region, where they continued their enterprises by maintaining garrisons and importing settlers. While the Stroganovs prospered from such colonization, the indigenous Siberians of the Kama region, led by their nominal khan, resisted it. In 1579, the Stroganovs sent an expedi-

FIGURE 14.4 The Conquest of Siberia as an Evangelizing and Civilizing Mission.

Portrayed in the Remezov Chronicle of 1700, the conquest is depicted as the rays of light of gospel texts reaching Siberian communities, rather than politically or economically motivated.

SOURCE: Library of the Academy of Sciences, St. Petersburg, Moscow.

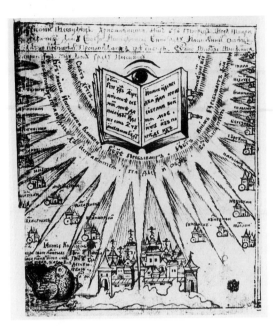

tion led by a professional soldier, the Cossack Yermak, across the Urals. Yermak successfully attacked the indigenous khan, who abandoned his lands to him. Yermak's success attracted the attention and favor of the Muscovite Tsar, Ivan IV (r. 1533–1584), and set a pattern for Russian expansion toward the Pacific.

Soon after Yermak's expedition, thousands of individual Russians, attracted by the potential wealth of the fur trade, crossed into Siberia to explore, build houses in the wilderness, and settle down. They were joined in time by refugees from serfdom (bondage to the land), military conscription, or religious persecution. Immigration of nonconformist religious communities into Siberia began as early as 1658. Such communities settled in the almost inaccessible forests and vast steppes of Siberia, even on territory claimed by the Chinese.

Government Colonization The extension of Russian frontiers eastward was also a matter of government policy and control. With the rise of Moscow to dominance, the Russian government adopted severe measures against individuals or "runaways" who crossed into Siberia, though the flow was difficult to stop. Official government settlement of Siberia was highly planned as a means of controlling resources and populations. Government colonization was carried out in part by parties of Cossacks sent to settle on the frontier, in part by bound (contracted) peasants who were required to settle at appointed places and maintain communication along the routes, and in part by convicts who were transported to internment camps (gulags).

Siberia as a Penal Colony Penal exile began the first years following Yermak's expedition and always remained a feature of the Russian Asiatic frontier, although the number of convict exiles to Siberia was always limited. Along with the garrisoned forts and the settlers who clustered around them, Russian authority was represented on the frontier by a special organization entrusted with the maintenance of horses for postal communication, required for centralized control over the distant Asian frontier.

Centralized governmental jurisdiction over the distant Siberian frontier was difficult to maintain, which meant that resident Siberian administrators often exercised a great deal of power. Control by Moscow overlapped with that by other institutions, not the least of which was the Church, which established an archbishopric in Siberia as early as 1621. Neither state nor Church policy in Siberia made brutal demands. Indigenous peoples were not forcibly baptized, though if they became Orthodox Christians they were treated as Russians and excused from paying various taxes levied on foreigners.

Impact on Indigenous Peoples Indigenous peoples were directly and powerfully affected by the extension of the Russian frontier eastward which was accompanied by considerable brutality. Siberia was thinly settled in the north (the first route of Russian encroachment), while central Siberia, both east and west, was chiefly inhabited by Mongols, who supported themselves mainly by stock breeding and trade. Numerous pastoral and agrarian Ural-Altaian peoples (among whom were Mongols, Turko-Tartars, and many others) were scattered over more densely populated southern Siberia to Lake Baikal. In the Amur basin and along the Pacific coast were Chinese, Manchurians, and Koreans.

Fur Economy The bounty of Siberian furs, which had been a powerful initial attraction drawing Russians east of the Urals, became important to Muscovite finance and foreign trade, and this provided an early example of the Russian impact on the scattered indigenous peoples of northern Siberia. Since control was military, Russian rule spread among them, government authorities made great efforts to limit private acquisition of furs and non-Russians were required to pay a tax in furs. Indigenous populations were deprived of their hunting and grazing privileges and forced to resort to agriculture. They were compelled to settle in less favorable regions, and poverty was common among them.

Absence of Serfdom in Siberia Since Siberia was scantily populated and usable space limited (except in Western Siberia), serfdom did not take root there. Nor was legalized slavery permitted, though indigenous peoples, ruined by the intrusion of agrarian colonists and the exactions of government officials, fell into what was practically a kind of slavery to merchants. By becoming nominally Orthodox—and missionaries were concerned principally about nominal Christianity—Siberians could be "assimilated" as Russians, while actual assimilation was a result of intermarriage, which was common between Siberians and Russian colonists. Despite forced exile and gulags and the cultural disruption that was a result of the Russian presence in Siberia, a social system that was in many ways freer than what existed west of the Urals took shape in what became known as the Russian "Far East."

Though government colonization might fill Siberia with forts, free colonization filled the intermediate space, and both the official and private advance of the Asian frontier were rapid. By the first half of the seventeenth century, Russians reached the Amur River (the border with China) and the Pacific. Russians explored as well as settled Siberia. Beginning with Peter the Great (r. 1682–1725), important expeditions mapped the frontier and collected information about the geography, geology, mineralogy, zoology, ethnography, and philology of the regions. This scholarly activity, including the first Academic Expedition, 1733–1742, defined the Russian Asian frontier and had practical value to settlement there.

THE ALASKAN FRONTIER

The Russian frontier reached the North Pacific realm in 1648, when a Russian expedition sailed along the northern Arctic coast of Russia and rounded the northeast tip of Siberia, passing into the North Pacific through what came to be called the Bering Strait. Other Siberian expeditions reached the shores of the North Pacific, penetrating the Kamchatka peninsula in 1696. A Russian expedition in the early half of the eighteenth century undertook the task of mapping the North Pacific shores of Siberia. Vitus Bering, a Dane in the employ of Tsar Peter the Great, commanded an expedition that in 1728 charted the strait dividing Asia and North America that bears his name.

Russians discovered Alaska in 1732, and on a second expedition (1740) to explore the American side of the strait, Bering sighted Denali, the highest peak in North America, and sailed among the Aleutian Islands. Russian expansion into North America accelerated during the reign of Alexander I (r. 1801–1825). New forts and trading stations were built in Alaska and even as far south as northern California, where Fort Ross was erected in 1812.

FIGURE 14.5 *Dutch Arctic Whaling Scene,* by Sieuwart van der Meulen, 1699.
Commercial whaling lured many to the North Pacific. The artist's interpretation of a polar bear was based on the Siberian brown bear given as a gift by Peter the Great.

SOURCE: The Kendall Whaling Museum, Sharon, Massachusetts.

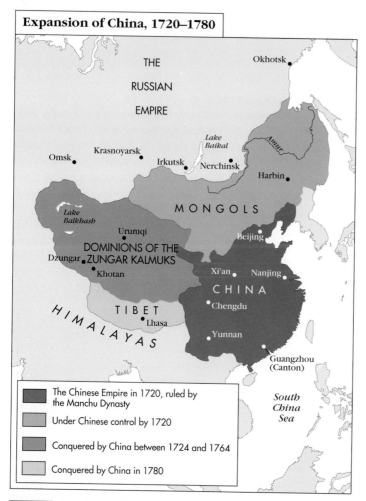

Expansion of China, 1720–1780

MAP 14.2 Frontiers of Russian and Chinese Empires.

SOURCE: Greaves et al., *Civilization of the World* (New York: Harper & Row, 199), p. 451. *with* Martin Gilbert, *Atlas of Russian History* (Dorset Press, 1972), p. 44.

As Russians reached Pacific shores, Alaska was colonized by them in the first half of the eighteenth century, the only part of the Russian empire in the Americas. But the Russian North American frontier ran into British, Spanish, and American frontiers, and these fellow European powers proved more fatal to Russian interests in Alaska than the indigenes there had been.

In contrast, eastward expansion on the Eurasian continent brought the Russian Empire into contact with China. As the Russians expanded in the eighteenth century and began pressing the borders of the Chinese Empire, they also came up against the Muslim states of Central Asia, the frontier of the Islamic world.

■

THE "ABODE OF ISLAM": BOUNDARIES AND FRONTIERS IN THE ISLAMIC WORLD

The boundaries of the Islamic world were clearly delineated in Islamic thought: the Dar ul-Islam was the "abode of Islam," the world of Muslim believers who followed Islamic law, and the Dar ul-Harb was the world of infidels who lived outside the law of God. These were religious boundaries that transcended the politics of empires. But the sixteenth-century Islamic political world was complicated by its division into three distinct empires in a zone stretching from North Africa to the Indian subcontinent: the Sunni Ottomans in West Asia and North Africa, the Shi'ite Safavids in Iran and Afghanistan, and the Mughals in India. Each of these empires dominated culturally distinct regions, and each was a composite of languages, cultures, and ethnic groups. Within the Dar ul-Islam, there were not only religious boundaries between Sunni, Shi'ite, and Sufi Islam but also cultural and political frontiers within each Islamic empire. The Mughals incorporated Hindu culture, language, and religion within their empire (see chapter 13), and the Ottomans expanded the boundaries of Islam to confront both Christianity and European states.

EUROPEAN AND ASIAN FRONTIERS IN THE OTTOMAN WORLD

In addition to representing Dar ul-Islam in the regions it controlled from North Africa to West Asia, the Ottoman Empire straddled both the European and Asian worlds; and although the boundaries between Dar ul-Islam and Dar ul-Harb were distinct, they were not impenetrable. With the conquest of Constantinople in 1453, the Ottoman Empire began to intrude on Europe's boundaries. The Ottomans took over the heritage of the Byzantine Empire along with that of the Abbasid caliphate in Baghdad. This was most visible under the

FIGURE 14.6 Selim III, Ottoman Sultan during the Siege of Vienna, by Hippolyte Berteaux.

Selim III (r. 1789–1807) is portrayed in the regal and heroic style of a European monarch, though his apparel identifies him as an Asian potentate.

SOURCE: Topkapi Sarai Museum, Istanbul. Photo by Sonia Halliday.

reign of Suleyman the Magnificent (r. 1522–66), the height of Ottoman power, when the Ottoman Empire controlled perhaps a quarter of Europe in addition to the entire eastern Mediterranean coast.

Piri Reis and Ottoman Cartography Islamic and Christian worlds competed for knowledge and trade goods. Cartography flourished in the sixteenth-century Ottoman Empire as it did in Europe. Like their European counterparts, Ottoman cartographers were closely allied to seafaring explorers. The cartographer and admiral Piri Reis (ca. 1470–1554) served in the Mediterranean during the Ottoman and Venetian wars between 1499 and 1502. At the time of the Ottoman capture of Alexandria (Egypt) in 1516 to 1517, he drew a map of the Nile Delta, the earliest of his surviving maps. In 1547, Piri Reis was appointed the commander of the fleet responsible for defending the Red Sea, Persian Gulf, and Indian Ocean from attacks by competing Portuguese ships. His failure to do so led to disfavor at court and eventually to his execution. However, several other maps attributed to Piri Reis and his major navigational text have survived. His world map, created sometime after 1517, included China and the discoveries of Columbus and reflected Ottoman access to new maps from both parts of the world. Despite the barriers between the exchange of certain kinds of knowledge such as printing and astronomy, the Islamic-Christian frontiers were not impermeable.

The Ottoman Empire as a European Power The greatest military power known to early modern Europeans was the Ottoman Empire, which straddled the Balkans, the Levant, and much of North Africa. Its warships dominated the Mediterranean (until the Battle of Lepanto in 1571), the Black Sea, the Red Sea, and the Persian Gulf. In 1528, Ottoman forces, in their quest for territory, advanced into central Europe, getting close to the Austrian capital city of Vienna before they were stopped. As Ottoman expansion into Europe continued in the sixteenth and seventeenth centuries, the Ottoman Empire increasingly became part of the European state system, adapting its diplomacy and military strategies to European power politics.

In 1683, when the Ottomans made a second unsuccessful attempt to capture Vienna, they found the Austrians a powerful military opponent who succeeded in forcing them out of much of the Danube Valley. In the treaty ending the conflict in 1699, the Ottomans were forced to cede large parts of central Europe, including Hungary and the Balkans, to the Hapsburg emperor of Austria. A new enemy also appeared to the north of the Black Sea. Peter the Great, the powerful and ambitious ruler of a resurgent Russia, was determined to acquire a port on the Black Sea and, if possible, the Bosporus and the Dardanelles strait, as a means of gaining an ice-free outlet to global seas. In part due to its involvement in European power politics through such engagements, by the eighteenth century the identity of the Ottoman state shifted from a West Asian to a more European one, though it remained in essence an Islamic empire.

The Ottomans and Safavids The Sunni Ottomans were further weakened by frequent wars waged on their eastern frontier against the Shi'ite Safavids of Iran. In 1722, as a result of persecution of its Sunni subjects in the area of modern Afghanistan, revolts broke out in Safavid Iran. The leader of the Afghan revolts invaded Iran and forced the last Safavid shah to abdicate. By the end of the eighteenth century, the Qajar dynasty took up the legacy of the Safavids and ruled for the next two centuries. Though the borders of Islamic empires, such as that of the Ottomans, defined the political boundaries of Islam, many Muslims dwelled outside these boundaries, from Africa to Asia.

■ BOUNDARIES AND FRONTIERS OF THE CHINESE EMPIRE

Muslims were incorporated into the Chinese Empire, a political and cultural framework that integrated vastly different peoples, languages, and cultures much as the Ottoman and Mughal Empires did. From the perspective of the Chinese Empire, the East Asian world shared a common culture with regional variations. Japan, Korea, and Vietnam were all part of this Chinese cultural world, influenced to varying degrees over centuries by Chinese ideas and institutions. The boundaries of Chinese culture, as perceived by Chinese, lay not with distinctions drawn between what was Chinese, Korean, Vietnamese, or Japanese but between Chinese "civilization" and the "barbarians" of the steppes.

For centuries the Great Wall had defined the boundary between the pastoral peoples of the steppes and grasslands and the settled agrarian population of China. Alternating patterns of trade and warfare characterized the relations between these two ways of life; and the periodic invasions of nomadic warriors from the north culminated in the thirteenth-century Mongol conquest, when China became part of a Eurasian empire.

CHINA'S TWO FRONTIERS

With the restoration of native Chinese rule in the fourteenth century under the Ming dynasty, the boundaries of Chinese civilization were redefined and two frontiers emerged: a maritime frontier and an inland frontier. The seven voyages undertaken by the Chinese Muslim admiral Zheng He between 1407 and 1433 bore witness both to the seafaring capabilities of the Chinese navy and to the Ming court's desire to command the maritime frontier.

Zheng He's Voyages Zheng He's Muslim background made him well suited for the task, ▓▓▓▓▓▓▓▓▓▓▓▓▓▓ since many of the countries visited by the expeditions were Muslim. Hailing from the southwestern province of Yunnan ("south of the clouds"), both Zheng He's father and brother were devout Muslims who had made the pilgrimage to Mecca.

The expeditions were huge in scale: 62 ships, more than 200 support vessels, and nearly 30,000 men made up the first contingent. The final voyage sailed more than 12,000 miles, and altogether the series of expeditions visited at least thirty countries around the rim of the Indian Ocean. Financed and supported by imperial patronage, Zheng He's voyages were designed to display the power of Ming China and to confirm its place as center of the world, even though they discovered that the world beyond China was larger and more diverse than ever before imagined. Ma Huan (ca. 1380–after 1451), who accompanied Zheng He on the voyages, wrote an account of them to record information about the lands and peoples encountered, thus enriching Chinese knowledge of the world.

Unlike their European counterparts later in the century, however, the purpose of the voyages was not to establish a presence in foreign lands nor to seek either goods or markets but to confirm the basic order of tributary relations by taking gifts from the Chinese emperor to rulers of other lands and accepting tribute in return. When the winds shifted at court under a new emperor, funding for the voyages was halted because of their great expense and because

FIGURE 14.7 East African Giraffe at the Emperor of China's Court, 1415; drawing by Shen Tu.

Many exotic goods, including this gift of an African giraffe, found their way to the Ming emperor's court by the time of the voyages of Zhenge He in the early fifteenth century.

SOURCE: National Palace Museum, Taiwan, Republic of China.

of distrust of maritime commerce. The government's interest turned instead to the country's inland frontiers and to the consolidation of Chinese civilization in its land-based realm.

The Chinese Diaspora In the sixteenth century, the Ming government limited the size of ▬▬▬▬▬▬▬ seagoing vessels and declared harsh punishments for private traders who put to sea in defiance of imperial injunctions. One of the reasons for this was the activities of Sino-Japanese pirates along the southeast coast. Despite imperial prohibitions, however, private maritime trade continued to expand alongside state-controlled trade into the early 1600s, enriched by Spanish silver transported from Acapulco to Manila, where Chinese merchants received payment in silver for silks, porcelains, and other luxury goods.

Zheng He's expeditions had stimulated the emigration of Chinese to all parts of Southeast Asia; by the sixteenth century, Chinese merchant communities were operating in port cities throughout Southeast Asia. Like the injunctions against engaging in maritime trade, prohibitions by the imperial government against emigration were seldom heeded by those who sought profits from trade abroad or were lured by the promise of economic opportunities. The diaspora of Chinese merchants created new commercial frontiers that expanded far beyond China's territorial boundaries and brought Chinese into direct encounters with both Southeast Asians and Europeans.

Land Frontiers A failed invasion of Vietnam in the early fifteenth century and an expensive ▬▬▬▬▬▬▬ war in Korea against a Japanese invasion in the late sixteenth limited the ability of the Ming state to exert its political control over countries regarded as part of its zone of cultural dominance. More dangerous, however, than the securing of its position in

Vietnam and Korea was the threat from beyond the Great Wall. In the mid–sixteenth century, as Sino-Japanese pirates harassed the coastline, a powerful coalition of Mongol tribes threatened the northern frontier.

It was the northeastern frontier, however, that produced the threat that dealt the final blow to Ming rule in the seventeenth century. Like the Mongol conquest in the thirteenth century, the Manchu conquest in the seventeenth century was a culmination of centuries of cultural, political, and economic interaction across frontiers. The Manchu Qing dynasty (1644–1910) brought about the integration of two distinctly different ways of life under the military domination of peoples from beyond the Great Wall, the Manchus from the northeast.

CULTURAL BOUNDARIES: MANCHUS AND CHINESE

The Manchus were an ethnic group whose homeland lay beyond the Great Wall in the region of modern Manchuria. When they conquered China in the seventeenth century, they carried out policies designed to maintain their ethnic distinction, such as forbidding intermarriage between Chinese and Manchus and prohibiting Manchu women to bind their feet in the manner of Chinese women. The Manchus also maintained a homeland beyond the Great Wall that was closed to Chinese immigration in order to preserve their purity as a people separate from the Chinese.

Over time, however, Manchus did intermarry with Chinese, and they gradually lost much of their language and culture. Manchu emperors learned Chinese, and in the eighteenth century the great Manchu emperors were skilled calligraphers, poets, painters, and patrons of the arts. Emperor Kangxi (r. 1662–1722), who was adept in the scholarly skills admired by Chinese while maintaining his equestrian abilities, despaired over his sons' losing their skill at horsemanship and command of the Manchu language.

The Multiethnic Manchu Empire By the eighteenth century, the Manchu Chinese Empire was the largest state in the world, covering nearly 13 million square kilometers (5 million square miles), stretching from the Himalayas to the East China Sea and from the Mongolian border with the Russian Empire to Southeast Asia. It encompassed a vast range of territories and peoples and incorporated into its government apparatus bilingualism, since government documents were written in both Manchu and Chinese, as well as sometimes Mongolian, and both Manchus and Chinese held high offices in the state bureaucracy. A vast array of languages was spoken within the realm of the Manchu Chinese Empire, including (in addition to Manchu, Chinese, and Mongolian) Uighur, Miao, Tibetan, Zhuang, Arabic, and Korean, and there were a great many religions as well. Besides Confucianism, Buddhism, and Daoism, Tibetan Buddhism or lamaism, Mongolian shamanism, Christianity, and Islam were all practiced by believers scattered throughout the empire. Although political boundaries were relatively fixed, within the empire, cultural and religious boundaries were fluid and highly permeable.

ETHNIC, RELIGIOUS, AND POLITICAL BOUNDARIES IN MONGOLIA, CENTRAL ASIA, AND TIBET

The Manchus had been successful in conquering China in part because they gained the support of Mongol tribes that had threatened Ming northern borders in the sixteenth century.

The Mongols' alliance with the Manchus, however, aroused the enmity of other peoples to the west, especially the Dzungars, who conquered the Islamic oasis states in the far northwestern regions bordering China. This was home to Muslim people of largely Turkic ethnic background, descendants of the Uighurs, who formed a powerful state in the eighth and ninth centuries.

Dzungars After their conquest of the northwest border region of China, the Dzungar leader Galdan (1644–1697) brought his people to the verge of establishing a large nomadic empire in Central Asia, an obvious threat to the Manchu order. Despite their defeat by the Manchu Qing in 1720, when Manchu troops moved into Tibet and expelled the Dzungars from the religious center of Lhasa, the Dzungars under Galdan's nephew succeeded in creating a vast empire in Central Asia that stretched from southern Siberia to the frontiers of Tibet and included the valley of the Ili River, south of Lake Balkhash, and the western part of Mongolia. The Dzungars were finally crushed and eradicated by Qing military campaigns in the mid–eighteenth century, as the Manchus expanded the Chinese Empire into the Islamic oases of the Tarim basin, from the Silk Road city of Dunhuang to the Pamirs, and from the Altai mountains to the Kunlun range. This newly incorporated region was called Xinjiang, the "new territories"—China's northwestern frontier.

FIGURE 14.8 Muslim Captives Awaiting the Chinese Emperor, 1760, after a Victory on the Frontier. The painter Lang Shih-ning (Giuseppe Castiglione, born in Milan) was court painter to Emperor Qian-Long (r. 1736–1796). He brought a European style to the portrayal of imperial scenes such as this.

SOURCE: Private Collection. Photo by Wan-go Weng.

Xinjiang A lengthy period of colonization of these "new territories" took place in the eighteenth century. A frontier where Indo-Iranian, Islamic, Turkish, Mongol, Tibetan, and Chinese influences had mingled for centuries, Xinjiang initially was a land of exiles for both political and common criminals; only in the late nineteenth century did it become a province within the administrative structure of the Chinese empire. The exiled Chinese scholar Ji Yun, for example, made his journey to Xinjiang in 1769, remarking that he felt as though he had entered another world, one dominated by Uighur merchants in strange clothes and unusual foods and smells. Still, the capital, Urumchi, had a bookstore that sold Chinese classical texts, and Ji Yun found other things to admire and give pleasure, such as the huge chrysanthemums and marigolds he was able to grow in his garden there. Like other frontiers, Xinjiang was a place where people could make miraculous changes in their lives: an emancipated convict made a fortune in 1788 by opening a shop in the city of Ili selling delicacies native to the Yangzi delta region.

Tibet In the course of this consolidation and extension of the Qing Empire, Tibet was brought under Chinese control, and the borders of the Chinese Empire reached as far as Nepal. Earlier, the Mongol tribes had cultivated Tibetan leaders by honoring the Dalai Lama, the leader of Tibetan Buddhism. The Manchus followed suit and invited the Dalai Lama to Beijing in 1652 for an imperial audience. The Manchus supported the translation and printing of Tibetan Buddhist texts into Mongol and Manchu. In 1732, the reigning Manchu emperor even converted his palace in the capital of Beijing to a Tibetan Buddhist temple.

Ethnic Frontiers in the South The southwestern provinces of Yunnan, Sichuan, and Guizhou had previously been brought under control by the Manchus but remained frontiers of complex ethnic and cultural mixes. The Miao people of Guizhou, for example, inhabited a region that was discovered to have rich mineral deposits and was consequently colonized and developed by the Chinese. The Dai people of Yunnan shared a common ethnic background with the Thais across the border in Southeast Asia, as did mountain-dwelling people, the Meng, who also lived both within China's borders and in Southeast Asia.

■
PIRACY, TRADE, AND THE POLITICS OF FRONTIERS

We have seen that armies, commerce, people, and ideas crossed boundaries and created new frontiers. Piracy around the world reveals the ineffectiveness and fluidity of boundaries as much as the defiance of authority. Piracy may be seen as a form of trade in which individuals exact profits by acting as middlemen between merchants or by forcibly confiscating goods for sale or trade. In East Asia, the Chinese state's official restrictions on maritime commerce often gave rise to illicit trade conducted outside the formal framework of state authority. Piracy everywhere signaled the existence of frontiers—zones of interaction—that emerged where political controls weakened. Vulnerable frontiers were often on the edges or seams of large polities. Piracy was a part of larger economic systems; it reflected instability, disorder, and chaos on the frontiers as much as it created them. At times piracy could also be sponsored by rulers or rebels who sought to use pirates as mercenaries to achieve political ends.

PIRACY ON CHINA'S BORDERS

Not only the nomads of the northern steppes threatened the borders of the Chinese state; during the sixteenth century, pirates plagued the southeastern coast of China. As Ming power weakened, central authority was less able to exercise control over local areas. The only officially sanctioned trade was the tribute system, which was under state control. However, local officials often participated in illicit private trade (behind the backs of state authorities) to enrich themselves and were thus reluctant to impose stringent sanctions against pirates.

Initially, small bands of pirates—many of them common people who were excluded from the state trade and forced into piracy by economic circumstances—sporadically raided coastal settlements. Eventually, these groups organized into larger and more effective forces that could undertake private overseas trade in spite of the official sanctions that prohibited it. Their armed fleets plied the coastal waters, and one pirate leader was said to have commanded more than fifty large ships.

Wako: "Japanese" Pirates   By the mid–sixteenth century, the prosperous Yangzi delta region was being harassed by *wako,* "Japanese" pirates. Despite being labeled "Japanese," most *wako* were Chinese, although some Japanese warrior bands did raid the coast. There was also fierce competition among powerful Japanese lords for domination of the official trade with China. The disgruntled losers in this competition often resorted to piracy to vent their anger and make a profit.

Japan, like other Asian states, was bound in its economic dealings with China by the tribute system; but this system broke down in the sixteenth century, and the covert private trading relations between Chinese and Japanese merchants expanded. Attempts by the Ming government to restore its control of overseas trade were largely unsuccessful. Policies favoring elimination of the causes of piracy—poverty, disorder, excessive restrictions on trade—were not followed consistently. Efforts were made to destroy the pirates themselves, rather than to remove the conditions that encouraged their existence.

During the sixteenth century, when piracy grew to be a serious problem in China, Japan was divided among warring lords. Bands of warriors in service to these lords periodically raided the Chinese coastline. But shortly after the unification of Japan in 1600 by the Tokugawa shogunate regional lords were prevented from independently initiating or allowing trading relations apart from those officially conducted at the southern port of Nagasaki under the authority of the shogunate. Thus, the threat of Japanese piracy was virtually eradicated by the time of the Manchu conquest of China.

Koxinga: Politics and Piracy   After the Manchu invasion and conquest of north China in the mid–seventeenth century, the remnants of the Ming court sought refuge in the south. Bolstered by other exiled supporters, the Ming emperor and his court attempted to stave off Manchu conquest of the south and to restore Ming rule. The deposed emperor was aided in this enterprise by Zheng Chenggong (1624–1662), who eventually became one of the most flamboyant and popular figures in the Chinese folk tradition. Known by the Latinized name of Koxinga, given him by the Dutch, he was the son of a Chinese father, who had been baptized a Christian by the Portuguese at Macao, and a Japanese mother from the southern Japanese port of Hirado. In addition to his contacts with the Portuguese and the Japanese, Koxinga's father also dealt with the Spanish at Manila.

A supporter of the Ming against the Manchus, Koxinga controlled much of the south-eastern coastline for over a decade in the mid–seventeenth century. The Manchu strategy to defeat Koxinga relied on policies adopted by the Ming in their attempts to eradicate coastal piracy: the restriction of foreign trade. In 1661, Koxinga was forced to retreat to Taiwan, where he expelled the Dutch. Originally named "Formosa" by the Portuguese, Taiwan had become part of the trading empire of the Dutch East India Company earlier in the seventeenth century. It was also the home of Chinese immigrants from Fujian along the southeast coast, but it had not been integrated into the Chinese Empire during the Ming.

After Koxinga's death, a Dutch fleet aided Manchu assaults on Koxinga's Taiwan base, then under the leadership of his son. Harsh tactics were employed by the Manchus to destroy this base; they evacuated the population along the Fujian coastline to close off Taiwan's access to human and material resources there. This strategy was effective, and Taiwan was finally occupied by Manchu forces in 1683, completing the consolidation of Manchu rule. In time, however, the Manchu rulers of China would face their own piracy problems related to the breakdown of control in "peripheral" areas.

The Cantonese "Water World" In the Cantonese "water world," a maritime zone that straddled the seacoast from the Pearl River delta at Canton to the Red River delta in northern Vietnam, piracy became more than a temporary survival strategy for impoverished fishermen. As political events in Vietnam intersected with ongoing ecological changes (overpopulation, land shortage, increased trade), they produced an intensification of piracy and large-scale collective action in the form of pirate confederations. The Sino-Vietnamese coastline was a "water world" inhabited by pirates who became mercenaries in the service of leaders of the Tay-son Rebellion, which captured power from the reigning Nguyen dynasty in Vietnam between the 1770s and 1790s.

When the Tay-son Rebellion was finally suppressed at the end of the eighteenth century, Chinese pirates who had served the Tay-son leaders returned to China and formed a confederation under the leadership of a man named Zheng Yi. By employing his male relatives as squadron leaders under his command and by marrying his female relatives to his supporters, Zheng Yi merged family loyalties and political power. By 1805, he commanded a confederation of between 50,000 and 70,000 pirates that controlled the coastal trade and fishing industry of the southeastern province of Guangdong, where the major foreign trading port of Canton was located.

Chinese Women Pirates At Zheng Yi's death in 1807, his wife, known only as Zheng Yisao (wife of Zheng), took over her husband's position. She moved rapidly to create personal ties that would bind her husband's followers—especially Zhang Bao, the adopted son of Zheng Yi—to her. A former fisherman's son who had been captured by pirates at age fifteen, Zhang Bao was initiated into piracy by means of a homosexual union with Zheng Yi and rose rapidly through the pirate ranks. To assure Zhang Bao's loyalty to her after her husband's death, Zheng Yisao took him as her lover and eventually married him. Zheng Yisao also negotiated on behalf of the pirate confederation with both the Chinese authorities and Europeans, eventually obtaining favorable terms of surrender for the pirates.

Zheng Yisao's ascent through marriage was in keeping with tradition. Other women rulers and rebel leaders in Chinese history often gained their position through marriage and the manipulation of political ties through their husbands. Zheng Yisao's career as a pirate

FIGURE 14.9 Zheng Yisao, Chinese Woman Pirate in Action.

Under her leadership, a community of 50,000 pirates flourished on the South China sea coast, ca. 1807.

SOURCE: National Maritime Museum, Greenwich, England.

leader, however, also openly defied Confucian mores and behavioral norms. Other women also participated fully in the life of the pirate confederation, though they did not attain the powerful position Zheng Yisao did. With their unbound feet, women pirates were active and mobile, able to hold rank and command entire junks by themselves. During one engagement in 1809, the wife of a pirate managed to wound several assailants while holding fast to the helm and defending herself with a cutlass.

Piracy in East Asian waters was a product in part of Chinese attitudes toward foreign trade. It was seen largely as a dimension of the tribute system, which ordered relations among states in East Asia under the domination of the Chinese emperor. Commerce was viewed as a necessary evil to be controlled and to be used as a source of profit for the state. Foreign trade was not to be conducted for the private interest and enrichment of individuals, either merchants or officials. Nevertheless, both merchants and officials engaged in foreign trade, surreptitiously at times and openly at others, and piracy flourished whenever weakened central authority allowed it and economic conditions encouraged it. Political patronage also shaped the growth of piracy, as governments or rebel leaders made use of pirate forces to further their own causes. Some pirates, such as Koxinga, were themselves political leaders, with goals that went beyond economic gain to political power.

PIRATES AND PRIVATEERS IN THE MEDITERRANEAN AND EUROPE

In other parts of the world, piracy similarly flourished on the boundaries and frontier zones between cultures. Piracy reached its peak in the Mediterranean during the sixteenth and seventeenth centuries, where not all pirates opposed state controls. Privateers were pirates licensed by the state. Under the guise of privateering, two equally backed groups, the Barbary Corsairs and the Knights of the Order of Saint John, acted as warriors in an extension of the holy war between the Ottoman Turks and Catholic Spain. Actually, these two privateer forces carried out an exchange of goods between Muslims and Christians that would otherwise have been impossible. So integral were these pirates to the Mediterranean economy that the Ottoman sultan in Constantinople acquiesced to their trade by first appointing the Barbary leader to the post of governor-general of Algiers in 1518 and later making him high admiral of the Ottoman fleets in 1535.

Elizabethan Privateers Not unlike the close collaboration between pirates and governments in the Mediterranean, wide-scale backing by the elite who lived along the coastline supported piracy in the English Channel during the Elizabethan era (named after Elizabeth I, r. 1588–1603). Throughoutthe sixteenth century, British gentry along the southern coast turned quick profits by marketing the prizes of local marauders. These conditions accorded well with the monarchy's aspirations at the time: war with Spain was the prevailing international concern of the Tudor sovereign, but waging war was a problem because the monarchy was still dependent on voluntary forces. By sanctioning the pirates and transforming them into privateers—ships whose captains, during wartime, were given governmental authorizations to attack enemy ports and ships—Elizabeth gained an inexpensive navy at a time when the English monarchy was unable to support its own.

PIRATES AND PRIVATEERS IN THE ATLANTIC WORLD

European hegemony and fierce competition during the eighteenth century crossed the Atlantic into the Caribbean, where it was played out against a background of constant piracy and privateering. Not all piracy was profitable. One of the first pirates to traverse the Atlantic was Palmier de Gonnville, who successfully seized goods from the Spanish, but was not able to recover the costs of his expedition. Merchants and ships had to defend themselves from pirates and privateers. Privateer status also meant that if they were caught by the enemy, pirates enjoyed the rights of soldiers. If captured, they would be made prisoners rather than hanged as criminals.

Pirates of the Caribbean In the eighteenth century, Caribbean islands were considered valuable both as sugar production sites and as fortified bases from which to conduct warfare. Competition and warfare resulted in the constant reconfiguring of political boundaries, as islands changed hands through diplomatic bargaining in Europe. The relatively large number of pirates reflected the political chaos of the region. Piracy sometimes ignored and often took advantage of the political boundaries that had been drawn on another continent, as pirates constantly threatened the peace and political controls established by European states in the Caribbean and also interrupted the steady growth of European commercial profits.

Criminals and buccaneers, or runaway bond servants, escaping from their contracts of servitude, found safety from exploitation by their masters and profits by becoming pirates in the Caribbean. Buccaneers began as hunters of runaway cattle in Santo Domingo (where they took their name from the *boucan,* a wooden grill for smoking meat), and they soon began to combine hunting with piracy. Buccaneers traversed the Caribbean and Atlantic and reached as far as Madagascar in the Indian Ocean, where they established the Pirate Republic of Libertalia.

Not all pirates remained independent of legitimate political entities. Like their counterparts from Asian and Mediterranean waters, pirates of the Caribbean often enjoyed political

FIGURE 14.10 Pirates in the Caribbean Included Free Africans and Escaped Slaves and Bond Servants.

Left front is Charles Gibbs from Rhode Island, who was eventually hanged in New York.

SOURCE: National Maritime Museum, Greenwich, England.

patronage. Indeed, it was often difficult to discern contraband from legitimate commerce, so unorthodox and unscrupulous were the dealings of merchants and pirates alike. The famous late-seventeenth-century buccaneer Henry Morgan sailed under orders from the governor of Jamaica, a British colony. His last expedition was an attempt to seize and pillage Panama City, despite agreements between Spain and England to cease such lawlessness. More devastating to piracy than the British Navigation Acts, which limited trade to British ships, was the 1692 earthquake at Port Royal, Jamaica. The earthquake and subsequent tidal waves pushed this coastal center of piracy, known as the "wickedest city on earth," under the sea.

Crossing Gender Boundaries: Women Pirates As in the Cantonese water world, women pirates were not all that unusual in the Caribbean frontiers. Two such women in the Caribbean were Mary Read and Anne Bonny, brought before the governor of Jamaica in 1720, convicted of piracy, and sentenced to hang. Women went to sea as passengers, servants, wives, prostitutes, laundresses, cooks, and, less frequently, as sailors. To avoid controversy and seize what was regarded as male liberty, the women pirates often cross-dressed, wearing men's jackets and pants and carrying pistol or machete or both. Read and Bonny also cursed and swore like any other sailors. Both came out of unconventional households, excelled in their chosen pursuits, and were recognized as leaders on their pirate ships. Such "warrior women" were celebrated around the Atlantic world in popular ballads, suggesting that their impact was both economic and cultural.

■

FRONTIERS OF THE ATLANTIC WORLD

The Caribbean was not only a site of piracy but also the destination of slave ships originating in West and Central Africa. On the African side of the Atlantic world, large and small states originated in response to the dangers and requirements of the trade in slaves and manufactured goods, including guns. On the edges of these states in the new African frontier, chaos reigned and new cultural identities emerged.

FRONTIER COMMUNITIES IN AFRICA AND THE AMERICAS

From the slave trade's sixteenth-century beginnings, many of the slaves originated as war captives. Warfare was fed by fierce economic competition and political rivalry. The slave trade was so lucrative that not only did African states sometimes agree to participate, but freelance African kidnappers and mercenaries also attempted to acquire prisoners of war. Political enemies who were potential slaves and slaves who managed to escape fled the cities and towns near the African coast, taking refuge in less accessible mountains and hills of the interior.

These refugees from the slave trade existed on the frontiers of coastal communities. They organized themselves around powerful lords who preyed on the weak and vulnerable in opposition to the traditional authority of kings and nobility. Out of the amalgam of fringe populations speaking many different languages, they came to construct a new and distinct cultural identity called "Jaga" or "Imbangala." Sent to the New World, troops of "Black Jaguars" fought as mercenaries for the European settlers, gaining a reputation for their fierceness in battle.

Quilombos and Maroon Communities of Brazil and the Americas

The transfer of African resistance across the Atlantic occurred when runaway slaves formed communities on the fringes of plantations. Successful communities of runaway slaves (called maroons) functioned much like the scattered communities on the edges of slaving frontiers in Africa. Sometimes they destabilized the authority of would-be oppressors; other times they accommodated and adapted to their new world of living apart. Moreover, runaway slaves often took African patterns of resistance as their organization model. The *quilombos* of Brazil were palisaded war camps modeled on the Jaga structures of Central Africa. These independent settlements followed African political and social exaples, using their African identity to instill pride and possibility on the margins of European control.

Resistance in North America: Seminoles and Creeks

Not all Spanish conquest in the Americas was directed at the centers of large empires, such as that of the Aztecs or Incas. In the frontier that would become the southeastern United States, the conquistador Hernando da Soto explored and plundered the territory and peoples of

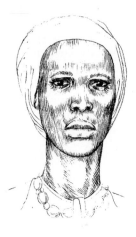

FIGURE 14.11 Nanny, Maroon Leader of Jamaica.

The Maroon woman known as Nanny was an eighteenth-century resistance leader with military, political, and spiritual authority.

SOURCE: Courtesy of the National Library of Jamaica. NLJ photo.

wealthy chiefdoms between 1539 and 1540. The resulting decimation of the indigenous population resulted in a pattern of European advance and Indian retreat, creating a frontier of resistance that lasted into the nineteenth century. Native American survivors, forced to relocate, became known as Creeks and Seminoles (or Muscogulges). They turned from agriculture to commercial hunting, selectively adopting parts of European culture while coexisting with other indigenous groups and sometimes with immigrant Africans who had escaped slavery.

Even in North America, where the ratio of European to African favored the dominant white community, the mixture of African and Native American resistance formed blended communities of common cause and purpose that ultimately evolved into formidable political and cultural opposition to European hegemony, including military warfare. One strategy of resistance was to capitalize on European rivalries. The year 1763 was decisive for the Creeks and Seminoles; the defeat of Spain and France by Britain in the Indian and French Wars decided which territories would be kept and which given away. The result was the encircling of Indian lands by British settlement. As other Native American peoples disappeared as a result of European pressures or were absorbed by the Creeks and Seminoles, the Creeks and Seminoles became the key representatives of Indian sovereignty and land rights on the shifting southern frontier of North America. After fighting on the side of the Loyalists in the War of Independence, many fled to the Bahamas with European loyalists in 1794.

CULTURAL BOUNDARIES AND FRONTIERS IN THE CARIBBEAN

The circum-Caribbean region was also the destination of most European slave ships out of Africa, and that region remained subject to changes wrought by constantly shifting political boundaries. In contrast to East Asians' resistance to penetration by Europeans prior to the nineteenth century, Caribbean boundaries remained fluid and permeable. "Fluid boundaries" and "shifting frontiers" can also be used to describe the nature of social realms. After the initial European intrusion into the Caribbean decimated or sent into exile most of the indigenous populations, Africans and Europeans dominated the social interactions of the region. They were joined by other Amerindians and by Asians, as well as by the descendants of marriages between persons of various cultures. *Creole* populations, people born in the Caribbean of admixtures of Hindi, Yoruba, Dane, French, Kongolese (of Central Africa), Ewe and Fon (of coastal West Africa), British, Arawak, Carib, and other cultures, were created by these interactions.

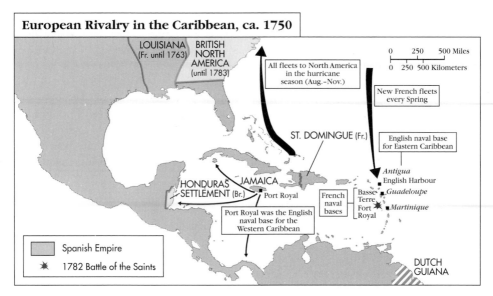

MAP 14.3 European Rivalry in the Caribbean, ca. 1750.

SOURCE: Peter Ashdown, *Caribbean History in Maps* (Trinidad: Longman Caribbean, 1979), p. 20.

Soon after the establishment of European hegemony in the Atlantic-based systems of plantation slavery, African-derived populations outnumbered all others by ratios of thirteen or more to one. The tenacity of African-derived religions, technologies, and other cultural artifacts limited European influence and control. Despite the oppressive and tyrannical system of plantation slavery in the Caribbean, African cultures survived and African identity itself became synonymous with resistance to European hegemony.

Between the sixteenth and eighteenth centuries, after Spanish power grew weak and Spain no longer controlled the entire region awarded it by the Treaty of Tordesillas, European rivalry increased. Conflicts, which were usually fought on European soil, involved the exchange of territories in the Caribbean from vanquished to victor in a game of diplomatic "chess." Some Caribbean islands changed sovereignty more than a dozen times over these centuries. The patterns of instability were sharpened by the constant guerilla warfare waged by maroons and by the general atmosphere of African resistance on the plantations.

Plantation Boundaries The history of plantation life in the Caribbean reveals the changing boundaries of town and country, as well as the complex and shifting lines that distinguished race, ethnicity, and gender as the Atlantic world came into being. By the eighteenth century, land surveyors and cartographers were important instruments of those who ruled over estates, and they played key roles in the settlement of boundary disputes between claimants.

Some eighteenth- and nineteenth-century surveyors, such as Thomas Harrison (ca. 1823–1894) of Jamaica, were well versed in botany; they noted their keen observations about fencing materials or agricultural crops on the maps they produced, thus recording valuable historical information. After about 1700, surveyors used a standardized compass and chain, actually 100 metal links that were 66 feet in length and joined with brass rings and counters marking off every ten links. Harrison's cadastral (land survey) map of Jamaica, dating from 1891, required decades of measurements and individual plantation surveys. Such precise lines of demarcation contrast with the complexity of social and cultural interactions that characterized the plantation economy and its society.

Crossing Boundaries Official maps were based on a European ideal notion of plantations and ▬▬▬▬▬▬▬▬▬▬ colonies as rigidly ordered and geometrically conceived landscapes. Plantation operations, however, reveal the ambiguity and limited usefulness of such an understanding. Plantations were international, multicultural zones with permeable boundaries. Most inhabitants and workers were non-Europeans, the majority of them African, whose different cultural backgrounds determined their use of space.

Slave provision grounds where Africans grew crops to supplement their diets and the maroon communities living independently in the mountains ran counter to the European maps. African land use patterns followed natural contours of the land and traditional African-derived organizational principles of settlement planning around a center courtyard, market area, or other communal space. Maroon thieves and marauders easily traversed the boundaries of field and farm; on occasion they even left the sanctuary of the territories they had won from the colonizers and appeared in towns, where they stole or traded for the goods they required for their survival. Sometimes maroons were employed by the estate elite as mercenaries and bounty hunters to capture runaway slaves in exchange for their own survival.

The contrast between the plantation Great House (the residence of the slave master) and the slaves' houses was great. Building materials for the great house were brought from abroad to re-create local versions of the houses of European aristocrats, while slaves houses resembled West and Central African structures in their style and construction out of tropical materials. Persons of African descent who entered the Great House crossed a cultural boundary, as did the few who labored as house servants or became mistresses of the European masters.

Lady Maria Nugent Relatively few European women accompanied their husbands to the ▬▬▬▬▬▬▬▬▬▬ Caribbean. One of them was Lady Maria Nugent (1771–1834), wife of the governor of Jamaica. Her *Journal* was first published in 1839 and records household life during a period of four years' residency on the island (1801–1805), when she was in her early thirties. During the course of her residence in Jamaica, Lady Nugent traveled the island without ever meeting another white woman. She records her interactions with "coloureds," mostly women of mixed descent and lower social rank than those born in Europe, whom she received in her bedroom and encountered on numerous social occasions. Lady Nugent also describes the cultural expressions of African slaves, writing about their Christmas celebrations, which crossed the usual boundaries of slave and master: "[They] . . . were most superbly dressed, and so were several of their friends, who came to join the masquerade; gold and silver fringe, spangles, beads, etc., etc." For Lady Nugent, recognition of class superseded the significance of differences of color.

Economic Boundaries The fluidity and permeability of boundaries were equally visible in the is-▬▬▬▬▬▬▬▬▬▬ lands' informal economies. Internal marketing systems transcended state and plantation controls. Slave-crafted pottery and other goods, including foodstuffs from slave provision grounds, were exchanged among plantations and islands, producing a money economy to the extent that some observers complained about the fact that the smaller denominations of local currencies were almost entirely in the hands of slave marketers and higglers (bargainers). The interplantation access permitted communication across islands and even regions and no doubt increased the effectiveness of slave resistance before the abolition of slavery in the 1830s.

■

BOUNDARIES AND ENCOUNTERS IN THE PACIFIC

In contrast to the Caribbean, which was quickly brought under European political hegemony, the vast Pacific remained contested territory despite the European presence. First circumnavigated by Magellan in 1520 to 1521, the Pacific—from Chile to Guam—was far more difficult to explore and exploit. During Magellan's pioneer voyage, the explorers nearly starved on a diet of putrid water and wormy biscuit "which stank strongly of rat's urine." The Hawaiian Islands were reached by Andrés de Urdaneta in a remarkable voyage in the sixteenth century but are not known to have been visited again until the time of Captain James Cook in 1779.

EUROPEAN EXPLORATION IN THE SOUTH PACIFIC

The first permanent European presence in the South Pacific was Dutch. From their base at Batavia (modern Jakarta), the Dutch sailed southward and in 1597 advanced claims to what was known as "Terra Australis" (Australia). These claims were substantiated by a description of the landing and circumstantial details of the relationship of Australia to New Guinea, which lay to its north. Throughout the seventeenth century, a number of Dutch ships sailed southward from Java. Voyages in 1616 and 1622 made discoveries along the southwest coast of Australia and explored the Gulf of Carpenteria. These expeditions met Aboriginal resistance, but succeeded in providing the earliest descriptions of Australia, where the names given by the Dutch to prominent physical features have been retained, suggesting the outcome of European and Aboriginal conflicts thereafter.

Tasman One of the best known of the Dutch explorers, Abel Janszoon Tasman (ca. 1603–1659), was sent on a "South Land" expedition in 1642, part of the cherished scheme of Governor-General Anthony van Diemen of the Dutch East Indies for extending the Dutch colonial empire. During his voyage, Tasman sighted and took possession of an island off the south coast of Australia that he named "Van Diemen's Land," though the name was later changed to "Tasmania."

Tasman also gave his name to the indigenous inhabitants of this island, Tasmanians, who were culturally distinct from peoples encountered elsewhere. In little more than two centuries after their "discovery" by Europeans, the last surviving Tasmanian died and her people became extinct. Parallel ecological destruction resulted in the disappearance of the wildlife native to the island.

When Tasman left Tasmania, he steered eastward for the Solomon Islands and encountered New Zealand (which he named Statenlandt), then Fiji, before returning westward to Batavia in June 1643. During his ten-month voyage, Tasman had made remarkable discoveries, not the least of which was to prove by his circumnavigation of Australia that the island continent did not stretch all the way to the South Pole. As a result of Tasman's voyages, by 1660 the Dutch had rough charts and tangible claims to Australia, to which they gave the name "New Holland."

Dutch claims to Australia were successfully challenged by the British, beginning in 1688 when the first English long-distance navigator, William Dampier (1652–1715), sighted Australia. That the continent ultimately became British is due less to Dampier than to Captain James Cook (1728–1779), whose three voyages into the Pacific made him the most significant of all European explorers of the Pacific.

The Cook Expeditions Cook, whose maritime apprenticeship was served in North Atlantic trade, had gained experience in geographic exploration in North America, surveying, sounding, and mapping the Saint Lawrence River and the coasts of Newfoundland and Labrador. In 1768, he was chosen to head a research expedition to compile geographical and astronomical information in the South Pacific. Sailing in the *Endeavor* with several scientific colleagues, Cook reached Tahiti; New Zealand, which he circumnavigated and charted accurately for the first time; and then the east coast of Australia, which he accurately surveyed, named New South Wales, and claimed for Great Britain.

During his first (1769) Pacific voyage, Captain Cook coasted along the eastern shores of the Australian continent, and in April 1770 he hoisted the British Union Jack at Botany Bay, claiming what he named New South Wales for England. Following Cook's voyages, the next English to appear in Australia in 1788 were a fleet of settlers who started a British penal colony at Port Jackson on the shores of Botany Bay. Beginning with this settlement, Australia was to retain the character of a penal colony for the next half century, until transportation of convicts from Great Britain was virtually suspended in 1839.

Cook's second expedition, in 1772, went around the Cape of Good Hope at the southern tip of the African continent, across the Indian Ocean to New Zealand, and thence to Tierra del Fuego at the southern tip of South America, around Cape Horn into the Atlantic, and northward to England. This circumnavigation of the globe was a voyage of massive proportions, and the work that Cook did in mapping and sounding made clear the main outlines of the southern portion of the globe substantially as they are known today.

European Settlement European settlement of New Zealand took place in the late eighteenth
in New Zealand   and early nineteenth centuries, following Cook's second expedition. The earliest, unofficial settlers were escapees from penal colonies in Australia, and sealers and whalers who made their headquarters on the North Island. They were joined by traders who came for the long timbers of New Zealand forests and the flax grown by the Native Maoris. The earliest official colonizing attempt, a French Roman Catholic mission, was unsuccessful, though it alarmed the British, who feared the French might dispute British claims to the islands, and spurred them on to establish official settlements, some of which were Protestant missionary efforts. Such efforts suggest one of the major cultural impacts that European colonization was to have on the peoples of the Pacific: the forced introduction of Christianity.

Maori Resistance The idea of political rivalry among Europeans over the control of resources in newly explored territories was not unique to Europeans. Before European contact, Polynesians competed in fierce battles to increase their authority and power, sometimes over the course of years or even generations. Europeans' technology, especially guns, quickened the pace of consolidation, but the impact of other aspects of their culture was more divisive. The Maoris of New Zealand in particular gained a reputation for warlike aggression in the face of European intrusion. European artists such as William Hodges, who accompanied Cook's second voyage, repeatedly portrayed Maoris emerging from their war canoes with harsh features and menacing manner, defiantly waving war clubs.

There was no doubt remaining as to the rumors of cannibalism among the eighteenth-century Maori when one Maori man brought a human head and some broiled meat on board Cook's ship *Resolution* and ate it before the ship's crew. The European sailors failed to see the parallels to Christian Holy Communion (drinking the blood and eating the body of Christ in the form of red wine and wafer) in the Maori ritual practice of consuming the power of one's enemy. Such traditional displays of power, while providing Europeans with evidence of "savagery" and thereby justifying their own cruelty, also served to fuel indigenous resistance.

Cook's Last Expedition Cook's final expedition in 1778 took him to the North Pacific in search of the long-sought Northwest Passage that would connect the Atlantic with the Pacific. On this voyage Cook reached the Hawaiian Islands, which he named the "Sandwich Islands" and claimed for Great Britain. From the first voyage to Hawaii he sailed up the northwest coast of North America, sighting land along the Oregon coast and sailing northward to the Bering Strait between North America and Russia, before returning to Hawaii where he met his death.

EUROPEANS IN THE NORTH PACIFIC

The earliest Western European overland intrusion into the North Pacific realm was that of the expedition of Alexander Mackenzie (1763–1820), who reached the Pacific shores of present-day British Columbia in 1793. This expedition, and Captain Cook's voyages into the North Pacific, confirmed the North Pacific rim as a British frontier. Spanish claims to a North Pacific frontier in Alta California date from the sixteenth century, when Hernán Cortés sent an expedition there and Juan Cabrillo sailed along its coast. Spanish colonization of the region began with the founding of the mission of San Diego de Alcala (1769) by Father Junipero Serra. In the next half century, twenty other mission settlements stretched northwards along the California coast.

The Pacific powerfully attracted the French in the Saint Lawrence Valley and the English along the Atlantic seaboard from the time they arrived and settled in North America in the late sixteenth and early seventeenth centuries, respectively. Initially, they sailed westward in the hope of reaching Asia, and though this proved impossible, it did not end the quest for the Northwest Passage, which continued into the nineteenth century. The quest for furs, for land, and in time for natural and human resources, including labor necessary to fuel the ever-developing and -expanding market economy, would result in continued European expansion across North America to the Pacific.

The Fur Trade The furs of sea animals were valued both in Europe and China, with the luxurious soft, warm fur of the North Pacific sea otter being particularly favored. The Canadian Hudson's Bay Company was at the forefront in supplying the European market from the vast territories it claimed, stretching from Hudson's Bay to the Pacific and down into the Oregon Territory; but after Captain Cook's third voyage across the Pacific in 1778, possibilities loomed for British fur trade in China. From 1785, vessels of the British East India Company visited the Northwest Pacific coast of North America and stocked up on furs for the China trade. Between that time and 1825, the peak period of the China fur trade, some 330 British vessels traded iron, cloth, blankets, and ultimately rum, tobacco, and firearms for sea otter skins to be transported to China.

The Pacific fur trade attracted the attention of other European powers, with which the British found themselves in heated competition. The Spanish had, in fact, made the first European contact with the inhabitants of the northwest Pacific coast. In 1774, the Spanish galleon *Santiago,* sailing the Columbia River, traded clothes, beads, and knives with a group of Haida on the coast of modern British Columbia for otter furs and native artifacts. It was the Russians, however, who gave the British their stiffest competition.

Russians in the North Pacific Russian expansion eastward across Siberia had been in part generated by the search for furs, and Russian expansion into the North Pacific was motivated by the same quest. Sea otter furs found early favor in Russian court circles, and a state trading company was developed to exploit the trade. In the 1730s and 1740s, Russians from permanent settlements on Kamchatka were seeking furs in the Kuriles and Aleutians. Initially the Russian fur trade was a form of tribute, with indigenous people providing government agents payments of pelts as tokens of political subjugation. By

DAILY LIVES

FIRST CONTACT, 1792

Alexander Mackenzie, fur trader and explorer, was the first European to cross the entire North American continent by land. Other fur traders and explorers had moved westward across the continent toward the Pacific and had made contact with indigenous inhabitants, but none had taken the route Mackenzie did, and so he encountered people who had never had contact with Europeans. The following is an account of Mackenzie's meeting with a group of Sekanis, inhabitants of the bleak northern forests whose meager livelihood supported only a small population:

> June 9 [1793] The rain of this morning terminated in a heavy mist at half past five, when we embarked and . . . perceived a small of fire, and in a short time heard people in the woods, as if in a state of great confusion, which was occasioned, as we afterwards understood, by their discovery of us. At the same time, this unexpected circumstance produced some little discomposure among ourselves, as our arms were not in a state of preparation, and we were as yet unable to ascertain the number of the party. I considered, that if there were but a few it would be needless to pursue them, as it would not be probable that we should overtake them in these thick woods; and if they were numerous, it would be an act of great imprudence to make the attempt, at least during their present alarm. I therefore ordered my people to strike off to the opposite side [of the river], that we might see if any of them had sufficient courage to remain; but, before we were half over the river,

which in this part, is not more than a hundred yards wide, two men appeared on a rising ground over against us, brandishing their bows and arrows, and accompanying their hostile gestures with loud vociferations. My interpreter did not hesitate to assure them, that they might dispel their apprehensions, as we were white people, who meditated no injury, but were, on the contrary, desirous of demonstrating every mark of kindness and friendship. They did not, however, seem disposed to confide in our declarations, and actually threatened, if we came over before they were more fully satisfied of our more peaceful intentions that they would discharge their arrows at us. This was a decided kind of conduct which I did not expect; at the same time I readily complied with their proposition, and after some time had passed in hearing and answering their questions, they consented to our landing, though not without betraying very evident symptoms of fear and distrust. They, however, laid aside their weapons, and, when I stepped forwards and took each of them by the hand, one of them, but with a very tremulous action, drew his knife from his sleeve, and presented it to me as a mark of his submission to my will and pleasure. On our first hearing the noise of these people in the woods, we displayed our flag, which was now shewn to them as a token of friendship. They examined us, and everything about us, with a minute and suspicious attention. They had heard, indeed, of white men, but this was the first time that they had ever seen a human being of a complexion different from their own.

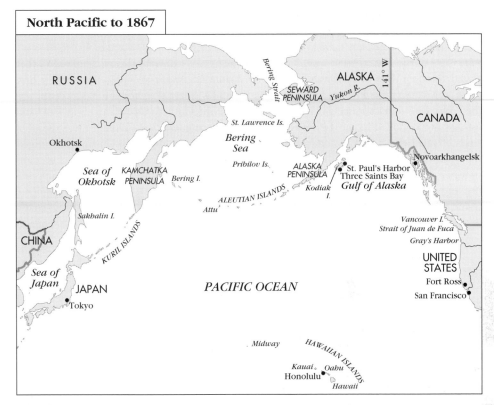

MAP 14.4 Russian and North American Frontiers in the North Pacific.

the end of the eighteenth century private trade was allowed and merchants were increasingly important, especially in trading furs to China in return for Chinese tea, silks, and linens, which the Russians favored almost as much as the British did.

SUMMARY

Changing frontiers and boundaries indicate the extent, dynamics, and impact of global political and cultural interaction, often initiated through trade, beginning in the fifteenth century. The Atlantic era ushered in a new global system, reorganizing the old patterns of trade and social life in many parts of the world. Perhaps the greatest impact on individuals and communities was felt along the frontiers and edges of polities, sites of great instability and potentially dramatic trans-formations. The outcomes of these interactions were varied: peoples were exterminated or assimilated, alliances were forged and reforged in the social mobility and intense competition of frontier zones. While the creation of the new Atlantic system initiated a long period of European hegmony over many parts of the world, the Europeans' presence did not immediately nor even inevitably lead to domination or change in other regions. Their presence and degree of political andeconomic control was met with resistance, and their legacy was often tenuous and thus ambiguous.

It was trade with Asia that persistently attracted Europeans eastward. From the seventh to seventeenth centuries, Muslim states in West Asia controlled the lucrative trade between Europe and Asia, especially China. The main impetus for Columbus's voyages was to discover a sea route to the "Indies" that would allow Europeans to circumvent the overland routes that passed through West Asia. Columbus took with him an Arabic-speaking Jew to help him communicate with the Muslim trading communities he expected to find. More successful was the Portuguese captain Vasco da Gama, who rounded the southern cape of Africa in 1497 and reached India, guided in part by an Arab pilot. The Portuguese then proceeded to establish a series of small commercial colonies that were to stretch from Arabia to China. They forged the way for the British, French, and Dutch, and in the seventeenth century these European states established footholds in India and Southeast Asia, all around the Indian Ocean, outflanking the Muslim states of West Asia. The long-term consequences of these establishments would take two centuries to develop. In the final chapter of Part III, we discuss cultural continuity and transformation in Europe, Africa, Asia, and the Americas, both independent of and connected with the emergence of a new global system dominated by Europeans.

ENGAGING THE PAST

THE DEATH OF CAPTAIN COOK

When Captain Cook returned to Hawaii during his 1779 expedition in the Pacific, he was stabbed and clubbed to death by islanders who, by traditional accounts, had taken him to be their god Lono, whose return was mandated as part of a ritualized cosmic cycle. When Cook first appeared on this second visit, he was treated as a god with great ceremony, but when his departing ship had problems and he returned to shore to make repairs, the islanders killed him because his unpredicted return symbolized cosmic chaos.

This explanation of Cook's death has been criticized as a European invention that sees the notion of Cook as a European "god" as a manifestation of European mythmaking in the process of conquest and a denigration of the practical rationality and logic of the islanders. In other words, Europeans projected their own sense of superiority and justified their conquest of other peoples by seeing themselves as gods in the minds of those they conquered. Modern anthropologists and historians have explored this process of mythologizing conquest. Some contest the view of Cook's death as a product of Hawaiian cosmology, arguing that explaining the cultural encounter in this way derationalizes the native culture in contrast to the assumed rationalism of Europeans.

Filtered through the lenses of contemporary observers and later accounts, there is no sure way to know exactly what the encounter with Cook meant to Hawaiians or what the true motives for his killing were. But the event of Cook's death symbolizes the essence of such encounters as they took place between Europeans and "others" in the course of European expansion in the Pacific and elsewhere.

A similar encounter with a very different immediate outcome can be found in the writings of Bernardino de Sahagún (ca. 1499–1590), a Franciscan missionary from Spain who arrived in Mexico in 1529. Having acquired facility in the Aztec language, Sahagún was able to compile a record of the Aztec people and their culture by collecting oral and pictorial sources that became the basis of his *General History of the Things of New Spain*. In this work the Aztec ruler Moctezuma is portrayed as awaiting the arrival from the sea of what the Aztec people believe to be Topiltsín-Quetzalcoatl, a legendary fair-skinned, bearded god-king prophesied to reappear after five centuries in 1519. When Cortés arrived, the prophecy seemed to be fulfilled, though the European "god" brought death and destruction, as, ultimately, returning Europeans in the wake of Cook's death brought change to the Hawaiian Islanders.

FIGURE 14.12 *The Apotheosis of Captain Cook* Depicts European Mythmaking in the Pacific.

This painting idealizes the European view of Cook as the great civilizer. Cook is depicted in his ascent hovering in the clouds above Kealakekua Bay, Hawaii, where he was killed.

SOURCE: *The Apotheosis of Captain Cook.* ca. 1794. Bishop Museum Honolulu.

SUGGESTIONS FOR FURTHER READING

E. Kofi Agorsah, ed., *Maroon Heritage: Archaeological, Ethnographic, and Historical Perspectives* (Kingston, Jamaica: Canoe Press, 1994). Multiple perspectives on resistance and continuity in the Caribbean.

Fernand Braudel, *The Mediterranean and the Mediterranean World in the Age of Phillip II*, 2 vols., trans. Sian Reynolds (London: 1972–1973). The now-classic study of the Mediterranean world in the six-teenth century, encompassing geological time, long-term cyclical changes in economy and society, and political events.

David Cordingly, *Pirates: Terror on the High Seas—From the Caribbean to the South China Sea* (Atlanta, GA: Turner Publishing, Inc., 1996). A colorful history of more than four centuries of piracy.

Howard Lamar and Leonard Thompson, eds., *The Frontier in History: North America and Southern Africa Compared* (New Haven, CT: Yale University Press, 1981). Pioneering work on comparative frontier history.

Dian H. Murray, *Pirates of the South China Coast, 1790–1810* (Stanford, CA: Stanford University Press, 1987). A lively scholarly study of piracy in the Cantonese water world at the end of the eighteenth century.

Norman Thrower, *Maps and Civilization: Cartography in Culture and Society* (Chicago: University of Chicago Press, 1996 [1972]). A stimulating social and cultural survey of maps and map making.

Eric R. Wolf, *Europe and the People without History* (Berkeley: University of California Press, 1982). Euro-pean expansion from the perspective of Asian, African, and American participants in this world historical process.

Crucibles of Change: Landscapes, Material Culture, and Social Life after 1500

In 1492, just as Columbus thought he was discovering the material riches of Asia, the Chinese painter Shen Zhou (1427–1509) inscribed the following on a painting he did, revealing the artist's ambivalence about material things:

> My outward form is slave to external things, and my mind takes its direction from them. Hearing is obscured by the sounds of bell and drum; seeing is obscured by patterns and beauty. This is why material things benefit people seldom, harm them often. Sometimes it happens, though, as with tonight's sounds and colors, that while they do not differ from those of other times, yet they strike the ear and eye all at once, lucidly, wonderfully becoming a part of me. That they are bell and drum sounds, patterns and beauty, now cannot help but be an aid to the advancement of my self-cultivation. In this way, things cannot serve to enslave man.

Shen Zhou wrote these words in a world that was becoming increasingly fixed on material things. By the sixteenth century, Chinese society was highly commercialized and urbanized, and collecting material things was a way to translate wealth into elite status. The ability—both financial and aesthetic—to collect prized objects was one criterion of upper class identity and a way to gain access to the social world of the literati, the scholarly elite. Where once the ability to manipulate words and images—mastery of classical texts, painting, and poetry—was the defining mark of the scholarly elite, increasingly the ownership of things was an indication of cultural refinement. Some years after Shen Zhou's death, a late-sixteenth-century writer recorded that the value of Zhou's paintings had "shot up tenfold," ironically making his works the object of the very materialism he had questioned. However, tensions between the values of materialism and those of scholarly achievement and cultivated taste persisted in seventeenth-century China.

In seventeenth-century Europe, similar tensions between the world of commerce and the world of the court nobility set the stage for the career of Johann Joachim Becher (1635–1682), who served some of the most powerful German princes of his time as court physician and adviser. In his role as adviser, Becher made use of his wide-ranging knowledge, which included training in the arts of alchemy. Alchemists sought to transform base metals into precious ones, a means of producing wealth. Alchemy provided Becher with a language to express the idea of material increase and thus enabled him to validate commercial activities to his princely masters. In a remarkable parallel with the traditional Confucian notion that commerce

FIGURE 15.0 Jan van Kessel, Kunstkammer with Venus at Her Toilet, 1659.

Oil on copper, showing mix of objects from New World and Old. The *Kunstkammer* was traditionally filled with products of artisans from rich trading cities and served as a representation of its owner's power. This depiction includes rare objects, people, and animals jumbled together in such a room, forming an image of the unknown, but one that was constructed within the confines of the Old World.

SOURCE: Staatliche Kunsthalle, Karlsruhe.

was an unproductive activity that merely took advantage of the goods produced by others, in Becher's world commerce was also viewed as parasitic, since merchants profited from the labors of others.

Becher, however, believed that, like alchemy's transformation of matter, commerce could transform material things into power by producing wealth, a source of power as great as arms and noble rank. With this in mind, Becher tried to acquire a strip of coastal land in what is now French Guiana from the Dutch West India Company on behalf of his employer Count Friedrich Casimir of Hanau (1635–1682; ruled from 1647); Becher hoped that acquisition of the West Indian colony, which produced sugar, coffee, and curiosities, would both enrich and empower the count. To gain the count's support in this venture, Becher supplied exotic goods associated with the colony for the count's *Kunstkammer,* a treasure room whose cabinets were filled with material objects that displayed the wealth and power of its owner. In turn, when Becher went to Amsterdam to negotiate the purchase of the colony, he took precious items, including a pair of ivory pistols and a jewel-encrusted hunting knife, from the *Kunstkammer* as gifts to officials of the Dutch West India Company to convey the count's regards as well as to display his nobility.

Though Becher's new world investment scheme failed, his efforts in this episode reflect the central issues of his time and the theme of this chapter. The West Indian colony that Becker hoped to secure as a source of wealth for his employer was one of many distant places that were increasingly connected to the material lives of seventeenth-century Europeans. The landscapes of the new world were becoming familiar to Europeans even as they changed them by their presence and by their commercial enterprises. European goods altered the material culture of peoples around the world through commerce, and material life in Europe also was profoundly changed by the goods produced by overseas colonies. The sugar and coffee produced by the Dutch colony, for example, contributed to substantial changes in the European diet during the seventeenth century.

Social life in Europe and across the globe in turn was transformed in the centuries between 1500 and 1800 by changing material conditions. Landscapes, material culture, and social life can all be thought of as crucibles, containers in which substances are altered or transformed. The seventeenth-century European alchemist Johann Joachim Becher was well-versed in the use of such containers; he even constructed a portable alchemical furnace, a crucible, so that he would be able to carry with him wherever he went the means of transforming matter, the key to wealth and power.

■

INTRODUCTION

Like Johann Becher's alchemical furnace, the crucible is a place where different elements meet and, under certain conditions, are changed in form and matter. This chapter uses the image of the crucible to explore transformations of the material world after 1500: historical crucibles were points at which cultural and social change occurred. Cultural and social transformations were expressed in physical landscapes, including cities. In these crucibles daily life, material culture, the pursuits and identities of individuals and their communities, and the human body changed.

Cities and towns were increasingly important as sites of transformation, where the effects of economic change were intensified and felt most keenly in the lives of individuals. Urbanization took place on a global scale, although more people continued to live in rural areas than in cities until well into the nineteenth century. Some ancient cities grew in size and complexity while others lost population, wealth, and power to new urban centers. As commercial capitalism grew in Europe and across the globe through European expansion, new cities emerged as commercial systems that linked producers in town and countryside with global markets and changed people's daily lives in the process. Commercial capitalism also affected rural communities. They increasingly produced goods for urban markets, and their economies were focused on cities through which they, too, participated in the global economic system. Not all cities were shaped exclusively or even in part by the new global economy, but more and more people lived within or in relation to cities.

The economic expansion of Europe made possible the distribution of goods to markets around the world, thus creating a shared global material culture. Though after 1500 the processes of change throughout the world were increasingly knit together, some parts of the globe were profoundly affected by the economic expansion of Europe, while others were not; some were highly urbanized, while others were not. Regardless of the relationship with Europe or the degree of urbanism, transformations experienced at the levels of individual and community throughout the world in the centuries after 1500 were expressed in physical landscapes, material culture, and social life.

■ LANDSCAPES OF CULTURAL IDENTITY

The most concrete sites of transformation were the physical landscapes in which people lived, worked, and played and across which they traveled. Dynamic cultural patterns altered by historical change shaped the ways that people understood the landscapes they inhabited and how they represented these landscapes in visual arts and in narrative forms (myths, stories). As crucibles of change, the landscapes of the period after 1500 may have been linked together in a new global way through the expansion of Europe, but people continued to experience and understand them largely according to distinct cultural orientations.

CHINESE LANDSCAPES

The commercial revolution in twelfth- and thirteenth-century China (see Chapter 11), including the development of the iron and steel industry, brought about a physical change in the landscape through deforestation as a result of the search for fuel to fire blast furnaces, mining, and such things as the dredging of canals for transportation. The Chinese response to these changes in the landscape was shaped by concepts deeply rooted in early thought and shared by people at all levels of society.

Geomancy   From early times in China, a belief in systems of correspondence between the human and natural worlds governed Chinese understanding of the place of humans in the cosmos and how humans might achieve harmony within it. By the Han dynasty (206 B.C.E.–220 C.E.), ideas about correspondence between the physical forms of the earth and the siting of human dwellings, graves, and temples were systematized into what is known as "geomancy." The idea of correspondence in geomancy meant that, for example, rocks were regarded as "kernels of energy, bones of earth" and waterways were likened to the arteries of the human body. Geomancy greatly influenced decisions people made about important matters—where they lived, where they buried their dead—at every level of society. Though some scholars criticized the superstitious nature of geomantic beliefs, geomancy remained an essential component of the Chinese worldview into modern times.

Fundamental to geomancy is the notion that propitious siting of human dwellings, graves, and temples enables people to use the positive energy embedded in the topographical patterns of the earth. Similarly, it is believed that misplacing graves will ensure misfortune for the heirs of the deceased. The proper location of the imperial palace enabled the emperor to tap the energy pattern of the entire empire. Mountains (*shan*) and water (*shui*) were the key elements in establishing the geomantic reading of place: the topographical composition of mountain and water revealed sites where humans could access power concentrated in the earth. These two terms used together, *shanshui,* came to refer to landscape painting.

FIGURE 15.1 Walking with a Staff, Hanging Scroll by Shen Zhou, (ca. 1485).

The fifteenth-century Chinese scholar-artist Shen Zhou spent his life close to home in the garden city of Suzhou. In contrast to that urban environment, this classic landscape shows a tiny human figure (lower portion) making his way along a lonely path in a spare but dramatic rural mountain landscape, suggesting the solitude sought by the recluse and idealized by both painters and poets.

SOURCE: Collection National Palace Museum, Taiwan, Republic of China

Landscape Painting Landscapes had been the dominant genre of painting in China since its development in the early centuries of the first millennium. Landscape painting, and painting in general, was closely related to the arts of poetry and calligraphy, since poems in elegant calligraphy were often inscribed on paintings and calligraphy itself was regarded as an art. In the late fifteenth and sixteenth centuries, the city of Suzhou in the Yangzi delta was the home of a famous school of landscape painting, as well as noted poets and calligraphers. In addition to regional schools of painters whose work focused on particular local landscapes, both literary imagination—recalling famous poets or poems with visual images—and the imitation of earlier masters were characteristic of landscape painting in the fifteenth and sixteenth centuries. Imitation, however, was more than merely copying: it meant grasping intuitively the spirit of the ancient painting and reproducing that spirit, rather than an exact copy of the original.

Gardens In addition to being the center of a famous regional school of landscape painting, the city of Suzhou in the sixteenth and seventeenth centuries was also famed for its gardens. Landscape painting and the construction of gardens were closely related. Gardens were attempts to capture all the elements of nature in a microcosmic setting, with rocks representing mountains and small streams representing rivers. Plants and flowers were juxtaposed with pavilions, bridges, and other buildings to create a harmonic composition, much like the composition of a landscape painting. Both gardens and landscape paintings were representations of nature as interpreted by humans, not realistic depictions of the natural world.

The urban material world contrasted sharply with the controlled perfection and harmony visualized in the nature of enclosed gardens. Like landscape painting, during the Ming

(1368–1644) gardens were associated with the culture of the literati, who were often amateur painters as well as connoisseurs of garden design. Though the building of private gardens originated in the Han and became somewhat prevalent in the Song (960–1279), a mania for garden building swept through centers of urban prosperity in the Ming (1368–1644). Retired officials, merchants, and local gentry spent enormous sums to hire designers, purchase exotic rocks and plants, dredge ponds, and wall in properties for garden display. Though gardens were meant in one sense to provide seclusion from the noise and bustle of the city and the public world of official life, they also became sites of social interaction. Writing about gardens proliferated in the Ming as owners drew up guides to their gardens and encouraged their friends to compose verses to commemorate the gardens. Poetry readings were held in gardens along with viewings of paintings and other prized possessions, such as jade, antique bronzes, and porcelains.

By the sixteenth century the material prosperity and accumulated commercial wealth of Ming merchants enabled them to construct expensive gardens that could display their refined taste and cultural sensibilities to the literati, whose cultivated style and status the merchants desired to emulate. The enclosure of nature in a walled urban garden was a way for wealth in property to be made acceptable by its transformation into art. By procuring expensive rocks and plants and hiring artisans to design a garden, a merchant could take part in cultural ac-

FIGURE 15.2 Enjoying Antiquities, Hanging Scroll (Detail by Du Jin ca. 1465–ca. 1509).

Ming Literati are shown here pursuing a favorite pastime in an elegant garden setting, examining antique bronzes and fine ceramics. Women at the back engage in domestic activities and servants attend them in the foreground.

SOURCE: Collection National Palace Museum, Taiwan, Republic of China.

tivities associated with literati life and gain access to their social world. By such means merchants could aspire to translate commercial wealth into social acceptance.

Real and Imagined Landscapes In other ways, too, culture shaped the landscape. Literati who ▩▩▩▩▩▩▩▩▩▩▩▩▩▩▩▩▩▩▩ traveled to famous places associated with important cultural and historical figures and to religious sites such as temples, shrines, or sacred mountains produced travel diaries and accounts of pilgrimage sites, both maps and drawings. On the other hand, literati artists often painted famous mountains or other sites they had never visited, and the representation of such a site was enriched by meanings embedded in calligraphic renderings of poems on the painting itself. These paintings, which could be considered imagined landscapes, often bore little or no relationship to the actual physical space they were said to represent.

EUROPEAN LANDSCAPES

Landscape painting flourished in Europe by the late seventeenth and eighteenth centuries, though it was never the dominant genre that landscape painting was in China and had very different themes and motifs. Chinese landscapes portrayed huge mountains and misty clouds, distant vistas with spare detail; human figures were miniscule if they were shown at all. European landscapes of the seventeenth and eighteenth centuries, represented by the paintings of the French artist Claude Lorrain (1600–1682), were often imaginative reconstructions—not unlike their Chinese counterparts—but they were inspired by very different ideas and sources. Claude Lorrain painted scenes of idealized nature drawn from inspiration in the antique ruins and scenery of the Roman countryside, where he spent much of his life. He combined different elements of scenes around Rome and added to them classical Greek and Roman or biblical figures dressed in pastoral or antique costumes. Integrating human figures into an idealized landscape painted in careful detail, Claude Lorrain showed nature as a harmonious and serene setting for human activities.

The eighteenth-century French painter Francois Boucher (1703–1770) painted rustic themes for the entertainment of the French court, providing diversion from the formality of court life by portraying court ladies as shepherdesses in natural settings. Boucher's paintings were thus idealized rural scenes where members of elite society could imagine themselves as Boucher portrayed them free of the restraints of court life. Eighteenth-century European landscape paintings, exemplified by Boucher, were compositions of artists created by selecting the most beautiful elements in nature. Similarly, Chinese landscapes were artistic compositions that were often constructed through the use of imagination or literary memory; they were not realistic depictions of scenes in nature, even when they represented a specific place.

Far more typical of European painting were portraits of people and scenes from daily life. Already in the Renaissance, for example, wealthy merchants could commission a portrait as easily as an aristocrat or a ruler could. As urban landscapes began to be transformed by new social classes, artistic interest in rural scenes and peasant life continued. Paintings such as *Lute Player* and *Card Players* by the Italian Michelangelo da Caravaggio (1573–1610) or *Dice Players* and *Young Fish Seller* by the Spaniard Bartolome Murillo (1617–1682) portrayed ordinary life and pastimes, as did works by the Dutch painter Peter Paul Rubens (1577–1640). In France several members of the artistic Le Nain family (late sixteenth-late seventeenth century) produced remarkable paintings of peasant life.

FIGURE 15.3 Claude Lorrain, *The Rest on the Flight to Egypt* (ca. 1635).

The idealized landscape is portrayed as an extension of the religious subject of this painting.

SOURCE: Noortman (London) Ltd./The Bridgeman Art Library.

When the middle class in Europe replaced popes and aristocrats as patrons of artists in the seventeenth century, portrait painting flourished. Dutch portraits of middle class culture and interior landscapes by masters such as Rembrandt van Rijn (1616–1669) or Jan Vermeer (1632–1675) contrasted with the urbanized and industrialized physical landscape outside the domestic interiors of family life. In contrast, landscape painters such as Claude Lorrain sought to recapture an idealized natural world that was increasingly disappearing (or never existed in quite the way he depicted it).

CROSS-CULTURAL LANDSCAPES

As changes in landscapes became more evident in Europe, interest in the construction of gardens became a popular expression of artistic and cultural interests, much as the fad for garden construction in sixteenth- and seventeenth-century China corresponded with increased material prosperity in urban settings. Unlike Chinese gardens, however, eighteenth-century European gardens reflected global contacts, by the use of plants from Africa, Asia, and the Americas and by foreign influences on landscape styles. The botanical gardens that opened at

Kew in 1760 played a singularly important role in encouraging the identification of the new species of plants arriving from ports around the world.

Chinese gardens influenced European landscape architecture. In 1687 Sir William Temple, in his *Gardens of Epicurus,* praised the intricate irregularity of Chinese gardens that he had visited. Temple's work, together with Batty Langley's *New Principles of Gardening* (1728), ensured that Chinese plans would influence European gardens. Sir William Chambers's *Designs of Chinese Buildings,* published in 1757, introduced Chinese styles to English architecture. The best-known example of Chambers's work is his pagoda in Kew Gardens near London.

Chinoiserie The fashion for *chinoiserie,* the elements of Chinese style adapted to European material culture in elegant garden structures and bridges, produced a design that derived from the idea that a landscape should follow the natural undulations of land and the meanderings of streams to provide moods of enchantment and awe. This style spread all over Europe. In 1774 the French king Louis XVI made an Anglo-Chinese park for his queen, Marie Antoinette, at Versailles; the park's central feature was the serpentine wanderings of a stream. However, the place where the elegant style took most permanent root was perhaps Sweden. At Drottningholm Palace near Stockholm a magnificent Chinese pavilion built in 1766 with a pagoda and surrounding gardens reflect careful study of Chinese landscape models.

European gardens had far less influence on Asian landscape gardening, but Jesuit fathers attached to the Chinese court in the eighteenth century oversaw the construction of several pleasure pavilions in the Italian baroque style. They also added towers and fountains in the European manner to imperial gardens on the outskirts of Beijing.

AFRICAN LANDSCAPES: METALLURGY AND CULTURE

Few things have transformed natural or cultural landscapes more than metal technology. Both figuratively and literally, metallurgy provided crucibles of change. The environmental impact of metalworking activities contributed to the awesome powers often associated with blacksmiths and metallurgists around the world. By the sixteenth century few parts of the world had not felt the tremendous effects of smelting, casting, and smithing operations, which seriously deforested vast regions. With few exceptions these technologies required large quantities of charcoal fuel, made from particular species of hardwood trees. Such trees provided the requisite high temperatures, but they were slow growing and not easily replaced within each generation.

Deforestation Deforestation was the inevitable consequence of industrial expansion. In Europe metalworkers and other artisans sought alternative fuels as early as the twelfth century. In China coal was used even earlier, though selectively, as a replacement for charcoal when wood charcoal became scarce. In most regions of the African continent, iron smelting had similarly deforested large tracts of land and thus contributed to population movements and eventually to the need to import cheap metals, since suitable coal supplies were not available for smelting. Production of pottery, glass, and other household needs also taxed the available fuel supplies as African urban populations increased in density.

African societies after about 1650 were witnessing their own transformations, especially environmental. In general, deforestation as a consequence of traditional iron industries and the violent depopulation of sub-Saharan Africa during the slave trade destroyed the conditions necessary for agricultural growth and indigenous technological innovation. Forests gave way to deforested landscapes, and urbanization increased in coastal areas, which functioned as magnets for Afro-European commercial growth and dense settlement. Cultural forms, however, remained vibrant and syncretic, blending the old and new elements in crucibles of change.

Many African societies perceived landscapes as dynamic social and spiritual as well as physical spaces. Specific landscapes were identified with family and ethnic history, since ancestors were believed to reside in the earth. The landscapes important to blacksmiths, who used huge quantities of specialized trees for charcoal fuel, were particularly subject to transformation. Mande blacksmiths in West Africa used their knowledge of the physical world and skills to intervene in and influence certain types of political situations.

Jiridon is the Mande term for knowledge or science of the trees, a specialized knowledge of the principles related to spiritual, medicinal, and natural energy that smiths could harness to create change, balance, and harmony. The activities of blacksmiths, making iron tools and weapons, created the forces of civilized space. Human-built and natural landscapes were thus altered through the practice of their technology. Iron tools such as hoes and spades were used to move earth, convert forests to fields, and literally transform African landscapes. Metals and metal objects imported after 1500, during the era of Atlantic trade, threatened to transform these links. Above all, the profound impact of technological changes in the period reflects the growing recognition of interconnectedness between Europeans and non-Europeans experienced by global societies as a consequence of the European industrial revolution.

■

EUROPEAN LANDSCAPES OF CHANGE: THE INDUSTRIAL REVOLUTION

Many global changes in material culture after 1500 can be linked to the rise of industrialism. At the heart of these material transformations were profound changes in the ways people perceived themselves in relation to the natural world. Dramatic technological changes and equally dramatic economic transformations resulted in changes in the physical and social organization of life. While many of these changes occurred first in Europe, their impact was not limited to European territory. Around the globe the products and impact of industrialism altered everyday lives.

Practical applications of most early European scientific knowledge were few and far between, but the scientific revolution led to a new habit of mind: the way of analyzing particular problems to solve them. Technological innovations took place in spheres far removed from the rarefied and well-educated arenas of abstract scientific philosophy and theory, but they also relied on the research and reasoning skills of science. For example, potters and machinists were members of the British and French Academy of Science, and they used scientific reasoning to solve major technological problems related to commercial production and overseas commerce—from reproducing Chinese porcelain to constructing clocks and mechanical toys. Innovations that materially transformed Europe sometimes developed in the workshops of uneducated craftsmen. Such innovation was not based on abstractions or theory, but on the commoner elements of base metals and sooty fuel.

IRON AND THE INDUSTRIAL REVOLUTION

Among important European technological changes that accompanied the development of theoretical science were those in metallurgy, especially the production of iron. Innovations in iron production supported the advances that made possible the European industrial revolution, but the association of iron with power was not unique to Europe.

Iron and Power   In China, for example, the technology of iron and steel production had been central to the commercial revolution of the Song (960–1279), and by the late imperial period (Ming [1368–1644] and Qing [1644–1911]) metallurgy was a well developed technology that generated philosophical observations. According to a sixteenth-century Chinese thinker, when observing the molten metal in the great blast furnace, one understood the origin of heaven and earth. For him, the fusion inside the furnace was like the beginning of the formless embryo, and its solidification was like the attainment of form. Similarly, the power of women to give birth was ascribed to the many African furnaces, including those of Bassari blacksmith smelters (1300–1800). Their furnaces, believed to be female, gave birth to red, glowing metal. In the eighteenth century European depictions of blacksmiths and fiery furnaces provided imagery of the impact of the technology and its fearful, inferno-like qualities. Such imagery came to be synonymous with modern industrial life.

The Problem of Fuel   The demand for iron and steel accelerated in Europe after about 1000 because of an increased demand for weapons of war and conquest and a growing population's need of more implements for farm, house, and industry. As a result, the scarcity of wood for charcoal, an essential ingredient of the smelting process, soon jeopardized the English and other European iron industries. One effect of the charcoal shortage was to shift the center of iron metallurgy from one country to another. Sweden, for example, which had plenty of trees as well as iron ore, became the leading European iron producer by the eighteenth century, replacing Germany and France. In countries such as Great Britain, the shortage of trees resulted in the replacement of charcoal with pit coal, which was abundant there.

   The key to increasing the production of iron and steel, once the major processes were in place, was clearly fuel, but the use of coal presented complicated problems. At all stages of iron making and steelmaking, the use of coal tended to impair the quality of the product. In 1614 a method was discovered for using coal in converting bar iron into a high-carbon product (steel), but for almost 100 years no advance was made toward the use of coal in the all-important blast furnace in which iron could be smelted in huge and continuous quantities.

Brewing Change   In the seventeenth century some brewers in Derbyshire, England, tried using coal to dry their malt. The presence of sulfur in coal ruined the taste of their beer, but when they refined the coal by heating it to produce coke, a new coal fuel, they got rid of the sulfur and brewed a famous beer. This industrial tale did not escape charcoal-short, thirsty iron makers. The first successful experiment in coke iron making was conducted at Coalbrookdale, Shropshire, England, in 1709 by Abraham Darby (1677–1721), who had served his apprenticeship in the malt mill of a brewery. Darby's use of coke in his blast furnace was not taken up quickly by others; because it remained an expensive process until the

FIGURE 15.4 Blast Furnaces in Coalbrookdale, Shropshire, Where Abraham Darby Was the First Industrialist to Use Coke as a Fuel in England (1709).

By the mid-eighteenth century Coalbrookdale had become an industrial center as a result of improved techniques in production.

SOURCE: © Armand Colin, Paris.

application of steam power, only six other coke furnaces were built in Great Britain in the next half century. Coke smelting gradually opened a new phase in iron technology and ranks with the steam engine as a major component in the European industrial revolution, which occurred between 1750 and 1850.

NEW TECHNOLOGIES AND THE INDUSTRIAL REVOLUTION

The acceleration of European technology in the eighteenth century was termed an "industrial revolution," and like other clustered innovations in world history, it provided new materials and means of production. Eighteenth-century technological innovations coupled with expanding capitalism to revolutionize European societies and their relationship with the non-European world. The industrial revolution also introduced new iron technology; indeed the parameters of the revolution may be set by the introduction of coke as a substitute for charcoal in the smelting process (eighteenth century) and the perfection of a new and successful process for steelmaking (nineteenth century). The scope of European technological achievements that begin in the mid-eighteenth century, their relationship to global economic changes, and their broad impact perhaps justify the use of the term "industrial revolution."

Steam Power: Technological innovations in eighteenth-century Europe took place principally ▨▨▨▨▨▨ in industries such as mining, metallurgy, and textiles. Most industrial innovations were produced by mechanics, craftsmen connected with the enterprises their innovations helped transform. Steam power was a dramatic leap from harnessing the power of water, horses, or heat; harnessing steam required a mechanical application. Since steam power is so much associated with the eighteenth-century revolution, the building of a steam engine in 1712 by Thomas Newcomen, a mechanic, may be taken as its inaugural event: all modern engines, either in factories or applied to locomotion, are descendants of Newcomen's engine. The earliest steam engines were solely pumping engines, restricted to coal mines; they were not very efficient and were expensive to operate. Eventually, however, their applications would create powerful tools for the expansion of Europe.

Subsequent eighteenth-century improvements made engines more useful and efficient that they became a basic ingredient of the revolution in production. James Watt (1736–1819), a Scottish instrument maker and repairer, is credited with perfecting Newcomen's engine. Watt completed its transformation in 1781–1782. All that remained was to make it generally available, which was achieved when Watt entered into partnership with Matthew Boulton, a wealthy hardware manufacturer in Birmingham, England, who had profited from an expanding export trade overseas. This exemplary marriage of Boulton's venture capital to Watt's inventive skill may be considered a model for subsequent industrial development. Watt's engine was efficient and cheap; embodied rotary motion, the basis of all subsequent machinery; and offered a continuous source of power.

The Textile Industry Equally significant was the use of the Watt engine for industrial, especially textile, production. Earlier in the eighteenth century, machines were being made that had the potential for transforming spinning and weaving from processes that had remained unchanged for centuries. As early as 1718 Thomas Lambe opened a silk factory with complicated machinery, the plans for which had been purloined from Italy. The hope was to manufacture silk textiles locally to sell in the lucrative African textile market and avoid having to buy them from Asian merchants. Similarly, competition with cheap, finely spun Indian cotton stimulated the desire to find a new means of producing cotton.

Before the textile revolution, cloth was produced by workers at home, using raw materials provided by merchants, who then gathered the completed cloth. Women spun thread and men generally did the weaving. The location, organization, and output of the industry changed dramatically during the industrial revolution. John Kay's flying shuttle (1733)—a device that allowed weavers to work individually rather than in pairs—hastened the weaving process and stimulated further development of spinning machinery. James Hargreaves's spinning jenny (1767), which produced large quantities of strong yarn from multiple spindles, was the first example of mass production in the textile industry. Weavers were then challenged to keep up with the output of spinning jennies.

Improved spinning produced finer, stronger yarn faster than traditional weavers could use it, and in 1785 Edmund Cartwright invented the power-driven loom, which restored the balance. Many other machines accompanied the development of spinning and weaving machinery, not the least of which was the cotton gin for processing raw cotton. It was built in 1792 by Eli Whitney, a Yankee schoolmaster, from plans suggested by workers at the Georgia plantation where he taught.

FIGURE 15.5 A Weaving Workshop in Eighteenth-Century England, by William Hogarth.
William Hogarth (1697–1764) used art to tell a story or impart a lesson. This typical engraving shows a weaving workshop such as would be replaced by the textile revolution and the factory system.

SOURCE: © British Museum.

The Textile Revolution New machines created a textile revolution, but not until they were harnessed to the Watt engine. The new power-driven machinery, which was responsible for increased textile production, depended on the increased availability of metal, particularly iron. Thus the innovations in metallurgy were as important as the steam engine in generating the industrial revolution. The substitution of coke for charcoal provided fuel for the full-scale application of steam to industry without which there might not have been an industrial revolution. Without the increased supplies of iron, Watt and Boulton could not have produced steam engines on a commercial scale, and without steam engines the European transformation from domestic industry to the factory system is difficult to imagine. Equally important were the sources of capital, labor, and raw materials and the markets that consumed the increased production. Underpinning all these innovations was the Atlantic slave trade, which provided labor and markets and produced capital for investment in industry.

Impact of the Factory System The introduction of new spinning and weaving equipment in Europe early in the eighteenth century began the process of moving textile production from the home to factories. In the case of textile production, the new machinery not only took work out of the home and agricultural villages but also (sometimes) reversed traditional gender-based tasks: in the industrialized factory, spinning became men's work, rather than women's work as before. The factory replaced the home as the workplace, requiring large numbers of workers to travel daily to the city or move there. Cities became clusters of factory sites—urban crucibles of change.

■

URBAN LANDSCAPES IN EUROPE

Commercial and technological changes in Europe had their most powerful impact in cities. As centers of population, production, and consumption of material goods, cities were sites of transformation. They acted as magnets, drawing population from the countryside and mixing people of diverse classes, regional backgrounds, and cultures. Cities were technological and artistic centers where material goods were produced in profusion. At the same time cities were centers of consumption that provided huge markets for consumer goods produced with increasing efficiency by regional specialization and transported with relative speed along well-maintained highway networks. Cities were also cultural centers that provided entertainment and cultural activities for residents and visitors, and thus significant sites of transformation.

URBAN MATERIAL WORLD: THE LABOR OF MANY, THE WEALTH OF FEW

The late eighteenth century witnessed the rising cost of urban subsistence as social benefits declined and workers were exposed to greater exploitation. The decline of urban cohesion was most clearly noted in the widening distinction between laborers and well-to-do employers. The eventual fusion of urban well-to-do with aristocratic culture was achieved in part as the result of the labor and misery of the working class, which was largely excluded from urban life's defining characteristics of wealth, leisure, and opportunities for advancement. Taking elements from the old landed aristocratic lifestyles to which they aspired, the well-to-do urban middle class constructed its material life.

Urban middle-class culture included well-built town palaces, in which tablecloths, napkins, fine china, and crystal could be found. Imported foods and wines were served to the middle class by household servants. With success, rich burghers took to wearing silks and velvets as aristocrats did. Yet their values were fundamentally different: they emphasized attitudes of social acquiesence and personal dedication to the "spirit of capitalism," the capacity to work hard, save, and invest. They became a true "middle class" between workers and aristocracy with its own culture.

Urban Poor While the lure of urban life offered the possibility of material benefits, cultural variety, and excitement, as well as economic gain, for many people European cities were synonymous with poverty and homelessness. Traditionally, the Church had taken a primary role in providing relief to vagabonds and homeless persons, but gradually this role was taken over by the state. "Poor laws" passed in sixteenth-century England required local government officials to register the poor of each parish and forbade unlicensed beggars. This legislation also empowered local governments to levy taxes called "poor rates," which were intended for the support of the community's poor. In England a 1601 law created overseers of the poor and established poorhouses, workhouses for the able-bodied. By the time the industrial revolution was in full swing, the poorhouse was institutionalized and served as a supplier of child and female labor for the new factories.

Mary Saxby: Homelessness
in the Eighteenth Century
The life story of the London-born woman Mary Saxby (1738–1801) illustrates how difficult it was for many women to survive the urban experience at the end of the eighteenth century. After her mother died, Mary was forced, at the age of about 10, to run away and hide in towns, sleep under shop stalls, and eat rotten apples and cabbage stalks found in markets. In the time of Mary Saxby, homelessness and poverty were associated with spiritual failure. According to Mary, "My companion [another vagabond woman] not being so hardy, and perhaps not so wicked as I, soon returned [to her home], and I was left alone." When Mary Saxby became older, she took to singing in alehouses and at feasts and fairs. Her vagabond life temporarily ended when she was briefly married. The plight of Mary Saxby was not isolated; cities became centers for the abundance of material goods, but access to the riches of industrial life was extremely limited.

POPULATION AND PRODUCTION

The eighteenth-century industrial revolution was accompanied by rapid demographic growth, and cities in most places expanded accordingly. The populations of many large European cities tripled in the period between about 1600 and 1750. During the eighteenth century Britain's population increased by 80 percent, from about 5 million to 9 million. Life in cities and towns began to replace rural experience as the determining feature of cultural life. Cities in Europe had to deal with such issues as public sanitation on an unprecedented scale. Indoor toilets were not introduced until the nineteenth century; heavy pollution from industrial activities, including manufacturing and the burning of coal, together with urban waste, contributed to the unpleasantness of city life. The new market economy produced larger urban populations and larger groups of urban poor as the forms of agrarian self-sufficiency and communal life gave way to smaller and more mobile family units.

The new forms of technology and production relied on larger and more highly organized forms of labor. Factories provided employment for large numbers of otherwise homeless or poor, including women and children. The evolution of the welfare system in Britain began with the utilization of factory space as temporary poorhouses. A new market agriculture was required by the expanding urban centers. The profitability of industrialization increased the accumulation of capital in the centers of production and attracted even larger numbers of people to these frontiers of opportunity.

■

NORTH AMERICAN LANDSCAPES: CONQUEST AND CHANGE

European views of the landscape of North America, particularly what would be known as New England, illustrate both a lack of ecological understanding and a desire to create commodities from the abundance European settlers observed there. While Native Americans, greatly reduced in numbers by genocide and disease, were forced onto less desirable agricultural lands, the Europeans who supplanted them wrought great changes to the landscape. Lands became bounded by concepts of property rights in the forms of fences and maps; forests were cleared to plant crops and to permit the Europeans' domesticated cattle and sheep to graze. The abundant animal wildlife rapidly disappeared. Dandelions and rats from Europe and Asia were introduced to the North American continent, and they and other pests and crop diseases spread in the cleared areas of European settlement.

THE IMPACT OF HORSES AND GUNS

The impact of European technology reached indigenous American cultures in landscapes far beyond the territories actually conquered and settled by the invaders. Horses and guns were essential in extending the conquest across continents. Horses had died out in the Americas 8000 to 10,000 years before Europeans arrived. They were returned to the Americas by Columbus on his second voyage, in 1493, and were subsequently carried wherever Europeans went. As the Europeans conquered, they also introduced firearms to the Western Hemisphere. Though the Spanish sought to prohibit indigenous peoples from riding horseback or carrying firearms, these prohibitions were difficult to enforce.

Horses thrived and propagated rapidly, spreading everywhere. Wild horses moved north from Mexico and by the eighteenth century had spread across the Great Plains and into Canada, a process encouraged by traders and native raiders. Horses were also carried to the Atlantic seaboard by traders and colonists; in South America, where a thriving horse trade with Africa developed, horses flourished as they spread inland from coastal Argentina and Brazil. The spread of guns among natives of both the Americas may have lacked the biological impetus and speed of the spread of horses, but it had an equal and deadly importance in changing their lives.

Horses and guns gave Europeans advantages; they also transformed the cultures of the peoples the Europeans encountered by giving the indigenous populations mobility, power, and military might and changing the social and economic bases of their lives. For example, before the European introduction of the modern horse, the economy of the peoples of the Great Plains of central North America was based on gathering-hunting and agriculture. Women raised crops and gathered wild foods and provisions; men hunted on foot and devised schemes for capturing their prey, such as driving animals over a cliff or into a compound. The Plains peoples lived relatively sedentary and stable lives with little antagonism or class distinction. Plains communities were bound by mutual aid, as people protected and supported one another for economic and religious reasons.

Changes in Plains Culture By the mid-eighteenth century the introduction of horse and gun had substantially changed Plains culture from communal societies in which individual profit making was uncommon and all people were relatively equal in rights and benefits into one of competition, inequality, profit, and increasing hostility. The horse gave Plains peoples mobility, and firearms gave them hunting efficiency and military prowess. Mobility and trading opportunities brought new people onto the Plains from its fringes and led to a richer, less isolated, and more flamboyant culture. Hunters had greater success when they could roam over vast areas, and agriculture declined as greater emphasis was placed on the hunt. The result was major ecological change: buffalo, once joint residents of the Plains with humans, diminished rapidly as they were successfully hunted and virtually disappeared.

Great Plains peoples became primarily nomadic; and trade, especially in guns and horses, developed between them. They became fur trappers and traders who killed not for food but for profit, exchanging furs that were in excess of individual needs for imported goods. As competition for profit replaced sharing for common welfare, hostilities among the Plains peoples, and between them and Europeans, increased. European epidemics and violence may have reduced the numbers of Plains peoples, but European horses, guns, and trade destroyed their traditional life.

■

URBAN LANDSCAPES IN THE AMERICAS

The most profound transformations of native cultures in the Americas took place in the crucibles of urban life. Spanish conquest resulted in the imposition of European urban patterns that transformed the lives of the indigenous peoples of Central and South America and in the Caribbean. From the time of their arrival, the Spanish replaced pre-Columbian towns and cities with new ones organized and functioning on the Spanish model. For example, Cuzco, capital of the Incan Empire, gave way to the Spanish imperial city of Lima. Central to these new Spanish urban centers were European economic and cultural systems, values, and moral judgments, which were forced upon the conquered peoples.

SPANISH-AMERICAN COLONIAL CITIES

Cities were the most conspicuous feature of colonial Spanish America. As early as 1494 Santo Domingo, the first seaport-stronghold-capital of the Spanish conquest, became an example of what was to follow. This remote outpost of Iberian culture became the earliest focus for Spanish America. Replications and rivals soon followed: in less than a century, there were some 200 colonial towns in Spanish America; by 1600 there were 250; by mid-seventeenth century aristocratic and luxurious Lima, with a population of 170,000, had become the largest city in Spanish America. When the Spanish conquest was completed by about 1700, an urban-dominated imperial system was in place.

Spanish colonial cities were distinguished by grants of land (four square leagues or 18,000 acres) and by groups of 10 to 100 Spanish heads of families who settled on the grants. As cities grew, they became centers of European culture set down in the Americas. Like towns in Spain, each had its own plaza, parks, imposing churches and monasteries, schools, and substantial government buildings. Within a decade of its founding, San Domingo had become a thoroughly Iberian city with convents, schools, and a bishopric, which by European definition was what made a city. Though its importance was to decline as a result on Spanish expansion on the mainland, San Domingo maintained a sort of general cultural primacy. As late as the mid-eighteenth century, its University of San Tomas (founded in 1538) attracted students from all over the Caribbean basin and supplied teachers for other Spanish-American universities and missionaries to convert the natives from Mexico to Peru.

Spanish Urban Imperial System The Spanish urban imperial system resulted in basic economic, social, and cultural changes in the lives of conquered peoples. Crown officials, and especially the clergy, became nothing less than agents of social control in charge of the lives, labor, education, and souls of indigenous peoples. The Spanish forced the peoples they conquered to till the land, mine its wealth, sell its products, and work for wages, a regime that often clashed violently with customary ways of life. The shock was as severe for the more politically centralized Maya, Aztec, and Inca peoples as it was for the

Caribbean islanders, but the Spanish had their way against most. Rural natives within reach of the imperial system were initially placed in the semifeudal *encomienda,* where they provided the cheap forced labor by which Spanish landlords, both laymen and clergy, were able to fully enjoy the benefits of the lands they had conquered. With forced labor and without either incentive or need for technological improvements, the Spanish conquerors were able to achieve a life that was both wealthy and easy.

Spanish Colonial City Life For indigenous peoples life in the colonial cities was only marginally better than rural life. City life certainly offered them greater freedom and mobility than people on the *encomienda* enjoyed, but it did not mean less labor. In the craft workshops of the towns, people were transformed from tillers of the soil to wage earners and were potentially liberated from the servile status to which conquest and the *encomienda* economy had assigned them; city workers earned higher cash wages than rural manual workers, but they also had higher living expenses. Women worked outside the home in both rural and urban Spanish America. Some skilled textile manufacturing was completely in their hands, and in Mexico City, as early as the sixteenth century, there were female guilds and guild officers.

Much of the art and architecture in Spanish America was ecclesiastical, and people were trained to quarry stone for churches, monasteries, and schools and to become the masons who erected them. They were trained as carpenters and cabinetmakers, sculptors and painters, musical instrument makers and performers, all in the service of religion.

FIGURE 15.6 **View of the Old Square, The Principal Marketplace of Havana; Eighteenth Century.** This Caribbean city reflected the blend of transplanted European architecture (modified for a tropical climate) and diverse peoples who met and interacted in a marketplace as typical of Africa.

SOURCE: Bibliothèque Nationale de France.

NORTH AMERICAN COLONIAL CITIES

Urban society was a feature of the first European colonies in North America. Urban attitudes were a part of the cultural baggage of many seventeenth- and eighteenth-century migrants. Communities were small in size but culturally diverse. Even early village settlements performed urban functions, including the exchange of goods, services, and ideas from the global economy. In the seventeenth century colonists established small urban centers extending the length of the Atlantic coastline and into the Saint Lawrence Valley. Some colonial cities grew out of the fortified outposts that protected inhabitants from indigenous peoples or competing European powers. Other towns were established with the support of governments or joint-stock companies to increase profits by more efficiently exploiting hinterland resources. Still other cities, such as Philadelphia or Baltimore, were communities established on the basis of religious beliefs.

Boston Colonial cities were coastal settlements, small by contemporary standards. Boston, the largest seventeenth-century town in British North America, hardly surpassed a population of 7000. Contemporary Philadelphia and New York scarcely reached 4000, though in the next century they surged ahead. By the end of the eighteenth century, Philadelphia had 40,000 inhabitants, making it one of the four largest cities in the British Empire. The coastal position of the new North American towns enabled them to participate in global trade routes, to which they supplied fish, furs, wheat, rice, tobacco, indigo, and lumber. Shipbuilding expanded to support the urban mercantile base. By 1720 Boston boasted fourteen shipyards and produced more than 200 ships annually.

The global position of the colonies in relation to the Atlantic economy also influenced the development of colonial urbanism. Though the Puritan colony at Boston began as a reformist religious community that was not dissimilar to Calvin's Geneva, the expansion of trade after 1650 weakened Boston's social homogeneity and ultimately undermined the power of the Puritan community's leaders. The growth of maritime commerce affected all elements of the city. Though as late as the last quarter of the seventeenth century small farmers still cultivated much of the peninsula on which the city was situated, new immigrants from Africa and Europe crowded together along the waterfront.

Philadelphia The city of Philadelphia also began as a religious community. Like Bostonians, Philadelphians were unable to stem the tides of secularism that derived from a steady prosperity. Founded in 1682 under William Penn's liberal instructions, Philadelphia was first settled by Quaker artisans and merchants seeking religious tolerance and political and economic freedom. The settlement soon became a city of entrepreneurs, craftsmen, and storekeepers. Those connected with maritime commerce clustered around the Delaware River, and industrial quarters soon became clearly discernible.

Quebec and Montreal Two very different cities, Quebec and Montreal, illustrate the variety of urban sites in French North America. Quebec was established in 1608 by Samuel de Champlain. The only walled city in North America, Quebec took on military, governmental, and cultural roles. It became the center of the diocese of New France and accordingly became a city by European definition. The site of Montreal was originally the Indian village of Hochelaga, reached by the French explorer Jacques Cartier in 1535. As the seventeenth-century French came to dominate the settlement, it became a key trading port for the continental interior. Both internal and international commerce were responsible for Montreal's growth. Like other far northern cities, it was a rather grim place with houses and public buildings made of cold grey stone. Montreal did not get drinking water from public aqueducts until 1801. The city's narrow streets were sullenly lit with oil lamps, and policing consisted of a few constables and a night watch. Though enormous profits were made from the fur trade, most of the wealth was funneled through Montreal to Europe.

■
URBAN LANDSCAPES IN AFRICA

In the first three centuries of African-European interaction, between 1450 and 1750, intensification of commercial activity and the consequent impact of Western culture was largely carried out by Africans who acted as agents of existing African states and corporations. Their adoption of European languages and dress became signs of the new merchant culture and status symbols. Manchester cottons and Chinese silks could be found in almost every village, just as Moroccan leather and West African gold regularly made their way to the markets and fairs of Normandy and Britain. As coastal markets and their communities grew in size and complexity, the urban centers became sites of cultural and social transformations.

WEST AND CENTRAL AFRICAN CITIES

Ancient African cities were typically political, religious, and economic centers; after European contact, cities continued to perform some or all of these functions. For example, the cities of Ife and Benin (both in Nigeria) were built around the ruler's palace, where industrial and economic activities took place and public rituals were performed. The palace was the hub of the city, and all roads to its hinterland radiated out from the city center.

Although new cities emerged after 1500 as coastal markets for the trade in slaves and other goods, centers such as Ife and Benin became sites of contested economic and political

FIGURE 15.7 Benin Bronze Figure of a Royal Messenger (Sixteenth Century).

This figure wears a cross and cap, emblems of royal authority, and carries a staff. Royal insignia enabled messengers to travel out of the city center and represent the king.

SOURCE: Nigerian National Museum, Lagos. © Dirk Bakker, 1978.

autonomy where the African rulers struggled to maintain control over the production of exports and the price and demand for imports in the rulers' dealings with Portuguese, Dutch, and English traders. One of the palace associations of specialists or guilds, *Iwebo,* was appointed by the Benin king to conduct affairs with the Europeans, and to this day its members speak a secret language they claim is derived from Portuguese, the language of the first Europeans. City artisans at Benin and other West African trading centers carved ivory objects as tourist art, which they sold to merchants and sailors. The Benin ruler also commissioned and collected items of material culture in his palace, according to the earliest European description:

> The king's court is square, and is certainly as large as the town of Haarlem [in the Netherlands], and entirely surrounded by a special wall, like that which encircles the town. It is divided into many magnificent palaces, houses, and apartments of the courtiers, and comprises beautiful and long square galleries, about as large as the Exchange at Amsterdam, but one larger than another, resting on wooden pillars, from top to bottom covered with cast copper, on which are engraved the pictures of their war exploits and battles, and are kept very clean.

The Lunda of Central Africa had established their capital, an elaboration of the royal enclosure (*musumba*), in open woodland east of the Kasai River. European visitors who saw several *musumbas* during the nineteenth century were impressed with their structures, orderly roads, and open public squares and with the cleanliness and hygiene of their communities. In contrast, European travelers described the Portuguese city of Luanda as small and squalid. The marginal placement of European traders in separate quarters for visitors was a widespread and traditional strategy for organizing the inhabitants of settlements according to ethnic affiliation, historical placement, and local importance.

■

ISLAMIC LANDSCAPES: TECHNOLOGY AND ARCHITECTURE

Urban populations everywhere struggled to harness technology to improve their living conditions. In light of the general aridity of much of West Asia and its relative lack of water, an enormous amount of energy there went into the construction of irrigation works and hydraulic machines. Large cities as well as fertile fields required an enormous amount of fresh water. After the Ottoman Turks captured Constantinople in 1453, they devoted considerable resources to building an elaborate complex of cisterns, dams, reservoirs, locks, and aqueducts to supply water to their new capital. This system is still in use. One section of it is a beautiful aqueduct 500 feet long with eleven pointed arches.

Dome Architecture   In addition to water systems, there were other public works projects whose construction required skilled engineers, such as bridges and domed buildings. Engineers and architects combined their skills to produce arches and domes for both practical and aesthetic purposes. Although the dome was in use in West Asia before the Arab conquest, the Muslims subsequently and on many occasions raised this device to monumental proportions. The purpose of a dome was to cover a great space while avoiding the need for rows of pillars to support the roof.

By the early modern period, hundreds of domed structures, above all churches and mosques, had been constructed throughout Europe, West Asia, and North Africa. Localized styles of architecture date to the division of West Asia among the Ottomans in Turkey, the Safavids in Iran, and the Mamluks in Egypt. The Ottoman style was symbolized by the immense domed mosques of Istanbul with their sleek pencillike minarets; the Safavid Persian style by the dazzling, tile-covered mosques of Isfahan with their bulbous domes; and the Mamluk Arab style by the intricately carved and joined stone domes of the tombs of the sultans in Cairo.

Suleymaniye Mosque The dome crowning the Suleymaniye Mosque in Istanbul epitomized ▬▬▬▬▬▬▬▬ the large-scale dome. It was designed for Suleyman the Magnificent by Sinan (d. 1588), the greatest Ottoman architect and a worthy rival of his close European contemporary Michelangelo. Completed in 1557 after seven years of labor, the Suleymaniye dome has a diameter of 80 feet and floats 160 feet above worshipers' heads. It rests on four massive piers and is extended at the front and back of the mosque by two half domes of equal diameter and 120 feet high. Even today the visitor is overwhelmed by the achievement.

INDO-ISLAMIC ARCHITECTURE IN MUGHAL INDIA

Mughal culture in India was the product of Persian-Islamic and Hindu influences, and Mughal architecture reflected this cultural blend. The city of Agra was dominated by the Red Fort, built by the sixteenth-century Mughal emperor Akbar. Shah Jahan's version of this building was his Red Fort in Delhi (1638–1648), which was based in part on a Mughal adaptation of classic Persian-Islamic architectural lines, though the shape of the emperor's pavilion in the hall of public audience imitated in marble the peasant dwellings of Bengal, the "rice bowl" of India.

Taj Mahal The most famous monument of Mughal architecture is the Taj Mahal, built as a ▬▬▬▬▬ mausoleum for Shah Jahan's wife Mumtaz Mahal after her death in childbirth in 1631. Designed by two Persian architects, it took more than 20,000 workers over 20 years to build. It has been called the greatest single work of Safavid art, but in its dependence on Indian materials and craftsmen, it can be seen as an excellent example of Mughal cultural syncretism, rather than as a Persian import. The Taj Mahal, however, can also be viewed as a symbol of oppression. Mumtaz Mahal died in the Deccan, a region of India that her husband waged costly wars to bring under control following the decimation of the local peasant population through one of India's worst recorded famines. Shah Jahan spent only 5000 rupees of imperial funds each week to help relieve widespread misery and starvation in Deccan; not long after that, he lavished billions on a peacock throne and his wife's mausoleum, the Taj Mahal.

■

URBAN LANDSCAPES IN THE ISLAMIC WORLD

The cultural encounter with Europe altered and transformed many parts of the world, but it was not the only source of global interaction and syncretism. The vast interactive sphere of the Islamic world depended on the existence of large cities and flourishing trade. The creation of Muslim empires led to the growth of large cities. The complexities and demands of urban life gave direction and impetus to long-distance trade that served the populations of cities.

FIGURE 15.8 The Taj Mahal

This classic example of Mughal cultural syncretism was designed by Persian architects, but constructed in India by Indian craftsmen using local materials.

SOURCE: Gerard Champlong/The Image Bank

ISLAMIC CITIES

The great Islamic cities were centers of trade and manufacturing, though the growth of European textile industries and the growing markets for East Asian goods were reducing the importance of Muslim manufactures in international trade. Surrounding the stable urban population of merchants, shopkeepers, and craftsmen was a larger population of unskilled workers, peddlers, street cleaners, and the semiemployed, a stratum that included a large proportion of rural immigrants. The line between country and city was not sharply drawn: market gardens surrounded and intruded into the city, whose outskirts attracted the floating rural population, which greatly increased in number in times of need and disorder.

The structure of Islamic cities reflected their purposes: trade and manufacturing, religion and scholarship, government and justice. Two or more complexes of major buildings were part of every Islamic city. One complex was the main mosque, surrounded by the chief courts, schools of higher learning, shops that sold objects of piety, and possibly the shrine of a saint identified with the life of the city. Another complex included the central market place (the main point of exchange), offices of money-changers, storehouses, and shops that sold locally made or imported goods. A third complex might be government offices. The power of government was present in everyday urban life (as watchmen, market supervisors, and police), but it was expressed as well in large and sometimes ostentatious public buildings.

Wealthy traders, merchants, and craftsmen resided near their complex, and scholars and religious leaders near theirs, but most of the urban population lived outside the center in quarters that were a mass of small streets and cul-de-sacs. Each quarter had its mosque (or shrine or church or synagogue), local market, and public bath. The tendency was for each quarter to reflect common links: religious, ethnic, and regional. Farthest from the center, near or beyond the walls of the city, were the poorer quarters of rural immigrants and the workshops of noisy or malodorous crafts (such as tanning or butchering). Also outside the city walls were cemeteries.

Urban Society   Non-Muslims in Islamic cities were set apart from the families of believers. They paid a special tax (*jizya*), and Islamic law required that they show signs of their difference by dressing in special ways and avoiding colors (especially green) associated with Islam. They were prohibited from carrying weapons or riding horses (much as native populations in Spanish America were) and could not build new places of worship or repair pre-Islamic ones without permission. Laws about marriage were strictly enforced: non-Muslims could not marry or inherit from Muslims. And though Christians or Jews might occupy positions of importance in certain economic activities such as the arts, they were virtually excluded from others such as food preparation.

URBAN TRANSFORMATIONS IN WEST ASIA AND NORTH AFRICA: ISTANBUL AND CAIRO

Istanbul began as a center of government, religion, and commerce. By the time it was conquered by the Ottomans, it was larger than any European city, a position it held for a thousand years. Istanbul was also fabulously rich, thanks to its advantageous location at the crossroads of trade between Europe and Asia, east and west, north and south. Once Istanbul became a part of the Islamic Empire, its economic well-being was essential to the Ottoman regime. Continued Ottoman expansion supported urban development.

The city's capture began a process of Islamization, including the painting over of Christian mosaics in the great church of Holy Wisdom, Hagia Sophia, and the addition of four minarets to it. Schools, hospices, hospitals, and public baths were built. On the hill overlooking the city, a vast government complex was built around Topkapi Palace, an inner city with thousands of inhabitants.

Like Istanbul, Cairo's importance as an ancient African city increased as a result of Muslim conquest. By the fourteenth century, when the Ottomans gained control of Egypt, Cairo had become a major world city with 250,000 inhabitants. Its population was estimated at 300,000 by the end of the seventeenth century, and it continued to be a vigorous center of trade and cultural exchange among Africa, West Asia, and Europe.

URBAN TRANSFORMATIONS IN MUGHAL INDIA

Urban culture on the Indian subcontinent also had ancient roots and was greatly affected by repeated conquests. Traditional (pre-Mughal) Indian cities of all sizes had two focuses: the palace and the temple. Palaces tended to be in or near the city center; they were often defended by fortifications and became citadels for the whole urban complex. The temple was much more than the focus of religious activities. Temples owned lands and employed priests, scribes, craftsmen, traders, laborers, and female dancers. They also maintained schools and hospices, dispensed charity to beggars, and relieved citizens in times of distress and famine.

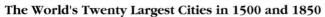

The World's Twenty Largest Cities in 1500 and 1850

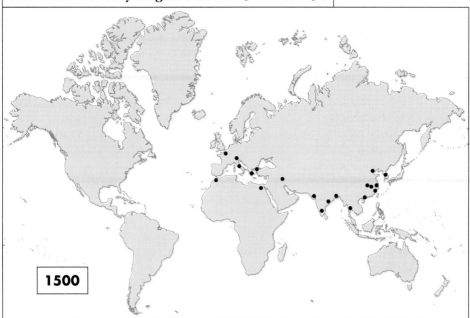

1500

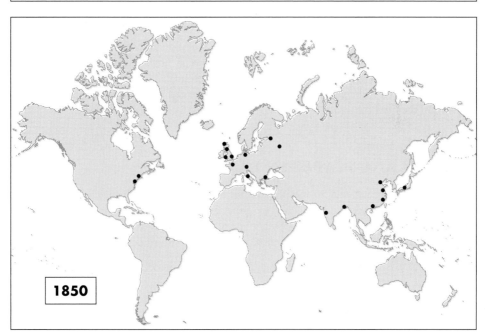

1850

MAP 15.1 The Shift of Global Population from Asia to Europe and North America.

The homes of the urban poor were humble huts of wood, reed, and mud brick, thatched with straw. Many urban poor had no shelter and slept in corners of the city. Both temples and palaces were often surrounded by open areas that featured trees and expanses of water—lakes, pools, and basins. Fortified cities were encircled by moats, some of which contained earthworks covered with spiny shrubs, and by high walls with numerous towers and balconies for defending troops.

Delhi The ancient Hindu city of Delhi was first altered by Muslim invasions between 1000 and 1200 C.E. During the Muslim sultanate (1206–1526) that chose Delhi as its capital, one of the most noticeable alterations of the city was the destruction of Hindu temples, the materials of which were used to build the mosque and the citadel. In 1556 the Mughal emperor Akbar conquered Delhi; the new capital city was located near Agra. As Mughal power declined in the eighteenth century, Delhi was subject to attack by rival noble factions and by foreign invaders: Persian, Afghan, and, finally, the British.

European Influences From the seventeenth century onward, European influences were most marked in certain Indian urban centers, especially Bombay, Madras, and Calcutta. These cities became "presidency cities," an urban tripod on which the British East India Company based its monopoly of power. At each center the company erected a fort around which an urban complex expanded, attracting Indians as agents or servants of company officials. Each British community consisted of only a few hundred men, merchants, administrators, and troops, at least until the end of the eighteenth century. At first the British residents clung to European culture and isolated themselves, closing the great gate at night. Eventually, cultural interaction won out, and many European merchants lived with Indian women, wore Indian-style clothing, and ate Indian foods. A further cultural layer was added in the case of Madras and Calcutta, where a Hindu mercantile elite provided the continuity between the precolonial city structure and the presidency and also helped maintain ritual resources and the traditional sacred order until the nineteenth century.

■

URBAN LANDSCAPES IN EAST ASIA

Urban cultures were not new in the period after 1500, but their influence was changing as they shaped lives around the globe. With a population of more than half a million, Edo (modern Tokyo) was the world's largest city by the end of the seventeenth century, while the populations of Osaka and Kyoto approached those of sixteenth-century London and Paris, the two largest cities in contemporary Europe.

POPULAR AND URBAN CULTURE IN TOKUGAWA JAPAN

Despite the influence of Confucian thought that idealized the labors of the peasant farmer and the cult of the samurai (*bushido*) that praised the warrior in seventeenth- and eighteenth-century Japan, commerce flourished, merchants prospered, and expanding urban areas became the centers of a lively popular culture. The urban culture of the Tokugawa period presents a dramatic contrast to the aristocratic court culture, shogunal patronage of the arts, and the religious concerns of earlier eras. Concentrated in the cities of Osaka, Kyoto, and the capital of Edo, this new urban culture was a product of merchant patronage.

Merchant Culture and Society Merchants who patronized the arts in urban Japan under the Tokugawa did so as members of a lowly social class that was without political power. The children of merchants, for example, were forbidden to marry children of samurai. The legally defined class system of the Tokugawa has sometimes been referred to as a "caste system," somewhat similar to the rigid social order of South Asia. Merchant wealth was not translatable into either political power or higher social status, but it could be used to patronize artists whose work portrayed the lives and world of the urban townspeople. The new urban culture of Tokugawa Japan patronized by merchants included the colorful *kabuki* theater, the sophisticated and elaborate puppet theater (*bunraku*), woodblock prints of the *ukiyo*—the "floating world" of the urban pleasure quarters—and popular fiction.

Like theatrical or literary representations of the lives of townspeople in the works of Chikamatsu (1653–1725) or Saikaku (1642–1693), the new technology of woodblock prints visually illustrated the lives of urban townspeople. This technology developed as an art form that was affordable and accessible to a popular audience, since prints could be reproduced relatively easily and cheaply, unlike the ink paintings of court-patronized artists. Portraying both urban and rural landscapes, as well as actors and high-class entertainers known as *geisha,* woodblock prints vividly expressed the new popular culture of Tokugawa Japan. Guides to pleasure quarters such as the Yoshiwara ("Nightless City") in Edo were illustrated with the new technique, as were stories of urban life.

FIGURE 15.9 **Angyusai Enshi c. 1792. Fireworks at Ryoguku Bridge,** *View from the Balcony of the Yamashiro Teahouse.* (Edo or Modern Tokyo).

Two men, surrounded by courtesans and *geisha* (entertainers), are enjoying the view of the Sumida River from the teahouse balcony, while other courtesans arrive in a water taxi.

SOURCE: Art Institute of Chicago. Clarence Buckingham Collection, 1937.498. Photo © 1996, The Art Institute of Chicago. All Rights Reserved.

CHINESE CITY LIFE

Despite the rapid growth of urbanization, before the nineteenth century most people lived in rural areas and engaged primarily in agriculture. However, the rapid rate of increase in urban populations in the early modern era (1500–1800) is significant. The fact that the lives of even rural villagers were increasingly tied to the commercial economy and cultural life of cities is even more important. By late imperial times in China, people in the countryside everywhere were influenced by what went on in the cities. Though there was no increase in the general rate of urbanization in the eighteenth century, a hierarchy of central places became more widely developed and refined throughout every region of the Manchu Empire. Marketing networks and regional merchant associations tied rural markets to the cities.

By the seventeenth century the city of Nanjing, a national cultural center, had been eclipsed by Yangzhou, Suzhou, and Beijing. Like Nanjing, Yangzhou and Suzhou were cities of the Yangzi delta, whereas Beijing, like Edo in Japan, was the capital and thus distinct from other urban centers. These cities attracted educated men of both landed gentry and mercantile backgrounds who built gardens, formed literary societies, patronized the arts, and practiced conspicuous consumption. Surrounded by walls and moats, with drum and bell towers where watchmen signaled the opening and closing of the gates, cities enclosed markets; Confucian, Buddhist, and Daoist temples; and shrines to local gods, along with government offices, examination halls, the dwellings of wealthy members of the elite, shops, restaurants, and military barracks.

Beijing The Manchus built their capital at Beijing in the north on the base of the Ming and ▬▬▬▬ the earlier foundation of the Mongols, who originally inhabited the site as their capital. The imperial palace, known as the "Forbidden City," was approached through a series of ascending steps, from outer to inner chambers, paralleling the hierarchy of space with the hierarchy of status. The Son of Heaven was approached only at a great distance, even by his closest intimates, and never by the common man or woman. Like other Chinese cities, Beijing was surrounded by a wall, with gates that guards opened and closed on a regular schedule.

Cities apart from the capital, however, were less rigidly ordered. Cities such as Suzhou, which, somewhat like Venice, was known for its canals, grew from the natural demands of population growth in conditions of economic prosperity, not because of the administrative needs of the government. In the sixteenth century a Spanish priest noted in his account of China that the houses were as grand as those in Rome, the interiors were painted in brilliant colors and burnished gold, and all fine houses had ornamental pools and gardens.

■

CHANGING WORLD LANDSCAPES: TRADE, TECHNOLOGY, AND MATERIAL TRANSFORMATIONS

The frontiers of opportunity created by industrial expansion were not limited to European shores. The period between 1500 and 1800, the era of the European intrusion into Africa, Asia, and the Americas, saw the gradual expansion of world commerce. Until the end of the sixteenth century, Portugal (through Macao) and Spain (through Manila) were the principal providers of Asian wares to Europe. Then came the English East India Company (1600) and the Dutch, who opened a trading factory at Nagasaki, Japan, in 1600. Successful French efforts date from the reorganized French East India Company in the 1720s, but transshipment in Europe made Asian goods available to the French earlier.

Raw materials and manufactured goods from Asia and Europe were transshipped to Africa and the Americas, creating global access to commodities. Trade provided products that first introduced Europeans to the features and styles of African and Asian arts, just as Africans and Asians were introduced to European goods and styles. Increased production relied on expanding markets in Africa and Asia. Along the Atlantic coasts, new cities emerged to serve these markets, and these cities became centers for the diffusion of European technology.

In many parts of the world, power continued to be derived from control over technology and the valuable trade items that technology produced. Sometimes technological innovations were stimulated by the expansion of markets; elsewhere, artistic styles and innovation were valued for their own contribution to sumptuous urban life as well as to individual or social identity. Technological innovation and tradition helped create luxury goods for global distribution. The movement of material goods reflected the beginnings of a shared global culture.

CONSUMING CULTURES: EUROPE AND THE WORLD

The development of world markets significantly involved Africans, increasingly so after the seventeenth century. Early exchanges between African and European merchants were limited to coastal interactions in which Europeans were interlopers in preexisting trade patterns. Some cultural expressions developed specifically from the interactions. West African tourist art was produced from Sierra Leone to Nigeria: intricately carved ivory saltcellars made their way via European sailing ships to great dining halls in Europe. Elsewhere there were early signs of cultural resistance to European imports.

Reweaving the Threads of Culture   According to one Portuguese observer in 1505–1508, the first Europeans in the area of southeast Nigeria bought locally made textiles and other products, and only later did Europeans sell imported cloth to Africans. Even after 350 years of European trade, it was possible to find an extensive weaving tradition remaining in Igala, an Ibo community. A later British colonial official, writing in 1854, identified "country cloth ornamented with perforations . . . done during the weaving," a reference to the elaborate openwork cloth handwoven by women on vertical looms. Their named patterns referred to ancient titles of rank, and cloths were custom-made for specific individuals or ritual uses. This example suggests the importance of the individual cultural contexts into which items of European material culture and technology were selectively introduced.

Continuities in the meanings and use of material goods were maintained even when the goods themselves changed. Imported goods were often incorporated into local culture. For example, European merchants in the seventeenth and eighteenth centuries sold vast quantities of Asian silks and brocades on the Gold Coast to Akan weavers, who unraveled them and rewove the silken threads into the named patterns of traditional Akan *kente* cloth. The blacksmiths of northern Ghana raised their forges in a European style for the repair and manufacture of guns first introduced by European traders, but they built those raised forges to resemble female bodies, similar to the traditional smelting furnaces, which gave birth to iron.

Kingdom of the Kongo   In the kingdom of the Kongo, early European traders found an elaborate court life, richly enhanced by locally manufactured textiles and other material culture. The availability of European trade goods after the fifteenth century provided a new set of status markers for Kongolese royalty and their dependents. The fabrics brought by Portuguese traders were worn by their African wives and female trading partners in ostentatious displays of wealth. An early sixteenth-century European traveler in the Kongo described the variety of textiles available, including velvets, tissue, satins, taffetas, damasks, and raffia palm cloth. Local velvets made of palm fibers were replaced by foreign brocades and silks. By the end of the sixteenth century, a new elite culture had emerged from the commerce and ideas of the foreigners, blending Kongolese and European sources of wealth and power.

ASIAN CERAMICS AS CULTURAL COMMODITIES

In both East and West Asia, the skilled production of fine ceramics provided highly valued commodities of trade. Evidence of both technological and artistic achievement, such cultural commodities eventually became part of a shared global material culture. During the late imperial period in China (Ming [1368–1643] and Qing [1644–1911] dynasties), private kilns produced fine wares in traditional styles characteristic of earlier eras, such as the celadon (pale green), white, or colored glazes of the Song (960–1279) and Yuan (1279–1367) eras. But it was the imperial kilns, such as the one at Jingdezhen in the southeast, that stood at the forefront of technical and artistic development. By the early fifteenth century, the production of blue-and-white ware had reached a peak. Imperial kilns, which were protected by an order prohibiting private sale of this ware, enjoyed a monopoly on its production. Ming blue-and-white ware stimulated imitation in Persia, where the cobalt blue glaze originated, and Holland. During the fifteenth century the color range broadened and white porcelains were decorated with various enamel colors.

By the eighteenth century the height of elaborate design and rich color was reached. Vast quantities of vessels in different shapes and colors were produced by the imperial kilns and housed in the palaces of both the Manchu and the Chinese aristocracy. Designs included writhing dragons in blue on a white background, elegant multicolored flowers and figures in hues of rose, green, and yellow, and "oxblood" vessels, highly prized for their deep, pure dark red glaze. China was the world's leading porcelain producer before the eighteenth century, and the imperial kilns at Jingdezhen and Dehua in the southeast occupied the premier position in manufacture and export by the state. The scale of the Chinese porcelain industry greatly exceeded that of other regions, and Chinese export porcelain dominated Asian markets.

West Asian Ceramics West Asian pottery was affected by Chinese influence, which reached its height under the Mongol Empire. West Asian pottery was often extremely fine, with vessels so thin and delicate that they seemed translucent. Decoration included floral patterns, various styles of Arabic calligraphy, and human and animal figures. The colors were brilliant: scarlet, flaming yellow, turquoise (French for "Turkish" blue). The cobalt blue-and-white pottery that was believed to have first been made in China actually originated in Iran. Blue-and-white ware was also a favorite of the Ottomans.

In the sixteenth century Ottoman kilns at Iznik in western Anatolia produced a beautiful series of large dishes, mosque jars, ewers, and bowls in these colors. In the following century a

FIGURE 15.10 Turkish Ceramic Jar from Iznik (Fifteenth Century).

Iznik became an Ottoman center for production of high-quality ceramics, whose fine design and decoration influenced artisans in Asia and Europe.

SOURCE: Victoria & Albert Museum, London/Art Resource, New York.

lively red was sometimes added. In addition to vessels, potters in Iran and Anatolia also specialized in making glazed colored tiles, beginning in the thirteenth century. They were especially used to cover the walls, domes, and prayer niches of mosques; the domes and walls of tombs; and the walls of *madrasas* and palaces. Outstanding examples dating from the sixteenth to eighteenth centuries can today be found in Isfahan and Istanbul.

TRADE AND TRANSFORMATIONS

There was great demand in Europe, Africa, and Asia for high-quality imported ceramics. Chinese glazed ceramics and their European derivatives, which were major trade items, were carried over long distances and were considered items of great value and status. In West Africa, members of royal families acquired German and English-made china, even broken pieces, and incorporated them into the architectural features of their houses. Chinese celadon has been excavated from eastern and southern African archaeological sites such as Great Zimbabwe dating from the twelfth to nineteenth centuries. Porcelains produced in Southeast Asia, especially in Thailand and Vietnam, occupied a major place in Southeast Asian trade, supplying a substantial portion of the market in better quality imported ware.

Imitation China Soon after Asian goods became plentiful in Europe, Chinese porcelain became so much in demand that Europeans began to imitate it. To this very day, porcelain is called "china" in English. By the mid-seventeenth century both the Dutch (by 1614) and the French (by 1640) were decorating faience, a glazed earthenware, with Chinese motifs, and these designs quickly spread throughout Europe. Within a century Japanese porcelains were also being copied in Europe. The great German porcelain factory at Meissen opened in 1710, and its earliest wares were decorated in the Chinese style.

European production did not curtail importation of large quantities of porcelain from China and Japan. At the same time that European potteries were imitating East Asian motifs in response to the eighteenth-century taste for the quaint and exotic, Asians produced porcelain in European shapes, decorated in the Western manner with Western scenes. Similarly, the styles and demands of distant world markets from Accra to Zanzibar dictated the shapes of British iron implements and other European manufactured goods.

Lacquerware and Wallpaper Lacquerware was another import from Asia that had great influence on European art and crafts. Much was imported, but it was soon also being copied in Europe. The Dutch and the English made lacquerware furniture decorated with Chinese motifs, and the Martin workshop in France, famous for its imitation of Chinese lacquer, became a state factory in 1748. Martin lacquerware was so admired and in demand that a branch of the factory opened in Berlin. Chinese wallpaper was another import in such great demand, especially in England, that it had an important impact on European crafts.

TECHNOLOGY, TEXTILES, AND TRADE IN ASIA

More than European technology helped to determine many of the qualitative aspects of human experience around the globe. In many parts of the world, power continued to be derived from control over technology and the valuable trade items that technology produced. Sometimes technological innovations were stimulated by the expansion of markets; elsewhere, artistic style and innovation were valued for their own contribution to sumptuous urban life as well as to individual or social identity. Technological innovation and tradition helped create luxury goods for global distribution. The movement of material goods reflected the beginnings of a shared global culture.

The biggest imports to Europe from Asia were raw and woven silk from China and linens and cotton muslins from India. The fast colors, fine weaving, and especially the imaginative designs of "Indian cloths," as all Asian fabric came to be known in England, made it popular and subject to imitation all over Europe. The influence of Asian fabric designs extended far beyond silk, linen, and muslin.

Chinese Silk In China sericulture, or silk production, was the major textile industry. There was a high demand for silk, not only by the court aristocracy but also by wealthy merchants who populated the prosperous cities of the Yangzi delta region. Picture patterns were woven on silk, and silk garments were highly prized. The organization of labor in the Chinese silk industry was specialized and had some similarities to that of the European textile industry. The textile industry in Europe was directly fed by merchants who had capital at their disposal and would use it to advance raw materials to craftsmen. In China such capital support was most visible in the silk industry, which needed costly raw materials. In a typical Chinese silkweaving workshop, the workers might be members of a household who received yarn from wealthy commercial firms; or they might weave as either piece-rate workers or with their own materials. By the eighteenth century commercial forces in the Chinese silk industry had reduced many highly skilled urban weavers almost to the status of daily wage workers completely dependent on export demand.

West Asian Textiles In West Asia, in addition to the interest in ceramics, enormous attention was also given to the production of textiles, especially after 1500. Silk, linen, cotton, and wool were the raw materials. Satin, brocade, and velvet were the products. From diaphanous gowns to thick felt cloaks, the choices, as reflected by a vast technical terminology, were astonishing. Clothing and fabric became major items of international trade during the expansion of maritime commerce after 1500. This trade brought to other parts of the world such words as damask, sash, muslin, chiffon, cotton, and taffeta. Cotton and silk woven in all major urban areas of West Asia were supplemented by a woolen industry based on the manufacture of carpets and coarse materials.

Carpets After the Turkish invasion of West Asia, carpets became major items of international trade. In their homes most West Asians sat on stools or sofas covered with textiles and ate and slept on the floor, making themselves comfortable with carpets, cushions, and mattresses. The textile industry therefore provided important products for daily life. Carpets in particular were utilitarian as well as decorative. The appearance of Turkish carpets in European paintings from the fifteenth and sixteenth centuries demonstrates their significance as an item of trade. Persians rapidly adopted the art of carpet making from the Turks and then made their own innovations, producing some of the finest carpets ever made. The Persians, in turn, stimulated carpet production in Mughal India.

From the sixteenth century on, Iran and Ottoman Turkey emerged as producers of highly prized wool or wool and silk rugs and carpets, which were produced not as part of the nomadic economy but as an urban industry, located especially in Bursa, Tabriz, and Isfahan. A similar pattern of regional concentration of textile industries was found in the Indian subcontinent, which remained one of the greatest exporters of cotton goods to the world market. The four significant industrial regions of India specializing in the manufacture of cotton fabrics for the world market were Punjab, Gujarat, the Coromandel coast, and Bengal.

Southeast Asian Textile Trade Situated between the world's two major sources of fine cloth—India for cotton and China for silks—Southeast Asia became known as a consumer rather than producer of textiles. There was high demand for Indian cotton textiles in Southeast Asia, though cloth was still Southeast Asia's major item of manufacture, and cotton was the leading agricultural product after foodstuffs. European traders showed great interest in the dyestuffs of both Southeast Asia and parts of Africa, importing indigo and other techniques for their own textile industries.

The Indian Calico "Crisis" Synonymous with changing European cultural values in the late seventeenth century was the increasing popularity of Indian calicoes, printed cotton textiles manufactured in India and imported into England. Indian calicoes looked like the elite fabrics of Europe, but they were more practical: they were easier to wash, and they were cheaper. Furthermore, they were popular with all classes. This worried local textile manufacturers in England, and many called for restraint in the purchase of foreign imports. By 1719 mutinous weavers in London rioted and actually went through the streets tearing calicoes off the women's backs. In 1720 the British government passed a bill to prohibit the consumption of multicolored printed cotton fabric. In spite of this act, the taste for calicoes continued. Imported Indian calicoes were smuggled into England and worn by stubborn and fashionable women until the British textile industry finally succeeded, later in the eighteenth century, in developing mass production and the complex printing and dyeing technology needed to produce the desired fabric.

■

SOCIAL LANDSCAPES: TRANSFORMATIONS IN COMMUNITY AND CULTURAL LIFE

Performance arts, performed types of cultural expression such as drama, dance, and festival, were powerful reminders around the globe that however individualistic the new urbanized, industrialized world encouraged people to be, the weaving and reweaving of the social fabric was a communal undertaking. Shared values continued to be constructed and reconstructed in the face of changing material conditions brought about by global trade or commercialization and industrialization. The successful maintenance of community was even more necessary as the density and diversity of populations increased in urban environments. There were many forms of social interaction in which peoples around the world found amusement and entertainment and through which individuals redefined themselves in relation to the changing material world.

EUROPEAN POPULAR CULTURE AND COMMUNITY LIFE

The various ways in which ordinary women and men expressed and amused themselves in the early modern era were, like almost everything else in Europe, influenced by institutional Christianity and changed as that influence waned. Individuals tended to amuse themselves differently in their homes and with their families than they did in their communities, in public, although at times the distinction between public and private activities became blurred. In European cities and towns, both new and traditional cultural forms shaped the social time enjoyed by their inhabitants.

Games and Amusements The most widespread and common examples of popular culture were games and similar amusements in which Europeans participated as individuals. The community festivities were occasions by which Europeans jointly marked and celebrated annual events. Aspects of both forms of popular culture were variously gender and age separated. The games and pastimes of individuals or families remained fairly constant over the centuries. They ranged from sedentary activities, such as storytelling and being read to or reading, to games requiring skill or luck and activities of a physical nature.

Oral recitation was the most common form of popular literary activity and remained a fashionable genre even after printing made books more available. It did not require literacy, only attention; informative as well as amusing, it was a major means of influencing and educating ordinary people. Gambling and games of chance, especially playing dice, were popular amusements, as was dancing. People of all ages played games that provided physical exercise, such as hide-and-seek, blindman's bluff, and the frog game, a game of catching those who pushed a seated player around. More vigorously physical activities, such as wrestling and racing, were primarily the province of able-bodied males. Otherwise games were not gender restricted on the whole: both men and women danced, gambled, and listened. Nor, after the sixteenth century, were there age restrictions on most forms of popular culture: adults and children played the same games, together and separately.

Elite amusements were transformed during the post-Columbian era. During the reign of King James in the early seventeenth century, the British monarchy supported elaborate productions, keen on demonstrating the pinnacle of worldliness, military prowess, and technological achievement over which they ruled. In 1613 on the Thames in front of Whitehall Palace, the poet John Taylor staged mock battles featuring a wood and paper version of the North African port of Algiers, Turkish galleys, Venetian caravels, and fireworks, to the delight of James and the huge crowds on the riverbanks.

Religion and Popular Culture Though gender and age may not have influenced individual participation in popular activities, both social position and organized religion did. Both Catholic and Protestant churches condemned games of chance as immoral and parlor games as indecent; they closed theaters and banned dancing and brutal physical sports, which often did degenerate into brawls. In sixteenth-century Geneva, under the influence of the religious ideals of the Protestant leader John Calvin, expressions of popular culture such as dancing, gambling, drunkenness, profanity, singing bawdy and licentious songs, and reading immoral secular books were considered misdemeanors and punished by censure, fine, or imprisonment.

Such prohibitions sometimes had an economic impact as well. In the sixteenth-century German city of Strasbourg, when Martin Luther closed down the brothels, prostitutes petitioned against this decision on the basis that they pursued their profession for bread, not because they liked it. In England Cromwell's government (1649–1660) used military patrols to control traditional forms of popular culture and enforce a rigid code of Puritan morality. Horse racing, cock fighting, and bear baiting were strictly forbidden; noisy gatherings on the Sabbath were broken up; use of profane language was punished; and strolling minstrels and stage players were arrested.

FIGURE 15.11 European Courtly Masquerader, Eighteenth-Century France.

Fanciful European costumes such as this "Coiffure, ou le Triomphe de la Liberte" influenced African and Caribbean masquerades

SOURCE: John Nunley and Judith Bettelheim, *Caribbean Festival Arts* (Seattle: University of Washington Press, 1988).

Communal popular culture was closely tied to institutional religion until at least the eighteenth century, though religious control and influence tended to diminish in proportion to the growth of secularism. For example, the Church originally monopolized and utilized the theater, sponsoring mystery plays as effective instruments of popular religion. As theater became more secularized, both Catholic and Protestant churches opposed and became hostile towards it. Actors were denied the sacraments and thus excluded from the body of believers; in some Protestant communities, such as Calvinist Geneva, theaters were closed and actors prosecuted. Yet theater continued as a major form of popular culture, the seventeenth century being an especially great age for drama. The flourishing of theater, performance, and opera was a reflection of the vigor of an increasingly secular society that enjoyed this form of popular culture and of powerful rulers who not only enjoyed it but also patronized and protected it.

Festivals of various sorts, relying on collective social bonds, were frequent, with all members of a community—children and adults, rich and poor, urban and rural—often taking part on equal footing. In Europe the most common expressions of collective popular culture were Twelfth Night (much more celebrated than Christmas until modern times), Shrove Tuesday and Mardi Gras (pre-Lenten celebrations), and All Souls Day (which is celebrated as Halloween in modern America). In rural areas special events revolved around seasonal activities such as harvests and also reflected the church calendar; urban festivals were connected with the specific guilds that organized and sponsored them and, since each guild had a patron saint, with the Church calendar as well.

These popular festivals took a variety of forms, such as masquerades, parades, and carnivals. They might last several days and were means to release social tensions as well as being sources of entertainment, frivolity, and popular activities. These community events were occasions for role-playing, cross-dressing, and generally inverting the social order. Carnival goers frequently became unruly, angry, and violent, thus giving the carnivals the character of popular social and political protest.

COMMUNITY AND CULTURAL PERFORMANCE IN WEST AFRICA

Performance arts helped to define—and sometimes expand—the cultural boundaries and conventions of society. For example, in West African masquerades such as the Yoruba *gelede,* men assumed the roles of women and demonstrated aspects of proper and acceptable behavior in their dramatic performances. Masquerades also functioned as sites of cultural transformation. In the context of traditional community events, people gave interpretive performances of the transformations they were experiencing in their changing cultural and social landscapes. West African masquerades register the processes of borrowing in their incorporation of cultural items ranging from dress to musical instruments to dance styles. These masquerades involved pantomime, acrobatics, costume, sculpture, dance, poetry, satire, reverence, and resistance; they served a variety of social, religious, and political purposes and provide historians with valuable information about how people viewed their changing world.

African-Caribbean Cultural Performance An example of the process of cultural borrowing and transformation is the popular Caribbean masquerade known as *Jonkonnu,* which dates to at least the eighteenth century. From Jamaica to the Bahamas, colorful, costumed dancers in street celebrations and African-derived festivals of harvest and new year combined with the Catholic pre-Lenten carnival form of European origin. The far-flung fame of John Konny, an African trader born in West Africa in the 1660s, may also have inspired the original masquerade.

CULTURAL PERFORMANCE IN EAST ASIA

Performances of dramas set to music—operas—were popular with audiences in China's towns, cities, and countryside. By the late imperial period, many forms of folk songs and local traditions contributed to distinctive regional operatic forms. Highly stylized makeup and acting, along with high-pitched, emphatic singing, evolved into the familiar Chinese or Beijing opera of modern times. The drama of the commercial urban theater, which first grew out of local opera troupes that performed without fixed scripts or theaters, was combined with regional opera traditions. There was a continuous transmission of urban drama into the countryside, as opera troupes performed at temple festivals. Drama was an important means of cultural integration and transmission between urban areas and the countryside. Both the themes, which were based largely on historical fiction, and the performances themselves were related in an interlocking way with storytellers, acrobats, and other kinds of street entertainers, who used some of the same story cycles.

Gender and Theater   By the early eighteenth century, actors had their own guild in the capital, and public theaters were open to audiences from all classes of society. Both imperial and merchant patronage played key roles in the growth of theatrical institutions, but in China as elsewhere actors and the theater were often subject to social, or even legal, restrictions by moralizing censors. Like the *onnagata,* the female impersonators of the Japanese *kabuki* drama, female impersonators in Chinese opera could be immensely popular with male audiences, and the sexual overtones of dramatic performances evoked moral outrage from some critics. The popularity of female impersonators in the eighteenth century conferred a new stylishness on homosexual relationships. In contrast, the Tokugawa state in Japan, fearing homosexual and heterosexual promiscuity and prostitution, tried to control the social influence of the theatrical world by passing legal prohibitions against the participation of male youths or women.

Cultural Continuities   Cultural performances also provided an expression of the continuities of traditional forms of authority and power relations, including those of gender. Whether in urban settings or in rural villages, people in China marked the passages of life with specialized rituals and ceremonies. Weddings and funerals were the most important of these, and both were carried out by wealthy elites according to elaborate Confucian prescriptions carefully recorded in ritual texts, though in the countryside and among the poor much simpler forms naturally prevailed.

Community holidays were celebrated at the New Year and at other seasonal occasions, such as the mid-autumn festival celebrated on the fifteenth day of the eighth month by eating "moon cakes" and viewing the moon. The spring festival was a time for people to visit and tend family graves, thus renewing their link with their ancestors. In contrast, a festival held in the seventh month to appease the spirits of the untended dead was a community event and required the services of both Buddhist and Daoist priests.

Japanese Drama Merchant patronage in urban centers such as Osaka in eighteenth-century
Japan supported the development of popular dramatic forms that drew large
audiences. Unlike the "Punch and Judy" puppet shows in Europe, *bunraku* is serious drama,
not comedy, in which three highly skilled and trained puppeteers manipulate elaborate and
lifelike puppets. Like Chinese opera and in contrast to the religious-inspired Noh drama that
developed in the fourteenth and fifteenth centuries, the *kabuki* theater makes use of flamboyant costuming and elaborate makeup (rather than masks as in Noh), as well as exaggerated
gestures and vocal effects to dramatize the feelings and responses of characters in the stories.
The dramas performed in both *bunraku* and *kabuki* theater were based on themes that ranged
from historical events to domestic tragedies drawn from the everyday life of the townspeople;
these dramas had the power to move audiences composed of samurai, merchants, and commoners.

CULTURE AND COMMUNITY IN SOUTHEAST ASIA

Community festivals in Southeast Asia had many features in common with festivals in other
parts of the world—a religious core, sense of community, gambling, theater, buffoonery, and
the lifting of usual taboos. In contrast to other parts of the world where festivals were an opportunity to alter temporarily the order of things, the public festivals of Southeast Asia appear to have reinforced, rather than challenged, traditional hierarchies. Disorder, sexual license, and social mixing might occur around the periphery of festivals, but there is little
evidence of the structured role reversals that are observable elsewhere.

Royal and religious festivals were occasions for political authority to reinforce its power
through displays of pomp and grandeur. In Southeast Asia the display of high status was accomplished with processions of elephants, horsemen, soldiers, and slaves. Leather shadow
puppets were used for more humble entertainment, telling the stories of the Hindu gods and
heroes in the Mahabharata or Ramayana. Music was a permanent presence in theater spectacles as well as in royal processions. Varieties of percussion instruments as well as stringed instruments made up orchestras for the performance of folk music as well as royal ceremonial
music.

■

THE CHANGING LANDSCAPE OF THE HUMAN BODY

The most intimate site of cultural transformations was the human body itself. The human
body's physical shape and requirements constituted the common experience of the human
species; at the same time, the body was in some ways the site of the most profound cultural
differences. Through such things as diet, dress, and sexual practice, the human body changed
in response to transformations in the material world while displaying continuities with inherited cultural practices.

THE BODY AS COMMODITY

Prostitution, which began to appear in major Southeast Asian cities in the late sixteenth cen-
tury, was slave prostitution and may have been stimulated by demand from Europeans and
Chinese who were not familiar with the custom of temporary marriage as practiced among
Southeast Asians. It may also have been a response to Muslim concern over the impropriety of

temporary marriages with foreigners and nonbelievers. Women who engaged in prostitution were unmarriagable.

In West and Central African urban centers, during the era of the trans-Atlantic slave trade, prostitution increased dramatically, a direct result of the commercialization of values and the demands of a European-driven cash economy. The mentality of the cash economy in which goods and services became commodities that could be bought and sold infused a widening realm of economic and social transactions. By the end of the eighteenth century, the effects of slavery devalued human worth and stereotyped Africans as different from Europeans. These two effects in turn contributed to the birth of myths concerning the sexuality of Africans and to some extent all non-Europeans. But Africans, as slaves, were particularly subjected to the most invidious bias and distortion based on contemporary European beliefs in the inferiority of blacks. Travelers' tales of promiscuity and lasciviousness among Africans became firmly entrenched notions that condoned and encouraged exploitation—both sexual and economic.

CULTURAL MODIFICATIONS OF THE HUMAN BODY

Cultural differences in food, clothing, and body art fascinated Europeans and other world travelers. Some voyages of exploration carried with them artists who recorded the fantastic sights they encountered. For example, sketches and paintings of Polynesian life by the artist John Webber, who visited Tahiti in 1777, included the portrait of a Ra'iatean chieftainess Poetua, whose body was covered with delicate tattoo patterns and traditional bark cloth.

Tattooing Tattooing, body painting by surgically introducing dyes under the skin, was also widely practiced in Southeast Asia, where some scholars believe that the influence of Islamic prohibitions on the practice led to it being replaced by the technique of batik, or cloth painting, as a religious statement and status indicator. European travelers copied the practice of tattooing, and some exhibited themselves in circuses and fairs. One of the first Europeans to do so was Jean-Baptiste Cabri, who had jumped ship in 1799 in the Marquesas and whose tattooed skin was preserved and exhibited in Europe after his death.

Scarification and Dress in Africa Africans used various means to enhance their natural beauty: scarification (intentional cuts in the skin, said by the Yoruba to be like the civilizing lines of patterned agricultural fields); chipping or filing of teeth; piercing and stretching of lips, nose, and ears; body painting; tattooing; and elements of dress and coiffure. Dress marked ethnicity, gender, status, rank, occupation, accomplishment, and age. Certain hairstyles were worn only by slaves. Certain dress or cloth patterns were appropriated by persons of wealth and power and prohibited to others of lower status.

The European traveler John Barbot (1732) described the clothing of Senegalese noblemen as consisting of a shirt, wide breeches, and cap. Commoners wore a loincloth or wraparound skirt and at times draped a cloak or mantle around one or both shoulders. It is likely that then as now the individual cloth patterns were named and associated with proverbial meanings. The successful merchant traders of West and Central Africa wore layers of imported cloth and sometimes feathered top hats and canes to express their distinctive, albeit intermediary, cultural position. More hidden expressions of personhood such as circumcision or pubic beads worn below the waist also contributed to individual identity and helped to sustain tradition amidst the overlay of imported textiles.

FIGURE 15.12 The Marquesan Tattoos of European Jean-Baptiste Cabri, ca. Late 1700s.

SOURCE: From *Voyages in Various Parts of the World 1813–14.* Volume 1. By Johann Langsdorff. New York Public Library, General Research Division, Astor, Lenox and Tilden Foundations.

Dress and Identity in Japan In Japan dress defined a person's identity geographically and historically and linked that individual to a specific community. People of all ages wore the same basic shape and style of Japanese robed garment known as the *kosode,* but drastic variations in the fabric's inward-facing pattern represented subtle reminders of distinct gender, social status, and cultural values.

During the Tokugawa period, large pictorial patterns became associated with women's garments, and men's robes became increasingly subdued and limited to stripes or small, patterned geometric figures. Wealthy people with high status had large wardrobes, and each class in the social hierarchy was distinguished by certain dress patterns. The widespread value placed on literacy for seventeenth-century women resulted in the incorporation of written characters, literary allusions, and riddles into the design of their inner garments, a practice that suggested that women should express their learning with subtlety and indirectness.

Dress in Southeast Asia To early European travelers, Southeast Asians appeared practically naked, since both men and women often left their upper bodies bare. This condition was natural because of climate, but it also reflected the belief that the body itself was a work of art and needed little adornment. Southeast Asians did not find it necessary to create artificial markers of gender through dress, hairstyle, or speech patterns, unlike many other societies which stressed such distinctions. An unsewn strip of cloth wound around the body was used by both men and women for clothing. Between the fifteenth and seventeenth centuries, this basic pattern of dress was transformed partly by the influence of Islam and later by European customs. A frequent innovation was the wearing of a jacket of European or West Asian design over an expensive cloth used as a sarong, the traditional draped garment.

Dress in India Religious ideology and practice in some cultures dictated certain standards of dress and decoration of the body. In India, Sanskrit religious law (*dharmasastra*) was presented in the eighteenth century as a manual for orthodox Hindu women in the form of a text titled *Guide to the Religious Status and Duties of Women* (ca. 1720–1750). This wide-ranging digest of rulings included prohibitions against the nakedness of women during the day and against the wearing of heavy earrings during lovemaking. The rulings stated that a woman should not show her breasts or navel and that her clothing should reach her ankles (obviously directed at women who did not work in the fields). Women made a distinctive forehead mark (*tilaka*) with saffron as a sign of marital happiness; by this it was suggested that a woman's religious devotion should be directed to her husband.

Dress in Industrial Europe In a similar vein, Christian European urban dress bound female forms, restricted movement, and represented increasing levels of male control after 1500. Tight sleeves on women's apparel "protected" the wearers from kitchen hazards. Men's dress emphasized their military role. Until the seventeenth century female dress was linked to devotional and virtuous roles and meanings, with sexuality hinted at but not expressed. An important part of dress included the use of lace made by women in convents. By the early seventeenth century, the secularizing influence of commerce on class and gender was visible, French necklines had plunged, and fashion, even that of the king, used abundant lace.

Differentiation of dress in Europe was also determined by status, position, and rank. Women and men who labored dressed very much alike: their clothes were of sturdy fabric (usually woolen) in somber colors, and their wardrobes were limited. The privileged could be recognized by their elaborate, colorful fabrics, embroidered gold and silver threads, and jeweled embellishments. Privileged men and women wore padded clothes and corsets; wigs or elaborately coiffed and powdered hair; and carried handkerchiefs, fans, canes, and purses. Both genders were fashion-conscious consumers of textiles in the global marketplace.

Changing Dress in the Americas The textile trade established important economic and technological connections between parts of the new global order. Sometimes the arrival of new goods set up new patterns of consumption; sometimes a new conceptual framework was needed. Among the peoples of the Inca Empire, for example, cloth had a cultural meaning and was used as a political statement. The cloth (*aqsu*) that wrapped the female body was believed to be a second skin and so was directly associated with self-identity and genealogy. This cultural concept of cloth was used to legitimize political authority, which was believed to descend from the first people who had emerged into life fully clothed. After the Spanish invasion, dress styles changed as the Incans lost political and cultural autonomy.

ALTERING THE HUMAN BODY: CHANGING DIETS

The availability of new foods and attendant changes in diet also significantly transformed human physiology, identity, and well-being. The global exchange of foods and crops altered traditional patterns of consumption.

Travelers' Diets Some of the first dietary changes were experienced on the very ships that transferred the new crops from one continent to another. From their earliest voyages, European sailing ships carried their own supplies of foodstuffs, relying on dried, un-leavened bread ("biscuit"), which was subject to weevils, and dried, salted cod and other pre-served meats, some of which became so dried that sailors carved them as souvenirs rather than challenge their teeth. The uncertainties of long sea voyages such as those across the Atlantic occasioned the need to eat shark meat or seabirds or to buy rats at exhorbitant prices from the ship's rat catcher. More than half of Vasco da Gama's crew died of scurvy, as did countless other sailors, until seafarers recognized the link between deficiency diseases and citrus fruits and greenstuffs. By 1601 the East India Company ships were stopping in Madagascar to ob-tain citrus fruits for their voyages.

Consuming Cultures Alcoholic beverages, such as fermented wines, ales and beers brewed from grains, and distilled liquors, and other drinks from fruits, flowers (such as the Arabic rosewater), and grains, were found in various forms wherever they were not outlawed by religious law. Some drinks, such as West African palm wine, were tapped fresh from the source and then allowed to ferment into an alcoholic beverage. The manufac-ture of palm wine was no doubt common in ancient times in West Africa as elsewhere, since the theme of drunkenness runs throughout historical tales and is even found in creation myths of the Yoruba.

DAILY LIVES

THE DAILY LIVES OF TRAVELERS AND MERCHANTS

When the crew members of Columbus's ship were washed ashore, they became accidental tourists of a sort. However, most travel encounters were more intentional, and they served as collecting points for the exchange of objects, songs, and ideas. In Europe official town delegations in-cluded wealthy merchants and artists. For exam-ple, the 1520 entourage arriving from Nuremberg for Hapsburg Emperor Charles V's coronation in-cluded the artist Albrecht Durer. Like any tourist, he did some shopping along the way, keeping a careful account of his expenses:

> I have bought a tract of Luther's for 5 weisspfen-nigs. And I spent another weisspfennig for the Condem-nation of Luther (that pious man). Also 1 weisspfennig for a rosary . . . I gave 2 weisspfennigs for a little death's head. I spent 1 weisspfennig for beer and bread.

In coastal West Africa tourism was big busi-ness during the Atlantic era. Ivory saltcellars in the Senegambia were carved locally and sold to sailors, who carried them back to Europe. The elaborate scenes depicted sixteenth-century Por-tuguese and Africans in distinctive dress of the day. In the seaports and on board ships, trade lin-gos (partial languages called pidgins and creoles) provided one means of exchanging goods and ideas. Sea shanties—the "ditties" sung by sailors while working and relaxing—were heard daily by African slaves and workers, who incorporated these musical styles into their own traditions.

And how might we interpret the circa 1678 wampum—beads made from shell and sewn into patterns on a leather strip used by Iroquoian peo-ple to record significant events in symbolic form—in the design of a votive belt to the Virgin Mary? Was it Indian devotion or a tourist art mar-ket of French Jesuits that led to its manufacture and transport across the Atlantic to the Cathedral at Chartres? The contradictions and complexities of the objects of material culture serve as vivid re-minders of the contradictions and complexities of daily life.

SOURCE: Lisa Jardine, *Worldly Goods: A New History of the Renaissance* (New York: Nan A. Talese/Doubleday, 1996), pp. 333–4.

Foods and drugs used for religious experiences and medicinal cures constantly circulated between cultures. Whether an item was considered medicine, foodstuff, or recreational drug largely depended on its availability and use, as is illustrated by the changing available quantity, value, and use of opium, which was once a women's tonic, or by similar changes in the status of sugar, which was originally considered a spice. By the 1670s the Dutch were willing to trade New York to the British in exchange for the sugar-producing territories of Surinam.

Columbus carried tobacco, originally a substance cultivated by indigenous peoples of the Americas for use in religious ceremonies, to Europe, where its use as a cure for migraines and its initial condemnation by King James I in 1604 and by Pope Innocent X in 1650 were soon overcome by exceedingly popular recreational use, though this indulgence was a male prerogative. European trade spread the knowledge of (and vocabulary for) tobacco from Lapland to Africa, where both men and women smoked pipes and inhaled other substances for recreation and for the hallucinogenic and religious experiences that resulted. By the 1790s tobacco and opium were routinely smoked together in China, despite prohibitions of the Ming era. The Spanish began to use other substances, such as quinine, extracted from the bark of the South American cinchona tree, against malaria by 1638. The resulting protection and curative effects subsequently enabled Europeans to expand into more tropical parts of the world.

Coffee, Tea, and Chocolate The era between 1500 and 1800 introduced new foods and beverages, including coffee from Africa and the Ottoman Empire to North Africa and Europe. The first coffeehouse in Constantinople was established in 1554 and in Oxford, England, in 1650, both parts of the world relying on beans from Mocha, near Aden, at the southern tip of the Red Sea, for their supplies. In the eighteenth century, the Dutch began to grow coffee in Java, as did the English in the Caribbean. Chinese tea was known for some time before it was eagerly adopted in Japan and Russia and first sold in England in the mid-seventeenth century. One pound of tea leaves could produce almost 300 cups of the drink; by the end of the eighteenth century, 1.8 million pounds of tea were consumed annually in England.

From the opposite direction, chocolate traveled from the Americas to Europe, and its trade was initially monopolized by Spain and Portugal. In Aztec society, cacao was a luxury item; the beans were used as currency and prepared in many different ways. In sixteenth-century Mexico cacao beans were dried, roasted, and then pounded to a paste with water; spices were added, and the mixture was shaken into a froth. The concoction was offered to early Spanish visitors at a banquet; they confronted the mixture with apprehension and fear. However, popular European opinion soon agreed with Bernardino de Sahagun, a Jesuit observer, who stated that "it gladdens one, refreshes one, consoles one, invigorates one."

Foods from the Americas The increasing populations of Europe, Africa, and Asia selectively embraced other crops from the Americas: the potato, the tomato, and maize. The potato reached England via Drake's voyage from Colombia, and it was immediately put into cultivation, though at first as an ornamental plant rather than as a food. As late as 1774, Prussian famine victims of Kolberg refused to touch a wagon load of potatoes sent by Frederick the Great. The potato, which originated in the Andes, enabled a huge population expansion to occur in Ireland after it was accepted there. The Irish reliance on the potato as a staple, however, created a devastating dependence, as nineteenth-century famines made abundantly clear.

Population in China increased dramatically thanks to the introduction of maize, sweet potatoes, and peanuts after 1500. In West Africa the introduction of the groundnut (peanut), chili pepper, cassava, tomato, and maize from the Americas provided the basis for agricultural production on marginal lands and population expansion and supported diets during the transshipment of slaves. By the end of the eighteenth century, these foods had become defining staples of local cuisine and were demanded by slaves on trans-Atlantic voyages, even while eschewed by their European masters.

Changing Asian Diets Similarly, the story of flat noodles originating in China is an example of Asian foods introduced through overland commercial connections. The noodles were carried by Indians and Arabs to the Mediterranean trade cities of Venice, Genoa, and Florence. By the fifteenth century Chinese-influenced Mongols working in Italian kitchens served the fare.

South Asian diets were also significantly transformed after 1500. The establishment of Mughal rule in India brought new everyday foods and methods of food preparation. Kebabs made of bite-sized meats grilled on spits, pilafs (dishes of rice with shredded meat), fruits served with meats, nuts (sweetmeats), and the wrapping of foods with delicate sheets of hammered gold and silver (easily absorbed by the body) all created a sumptuous and distinctive cuisine. The introduction of peppers from the Americas forever altered the taste of curry blends of spice mixtures, which were in turn carried from the Indian subcontinent to the markets and cuisines of Africa and other parts of Asia, and eventually back to the Caribbean.

Ironically, while certain foods became common to multiple regions, they also came to be used more and more distinctively as forms of cultural expression. One aspect of a diverse city life was its embrace of sojourners and the opportunities for eating out. In India, buying food on the street was rare, but elsewhere streets and compounds catered to visitors. In eighteenth-century Qing China, city restaurants served banquets for all levels of clients and catered to Muslim diets by excluding pork or by taking into account the Central Asian preference for beef and lamb. Regional tastes and dietary practices continued to be expressed. Only the world's urban elites participated in anything like an international cuisine, as their access to global connections allowed.

SUMMARY

The expansion of Europe after 1500 had profound effects on landscapes, material culture, and social life around the globe. As technology transformed the physical landscapes and trade transformed the material world, people experienced these changes and responded to them in culturally distinctive ways. The material advantages that resulted from exploration, conquest, and the establishment of overseas empires was quickly apparent to Europeans. Contacts in Asia made fortunes for those engaged in the spice and tea trade. The European-African-American Atlantic connection and its subsequent extension into the Pacific opened a colonial treasure chest of natural resources such as precious metals (especially silver), furs, fish and timber, and the products of slavery and plantation production, such as sugar, tobacco, and cotton.

At the level of daily life, global contacts provided ordinary Europeans such mundane things as new foods: tea from China and coffee from Africa; potatoes, tobacco, maize, chocolate, tomatoes—altogether more than 100 crops—from the Americas. The material results of European global expansion obviously contributed to reshaping the lives of all Europeans. In

East Asia, however, contact with Europe had relatively little real impact, apart from the indirect, though long-lasting and profound, effects of new food crops. In other parts of the world, such as West Africa or the North American continent, contact with Europeans brought new goods that were integrated into the cultural and social worlds of inhabitants or new technologies that altered traditional patterns of life, such as horses and guns for the peoples of the Great Plains.

After 1500 the growing importance of cities across the globe and the expansion of trade transformed the way people thought about themselves and the world they inhabited. The changes experienced by people living in urban environments were not simply changes in the economy and scale of community; they constituted qualitative transformations in the individuals' daily lives. The industrial revolution recast the role of the individual as a participant in communal life. Workers became interchangeable, anonymous individuals in urban landscapes, though they continued to participate in communal rituals and festivals that evoked preindustrial times. For pioneers on the frontiers of the new global society, such as the sailor or merchant, life could be lonely, but also full of opportunity for social and economic mobility that could reduce the constraints of birthright and predetermined status.

These cultural changes are sometimes obscured when compared with the historical impact of commercial, and later industrial, capitalism. When considered together, however, cultural and commercial changes provide the context for seeing how individuals and their communities were redefined at the levels of daily life and experience. In the following chapters, we focus on changing structures of political authority, their ideological underpinnings, and the impact of these changes on the lives of men and women from the late eighteenth to the end of the twentieth century.

FIGURE 15.13 The Rituals of the New Beverage Coffee, Shown Here in a Coffeehouse at the Kuchen Garden, Gaststate, Were Satirized in Bach's *Coffee Cantata.*

SOURCE: Lebrecht Collection.

ENGAGING THE PAST

IN THE COFFEEHOUSE

The Parisian cafe Le Procope, the oldest coffee-house on the Left Bank, welcomed the likes of Voltaire, Rousseau, and other Parisians who went there in the eighteenth century "to mingle the attractions of the spirit with those of the palate." The centerpiece of the cafe was coffee mixed with conversation. Patrons, mostly men, debated the ideas and issues of the time while sipping their steaming drinks. Though historians may never know the contours of the conversations, their context—that is, the coffee house itself—was most certainly an occasion of debate when the cafe opened in 1686. Many Europeans felt that coffee undermined family life, distracted women from wifely obligations, and consumed time otherwise spent more productively. In Leipzig one of coffee's most ardent defenders was the composer Johann Sebastian Bach. His *Coffee Cantata* was a satire on the benefits of the controversial beverage.

The plant *Coffea arabica* was first domesticated on the plateaus of central Ethiopia, and its use spread to Yemen and the Islamic world before 1000 C.E., where it was first ingested as a medicine and then later as a beverage during meditation and the religious exercises of dervishes. European visitors first encountered the drink in coffeehouses in Cario and Mecca in the sixteenth century, and it quickly became a luxury item imported from Mocha (Yemen) and Java, where it had been propagated from seeds the Dutch had

carried from Malabar, India. The Dutch are also credited with providing a coffee tree to King Louis XIV of France in 1715. This plant became the centerpiece of the first greenhouse in Europe. An offshoot reached Martinique in 1720 via the French, who tried to guard other nations from access to the plant. The blockade was broken when the wife of the governor of French Guiana shared plants and seeds (and probably her ardent devotions) with the charming Brazilian Don Francisco de Melho Palheta in 1727, when he traveled to the French territory in search of a specimen plant. The West Indies and Brazil thereafter supplied coffee for much of Europe.

The drinking of coffee in public coffeehouses spread to Europe from the Ottoman Empire, where the first coffeehouse was established in Constantinople in 1554, after which reports began to circulate that coffee prevented its drinkers "from feeling drowsy. For that reason, students who wish to read into the late hours are fond of it." People flocked to the first coffeehouse in Oxford, the English university town, where curiosity drew patrons in 1650 to try the exotic, hot, unintoxicating drink they had read about in travel books. By the time of Rousseau, the European coffeehouse had become the place of intellectual debate and an enduring symbol of the global exchanges underway.

SUGGESTIONS FOR FURTHER READING

K. N. Chaudhuri, *Asia before Europe: The Economy and Civilization of the Indian Ocean from the Rise of Islam to 1750* (Cambridge: Cambridge University Press, 1990). Material culture of the Indian Ocean world, including food, dress, architecture, urbanization, and economic organization.

Jeffrey and Susan Jellicoe, *The Landscape of Man: Shaping the Environment from Prehistory to the Present Day* (London: Thames and Hudson, 1987). A beautifully illustrated examination of how the social and intellectual characteristics of twenty-six cultures are expressed in the landscapes they have molded.

Anthony Reid, *Southeast Asia in the Age of Commerce, 1450–1680 Volume One: The Lands Below the Winds* New Haven, CT: Yale University Press, 1988. A rich resource on the material culture and social life of Southeast Asians in the era of early European contact.

Simon Schama, *Landscape and Memory* (New York: Alfred A. Knopf, 1995). Suggests the links between real and imagined landscapes and their impact on European history.

Robert Farris Thompson, *Flash of the Spirit: African and Afro-American Art and Philosophy* (New York: Random House, 1983). Landmark treatment of African transformation and continuity in the Atlantic world.

Cultural Creativity and Borrowed Art

The creative spark that is said to inspire artists originates with both internal sources (sometimes called "inspiration") and external influences. Or as the French poet Baudelaire (1821–1867) put it, "[pure art] is the creation of suggestive magic which simultaneously contains object and subject, the world outside the artist, and the artist himself." As global trade became increasingly important after 1500, commercial connections provided new ideas and objects that artists borrowed and imitated. The demand for foreign works of art as prestige items became widespread. Artisans in Europe, Africa, Asia, and the Americas copied objects, techniques, motifs, and themes according to local demand and for foreign export. Many goods were produced in Africa and Asia by artists and craftsmen for the European market, and European artisans were also influenced by foreign designs and techniques.

TRADE AND TOURIST ART

Sailors and merchants were among the earliest tourists. Like modern tourists, they sought souvenirs in the foreign places they visited and their presence as foreigners inspired the production of specific objects. For example, European travelers' descriptions of patronage by tourists

FIGURE CI-2.1 Ivory Pedestal Bowl (Saltcellar or Container for Spices), Bulom, Sierra Leone
West African artists used local styles to create objects for sale to European tourists.
SOURCE: National Prehistoric and Ethnographic Museum, Rome. Index. Photo by L. Pignori.

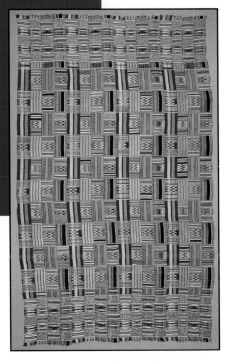

FIGURE CI-2.2 Kente Cloth, Asante (Silk, Twentieth Century) The "oyokoman ogya da mu" pattern was only worn by royalty. SOURCE: National Museum of African Art and National Museum of Natural History, Smithsonian Institution. Purchased with funds provided by Smithsonian Collections Acquisition Program. 1983. 85. Lamb EJ10583. Photo by Frank Khoury.

along the West African coast in the sixteenth century suggest that visitors actually provided African ivory carvers with drawings to describe what they desired to purchase. According to the Portuguese observer Valentim Fernandes, "In Sierra Leone men are most able and ingenious in doing ivory works truly wonderful to behold of all things they are ordered to make, some make spoons, others salt cellars, others hilts for daggers, and any other refined object . . . And of whatsoever thing they are given a drawing, they carve it out of ivory."[1] African artists created foreign objects, in which they portrayed aspects of Portuguese culture using local carving styles.

REWEAVING THE THREADS OF CULTURE

The magnificent textiles known as *kente* cloth provide vivid examples of the Akan (Ghana, West Africa) process of selectively borrowing foreign elements. *Kente* cloth was woven on horizontal looms with Indian cotton imported from the Islamic world by West Africans, who were situated on trade routes that linked them across the Sahara to North Africa and beyond to India. By the seventeenth

[1]Monod, et al., *Description de la cote Occidentale d'Afrique* (Bissau: Centro de Estudos da Guine Portuguesa, mem. 11, 1951): 96, 104; quoted in Vinigi L. Grottenelii, "Discovery of a Masterpiece: Sixteenth-Century Ivory Bowl from Sierra Leone," African Arts, 8 (4) 1975:22 (translation by the author).

FIGURE CI-2.3 "Virgin of Guadalupe," Pedro Antonio Fresquis, c. 1800 SOURCE: National Museum of American Art, Washington D.C. Art Resource, NY.

century in the Akan region of Ghana, narrow strips of cloth were woven separately and sewn together to create impressive textiles. Using threads unraveled from Chinese silks imported through the European coastal trade, weavers produced familiar patterns. *Kente* patterns were recognized and associated with local historical events or cultural proverbs. For example, the cloth illustrated here was known as *oyoko-man ogya mu* ("there is a fire between two factions of the Oyoko clan"), a reference to the Asante civil war after the death of the ruler Osei Tutu around 1730. Textiles combined elements borrowed from the past and from foreign sources, literally reweaving their borrowed inspiration into a culturally meaningful and vibrant pattern.

CULTURAL INTERSECTIONS IN THE AMERICAS

Soon after Columbus, the Americas became a meeting place of world cultures. Cultural forms were sometimes imposed by European colonizers through religious conversion and artistic endeavors were influenced by new religious and cultural ideals. Colonies also became sites where cultures converged and new hybrid forms of art and identity emerged. Probably the most profound cultural transformations were visible in religious syncretism, the blending of indigenous and Christian beliefs. The image of the Virgin of Guadaloupe portrays the dark-skinned Virgin with roses, who miraculously appeared in 1531 soon after the Spanish conquest, to the recent convert Juan Diego at Tepeyac, Mexico, the sacred site of the Aztec mother goddess. The Virgin of Guadaloupe's image, which appeared on Diego's coat, became the basis for the most important cult in American

FIGURE CI-2.4 Greeting the Arriving Portuguese Detail from a pair of six-fold screens attributed to Kano Naizen; colors on paper. SOURCE: Laurie Platt Winfrey, Inc. Kobe City Museum of Namban Art.

FIGURE CI-2.5 Indian Village Biombo (Japanese Byobu, Folding Screen) from Mexico
The screen depicts Corpus Christi ceremonies, featuring flying men (mid-seventeenth century, painted in Mexico probably by an artist of Asian descent). These 10 panels (oil canvas, mounted on wood) illustrate a Catholic religious festival with indigenous cultural elements.
SOURCE: Museo de America, Madrid. Oronoz

FIGURE CI-2.6 Interior of a Porcelain Shop. Artist unknown. ca. 1820–1830. Gouache on paper, one of a set of thirteen. SOURCE: Peabody Essex Museum. Salem, Massachusetts. Photo by Mark Sexton.

Catholicism. Copied time and again by devoted artists, it was also taken up as a symbol of revolution under the Mexican insurgent Miguel Hidalgo in 1810.

In the sixteenth century, Japanese artists working in traditional modes painted ornate, brilliantly colored screens depicting the Portuguese, the "southern barbarians" (*namban*). *Namban* art portrayed the Portuguese in their traditional costumes with often grotesque features, the way they appeared to the Japanese. As Christianity gained ground in sixteenth- and early seventeenth-century Japan, Japanese artists using Western techniques painted Western subjects such as the Jesuit missionary Saint Francis Xavier.

Japanese folding screens were also popular with the Spanish elite and creole populations of New Spain. These easily transportable screens were painted in China and Japan in European styles for export across the Pacific. After a colony of Japanese converts to Christianity and Chinese slaves, including some artisans, developed in Mexico around 1618, screens were also painted locally. Their subject matter consisted of both Christian and indigenous cultural and

FIGURE CI-2.7 Portrait of Howqua, a Rich Chinese Merchant
Oil color by anonymous Chinese painter after George Chinnery; early nineteenth century.
SOURCE: Bequest of W. Gedney Beatty, 1941. (41.160.405) Photograph © 1979 The Metropolitan Museum of Art.

historical events. The folding screens were Asian in origin, but their imagery represented the European perspective of the intended owner and patron.

CHINOISERIE AND THE CHINA TRADE

The movement known as *chinoiserie* (Chinese style) in Europe was an attempt by Europeans to capture the exotic images and forms of China beginning in the eighteenth century. For example, the German porcelain factory at Meissen produced wares decorated in the Chinese style, and the Martin workshop in France became famous for its imitation of Chinese lacquer (see Chapter 15). The fad of *chinoiserie* in eighteenth-century Europe produced gardens that were modeled on traditional Chinese designs and decorative arts such as wallpaper that depicted idealized Chinese scenes, much as Voltaire and other French Enlightenment intellectuals idealized Chinese government. With the increase in commerce between China and Europe in the eighteenth century, fostered by the high demand for tea in Europe, Chinese craftsmen began to produce ceramics and fine furniture for the export market.

The eighteenth-century North American China trade from New England inspired a large number of paintings in the Western style by both European and Chinese artists. The first Chinese painter known to have painted in oil on canvas—in contrast to the traditional water and ink on silk—was a man known to the West as Spoilum, who painted a number of portraits of American and English sea captains and merchants in the late eighteenth century. Among Spoilum's successors in the nineteenth century were Chinese students of the English painter George Chinnery, who was born in London in 1774 and traveled to Macao and Canton in 1825. Along with the English painter J.M.W. Turner, Chinnery had been a student of the famous English painter Sir Joshua Reynolds, and he became a well-known portrait artist along the China coast, influencing native Chinese artists.

ORIENTALISM

The "exotic" East provided new subject matter that inspired nineteenth-century European painters who romanticized both landscapes and peoples encountered through the exploits of imperialism. Images of desert caravans, bazaars, luxurious palaces, and sensuous dancers rich in historical and imagined detail contrasted sharply with the increasingly industrialized European world. Artists such as

FIGURE CI-2.8 "The Dancing Girl"
By Giulio Rosati (1858-1917). Orientalist painting by a European artist.
SOURCE: Christie's Images
Bridgeman Art Library, London.

FIGURE CI-2.9 Odalisque with a Parrot (Mughal,
Lucknow or Delhi, early nineteenth century)
Opaque watercolor on paper.
SOURCE: Reproduced by/and permission of the Trustees
of the Chester Beatty Library, Dublin (ms. 69, no 19).

Ingres (1780–1867) portrayed non-European subjects in paintings of
the *odalisque* (harem women). This vision was adapted by Indian
painters under the Raj. Just as the sixteenth- and seventeenth-
century Mughal emperors Akbar and Jahangir had urged their court
painters to borrow European exoticisms from imported works of
art, nineteenth-century Indian artists working under the Raj used
motifs drawn from European paintings.

BORROWED TIME
Borrowing occurred not only through the meeting of distinct cultures. Artists around the world also sought inspiration from earlier
periods within their own cultural traditions. European Renaissance
artists reinterpreted religious themes and subjects with new artistic
styles and techniques that reflected the humanistic concerns of
their own time. At the same time, Renaissance art reflected the con

temporary commercial transactions between patron and artist that supported artistic undertakings. Renaissance artists also crossed cultures. Artists were sometimes loaned by their patrons, as in the example of the Venetian painter Gentile Bellini who was loaned by his benefactor to the Ottoman court in Istanbul in 1479. His portrait of the Sultan Mehmet II uses borrowed composition and incorporates details of foreign dress, reflecting the aesthetic sensibilities of his patron.

Neoclassicism was a nineteenth-century movement that used as its subject matter sources from ancient history and classical myth, typified by Jacques Louis David's "Death of Socrates" (see Chapter 4). Though European neoclassicism portrayed classical subjects in a style that increasingly suggested romanticism by its intense expression of emotion, imitation of the past in both style and subject matter was a hallmark of traditional Chinese painting. The imitation of earlier artists was not considered copying, but appropriate acknowledgment and reverence of past masters.

FIGURE CI-2.10 "Sultan Mehmet II"
By Gentile Bellini, 1479
The Venetian painter adapted the aesthetic style of his Ottoman patron.
SOURCE: Reproduced by courtesy of the Trustees, The National Gallery, London.

REPRESENTATION AND REALITY

Production of art was inseparable from the dramatic technological changes witnessed by world societies after 1500. The printing of illustrated books and distribution of printed materials increasingly commercialized artistic endeavors. Semiliterate and newly literate citizens of the world eagerly acquired books, relying heavily on their illustrations to comprehend the new worlds being opened to them (see Chapter 13).

Even before the mid-nineteenth-century invention of photography, artists began to consider more closely issues of realism and representation. Exploration of the limits of descriptive accuracy since the Renaissance took the form of *camera obscura* (Latin for "dark chamber"), a dark box or room with a lens through which light passed and an exact image of the landscape behind was projected on the opposite wall. The camera's ability to "see" and represent the world caused painters to question the roles of individual impressions of reality, creative expression, and artistic license to convey feelings and opinions about the subjects of their work.

IMPRESSIONISM AND MODERNISM

Impressionism was a movement in European painting that rejected the realistic depiction of a subject in favor of using stylistic conventions, especially the shifting play of light on the painting's surface and the artist's eye, to convey feelings about a particular place and time. From the beginning of the twentieth century, works by impressionist and postimpressionist artists were exhibited and debated by westerners in the same way and sometimes even the same forum that primitive and erotic sensibilities were being explored. Modernism became the movement toward abstraction and nonrepresentational art. It was also an acknowledgment of the multiple ways of seeing the world.

THE ENCOUNTER BETWEEN EAST AND WEST

The conflicts between tradition and modernity were particularly acute in Japanese art in the late nineteenth and early twentieth centuries as Japanese artists struggled to retain a distinct cultural identity under Western influence. Japanese artists also had a persuasive

and powerful influence on modern European painting. After the eighteenth century, many Japanese artists abandoned traditional motifs and Chinese influence, and produced woodblock prints whose form and content were popular in nature. Woodblock print artists portrayed *geisha* or *kabuki* actors, inhabitants of the pleasure quarters of the urban centers of Osaka and Edo, scenes of urban domestic life or famous rural landscapes. When Japan was forced to open up to the West in the second half of the nineteenth century, these prints, not highly valued in Japan, appeared in the West, often as padding and wrapping for trade goods. They were easily and enthusiastically picked up and had a powerful and fruitful artistic impact on Europeans.

French Impressionists, in particular, in their quest for new motifs and color schemes, were passionately attracted to these colorful Japanese woodblock prints. Artists such as Edouard Manet (1832–1883), Edgar Degas (1834–1917), and their circle were among the first to appreciate and collect them. They felt they had found allies and models for their own goals in the works of Japanese masters such as Hokusai (1760–1849) and Utamaro (1753–1806). The enthusiasm of the French Impressionists for Japanese prints was shared by James Whistler (1834–1903), an American working in Great Britain. The Dutch artist Vincent Van Gogh (1853–1890), who

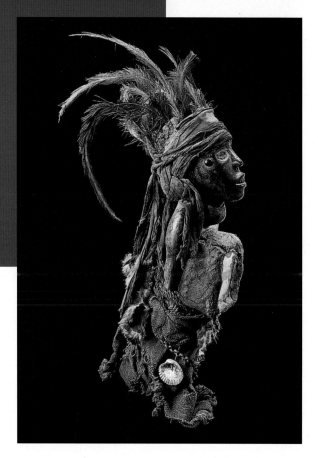

FIGURE CI-2.12 Reliquary Guardian (nlo byeri), Fang, Gabon (Central Africa, Nineteenth Century) Sculptures obtained in European colonies in Africa and Oceania were collected by museums and individuals in the late nineteenth century. In its African cultural context, this was an empowerment object. SOURCE: Museé Dapper, Paris.

worked in France, wanted his paintings to show the influence of the Japanese prints he admired. Mary Cassatt (1845–1926), an American working in Paris, used colored drypoint and aquatint to capture and carry forward the lightness and calm energy of Japanese artists.

BORROWING THE ART OF THE "OTHER"

Some of the most significant examples of cross-cultural influences took place in the art salons of Paris in the first few decades of the twentieth century. Here artists such as the Spanish painter Pablo Picasso encountered highly conceptual examples of African sculpture, which in turn empowered them to develop abstract and nonrealist modern art. Just as Asian and African artists traveled to Europe and were influenced by European styles, a few European painters actually traveled to other parts of the world, where they encountered non-European art in its own cultural context. The French painter

Paul Gauguin spent many years living in Polynesia, where he not only painted its cultural scenes as viewed through European eyes, but also incorporated its artistic principles and symbols on his own canvases.

Imperialism provided a variety of objects and multiple opportunities for seeing and knowing the world, as well as for appropriating the cultural styles of "others." In a series of paintings, the Euro-Canadian artist Emily Carr depicted the cultural landscapes of Native Americans. Her sensitive reproductions appropriatied cultural design elements that were part of a disappearing landscape. The 1907 painting by Pablo Picasso "Les Demoiselles d'Avignon," both marks the debut of modern art and reflects foreign cultural influences. In Picasso's rendering of women in a brothel in the red-light district of Barcelona, the cubist style of faces and body forms derives directly from West and

Central African sculptures and masks. Picasso's borrowing of the conceptual basis and formal abstraction of African art has been termed primitivist, and it is echoed in the twentieth-century works of Max Ernst, Henri Matisse, Paul Klee, Braques, Brancusi, Giacometti, Calder, and others.

FIGURE CI-2.13 "The Call (L'Appel)"
By Paul Gauguin, 1902 Oil on canvas, 130.2 × 90.2cm.
SOURCE: The Cleveland Museum, Gift of the Hanna Fund, 1943. 392.

FIGURE CI-2.14 "Indian House Interior with Totems"
Oil on canvas by Emily Carr.
SOURCE: Vancouver Art Gallery. Photo, T. Mills.
VAG 42.3.8.

But the "primitive" and "modern" did not speak to one another as
equals. African art was taken out of the social and political contexts
that infuse its abstraction and surrealism with meaning, stylistic conventions that were merely intuited by the European art community.
Picasso was also drawn to ancient images of his own culture, having
studied fifth- and sixth-century B.C.E. sculptures excavated from the
Pyrenees region of Spain. In "Les Demoiselles d'Avignon," Picasso's
female figures are flattened, angular, and hostile confrontations between the terrors and desires he imagines to be communicated from
behind their masks.

ART AND IDENTITY

The global exchanges that took place in artistic influences after 1500
were complex cross-cultural experiences. Artists and craftsmen interpreted traditional styles and forms in new ways that were subject to
influences not only from other cultures but from reinterpretations of
their own cultures in the light of profound transformations that occurred with the knitting together of the globe after 1500. Influences

went back and forth in creative surges that produced vibrant and powerful expressions of new identities. Modern art in the West has tended to reject history, to challenge the power of the past. In other cultures subject either to colonialism or the forceful model of commercialism and industrialism, artists have sought ways to integrate the past with the present, to incorporate tradition in ways that smooth the connection between past and present instead of disrupting it.

One of the most dynamic zones of cultural interaction is Southeast Asia, where Indian, Chinese, and later Islamic influences blended with indigenous Southeast Asian traditions. European colonialism added yet another layer to this rich blend. In modern times artists have drawn inspiration from these cultural encounters and produced remarkable renderings of the complexities of these interwoven traditions and the tensions between past and present, East and West. A powerful evocation of these themes appears in the form of a mural painted on the walls of a Thai Buddhist temple not far from the All-England Lawn Tennis Club at Wimbledon. A contemporary Thai artist, Panya Vijinthanasarn (b. 1956), who was educated in Bangkok and London, painted much of the mural. It portrays Mara Wasawadi, the temptress in Buddhism, riding on an elephant accompanied by soldiers armed with machine guns, rocket launchers and bazookas. The nineteenth-century Dutch artist, Vincent Van Gogh falls off a ladder while a Thai

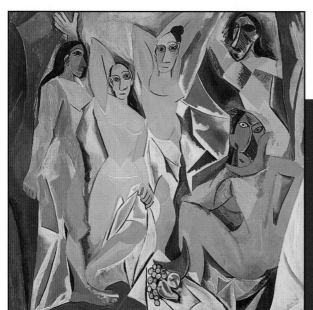

FIGURE CI-2.15 "Les Demoiselles d'Avignon" By Pablo Picasso, 1907. Oil on canvas.
SOURCE: Museum of Modern Art, New York Acquired through Lillie P. Bliss Bequest. Photograph © 1998 Estate of Pablo Picasso/Artist Rights Society, (ARS) New York.

International Boeing flies above Big Ben. The juxtaposition of these images—traditional Buddhism, a Western artist, weapons, and modern technology—vividly evokes the confusion and the complexity of modern global identities.

FIGURE CI-2.16 Panya Vijinthanasarn (b. 1956), "The Defeat of Mara and Enlightenment" (detail). Acrylic and spray paint, 1984–1987.
SOURCE: The Ordination Hall, Wat Buddhapadima, Wimbledon, England. Photo, A. L. Cooper, Ltd.

PART IV Balance

| Asia | | | |
East	South	Southeast	West
1700 Qing Empire (1644-1910)	Mughal Empire	Islamic States	Ottoman Empire
Manchus			
Tokugawa Japan (1600-1868)	British in India (1763)		
1800 Opium War (1839-1842)			
	Sepoy Mutiny (1857)		
Meiji Restoration (1868-1912)			1869 Suez Canal Opens
	Indian National Congress (1885)	British and French Colonialism	
1900 Boxer Rebellion			European imperialism
1911 Republican Revolution	Gandhi (1869-1949)		Independence Movements
	1914-1918 World War I		
1919 May 4th Movement	1919 Amritsar Massacre	Nationalist Movements	
1945 Atomic Bomb	1939-1945 World War II		
	Cold War 1949-1990		
1949 Chinese Revolution			
Mao Zedong (1893-1976)	1947 Independence: India and Pakistan		
		1954-1975 Vietnam War	1979 Iranian Revolution
2000			

The philosopher Thomas Kuhn (1923–1996) was once asked whether he was a realist. After replying that he was, the questioner went on to ask, "But do you believe that whenever theories change, the whole world changes?" "Of course," Kuhn reportedly replied. Inexorably and increasingly after the onset of revolutions at the end of the eighteenth century, both the recognition and experience of change became regular features of human life.

Kuhn believed that the nature of change was not an orderly progression, but an abrupt rupture. Change involved the accumulation of anomalies—the seemingly irrational confusion of contradictions, informational misfits, and exceptions—that eventually demands a shift in the generally accepted framework of basic concepts about the world. Kuhn called this a paradigm shift. This pattern is then repeated as the accumulation of anomalies according to the new paradigm eventually requires an abrupt shift to a competing paradigm that subsequently becomes dominant.

Although Kuhn's views pertained to the nature of scientific revolutions, they have also been applied to other realms of knowledge such as

Europe	Africa	Americas/ Pacific
British East India Company Enlightenment	Era of Merchant Princes	European Colonies in No. America Spanish Empire in Americas
Capitalist Industrial Revolution (ca. 1750)	Napolean Invades Egypt (1798)	1776 American Revolution
French Revolution (1789-1799)	Famine in Southern Africa	European Colonialism
Napoleon (r. 1799-1815)	Jihads in Western Africa	in the Pacific
Crimean War (1854-1856)	European Abolition of Slavery (1807-1865)	Independence Movements
Karl Marx(1818-1883)		
Charles Darwin's Origin of Species (1859)	Era of Legitimate Commerce Great Trek (S.Africa)	
1870 Franco-Prussian War	Suez Canal (1869)	American Civil War (1861-1865)
	Berlin Conference (1884-1885)	Transatlantic Cable
Berlin Conference (1884-1885)	Anglo-Boer War 1899-1902	1898 U.S. Annexation of Hawaii
	Maji-Maji Rebellion (1906)	Australia and New Zealand in British Commonwealth Panama Canal (1914)
1914-1918 World War I		
1917 Bolshevik Revolution	Ibo Women's War (1929)	Great Depression (1929-1932)
1939-1945 World War II		
Cold War 1949-1990		Computer Age (c. 1946)
	Independent Africa: 48 Nation States Created (1951-1980) Apartheid (1948-1994)	Moon Landing (1969)

philosophy and history. While the notion of a paradigm shift remains controversial, Kuhn's work has challenged a whole generation to reconsider the issue of objectivity and the dynamics of change and uncertainty in the modern world. The embrace of global history, replacing the Eurocentric history of a past generation, is an example of a paradigm shift. While many modern historians might contend that historical truth exists, few would deny that the shape of that truth depends on the place and identity of the observer.

The theme of "Balance" shapes Part IV, the final part of this book, as we examine shifting cultural and political identities after 1750, and trace the desire of individuals to maintain balance amidst the moving forces of change. Sometimes revolutionary change took place within individual societies and cultures (Chapters 16 and 19); after 1800, change was increasingly global (Chapters 17 and 18). Even resistance—whether registered as reluctance to change (adherence to the old paradigm) or as the impetus toward change and against the status quo (Chapter 19)—augmented the modern individual's sense of social and political balance and need for redefinition and rebalance. In the final chapter (Chapter 20), we consider the swinging pendulum of uncertainty and the inevitability of change at the end of a millennium.

Dual Revolutions: Capitalist Industrialism and the Nation State

R eflecting on the state of the world in the late eighteenth century on the eve of the American Revolution, the Scottish economist Adam Smith (1723–1790) observed in *An Inquiry into the Wealth of Nations* (1776):

> The discovery of America, and that of a passage to the East Indies by the Cape of Good Hope, are the two greatest and most important events recorded in the history of mankind. Their consequences have already been very great; but in the short period of between two and three centuries which has elapsed since these discoveries were made, it is impossible that the whole extent of their consequences can be seen. What benefits, or what misfortunes to mankind may result from these great events, no human wisdom can foresee.

Like his predecessor, the English scientific thinker Francis Bacon, who claimed that the invention of the magnetic compass, gunpowder, and printing—all attributable to the Chinese—had irrevocably and profoundly changed the world, Adam Smith's pronouncements accurately predicted the enormity of the impact that Europe's global expansion would have on the world.

What Adam Smith could not foresee were the dramatic transformations in European life and society that were beginning to take place with the industrial revolution and the rise of the nation state, processes already underway in his lifetime that would change the world. By the late eighteenth century, an industrial revolution (see Chapter 15) was taking place in Europe, and political changes that laid the foundations of modern nation states accompanied this revolution. English historian Eric Hobsbawm has referred to the combined force of these two historical processes as the "dual revolutions," stressing the interaction and interdependence of the two processes of economic and political change.

■

INTRODUCTION

The dual revolutions of capitalist industrialism and the nation state profoundly altered the identities of individuals in Europe and the Americas by transforming the means by which they earned their livelihoods, the nature of the communities in which they lived, and their relationships to political authority. Changes in the mode of production from rural agriculture and handicraft industries, embedded in community life and characterized by personal relationships, to the industrial revolution's relatively impersonal and urbanized factory system had a dramatic effect on individual and family life. The political transformations associated with the rise of the nation state, whether by revolutionary or by more evolutionary means, reshaped the relationships of individuals, families, and communities to state authority.

The industrial revolution was closely tied to the economic system of capitalism, the use or investment of money to make profits. The earliest form of capitalism was agricultural, where wealth was both made from the land and invested in its improvement and expansion. Localized, self-sufficient agriculture was only gradually replaced with market-oriented agriculture, which required capital investment. Commercial capitalism developed with the late-medieval revival of cities and trade and flourished as a result of global exploration, trade, and colonization beginning in the sixteenth century (see Chapters 11 and 12). Before the sixteenth century, the power of monarchs depended on their relationship with an agrarian-military aristocracy; with the development of commercial capitalism, monarchs were supported by their merchant partners in mercantilism (see Chapter 12).

By the late eighteenth century, the investment of capital in industry, much of it derived from commerce and agriculture, began the vast expansion that would make industrial capitalism the dominant form of capitalism by the end of the nineteenth century. Older forms of capitalism were gradually subsumed in finance capitalism, in which bankers and financiers invested in industry, commerce, and even agriculture. Finance capitalists combined huge corporations and immense concentrations of money in economic activities that were increasingly global and intertwined with the expansion of European nation states in the Americas, Asia, and Africa (see Chapter 17).

The term "state" is derived from the word "estate," which reflects the fact that the monarchical governments of the eighteenth century originated in an earlier era when rulers did not distinguish between their private and public domains. Absolute monarchs of the seventeenth and eighteenth centuries, such as Louis XIV of France (r. 1642–1715), thought of themselves as the embodiment of the state. The concept of proprietorship continued to be embodied in the notion of the state: not only did the state "belong" to the monarch, but many of its institutions and much of its wealth was still the property of private persons, and social and political power were virtually indistinguishable.

The redefinition and transformation of the state took place in a variety of ways. The evolution of the modern nation state in England was catalyzed by revolutionary changes in the seventeenth century, and the American and French Revolutions in the eighteenth century produced modern nation states in the United States and France. These political transformations were based on the concept of the state as a social contract, the idea of a compact between rulers and ruled as the basis for the state. States based on the social contract can be distinguished as nation states, those in which the state is the property, not of the ruler alone, but of all people who make up the nation. The nation state thus represents a common historic and cultural identity of ruler and ruled. That identity, however, was persistently transformed over time and profoundly reshaped by the late nineteenth century under the impact of capitalist industrialism as economic dimensions of the social contract became increasingly important.

■

THE TRANSFORMATION OF THE ENGLISH MONARCHY: CIVIL WAR AND REVOLUTION

The transformation of the English monarchy from absolutism to constitutional monarchy, in which the king shared power with a representative body called parliament, was a long-term process that encompassed evolutionary change, civil war, and revolution. The Magna Carta, granted by King John in 1215, declared that the king was subject to the same laws as those he ruled and could not arbitrarily impose his will. In 1295 Edward I summoned the first or "model parliament," an assembly of nobles and representatives from the cities, to lend support for his war with France. Over the centuries the summoning of parliaments became regularized, though they remained elite bodies whose role in governing was controlled by strong kings. For example, Tudor monarchs, such as Henry VIII (r. 1509–1547) or Elizabeth I (r. 1558–1603), could not dispense with parliament; but by their use of political pressure and economic favors, they were able to manipulate parliament so that it interfered very little with their absolute power.

PARLIAMENT AND CIVIL WAR

Like their sixteenth-century predecessors, seventeenth-century Stuart monarchs of Great Britain held a paternalistic and absolutist view of the role of the king. James I (r. 1603–1625) buttressed his authority by proclaiming that kings ruled by divine sanction, though both James and his successors found themselves increasingly at odds with their parliaments. Disagreement with Charles I (r. 1625–1649) led parliament to draw up a Petition of Right (1628) requiring the king to address grievances such as arbitrary taxation and imprisonment. Though Charles assented to the petition, he paid little attention to what he considered an interference with his rights. When parliament challenged him again, he dissolved it, governing for the next eleven years without summoning a parliament. When political and financial troubles forced Charles to summon a new parliament (1640), the confrontation between him and parliament was renewed. This confrontation was ultimately resolved by a dramatic civil war (1642–1649) that culminated in the capture, trial, and execution of the king by parliamentary armies (1649).

Parliament's victory was a frontal assault on the divine-right monarchy, and for a decade parliament and its army under the leadership of Oliver Cromwell (r. 1653–1658), himself a member of parliament, governed England. During Cromwell's interregnum, parliament was transformed into a permanent institution. Though the monarchy was restored in 1660, when parliament called Charles II to the throne, it was monarchy with a difference. Two factors circumscribed the powers of the later Stuarts (Charles II [r. 1660–1685] and James II [r. 1685–1689]): first, the trial and beheading of Charles I by parliament demonstrated that body's power; second, Charles II owed his throne to parliament.

THE "GLORIOUS REVOLUTION"

The reign of James II, a Roman Catholic monarch who sat on the throne of a country that was increasingly Protestant, further clarified the role of king and parliament. When the birth of a son to James's second, and Catholic, wife presented the prospect of a Roman Catholic Stuart dynasty in Protestant England, dynastic tradition gave way to religious prejudice. Parliament took up arms against the king again, exerting its right to determine the religion of the ruler. Parliament offered the throne to the Protestant daughter of James's first marriage, Mary Stuart, and her husband, the Dutch William of Orange, who landed in England in November 1688 to help drive James out of England. This event came to be known as the "Glorious Revolution."

By defeating James (who left for exile in France) and choosing his successor, parliament had made an emphatic statement of its dominant role in the governance of the kingdom. The Glorious Revolution of 1688–1689 clearly and irrefutably defined the relation of king and parliament in Great Britain. That relationship is best described by the concept "king in parliament," according to which the king was expected to act in and through parliament and only with parliamentary approval and support. Among the legislation resulting from the Glorious Revolution was a Bill of Rights, the earliest guarantee of individual rights and liberties.

John Locke and the   The Glorious Revolution inspired the English philosopher John Locke
Glorious Revolution   (1632–1704) to suggest that anyone in authority who exceeds the
▬▬▬▬▬▬▬▬▬▬   power given to him by the law or who encroaches on the rights of individuals forfeits the right to rule. Having done so, he may be opposed and resisted just as "any other man who by force invades the right of another." In this way Locke justified the Glorious Revolution and provided a justification for revolution in general.

As a result of Cromwell, the Glorious Revolution, and legislation making up the Revolutionary Settlement (1701), by the eighteenth century the roles of parliament and the king were clearly defined in England. During the eighteenth century, parliament, including the hereditary House of Lords and the elected (by a very limited franchise) House of Commons, worked out the political mechanisms of government. Because George I (r. 1714–1727), the first of the German Hanoverian dynasty who succeeded to the English throne in the eighteenth century, spoke no English, had little interest in or understanding of English politics, the ministers he chose in effect governed for him. Between 1721 and 1742 the council of ministers or cabinet was headed by Sir Robert Walpole, who became the first or prime minister, though he never held that formal title. Walpole's authority—and that of his successors as prime minister—rested on his command of the support of a majority of the members of the House of Commons and the favor of the king. This dual source of authority defined parliamentary government in England, though parliamentary support ultimately became more important than royal favor.

■

THE AMERICAN REVOLUTION AND THE NATION STATE

While the forms of parliamentary government were being worked out in England, British colonists in the Americas rebelled against English rule in what became known as the American Revolution (1776–1783). The American Revolution occurred soon after the apex of British imperial power in the Americas was reached in the mid-eighteenth century when the British gained control of most of the North American continent by their victory over the French (1763).

COLONIAL CONFLICTS

The thirteen British colonies along the Atlantic seaboard flourished in the eighteenth century. They were as populated as most European states at the time and soon began to expand their borders westward toward the Appalachians. When the British government closed the area west of the Appalachians to settlement by the seaboard colonists, they were frustrated. The colonists were further angered by treaties that the British negotiated with Native Americans of the trans-Appalachian area and by the Quebec Act (1774), which reserved the Ohio Valley for the French communities of Quebec and which the seaboard colonists interpreted as a southward extension of Canadian frontiers that would block their own westward expansion.

Discontent mounted as innumerable specific incidents further exacerbated relations between the seaboard colonies and the British imperial government. Discontent fueled resistance, and resistance became rebellion. Colonists became more radical as they convinced themselves that the liberties they believed belonged to them as British subjects were endangered. They embraced the concepts of the social contract proposed by Locke and were influenced by such Enlightenment thinkers as Montesquieu and Benjamin Franklin, one of their own.

The Atlantic seaboard colonists and the imperial government in London had incongruent economic interests and differing opinions as to how North America should be governed. The British monarchy, assuming that the colonists should pay their proper share of the costs of defense and common imperial concerns, undertook to impose new tax measures to assure this (a stamp tax and duties on paper, glass, and tea). Many colonists, particularly those in the towns involved with trade, saw these as unilateral acts by an imperial legislature, an assault on their custom of raising revenues by their own colonial assemblies. Thus the issue of whether the legislative sovereignty of the British parliament also extended to the colonies came into focus.

Americans who took the lead in the debate, and some British politicians, assumed the position that no taxes should be levied on the colonists by a legislature in which they were not represented. Their rallying cry, "No taxation without representation," produced boycotts and riots, such as the famous Boston Tea Party—largely a protest against British mercantilism—in which colonists dumped tea into Boston harbor in defiance of the tea tax. The issue of whether parliament in London could enforce laws in the colonies got out of hand as neither side was willing to compromise or retreat.

THE CONTINENTAL CONGRESS

In September 1774 the colonists summoned a Continental Congress to which twelve of the thirteen colonies sent delegates (only Georgia held back). The brightest of colonial leadership assembled in Philadelphia amidst ceremony and banquets. Though the delegation from Massachusetts was regarded with suspicion on account of its radical views, the congress approved the Massachusetts resolutions refusing obedience to objectionable acts passed by the London parliament and detailing ways to defy them. Before the congress dissolved, it also agreed to sever commercial relations with Great Britain by adopting a policy of nonimportation and nonexportation. A "continental association" was set up to facilitate communication between the colonies and to enforce the congress's decisions.

The gap between the British imperial government and the colonies widened. Parliament responded to the actions of the Continental Congress by hurrying through a Restraining Act that forbade the colonists to trade with each other or with any British dominion. Boston was heavily occupied by British troops, and in the Massachusetts countryside militiamen drilled and stored military supplies. On the night of April 18, 1775, the British sent an expedition to seize and destroy military stores at Concord, twenty miles or so from Boston. Along the way 700 British infantrymen were met at the village of Lexington by a line of minutemen, 75 volunteer militiamen determined to resist the British advance. A shot—the "shot heard around the world"—was fired (by which side is unknown), and the first action of the American Revolution had taken place.

THE WAR FOR AMERICAN INDEPENDENCE

The war between the colonists and Great Britain flared up simultaneously in several places, and on May 10 a second Continental Congress met to organize the conflict and make sure that all the colonies had a stake in it. The long and difficult struggle might have had a different outcome had the colonies not received foreign aid. After two years of indecisive campaigns, the Americans were joined by European powers who saw in the struggle an opportunity to weaken British global power.

France, eager to revenge its defeat in the mid-century wars, joined the Americans in 1778, followed by Spain (1779) and the Netherlands (1780). The British were unable to maintain a successful struggle against such a coalition, and in 1781 at Yorktown, Virginia, they surrendered. Peace negotiations at Paris, concluded in 1783, recognized the independence of the thirteen colonies. The British had lost the war because of geographical factors (distance and inability to adapt their military strategy and tactics to the American environment), thanks to the aid the Americans received from Great Britain's European opponents, and perhaps because it was difficult to wage a total war against the colonists whom many English considered to be fellow countrymen.

Declaration of Independence The Americans made their case in a Declaration of Independence approved by the Continental Congress on July 4, 1776. Drafted by Thomas Jefferson (1743–1826) of Virginia, this document distilled eighteenth-century ideals of rights common and equal to all and the concept of the social contract: "all men are created equal . . [and] endowed with certain inalienable Rights, that among these are Life, Liberty and the pursuit of Happiness. . . Governments derive their just powers from the consent of the governed." The Declaration explicitly justified the American rebellion: "To secure these rights, Governments are instituted among Men . . . whenever any Form of Government becomes destructive of these ends, it is the Right of the People to alter or abolish it, and to institute new Government." Jefferson's words became the ideological base on which the new American nation state was to rest.

It took the Americans nearly a decade to agree upon the principles and structures for their nation and embody them in a contract, the Constitution of 1789. Like the Declaration

FIGURE 16.0 George Washington in Masonic Dress

Many revolutionary leaders were Masons and symbols from the secret, fraternal organization were retained as part of the design of U.S. currency.

SOURCE: Alexandria Washington Lodge #22.

of Independence, the Constitution reflects eighteenth-century ideas and ideals, such as separation of church and state (secular rationalism) and the separation of powers suggested in Montesquieu's *Spirit of Laws* (1748). The makers of the Constitution seemed to realize that it was not a perfect document, and so they provided means for amending it. This first phase in the construction of the American nation state occurred from 1776 to 1815, roughly from the time of the Declaration of Independence to the end of the War of 1812 between Great Britain and the United States, a brief struggle that confirmed American independence.

■ THE FRENCH REVOLUTION AND THE NATION STATE

John Locke's justification of revolution not only supported the American revolutionaries who sought independence from England and its king but also foreshadowed the upheavals of the French Revolution at the end of the eighteenth century. Though the first French parliament, known as the "Estates General" and representing the three "estates" of clergy, nobility, and commoners, was summoned at about the same time as the English model parliament, the French parliament never evolved into a body that actively participated in governing. When it questioned royal policy, it was simply dismissed; following the dismissal of the Estates General of 1614, the body was not called for another 175 years.

Louis XIV and Absolute Monarchy   Though royal power was often hampered by powerful aristocrats, ambitious kings such as Louis XIV (r. 1643–1715) sought to extend their authority by keeping the aristocracy at court where they could be controlled more easily and by creating a new aristocracy drawn from the lesser nobility or wealthy commoners who could buy offices that ennobled them. The phrase "L'etat c'est moi" ("I am the state"), attributed to Louis XIV, expressed the king's ambition—though not necessarily the reality—that all political authority in France emanated from him.

Following Louis XIV's reign, the political power and rights of the aristocracy, against which he had struggled, continued and broadened, as those who purchased noble rights were as jealously protective of them as were the hereditary aristocracy of theirs. During the reigns of Louis XV (r. 1715–1774) and Louis XVI (r. 1774–1793), the aristocracy attempted to shape institutions such as the courts (*parlements*) to protect privilege and power, especially the exemption of nobles from taxation. Wars and uncontrolled expenses of the court strained the royal treasury and pitted the aristocracy and the government against each other. The tensions were exaggerated by demographic and economic crises. A series of bad harvests and growing fiscal difficulties forced Louis XVI in 1789 to do what no king had done since 1614: summon the Estates General.

THE ESTATES GENERAL OF 1789

The traditional purpose of the Estates General was to advise the king on the state of the kingdom and to support such measures as he should propose to it. The serious fiscal crisis that led Louis XVI in 1789 to summon the Estates General to Versailles offered the opportunity for expanding the role of the Estates General and for examining the whole nature of the French state. Deputies of the "third estate," generally young and ambitious commoners, were quick to take advantage of this opportunity.

From its initial session the Estates General of 1789 clearly had no intention of conforming to the king's expectation that it would limit itself to dealing with the fiscal crisis. The earliest indication that the Estates General intended to go far beyond its stated purposes occurred when it declared itself to be a National Assembly (June 10, 1789). This act was a major step in replacing the traditional monarchy in France with a nation state based on the principle of the social contract. Outside the halls of the Estates General, increasing public action constituted a popular revolution to which both the king and deputies had to pay heed. Such popular revolutionary action as the storming of the Bastille prison in Paris (July 14, 1789) in search of arms and gunpowder or the women's march on the royal palace at Versailles (October 1789) which demanded bread and resulted in the removal of both the king and the deputies to Paris, where they were henceforth under the watchful eyes of the citizens of Paris, moved the revolution in more radical directions.

Rousseau and the Social Contract The most powerful ideas underlying the actions of the deputies of the third estate came from the writings of Enlightenment thinkers such as Montesquieu (1689–1755) and, above all, of Jean-Jacques Rousseau (1712–1778), whose *Social Contract* became the guiding principle of the third estate. Rousseau argued that the social contract between rulers and ruled required rulers to obey the "general will" of the people. If they failed to do so, then the people had the right to overthrow them. These ideas were embodied in the Declaration of the Rights of Man and the Citizen, which was adopted on August 26, 1789. This "solemn declaration of the natural, inalienable, and sacred rights of man" declared that sovereignty is located in the people who constitute the nation, and that "no body, no individual can exercise authority" unless it is granted by the people. Frenchmen, the declaration proclaimed, "are born and remain free and equal in rights," and it proclaimed that the purpose of law, which was defined as "the expression of the general will," was to preserve the rights of Frenchmen, those rights being defined as "liberty, property, security, and resistance to oppression."

FROM CONSTITUTIONAL MONARCHY TO REPUBLIC

The Declaration of the Rights of Man and the Citizen was the reference point for various efforts during the revolution to create a new French social contract. The first effort, the Constitution of 1791, was invalidated by continued tension between the king, who was not committed to it, the deputies, who were divided among themselves, and the many elements of the population who felt themselves excluded by it (for example, women, the poor "passive citizens," who were denied full civic rights because they did not own property) and whose conditions were not improved.

The war between revolutionary France and traditional European monarchies that broke out in March 1792 (and would last with only brief intermissions until 1815) brought the problems of the constitutional monarchy created in 1791 to a crisis. On August 10, 1792, as

 DAILY LIVES

REVOLUTIONARY VIOLENCE AND SENSATIONAL JOURNALISM

Collective violence such as the storming of the Bastille or the women's march on Versailles was the expression of class hatred generated by the institutionalized violence of royal and aristocratic power. The summer of 1789 offered a plentiful display of spontaneous popular violence, and the many newspapers that flourished at this time discovered its shock appeal. Among the most successful of them was the *Revolutions de Paris*, published by Elysee Loustalot, a 27-year-old lawyer. Loustalot understood that readers wanted less tiresome recitations of political debates and more graphic reporting of events in Paris and the provinces. He gave them eyewitness accounts of popular violence, such as the lynching of Bertier de Sauvigny, a royal official, by a crowd on July 22, 1789. Held responsible for popular discontent, Bertier was led to the town hall amidst a crowd playing fifes and drums and was presented with the head, recently removed, of his father-in-law. According to the report, when the head of his father-in-law was thrust in his face, "Bertier shuddered and for the first time, perhaps, his soul felt the twinges of remorse. Fear and terror seized him." Loustalot described the scene inside the town hall where the authorities had been unable to prevent the crowd from seizing Bertier:

Already Bertier is no more; his head is nothing more than a mutilated stump separated from his body. A man, O gods, a man, a barbarian tears out his [Bertier's] heart from his palpitating viscera . . . His hands dripping with blood, he goes to offer the heart, still steaming, under the eyes of the men of peace assembled in this august tribunal of humanity. What a horrible scene! Tyrants, cast your eyes on this terrible and revolting spectacle. Shudder and see how you and yours will be treated. This body, so delicate and so refined, bathed in perfumes, is horribly dragged in the mud and over the cobblestones.

Frenchmen, you exterminate tyrants! Your hatred is revolting, frightful . . . but you will, at last, be free. I know, my dear co-citizens, how these revolting scenes afflict your souls . . . but think how ignominious it is to live as slaves.[*]

As Loustalot so graphically portrayed it, collective violence provided much of the revolutionary energy that shaped events in 1789, and eager reading audiences shared events in which they had no part.

[*]Simon Schama, *Citizens: A Chronicle of the French Revolution* (New York: Knopf, 1989), pp. 446–7.

a result of popular insurrection in Paris, the king was overthrown and, following the defeat of invading Austrian and Prussian armies, a new assembly, the Convention, proclaimed the first French Republic. The first business of the Convention was to try Louis XVI, who was condemned to death and executed. The Convention then drew up a new constitution, one much more closely reflecting Rousseau's concept of a social contract based on the general will. The Constitution of 1793 provided universal male suffrage, freed slaves in France and its territories, and gave citizens the right to work and the right to revolt.

THE JACOBINS AND THE REIGN OF TERROR

The 1793 constitution reflected the vision of Rousseau's social contract held by revolutionaries known as "Jacobins" (named after the hall where they met), whose spokesman was Maximilien Robespierre (1758–1794). The imposition of the Jacobin constitution on France produced a power struggle that led to the expulsion of more moderate factions from government and the concentration of power in Jacobin hands. The needs of prosecuting the war against European monarchies (including England, which had joined following the execution of Louis XVI) consolidated Jacobin control, but competing interests and power conflicts remained. The conduct of the war, economic tensions, and personal ambitions all tested Jacobin leadership. In order to maintain their control and impose their version of the general will, Robespierre and his associates resorted to force and violence against their opponents during the period of the revolution known as the "Reign of Terror" (1793–1794).

Journees Reaction against the Jacobin government reached its height in the spring of 1794; it was finally toppled by the *journees* (days of insurrection), which resulted in the execution of Robespierre and other Jacobin leaders and in turn led to the creation of yet another republican constitution (1795). *Journees*, as instruments of the popular revolution, consistently influenced the direction the revolution was to take; they helped account for the Jacobin triumph in 1793 just as they contributed to the Jacobin overthrow in 1794.

WOMEN IN THE FRENCH REVOLUTION

Though women were denied civic rights and equality with men, even in the more radical Jacobin constitution of 1793, they took active roles in the popular revolutionary *journees*, which were often inspired by hunger and began as bread riots led by women. For example, the October 1789 women's march on Versailles brought the royal family—popularly referred to as "the baker, the baker's wife, and the baker's son"—back to Paris. Participation in *journees* provided women with political opportunities and experience. Militant women responded to being shut out of the political process by organizing political clubs and exerting pressure by speaking out at rallies and during riots. One militant woman revolutionary, Olympe de Gouges (1748–1793), responded to the Declaration of the Rights of Man by publishing a Declaration of the Rights of Women (1791), which proclaimed that "woman is born free and lives equal to man in her rights."

When the Constitution of 1793 did nothing to extend full rights to women, militant women felt betrayed and turned on the Jacobin leadership, who responded by trying to discredit them, attacking their personal lives, and forbidding their political activities. Olympe

FIGURE 16.1 Revolutionary Parisian Market Women Marching to Versailles in October 1789

SOURCE: Musee de la Ville de Paris, Musee Carnavalet/Giraudon/Bridgeman Art Library.

de Gouges was sent to the guillotine in 1793; she and other radical women like her were accused of overstepping the bounds of feminine decency with their radical political activities.

THE COUNTERTERROR

The Jacobin effort to create a state based on its interpretation of the general will ended in failure. It was followed by a movement known as the "counterterror," by which many whom the Jacobins had dispossessed and silenced regained control of the republic. The men who gained control of France in 1794 expressed their vision of the social contract in the Constitution of 1795, a document much less advanced than that of 1793. The Directory, established by the constitution, concentrated authority in men of property, who proved less successful than the Jacobins in solving continuing domestic problems—economic difficulties, taxes, efficient administration—and in dealing with the republic's external enemies. Popular support for the Directory rapidly eroded, and it was attacked by a continuous series of *journees*.

Robespierre and his Jacobin associates had shown that a single voice could be imposed on the state, that the general will need not rise from universal and common consent, but could be extracted by strenuous pressure and violent enforcement. It was a message understood by Napoleon Bonaparte (1769–1821), a young Corsican artillery officer, as he witnessed the disintegration of the republic in the years following the adoption of the Constitution of 1795. Internal struggles and the dangers posed by external enemies—revolutionary France had been at war with the rest of Europe since March 1792—offered Napoleon his opportunity to seize power. As a result of an insurrection in October 1799, Napoleon (r. 1799–1815) assumed power. He was the ultimate co-opter of the "general will."

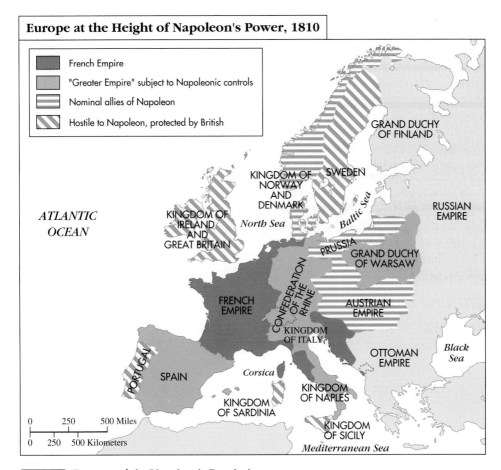

MAP 16.1 Europe and the Napoleonic Revolution

THE NAPOLEONIC REVOLUTION

Napoleon was a child of the French Revolution. He paid lip-service to the ideals on which the revolutionary French state was based while modifying them to his own ends. Napoleon's control of the army enabled him to control the state and even to convert it from a republic to an empire, but he accepted the revolutionary ideal that "sovereignty is located in essence in the nation" and that "law is the expression of the general will." Recalling the period of Jacobin control, Napoleon also realized that neither sovereignty nor law had to originate in the nation, rather that the nation could merely be asked to ratify law and confirm sovereignty. Accordingly, Napoleon based his rule on universal male suffrage, but his rule did not include popular participation. Napoleonic France was governed by plebiscite, popular referenda on laws that were presented to the electorate, rather than originating from them.

Napoleon used his power and popularity to deal effectively with major domestic problems unresolved by and inherited from ten years of revolution. Among his many achievements were the establishment of fiscal stability, the codification of laws, the creation of efficient administrative systems that would remain a permanent fixture in France, and the making of peace with the Church. Thanks to his political achievements and his continued military success, Napoleon received approval by plebiscite in 1804 for transforming the revolutionary French republic into a hereditary empire. The Napoleonic empire was not, however, a traditional monarchy. The codification of French law in 1804, later known as the "Napoleonic Code," confirmed revolutionary ideas such as legal (male) equality by which all men were equal before the law and could compete for jobs, rewards, and power on the basis of talent rather than birth or wealth.

Napoleon's twofold achievement was to define and institutionalize a social contract for France by resolving the conflicts of ten years of revolution and to protect France from external enemies. Though he had consistent success in his campaigns against other European powers, Napoleon was finally defeated and exiled in 1814. When he returned to power from exile in 1815, he was again defeated and sent to the rocky South Atlantic island of St. Helena, where he died in 1821.

■

REVOLUTION AND NATIONALISM IN THE CARIBBEAN: THE HAITIAN REVOLUTION

Across the Caribbean region, from Brazil to Hispaniola, earlier Spanish and Portuguese hegemony had been challenged in the seventeenth and eighteenth centuries by other European imperialist powers, especially the Dutch, French, and English. These territories were linked together by the commonality of their experience of plantation slavery and colonial rule. The indigenous Caribbean peoples and the Africans who were forcibly brought to the area also experienced the effects of European domination and were influenced by revolutionary changes in Europe.

THE INFLUENCE OF THE FRENCH REVOLUTION

Eighteenth-century European ideals, such as "men are born free and equal in rights," and "liberty, equality, and fraternity," (the rallying cry of the French Revolution) promptly reached Caribbean shores, where they were translated into the issues of property, labor, and race. Soon after the outbreak of the French Revolution (1789), white planters in St. Domingue (the western third of the island of Hispaniola) were given control of colonial assemblies and a large measure of autonomy. Then in 1791 the National Assembly in Paris, responding to pressures from a European abolitionist society, *Les Amis des Noirs* ("The Friends of Blacks"), further extended rights to all free persons, including mulattoes (those of mixed race), decreeing that "persons of color, born of free parents" should have voting rights in the colonial assemblies. White planters demanded the law be repealed and threatened to join the British Empire if it was not. Both whites and mulattoes began to arm themselves, and the conflict that broke out between them offered slaves their opportunity to revolt.

The potential threat of slave revolt on St. Domingue was great. Most of the slaves were African born, and they formed the majority population, outnumbering other ethnic groups

FIGURE 16.2 French Depiction of the Slave Uprising in St. Domingue (Haiti) in 1791

The Haitian Revolution was the largest war of liberation in the western hemisphere and was discussed in Europe and the Caribbean

SOURCE: The Granger Collection, New York.

by a ratio of thirteen to one. Since the colony's mountainous interior afforded ample inaccessible hiding places, there were numerous maroon (freedom-fighter) communities. Common beliefs, such as the African-derived religion of Vodun, and shared myths and heroes united diverse slave populations. Heroes, such as the martyred Francois Machandal, who had plotted to contaminate the water supplies of the white plantocracy (ruling class) provided inspiration and example for slaves. Machandal was burned alive, but a legend surrounding his death held that he had actually escaped by changing into a mosquito and flying away. The oppressed believed that the mosquitoes that long afterward plagued French troops (and caused death by spreading malaria) constituted the vengeance of their hero.

TOUSSAINT L'OUVERTURE AND THE SLAVE REVOLT

In August 1791 slaves in northern St. Domingue demanded their own liberty and rebelled; during much of the period from 1791 to 1792, slave strikes and revolts spread across the island. Reluctantly, France sent troops in. Attempts at negotiation to restore colonial order failed to gain the support of slaves. In 1793 the French National Assembly granted emancipation to the slaves, an act further angering both the planters and the free coloreds, who accepted aid from the British (who were alarmed at the possibility that the slave rebellion might spread to their colonies) against the rebellious slaves.

More than 100,000 slaves participated in the rebellion under the leadership of Toussaint L'Ouverture (ca. 1746–1803), the educated son of African slave parents. In his efforts to liberate his fellow black slaves, Toussaint fought for a decade against intervention and blockades by slave-owning nations (France, Britain, Spain, and the United States) and even against mulatto opposition. By 1801 he controlled the entire island of Hispaniola, but many more battles were fought before a final victory established the independent nation state of Haiti.

Once Napoleon was firmly in control, he dispatched a huge army to invade St. Domingue. L'Ouverture was induced to meet with the French, treacherously seized, carried to Europe, and imprisoned, where he died in 1803. Jean-Jacques Dessalines and Henri Christophe continued the struggle in Haiti, and black strength and yellow fever defeated the massive French effort to regain control of St. Domingue. The failure of Napoleon's design for restoring a French empire in the Americas made him agreeable to selling the Louisiana Territory to the United States.

HAITIAN INDEPENDENCE

On January 1, 1804, the independence of the western half of Hispaniola was proclaimed, and the new nation was given the name Haiti. But the only successful slave revolution came at a high price. By this time the country was bankrupt, its population cut by 25 percent, plantations destroyed, the ecology damaged, and the economy staggered. The pattern of civil war, instability, and outside intervention has continued relentlessly for almost 200 years, and even today jeopardizes the stability and development of the Haitian republic.

Language and Revolution The language of the Haitian revolution provides historical insight into its complexity. Toussaint L'Ouverture, it is claimed, spoke French and was literate, but Generals Dessalines and Henri Christophe were not literate. Some of the most famous rhetoric of the revolution attributed to Dessalines was contained in a document written in French by his secretary-general. Dessalines probably spoke Creole, a blending of French, English, Spanish, and Taino (a Native American language) with African-derived vocabularies and syntax from multiple sources. Creole was imposed as the national language, and Dessalines, rather than the francophile Toussaint, was canonized by the indigenous Vodun religion (he is the deity Papa Dessalines). Furthermore, Dessalines reportedly went into battle covered with talismans believed to be magical substances to make him invulnerable. Upon independence he tore out the white of the French flag. He called the new nation "Haiti," after the Amerindian word for the island (*Ayti*) that referred to the mountainous landscape. Although the experience of the French Revolution was the catalyst for events in Haiti, the language was the polyglot of resistance.

■

NATIONAL REVOLUTIONS IN SPANISH AMERICA

The language of Central and South America may have been more uniformly divided between the colonizers' Spanish and Portuguese, but the region's experience of revolution and nationalism was just as complex a mix of issues and injustices as that of the Caribbean. Like the

Colonial Latin America: Political Organization

Disputed by
England, Russia,
and Spain

NEW FRANCE

Effective Frontier
of Spanish Settlement

ENGLISH COLONIES

Mississippi R.

ATLANTIC
OCEAN

VICEROYALTY
OF NEW SPAIN

Mexico City

HAITI
(ceded to France, 1697)

Santo Domingo

JAMAICA
(conquered by
English, 1655)

1494 Line
of Tordesillas

Original boundary between
viceroyalties of New Spain
and Peru

Caracas

VICEROYALTY
OF NEW GRANADA
(established 1717, 1739)

Spanish
Port.

Bogotá

GUIANA

MARANHÃO

Quito

GRÃO PARA

PERNAMBUCO
(held by Dutch,
1630–54)

VICEROYALTY
OF PERU
(established 1543)

MATO
GROSSO GOIAS

Lima   Cuzco

BAHIA

Bahia
(Salvador)

PACIFIC
OCEAN

MINAS
GERAIS

SÃO
PAULO

Rio de Janeiro

VICEROYALTY OF
RIO DE LA PLATA
(established 1776)

RIO DE JANEIRO

Santiago

Buenos Aires

Spanish America: Viceroyalties

Portuguese America (Viceroyalty
of Brazil): Captaincies-general ca. 1780

MAP 16.2 The Claims of Conquest and Diplomacy in Latin America, 1494–1780

British colonists in North America who rebelled against the British imperial government in the late eighteenth century, descendants of Spanish colonists and Native Americans rebelled against Spain beginning in the early nineteenth century.

THE SPANISH AND PORTUGUESE IMPERIAL SYSTEMS

In the sixteenth century, a century before the English, French, and Dutch colonized North America, Spanish and Portuguese conquistadors established themselves in a wide geographic range, from the southern parts of North America to the tip of South America. Following the conquests of Mexico and Peru, a well-organized colonial administration, which was controlled from Spain by the Council of the Indies, supported the mercantilist goals of the kingdom, selling goods in America and shipping to Spain as much precious metal as possible.

By the eighteenth century, the Spanish monarchy had established "viceroyalities," administrative units presided over by the king's representative (the viceroy), in New Spain (Mexico); New Granada (Colombia, Ecuador, and Venezuela), from which one for Peru was separated; and finally Argentina (1776). Viceroys, responsible to the Council of the Indies and the European king, headed the well-defined hierarchical system with an easily recognizable chain of command. A similar system was set up in Portuguese Brazil, though the Portuguese monarchs were more prone to appoint Brazilians to high office in the viceroyalty of Brazil than Spanish monarchs were willing to name Americans to elevated offices in Spanish America. And because Portugal had fewer resources to devote to its Brazilian viceroyalty, it granted captaincies to private persons and permitted them to exploit the region.

Colonial Society The viceregal and mercantilist system by which Spain and Portugal controlled their American colonies tended to create a European elite in Latin America, consisting of *peninsulares* (those who had come to America from the Iberian peninsula) and creoles (Iberians who were born in America) who controlled wealth and exercised power, neither of which they willingly shared with mestizos (a "new race" resulting from European and native American unions). Both the European monopoly on wealth and power and the complicated relations between the native populations of South America and the Europeans became important components in the nationalist struggles in Latin America during the nineteenth and twentieth centuries.

Bourbon Reforms in Spanish America Change in Spanish America began partly as the result of the ascent of a new dynasty to the Spanish throne. When the last Spanish Hapsburg died in 1701, his Bourbon successors undertook programs bearing the hallmarks of eighteenth-century "enlightened" ideas, and changes in Spain included attempts at reform in the colonies. The Spanish Empire was reorganized: the two earliest viceroyalties (New Spain and New Granada) became four, and the closed mercantilist commercial system was relaxed.

Traditionally, only Spaniards were allowed to trade and settle in Spanish America; the eighteenth-century reforms limited the Spanish monopolies and allowed controlled access to Latin American trade to other Europeans. The latter change may have been a means to prosperity for the Spanish colonies and profits for other than Spanish merchants, especially the British, but it also loosened Spanish political dominance by introducing the possibility of political influence and ideas from other countries.

The efforts to reform the Spanish Empire did not correct all the tensions and ills, and during the eighteenth century, a series of insurrections threatened Spanish control. To meet them, the imperial government had to arm colonials, a development that touched upon one of the most fundamental problems of colonial society, the deep division that existed between *peninsulares*, whose loyalties were primarily to Spain, and creoles, who, being born in Latin America, had divided loyalties and a strongly independent streak. Arming the creoles and providing them with military training may have been necessary to defend Spanish control against mestizos and foreign intervention, but it also created a force that could be used against the Spanish Empire. The possibilities of being armed and trained was not lost upon the creoles, many of whom found inspiration in the revolutions in North America and France.

INDEPENDENCE IN LATIN AMERICA

The turmoil of the French Revolution and Napoleonic decades led to the collapse of the Spanish Empire in the Americas. By the beginning of the nineteenth century, Spain was severely weakened in Europe as well as in its colonial possessions in the Americas. In 1807 Napoleon invaded the Iberian peninsula, causing the Portuguese king to seek refuge in his Brazilian colony and replacing the Spanish king with Joseph Bonaparte. Spain's sea power had been destroyed, a development fatal to an overseas empire and one that gave especially the British the opportunity to expand their commercial intrusion into Latin American trade.

The disarray of the Spanish monarchy enabled Latin Americans to liberate themselves from Spanish control. Many leading creoles whose loyalties to the lands of their birth were greater than to Spain and who saw independence as a chance to replace *peninsulares* in power, took leading roles in the uprisings that became wars of independence. The Spanish government was unable to win over the rebels by either compromise or force, and a number of Latin American revolutions substantially ended Spanish imperial control in the Americas.

Bolivar   Simon Bolivar (1783–1830), educated in Caracas, Venezuela, and in Spain, was one of the heroes of the struggle for South American independence from Spain. Like so many of his contemporaries in North America and Europe, Bolivar was influenced by Enlightenment ideas such as the social contract of Rousseau; these ideas inspired his efforts to achieve independence for his homeland. In his fight against Spain in Venezuela, Bolivar was defeated many times before independence was finally achieved in 1817. During the struggle against Spain, he visited Haiti seeking support, and while living in temporary exile in Jamaica in 1815, Bolivar composed a letter to the island's British governor in which he eloquently stated his views on independence:

> Americans either defend their rights or suffer repression at the hands of Spain, which, although once the world's greatest empire, is now too weak, with what little is left her, to rule the new hemisphere or even to maintain herself in the old. And shall Europe, the civilized, the merchant, the lover of liberty allow an aged serpent, bent only on satisfying its venomous rage, devour the fairest part of our globe?. . .
>
> [I]f she [Spain] will fix herself on her own precincts she can build her prosperity and power upon more solid foundations than doubtful conquests, precarious commerce, and forceful exactions from remote and powerful peoples.

Two years later Bolivar led his army across the Andes to liberate Colombia, which was then united with Venezuela. In 1822 Ecuador was liberated, followed by Peru, the southern part of which was named Bolivia.

Bolivar was aided in the liberation of Latin America by others, such as Jose de San Martin (1778–1850), an Argentine who led an army of liberation across the Andes in 1817 and with the Chilean leader Bernardo O'Higgins (1778–1842) freed Chile in 1818, invaded Peru,

Latin America in 1830

OREGON COUNTRY (Joint U.S.-British Occupation)

UNITED STATES

BRITISH NORTH AMERICA (Great Britain)

Mississippi R.

Colorado R.

Rio Grande

San Antonio

MEXICO 1821

Gulf of Mexico

Mexico City • Veracruz

BAHAMA ISLANDS (Great Britain)

CUBA (Spain)

HAITI 1804

PUERTO RICO (Great Britain)

BRITISH HONDURAS (Great Britain)

JAMAICA (Great Britain)

Caribbean Sea

Guatemala

GUATEMÁLA

Panama

Caracas

VENEZUELA

TRINIDAD (Great Britain)

BRITISH GUIANA (Great Britain)

DUTCH GUIANA (Netherlands)

FRENCH GUIANA (France)

GRAN COLOMBIA 1819–1830

• Bogotá

GALÁPAGOS ISLANDS

• Quito

ECUADOR

Amazon R.

ATLANTIC OCEAN

EMPIRE OF BRAZIL 1822

Lima •

PERU 1821

BOLIVIA 1825

• Sucre

PACIFIC OCEAN

CHILE 1817

PARAGUAY 1811

Parana R.

Rio de Janeiro

São Paulo

UNITED PROVINCES OF LA PLATA

Santiago •

URUGUAY 1828

ARGENTINA

Buenos Aires •

• Montevideo

PATAGONIA (Disputed between Argentina and Chile)

ISLAS MALVINAS (FALKLAND ISLANDS) (LA PLATA)

0   500   1,000 Miles

0   500 1,000 Kilometers

MAP 16.3 Polities of the Western Hemisphere

and captured Lima in 1821. Bolivar had a vision of a united Latin America and tried to achieve political unity among the territories he liberated from the Spanish. His dream was destroyed by political factionalism and rivalry between liberation leaders, by tension and suspicion between Latin Americans of European origin and native Americans and also between classes (creoles and mestizos, for example), all of which were inherited from the colonial era. The idea of a Latin American state collapsed, and Bolivar died a disillusioned leader.

Brazilian Independence Portuguese Brazil, like Canada in North America (see Chapter 17) and unlike its South American neighbors, did not break away from its imperial master as a result of a nationalist revolution. When the French invaded the Iberian peninsula in 1807, the Portuguese government simply moved to Brazil, and Rio de Janiero, instead of Lisbon, became the seat of Portuguese government. In 1815 King Joao declared the viceroyalty was a kingdom and decided to remain in Brazil even though the French occupation of Portugal had ended. In 1820 leaders of a revolution in Portugal demanded that the government return to Lisbon and that Brazil be reduced to colonial status. When Joao returned to Lisbon, he left his son, Pedro, to continue Portuguese control; but in 1822 when independence was declared, Pedro became emperor of Brazil, which kept the monarchical government until 1889.

Mexican Independence The liberation of Mexico from Spanish control was considerably more complicated than that of the South American republics established in the first decades of the nineteenth century. Miguel Hidalgo (1753–1811) was a priest who devoted himself to improving the conditions of his mainly native American parishioners. In 1809 he joined a secret society dedicated to overthrowing the Spanish colonial government; in 1810 holding aloft a banner of Our Lady of Guadalupe, the patron saint of Mexico who had revealed herself to an Indian peasant, Hidalgo led a crusade that captured the towns of

FIGURE 16.3 *Panel of the Independence–Father Hidalgo,* by Juan O'Gorman (1960–61)

The priest is depicted carrying the image of Mexico's patron saint and leading a diverse group of people to independence.

SOURCE: Schalkwijk/Art Resource, New York.

Guanajuato and Guadalajara. His peasant army was routed by Spanish soldiers, and Hidalgo was captured and executed. After Mexican independence was finally achieved (1821) and a republic established, Father Hidalgo was revered as a martyr for independence.

Juarez The next generation of leaders in Mexico is represented by Benito Juarez ▬▬▬▬ (1806–1872), a Zapotec Indian who was educated as a lawyer and became governor of the state of Oaxaca in 1847. When the Mexican general Santa Anna seized the national government in a coup in 1853, Juarez fled to Louisiana, but he returned to Mexico in 1855 to take part in the revolution that overthrew Santa Anna, which was followed by a civil war. When Juarez was elected president of Mexico in 1861, he faced the fiscal chaos that was the result of years of revolution and civil war. When he suspended payments to foreign creditors, the major European powers to whom Mexico was indebted—France, Spain, and Great Britain—intervened, and the French dispatched an army that marched inland and captured the capital, Mexico City.

The French set up a puppet empire in Mexico and installed Maximilian, an Austrian archduke, as emperor. Juarez assumed a leading role in Mexican resistance to Maximilian. When the French withdrew, the puppet regime was easily overthrown and Maximilian was executed (1867). Juarez, who had become a national hero, returned to serve a second term as president (1867–1872). Like the priest Hidalgo, the lawyer Juarez is venerated as one of Mexico's greatest national figures. Among Juarez's notable achievements during his terms as president was the subordination of church and army to a secular state. Both Church and army resented the government's policy, and though the Church reluctantly acquiesced, the Mexican republic, like other Latin American countries, continued to be troubled by political interference from the military. National revolutions in Mexico and South America established independent nation states and freed the region from the political bonds of the Spanish Empire, but not from cultural, social, and economic ties to the colonial past.

■

THE REVOLUTION OF CAPITALIST INDUSTRIALISM IN THE ATLANTIC WORLD

Political revolutions that created new nation states in England, France, North America, and the Caribbean in the eighteenth century were shaped as much by economic ideas and practices as by ideals of the social contract and political action. The redefinition and transformation of the state was the counterpart of capitalist industrialism in the dual revolution that reshaped European economic, political, and social life between the seventeenth and nineteenth centuries. During this period individual identities began to shift from family and community to factory and state.

Capitalist industrialism took shape in the late eighteenth and early nineteenth centuries along the Atlantic frontier of western Europe and, perhaps earliest and most successfully, in England. The two decades of political upheaval that began in Europe with the French Revolution in 1789 and lasted until Napoleon's exile to St. Helena in 1814 especially affected processes of capitalist industrialization in England and to a somewhat lesser degree in France. Demands made by the lengthy war in which they (and the rest of Europe) were engaged between 1792 and 1815 encouraged expansion of the industrial sectors of both countries.

Capitalist industrialism was the result of many factors, including government-encouraged economic growth, new large-scale marketing, the availability of surplus capital, and technological innovations that had cumulatively developed since the sixteenth century. It developed earliest in industries such as machine tools, which are basic to all forms of industrial production, and textiles, which supply vast market demands. Enterprises such as mining and metallurgy that were ancillary to machine-tool or textile production were also involved in early capitalist industrial development.

Many of the factors responsible for capitalist industrialism, such as population growth and demographic shifts, technological innovations, and the accumulation of capital for investments in new and risky enterprises, date from the late seventeenth century, a time when the political transformations of the English Civil War and the Glorious Revolution were ushering in profound changes in the English nation state. These political and economic developments were intertwined, and by the eighteenth century, the impact of the industrial revolution was producing dramatic changes in the ways people lived and how they experienced the world around them.

DEMOGRAPHIC CHANGES: AGRICULTURE AND URBANIZATION

An increase in births and a decline in deaths increased the population of England by about 3 million (to 8 million) in the eighteenth century. Population growth evident in his own lifetime led the Reverend Thomas Malthus (1776–1834) to despair in his *Essay on the Principle of Population* (1798) that "the power of population is infinitely greater than the power of the earth to produce subsistence for man." Increased numbers required increased food production, and the innovations and rapid changes that took place in eighteenth-century agricultural practices constituted what can be called an "agricultural revolution."

Agricultural Revolution One aspect of this revolution, the culmination of a long process, was the consolidation of agricultural estates by engrossing (combining smaller into larger parcels of land) and enclosure (which converted arable land into pastures for sheep). Enclosure was vigorously pursued in eighteenth century England when people with capital and influence were able to take over common lands, dispossess small farmers, and consolidate their holdings to create landed estates that were more efficient and that could supply wool for the expanding textile industry. By the early nineteenth century large, landowning, agricultural capitalists were sufficiently powerful to persuade the government to pass a general enclosure act (1801), providing a formula that standardized, simplified, and thus accelerated the process.

Urbanization New agricultural machinery, which reduced the need for human agricultural labor; new crops; and new methods of improving fields and cultivation were as important as enclosure in responding to the market needs of expanding populations and increasing urbanization. Increased numbers of people dispossessed of their lands by the agricultural revolution sought employment in the cities. The marked increase in urban populations in the second half of the eighteenth century complemented industrial expansion by providing a useful supply of labor and by increased market demand for manufactured as well as agricultural products. The inability of traditional modes of production to satisfy the growing needs of expanding populations led to the investment of capital in the technology and organization of industry as well as agriculture.

TECHNOLOGY AND CAPITAL

Many of the technological innovations essential to the capitalist industrial revolution were the result of experiments and tinkering by craftsmen and artisans. Consistent developments of textile machinery, beginning with an improved loom (John Kay, 1733) and continuing with swifter methods of spinning (James Hargreaves, 1764) provided the basis of the revolution in textile production. The distinctive technological feature of the capitalist industrial revolution, however, was the rotary steam engine perfected by James Watt (1736–1813), a trained instrument maker. The combination of such technological innovation with the investment of wealth—some of which was rooted in the Atlantic plantation economy and slavery—was essential to the capitalist industrial revolution and helps explain why it was first successfully launched in England.

The use of power-driven machinery under factory conditions, a feature that characterizes the industrial revolution, was made possible by venture capitalists who were willing and able to invest substantial sums in innovations and take risks in the quest for profits. Not all capitalists, however, were willing to take risks involved in developing new modes of production. As long as the traditional, labor-intensive methods of production were profitable, most capitalists continued to invest in them, rather than in machine-operated factory production. Labor-intensive industry remained a major mode of production well past 1800, even as machine production increased.

THE FACTORY SYSTEM

The distinctive institution of the capitalist industrial revolution was the factory system of production, whereby workers were herded together in buildings for fixed hours of labor at power-driven machines. Factories were, however, slow to replace domestic industry, where workers spun and wove in their own homes, using their own spinning wheels and looms. Except in cotton spinning and weaving, as late as the 1830s many employers continued to find domestic industry more profitable and to prefer small shop production to large factory enterprise. Traditional workers also tended to resist the reorganization of the workplace.

As factories multiplied, younger trainees, many of them women, who had no commitment to older modes of production, replaced traditional artisans and older workers. Factory work meant a loss of the artisan's independence and often a readjustment of family relationships, since production moved outside the home and altered the roles of individual workers. In 1831 a government committee in England investigating child labor in the textile industry uncovered the grim circumstances of daily life for many young children condemned to work in the mills to supplement family income. Twenty-three-year-old Elizabeth Bentley described her work in a textile mill at the age of 6, laboring from 5:00 in the morning to 9:00 at night, with meager portions of poor quality food to sustain her.

Many people compared the factory to the workhouse, where people were sent to work off debt. Many factory owners, who believed themselves morally as well as physically justified in controlling and disciplining their workers, introduced strict work codes that regulated every aspect of the factory day as well as after-hours activities. Despite the reluctance of some entrepreneurs and the resistance of some workers, by the middle of the nineteenth century the factory system had become the common mode of production, and capitalist industrialists who owned the factories organized and controlled the economic, cultural, and even religious life of factory communities.

TRANSPORTATION AND COMMUNICATION

Improvements in transportation affected industrial production of every type. Efficient and cheap movement of goods was instrumental in providing supplies necessary for the growth of production and satisfying the market demand necessary to sustain it. For example, landed aristocrats who wanted to profit from mineral deposits on their land and needed a way to transport the minerals often funded extensive canal building programs in England from 1760 onward. Canals decreased the costs of transportation, and similar improvements in roads, bridges, and harbors furthered the success of English industrialism in the eighteenth century. The English transportation network was superior to that of continental Europe, where internal tolls also hindered the movement of goods. Such tariffs had disappeared in England well before the beginning of the nineteenth century, but they were not eliminated in France until 1790 or in Germany until 1834.

FIGURE 16.4 Women at Textile Machinery in a New England Mill, ca. 1850
This early photograph depicts the discipline and grim conditions faced by women factory workers.

SOURCE: Courtesy George Eastman House.

By 1829 a practical steam locomotive was developed by George Stephenson in England, and shortly thereafter railway construction proceeded rapidly. In England alone railway mileage grew from 49 miles in 1830 to 15,300 in 1870. By the end of the century, Europe was knit together by a network of rail lines, and by 1905 travelers could go from Paris to Moscow and on to Vladivostok on the Pacific via the lengthy trans-Siberian railway.

Equally important to industrial growth in Europe was the development of practical ocean-going steamships, which made non-European parts of the world readily available as sources of raw materials and markets for finished products of European factories. As early as 1785, a steamboat had plied the Potomac River in the United States, but it was the success of Robert Fulton's *Clermont* on the Hudson River in 1807 that proved the feasibility of the commercial steamboat. In 1819 the *Savannah*, using steam power as a supplement to its sails, crossed the Atlantic to Liverpool, and in 1840 Samuel Cunard inaugurated a regular trans-Atlantic passenger steamship line.

Rapid transportation was accompanied by even more rapid means of communication, as people began to gather news of events from every part of the world and with increasing synchronicity. As early as 1820 André-Marie Ampère (1775–1836), a French physicist, used electromagnetism to send a message over wire; by 1837 Samuel F. B. Morse (1791–1872) patented a practical system of electric telegraphy in the United States. In 1851 an undersea telegraph cable across the English Channel provided instantaneous communication between London and Paris, and in 1866 a trans-Atlantic cable successfully established telegraphic communication between Britain and North America. Ten years later, the Canadian Alexander Graham Bell successfully exhibited his telephone and, with improvements and modifications, it was adopted throughout America and subsequently in Europe.

TECHNOLOGY AND INDUSTRIALIZATION

Demands for supplies and for finished goods doubled every few years with the expansion of global markets. For example, iron production, basic to the machine age, increased 100-fold in the nineteenth century. Innovations in metallurgy, an important aspect of the eighteenth-century beginnings of capitalist industrialization, continued in the nineteenth century. An English engineer, Henry Bessemer (1813–1883), patented a process for the efficient conversion of iron to hard steel in 1856, and about the same time William Siemens (1823–1883), a German who had settled in England, perfected an alternative process. Steady progress in discovering and using new technologies was essential to increasingly mechanized industrial production in the latter part of the nineteenth century.

Many new industries appeared in the decades after 1850, and this tendency accelerated in the twentieth century. Innovations resulted in the alliance of industry with science and engineering, and technical schools and institutions of applied science became widespread. Precision tools and implements multiplied on demand, and new processes led to a proliferation of market products, some specifically connected with heavy industrial production but many, and increasingly, geared to the consumer market.

Among the more important new industries appearing in the second half of the nineteenth century were those connected to new sources of power such as electricity. Dynamos and motors were improved and multiplied, and new kinds of engines resulted in the development of industrial production unheard of during the initial eighteenth-century phase of the capitalist industrial revolution. This status was especially true of the internal combustion engine, which would result in the twentieth-century triumph of motorized vehicles and, among other things, cause the world production of petroleum to leap 1000 percent in the first thirty years of the twentieth century.

Consumer Industries   At the same time a conspicuous growth of essential consumer industries occurred, producing aids to individual comfort that greatly improved both the style and standard of material life, first in much of the western world and ultimately around the globe. For example, in 1879 Thomas A. Edison (1847–1931) patented the greatest of his inventions, the incandescent lamp, which would rapidly become a necessary luxury. Artificial fabrics, such as rayon, patented by the French chemist Hilaire Chardonnet (1836–1924), and artificial dyes made finery widely and cheaply available.

Refrigeration, first used on ships in 1877, added immeasurably to the availability and variety of foodstuffs. The world became the garden for urban industrial workers who could not raise their own food in rapidly expanding cities where they were confined. An Englishman might sit down to a meal gathered from five continents, and commoners who could afford to do so indulged in foods and supplies that even kings of an earlier age could not have imagined. Coal- and oil-burning furnaces kept people warm and comfortable, and trains, ships, trams, bicycles, and in time the automobile kept the population mobile.

FINANCE CAPITALISM

Expansion of industrial production would not have been possible without continued improvements in agriculture and finance capital. Capital accumulation by partnerships or joint-stock companies, sufficient to finance early capitalist industrial enterprises such as metallurgy and textiles, was inadequate for the demands of later industrialization and trade. New means of augmenting capital were devised, leading to the formation of trusts or cartels (as trusts were designated in Germany).

Trusts and Cartels   Trusts and cartels were permanent, legally agreed upon combinations of businesses (industries, financial institutions, merchants, and the like) seeking to establish monopolies that would eliminate competition and control production and marketing. Such financial and legal combinations promised reduction of overhead expenses, increased the amount of capital available for investment, and expanded profits for those who had a share in them. Capitalist industrialism approached its apex by the end of the nineteenth century when trusts and cartels became increasingly global in their structure and operations, enabling businessmen to gather requisite financing for industrial growth by continuously increasing profits.

■

THE CONSTRUCTION OF NATIONAL IDENTITIES IN NINETEENTH-CENTURY EUROPE

As the impact of the revolution of capitalist industrialism was being experienced across the Atlantic world and new national identities were being created through revolutions in the Americas, representatives from European states met to reconstruct Europe after the two decades of disruption stemming from the French Revolution and Napoleonic Wars. From September 1814 to June 1815, representatives from European states met in Vienna to redraw the map of Europe and restore the balance of power following Napoleon's final defeat at the Battle of Waterloo (June 1815). The Congress of Vienna was dominated by the major European monarchies that had most persistently resisted the French Revolution and Napoleon: Great Britain, Russia, Prussia, and Austria. Their participation ensured that the restoration of order would reflect the interests of these "old regimes," not those of new national identities inspired by the French Revolution and Napoleon.

At the Congress of Vienna territories conquered and annexed by Napoleon were removed from French control, and a new balance of power was established among the European states. The principal desire of key diplomats, especially the Austrian prime minister, Prince Metternich (1773–1859), who acted as the presiding official of the congress, was to suppress revolutionary nationalism throughout Europe. Though the French were defeated and the Napoleonic Empire was dissolved, the example of the revolutionary French nation state based on liberty, equality, and fraternity had spread throughout Europe as the French gained control of the continent during the Napoleonic era.

Despite the efforts of Metternich and the Congress of Vienna, the example of the French nation state and the ideas that it embodied continued to influence other Europeans—Germans, Italians, Spanish, and subjects of the Hapsburg emperor. By 1820 revolutions against restored Bourbon kings had broken out in Naples and in Spain and a revolution against Turkish rule in Greece became a struggle for Greek independence (1821–1829). It was clearly difficult to curb the influence of the ideas and example of the French Revolution, and for most of the nineteenth century attempts to create nation states based on contractual constitutions were made all over Europe, from the Baltic eastward to the Black Sea and south to the Mediterranean.

RESTORATION AND REVOLUTION IN FRANCE

Following the downfall of Napoleon, though the French restored their traditional ruling family, the effects of the Revolution on the nature of the French state could not be erased. The last Bourbon monarchs (r. 1814–1830) were forced to accept a constitutional charter that established their contractual position as rulers. Implicit in the restoration of the Bourbons to the French throne was the right of French citizens to terminate their political contract with the dynasty. The citizens exercised this right in 1830, when a revolution removed the last Bourbon, Charles X (r. 1824–1830), following his attempt to deprive nonaristocrats of the vote. Charles was replaced by Louis Philippe (r. 1830–1848), who referred to himself as the "citizen king" and whose reign was terminated by another revolution.

The revolution of 1830 not only removed the Bourbons but also increased the role of the urban bourgeoisie who, with the landed bourgeoisie, constituted the governing elite during the reign of Louis Philippe. This coalition jealously guarded its position in the face of changes that accompanied growing social and economic uncertainties resulting from economic difficulties and industrial growth. Workers, peasants, and bourgeois democrats began to demand general enfranchisment and social and economic equality; where the governing elite resisted change, rallies and the government's attempt to limit public assemblies in February 1848 set off the revolution that sent Louis Philippe into exile.

Following Louis Philippe's abdication, a provisional government undertook to address the needs and demands of working class revolutionaries by setting up national workshops to

FIGURE 16.5 *Liberty Leading the People, July 28, 1830*

This preliminary sketch for a larger painting by Eugene Delacroix (1798–1863) expresses the spirit of revolutionary forces. Though women were excluded from power in the aftermath of the French Revolution, the romantic representation of such ideals as liberty was usually female. The French government purchased the painting from Delacroix, but refused to allow public viewing because of its inflammatory nature, until forced to show it after the Revolution of 1848.

SOURCE: Louvre, Paris/Giraudon/Bridgeman Art Library.

provide jobs and income for the urban poor. When the national workshops were closed as a result of conservative bourgeois pressure, a new insurrection broke out in Paris (the June Days) between radical workers, peasants, and democratic-socialist leaders on one side and the bourgeois elite who used the army to brutally suppress the rebels on the other. Following the suppression of the June uprising, a constitution for a Second French Republic was drawn up. This document left power in the hands of a political and economic elite while promising universal male suffrage and social and economic reforms.

Prince Louis Napoleon Bonaparte, elected president of the conservative republic in December 1848, was a stronger supporter of general male suffrage, not because he was a democrat but because, like his famous uncle, he understood the political expediency and value of championing popular causes and using popular approval to validate power. Accordingly, like his uncle, the prince president would later (1851) subvert the Second Republic and transform it—with plebiscitary approval—into the Second Empire, with himself as Emperor Napoleon III (r. 1852–1870).

THE REVOLUTIONS OF 1848 AND NEW NATIONAL IDENTITIES

Revolution also occurred in 1848 throughout the Austrian (Hapsburg) Empire: in Vienna, where reformers demanded a constitution; in Prague, where Czechs demanded autonomy and their own parliament; in Budapest, where Magyars sought to establish a Hungarian state free of Germanic dominance. Southern Slavs proclaimed a southern Slavic state of Croats and Serbs; Italians were in revolt, seeking their rights and freedoms. As Metternich had feared, the traditional Hapsburg monarchy, a composite of peoples held together by a common dynasty, was seriously endangered by a combination of ethnic desires and the ideal of the contractual nation state. The 1848 revolutions in the Austrian Empire failed and Hapsburg power was restored, but the days of traditional dynastic monarchies in Europe were numbered. At the end of the reign of the Hapsburg emperor Franz Joseph, which began in 1848, the Hapsburg monarchy collapsed and broke apart (1918).

The unification of Italian territories into the kingdom of Italy in 1861 and the creation of the Second (the first existed in medieval times) German Reich (empire) in 1871 were products of nationalist movements that developed during the Napoleonic era as a result of both admiration of what the French had achieved and resentment at French occupation and control under Napoleon.

Unification of Italy Once the French were expelled, a nationalistic movement, the *Risorgimento*, aimed to make Italy more than a mere "geographical expression" by reforming and unifying the peninsula. Various patriotic movements and leaders attempted to expel foreign (meaning, principally, Austrian Hapsburg) influence and create an Italian nation state, but they failed in 1820 and again in 1830. In 1835 the Italian nationalist and patriot Giuseppe Mazzini (1805–1872), who mobilized Italian national aspirations, expressed his understanding of nation: "A nation is an association of those who are brought together by language, by given geographical conditions or by the role assigned them by history, who acknowledge the same principles and who march together to the conquest of a single definite goal under the rule of a uniform body of law."

After the failure of the revolutions of 1848, Italian nationalists found a realistic leader in the person of Count Camillo di Cavour (1810–1861), the chief minister of the Italian Kingdom of Sardinia. Cavour engaged the support of the French in freeing Italy from Hapsburg domination. The next step toward completion of Italian unification came under the leadership of Giuseppe Garibaldi (1807–1882) and his followers, who continued Cavour's efforts to unite Italy by adding more territory. The kingdom of Italy was proclaimed in 1861, and unification was completed in 1870 when Romans voted overwhelmingly for incorporation into the kingdom of Italy.

The Unification of Germany Following the Congress of Vienna, which left Germany a far-from-unified confederation of thirty-eight states, nationalist aspirations flourished. Metternich strongly supported efforts by German monarchs who had been restored by the Congress of Vienna to fetter opinion, rights, and nationalist aspirations. Nonetheless, the hopes of Germans to achieve unity and constitutional government remained alive and in 1848 resulted in a series of revolutions in German states, including Prussia, the most powerful one. Though progress had been made in economically unifying Germany by the creation of a tariff union (*Zollverein*, 1834), this union proved more important in stimulating German industrialization than it did in creating a single German state. After the 1848 failure to unify Germany, many German patriots concluded that the way to unification was by force—"blood and iron"—and the "politics of reality" (*realpolitik*).

The state best able to use such means was Prussia, and in the end, German unification became a process of the growing dominance and control of Prussia. Prussian dominance hinged on expelling Austrian influence, and the Prussian statesman, Prince Otto von Bismarck (1815–1898), directed the process. Bismarck's victory in a series of three wars fought between 1864 and 1870 unified Germany under Prussian leadership, and the Prussian defeat of France in the Franco-Prussian war of 1870 completed the process. Bismarck's *realpolitik* had been successful; it ended centuries of French hegemony and created a new European balance of power. By the end of the nineteenth century, as a result of unification and the rapid progress of industrialization that followed it, Germany became not only a single nation state but also the major continental power in Europe.

■

THE CONSTRUCTION OF AMERICAN NATIONAL IDENTITY, 1815–1865

The American nation state originated with the military struggles of 1775–1781; it was redefined and reaffirmed in another military struggle, the Civil War (1861–1865). The construction of American national identity through the Civil War era encompassed compromise, conflict, and conquest. American expansion accompanied and inspired the growth of American nationalism, and by the end of the nineteenth century the United States dominated the North American continent, as Germany dominated Europe.

"MANIFEST DESTINY" AND AMERICAN EXPANSION

The expansion of territories across the Appalachians and on to the Pacific got a tremendous boost when in 1803 President Thomas Jefferson (in office, 1801–1809) purchased the Louisiana Territory from Napoleon following the Haitian revolution. The possibilities that this territory offered Americans was made clear by the Lewis and Clark expedition (1804–1805), which Jefferson promptly commissioned to explore it.

American territorial expansion also involved conflicts with Great Britain (the War of 1812) and Mexico (the Mexican-American War [1845–1848]); the possibility of renewed conflict with Great Britain (over the Oregon Territory and possible invasions of Canada); voluntary annexation (Texas, 1845); and purchase (Alaska from Russia, 1867). In this way America's Manifest Destiny "to overspread the continent allotted by Providence for the free development of our yearly multiplying millions," proclaimed in 1845 by the journalist John L. O'Sullivan, was forged.

NATIVE AMERICANS AND NATIONAL IDENTITY

Along with territorial gains through war, annexation, or purchase, removal of Native Americans from their lands was equally part of the policies of Manifest Destiny. During the Jefferson presidency, for example, Indians were pressed into ceding over 100 million acres of land

FIGURE 16.6 *In the Yosemite Valley* (1867, by Albert Bierstadt). Oil on canvas (35⅛ × 50″).

This painting presents an idealized European vision of the vast American West. The image of a landscape devoid of indigenous people served the ideology of expansionism.

SOURCE: Wadsworth Atheneum, Hartford. Bequest of Elizabeth Hart Jarvis Colt.

in the Ohio River Valley to white settlers. Jefferson encouraged the policy of selling goods on credit in order to lure Indians into debt and force them to cede land. In the face of pressures from the expansion of white settlers westward, some Indian leaders, such as Chief Black Hoof of the Shawnees in Ohio, supported accommodation, while others organized resistance. In the early 1800s a Shawnee known as the "Prophet" led a religious revival and urged a return to traditional ways of life (such as hunting with bows and arrows) that had been shattered by alcohol and dependence on trading goods (such as guns) acquired from white settlers. The Prophet's older brother Tecumseh adopted political and military strategies to confront white encroachment on Indian lands, establishing a confederacy of tribes through a message of Pan-Indian unity.

The Cherokees, led by the mixed-blood (with both white and Indian ancestry) John Ross, followed a policy of accommodation. In 1827 the Cherokees adopted a constitution modeled on that of the United States; they developed their own alphabet and even published their own newspaper, *The Cherokee Phoenix*. Some Cherokees, particularly those of mixed blood, became wealthy planters and slaveholders and supported acculturation to such an extent that they adopted the same attitudes toward African American slaves that white society adopted toward Indians.

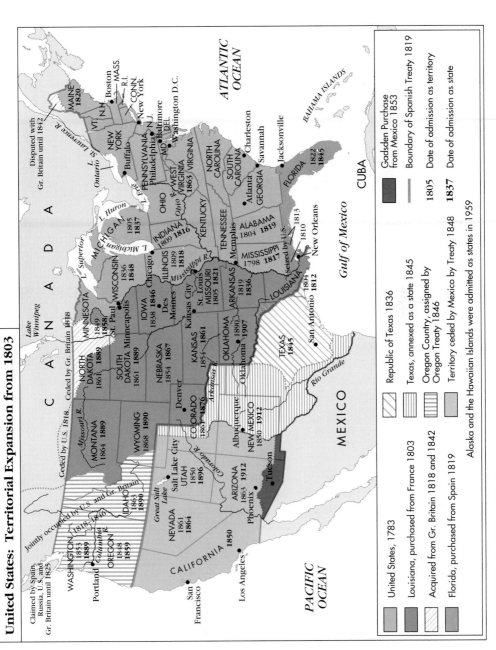

United States: Territorial Expansion from 1803

ATLANTIC OCEAN

PACIFIC OCEAN

Gulf of Mexico

CANADA

MEXICO

CUBA

BAHAMA ISLANDS

Disputed with Gr. Britain until 1842

Claimed by Spain, Russia, U.S. and Gr. Britain until 1825

Ceded by Gr. Britain 1818

Ceded by U.S. 1818

Jointly occupied by U.S. and Gr. Britain 1818–1846

Serzed by U.S.

Lake Winnipeg

L. Superior

L. Huron

L. Michigan

L. Erie

L. Ontario

L. St. Lawrence R.

Missouri R.

Columbia R.

Great Salt Lake

Colorado R.

Rio Grande

Arkansas R.

Mississippi R.

Ohio R.

MAINE 1820

MASS.

R.I.

CONN.

N.H.

VT

NEW YORK — Boston

N.J.

PENNSYLVANIA — Philadelphia — New York

DEL.

MD. — Baltimore — Washington D.C.

WEST VIRGINIA 1863

VIRGINIA

NORTH CAROLINA

SOUTH CAROLINA — Charleston

GEORGIA — Atlanta — Savannah

FLORIDA 1822 **1845** — Jacksonville

OHIO

INDIANA 1809 **1816**

MICHIGAN 1805 **1837**

WISCONSIN 1836 **1848**

ILLINOIS 1809 **1818** — Chicago

KENTUCKY

TENNESSEE — Memphis

ALABAMA 1804 **1819**

MISSISSIPPI 1798 **1817**

LOUISIANA 1804 **1812** — New Orleans

1813

1810

MINNESOTA 1849 **1858** — St. Paul — Minneapolis

IOWA 1838 **1846** — Des Moines

MISSOURI 1805 **1821** — St. Louis

ARKANSAS 1819 **1836**

NORTH DAKOTA 1861 **1889**

SOUTH DAKOTA 1861 **1889**

NEBRASKA 1854 **1867**

KANSAS 1854 – **1861** — Kansas City

OKLAHOMA 1890 **1907** — Oklahoma

TEXAS 1845 — San Antonio

MONTANA 1864 **1889**

WYOMING 1868 **1890**

COLORADO 1861 – **1876** — Denver

NEW MEXICO 1850 **1912** — Albuquerque

IDAHO 1863 **1890**

UTAH 1850 **1896** — Salt Lake City

ARIZONA 1863 **1912** — Phoenix — Tucson

NEVADA 1861 **1864**

CALIFORNIA 1850 — Los Angeles

WASHINGTON 1853 **1889** — Portland

OREGON 1848 **1859** — San Francisco

Legend

	United States, 1783
	Louisiana, purchased from France 1803
	Acquired from Gr. Britain 1818 and 1842
	Florida, purchased from Spain 1819
	Republic of Texas 1836
	Texas, annexed as a state 1845
	Oregon Country, assigned by Oregon Treaty 1846
	Territory ceded by Mexico by Treaty 1848

Alaska and the Hawaiian Islands were admitted as states in 1959

	Gadsden Purchase from Mexico 1853
	Boundary of Spanish Treaty 1819
1805	Date of admission as territory
1837	Date of admission as state

MAP 16.4 Westward Expansion in the Nineteenth Century

699

FIGURE 16.7 *The Natchez,* by Eugene Delacroix

Oil on canvas, nineteenth century. Romanticism was not limited to European subjects. The French painter Delacroix romanticizes a Natchez Indian family as they were before their decimation by the French in the Mississippi Valley. This event served as a prelude to the dispersal of the Cherokee and other Native American peoples by the United States federal government in the nineteenth century.

SOURCE: The Metropolitan Museum of Art, Purchase, Gifts of George N. and Helen M. Richard and Mr. and Mrs. Charles S. McVeigh and Bequest of Emma A. Shaefer, by exchange, 1989 (1989.328).

The Cherokee Removal Despite the accommodation strategies of the Cherokees, during the 1830s the United States government began a policy of systematic removal of Indians (including the Cherokees) from lands east of the Mississippi River. First came the Choctaws, who were dispossessed of their lands in what is now the state of Mississippi, and then the lands of the Cherokees in Georgia were "legally moved into the market." The Cherokees resisted and refused to abandon their homes and lands. More than 15,000 Cherokees signed a protest petition to Congress. The federal government ignored it and ordered the army to move the Cherokees west of the Mississippi to the Oklahoma territory. By the time they reached their new lands, more than 4000 people, a quarter of the Cherokee nation, had died on what they bitterly remember as the "Trail of Tears." Some Seminoles in Florida, under the leadership of Osceola, for a time were able to resist removal, but were finally subdued at a cost of $50 million and more than 1500 soldiers' lives.

The demographic pressure of high birth rates and aggressive expansion on the part of Anglo-Americans ensured conflict between the two cultures. Federal government policy contributed to the construction of American national identity by contrasting the seminomadic culture, society, and economic livelihood of Native Americans to those of agrarian Anglo-Americans and thereby justifying the removal of Indians from their lands so that Anglo-Americans could claim them.

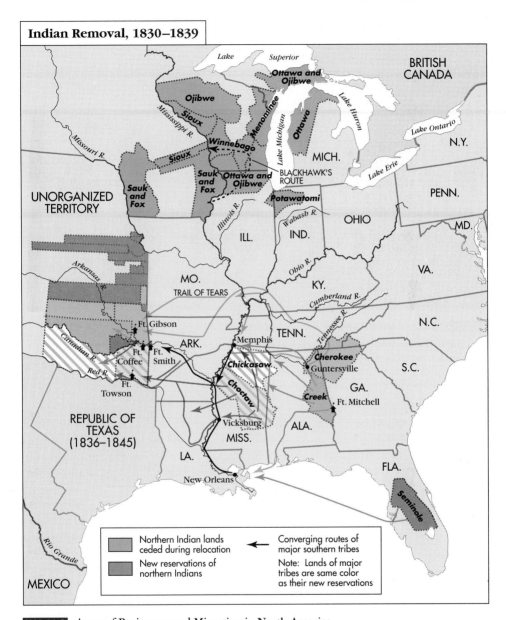

Indian Removal, 1830–1839

MAP 16.5 Areas of Resistance and Migration in North America

THE GROWTH OF A NATIONAL MARKET ECONOMY

The expansion of Anglo-Americans onto Indian lands in such places as the rich Ohio River Valley provided the basis for stable agriculture with surplus production, which in turn gave rise to commerce that transcended local and barter exchange. The major agents of the expan-

FIGURE 16.8 *The Trail of Tears,* by Robert Lindneux (1942)

This painting shows the Cherokee being forced from their homeland in Georgia to reservation lands in the West.

SOURCE: Woolaroc Museum.

sion of production and trade were merchants and bankers of the Northeast. By about 1830 merchants were handling trade beyond local communities, and banks controlled money, essential for wage labor, large scale manufacturing, increased production, and expanding trade. The growth of cities indicated the emergence of a national market economy, which was successfully launched between 1815 and the Civil War.

At the heart of this process was a self-generating triangular relationship between the South, which produced surplus cotton, tobacco, and other products of an expanding market oriented agrarian economy; the Northeast, where textiles were finished and trade and banking flourished; and the West, which produced food for both. It was an integrated, interdependent national economy, but one in which regional differences were sharpened. Differences between urban wage labor in the Northeast, the cotton slave culture in the deep South, and farmers in the West became exacerbated.

As the institution of slavery became deeply entrenched, the economy of the deep South became less and less attuned to and integrated into the emerging national market economy dominated by the Northeast. Technological change in the South lagged behind other regions, and the South remained in many ways self-sufficient and relatively isolated, continuing many of the characteristics of British colonial society. Northeastern merchants controlled the markets for the products of Southern agriculture, especially cotton; manufactured goods came principally from the North; and labor in the south was often owned rather than employed. In many ways the deep South remained an economic colony, but of the Northeast rather than of Great Britain.

SECTIONALISM, SOVEREIGNTY, AND AMERICAN NATIONAL IDENTITY

By the mid-nineteenth century, conflicting views of the nature of the new American nation state became increasingly apparent. Northeastern merchants and manufacturers and western freehold farmers adhered to one view, based on private property, individualism, and free labor. The agrarian, slaveholding South had another view, locally determined and maintained, in which the American nation was plural—interdependent perhaps, but not integrated as a single political system. This distinction was derived from one interpretation of the Lockean idea of "popular sovereignty," that all power derives from the people and that the people have the right to determine the nature of government and to alter government at will. The Southern interpretation of the nation carried in it the right of revolution; it increasingly conflicted with the northeastern and—in different ways—the western understanding. These differing interpretations of the American nation state were to produce a second American revolution, the Civil War era (1819–1865), that was finally to define American national identity.

The sovereign right of the people to revolt came to hinge on the question of who "the people" were, and this definition depended on contrasting views of who made up the nation. Did the United States consist of a nation of individual white male citizens whose citizenship and loyalty were national rather than local? Or was it a collection of autonomous and differing states by which citizenship and loyalty were locally determined? Those who held the former view were nationalists; those who held the latter view, prevalent in the South, believed the nation was a collective of independent sovereign units, the states. For them the nation as a

FIGURE 16.9 *Liberty, Equality, Fraternity, Dedicated to the Smartest Nation in All Creation*

An 1848 English cartoon points out the "masquerade" of American liberty in the contrast between American democratic ideals and the realities of the slave system.

SOURCE: Mansell/Time, Inc.

LIBERTY, EQUALITY, FRATERNITY,
DEDICATED TO THE SMARTEST NATION IN ALL CREATION.

whole possessed only the powers given to it by the sovereign states. By the 1850s Southerners concerned with the protection of slavery and their right to extend it into western territories argued that there was, in fact, no American nation as such; rather, the United States was a collective of sovereign independent states. This theory was a means of guaranteeing slavery, but its implications ran counter to the nationalist interpretation of the United States, and it was an important factor in the outbreak of the Civil War in 1861 between the slave-holding South, the Confederacy, and the North, the Union.

The Impact of the Civil War The Civil War resolved the fundamental issues that caused it— sectionalism, slavery, and sovereignty—and confirmed American national identity. The defeat of the South resulted in the official rejection of the doctrine of state sovereignty. The confirmation that the United States was a union, rather than a collection of regions, was reflected in American linguistic usage. Before the Civil War, citizens referred to the nation (especially in the South) in the plural: "The United States *are*"; following the war, it was possible to refer to the country only in the singular: "The United States *is*."

African Americans An important part of the definition of American national identity that was accomplished by the Southern defeat was the abolition of slavery (1863) and the Fourteenth Amendment to the Constitution, which confirmed the constitutional rights of African Americans. Knowing that these were the stakes, many blacks enlisted as soldiers for the Northern cause, while Southern slaves were forced to assist their Confederate masters. The eighteenth-century ideals of equality, popular sovereignty, and the social contract, which were the bases for the American Revolution and the nation state that resulted from it, were in theory legally recognized for all Americans. In practice, it took more than a century for African Americans to begin to realize the rights recognized in the Fourteenth Amendment.

The shift in the way Americans defined their national identity suggests a pattern to the progress of American nationalism in the nineteenth century. Before 1815 Americans defined themselves primarily in local terms, as Charlestonians or Bostonians, for example; between 1815 and 1865 they used regional terms such as Southerners or westerners. Increasingly in the post–Civil War period, most Anglo-Americans thought of themselves as Americans first. What remained to be resolved was the role of Native Americans and African Americans in post–Civil War American national identity.

■
THE CULTURAL CONSTRUCTION OF NATIONAL IDENTITIES

The inhabitants of every state identify with it in a number of tangible ways, whether (as in constitutional nation states) as citizens, partners in a social contract, or (as in traditional dynastic monarchies) as subjects of a hereditary ruler. Subjects in traditional monarchical states had a sense of being a part of the ruling family, such as the Russian conception of the czar as "little father." Flags are recognizable symbols of a nation around which its members rally in

FIGURE 16.10 Battery "A," Second Colored Artillery (light), Department of the Cumberland, 1864. Photographer unknown. Black Troops in the American Civil War Man Union Guns

SOURCE: Chicago Historical Society. ICHi-07774.

war and peace. In traditional dynastic states, flags bore the coats of arms of the ruling family: under the Hapsburgs, the double-headed eagle was the center of the flag of the Austrian Empire; and a golden fleur de lis on a white field, the coat of arms of the Bourbon dynasty, was the French flag before the Revolution.

Nationalism is the expression of a common sense of belonging to a nation, which is constructed of a combination of ethnic, linguistic, religious, historical, and cultural identities. Nation states as they evolved in the nineteenth century had to develop new symbols, unconnected with the person or family of the ruler, that became the means by which citizens identified with them. Popular manifestations of nationalism, such as flags and the veneration and glorification of national heroes, such as Simon Bolivar, Napoleon, Marcus Garvey, or Abraham Lincoln, all contributed to the shaping and expression of national identities, as did theater, festivals, and mass celebrations.

The Invention of Tradition The construction of national identities took many forms and, according to historians Eric Hobsbawm and Terence Ranger, even involved the "invention of tradition." Swiss nationalism, for example, was promoted in the nineteenth century with the formation of the Swiss federal state by adapting traditional customs for new national purposes. The traditional hero William Tell became associated with the Swiss nation, and marksmanship and other physical contests were used in the service of nationalism. Folk songs and musical styles, too, were adapted to promote national feelings by using new words in traditional tunes or new styles that reflected a common sentiment and identity.

HISTORY AND NATIONAL IDENTITY

The notion of a shared past played a vital role in shaping national identities, so views of history—what it meant, how it was practiced, and how it was used—were critical in the formation and maintenance of nationalism. History became a formal and structured discipline in nineteenth century Europe, and its development was closely connected with the emergence of the European nation state and nationalist ideology.

Leopold von Ranke (1795–1886), a German historian, played a defining role in the creation of history as a modern academic discipline. According to Ranke, the task of the historian is to reconstruct the past as objectively and comprehensively as possible, to present the past *wie es eigentlich gewesen* ("as it actually was"). The historian does this task through the critical use of evidence contained in written texts collected in archives, or official repositories of documents.

The archival sources that Ranke and his followers relied on were largely official documents dealing with political affairs that governments assembled and stored in national archives. Such sources naturally validated official views of national histories. Archival collections, along with national biographical dictionaries and collections of folklore and law, legitimized the nineteenth-century nation state.

Repositories of historical sources, such as personal royal libraries and archives, were transformed into national collections. For example, the *Bibliothèque nationale* and the *Archives nationale* in Paris date from the French Revolution, and the National Archives in Washington, D.C., dates from the beginning of the American republic. As nation states proliferated, so did archival collections. Since archival research governed the content of Rankean history, it also determined the nature of historiography, making the nation state the subject of historical narrative: history was telling the "story" of the nation.

As the study of history became professionalized, historians became increasingly connected with academic institutions. In France and Germany academic appointments were state appointments, and some famous and successful professors of history were even named national historians. Heinrich von Treitschke (1834–1896) fully accepted and utilized the possibilities of writing history as nationalistic propaganda, validating Prussian Germany. Jules Michelet (1798–1874) reified "la Belle France," and Thomas Macaulay (1800–1859) in England praised seventeenth-century English politics as the paradigm for human political achievements. Francis Parkman (1823–1893), James Ford Rhodes (1848–1927), and Frederick Jackson Turner (1861–1932) praised the American experiment and its achievements, supporting and justifying the doctrine of Manifest Destiny.

ETHNICITY, RACE, AND NATIONAL IDENTITY

During the nineteenth century ethnic identity emerged as one of the principal rally points of nation states. This was particularly true in central Europe when many ethnic communities sought independence from the Germanic Hapsburg control in the multiethnic Austrian Empire or when the Poles tried to liberate themselves from Russian dominance. Though these efforts were frequently unsuccessful (only the Magyars gained some degree of autonomy with the creation of the Austro-Hungarian dual monarchy in 1867), ethnic identity continued to be a rallying point for nationalists, who encouraged it in both political and cultural ways.

Slavic peoples in the Hapsburg Empire created Slavic associations dedicated to their ethnic identity. Some, with overtly political goals, sought support from Slavs outside the Austrian Empire, such as the Russians; others stressed Slavic culture as the best means of preserving ethnic identity until Slavic nation states could be formed. In the latter part of the nineteenth century, Slavic dictionaries were created and Slavic literature and folklore revived.

Some used religion as a means of preserving cultural identity. While this was true of the Poles, for whom their Roman Catholicism was a rallying point against the domination of Eastern Orthodox Russians, religion was the very essence of Jewish ethnicity. A minority in Europe, subject to organized persecution and killing (pogroms) especially in Russia, many nineteenth-century Jews adopted a policy of assimilation. While adhering to their faith, assimilated Jews gave up many distinctive Jewish ways of life as a means of entering business or professions, becoming citizens like gentiles, and freeing themselves from discriminations that had been imposed on them for centuries.

Darwin and Social Darwinism Ethnicity and racism became closely associated as a result of the adaptation of the theory of evolution that Charles Darwin (1809–1882) proposed in *The Origin of Species* (1859). As a young scientist Darwin had sailed around the world collecting specimens and fossils that supported his evolutionary theory: species evolve as a result of adaptation to change, and only those that are able to adapt can survive in the natural environment of competition and conflict. Darwin made it clear that his theories applied only to individual biological species, not to ethnic or other groups, but his stipulation did not stop others from distorting his ideas in this way. The broader application of Darwinian ideas began with their popular propagandization by Herbert Spencer (1820–1903), whose "social Darwinism" used such Darwinian concepts as "natural selection" and "survival of the fittest" to suggest that certain human social groups were superior to others and that this "natural superiority" explained their dominance.

Social Darwinism fit well with the atmosphere of *realpolitik* that characterized European politics and imperialism in the second half of the nineteenth century by supporting concepts of ethnic, racial, and national superiority. A virulent literature of racial prejudice emerged, perhaps the most notable example being the *Essay on the Inequality of Races* by Comte de Gobineau (1816–1882). Racist ideas became easily associated with the glorification of violence proposed by writers such as Georges Sorel (1847–1922), who argued that conflict, rather than compromise, was both natural and the agent of progress, since the superior survives through struggle. Such views justified the dominance of the nation state over minority ethnic groups and ultimately the dominance of one nation state over another, supporting the notion that domination was the result of a natural process often achieved through violence.

SLAVIC CULTURE AND RUSSIAN NATIONAL IDENTITY

European and yet not European, the Russian Empire lay on the borders of Europe and shared cultural, political, and economic ties with Europeans. But Russian's Asian borders were even more extensive, and the diversity of peoples within the Russian Empire included Mongols and Turks. Russian Orthodox Christianity was inherited from Byzantium and thus different from the Christianity—either Catholic or Protestant—practiced in Europe. In the late seventeenth and early eighteenth centuries, as English monarchs struggled to maintain their authority and independence from parliament, but well before the American and French Revolutions, Czar Peter the Great (r. 1689–1725) extended Russian territorial claims and carried out a series of reforms to modernize Russia.

Peter the Great and Westernization
By his defeat of Sweden in the Great Northern War (1699–1721) and the terms of the Treaty of Nystadt that ended it, Peter the Great opened a window to the West. He established a new capital called St. Petersburg close to the European frontier to replace Moscow in the interior, and he renamed the Czardom of Muscovy the "Russian Empire," using the Latinized form of the ancient term "Rus." His Westernizing reforms included the creation of a huge standing army and a new navy, along with compulsory education for the Russian nobility in mathematics and geometry, two subjects deemed essential for the Russian ruling elite to master. Students were also sent abroad to study subjects that would be useful to the state, such as navigation. Peter himself visited Europe and recruited Europeans as teachers and as skilled professionals in such fields as architecture.

Peter the Great's enthusiasm for European ideas, technology, and people was not shared by all his countrymen. His program of Westernization met opposition from people who believed that adopting Western ways would undermine Russian cultural identity and betray the Russian people. Those who opposed and critized Peter in this way launched a debate about Russian national identity and its relationship to the West that lasted well into the twentieth century. In the mid-nineteenth century opponents of Western ideas and defenders of tradition were known as "Slavophiles," and in the late nineteenth century a Pan-Slav movement developed that was dedicated to uniting Slavic peoples no matter what political borders separated them. This idea was threatening to the Hapsburg Empire, for example, as Slavs sought ties with their ethnic brethren in the Russian Empire.

HISPANISMO: CULTURE AND NATIONAL IDENTITY IN LATIN AMERICA

The relations between creoles and *peninsulares* had been tense in the colonial era and were an important element of nineteenth-century independence movements, when creoles saw the opportunity to replace the *peninsulares* as the elite in Latin America. Even so, the two groups shared a common ethnicity and culture that distinguished them from the Native American and mestizo majority. In the late nineteenth century, the European ethnic elites in Latin America embraced the ideology of *Hispanismo*, a nostalgic desire to recover their Hispanic cultural past.

The rejection of the Spanish Empire by nineteenth-century independence movements was reevaluated in the context of the turbulent, postcolonial political life in many Latin American societies. Though *Hispanismo* provided a limited and romantic view of colonial Latin America, it served Latin Americans of European background with a heritage that supported their privileges and power and that continued accordingly to shape individual nations within the hemisphere. *Hispanismo* continued the dialectic between past and present, between the legacy of a colonial empire and the realities of independent nation states in Latin America.

■
THE IMPACT OF CAPITALIST INDUSTRIALISM ON SOCIETY

The concentrated impact of mature capitalist industrialism on the lives of average people in the centers of western European culture was clearly discernible by the early twentieth century. A century earlier farmers had plowed their fields much as they had done for 2000 years. The horse was the swiftest means of land transportation, and the sail served for speedy water travel. The swiftest way to send a message was by signal from one hilltop to the next. These traditional practices were as widespread as they were aged, but they were rapidly replaced by nineteenth-century innovations in transportation, communication, and production.

URBAN INDUSTRIAL SOCIETY

By the end of the nineteenth century, the integration of manufacturing processes, enlargement of factory units, and the amalgamation of firms into virtual monopolies held a decisive grip on industrial societies. As a result, urbanization continued at an increasingly rapid rate. In 1870 there were only about 70 cities in Europe of over 100,000 in population; by 1900 there were nearly 200. London and Paris were joined by Berlin, Vienna, Moscow, and St. Petersburg as cities of a million or more inhabitants.

Urban capitalist industrial society became hierarchically complex, and imbalance appeared between the managers and owners of production who controlled profits and the workers, producers of goods without which there would be no profits, whose only share of profit was a wage determined by management. Wealth and expanded productivity had made material existence vastly more comfortable, luxurious, and amusing, but only for some and in some places.

The Middle Class   As productivity expanded and wealth increased during the nineteenth century, a European (and American) urban middle class secured its position between wage-earning workers and their employers. The middle class consisted of professionals, small businesspeople (merchants and specialist manufacturers), and service providers. The middle class enjoyed the profits of expanding markets and wealth though it tended to be protective and unadventurous with its profits.

The middle class was an important source of increasing demand that encouraged the expansion of production and markets, since it was both willing and able to take advantage of the new products, both manufactured goods and agricultural products. Accordingly, the standard of living of the middle classes of western and central Europe and the United States seems to have steadily improved in the nineteenth century. The middle class was, however, as subject to the uncertain fluctuations of productivity and market conditions as wage earners were, and it was not uncommon for some middle-class people to be forced to become wage earners.

The Working Class   Wage earners, crowded into rapidly growing urban centers, experienced lives of degradation. In 1839 French socialist Flora Tristan (1803–1844) described conditions in the slum area of St. Giles in London, known as "Little Dublin," where 150,000 people lived in the neighborhood at the center of the city:

Picture, if you can, barefoot men, women, and children picking their way through the foul morass; some huddled against the wall for want of anywhere to sit, others squatting on the ground, children wallowing in the mud like pigs . . . I saw children *without a stitch of clothing*, barefoot girls and women with babies at their breast, wearing nothing but a torn shirt that revealed almost the whole of their bodies; I saw old men cowering on dung hills, young men covered in rags.

Though urban life in Great Britain began to improve after mid-century, when parliament passed local government and public health legislation, conditions for the urban industrial working class improved slowly. As late as 1883 a pamphlet described the degradation of working people who lived in the heart of London in "pestilential human rookeries . . . where tens of thousands are crowded together amidst horrors which call to mind what we have heard of the middle passage of the slave ship."

Improvements in the lives of workers that resulted from increased wages and the availability of more products were compromised by the rising cost of living. Real wages improved only slightly and continued to fluctuate in response to market forces (costs and profits). The uncertain and difficult lives of the laboring majority (urban workers and peasants) improved only slowly.

Inequalities multiplied and were reflected in the vastly different perceptions and experiences of those affected by capitalist industrialism. The benefits of capitalist industrialism were more readily available to businessmen, financiers, and industrialists than to laborers;

FIGURE 16.11 *The Houses of the Poor Are Not the Palaces of the Rich,* by Gustave Dore (ca. 1880)
This engraving depicts the grim and crowded lives of urban poor in London.

benefits were more apparent to Europeans than to others who lived outside of Europe. Expansion of industrial capacity allied with fuller exploitation of global raw materials led to severe bouts of overproduction: from 1873 to 1893 there was a severe depression in prices and a crisis in profits, investment, and growth. This global depression was a retardation rather than a reversal of overall growth, but it highlighted clear difficulties in urban capitalist industrialism, notably the surplus of workers in times of recession and the human costs of underemployment.

Industrialization and Emigration Unemployment and underemployment were related to demographic as well as economic factors. The population of Europe doubled between 1750 and 1850, and it continued to expand. Improved production encouraged

DAILY LIVES

FACTORY LIFE, FAMILY LIFE, AND DIET

The demands of factory work schedules dramatically altered the diets of European workers and their families. Working hours divided the workers' days into segments rigidly fixed by the time clock, in contrast to the more natural rhythms of agrarian life. Breaks for eating and drinking served not just to appease hunger and thirst, but also provided almost the only interruptions, however brief, in a monotonous and lengthy workday.

Even as late as 1885, Fridolin Schuler, a factory inspector in the textile industry in the upper part of the Zurich canton in Switzerland, reported on the disruptive effects of factory work on families:

> Traditionally, the housewife remained at home. She left home only to work in the field, and if for some reason she occasionally did not have time to cook a proper meal, older girls would take her place in the kitchen. Nowadays, the entire family works in the factory. In the morning, the wife must get to the kitchen very early—one of the children may have to report to the factory, a half hour away, by six o'clock even in the winter—so breakfast has to be fixed in a hurry. A half hour before the noon meal, the mother leaves her job in the factory, rushes home, and cooks as quickly as possible, for soon the family will be home to eat and will complain if the steaming bowl is not already on the table. An hour later, the whole family will be back on the job in the factory. Where can she find time for any proper cooking and where will her daughter learn to cook if she is constantly working in the factory?*

Schuler found the worker's diet poor and deficient. The morning meal usually consisted of potato hash, a great deal of chicory coffee containing a few real coffee beans, and some milk. At noon, since time was short, there was buttered bread and cheese—and on good days a flour or potato soup with vegetables—and more of the same coffee. Swiss working-class families ate great quantities of baked or cooked pastry, often baked in a great hurry so that it might be undone on the inside and burned on the outside. Children ate the same food as adults.

As food deteriorated, Schuler reported, the temptation of alcohol became greater. Cheap liquor had to make up for inadequate food. In this way many families were caught in a vicious cycle: the lack of work opportunities forced entire families to work in factories. The absence of wife and daughters from home brought about a deterioration of the food eaten by the whole family. The poor diet in turn led to an increased consumption of liquor, and the resulting malnutrition and alcoholism led to reduced incomes, loss of jobs, and personal tragedies. The way out of this cycle lay in the distant future, in the rising real wages for all, decline in female and child labor, and increase in factory canteens.

*Elborg and Robert Forster, eds., *European Diet from Pre-Industrial to Modern Times* (New York: Harper and Row, 1975), pp. 81–83.

population growth, but basically it resulted from a declining mortality rate associated with respite from widespread and terrible epidemics. Increasing numbers of Europeans began to emigrate abroad by the middle of the nineteenth century (more than 375,000 annually, most of them going to North America, but some going to South America, Australia, and South Africa). The exodus reached its peak during and following the 1873–1893 depression, with more than 900,000 Europeans leaving their homeland each year. This emigration alleviated European population pressures somewhat; it also resulted in the spread and increase of Europeans around the world: from a global percentage of 22 percent of all emigrants in 1800 to a peak of 35 percent in 1930.

RESPONSES TO CAPITALIST INDUSTRIALISM

In England the concepts that would become basic to capitalist industrial development in the nineteenth century were contained in the *laissez-faire* ("let it alone") ideas of Adam Smith. In his *Wealth of Nations*, Smith asserted that a free-market economy determined by supply and demand would produce an abundance unimaginable under the controlled economy of mercantilism. Smith also suggested that specialization, or assigning different tasks to different production units, was one way to increase production, an idea that was reflected in the industrial factory.

The Manchester School David Ricardo (1772–1823) was the leader of the Manchester School, a group of critics whose "gloomy science" of economics sought to explain and justify the impact of English capitalist industrialism. By accepting Smith's belief in a free market economy and Malthus's belief that the size of a population was related to the level of subsistence, Ricardo concluded that the dilemma of the industrial revolution—the rich growing richer and the poor growing poorer—was inevitable, since the number of workers in a free market economy was always sufficient to keep wages low and profits high. Ricardo's "iron law of wages" asserted that wages would stabilize at the subsistence level because increased wages would lead to an increase in the working population, which in turn would cause increased competition in the labor market and drive down wages.

Robert Owen's Industrial Community Robert Owen (1771–1858) was a practicing and successful capitalist industrialist who sought to mitigate the most disturbing effects of capitalist industrialism: a decline in personal contact between employer and employee that characterized the factory mode of production and resulted in the alienation of laborer from employer. Owen's solution was not to return to precapitalist, preindustrial society, but to create a paternalistic industrial communalism based on the mutual interests of workers and employers. His scheme was implemented in communities such as New Lanark in Scotland and New Harmony in Indiana. The New Lanark factory community contained a mill and cooperative housing and stores. Free schooling was provided, for Owen believed that educated workers were better workers. Though inadequate leadership and internal dissension led in time to the failure of Owen's experiments, his ideas and efforts, which deviated from the strict *laissez-faire* ideals of the Manchester School, indicated possibilities for closing the gaps between employers and their employees.

John Stuart Mill John Stuart Mill's (1806–1873) father had been a fanatical disciple of Jeremy Bentham (1784–1832), the formulator of the philosophy of Utilitarianism, which argued that the goal of society should be the greatest good for the greatest number of people. Utilitarianism attacked unrestrained capitalist industrialism, and Mill in turn continually questioned the economic structure and social patterns of nineteenth-century England. In opposition to the Manchester School, he approved of labor unions as a means by which workers could improve their conditions through collective bargaining. Mill proposed that more equal distribution of property and wealth could be accomplished by heavy taxes on land and by levies on inherited wealth. Progress, Mill insisted, lay in a better distribution of material goods and in social justice, including equal rights for women, which he championed.

French Social Critics One of the early French critics to begin a dialogue on achieving justice in capitalist industrial societies was Count Henri de Saint-Simon (1760–1825). He accepted that an economy based on industrial production would ensure a future of abundance that would put an end to human want. Though of an ancient noble family, Saint-Simon viewed the aristocracy as an idle class whose privileges were unjustified. For him, privilege should belong only to those who work to produce, those whom he called *industriels*—agriculturalists, manufacturers, and merchants. Society, he proclaimed, should be organized for the promotion and well-being of the most numerous and poorest class. In his last work, *The New Christianity* (1825), Saint-Simon undertook to reform society on the basis of Christian ethics.

Among those strongly attracted to Saint-Simon's ideas were professionals, including bankers and engineers; intellectuals; and some working-class women. By the 1830s about 200 women identified themselves as Saint-Simonians, an early example of the appeal that alternative visions of industrial society had for women, who were often its most oppressed victims. In 1832 a group of Saint-Simonian women published their own newspaper, *The Free Woman*, which printed only articles written by women and declared that "With the emancipation of women will come the emancipation of the worker." Although their movement collapsed, other feminist movements continued to offer criticism and alternatives to capitalist industrialism in the later nineteenth century.

Charles Fourier (1772–1837), another French critic of capitalist industrialism, differed from Saint-Simon by rejecting industrialism. Fourier proposed a visionary reorganization of society as an alternative to the industrial society that Saint Simon sought to make just and rational. Particularly alarmed by large-scale centralized production, which he saw as a threat to small enterprise, Fourier proposed as a substitute his own conception of a community based on an agrarian handicraft economy. In his vision labor would be necessary but also attractive and joyous, and life would be long, attractive, and happy.

The utopian vision of society proposed by Saint-Simon and Fourier did not have the wide appeal to the working masses that other more practical strategies did. Pierre-Louis Proudhon (1809–1865), a self-educated printer who wrote *What Is Property?* in 1840, was a working-class critic of capitalist industrial society. For Proudhon, property was theft, profit stolen from the worker with the connivance of the state. Proudhon proposed a cooperative society of independent equals based on common ownership. Because he rejected private property, he was called a socialist, and because he rejected the state in favor of cooperative organizations, he was called an anarchist.

Bakunin and Anarchism   One of Proudhon's admirers was the Russian anarchist Mikhail
■■■■■■■■■■■■■■■■■■■■   Bakunin (1814–1876), who believed that the state was the cause of
the common man's afflictions. Bakunin, who espoused and engaged in terrorist action against
the state, was an exile from Russia and familiar with the inside of many European jails. From
his base in Switzerland, Bakunin continued to work for revolution against the social order in
which he found himself. The true revolutionary, he wrote, "has severed every link with the social order and with the entire civilized world." Bakunin believed that industrial workers constituted a vanguard of revolutionary activity that would lead to the replacement of capitalist
industrial society. Two other Russians, Prince Peter Kropotkin (1842–1921) and Count Leo
Tolstoy (1828–1910) also contributed to criticism of capitalist industrial society. They, like
many Russian intellectuals and similar to Fourier, saw small rural communes as a basis for an
alternative society.

THE MARXIST CRITIQUE OF CAPITALIST INDUSTRIALISM

The critique of capitalist industrial society that would have the greatest impact appeared in
the half century following the 1848 revolutions. Two Germans, Karl Marx (1818–1883) and
Friedrich Engels (1820–1895), presented their case against capitalist industrial society in
their *Communist Manifesto* (1848) and in Marx's *Capital* (published between 1867–1883).
These two works became the basic scriptures of "scientific socialism" or communism. Indebted to earlier German and French thinkers and based on his study of history, Marx's critical analysis of the capitalist industrial state was one of the most forceful attacks on the society
of his time.

Marx definitively shaped his view of history once he had joined Engels in England. He
believed that events over time were the result of material factors, such as modes of production
(slavery, serfdom, the factory system), and that all other activities (politics, social patterns,
ideas, culture in general) were determined by the forces of production. Accordingly, changes
in modes of production were the basis for all other changes in history. Changes in modes of
production, and thus society in general, proceeded in a dialectical fashion. That is, every innovation provoked a reaction that was resolved in a synthesis, a combination of elements of
old and new modes of production, which itself became subject to innovation and change.

Marx's analysis of history provided a rational basis for understanding the problems and
conflicts of his own time. Throughout history, changes in modes of production had resulted
from conflict between producers and the owners of the means of production. The characteristic conflict of the ancient world was between slave and master; that of the feudal age was between peasant and landowner; and that of capitalist industrial society was between those who
worked in factories (wage earners whom Marx labeled the proletariat) and the capitalists who
owned the factories.

Class Theory   Marx introduced the concept of "class," divisions of society arising from eco-
■■■■■■■■■■■■■■   nomic and social differences. He thought that the widening gap between capitalists and proletariat had produced a heightened class consciousness in both classes and that
the outcome of the conflict between them would produce a final synthesis in which the proletariat would be victorious. The outcome of the victory of the proletariat would ultimately be
a classless society, one in which conflict would disappear, since producers themselves would
own the means of production.

The Labor Theory of Value   Marx analyzed nineteenth-century contests between workers and
━━━━━━━━━━━━━━━━━━━━━ capitalist industrialists on the basis of a labor theory of value.
The true value of an object, he argued, is determined by the labor that goes into it. The difference between the cost of production (wages and material) and the market price is the surplus value, of which those who own the means of production (capitalists) rob those who produce (the proletariat). Keeping surplus value for themselves permits capitalists to get richer
while the proletariat grows poorer as a result of rising costs and stagnant wages. This widening gap between capitalists and the proletariat increased class consciousness and the hostility
between capitalist industrialists and the proletariat that culminated in increasing conflict.

As the unsavory aspects of capitalist industrialism—urban blight, economic cycles, the
slow progress of change by political processes—became common in the second half of the
nineteenth century, Marx's vision gained widespread appeal in Europe and ultimately found
wide acceptance outside Europe. In a world that increasingly valued science, Marx's claim
that his views were based on a scientific analysis of history and were inevitable was a powerful
one. At the same time vagueness in Marx's thought allowed for conflict among his followers.
Marxism came to incorporate competing versions of Marx's ideas, many of which were often
far removed from his intentions.

■

CAPITALIST INDUSTRIALISM AND
THE NATION STATE

In the first half of the nineteenth century, capitalist industrial elites gradually replaced the
traditional landed aristocracies as the dominant economic power in western Europe. They also
began the slow process, which continued on into the twentieth century, by which they shared
political power and even social position with the aristocracy. The rise of control by urban
wealth was accompanied by the even slower growth of political influence and power by the
middle and working classes, though social differences and a wide economic gap between the
working and wealth classes remained.

POLITICAL AND SOCIAL DEMOCRACY IN GREAT BRITAIN

In Great Britain the growth of the urban industrial working classes resulted in further evolution of the idea of the state as a social contract that John Locke had introduced in the seventeenth century. During the first half of the nineteenth century, as the traditional political monopoly of landed aristocracy was challenged, an urban capitalist industrial ruling class began to
take control of British political culture. Further broadening of the political process, which followed in the second half of the century and continued into the twentieth, completed the transition from a traditional dynastic monarchy to a national monarchy with a broad social base.

The Great Reform Bill   Realization of a fully democratic social contract in Great Britain was
━━━━━━━━━━━━━━━━━━━━━ a result of the expansion of suffrage to all males, and later to all females. The process of achieving political democracy began in 1832 with the passage of the
first Reform Bill, which sought to redefine and broaden male suffrage. Before 1832 the right
to vote (and thus to be elected to parliament) was a virtual monopoly of privileged landowners (including industrialists) by virtue of their property and influence over electoral districts.

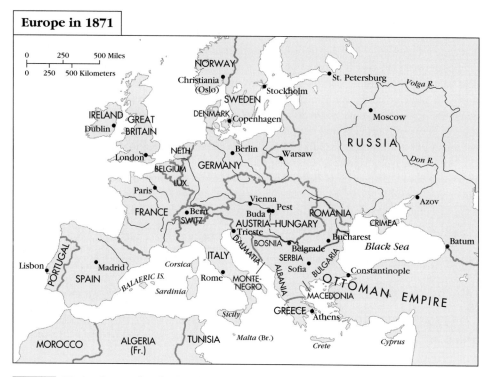

Europe in 1871

0   250   500 Miles

0   250   500 Kilometers

NORWAY

Christiania (Oslo)

St. Petersburg

Volga R.

Stockholm

SWEDEN

DENMARK Copenhagen

Moscow

IRELAND GREAT

Dublin BRITAIN

RUSSIA

NETH. Berlin

London Warsaw

Don R.

BELGIUM GERMANY

LUX.

Paris

Vienna

Azov

FRANCE Bern Buda Pest

SWITZ. AUSTRIA–HUNGARY ROMANIA CRIMEA

Trieste Bucharest

DALMATIA BOSNIA Belgrade Black Sea Batum

ITALY SERBIA

Lisbon Madrid Corsica Sofia Constantinople

PORTUGAL SPAIN BALEARIC IS. Rome MONTE-NEGRO ALBANIA BULGARIA OTTOMAN EMPIRE

Sardinia MACEDONIA

Sicily GREECE Athens

MOROCCO ALGERIA (Fr.) TUNISIA Malta (Br.) Crete Cyprus

MAP 16.6 Nation States after the Dual Revolutions

Even wealthy inhabitants of the many cities, especially those that had grown as a result of the industrial revolution, were unable to vote or become candidates for parliament.

The Great Reform Bill, which gave the vote to urban men of wealth and property, was a recognition of economic and demographic changes that had taken place as a result of urban and capitalist industrial growth. Industrialists, who soon exerted influence on government that rivaled and replaced that of the landed elite, lost no time in jealously guarding their new power. For their purposes and interests, the vote had been extended far enough, and they ignored the demands of those who had supported the 1832 reform, but who lacked the property qualification to be enfranchised by it. The beneficiaries of the Great Reform Bill, imbued with laissez-faire economic ideals, used their political power in Parliament, which they dominated for more than two decades, to keep the disenfranchised from satisfying their political and social needs.

The Chartist Movement   Portions of the population, particularly the urban portion, who remained disenfranchised, had learned from their involvement in the 1832 reform movement how to make their voices heard through mass pressure and public action. Men who had not gained the vote in the Reform Bill of 1832 organized to exert pressure on parliament for further reform. Their demands were met only by palliative legislation, and this situation led to a massive public demonstration in London in 1848, during which a people's charter, embodying political demands such as universal male suffrage, was presented. The "Chartist movement" ended in failure, but it did prompt Parliament to address some of

FIGURE 16.12　Massacre at St. Peter's or "Britons Strike Home", 1819

Political cartoon depicts the events in which 80,000 people demonstrated for universal male suffrage and more representation for the poor and working classes at St. Peter's Field, Manchester. They were fired upon by government troops, who killed 11 demonstrators and wounded 400, including 113 women. Radical critics derisively dubbed this the "Peterloo Massacre," making ironic comparison with the Battle of Waterloo in which the British defeated Napoleon.

SOURCE: Mansell/Time, Inc.

the more immediate material needs of those still unable to vote. More important, it emboldened the disenfranchised to continue their pressure for political democracy, which they believed in the long run would lead to social democracy.

Later reform bills gradually extended suffrage to larger portions of the adult male population, though not until the twentieth century was universal adult male suffrage achieved. During the lengthy process by which Great Britain attained political democracy, traditional parties (Conservative, generally associated with the landed privileged, and Liberal, generally supported by the urban elite) exercised political power. The British combination of political democracy controlled by privilege classes worked without major change until the end of the nineteenth century.

By the early twentieth century, organized labor entered the political arena as the Labour Party and allied with the Liberal Party. This coalition succeeded in using the parliamentary system to achieve goals of the working classes, such as workmen's compensation for job-related injuries, old-age pensions, strengthening the position of unions, setting up labor exchanges to relieve unemployment, and arbitration boards to settle disputes. The nature of the social contract had altered dramatically since the seventeenth century, reflected in the growth of the nation state as a source of identity and the impact of capitalist industrialism on the making of the English working classes.

POLITICAL AND SOCIAL DEMOCRACY IN FRANCE

Following the defeat of France and the collapse of the empire of Napoleon III in the Franco-Prussian War of 1870, France was plunged into an often violent struggle over its future. Between March and May of 1871, the provisional national government was locked in a civil war with the commune, the revolutionary municipal government in Paris, which refused to accept the national government's authority. The Paris commune proclaimed a republic before the idea was acceptable to much of the rest of France, particularly conservative, rural France. The provisional national government, located in Bordeaux, brutally suppressed the Paris commune and similar communes in other cities. Exemplary retribution was taken on the communards; 20,000 were put to death and 7500 were exiled.

Once the commune was suppressed, there was much political maneuvering before a new constitution (1875) inaugurated the Third French Republic. The Third Republic continued the tradition of general male suffrage in France, though the right to vote, as past experience had shown, did not guarantee to all a full and equal participation in French society. Universal male suffrage in the Third Republic was limited in its effect, since men of wealth and property controlled elections in the countryside and the numerous conservative deputies from the provinces could maintain control by outvoting more radical urban deputies.

Because the men who dominated the Third Republic were economically and politically conservative, the government was slow to respond to the needs and demands of the working class. It was not until 1884, for example, that the Chapelier Law, governing the rights of labor, was repealed. The Chapelier Law, which dated from the early days of the French Revolution (1791), forbade strikes and all worker associations. Its repeal removed a major obstacle to political action by the working class. Now that unions and direct action by labor were legal, the working classes had a means to show their strength and to move the government in their interests.

The Dreyfus Case In the last years of the nineteenth century, the Dreyfus affair provided the French working classes through their organizations with an opportunity to expand their role and influence. In 1894, when a young Jewish army captain, Alfred Dreyfus, was accused of selling confidential documents to the German military attache, anti-republican elements in the army, the church, and among monarchists turned the case into an attack on the Third Republic. Dreyfus's family, never doubting his innocence, enlisted the support of prominent republicans and intellectuals, such as the novelist Emile Zola (1840–1902), who rallied in support of Dreyfus and in this way sought to defend the republic from its opponents.

What had begun as a minor military scandal became by 1898 a major national issue that divided and endangered the republic and highlighted anti-Semitic sentiments in France. The opponents of the Third Republic condemned Dreyfus as representative of the "syndicate" of Jews, freemasons, and friends of Germany whom they believed were undermining France, whereas those who believed in his innocence saw the Dreyfus case as the means of undermining the republican government with accusations of corruption and weakness. Powerful support for Dreyfus and the republic came from the working classes, through their unions, and from socialist movements that had grown up during the Third Republic. Socialists in parliament, who grew steadily in number in the 1890s, joined in a Cabinet of Republican Defense that was created to deal with the Dreyfus crisis. Between 1901 and 1905 the government, strengthened by the upsurge of support for the republic, declared Dreyfus innocent and weakened the power of antirepublican groups.

One effect of the active involvement of the working class and socialist movements in support of the republic during the Dreyfus affair was to advance France in the direction of social democracy. The political success of the socialists and the growth in membership and power of unions willing to use direct action such as strikes to achieve their goals curtailed the government's ability to ignore the needs and demands of the working classes.

SOCIAL DEMOCRACY IN GERMANY, ITALY, AND RUSSIA

Capitalist industrialism expanded rapidly and successfully in Germany after unification and more slowly and less generally in Italy and Russia in the second half of the nineteenth century. Political and economic development in these three countries assured change, but the benefits for working classes that emerged in Germany, Italy, and Russia were more the result of authoritarian paternalism than of the democratic political processes that had taken place in Great Britain and France.

Germany Before unification, capitalist industrialism had not been able to make rapid headway in Germany, despite efforts that began as early as 1834 to establish economic cooperation through a pan-German tariff union. By 1871 Germany was a federated empire, and German business discovered the economic benefits of a common government in terms of market expansion and regulation; government support; and unified transport, communication, and tax systems. By 1900 German economic growth, greatly aided by scientific and technical progress, was unparalleled and in many areas had overtaken and exceeded that of Great Britain, the most highly industrialized nation in the world.

The rapid progress of capitalist industrialism in Germany was accompanied by problems of rapid urbanization, changing working conditions, and disparity in wealth. The autocratic new German Reich dealt with them in its own way. The imperial government neither represented the German people as a whole nor was responsible to them. The Reichstag (parliament), elected by universal male suffrage, had little power. The ministry and its head, the chancellor, were the effective government of the empire. They served at the will of the emperor (Kaiser) and were responsible neither to the parliamentary majority nor to the electorate. Since voting had little influence on policy and proved largely frustrating to the German working classes, they looked to trade union organizations and socialist movements to extend and protect their rights and interests.

In general the German socialist movements, like those in France influenced by Marx, were divided among those who aimed at overthrowing existing government and those who were dedicated to improving working class conditions through the use of existing political institutions. In 1875 these two factions united into a single Social Democratic Party hostile to the oligarchical government of the empire. The Social Democrats alarmed Chancellor Bismarck, who was determined to end the organized socialist movement before it became an effective menace to the state. He undertook to cripple the Social Democratic Party by censorship and other repressive measures: prohibition of publication or propagation of radical social and political ideas, limitation of public meetings and the right of assembly, and arbitrary arrest.

To placate the German working classes, Bismarck proposed legislation that would satisfy their material needs and concerns; he introduced a comprehensive program of social insurance: a Sickness Insurance Act (1883); an Accident Insurance Law (1884); and an Old Age Pension Act (1889). This legislation, a product of governmental paternalism, provided Germans with a comprehensive social program more than twenty years before democratic parliamentary processes produced anything equivalent in Britain or France. It met the needs of the German working classes and contributed to the productivity and prosperity of the German state.

Italy The kingdom of Italy as completed in 1870 was in theory a parliamentary democracy, but in practice a conservative military bolstered the king's authority and parliament served the interests of the rural and urban wealthy. The middle class was small, and the agrarian majority was powerless. A small industrial working class only gradually found its voice as it slowly grew in size; discontent made workers receptive to radical ideas associated with unions and socialism. Political life was infused with the strong national emotions that had contributed to the lengthy process of unification. Nationalists were proud of the new Italy; the Church and the feudal aristocrats, especially in Naples and Sicily distrusted it; and urban workers in the industrial north, influenced by Marxist and other socialist ideas, felt it was unresponsive to their needs and were willing to use violence to change it.

The government, though faced with political division and growing unrest, turned to imperialist ventures, hoping nationalist enthusiasm would quell discontent. The failure of Italy to conquer Ethiopia in 1896 (see Chapter 17) was an embarrassment to the state and solved none of its problems. In 1898 slow economic expansion and growing unemployment led to riots and insurgency to which the government responded by declaring martial law and installing a brief military dictatorship. By 1900 the crisis had passed, but the threat of revolution continued to loom. To deflect unrest, a series of reform government introduced universal male suffrage, greatly increasing the number of voters (from 3.5 million to 8 million).

Following the electoral reforms, trade unions and collective bargaining were legalized, hygienic working conditions were standardized, minimum wages were established, and working conditions for women and children were improved and regulated. The state's economic role was expanded when railroads were nationalized. But there was no agrarian reform and no laws reapportioning land, and universal male suffrage meant very little to peasants in a region dominated by landlords and the Church. The division between the industrial, urban north and the agricultural south hindered economic development in the kingdom, and made it difficult for parliamentary democracy to function and social democracy to benefit all.

Russia In the first quarter of the nineteenth century, reform and revolutionary movements developed in Russia among intellectuals and young army officers who had become influenced by French ideas during the Revolution and Napoleonic decades when France dominated Europe. The first attempt at revolution occurred in the Decembrist revolt of 1825, when confusion over the succession to the throne of Nicholas I (r. 1825–1855) offered opponents of the traditional absolutist monarchy an opportunity to institute a constitutional monarchy in Russia. The Decembrist revolt, little more than an attempted palace coup which failed, was the basis of a Russian revolutionary tradition that became an increasingly powerful force throughout the nineteenth century.

By the mid-nineteenth century the defeat of Russia in the Crimean War (1854–1856) contributed to an emerging revolutionary movement in Russia. The failure of Nicholas I to win the war discredited the traditional autocracy and raised the issue of reform. The most important change made by Nicholas's successor, Alexander II (r. 1855–1881), was to ending serfdom, which had developed in Russia after it had begun to disappear in western Europe. Emancipation of serfs (1861) was followed by a remarkable decade of further reform, by which, among other things, the newly freed populace was given some local self-government.

The reforms decreed by Alexander II, the "czar liberator," as he became known, rather than dampening pressures for more radical change, actually encouraged revolutionary movements. When Alexander, under pressure from the landed aristocracy, began to qualify and retreat from reforms, it was too late: radical movements and revolutionary societies, had already appeared. Some of these movements were ideologically inspired by non-Russian ideas such as socialism while others seemed uniquely Russian. One such movement was nihilism, predicated on the belief that all institutions, political, social, or economic, were so bad that they required destruction by any method possible, including terrorism.

Alexander II, who strove to crush the radicals, fell victim to a terrorist bomb in 1881, and his successors halted further reform and outlawed and persecuted revolutionary societies. In the long run, efforts at repression were unsuccessful. Rather than disappearing, revolutionary movements went underground and, as a result of the progress of urban industrialization that began to accelerate after 1890, found new support and strength (see Chapter 18).

SUMMARY

Beginning with the transformation of the English monarchy in the seventeenth century and the American and French Revolutions in the eighteenth, the personal ties that bound the privileged aristocracy to their rulers in dynastic states were replaced in nation states by the abstract ideal of a constitutional contract regulating the relationship between ruler and ruled. In the economic sphere, guild production, where masters lived in close daily contact with their journeymen (day laborers) and apprentices, and the domestic system, where entrepreneurs who provided raw materials had personal contact with those whose finished products they marketed, gave way to the impersonal and shifting relationships of the factory mode of production.

The contractual nature of society was acknowledged by political guarantees of legal equality and personal freedom, though gender and social class often determined the extent to which these principles were enacted. The factory mode of production, with clear distinctions between employer and employee, and increasing demographic mobility and urbanization created conditions that necessitated other forms of contract to assure that the ideals of equality and freedom were not confined to certain economically privileged groups in society.

From the seventeenth through the nineteenth centuries, Europe was transformed by dual revolutions: changing modes of production accompanied capitalist industrialism and nation states replaced dynastic states. Although both aspects of the dual revolution became increasingly interdependent throughout the nineteenth century, their effects were not uniform and did not occur at the same time. Capitalist industrialism depended on the nation state to succeed and supported the efforts of nation states in Europe (and the United States) to extract wealth from other parts of the globe and reinvest it. National revolutions in Latin America were tied both to Europe and to independence movements directed by indigenous leaders. The complex intersection of the dual revolutions of capitalist industrialism and the nation state constitutes a global theme that will be pursued in Chapter 17. The following chapters show how European and American capitalist industrialism and the nation state expanded across the globe through the interdependent political and economic systems of imperialism.

ENGAGING THE PAST

MARX AND MATERIALISM

In contrast to earlier European views of history, which were shaped initially by Judeo-Christian faith and later by Enlightenment reason, Marx's understanding of historical change rested on two basic principles: materialism and the dialectic. By materialism, Marx meant that material conditions—including technology, natural resources, and economic institutions such as landholding systems—determine the structures of human societies. Political and social institutions, laws, values, religion, and culture are all "superstructures" determined by "modes of production," Marx's term for economic systems and the relations between producers and consumers characteristic of them. Human consciousness, according to Marx, is formed from these material conditions; for example, the thought of an industrial worker will differ from that of a farmer because each is part of a different mode of production.

Historical change was driven by changes in the modes of production and resulting class struggle, the "engine" of historical change. Marx's view of struggle was inspired by the dialectic, the search for truth through contradiction of statement and counterstatement, which was basic to the thought of the German idealist philosopher, Georg W.F. Hegel (1770–1831). Hegel believed in mind over matter, that ideas dominated the material. Marx stood Hegel on his head by placing matter over mind, though he adopted Hegel's concept of the successive stages of the dialectical process—thesis met by antithesis and then resolved by synthesis—to explain change in history.

Though he never used the term, Marx's version of the Hegelian dialectic is known as "dialectical materialism." According to dialectical materialism, for example, in medieval European society there were landholding classes produced by feudal-manorial conditions and a growing commercial bourgeois class that was the result of urban modes of production such as handicrafts and trade. Conflict between these classes developed in the form of bourgeois revolutions against feudal interests—in England in the mid-seventeenth century, in France in 1789, and in Germany in the mid-nineteenth century. As the "bourgeoisie," defined as owners of capital and the means of production, succeeded, another class, the industrial working class or proletariat came into being. In turn, struggle ensued between the bourgeois owners of the means of production and the workers who produced surpluses through their labor.

Marx believed that the dialectic of historical change would end when private property was abolished and the means of production was transferred to the control of those who used them. The result would be a classless society with none of the institutions characteristic of earlier stages. Marx's ideas themselves could be said to have emerged directly from observation of the transformations wrought in nineteenth-century Europe by the dual revolutions of capitalist industrialism and the nation state. Marx also wrote about non-European parts of the globe, though with less sophistication and often no firsthand knowledge. Still his writings were to have a profound impact on later developments far beyond Europe's borders, suggesting ironically perhaps that ideas *can* be "engines" of historical change.

SUGGESTIONS FOR FURTHER READING

Benedict Anderson, *Imagined Communities: Reflections on the Origin and Spread of Nationalism* (London: Verso, 1983). Path-breaking work on the narration and representation of the nation, tracing cultural sources of nationalism.

James Anderson, ed., *The Rise of the Modern State* (Atlantic Highlands, NJ: Humanities Press, 1986). A series of essays on how states became "modern" by contrasting them with earlier forms of the state.

Hugh Brogan, *The Pelican History of the United States of America.* (Harmondsworth: Penguin Books, 1985). A stimulating and provocative look at American history by an Englishman who teaches it.

Joan Dayan, *Haiti, History, and the Gods* (Berkeley: University of California Press, 1995). A well-written, cultural history of the island's intertwined ritual and political past.

William Doyle, *The Oxford History of the French Revolution* (Oxford: Oxford University Press, 1988). A brief, clear analysis of the French Revolution based on current scholarship.

Sarah Shaver Hughes and Brady Hughes, *Women in World History*, vol. 2, *Readings from 1500 to the Present.* (Armonk, NY: M.E. Sharpe, 1997). Selected secondary sources on women in world history since 1500.

John Hutchinson and Anthony D. Smith, eds., *Nationalism* (Oxford: Oxford University Press, 1994). A selection of sources on various aspects of nationalism, from the theory of the nation to the political and cultural histories of modern nation states.

Simon Schama, *Citizens: A Chronicle of the French Revolution* (New York: Knopf, 1989). A dramatic and vivid reexamination of the first five years of the French Revolution.

The Tentacles of Empire: The New Imperialism and New Nationalisms in Asia, Africa, and the Americas

The Caribbean writer Aime Cesaire was one of many twentieth-century critics who tried to define the forces and interests that shaped the encounters between Europeans and other peoples (in *Discourse on Colonialism*, 1955). Imperialism and colonialism were complex and difficult to define, but Cesaire's attempt projects great clarity and power in its directness and simplicity:

> In other words, the essential thing here is to see clearly, to think clearly—that is, dangerously—and to answer clearly the innocent first question: what, fundamentally, is colonization? To agree on what it is not: neither evangelization, nor a philanthropic enterprise, nor a desire to push back the frontiers of ignorance, disease, and tyranny, nor a project undertaken for the greater glory of God, nor an attempt to extend the rule of law. To admit once and for all, without flinching at the consequences, that the decisive actors here are the adventurer and the pirate, the wholesale grocer and the ship owner, the gold digger and the merchant, appetite and force, and behind them, the baleful projected shadow of a form of civilization which, at a certain point in its history, finds itself obliged, for internal reasons, to extend to a world scale the competition of its antagonistic economies.
>
> That being settled, I admit that it is a good thing to place different civilizations in contact with each other; that it is an excellent thing to blend different worlds; that whatever its own particular genius may be, a civilization that withdraws itself atrophies; that for civilizations, exchange is oxygen; that the great good fortune of Europe is to have been a crossroads, and that because it was a locus of all ideas, the receptacle of all philosophies, the meeting place of all sentiments, it was the best center for the redistribution of energy.
>
> But then I ask the following question: has colonization really placed civilizations in contact? Or, if you prefer, of all the ways of establishing contact, was it the best?
>
> I answer no.
>
> And I say that between colonization and civilization there is an infinite distance; that out of all the colonial expeditions that have been undertaken, out of all the colonial statutes that have been drawn up, out of all the memoranda that have been despatched by all the ministries, there could not come a single human value.

INTRODUCTION

This chapter explores the motivations and impact of imperialism and colonialism in Africa, Asia, Europe, and the Americas. Defined broadly as the systematic domination of one state or people over another, imperialism can

Dayr el Medeeneh, Thebes, Color Lithograph by David Roberts (1796–1864)

Roberts, A Scottish artist who accompanied an expedition to Egypt in 1838–1839, altered proportions, added decorative elements, and repositioned stones and monuments to achieve his visually impressionistic portrayal of the ancient world.

SOURCE: Huntington Library and Art Gallery, San Marino, CA.

be found throughout history in many parts of the world. However, beginning in the nineteenth century, the "new imperialism" refers more specifically to the expansion of Europe, including Russia, and to both the United States and Japan beyond their own borders from the mid-nineteenth century to the beginning of World War I (1914). The counterpart of imperialism is colonialism: the economic, political, cultural, and social structures imposed on peoples by the forces of imperialism.

As Cesaire suggests in the introductory passage, from the perspective of the colonized, the era of European imperialism was largely about "appetite and force." The dual revolutions of capitalist industrialism and the nation state in Europe fueled the hunger for global expansion in the nineteenth century. Europeans constructed a new global order through the creation of colonies in some parts of the world and through less visible, though no less potent, means of domination in others.

During the eighteenth century conflicts among nation states in Europe were closely tied to imperial ambitions in far-flung corners of the globe; sometimes struggles over colonial territories even precipitated or preceded conflicts in Europe. The French and Indian War in

North America between Britain and France actually began in 1754, two years before the Seven Years' War (1756–1763), a struggle among European nation states that took place in Europe as well as in colonial North America and in India between Britain and France. The defeat of France by Britain in this conflict resulted in the French surrender of its territory in North America (Canada) and India, which substantially enlarged the growing British Empire and partially made up for the loss of other British colonies with the American Revolution. By the mid-nineteenth century, the French were beginning to reassert their claims to empire in Africa, the Americas, and Asia. The term *imperialism* was, in fact, first applied to the actions of Napoleon III (r. 1852–1870), who "pacified" Algeria, sought to create a satellite empire in Mexico, and began French penetration into Southeast Asia.

Many factors motivated expansion and imperialism in the nineteenth and twentieth centuries. Nothing stimulated imperialism more than national rivalry, as new nation states competed for power and territory. The new economic forces unleashed by capitalist industrialism stretched the tentacles of empire around the globe and heightened this rivalry. Industrialized European nations in the nineteenth century, and Japan and the United States in the twentieth, required expanding markets and cheap raw materials. Some historians have argued that the expansion of markets and exploitation of resources from the colonized world fueled the engine of capitalist growth. Contemporary observers, including the economist J. A. Hobson (1858–1940) and the Russian Marxist V. I. Lenin (1870–1924), even went so far as to claim imperialism to be the inevitable consequence of capitalism and part of its ultimate extension worldwide.

As the growth limits of capitalist industrialism began to be felt in European economies during the second half of the nineteenth century, alternative markets and resources had to be found overseas. While there were still a few possibilities for more intensive utilization of European resources, increasingly Europeans turned to the exploitation of other parts of the world. Late nineteenth-century European imperialism completed the process of European domination of the world that began with the opening of the Atlantic frontier in the sixteenth century. Engendered by capitalist industrialism and the nation state, the new imperialism spread both industrialism and nationalism around the world. Europeans little realized, and less expected, that both might be used eventually by non-Europeans to challenge and readjust Europe's position in the world.

The principle of balance of power among European nation states—that is, no single state should be allowed to dominate territory or economic control—guided the diplomatic and political decisions underlying global expansion through imperialism. As European nation states created empires and colonies, the balance of power came to be applied on a global scale. As a global balance among European nations was sought, however, the imbalance between European powers and those they colonized was heightened. Between 1800 and 1914 the dissolution of old empires and states produced new nationalisms around the world that would eventually alter the global balance of power in the twentieth century.

■

EUROPE AND THE OTTOMAN EMPIRE

Beginning with the conquests of Napoleon Bonaparte at the end of the eighteenth century, European nation states confronted an old adversary, the Ottoman Empire. The process that led to the weakening and disintegration of the Ottoman Empire pitted the rising forces of

European Colonial Empires, ca. 1750

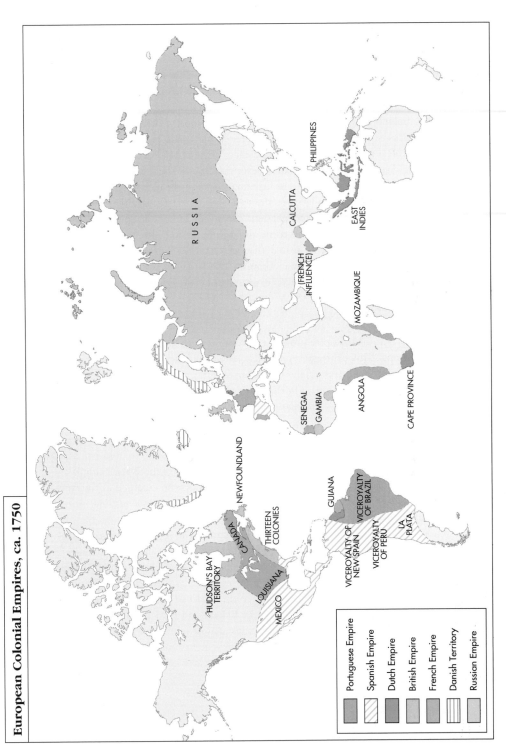

RUSSIA

PHILIPPINES

CALCUTTA

(FRENCH INFLUENCE)

EAST INDIES

MOZAMBIQUE

SENEGAL

GAMBIA

ANGOLA

CAPE PROVINCE

NEWFOUNDLAND

GUIANA

VICEROYALTY OF BRAZIL

CANADA

THIRTEEN COLONIES

VICEROYALTY OF NEW SPAIN

VICEROYALTY OF PERU

LA PLATA

HUDSON'S BAY TERRITORY

LOUISIANA

MEXICO

	Portuguese Empire
	Spanish Empire
	Dutch Empire
	British Empire
	French Empire
	Danish Territory
	Russian Empire

MAP 17.1 **Distribution of European Colonial Claims**

European nationalism against the once powerful Ottomans, who adapted to the European nation state system, though too little and too late. By the eighteenth century the Ottomans were no longer the formidable enemy that had threatened Europe for centuries. Major European powers, in fact, were expanding while the Ottoman Empire entered a long period of contraction. Henceforth, it was Europe that threatened the Ottomans, and territorial expansion was justified on the basis of protecting the balance of power.

In 1798 Napoleon invaded Ottoman Egypt in an attempt to cut British communications with India. The British were able to force the French out a few years later and in 1802 returned Egypt to the sultan. The obvious weakness of the Ottoman Empire encouraged some of its Muslim subjects to break away. Shortly after the British drove the French from Egypt, the Ottoman Empire's largest province, an Albanian adventurer named Muhammad Ali became viceroy of Egypt (*Khedive*) under the sultan's authority. By 1820, after crushing all local opposition, he established virtually independent control of Egypt; in 1831 and 1839 he rebelled against the Ottomans and led his army through Syria and into central Anatolia. Only the intervention of the British, who feared that an Ottoman collapse would play into the hands of the Russians, saved the Ottoman Empire. The British navy forced Muhammad Ali to withdraw to Egypt where he was allowed to establish his own dynasty.

THE EASTERN QUESTION

The decline of the Ottoman Empire provided Europeans with what was known in Europe as the "eastern question." This expression referred to the diplomatic moves that were meant to prevent the disorderly dissolution of the Ottoman Empire, which, it was feared, would disrupt the balance of power in Europe. On the other hand, diplomacy was also intended to ensure a fair division of the spoils—Ottoman territory—by Britain, France, Austria, and Russia if the empire did collapse.

This episode convinced the British that the integrity of the Ottoman Empire was of major importance to their own growing imperial system and a buffer to Russian expansion. Thus, when the Russians resumed their southward expansion after the Napoleonic Wars, they met the opposition of not only the Turks but also the British, who emerged as the chief competitors of Russia in West Asia. Throughout the nineteenth century a cardinal principle of British foreign policy was to support the Ottoman Empire against Russia.

The French Revolution and Napoleonic era had spread the ideas of national and popular rights throughout Europe, and the disintegrating Ottoman Empire in the nineteenth century was not immune. The Christian subjects of the Ottomans proved to be highly receptive to these revolutionary ideas. Encouraged by both European and later American missionaries and governments, one by one each Christian ethnic group launched a struggle for national independence, beginning with the Serbs (1804–1813). Britain and France, of course, not to mention Russia, could not go to the aid of the Ottomans against fellow Christians. Russia in particular took advantage of Christian independence movements to intervene in the Ottoman Empire, frequently as the protector of Greek Orthodox Christians, and France later claimed to be the protector of Roman Catholics.

THE CRIMEAN WAR

The Crimean War (1854–1856), which pitted Russia against the Ottoman Empire, Britain, France, and Sardinia and was a major turning point in the political history of post-

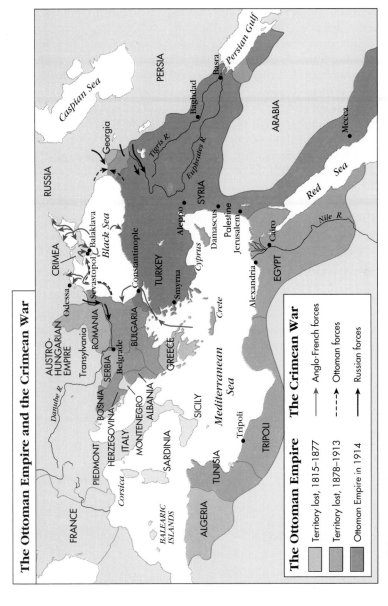

The Ottoman Empire and the Crimean War

The Ottoman Empire

	Territory lost, 1815–1877
	Territory lost, 1878–1913
	Ottoman Empire in 1914

The Crimean War

⟶	Anglo-French forces
⤏	Ottoman forces
⟶	Russian forces

MAP 17.2 Decline of the Ottoman Empire

Napoleonic Europe, began as a dispute between Russia and France over control of the Christian holy places in Jerusalem, in Ottoman Palestine. The Ottoman sultan's backing of the French position supporting Roman Catholics against Orthodox Christians aroused the Russian czar Nicholas I to make efforts to protect the rights and interests of Orthodox Christians. Though this issue was settled, Russian pressure on the Ottomans continued.

When Russia occupied Ottoman territories in the Danube basin, the Ottomans declared war on Russia. When most of the Turkish fleet was lost, Britain, France, and eventually Sardinia joined the Ottomans, ostensibly to protect them from the Russians, but, in fact, to keep Russia from gaining control of the Bosporus and thus access to the Mediterranean. The Treaty of Paris (1856), ending the Crimean War, was a major setback for Russia, which was defeated and lost Ottoman territory it had claimed; but it also deprived the Ottomans of much territory in the Danube basin. Protection of remaining Ottoman territories by the Great Powers (as Great Britain, Austria-Hungary, Germany, and France were known) helped ensure the empire's survival until World War I. The long-term significance of the Crimean War and its outcome lay in the collapse of the post-Napoleonic alliance among Britain, Russia, Austria, Prussia, and the exposure of Russian vulnerability.

THE SUEZ CANAL

Though European interest in Egypt was evident in Napoleon's invasion in 1798 and the British expulsion of the French in 1802, it was not until mid-century that both the British and French paid serious attention to Egypt. London's interest was drawn to Egypt in 1856

FIGURE 17.1 Procession of Ships at the Opening of the Suez Canal, 1869

The canal become a symbol of economic and technological triumphs to the British and a symbol of colonial domination to the Egyptians.

SOURCE: Mary Evans Picture Library.

when the French engineer Ferdinand de Lesseps acquired a concession from the Egyptian ruler Ismail Pasha to build a canal through the Suez isthmus connecting Africa and West Asia. Such a canal would allow for the most direct naval communications between Europe, India, and East Asia. A few years after this waterway was completed in 1869, the British bought out Ismail's interest in it. The subsequent British commercial penetration of Egypt led to local resentment and civil unrest. In 1882 the British occupied the country by force.

By this time the canal was being used to capacity, with 3,000 ships annually—80 percent of them sailing under the British flag—choosing the new passageway between the Mediterranean and the Indian Ocean. One of the most important consequences of the building of the canal was to shorten the distance and reduce travel time and costs between Europe and Asia. The Suez Canal made a major contribution to the development of world trade and helped make the region one of great strategic importance.

OTTOMAN REFORMS

During the eighteenth century, the enormous confidence that had characterized the invincible and expanding Ottoman Empire gradually eroded. Previously the continuous victories of the Ottoman armies were regarded as proof that God favored Muslims over Christians. But now the victories had ceased, and Muslims were on the defensive. Had they lost God's favor? Many Muslims in the Ottoman Empire viewed their reversal of fortune as punishment from God and called for a return to "true" Islam. Others, especially those in the government, took a more pragmatic approach. They were convinced that the empire could return to its former power and influence only if systematic reforms were introduced to eliminate corruption and modernize the government and the armed forces.

The Tanzimat The path to reforms proved difficult. Selim III (r. 1789–1807), the first Ottoman ruler to initiate a series of reforms, was overthrown by conservative elements. Mahmud II (r. 1808–1839) was more successful, although the revolt of Muhammad Ali in Egypt interrupted these efforts. His successor, Abd al-Majid (r. 1839–1861), went so far as to launch an era of reforms that were overtly Western in origin and purpose. This era was called "the Tanzimat" (which means "reorganization").

Most European states, including Britain, actually supported the reforms as a means of strengthening the Ottoman Empire and guaranteeing special rights for Christian minorities. Europeans tended to encourage the national aspirations of these minorities, and this stance caused resentment among Muslims, thus adding to the forces opposing the state. The Tanzimat continued for the remainder of the nineteenth century. Europeans were invited to help streamline the government, teach in technical schools, train the army and navy, and improve the state's infrastructure. Unfortunately, all of this activity cost money, which had to be borrowed heavily from Europe. When the Empire went bankrupt, it was forced to surrender its finances to European governments and bankers.

Forging a National Identity As more and more Turks and other peoples in the Ottoman Empire were trained by Europeans or exposed to their ideas, there arose a literary intelligentsia that popularized Ottomanism, patriotism, Islamic modernism, and constitutionalism. One member of this group, Midhat Pasha, rose to become vizier (prime minister) and in 1876 deposed the sultan and replaced him with Abd al-Hamid II

(r. 1876–1909), who was believed to be more sympathetic to parliamentary government. Once firmly in power, however, Abd al-Hamid arrested Midhat, suspended the constitution and began to rule despotically. Nevertheless, he carried out major reforms in education, transportation, and communications.

The Young Turk Movement While Abd al-Hamid worked to centralize power in his own hands, a group of young "Westernized" Turks formed a clandestine organization, the Young Turk Party, which spread among the intelligentsia and the army. In 1908 the party engineered a coup d'etat and forced the sultan to restore the constitution. This event opened a brief period of political freedom in which the roles of Turkism, Arabism, Islam, and Westernization were intensively discussed. In short, the Turks and other Muslims tried to reach a consensus on their identity and the direction of the state. At the very least the empire had to continue to modernize its infrastructure and technology, even though modernization meant Europeanization. For the Christians of the empire, the choice was easy, but for most Muslims it meant abandoning their heritage and, not surprisingly, they balked.

During this period the Young Turks began to equate "Ottoman" with "Turkish." Furthermore, Turkish-speaking provinces seemed to dominate parliament, and there was pressure to make Turkish the common language of the empire. Finally, as debate continued over the future of the empire and European powers again chipped away at its territory, the Young Turks seized power for themselves in another coup in 1913. The new government leaned toward Germany, which appeared to be a model of modernization and seemed to have no designs on the Ottoman Empire (see Chapter 18).

■

BRITISH AND RUSSIAN IMPERIALISM IN IRAN AND CENTRAL ASIA

At the beginning of the eighteenth century, West Asia was divided between the Ottoman Empire in the west and Iran under the Safavid dynasty in the east. In 1722 a small Afghan army invaded Iran and overthrew the Safavids, touching off a series of struggles for leadership that ended finally with the establishment of the Qajar dynasty (1794–1925). From the beginning of the nineteenth century, the Qajars fell increasingly under the shadow of Russia in the north and Britain in the south and east. Russia sought a warm-water port both on the Black Sea and on the Persian Gulf. While pressing on the Ottomans in the Crimea, Russia also pressed on the Qajars in the Caucasus. After a series of wars, Iran ceded, in 1813 and 1828, all of its Caucasus territory to Russia.

At the same time the Russians expanded east into Central Asia, toward both China and India. One by one, they conquered the mostly Turkic peoples of that vast area. In an advance reminiscent of the American conquest of the North American continent, the Russians marked their progress by building a line of forts that provided security for traders and settlers who took the most fertile lands. The Turkish nomads could not match the Russian weapons. The power of the tribal chiefs was liquidated, and the cities were subdued. The final thrust into Turkistan began in 1855, and in 1865 Tashkent fell. The minor principalities of Bukhara (1868), Khiva (1873), and Kokand (1876) were then captured in turn. A Russian army met its greatest resistance at Gok Tepe in 1879, but by 1884 all effective resistance was crushed. The Russians then incorporated Central Asia into their empire and adopted a colonial policy toward its Turkish population.

The British watched the course of Russian expansion very closely. They began to view Qajar Iran, and then Afghanistan, as a buffer between Russia and British India. In 1885 Britain and Russia delineated borders that confirmed a buffer role for Afghanistan. Meanwhile, competition between Britain and Russia in Iran itself intensified. Nasir ad-Din Shah (r. 1848–1896) granted wide-ranging concessions to European powers for fairly small amounts of money to satisfy his immediate needs. This move eventually gave Europeans effective control of the country's economy and infrastructure.

An example of European control was the sweeping concession given to Baron Julius de Reuter, a British subject, in 1872. Among other things, he acquired the exclusive right to exploit all minerals and forests in Iran, build all railways and canals, create a national bank, and even control customs. This arrangement was too much for the Russians, who succeeded in forcing the shah to cancel it. The Iranian people themselves became resentful of such special grants to foreigners, and this resentment was soon manifest in the streets. In 1890 a British company was given a 50-year monopoly on the curing and sale of Iran's entire tobacco crop in return for an annual fee. Because most Iranians used tobacco, this concession brought home to the common people the extent to which Europeans were controlling the country. The religious class, led by the *mullas* (clerics), organized demonstrations and forced the shah to retract the tobacco concession.

As with the Young Turk movement under the Ottomans, growing discontent with foreign political pressure, economic control, and government corruption at the beginning of the twentieth century provided fertile ground for a budding nationalist and constitutional movement in Iran under the Qajar dynasty. Inspired in part by events in the Ottoman Empire, the religious and commercial classes led a revolutionary movement in 1905 that forced Muzaffar ad-Din Shah to proclaim a constitution and establish a parliament (*majlis*) in 1906. When Muhammad Ali Shah (r. 1907–1909) came to the throne, in 1907, he tried his best to subvert the innovations. The ensuing struggle between him and the nationalists played into the hands of Russia and Britain.

Iran Divided   Concerned for the security of their respective empires and anxious to protect their concessions in Iran, Russia and Britain negotiated the Anglo-Russian Convention of 1907. According to its terms, Iran was to be divided into a Russian sphere of interest in the north and a British sphere in the south, separated by a neutral zone. The British sphere of influence proved to be of great importance to London the following year when oil was discovered in the southwest. Meanwhile the struggle between the shah and the nationalists resulted in civil war. Muhammed Ali was deposed and his 11-year-old son Ahmad was proclaimed shah. In 1911, however, Russia intervened, occupied Tehran, and closed the new parliament. Thus began an enduring focus of conflict between the forces of imperialism and nationalism that has lasted well into the twentieth century.

THE TECHNOLOGIES OF IMPERIALISM

The Suez Canal was but one of many technological achievements that furthered the course of imperialism on a global scale. Like earlier technological innovations that enabled the expansion of Europe in the sixteenth century, nineteenth-century advances in shipbuilding, transportation, communication, medicine, and science served as "tools of empire" in the age of the new imperialism.

TRANSPORTATION AND COMMUNICATION TECHNOLOGY

Perhaps nothing so distinguishes the late nineteenth and twentieth centuries as rapidity of movement, the speed with which material things, ideas, and human beings move about the globe. Increasing speed and lowering costs of transportation shrank the planet, and distant continents became as accessible as contiguous states had been before the nineteenth century. Significant changes in transportation derived from the eighteenth-century development of the steam engine.

The Steamboat Global transportation and communication were expedited by the development of the steamboat. During the 1850s the substitution of screw propellers for paddlewheels and of iron for wood in ship construction permitted vessels that moved rapidly and independent of the whims of the weather to link Europe with the non-European world. As late as the 1830s, when an Englishwoman wrote her officer husband stationed in India, her letter was carried by sailing ship from England to Africa and on to India, reaching its destination in about six or eight months. Because of the monsoon winds, a reply might reach England two years after the original correspondence. Two decades later, by the 1850s, the full impact of steam meant that the letter went by ship from London to France, by train across France, by steamer across to Alexandria and Cairo, by camel across to Suez, and then by steamer to Bombay or Calcutta, reaching its destination in thirty to forty-five days.

The Railroad Like steamships, trains were powerful machines and highly visible symbols of the conquest of the globe. The steam-powered locomotive was joined by other types, such as the electric locomotive (developed in 1851) and the internal combustion diesel locomotives, which replaced the steam engine in the twentieth century.

Railroads were boom enterprises throughout the nineteenth century and they interconnected vast territories of the world, including Asia and Europe. The east and west coasts of North America were joined by rail lines across Canada and the United States, with most projects completed in the second half of the century. One of the dreams of British imperialists

FIGURE 17.2 East India Railway in India, 1863

The railroad opened up the interiors of Asia and Africa to European penetration. The impact on India was particularly significant, since passenger trains such as the one depicted crowded Indians of different castes together and began a process that would eventually lead to Indian national unity in opposition to the British Raj, which originally built the railway.

SOURCE: Mary Evans Picture Library.

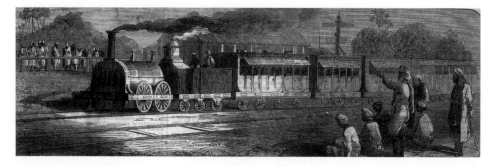

such as Cecil Rhodes was a Cape Town to Cairo railway across the African continent, an ambition more linked to nationalist pride than to practical need and one that was never fully completed. In South America, Australia, and India railroads rapidly became the customary way to move people, raw materials, and finished goods cheaply and quickly over great distances—even across such barriers as the Andes.

The Wireless Communication also speeded up in the second half of the century, and not just because of faster transportation. After 1870, the telegraph cable not only provided instantaneous communication between London and Paris, and connected Britain and America, but also joined colonies to their metropoles. Alexander Graham Bell's invention in 1876 provided the world with telephone connections. When these technologies became wireless (the telegraph and radio in 1895 and the telephone in 1899), their general use was greatly expanded. Such technologies enhanced the ability of the imperial center to control communications with its colonies.

■

THE IDEOLOGIES OF IMPERIALISM

Many ideas emerged in the nineteenth century in support of imperialism and were even driving forces behind it. Scientific and pseudoscientific knowledge had a tremendous impact on the language of imperialism and offered justification for it. One of the most influential ideologies of imperialism came in response to the evolutionary theories of Charles Darwin as adapted by Herbert Spencer, known as social Darwinism (see Chapter 16). Spencer and others

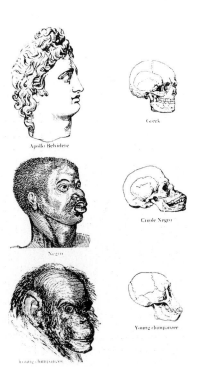

FIGURE 17.3 *Scale of Human Races and Lower Relatives,* by Nott and Glidden (1868)

Drawing in which the chimpanzee skull is falsely inflated and the Negro jaw extended to give a false impression that blacks might rank lower than the apes. The mismeasurement of heads and their comparison was a pseudoscientific pursuit of Social Darwinists in the nineteenth century.

SOURCE: From: *Indigenous Races of the Earth,* by J.C. Nott and G.R. Glidden, 1868. General Research Division, New York Public Library, Astor, Lenox and Tilden Foundations.

used pseudoscientific ideas of racial inferiority on the basis of skin pigmentation and other physical characteristics (such as head size and shape) to justify imperialism. Accordingly, people were classified as separate "races" along an evolutionary scale, and the subjugation of peoples of color was considered the inevitable consequence of the superiority of white men. While by no means all Europeans adopted the stance of racial superiority dictated by social Darwinists, the pseudoscientific origins of racism were to have a virulent and long-lasting impact around the globe.

CHRISTIANITY AND THE MISSIONARY ENTERPRISE

Though Catholic missionaries—Jesuits, Dominicans, and Franciscans—accompanied the sixteenth-century expansion of Europe and had a lasting influence in Asia and Africa, they were most successful in the Americas. In the nineteenth century, however, the Protestant missionary movement provided ideological support for the new imperialism, especially in Asia and Africa. The biblical command "Go ye into all the world, and preach the gospel to every creature" was literally taken up by Protestant men and women as they moved out from their homes, cultures, and societies to make their own particular contributions to the new imperialism through evangelization, converting other peoples to Christianity.

While dedicated to converting the "heathen" unbelievers of the non-European world to the saving grace of Protestant Christianity, many missionaries engaged as well in medical work and teaching, setting up hospitals and schools as bases for their evangelical activities.

FIGURE 17.4 **Deaconess Ellen Mort, an Australian Missionary in China Preparing to Begin Her Rounds (ca. 1900)**

SOURCE: Church Missionary Society.

The motives of missionary men and women were complex and diverse. Many European and American women simply accompanied their husbands on missions, but others went as single women for whom the mission was an attractive alternative to marriage or spinsterhood at home. The missionary life was also one of the few adventurous opportunities available to women and offered a perfect female vocation when coupled with either an intense experience of religious conversion or a steady background of religious training in family, school, and church.

Though by the late nineteenth and early twentieth century, most missionary volunteers came from the rural Midwest, the American missionary movement began in New England, coordinated by the American Board of Commissioners for Foreign Missions, headquartered in Boston. In 1819 the first mission destined for the Sandwich Islands (the Hawaiian Islands) left Boston harbor on the *Thaddeus.* When the ship arrived on the big island of Hawai'i five months later, the missionaries on board ship were approached by islanders bringing articles for trade. One of the missionary wives, Sybil Bingham, was appalled by the nakedness of the men, crying out, "O, my sisters, you cannot tell how the sight of these poor degraded creatures, both literally and spiritually naked, would affect you!"

At the turn of the century, Emma and Elizabeth Martin and many other young women from the rural American Midwest, dedicated their lives to saving the world in their own generation. Aged 30 and 27, Emma and Elizabeth left their family home in Otterbein, Indiana,

FIGURE 17.5 The Methodist Missionary T. B. Freeman presenting an exotic gift (a carriage) to the Asantehene at Kumase in the Gold Coast (Ghana) in 1841.

SOURCE: From: *Journal of Various Visits to the Kingdom of Ashanti, Aku and Dahomi in Western Africa,* by T.B. Freeman, 1844. General Research Division, New York Public Library, Astor, Lenox and Tilden Foundations.

in the spring of 1900 for missionary work in China. Both women were college graduates, and Emma had studied medicine at Chicago Woman's Medical College. But their education did not prepare them for the challenges of the train trip across the United States, let alone for the rigors of life in China at the turn of the century. They arrived in time to experience the Boxer Uprising.

European and American women often saw their role as one of uplifting women in foreign lands both spiritually and socially and working to improve their treatment by men, though at times missionary women found themselves in societies where women had more power than in the missionaries' own. Both sincere and corrupt Christians, some with little education, spent much of their lives in foreign lands. Most were tolerated, and some of the European travelers became popular in their adopted cultural settings and are still remembered with affection by the communities in which they resided. One of the most famous missionaries in Africa, David Livingstone, spent decades in Southern Africa and had only one convert.

Some missionaries also recognized the great difficulties inherent in trying to accommodate Christianity to vastly different religious and cultural traditions and devoted much of their time to translation work and educating themselves in the cultures of the peoples they sought to convert. They recorded local customs and cultural traditions, including languages. For example, the British missionary James Legge, working at the China Inland Mission in the late nineteenth century, made translations of the Chinese classics that are still widely used today. Missionaries in Africa recorded languages, history, and cultural observations. Missionary accounts of the persistent slave trade in Africa figured heavily in the antislavery movement in the United States. On occasion they deliberately exaggerated and invented cultural practices attributed to African peoples in order to sway congregations back home to support missionary efforts.

The very nature of the missionary enterprise reinforced the goals of the new imperialism. Missionaries provided essential information needed for conquest. They served as critical communication links in areas remote from the colonial centers. Their mission stations were key trading points for the transfer of European manufactured goods, as well as ideas. To the missionaries, conquered peoples were "sinners to be saved." By justifying conquest of other peoples with the purpose of converting them to Christianity, the goals of missionaries dovetailed with the political and economic goals of European and American nation states. As the American missionary and China scholar S. Wells Williams put it, the Chinese "would grant nothing unless fear stimulated their sense of justice, for they are among the most craven of peoples, cruel and selfish as heathenism can make men, so we must be backed by force, if we wish them to listen."

■

THE NEW IMPERIALISM IN AFRICA

Expansion fueled by capitalist industrialism and nationalism brought previously unsubjugated lands under European control during the nineteenth century. At its height the British Empire alone consisted of over a quarter of the world's land mass and people. By 1914 Europe together with its colonial possessions occupied more than 80 percent of the globe. The conquest of Africa provided perhaps the clearest example of what is sometimes called the "new imperialism," an era roughly beginning in Africa in the 1880s and continuing into the twentieth century.

EUROPEAN IMPERIALISM AND THE BERLIN CONFERENCE

Africa, which Europeans called the "dark continent" because its interior was still virtually unknown to them, was colonized by conquest from one end of the continent to the other. The British spread southward from Egypt, where they had established themselves by 1875 and assumed a protectorate (controlling authority) by 1882, while they moved northward from Cape Colony in South Africa, which they had held since 1815. A column of British-claimed territories that stretched up the entire east coast of Africa was interrupted by German acquisition of East African territory in 1885.

The trans-Atlantic slave trade had been central to capitalist development and growth in West and Central Africa. Even after the abolition of slavery by European powers beginning about 1807, African societies continued and, in some instances, even deepened their dependence on slave labor. The slave trade era was followed by the era of "legitimate commerce," a period between about 1800 and 1870 during which African-European economic enterprises were forced to find other products to replace illegal human cargoes. In almost all instances the products sold to international markets were agricultural or forest products grown or collected for export to Europe. They included timber, rubber, palm oil, minerals, and ivory. Even when slaves were no longer exported, slavery and other forms of coerced labor remained essential to the production and transport of commodities. The era has also been termed a period of informal empire, suggesting that the economic relations characteristic of the subsequent formal empires of the colonial era were well underway by the end of the nineteenth century.

The Berlin Conference At the Berlin Conference in 1884–1885, European powers and the United States met to protect their "spheres of influence" (areas of special economic and political interests) and to establish mechanisms for making new territorial claims. The scramble for African territory was underway. An earlier catalyst for the scramble for territories came from King Leopold II of Belgium (r. 1865–1909). Motivated by greed and ambition to expand the wealth and territory of his small European kingdom, Leopold undertook what he called a crusade to acquire the Congo Free State (later, Zaire). The relatively swift imposition of European colonial rule in Africa following the Berlin Conference also needs to be understood against the backdrop of several centuries of the Atlantic slave trade, the rise of an African merchant class, and the penetration of merchant capital prior to 1900. These forces undermined the earlier systems of authority on the continent and prevented African societies from dealing with the European presence in any unified way.

EUROPEAN TERRITORIAL CLAIMS IN AFRICA

The distribution of European-dominated territory on the West and Central African coast was more scattered than other regions, and European trade competition, especially between Britain, France, Germany, and Belgium was more fierce. Before the outbreak of World War I (see Chapter 18), the lower Niger valley had become Nigeria, a British protectorate, as had Sierra Leone and the Gold Coast, but German imperialist activity checked British interest in the coast above Cape Colony. A German protectorate, established over Southwest Africa in 1884, was a sharp blow to British designs. Despite such frustrations, Great Britain had staked out claims to a great share of African territory.

French territorial acquisitions in Africa were equally staggering. From about 1830, the French began to re-create the empire they had lost in 1763 (when they surrendered Canada and India to Britain) with a campaign to conquer Algeria. Using piracy as an excuse, the French began their African expansion with an expedition of troops to Algeria in 1830, leading to a lengthy and violent assault (termed a "pacification" by the French) that resulted in its mid-century integration as three departments of metropolitan France. France, in claiming lands and peoples previously unclaimed by Europeans, was setting the pattern for a general European imperialist race that resumed after 1870. The annexation of Algeria was an inaugural step toward realizing a French dominance of Africa north of the equator. The next step was the annexation of Tunisia (1881). In 1904 an agreement with Great Britain provided English support for rounding out French holdings in northwest Africa by establishing a protectorate over Morocco (1912), despite German opposition.

In equatorial Africa the French established themselves on the Kongo, and in West Africa in Senegal. As early as 1885 these colonies were linked across the Sahara to French North African territories, thus consolidating the vast African territory north of the equator and west of Egypt and the Sudan. With French acquisition of the island of Madagascar in 1896, their African territories exceeded those of Great Britain, though the colonies most strategic to the French lay along the Mediterranean shore of North Africa, closest to France itself.

What the British and French left unclaimed in Africa was taken by the Germans, Italians, Belgians, Portuguese, and Spanish. Taken together, these holdings meant that only two areas of Africa remained unclaimed by Europeans by the time of the outbreak of World War I: Liberia, a territory that was partly settled by repatriated African and African-American slaves from the Americas and virtually a dependency, however unacknowledged and ignored, of the United States; and Ethiopia, which retained independence only by defeating the 1896 Italian effort at conquest. This comprehensive European hegemony over Africa, once completed, proved to be surprisingly short-lived, though no one would have supposed so before World War I.

The Economic Advantages   In some important ways the era of colonial rule was fundamentally different from what had preceded it. Before colonial rule Africans were independent, if not always equal, trading partners. After colonial rule, this African economy became a European-dominated economy. Under post–Berlin Conference colonial rule, African political economies controlled by colonial powers—such as Great Britain, France, or Germany—were rapidly establishing Western-based capitalism that would inevitably reduce the power and economic opportunity of the African participants. While production remained largely in Africa hands, Europeans controlled colonial credit and trade tariffs. Few Africans prospered during this era; colonial controls hampered the development of free enterprise, and European governments offset the high costs of extracting raw materials and transporting them to European-based manufacturing centers by providing price supports.

European economic and political hegemony depended on the development of the colonial system. African colonies supported many European industries that otherwise could not have been profitable. For example, the textile industry of France depended on the cheap cotton supplied by French West African colonies to remain competitive with technologically more advanced manufacturing in Great Britain and the United States. The other side of the colonial relationship was of course the development of markets in Africa. African markets continued to support the patterns of Western industrial growth as Africans became dependent consumers of European textiles, iron pots, agricultural implements, soap, and even foodstuffs.

Political Conquest There was another way in which the industrial achievements of the colonizers wrought a hefty price from the colonized: political independence
was lost as one territory after another was conquered. Although post–Berlin Conference colonial rule followed decades and even centuries of involvement, its imposition was swift. The
use of military force as necessary everywhere to establish and maintain European control of
African territories. The European tools of empire, from quinine (to treat malaria) to the
steamboat, railway, and machine gun, all enabled the penetration and conquest to be complete. In some places, such as the Benin kingdom of Nigeria in 1897, Europeans forcibly removed the local rulers (the *oba* and his chiefs) from power and sent them into exile. Cultural
treasures that expressed power and recorded the Benin kingship's historically sanctioned le-
gitimization were stolen and taken to Europe, where they were auctioned to offset the costs of
the expedition. Accordingly, the Benin bronzes and ivories are found today in world museums, from Berlin to London and New York.

THE COLONIAL SYSTEM

The colonial systems differed in strategy and form under British, French, Belgian, German,
and Portuguese rule. The British policies were termed "indirect rule," and they required
British district officers to be supported by local chiefs and puppet administrators drawn from
local circles. French rule was termed "direct rule" and utilized the French themselves as colonial officials in the field; under French assimilationist policy, Africans who adopted the culture (language, dress, and lifestyle) of French nationals were allowed to become French citizens. The repercussions of such distinctions had a lasting impact on the relations between the
former colonial power and its colonized peoples.

  The purpose of the colonial system, regardless of the type of rule, was exploitative, seeking to harness the resources of land and people for the benefit of the metropole (the European
capitals). Profits from the unequal and often brutally enforced economic relations were returned to Europe while African markets were created to consume European manufactured
goods. Colonial laws, imposed by force, invaded peoples lives, from their rights to work and
live in certain places and travel freely to their rights to read or speak their own languages or
practice their traditional religions.

  Although many Europeans complained bitterly about the costs of the colonial enterprise
(the British author Rudyard Kipling called this the "white man's burden"), some segments of
European and other industrialized societies were enriched by their colonial ties. For example,
some French industries were absolutely dependent on the cheap raw materials, labor, and consuming markets of their colonial partners. Large multinational concerns eventually emerged
from the colonial enterprises, including Lever Brothers, Lloyds of London, and many other
companies that began as commercial organizations during the slave trade and the subsequent
era of legitimate commerce.

■

AFRICAN RESISTANCE TO THE NEW IMPERIALISM

Conquest and exploitation through the use of force brought about immediate resistance in all
parts of the colonized continent. In 1890 in southern Tanganyika, the main opponents were

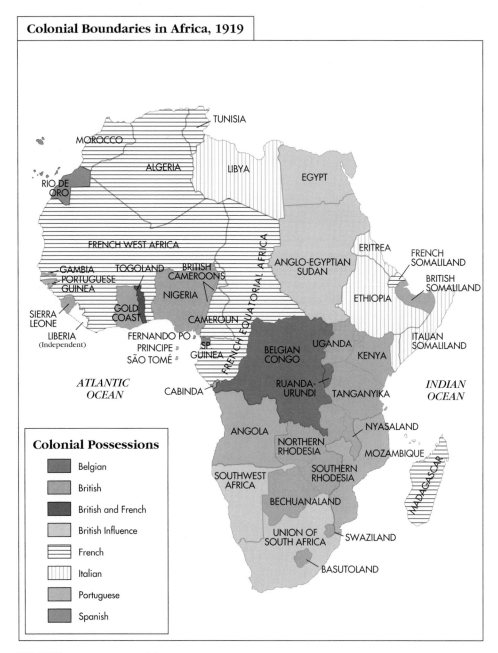

Colonial Boundaries in Africa, 1919

TUNISIA

MOROCCO

ALGERIA

LIBYA

EGYPT

RIO DE ORO

FRENCH WEST AFRICA

ERITREA

ANGLO-EGYPTIAN SUDAN

FRENCH SOMALILAND

BRITISH SOMALILAND

GAMBIA

TOGOLAND

BRITISH CAMEROONS

PORTUGUESE GUINEA

NIGERIA

ETHIOPIA

SIERRA LEONE

GOLD COAST

CAMEROUN

LIBERIA
(Independent)

FERNANDO PO
PRINCIPE
SÃO TOMÉ

SP. GUINEA

FRENCH EQUATORIAL AFRICA

BELGIAN CONGO

UGANDA

KENYA

ITALIAN SOMALILAND

ATLANTIC OCEAN

CABINDA

RUANDA-URUNDI

TANGANYIKA

INDIAN OCEAN

ANGOLA

NORTHERN RHODESIA

NYASALAND

MOZAMBIQUE

MADAGASCAR

Colonial Possessions

■	Belgian
■	British
■	British and French
■	British Influence
≡	French
▥	Italian
▤	Portuguese
■	Spanish

SOUTHWEST AFRICA

SOUTHERN RHODESIA

BECHUANALAND

UNION OF SOUTH AFRICA

SWAZILAND

BASUTOLAND

MAP 17.3 Imperialism in Africa

the German commander Hermann von Wissman and Macemba, ruling chief of the Yao people. When Wissman demanded subordination by Macemba, the African ruler replied by way of a letter written in Kiswahili:

> I have listened to your words but can find no reason why I should obey you—I would rather die first . . . I look for some reason why I should obey you and find not the smallest. If it should be friendship that you desire, then I am ready for it, today and always; but not to be your subject, that I cannot be. If it should be war you desire, then I am ready, but never to be your subject. I do not fall at your feet, for you are God's creature just as I am. I am sultan here in my land. You are sultan there in yours. Yet listen, I do not say to you that you should obey me; for I know that you are a free man. As for me, I will not come to you, and if you are strong enough, then come and fetch me.

Macemba's reply was characteristic of a great many African responses. Some resistance also amounted to revolts of despair over the dispossession of lands or European brutalities.

For example, the Maji Maji rebellion covered a large area of central and southern Tanganyika in 1906, where labor coercion by German colonizers was particularly intense. The movement was an attempt to overcome the superior military technology of the Germans. Resisters sprinkled their bodies with protective magic water known as *maji-maji* and believed to turn the enemy's bullets into water. The use of spiritual beliefs helped foster African unity, and although thousands were killed by machine gun fire, the Germans ultimately reduced their use of violence in order not to provoke another mass uprising.

Other kinds of resistance were more successful, long-term strategies that undermined colonial rule and sometimes targeted the collaborating African elites. About the same time that German East Africa was threatened by the Maji Maji, the British were facing uprisings in Nigeria. Using the traditional *jihad* or holy war waged against nonbelievers from Islamic regions, peasants challenged British colonial authority.

With no technological match for advanced European weaponry, the failure of African resistance was endemic, until well into the twentieth century, when the educated elite and masses eventually found common political and sometimes even nationalist grounds. The one exception to the pattern of extracting raw materials without furthering local African processes of industrialization occurred in South Africa, the southern-most territory of European settlement on the continent and the site of persistent African resistance. Even in South Africa, colonial development had uneven benefits for the colonizer and the colonized.

IMPERIALISM AND RESISTANCE IN SOUTH AFRICA

In South Africa, European settlers claimed African territories that they eventually considered as their own homelands. There were European settlers in other parts of the continent, the Kenyan highlands, for example, but only in South Africa had the European presence taken root as early permanent settlement and in such a peculiar way. Isolated from their European roots and marginalized by shifting global relations, these "white" settlers—the Afrikaners—found themselves competing with Africans and European empires for control over territory and resources. They were descendants of early Dutch settlers who began arriving only in the seventeenth century; by the nineteenth century they displayed a language and culture born of centuries of interaction with African populations and began to develop a cultural nationalism that would eventually turn political.

Excluded from the same political process, Black South Africans created separate nationalist movements, which shared some tactics and visions with the anticolonial revolutions in neighboring African territories. The Black South African nationalist leader, Anton Lembede, once repeated a quote that he attributed to Paul Kruger, the father of the white Afrikaner state. Lembede said: "One who wants to create the future must not forget the past." It is interesting, but not surprising, given the role of history in shaping the unique landscape of people and power, that the two leading figures in parallel nationalist movements in the same land should have both invoked a reverence for the historical past. However, Lembede and Kruger probably would have disagreed on the meaning of that past.

Competing Histories For the Afrikaner the history of South Africa began in 1652, the year of the first permanent settlement in the Cape. From that century onwards, their history took on mythic proportions. With motives they considered of divine origin and therefore pure (the claiming of lands by God's chosen people) and with their God's protection, the descendants of these early European settlers found themselves pitted against two traditional sets of enemies: the British, who acquired control over Cape Colony in 1815, and the Africans. In the Afrikaner view of history, the central saga is the so-called Great Trek, the era of the Afrikaner migration northward out of the Cape when both sets of enemies opposed the expansion of the Afrikaner state.

From the African point of view, the central theme of recent history—merely the last several hundred years out of many millennia—was white conquest and the expropriation of African lands. The quarrels between the British and the Afrikaner Boers were of little concern. What both African and Afrikaner historical traditions might agree upon is the critical importance of the century between about 1790 and 1890. This was a period of devastating transformations in African and European societies coexisting in the southern-most part of the African continent.

By the end of the eighteenth century, the players in the historical drama that was about to unfold were in place or, as in the case of the expanding farmers of Dutch descent (*trekboers*), moving into place. The geography of southern Africa had determined to a large extent the nature of population movements and the ultimate distribution of pastoralists, mainly Boers moving north and eastward from the Cape Colony, who were blocked by mountains and attracted by pasturelands for their cattle. To the west expanding populations of Sotho speakers spread across the plateau in search of pasture lands, from the Limpopo to the Orange rivers. The Tsawa were pushed by the farmers against the fringes of the Kalahari Desert in the west.

Zulu Imperialism The ecological balance that most Africans had attained through stock-keeping and mixed farming, including the cultivation of grains, was a delicate, if successful one. In Zululand, an area well-suited to its cattle-keeping cultivators, a system of exploitation of native grasses had developed, whereby the configuration of grass types available in different seasons and at different elevations affected the development of political and economic units. Territorial expansion took place to acquire seasonal pasturelands.

Nguni Militarization and Resistance The Nguni were one of a number of Bantu-speaking peoples whose ancestors had originated thousands of years earlier in the region of the Nigerian-Cameroon border of West Africa. Arriving in southern Africa during the Early Iron Age (by about 500 C.E.), these farmers with cattle had become the dominant group. Their expansion, often at the expense of herders, hunters, and gatherers, had resulted in the growth of villages and towns and the increasingly stratified society of the 1700s.

Southern Africa in the Era of the "Scramble"

GERMAN SOUTH WEST AFRICA

Limpopo R.

VENDA

BECHUANALAND PROTECTORATE

BOER REPUBLIC OF TRANSVAAL

PEDI

PORTUGUESE EAST AFRICA

Lourenco Marques

Johannesburg ●

Pretoria ●

SWAZILAND

Vaal R.

BOER REPUBLIC OF ORANGE FREE STATE

GRIQUALAND WEST

ZULULAND

Tugela R.

Orange R.

Kimberly ●

BASUTOLAND

NATAL

Durban

TRANSKEI

ATLANTIC OCEAN

CAPE COLONY

Fish R.

Kei R.

INDIAN OCEAN

● Cape Town

● Port Elizabeth

0   150   300 Miles

0   150   300 Kilometers

* Regions of rebellion and resistance

MAP 17.4 Imperialism and Resistance in South Africa

The traditional methods for dealing with ecological constraints—population movements in response to cycles of environmental degradation, concentrated grazing, overpopulation, shortages of resources and land—depended on the availability of pastures over the next hill. Famine and drought, if combined with overpopulation, could result in a crisis. Such was the time of *Madlathule,* a famine that devastated Zululand from the 1790s until about 1810.

Shaka and the Zulu Kingdom   The first half of the nineteenth century saw the rise and consolidation of the great Zulu kingdom. That the centralization of authority and increased expansionary efforts occurred following the great famine is not coincidental. During the famine larger villages were needed to defend grain storage from the attacks of marauders. The control of cattle over a larger area was also necessary to compensate for the decrease in palatable grasses. One great revolutionary leader known as Shaka (r. 1818–1828) exploited the crisis. Of enormous importance was Shaka's control over three factors of production: cattle, women, and marriage.

Some of the tremendous changes of Shaka's time were inevitable. Revolutions in military tactics (the use of a new weapon, the short stabbing spear, and a new formation, the cow-horn formation) included the conversion of the traditional age-grade system into a military organization. The system was an association of similar-aged males, who from boyhood to manhood created regiments in a unitary, nationalized army. Social changes also made the chief more powerful.

Through his control over marriage (and thus population and production), Shaka was able to revolutionize Zulu social relations. Marriage practices had potentially important economic and political consequences. As social and political transactions, marriages transferred wealth and created strategic alliances between families. Shaka, by delaying the marriage of his young soldiers, was able to control the movement of a significant proportion of the kingdom's power and production. With marriages delayed and warfare increased, Shaka was able to resolve the population pressures that the *Madlathule* had induced. To his enemies Shaka became a beastly and harsh ruler. He became a legend in almost every version of southern African history.

The Impact of the *Mfecane* The era after the famine came to be called the *Mfecane,* the "time of the crushing." The forces and peoples of the *Mfecane* transformed the region, and societies that could not resist Shaka's armies became starving, landless refugees. Survivors were highly militarized. Small political units were no longer viable; populations were dramatically redistributed across southern Africa. The Great Trek era (1836–1854) of Afrikaner history was the collision of Boer expansion with these forces.

The mid-nineteenth century presents a momentary balance of power: the independent states of the Zulu and other Africans, independent Boer "republics" (not much more than lumps of settlements), and British control over two southern African colonies, Cape and Natal. The *Mfecane* had left large unpopulated areas vulnerable to European imperialists. This was the eve of the country's mineral revolution: the European discovery of diamonds and gold in 1868 and 1886 dramatically altered the role of land and capital.

Gold, Diamonds, and the Mining Industry Mining spurred significant economic changes as southern Africa, unlike the rest of the sub-Saharan Africa, underwent the early stages of an industrial revolution. South African capitalist development intensified with the recognition of extensive mineral resources. British capitalists, backed by foreign finance and technology, succeeded in gaining the mining territories. The sudden influx of people and capital transformed the areas of the Transvaal and Orange Free State where the mining settlements were attracting a large number of immigrants and investments and creating urban crises. The land on which the gold and diamonds were situated had been easily expropriated from Africans. More complicated was the problem of attracting labor to the mines while industrializing the operations.

Eventually, the economy developed a dependence on cheap and temporary unskilled labor to work in the mines. Legislative initiatives in the colony and the ravages of the Anglo-Boer conflicts at the end of the century speeded up the process by which Africans and their labor were brought under control. Initially both African and Afrikaner were attracted by the opportunities for employment. The wide disparity between the earnings of skilled and unskilled laborers in the mining sector came to be entrenched along racial lines, as discrimination and color prejudice were used to give white workers advantages. Between 1913 and 1922, the government imposed a series of discriminatory legislation. For example, the Natives Land Act (1913) prevented Africans from acquiring certain lands and this restriction and later laws helped create an unsettled migrant labor pool. Thus industrialization set the standard for racial discrimination and for the racist presumptions that white, rural competitors (Afrikaners) brought to the new urban setting of the mines.

The Anglo-Boer War Conflicts over land and ideology erupted between farmers and capitalist interests. Known as the Anglo-Boer War (1899–1902), this period of conflict witnessed the birth of Afrikaner nationalism, which was based on a sense of shared religion and historical experience of the Boers. The civil religion and sacred history that came

FIGURE 17.6 Attending the Injured after the Battle of Driefontein

During the Anglo-Boer War (1899–1902), Africans fought beside white soldiers on both sides of the conflict.

SOURCE: Hulton Getty/Tony Stone Images.

to fruition in the twentieth century was first expounded by Paul Kruger, an Afrikaner leader in the Anglo-Boer conflict. Kruger was a *Voortrekker,* one who had been a part of the expansion from the Cape, and he was president of the South African Republic between 1881 and 1900. His thinking was influenced by the theology of John Calvin, whose emphasis on collective individualism, encouraging individual action on behalf of the collective good of the group, was useful in Kruger's development of nationalist sentiment among Afrikaner settlers. Afrikaner nationalism became the struggle among the white people of South Africa for political control.

In contrast to the Afrikaner "whites," who were a diverse and widely differentiated population of landowners, rich commercial farmers, professionals, and impoverished, unskilled workers, the Africans for the most part remained peasants and pastoralists for whom wage labor was occasional. After the 1880s and under the influence of capitalist economic forces, rural and urban whites sought and received privileged status. Parallel to this movement were the expropriation of African land and the incorporation of African labor into the South African process of industrialization.

The Anglo-Boer War was basically about who should dominate South Africa: the British, who controlled mining, or the Boers, who controlled politics. The conflict temporarily halted mining and capitalist development. When Africans resumed mining in post-war South Africa, the unity of whites resulted in black political exclusion. The blacks of South Africa began to feel the contradictions of white domination and their own increased economic participation. African political movements seized the opportunities provided by the forces of urbanization, industrialization, and the very tools of the European empire: western-style education and Christianity. In the end the tools would be turned against the imperialists here as elsewhere in Africa, where broad nationalism transcended both individual and ethnic differences.

IMPERIALISM AND COLONIALISM IN SOUTHEAST ASIA

The upheavals of the French Revolution and Napoleonic eras brought change to such distant parts of the globe as Southeast Asia, where the Dutch had dominated the East Indies while indigenous monarchies retained control on the Southeast Asian mainland. Conflicts between the British and Dutch erupted in the wake of the Napoleonic wars, resulting in a division of control between the two European powers in the East Indies. In 1819 the British Sir Thomas Stamford Raffles founded the free trade port of Singapore at the southern tip of the Malay peninsula, thus breaking the Dutch trading monopoly on the Straits of Malacca. In the 1840s the British James Brooke became the Rajah of Sarawak on the island of Borneo, ruling much as a native monarch.

French and British Colonies   In the late nineteenth century, France claimed colonial possessions on the mainland of Southeast Asia, known as French IndoChina. French interest in Southeast Asia dated from the beginning of the century when volunteers from the French navy helped put down a Vietnamese rebellion. French Catholic

DAILY LIVES

"MISTA COURIFER"

Adelaide Smith Casely-Hayford was born in Sierra Leone, West Africa, in 1868. She represented the aspirations of the creole elite in Sierra Leone and sought unity among competing races, classes, and cultures through recognition of common African values and culture. With her sister she established the Girls Vocational School in Freetown. In her writings Casely-Hayford explored the silent but invidious process of change across the cultural boundaries experienced by West Africans:

> Not a sound was heard in the coffin-maker's workshop, that is to say no human sound. Mista Courifer, a solid citizen of Sierra Leone, was not given to much speech. His apprentices, knowing this, never dared address him unless he spoke first. Then they only carried on their conversation in whispers. Not that Mista Courifer did not know how to use his tongue. It was incessantly wagging to and fro in his mouth at every blow of the hammer. But his shop in the heart of Freetown was a part of his house. And, as he had once confided to a friend, he was a silent member of his own household from necessity. His wife, given to much speaking, could outtalk him.

> Mr. Courifer always wore black. He was one of the Sierra Leone gentlemen who considered everything European to be not only the right thing, but the only thing for the African and having read somewhere that English undertakers generally appeared in sombre attire, he immediately followed suit. He even went so far as to build a European house. During his short stay in England, he had noticed how the houses were built and furnished and forthwith erected himself one after the approved pattern—a house with stuffy little passages, narrow little staircases and poky rooms, all crammed with saddlebags and carpeted with Axminsters. No wonder his wife had to talk. It was so hopelessly uncomfortable, stuffy and unsanitary.

> So Mr. Courifer wore black. It never struck him for a single moment that red would have been more appropriate, far more becoming, far less expensive, and far more national. No! It must be black. He would have liked blue black, but he wore rusty black for economy.*

*Adelaide Smith Casely-Hayford, "Mista Courifer," in Charlotte H. Bruner, ed., *Unwinding Threads: Writing by Women in Africa* (London: Heinemann, 1983), pp. 8–10.

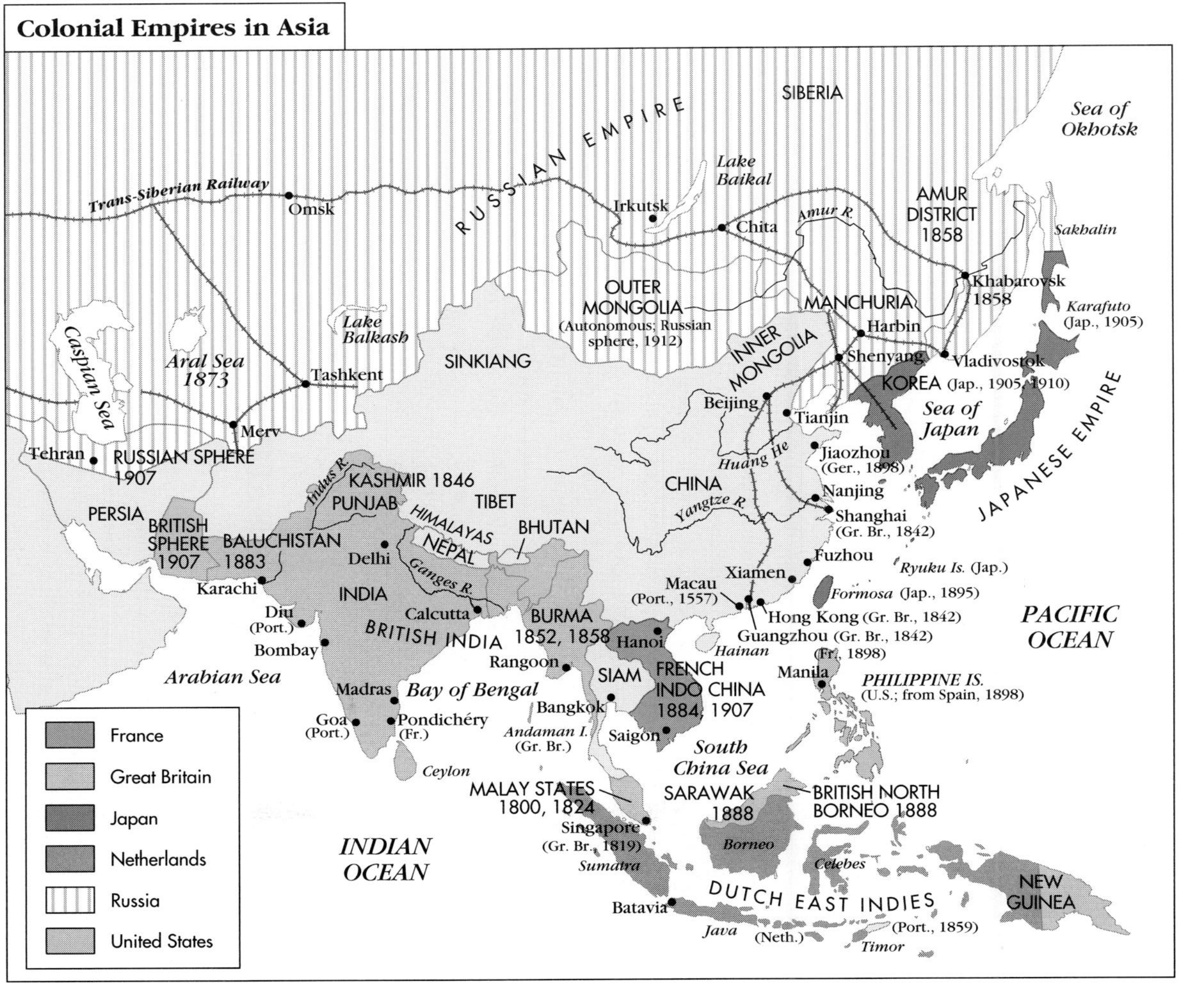

Colonial Empires in Asia

Sea of
Okhotsk

Sakhalin

Karafuto (Jap., 1905)

Khabarovsk
1858

AMUR
DISTRICT
1858

Vladivostok

JAPANESE EMPIRE

PACIFIC
OCEAN

NEW
GUINEA

SIBERIA

Chita

Amur R.

MANCHURIA

Harbin

Shenyang

KOREA (Jap., 1905–1910)

Sea of
Japan

Ryuku Is. (Jap.)

PHILIPPINE IS.
(U.S.; from Spain, 1898)

RUSSIAN EMPIRE

*Lake
Baikal*

Irkutsk

INNER MONGOLIA

OUTER
MONGOLIA
(Autonomous; Russian
sphere, 1912)

Beijing

Huang He

Tianjin

Jiaozhou
(Ger., 1898)

Nanjing

Shanghai
(Gr. Br., 1842)

Fuzhou

Formosa (Jap., 1895)

Hong Kong (Gr. Br., 1842)

Guangzhou (Gr. Br., 1842)

Manila

Hainan

BRITISH NORTH
BORNEO 1888

DUTCH EAST INDIES

Celebes

Timor (Port., 1859)

Java (Neth.)

CHINA

Yangtze R.

Xiamen

Macau
(Port., 1557)

FRENCH
INDO
CHINA
1884 1907

South
China Sea

Borneo

SARAWAK
1888

Batavia

Sumatra

Trans-Siberian Railway

Omsk

SINKIANG

*Lake
Balkash*

Tashkent

TIBET

BHUTAN

BURMA

Hanoi

SIAM

Bangkok

Saigon

Singapore
(Gr. Br., 1819)

MALAY STATES
1800, 1824

Merv

Indus R.

KASHMIR 1846

PUNJAB

HIMALAYAS

NEPAL

Ganges R.

Calcutta

Rangoon

Andaman I.
(Gr. Br.)

*Aral Sea
1873*

Caspian Sea

Tehran

PERSIA

BRITISH
SPHERE
1907

BALUCHISTAN
1883

Karachi

Bombay

Diu
(Port.)

Goa (Port.)

Delhi

INDIA

BRITISH INDIA 1852, 1858

Madras

Pondichéry
(Fr.)

Ceylon

Bay of Bengal

Arabian Sea

INDIAN
OCEAN

RUSSIAN SPHERE
1907

France

Great Britain

Japan

Netherlands

Russia

United States

MAP 17.5 European and Asian Colonizers

749

missionaries had gained enough converts that the Vietnamese emperor Minh-Mang's (r. 1820–1841) pursuit of anti-Catholic policies along with French commercial interests led to French intervention in Vietnam. In 1858 the French occupied Saigon, which they intended to use as a port to compete with the British ports of Hong Kong and Singapore. French territorial claims throughout mainland Southeast Asia continued into the late nineteenth century. Britain acquired control of Burma (1886) in connection with its colonial domination of India and Ceylon.

Thai Independence Only Thailand retained its independence, though at the cost of much territory. The British and Thai governments signed a commercial treaty in 1826, after which British influence increased. On his deathbed the Thai king Rama III warned his successor that "there will be no more wars with Vietnam and Burma. We will have them only with the West." According to Rama III, the British defeat of China in the Opium War signaled the end of an era and the beginning of a new international order.

Ruling as Rama IV, the former Buddhist monk King Mongkut (r. 1851–68) followed the advice of his predecessor and signed treaties with Britain and France. He also brought European advisers to his court to assist in carrying out legal, financial, and military reforms to modernize the country. The era of Mongkut's Western-style reforms was immortalized and romanticized in the musical *The King and I,* based on the account of an Englishwoman brought to tutor the king's children. Mongkut's son, Chulalongkorn (Rama V), continued the reforms of his father, especially encouraging Western education.

In 1893, though Thailand remained independent, the threat of European imperialism encouraged further political reforms. Disputes with France, whose colonial possessions bordered Thai territory, ended in the French takeover of Thai-controlled Cambodia and a portion of Laos. In 1904 and 1907 more Thai territory was ceded to the French, and in 1909 the British took over two Thai-controlled states on the Malay peninsula.

IMPERIALISM AND NATIONALISM IN EAST ASIA

European imperialism played a major role in the transformation of East Asia from the late nineteenth through the early twentieth century. European expansion into East Asia was fueled by economic and commercial growth that drew the attention of European merchants to the potential trading wealth of China and, to a much lesser extent, Japan. Japan alone retained both political and economic independence from Western powers, although the forces of Western imperialism precipitated change there as well. Unlike other parts of the world, however, neither China nor Japan were directly colonized by Western powers, although China was subject to substantial economic exploitation and political domination through the "spheres of influence," territories where individual European powers exercised commercial rights and political influence during the late nineteenth century.

CHINA AND THE WEST: THE OPIUM WARS AND THE TAIPING REBELLION

From the creation of the Canton system (1757), which restricted European traders to the port of Canton in order to limit and control their activities, until the 1830s, the balance of trade was in China's favor. British merchants plied their trade in tea, supplying the growing national market at home in Britain and paying for this and other goods, such as silks and spices, with silver. Silver was the basis of the Chinese monetary system and thus desirable as payment for Chinese goods. With the loss of access to sources of silver in the Americas, when the Atlantic seaboard colonies revolted against British rule in the late eighteenth century, British merchants had trouble paying in silver for the products they wanted. By the 1830s they turned to the illegal importation of opium produced in Bengal in British India to support their China trade.

The opium trade had a devastating impact on Chinese society and the Manchu Qing (1644–1911) government sought to control it. In 1838 the imperially appointed Commissioner Lin Zexu (1785–1850) was despatched to Canton to deal with the opium problem. The British refused to control the opium traffic, and in 1839 China and Britain engaged in armed conflict in the first Opium War (1839–1842). The humiliating defeat of China was documented in the Treaty of Nanjing (1842), which opened five treaty ports along the southeast coast, ceded the island of Hong Kong to the British, and established the concept of extraterritoriality, exempting foreign residents in the treaty ports from the rule of Chinese law. By the middle of the nineteenth century, missionaries, largely though not exclusively Protestant, had become active in the treaty-port cities; and with the conclusion of the second Opium War (1860), they began to establish missions in the Chinese hinterland as well as in coastal areas. Thus China was forcibly "opened" to Western trade and influence by the outcome of the Opium Wars.

The Taiping Rebellion The Qing government's problems were not only with foreigners. China's population exploded dramatically in the nineteenth century, nearly tripling from approximately 150 million in 1500 to 430 million in the mid-nineteenth century. Population pressures led to social and economic disruption and rebellions inspired by religious or ethnic disaffection coupled with socioeconomic crisis. The most significant of these was the Taiping Rebellion (1851–1864), which reflected not only the socioeconomic strains connected to the Opium Wars, but also the influence of Western ideas, particularly Christianity, resulting from missionary activity.

The Taiping leader Hong Xiuquan (1811–1864) was influenced by Old Testament ideas in a Christian missionary pamphlet given to him in Canton, where he had gone to take the civil service examination. After failing the examination for the third time, Hong had hallucinatory visions that he was the younger brother of Jesus Christ and was destined to lead the Chinese people back to the true God. Gaining support from other disaffected and alienated groups in Chinese society whose livelihoods had been disrupted by the Opium Wars, Hong led his rebel followers to capture the former imperial capital of Nanjing in 1853, where they attempted to establish the Heavenly Kingdom of Great Peace, a utopian social and political order that reflected their ideology of communalism and egalitarianism. Their radical vision of the ideal society presented such a profound challenge to the prevailing Confucian social order that the Chinese elite rose up in defense of the Manchu government. The Taipings were finally defeated by imperial troops in 1864, and little of their vision was ever accomplished.

Despite their eventual suppression, the impact of the Taiping and other mid-nineteenth century rebellions was enormous; historians estimate that 20 million people lost their lives in connection with the Taiping Rebellion alone. In other ways, too, mid-century rebellions brought about important changes with long-term impact. The most immediate of these changes was the militarization of local society, the result of people arming themselves and creating militias to protect their lives and property from the ravages of rebellion, and the rise of provincial armies with only tenuous loyalty to the Manchu court.

"SELF-STRENGTHENING" AND EUROPEAN IMPERIALISM IN CHINA

In the late nineteenth century, provincial leaders, with the implicit approval of the imperial government, adopted Western technology in an effort to strengthen China in the face of proven Western military and technological superiority. The "self-strengthening movement" resulted in such things as the establishment of schools that taught Western languages and learning, particularly mathematics and science, and the building of arsenals and shipyards.

Many self-strengtheners believed they could adopt Western technology for practical use (*yong*) and retain Chinese values as the basis of their culture (*ti*). So Western learning was initially confined to mathematics and science because they were of immediate practical use, and Western languages were studied only to enable Chinese to learn science and mathematics. But as the people learned Western languages, they also began to translate Western literary, political, and social writings. Yan Fu (1853–1921) translated the works of such major European thinkers as John Stuart Mill, Adam Smith, and Charles Darwin, and Chinese translations of Shakespeare and Charles Dickens were available by the turn of the century.

European Spheres of Influence By the 1880s Western imperialism was making further inroads on Chinese territory, and by the end of the century most of China was a foreign "sphere of influence," a territory where foreign powers had special economic or political privileges. The Sino-French War in 1884–1885 was fought over competing territorial claims in China's southwestern border regions. The victorious French extended their influence across the southern borders of China from their colony of Annam (Vietnam), creating a French sphere of influence in China's southwestern province of Yunnan. In 1897, using the excuse of the murder of two missionaries, the Germans sent troops to China and acquired the port of Tianjing on the Shandong peninsula as the base for a German sphere of influence in north China. The Russians penetrated into Mongolia and Manchuria, where they built and controlled the rights to the Trans-Siberian railway, and secured Port Arthur on the Liaodong peninsula (1898).

KOREA AND THE SINO-JAPANESE WAR

Korea had been heavily influenced early in its history by Chinese civilization and continued to exhibit many aspects of Chinese influence. China viewed Korea as one of its tributary states and part of a buffer zone of cultural influence and strategic interest. Even by the late nineteenth century, no European power saw Korea as sufficiently important to challenge China's influence there. However, as Japan became a formidable military and economic power in the region, the Japanese threatened China's historic domination of Korea, beginning in the 1870s with the Treaty of Kanghwa (1876), which on the surface guaranteed Korea's independent status but actually prevented Chinese interference with Japanese interests in Korea.

The Tonghak Rebellion The Tonghak (Eastern Learning) Rebellion (1893–1894) provided a pretext for Japanese intervention in Korea. Like the leader of the Taiping Rebellion in China, Ch'oe Che'u (1824–1864), the Tonghak leader, was a disaffected scholar. Unlike the Taiping leader Hong Xiuquan, Ch'oe did not lead an armed rebellion, but

FIGURE 17.7 Western Businessmen in China at a Rattan Factory, ca. 1875

Foreign commercial interests took advantage of cheap Chinese labor to produce goods for the markets in China and abroad. The word *rattan* is an English adaptation from the Malay *rotan*.

SOURCE: Daniel Wolf Collection.

he was still executed by the government. His successor roused Tonghak followers to open rebellion based on demands for political, social, and economic reform, including punishment of corrupt officials and nobles, reforms in the examination system, and the right of young widows to remarry.

Japanese troops were sent to aid the Korean government in suppressing this rebellion, and China sent its own troops to balance those of Japan. The Sino-Japanese War of 1894–1895, resulting from conflicts over domination of political events on the Korean peninsula, ended in the crushing defeat of China by its cultural disciple and former tributary state, Japan. The Treaty of Shimonoseki (1895) ceded to Japan the island of Taiwan and recognized Japan's paramount interest in Korea.

REFORM AND REBELLION IN CHINA

The loss of the war sent a profound shock wave through the educated elite in China, particularly Chinese scholar-officials who recognized the failure of the piecemeal approach of self-strengthening and saw the need for more fundamental reform of the political and social order.

Kang Youwei (1858–1927), an examination candidate at the capital in 1895, circulated a petition asking for the Manchu government to undertake reforms to respond to the crisis of the state symbolized in the defeat by Japan but dating from the beginnings of Western imperialism at the time of the first Opium War.

No lasting program of reform resulted from this request, but for a brief time during the summer of 1898, Kang led the 100 Days of Reform, during which the young Emperor Guangxu (r. 1875–1908) issued edicts calling for fundamental reforms in state, society, and the economy. The conservative empress dowager Cixi (1835–1908), Guangxu's aunt and the power behind the throne, canceled the reforms, placed the emperor under house arrest, and arrested the reformers, several of whom were summarily executed. Kang and others fled to Japan, ironically a haven for Chinese reformers and revolutionaries.

The Boxer Rebellion The popular counterpart to the reform movement of 1898 was the Boxer Rebellion (1898–1900). Even though the immediate inspiration for the 1898 reform movement was the defeat of China by Japan, the larger implications of this defeat were related to China's failed efforts to respond to the threats and realities of Western imperialism. The Boxers reacted to the tangible presence of Western imperialism in the form of missionaries, traders, and diplomats by attacking missions, residences, and foreigners.

The Boxer movement was an outgrowth of secret society organization, a brotherhood based on popular religious beliefs and martial arts traditions known as the "Boxers United in Righteousness." They believed they could make themselves impervious to Western bullets by magic rituals and incantations. Inspired by antiforeign and anti-Christian sentiments, the Boxers were active in the northeast, in the vicinity of the capital. Seeing the Boxers as a possible help in ridding China of foreign influence, the empress dowager aided them with imperial troops, which led to the Boxer siege of the Foreign Legation quarters in Beijing during the summer of 1900.

When an allied force of European, American, and Japanese troops finally reached Beijing, freed the hostages held in the Foreign Legation quarters, and thereby brought the Boxer Rebellion to an end, the Manchu government suffered yet another devastating blow to its authority. The Boxer Protocol, signed in 1901, called for China to pay compensation to the Western powers; but, in fact, many of these funds were used to pay for Chinese students sent to study abroad. Representatives of Western governments believed that Western education would help China to become a modern nation and reduce the likelihood of future conflicts with the West. In addition, the collapse of the Manchu government was not in the interests of Western nations, who restrained their demands in order to avoid the complete loss of power by the dynasty.

REFORM AND REVOLUTION IN CHINA

During the first decade of the twentieth century, in the wake of the elite-led reform movement and the populist Boxer Rebellion, the Manchu government undertook substantial reforms, many of which ironically recalled the reform movement of 1898. The most important of these reforms was the abolition of the civil service examination system in 1905, which severed the bond between the scholar-official elite and the imperial government. Elite status was traditionally tied to passing the government-administered examinations, which determined eligibility for holding government office. When the examination system was abolished, the government's role in confirming elite status was undermined and people turned to other oc-

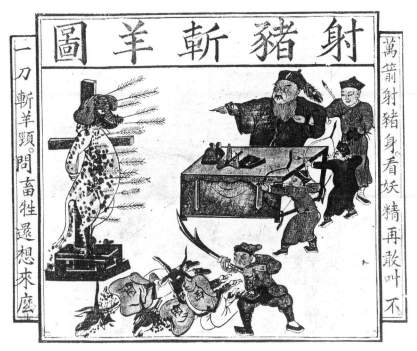

FIGURE 17.8 *Shooting the Pig* [Jesus] *and Decapitating the Sheep* [Disciples], Chinese Anti-Christian Woodcut, early 1890s

SOURCE: Church Missionary, Society Photo by Zoltan Wegner. Images such as these reflect the anti-Christian background of the Boxer Uprising.

cupations besides government service—such as the military or commerce—as ways to achieve power, status, and wealth.

Other reforms were carried out in the economic and political arenas. A bureau of commerce was created to encourage and manage the commercial sector of the economy. But when steps were taken to establish a constitutional monarchy, including the election of provincial assemblies in 1908 (with an electorate limited by property ownership and education) and the convening of a national assembly in 1909, it was already too late for reform. The speed of historical events had overtaken the ability of the Manchu government to effect change and maintain control.

Resistance to the Manchus In 1895 Sun Yat-sen (1866–1925), a Cantonese who studied in a missionary school in Hong Kong and was trained in medicine in Hawaii, organized the Revive China Society to overthrow the Manchu monarchy and restore China to Chinese rule in a republican form of government. By 1905 Sun had formed a new organization, the Revolutionary Alliance, bringing disparate elements together into one group by emphasizing anti-Manchuism as the basis for common interests and action. This organization led an abortive uprising against the Manchus in Canton in the same year, and Sun barely escaped with his life.

Despite the efforts of the Manchu government to implement reforms, there was a steady weakening of its authority and a flow of power into the hands of the provincial elite, people who formed the electorate and the candidates for provincial assemblies and who before the abolition of the examination system would have been examination degree holders seeking office in the imperial government. By the first decade of the twentieth century, provincial elites had begun to see their interests as separable from those of the central government and to distinguish their provincial loyalties from service to the imperial government, which had been humiliated and weakened by Western powers beginning with the Opium Wars and reflected most vividly in the spheres of influence.

In 1910 members of the provincial elite in Sichuan organized a Railway Protection League in opposition to the Manchu government's proposed plan to accept foreign loans for the construction of a railway in Sichuan. Provincial leaders were opposed to this plan because the use of foreign loans was seen as yet another manifestation of foreign imperialism. This movement symbolized the new sense of independence and autonomy that had spread throughout the provinces. On October 10, 1911, a unit of the new army mutinied in the central Yangzi Valley city of Wuchang, and by December of that year sixteen of the eighteen provinces of China had declared their independence from the Manchu government. The Revolution of 1911 led to the founding of the Republic of China on January 1, 1912.

Sun Yat-sen and the Republic of China Sun Yat-sen was declared the president of the republic, and he has often been credited for leading the Revolution of 1911. In fact, he was in Denver, Colorado, at the time of the Wuchang uprising, soliciting financial support from the area's Chinese residents, and returned to find that his dream had apparently been accomplished. However, the real forces that brought about the overthrow of the Manchu dynasty—regional militarization dating from the mid-nineteenth century and sociopolitical disintegration—had little to do with the revolutionary ideals espoused by Sun and his supporters.

Sun's political ideology, known as the "three principles of the people"—ethnic identity or nationalism, people's welfare or socialism, and people's rights or democracy—were adaptations of Western political concepts and had no grounding in traditional thought. Sun himself was a product of Western influences in the treaty-port society of Canton, the British colony of Hong Kong, and Hawaii, where he was educated in Western medicine. Sun's fragile republicanism could not survive the brutal political, economic, and social conditions of early-twentieth-century China.

Only one month after taking office, Sun turned over the presidency to Yuan Shikai (1859–1916), the head of the elite Beiyang army, whose support had been crucial in forcing the abdication of the Manchus and in consolidating support behind the new government. Following Yuan's death, the tenuous unity of the republic collapsed and regional warlords controlled the country behind the facade of a central government in Beijing. The social and political dismemberment of China was complete, and further cultural disintegration would take place before the reconsolidation of China as a modern nation.

JAPAN AND THE WEST: THE MEIJI RESTORATION

Although Russian encroachments on Japan began as early as the seventeenth century and British ships entered Japanese waters in the early nineteenth century, it fell to Americans to "open" Japan. In 1853 Commodore Matthew C. Perry, bearing a letter containing a request to the ruler of Japan from the U.S. president for the opening of diplomatic and commercial relations, steamed into Uraga Bay near Edo, the capital of the Tokugawa shogunate. Perry left without a reply, promising to return the following year. The shogun, who was responsible for both national defense and foreign policy, consulted with the territorial rulers (*daimyo*) about how to respond to the American "request," which was backed up by the armed ships that brought it. The act of consulting with the *daimyo* irrevocably undermined the authority of the shogun to decide foreign policy and led to the unraveling of the threads that bound the *daimyo* to the shogunate.

When Perry returned in 1854, representatives of the shogun believed their only alternative was to sign the Treaty of Kanagawa, which provided for the opening of treaty ports and establishing diplomatic ties with the United States. A further treaty in 1858 set up the framework for commercial relations. In the early 1860s the presence of foreign residents in Japanese cities and foreign ships in Japanese harbors incited extremist attacks by young samurai who identified this presence with the weakness of the shogunate as well as with the aggressive intrusions of outsiders.

Among the various responses to the perceived foreign crisis that reverberated throughout the country were calls to "revere the emperor" and others to open the country to foreign influence. By 1866 two of the most powerful *daimyo* domains formed an alliance against the shogunate, and in 1868 with the coming of a new emperor to the throne, a coup led by these and two other domains overthrew the shogunate. The coup leaders declared the "Meiji Restoration," the restoration of authority to the imperial line in the person of Emperor Meiji after more than 600 years of shogunal rule.

The cry of the Meiji Restoration was "enrich the nation, strengthen the army," and by 1873 a series of steps had been taken that fundamentally altered the social, political, and economic landscape of Japan. A new capital was declared at Edo, now known as Tokyo, and governors appointed by the Meiji leaders, who claimed to speak for the emperor, administered newly created prefectures (administrative districts) carved from former *daimyo* domains. The Meiji leaders adopted a national land tax base and organized a modern army. Westernization, guided by the Restoration leaders, in political and social institutions as well as in intellectual life became the hallmark of the Meiji era.

Less than a generation later, in 1894–1895 Japan proved the success of its endeavors by defeating China in war over domination of the Korean peninsula, and a bare decade later Japan defeated Russia in the Russo-Japanese War (1904–1905), a war generated by competing interests in Manchuria in northeastern China. In less than a half century, Japan had met the threat of Western imperialism with a revolutionary transformation into a modern nation state. Selective adoption of Western ideas, technology, and institutions, coupled with a strong national identity symbolized in the emperor, enabled Japan to weather the storms of Western imperialism and emerge unscathed.

■

IMPERIALISM, COLONIALISM, AND NATIONALISM IN SOUTH ASIA

Like other parts of the globe, India became a pawn of European politics and ultimately of the conflicting designs of imperialists. By the seventeenth century, the Mughal Empire, which once controlled large parts of India, had weakened so that it became easier for Europeans to make their presence felt. By this time the major European powers in India were France and

Britain, and the French lost their position (excepting a few coastal trading stations) and influence to the British following defeat in the Seven Years' War at the Peace of Paris in 1763.

BRITISH IMPERIALISM IN INDIA

From the outset the British did not govern India as conquered territory to be assimilated into their empire. An organization of traders, the British East India Company, chartered by Queen Elizabeth I in 1603, was responsible for British interests in India. That essentially private agency confirmed and expanded British control and exploitation of the subcontinent. The few settlers were mostly commercial and military agents. The European minority dominated the local population either directly, relying on their military and technological advantages after the decline of the Mughal empire, or indirectly through arrangements with Indian rulers.

After its victory over the French, the British government began to take steps to bring the activities of the East India Company more closely under its supervision, questioning the propriety of a commercial concern interfering in the affairs of a foreign land without supervision. Increasing government involvement formalized the process of creating a colony for the purpose of securing the state's commercial and strategic interests overseas. The India Act of 1784 set the standard for company rule up until 1858. It provided for a board of control that exercised considerable supervision over the company by sending directives straight to India and reviewing all the company's correspondence. The board appointed the governor general of the colony, though the company retained the right of nomination. This act considerably strengthened the British government's role in India and remained the operative mode of governing the colony until the mid-nineteenth century.

The Sepoy Mutiny In 1857 the native troops of India (called *sepoy*) were ordered to bite off the tips of greased cartridges of their new Enfield rifles. Indian Hindu and Muslim soldiers, believing that the grease was made of forbidden animal fat, refused to obey the orders because it was sacrilegious to have contact with cows (in the case of the Hindus) or pigs (in the case of the Muslims). Those soldiers who disobeyed were stripped of their insignia and sent home by the British. Violence eventually erupted and was quickly extinguished by the British government. Historians have debated the events of the Sepoy Mutiny (or "Indian War") of 1857. Some have represented the rebellious refusal of native soldiers to obey orders as simply an army affair; others have characterized the incident as a full-scale revolt against British rule, a demand for political freedom; and still others have seen the event as an expression of religious grievance.

However interpreted, the events showed officials in India and in London that a change in the informal manner of governance was needed. The 1858 Government of India Act and subsequent laws made India, part of the British Empire. The East India Company disappeared from the scene, and the governor-general became a viceroy representing Queen Victoria, who was proclaimed empress of India in 1876 and to whose imperial crown was thus added the "jewel" of India. The viceroy governed India with an executive council; laws were made by a legislative council, consisting of the executive council and other appointed members. Though some of the larger Indian states had their own councils, ultimate authority rested with the viceroy who represented the British government. In London, a secretary of state for India, with a full ministerial department, replaced the board of control.

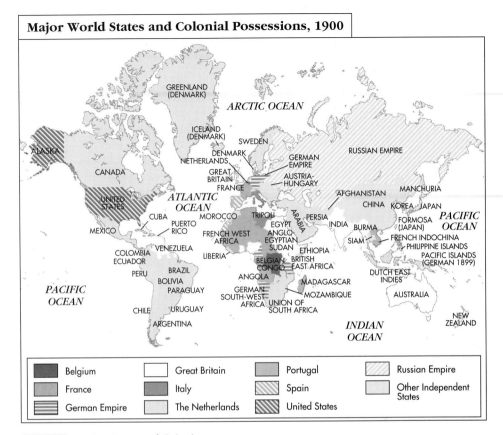

Major World States and Colonial Possessions, 1900

GREENLAND (DENMARK)

ARCTIC OCEAN

ICELAND (DENMARK)

SWEDEN

ALASKA

CANADA

DENMARK
NETHERLANDS
GREAT BRITAIN
FRANCE

GERMAN EMPIRE
AUSTRIA-HUNGARY

RUSSIAN EMPIRE

AFGHANISTAN

MANCHURIA

UNITED STATES

ATLANTIC OCEAN

CHINA

KOREA

JAPAN

CUBA
PUERTO RICO

MOROCCO

TRIPOLI

PERSIA

INDIA

BURMA

FORMOSA (JAPAN)

PACIFIC OCEAN

MEXICO

FRENCH WEST AFRICA

EGYPT
ANGLO-EGYPTIAN SUDAN

ARABIA

SIAM

FRENCH INDOCHINA
PHILIPPINE ISLANDS

COLOMBIA
ECUADOR

VENEZUELA

LIBERIA

ETHIOPIA

PACIFIC ISLANDS (GERMAN 1899)

PERU

BRAZIL

BELGIAN CONGO

BRITISH EAST AFRICA

DUTCH EAST INDIES

BOLIVIA

ANGOLA

MADAGASCAR

PACIFIC OCEAN

PARAGUAY

GERMAN SOUTH-WEST AFRICA

MOZAMBIQUE

AUSTRALIA

CHILE

URUGUAY

UNION OF SOUTH AFRICA

NEW ZEALAND

ARGENTINA

INDIAN OCEAN

Belgium	Great Britain
France	Italy
German Empire	The Netherlands
Portugal	Russian Empire
Spain	Other Independent States
United States	

MAP 17.6   Nation States and Colonies

THE EARLY STAGES OF INDIAN NATIONALISM

The agency of Indian nationalism was an organization called the Indian National Congress, which was formed in 1885. At first its demands were moderate, reformist rather than revolutionary, aiming to give Indians a voice in running their own country. Congress's practical suggestion for achieving this goal included reorganizing the Indian Civil Service to give Indians more opportunity to participate in the British-controlled government known as the "Raj."

The progress of the Indian nationalist movement was slow and fraught with regional and religious differences, of which the divisions between Hindu and Muslim were the most difficult. The leaders of the Indian National Congress also disagreed on how to bring an end to British rule. Congress became divided between extremists, the leader of whom was B. G. Tilak, and moderates, led by G. K. Gokhale. In 1905 Hindu-Muslim differences resulted in a separate Muslim League; in 1906, when Congress split between Tilak and Gokhale, the unity of the nationalist movement seemed ruined. Even so, antagonism toward the British was commonly shared, increased, and in time produced results.

Though the British were willing to take advantage of the division among nationalists in order to continue their rule, they also undertook several reforms, partly in the hope of defusing Indian nationalism. The India Councils Act of 1892 enlarged both the size and scope of the viceregal and provincial councils and allowed increased but nonofficial Indian membership. The new British order brought about by this act provided for an elected bicameral all-Indian parliament and for provincial legislative councils. Matters of local and lesser importance were entrusted to these bodies, but major decisions were still reserved for the British. The more radical Indian nationalists were already demanding independence, a demand that continued and was not appeased by further reform such as the Government of India Act of 1909. This act introduced indirect election and gave yet more Indian representation on councils, but it was still a far cry from even self-government, much less independence.

■

THE BRITISH EMPIRE: CANADA, AUSTRALIA, AND NEW ZEALAND

Responses to imperialism elsewhere produced nationalist movements like the Indian National Congress. Indigenous peoples, as well as immigrant communities of Europeans overseas responded to imperialism. Such communities not only extended European hegemony through conquest and colonization but also provided examples of the rise of new nationalist identities in conflict and competition with the old.

Settler colonies had come into existence during the early maritime expansion of Britain and other European nations, and immigrant ambitions had particularly significant consequences on vast land masses in the Americas and the Pacific. In North America, Australia, and New Zealand expansion came at the expense of the subjugation of indigenous peoples. Immigrant communities also struggled with conflicts between their new colonial identities and ties to their homelands. Both the resistance of immigrant communities to control by their home governments and the resistance of indigenous peoples to incorporation into the new colonial world were threads woven into the fabric of the new imperialism.

CANADA

Canada, like so much of the globe, became an arena for competing European imperial ambitions following the sixteenth- and seventeenth-century voyages of exploration and subsequent colonization. Because parts of this vast northern half of the North American continent were claimed, explored, and settled by both France and Great Britain, it became an extension of their competition for dominance in Europe. In 1763, at the Peace of Paris, the issue was resolved: Canada, including those parts claimed and settled by the French for 200 years, became wholly a part of the British Empire.

British North America, as Canada was officially known, provided legal and religious arrangements for the French settlers, who were concentrated in Quebec, that differed slightly from those for the widely scattered Anglo-Saxons. Even so, both French and British Canadians were integral parts of an empire controlled and governed from London. The often-strained relationship between French and Anglo-Saxon Canadians made the British Colonial Office a useful arbitrator-mediator. Canadians also looked to the imperial government for protection against the ambitions and power of the burgeoning and threatening American republic to their south.

Colonial Rule and Canadian Canadians eventually became restive with their status as colo-
Nationalism nial subjects. The desire to control their own destinies indepen-
dent of London became a motivating force in their politics and led to independence in the twentieth century. The Canadian insurrection of 1837, when large numbers of immigrants from the British Isles reinforced growing discontent with closed, oligarchical governments in both Lower (French) and Upper (Anglo-Saxon) Canada, occurred after a quarter century of expansion.

In 1838 Great Britain sent Lord Durham out to Canada to investigate the situation in the wake of insurrection. The result was a "Report on the Affairs of British North America" in which Durham argued that representative government was needed to restore and maintain harmony. Following the report an Act of Union (1840) united Lower and Upper, French and English, Canada, though Durham's recommendation for representative, majority government for the united Canada was evaded. Final responsibility for their own domestic issues was given to Canadians by Lord Elgin, who became governor general of the united Canada in 1849 when for the first time Canadian assemblies controlled local Canadian affairs.

The Impact of American The American Civil War was crucial to the Canadian nationalist
Imperialism desire for confederation. It once again aroused Canadian concern
with the threat from the south, and it reaffirmed the Canadian sense of dependence on England. Although the threat of American invasion subsided when the war was over, the danger of American competition and ambition continued. Three and a half million Canadians could hardly ignore 35 million Americans whose national energies and ambitions, finally freed from their internal conflict, turned toward western expansion. Canadian nationalism grew, too, as Canadians recognized that British government interest in and commitment to North America was waning. As a result, negotiations between Canadians and the British Colonial Office led to the creation of the Canadian confederation through the British North America Act of 1867, which officially declared the Dominion of Canada.

By promising to build a transcontinental, interprovincial railroad, the dominion gained the support of the maritime provinces and later the adherence of British Columbia. With British Columbia joining the confederation, Canadian claims to the northern Great Plains were confirmed and subsequently solidified with cross ties and rails. The railroad proved to be a material and psychological stimulant to the dominion; it provided an opportunity for profitable investment, which kept the English involved, and made settlement and exploitation of the interior infinitely easier.

Canadian Nationalism and The development of Canadian nationalism also took place against
Indigenous Peoples the background of expansionist claims against indigenous peo-
ples, those known in modern Canada as the "First Nations." As early as 1836 the Ojibwa and Ottawa people signed treaties with Upper Canada by which they surrendered some of their land to Europeans. The lieutenant governor of Upper Canada explained that the treaty was necessary due to "an unavoidable increase of white population as

well as the progress of cultivation" and that its purpose was "protecting you [the Ojibwas and Ottawa] from the encroachments of whites." The problem, explained the official, was that "in all parts of the world farmers seek for uncultivated land. If you would cultivate your land it would then be considered your own property . . . but uncultivated land is like wild animals, and your Great Father [the British monarch] . . . has now great difficulty in securing it for you from whites who are hunting to cultivate."

Despite opposition from religious organizations in both Britain and Canada, by the mid-nineteenth century, the Colonial Office and various Canadian provinces carried out policies designed to remove First Nation peoples to reserves (lands reserved for them) and to persuade them to become freehold farmers. By mid-century, treaties were negotiated with the native peoples of northern Ontario to extinguish their claims over vast territories, in advance of European settlement and in return for substantial reserves. Following the British North America Act of 1867, the dominion announced that its policy toward First Nation peoples was to "lead the Indian peoples by degrees to mingle with the white race in the ordinary vocations of life."

As the Canadian government took over the vast territories of the Hudson Bay Company and as European immigration to Canada increased, the government set up a massive round of new treaty negotiations with western indigenous peoples. Though the government boasted that Canadian treaty arrangements guaranteed that no difficulties with native peoples, such as those current in the United States, existed in Canada, some native peoples resisted agreeing to

FIGURE 17.9 Big Bear Trading at Fort Pitt, Hudson's Bay Company Outpost in 1884

Native American resistance in Canada led to attacks on Hudson Bay Posts by Cree followers of Big Bear.

SOURCE: National Archives of Canada.

Canadian terms and at least one important Plains chief, Big Bear (ca. 1825–1888), joined Métis (mixed) discontents in a rebellion (1885) against the encroachment of government policy and immigrants into the western Great Plains. The Big Bear-Métis rebellion was suppressed, and Indian policy remained directed by the interests of settlers. After 1885 First Nations were pushed out of sight of settlement, "pacified" on reserves from the Atlantic to the Pacific.

AUSTRALIA

Australia's history bore some similarities to that of Canada but also differed in ways that shaped its own distinctive experience of British imperialism and the growth of nationalism. The first British settlements in Australia during the late eighteenth and early nineteenth century were penal colonies for felons transported from Britain. The spread of European settlers into the interior of the continent destroyed the fragile ecology of the Australian aborigines, the indigenous people who were forced into the deep interior and whose way of life was virtually destroyed by the incursions of European settlement.

The growth of a world market in wool and technological advances in shipping and refrigeration contributed to a developing commercial economy. The largely British and European population remained predominantly in the major cities, especially Melbourne and Sydney, despite important mineral discoveries that led to gold rushes in the 1850s and again in the 1890s. The individual colonies of Tasmania, Western Australia, South Australia, Victoria, and Queensland were united into a federation as the Commonwealth of Australia in 1901, part of the British Empire.

NEW ZEALAND

Like Australia, the settlement of New Zealand dates from the late eighteenth century in the wake of the voyages of Captain Cook; and, like both Australia and Canada, New Zealand became a self-governing dominion within the British Empire in the early twentieth century (1907). As with other dominions in the British Empire, the settlement of New Zealand by Europeans came at the expense of native peoples. Britain claimed sovereignty over New Zealand and its native inhabitants, the Maori people, in the 1840 Treaty of Waitangi, though the terms of this treaty as understood by Maoris and British differed.

Granted a constitution in 1852, New Zealand was governed according to a British provincial system. In the 1850s an influx of European settlers into the colony led to disputes over land between the "Pakehas," as the Europeans were known, and the Maoris. In response to European demand for land, Maoris formed a pan-tribal antiland sales league known as the "Maori King movement." Land wars beginning in 1860 led finally to the confiscation of much Maori land, and in 1864 the Maoris were confined to reservations.

The Natives Land Act in 1865 and the Native Schools Act and the Native Representation Act in 1867 promoted the assimilation of the Maoris by education, some representation, and a Native Land Court. The individualization of land tenure was the outcome of the Natives Land Act, and the Native Land Court proved a difficult place for Maoris to confirm their claims to land through legal means. Many Maoris actually were forced to sell their lands to pay legal fees necessary to prove their claims to the land. By the 1890s the bulk of New Zealand had been shifted to Pakeha ownership, and many Maoris were left in poverty.

■

IMPERIALISM, COLONIALISM, AND CULTURAL IDENTITY IN THE PACIFIC

European territorial claims extended even to the scattered islands of the Pacific. Though Europeans first made contact with peoples of the Pacific islands in the sixteenth century, only in the late eighteenth century did European settlement take place, along with the growth of commerce and Christian missions. With the exception of Hawai'i, the numbers of European settlers were relatively small, which meant that European domination of smaller Polynesian tribal societies was less effective and complete than elsewhere.

HAWAI'I

Mission work began in Hawai'i in 1820 with the arrival of American missionaries. Up to 1820 Hawai'i and Tahiti were the principal sites of foreign contact in Polynesia, and substantial culture change occurred there before the rest of Polynesia felt foreign influence. Before the coming of missionaries, most of Hawai'i was under the control of Chief Kamehameha I. He saw benefits to be gained from foreign contact, including not only goods such as firearms that would support his military ambitions but also skills such as blacksmithing that the Hawaiians could learn.

After the death of Kamehameha in 1819, the increasing demand for Hawaiian sandalwood and Hawai'i's growing importance as a supply port for American whalers in the Pacific brought about economic, social, and even political changes in Hawaiian society. In the 1820s and 1830s, a steep decline in population caused by disease and male emigration threatened traditional communal patterns of economic organization and precipitated a crisis in Hawaiian society. Hawaiian rulers resolved the crisis by carrying out land reforms that enabled Hawaiians to retain their political identity by holding on to territory, but these reforms also severely undermined traditional social and economic organization by reassigning land to individual ownership rather than the traditional looser communal "ownership."

Although contact with Europeans may have initiated changes in Hawaiian society, the long-term impact of these changes was the product of the Hawaiian rulers' policies designed to preserve Hawaiian identity. Rulers such as Kamehameha and his successors sought to preserve their power as monarchs, and their policies sometimes undermined the common cultural traditions that held Hawaiian society together, particularly when these policies created economic dependence.

The role of missionaries in these changes was complex. As much as missionaries sought to reconstruct Hawaiian identity in the image of Christianity, in the 1820s and 1830s, missionaries and churches actually provided a focal point for traditional community life that was elsewhere disintegrating under the impact of land reform and other changes. Christian belief became incorporated into nineteenth-century Hawaiian identity, but the damage to Hawaiian political, economic, and cultural interests after 1860 with the imposition of the plantation economy was the factor that ensured Hawaiian subordination to American interests by the end of the nineteenth century.

POLYNESIA

In Tahiti European missionaries experienced earlier and more immediate success than elsewhere in Polynesia. In 1815 the principal Tahitian chief won a victory over his enemies and pledged his victory to the Christian God, thus effectively crushing local gods and winning new converts to Christianity. The French protectorate, established in 1841, actually maintained the Tahitian monarchy under French authority. Even after annexation by France in 1880, there were two sectors of Tahitian society: one that mixed with the foreign commercial community and one that remained traditional, isolated, and independent.

The people of Tonga in Polynesia resisted Christianity when it was first introduced in the 1820s, but by the 1830s there were mass conversions. Some senior chiefs were converted, and they led a movement for political reform that was couched in terms of a new moral order drawn from Christianity. Unlike Hawai'i, Tonga had discouraged foreign settlement, and through a series of reforms carried out by their own leaders, Tongans adopted a written constitution in 1875 and retained their independence.

Fiji became a British crown colony in 1874, when it was already home to about 2,000 European settlers. However, rather than strengthening and securing the position of resident

FIGURE 17.10 *No Te Aha Oe Riri; Why are you Angry?* **by the French Painter Paul Gaugin (1896) Oil on Canvas (95.3 cm x 130.5 cm).**

Gauguin lived much of his life in Polynesia. The painting captures specific Tahitian attitudes and gestures in his portrayal of the three central women.

SOURCE: Art Institute of Chicago, Mr and Mrs Martin A. Ryerson Collection, 1933.1119. Photo © 1996, The Art Institute of Chicago. All Rights Reserved.

foreigners, the imposition of colonial rule actually protected the political and economic traditions of Fijians, supporting a gradual development led by Fijians themselves. Western influence in Polynesia was intrusive and opportunistic and precipitated irrevocable changes in Polynesian societies. However, indigenous Hawaiian, Tahitian, Tongan, and Fijian leaders overwhelmingly determined the direction of those changes.

The highly competitive system of warfare in Samoan society meant that contact with foreigners was welcomed because it brought firearms that could be an advantage in war. The Samoans had extensive commercial contacts with foreigners, and by the time Samoans encountered Christian missionaries in the 1830s, they were reasonably receptive. But Christianity never penetrated below the surface of Samoan society, and traditional competitive practices continued, complicated by foreign intervention. Between 1868 and 1889 numerous attempts to establish a formal modern state to deal effectively with the problems of foreign penetration and chronic warfare failed. Britain, Germany, and the United States appointed a government that functioned for a decade; however, in 1900 chronic disturbances led to the partition of Samoa between Germany and the United States. By 1900 every Pacific island belonged to either Britain, France, Germany, or the United States.

LATIN AMERICA: NATIONALISM AND TRANSFORMATION

While European powers were scrambling to extend their empires through colonization at the end of the nineteenth century, Latin Americans rid themselves of colonial controls, though they were increasingly under the influence of the external forces of capital industrialism and the politics associated with it. Independence to Latin Americans meant the replacement of Spanish and Portuguese viceroyalties with a diverse collection of republics. The revolutions that ended imperial control produced a number of heroic leaders—San Martin, O'Higgins, and especially Bolivar, all of whom were gone by 1830—and politically independent nations that struggled to remain viable. The newly built nation states of Latin America found themselves above all else engaged in a struggle to redefine themselves in the age of the new imperialism.

CAUDILLO RULE

Some of these new nation states came under the control of a continuous series of leaders known as *caudillos,* independent politicians who relied on both personal charisma and military force, defying democratic politics and constitutional government. In this manner independence for the peoples of Latin America became a process of substituting one master, imperial Spain, for another, the *caudillos.* As they assumed control of Latin American republics, *caudillos* sometimes exercised power very much as imperial officials had, and the development of Latin American nationalism was shaped by the military forces that controlled politics under the leadership of the *caudillos.*

A classic example of the *caudillo* was Porfirio Diaz (1830–1915), a military leader and president of Mexico from 1884 to 1911. Diaz was a nationalist who stabilized the finances of the country, but who supported economic development with the aid of foreign capital. He ruled through a brutal tyranny and allowed foreign enterprises to exploit Mexico's natural resources. Lands of the Native Americans were increasingly concentrated in the hands of a few large landholders, whereas poverty and illiteracy were widespread. In Guatemala by contrast, the conservative caudillo Rafael Carrera (r. 1839–1865) ruled on behalf of the interests of the Indian majority population.

RACE, CLASS, AND GENDER

Continuities in social structure and economic dependence on foreign capital compromised prospects for the economic development of newly independent republics in nineteenth-century Latin America. Colonial divisions between privileged minorities and masses of peasants and workers continued, and in some cases grew sharper. The new power base was the hacienda, the landed estate, which although not economically productive was retained essentially as a social institution bound to the availability of cheap labor.

Though slavery was abolished in all Spanish-speaking republics in the 1850s, Portuguese Brazil was an exception: Brazil did not abolish slavery until 1888, and the African-Brazilian, like the majority of those of mixed ancestry there, remained at the foot of the economic ladder. Such groups often became tenant farmers on haciendas. Social and racial discrimination was theoretically prohibited by law after independence (1822), but this policy did not mean economic and social equality for many Latin Americans. Attempts to integrate Native Americans into national economies by dividing their communal lands among individual owners resulted in their being overpowered by their white neighbors.

Social structures remained virtually unaffected by independence. Kinship ties continued to be a means of consolidating the landholding interests of wealthy families. Women remained largely dependent on their fathers and husbands; marriage was early, and by the age of 15 most girls were also mothers, effectively ending any possibility for schooling. In urban areas, however, public education was increasingly extended to girls as well as boys. The education of Latin American women produced activists in the struggle for women's political rights by the end of the nineteenth century. Even without political or social equality, women played important economic roles in households, factories, and markets.

PROBLEMS OF ECONOMIC DEVELOPMENT

Following political independence, Latin American states under the leadership of elite *caudillos* embarked on the path of economic development. The common belief was that economic development would produce material goods, which would trickle down for the benefit of all. But progress resulting from development was accompanied by new tensions. The patterns of development often continued the preindependence process of exploitation, and some foreigners gained commercial benefits beyond the wildest expectations of the colonial era.

Economic expansion after independence was dictated by the growth of agricultural or mineral exports: bananas and coffee from Central America; tobacco and sugar from Cuba; copper and silver from Mexico; silver from Peru and Bolivia; and wool, wheat, and beef from Argentina. Not only did Iberians reap huge profits from investment in Latin American enterprises, but British, French, German, and North American investments wielded increasing influence in the decisions of Latin American nation states.

Railroads Nineteenth-century European and American exploitation in Latin America went ▬▬▬▬ far beyond trade goods. Railroads are a classic case in point. Financed by foreign, largely British, investment, they tended to serve principally industries in areas that provided the materials that the world market desired. Thus the modernization of Latin American transportation, like the technological changes of the African continent, primarily benefited capitalist and foreign investors even while they unified the region. The British financed the building of railroads in many parts of Latin America (as well as in Canada and the United States), especially in Brazil and Argentina, both for the profits to be made from investment in transportation systems and because it gave the investors some voice in locating the railroad systems. Accordingly, railroads were designed primarily to serve extractive industries for the benefit of external and domestic capitalists—and all too often at the expense of the environment and without regard to the needs of the local population.

EMERGENCE OF THE NEOCOLONIAL ORDER

The new flow of foreign investment between 1850 and 1880 created situations that, despite political independence, greatly resembled the dependency of colonial times. Foreign capital dominated both eras. Latin American had become the producer of raw materials for European markets, while Europe traded manufactured goods to Latin American cities. The landholdings in the countryside were increasingly consolidated in the interest of economic profitability, leaving rural people to struggle as displaced workers. In Chile some small farmers gained autonomy by paying rent to large landowners for the use of a plot of land that they could then cultivate. In Brazil, Argentina, and Uruguay, large-scale immigration provided labor, much as it did in North America. Chinese laborers were brought to Cuba and Panama to replace freed slaves, and their conditions were not a vast improvement over slavery.

A classic example of external economic imperialism occurred in Peru. In 1890, faced with imminent financial collapse, the Peruvian government sought to borrow money from a consortium of British bankers and the Grace Steamship Company. For the next seventy years, because of the debt owed them by the Peruvian government, these foreign capitalists exercised a great deal of control over Peru. Peru became a "Grace Steamship republic" in much the same way that Central American states, such as Nicaragua, were controlled by the United Fruit Company and were condescendingly referred to as "banana republics."

The Empire of Brazil In nineteenth-century Brazil political conflicts between the old and ▬▬▬▬▬▬▬ new orders highlighted characteristics of the age of global imperialism. The ties between this former Portuguese colony and the Atlantic economy were perhaps the most entrenched of the region. Slavery lasted longer and the ties to West and Central Africa were more numerous and enduring. Between 1850 and 1874 the number of slaves had been cut by more than half, but still remained about 1 million. When slavery was finally abolished in 1888, planters felt betrayed by the Brazilian monarchy; this opposition fueled the impetus for a military coup and the creation of a new republic. Its motto was "Order and Progress," and both were sought in the following generations as Brazil also joined the neocolonial pattern of Latin American economies.

Critics of Dependency Not all Latin Americans approved of the path of economic development ▬▬▬▬▬▬▬ ment that came to reflect foreign ties and dependencies. As early as

1856 the Chilean writer Francisco Bilbao (1823–1865) expressed his sense of a unique Latin American identity in contrast to its powerful North American neighbor, the United States. In the face of imperialist threats from the United States, Bilbao reminded his readers that, unlike most Latin American nation states, the United States had not yet abolished slavery:

> In our land there survives something of that ancient and divine hospitality, in our breasts there is room for the love of mankind. We have not lost the tradition of the spiritual destiny of man. We do not see in the earth, or in the pleasures of the earth, the definitive end of man; the Negro, the Indian, the disinherited, the unhappy, the weak, find among us the respect that is due to the name and dignity of man!
>
> That is what the republicans of South America dare to place in the balance opposite the pride, the wealth, and the power of North America.

The Complexities and Costs of Independence As was true before the nationalist revolutions that established early nineteenth-century republics in South America, economic and political power after independence was concentrated in the hands of the few. Although an individualistic republican society replaced colonial society, the pyramidal structure remained. Cities continued to dominate the countryside, landlords still subjugated the peasants, and there was little social mobility. Divisions that resulted from postindependence politics were added to traditional distinctions of class and birth. Those who were liberals, wishing to adopt new and "foreign" ways such as the parliamentary system or democracy, were bitterly opposed by conservatives, who wanted to keep as much as possible to the old ways. For some, progress lay in adopting the parliamentary system, while for others, it lay in North American republicanism; for some it was free enterprise, for others, socialism. These tensions and conflicts would continue to play out through the twentieth century.

■

THE UNITED STATES AND THE RISE OF THE AMERICAN EMPIRE

Between the end of the Civil War (1865) and the beginning of World War I (1914), Thomas Jefferson's dream of an American republic of small, independent farmers became a distant memory. The Civil War had clarified the nature of the federal union by uniting the continent's diverse communities in basic agreement about their national identity. By the end of the nineteenth century, an economic destiny matched the political one. Rapidly evolving technology, expanding and more diverse populations, and increasing urbanization were forces transforming the United States into what could be called a billion-dollar country, the most richly productive capitalist nation on earth.

Economic Expansion The late-nineteenth-century boom was based on the exploitation of human and natural resources by ever-larger units of production and new technologies that resulted in efficient, rapid, and increased production. The emphasis was on quantity, often at the expense of quality, and reduced labor costs. The outcome was the creation of a consumer economy structured around production of consumer goods for the market. This kind of economy produced great wealth (not always equally distributed) and increased material comfort (for many).

The economic and social transformation of the United States in the post–Civil War decades was accompanied by a readjustment and reassessment of the American role and place in world affairs. The result was the creation of an American empire. Up to the Civil War, American attitudes and policies toward other countries were determined by the Monroe Doctrine (1823), the idea that the United States would keep out of European affairs, so long as Europeans kept out of the Western Hemisphere. The United States would keep its hands off Canada or Latin American countries except when Manifest Destiny (see Chapter 16) demanded otherwise, as in the Mexican War (1846–1848).

THE "ASSIMILATION" OF NATIVE AMERICANS

The resolution of the Civil War may have formally ended slavery for African Americans, but it did not resolve the conflicts between Native Americans and European Americans represented by the federal government. The Cherokee removal of the 1830s (see Chapter 16) was the beginning, not the end, of federal military policy against Native Americans. By the 1860s and 1870s, the railroad and white hunters destroyed the bison herds that were sustenance to Great Plains peoples, and by the 1880s bison had nearly disappeared. Mining and farming likewise altered the familiar landscapes of Native American livelihood.

The Nez Perce In 1877 the Nez Perce War broke out when, following a decade and a half of white settlers' encroachment, the federal government decided to take away Nez Perce ancestral lands in the northern Rocky Mountains. Like the Cherokees, the Nez Perce were defeated and deprived of their lands. When he surrendered, Nez Perce Chief Joseph reported: "Our chiefs are killed . . . The old men are all dead . . . It is cold and we have no blankets. The little children are freezing to death . . . I want to have time to look for my children and see how many of them I can find. Maybe I shall find them among the dead . . . I am tired; my heart is sick and sad."

The Sioux In the mid-1870s the Sioux also struggled with the United States federal government and lost. Though the Sioux chief Crazy Horse and medicine man Sitting Bull confronted and slaughtered General George A. Custer and his men at the battle of the Little Big Horn in the Black Hills of South Dakota in 1876, the federal government ultimately defeated the Sioux and their allies, the Cheyenne, and they were confined to reservations. In the 1880s the United States government tried to assimilate the Sioux and other Indians to "Americanism," as defined by the outcome of the Civil War. The Indian Rights Association (IRA), founded in 1881, was the agency of this assimilation policy. Following his visit to the Great Sioux Reservation in 1881, William Welsh, the founder of the IRA, stated that the Indian had to be "taught to labor, to live in civilized ways, and to serve God." In order to embrace these values, they needed to unlearn communal values, give up their "pagan" beliefs, and become more individualistic. Assimilation meant that traditions and customs such as the shuffling and chanting of the Sun Dance, a cornerstone of Lakota belief, had to be given up. Secretary of the Interior Henry M. Teller ordered agents to suppress this custom in 1883.

Linking the private ownership of property to advanced civilization, the IRA also promoted the division of the Great Sioux Reserve, which ironically fit with the desire of land speculators and white settlers to acquire Sioux land. In the Sioux Act of 1889, Congress partitioned the Great Sioux Reservation, allotting 320 acres to each Sioux family head and opening about half the reserve for sale to whites. Though Sioux leaders were assured that accep-

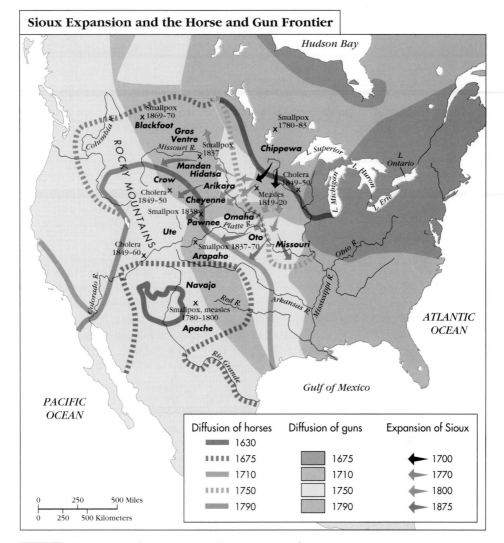

Sioux Expansion and the Horse and Gun Frontier

Hudson Bay

Smallpox
x 1869–70
Blackfoot

**Gros
Ventre**
Smallpox
x1837

Smallpox
x1780–83

Chippewa *L. Superior*

Cholera
1849–50

L. Ontario

Columbia R.

Missouri R.

**Mandan
Hidatsa**

Crow

Arikara

x

Measles
1819–20

L. Michigan

L. Huron

L. Erie

Cheyenne

Cholera
1849–50

Smallpox 1838x

Pawnee *Platte R.*

Omaha

Ute

Oto

Missouri

Ohio R.

Cholera
1849–60 x

xSmallpox 1837–70

Arapaho

Mississippi R.

Navajo

Red R.

Arkansas R.

x
Smallpox, measles
1780–1800

Rio Grande

Apache

**ATLANTIC
OCEAN**

Gulf of Mexico

**PACIFIC
OCEAN**

Diffusion of horses	Diffusion of guns	Expansion of Sioux
1630		
1675	1675	1700
1710	1710	1770
1750	1750	1800
1790	1790	1875

0   250   500 Miles

0   250   500 Kilometers

MAP 17.7 The Impact of Technology and Imperialism, 1630–1875

tance of this land division would not result in a reduction in ration allotments (which they were due for having been displaced from their source of livelihood) from the federal government, Congress slashed appropriations for rations. By the end of 1889, the death rate at Pine Ridge in South Dakota was 45 people a month in a population of 5,550.

The Wounded Knee Massacre The final tragedy took place at Wounded Knee Creek in South Dakota in 1890. Following the killing of Chief Sitting Bull for his resistance to federal attempts to force the Sioux onto reservations, federal troops, fearing an uprising, forced a group of 120 men and 230 Sioux women and children into a tent camp. When the soldiers sought to disarm the Indians, one warrior, apparently deaf, appeared to resist. The soldier opened fire with automatic rapid firing Gatling guns; 153 Indians lay dead, and dozens more crawled away to die in the bush. The genocide of the Native Americans which had begun in 1492 culminated at Wounded Knee nearly 400 years later.

THE UNITED STATES IN WORLD AFFAIRS

Following the Civil War, the United States took a more forceful role in international affairs, a role compatible with and encouraging of economic growth. The United States, whose only tangible territorial connection with Africa was the state of Liberia (founded by American slaves), attended the Berlin Conference (1884–1885), which redrew the map of the continent for the benefit of Europeans. In 1905 President Theodore Roosevelt (in office 1901–1909) offered his good services to the Japanese and Russians to negotiate the Treaty of Portsmouth (New Hampshire) ending the Russo-Japanese War. In 1906 representatives of the United States attended a conference on African affairs, at Algeciras, Spain, when Morocco was handed over to the French.

Territorial Expanison The abandonment of American isolation based on the Monroe Doctrine was indicated more forcefully by its territorial expansion. The territory north of the Rio Grande taken from Mexico in 1848 may be viewed as a (large) part of the realization of Manifest Destiny. The purchase of Alaska from Russia (1867), referred to at the time as "Seward's Folly" (after the secretary of state who arranged the purchase), was in fact a shrewd extension of American commercial interests in the Pacific.

FIGURE 17.11 *Queen Liliuokalani*

The Hawaiian monarch was deposed in 1893 and her territory annexed by the United States in 1898. The queen is shown here in Victorian dress posed before the backdrop of a traditional royal feathered cape.

SOURCE: Brown Brothers.

The acquisition of Hawaii came next. In 1875 the United States established a protectorate over the islands, guaranteeing Hawaiian independence against any third party in return for trading privileges and the use of Pearl Harbor as a naval base. Americans quickly established huge, profitable sugar and pineapple industries in Hawaii, and by 1891, when Queen Liliuokalani came to the throne and endangered their interests by trying to check Americanization, they overthrew her and set up an independent republic that soon sought annexation to the United States. After some hesitation the Hawaiian republic was annexed in 1898.

DAILY LIVES

LIFE ON A MILITARY OUTPOST

Historians studying military outposts usually focus on soldiers, rather than on families. The diary of Harold D. Corbusier offers documentation of daily life at a nineteenth-century fort on the Canadian border of the United States from the perspectives of a 10-year-old child and then an 18-year-old man at Fort Mackinac, Michigan, during the 1880s and 1890s. Corbusier was born into an Army family at Camp Date Creek, Arizona Territory, in 1873. As a child he lived at outposts in North and South Carolina, Tennessee, and Nebraska, among the Ogalala Sioux, at Fort Washakie, Wyoming, and finally, Fort Mackinac on Lake Huron. Henry went on to graduate from the University of Michigan in 1899 with a degree in medicine. As an Army surgeon he served in China and the Philippines, on the Mexican border, and after World War I, became a colonel in the medical reserves. His lifetime epitomizes the dedication and service that was also a part of the age of imperialism. Between 1883 and 1892 his diaries provide invaluable historical information about American social life on the edge of the empire during childhood and adolescence:

> 4th July, 1883 (at age 11)
> It has been a pleasent day. They fired a sulute of thirty-eight guns at noon we have had a very nice time today down town they had go-as-you-please races, walking maches, pony hurdle, row boat races, greased pole, tub races. Jumping matches. Mama Mrs Sellers, Miss Duggan and Mr. Duggan went to the Point on the Algomah.
> 5th.
> Last night we set off a great many fire works. Claude hurt his hand very badly last night.
> 11th.
> It has been a very disagreeable day Capt. Ward Inspector on Genl. Hancock staff inspected the post today.

> Sept. 23rd
> I have a very bad coald. Papa thinks it is because I had my hair cut on saterday.
> 4th July, 1892 (at age 18)
> They had a few country races & other amussements (?) down in the village today besides these there has been no unusual excitement. The usual salute was fired from the fort & they had a pretty good game up there. The Fort Wayne nine played the Fort Mackinac. The score was 3 to 1 in favor of Fort Wayne. There was a hop at the Grand Hotel this evening. I danced twelve dances. I am beginning to waltz a little.
> 5th.
> We went on a picnic today with mother & Mrs. Bailey. We got a three seated rig & drove out to the North side of the Island. We found a cave which we expect to explore tomorrow. We are all quite tired after our tramp. Went to a hop at the Astor House this evening danced about eleven dances.
> 6th.
> Quite stiff this morning but we all started about eleven o'clock to explore the cave that we found yesterday. Two of the soldiers went with us. I went down into the hole, with a rope fastened around me, for about 20 ft. then the rest came down & we went a little farther following a large crack which crossed the cave . . . There was a hop at the Grand tonight but I did not go but went to the Mission House where a number of young people assembled to spend the evening. We came home about eleven after playing the banjo and singing (?) most of the evening. Mrs. Rome Wendell was there. I used to know her when she was a little girl. Her sister is now Mrs. McKinnen.*

Source: *Phil Porter, ed. *A Boy at Fort Mackinac: The Diary of Harold Dumbar Corbusier, 1883–1884, 1892.* Mackinac Island, MI.: The Corbusier Archives and Mackinac State Historic Parks, 1994: 50, 56, 85, 86.

MILITARY INTERVENTIONS

Americans also used force in the late nineteenth century in their quest for noncontiguous territory, most of which they acquired for economic reasons. The use of force rather than cash as a means of expansion is most clearly seen in interventions in the Caribbean and Latin America, where the United States steadily undertook to establish its hegemony. In 1895, invoking the Monroe Doctrine, President Grover Cleveland (in office 1885–1889; 1893–1897) intervened in a border dispute between British Guiana and Venezuela, forcing the British to accept American arbitration.

Roosevelt Corollary In 1904, when Venezuela's default on a debt payment offered Europeans an opportunity to intervene there, President Theodore Roosevelt declared the American right to exercise "international police power" in the Western Hemisphere. The Roosevelt Corollary of the Monroe Doctrine summed up the direction of an aggressive imperialist policy, vigorously pursued on many fronts and in many ways.

The Spanish-American War The Roosevelt Corollary was an effective means of furthering American economic and political interests. So was war, as the brief Spanish-American War (1898–1899) made clear. Revolutionary disturbances in Cuba and Puerto Rico, all that remained of the once vast Spanish-American empire, won support from Americans anxious to protect and extend their considerable investments on the two islands and disturbed by the forceful efforts of Spanish authorities to suppress the independence movements.

The unexplained sinking of the American battleship *Maine* in Havana harbor resulted in outright war between the United States and Spain. Spurred on by a mixture of humanitarianism, greed, and dreams of martial glory, the Spanish-American War (from which Theodore Roosevelt emerged as a hero) was a brief conflict easily won by the United States. Puerto Rico was annexed, and a veiled protectorate was established over Cuba by means of the Platt Amendment, which gave the United States broad rights of intervention in matters of "life, property, individual liberty" and "Cuban independence." In Asia, the Philippines and Guam became American protectorates as result of the Spanish-American War.

The Panama Canal In 1903, when Colombia faced a revolution in its isthmus of Panama, Roosevelt intervened. Supporting the revolutionaries, he immediately recognized Panama as an independent republic and thus created an ally sympathetic to an American desire to build a canal across the isthmus. The idea of such a canal came from Ferdinand de Lesseps, who had built the Suez Canal, but whose French Panama Canal company went bankrupt in 1880. The United States bought French rights and assets associated with the canal project in 1887, and in 1904 the United States leased the canal zone, subsequently fortified, which bifurcated its client state in Panama. American capital financed the construction of the Panama Canal, which relied on labor from the Caribbean region. Ten years after work resumed, the canal was completed (1914), and the strategically valuable connection between the Atlantic and Pacific oceans was under the control of the United States.

THE EXPANSION OF AMERICAN INFLUENCE

The rapid spread of American influence and empire into the Caribbean and Latin America, across the Pacific, and into the diplomatic councils of Europe was also symbolized by President Theodore Roosevelt's advocacy of a large American navy, one appropriate to the position of the United States in the world. The American president, like his British and German contemporaries, was not unaware of the highly regarded and influential *Influence of Seapower upon History* by the American admiral Alfred Thayer Mahan (1840–1914). Roosevelt's entry into the naval race that was gripping Europe was to dispatch his "great white fleet," a flotilla of American naval vessels, on a world tour, a powerful—and no less powerful by being symbolic—indication of the position the United States would assume in world affairs in the twentieth century.

Latin America and In Central America, in addition to the protectorate established in
the Caribbean Panama, the United States naval intervention in Nicaragua (1909) (associated with internal political changes) was followed by an extended occupation by Marines (1912–1925), during which the Americans secured rights to build a canal across Nicaragua (1916). Imperialism in Central America was very closely connected to the exploitation of that area by such American enterprises as United Fruit Company. The interlocking nature of commercial and political ties made it difficult to distinguish between "dollar" (guided by economic interests) and "gunboat" (determined by military force or threat of force) diplomacy. American military action south of the border also included forays to Mexico, where political instability resulting from the Mexican Revolution (1911–1913) provided opportunities for intervention in 1914 and again in 1916–1917. In the Caribbean, the United States occupied the Dominican Republic from 1916 to 1934, and direct rule was added to the United States control of customs receipts in Haiti from 1915 to 1934.

North America The establishment of dominance in the Caribbean and Latin America is not the only example of American expansionism. Normally peaceful relations with Canada were aggravated by a boundary dispute between British Columbia and Alaska that was brought to a crisis by the gold rushes in that area. This dispute, settled in 1903 in favor of the United States when the British member of the arbitration commission voted with the American, confirmed the Alaska panhandle as American territory, revived suspicions of American expansionism in Canada, and further disillusioned Canadians with Great Britain, fueling their own break with imperialism.

■

THE CULTURE OF IMPERIALISM

The expansion of imperialism in the nineteenth century was reflected in complex, often subtle, ways in the works of writers, artists, and composers. Those who colonized relied also on the processes of acculturation, the transmission of Western culture to the colonies, to create a culturally unified empire. Sometimes the cultural forces of imperialism were as effective as any military conquest.

CLAIMING AND CONSTRUCTING CULTURES

When Napoleon invaded Egypt in 1798, he was accompanied by French scientists who produced a lengthy work (twenty-four volumes!) called *The Description of Egypt*. This work details the splendor of Egypt's past as preparation for the appropriation of that past by European powers. The Franco-Prussian War (1870) led to an increase in French geographical societies, which linked geographical exploration to the imperial enterprise. Some armchair travelers never left their own cultures but still produced imaginative renderings of life and monuments. Later in the nineteenth century, as European expeditions became more common, many travelers to Egypt and other parts of the world recorded what they saw with great accuracy.

Imagining the Past The Italian grand opera *Aida* by Giuseppe Verdi was commissioned by ▨▨▨▨▨▨▨▨▨▨ the Khedive (the hereditary title granted to Egyptian rulers by the Ottomans) of Egypt to celebrate the opening of the Suez Canal and was first performed in Cairo in 1871. Set in ancient Egypt as imagined by Verdi, *Aida* tells the story of the Ethiopian princess Aida and her tragic love for Radames, the Egyptian warrior. Aida innocently betrays her lover, who is condemned to death for treason, and in the final act both Aida and Radames die entombed together. The historical background of the story is the conflict between Egypt and Ethiopia, but the contemporary setting was that of Anglo-Egyptian rivalry in East Africa during the mid-nineteenth century.

    Aida represented an imagined Egyptian past reconstructed by Europeans and ironically commissioned for the opening of the strategically important Suez Canal, the control of which would continue to be contested between Europeans and Egyptians over the next century. The

FIGURE 17.12 Scene from Verdi's *Aida*. ca. 1879 at Her Majesty's Theatre

This engraving of a scene from Verdi's opera shows a romantic depiction of the Egyptian past. The Italian opera was first performed in Cairo in 1871 as part of the Suez Canal celebrations.

SOURCE: Hulton Getty/Tony Stone Images.

Suez Canal was a vital link in the economic web of imperialism, providing for the rapid and efficient transportation of goods and people between Europe and its African and Asian colonies. The city of Cairo itself mirrored European cultural and political presence juxtaposed with the Egyptian past. The east quarter of the city was still a native preindustrial city, where itinerant water peddlers controlled the water supply and the homes were plunged into darkness at nightfall. The western part of Cairo, the colonial city, was home to Europeans; the water supply came from a network of conduits connected with a steam-pumping station near the river, and the streets were illuminated with gaslights at night. The opera house where *Aida* was staged was built by the Khedive; it faced the colonial city and was part of the imported landscape.

Collecting Cultures   The mapping and description of the world was a responsibility of colonial governments, which employed scientists, linguists, and other scholars to carry out the tasks of recording, collecting, and preserving knowledge and artifacts. Archaeology and anthropology flourished in the context of nineteenth-century imperialist ventures. Recovering the artifacts of antiquity was an undertaking financed by imperialism and carried out by European archaeologists, who employed "native" guides and workers, but who gained fame and wealth for themselves from the artifacts they unearthed. Through their observations and study of other peoples and cultures, European anthropologists heightened the popular awareness of cultural differences and often presented other cultures as museum pieces, unchanging and passive, in contrast to the dynamism of European culture.

Those who collected knowledge and artifacts were both trained specialists and ordinary travelers, including both men and women, some of whom found conventional life in Europe so stultifying that they fled its restrictions and expectations for the freedoms of colonial territories. Others acted as officials of governments or institutions, as did the Hungarian Emil Torday (1875–1931), who left Europe for the Belgian Congo in 1900, employed first by the Belgians and later by the British Museum. He eventually learned local languages and came to adopt an informed understanding of the African peoples (including the Kuba) he befriended and admired. As Torday later wrote, "I had not the slightest desire to see Europe again, and if it had been possible I would have stayed on for the rest of my life." Emile Torday collected nearly 3,000 objects and established standards of ethnographic research techniques using oral interviews, a strong historical framework, and extensive field documentation. The collections of arts from Africa and Pacific Oceania made by Torday and others found their way from British, German, French, and Belgian territories to the museums of London, Paris, Berlin, and Brussels.

THE LITERATURE OF IMPERIALISM

In eighteenth- and nineteenth-century Europe, the development of the novel accompanied the emergence of nationalism, and imperialism is likewise woven into the fabric of literary works like a glittering gold thread illuminating sources of wealth that supported the aristocratic social life portrayed in the works of such authors as Jane Austen (1775–1817), the Bronte sisters, Charlotte (1816–1855) and Emily (1818–1848), and even Charles Dickens (1812–1870). The household economy of Thomas Bertram portrayed in Austen's *Mansfield Park* (1814) depends on plantations on the distant Caribbean island of Antigua, and this consciousness intrudes ever so subtly into the novel. Acknowledgment of economic dependence produces a kind of cultural, and even racial, repugnance, juxtaposing orderly, white European society with the dark, chaotic forces of foreign places and peoples.

In Charlotte Bronte's *Jane Eyre,* Mr. Rochester's wife, the mad Bertha Mason, has a Jamaican mother who was said to be insane. In Jamaica to make his fortune, the young Rochester innocently married Bertha Mason there, and after returning to England was tormented by her until her own suicide, which also resulted in the maiming and blinding of Rochester. Emily Bronte's great novel, *Wuthering Heights,* features the wild and passionate character Heathcliff who is said to have had a black father. Heathcliff was found by the father of the heroine, Catherine Earnshaw, in Liverpool, a leading slave-trading port in late eighteenth- and early nineteenth-century England. Wealth derived from the slave trade provided the income for rich families whose homes were spread across the north of England. When the products of the slave trade or of plantation economies in the West Indies intrude on English life, they represent the forces of darkness, chaos, and tragedy.

Not only foreigners figure in the complexities of interaction between the imperial center and its colonies: Europeans who have fallen into the lower tiers of society as criminals are exiled to colonies where they can make new lives for themselves while they extend the power of empire over indigenous peoples in colonial territories. In Dickens's novel, *Great Expectations* (1861), the hero, Pip, early in his life befriends a convict, Abel Magwitch, who is transported to a penal colony in Australia. Later Pip is the recipient of wealth bestowed on him by Magwitch, but mistakenly believes his benefactor to be the mysterious and elusive aristocrat Miss Havisham. When Magwitch returns illegally to England, Pip initially rejects him because of his unsavory background (including his Australian penal exile) but finally reconciles with his surrogate father. Pip ultimately bestows on Magwitch the acknowledgment of fictive kinship, as Australia was wrapped in the protective embrace of England and the dark forces of aboriginal life there were pushed further into the interior, away from the civilized spaces of cities such as Melbourne.

The British Empire became more than a tangential factor alluded to in references to plantations in the West Indies or the backgrounds of characters in the writings of Rudyard Kipling (1865–1936). *Kim* (1901) is perhaps the quintessential novel of the empire, the story of an orphaned white boy who grows up as a native in the streets and bazaars of Lahore. At least part of *Kim* is semiautobiographical: Kipling was born in Lahore, grew up speaking Hindustani, and lived as any other native speaker until he was sent to school in England. Kim becomes involved in international espionage in India but is eventually sent away to school and returns to take up service in the British colonial government. Much of the power of *Kim* derives from the young man's interaction with an old Tibetan monk who is searching for the river that will cleanse him of sins. Kim becomes the monk's disciple and returns to him at the end of the novel, when both discover what they have been seeking: the monk, his river; and Kim, his destiny. The most poignant and remarkable feature of *Kim* is the sympathetic treatment of Indian culture that still does not contradict the legitimacy of British imperial power. Kim's (and Kipling's) view of India is a deeply ambivalent one: each finds something precious there, but the view remains one of the colonial power benevolently patronizing the peoples it conquers.

Another European writer whose work is grounded in imperialism is the Polish-born English writer, Joseph Conrad (1857–1924), the author of *Heart of Darkness* (1898–1899). As a young man, Conrad spent his life at sea, and the settings of his novels derive from his experiences in the South Seas, Central Africa, and Asia. Conrad was deeply ambivalent about imperialism and extremely adept at portraying the dark side of European exploitation of colonial lands and peoples and the attitudes imperialism fostered among both exploiter and exploited. In *Heart of Darkness* Conrad exposed the dark underpinnings of the imperialist venture in characters whose souls are blighted by their experiences. He probably based his characters on the actions and beliefs of real persons in the Congo. In *Nostromo* (1904) Conrad showed the economic exploitation of a fictional independent Central American republic, dominated by foreign interests because of a rich silver mine. The intertwining of economic and cultural imperialism in Conrad's eyes provides a rich source of literary complexity that universalizes his characters' dilemmas to the heart of modern humanity.

By the early twentieth century, deep ambivalence characterized modern European writers who confronted the dehumanization of imperialism but were themselves caught in its web. For indigenous peoples in colonized territories, the ambivalences were different, but just as troubling, in their confrontation with the world constructed by European expansion in the nineteenth century. The adoption of European culture and institutions—Westernization— was at once a means of empowerment, enabling former colonies to assert their independence, and a source of profound anxiety about their own cultural identity. At the same time the dynamic interaction between European and non-European peoples and cultures produced a rich confluence of cultures reflected in musical forms, art, literature, and aspects of material life such as food and clothing. Similarly, the tension between European and non-European cultural forms has its counterpart in the tensions between tradition and modernity that shaped music, art, and especially literature in the twentieth century.

Imperialism knit the world together as an extension of Europe, but Europe's exposure to other peoples and cultures also contributed in important ways to the reconstruction of European identity in the twentieth century. As the world has become technologically interconnected, the emerging global culture has been constantly and rapidly transformed, producing increasingly unstable, fragmented, and ambiguous cultural and social identities, but also bearing the imprint of a rich sense of possibility produced by the dynamic interaction of cultures in much the way Aime Cesaire imagined in the opening section of this chapter.

SUMMARY

"The sun never sets on the British Empire" was a favorite expression that symbolized the great geographical reach of that empire in the nineteenth century. Just as this phrase symbolized Britain's empire, so the image of the rising sun symbolized Japan's new nationhood as it was formed in the nineteenth century. As the dual revolutions of the nation state and industrial capitalism gave rise to imperialism, in turn European imperialism stimulated non-European nationalisms, such as that of Japan, that fed revolutions both against European nation states and against traditional dynastic states.

Innovations following the first industrial revolutions made technological change a global issue. Technological advances made possible European expansion across the globe, and profound cultural transformations in Europe, Asia, Africa, and the Americas were the result of encounters produced by imperialism. The tools of empire, including such things as the steam boat, railroad, and telegraph, furthered communications and the transportation of goods between the colony and the imperial center and thus facilitated exploitation of resources. All imperialisms were not the same, just as the "responses" to European imperialisms differed according to distinctive cultural and historical experiences in widely varying parts of the globe.

In documenting the emergence of nationalisms around the world, we have emphasized not only the influence of the European nation state but also the complex historical and cultural patterns at work in the many definitions of "nation." In many non-European parts of the world, European imperialism stimulated indigenous nationalisms, which often led to revolu-

ENGAGING THE PAST

CHRISTIANITY, COLONIALISM, AND CULTURAL IDENTITY

The role of Christianity in colonialism and the impact of both Christian missionaries and colonial governments on the cultural identities of peoples in Asia, Africa, and the Americas is frequently assumed to have been overwhelmingly negative and destructive. Without denying the oppressive nature of colonial and semicolonial systems in the age of the new imperialism, some historians argue that it is important to understand the complexities of such cultural encounters as they were experienced by both colonizers and colonized.

Deliberate policies such as amalgamation or assimilation that were adopted by colonial governments aimed to "civilize" colonized peoples by forcing them to live as Europeans and adopt European religious, cultural, and social values. To what extent did such policies work? To be sure, some portions of indigenous populations cooperated with colonial officials, collaborating in the hope of gaining benefits and opportunities. But others resisted, refusing the cultural offerings imposed by European colonizers. At times the dividing line between collaboration and resistance was blurred, as individuals came under the influence of contradictory forces. Both resistance and acculturation often spawned religious movements and contributed to the creation of new cultural identifies that reflected the fusion of old and new, of indigenous tradition and imported ideas.

In New Zealand, one Maori response to conflicts with Europeans and the oppression of the colonial government took the form of a religious movement known as the Pai Marire ("The Good and the Peaceful"), also called Hauhauism after its founder Te Ua Haumene. Te Ua had been baptized by a Christian missionary and had also been a follower of the Maori King movement that opposed land sales to Europeans. In 1862 Te Ua

claimed to have had a vision of the angel Gabriel who told him to reject war. Te Ua preached a blend of New Testament Christianity and traditional Maori beliefs, including "peaceful arts" such as song, dance, and tattooing, that culminated in a millennarian prophecy of a new world free from pain, suffering, and oppression. When it peaked in the mid-1860s, approximately one-fifth of the Maori population were followers of the Pai Marire movement. Though its leader preached peace and virtuous behavior, more radical elements of the Pai Marire engaged in violence against Europeans, leading to divisions within Maori society between those who resisted European encoachment and those who cooperated with the Europeans and gained some benefits as a result.

A series of catastrophes in the eastern Cape province of South Africa left the Xhosa, whose ancestral lands had been annexed to the British Empire in 1847, landless migrant laborers. An epidemic of disease destroyed nearly 100,000 head of cattle, the mainstay of Xhosa livelihood and traditional culture. One response to these desperate circumstances came in the form of a cattle-killing prophecy revealed in a vision experienced by a 15-year-old Xhosa girl named Nongquwase, who claimed that "the whole nation will rise from the dead if all the living cattle are slaughtered because these have been reared with defiled hands, since there are people who have been practicing witchcraft."[*] Also embedded in the visions of the young girl were notions of hastening change through sacrifice.

Since the London Missionary Society established its first station in Xhosaland in 1817,

[*]J. B. Pieres, "The Central Beliefs of the Xhosa Cattle-Killing," *Journal of African History,* 27 (1987): 43.

tions, many of which began as anti-European, anti-imperialist movements. Not all non-European nationalisms took revolutionary directions, though many adopted as models institutions derived from the West. In Chapter 19 we will return to the theme of nationalism in the context of resistance to imperialism and movements of national liberation in the twentieth century. The following chapter deals with the outcome of European nation state rivalry and its impact on the world in global war.

Christian ideas had penetrated Xhosa beliefs. Nongquwase's prophecy represented an amalgam of traditional Xhosa beliefs in the omnipresence of the spirits of dead kinsmen and Christian and African ideas of sacrifice to achieve a desired end (resurrection in Christian terms, but political change in Xhosa tradition). Most Xhosa followed Nongquwase's instructions, and by the end of 1857 more than 400,000 head of cattle had been destroyed with the result that more than 40,000 Xhosa died of starvation. In the aftermath of this tragedy, the Xhosa were divided into those who believed in following traditional ways, despite the devastation caused by the cattle killing, and those who were now without any recourse and ready to seek opportunities from the colonial presence and opposed the cattle killing as senseless.

The ideology of the Taiping Rebellion in mid-nineteenth century China was a blend of Old Testament Christianity and a Chinese utopian tradition that envisioned a world of perfect harmony and peace, the "great peace," from which the Taipings took their name. The Old Testament ideas of the Jews as a "chosen people" whose suffering distinguished them as children of God fit well with the sense of disaffection among Chinese whose livelihoods had been disrupted by the effects of the Opium Wars. The Boxers at the turn of the century, in contrast, used traditional religious beliefs and practices to resist the foreign presence in China, most visible to rural, disaffected, and uneducated Chinese in the form of Christian missionaries. In both cases, whether influenced by Christianity or drawing on traditional beliefs in opposition to Christianity, religious movements were inspired by specific social and economic conditions.

Similarly, desperate economic conditions on the Great Sioux reservation in the winter of 1889 led the Sioux to turn to the Ghost Dance religion, based on the teachings of Wovoka, a Paiute shaman from western Nevada. In the 1880s, under the influence of Protestant evangelists, Wovoka had seen a vision of the reunion of the living and dead. Wovoka commanded his followers to perform the round (or ghost) dance in which men and women joined in a circle with fingers interlocked as the key to the regeneration of the world. Federal agents saw the Ghost Dance movement as threatening and moved to suppress it among the Sioux, with the result that some Ghost Dancers became militant. Conflict erupted between the federal government and the Lakota Sioux, climaxing in the massacre at Wounded Knee in the winter of 1890.

While personal charisma and fanaticism may have characterized some of the leaders of these movements, the power of their ideas to move people and gather followers can only be explained in the broader context of the economic, social, and political impact of imperialism. These multiple examples, drawn from vastly differing cultural and historical backgrounds, illustrate both the cultural resilience of colonized peoples and the unpredictable consequences inherent in cross-cultural encounters that shaped the cultural identities of Europeans as well as non-Europeans. Cultural identity is the product of ongoing processes of transformation. Imperialism and colonialism forced a redefinition of cultural identities among peoples from Africa to the Americas, Asia, and the Pacific. The transformation of cultural identities however, was at least in part the product of conscious agency through revitalization movements that drew on foreign ideas such as Christianity as well as indigenous traditions.

SUGGESTIONS FOR FURTHER READING

Patricia Grimshaw, *Paths of Duty: American Missionary Wives in Nineteenth-Century Hawaii* (Honolulu: University of Hawaii Press, 1989). The cultural encounters experienced by women who accompanied their spouses on missions to Hawaii beginning in the early part of the nineteenth century.

James O. Gump, "A Spirit of Resistance: Sioux, Xhosa, and Maori Responses to Western Dominance, 1840-1920," *Pacific Historical Review* vol LXI, no.1 (February, 1997), pp.21-52

Daniel R. Headrick, *The Tentacles of Progress* (New York: Oxford University Press, 1988). Examines the impact of technology from the nineteenth century into the mid-twentieth.

Daniel R. Headrick, *The Tools of Empire* (New York: Oxford University Press, 1981). Examines the relationship between technology and imperialism.

Jane Hunter, *The Gospel of Gentility: American Women Missionaries in Turn-of-the-Century China* (New Haven, CT: Yale University Press, 1984). A rich study of American women who committed their lives to become Christian missionaries in China.

Walter Rodney, *How Europe Underdeveloped Africa* (NJ/Trenton: Africa World Press, 1974). A provocative perspective on the role of Africa in world capitalist development.

Edward W. Said, *Culture and Imperialism* (New York: Vintage, 1994). A stimulating and provocative discussion of the cultural components of imperialism, particularly from the perspective of literature.

Kevin Shillington, *History of Africa* (New York: Macmillan, 1989). A readable account of conquest and colonization in Africa.

Robin W. Winks, *The Age of Imperialism* (Englewood Cliffs, NJ: Prentice-Hall, 1969). A rich source for documents, mostly from the European colonizer's perspective.

Stanley Wolpert, *A New History of India,* 4th ed. (New York: Oxford University Press, 1993). A solid and comprehensive overview of Indian history through the modern period.

Culture, Power, and Perspective: War and Peace in the Twentieth Century

I n 1893, during the high tide of the new imperialism, the Chicago World's Columbian Exposition opened to commemorate the 400th anniversary of Columbus's arrival in the New World. The midway of the exposition displayed exotic cultural exhibits from around the world, including the street in Cairo, the Algerian village, the Persian palace, and the Turkish theater, along with Innuits (called "Esquimaux") from North America and Dahomeyans from West Africa. As one journalist described his visit to the midway:

> you met people of all nations, all stations, all classes and all dressed in holiday attire. There were Turks in European costume, with red fez, and Turks in all the glory of rich silk turbans, purple silk mantles and yellow silk trousers; Arabs in long, pale, tan-colored robes, embroidered in gold, and in long silk robes, covered with gold lace.

While the Turks and Arabs could be viewed with pleasure and appreciation for their rich exoticism, colorfully and luxuriantly dressed in silks and gold, the Innuits and Dahomeyans exemplified what Americans and Europeans considered to be the "primitive" cultures of the world who were viewed with curiosity and the confidence of cultural superiority. Visitors were asked to note the Dahomeyans' "regretful absence of tailor-made clothes." In contrast, Innuits attired in native fur costume were made to perform with their dogsleds, though the hot and humid Chicago summer made physical activity in such apparel almost unbearable. The Chicago Columbian Exposition, a vivid expression of the view of the world through the lens of imperialism, trumpeted the virtues of the American nation at the same time that it exposed the suppression of the rights of African Americans, women, and the conditions of immigrant workers and others of the laboring classes.

Nearly half a century later, the planners of the New York World's Fair that opened in 1939 attempted to create a futuristic vision of the union of science, technology, and industry in the World of Tomorrow. Like the city of Oz in the firm *The Wizard of Oz* that opened the same year, the fair's planners dazzled visitors with its constructed vision of an imagined world clothed in color:

> From almost any point of entrance, the New York World's Fair assaults the beholder as a carnival of color in architecture. Great stretches of eye-filling hues, canary yellow, orange, blue, green, and rose, carry the eye along unbroken wall surfaces, set among fountains and lawns, and softened by long vistas

FIGURE 18.0 The Woman's Building at
the Gateway to the Midway,
Chicago World's Columbian
Exposition, 1893.

SOURCE: Culver Pictures.

of tree-lined avenues. From the central axis, dominated by the pearl-white perisphere and the slen-
der, sky-piercing trylon, more than five hundred graduated tints and shades contribute to the
palette which the fair has devised to depict the World of Tomorrow.

Despite the colorful fantasy and glamorous future envisioned by the planners, the fair was not
immune to the realities of world politics. In January 1939, before the fair's official opening,
the Spanish government fell, and the Spanish pavilion was closed. In March, Hitler's Germany absorbed Czechoslovakia, and Czech immigrants took over the Czech pavilion. Poland
was invaded by Germany in September, and the Polish pavilion closed. In the spring of 1940,
Denmark, Norway, Belgium, the Netherlands, and France fell to German forces, and their
participation in the fair ended. Just as the Chicago Columbian Exposition was the product of
imperialist fantasy and yet reflected the realities of imperialism, the 1939 New York World's
Fair on one level bore little resemblance to the real world and yet on another level revealed
sharply the dissonances of that world on the eve of the second global war of the twentieth
century.

■
INTRODUCTION

In the twentieth century, conflicts among European nation states reflected in imperialist rivalries in the non-European world twice led to global war. European nationalisms forged in the aftermath of the Napoleonic wars in the nineteenth century fed the fires that led to global conflagration in World War I. The new national boundaries drawn after the war split groups that were bound by language and culture and heightened tensions to the point that sparks flew and lit the tinderbox of competing national identities and their economic interests.

The dual economic and political revolutions, ongoing since the seventeenth century, that had produced capitalist industrialism and the nation state, also created a political environment in Europe in which war was viewed as an instrument of state policy used to maintain the balance of power within a system of rival states and to protect national economic interests. Coalitions were built, dismembered, and rebuilt in response to perceived threats of power concentrated in the hands of one state. Political power was widely understood from the perspective of alliances and diplomacy.

Industrialization expanded the notion of power to include economic interests and by the twentieth century industrialization would also change the nature of warfare and its impact on society. Mechanization and mass production techniques that grew out of the industrial revolution were applied to the weapons of war. The American Civil War was the first armed conflict in which technology produced by the industrial revolution—railroads, telegraph, rifled weapons, and armored ships—was used extensively. The two world wars of the twentieth century expanded industrialization and the development of new industrial technology on a global scale. The continued industrial expansion in the postwar era provided seemingly limitless numbers of consumer goods and invoked changes in material culture and social life.

On the political front challenges to the power of rulers and their governments took the form of mass demands for more democratic political institutions; states were compelled to respond to these demands with promises of greater material rewards or political rights. War was one way to channel mass discontent, and patriotic fervor in a nationalistic cause such as territorial struggle with a neighboring state could deflect criticism of domestic political, social, and economic conditions.

In this chapter we will examine the struggle of war and peace in the twentieth century and the political, cultural, and social dimensions of change related to this struggle. Both World War I (1914–1918) and World War II (1939–1945) began in Europe, pitted the German nation against a coalition of allies, and ended with the defeat of Germany. But the two global conflicts also demarcate a shift from a world dominated by Europe, a condition dating from the sixteenth century, to one dominated by the United States and increasingly by new nations born from the dismantling of European imperialism worldwide. The impact of these struggles ranged from the diplomatic and political arenas of nation states to the intimate, daily lives of individuals.

■
THE ROOTS OF GLOBAL WAR

The unification of Italy and Germany by 1871 and the defeat of France in the Franco-Prussian War (1870–1871) set the stage for tensions to erupt on the European continent (see Chapter

16). By replacing France as the dominant continental power, the new German empire disrupted the established balance of power in Europe. Germany's rapid development into a major industrial power challenged the economic dominance of Great Britain in industrial production, access and control of foreign markets, and even the acquisition of colonies.

By the beginning of the twentieth century, the major European powers were grouped into two hostile military alliances created by diplomatic strategies stemming from late nineteenth-century power politics and imperialism. The Triple Alliance was made up of Germany, Austria-Hungary, and Italy; the Triple Entente (or Entente Cordiale) included Great Britain, France, and Russia. Tensions among these nations extended beyond Europe. From the end of the nineteenth century to the outbreak of World War I, economic rivalry in Africa—the Sudan, East Africa, Morocco—fueled tensions that on several occasions nearly led to war between France, Great Britain, and Germany. Economic and political rivalries, military expansion, the maintenance of large standing armies, and naval competition provided the volatile background for war in 1914.

The immediate cause for the outbreak of war, however, was Slavic nationalism in the Balkans, where Serbians wanted to annex fellow Slavs from the Ottoman Empire into an enlarged Slavic state. Serbia saw its opportunity when internal political problems in the Ottoman Empire in the first part of the twentieth century offered Slavs the chance to liberate themselves from centuries of Ottoman control. Dreams of a Slavic state were frustrated in

FIGURE 18.1 *For What,* **by V.H. Varley (ca. 1918)**

The painting depicts the hopelessness and devastation of twentieth-century global warfare.

SOURCE: © Canadian War Museum. Cat. No. 8911. Photo by William Kent.

1908 when the Austrians annexed Bosnia and Herzegovina, which had Slavic populations, an event that infuriated the Serbs.

The Balkan Wars of 1912–1913, in which the Ottomans were all but expelled from Europe, temporarily revived Serbian aspirations for a Slavic state. But these hopes were once again dashed when separate Slavic states, such as Albania, were created as an outcome of these wars. The nationalistic frustration of the Serbs was focused on Austria, and the event that precipitated hostilities in 1914 was the assassination of Archduke Franz Ferdinand, heir to the Austrian and Hungarian thrones, by a 19-year-old Serb nationalist at the Bosnian capital of Sarajevo.

The Great War, as it was known to Europeans, began in 1914 as a local European war waged between Austria-Hungary and Serbia. This central European conflict quickly extended into a general European war because of the two opposing systems of alliances into which Europe was divided. Germany honored its pledge to come to the aid of Austria, and Russia rallied to the aid of Serbia, which also involved Russian's French and British allies. Britain's participation in turn involved Japan as an ally.

The war eventually spread beyond Europe and involved thirty-two nations, including the European colonies in Africa and Asia. Twenty-eight nations, known as the Allies, including Great Britain, France, Russia, Italy (which joined the Allies in 1915), and the United States (which did not enter the war until April 1917), opposed the coalition known as the Central Powers, consisting of Germany, Austria-Hungary, the Ottoman Empire, and Bulgaria. Though precipitated by a political assassination, it was the intense nationalism rampant in nineteenth-century Europe, together with economic competition stemming from the growth of capitalist industrialism and its extension through imperialism, that lay at the heart of the conflict that engulfed Europe and other parts of the world in the early twentieth century.

■

WORLD WAR I

For European diplomats the outbreak of World War I provided an opportunity for rallying nationalist pride and patriotic loyalty. Both alliances assumed that the war would be short and that victory would be swift. Both were mistaken. The war lasted four years, and after initial rapid advances, the struggle became virtually fixed along a series of fronts: a western front in France; an eastern front along the frontiers of Russia, Germany, and Austria, and a southern front along the Austrian-Italian frontier. Industrial technology supported the expansion of the conflict into a global war of unimaginable material destruction and human pain.

For the first time in history, warfare became global in scale and impact. The war on the western front began with the rapid advance of German armies through Belgium into northwestern France until they reached the Marne River, dangerously close to Paris, in early September 1914. Here they were stopped by French forces, and the war of movement on the western front became a long war of siege.

TRENCH WARFARE

The Germans constructed a labyrinth of trenches, which were complicated ditches designed to provide cover for troops. The French and their British allies in turn ordered trenches as defense against the possible German advances. The digging of trenches, some of them 4 feet deep, meant that soldiers were held fixed in their defensive positions, awaiting face-to-face combat and death. In the meantime they lived through cramped, miserable, unhealthy, and dangerous days and nights of constant gunfire and bombardment, relieved only by the even more dangerous efforts to break through the lines and advance.

The horror of trench warfare was dramatically evoked by the German author Erich Maria Remarque (1898–1970) in *All Quiet on the Western Front*, a powerful indictment of war published in 1929. Remarque was drafted into the German army at the age of 18 and wounded on the western front, where he observed the horrors he later described in his novel: "The sun goes down, night comes, the shells whine, life is at an end. Still the little piece of convulsed earth in which we lie is held. We have yielded no more than a hundred yards of it as a prize to the enemy. But on every yard there lies a dead man." Remarque's book was a plea for peace, but for those engaged in the war the mechanisms for peace held little hope as they lived through endless days of misery and bloodletting in the muddy trenches and scorched landscapes of Europe. Nearly 9 million lives would be lost, and the lives of many more on battlefields and homefronts around the world permanently scarred.

THE IMPACT OF TECHNOLOGY

Innovations in military technology multiplied the misery of trench warfare in World War I. Improvements in mass-produced weapons and new experimental weapons intensified the conduct of the war, sometimes with unpredictable results. For example, the lines of barbed wire used to protect soldiers in trenches also ensnared and impaled them when they tried to advance.

Each side introduced new weapons to try to gain an advantage, but many of them had not been perfected. The Allies introduced tanks in 1916 as a means for spearheading advances into German-held territory. These new armoured, motorized vehicles provided mobile fire power, but they also broke down frequently and could be easily trapped in trenches. The Germans developed flamethrowers to attack the mobile tanks. The military prototype of the Wright brothers' 1903 airplane proved to be of problematic military use until pilots could figure out how to shoot without hitting the propellor blades. Accordingly, despite the fame of "ace" fighter pilots such as the German Baron Richthofen, air warfare was basically ancillary to land fighting. Airplanes provided reconnassiance behind enemy lines and served as a substitute for artillery, attacking and bombing the enemy far beyond the front lines.

The most terrifying new weapon was poison gas, first used by the Germans in April 1915. The use of poison gas was unpredictable: it could drift back and kill or disable those who launched it as well as those for whom it was intended. Even the invention of gas masks provided little protection from the searing, blistering chemicals. The British poet Wilfred Owen (1893–1918), who was killed just before the end of the war, described from personal experience the horror of poison gas:

> the blood
> Come gargling from the froth-corrupted lungs.
> Obscene as cancer, bitter as the cud
> of vile, incurable sores on innocent tongues.

Other weapons were more controllable but equally deadly. Rifles fired quickly and accurately. The Gatling gun, first used in the American Civil War, could fire several rounds of ammunition a minute, but the machine gun, invented in 1884 by Hiram Stevens Maxim (1840–1916), had proven superior during the British conquest of Africa. Bullets were fed into this new weapon by a belt that contained thousands of rounds of ammunition. Maxim manufactured and sold his machine gun to the leading nations of the world, and it became the major weapon of World War I. The Germans developed efficient, long-range cannon that could effectively bombard the enemy from a great distance behind the front lines. The most famous cannon of World War I, known as "Big Bertha," was produced by the Krupp munitions works, the chief German arms supplier. It was able to hurl 1-ton shells a distance of more than 15 kilometers (9 miles).

NAVAL TECHNOLOGY AND POWER

Improvements in maritime technology affected the war at sea. By the end of the nineteenth century, German efforts to build a navy competitive with that of Great Britain resulted in a race to construct new fleets of heavily armoured and heavily armed battleships. In 1914 Britain and its allies were still ahead in the naval race. When Britain declared a blockade of enemy territory, it had the naval means to make the blockade effective. This tactic forced the Germans to retaliate, which they did by using submarines, thus beginning a new chapter in the history of naval warfare. The development of the submarine from a short-range vessel for coastal protection to an ocean-going vessel enabled Germany to retaliate against the British blockade with terrible effectiveness. It also extended the war across the world's oceans.

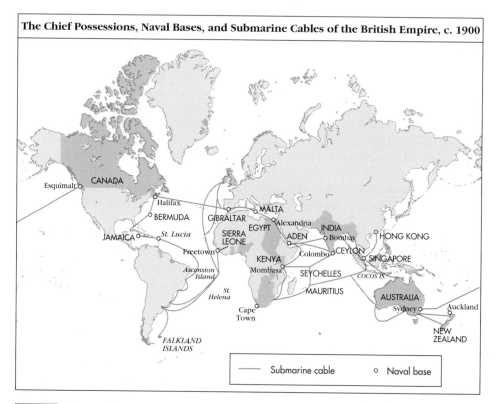

The Chief Possessions, Naval Bases, and Submarine Cables of the British Empire, c. 1900

— Submarine cable   ○ Naval base

MAP 18.1 The World Linked by British Naval Power and Technology, ca. 1900

The Germans declared the British Isles a "war zone" in which any Allied merchant ship might be sunk by torpedoes fired from a submarine or U-boat. German U-boats began to sink British ships almost daily, including the giant liner *Lusitania* with a loss of nearly 1200 people, many of whom were Americans and other neutrals. Though such actions failed to stop the flow of Allied commerce, they inflamed neutral opinion against the Central Powers.

AMERICA ENTERS THE WAR

After the sinking of the *Lusitania*, strong protests, especially from the Americans, forced the Germans to modify their U-boat campaign until January 1917, when they announced the resumption of unrestricted submarine warfare. This decision, and the fact that American financiers and industries wanted to protect the $1.5 billion they had advanced to the Allies, brought the United States into the war on the Allied side (April 6, 1917). America's entry into the war came shortly after the revolution that broke out in Russia (February 23, 1917) put an end to effective Russian participation in the war.

Faced with the withdrawal of Russia and the fact that it would take the United States considerable time to train and transport large forces to Europe, the Germans undertook new offensives against the Allies. But the failure of German food supplies, the strain on finances, and the withdrawal of Germany's allies from the war signaled its end. The collapse of the Ottoman Empire, a result of Arab rebellion and British intervention, had begun as early as September 1917, and the Austro-Hungarian Empire, faced with revolts among its many subject peoples and the failure of its armies, capitulated on November 4, 1918. The Germans surrendered on November 10, and firing along the western front ceased the next day.

THE WAR AT HOME

World War I was also fought by people not at the front. Since those who did fight were citizen soldiers, their mobilization had a major impact on the society of the countries engaged in combat. Those left behind suffered shortages and famines. As the productive forces of industrialized societies were turned to military goals, states seized greater control over economic and social activity. Family life was disrupted for more than four years; women assumed the charge of households and children, whose fathers were at war, were raised by mothers and grandparents. The revisioning of new social and economic roles did not stop there.

Women at War The occasion of global war provided opportunities for women around the world to challenge gender roles. Women took over customarily male jobs so that men could go to the battle fronts. Factories employed women, and their work in the munitions industry was a major contribution to the war effort. Women also assumed a variety of service and administrative jobs in transportation, worked in offices, and entered teaching and government to lead more public lives.

In Russia a "battalion of death" made up exclusively of women (80 percent of whom were killed) was sent to the front in 1917. Women also served in combat as nurses and ambulance drivers for military hospitals. A generation of young women remained unmarried or were widowed, childless, or single parents. The contributions of women to the war efforts led some postwar societies to reconsider their roles. In Great Britain, where a massive women's suffrage movement in the decade before 1914 had failed to get women the right to vote, women over the age of 30 were given the right to vote in 1919. In the United States, President Woodrow Wilson (in office 1913–1921) recommended that women be enfranchised as a war measure.

Opposition to the War Many women did not support the war. Between 1890 and 1920 a ▨▨▨▨▨▨▨▨▨▨▨ woman's rights movement had spearheaded a wave of political activism. Womanhood was no longer defined solely as the ideal of motherhood in the context of private, family-oriented domesticity. Politicized women supported progressive causes that were critical of the plight of urban and rural families and fought for social reform, economic justice, and international peace.

PACIFISM

Opposition to war was not new in the twentieth century. From their origins in the seventeenth century, people of the Quaker religion were committed to peace. Secular peace groups were established in New York and London in the aftermath of the Napoleonic Wars. But it was the end of the nineteenth century that saw the formation of a viable peace movement. Its political ideology was broad based, including progressive reformists, anarchists, and socialists, and its members were mostly women, many of whom worked through the American Union Against Militarism (AUAM), a lobbying group that attempted to keep America out of the war. The link between growing pressure for women's rights and the peace movement was

FIGURE 18.2 Women March Down Fifth Avenue, New York City, in an International Protest Against the War, 1915

SOURCE: Brown Brothers.

symbolized in the organization of a Women's Peace Party in January 1915 in Washington, D.C., led by suffragists and social reformers such as Jane Addams.

Delegates from the Women's Peace Party joined European women at an international conference in The Hague in April 1915. Though vilified by the press and called "hysterical women" by Theodore Roosevelt, the Women's Peace Party persisted. The traumas of World War I gained support for the peace movement, and in 1919 the International League for Peace and Freedom was founded to promote the goals of the 1915 International Women's Congress. At the end of the war, one of the leading suffragists, Carrie Chapman Catt, established the National Conference on the Cause and Cure of War.

■

PEACEMAKING

Two contradictory conceptions of peacemaking dominated the negotiations in Paris that ended World War I. One was the traditional idea that "to the victor belongs the spoils," the assumption that a defeated state would have to sacrifice territory and wealth to the victor. Contrary to this in spirit and content was the peace envisaged by President Woodrow Wilson, a "peace without victors or vanquished." In presenting his war aims in January 1918, Wilson proclaimed that the war was being fought "to make the world safe for democracy," and that it would be a war to end all wars if the self-determination of all major nationalities were the basis for peace. Wilson's ideal of self-determination of peoples as a means for achieving lasting peace and democracy ran counter to the realities of postwar Europe where the claims of victors had to be satisfied along with those of new nations created out of the disintegrating Austrian, Russian, and Ottoman empires.

Wilson believed that peoples, granted national and democratic rights, would never again support militaristic leaders who would lead them to war. Wilson embodied these ideas in his Fourteen Points, which concluded with a proposal for a League of Nations, "a general association of nations must be formed under specific covenants for the purpose of affording mutual guarantees of political independence and territorial integrity to great and small states alike," a world organization that would guarantee peace. Wilson's idealism appealed to ally and foe alike and was assumed by the Germans to be the basis on which the peace would be created.

The peace negotiations with the Central Powers were carried on in various suburbs of Paris, including Versailles, where the treaty with Germany was drawn up. The sessions were dominated, but not controlled, by the American delegation; Wilson's influence was great, for he was at the peak of his popularity in Europe, and all politicians recognized that economic aid from the United States was essential for postwar recovery. In the hard work of peace negotiations, however, the American role was limited by the determination of the European victors that the peace should, after all, be a victor's peace. Clashes at the conference, reflecting national interests and patriotic fervor heightened by four destructive years of war, were resolved in a peace treaty that was harsh and vindictive.

The Versailles Treaty The Versailles treaty with Germany inflicted significant territorial and ▓▓▓▓▓▓▓▓▓▓▓▓▓▓▓ material losses on Germany. Germany was forced to dismantle its armed forces, to surrender most of its merchant fleet, and to agree to extensive reparations, compensation for economic damages done by Germany to the Allies during the war. Such indemnities, with which all the defeated powers were saddled, reflected a moral assumption of the Central Powers' war guilt, a direct statement of which German negotiators were forced to acknowledge when they signed the Treaty of Versailles (June 28, 1919). The Versailles treaty with Germany was the model for other treaties made with Germany's allies, beginning with the Treaty of St. Germain with Austria (September 10, 1919) and concluding with the Treaty of Sevres with Turkey (August 10, 1920).

The League of Nations Wilson's firm belief that an association of nations would assure world peace made him adamantly determined that each peace treaty should contain a covenant of the League of Nations that would allow admittance of the defeated country to the world assembly. The League of Nations was, in fact, the chief innovation of the peacemaking in Paris. The British and French delegations tended to view Wilson's ideal skeptically. But skepticism did not preclude acceptance, and the League of Nations was the first attempt in history to institute a formal rule of law among all nations.

In addition to transformations of the European political map and international relations, World War I also hastened the demise of two empires on the fringes of Europe and the creation of two new nation states. The Russian Empire fell, and the Bolsheviks led a war-weary Russian people to revolution. As the Ottoman Empire weakened and disintegrated in the aftermath of World War I, a new leader rose and found modern Turkey.

■

THE RUSSIAN REVOLUTION

As industrialization accelerated in late-nineteenth-century Russia, reformist and radical revolutionary groups proliferated and grew stronger. Several groups gained prominence: the Social Democrats (SD), who enlisted urban workers nursed on Marxism (their 1903 split into Bolsheviks and Mensheviks did not diminish their importance); the Social Revolutionaries (SR), who represented the hopes and concerns of the rural, agrarian population; and the less radical Constitutional Democrats (Cadets), who represented Western-style parliamentary government. The growth of urbanism and heavy industry and a great advance in railroad building (the trans-Siberian railroad was built between 1891 and 1904) signaled modernization, the rapid pace of which made cities like St. Petersburg and Moscow seedbeds for revolutionary movements seeking radical change.

THE 1905 REVOLUTION

During the winter of 1904–1905, an unsuccessful war with Japan over domination of Manchuria in Northeast China intensified internal unrest and made clear the weakness of autocratic rule under Czar Nicholas II (r. 1894–1917). On Sunday, January 22, 1905, a large crowd gathered before the Winter Palace in St. Petersburg to petition the czar for a national assembly, civil liberties, and labor reforms. Troops fired into the crowd, killing and wounding hundreds. "Bloody Sunday" set off the next episode in an emerging Russian revolutionary tradition, an epidemic of strikes and protests accompanied by considerable violence and disorder. Sailors mutinied and seized the battleship *Potemkin*, and in October a general strike paralyzed the country.

Nicholas II found it expedient to promise far-reaching reforms, which implied a transformation of the autocracy. His October Manifesto called for a legislative body, a Duma, elected by a broad franchise and other popular reforms, but by 1906 this "revolution" had run its course. The autocracy began to rally its strength to resist effective implementation of the promised reforms. The spirit, if not the letter, of the October Manifesto was violated, and effective resolution of the tension between change and tradition, between reform and reaction, had not been achieved. When World War I came, problems had been eased but not resolved and major crises soon arose.

WORLD WAR I AND THE BOLSHEVIK REVOLUTION

During World War I Russia literally began to break down: military defeats went hand in glove with the breakdown of transportation, and shortage and need became endemic. As in the west, Russian women began to take over jobs in the workplace that had been dominated by men before the war. During 1916 the power to resist the Germans and the ability to deal with mounting domestic problems had for all purposes collapsed.

Women and the Revolution   By the beginning of 1917, more women than men worked; women faced persistent hunger and great hardships, often working thirteen-hour days in gloomy and unsafe conditions alongside their children. On March 8, 1917, more than 7000 women workers went on strike in the city of Petrograd in acknowl-

FIGURE 18.3 *Lenin Speaking,* Painting by the Russian artist I.A. Serebryany.

SOURCE: Sovfoto/Eastfoto.

edgement of International Women's Day, an event initiated in the United States. The protesters took to the streets, where they were joined by tens of thousands of other workers by the end of the day, all of whom were calling for bread and peace and an end to the czardom. Even the czar's soldiers mutinied, rather than confront the wives and sisters of fellow soldiers away at the front. Czar Nicholas, faced with domestic discontent, strikes, and demonstrations, and with the fact that the army would not support him, was forced to abdicate. A provisional government was set up by leaders of the Duma in conjunction with representatives of worker groups in St. Petersburg.

Dual Power The provisional government essentially aimed to realize the promises of the 1905 revolution, hoping to evolve the traditional autocracy into a constitutional parliamentary state; it also determined to continue Russia's participation in the war. Neither hope was fulfilled. The failure of the war effort and the expanding needs and demands of the peasants and the organized urban, industrial working class frustrated the provisional government, which was unable to provide the most basic needs of the Russian people: peace, bread, and land. The government's failure played directly into the hands of the most disciplined and organized radical group, the Bolshevik faction of the SD party. Bolsheviks took control of worker and soldier-sailor organizations (soviets) and adopted the slogan "Peace, Bread, and Land."

Lenin, Trotsky, and the Bolsheviks In Vladimir Lenin (1870–1924) and Leon Trotsky (1879–1940), the Bolsheviks found formidable leaders. On November 7, 1917, the Bolsheviks struck, and the provisional government fell. Insofar as possible, the promise made to the women and their families, of bread, land, and peace, was rapidly made good. On November 8 land was nationalized and given to the peasants; on November 29 control of factories passed to workers; on December 15 a truce was signed with the Germans, leading to the Peace of Brest-Litovsk in March 1918. Bread proved more difficult to provide.

COMMUNISM IN RUSSIA

The Bolsheviks, whose ideology was based on the ideas of Karl Marx, replaced the parliamentary state that the provisional government had established after the fall of the monarchy in 1905 with their own revolutionary state in 1917. After the Bolshevik Revolution of 1917 in Russia, the disruptions of war and revolution played havoc with the economy and productivity. A civil war between the Bolsheviks and their opponents, during which the czar and his family were killed, along with intervention by Russia's wartime allies—in 1918 Great Britain, France, the United States, Japan, and ten other nations sent trops to Russia in the effort to keep Russia in the war and protect Allied supplies there. Some Allied troops remained until 1922—further disrupting Bolshevik efforts, but justifying increased centralization and control.

The New Economic Policy By 1921 efforts to create a new communist society seemed to fail. The pragmatic Lenin saw the necessity to abandon "War Communism," a program for rapidly establishing a communist society in Russia, and reverted to a compromise New Economic Policy, "one step backwards in order to take two steps forward," as he described it. This policy, which allowed peasants to keep land, small private business to continue, and prewar managers to run factories, continued in force until 1929, when the first of an ongoing series of five-year plans signaled a return to the aggressive pursuit of a revolutionary communist society.

Stalin Following Lenin's death in 1924, a power struggle ensued between the revolutionary ▬▬▬▬ Leon Trotsky and Joseph Stalin (1879–1953), the secretary-general of the Bolshevik Party. Stalin emerged supreme, and his triumph revealed several things about the changes that had occurred in Russia. First, it fixed the source of authority in the Bolshevik party infrastructure: control of the party was necessary for control of the nation. The monolithic exercise of power by the Communist Party in the Soviet Union was comparable to the practices of all totalitarian (total power concentrated in the state) systems that appeared in the first half of the twentieth century. Each system acknowledged liberal ideals and procedures—constitutions promised elections and legislative bodies—but proved a facade for the reality of concentrated political power.

Second, the leaders of the Bolshevik Revolution clearly intended it to be an economic as well as a political reshaping of Russian society. Lenin's New Economic Policy relaxed the government control of the economy, but in 1928 Stalin resumed the Bolshevik plan for using rigid government regulation and supervision with the first of a series of five-year plans. These plans aimed at the rapid industrialization and the restructuring of Russian agriculture; it was expected that agricultural growth would support investment in industry. The five-year plans, which also aimed to improve literacy, health, and the standard of living, achieved many of their goals. Though heavy industry expanded, by the mid-1930s it was increasingly devoted to military production, and the promise of more and better consumer goods was not realized. The collectivization of agriculture not only failed to achieve its economic goals but also caused considerable social disruption.

The Reforms Collectivization, the consolidation of small private farms into collectives where ▬▬▬▬▬▬▬▬ farmers would labor together on commonly owned lands, resulted in the nearly complete destruction of the *kulaks*, the better off pesants. Many *kulaks* slaughtered their own livestock and destroyed agricultural equipment rather than join a collective. *Kulaks* who resisted collectivization were arrrested and executed or sent off to labor camps (*gulags*) in Siberia or northern Russia, where many died.

Under Stalin the goals of the Russian Revolution became less ideological and more brutally pragmatic, less interested in international socialist solidarity and more concerned with Russian nation interests. During the 1930's Stalin created a climate of terror in a campaign of purges carried out by his secret police. Millons were sent to labor camps, and many were put on trial on trumped-up charges of treason, which could stem from something as petty as the jealousy of a coworker. This human tragedy of huge proportion extended the turmoil and distress of wartime into peacetime. At the same time, by the end of the 1930s the Soviet Union was the third-largest industrial economy in the world, and a powerful Russian nationalism was resurgent.

■

THE OTTOMAN EMPIRE AND MODERN TURKEY

Threats to the Ottoman Empire by Britain, France, and Russia led to the signing of a treaty of alliance with Germany in August 1914. The Ottoman Empire thus joined the camp of the Central Powers against the alliance of Britain, France, and Russia. The major war aims of the Ottoman government were the Turkification of the empire, an end to Western intervention, reconquest of territories lost to members of the Entente, and liberation of the Turkish areas of the Caucasus and Central Asia that had been conquered by Russia.

These grandiose goals were unrealistic from the beginning. The Ottoman Empire was economically and militarily weak, and division among its many ethnic elements was growing. Turks and Arabs each constituted about 10 million of its 25 million inhabitants. The remaining 5 million were Kurds, Greeks, Armenians, and others. The Greeks and Armenians were already infected with nationalist ideas, and the Arabs were beginning to succumb to them as well. When hostilities opened in November 1914, the government could only count on the Turks as being absolutely dependable.

In 1916, with the encouragement of the British, the Arabs in the Hejaz of western Arabia revolted. Their objective was to create an Arab state in Arabia and the Arabic-speaking regions of the Ottoman Empire lying between the Mediterranean and Iran. The British also made promises to the Zionists, Jewish nationalists in the West who hoped to create their own state in Palestine. The Zionists wanted the Entente to recognize Palestine as a Jewish commonwealth if the Ottoman Empire were defeated.

Palestine and the Balfour Declaration In 1917 two events occurred that proved critical to the Zionist cause: the Bolshevik Revolution in Russia and America's entry into the war. Because Jews were prominent in the revolution in Russia, the British believed that it was essential to obtain their good will in order to keep Russia in the war. At the same time London believed that the support of American Zionists was important for gaining the full cooperation of the United States in the conflict. Therefore, on November 2, 1917, the British foreign secretary, Lord Balfour, announced that his government favored the establishment of a national home for Jews in Palestine. Earlier promises to the Arabs that Palestine, then overwhelmingly an Arab region, would be included in a future Arab state were downplayed. This set the stage for a struggle over Palestine between the Zionists and the Arabs, above all Palestinian Arabs, which has lasted to the present day.

Despite some military successes, the Ottoman Empire could not hold out against the Allies; incompetent leadership in the Turkish government and the nationalst insurrection of many Arabs contributed to its collapse. On October 31, 1918, the Ottomans and the British signed an armistice ending hostilities in West Asia. The Allies took control of Istanbul and occupied parts of Anatolia, Palestine, Syria, and Iraq.

THE DISMEMBERMENT OF THE OTTOMAN EMPIRE

In addition to the promises made by the British to the Arabs and Zionists, a number of secret agreements had been reached during the war among the British, French, Russians, Italians, and Greeks for a division of the spoils if the Ottoman Empire were defeated. The United States was not a party to these secret agreements; in Russia the Bolsheviks, after they came to power and took that country out of the war, denounced them. Thus when the victors met at Versailles in 1919, it was the British, French, Italians, Greeks, Zionists, Arabs, Armenians, Kurds, and other ethnic groups who submitted claims.

All Arab regions were detached from the Ottoman Empire. The Hejaz in western Arabia became independent, while the fate of Palestine, Syria, Iraq, and the Gulf was to be decided later by Britain and France. Western Thrace and certain Aegean islands were given to Greece.

The Dodecanese, including Rhodes, were given to Italy. An independent Armenian state in the Caucasus was recognized. The Kurdish area of eastern Anatolia was given autonomy. The straits were internationalized and demilitarized. Turkish finances were to be controlled by Britain, France, and Italy. Special extraterritorial commercial and judicial concessions for Europeans, known as "capitulations" and which dated from before the war, were to be maintained, and the rights and privileges of all minorities had to be respected.

The Allies, who took control of the Ottoman capital of Istanbul on November 13, 1918, reduced Ottoman territory to the city and its environs, along with a stump of Anatolia. Soon even that was threatened. It became apparent that the sultan, Mehmet VI (r. 1918-1922), and his government were only puppets and that the Allies would carve up Anatolia when they agreed on how it should be done. On May 15, 1919, Greek troops had landed at Smyrna (modern Izmir) on the Aegean coast of Anatolia as part of the occupation army. In June 1920, with the approval of the British and the French, Greece launched an offensive into Anatolia to take possession of what it had been awarded by the Paris Peace Conference. On August 10, 1920, the Treaty of Sevres, the peace treaty between the Allies and the Ottoman Empire, was concluded. It thoroughly humiliated the Ottoman Empire and then effectively dissolved it. Organized Turkish resistance soon found a leader in the person of Mustafa Kemal (1881–1938), a general in the Ottoman army who had earlier been associated with the reformist Young Turk movement against the autocratic rule of the Ottomans.

ATATURK AND MODERN TURKEY

Shortly after the Greeks landed at Smyrna, Kemal, who had been assigned to superivse demobilization of the former Ottoman army on the Black Sea, resigned his commission, took command of what remained of the army, and called upon all patriotic Turks to defend their homeland. A magnetic personality and organizing genius, Kemal succeeded in rallying his countrymen, to whom the idea of becoming subject to Greece was especially distasteful. Several congresses were held in eastern Anatolia and laid the foundation for the Turkish national movement. It sought to transform all of Anatolia and Istanbul into a Turkish state.

In April 1920 the first Grand National Assembly was held in Ankara. It challenged the authority of the Ottoman government and subsequently rejected the Treaty of Sevres. Then, making brilliant use of military forces and diplomacy (taking advantage of the more pressing problems the Allies had elsewhere and their mutual suspicions), Kemal drove out the occupiers of Anatolia one by one. The last to go were the Greeks, against whom Kemal turned his full attention in August 1921 when they threatened Ankara.

A year later, after a dazzling campaign, the Turkish army stood on the shore of the Aegean. Immediately afterward, the Grand National Assembly proclaimed the abolition of the sultanate, which had lost virtually all popular support and authority. In effect, the assembly announced the end of the Ottoman Empire. The last sultan fled on a British ship. On July 24, 1923, Greece and the Ankara government signed the Treaty of Lausanne, effectively providing international recognition for the new nation state of Turkey. The treaty recognized the integrity of the ethnic Turkey more or less within its present borders. It instituted a compulsory exchange of the minority Greek and Turkish populations between the two states and abolished European control of finances and the capitulations.

In October 1923 the Grand National Assembly proclaimed the Turkish Republic and elected Kemal its first president. It then adopted a remarkable series of measures aimed at changing Turkey into a modern Western country. Kemal, who acquired the honorific title "Ataturk" (Father Turk), and the Turkish nationalists believed that modernization was essental for their country's survival and prosperity. They demanded that Turkey be coequal with the leading European states in almost every respect.

The Secularization of Turkey   The Grand National Assembly took many actions concerning religion: it abolished the caliphate (the religious leadership of the Muslim world that had generally been appropriated by later Ottoman sultans); replaced religious courts with civil courts and civil law based on European models; disbanded the religious brotherhoods; abolished the fez (male headgear) and veil for women, which were symbols of religious conservatism; replaced the Muslim calendar with the European calendar; and officially disestablished Islam as the state religion. Turkey became the first, and is still the only, secular Muslim state.

Other measures were equally far-reaching. The Latin alphabet replaced the Arabic alphabet. Polygamy was abolished, and women were given the right to vote and hold all public offices and professions in the country. A system of public schools and universities was established. Even the Western youth organization, the Boy Scouts, was introduced. Foreign-owned railways were bought out and expanded. Industrialization was stressed, and a balance was struck between private enterprise and a few state monopolies. European and American experts were invited to give advice in a large number of enterprises, such as mechanized industry and transportation.

FIGURE 18.4   **Ataturk Arriving in Istanbul from Ankara**

Both Ataturk and his entourage are wearing Western attire and the women are unveiled, showing Ataturk's commitment to Westernize Turkey.

SOURCE: Hulton Getty/Tony Stone Images.

From 1923 until his death in 1938, Ataturk ruled Turkey as a kind of benevolent dictator through a one-party government. The lack of organized political opposition made it easier for him and his nationalist supporters to implement their fairly radical program of Westernization. Though conservative elements and others expressed their opposition from time to time in civil disturbances, Westernization which could be traced back to Selim III in the late eighteenth century, finally took firm root under Ataturk.

■

THE ARAB WORLD

At the end of World War I, the independence of the Hejaz, ruled by Sharif Hussein of Mecca, leader of the Hashimi dynasty that has ruled the region for several centuries under the Ottomans, was recognized. However, Hussein had rivals elsewhere in the peninsula, above all the Saudi dynasty in the central and northeastern part of the country. Rooted in a puritanical Muslim reformist movement of the eighteenth century popularly called the "Wahhabiyah", the dynasty's leader, Abd al-Aziz, like Hussein, became allied with Britain during the war. Afterward he united all of northern and central Arabia. In 1924 Abd al-Aziz defeated Hussein and in 1930 was proclaimed king of a new state, Saudi Arabia. Yemen alone remained independent while all of Arabia's southern and Persian Gulf coastal lands became British protectorates.

For Europe, most of West Asia, and the rest of the world, the Arabian Peninsula, on the whole a vast and arid land with few inhabitants, was of little consequence except for the holy cities of Mecca and Medina, the focal points of the Muslim world. Only Britain, always concerned for its communication with India and anxious to preserve its Gulf oil monopoly, paid any attention to it and thus became the dominant outside power there. However, beginning in the 1930s, American oil companies obtained concessions, first in Bahrain and then in Saudi Arabia, successfully challenging Britain's position. These concessions were a harbinger of things to come.

SYRIA AND PALESTINE

The people to the north of Arabia attracted more immediate interest. With no significant army of their own and their territory effectively occupied by the British after 1918, people in this region found themselves very much at the mercy of the great powers, that is, Britain and France. In May 1919 President Woodrow Wilson sent a delegation, the King Crane Commission, to Syria and Palestine to determine the wishes of their people. The commission also met with representatives of Iraq. They were unanimous in their desire for independence and were firmly opposed to Zionist colonization of Palestine. The commission's report was ignored at Versailles because it conflicted with the secret wartime agreements and because Wilson returned to the United States and did not push it.

Subsequently, on April 24, 1920, the Peace Conference met at San Remo in Italy and assigned to Britain and France "mandates"—a form of temporary administration ostensibly leading to independence—over the occupied Arab provinces of the defeated Ottoman Empire. Britain was given Palestine (including Jordan) and Iraq. France received Syria. Wilson's principle of self-determination was rejected. Britain and France then set about establishing the borders of their mandates and encouraging cooperative elements among their inhabitants.

Historically, and to some degree culturally and politically, this region fell into two zones—Syria to the west and Iraq to the east. Palestine was detached from Syria to allow Britain to fulfill its promise to the Zionists, the mandate for Palestine included in the Balfour Declaration. In 1928 Britain detached Jordan from Palestine and made it a separate monarchy. One reason for this action was strategic: to link Britain's de facto protectorate of Egypt with its new mandate, Iraq. The British also imposed a monarchy on Iraq. The kings of Jordan and Iraq were, in fact, brothers, sons of Sharif Hussein. In what remained of Syria, the French carved Lebanon out of its west coast in 1936 to create a separate state for Christian Arabs, although they were barely a majority in this enclave.

The mandates had the effect of denying the nationalist aspirations of their inhabitants. At the same time these agreements opened Palestine to large-scale colonization by Zionist immigrants whose goal was to create a Jewish state in that territory. From the beginning of the mandates, the Arabs struggled for independence and tried to resist Zionism. Iraq became independent in 1932, Lebanon and Syria in 1945, Jordan in 1946. In Egypt, which had become independent in 1922, Britain retained special rights, including "the security of communications for the British Empire in Egypt," that is, the Suez Canal.

Arab independence only intensified opposition to the Zionist state in Palestine. In 1948, after torturous negotiations over the fate of Palestine, Britain withdrew from that region in exasperation at trying to reconcile Zionist and Arab goals. The Zionists, benefiting from Western support and concern for the fate of the Jews following the Holocaust and a major influx of European refugees, especially women and children, immediately went to war against Arab forces from Palestine, Syria, Jordan, and Egypt, which were intent upon regaining Arab control of Palestine, defeated them, and proclaimed the state of Israel.

■

IRAN

Iran was neutral during World War I, but Russian and British troops occupied the country, reflecting pre–World War I imperialist struggles over Iran between Russia and Britain. The central government went bankrupt and lost its authority over the provinces. After the Bolsheviks seized power in Russia, they attempted to establish a Soviet republic in the Russian sphere of northern Iran, but the plan quickly failed and the Russians left the country in 1921. The British who faced enormous opposition withdrew in the same year. In 1921 a military coup led by the resolutely anti-British Colonel Reza Khan took over the weakened government of the shah. In 1925 the Qajar dynasty that had ruled Iran since the eighteenth century was officially ended, and Reza Khan assumed the throne, founding the Pahlavi dynasty.

Like Ataturk, Reza Shah, as he was now entitled, was determined to bring his country into the modern world. He began a program of Westernization and centralization in which many Islamic institutions were abolished or changed. For example, he introduced civil law codes and public education (for both sexes). Faced with a far less homogeneous population, however, Reza Shah was not as radical as Ataturk and did not try to create a secular state, much less a republic. The religious opposition was too strong. On the other hand, the new shah used oil royalties and increased taxes to build railroads, improve communications, and begin some industrialization.

The shah essentially carried out these reforms by decree and used parliament to rubber-stamp his decisions. Increasingly despotic, Reza Shah tried to change Iran from the top without winning the confidence and full support of the people. The Ottoman Empire had actually buffered Iran from intense, direct, and continuous European influence for centuries. Westernization was thus a greater shock to Iran than it was to the Ottoman Empire because previous exposure to European culture and institutions had been quite limited and of short duration. The tensions created by rapid Westernization imposed from the top would eventually topple the rule of Reza Shah (see Chapter 19).

■
THE WORLD BETWEEN TWO WARS

The two decades between the Paris peace treaties that ended World War I and the outbreak of World War II (1919–1939) were years of growing tension and uncertainty that undermined domestic order nearly everywhere and contributed greatly to the collapse of international cooperation and peace that the League of Nations had attempted to ensure. The failure of hopes and expectations at home and abroad produced among Europeans a general sense of disillusionment and despair that had many roots, some of them unique to individual nations and some common to all. Basic to the common problems of the interwar decades were political problems resulting from the failure of the peacemaking after World War I and economic problems that resulted from the Great Depression that gripped the capitalist world in 1929.

THE GLOBAL ECONOMY AND THE GREAT DEPRESSION

In no arena of interaction was global interdependence more apparent than in economic relations. The construction of an interdependent capitalist world economy under the domination of Europe, in progress since the sixteenth century, meant that coffee growers in Brazil, wheat farmers in the United States, sugar producers in Java, and silkworm cultivators in China were knit together by their common dependence on supply and demand determined by the world market in commodities. This economic system was a complex and interlocking mechanism, with banking, stockholding, and corporate direction increasingly global and interdependent. A shift in almost any part of it could have a powerful impact on the entire system. The smooth operation of the world market depended on the mutual confidence in the system by investors and on the continuity of mutual exchange.

In the aftermath of World War I, a boom of prosperity from 1924 to 1929 was fueled by international trade, new building construction, and new industries. The automobile became an article of mass production after the war. Widespread use of the automobile increased demand for oil, steel, rubber, and electrical equipment, along with the rebuilding of roads. All this activity stimulated new secondary professions such as mechanics. Other kinds of consumer goods such as radios were produced for a mass market. But unions remained weak, salaries and wages did not keep pace with profits and dividends, and mass buying power fell behind production.

It was in the agricultural sector, though, that problems were most severe. The overproduction of wheat in the mid-1920s caused by mechanization, the expansion and recovery of arable lands for growing wheat, and other improvements led to a collapse in the world market for wheat, demand for which was relatively inelastic since people could eat only so much bread. In 1930 the price of a bushel of wheat, calculated in the world market standard of gold, fell to its lowest price in 400 years. The prices for such commodities as cotton, corn, coffee, cocoa, and sugar similarly collapsed, causing great distress to farmers all over the world whose livelihoods depended on these crops.

The Illusion of Economic Power   The Great Depression of 1929 ended several years of unprecedented boom in Western capitalism. By the mid-1920s, unregulated investment resulted in massive speculation, "playing the market" by buying stocks largely on credit in hopes of quick resale at huge profits. Buyers paid only a fraction of the cost in cash and borrowed the balance (sometimes even the cash payment as well) from lending banks. Similarly, consumer goods—automobiles, refrigerators, radios—were in increasing demand because they too could be financed on borrowed money.

Eventually, when shrewd investors began to sell their holdings in the fear that the expanding market might contract, the bubble burst. The doubts of investors became fact: declining confidence led to dropping stock values and losses. Those who borrowed from banks were unable to repay loans. Major financial institutions, like the Credit Anstalt of Vienna, were unable to collect their investments and failed. The trend reached catastrophic proportions with the crash of the New York Stock Exchange in October 1929. Thousands of American and foreign banks closed their doors. Capital was no longer available for investment or borrowing; market demand slowed, industrial production declined, and factories closed, leaving millions unemployed and penniless.

DAILY LIVES

SPRING SILKWORMS

In his novella *Spring Silkworms* (1932), the writer Mao Dun (pen name of She Dehong, b. 1896) evocatively described the plight of Chinese peasants whose economic dependence on the cultivation of silkworms tied their livelihood to world market forces well beyond their grasp and control:

> Old Tung Pao had heard Young Master Chen—son of the Master Chen who lived in town—say that Shanghai was seething with unrest, that all the silk weaving factories had closed their doors, that the silk filatures here probably wouldn't open either. But he couldn't believe it. He had been through many periods of turmoil and srife in his sixty years, yet he had never seen a time when the shiny green mulberry leaves had been allowed to winter on the branches and become fodder for the sheep. Of course if the silkworm eggs shouldn't ripen, that would be different. . .From the time foreign goods—cambric, cloth, oil—appeared in the market town, from the time the foreign river boats increased on the canal, what he produced brought a lower price in the market every day, while what he had to buy became more and more expensive. . .

Last year something had happened that made him almost sick with fury: Only the cocoons spun by the foreign strain silkworms could be sold at a decent price.

Though the silkworms that year did ripen, and everyone in Old Tung Pao's village worked furiously to make that happen, the silkworms they raised were considered inferior to foreign ones, and so they actually lost money they invested in feeding and cultivating the silkworms:

> Because they raised a crop of spring silkworms, the people in Old Tung Pao's village got deeper and deeper into debt. Old Tung Pao's family raised five trays and gathered a splendid harvest of cocoons. Yet they ended up owing another thirty silver dollars and losing their mortgaged mulberry trees—to say nothing of suffering a month of hunger and sleepless nights in vain!*

*Patricia B. Ebrey, ed., *Chinese Civilization and Society: A Sourcebook* (New York: Macmillan, Free Press, 1981), pp. 310–11; 320.

The global repercussions of this financial collapse were devastating. The export of American capital once important to investment in foreign enterprises came to a halt, the foundations of the postwar economic recovery in Germany crumbled, and the effects of this economic calamity extended throughout Europe. Between 1929 and 1932, as investments in business dried up, world production was estimated to have dropped by more than one-third, and international trade fell by two-thirds. Shortages were quickly felt in markets around the world, including those in African, Caribbean, and Asian colonies.

CULTURAL VOICES DURING THE INTERWAR YEARS

Popular music and literature during the 1930s registered the misery and confusion that resulted from hard times. Writing in China in the 1930s, Mao Dun had expressed the plight of rural peoples at the mercy of the uncaring world economy. In the British Caribbean colony of Trinidad, the 1930s context of urban hunger, unemployment, worker militancy, and social upheaval found expression in the island's musical form known as calypso. The lyrics of songs like "Depression" (1938), with its humorous facade and dark undertones, suggest the spirit of the times:

> Work, work, you gone and leave me
> Why did you treat me so?
> Once we were married but now, of course,
> It seems as if me and you divorce.

West Indian men unable to support their families felt the impact inside their households, in marriages, and from the perspective of relationships, where gender roles and expectations registered in the lyrics of contemporary calypsoes. The calypsonian who called himself Atilla the Hun blamed the social upheaval on cultural change in "No Comparison" (1938):

> All the old-fashioned girl asked of life
> Was to be help-mate, mother and wife
> But the modern girl thinks more of sport
> Cigarettes, high balls and the divorce court
> I don't know if the cause is the cinema
> Or the looseness of modern literature

Atilla's calypso from 1935 "Women Will Rule the World" also warned men to beware of the modern woman and suggested the calypsonian's perception of the relationship between work and male esteem:

> If women ever get the ascendancy
> They will show us no sympathy . . .
> And in the nights when they go out to roam
> We'll have to mind the baby at home

American writer John Steinbeck's twentieth-century classic novel *The Grapes of Wrath* told the poignant and powerful story of a family's struggle in the Depression years, as expressed through the genre of the long journey through hardship and labor. It was made into a popular film by John Ford in 1939, the same year that Charlie Chaplin starred in *The Great Dictator* and *The Wizard of Oz* delighted audiences with its fantasy world above the harsh landscape of rural America.

FIGURE 18.5 The Shacks of the Unemployed in Hooverville, Near Seattle, Washington, During the Depression (1933)

SOURCE: University of Washington Libraries, Special Collections Division, Seattle.

Cinema also pondered the altered power relationships of the interwar years. A film version of Remarque's *All Quiet on the Western Front* (1930) relived the psychological drama and great battlefields of World War I. The musical number "My Forgotten Man" from the film *Gold Diggers of 1933* was a passionate statement of Depression resentment. In *La Grande Illusion* (1937), French film director Jean Renoir considered the end of an era that the interwar years seemed to represent, the collapse of the old and uncertainty of the new through the subtle and complex social and psychological relationships that develop among a group of French officers who are imprisoned in a German fortress. The German productions *The Blue Angel*, 1930, and Bertold Brecht's *Three Penny Opera*, 1931, became two of the era's most famous films exploring war from the perspective of societies at peace, but experiencing social turmoil.

The Perspective of Crisis and the Search for Security   Given the widespread commitment to peace, the struggle for prosperity, and the reluctance to do anything more than revisit the drama of wartime on a distant moviescreen, how did the world return again to the brink of global warfare in 1939? Modest economic revival in many industrialized nations during the mid-1930s was due in part to the rearmament movement, which also adopted policies of economic nationalism in the form of high tariffs and other protectionist regulations in attempts to provide economic security for their citizens. One long-term impact of the Great Depression was to make nations reluctant to become dependent on international trade and to be subject to whims of the global market that were beyond the power of any individual nation to control. The worldwide economic crisis of 1929–1932 also had serious repercussions for international politics. The economies of both Germany and Japan were severely and negatively affected as the world economy disintegrated into fiercely competing national economic systems.

THE UNITED STATES BETWEEN THE WARS

The late entry of the United States into World War I was a reflection of the American reluctance to become involved in European affairs that was implicit in the Monroe Doctrine (1823), the ideological cornerstone of American policy since the early nineteenth century. As late as 1916 President Wilson had justified his bid for a second term on the grounds that he had kept the United States out of war.

After the war isolationist sentiments were rampant among members of Congress. Senator Warren Harding of Ohio, who succeeded Wilson as president, said in an attack on Wilson's plan for a League of Nations, that what the United States needed was "not submergence in internationality but sustainment in triumphant nationality." Such views, which lead to American rejection of the League of Nations, had their domestic component as well. Americans wanted to forget great ideals and crusades, to lay down their arms and be left alone.

The "Red Scare"   Postwar isolationist sentiments reached a hysterical peak in xenophobic attacks on foreigners known as the "red scare." Like peoples in all capitalist countries, Americans looked with fear at the success of the Bolsheviks in taking over Russia and communism became in popular (and in some official) minds a danger and the root of all problems. During the last month of World War I, Congress passed a law authorizing the arrest and deportation of any aliens who advocated revolution or belonged to a revolutionary organization. Efforts to deport aliens intensified once the war was over, and in January 1920 coordinated raids by government agents in thirty-three cities swept up anyone found in the offices of revolutionary organizations, alien or not. Artists and common folks alike were hunted down. Altogether more than 5000 people were arrested, of whom only 556 were deported. When the hysteria died down, steps were soon taken to prevent it from happening again.

American Foreign   United States involvement in foreign affairs during the 1920s reflected
Policy in the 1920s   the decline in American xenophobia. Though the United States refused
to join the League of Nations, it worked with its auxiliary bodies, such as the World Health Organization and the World Court, and it made several separate efforts to support the aims of the international body, particularly arms control. During 1921–1922, for example, the Washington Naval Conference reduced the size of major navies (and also established American naval parity with Great Britain). In 1928 Secretary of State Frank B. Kellogg, responding to a bid from the French prime minister, Aristide Briand, for a treaty outlawing war between the two countries, proposed instead a multilateral treaty by which all countries would renounce war as an instrument of policy. The Kellogg-Briand Treaty (offi-

cially the Pact of Paris) was more an expression of hope than an instrument of policy, as events ten years after its signing proved.

The Great Depression in the United States In October 1929 the crash of the stock market, which had advanced rapidly for two years as a result of excessive speculation, was a severe blow to American confidence and sense of security. The statistics of bank closures, business failures, and soaring unemployment told the story as the United States slid ever deeper into depression. When Franklin Roosevelt was elected president in 1932, national income had fallen by 50 percent since 1929 and 12 million workers were unemployed. Roosevelt had no coherent ideology or firm commitment, but he did have a pragmatic determination to end the depression by all possible means and as quickly as possible. What evolved was a program of recovery and reform called the New Deal, which was predicated on broadening the government's role in solving social and economic problems.

The New Deal Some of Roosevelt's first acts were aimed at stabilizing the banking system and currency. The next priority was relief for the unemployed and destitute. A federally funded Works Progress Administration (WPA) was set up to direct a program of public spending and construction to provide jobs for the unemployed; and a Civilian Conservation Corps was formed to employ young men at planting trees, building dams, and otherwise enhancing the country's natural resources. The Tennessee Valley Authority (TVA) was aimed at the erection of a series of dams in the Tennessee Valley both to control floods and to produce cheap electricity for manufacturing and lighting. The Bonneville Power Administration provided essentially the same services for the Pacific Northwest.

A major item of the New Deal was the federal Social Security Act (1935), designed to aid the unemployed, aged, disabled, and dependent, addressing needs that had been assumed by European governments since the end of the nineteenth century. The New Deal also addressed other needs affecting working people. Legislation was passed (1935) to guarantee and protect workers in their right to organize unions and bargain with employers. A minimum wage and a forty-hour work week were established and child labor prohibited (1938). Farm prices were stabilized and patterns of cultivation subjected to federal controls (1933).

New Deal Isolationism Throughout most of Roosevelt's first two terms (1932–1940), domestic problems occupied most of the government's attention. Events in Europe—where Hitler was coming to power and Germany began rearming—or in Asia—where Japan violated the territorial integrity of China by occupying Manchuria—were reacted to in a determinedly isolationist way, one that seemed justified when congressional investigations concluded that bankers and munitions makers had been responsible for American entry into World War I.

Between 1935 and 1937, Congress adopted neutrality legislation designed to insulate the United States from any future involvement in foreign wars. As the possibility of war became more and more obvious, Roosevelt had to find ways of guiding American foreign policy through the atmosphere and legislation of isolationism. Unable to abandon neutrality legislation overtly, Roosevelt developed such policies as Lend-Lease, by which the United States provided ships and military supplies to Britain in return for leases on British territories where American bases were built. In such ways he quietly began to prepare the United States for war while aiding those in Europe and Asia who engaged in trying to stop aggression.

EUROPE BETWEEN THE WARS

The struggle for the economic recovery of Europe took place between the pillars of hope and despair. The industrial "progress" of the century's early decades had provided the means to wage a brutal war. Yet industrial growth was a key to economic recovery and viewed by many as a necessary step in the search for security. The war had left behind a wave of destruction, debts, and economic hardship. Political fragmentation and abrupt changes of government plagued the nation states in Europe as each struggled to find solutions for recovery. Ultranationalist sentiments increased. International cooperation seemed even more elusive.

British Social Democracy British social democracy, which had begun so promisingly in the decade before 1914, was slowed down in the twentieth century by the two world wars and the economic depression that occurred between them. Following World War I, the increasing industrial progress of other nations, and even of states within the British Empire, caused serious problems for Great Britain. Japanese textiles successfully competed with British fabrics in Asia, and American goods were rapidly replacing British products in South America. The export of coal and industrial and transportation machinery, long a source of British wealth, declined rapidly. The result was that throughout the 1920s the British economy remained sluggish and unemployment was high: during the decade, as the economy ebbed and flowed, unemployment varied from 775,000 to 3 million. Unemployment was an acute social problem and put a severe fiscal strain on the state which, under the social insurance acts passed before World War I, was responsible for relief.

Matters grew worse following the Great Depression. As a result of the worldwide "economic blizzard," unemployment continued to rise while productivity and government revenues declined. The government was forced to take measures that seemed to some to dismantle the social welfare program. A 10 percent cut in unemployment insurance was enacted, and drastic cuts were made in the salaries for all government employees from cabinet ministers to policemen and school teachers.

After a century of free trade, tariffs were imposed to protect British goods, an example of the sort of economic nationalism that all countries engaged in during the Great Depression. Despite the slowdown of the British program of social democracy during the depression, the idea of the state's responsibility for the well-being of all its citizens was not abandoned. During the midst World War II, when British survival was in doubt, programs for expanding and inaugurating the social welfare program were drawn up.

The economic challenges of the interwar decades also hampered Great Britain's ability to play a decisive role in international affairs. The increasing impotence of the British weakened the League of Nations in which the British had played a dominant role. Nor was cooperation with her wartime ally France any more effective, since both countries were consumed with their own problems, which were intensified by the devastating impact of the worldwide depression.

French Reconstruction During the 1920s the French were preoccupied with the work of reclamation and reconstruction of wartime damage, which they expected German reparations to pay for, and with the creation of a system of alliances by which they expected to isolate Germany and keep her weak. Neither plan worked very well. Reparation payments were so punitive that it was impossible for the Germans to fulfill them. International efforts, under American guidance, to resolve the reparations issue did not succeed before the depression forced a moratorium on all intergovernmental debts.

The major impact of the reparations issue was to heighten tension between France and Germany and to intensify French efforts to find security in a series of alliances with central and eastern European states—Poland (1921), Czechoslovakia (1924), Yugolslavia (1927)—and by spending billions of francs for the construction of defenses along the German border.

The Popular Front The Great Depression, the effects of which were felt in France somewhat later than in other European countries, caused domestic problems that added to French insecurity. In the face of the economic crisis, criticism of the state was coupled with demands for expanding social legislation. In 1936 a Popular Front government was formed to deal with the crises in French society. This coalition, led by Leon Blum (1872–1950), was the first government in France headed by a Socialist, and Blum's main concern was social reform.

Faced with widespread strikes, the Blum government induced French industrialists to make a number of concessions, among them compulsory collective bargaining between unions and employees, a forty-hour work week, paid holidays, and wages increased up to 15 percent. The Blum government also took control of the Bank of France and its credit policy. Opposition was strong and problems, such as inflation and decline of the franc, were many. Blum was forced to retreat, to take a breathing spell from his reforms, but this respite did not satisfy his opponents. His tenure as prime minister was brief: his Popular Front government fell from power in 1938.

A series of unstable and shifting coalitions replaced the Blum government, and the advance of social democracy in France was halted until after World War II. Governments became consumed with the menace of a resurgent Germany. As the German threat grew, domestic differences were exaggerated and further weakened France's ability to deal with the Germans. Political differences became schisms. The Popular Front, which received support from the French Communist Party, was viewed by its opponents as a front for Moscow. Some openly declared "Better Hitler than Blum," a veiled double insult to the Jewish Socialist leader, and went so far as to conspire against the government and receive financial and propaganda aid from Hitler and Mussolini. In this divided situation the French search for security was doomed to failure.

Fascism in Italy The specter of socialism also reared its head in disillusioned Italy. Italy had joined the Allies in 1915 but experienced great hardship, loss, and humiliation in the war and emerged with only a small portion of what the Allies had promised as the price of its participation. Postwar bitterness, inflation, and unemployment increased general discontent and, inspired by events in Russia, encouraged the spread of radical ideas. Out of this morass of confusion and disillusionment, Benito Mussolini (1881–1945) offered himself as a national savior who would protect Italians from both Bolshevism and the bankruptcy of nineteenth-century precepts of liberty and democracy.

The term "fascism" (state dictatorship over society) was coined by Mussolini in 1919 and referred to the ancient Roman symbol of power, the *fasces,* a bundle of sticks bound to an axe. Using propaganda and violence, Mussolini's Fascist party abandoned parliamentary democracy. Industrialists and landowners who rallied behind the Fascist government and supported Mussolini were eventually joined by the Catholic leadership, to whom Mussolini made concessions that restored peaceful Church–state relations.

Guernica by Pablo Picasso, 1937

Picasso completed this painting depicting the anguish and horrors of war in response to the devastating bombing of the Spanish town of Guernica y Luna by German planes. Guernica had been a Loyalist stronghold during the Spanish Civil War.

SOURCE: Museo del Prado, Madrid/Art Resource, NY. © 1998 Estate of Pablo Picasso/ArtistsRights Society (ARS), New York.

Italian Imperialism in Africa   The easing of social and economic tensions in Fascist Italy was accomplished by the dictatorship's complete control. As stability was established and the Fascist regime seemed financially trustworthy, Italian and foreign capital was freely invested and Italian economic life was stimulated, resulting in improvement in the quality of Italian life. Domestic security enabled Mussolini to embark on an increasingly bold and adventurous foreign policy across the Mediterranean, in the Horn of Africa. Using aerial bombing and poison gas, Italy attacked the nation of Ethiopia ruled over by the traditional monarch Haile Selassie I, a descendent of African Christian rulers since the fourth century C.E. Mussolini's successful invasion of Ethiopia in 1935 received worldwide condemnation and demonstrated as much as any other action the ineffectiveness of the League of Nations.

The Spanish Civil War   About the time that Mussolini seized power in Italy, Primo de Rivera overthrew the Spanish monarchy and established a dictatorship (1923). The monarchy, weakened by the loss of most of the remnants of its once-vast empire in the Spanish-American War at the end of the nineteenth century, mistakenly undertook the subjugation of rebels in Spanish Morocco, an attempt that was so ruinous in costs and defeats that it resulted in the coup d'etat that placed Rivera in power for eight years.

A revolt against Rivera broke out in 1931, and a constitution was drawn up. Republicans, who believed that the Catholic Church was the bulwark for the old regime in Spain, undertook a concerted attack on the Church, confiscating its property, expelling religious orders, and forbidding religious instruction in schools. The anticlericalism of the government alienated many pious Spaniards, but its formula for dividing large estates for distribution to impoverished peasants and its efforts to curb the power and influence of the army turned the three most powerful elements in Spanish society—clerics, landowners, and the military hierarchy—against the republic.

In 1936 a group of army officers organized a revolt against the Republican government. Under the leadership of General Francisco Franco (1892–1975), the "Nationalists," as they called themselves, expected an easy victory. Instead they met fierce resistance from the Republicans, and the bloody civil war continued for three years, until 1939. The Nationalist victory was assured by support from both Italy and Germany, both countries welcoming an opportunity to test their arms and methods of warfare.

Neither Britain nor France, bogged down in uncertainty and their own domestic affairs, came to the support of Republicans. The Russians sent experts and some tanks, planes, and supplies; while corporations in the United States sent fuel and supplies to the Nationalists, American volunteers (the Abraham Lincoln Brigade) joined in what became an international struggle against the Nationalists. The Spanish Civil War ended with the fall of Madrid (March 1939) to the Nationalists and at a cost of 775,000 lives. The republic was replaced with a militaristic totalitarian state controlled by Franco for the next thirty-five years. Events in Spain were a preview of things to come in the rest of Europe.

WEIMAR GERMANY AND THE RISE OF NAZISM

The victory of the Allies in World War I was as surprising as it was difficult to achieve, and none could have expected it less than the Germans. This fact, along with the harshness (also unexpected) of the Versailles peace treaty, had a profound effect on Germany. The terms of the peace treaty were accepted by the new German republic, proclaimed at Weimar in 1919.

The Weimar Republic   The new government, which took shape under the shadow of unexpected defeat, was immediately stigmatized by having to accept what Germans felt to be the humiliating Versailles treaty. Although mired in an atmosphere of disgruntled nationalism, disillusionment, and social distress, economic recovery remained the central goal of the government's policy. The difficult problems of bitterness and political discontent were complicated by economic distress. The cost of the unsuccessful war and the challenges of postwar adjustments made the balance of the economy so fragile that the punitive reparations payments with which Germany was saddled became a crushing bruden. The inexperienced and unpopular government faced grave unemployment, disoriented production and trade, and runaway inflation. Conditions improved somewhat after 1925, but suffered a sharp reversal as a result of the economic crash of 1929.

Hitler and the Nazi Party   Among the serious problems the Weimar government had to face was Adolph Hitler (1889–1945), who became the agent by which the German republic was transformed into a totalitarian state. Disillusioned by German defeat and embittered by the Weimar government's acceptance of the Versailles treaty, Hitler joined with other unemployed and like-minded veterans to form a National Socialist German Workers (Nazi) Party (1919) and shortly thereafter became its leader (*Fuehrer*).

The international economic crisis that began in 1929 was a godsend for the Nazi movement. Looking for a solution to their problems, Germans found Hitler more than willing to act as guide and his party grew in electoral strength. By 1932 it emerged as the strongest in Germany. In January 1933 aging President Hindenburg was persuaded to name Hitler chancellor, though the Nazis lacked the majority needed to form a government.

FIGURE 18.7 Antisemitic Political Cartoon (1933) from a Catholic Student Newspaper, Netherlands.

Titled "The Death Cure," the cartoon depicts a Jew being driven across the border by the fascist German leader Hitler.

SOURCE: From: Mozes Heiman Gans, *Memorbook: History of Dutch Jewry from the Renaissance to 1940,* Baarn, Bosch & Keuning, 1971.

Once in power, Hitler proceeded to establish a totalitarian dictatorship predicated on the theory of permanent emergency. Evoking emergency clauses of the Weimar constitution, he suspended civil liberties and all forms of opposition, including newspapers and the Communist Party, were suppressed. An Enabling Act passed by the German Reichstag gave Hitler the power to rule for four years by decree. Federalism was ended, and the central government assumed direction of all local economic, social, and political institutions. After 1933 Germany was a totalitarian state dominated by the Nazi Party. Hitler stressed struggle and violence as positive virtues; militarism was glorified, and the secret police (SS) conducted sporadic reigns of terror designed to subdue opposition and purify the German nation. The rural and bucolic were extolled, paradoxically at the very time that Germany was becoming increasingly industrialized and urbanized.

Propaganda, Racism, and Culture While there was no doubt that Hitler was helped along by financial support from German industrialists on the one hand and by continued economic uncertainty on the other, his ideology clearly rested with the deepening divisions between class, culture, and race. Masterfully served by Hitler's publicist, Josef Goebbels (1897–1945), the Nazis bombarded Germany with propaganda, which played upon such sensitive issues as the treasonous "stab in the German back" that concluded World War I, the fear of Bolshevism, rampant racism, and economic distress and uncertainty.

Nazi ideology was infused with ideals of racism and violence. Pseudoscientific and false historical notions of German descent from white "Aryan" and racially pure stock were derived from widespread nineteenth-century racist assumptions about the superiority of some people and the inferiority of others based on inherited qualities. The ultimate expression of this vision of supremacy was contained in the Nazi propaganda films by Leni Riefenstahl, *Triumph of the Will* (1936), the record of the Nuremberg Nazi Party rally of 1934, and *Olympia* (1938) a documentary on the Olympic Games of 1936, in which the Nazi leaders were extolled as a superhuman pantheon.

But Hitler went beyond the glorification of white culture embraced by the Nazi Party, its supernationalism, and symbol of the swastika (cross). He identified representatives of cultural, racial, and other difference as scapegoats and justified their exclusion from society. Hitler seized the attention of the masses with propagandistic rhetoric and began to expound a policy of action against those who were not members of the "pure" race. Non-Aryans—Jews, Gypsies, Slavs, those of mixed racial backgrounds—and those whose behavior and, therefore, genetic makeup were considered socially unacceptable, such as homosexuals, the mentally ill, alcoholics, or political resisters, were declared undesirable and subject to scorn and destruction.

Persecution of Jews Jews, whom Hitler transformed into scapegoats for the German defeat in World War I, were the Nazis' particular targets. Beginning in 1933, the Nazi government enacted discriminatory legislation, outlawed marriage and sexual relations between Jews and citizens "of German blood," destroyed businesses belonging to Jews, and denied them employment. In the Nuremberg Laws (1935), a Jew was defined as any person with one Jewish grandparent and their German citizenship was stripped. By the night of November 9, 1938 (known as "Kristallnacht"), when synagogues were destroyed and books and property of Jews were burned, anti-Semitism had become a permanent part of the ideology and culture of the Third Reich.

Thousands of Jews and others began to disappear; men, women, and children were marked with yellow armbands bearing the Star of David. State-sponsored organizations for Nazi youth, men, and women supplied pressure to conform to the party's ideology, and their strong ties among members cut across and began to replace the bonds and loyalties of the family. Abortions among the racially pure Germans were outlawed, and women were pressured to increase the size of their families. Yet even while motherhood was extolled as virtuous and patriotic, the productive capacities of women were being directed toward war preparations.

Military Industrialism Total disarmament of the German state was a condition of the Versailles peace treaty. Between the 1920s and 1933, the Germans secretly rearmed in violation of the treaty. The alliance between industry and the state in war is exemplified in Germany by the history of the Krupp family firm. After the unification of Germany in 1871, the Krupp firm became the chief arms supplier for the German state, often keeping ahead of the military in the development of new weapons, such as its cannon "Big Bertha." Following World War I, the Krupp family firm turned from weapons to nonmilitary production, from railroad equipment to stainless steel dentures. During the interwar years, however, the Krupps also secretly manufactured weapons banned by the Versailles Peace

Treaty and developed new ones. Not only did they participate in Hitler's rearmament of Germany in the 1930s, but during World War II, 70,000 forced laborers and concentration camp inmates toiled in Krupp factories on behalf of Hitler's armies. The relationships between military industrialism, armament, and security were ones with which the world, teetering between war and peace in the twentieth century, would continue to wrestle.

JAPAN: NATIONALISM, FASCISM, AND WAR

The Japanese victory in the Russo-Japanese War (1904–1905), fought over domination of Manchuria, shocked the Western world. Though Japan had signed a treaty of alliance with Britain in 1902, there were signs that Japan had not really been accepted into the "white men's club" of European imperial powers. Its victory over Russia awakened Europeans to the potential threat of the Asian power. Japan's victory in the Russo-Japanese War had a profound impact at home as well as abroad. Japan incurred great losses in this conflict with Russia. The large number of casualties brought the war home to rural Japan, the source of many recruits, in a way that worked to instill a sense of nationalism among farmers in rural society who had not hitherto been associated directly with the goals of "enrich the country, strengthen the army," other than as the reason they were being taxed.

Soon after the beginning of the Taisho era (1912–1926), as the ideal and practice of democracy took form in the growing strength of political parties in the Japanese parliament (Diet), Japan formally entered World War I as an ally of Britain and occupied former German concessions on the Shandong peninsula in China. World War I also allowed Japan to expand its markets abroad, as European nations were engaged in war and unable to concentrate their economic efforts on marketing consumer goods. Japan began to see the need to develop its own area of domination in Asia both for markets and for access to important natural resources that Japan lacked.

Beginning in 1915 with the Twenty-one Demands for economic concessions issued to the Chinese republic, which was too weak to resist, Japan carried out a steadily escalating policy of encroachment on Chinese sovereignty. The loss of autonomy culminated in 1919 with the outcome of the Versailles Peace Conference, which formalized Japan's special rights on the Shandong peninsula, rather than returning the German concessions there to Chinese sovereignty. Japan became a member of the League of Nations in 1924, but in that same year, the American Congress passed legislation restricting Japanese immigration into the United States, illustrating the contradictions in Japan's international position. Further heightening tensions, the economic boom of World War I had come to an end by 1920, and at the close of the decade the worldwide depression severely affected Japan, which had become dependent on its export trade in textiles, particularly raw silk.

The Growth of Militarism The Japanese army and navy were increasingly unhappy with policies adopted by the civilian government, which was at times led by prime ministers who were heads of the majority party in the Diet. At the Washington Naval Conference in 1921, Japan's naval strength in the Pacific had been restricted by the United States and Britain; and at the London Naval Conference in 1930 this strategic imbalance was only slightly improved. In 1931 units of the Japanese army in Manchuria, responsible for overseeing Japan's interests in the region following the Russo-Japanese War, utilized a pretext to launch an invasion of Manchuria. The civilian government in Tokyo was helpless to control the situation, and in 1932 the Japanese puppet state of Manchukuo was declared.

In 1933 Japanese troops made further advances into China, and in the face of international criticism, the Japanese delegate walked out of the League of Nations. The Japanese government issued its Amau Statement in the following year, a document that has been likened to the Monroe Doctrine because it stated Japan's primary interests in the Asian continent and its right to protect those interests just as the United States had declared its paramount interests in Latin America as early as 1823. On July 7, 1937, an incident between Chinese and Japanese soldiers at Marco Polo Bridge on the outskirts of the Chinese capital, Beijing, provided a pretext for Japan to launch a full-scale invasion of China. This action was the beginning of the Sino-Japanese War (1937–1945), and by 1938 the Japanese controlled most of the commercial and industrial infrastructure of China along an axis from Beijing in the north to Canton in the south.

CHINA: NATIONALISM, COMMUNISM, AND WAR

As in many parts of Europe, especially Germany, the resolution of World War I in East Asia carried the seeds of further turmoil. The awarding of former German possessions in the Shandong peninsula to Japan by the terms of the Treaty of Versailles sparked student demonstrations beginning on May 4, 1919, that spread from Beijing University to other urban centers among members of the educated elite and a growing nationalist bourgeoisie. This protest became known as the "May 4th Movement" and marked the first major stage in the evolution of modern Chinese nationalism. Although the nationalism of the May 4th Movement was not limited to intellectuals—primarily university students and faculty—but included urban workers and merchants as well, it still was concentrated in the urbanized, Westernized, modernized sectors of society. Nationalism had not yet begun to penetrate to the great masses of the peasant population.

Warlordism and the Republic of China The May 4th Movement took place in the political context of warlord control of China. Following the 1911 Revolution and the establishment of the Republic of China, the fragile republic shattered into zones dominated by warlord generals. From political exile Sun Yat-sen formed the Nationalist Party (Guomindang) in 1914, gained the military support of certain warlords, and reemerged in the 1920s as the key political leader of the Republic of China. Lacking any substantive support from Western democracies, Sun responded positively to overtures from the Soviet-based Communist International (Comintern) for aid in political organization. At the same time the Comintern was heavily involved in the organization of the Chinese Communist Party (CCP), which had been founded in 1921. In 1924 Comintern representatives convinced both the CCP and the Nationalists to cooperate in a United Front to carry out a democratic nationalist revolution that would wrest control of the country out of the hands of warlords and create a unified nation.

The newly formed Nationalist Army under the leadership of Chiang Kai-shek was the agent of the reunification of the country. Chiang led the Nationalist Army in a two-year campaign (1926–1928) to subdue the warlords and established himself as the leader of a unified Republic of China. However, Chiang had no intention of including Communists in his government. In March 1927, as the Nationalist Army neared Shanghai, midway through its campaign to unify the country, Communist labor organizers called a general strike that brought the city under control for delivery to the Nationalists. But Chiang ordered a surprise attack on the Communists, and hundreds were summarily executed as they tried to flee.

This blatant betrayal of their alliance ended the first United Front between the Nationalists and the Communists, and the Communists went underground. In 1928 Chiang established the Nationalist government at the old imperial capital of Nanjing. He continued to rule from there until the Japanese invasion in 1937 forced the removal of the government to a wartime base deep in southwestern China.

The Chinese Communist Party and the Peasants   Between 1927 and 1934 Communist Party policy gradually shifted from the orthodox Marxist and Soviet model of organizing urban workers to the mobilization of the rural peasantry. A young man named Mao Zedong (1893–1976) emerged during this period as the party's leader, a visionary political strategist who recognized that Marxist dogma about the industrial proletariat had little relevance to the resolution of China's fundamental agrarian problems, particularly the issue of land reform. By 1930 Mao and his followers, including the nucleus of the growing Red Army, had established a government in the province of Jiangxi. Between 1930 and 1934 they administered a population of about 6 million, carried out moderate land and other reforms, and provided a base for the CCP.

The Long March   The Nationalist government at Nanjing launched a series of "extermination campaigns" against the Communist base in Jiangzi, the fifth of which in 1934 forced the strategic retreat that became known as the "Long March." Between October 1934 and October 1935, the Red Army moved out of its base camp in Jiangxi on a circuitous route that took it finally to its wartime base in northwestern China, Yan'an, where the Red Army would organize an effective strategy of guerrilla warfare against the Japanese. It was during this historic march, one that attained the status of epic myth, that Mao achieved his position as official leader of the CCP.

THE SINO-JAPANESE WAR

After the Japanese invasion of Manchuria in 1931 and the creation of the puppet state of Manchukuo in 1932, by 1933 Japanese forces began to press southward. In 1936 intellectual and political leaders, such as the writer Lu Xun (1881–1936) and Sun Yat-sen's widow, formed a National Salvation Association. These leaders argued for the Nationalist government to cease persecution of the Communists and turn its attention to the struggle against Japan, which was intensifying daily. In 1937 Chiang was finally forced to declare war on Japan and flee with his government and army to Chongqing in the southwestern province of Sichuan; later that year the Nationalists and the Communists declared a second United Front in their struggle against the Japanese. The Sino-Japanese War was the first phase of the global conflict known as World War II.

■

WORLD WAR II

Neither the League of Nations nor individual nations were able to stop the Japanese attack on China, German rearmament, remilitarization of the Rhineland and absorption of central European states, Italy's invasion of Ethiopia, or the Spanish Civil War. Japan, Germany, and

Italy, had embarked on similar designs backed by similar government ideologies and policies. They consolidated their assault on international law and order by joining in an alliance known as the Axis. The classic example of response to Axis actions came in 1938 when the British and French prime ministers met with Hitler, poised to attack Czechoslovakia. Their diplomatic effort to check German aggression without the risk of armed resistance was an approach that came to be known as "appeasement." As a policy, appeasement was as much dictated by British and French domestic politics and economic realities as it was a reflection of the hope for a conciliatory and reasonable response to demands made by the Axis, and a policy that would continue the noble aim of the peacemakers after World War I.

THE WAR IN EUROPE

The faulty idealism of the policy of appeasement applied to Hitler was revealed when Hitler gained British and French approval for annexing the Sudeten region of Czechoslovakia, which was inhabited by Germans. In return Hitler promised to halt his plans to annex all of the Czech republic, a promise that lasted only until March 1939 when the remainder of Czechoslovakia was occupied. Six months later, following a Nazi-Soviet nonaggression pact, Germany and its new ally, the Soviet Union, invaded Poland. Britain and France abandoned appeasement and declared war. World War II in Europe had begun.

FIGURE 18.8 Jewish Children Transported for Safety from Berlin to Palestine, ca. 1930s, Became Refugees

SOURCE: From: Mozes Heiman Gans, *Memorbook: History of Dutch Jewry from the Renaissance to 1940,* Baarn, Bosch & Keuning, 1971.

Within two months Germany invaded and occupied Denmark, Norway, the Netherlands, Belgium, and France in a rapid effort to confirm its hegemony over the continent. The two-thirds of France in German hands became a part of Hitler's Reich; what remained was the collaborationist Vichy government, a German puppet state that maintained a tenuous independence until 1942 when it too was absorbed by Germany.

The Holocaust From 1942 the Nazi language of elimination ("the final solution") and genocide became a gruesome reality when the victims of propaganda and discrimination were branded with ink identity numbers and herded into camps to be removed from German cities and occupied territory, enslaved or killed. For years Jews and members of other groups attacked by the Nazis were forcibly detained by the state. Between 1942 and 1945 Jews were sent to concentration camps, where those who were strong enough were used as slave labor and the weak were gassed to death by assembly-line methods or "eliminated" in other ways. The largest of the camps was Auschwitz, where more than 1 million Jews died.

The full impact of the horrors of the concentration camps only became evident to people around the world when the camps were liberated at the end of the war. More than 15 million people were exterminated in the Holocaust (from the Greek *holo*, "whole"; *caustos*, "burned"), including Jews, Gypsies, Slavs, and homosexuals. The complicity of those who watched the killings in silence or knew about them and did nothing remains the most troubling and unexplained aspect of the century's history. It is a history that could not be silenced.

The Battle of Britain With the fall of France, Great Britain faced Germany alone. Since the English Channel separated the British Isles from the continent, Hitler had to rely on the German air force as the primary weapon with which to assault England.

DAILY LIVES

DAILY RECORDS OF THE HOLOCAUST

The painful recording of the daily lives of Holocaust victims and survivors took many forms. Perhaps the most famous source is the 1942–1944 diary of Anne Frank, a young Jewish girl in hiding in the Netherlands during the German occupation. Also remarkable is the record of the daily life of a community of Dutch Jews in Oude-Pekala kept by the recording secretary or "rebbe" Abraham Toncman. His was a sacred position, although the Jewish faith declares each Jew to be a historian, responsible for passing down the culture's traditions. Handwritten pages that were found in the ruins of Abraham Toncman's synagogue describe the eventual destruction of his community of 125 Jews up to the very last moment, recording who was condemned to death, which person had gone into hiding, one by one, until almost all had disappeared:

For we are left but a few of many: we are counted as sheep for the slaughter; to be killed and to perish in misery and shame. Many enlargement and deliverance arise to the Jews. Speedily in our days, Amen.

> Oude-Pekela, 31 December 1942
> Abr. Toncman*

A Jewish proverb says "The community does not perish." The community lives as long as its history survives to be told. Still, for the millions of Jews who experienced the horrors of the Holocaust, "the community" came perilously close to extinction. For the world, human values by any standard were swallowed by the darkness.

*Moses Heiman Gans, trans. Arnold J. Pomerans, *Memorbook: The History of Dutch Jewry from the Renaissance to 1940* (Baarn, Netherlands: Bosch and Kewning, 1977), p. 820.

FIGURE 18.9 *Tube Shelter Perspective,* Drawing in Chalk, Pen, Watercolor by Henry Moore (1941)

Moore conveys the fear and common humanity in civilian bomb shelters during the Battle of Britain, 1940.

SOURCE: Tate Gallery, London. Art Resource, NY. Reproduced by permission of the Henry Moore Foundation.

Within six weeks of the fall of France, Hitler launched a massive air campaign against the British Isles that is known as the Battle of Britain. Between August and October 1940, the Battle of Britain involved indiscriminate massive day and night bombing designed to destroy British production and demoralize the public. Civilians, including women and children, huddled together in cold and dark underground shelters listening to the air assault.

The foremost obstacle to German success was the British Royal Air Force (RAF). Not until the Battle of Britain did the RAF, significantly aided by technological innovations like radar, show its greater skill and quality against the experience and strength of the German air force. The success of the RAF greatly bolstered British morale and saved British industry.

The Great Patriotic War   As fatal to German plans as the RAF was Hitler's unannounced attack on his Russian ally. Believing that the Soviet Union constituted a threat to German security and ambitions, and anxious to gain control of food supplies and raw materials, especially oil, in the Soviet Union, the Germans launched their invasion on June 22, 1941. Great Britain no longer stood alone, and when the United States joined Britain and Russia against the Axis powers in late 1941 following the Japanese attack on Pearl Harbor in the Hawaiian Islands, the second phase of World War II commenced what was known to the Russians as the "great patriotic war." Within four months the Germans reached the vicinity of Moscow, when a combination of the extreme Russian winter and a Soviet counteroffensive checked them. In the following year the Russians halted a German offensive into the Ukraine in a bitter siege at Stalingrad.

The Battle for Africa While an air war raged over Britain and the Germans and Russians struggled for control of the Soviet Union, the British fought the Axis in North Africa. It was essential for the British to protect the Suez Canal, their life line to India, Australia, and New Zealand. From the beginning of the war, they established their line of defense at the western border of Egypt in order to prevent Axis armies from moving eastward from the Italian colony of Tripolitania (modern Libya).

In October 1942 the British undertook an offensive against the Italians in conjunction with the landing of British and American troops in Morocco and Algeria. The aim was a joint attack from east and west that would drive the Axis out of North Africa. The costly campaign shifted back and forth across the deserts of North Africa, but by the spring of 1943, following the Axis loss of Tripolitania, the Axis "Army Group Africa," by now dominated by the Germans, surrendered. The southern flank of Europe, across the Mediterranean, was open for Allied assault.

The Assault on Europe Russian demands that the Americans and British come to their aid by launching a second-front assault on Hitler's "Fortress Europe" were answered soon after the surrender of Axis armies in North Africa. In the summer of 1943, British troops landed in Sicily and Americans at Salerno on the mainland to begin a slow and destructive attack on Italy. As Allied forces fought their way up the peninsula, Mussolini was removed from power. The Germans took over Italy and continued to offer strenuous resistance until an Allied offensive achieved a breakthrough that brought about the capitulation of German forces in Italy by the beginning of May 1945.

The Allies opened up an even more significant second front in western Europe on June 6, 1944, when the invasion of France began. Despite desperate German resistance, Paris was liberated in a little more than two months. The Allies reached the borders of Germany and the Netherlands in the fall of 1944 and commenced a three-pronged invasion that carried them deep into German territory by spring 1945, at the same time that a major Soviet offensive brought their troops into contact with the Allies. On April 30 Hitler committed suicide, and on May 7, at Reims in France, representatives of a German provisional caretaker government signed an unconditional surrender; the following day the Germans repeated the act of capitulation at Soviet headquarters in Berlin. The war in Europe was over.

NAVAL TECHNOLOGY AND THE WAR AT SEA

The war in Europe had been primarily fought on the land and in the air, though Allied control of the sea was no less important to victory in World War II than it had been in World War I. Naval warfare was waged on the surface and under the seas, and even in the air. The identical pattern of conflict between small groups of highly trained fighting men manipulating complex weapons systems, of competing technologists, and of commanders exercising control at a very long distance, though not new, emerged with the development of war in the air as it had at sea. An important innovation in naval warfare was the introduction of the aircraft carrier, which enabled aircraft, taking off on the high seas, to take part in naval battles, provide cover for troop landings from ships, and engage in long-distance bombing of targets on land.

But it was the submarine, which had proved its worth in World War I, that was the major weapon in the war at sea in World War II. German U-boats, in conjunction with the German air force, were extensively employed in the effort to defeat Great Britain quickly after the fall of France. The U-boat campaign against British shipping produced a successful Allied response from Britain and the United States. In the United States, ships were constructed in such numbers and so speedily that a "bridge of ships" was maintained, enabling Britain to keep up her struggle against Germany. Large convoys of merchant ships carrying supplies sailed under the protection of battleships skilled in antisubmarine combat. Sensitive electronic detection devices, known as sonar, were perfected, and effective depth bombs neutralized the U-boat menace. About 700 German submarines were destroyed while Allied shipping losses attributed to U-boats amounted to an incredible 21 million tons.

Navies and merchant marines made definite contributions to the mobility characteristic of World War II. Large numbers of men and heavily mechanized equipment could best be transported to distant battle zones by ship, despite great advances in air transport, which was faster and increasingly used as the war persisted. Nowhere were naval power and air power more significant than in the struggle in the vast Pacific.

THE WAR IN ASIA AND THE PACIFIC

Victory in Europe did not mean that the war was over. Though Germany and Italy had been defeated, Japan was still an active and potent enemy, despite the fact that domestic conditions in Japan were desperate. Throughout the war, opposition to militarism and Japan's pursuit of empire festered, though it was suppressed by the government's "thought police" (*kempeitai*). Anonymous graffiti collected from the walls of private and public places by the thought police between December 1941 and early 1944 bear mute testimony to the hidden opposition to the war: "Look at the pitiful figures of the undernourished people. Overthrow the government. Shoot former Prime Minister Konoe, the traitor (December 1941); No rice. End the war. Give us freedom (June 1942); Anglo-American victory, Japanese German defeat (October 1943).

Following the invasion of China in 1937–1938, Japan had moved into Southeast Asia and occupied territory from Burma to Singapore on the Asian mainland and a vast array of islands stretching from Indonesia and the Philippines into the central Pacific. Japan's expansion on the Asian continent, beginning in 1931, was stimulated by demand for raw materials and markets; its continuing advance into Southeast Asia was driven by increasing needs for oil, tin, and rubber, which Southeast Asia had in abundance. Critics later called this cycle the "China Quagmire," referring to the idea that Japan was sucked deeper and deeper into war as each advance demanded more resources to sustain it. Japanese propagandists justified Japan's role in Asia as exercising beneficial political and economic leadership for Asian countries through the "Greater East Asia Co-Prosperity Sphere;" however much Southeast Asians resented European colonial powers, few were taken in by the Japanese claim that their imperial goals worked for the benefit of Asians.

Because the long struggle in Europe had exhausted its allies, the burden of the campaign to defeat Japan fell on the United States. It was a campaign of naval warfare, "island hopping" whereby the Japanese had to be driven from one after another of the many Pacific islands they had occupied, and air power. On the Asian mainland the Japanese put up stiff resistance. In support of the land campaigns, the Americans took the war to Japan itself by an air offensive—launched from bases in China, liberated Pacific islands, and aircraft carriers—designed to destroy Japanese industrial centers and morale.

FIGURE 18.10 Japanese Troops Entering the Chinese City of Nanjing, December, 1937.

SOURCE: Keystone/Sygma, New York.

The Atomic Bomb Despite land, sea, and air efforts, Japan showed no signs of ending the war quickly. Toward the end of the sixth year of World War II, an air raid by the United States on the Japanese main island dropped an atomic bomb on the city of Hiroshima (August 6, 1945), destroying military targets and killing outright 80,000 civilians. The detonation of a second atomic bomb over Nagasaki on the southern island of Kyushu (August 9, 1945), before the effects of the first were properly registered, brought about Japanese surrender (September 2, 1945). World War II ended exactly six years after it had begun, and nuclear warfare had become a global reality.

Secretly developed by an international team of scientists working for the U.S. government in various laboratories and tested in the deserts of New Mexico, the atomic bomb was a weapon of incredible terror and destruction. The question of whether the bomb should have been used, or even developed, raises an issue that has never been resolved. Military justification for the dropping of the bomb, that it would put a quick end to a seemingly interminable war and accordingly save lives, particularly Allied lives. Nevertheless, much of the world continues to ask: Could not other means, such as stringent blockading, have accomplished the same ends? Was it necessary to drop the bomb on a city? Above all, why was it necessary to drop a second bomb? What of the environmental results of atomic explosions? Peace replaced war at the cost of enormous uncertainty and questioning.

PEACEMAKING

In yet another way World War II recapitulated the experience of World War I. While both conflicts raged, attention was given to the shaping of the postwar world. After two global wars, the planet was conflict oriented, its nations suffering deepening divisions between classes, cultures, and races. President Wilson had pinned his hopes on a League of Nations that would guarantee a peace without victors or vanquished and "make the world safe for democracy." The Allied vision of the postwar world, reflecting the powerful influence of President Franklin Roosevelt, was perhaps less idealistic and more pragmatic. It was formulated in a series of wartime conferences, beginning with the meeting of Roosevelt and Churchill at Casablanca in Morocco in January 1943, where they declared a policy of unconditional surrender as basic to any peace agreement. They were joined by representatives from Russia and other countries in a series of conferences held to design a peace based on victory that would deal harshly with the vanquished. At a meeting held in Cairo, Egypt, in November 1943, the fate of the Japanese empire was agreed upon, and at a meeting at Yalta in Soviet Crimea, agreement on the future of Germany and eastern Europe was arranged.

Like Wilson, Roosevelt believed that an international organization would help establish and maintain a rule of law among nations, and once again the United States took a leading role in creating such an organization. Roosevelt's proposals, which were less skeptically received than Wilson's, resulted in the San Francisco Conference (April–June 1945) that created a United Nations organization even before the war in Europe was completed, though not before Roosevelt's death in 1945. The new international organization came into existence before and apart from subsequent peace treaties. Fifty years after its creation, the United Nations continues to wrestle with the maintenance of international order in a global climate of rapid change and instability.

■

THE BALANCE SHEET PERSPECTIVE ON GLOBAL WAR: HUMAN AND MATERIAL COSTS

In contrast to nineteenth-century conflicts such as the Crimean and the Franco-Prussian Wars, which were relatively brief and had fewer casualties, the global wars of the twentieth century were of long duration and exacted heavy tolls in human lives and resources. Loss of lives among civilian populations could not be immediately nor easily estimated, and measuring the spiritual anguish and emotional dislocation caused by the war and its effects was virtually impossible.

World War I was unique in the numbers participating in and affected by it. Previous wars, such as the French Revolution and Napoleonic Wars, had required the active participation of large portions of the population, but never before 1914 had war so extensively called into play all the human and material resources of the participating nations. In World War I more than 10 million soldiers perished and twice as many were wounded, many permanently crippled and unable to return to normal peacetime lives. In World War II conscription and the displacement of people fleeing war or persecution made huge demographic changes across the European landscape. Between September 1939 and early 1943, at least 30 million Europeans were deported or fled from their homes. By recent estimates close to 60 million men, women, and children lost their lives in World War II, and many millions more suffered the indelible pain of loss and hardship. Twenty million people are estimated to have succumbed to war and its effects in the Soviet Union alone.

World War II in the Asian Pacific

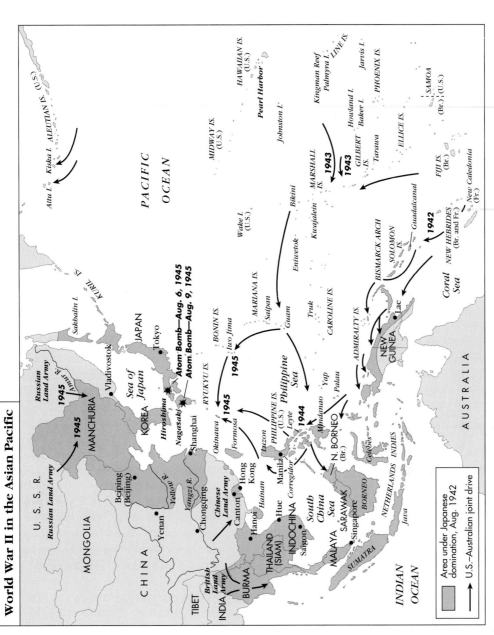

MAP 18.2 The Continuing War in Asia and the Pacific

Material costs were also too vast to be readily comprehended. Combatant nations in World War I spent at the rate of $10 million an hour, and the grand total of war expenditure (including property damage) has been estimated at $186 billion. World War II cost the United States $341 billion and cost Japan $562 billion; the Soviet Union lost approximately 30 percent of its national wealth. These staggering figures take on true meaning only in terms of what might have been accomplished by the expenditure of so much energy, effort, and money for peaceful purposes such as feeding, housing, and clothing people.

HOW WAR CHANGED SOCIETY

War tends to encourage the growth of state power for the mobilization of resources and the mobilization of citizenry. Control of the economy, government regulation and planning, and even requisitioning and rationing were necessary in the pursuit of wartime goals. The demands of technological innovation and the expense of new technology showed that the concentration of power in the hands of political leaders was an effective and essential way to increase production and contribute to national power through military successes.

Both World War I and II depended heavily on conscripted manpower. The mass production of weapons required the mass production of soldiers. By World War II fighting units were highly diversified, and the new dependence on technology required many units dedicated to servicing and supplying that technology. The traditional division between soldier and civilian disappeared, as mechanics were as necessary as other soldiers to the war effort. The importance of scientists and engineers grew as the realization dawned that new weapons could tip the balance quickly in favor of one belligerent over another. During World War II, European refugee scientists fleeing Hitler's Germany persuaded the British and American governments to mount an effort for research and development that produced the first atomic bomb. Science and other aspects of culture were harnessed to serve the nationalist goals of societies.

The Impact On Daily Life People felt the impact of war in many ways. Rationing of sugar, gasoline, tires, automobiles, coffee and other goods, shortages, and inflation were endured by millions. Welfare measures and expanding roles for labor unions in the organization of the labor force were utilized in the interests of the war effort. The war permitted the intrusion of states into the daily lives of individuals and families, sometimes legislating motherhood. Managed health care likewise was a product of the need to ensure workers' health so that they could achieve maximum productivity. In the postwar era technology that had been created to meet military demands was applied to the production of consumer goods.

OCCUPATION, COLLABORATION, AND RESISTANCE MOVEMENTS

World War II subjected most of Europe and much of East Asia to foreign military occupation. The responses of occupied peoples varied from one place to another and among peoples—sometimes even among members of the same family—in the same community. In the colonized Dutch East Indies, the Japanese invaders were welcomed as liberators. In Norway most citizens resisted both the Nazis and a handful of Norwegian collaborators set up by the Nazis as a puppet government. Sometimes the path of resistance offered impossible moral dilemmas. For example, those who spied for the enemy or hid Jewish children and other refugees were often required to act in ways that endangered their own lives and the lives of their families.

Resistance Movement   Not all resistance occurred as individual acts of moral conscience. Following the fall of France in 1940, two forms of French opposition to the Germans emerged. French patriots led by General Charles de Gaulle (1890–1970) organized resistance to the Germans from abroad. Within France and outside France in French North African territories, a secret, underground resistance movement operated with much success to hide Jews and downed British and U.S. airmen, and to help some of them escape from the German authorities. Many men and women gave their lives in the Resistance. There were also resistance movements in communities in Denmark and the Netherlands. In Yugoslavia resistance took the form of guerrilla warfare against German and Italian occupation forces conducted by two groups: loyalists to the monarchy and "partisans" supported by the Soviet Union and led by Josef Broz (1892–1980), known as Tito. Resistance movements within both Germany and Italy opposed the Nazis and Mussolini's Fascists.

The Warsaw Uprising   Jewish resistance was extremely difficult in the heavily guarded camps, though there were isolated but remarkable instances of rioting. In the Warsaw ghetto, where thousands of Polish Jews were confined to one quarter of the city and subjected to overcrowding and starvation, an armed rebellion broke out in 1943. The resisters received no outside backup, and most were ultimately exterminated by the Nazis.

Not all responses to the Nazi occupation were easily explained as rational, nor would they be judged morally acceptable at the end of the war. Europeans who collaborated (for example, the Dutch) suffered from semistarvation as often as those who acquiesced or resisted (for example, the fiercely independent Greeks who waged civil war and died of hunger by the tens of thousands). Industrialists collaborated commercially and made huge profits during the war by manipulating prices and selling to enemy and ally alike. While resistance by individuals did little to thwart the enemy, it did provide the basis for community in the most inhumane of modern times.

Resistance and Responsibility   The countless documented (and undocumented) individual acts of heroism were cumulatively insufficient to alter the course of events. Resistance by communities is even more difficult to measure and judge. At what point do the actions of leaders and their governments represent the intentions of entire communities and cease to be the accountable acts of individuals? To what extent can societies and individuals be held accountable for the rise of Nazism and its devastating consequences? The White Rose was the name of a small group of German students, professors, and intellectuals who opposed the war and distributed pamphlets urging the German people to resist the Nazis and the war effort. Two students and a professor at the University of Munich were executed in 1943 for their activities with the White Rose society.

Documentation of large-scale resistance to the Nazi government in German society is harder to find. One example of mass resistance by German women did occur in 1943, when about 600 unarmed women marched on a building near Gestapo headquarters in Berlin and demanded the release of prisoners who had been rounded up as a result of the laws restricting marriage between Jews and non-Jews. The women protestors succeeded in securing the release of those accused; their actions saved the lives of many Germans. Does acknowledgement of the effectiveness of such mass resistance point to the culpability of other German communities that did not oppose and might have prevented the injustices and crimes of the Fascist government?

WOMEN IN WAR

Women served the war efforts in both global conflicts. As early as the French Revolution, the services of women had been requisitioned during wartime, but at no preceding time had the role of women in war been so organized, planned, and complete as in World War I. Their contributions were significant enough to warrant postwar "rewards," such as the extension of suffrage to English women who had been refused it despite vigorous campaigns before the war. Women found release from domestic occupations in jobs never before open to them and in auxiliary roles in combat.

During World War II women aircraft workers such as Rose Will Monroe (1920–1997), known as "Rosie the Riveter," became celebrated symbols of the United States patriotic womanhood. There were actually many "Rosie the Riveters," women for whom gender boundaries were temporarily lifted, allowing them full access to jobs and skills normally available exclusively to men. The Rosie the Riveter who appeared in wartime films and posters promoting war bonds worked in an aircraft parts factory in Ypsilanti, Michigan. The Ford Motor Company's bomber plant recruited women for delicate technical work. A pamphlet claimed: "The ladies have shown that they can operate drill presses as well as egg beaters." Some firms made deliberate efforts to recruit the wives and daughters of servicemen whom they had employed before the war so as not to encourage the women to consider their jobs permanent. But war also created new kinds of hardship and oppression for women as well.

Combat Roles   Women also served in combat roles. In 1939 the Soviet Union drafted women for the first time, mostly to take support jobs. After the German attack in 1941, many women took part in combat. Of the million women serving in the Red Army and the Soviet navy, about 800,000 of them saw combat. Over 100,000 won military honors and 86 earned the coveted rank "Hero of the Soviet Union." Female pilots in the Soviet Union flew numerous combat missions. One fighter regiment had only female pilots, navigators, mechanics, and handlers of munitions; it was so successful in its bombing raids over Germany that the Germans called its pilots "night witches."

The Heroism of Motherhood   At the same time that new roles for women and new opportunities were created by the demands of wartime, traditional roles were promoted by the policies of some leaders. Hitler, who viewed the role of women as confined to the domestic sphere, encouraged motherhood as the fulfillment of a woman's destiny and her duty to the Nazi state and society. On Mother's Day in 1939, 3 million women were given the "Cross of Honor of the German Mother" for having four or more children. On the opposite side in the war, but with similar goals to raise the birth rate, in 1936 the Soviet Union drafted a new law prohibiting abortion, supported by fines and prison sentences. In 1944 the Soviet government launched the "mother-heroine" campaigns that awarded cash bonuses to women who bore more than two children, with the amount increasing as each additional child was born.

"Comfort Women"   Women also served in the war in roles associated with traditional modes of oppression outside the family. Young Japanese girls from impoverished families had been sold to brothels in the prewar period to help support their families or pay off debts. As the Japanese empire expanded in the early twentieth century, Japanese brothels

FIGURE 18.11 1943 British Cartoon Depicting the Japanese Enemy during the War as Part Superman and Part Ape

SOURCE: Daily Mail/Solo.

were established all over Asia, including Siberia, Korea, China, Manchuria, Hong Kong, Singapore, and Southeast Asia. Often tricked into servitude and sexual slavery by promises of lucrative jobs in foreign places, the Japanese women were called *karayuki* ("going to China," i.e., abroad). Cut off from home and family and lured into prostitution, they lived their lives without any comfort or hope.

World War II created a new and more miserable extension of prostitution for women in Japanese colonies such as Taiwan and Korea who were forcibly sent to provide sexual services for Japanese troops stationed all over Asia. In 1941 Japanese authorities conscripted Korean women as "comfort women" for Japanese troops in Manchuria. With the beginning of the Pacific war, between 50,000 and 70,000 Korean girls and women were sent as unpaid prostitutes or sexual slaves to Japanese troops throughout Asia. During the course of the war, other women in areas occupied by Japan, such as the Philippines, were also forced into state prostitution by the Japanese army.

■

CONFLICT IN THE TWENTIETH CENTURY

As the engagement of almost all the nations of the world in global warfare suggests, the twentieth century reflects the widespread and deep cultural divisions among societies. The goals of the major combatants and their alliances in World War II were complex and diverse, but the governments, if not the entire populations, were ardently committed to the justness of their causes and devoted enormous energy in propaganda efforts to convince both their own people and sometimes the enemy that they were right. Technological innovation, bureaucratic expansion, the ideological fervor were all characteristics of participants in World War II, which only temporarily, if at all, masked the divisions of race, class, and gender emerging in societies around the world.

PROPAGANDA

Propaganda was an important strategy that all sides used to help win the war. Hitler created a Ministry of Propaganda under the direction of Joseph Goebbels (1897–1945), who orchestrated mass demonstrations of Nazi supporters and coordinated the use of Nazi symbolism such as the swastika while crafting negative images of Jews and others in contrast to the ideal of Germanic nationhood. After the United States entered the war following the Japanese attack on Pearl Harbor, vivid imagery and powerful stereotypes emerged on both sides of the Pacific.

Just as the films of Leni Riefenstahl were useful propaganda for the Nazis, the forces of Hollywood created a propaganda campaign to convince American troops that they were fight-

DAILY LIVES

I SO MUCH WANTED TO STUDY

Among the many casualties of war, the lives of comfort women were ruined by enforced prostitution and lost opportunities for education and family life. A Korean women, Mun P'ilgi, recounts the story of how she ended up in a "comfort" station in Manchuria:

> I was born in 1925 . . . My parents kept a small shop selling potatoes, fish, fruits, and sweets . . . There were eleven of us children . . . I wasn't allowed to go to school. When I was nine, mother sold about 10 kg of rice to pay for my tuition and bundled me off to school. My father soon found out. He said that if a girl studied she would become too foxy. He rushed into my classroom, dragged me home and burnt all my books. That was the last of my education . . . He beat me and threw me out of the house . . . It was only after I promised that I would never go to school again that I was allowed to return home.[*]

Mun P'ilgi goes on to describe how a village neighbor, who was an agent for the Japanese, told her he would help her get an education and lured her to Manchuria, where she joined other Korean girls similarly abducted as inmates of a comfort station.

Yi Tungnam was born in 1918, the eldest daughter in a poor farming family. Her story shows the same pattern of mother encouraging daughter to go to school while the father opposes it and her own desire to seek opportunity that ended with her sexual enslavement:

> When I was nine, my mother placed me in a school without letting my father know. One morning he caught me going out to school. He stared and said, "A girl, studying?" He snatched my school things and threw them on to a fire. He repeated this a number of times, but my mother continued to send me off to school. She said that girls, not just boys, should be able to open their eyes to the affairs of the world. But I found it very difficult to keep up with school work, for I had to try to avoid being caught by my father and needed to help with housework. I gave up school after something like two years.[*]

Yi Tungnam eventually ran away from home to her aunt's cafe in Manchuria where she helped out until she was seduced into leaving for a better job in 1939 by a Japanese man who forced her into sexual slavery for Japanese troops in China. In 1942 she was transferred to Sumatra to another comfort station and in 1945 finally returned to Korea.[*]

[*]Keith Howard, ed., *True Stories of the Korean Comfort Women* (New York: Cassell, 1995), pp. 80–87; 134–42.

ing for their way of life. The director Frank Capra was called in by the U.S. government to prepare a series of documentaries to be distributed to American troops. These films were called *Why We Fight* and portrayed Japan as a demonlike enemy that represented the annihilation of civilization. Political cartoons showed Japanese soldiers with simian features, at once powerful and superhuman and pathetic and subhuman. Either image dehumanized the Japanese soldier. The Japanese used similar dehumanizing imagery in portrayals of American soldiers to strengthen the Japanese soldiers' will to fight.

RACISM

The Axis powers, particularly Nazi Germany, were committed to building a modern society based on racial purity; to this end they dedicated energy and resources to eliminating those human beings who did not fit their description of racial purity, including Gypsies and other minorities, along with the 6 million Jews who died in the Holocaust. The racism of the Nazis, widely criticized by the Allies but only reluctantly acted on, found echoes in racial discrimination that was part of both American and European societies. While the U.S. government critized Nazi policies, anti-Semitism and segregation laws that demeaned African American citizens were widely practiced in American society.

Mobilization for the war effort also brought jobs to many African Americans. In Detroit, where auto factories first hired minorities in large numbers, hate strikes erupted in the plants and a race riot occurred in 1943. Unlike the women workers whose presence had been tolerated because it was assumed to be temporary, the black workers stayed after the war and Detroit became a center of the Civil Rights movement.

The U.S. military establishment was segregated, and racial discrimination extended to the defense industry. Despite the fact that African-American troops saw heavy combat in which they valiantly laid down their lives, they remained segregated in most situations and were frequently discriminated against by white soldiers. Even the elite corps of black American bomber pilots known as the Tuskegee Airmen were subjected to racism by their fellow white soldiers. American armies also included Native Americans and Chicanos. The only secret U.S. military code never to be deciphered by the enemy was based on a Native American language.

War in the Colonies European armies included many thousands of colonized peoples from Africa, Asia, and the Americas who fought alongside their colonizers. Support for the war effort was not unanimous. For example, in the British colony of Trinidad, where an American military base was situated, many saw the class struggle as more important and resisted fighting in the war. Black activist Elma Francois, whose occupation was clothes washer, was tried for sedition in 1937, and she spoke for many oppressed peoples when she claimed: "The only war we will fight in is the fight for better conditions, peace, and liberty." But many in the colonies did see combat. Their wartime experiences forever changed the era's understanding of colonial notions of "civilization" and "barbarism."

Japanese American Internment Throughout the nineteenth and twentieth centuries, U.S. immigration policy was severely biased against nonwhites, except for purposes of importing workers for hard labor. After Pearl Harbor the summary incarceration of more than 110,000 persons of Japanese birth or ancestry on the Pacific coast in either relocation (for the general population) or internment (for suspected Japanese loyalists or troublemakers) camps between March and mid-August 1942 demonstrated the difference in the ways that European and non-European immigrants were viewed.

A U.S. Supreme Court decision in 1943 (*Hirabayashi* v. *U.S.*) upheld the right of the military to treat Japanese Americans as enemy aliens, despite protestations of loyalty and actions that confirmed loyalty. One example of this was the all–Japanese American U.S. Army Unit 442, which fought bravely on World War II battlefields and became the most highly decorated unit in the army's history. Japanese Americans also served the United States during the war as translators. The 150,000 Japanese living in Hawaii were not sent to internment camps because their labor was needed in agriculture and to rebuild the shipyards, unlike the West Coast Japanese whose confiscated agricultural lands and small businesses were desirable assets coveted by others.

Pan-Asianism   The Japanese heralded Pan-Asianism in their Greater East Asia Co-Prosperity Sphere, a plan aimed, however hypocritically, to unite Asians against their white European colonial oppressors. When the Japanese invaded Southeast Asia in 1941–1942, they claimed to be liberators from European colonial aggressors, and in India, Burma, and Indonesia the Japanese were met with support from local nationalists seeking to overthrow their European colonial masters. But the Japanese, like their Nazi allies, also had a strong sense of their own superiority and ultimately proved to be as oppressive as the Europeans they displaced, forcing other Asians to labor in factories and to serve their Japanese rulers as they had Europeans. Pan-Asian unity was as much a myth as that of the Aryan nation promoted by the Nazis.

WAR ATROCITIES AND WAR CRIMES TRIALS

Atrocities were carried out by Japanese soldiers in China as elsewhere, though perhaps the most dramatic was the "Rape of Nanjing" in December 1937, when Japanese troops engaged in random and merciless slaughter of an estimated 200,000 civilians in Nanjing and the surrounding area over a period of six weeks. The secret documents of Unit 731, a Japanese military unit in Manchuria whose doctors and scientists performed institutionalized murder in the form of lethal medical experimentation, only came to light publicly long after the end of the war. Such experiments as spreading bubonic plague virus among the local Chinese population or the vivisection of captured U.S. airmen at Kyushu Imperial University in 1945 mirror Nazi medical experiments on the inmates of concentration camps.

No side was immune to accusations of atrocities. Toward the end of the war in Europe, the British put the German city of Dresden to the torch in a massive incendiary raid that killed 135,000 people, many of whom had fled westward from the Soviet advance. The firebombing of Tokyo in spring 1945 razed 16 square miles of the capital city and killed between 80,000 and 100,000 civilians, who were "scorched and boiled and baked to death" in the words of U.S. General Curtis LeMay, the architect of the bombing raid. The atomic bombs were dropped only a few months later on Hiroshima and Nagasaki. The Nuremberg and Tokyo War Crimes Trials were held after the war ended to seek legal redress against war criminals. Some were sentenced and a few individuals were executed, but these people, while guilty as charged, were also scapegoats for the responsibility of many more.

FIGURE 18.12 *Holy Mountain III,* 1945, by African-American painter Horace Pippin

Horace Pippin fought in World War I in the 379th U. S. Army (African-American) unit and painted this peaceful scene in the aftermath of World War II.

SOURCE: Hirshhorn Museum and Sculpture Garden, Smithsonian Institution, Gift of Joseph H. Hirshhorn, 1966. Photo by Lee Stalsworth.

Universal Human **The two world wars focused attention on the extremes of human behavior**
Rights and Values and values and on the different interpretations of "human rights" that cultures and governments constructed to promote domestic or international interests. After World War II organizations dedicated to international peace and order began to discuss universal human rights—basic human needs, decencies, participatory rights, and liberties. Could peoples from vastly different cultural and political perspectives agree on a basic covenant of human rights?

■
THE POSTWAR ORDER

After 1945 the United States constructed a system of interlocking alliances and organizations that were designed to protect its national interests globally and to further economic ties. The most important of these was the North Atlantic Treaty Organization (NATO), the principal organizational link between the United States and Europe. Other alliances formed by the United States in the postwar period include the Organization of American States (OAS), the defense treaty with Australia and New Zealand (ANZUS), and the Southeast Asia Treaty Organization (SEATO). The Soviet Union similarly concluded the Warsaw Pact in postwar Europe to seal its relations with its allies and client states in eastern Europe. Seemingly little had changed in the perspectives of power. Status in the world community continued to be based on strategic military strength and the global reach of political and economic influence.

THE COLD WAR

The emergence of the two superpowers, the United States and the Soviet Union, is the clearest example of this postwar continuity of international relations. Their rivalry and competitiveness resulted in the era known as the "Cold War," a period between the end of World War II and 1990, in which arms and security continued to play a defining role. During the Cold War, suspicion and insecurity ran rampant. Russian distrust of the capitalist west and western distrust of radicalism had existed since the Bolsheviks tooks power in 1917. Russian and Allied self-interest, rather than mutual trust, had prevailed during the war.

The Cold War was a global political chess game of moves and countermoes in which tensions between the two superpowers varied in intensity. The division of Germany into Allied and Soviet zones of occupation after the war created the frontline of the Cold War in Europe, which persisted in the division of the city of Berlin and the two Germanys, East and West, until the fall of the Berlin Wall in 1989. The division between the United States and the Union of Soviet Socialist Republics (USSR) deepened as a result of the Marshall Plan, by which the United States provided about $22.5 billion to aid the recovery of western Europe between 1948 and 1952. The Soviets perceived the 1949 military alliance of western governments (NATO) as a threat to their security. They responded with the economic integration of central European satellite states and the Warsaw Pact, a counter military alliance. From West Asia to Ethiopia to South Africa, the superpowers extended their perspectives through conflicts and strategies involving "national security interests." The Cold War found expression in technological ventures, including the space race to the moon, and in the continued development in military arms and nuclear capability. The Cold War became global in scale; no part of the world could be uninvolved.

The Occupation of Japan   In theory an Allied operation, the Occupation of Japan was in reality an American undertaking. General Douglas MacArthur, the supreme commander of the Allied Powers (SCAP), was in control of the Occupation forces. Initially, members of political parties and labor union organizers released from jail were allowed to recreate their organizations in the interest of creating a "democratic" Japan. Officials and bureaucrats identified with the militaristic ultranationalism of the war were removed from office, and some military figures were tried for war crimes. The goal of the democratization and demilitarization phase of the Occupation was to destroy the foundations of the Japanese empire and to prevent its resurgence.

By 1947 the direction of Occupation policy began to shift. A general strike called by the newly reorganized labor unions was prevented by the Occupation authorities, and gradually former bureaucrats regained positions in the economic and political hierarchies of the Japanese government. Growing fears on the part of the United States that Communism was going to overwhelm Asia influenced the policies of the American Occupation. American authorities began to see Japan less as a defeated enemy to be controlled and more as a potentially important strategic ally in Asia. Reform and recovery became the key concerns of the Occupation after 1948 as the tide turned clearly in favor of Communist victory in China.

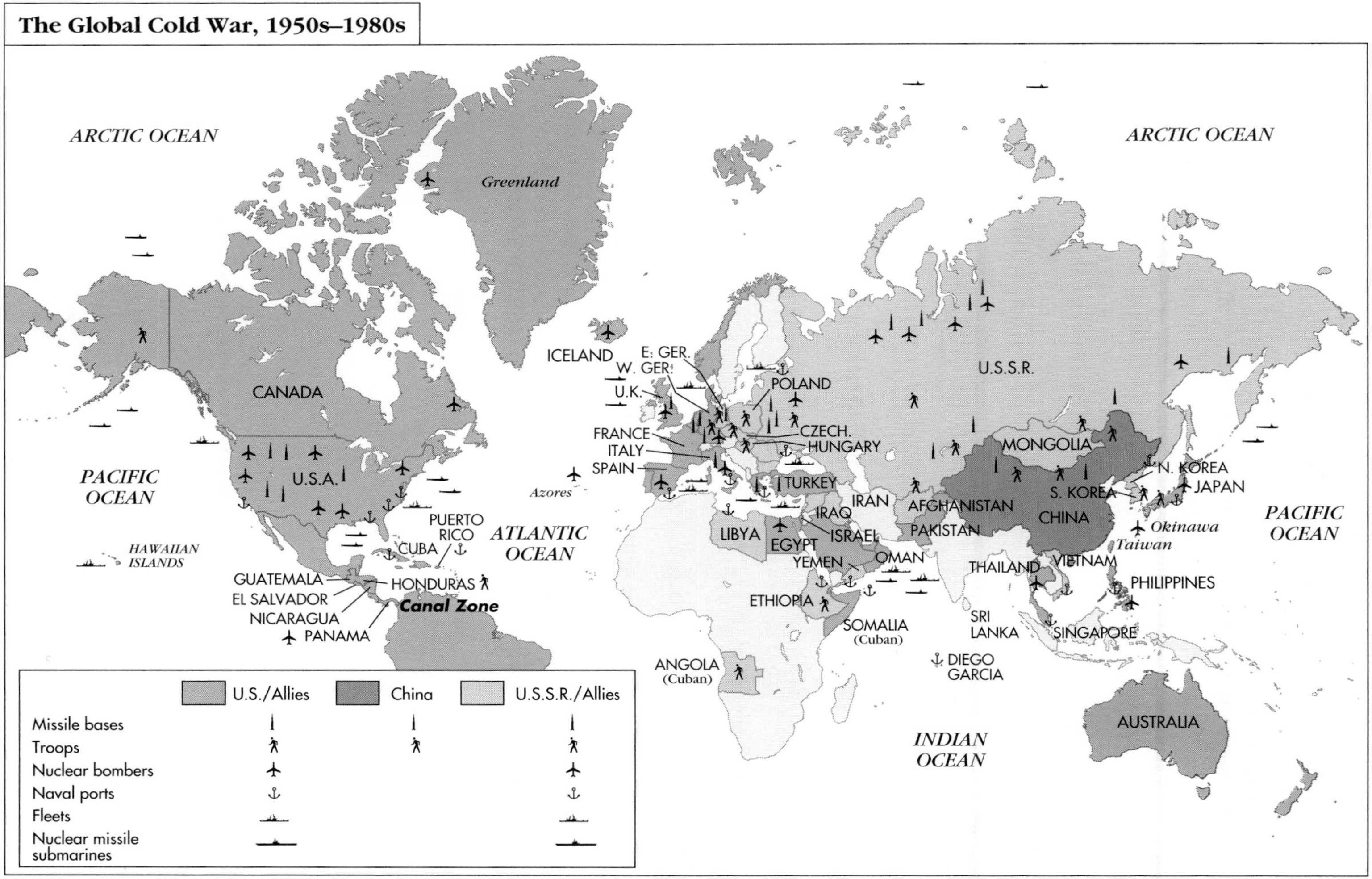

The Global Cold War, 1950s–1980s

MAP 18.3 Strategic Cold War Sites

Legend:

Missile bases
Troops
Nuclear bombers
Naval ports
Fleets
Nuclear missile submarines

U.S./Allies

China

U.S.S.R./Allies

ARCTIC OCEAN

PACIFIC OCEAN

ATLANTIC OCEAN

INDIAN OCEAN

Greenland

CANADA

U.S.A.

HAWAIIAN ISLANDS

PUERTO RICO
CUBA
HONDURAS
Canal Zone
GUATEMALA
EL SALVADOR
NICARAGUA
PANAMA

Azores

ICELAND
U.K.
E. GER.
W. GER.
FRANCE
ITALY
SPAIN
POLAND
CZECH.
HUNGARY
TURKEY
LIBYA
EGYPT

U.S.S.R.
MONGOLIA
CHINA
N. KOREA
JAPAN
Okinawa
Taiwan
S. KOREA
PHILIPPINES
VIETNAM
THAILAND
SINGAPORE
SRI LANKA
DIEGO GARCIA
AFGHANISTAN
PAKISTAN
IRAN
IRAQ
ISRAEL
OMAN
YEMEN
ETHIOPIA
SOMALIA (Cuban)
ANGOLA (Cuban)

AUSTRALIA

When the Occupation ended in 1952, the United States had signed a peace treaty with Japan linked to the U.S.-Japan Security Pact, which provided for United States defense of Japan and the right of the United States to station troops in Japan. Part of the new Japanese constitution concluded in 1947 was a prohibition against maintaining armed forces capable of aggression. The United States demanded the inclusion of this article as a means to prevent Japan from launching another aggressive war. Because of this prohibition and because of U.S. interest in maintaining a strategic Asian ally, the United States has continued to maintain bases in Japan. Although there was considerable opposition to the U.S.-Japan Security Treaty, both domestically and abroad, and serious demonstrations against the renewal of the treaty in 1960 forced the resignation of the prime minister and the cancellation of a visit by the United States president, it was renewed every ten years.

The Korean War   The Korean War erupted in 1950 as tensions between the United States and the Soviet Union heightened on the Korean peninsula following the postwar drawing of a line at the 38th parallel demarcating the Democratic People's Republic of Korea in the north from the Republic of Korea in the south. An ally of the Soviet Union, the People's Republic of China felt threatened by the landing of United Nations troops led by the American general Douglas MacArthur, who advocated crossing the northern border of the Yalu River into Chinese territory and eradicating the specter of Communism in Asia. The Korean War, which ended in 1953, symbolized the growing strategic concerns of the United States in Asia, reflected in the shift of Occupation policy toward Japan, and the division of Korea paralleled the division of postwar Germany and later of Vietnam between the two superpowers and their client states.

After the Cold War   The collapse of the USSR and the fragmentation of Eurasia in the closing decade of the twentieth century ended the Cold War. The costs of this "war" were higher than those of any other global conflict. Human, capital, and technological resources were drawn into the worldwide competition of the superpowers for political influence and strategic advantage. World military spending from 1960 to 1990 was $21 trillion. Despite major arms reductions (especially after the Strategic Arms Reduction Talks in 1991), the international perspectives on the role of weapons in creating security have not altered. Nuclear dangers persist. Japan's economic achievement and the united postwar European economic community, as examples of successful transformations in which global interdependence is balanced with limited military spending, are exceptions to the pattern of conflict and development. The persistence of world poverty among 1 billion of the planet's peoples and the oppression of many more reminds us that "global politics in the human interest" reaches beyond the dualistic and perhaps oversimplistic perspectives of war and peace.

SUMMARY

The two world wars of the twentieth century began as European conflicts between nation states. They eventually became global in scope and impact; World War II included most nations of the world. Their conclusion created new national identities. Between World War I in the early twentieth century and World War II at mid-century, as Europe struggled with political conflicts among nation states and the economic impact of a worldwide depression, their overseas colonies in Asia and Africa began the long, painful, and often violent process that would eventually free them of the tentacles of empire.

Post–World War I Europe was split among three competing ideologies. In appearance 1918 saw the triumph of nations who adhered to principles of liberal democracy, who proposed to use their victory to establish an international rule of law and to renounce war as an instrument of policy. These were ideas that flowered particularly in Great Britain and the United States. But in practice, by destroying so much of the traditional framework of European society, World War I had greatly strengthened revolutionary politics on both the left and the right. The effects of World War I and the collapse of capitalism in the Great Depression of 1929 transformed disillusionment with liberal politics—represented by ideals of constitutional democracy—into rejection. In some countries, such as Germany, Italy, and Russia, this political climate took the form of revolution against the ideals and practices of the nineteenth century, leading to the rise of both fascism and communism. These political ideologies were radically opposed to each other in terms of the ideals they proclaimed, but both gave totalitarian power to the state to order society and the lives of individuals.

Japan, which had modeled itself on European nation states such as Prussia in the nineteenth century, like its European allies Germany and Italy in World War II, rejected parliamentary government and came under the dominance of the military in a Japanese form of fascism. China, after undergoing a century of upheaval, established a communist state after World War II and a brief civil war, like that of the Soviet Union founded after World War I. In European countries such as Great Britain, France, and Sweden, continuities with the English and French models of the state as a product of the social contract led to revisions of the role of the state in society, creating a new model of the social welfare state. Like fascism and communism, though to a lesser degree and with different goals, the social welfare state also increased the power of the state in society.

The rise of these conflicting models of the state in an international context set the stage for global conflagration at mid-century in World War II. Despite its origins as a European conflict, World War II truly engulfed nearly the entire globe because of connections among Europe, Asia, Africa, and the Americas created by imperialism. Japan's rise as a modern nation state and its role as a powerful player in both Asian and global politics by the early part of the twentieth century is a potent reminder of the influence of European imperialism as a model. Japan adapted rapidly to the developing global system of nation states and emerged as an Asian imperialist power by World War I, becoming a world player in World War II as a major ally of Germany and Italy.

World War I was the end product of industrial and technological changes that expanded conflict-oriented nation state rivalry and competition into a global war. Even more than World War I, World War II was a total war. It showed how effective an alliance among industry, science, and nationalism could be in the creation of wartime culture and its instruments of mass destruction used in the interests of the state. Though the era of mass armies supported by the fanatical nationalism of the civilian population had passed, World War II was a conflict between entire societies and cultures. The dropping of two atomic bombs on the cities of Hiroshima and Nagasaki in August 1945 marked the end of the world war, but not the end of the perspectives that saw the world in terms of war and peace. Soon thermonuclear weapons, containing more destructive power than used by humans in their entire recorded history, made mass warfare utterly and completely obsolete. The powerful forces of resistance and revolution, however, were not.

ENGAGING THE PAST

MORALITY AND WAR

Global wars in the twentieth century resulted in the deaths of approximately 100 million people. While most of those were casualties of war, both military and civilian, some were the result of deliberate policies of genocide, the systematic killing of members of a group. From the slaughter of 2 million Armenians by the Turks in 1915 to the 15 million Jews, Gypsies, Slavs, and homosexuals murdered by the Nazis during World War II, genocide was practiced by governments and by people who bore responsibility for carrying out these acts of institutionalized murder. Though genocide was not unique to the twentieth century, technology made it more efficient, as the gas chambers of German concentration camps bore witness. At Auschwitz as many as 12,000 victims a day were gassed to death.

The Nuremberg and Tokyo War Crimes Trials at the end of World War II attempted to assign guilt and to punish those who had transgressed the bounds of civilized human behavior in the conduct of war as defined by the international community in such forums as the League of Nations. The Geneva Convention, for example, established rules for the humane treatment of prisoners of war, though these were nonetheless violated by belligerents in World War II. One particularly gruesome example is the vivisection of eight captured U.S. airmen by Japanese doctors at Kyushu Imperial University in 1945.

The dropping of two atomic bombs on Hiroshima and Nagasaki ostensibly to bring about a rapid capitulation by Japan brought moral questions sharply into focus. Yet numbers of those killed in the atomic holocaust or the Nazi Holocaust quickly become numbing statistics, just as photographic records by their very clarity and objectivity make us all too familiar and comfortable with the grim realities of war and human inhumanity. The German-born American political philosopher Hannah Arendt (1906–1975) wrote of the "banality of evil," the idea that evil is commonplace and that trying to define it as something atypical of human behavior is fruitless. Nevertheless, in the aftermath of World War II, though neither genocide nor war ended in 1945, people continued to question the morality of war, to oppose it, and to struggle to prevent it.

SUGGESTIONS FOR FURTHER READING

John W. Dower, *War Without Mercy: Race and Power in the Pacific War* (New York: Pantheon, 1986). A powerful study of race, propaganda, and culture in wartime, focusing on Japan and the United States.

Paul Fussell, *The Great War and Modern Memory* (New York: Oxford University Press, 1977). A vivid recreation of World War I through the eyes of major literary figures who fought in it and whose literary works were shaped by their wartime experiences.

Paul Fussell, *Wartime* (New York: Oxford University Press, 1990). A description of twentieth-century war and its effects on combatants and civilians, supported by recollections from both.

Wendy Z. Goldman, *Women, the State, and Revolution: Soviet Family Policy and Social Life, 1917–1936* (Cambridge: Cambridge University Press, 1993). Women and family life in Soviet society between the wars.

Thomas R. H. Havens, *Valley of Darkness: The Japanese People in World War II* (New York: W.W. Norton, 1978). A close study of the war at home for the Japanese.

John Keegan, *The Battle for History: Re-Fighting World War II* (New York: Vintage, 1996). A thoughtful review of the historical literature and perspectives on World War II by a leading military historian.

Linda K. Kerber and Jane Sherron de Hart, *Women's America: Refocusing the Past*, 4th ed. (New York: Oxford University Press, 1995). Selected primary and secondary articles on the historical experience of American women.

William McNeill, *The Pursuit of Power: Technology, Armed Force, and Society since A.D.1000* (Chicago: University of Chicago Press, 1982). A survey of the relationship between technology and war from medieval through modern times by one of the most distinguished world historians.

John Modell, ed., *The Kikuchi Diary: Chronicle from an American Concentration Camp* (Urbana, IL: University of Illinois Press, 1973). The diary of a young man's experience with the internment of Japanese Americans during World War II.

Leni Yahil, *The Holocaust: The Fate of European Jewry, 1932–1945* (New York: Oxford University Press, 1990). Detailed history of the attempt to exterminate European Jewry in the interwar period and World War II.

19 Resistance, Revolution and New Global Order/Disorder

W hen reggae music legend Bob Marley (1945–1981) sang "Get Up Stand Up," it was a call to arms. Reggae had become the anthem of resistance in Jamaica, a former British colony where color, class, and capitalism churned in an urban crucible of poverty and underdevelopment. The song's lyrics rang true for many people far from the Caribbean:

> Get up, stand up,
> Stand up for your rights,
> Get up, stand up,
> Don't give up the fight.

In its Jamaican homeland, reggae was linked to the Rastafarian religion, an African-derived philosophy that combined Christian biblical teachings with beliefs rooted in the historical crowning of the last Ethiopian Emperor Haile Selassie I (r. 1930–1974) as the living god of black people. Freedom songs were "songs of redemption." Emerging from Jamaican folk traditions and embracing multiple musical styles from local and imported sources, reggae music was also rooted in historical consciousness. Marley's song "War" was taken almost entirely from a speech by Haile Selassie. Other music sang of histories silenced by those in power; through the lyrics in "Buffalo Soldier," about the forgotten African American soldiers who were freedom-fighters in the United States, Marley reminded his listeners that "If you'd know your history, then you would know where you're coming from."

Marley's artistry attracted the attention of Jamaica's political establishment, who were forced to take seriously the poor, mostly black underclass on the island. But reggae's message transcended political and religious boundaries. Bob Marley sang to the hopes and aspirations of the downtrodden and a new generation of young people and revolutionaries searching for alternative philosophies to challenge the status quo. He called for personal freedom through revolution. His songs hit the music charts in every part of the world and came to be associated with the struggles for black political independence. In 1980 Bob Marley was invited to Zimbabwe to perform at the African nation's independence ceremony. Although Marley died the next year, the political authenticity of reggae music provided a model for revolution and resistance beyond Jamaica in the 1970s.

FIGURE 19.0 *Economic Protest,* Etching
Mexico, ca. 1900, by José
Guadeloupe Posada
(1852–1913)

Depicts the protest over high food prices by
irate housewives, threatening a foreign merchant.

INTRODUCTION

Two world wars and a global depression undermined European hegemony, and resistance
movements throughout the colonized world challenged European political, economic, and
cultural domination. This chapter explores the varieties of cultural and political resistance
that contributed to the end of European hegemony in Asia and Africa. Responses to European
imperialism varied greatly, ranging from nationalist movements in colonial territories that
eventually gained independence, exemplified by the experience of India, to revolutionary
movements in the postwar era that overthrew traditional rulers while expelling European and
other foreign powers, as was the case in some former colonies in Africa and Southeast Asia.

In East Asia the Chinese revolution went through two stages: a nationalist revolution
that marked the end of the traditional monarchy (1911) and a social revolution (1949) that
replaced a nationalist military elite with a Chinese Marxist government committed both to
Chinese nationalism and to the creation of a socialist society. In contrast, Japan's emergence as

a modern nation state began in the mid-nineteenth century with the overthrow of the military government that had ruled for 600 years. The "restoration" of power to the symbolic authority of the emperor was in fact the vehicle for rapid transformations in political, social, economic, and cultural life. Although the political and social background of the Meiji Restoration (1868) was complex, it can be seen as a "revolution from above," revolutionary change carried out by a traditional elite. Like both China and Japan, Korea was influenced by Western ideas and powers, but Korea was also the site of political conflicts between its two powerful neighbors. Korea's modern history encompassed resistance to both Western and Japanese imperialism along with struggles for national independence.

Latin America presents yet another, in some ways more complex, scenario of resistance and revolution that was conditioned by its past. As detailed in Chapter 16, independence movements in the early nineteenth century had freed Latin Americans from the Spanish Empire, but independence had not eradicated colonial social structures and economic dependence a century later. The lingering dependencies created a neocolonial order, which many resisted through revolutionary action.

In this chapter we will explore the ways in which resistance movements of national liberation from colonialism were shaped by the particular historical experiences of peoples in Asia, Africa, and the Americas. We will also examine revolutionary change in the non-European world that was influenced by diverse experiences and models, from the American and French Revolutions to Marxism. We will consider the case of Ireland as an example of imperialism and colonialism within Europe. We will explore the concept of resistance expressed in the form of organized labor in both Europe and the United States, though organized labor also played a critical role in resistance and revolutionary movements across the globe. We will examine gender resistance in both its colonial contexts and in the context of twentieth-century liberation movements across the globe. Finally we will consider resistance movements in the United States, such as the African American civil rights campaign, based on ethnic identity and rooted in the experiences of labor and political movements across cultural boundaries.

■

MARXISM AND MODELS FOR REVOLUTIONARY CHANGE

As suggested by the enduring music of Bob Marley, the ideas and circumstances that inspired revolutionary change in the twentieth century were found both in the experiences of oppressed peoples around the globe and in the historical examples of other resistance movements. History told from the viewpoint of those in power could be a tool for silencing other pasts; but historical memory could also be a means of empowerment for those who sought social and political changes.

Models for revolutionary change in the twentieth century begin with the American Revolutionary struggle for independence from Britain; the eighteenth-century popular uprisings of the French Revolution; and the cultural, ethnic, and political complexities of the Haitian Revolution (see Chapter 16). The revolutions of 1848 in Europe inspired Karl Marx's ruminations on the relationship between capitalist industrialism and the nation state and led to the formulation of the Marxist model of revolutionary historical change (see Chapter 16). According to this model, modes of production or economic systems and the class relationships they generate provide the dynamic forces that propel and direct historical change. The first major impact of Marxist political ideology came with the Russian Revolution, interpreted through the lens of Lenin's thought. When Marx created his model of historical change based on observation of mid-nineteenth century European capitalist industrial society, he was dismissive of the non-European world and even of Russia, which was "backward" in comparison with western Europe at the time. He saw in parts of the non-European world such as India and China examples of what he called the "Asiatic mode of production," which was based on feudal landlord-tenant relations.

Marx assigned no revolutionary role to peasant cultivators in any society, including that of Europe, arguing that because farmers were by the nature of their livelihood isolated, individualistic, and self-interested—concerned only with what they could produce on their own plots of land—they lacked consciousness of their condition of oppression as a class and would remain a conservative force in society. In contrast, the urban proletariat, the industrial working class, by the nature of their labor in factories, subject to the oppressive management of capitalist entrepreneurs who exacted surplus value from their labor, would develop the class consciousness necessary for revolutionary change.

IMPERIALISM, COLONIALISM, AND REVOLUTION

Marx knew little about the non-European world, and he could not foresee the impact of imperialism and colonialism on the capitalist industrialism he was familiar with in Europe. In the generation after Marx, in the backwater of the European industrial revolution that was Russia at the turn of the century, Lenin saw beyond Marx's vision to the realities of his own time. While World War I was in progress, Lenin wrote *Imperialism, the Highest Stage of Capitalism* (1916–1917), arguing that imperialism had extended the life of capitalism by improving conditions for the proletariat in the advanced industrialized nations and therefore enabling capitalist societies to avoid revolution.

According to Lenin, Marx's prediction that the worsening condition of the working classes in advanced industrial societies would lead to revolution had not come true because imperialism had allowed the expansion of capitalist economies. Even though harsh economic inequities persisted, overall growth meant that conditions for the working classes had not worsened and may even have improved. Lenin concluded that Marx was not wrong about the process, only the timetable, since the unforeseen effects of imperialism had provided the means to extend the life of capitalism. However, in Lenin's view, imperialism carried within it the seeds of its own destruction. He believed he was witnessing this destruction in World War I, the result of the clash of imperialist rivalries that led to militarism, war, and widespread popular discontent. Lenin appeared to be right about Russia at least. World War I contributed significantly to the breakdown of the Russian monarchy and the opportunity for the Bolsheviks to seize power (see Chapter 18).

TWENTIETH-CENTURY AGRARIAN REVOLUTIONS

The success of the Bolshevik Revolution impressed many Chinese intellectuals and attracted them to the study of Marxism. The model of the Russian Revolution was exported to China in the early 1920s, when Russian and other agents of the Communist International (Comintern) helped to organize the fledgling Communist Party. Because of its ideological focus on the urban proletariat and the necessity of an industrial base, the Russian Revolution had limited applicability to the Asian and African worlds, which were overwhelmingly agricultural. The Mexican Revolution (1910–1913) yielded a very different model of revolutionary change: agrarian reform, the redistribution of land as the basis of wealth. This model of revolutionary change, flawed though the outcome was in Mexico, provided an example for ongoing revolutions in much of the colonized and semicolonized world in the twentieth century, where land reform was still the key issue for most of the disenfranchised population.

The key transformation in Marxist ideology that made Marxism into a model of revolutionary change for agrarian societies took place in China where the urbanized, industrialized sector of society was far smaller even than that of Russia and where the peasantry was the vast majority of the population. Though early Chinese Marxist revolutionaries were inspired by the Russian Revolution, guided by Russian mentors, and looked to an urban proletariat for support, the young Mao Zedong (1893–1976) challenged Marxist dogma focused on the revolutionary consciousness of urban industrial workers with his own vision of the peasantry as the key to revolutionary change:

> A revolution is an uprising, an act of violence whereby one class overthrows another. A rural revolution is a revolution by which the peasantry overthrows the authority of the feudal landlord class. . . . If the peasants do not use the maximum of their strength, they can never overthrow the authority of the landlords which has been deeply rooted for thousands of years. . . .
>
> In a very short time. . . several hundred million peasants will rise like a tornado or tempest, a force so extraordinarily swift and violent that no power however great will be able to suppress it.

Written in 1927, Mao's words echo the revolutionary violence of the French Revolution, distant in time, context, and outcome though it was.

FIGURE 19.1 The Young Mao Zedong Chatting with Peasants in the Red Army's Wartime Base of Yan'an in northwest China

SOURCE: Sovfoto/Eastfoto.

Everywhere that European imperialism had penetrated, whether through colonization or in less structured ways such as the "spheres of influence" in China, revolutionary change took the form of nationalism. Whether it originated in response to imperialism alone or in tandem with resistance to the traditional state, nationalism could become either a revolutionary force that overturned the traditional social order or it could overthrow the old state structure but not those in power. Revolutions tended to recreate hierarchies of power within the revolutionary state, which in turn generated resistance to the revolutionary leadership.

■

THROWING OFF THE YOKE OF IMPERIALISM: ANTICOLONIAL MOVEMENTS AND NEW NATIONS

From the onset of European conquests and colonization, resistance and revolts by subjugated peoples were as persistent and commonplace as they were unsuccessful. Closest to home, in the very bosom of British imperialism, the Irish struggle provides a distinctive case—because it is European—even while it illustrates common themes in the history of resistance.

BRITISH DOMINATION AND IRISH RESISTANCE

Ireland was the earliest example of English conquest and colonization. Centuries before the British colonized North America, Ireland was given to King Henry II (r. 1154–1189) as a fief by the papacy. Irish resistance to English colonization and control was persistent from the beginning, and following the establishment of Protestantism in England, Irish resistance took on the character of a religious conflict between the Roman Catholic Irish and the Protestant English. English control was not consolidated until the seventeenth century, and in 1707 Ireland was incorporated into the United Kingdom (England, Scotland, and Ireland).

In the nineteenth century continued Irish resistance to British control, in forms ranging from boycotts to violence, led to consideration of "home rule" for Ireland, whereby the Irish would have their own parliament and control of their own affairs except for foreign affairs, the military, and customs, matters that were reserved for the British crown. Parliament passed an Irish Home Rule bill in 1914, but the outbreak of World War I delayed its implementation. Irish resistance made headway during the war under the leadership of the Sinn Fein ("We Ourselves") movement, which aimed at nothing less than complete self-government—not just home rule—for Ireland.

The Easter Uprising   Serious resistance came in Dublin where a full revolt broke out during Easter week 1916. During this Easter uprising, the Sinn Fein insurgents seized the greater part of the city and proclaimed a republic. The British sent in troops and fierce fighting raged before the rebellion was suppressed. Some 2000 insurgents were imprisoned and 15 were executed. The protracted process of the executions, which dragged out over nine days, resulted in a wave of fear and outrage among even those Irish not sympathetic to Sinn Fein, whose defeat in the uprising was therefore transformed into broadening support.

Following the end of World War I, resistance continued in the form of bitter guerrilla fighting, and the Irish nationalists proclaimed a new Irish republic in 1919. Three years later, the British instituted the Irish Free State, granting Ireland (minus six northern counties with significant Protestant populations, which remained a part of the United Kingdom) dominion status, such as Canada and Australia had earlier achieved within the British Empire. The Irish continued, however, to demand total independence and the union of the six northern counties with southern Ireland. Independence came in 1949 when the Republic of Ireland (Eire) was proclaimed, after which it withdrew from the Commonwealth, the association of former members of the British Empire.

The fate of the six counties of Northern Ireland continues to persist as a problem, geographically, politically, and religiously dividing Ireland and resulting in continued resistance to the British presence. The Irish are split between those who want to heal the wounds of the long conflict with Great Britain, and those, particularly the Irish Republican Army, the militant arm of Sinn Fein, who want to continue resistance and are willing to use violent means to bring Northern Ireland into the republic and expel the British from Ireland. Their efforts are matched by the Protestant Ulster Unionists, equally determined to keep the northern counties as part of the United Kingdom.

NATIONALISM AND DECOLONIZATION IN SOUTH ASIA

Because India was in many ways the jewel in the British Empire's crown, the eventual rejection of European domination there had repercussions far beyond the single event that came to characterize colonial resistance. Indian independence from Britain was rapidly followed by the collapse of European control in Southeast Asia and Africa. As European empires disintegrated in Southeast Asia and Africa, they were replaced by new nation states in which the legacy of colonialism contributed to conflicts that have shaped the subsequent political history of ethnically and culturally diverse former colonies, whose maps were drawn by Europeans and whose unity was defined by colonialism.

Gandhi Despite the violence that accompanied European conquest and colonization, not all resistance was violent. Gandhi's tactic of resistance to the British Raj was known as *satyagraha* (literally, "truth-force"), noncooperation and passive resistance. Gandhi's strategy of nonviolent resistance was influenced by such diverse sources as Jesus Christ, the Russian writer Count Leo Tolstoy (1828–1910), and the American writer Henry David Thoreau (1817–1862), whose most famous essay was "On Civil Disobedience." Though civil disobedience on occasion went beyond Gandhi's control, it was a strategy that proved remarkably effective, leading the British finally to accept the Indian demand for an end to British rule.

The young Indian lawyer Mohandas K. Gandhi (1869—1948) went to South Africa in 1893, where he developed his philosophy of nonviolence and many of his techniques of civil disobedience. In South Africa Gandhi experienced discrimination, including beatings by white South Africans, and was even thrown off a first-class passenger train because of his skin color. When he returned from South Africa in 1906 to attend the Indian National Congress, he incorporated his South African experiences into a deeper understanding of resistance to injustice. Gandhi began to wear the Indian *dhoti* (dress), rather than an English-tailored suit, and adopted the diet of a poor Indian peasant. He used techniques such as boycotts, defiance, strikes, and marches to protest British rule.

Swadeshi One particularly effective boycott that Gandhi supported through his symbolic wearing of the dhoti was the *swadeshi* ("of our own country") movement, which originated in 1905 in Bengal in opposition to the British partition of Bengal into Hindu and Muslim majority areas. This boycott of British goods was intended to support the indigenous textile industry as well as to protest the partition of Bengal. Beginning with petitions and pleas, the *swadeshi* boycott turned into a widespread nationalist movement, with bonfires burning British-made *saris* (Indian women's dress). By 1908 the boycott was so successful that textile imports were down by 25 percent.

The Swaraj Movement   When the Indian National Congress met in 1906, it adopted the goal of self-government, *swaraj;* as Gandhi used the term, it meant political independence, economic independence, and personal psychological self-control. At first Gandhi pursued discussions about India's future status with British statesmen, but many nationalists grew impatient with the slow process of negotiations for independence.

When the Raj adopted a new policy in 1919 aimed at controlling political activities, a demonstration against this new policy at Amritsar, a center of Indian resistance to British rule as well as the holy city of the Sikhs, brought about a confrontation between Indian demonstrators and British troops. When the troops fired on the crowd, 400 demonstrators were killed. The Amritsar Massacre intensified Indian resistance to British rule and pressure for independence; it also galvanized support throughout the country for Gandhi's movement.

FIGURE 19.2   **Passive Resistance by Gandhi Challenged British Rule in India**

Shown here is the famous salt march to the sea in 1929.

SOURCE: "PA" News Photo Library.

One of Gandhi's most famous protests came in 1930, in a peaceful march against British taxation, especially the salt tax, which he had encouraged his followers to refuse to pay. On the anniversary of the Amritsar Massacre Gandhi and hundreds of his followers marched over 200 miles to the sea. When they reached the sea, Gandhi waded into the surf and picked up a lump of natural salt. By this act, Gandhi and his followers openly defied the British salt monopoly, which forbade the independent manufacture or sale of salt, an essential commodity. The British responded to this challenge to its authority with violence, arresting and imprisoning tens of thousands of nationalist leaders and followers, including Gandhi himself. The Indian Independence League proclaimed their conviction that the only resolution to the situation of intensified conflict and violence lay in prompt and complete independence from British rule.

The Issue of Caste   The breakdown of the caste system illustrates one of the ambiguities of colonialism. The questioning of caste began to take place under the British, as people of different castes were thrown together everywhere—on trains, in the British Indian army, and even in British prisons. Christian missionaries also encouraged Hindu leaders to examine their social beliefs. In 1921 Gandhi linked the abolition of untouchability to the goal of *swaraj,* saying "*Swaraj* is a meaningless term if we desire to keep a fifth of India's population [the untouchable caste] under perpetual subjection."

Because he believed that Gandhi was not as determined to eradicate the caste system as he should be, the untouchable leader, Dr. B. R. Ambedkar (1891–1956), opposed Gandhi by insisting on separate electorates for untouchables in order to protect their rights. Ambedkar persisted in this demand until in 1932 Gandhi fasted and finally gained Ambedkar's agreement to a communal electorate. Abolition of untouchability then became a principle of the Congress Party.

Independence   A new Government of India Act in 1935 showed only modest efforts at meeting the demands for independence. This act created a constitution and attempted an Indian federation of princely states and provinces ruled by elected legislatures; both were to send delegates to a central legislature. Domestic affairs were to be turned over to Indians, but the British retained control of defense and foreign policy. When this act went into effect in 1937, it failed to meet the demands of many Indian nationalists.

With the outbreak of World War II, England was unable to count on wholesale Indian support and loyalty. The Indian National Army was formed to support the Japanese effort to overrun British Asian possessions and it assisted in the Japanese occupation of British Burma. Many Indians apparently believed that if they must be subjects of foreign imperial rule, Asian rule was preferable to European. The destructive effects of World War II on Great Britain enabled Indian nationalists to realize their dreams at last. An Indian Independence Act was finally adopted by the British government in 1947.

Partition   Independence, however, did not bring peace, but violence and partition. The subcontinent was partitioned between India, a Hindu state, and Pakistan, which was Muslim, a compromise carved from the religious and ethnic divisions that had plagued Indian nationalism from its beginnings. The two countries chose to become members of the loose economic and cultural organization known as the British Commonwealth of Nations. British authority in India formally ended on August 15, 1947 when the Union Jack was hauled down and replaced with flags of the two new states.

As part of the partition, the Indian state of Bengal, including the city of Calcutta, was partitioned into West Bengal, part of India, and East Bengal, or East Pakistan, part of the new nation of Pakistan. In 1971 the strength of Bengali culture in East Pakistan led to the successful creation of an independent state of Bangladesh (Bengali for "Bengal nation"). The birth of Bangladesh came about when Pakistani repression of the Hindus in East Pakistan brought Indian support for Bangladeshi guerrillas, though the state religion of Bangladesh is Islam, with 85 percent of the population belonging to the Sunni branch of Islam.

Jawaharlal Nehru (1889–1964), head of the Congress Party and first prime minister of India, was eventually succeeded in 1975 by his daughter, Indira Gandhi (1917–1984). Though she initially supported democratic institutions, she ultimately declared a national emergency and ruled by decree, effectively silencing opposition. Amritsar, center of opposition to the Raj before independence, once again became the site of a massacre in 1984, when the Indian government sent troops to occupy the Golden Temple, the sacred Sikh shrine in Amritsar, in a effort to quell Sikh terrorism and demands for greater autonomy for the Punjab. Hundreds were killed, and in retaliation for this massacre, Indira Gandhi was assassinated by a Sikh bodyguard in the same year. Her son, Rajiv Gandhi, succeeded her, but was killed by a terrorist bomb in 1991. Ethnic divisions and religious tensions, as well as economic woes, have continued to plague Indian democracy. In 1996 the power of the Congress Party was threatened with the electoral victory of the Hindu nationalist Bharatiya Janata Party, raising fears of intensified ethnic and religious conflict on the subcontinent.

Ceylon/Sri Lanka and Burma/Myanmar

Both Ceylon and Burma, which had been administered by the British together with India, became independent in 1948. Ceylon's first decade of independence from Britain was marked by conservative rule, but in 1956 S. W. R. D. Bandaranaike came to power with a populist program designed to appeal to the rural masses. Bandaranaike was assassinated in 1959; his widow came to power in 1970 and instituted a period of radical reform, including recognition of the Buddhist religion and renaming the country Sri Lanka, after its traditional Sinhalese name.

In British Burma, the Burmese Independence Army, supported by the *Thakin* (master, a term previously applied to the British) movement of former students who agitated for a truly independent Burma, aided the Japanese occupation of Burma in 1942. This nationalist movement, however, later resisted Japanese rule at the end of World War II. After the end of the war, its leader, Aung San, negotiated with Britain to gain Burma's independence, but was assassinated in 1947 by a political rival.

Military rulers tried to assert independence and nonalignment and to experiment with socialism in the economy. Beginning in the 1950s General Ne Win assumed control of the country, and during the 1960s and 1970s sought to establish legitimacy for his rule and international recognition as a nonaligned nation. In 1989 the name of the country was officially changed to Myanmar, drawing on traditional associations, much as Ceylon was renamed Sri Lanka.

Elections in 1990 showed overwhelming support for the democratic opposition to the military government, led by Aung San's daughter, Aung Sun Suu Kyi, who had been placed under house arrest and held incommunicado since 1989. Like Indira Gandhi, Madame Bandaranaike, and Benazir Bhutto (b. 1953) of Pakistan, who led her executed father's political party to power as prime minister in 1988, Aung San Suu Kyi became a political leader through her father's (or husband's, in the case of Mme. Bandaranaike) position. Rather than holding power in the government, she has remained a symbol of resistance to the military regime. In 1991 Aung San Suu Kyi was awarded the Nobel Peace Prize for her peaceful opposition to the Burmese government, which has continued to deny her the legitimacy she won in the 1990 election.

Ethnic insurgency movements in both Myanmar and Sri Lanka have continued to plague both nations. In Myanmar the Karen, the Kachin, and the Shan peoples have agitated for greater autonomy or even independence, claiming control of large areas of the country. In Sri Lanka the Hindu minority have carried out terrorist activities through the group known as the "Tamil Tigers," claiming ethnic, linguistic, and religious links to the southern Indian state of Tamil Nadu. Since 1972 Tamil leaders have demanded a separate state in a loose confederation with the Buddhist Sinhalese majority. As in India, ethnic and religious conflicts have shaped the postcolonial histories of both Sri Lanka and Myanmar.

AFRICAN NATIONALISM AND RESISTANCE IN THE ERA OF DECOLONIZATION

In much of the African continent, the notion of nation state became a charged and almost magical concept, attached to a variety of political aspirations. It was hoped that independent African states would erase ethnic quarrels and antagonisms, as well as abolish class differences that were exaggerated by colonialism. Between 1951 and 1980, no fewer than forty-eight independent nation states were created in Africa, the products of many successful nationalist movements. The roots of African nationalism in these fledgling twentieth-century nations are to be found in nineteenth-century Africa, in the reaction of Africans against colonialism. In Africa, as in many other parts of the colonized world, nationalist forces were not always revolutionary. Unifying political forces were as often reactionary in spirit, using the past as a model for revolutionary change.

Resistance to Colonial Injustice   Colonial rule began with the threat and use of violence. African peoples, particularly those belonging to state structures, rarely surrendered to the imposition of external political rule without resistance. With brutal force, European expeditions into interior regions attempted to establish territorial sovereignty in order to exploit resources. The productive potential of the colony was claimed by the colonizers through the appropriation of land and the taxation of African labor. Africans were compelled to migrate to urban centers in search of wage-paying jobs to pay the taxes demanded by colonial officials. Forced labor was common, while colonial laws forbade the exploitation of local resources except by the colonial government. Africans were conscripted into work gangs and armies. Armed revolts and more subtle forms of resistance, including work stoppage and flight, were immediate responses to colonialism.

Primary resistance movements were military responses to economic and materialist grievances; sometimes they also represented an attempt to reclaim African lands. They have been understood as essentially backward-looking struggles in the early development of nationalism, since rather than imagine a new world, they sought to return to the past. Their leaders were forced to adopt the colonists' violent tactics, negotiate with the foreign powers who occupied their territories, and accept the territorial boundaries determined by cartographers and politicians a continent away. The first generation of African resisters frequently wrung concessions and brought about alliances between the colonial administrations and African societies. Importantly, the memory of resistance would shape the thoughts and environment of a later generation.

The Impact of Global Events The decolonization of Africa should also be viewed in relation to two global events of the twentieth century: the Great Depression and World War II. Both shifted world political economy, and both initiated social and economic transformations that affected the lives of Africans. The global depression of the 1930s was a period of economic stagnation and severely questioned the economic profitability of the colonial enterprise. During the military confrontations of the twentieth century, rapid change and urban growth occurred. Britain and France relied heavily on African resources and troops. Colonial enterprises used forced labor in Kenya, Tanganyika, Nigeria, and French West Africa. Africans mined resources and constructed railways; they suffered massive food shortages and famine conditions that developed from the economic orientation of the colonizers' war economy. The need for reforms became painfully visible in the postwar era, as the food and shelter requirements of urban populations became a concern of the colonial states and peasant masses alike.

Changing economic and social conditions created a context more favorable to African political movements. In particular, the forces of urbanization and industrialization increased exposure to Western education, and even conversion to Christianity provided broad opportunities for nationalism. Thus it was in the cities and towns of Africa that an urban elite began to vocalize its discontent with the unfulfilled promises of Western ideology and the colonial order. Especially after the world economic crisis of the 1920s and 1930s, educated Africans found their lot to be without opportunity in a stagnating and oppressive colonial regime. Dramatic changes in the global political economy convinced increasing numbers of Africans of their vulnerability—as producers for foreign markets and consumers of foreign goods—to political events and economic problems beyond Africa, such as the two world wars, the subsequent Cold War era, repeated economic depressions, and soaring inflation.

African Nationalism and Religion In many parts of the continent, African resistance to colonial rule formed a lasting legacy and was translated into a subsequent generation of resistance in the form of nationalist movements. Also during the early twentieth century, the radical leadership potential of African religious movements was beginning to be recognized in rural and urban areas. Independent churches were highly nationalistic. One founded by John Chilembwe led to an armed nationalist uprising in Nyasaland (Malawi) in 1917. Chilembwe had founded his own African Christian mission in an area of white settlement and used it as a base for rebellion against colonial injustice. Women spiritual leaders, visionaries, and movement members also presented radical alternatives to the political systems in which men participated. African women, by virtue of their marginality, found themselves in positions to act as truly revolutionary voices for change, to transcend the anticolonialist spirit of an earlier generation, and to envision a new era.

Ibo Women's War of 1929 The Ibo Women's War of 1929 was a protest against one of the basic mechanisms of colonial rule: taxation. Led by approximately 10,000 women of southeast Nigeria, the war was actually a traditional response to injustice experienced by Ibo women, a response known as "sitting on a man." When an individual woman could not resolve a conflict with a man, she utilized marketing and kinship-based organizations to spread the word about the grievance and produce the participation of other women in solidarity with her.

The specific grievance in 1929 was begun by an African assistant to the local colonial officer, who had been sent to count a certain woman's goats. Fearing that this inventorying of her property would mean eventual taxation, the woman refused to cooperate and was eventually struck by the colonial employee. Shortly after the incident, thousands of nude women carrying men's weapons (sticks and spears) surrounded the houses of the accused parties and sang ridiculing songs in the ritual of "sitting on a man". This protest traditionally would have effectively isolated the accused until he provided reparations. However, the British response to the peaceful assembly of women was swift and violent, and about fifty women were killed or injured. Eventually the tax was imposed.

The British won the war, and their language prevailed in the way in which the event was known. In colonial documents, the "war" was termed "Aba Riots" by the British, even though the event was neither chaotic nor was it confined to the single village of Aba. The African women were "invisible" in the British terminology. One of the consequences of colonial rule was that the colonizers controlled the language and content of history. However, traditional forms of resistance such as sitting on a man survived in the inspirational oral history of Ibo women. Their strategy of resistance also survived into the 1990s, when it was witnessed by corrupt government officials in postindependence Nigeria. The widespread resistance to the violent imposition of colonial rule was not successful but had a lasting legacy.

Urban Protests Economic and political forces in the interwar years also brought Africans to ▪▪▪▪▪▪▪▪▪▪ towns where the woefully inadequate social provisions of colonial administrations were fuelling economic grievances. Urban centers attracted migrant (male) labor as Africans sought cash to pay taxes and buy imported goods. By the 1940s an era of rapidly growing wage-labor and labor unrest in the cities was under way, joining an equally threatening period of rural discontent. Only the coalition of these forces—urban intelligentsia, organized urban laborers, and rural mass protest—could create successful nationalist movements in postwar Africa. They did so in the form of dockworker and railway strikes in Dakar (from 1922 to the 1940s) or the cocoa boycotts and protests in Ghana (1930 and 1938). Resistance before this time rarely had anything to do with sovereignty or racial identity; rather it resulted from crises in the Africans' material world and was related more closely to cracks in the colonial construction of class and its painful social reality.

Algeria The contradictions of the postwar world, in which colonized Africans were denied ▪▪▪▪▪▪▪▪ the rights and freedoms for which they had fought in the European-driven conflicts, required both political and social reform. Africans were not unaware that the war had swept away European colonialism in Asia. Popular resistance to the colonial state after 1940 made African colonies increasingly difficult to administer. A key symbol of European hegemony in Africa was Algeria, a French colony since the mid-nineteenth century. Nationalist struggles there led to nearly a decade of civil war. Algerian independence in 1962 represented the culmination of mass political party activities of the Front National de la Liberation (FLN) beginning in the period of 1937–1946. Algerian women, socially and politically marginalized by traditional society, played critical roles in the revolution. They were spies, smugglers, and even took on combat roles. The escalation of the struggle in Algeria, where as many as 2 million French settlers resided, forced the French government to negotiate independence there and in other territories.

French and British Africa   As early as the late nineteenth century, Samory Toure led an armed rebellion against the zones of French expansion in West Africa. Samory's opposition was both cultural and political, and his guerrilla warfare tactics succeeded in resisting the French occupation for more than fifteen years. Collaboration between Europeans in British and French colonies and superior weapons eventually led to the defeat of all African military responses. In French West Africa, African political activity eventually included representation in the National Assembly in Paris after 1946. Labor organizations became increasingly political and the organized strikes and boycotts by African workers brought about the collapse of the colonial system. In the Gold Coast, which was British, Kwame Nkrumah returned from his education in the United States in 1949 and formed the Convention People's Party (CPP), which would become a mass party and the catalyst of the independence movement producing sub-Saharan Africa's first independent nation state (Ghana) in 1957. Nkrumah's philosophy of pan-African unity found sympathy across the continent.

The emergence of independence movements brought an end to most of the traditional, aristocratic leadership that had predated the colonial era. Already undermined by the merchant middle class and the missionary- and colonial-educated elites, few traditional African leaders remained. The survivors became symbolic targets for mass political action, such as in the example of the armed Mau Mau revolt in Kenya between the 1940s and 1955, which began with the assassination of the senior chief, Waruhiu, and the onset of an intense period of grassroots guerrilla warfare. During the Mau Mau struggle, violent rural action attempted to frighten British settlers, who had been given lands taken away from African farmers. Although the freedom fighters were defeated, the struggle convinced the British to accept the principle of African majority rule over the protests of white settlers. Elsewhere the targets of resistance were employees of corporations, such as the concessionary rubber-gathering firms of the Congo Independent State, whose African military units had used force to rule over the Central African political economy since the 1920s.

The Struggle in the Congo In other regions the legacy of colonial rule has continued through the second half of the twentieth century. Excessive reliance on expensive bureaucracies and military might, and the continuing dependency on foreign technology and capital, coupled with elite corruption, have severely curtailed the achievement of political stability. Elsewhere, such as the former Belgian Congo (and former Zaire), a deadly combination of these forces of underdevelopment and covert and overt foreign intervention into African political affairs, ushered in a half century of violence and moral and economic decay following independence.

Rapid Belgian decolonization in the Congo reinforced European cultural and economic dominance of urban and mining regions. Racist insensitivity and continuing interference also furthered the cause of resistance. The speech by the Belgian king, Baudouin, on Independence Day in 1960 blithely celebrated the colonial past. His words infuriated many Africans, including Patrice Lumumba (1925–1961), a radical nationalist, who became a martyr of independence. In his struggle for total independence, Lumumba passionately enumerated the grievances against the colonial regime; civil unrest, riots, and strikes followed.

FIGURE 19.3 *Lumumba Makes His Famous Speech,* Genre Painting by Zairian Artist Tshibumba Kanda Matulu, ca. 1973–74

Lumumba's 1960 speech was a direct renunciation of a painful past delivered while the Belgian king listened (in the background).

SOURCE: From: *Remembering the Present: Painting and Popular History in Zaire* by Johannes Fabian. University of California Press, 1996. Photo courtesy of the author.

Civil war soon broke out in the huge territory, as the nation state struggled to hold together the diverse cultural and economic aspirations of its peoples. After being briefly incarcerated by the colonial rulers, Lumumba was freed, but foreign powers eager to maintain their control over the country's strategic minerals feared his radical message. Lumumba's political quest for unity in his country was cut short when he was assassinated after secret orders reportedly issued by the United States Central Intelligence Agency. Lumumba became a national hero, while covert military and economic assistance from the United States and European governments supported subsequent revolutionary regimes, including that of Mobutu Sese Seko Nkuku Ngwendu wa Zabanga, leader of the Popular Movement of the Revolution, in order to protect United States mining profits in the rich Shaba (Katanga) province. In 1997 Mobutu was finally deposed, and a democratic republic renamed the territory as the Congo.

The Decolonization of the Mind   The final front of the anticolonialist and nationalist battles was the historical front. Because the appropriation of knowledge and history was as necessary to the maintenance of colonial rule as any gun, European colonizers, through their control over education and language, had attempted to steal African history, together with the continent's palm oil, peanuts, and gold. It was thought that without a past, a people could be more easily exploited. Accordingly, colonialism never brought literacy in European languages to more than a small number of Africans, who formed an elite class.

Historians must look to the oral and literary traditions of resistance to forge a balanced historical understanding of the period. African novelists such as Chinua Achebe (b. 1930) of

Nigeria or his East African counterpart Ngugi wa Thiong'o wrote personal, almost autobiographical accounts of the events of their lifetimes from their African perspectives. Achebe's *Things Fall Apart* (1959), for example, was an attempt to tell the story of the colonial past in a personal way at a time when virtually no written African histories existed. The oral poetry of combat between nationalist and European forces records more than the linear pattern of events.

Independence was not "given" to the colonies by the European powers, nor was it the "happy ending" to the struggles of the twentieth century. Independence was achieved by Africans who opposed the giant and controlling interests of foreign colonizers, but those interests were not altered by independence. Not long after achieving independence, many Africans realized that the era of colonial rule had evolved into neocolonialism, a "newer imperialism," in which the authority and class structure prevailed under the essentially same global system of capital, finance, and control by multinational corporations. No experience exhibits this continuing struggle against a global system more clearly than that of resistance in South Africa.

RESISTANCE AND REVOLUTION IN SOUTH AFRICA

The political and cultural path of South Africa differed greatly from that of the rest of the African continent, where European settler populations were limited by the climate and geography. The South African economy had been industrialized since the late nineteenth century, owing to the impact of the discoveries of diamonds and gold. Mineral exploitation in turn spurred the British imperialist expansion into the interior of South Africa, where it met with the resistance of Africans and Boers, the descendant "white" farmers from Dutch and racially mixed frontier mercantile and farming societies at the Cape.

This conflict resulted in the Anglo-Boer War (1899–1902) and set the stage both for the social, political, and economic reconstruction after British victory in 1902 and for unitary white rule under the British crown in 1910. British and other foreign investment in agricultural production further removed Africans from their landholdings in an era of expanding foreign capital. Against this background customary policies of segregation and discrimination became entrenched in laws between 1905 and 1945. Black Africans continued to be denied participation in the machinery of government; they could neither vote nor hold office.

The Apartheid Election of 1948   A major turning point in South African history was the national election of 1948 through which the Nationalist Party came into power. The discriminatory labor laws and practices of the diamond and gold mining industries and agricultural sectors became rigidly defined between 1913 and 1922. After 1948 they were expanded by a national policy of segregation and oppression, known as "apartheid." Apartheid policies enforced a color code that favored whites over all others and dictated where the majority African populations could live, travel, and work. Blacks were systematically excluded from holding political office and from voting, yet their labor was essential to the processes of industrialization. Black Africans were required to carry identity passes that revealed their racial classification. The white minority enacted "pass laws" to restrict African movements and particularly to control the influx of workers from rural to urban areas. Internal security acts legalized the violent repression of resistance to gross human rights violations.

Strategies of Resistance   Among those who actively opposed the government and apartheid
▬▬▬▬▬▬▬▬▬▬   were two men who eventually became Nobel Peace Prize winners:
Albert Luthuli (1898–1967) and Nelson Mandela (1918–). Chief Albert Luthuli led a lifelong, nonviolent struggle against racial discrimination and injustice. His doctrine of a multiracial society resulted in Luthuli's imprisonment and exile. Nelson Mandela was also active
in the struggle against economic and political injustice through his leadership position
within the African National Congress (ANC). Founded in 1912 on principles of noncooperation, the Congress initially worked through nonviolent techniques of mass resistance and
eventually adopted a program of terrorism directed against the repressive South African state.
The aims of the ANC and other labor union and political leaders fueled worldwide condemnation of the government of South Africa; a global antiapartheid movement spread across the

DAILY LIVES

SOUTH AFRICAN WOMEN PROTESTS: "We are now the men"

African women's experience of colonial rule was fundamentally different from that of African men. It was primarily men's labor that was demanded for the mines, often leaving women alone to raise children and provide both domestic labor and agricultural production. Their daily lives were harsh, with few opportunities for change. For Zulu-speaking women in South Africa in the 1920s, subjugation was at the hands of both African men and the colonial system. The depth of women's experience of social, political, and economic injustice was clearly visible in widespread protests in 1929.

By 1929 the traditionally female activity of brewing beer (*utshwala*) was severely curtailed and eventually outlawed by the Native Beer Act of 1908 and the 1928 Liquor Act. These colonial laws made illegal the selling of beer (one of the few sources of female earnings) and even stripped women of the right to consume government-licensed alcohol by barring them from canteens and beerhalls. The men who did legally frequent the government canteens squandered their rent money on beer to the benefit of colonial coffers, not the African community. Many women were outraged, and their protests became increasingly strident, much to the surprise of white magistrates. Spreading from the countryside to urban centers like Durban, the women's beer protests seized the traditional Zulu male perogative of violence.

According to eyewitness accounts, the protests consisted of groups of 60 to 100 militant women, many of whom, shunning European dress, carried sticks and wore cow tails and feathers; some even wore male loincloths, the war dress of Zulu men. From August to November, women attacked canteens, bit and stoned police, stamped, danced, and sang. Many women were imprisoned for the clashes with the police and male drinkers. Their incarceration produced an additional hardship on the men, who were left to mind small children and reluctantly supported the women's cause.

When a white magistrate told a group of women that their demands were illegitimate, he said, "This is a matter for the men to make a representation to me."

The spokeswoman Matobana Mjara responded, "We are now the men and that is why we have come to you."[*]

The women protesters used traditional forms of political expression but also inverted the gender roles available to them. They were powerful reminders of the critical economic roles in which African women served. It would take another generation of resistance for South African women and men to regain control of their daily lives.

[*]Helen Bradford, ""We are now the men:" Women's Beer Protests in the Natal Countryside, 1929," in Belinda Bruzzoli, ed., *Class, Community, and Conflict*: South African Perspectives (Johannesburg: Rawan Press, 1987), p. 292.

industrialized world and even targeted multinational corporations for their support of the racist regime.

Capitalism and Apartheid   That the struggle in South Africa lasted so long was in part a consequence of how entrenched the South African economy had become in the world capitalist system. The interests of the world economy benefited those in power, committed to economic growth at the expense of social justice. But the opposition prevailed and expanded to include women and children, labor, and sources of international support. Mandela, imprisoned for more than twenty years on charges of treason, eventually gained world support for the fight against the apartheid system and its racially based disenfranchisement of the black majority. Released from prison in 1990, Mandela led the ANC to political victory and the end of the apartheid era. As the first African elected president of South Africa, Mandela remains one of the world's most celebrated resistance fighters against twentieth-century tyranny.

DECOLONIZATION IN SOUTHEAST ASIA

Clashes between nationalist insurgents and colonial government forces took place in the aftermath of World War II in almost every state in Southeast Asia. In those parts of Southeast Asia that had been colonized by the French, nationalist leaders challenged French colonial authority and worked to overthrow traditional political and social orders. Elsewhere in Southeast Asia, such as in Malaysia and the Philippines, the combination of colonial legacies with complex ethnic and religious compositions shaped new political and social orders.

Vietnam   In Vietnam, a French colony since 1857, a nationalist movement began in the early twentieth century, inspired by the success of the Japanese in defeating Russia in 1905, the 1911 revolution in China, and the Russian Revolution in 1917. Opposition to French colonial rule was galvanized by the military leadership of Vo Nguyen Giap and the political leadership of Ho Chi Minh (1890–1969), who was introduced to Marxism as a student in France. Ho played a role in the founding of the Vietnamese national independence movement, the Viet Minh, which fought the Japanese occupation in World War II and was determined to resist the restoration of French colonialism after the war's end.

When Japan surrendered in 1945, the Viet Minh captured the capital of Hanoi, forced Emperor Bao Dai to abdicate, and declared the Democratic Republic of Vietnam with Ho Chi Minh as its president. Although France initially recognized the new state, armed conflict between the French and Vietnamese erupted at the end of 1946 when negotiations over the political and economic relationship with France broke down. In 1949 the French set up a separate state, South Vietnam, with its capital at Saigon and its ruler the deposed emperor Bao Dai.

Fearing the spread of Communism in Asia, especially in the wake of the Korean War and the build-up of the Cold War, the United States supported the French until the French defeat at Dien Bien Phu in 1954. An international meeting in Geneva following the French defeat partitioned Vietnam at the 17th parallel, with North Vietnam under the Communists and South Vietnam controlled by the Saigon government. The United States backed the government of the south under Ngo Dinh Diem, a Catholic collaborator with the French. During the next two decades, U.S. involvement in Vietnam steadily escalated, from sending military advisers and material support to committing thousands of troops.

Domestic opposition in Vietnam to the Diem government crystallized in the opposition of Buddhist monks to the Catholic-led government, some of whom burned themselves alive to demonstrate their resistance. But the guerrilla activities of the Vietcong, Communist sympathizers who infiltrated the south in increasing numbers, were by far the most serious threat to the South Vietnamese government. In 1963 Diem was overthrown in a military coup that the U.S. government knew to be imminent, but did not stop. Succeeding Vietnamese military governments were dependent on U.S. aid to prop them up.

The Vietnam War delivered the United States its first military defeat, at high cost to both Vietnamese and Americans. More bombs were dropped on Vietnam than were used by

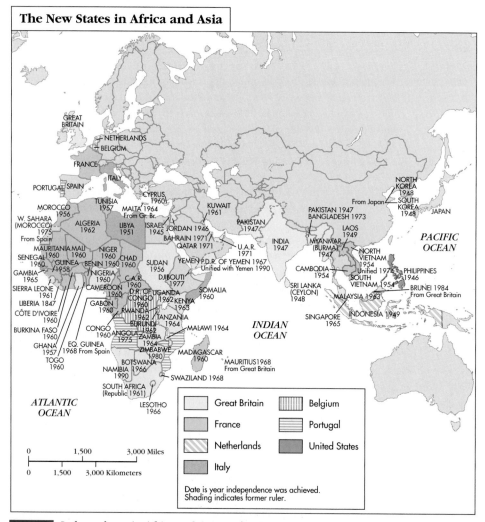

MAP 19.1 Independence in Africa and Asia, 1847–1990

the Allies during World War II, and the use of defoliants to clear jungle vegetation that provided enemy ground cover left widespread destruction and pollution of the countryside.

The Vietnam War's reliance on guerrilla combat and the use of the helicopter in difficult terrain marked a major turning point in modern warfare. Guerrilla warfare also made it a "people's war" because there was no clear division between the civilian and the military populations. Vietnam proved the strength of guerrilla war on home territory against even such a powerful force as the United States, with its tremendous financial, material, and human resources. The Vietnam War also fragmented American society as conflicts erupted between the generation that remembered World War II with its clear enemies and the generation of the 1960s whose Peace Movement protested a seemingly hopeless and pointless war.

Laos and Cambodia   Other parts of French Indochina were drawn into the Vietnam conflict and underwent similar experiences with Communist movements tied to campaigns for national liberation in the wake of Japan's surrender at the end of World War II. Both the legacies of traditional monarchies and the power of newly emergent military leaders complicated the struggles for national liberation. For example, Laos, a French colony from 1896 until 1953, retained its monarchy though a series of military coups in the 1950s and 1960s which led to civil war. In 1975 the monarchy was abolished under the Pathet Lao, a Laotian Communist movement.

Cambodia, a French colony since 1856, similarly gained its independence from France in 1953. Prince Norodom Sihanouk, who had come to power in Cambodia in a government installed by the Japanese in 1945, was ousted from power in a military coup by the general Lon Nol in 1970, who wanted to fight Vietnamese Communists, the Viet Cong, who had made inroads into Cambodian territory.

With the fall of South Vietnam in 1975, a Cambodian Communist movement, the Khmer Rouge ("Red Khmer") captured Phnom Penh and ended the 600 year old monarchy, calling the country by the traditional name, Kampuchea. The Kampuchean regime of Pol Pot carried out a massive reordering of Cambodian society, bringing about the deaths of more than 1 million people through forced labor, migration, and execution. In 1979 Vietnam invaded Cambodia and installed a puppet regime. After more than a decade of struggle between Vietnamese elements and the Khmer Rouge, Prince Sihanouk was restored as a leader of a new coalition government in 1993.

Thailand   Thailand had remained independent throughout the colonial era in Southeast Asia, though it lost much territory to European powers, especially the French (see Chapter 17). The traditional Thai monarchy was formally brought to an end by a coup in 1932, which established a constitutional monarchy. The grandson of King Mongkut came to the throne in 1946 and celebrated his fiftieth anniversary as an extraconstitutional symbol of authority in 1996. Throughout his fifty years on the throne, the king has served as the symbolic figure of the Thai nation, providing a source of continuity through fifteen constitutions, seventeen coups, and twenty-one prime ministers. Buddhism is another source of continuity and stability in Thailand.

In recent years Thailand has emerged as an economic "miracle" of development, though the capital of Bangkok displays the dismal effects of unsupervised development in the worst air pollution and the most congested traffic conditions in all of Asia. Along with non-Communist Thailand, Communist Vietnam has begun to emerge as a site of rapid economic development, following a mixed pattern of socialism and capitalism in a burgeoning market economy.

Malaysia The Malayan peninsula gained its independence from Britain in 1957 and became ▬▬▬▬ Malaysia in 1963, incorporating the states of Sabah and Sarawak on the island of Borneo. Tensions between Muslims, who are in political control, and ethnic Chinese, who dominate the economy in Malaysia, have contributed to continuing violence, though it remains a multiethnic Islamic state.

Singapore Founded by the British colonial administrator Thomas Stamford Raffles in the ▬▬▬▬ nineteenth century, the city state of Singapore gained independence from Malaysia in 1965 and has since become one of the Asian economic success stories of the late twentieth century. Subject to strict authoritarian political control and repressive social policies carried out in the 1970s and 1980s, by its Chinese leader, Lee Kuan Yew, who drew on an authoritarian variety of traditional Confucian values to exert social control, Singapore remains politically and economically dominated by Chinese.

Indonesia A movement for Indonesian independence from Dutch rule began in 1927 with ▬▬▬▬ the establishment of the Indonesian National Party, headed by a young engineer named Sukarno (1901–1970). Dutch repression of Indonesian nationalism reached a peak in 1940 when Dutch colonial authorities prohibited the use of the name Indonesia. During World War II when Indonesia was occupied by the Japanese, the extent of opposition to the Dutch surfaced in the relatively passive acceptance of Japanese rule, which was regarded as no worse, and perhaps better, than Dutch rule. Though Indonesian independence was declared by a puppet government of the Japanese in 1943, and again at war's end in 1945 by Sukarno, Dutch recognition of Indonesian independence came only in 1949. In turn, the new Indonesian government suppressed the declaration of independence by the Moluccas (formerly the Spice Islands) in 1949, but Moluccan terrorists have continued to carry out attacks on both Dutch and Indonesians. The attempted Communist coup in 1965 against the government of President Sukarno ended in enormous bloodshed (estimated deaths run from a low of 100,000 to as many as 750,000), repression, and the establishment of military rule. Rebels on the island of Timor have pursued a civil war since 1975 to establish their independence from the Indonesian government.

New nations such as Indonesia, created from the anticolonial resistance of the postwar era, have in turn spawned resistance movements to authoritarian regimes buttressed by the military. Resistance has taken the form of either internal opposition to the government, as in Communist uprisings, or in movements for independence from the nation, as in Timor.

Philippines The complex colonial legacy of the Philippines includes Spanish domination be-▬▬▬▬ ginning in the sixteenth century, followed by American hegemony after the Spanish-American War in 1898, and finally Japanese conquest during World War II. Resistance to American control surfaced under the leadership of Emilio Aguinaldo (1869–1964) between 1899 and 1902. The reconquest of the Philippines from the Japanese took place with the help of guerrilla groups such as the Communist Hukbalahap (from words in the Tagalog language meaning "People's Army against the Japanese") movement. The Huks, as

FIGURE 19.4 Emilio Aguinaldo (Bottom Center) and Comrades

Aguinaldo led a Filipino insurrection against the United States and was defeated only when 70,000 American troops were sent to suppress the insurrection (ca. 1900).

SOURCE: New York Public Library.

they were known, represented an important rural resistance movement that challenged traditional social and economic hierarchies in the countryside and championed the interests of poor tenant farmers.

After Japanese defeat and despite the declaration of independence for the Philippines on July 4, 1946, U.S. political and economic influence remained strong. Direct leadership alternated between presidents from the two major postwar political parties, the Liberals and the Nationalists. The Huks continued their opposition to the government but were defeated by the mid-1950s, seemingly along with hope for resolution of the deeply embedded problems of the rural and landless poor. Ferdinand Marcos (1917–1989) was elected president in 1965, and though he came from a poor rural background, he did nothing to break up the power of the landed aristocracy and to relieve chronic agrarian unrest.

The Marcos government instituted martial law in 1972 in response to popular opposition, but even such strong tactics failed to halt the progress of the New People's Army, a guerrilla force active throughout the Philippines, organizing farmers, pressuring landlords to reduce rents, and at times engaging in open warfare. The New People's Army attracted thousands of Roman Catholics, while the southern islands of Mindanao and Palawan became strongholds of the Moro Liberation Movement, a Muslim guerrilla force.

In contrast to the failure of resistance to the Indonesian military government during the Communist insurgency in 1965, the Marcos government, which was propped up with U.S. support, was finally overthrown in 1986 by the electoral victory of the People's Party, headed by Corazon Aquino, widow of a slain reformer. Aquino was defeated for reelection in 1992 by her defense minister and military chief, Fidel Ramos. The legacy of both the colonial past and the postwar past remain as challenges to Ramos and his successors: the relationship between civilian government and the army; the traditionally powerful Roman Catholic Church; and the conflicts between wealthy landed interests and poor farmers.

Although U.S. hegemony has by no means disappeared from the Philippines, the victory of the People's Party in 1986 demonstrated the potential strength of mass resistance to authoritarian political regimes propped up by the military and even by such powerful foreign influence as that of the United States. The resistance of mass and revolutionary nationalism in Vietnam, which defeated the might of the U.S. military during a protracted guerrilla war, similarly proved that resistance movements with a strong base of support among the people can overcome even the most powerful nation in the world.

■

RESISTANCE AND REVOLUTION IN LATIN AMERICA

In their quest for economic development and political autonomy, Latin Americans struggled between reformist and revolutionary options. Especially when institutional reforms failed, frustrations with the status quo led many Latin Americans to choose the violent substitution of old, discredited paths by new directions. Ongoing revolutionary struggles took place across several generations in twentieth-century Latin America: in Mexico, Guatemala, Nicaragua, Cuba, Bolivia, Peru, Chili, and Argentina. What these very different revolutions had in common was their highly nationalistic tone and their objective goal of reducing dependency. All tried to change old institutions, eradicate injustice, or create meaningful economic patterns that support self-reliance and forces of development favorable for the majority of the people. None have succeeded in achieving all their goals.

MEXICO

The culmination of the nineteenth century struggle for independence from Spain and for control of Mexican politics came with the presidency of a mestizo strongman, Porfirio Diaz (1830–1915). The dictatorship of Diaz (r. 1876-1911) saw political stability, spectacular economic progress for landed and commercial elites, and great profits for foreign capitalist investment, but abject poverty for the masses of the landless population. Resentment over the inequities caused by such uneven economic growth that benefitted only the smallest minority led to a revolution that overthrew Diaz in 1910. The leader, Francisco Madero (1873–1913), crossed the frontier from the United States to become the new president in 1911. Madero was at first supported by Emiliano Zapata (1877–1919), who became one of Latin America's most popular and influential agrarian leaders, but the support was short-lived.

Zapata and Villa Zapata, like many of those for whom he spoke, began life as an illiterate tenant farmer of Native American descent. He advocated transferring land to the landless peasants. Zapata rallied Native Americans to Madero's cause in 1910, as Francisco "Pancho" Villa (1877–1923), also the illiterate son of a farm worker, led north Mexican troops in support of the revolution against Diaz. Zapata eventually lost confidence in Madero's policies when it became clear that social and economic reform would not occur. Zapata formulated his own plan for agrarian reform, called the Plan of Ayala, in 1911. He and his followers demanded land for peasants and seized the haciendas of many wealthy elites. During the Huerta and Carranza regimes that followed Madero, Zapata continued his resistance to the government, extending his power throughout southern Mexico, while Villa directed the revolution in the north. After marching on Mexico City three times in 1914, Zapata was forced to withdraw and five years later was murdered by an agent of Carranza; his co-revolutionist Villa was assassinated in 1923. The agrarian revolution and attempts at reform did not end there, however.

1917 Constitution A new constitution in 1917 expropriated religious property, restored communal lands to Native Americans, and promised a variety of radical social and economic reforms. Crucial to the political success of the National Revolutionary Party (PNR), which came to power with the Mexican Revolution, was negotiation with U.S. oil companies, and the issue of control over Mexico's oil resources continued to plague Mexico's leaders. Under President Lazaro Cardenas (in office 1934–1940), the redistribution of land was accelerated. Railways were nationalized in 1937, along with the subsoil rights of foreign oil companies. After labor disputes in 1938, foreign oil properties were expropriated and the rights of urban workers upheld. Though dependent on the sale of oil to Germany, Italy and Japan, after World War II erupted, Mexico joined the United States against the Axis powers in 1942.

Since the end of World War II, the Institutional Revolutionary Party (PRI), renamed from the prewar PNR, has dominated the government, rather than the government being controlled by powerful individuals. Economic struggles and political corruption have continued to plague Mexican politics. In the 1990s former president Carlos Salinas became embroiled in a corruption scandal that threatened the rule of the PRI. In 1994 the Zapatista National Liberation Army, named for the revolutionary hero Zapata, captured towns in the southern Mexican state of Chiapas, continuing the demand for land reform and recognition of the rights of Native Americans.

CENTRAL AMERICA AND THE CARIBBEAN

The twentieth century also produced resistance movements that, without becoming full-blown armed revolutions, unsuccessfully challenged states formed from the independence movements of the nineteenth century. Many of these resistance movements have not been successful in unseating military rulers or in opening up the political process beyond one-party government for more than a brief period of time. Eventually, violence gave birth to more violence. As in parts of Southeast Asia, the effects of resistance, coupled in the case of Latin America with the overt and covert intervention of its powerful North American neighbor, the United States, often produced stronger concentrations of authority in the hands of the military.

Trinidad In Trinidad, from the early part of the twentieth century, the oil industry speeded that country's industrialization. Because of Trinidad's strategic Caribbean location, the island and its resources attracted the attention of the United States, especially during World War II. The U.S. military presence provoked the mocking lyrics of the calypso "Rum and Coca Cola," a song that became popular in the United States during World War II, but that actually criticized American soldiers for assaulting Trinidadian women.

Contemporary Latin America

UNITED STATES

ATLANTIC OCEAN

MEXICO

Mexico
City•

Havana•

CUBA

JAMAICA

HAITI DOMINICAN REPUBLIC

PUERTO RICO

Port-au- Santo
Prince Domingo

BELIZE
HONDURAS

GUATEMALA

Guatemala•

San Salvador•

EL SALVADOR

•Tegucigalpa

•NICARAGUA

Managua•

Panama•

San José•

COSTA RICA

PANAMA

Caracas•

VENEZUELA

TRINIDAD

GUYANA

FRENCH
GUIANA

Bogotá•

COLOMBIA

SURINAME

Quito•

ECUADOR

PERU

Lima•

BRAZIL

•Brasília

BOLIVIA

•La Paz

PARAGUAY

CHILE

Asunción•

PACIFIC OCEAN

Santiago•

ARGENTINA

URUGUAY

Buenos Montevideo
Aires•

ATLANTIC OCEAN

FALKLAND IS.

0   500   1,000 Miles

0   500   1,000 Kilometers

MAP 19.2 Nation States in Latin America and the Caribbean

Panama The Panama Canal had great strategic importance in World War II and provided ▬▬▬▬ enormous economic benefits to the United States, which controlled it. In the 1960s and 1970s, opposition to U.S. control of the Panama Canal Zone led to a new treaty in 1978, agreeing to the transfer of the Canal Zone to Panama and the end of the U.S. military presence by the year 2000. However, political instability in Panama, in which the drug-trafficking general Manuel Noriega played a large role, provided the pretext for a U.S. invasion of Panama in 1989. While the motives for the move against Noriega remain confused, the transformation of Panama from a client state of the United States to a symbol of Latin American nationalism reflected the depth of anti-imperialist sentiment in the region.

The Cuban Revolution Between 1953 and 1959, the Cuban revolutionary Fidel Castro ▬▬▬▬▬▬▬ (b. 1927) led a rebel movement with popular support to overthrow the dictator Fulgencio Batista. The movement's goals were nationalistic: sovereignty, development, and cultural autonomy. The tradition of rural unrest was especially strong in eastern Cuba, and peasants there formed the basis for the outright revolution against the past that had created hardships suffered by all but the wealthy few. A moderate leftist at the outset, Castro became increasingly hostile to the United States, which frequently intervened in Cuban affairs and had supported Batista, who opposed reforms. Castro's seizure of American-owned companies enraged the United States, which launched an unsuccessful invasion of Cuba in 1961.

Castro became increasingly dependent on the Soviet Union in the 1960s and gave active support to revolutionary movements throughout Latin America and in Africa. Cuba became the first Western Hemisphere nation to align itself totally with the Soviet Union. The Argentine revolutionary theorist and guerrilla leader, Che Guevara (1928–1967), aided Castro in his rise to power and actively supported peasant-based revolutionary movements in developing countries, including Angola, Portuguese Guinea, Mozambique, and the Congo. He became an insurgent leader in Bolivia, where he established a training camp for his followers in 1966. The following year he was captured and executed by the Bolivian army, with support from the United States Army.

Though U.S. policy worked against everything Guevara and Castro stood for, both became heroes to New Left radicals of the 1960s in the United States and to oppressed peoples around the world. Because the causes of the Cuban revolution were found widely in the poverty, underdevelopment, exploitation, and dependency of the Third World, the revolutionary solutions appealed to many in distant parts of the globe. The Cuban revolution's other success has been in promoting women's rights and making education and health care available to most of its peoples.

The Nicaraguan Revolution The forces of revolution in the Central American nation of ▬▬▬▬▬▬▬ Nicaragua emerged as early as the 1930s in the struggle against imperialism. The roots of grievances and resistance date to the earlier part of the twentieth century (1909–1933) when the United States occupied the nation and engaged in combat with guerrilla fighters led by Augusto Cesar Sandino (1893–1934). Sandino's demands for political independence from foreign interference, sovereignty, and economic recovery for the benefit of all were again taken up in 1961 by the founders of the Sandinista Front for National Liberation (FSLN). The Sandinistas did not take seriously the historial and cultural differences between Atlantic and Pacific coast ethnic groups, and rural and urban interests. Military opposition was supported by foreign capital. While the revolution ultimately succeeded in seizing power in 1979 through violent means, it departed through the ballot box in 1990, when elections created a counter revolution in support of the opposition's commitment to capitalist economic growth.

DEPENDENCY, THE MILITARY, AND REVOLUTION IN SOUTH AMERICA

Like other parts of the emergent global economy, Latin American economies were drawn into world markets during the late nineteenth and early twentieth centuries, expanding production of certain commodities and exploiting resources to meet the demands of an international market. For example, in the late nineteenth century, Bolivia, Chile, and Peru battled over control of the nitrate deposits in the Atacama Desert because of world demand for nitrate. Chile won the dispute, but when the market for nitrate collapsed in the post–World War I era because of peace (reduction in demand) and synthetic substitutes, the Chilean economy was severely affected. The discovery of oil in Venezuela in 1914 led to extremes of wealth and poverty in that country. As in Mexico, oil in Venezuela became a nationalized industry.

Violence and revolutions were widespread in bringing about political changes in South America. In Chile the Socialist candidate for president, Salvador Allende (1908–1973), won the election in 1970, supported by a leftist coalition. Allende set out to transform Chile by nationalizing industries and carrying out social reforms but met with resistance from both the right and the radical left. He lost his life in a military coup supported by the United States in 1973, and Chile entered a long period of military rule under General Augusto Pinochet (b. 1915).

Under pressure of a 1988 plebiscite that rejected one-man rule by a resounding 55 percent to 43 percent, Pincohet, though remaining commander in chief of the army (until 1998), stepped aside in 1990, allowing free and open presidential elections. In 1993, Eduardo Frei, son of a president who preceded Allende, was elected president.

In Argentina nearly a half century of republicanism (1890–1930) came to an end when a coalition of military officers and aristocratic civilians seized power (September 1930). For the following half century, the military was in control of Argentina, culminating in the increasingly authoritarian rule of an army colonel, Juan Peron (1895–1974) who emerged as the strong man after World War II. During his first term in office (1946–1955), Peron increasingly shared his power with his charismatic wife, the actress Eva Duarte ("Evita"), perhaps the most politically powerful woman in the history of the Western Hemisphere. In 1955, a coup by the armed forces sent Peron into exile, from which he returned to power in 1973. When Peron died in 1974, his third wife, Isabel, became president; Argentina disintegrated into economic and political chaos during her presidency and in 1976 she was removed from office. The next few years saw a series of military juntas that violently repressed political opposition by a reign of terror that included the murder and disappearance of thousands of people. In 1982 the generals undertook to rally nationalistic support by attempting to retake the Malvinas Islands in the South Atlantic, over which Argentine claimed sovereignty, but which the British (who called them the Falkland Islands) occupied and ruled. The defeat of Argentina in the Malvinas/Falkland War produced disarray among the junta and lead to the promise of an election (1983) and return to civilian government (1984). Raul Alfonsin, who was elected president, was successful in prosecuting the generals responsible for the repressive and violent rule of the juntas, but it remained for his successor, Carlos Menem (elected 1989) to cope with Argentina's serious economic problems.

Peru similarly experienced alternation between military and civilian government, and with the election of Alberto Fujimori (b. 1938) in 1990, an austerity program to restore economic order led to intensified terrorist kidnappings and attacks by the Maoist rebels known as the Sendero Luminoso, the "Shining Path" guerrillas. A more recent indigenous rebel movement, the Tupac Amaru, takes its name from an eighteenth-century rebel against Spanish colonialism who was executed by the Spanish. Like the Shining Path guerrillas, the Tupac Amaru organize among the peasants and seek support for meeting the needs of Peruvian poor who have not shared in the economic gains of the postwar period. In 1996 their assault on the Japanese embassy in Lima and holding of hostages there for four months to support demands for the release of Tupac Amaru political prisoners resulted in an armed attack by the Peruvian army that killed all rebels and freed the hostages.

FOREIGN INFLUENCE AND RESISTANCE

Throughout Latin America and the Caribbean, the United States continues to use military force to protect its economic and political interests in the Western Hemisphere. The Organization of American States (OAS), founded in 1948, is one of many multinational organizations created in the aftermath of World War II to foster coherent regional development policies. But since it is dominated by the U.S., the OAS can also be seen as an extension of U.S. policy formulated in the 1823 Monroe Doctrine, which claimed the paramount interests of the United States in the Western Hemisphere.

In contrast to the increased U.S. political involvement in Latin America and the Caribbean, the decline of British investment and power has been consistent with the general reduction of the role of Great Britain in the post–World War II world, a role further damaged in Latin America by the 1982 Malvinas War between Argentina and Britain. As British influence and investment in Latin America declined in the postwar era, the influence of Asian nations such as Japan increased.

The remarkable recovery and development of Japan in the post–World War II era has enabled Japanese industrialists and financiers, who may seem in Latin American eyes to lack the stigma of historical imperialism attached to their North American equivalents, to make rapid inroads. Perhaps more willing to accept the aspirations and realities of indigenous Latin American politics than are North Americans, the Japanese have invested heavily in Brazil and Mexico in particular, and large numbers of Japanese immigrants have settled in most Latin American countries. Alberto Fujimori, the elected president of Peru, is of Japanese descent.

Resistance to state power in Latin America has taken many forms, from the guerrilla warfare of Che Guevara in Cuba and Bolivia to the Tupac Amaru in Peru. Resistance can also be linked to opposition to the continuation of the imperial hegemony of the United States in the Western Hemisphere, as well as to internal challenges to military rulers and one-party governments, which have often been characterized by financial corruption and the abuse of the human rights of their citizens.

LIBERATION THEOLOGY AND RESISTANCE IN LATIN AMERICA

Religion can be a source of inspiration for social and political change as well as a conservative force that opposes change and supports the status quo. Since the introduction of Catholicism during the European conquest in the fifteenth and early sixteenth centuries, the Roman

Catholic Church has played a sometimes contradiactory role in historical change in Latin America. Until recently, the Church opposed revolutions in Latin America, as its own institutional role had been closely aligned to European colonial control as an instrument of European power and to the neocolonial order that followed independence.

Beginning in the nineteenth century, Protestant missionaries made inroads, especially with the poor, though the Catholic Church continued to dominate Latin America. The victory of the Cuban revolution in 1959 brought home to the Church in Latin America (and its foreign supporters) the realities of the political and economic crises of the region. Gradually during the 1960s and 1970s, the role of the Church as defender of the state and the landed aristocracies began to be transformed. Pope Paul VI issued several papal encyclicals in the 1960s that significantly condemned capitalism and put forward a theory of development as part of the Church's mission to abolish injustice. The historic Medellin Conference of Latin American Bishops in 1968 went even further to declare that what was holding back development was oppression; liberation required political action to obtain the radical solution of socialism. Parallel developments occurred within the Protestant clerical community.

The more recent Christian involvement in revolutionary movements in Nicaragua, El Salvador, and Guatemala has been characterized as following a liberation theology, a Christian ideology that emphasizes the revolutionary and subversive power of the Gospel and the conviction that things in society can change. Liberation theology inspired political and social activism, including support for guerrilla warfare. As a consequence, many churches became enemies of the totalitarian states; church leaders, including archbishops, were martyred.

FIGURE 19.5 *The Torches,* Linocut, Mexico, 1948.

The artist Leopold Mendez (1903–1969) expresses the intensity and determination of villagers in a local revolt to control their own destiny.

■

RESISTANCE, REFORM, AND REVOLUTION IN THE ISLAMIC WORLD

Two responses to nineteenth-century Western domination in the Islamic world had been reform and revolution. By the early twentieth century, world power had passed into European hands, and the last of the great Muslim empires, the Ottoman, was no more. The shrinking of territory and influence ushered in a period of readjustment and reconciliation between Western science and technology, European imperialism, and Islamic cultural identity. The impact of modernist reform was experienced from North Africa to Central and Southeast Asia.

DECOLONIZATION AND ARAB NATIONALISM

Throughout West Asia and North Africa, the processes of decolonization led to attacks on traditional polities supported by European powers. An army coup in 1952 overthrew the Egyptian monarchy that had ruled Egypt since formal independence from Britain in 1922. British influence had continued, despite formal independence, because of the strategic importance of the Suez Canal, which Britain still administered. Egyptian groups agitating for removal of British authority over the Canal joined together with the only grass roots political movement, the Wafd. Gamel Abdel Nasser, who came to power in the 1952 coup and assumed the presidency in 1954, negotiated the evacuation of the British. When Nasser nationalized the Suez Canal in 1956, Britain, France, and Israel attacked Egypt. They were forced to withdraw by both the United States and the Soviet Union. Nasser, who had been pro-Western, turned increasingly to the Soviet Union, which helped to finance the Aswan Dam.

In 1958 Nasser engineered the union of Egypt and Syria in the United Arab Republic, the beginning of his dream of Pan-Arabism. But within three years this union disintegrated, and Syria declared its independence. The 1960s saw the growth not only of Arab nationalism but also of Arab socialism under Nasser. The promotion of socialism lost the support of conservative Arab states. In 1967 Egypt lost the Sinai Peninsula to Israel in the Six Day War, and Egypt began to shift from reliance on the Soviet Union to reliance on the United States.

The PLO and Israel Arab resistance to the state of Israel, formed in the aftermath of World War II, was organized and led by the Palestine Liberation Organization (PLO), founded in 1964 and headed by Yasir Arafat (b. 1929) since 1968. The Arab League, founded in Cairo in 1945, finally recognized the PLO as the sole representative of the Palestinian Arabs in 1974, and since that time Arafat has worked to gain international recognition for the PLO. In 1988 he proclaimed an independent Palestinian state, but at the same time recognized Israel's right to exist.

Islamism The Ikhwan al Muslimin (Muslim Brotherhood) was the leading Islamist force in West Asia and North Africa. Sometimes referred to as "fundamentalist," the movement was founded in Egypt in 1928 by Hasan al-Banna (1906–1949). It disagreed with traditional orthodoxy about modernization and called for a revivalist Islam as a means of resisting the economic and political injustices of secular states. Between 1948 and 1981 the Brotherhood was banned and suppressed by the successive colonial and postindependence

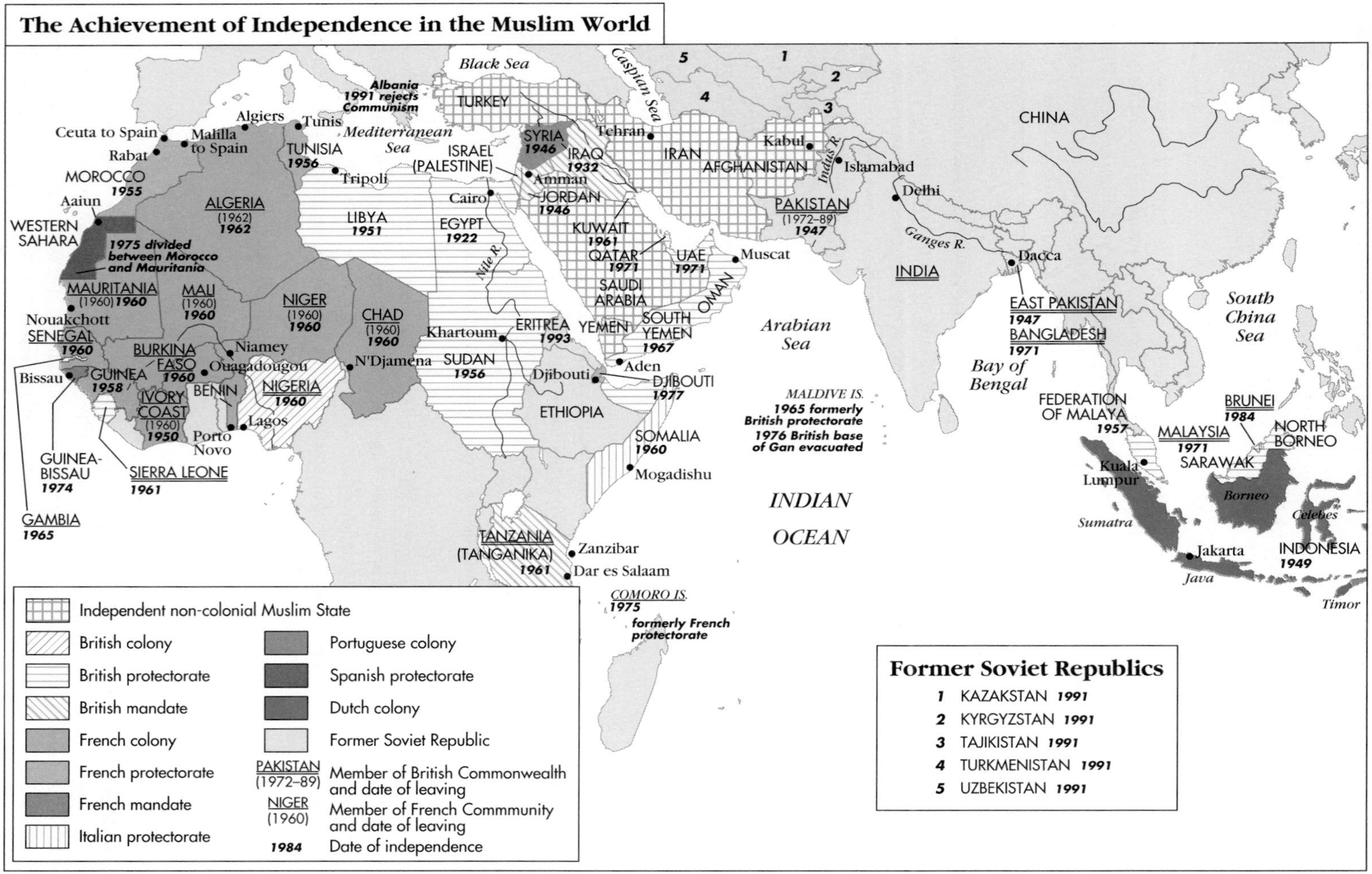

The Achievement of Independence in the Muslim World

Former Soviet Republics

1 KAZAKSTAN *1991*
2 KYRGYZSTAN *1991*
3 TAJIKISTAN *1991*
4 TURKMENISTAN *1991*
5 UZBEKISTAN *1991*

Independent non-colonial Muslim State

British colony

British protectorate

British mandate

French colony

French protectorate

French mandate

Italian protectorate

Portuguese colony

Spanish protectorate

Dutch colony

Former Soviet Republic

PAKISTAN (1972–89) Member of British Commonwealth and date of leaving

NIGER (1960) Member of French Commmunity and date of leaving

1984 Date of independence

MAP 19.3   New Nation States in the Muslim World

governments of Egypt. Syria, the Sudan, and Pakistan also struggled with Islamic forces. By the late 1970s all Muslim societies came to contain at least an Islamist wing that resisted the contamination of their communities by Westernization.

Divisions in the Arab World Divisions within the Arab world were more pronounced than ever after the 1970s. When Nasser died in 1971, he was replaced by a close associate, Anwar Al-Sadat, who presided over the Yom Kippur War with Israel in 1973. The Organization of Petroleum Exporting Countries (OPEC) placed an embargo on shipments of oil to countries that supported Israel, producing a world crisis because of the dependence of the West (and Japan) an oil. By the late 1970s Sadat began to work toward peace with Israel, signing the Camp David accords in 1978 and finally a peace treaty with Israel in 1979. Egypt was expelled from the Arab League for this action in 1979, and two years later Sadat was assassinated by a member of the Muslim Brotherhood for having supported peace with Israel. In the 1980s, however, other Arab states such as Jordan began to follow Egypt's lead, and in 1989 Egypt was readmitted to the Arab League.

Iran and Iraq Western influence had grown during the interwar years, beginning with the expansion of German political and economic interests in Iran. The ruler of the Pahlavi dynasty, Reza Shah, like the Young Turks in Turkey, saw Germany as an important power that had no imperial designs. In 1941, after World War II had begun, Britain and the Soviet Union demanded the expulsion of all Germans from Iran. They were concerned about the flow of oil and the ability of the Allies to provide war material to the Soviet Union, then under attack by Germany. Reza Shah refused and on August 25, 1941, British and Soviet forces invaded Iran. The shah abdicated and was succeeded by his son, Muhammad Reza, who ruled Iran until 1979 when he was overthrown in a popular Islamic revolution under the leadership of Ayatollah Ruhollah Khomeini, a Shi'ite cleric who had been in exile in France since 1963. Rejection of modernization based on Western models and resistance to the continuation of monarchical rule was at the heart of the Islamic fundamentalist movement that unseated the shah, a Westernized monarch whose policies favored the Western model of the state and rejected the Islamic ideal of the "community of true believers."

In the same year as the Iranian revolution (1979), Saddam Hussein (b. 1937) became head of Iraq. A member of the Arab Ba'ath Socialist Party since 1957, Hussein launched a far-reaching suppression of political opposition and put down a Kurdish rebellion. He also led Iraq in a costly war against Iran in the 1980s and invaded the neighboring oil-rich kingdom of Kuwait in 1990. That invasion led to the Persian Gulf War, which brought a coalition of forces led by the United States to the region and eventually forced Iraq to withdraw from Kuwait.

Religion and New States A broad spectrum of resistance movements and their interaction with new states formed by the overthrow of traditional monarchies characterized postwar developments in West Asia and North Africa. Islamic fundamentalism provided a key ideological source of resistance to Westernized authoritarian or one-party states, as Muslims rejected the Western notion of the social contract in favor of the Islamic belief in the "community of true believers" as the model for the nation state. Religion and state were to be a unified whole, and religious law was joined to state law. A similar issue has dogged Israeli politics since the creation of the state of Israel in 1948 as a homeland for the Jewish people: Should the religious laws of Judaism also be the law of the state?

■

NATIONALISM, RESISTANCE, AND REVOLUTION IN EAST ASIA

The experiences of nationalism, resistance, and revolution in East Asia were shaped by the forces of Western imperialism in the nineteenth century and by both Western and Japanese imperialism in the twentieth. As Western imperialism precipitated Japanese nationalism in the mid-nineteenth century, Japanese imperialism in China during World War II gave rise to Chinese revolutionary or mass nationalism. Though China was never directly colonized by any Western power, the impact of Western imperialism dating from the mid-nineteenth century began a century-long struggle for national independence against the forces of both Western and Japanese imperialism as well as traditional society.

NATIONALISM AND RESISTANCE IN MODERN JAPAN

Modern Japanese nationalism was a product of the 1868 Meiji Restoration, a "revolution from above" led by an elite that transformed the Japanese political, economic, and social order. Resistance to this new order, which eradicated the social position of the samurai and the hereditary feudal rights of *daimyo* to rule their domains, came first from the samurai. The Satsuma Rebellion of 1877 came about as a result of conflicts within the Meiji oligarchy (group of leaders in power) following the 1873 introduction of a conscript army. It focused on the demand of Saigo Takamori (1828–1877) and his followers to launch an invasion of Korea and divide up territory among the samurai as a way to make up for the loss of their special status. A brief military engagement followed the Meiji government's refusal, and Saigo and his followers were defeated.

Resistance to the new Meiji government came also from other groups in Japanese society such as farmers, who could identify with a legacy of resistance that dated at least to the Tokugawa period (1600–1867), which was peppered with peasant uprisings against the government of the shogun. These uprisings protested inhumane demands made on the peasant producers. The authors of the Meiji Constitution (1889) rejected the demands of the popular rights movement in the 1880s, which had agitated for more popular voice and representation in the governing of the country. Both before and after the promulgation of the Meiji constitution, however, resistance to the Meiji state persisted.

Rural and Urban Resistance In 1884 farmers in Chichibu (Saitama prefecture) who depended for their livelihood on raw silk production were hit by agricultural depression and organized a campaign for debt deferment and reduced taxes. When this effort failed, between 7000 and 10,000 rioters broke into homes and offices of moneylenders and took over the prefecture. The uprising was soon crushed, four of the leaders were executed, and 3000 participants were either fined or imprisoned.

The Hibiya Riots in 1905 took place in Hibiya Park in central Tokyo and protested the terms of the Portsmouth Treaty ending the Russo-Japanese War (1904–1905). Demonstrators attacked and burned public offices and buildings, including police stations. The army was called out, and martial law was declared in the Tokyo area. The Japanese government shut down newspapers and magazines that were critical of the government and prohibited demonstrations and political activities in downtown Tokyo close to the center of government.

Resistance of a different kind was expressed in demands that the Meiji government halt operations at the Ashio copper mine in Tochigi prefecture north of Tokyo, effluents from which were polluting rivers and thus jeopardizing the health and livelihoods of people in the area. Complaints began in the early 1880s, a resolution to close the mine was introduced without result in the Diet (parliament), and mass demonstrations took place in Tokyo in 1897. Anti-pollution legislation was passed, but it was inadequate, and the Ashio copper mine finally ceased operation only in 1973. Conflicting interests between the industrial benefits to the state of the production of the Ashio mines and the needs and welfare of local farmers were at the heart of this struggle, a harbinger of environmental pollution cases in the postwar period (see Chapter 20).

War and Resistance Other economic concerns fueled demonstrations of dissent, too. At the end of World War I, which Japan officially joined as an ally of Britain, Japanese housewives demonstrated in 1918 against the cost of rice, the price of which had risen in mid-1918 to about four times the prewar level. Wages had failed to keep pace with the inflationary boom of the postwar period, and so the escalating price of rice, the principal dietary staple, created hardships for urban workers as well as for poorer farmers and tenants in the countryside. Following a demonstration against rice hoarding by fishermen's wives in Toyama prefecture, discontent erupted in a nationwide wave of riots and demonstrations affecting over 300 places in thirty prefectures. Tens of thousands of people were arrested, many of them members of the *burakumin* (the "untouchables") minority who were severely discriminated against in Japanese society; some of those arrested received the death penalty. The government responded, however, by reducing the price of rice, increasing domestic production, and importing rice.

Resistance in Japan was directed at the powerful nation state that was shaped in the aftermath of the Meiji Restoration. Nationalism became a force that suppressed social revolution and strengthened the identity of individuals with the interests of the state under fascism in the 1930s. During World War II, resistance, though vigorously suppressed by the "Thought Police," persisted in opposition to the fascist state and to militarism. In postwar Japan resistance revived in the 1960s with demonstrations against the Japan-U.S. Security Treaty that allowed the United States to maintain military bases in Japan. In the late 1960s and 1970s, Japanese students joined their comrades in Europe and the United States in protest demonstrations against the Vietnam War (to which Japan was linked by its alliance with the United States) and other policies.

REVOLUTIONARY NATIONALISM AND THE PEOPLE'S REPUBLIC OF CHINA

Chinese nationalism evolved in two stages, elite and popular, and came to fruition only in the aftermath of World War II. Nationalism in China became a revolutionary force that overturned the traditional social order and provided the model of mass nationalism forged in the fires of the Sino-Japanese War (1937–1945). The May 4th Movement signalled the intellectual revolt against traditional society, culture, and politics and also gave birth to the Chinese Communist Party (CCP). Initially an elite movement of Marxist intellectuals, many of whom studied in Europe, the CCP under the leadership of Mao Zedong in the 1930s turned toward the peasantry as a source of revolution. In World War II Chinese Communist guerrillas fought the Japanese and gradually gained the support of the peasant masses. With the defeat of Japan in 1945, the Sino-Japanese War, the East Asian "theater" of World War II, ended. In China the end of global conflict marked the beginning of civil war. The nationalism inspired initially by Western imperialism, and later by Japanese imperialism, took a revolutionary form in the Communist movement. The Communists defeated their opponents in the civil war, the nominal "Nationalists," in large part because they were able to win the support of the majority of the Chinese people as nationalists representing China against the forces of Japanese imperialism.

The People's Republic of China   With the Communist victory in 1949, the founding of the People's Republic of China (PRC) was declared. The building of a socialist society was the goal of the newly formed government under Mao Zedong as chairman of the CCP and Premier Zhou Enlai. The most important international ally of the Chinese was the Soviet Union; the PRC and the Soviets signed a treaty of alliance and aid in 1951, cementing ties between two Communist giants of the postwar world. Ties with the Soviets shaped the initial stages of economic development in the PRC, determining that the Chinese would follow the Soviet model of centralized planning and industrialization.

The first external national crisis was the Korean War. Hostility on the part of the United States to the PRC and fear on the part of the Chinese that the United States would try to destabilize their government led to open conflict on the Korean peninsula, as Korea was divided in the postwar settlement at the 38th parallel. The threat from the United States in the Korean War had internal repercussions as an initially liberal policy toward professionals—managers, industrialists, bankers—shifted to persecution of professional elites identified with the former regime.

Many professionals in the early 1950s fled to Chiang Kai-shek's Republic of China on Taiwan, where he and the Nationalist Army had installed themselves as a government in exile after having bloodily suppressed the Taiwan independence movement. The Nationalists continued to rule Taiwan as a province of China, awaiting reunification with the mainland. Taiwan flourished economically, aided by the United States and by the economic infrastructure the Japanese built during their half-century colonial occupation (1895–1945).

By 1952, with the resolution of the Korean conflict, the new government on the mainland of China could turn its attention to issues of economic development and the socialist transformation of society. The Communists had gained strength under Mao's leadership as representing the interests of China's peasants, and land reform was one of the first programs that the new government carried out. Land reform had begun already in some areas in the late 1940s, and it was continued as a national policy after 1949. Peasants were grouped according to their material standing as rich, middle, or poor and allocated land confiscated from landlords on that basis. Despite the urban, intellectual background of the founders of the CCP in the 1920s, by the time they came to power as a national government in 1949, the CCP was alienated from China's urban development. It was much more difficult to resolve the problems of China's urban areas than to carry out land reform in the countryside.

The conflict between urban and rural development is one of the major themes that persists through the history of the PRC. This conflict can also be seen as one between the needs of agricultural development and industrialization. A Soviet model clearly inspired the First Five-Year Plan, adopted in 1952. Heavy industry was to be emphasized, and capital investment was to be drawn from the agricultural sector. The peasants, who had supported the Communists in their rise to power, were to pay for economic development.

The Great Leap Forward   Although industrialization proceeded, the conditions of the peasantry remained poor. In 1955 Mao called for the speeding up of the collectivization of agriculture, one of the primary steps toward the creation of a socialist society. Reorganizing individual peasant farms into cooperatives, collectives, and ultimately communes, agriculture was to lead the way to socialism. By 1958 Mao introduced a more radical series of policies in what became known as the "Great Leap Forward." These policies were designed to balance the needs of agriculture and industry, of urban and rural, by bringing industry to the countryside.

One of the most widely publicized and dramatic examples of this movement was the "backyard steel furnace," that required peasants to produce iron for industry during slack agricultural time. The economic consequences of these policies, as theoretically attractive as they may have seemed, were disastrous. As many as a million people may have died as a result of the economic disruption caused by the Great Leap Forward. The withdrawal of Soviet aid in 1960 intensified China's economic woes. The Soviets sharply criticized Chinese "revisionism" because it rejected the Soviet model of development, and tensions between the two grew along the Sino-Soviet border.

The economic failures of the Great Leap Forward weakened Mao's position in the party, and he withdrew from the political spotlight. Despite the economic problems of the Great Leap Forward, a new vision of socialist society had been created and large numbers of people had begun to participate in politics and managerial decision making as they never had before. Although Mao had lost power in the CCP, he still had enormous charismatic leadership strength among the people and a base of power in the People's Liberation Army (PLA). By 1964 a political campaign to "learn from the PLA" began using the army as a model much as it had been during the 1940s when the Red Army led a guerrilla war against the Japanese.

The Cultural Revolution   In 1965 a critical review of a play suggested that Mao was being criticized by the playwright, who presented Mao in the guise of a corrupt emperor. Mao responded by calling for a cultural revolution to attack the lingering remnants of the old culture, old society, and old values. The Cultural Revolution raged for several years, most violently from 1966 to 1968. The most radical expression of the Cultural Revolution were The Red Guards, youths inspired by Mao's call for a cultural revolution, who shut down the universities and traveled about the country smashing idols of the old culture. The Red Guards destroyed libraries, attacked teachers, ransacked temples, and wreaked havoc throughout the country. The Party lost control of the situation, and the Army also began to fragment, bringing China dangerously close to civil war. When it became clear to Mao that the Red Guards had outlived their usefulness and were in danger of becoming too disruptive and too powerful, he withdrew support and tried to restore order.

The Cultural Revolution took a devastating toll on China, not only economically because of the severe disruption in agricultural and industrial production but also socially and culturally. The disruption of schooling for nearly ten years virtually denied a whole generation access to higher education. Intellectuals, writers, and artists had been persecuted and attacked, some committing suicide in despair at their treatment.

The Four Modernizations   After the death of Mao in 1976, his widow and three others were ▨▨▨▨▨▨▨▨▨▨▨▨▨ attacked as the infamous "Gang of Four" for their extreme radicalism during the Cultural Revolution. The eventual winner in the political struggles following Mao's death was Deng Xiaoping (1904–1997), who constructed China's new strategy for development, the Four Modernizations: agriculture, science and technology, defense, and industry. Adopting some aspects of a market economy, and ultimately, of capitalism, China seemed headed toward an economic development model patterned far more after the capitalist West than Marxism. The idea of a centrally planned economy, symbolized in the five-year plan modeled after the Soviet Union, was gradually abandoned. Yielding to diverse economic demands and resources in different regional economies, the government allowed a measure of independence in planning.

China's economic future began to look bright, and following the normalization of relations with the United States in 1978, American aid and investment began to support the economic growth of the PRC. Accompanying the policies of the Four Modernizations, which generally set economic development as a priority and left the question of the socialist transformation of society in the background, a degree of liberalization was apparent in the relaxation of political restrictions on art and literature in the early 1980s.

Tian'anmen   But real political change was not forthcoming, and when students demonstrated ▨▨▨▨▨▨▨▨▨ for better conditions and more political freedom in May and June of 1989, the "Democracy Movement" was bloodily suppressed with the Tian'anmen massacre on June 4, 1989. Just as the Communists had led resistance to the dual forces of Western and Japanese imperialism, less than a half century after the founding of the P.R.C., some Chinese participated in organized resistance to state power represented by the entrenched government of the PRC. Many others agreed and were silenced by imprisonment or threat of arrest and unable to publicize or communicate their criticisms freely.

A Peasant Revolution?   Did peasants support the Communists because they believed in socialism or because they hoped to get their own land? Did peasants support the Communists because the Communists were perceived as nationalists fighting for China? Did the peasants really support the Communists, or were they manipulated into apparent support? The answers to these questions must take into account regional differences as well as conflicting goals among different groups in Chinese society. The underlying theme is echoed in the history of every developing country: the relationship between economic development and political rights, between economic development and social transformation.

When resistance becomes revolution as it did in twentieth-century China, political, social, and economic orders can be transformed, but as revolutionaries take power continuities with the old order persist in often subtle ways that can resurface with surprising swiftness. Tibet was a victim of Western imperialism in the nineteenth and early twentieth centuries; after the Chinese Revolution in 1949, the new Chinese government invaded and occupied Ti-

FIGURE 19.6 Tian'anmen Square, May 30, 1989

Chinese student demonstrators raise the "Goddess of Democracy," symbolizing their democratic aspirations, though mainly to themselves and the international media. Just five days later, the square was cleared in one night of bloodshed and violence by soldiers of the People's Liberation Army.

SOURCE: AP/Wide World Photos/Jeff Widener, File.

bet. In 1959 Chinese troops brutally suppressed a Tibetan uprising led by the Dalai Lama, who subsequently fled to India where he has presided over a Tibetan government in exile. Like Gandhi, the Dalai Lama became known for his nonviolent opposition to the Chinese occupation of Tibet and in 1989 was awarded the Nobel Peace Prize. Revolutionary nationalism in China engendered its own resistance movements, both internally and externally.

■

FORMS OF CULTURAL RESISTANCE AND REVOLUTION

Resistance remained a continuous thread in the fabric of European hegemony and in the post colonial world. Colonial governments controlled not only people but also language and history. The history of resistance to slavery, colonialism, and imperialism was often not recorded and sometimes was even silenced by those in power. If the responses of slaves and other oppressed peoples were not always part of the official history, they often did become part of rituals, oral traditions, and narrative fiction and film. Among the most powerful weapons of resistance are what might be called the rituals of rebellion. Forms of culture, including sports, music, dance, and the visual arts, all help create the solidarity of nationalism, incite revolution, and document the subtle, complex, and even unspeakable acts and events of the human experience.

THE LITERARY REVOLUTION AND REVOLUTIONARY LITERATURE IN CHINA

In twentieth-century China, literature became a tool of revolution that drew on Western models and used these models to critique Chinese society. By the late nineteenth century, Chinese translations of Shakespeare, Balzac, Tolstoy, Dickens, Cervantes, Ibsen, and other European authors began to appear, and their form and content influenced young Chinese writers in the early twentieth century.

Lu Xun Lu Xun (1881–1936) was educated in the classical literary tradition but exposed to Western ideas in China and later as a medical student in Japan. There Lu Xun became deeply conscious of the weak Chinese response to humiliation by Western powers, which led him to abandon medicine in favor of writing. Lu Xun believed that the souls of China's people needed "curing" far more than their bodies and that the pen was more effective an instrument than the scalpel. His most famous stories are "Diary of a Madman," and "Our Story of Ah Q," both of which are deeply ironic portraits of Chinese culture in the midst of rejecting its past and looking for its future. In "Diary of a Madman," the narrator suffers from severe paranoia, but it becomes evident that the cannibalism he fears is a metaphor for the hypocrisy of Confucian culture that has destroyed human lives as surely as if they had been eaten alive. The character of Ah Q is a metaphor for the Chinese nation, which Lu Xun portrays as living in a fantasy of its own superiority even as it is subjected to relentless degradation and humiliation.

Ba Jin (b. 1904) created his pseudonym from the first syllables of the names of the two famous Russian anarchists, Bakunin and Kropotkin, as a symbol of rebellion against his gentry family background. Like many other young intellectuals of the May 4th era, he studied in France. His most famous novel, drawn on his personal experience, is *Family* (1931). This novel presents the conflicts between generations in a Chinese gentry family as the sons come of age in a period of social and political upheaval. Age, gender, and class each play a role in the oppression of people portrayed in this novel. Even the most privileged characters, the sons in the family, are not free to follow their hearts or minds but must be slaves to the dictates of Chinese family tradition. Some rebel, but some do not.

Ding Ling The most famous woman writer of early twentieth-century China was Ding Ling (b. 1907). The vicissitudes of her career as a writer and her political fortunes—for the two were closely linked—mirrored shifts in Communist Party policies toward writers and the arts. She was influenced by European literature, and her early stories, such as "Miss Sophie," are shaped by romanticism and individualism. She joined the Communist Party in 1931 after her husband was executed by the Nationalists. But her independence caused her to come into conflict with the Communist Party at Yan'an in 1942, the year Mao Zedong made his famous speech on art and literature in which he defined the role of artists and writers as a fundamentally political one. Writers and artists were exhorted to live among the people to absorb and grasp the nature of society and only then create their works, which should serve the interests of revolution.

Ding Ling's novel *Sun Shines over the Sang-kan River* (1948) was a Stalin Prize in 1951. It describes land reform in a way characteristic of socialist realism, the Soviet-inspired literary theory that aims to realistically, but positively, depict the lives of workers, peasants, and other building socialism. In the mid-1950s Ding Ling became involved in the government-sponsored Hundred Flowers Movement to elicit criticism of the Communist Party from intellectuals, writers, and artists. When the government halted the campaign, many of those who had dared to express criticism were attacked. Both Ding Ling and her husband were accused of being "rightists" during the Anti-Rightist Campaign.

Literature largely stayed within Party-dictated confines until the relaxation of the late 1970s and early 1980s. A "new realism" appeared in the works of writers who published novellas and stories in that period. Many of these writers were women, and many of the works dealt with the particularly difficult roles of women in the new society, where they were expected not only to shoulder full work responsibility, like men, but also to conform to traditional roles of responsibility for household work and child care. Marriage and family were still the defining characteristics of women's lives, more than a generation after the revolution had declared them equal members of society and free from the traditional constraints imposed by the old culture. Writers in the 1980s explored previously forbidden topics, such as romantic love, earlier labeled "bourgeois idealism" by the political authorities.

A distinctive new kind of literature arose during this period of experimentation and liberalization. Called "reportage" (*baogao wenxue*), it was a slightly fictionalized, cross between muckraking journalism and fiction. The most well-known example of this genre is the work by Liu Binyan entitled "People or Monsters?" This damning indictment of official corruption is based on a real case that was typical of the abuse of position by Communist Party members. Literature was a means of expressing resistance both to the old society and to the oppressive power of the revolutionary state and its new elite, the Communist Party members.

LITERATURE AND RESISTANCE IN THE AFRICAN-CARIBBEAN WORLD

In colonized parts of the worlds, such as Africa and the Caribbean, European languages had initially represented an opportunity—through the use of a common language—for solidarity and unity leading to independence, but they also symbolized the continuing neocolonialism and cultural dependency experienced even after independence. In Jamaica the writer Louis Bennett brought street talk and African-derived patois along with oral storytelling devices to literary heights, empowering a new generation of writers and rappers.

Writing in the vernacular, the Jamaican poet Andrew Salkey (1929–1996) used the African-derived spider folk hero Anancy to express outrage over a brutal dictatorship in Guyana. Anancy takes on the garb of freedom-fighter and works his magic in Salkey's short book *The One*, by avenging the murder of the Caribbean historian and political activist Walter Rodney (1942–1980).

On the African continent Ngugi wa'Thiongo reverted to writing in his first language, Kikuyu, rather than the English language of the colonizer, because he believed the language itself colonized the mind. By contrast, the Nigerian Nobel Laureate Wole Soyinke used not only the English language, but particularly Shakespearean English, to ruminate on the twentieth-century Yoruba experience in *Death and the King's Horseman*, a book that few Nigerians can buy or even read today because the Nigerian government prohibits it.

The African writer Frantz Fanon suggested that the literature of the former colonial world first passes through a cultural nationalist phase that romanticizes the precolonial past. The trend among African novelists in the late twentieth century is away from romanticism and toward realism and even surrealism (beyond or above realism) to describe their late-twentieth-century worlds.

RESISTANCE IN MOTION: RITUAL AND DANCE

Dance and ritual, in parts of the world where they are integral parts of cultural politics, have also played a significant role in resistance. In ritual and in dance movements, bodies say what cannot be spoken. Responses to colonial rule ranged from the successful armed rebellions to forms of cultural resistance to active collaboration. African resistance to colonialism sometimes took the subtle and complex path of mimicry.

The Hauka Movement of West Africa   Beginning about 1925 the Hauka movement of West Africa embodied colonial resistance in the rituals and dances of spirit possession in which European colonizers were mocked. Members of dance troupes traveled around the countryside of Niger proselytizing and spreading messages of derision and rebellion. The dancers dressed like European soldiers and imitated their colonial behaviors. By appropriating the European style and form of body movement, Hauka members hoped to empower themselves in opposition to the French administration of their territory.

Historical Memory and Dance   Today the bodies of dancers also speak of their own complex history through the motions of samba, a singularly unique dance form that mixes Amerindian, African, and European dances in Brazil. The samba's three-count, between-the-beat, intricate movement of swaying hips and feet resisting the contrary two/fourth beat became a metaphor that celebrates the fusion of separate traditions. In Brazil, African (Kongolese) and Amerindian (Cariri Indian) syncopation and rhythm work against the strong beat. A kind of layering of movements allows one rhythm to resist and alternatively silence the others in the syncretic samba form. After the abolition of slavery in 1888, though some written historical documents pertaining to slavery were destroyed in attempts to eradicate a painful past, the stories have lived on in such forms as the samba.

In twentieth-century Brazil and other parts of the African-Caribbean world, the politics of resistance came to be performed as art and ritual just as they had under slavery. Dance and other performance arts were resistance in motion. The oppressed used religious expression to empower individuals, invert the social order, and sometimes even transform political identity. Whether in the danced rituals and other ceremonies of the African-derived religion known as *candomble,* the rituals and dance steps of carnival in Trinidad, the Brazilian martial arts form called *capoeira,* or in samba, which became the popular "national" dance of Brazil, elements of resistance and of cultural expression survived as intertwined cultural memories.

Dance steps and musical instruments had multiple meanings in a history of resistance. The Brazilian *berimbau,* a single-stringed bow with a resonating gourd attached, was played as an instrument and according to one musician, "in the hour of pain, it stops being an instrument and becomes a hand weapon." *Candomble,* a syncretic faith combining Catholic elements and Yoruba deities, originated in the violent cultural encounters of the Atlantic world. But it also emerged in the context of community and collective action. As creative expression dance was not only relevant to resistance, it remained at the core of historical identity. According to dance scholar Barbara Browning, "the insistence of Brazilians to keep *dancing* is not a means of forgetting but rather a perseverance, an unrelenting attempt to intellectualize, theorize, understand a history and a present of social injustice difficult to believe, let alone explain."

THE STRUGGLE FOR SOCIAL JUSTICE AND DEMOCRACY IN THE MODERN WORLD

Resistance movements were not limited to the non-Western world. As imperialism generated resistance movements throughout the colonized world, the impact of the industrial revolution on the conditions of people's lives produced resistance within societies in the Western world. Much as Karl Marx had predicted, the factory system method of production in the industrial revolution, one of the key markers of the modern world, stimulated consciousness of common interests among industrial workers and led to the organization of labor. In the nineteenth century active resistance to the subordinate status of women gave birth to women's rights movements, which were complicated by divisions of race and class. By the twentieth century, international resistance movements on the fronts of labor and gender intersected with political revolutions that took place across both cultural and political boundaries.

RESISTANCE AND ORGANIZED LABOR

In the early stages of the industrial revolution, governments prohibited workers from organizing to seek higher wages and better working conditions; with the expansion of male suffrage in the second half of the nineteenth century, European male workers were able to use their votes to reduce restraints on the organization of labor. Official recognition of labor unions came in England in 1871 and in France and Germany in the 1880s. The first nationwide American labor organization, the National Labor Union, was founded just after the Civil War (1866).

As membership in labor unions grew—2 million in England and 850,000 in Germany by 1900—their political influence increased. By voting as a bloc, labor was able to support candidates that represented the interests of working people. In 1906 the British Labor Party elected twenty-nine members of Parliament; after World War I, the Labor Party became the second major party in Great Britain. By the outbreak of World War I, German and French socialist parties supported by workers played major roles in parliamentary government.

When political representation of workers was inadequate and governments did not respond to the demands of labor unions, workers turned to the strike as a method to achieve their goals. However, the effects of economic depression—job loss and decreasing wages—precipitated more strikes than did the inaction or ineffectiveness of government. For example, depression in the United States in the mid-1870s produced the greatest labor confrontation of the century, the railroad strike of 1877; during the serious depression in England at the end of the nineteenth century, a London dock strike (1889) closed the port of London for the first time since the French Revolution a century earlier.

The Haymarket Riot   One of organized labor's most powerful tools of resistance is the general strike in which all workers abandon their jobs and bring society to a standstill. In 1886 union leaders in the United States called for a general strike in support of the eight-hour day. The specter of a nationwide strike frightened the public, though the strike, which began on International Labor Day, May 1, proved to be a fiasco. About 190,000 workers laid down their tools, but they were mostly in large cities such as New York and Chicago. In Chicago the situation was complicated by a separate strike against the

FIGURE 19.7 Shoemakers' Strike in Lynn, Massachusetts

Eight hundred women operatives marched in a snowstorm, followed by four thousand workmen and preceded by the band of the Lynn City Guards.

SOURCE: Corbis-Bettmann.

McCormick Harvester Company during which strikers clashed with police and one man was killed. A protest meeting was called in the city's Haymarket Square; when police appeared, someone tossed a bomb, killing one policeman and injuring others. The police charged into the crowd with guns firing. Eight "anarchists" were convicted, four were hanged, and a backlash against labor was the result of what became known as the "Haymarket riot."

Uprising of the 20,000   On a November night in 1909, thousands of shirtwaist makers gathered at New York's Cooper Union to protest working conditions and low wages in the city's garment industry. Mostly women and many of them immigrant women, the workers earned as little as $3.50 a week; some were forced to buy their own needles and thread and to pay for their own electricity. The meeting, called by the International Ladies Garment Workers Union (ILGWU), was orderly until interrupted by a young Russian woman, who stood to announce that she, too, had "worked and suffered," but she was tired of talking and moved that they go on general strike. By the next night more than 20,000 garment workers had walked off their jobs. Their plight received widespread sympathy. In rare cross-class solidarity, wealthy women's clubs, college students, and suffragists united with the garment workers. For the first time, women were at the forefront of a successful labor struggle in the United States.

Early European Labor Movements Attempts at general strikes in early twentieth-century Europe met with mixed results. General strikes in Italy (1904) and France (1911) ended in failure. The French strike began as a railroad strike; it was frustrated when the government, in order to keep trains moving, ordered military mobilization so that workers, who were subject to conscription, were forced to work under military law and command.

Following World War I labor everywhere had a difficult time retaining the gains and concessions it had achieved during wartime. In Great Britain the situation reached a climax in 1926 in the coal mining industry. A strike by coal miners led to a general strike supported by other British unions; about half a million organized workers in other industries left their jobs in solidarity with the coal miners. The government declared a state of emergency; army and navy personnel and middle class volunteers performed essential services, and the strike ended in failure. But the impact of labor organizations would continue in industrial and political realms, especially after World War II.

International Labor and Political Emancipation The international migration of labor and industries helped spread the impact of labor organizations around the world in the twentieth century. Labor and trade unions also became increasingly political. In European colonies the struggle of labor (the workers) against capital (the government and its industries) fueled anticolonial and anti-imperialist sentiments. In the British Caribbean colony of Barbados, Grantley Adams, the leader of the Barbados Labour Party and Workers Union, expressed the connection between labor and universal suffrage in a Labor Day speech in 1946:

> Today I want to make a special appeal to you. The day is long past when the working man—the Broad Street clerk or the water-front worker—can afford to stand by himself and hope to win the fight with capital . . . I want every one of you to look upon this day as a milestone on the road to democracy in industry . . . The people of this country make the wealth of the country, and it is for the organized might of this country to say how that wealth is to be distributed. For centuries it has been the practice of the capitalist class to amass wealth out of the toil and sweat of the labourers. If it has been the unfortunate lot of the labourers not to have a vote in this government, it is our duty to change that . . . If we stand solidly together, we can, and should, be masters of this country.

Barbados was not an isolated example of the link between economic and political empowerment. From Latin America to Africa and Asia workers were essential in the struggle for political and social justice.

The Labor Movement in East Asia The goals of organized labor were often as much political as economic, particularly in authoritarian political systems of either the left or right in which there was no effective institutionalized way to challenge state power. The student demonstrations that sparked the May 4th Movement in China in 1919 were supported by labor strikes and merchant boycotts in Beijing, Shanghai, and Canton, the major industrial and commercial centers. The organization of Chinese labor began with the May 4th Movement and intensified with the activities of anarcho-syndicalists, those who rejected working within the political system (anarchists) in favor of direct organization of workers to take over government (syndicalists).

In the early 1920s the principal focus of Communist Party activities—which were greatly influenced by the ideas of anarcho-syndicalism—was the organization of labor. The

FIGURE 19.8 Student Demonstrations, Tian'anmen, 1919

Striking workers in China's urban centers supported the protests of the May 4th Movement, and organized labor played a major role in the demands for political change in China.

SOURCE: Sovfoto/Eastfoto

success of these efforts was evident in the Hong Kong Merchant Seamen's strike in early 1922 when 40,000 sailors, supported by sympathy strikes throughout south China, won wage increases. In Japan during the same year, a strike of dockworkers at the port of Kobe demonstrated the potential of Japanese organized labor.

But in both China and Japan, early successes were compromised by failures that sharply revealed the weakness of organized labor in militaristic (warlord-controlled China) or unstable parliamentary (Japan) governments. A strike of 50,000 coal miners in north China in 1922 ended in failure, as did a strike in the silk spinning mills on the outskirts of Shanghai in the same year, though the latter was the first large strike by women in the history of China. Though it did not signal the beginning of a large-scale labor movement, a much earlier example of labor organization in the textile industry—key to the industrial revolution in England and elsewhere—was the strike of 100 women workers in the Amamiya silk mill in northern Japan in 1886. When the owners of seventy-three silk mills in the area formed an organization to tighten control over some 4500 female workers they employed, 100 women refused to work; the employers granted some concessions and the dispute ended.

One of the most tragic failures in Chinese labor history was the 1923 strike of the United Syndicate of Railway Workers of the Beijing-Hankou System, a line that served the territory of a warlord whose soldiers attacked the striking railway workers and killed sixty-five. Anti-union activity escalated in China during the next two years, but in 1925, when English police in the International Settlement in Shanghai fired on a group of demonstrators and killed ten, a general strike was organized in response to this brutality. The strike involved 150,000 workers, merchants, and students and lasted for three months, though sympathizers throughout China contributed money, boycotted foreign goods, and staged strikes for more than a year. This event became known as the May 30th Movement and was the peak of organized labor's success during this early period.

Labor Organization in Facist and Communist States
Labor union activity in many countries subsided during World War II. Labor unions in Japan were outlawed during the rise of fascism in the 1930s, and in Mussolini's Italy and Hitler's Germany, unions became instruments of national socialism, organizations that supported the interests of the state, which were identified under fascism as the interests of the masses. Postwar Japan experienced a resurgence of union activity under the Occupation, just as prewar political parties, which had been unified into the Imperial Rule Assistance Association in 1940, were revived after 1945. But as unions became more institutionalized in many countries where they had existed for a long time, they ceased to be instruments of resistance.

The potential of organized labor to bring about political change, however, was demonstrated in Communist Poland during the 1980s, when scattered strikes ballooned into a working-class revolt. A variety of unions united under the name "Solidarity," a national movement that used its focus on the economic ills of the country to rally support for the transformation of Poland from a state run by the Communist Party to one governed by the elected representatives of the people. By the summer of 1989, members of the Solidarity movement had been elected to parliament (previously controlled entirely by the Polish Communist Party). They became the first freely elected party in a Communist country. The use of organized labor to challenge government in a Communist state is particularly ironic, since in theory Communist states represent workers' interests.

GENDER AND RESISTANCE: THE "WOMAN QUESTION"

In the nineteenth century, women's rights—then known as the "woman question"—were widely debated in European society. Male intellectuals such as the English philosopher John Stuart Mill, who supported improving the status of women, and the German philosopher Friedrich Nietzsche, who expressed deeply misogynistic views, debated the issue and influenced popular ideas about the role of women in society. In the 1830s American women in the northern United States joined the antislavery crusade and were active in the abolition movement. This experience in public life helped prepare women for organizing the women's rights movement.

Although European women took part in the revolutions that swept Europe in 1848 (see Chapter 16), that year marked a turning point for women all over the world because of the women's rights meeting held at Seneca Falls, New York. Organized by Lucretia Mott (1793–1880) and Elizabeth Cady Stanton (1815–1902), this meeting of about 300 people was devoted exclusively to the problems of women and issued a document, "Declaration of Rights and Sentiments," that had a powerful impact on women's rights advocates in both the United States and Europe. Other meetings followed, and new leaders emerged. In 1851 a freed slave who called herself Sojourner Truth told a gathering in Akron, Ohio, that women were not the weaker sex, citing as evidence the conditions that black women endured under slavery.

Another important leader of the women's rights movement in the United States was Susan B. Anthony (1820–1906); Mott, Stanton, and Anthony worked for reform in higher education, employment, the status of wives, and suffrage. Following the Civil War, demands for full female suffrage began to increase; by the late nineteenth century, the issue of suffrage had become central to established politics because it was the key to bringing about political reform. The term "suffragette" popularly described any woman who demanded the right to vote. In early twentieth-century Britain, radical suffragettes such as Emmeline Pankhurst (1857–1928) chained themselves to buildings to make speeches advocating the right to vote or in other ways tried to gain the attention of people to support their cause. Some British radical women were imprisoned for their actions; Pankhurst ended up in Ethiopia where she lived in exile. New Zealand, colonized by the British, actually became the first country in the world to grant female suffrage (1893); South Africa granted African women the right to vote in the 1994 national election.

Elsewhere in Europe women were also active in movements to gain the right to vote. Women in the Hapsburg Empire organized to demand their right to engage in political activities and to vote. Socialist parties in Europe and the United States championed women's rights and supported female suffrage. Following the 1905 revolution in Russia, women became politically aware of their subjugation. Nadezdha Krupskaya (1869–1938), the wife of V. I. Lenin, was a strong supporter of her husband and wrote the first major Russian work on the woman question from a Marxist standpoint, *The Woman Worker* (1900). Alexandra Kollontai (1872–1952), born an aristocrat, was a radical advocate of women's rights who held positions in the Soviet government.

Race and class intersected with gender in the struggles for women's rights. For black women in the post–Civil War United States, discrimination on the basis of gender was complicated by racial discrimination. Black women leaders such as Ida B. Wells (1862–1931) worked for the female vote, but they also struggled for racial equality and justice. Middleclass women formed the backbone of the suffrage movement; working-class and poor women had neither the leisure nor often the education to participate in demonstrations or other activities that demanded time away from work and family.

After World War I women gained the vote in the United States, the Soviet Union, and many European countries. From the early 1880s women in Japan had been active in the popular rights movement, and some enlightened intellectuals of the Meiji period, such as Fukuzawa Yukichi (1835–1901), advocated the improvement of the position of women. Japanese women were active in temperance organizations and in efforts to abolish prostitution. But legislation in 1889 and 1900 forbade political activity by women, and female socialists attacked such restraints. Other women were less concerned with emancipation and turned to activities associated with a more traditional female role. For example, the Patriotic Women's Association, founded in 1901, assisted wounded soldiers and bereaved families who suffered as a result of the growing militarism and imperialism of the Meiji state. In contrast, the Bluestocking Society, founded in 1911, was a middle-class intellectual movement advocating self-awareness of women; it lasted into the 1930s when all such organizations were either absorbed or suppressed by the state. Although universal male suffrage was achieved in Japan in 1925, like France and certain other European countries, Japan did not extend the vote to women until after World War II.

THE UNITED STATES IN THE WORLD: THE CONTRADICTIONS OF DEMOCRACY ABROAD AND AT HOME

The struggle for justice on the home front was one of the most marked contradictions in the history of Western democracy. Throughout much of the twentieth century, United States foreign policy seemingly ignored the political aspirations of peoples around the world in the quest for capitalist expansion, continued access to profits, and perceived national security interests. In the postwar world, United States government policies tried to impose the values of democracy abroad, even while many citizens struggled for social and economic justice within the borders of the democratic nation state. Contradictions also characterized domestic socio-economic conditions that both attracted immigrants and led to great disparities between the wealthy and the poor.

The Civil Rights Struggle   The period following the end of the Civil War (1865) is called the Reconstruction era. Although slavery was abolished, African Americans were only beginning a long struggle for economic equity, social justice, and full political participation. One of the most important black leaders was W. E. B. Du Bois (1868–1963), who helped found the National Association for the Advancement of Colored People (NAACP). Harvard-educated Du Bois was an eloquent and skillful spokesperson for his vision of racial equality. The official publication of the NAACP was called *The Crisis,* and its title reflected the intensity of the struggle to realize in society the values of equality and justice fought for in the Civil War.

The Invisible Empire   A secret terrorist organization, the Ku Klux Klan, originated in Southern states during Reconstruction. It espoused beliefs in the superiority of white people and tried to terrorize public officials. In 1871 during the presidency of Ulysses S. Grant, the government implemented the 14th Amendment of the United States Constitution, guaranteeing the civil rights of all citizens (at least all males, white and black); in the same year President Grant called for all members of illegal organizations, including the Ku Klux Klan to disarm and disband. Although the organization went underground and its membership dwindled, its terrorist activities against blacks, Jews, and Roman Catholics did not cease. In the 1890s more than 1000 documented lynchings of African Americans occurred. Despite the terror and racism, many African Americans persevered in their efforts to achieve equality. Some few, called by Du Bois "the talented tenth" (one-tenth of African Americans), achieved an education and enjoyed economic gains. Racial pride began to swell, as suggested by the 2 to 4 million members in popular militant black leader Marcus Garvey's (1887–1940) United Negro Improvement Association (UNIA), founded in 1916. Garvey, born in Jamaica, espoused a black nationalist political agenda for political and economic development, and the agenda received support from Africa to Latin America. His impact was international, but short-lived; charges of business fraud led to his conviction and ultimate exile from the United States.

Despite the participation of blacks in both war efforts, discrimination and inequality continued. In Georgia about 1915, an organization called the Invisible Empire, Knights of the Ku Klux Klan, reactivated the name, rituals, and beliefs of the nineteenth-century Ku Klux Klan. For a time in the 1920s, the organization claimed 3 million members—white males from Florida to Oregon—an increase in response to black gains and urban migration, although violence and corruption quickly discredited the organization's leadership. Especially after World War II, black discontent grew as the victory over fascism abroad encouraged the struggle against racism at home.

Desegregation and   By the 1940s black leaders and religious pacifists began to apply the
Nonviolent Strategies   nonviolent techniques of the Indian leader Gandhi to the racial struggle in the United States, promoting nonviolent sit-ins. In 1954 a

FIGURE 19.9 Ku Klux Klan Women March down Pennsylvania Avenue, Washington, D.C., in 1928

Women used suffrage for a variety of political expressions.

SOURCE: National Archives.

unanimous Supreme Court decision in the *Brown* v. *Board of Education* case made racial segregation unconstitutional. The actions of a single black woman, Rosa Parks, who disobeyed a city law in Montgomery, Alabama by refusing to give up her seat on a city bus to a white man, sparked the Civil Rights movement.

The black leader Martin Luther King Jr. (1929–1968) used the arrest of Rosa Parks to organize a bus boycott, and Parks's action inspired King's lifelong commitment to civil disobedience and nonviolence. In 1963 King was jailed for participating in a demonstration against segregation. Written in solitary confinement from his jail cell on toilet paper, King's famous "Letter from the Birmingham Jail" challenged critics of his resistance movement: "Oppressed people cannot remain oppressed forever. The urge for freedom will eventually come. If his repressed emotions do not come out in these nonviolent ways, they will come out in ominous expressions of violence. This is not a threat; it is a fact of history."

Labor, Migration, and Ethnicity   As African Americans were forcibly brought to the Americas for slave labor in the eighteenth and nineteenth centuries, Asian (particularly Chinese) immigrants in the nineteenth and twentieth centuries provided labor to build the railroads and to mine gold. In the twentieth century male laborers from

Mexico were recruited to work in the United States as early as World War I (1917). When the United States entered World War II in 1941, the program to bring Mexican workers into the United States, the *bracero* program, was expanded to meet the demands of wartime production. Recruiters would cross the Mexican border into towns where they would seek men to come north and work as migrant laborers under short-term contracts.

The *bracero* program ended in 1964, but undocumented workers from Mexico continued to cross the border as part of a new wave of postwar immigration from Mexico and Puerto Rico and, in the case of Cubans, after the 1959 revolution that brought Castro to power. Like Asian immigrants who came from varied cultural backgrounds, Hispanic immigrants represented diverse political, economic, and social backgrounds. Cubans who fled the revolution tended to be wealthier professionals and settled in the urban center of Miami, while Puerto Ricans were concentrated in the barrios (Hispanic ghettos) of New York City. Mexican Americans were the largest segment of the Hispanic population, and though they originally were rural laborers in the West and Southwest, by the 1950s the process of urbanization had begun to affect them just as it did African Americans who moved to northern industrial cities.

Hispanic Resistance and the Chicano Movement   Hispanics became politically active in the civil rights movements of the 1960s. Mexican Americans called themselves "Chicanos," a shortened form for Mexicanos. Cesar Chavez (1927–1993) organized migrant laborers into the United Farm Workers, which the AFL-CIO officially recognized in 1966. In 1968 Chavez led a nationwide boycott of California table grapes and lettuce to achieve labor contracts for migrant laborers. By the late 1960s the formation of "La Raza Unida" (The Race United) demonstrated the growing ethnic and political consciousness of

FIGURE 19.10   Rosa Parks Sits in the Front of the Bus

Passengers in Montgomery, Alabama, where the bus boycott was organized experienced the civil rights movement in their daily lives.

SOURCE: Corbis-Bettmann.

Hispanic Americans and their efforts to achieve political goals within the system. The more militant "Brown Berets" were Hispanic activists whose methods mirrored the radical ideas of the African American Black Panthers.

Native American Resistance   Native Americans also became politically conscious and active during the 1960s with the founding of the American Indian Movement (AIM) by urban activists. In 1973 AIM organizers Russell Means and Dennis Banks took over the trading post at Wounded Knee, the site of the 1890 massacre of Sioux people by white cavalry on the Sioux reservation in South Dakota. Wounded Knee was a powerful symbol of the betrayals of Native Americans by the U.S. federal government, but it was also a symbol of divisions among Native Americans that the AIM claimed to represent. Various tribes pursued different agendas and strategies to achieve their goals, and by the 1970s more than 100 different organizations represented tribal interests.

Gender and Resistance   By the 1970s the second wave of American feminism made use of the Marxist concept of class to represent gender. In 1969 a manifesto of a group known as the "New York Redstockings" claimed that women were an oppressed class. At the same time sexual identity was becoming a political issue, and gay men and women began to organize to achieve social acceptance and equal rights. In the same year that the New York Redstockings issued their manifesto, police raided a gay bar in New York's Greenwich Village; because patrons fought back, unlike previous raids, this incident (Stonewall, after the bar's name) became the symbol of gay liberation. After Stonewall, activists called for gays and lesbians to publicly affirm their sexual identity and to reject the hidden lives they had led.

Events of resistance such as Stonewall or Seneca Falls, the Nicaraguan Revolution, Tian'anmen Square, or the Ibo Women's War became defining moments in the lives of their respective communities. Whether remembered by participants, the survivors, or their descendants, subsequent generations seized upon such events as rallying points to continue to effect change. Whether successful or not, the acts of resistance produced communities whose identities were profoundly revisioned.

SUMMARY

Resistance to European and American hegemony took many forms, from Gandhi's passive nonviolence to the aggressive militancy of PLO *fedayeen* (commandos). Resistance also took different courses, shaped according to the objects of resistance. In some cases the direct controls of colonialism were resisted, as in the Indian nationalist movement. In others resistance was directed at national governments, as in postwar Peru, where the Shining Path guerrillas carry out campaigns of terrorism to destabilize the Peruvian government.

In China resistance was first aimed at the imperial government, then at Western powers, and finally at the Chinese state under the control of the Nationalists. In each instance the goals of resistance were conditioned by the nature of the oppressive system: political reformers in the late nineteenth century wanted to transform the dynastic state into a constitutional monarchy; republican revolutionaries wanted to overthrow the monarchy and establish a republic in order to confront the West on its own terms as a modern nation state; and, Marxist revolutionaries demanded the overthrow of the republican state in the interests of the "people."

Finally demonstrators for democracy looked to the West, as had their early twentieth-century predecessors in the May 4th Movement, for models of resistance to the postrevolutionary Chinese government. The irony in 1919 was that although May 4th was sparked by opposition to treatment of China's sovereignty by Western powers, the ideas of May 4th—democracy and science—were Western ones. The irony of 1989 was of a different sort: Western democratic values were used to resist a postrevolutionary state that had gained power as the representative of an independent Chinese nationalism that had successfully resisted both Western and Japanese imperialism.

When revolutionaries become rulers, they almost inevitably become wed to the idea that their power is identified with the success of revolution; their leadership is often compromised by ties to powerful economic and political interests. This relationship was shown in Maoist China, under Daniel Ortega after the Sandinista victory in Nicaragua, and in the Philippines under Corazon Aquino. It is extremely difficult for political leaders to shed the bonds of powerful economic interests, as was demonstrated when the populist leader Corazon Aquino's regime was undermined by the persistence of wealthy landholders making demands on the political leadership.

As imperialism succeeded in threading together disparate cultures into single political and economic systems and capitalism spread its tentacles worldwide, the experience of vastly different parts of the globe led to the recognition of a common identity. This identity, called by Franz Fanon the identity of "the wretched of the earth," was also the beginning of a common determination to end all forms of oppression and injustice. International solidarity and links across class, culture, and color lines increased dramatically after 1910. Not only was the presence of any injustice viewed as a threat to all within the community, but the defeat of common enemies brought many causes into a single revolutionary vision. The export of revolutions across cultures not only has illuminated both cultural and historical diversities of experience but also has shown the commonality of concerns for justice and equality.

Twentieth-century technology has enabled individuals to be informed about and to participate in resistance and revolutionary struggles around the world. The earlier revolutions in America and Haiti would not have succeeded without the support of foreign allies. Through the solidarity of labor union activities, the Spanish Civil War had followers in Latin America and the Caribbean. Cubans fought in Angolan and Mozambiquan struggles. Viewers around the world watched and listened to and protested against events in China and South Africa.

The emergence of the European nation state and the parallel development of capitalist industrialism, the dual revolutions of the late eighteenth and nineteenth centuries, were the subject of Chapter 16. Chapter 17 carried the story forward into the late nineteenth and early twentieth centuries, examining responses in Asia, Africa, and the Americas to the product of the European dual revolutions: the "new" imperialism. Chapter 18 concluded with another result of the dual revolutions and of imperialism: global warfare, viewing war and peace in the twentieth century from the multiple perspectives of power and culture. This chapter (19) assessed the results of the collapse of European, and the rise of American, hegemony examined in the preceding two chapters. It traced the thread of resistance and revolution inherent in the multipolar, new world order that has begun to replace the old. The final chapter of this book (Chapter 20) considers the many sources of identity in twentieth-century societies. The concluding chapter also considers fundamental issues of global culture and changes in demography, the environment, and technology that continue to provide a basis for understanding the common human experience.

ENGAGING THE PAST

HUMOR AND HISTORY IN POLITICAL CARTOONS

Even before cartoons it was said that the pen was mightier than the sword. From wars to revolutions, those who write and draw humorous and satirical commentaries have targeted the most serious of political and social concerns. One consequence of the advent of printing and subsequent mass media has been the wider audiences for the visual presentation of popular protest. Political cartoons serve as a forum for political debate, resistance, and criticism of the status quo, and they also provide historians with more than a few good laughs. Cartoons are valuable historical documents. They lend rich social and cultural insights into the reality of past moments, and like any art, they can be "read" in multiple, complex ways.

Political cartoons around the world began with the introduction of newspapers and periodical journals, in most places in the nineteenth century. The cartoon strip format used a linear concept of storytelling, but at the same time plunged the reader/reviewer into separate frames or intervals of experience so that the art form appealed to all ages and cultures. Western models inspired most early published cartoons. For example, the leading satirical journal of Muslim India (1870s–1930s) *Awadh Punch* was derived from the British magazine *Punch,* popular in the Victorian era. The most successful comic strip magazine in the Arab world since its inception in 1979, *Majid* is revolutionary both because it uses the voice of a little girl and because of the actual content of its commentary on politics, religion, and other topics.

Many governments have issued their own propaganda cartoons in support of state policy while censoring the opposition. When publishing cartoons was outlawed or prohibitively expensive in the twentieth century, Chinese, Brazilian, and South African artists used woodcuts, linoleum cuts, T-shirts, and wall grafitti to distribute subversive cartoon commentary to their illiterate audiences.

Stories, films, and cartoons evolved from Edgar Rice Burrough's story character "Tarzan," the superhero of the colonial era between 1912 and 1947. The Tarzan myth constituted the most popular dissemination of stereotypes about the continent and racist notions of white superiority. Following independence, some countries banned Tarzan cartoons as seditious propaganda. Today many African newspapers instead carry the cartoon strip "Captain Dark," an African superhero who fights his own battles and may provide readers in independent Africa with the last laugh.

SUGGESTIONS FOR FURTHER READING

Hakim Barakat, *The Arab World: Society, Culture, and State* (Berkeley: University of California Press, 1993). An examination of how social and political history are interwoven in the Arab world.

Phillip Berryman, *The Religious Roots of Rebellion: Christians in Central American Revolutions* (Maryknoll, NY: Orbis Books, 1984). A personal account of liberation theology in Latin America.

E. Bradford Burns, *Latin America: Conflict and Creation* (Englewood Cliffs, NJ: Prentice Hall, 1989). The discussion of major themes in Latin American history provides a superb and succinct context for historical documents.

Barbara Evans Clements, *Daughters of Revolution: A History of Women in the USSR* (Arlington Heights, IL: Harlan Davidson, 1994). Concise survey of Soviet women's history.

Tulio Halperin Donghi, *The Contemporary History of Latin America* (Durham, NC: Duke University Press, 1993). An influential general history of Latin American periods of history since colonial times.

FIGURE 19.11 The Arab Comic Strip Magazine *Zakiyya al-Zakiyya* (Zakiyya the Clever)

This magazine is a source of revolutionary political commentary.

SOURCE: Courtesy Majed (Magazine for Children).

Sheila Fitzpatrick, *Stalin's Peasants: Resistance and Survival in the Russian Village after Collectivization* (Oxford: Oxford University Press, 1994). A study of the resistance strategies of the Russian peasantry to Stalin's collectivization policies.

Gail M. Gerhart, *Black Power in South Africa: The Evolution of an Ideology* (Berkeley: University of California Press, 1978).

John Iliffe, *Africans: The History of a Continent* (Cambridge: Cambridge University Press, 1995). A comprehensive and thematic approach to the vast African past.

Jacob M. London, ed., *Ataturk and the Modernization of Turkey* (Boulder, CO: Westview Press, 1984). Essays on various aspects of modern Turkey, including culture.

Robert W. Rydell, *All the World's a Fair: Visions of Empire at American International Expositions, 1876–1916* (Chicago: University of Chicago Press, 1984). An illuminating look at the representation of American power through international expositions.

Wieringa, Saskia, ed., *Subversive Women: Women's Movements in Africa, Asia, Latin America and the Caribbean* (London and New Jersey: Zed Books, 1995). A comprehensive look at women's movements from a non-European perspective.

The Crossroads of History: Culture, Identity, and Global Community

The Yoruba diviner Babalawo Kolawole Ositola sits before a carved wooden tray (*opon*) in the Porogun Quarter of the city of Ijebu-Ode, Nigeria. He begins the divination ritual in which he will explain the present and predict the future by invoking the past. First he traces the crossroads pattern, two lines that intersect at a right angle, in *irosun* powder on the surface of the tray. The crossroads symbolizes the meeting place of all directions, all forces. Like any busy intersection, the crossroads is a place of danger and confusion that arise with the opportunity to change direction. The Yoruba experience of the universe is expressed by the carvings on the *opon* and the words of the diviner that speak of continuous change and transformation, amidst the social realities of interaction and interdependence. The divination will become a dialogue with the ancestors and spiritual forces. The divine messenger, the deity Esu/Elegba, will be called upon to assist with the deeper truths about nature and the dangers and ambiguities of human communication. Yoruba divination sculpture reflects an ideal world of balance: humans are in the balance with nature and the unseen forces of agency and energy; the past is in balance with the future. According to the Yoruba scholar Robert Farris Thompson, "If there is anything to learn from [Esu] the god of the crossroads, it is that all is not as it seems to be."

In contrast to the Yoruba's acceptance of the potent ambiguity of the world illustrated in the work of the diviner, nineteenth-century Europeans believed in the possibility of understanding the world through scientific observation that would lead to discovery of the orderly, rational laws that made it work. Europe's domination of the world through imperialism reinforced confidence in European civilization. As the end of the nineteenth century approached, however, contemporaries considered the meaning of the past and made predictions about the future, not unlike the Yoruba diviner. For example, the term fin de siècle ("end of century") came to represent an attitude of despair, discomfort, and uneasiness that went far beyond the literal meaning of the term in French. The term suggested the possibility of tectonic shifts in cultural meaning and identity that could arise from a new era and an uncertain future; it also came to be associated with the perception of decaying moral codes.

At the end of the nineteenth century, the philosopher Friedrich Nietzsche (1844–1900) was one of many Europeans who made predictions about the age ahead. Writing in 1888, he warned that lives in the new century would be characterized by the onset of catastrophic wars beyond

imagination; by the death of god; and by feelings of self-loathing, skepticism, lust, greed, and cynicism. Certainly some twentieth-century survivors would see the fulfillment of Nietzsche's prophecy in the world wars; the threat of a nuclear holocaust; the dark night of fascism; and the contradictions, inequalities, and injustices exhibited in the twentieth-century world. Whether or not cultures view the human condition as inherently filled with contradiction and ambiguity, as in the world of the Yoruba diviner, there is no doubt that the history of the past century leaves humankind at just such a crossroads as the one overseen by the Yoruba deity Esu.

■ INTRODUCTION

Against the backdrop of wars, revolutionary violence, and rapid technological change, twentieth-century humans have often felt like victims, rather than participants, in an impersonal and fast-paced world. In the nineteenth and twentieth centuries, the transformations of industrialism, nationalism, imperialism, and global war have undermined the stability and security of both individuals and their communities. The collapse of certainties embedded in traditional cosmologies has produced anxiety about who "we" are and where we are going. The intrusion of constantly changing technology in our daily lives has created a sense of persistent unfamiliarity and alienation at the same time that the technology of communication has brought people closer together.

Such late-twentieth-century technology as infrared mapping, an ancillary product of satellites that record images of the earth from space, has altered perceptions of peoples and places. International boundaries have never been more accurately drawn than by space-age cartographers, yet these boundaries have also been made irrelevant in some ways by satellites, which invade the cultural and social space of even the most isolated corners of the globe on a daily basis. Telecommunications and computer technologies make possible intimate and immediate links between Los Angeles and Lahore, or London and Lagos.

Both the material bases of human cultures (including technology, environment, and demographics) and the resulting changes in the way people understand the world provide the sources of individual as well as community, national, or even global identity. This chapter focuses on how accelerated change has affected issues such as ethnicity, race, class, and gender in the lives of individuals and communities. We examine some of the dramatic transformations in the scientific, technological, social, and cultural arenas and consider their contributions to the age of uncertainty and our sense of global identity.

Never before have humans faced the possibility of extinction as a consequence of the meeting of the forces of technology and population. The combination of increasing population and advances in industrial technology has altered the physical landscape of larger and larger portions of the globe, and caused a growing imbalance in the relationship between nature and human life, while drastically reducing the resource base that supports life on the

FIGURE 20.1 *The Scream,* by Edvard Munch, 1895

The tensions and anxieties of modern life are portrayed in the swirling shapes of anguish and panic that embrace individual and landscape alike.

SOURCE: National Gallery, Oslo/Art Resource, New York.

planet. At the same time that technology has provided the means to raise the standard of living of a portion of the world's population while damaging the environment through deforestation and the pollution of water and air, progress in transportation and communication technology has brought the peoples of the globe closer and closer together, enhancing awareness of humanity's common fate and interests.

As the world has become technologically interconnected, the emerging global culture has been constantly and rapidly transformed; increasingly unstable, fragmented, and ambiguous cultural and social identities have been but one consequence. Another is a rich sense of possibility that the dynamic interaction of cultures has created. Culture, the patterns of behavior developed by societies in their efforts to understand, use, and survive in their environments, is a basic form of power, no less important than political or economic power, which it underscores and helps shape. Culture is also simply a people's "way of life," concerned with how people understand themselves, their communities, and their world, as well as how writers, artists, and musicians represent that world. In this chapter we explore the interaction of cultures through the development of global cultural idioms: literature in translation crossing national boundaries, music created from the cross-fertilization of different forms, and finally film as the art form of the twentieth century: the moving image that documents the speed of change, the richness and challenge of cultural diversity, and the universal concerns that shape the human condition at the late-twentieth-century crossroads.

■

UNCERTAINTY AT THE CROSSROADS: PHYSICS, PSYCHOLOGY, PHILOSOPHY

Advances in science and technology have been responsible for many transformations in twentieth-century life, ranging from the new theoretical view of the universe introduced by physicists early in the century to the uncertain benefits of atomic fusion at the end of the century. Such "advances" are responsible for invoking the sense of danger, confusion, and uncertainty of a twentieth-century crossroads. They can no longer be seen in terms of the simple progress of the nineteenth century; rather, scientific and technological change has been increasingly understood as adding an ambiguous complexity to twentieth-century lives, and the changed ways people comprehend their world are reflected in developments in psychology and philosophy.

THE CONTRIBUTIONS OF PHYSICS

In some ways physics has been the most successful science of the past 300 years. The modern ways of knowing the world and the very precise language used to describe that world were developed by physicists. The scientists Isaac Newton (1642–1727) and Robert Laplace (1749–1827) established the criteria of rational objectivity for natural science in which the scientist was a pure spectator. The classic expression of this was Laplace's image of the ideal scientist as the omniscient calculator, who, knowing the initial positions and velocities of all the atoms in the universe at the moment of its creation, would be able to predict and give running commentary on the entire subsequent history of the universe. Thus the nineteenth-century world was not only knowable, but it existed as a result of its past, which was the cause of its future. The physicist's cause-and-effect view of the universe was soon applied by many other disciplines besides physics, including history.

Einstein and Uncertainty   The problem with the cause-and-effect view, however neat and believable it may have been, was that it depended on an artificial construct: the separability of observer and observed, the belief in the scientist as an objective spectator. Take that away and, like a house of cards, all else would (and did) follow in a tumble of uncertainty and chaos. Among the scientists who created a post-Newtonian view of the universe, the most influential was Albert Einstein (1879–1955). Einstein assailed the concepts of the stability of matter, time, and motion that had been received wisdom since Newton. In 1905 Einstein proposed his theory of relativity, which made time, space, and motion relative to each other as well as to the observer, rather than the absolutes they had been believed to be.

Objectivity was no longer possible. According to Einstein, "this universe of ideas is just as little independent of the nature of our experiences as clothes are of the form of the human body." That is, theories about the world are like garments in that they fit the world to a greater or lesser degree, but none fits perfectly and none fits every occasion. And all are manufactured by humans. Einstein also said that we cannot even compare our theories with the real world. We can only compare our theoretical predictions with observations of the world, and these observations are subjective and therefore inherently uncertain.

Uncertainty was also suggested by the work of Joseph Thompson (1856–1940), Hendrick Lorentz (1853–1928), and Ernest Rutherford (1871–1937), who, by unlocking the secrets of

FIGURE 20.2   Two Scientists of the Twentieth Century: Robert Oppenheimer (right) with Albert Einstein (left) at Princeton University

SOURCE: Alfred Eisenstaedt, *Life* Magazine © 1947, Time, Inc.

Modern science has grappled with its own assumptions about knowable reality, a struggle personified in the lives of Oppenheimer (who critiqued atomic weapons) and Einstein (who rejected the distance between the observer and observed).

the atom, cast doubt on accepted beliefs about the nature of matter. Thompson and Lorentz independently discovered that the atoms of which all matter is composed are in turn composed of small particles, which Lorentz named electrons; Thompson and Rutherford imagined each atom as a miniature solar system consisting of a nucleus (the sun), electrons (the planets), and (mostly) space. They further suggested that the particulars of the atomic solar system might themselves not be matter at all, but energy: the positive and negative charges of electricity. Their work made possible the practical impact of twentieth century physics by bringing to light the details of the microscopic, subatomic universe. Devices such as transistors, silicon chips, integrated circuits, superconductors, and nuclear power all depended on knowledge of the electron.

Heisenberg's Uncertainty Principle   Another "card" that brought down the house of scientific certainty was the work of the physicist Werner Heisenberg (1901–1976), who is credited with conceiving the Uncertainty Principle, a principle that sought to explain the unlikelihood that science can know a predictable and orderly world independent of the observer. Heisenberg argued that what scientists observe is not nature itself but rather nature exposed to our method of human understanding.

Since the 1940s, more subatomic particles have been identified, including quarks. The set of scientific studies of the subatomic world since about 1925 is called "quantum theory," but while its impact has been great, it is hardly a finished story. Contrary to the Newtonian worldview, quantum theory implies randomness—the constant movement and unknowable arrangement of atoms—and a lack of predictability. During much of the nineteenth century, the mechanical universe of Newton had exuded confidence in an independent reality that existed essentially unchanged whether or not we observed it. In the twentieth century, quantum theory has transformed this certain world into chaos. Reality understood is reality changed, since the capture and perception of information is fundamentally flawed by the scientist whose presence intrudes on and changes the scene. In the world of physicist Niels Bohr, there are no atoms, only observations made by scientists. The atom according to Bohr is a creation of the human mind; science is imposed and fabricated order—humanmade, not natural. These scientific ideas questioned the very nature of matter and furthered a creeping sense of uncertainty, a sense that the more we learn, the less solid and reliable the natural world seems. As astronomers and astrophysicists continue to explore the origins of the universe and the way it works, new discoveries undermine previous assumptions about the infinite space that surrounds the planet and lend greater force to the sense of prevailing uncertainty.

THE IRRATIONALITY AND UNCERTAINTY OF KNOWING: PSYCHOLOGY

In the late nineteenth and early twentieth century, people working in the new field of psychology undertook the systematic study of human behavior, including relationships between mind and body. One of the first such psychologists was Wilhelm Wundt (1832–1920), who tested animal and human reactions in laboratory conditions. The Russian Ivan Pavlov (1849–1936), like Wundt, carried out controlled experiments on animals under the assumption that the results would be applicable to humans. One of his experiments with a dog resulted in "Pavlov's response," the concept that many human responses are not rational, but purely mechanically products of stimuli of which we are often unaware.

Freud and the Irrational The most considerable stir in understanding human nature in the twentieth century was created by the work of Sigmund Freud (1856–1939), the father of the method of investigation and treatment called psychoanalysis. Freud concluded that much of human behavior is irrational, unconscious, and instinctive. Conflict, he believed, not reason, is the basic condition of life. Freud believed that conflicts exist mostly on an unconscious level and begin in childhood. They cause frustation, which festers in the subconscious and results in neuroses and psychoses (mental disorders of varying degrees). Neuroses may be dealt with by making the neurotic person conscious of the facts and circumstances of the original frustration. Such consciousness was the objective of psychoanalysis. Freud's ideas have gone through three-quarters of a century of evolution, modification, and rejection. Despite criticism that Freudian ideas are time, place, and especially gender bound, psychoanalysis persists as one response to the confusions and fears of individuals living in the uncertain twentieth century.

Art, Uncertainty, and the Unconscious Systematic efforts to understand and interpret the twentieth century, the relationship of people to each other and to the universe they inhabit, have found various forms of cultural expression. A major aesthetic movement of the twentieth century, surrealism, grew out of a rejection of all aspects of Western culture, a rejection also associated with a cultural movement known as "Dadaism" (from the French for hobbyhorse, suggesting nonsense). Both of these movements emphasized the role of the unconscious in creative activity and were represented in literary and artistic works in which dream imagery and the unconscious play a large role.

FIGURE 20.3 Freud in His Study

This haunting potrait of Sigmund Freud shows him surrounded by antiquities and non-Western art, in which he recognized a more direct access to the non-sensory parts of the knowable world.

SOURCE: Corbis-Bettmann.

FIGURE 20.4 The Persistence of Memory, 1931, by Salvador Dali. Oil on canvas, 9 1/2″ x 13″

The Spanish surrealist Dali, mixing surprising and incoherent fragments of reality, painted with detailed accuracy a confusion in which objects merge and exchange places. The painting's title suggests the fragility and potential distortion of the human experience of time and meaning.

SOURCE: Museum of Modern Art, New York. Given anonymously. Photo © 1997 The Museum of Modern Art, New York. © 1998 Demart Pro Arte. (R), Geneva/Artists Rights Society (ARS), New York.

Surrealism   The work of the Spanish artist Salvador Dali (1904–1989) exemplifies surrealism in painting. His most famous painting is called *The Persistence of Memory* (1931), depicting limp, fluid watches strewn about a dreamlike landscape. Though based on the sixteenth-century artist Hieronymous Bosch's famous painting *The Garden of Earthly Delights,* Dali's work is a product of the twentieth century and suggests the breakdown of the certainties of the mechanical Newtonian universe (the limp watches sliding over the landscape) as well as the human perception of time itself. Surrealist writers, painters, and filmmakers extended the Western notions of reality beyond what was known and visible to the human eye or the eye of the camera.

PHILOSOPHY AND UNCERTAINTY

Philosophical responses to the changes of the twentieth century have been many and varied. European reactions have been often crouched in extreme pessimism, an insistence that European civilization has collapsed and is doomed. The German metahistorian Oswald Spengler

(1880–1936) put forth this argument in *The Decline of the West* (1918). For Spengler, World War I was the beginning of the end for European (German) civilization. The works of the Spaniard Jose Ortega y Gasset (1883–1935) express a similar sense of decay and crisis. His *Revolt of the Masses* (1930) is a lament for the dehumanization and decline of rational society, which he believed was the result of the rise of popular material culture and the tendency of the masses to use destructive force to achieve their goals.

Existentialism   Another reaction to twentieth-century uncertainty was Existentialism. Rooted ▬▬▬▬▬▬ in the disenchantment and anxiety produced by two massive twentieth-century wars, Existentialism became especially prominent after World War II. According to this philosophy, there were no absolutes or permanencies or universal truths, only personal inspiration and individual commitment. Existentialists argued that there is no ultimate meaning, rational or irrational, to existence. Individuals are simply born and exist. They are free and are responsible for the decisions they make and the actions they take. There are no final, ultimate rights or wrongs, so individuals must establish their own rules and standards and be responsible for living up to them. These personal rules are their blueprint for living, after which they die.

THE COMPUTER REVOLUTION: A WORLDWIDE CROSSROADS

The notion that machines could replace the human body and its functions was a powerful catalyst to the development of the computer, probably the most important invention of the twentieth century. The computer has revolutionized the speed of access to information. Many of the late-twentieth-century appliances and innovations, from telephone-answering machines to microwave ovens to air traffic control systems, would not have been conceivable without the development of the computer. No other invention has had such a revolutionary impact on global relations and daily lives.

DEVELOPMENT OF COMPUTERS

The first generation of computers relied on another innovation, the vacuum tube, the device that also enabled the invention of television. Early computers were enormous objects that filled entire rooms. Like many other technologies, the computer and its impact were shaped by its development in a military context.

The Computer's Language   Major developments in computer technology created an information ▬▬▬▬▬▬▬▬▬▬▬ tion age; some of these developments can be credited to United States Navy Rear Admiral Grace Murray Hopper (1906–1992), a mathematician recruited by the Navy to work on the Harvard University computer project. Dr. Hopper, who realized that most people communicate better with prose than with mathematical symbols, created and standardized what came to be known as COBAL, a common business-oriented language for computers. The use of complex, mathematical data to translate and manipulate words and concepts also made possible the mass communications revolution that interconnects the globe, while revealing the information storage and retrieval potential of the new computer technology.

From Reproducing to Connecting the World Whereas photography, the moving picture, and television provided a whole new technology for storing and displaying pictorial information and the telegraph, the telephone, the phonograph, the tape recorder, and the radio have given us new technology for storing and transmitting auditory information, the computer's evolution has been able to integrate all these technologies into one system. The computer is unique, however, in that it has the capacity for manipulating and transforming information without human intervention. There is no doubt that computers have increased human productivity, whereas the impact of computers on the nature of work and leisure and on the quality of life is still debated. Computer technology originated to meet the needs of the most nationalistic of twentieth-century institutions, the United States military, yet the information superhighway, a worldwide network of computer networks, now delivers computer-transmitted information instantaneously to a global community.

COMPLEXITY THEORY

Computer science has produced new ways of ordering and understanding reality in the face of Heisenberg's Uncertainty Principle and what has come to be known as chaos theory. One new field of inquiry is called complexity theory, and it is rooted in the notion that systems as diverse as economic, ecological, and immune systems, genetic codes, and computer networks are all characterized by extraordinary complexity. Some complexity theorists believe that, complex and diverse as these systems are, they may share some hidden order or common characteristics and interactions that will lead to the ability to anticipate the future, to learn and adapt in ways that we do not yet understand. Though controversial, complexity theory has been used, for example, to model the spread of AIDS. Complexity theory is built on computer models, which are essentially mathematical extrapolations, not on observation of the real world, but such models can lead to genuine insights about how things work. At the very least complexity theory is clearly a long way from nineteenth-century models of scientific inquiry.

For the last 400 years, science has advanced by reductionism, the idea that the world could be understood by examining smaller and smaller pieces—the component parts—of it. Scientists believed that mathematical laws could predict all natural phenomena. But in the last 100 years, reductionism and the mathematics on which it is based, have come under assault by new theories such as that of Kurt Godel, who proved that mathematical systems are always incomplete and cannot be relied on to describe nature. Scientists have begun to take a closer look at nature, finding that the world is filled with complex phenomena that do not behave in a linear fashion and that cannot be explained by reductionism.

Adding up the parts to understand the whole, according to complexity theorists, does not give a good picture of the whole; rather, the interactions within a given system are just as important as the parts. To understand this theory, a different kind of mathematics, using nonlinear approaches, is needed. Working on this new frontier requires the ability to reduce to its essentials a wide range of information as part of the process of building models of complex systems, but it also has an artistlike creative dimension, in that the researcher must rely on metaphors and analogies to summarize information. Creativity in science and poetry, as in mathematics and music, have much in common. Complexity theory is one aspect of new cosmology at the end of the twentieth century, a vivid reminder of the constant mutation and transformation of cosmologies throughout history.

■

CULTURAL CROSSROADS: GEOGRAPHY, HISTORY, AND REGIONAL IDENTITIES

People's understanding of the nature of their world (cosmology) can be transformed by technological developments such as the computer and its influence on complexity theory. Geography is another way of framing and organizing an understanding of the peoples, places, and environments of the world. Just as cosmologies are transformed by the ongoing dialogues in which connections are constructed between the present and the past and between cultures, connections are made within specific historical and geographical settings. Geography defines cultural identities and shapes the encounters of cultures that meet at its crossroads. Geography is a human science, the product of certain ways of conceptualizing the physical world, and therefore bears the imprint of human and historically created understandings of that world. The creation of regional geographies is also a historical process, suggesting the impermanence of cultural and political categories and identities in the twentieth century.

EAST ASIA: FROM FAR EAST TO PACIFIC RIM

For nearly two millennia, East Asia was characterized by a certain degree of cultural cohesion through the domination of Chinese civilization. When Europeans first encountered the societies of East Asia beginning in the sixteenth century, they identified individual countries by different names and acknowledged in their descriptions of these societies fundamental differences among them, just as there were differences among the Spanish, Portuguese, Dutch, and English. By the time of nineteenth century encounters, however, both Europeans and East Asians were homogenized to a degree in stereotyped perceptions of each other. Peoples who inhabited East Asia were conscious of being part of a world dominated by China. They were not conscious of being a region of the world as defined by Europeans, although increasingly they were precisely that through the expansion of the European economy to become *the* world economy.

European economic expansion into East Asia created a counterweight that first challenged and then overcame the original economic (and politico/cultural) core: China. The integration of East Asia into European capitalist economic formations began gradually during the sixteenth through the eighteenth centuries and then speeded up in the nineteenth. With economic integration came the European definition of the region as an expression of its relationship with Europe: spatially, the "Far East," and culturally, the "Orient."

The Pacific Rim The concept of the "Pacific Rim," referring to the countries rimming the Pacific Ocean, can be seen as a contemporary extension of the notion of the "Orient". Less weighted with cultural assumptions, since it includes Latin American, North American, and Asian countries, the idea of the "Pacific Rim" is based on connections established through common economic interests. It is important to recognize, though, that Pacific Rim is a historical construct and that it represents only a more recent version of earlier constructs that gave differing shapes to regional identity in this part of the world. From the sixteenth through the mid-nineteenth centuries, the Pacific was a "Spanish lake"; in the nineteenth century it became an "English lake." In the twentieth century it has been transformed into an "American lake," though increasingly the economic and military power of Asian

The Peters Projection Map of the World

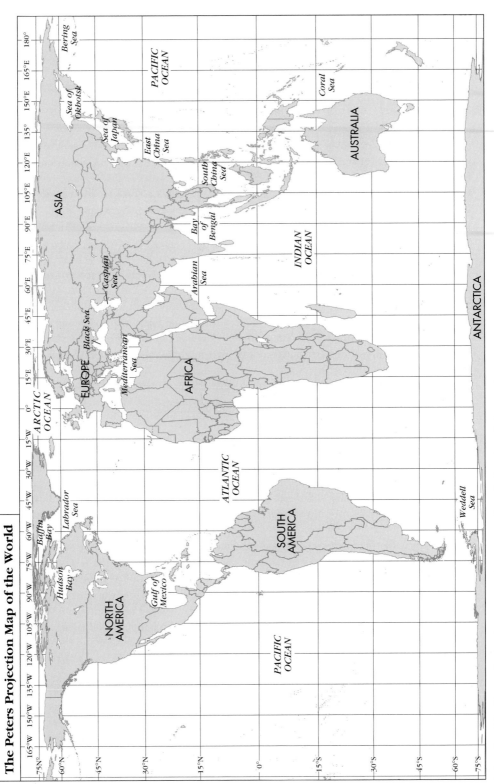

MAP 20.1   The Peters Projection accurately conveys the relative size of the continents.

nations such as Japan, and more recently China, have begun to alter once again the regional identity of the Pacific.

THE GEOGRAPHY OF COLONIALISM IN ASIA, AFRICA, AND THE AMERICAS

The extension of imperialism and the imposition of colonial rule resulted in the redrawing of boundaries of political and social interaction as the earth's surface was divided and controlled. Sometimes those boundaries traced old, familiar patterns of interdependence; more often they organized new ones. In this way geographical reconfiguring has emphasized the complexity of cultural interactions and the role of place in the construction of political and ethnic identities.

India Although there were periods in India's past in which much of the subcontinent was unified under powerful rulers, such as Asoka, the Guptas, or more recently, the Mughals, the idea of the modern Indian nation was in large part a product of its colonial experience under British rule. The extreme linguistic, religious, ethnic, and cultural diversity of the Indian subcontinent historically has produced centrifugal forces that made unity difficult to achieve, let alone maintain. The daunting problems that face Indian democracy in the latter twentieth century can be attributed in large part not only to the residue of the caste system, but also to the imposition of the idea of a unified nation by the British Raj on such a complex and diverse region. One observer has noted that considering India as a single nation is comparable to regarding Europe as a unified polity, with its many languages, cultures, and ethnic groups.

Africa The African continent has similarly been created as a singular geographic and cultural entity by its historical relation to other parts of the world, in particular, through its colonization by Europe. Not only were cultural and national boundaries created by the brutal imposition of colonial rule, but these European-drawn boundaries were profoundly reductionary: regions of immense cultural diversity and political history were "united" under false national flags.

In reality, the boundaries cut through the middle of cultural groups and families, collapsing hundreds of distinct African languages and ethnic groups into the false notion of a single "African" culture. Indeed, even the idea of a geographic unity, a single continent, has been imposed by those outside the continent, who drew maps deciding where Africa ends and the Arabian peninsula begins. North Africa has often been separated from the rest of sub-Saharan Africa and attached to the "Middle East," reflecting the influence of Islam in the region, as well as the legacy of the Ottoman Empire. The "Near East" was used in the same way as the "Far East," defining regions of the world by their proximity to Europe.

The Americas Similarly, the "New World" was new only to Europeans, not to the inhabitants of the Americas. The term "Latin America" reflects the impact of the Spanish empire and Hispanic culture on this part of the world, but since African, Native American, and other European influences also figure in the region's cultural history, the term is not the only category of regional identity appropriately applied to peoples of Central and South America. Like other regional identities such as the Far East, the notion of the "New

World" was a historically produced construct created by the movement of Europeans across the globe and encounters with other cultures and peoples brought about by demographic processes of migration as well as the expansion of Europe through imperialism.

■

POPULATION AT THE CROSSROADS: DEMOGRAPHIC PATTERNS OF THE TWENTIETH CENTURY

Issues of population, environment, and technology together provide the setting in which historical "events" and cultural transformations of the late nineteenth and twentieth centuries have unfolded. The most conspicuous trends in this period are the restructuring of identity in relation to place, the migration of peoples across the globe, the growth of world populations, and the concentrations of population in urban environments.

MIGRATION

Humans have always been mobile. Prehistoric migrations over vast areas by small numbers of peoples who, mostly traveling by foot on land or boats on water, populated the globe. As people settled, pressure of increasing population was a persistent factor in specific regions (such as the Nile Valley), leading to recurrent migrations. As the millennia passed human movement became easier; increasing numbers made it necessary. But never before the present has the whole world faced the prospect of the filling up of open spaces; the crowding of ever-expanding cities; the pollution of streams, lakes, and even oceans; and the amount of material equipment, the level of education, and the complexity of organization necessary to expand the output of goods and services at a rate sufficient to maintain existing standards of living.

In the nineteenth and twentieth centuries, population movements have been the result of a number of factors: pressure of numbers, the need for labor, the desire for land and jobs, and political and religious persecution. Vast increases in population necessitated the exodus of large numbers from their homelands; it was an important factor in the spread of European dominance around the globe, leading to the creation of European states in North and South America, Australia, and New Zealand and exerting great influence, if not permanent settlement and control, on every continent.

European Emigration Beginning in the mid-nineteenth century, the rapid spread of urbanization and industrialization resulted in an increased exodus from Europe. These migrations served to relieve population pressure, and they satisfied the need for labor, especially in industries. Most of these European immigrants came into areas already settled by Europeans. The United States provides a clear illustration of the pattern of nineteenth century immigration. Immigrants came in three waves: the first reached its high-water mark in 1854, when nearly 430,000 new arrivals were recorded; the second, starting in the 1870s rose to a height in 1882, when nearly 800,000 people arrived; the third brought in a average of a million people a year in the decade before World War I, after which immigration was limited by law.

Similar patterns, though lesser numbers, are found in Canada and Australia. The earliest nineteenth-century immigrants were northern European: Irish (some 2 million); German (1.5 million); and British (750,000). By the end of the century, southern and eastern Europeans had displaced northern Europeans. Without Italians and southern and eastern Slavic peoples, the great increase in numbers would not have been possible. For example, by the outbreak of World War I, 4 million Italians had left their homeland. Not all Europeans went to North America. Between 1890 and 1900 about 2 million Italians and Germans migrated to South America, many of them settling in Brazil and Argentina.

Indian Emigration Europeans were not the only peoples caught up in the labor migration. From the mid-nineteenth century on, Indians left the subcontinent in continuing numbers to escape overcrowding and to seek jobs. They scattered even more widely around the globe than Europeans, who tended to migrate to states of prior European settlement. Significant numbers of Indians, who were not always welcomed, have settled in South America, where half the populations of Guyana and Surinam is Indian; in the Caribbean, where 40 percent of the population of Trinidad is Indian; in the South Pacific, on Fiji (50 percent Indian); and on Mauritius (70 percent Indian) in the Indian Ocean. Indians also settled in nearby Asian countries such as Malaysia (10 percent) and in lesser numbers in more distance east and south African countries.

The Chinese Diaspora Beginning in the mid-nineteenth century, harsh economic conditions forced hundreds of thousands of Chinese to leave their homeland to seek employment abroad. Many of them went to nearby Malaysia or Singapore or islands in

FIGURE 20.5 Chinese Workers at a California Gold Mine, 1852

SOURCE: California History Section, California State Library.

the Pacific, but they also settled in South America (there were nearly 100,000 Chinese in Peru by the end of the nineteenth century); the Caribbean (Cuba and the British West Indies); Canada, especially British Columbia; and the United States. By 1930, 400,000 Chinese had crossed the Pacific, 77 percent of them settling in California. They were invaluable in building transcontinental railroads, and when that task was completed, they engaged in agriculture and small businesses. They took part in the search for gold in California, British Columbia, and Australia, and in South Africa industrialists imported more than 50,000 Chinese indentured laborers by the end of the nineteenth century to work in mines.

Migration   In smaller numbers other peoples moved around the globe in search of work, land, and security. Some returned to their homeland once they had made their fortunes, but most stayed and gradually and often painfully were integrated into the cultures of their new homelands. Full acceptance of immigrants, especially of those of color by countries with predominantly white populations, was slow coming. Countries like Australia and the United States undertook to limit the number of immigrants by establishing quotas. Quotas were in large part racially motivated, with nonwhite, especially Asian, immigrants singled out as undesirable.

World War II and   At the conclusion of World War II, a new redrawing of borders was in-
New Boundaries   strumental in shifting large numbers of peoples. For example, the creation of the new state of Israel resulted in the migration of Jews to western Asia, where Palestinians felt they were dispossessed of their homeland. The result has been a continuous ethnic and religious struggle. When the Indian subcontinent was divided between Muslims (Pakistan) and Hindus (India), each sought to clear their lands of the other, and the effect was not only large-scale human movement but also violence and massive loss of life. The redefining of borders after World War II especially affected the Poles, since Russia moved far west into former Polish territory. Poland was compensated by being given portions of eastern Germany.

The uprooting effect of human politics continues to be a major problem at the end of the twentieth century, especially when it accompanies the break up of nation states. Human mobility in modern times has all too often been a source of human pain, but whether voluntary or forced, whether resulting from economic or political or religious forces, it remains, as it was at the dawn of human history, a human imperative.

POPULATION GROWTH

The effect of human population growth has been debated since the eighteenth century. Thomas Malthus, in his influential *Essay on Population,* expressed the belief that population grew at a rate exceeding that of resources; this theory led many to conclude that surplus population means too many people and not enough resources. Others attributed the perception of over population to the inequitable division of resources in society. Nineteenth century capitalists, in contrast, welcomed increased numbers of consumers who created the expanded markets necessary for capitalist industrial growth.

Population growth was even encouraged by some political leaders in the twentieth century, such as Stalin in the Soviet Union and Mussolini in Italy, both of whom gave awards for motherhood. Mao Zedong during the 1950s urged his people to expand their already huge

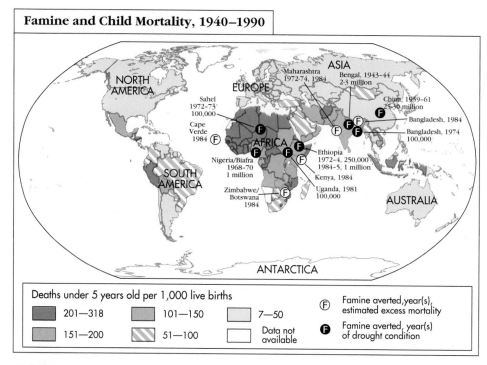

Famine and Child Mortality, 1940–1990

Sahel
1972-73
100,000

Cape
Verde
1984 Ⓕ

Maharashtra
1972-74, 1984

Bengal, 1943-44
2-3 million

China, 1959-61
25-30 million

Bangladesh, 1984

Bangladesh, 1974
100,000

Nigeria/Biafra
1968-70
1 million

Ethiopia
1972-4, 250,000
1984-5, 1 million

Kenya, 1984

Zimbabwe/
Botswana
1984

Uganda, 1981
100,000

NORTH
AMERICA

EUROPE

ASIA

AFRICA

SOUTH
AMERICA

AUSTRALIA

ANTARCTICA

Deaths under 5 years old per 1,000 live births

201—318	101—150	7—50
151—200	51—100	Data not available

Ⓕ Famine averted, year(s), estimated excess mortality

Ⓕ Famine averted, year(s) of drought condition

MAP 20.2 Global Patterns of Famine and Child Mortality

population, arguing that the country could make up in people what it lacked in industry and other resources. But this policy was dramatically reversed with the introduction of the "one child" policy in the 1960s, in which only one child was allowed per family, to slow China's devastating birth rate and population growth.

Tremendous postwar population increases were noted with alarm by many, including the biologist Paul Ehrlich, who described the "problem" of growth in his book *The Population Bomb* (1968), at a time when there were 3.5 billion human beings, five times the population of Malthus's world. With world population at 5.3 billion in 1990 and over 6 billion anticipated for the year 2000, three people each second, a quarter million each day, about 90 to 100 million each year of the coming decade will be added, according to the 1990 State of World Population Report/UN Population Fund. More than 90 percent of the current population growth occurs in the poorest countries of the world, and a billion of the current 5.3 billion inhabitants of the world, the "bottom billion," live in poverty, a fact that suggests that part of the crisis at the crossroads is political and economic.

URBANIZATION

In the twentieth century the process of urbanization has escalated, with the sharpest growth in non-European cities. In 1950 fewer than 30 percent of the world's people lived in cities; near the end of the century, nearly half do, and the number is steadily increasing. Tokyo is

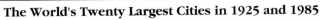

The World's Twenty Largest Cities in 1925 and 1985

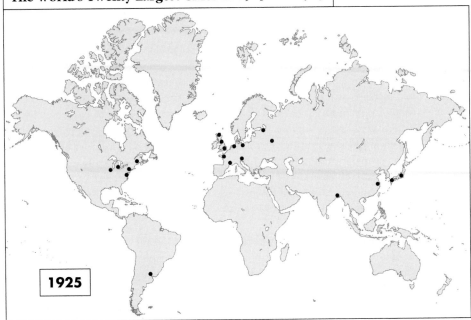

1925

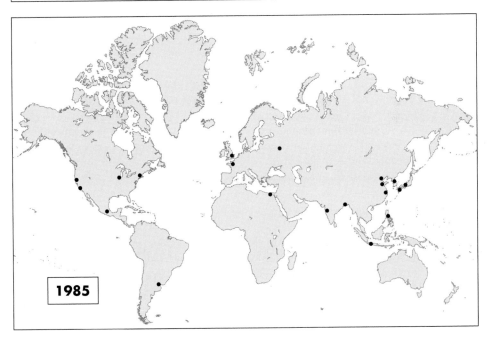

1985

MAP 20.3 Shifting Urban Centers in the Twentieth Century

currently the only city with a population of more than 20 million, but early in the next century it will be joined by Bombay, Lagos, Shanghai, Jakarta, Sao Paulo, and Karachi, with Beijing, Dhaka, and Mexico City close behind. By the year 2025, it is estimated that two-thirds of the world's population will be city dwellers.

Overcrowded and polluted cities, especially in less-developed regions of the world, are also sites of instability and tremendous social and economic change. Between 1950 and 1990 there was a fivefold increase in the number of urban residents in less-developed countries, a far more rapid increase than for the world as a whole. A U.N.-sponsored conference on cities met in Istanbul (population 10 million) in 1996, but U.N. elites cannot hope to solve the problems of third-world cities without paying serious attention to rural development and the reasons for urban migration. Prior to the nineteenth century, the vast majority of the world's peoples lived on farms, in rural settings, and their lifestyles, while culturally distinct, shared certain technological similarities. The gaps between highly industrialized and "developing" societies began to emerge during the colonial era, as capitalist industrialism spread and encouraged the growth of urban centers.

Capitalist Industrialism and Urbanization   Capitalist industrialism attracted people to urban centers, where markets and factories needed their labor while fluctuations in production and consumption also created large numbers of unemployed and homeless people. Urbanization also altered cultural patterns in parts of the world distant from industrial centers, where the contradictions of capitalist industrialism were experienced by colonized and marginalized peoples. Urban centers separated many peoples from their traditional means of subsistence, utilizing their labor to produce goods for world markets and transforming them into consumers of manufactured goods.

■

CRISIS AT THE CROSSROADS: TECHNOLOGY, MATERIAL LIFE, AND SOCIAL CHANGE

Technology has shaped both urban and rural environments and the daily lives of people who migrated to cities and those who remained in rural areas. Developments in technology altered the quality, conduct, and even length of daily life. Industrialization took place not only in factories, public transport systems or market places but also in the home.

ELECTRIFYING CHANGE

Although Michael Faraday built the first electric motor in 1831, more than half a century passed before Nicola Tesla, with the Westinghouse Company, successfully patented a small electric motor for use as an electric fan (1889). In the 1890s electric current was still a luxury discussed everywhere but generally agreed upon as being too expensive for common use. Inventors like Tesla, on the other hand, predicted that electricity would soon be used as casually as water. The electrification of the home took place in industrialized parts of the world first: electric lights rapidly replaced gas lamps between 1918 and 1928.

Changes in the lighting of community streets and individual homes were not the most profound effects of electrification. The advent of electric lighting increased the length of the work day and altered material life. In the United States and other industrialized parts of the world in the 1920s, electric irons and electric washing machines became widespread symbols of the industrial revolution in the home. Yet these and other innovations and appliances did not reduce the amount of household labor performed by women; the number of tasks multiplied and increased awareness of such things as germs and hygiene required more frequent washing as new standards imposed additional tasks.

The increased consumption of material goods created by industrial technology in turn brought women to the forefront of a consuming public. A study in Oregon in 1928 revealed that farm wives (many without electricity) spent 61 hours a week on housework; "electrified" town wives spent 63.4 hours. Just after World War II, economists reported that farm wives spent 60.55 hours on housework each week, women in small cities spent 78.35 hours, and women in large cities spent 80.57 hours, a trend that some historians have viewed as contributing to the women's liberation movement of the late twentieth century. In turn, inventions that rely on electricity, such as the radio, television, and computer have changed the nature of family and household life. Whereas listening to the radio in the 1940s or watching television in the 1950s was often a family ritual that linked isolated households to the larger community, technological changes have made these innovations more widely available to individuals, with the result that their use is less social. The proliferation of technological change has increased the awareness of its unpredictable interaction with social forces, and change contributes to an age of uncertainty. More than one cultural observer has commented that change has become the only global constant of the twentieth century.

LIVING ON THE EARTH: POPULATION, RESOURCES, AND TECHNOLOGY

Both technological innovations and the growth of population have had a profound impact on the consumption of resources and transformed the physical landscape. Though humans have altered their landscapes since prehistoric times through the use of fire and other manipulations of the environment, the human impact on the landscape has intensified dramatically in the past two centuries. The period between 1800 and 1914 witnessed an unprecedented expansion of agriculture and population growth throughout the world, both of which had devastating effects on world resources and the physical landscape. These forces can be held directly responsible for global deforestation beginning in the nineteenth century.

The Landscapes of Imperialism The Western attitude toward nature as a force to be controlled and exploited by civilization intersected with the powerful political ideas of imperialism in the nineteenth century. The Western attitude has increasingly become the model and pattern for non-Western peoples, and its global acceptance has brought humanity to the threshold of ecological disaster at the end of the twentieth century. For example, the British Raj exploited and destroyed the forests of the western Himalayas between 1815 and 1914 while building the most sophisticated forestry service in the colonial world. The colonization of nature was viewed as just as inevitable as the subjugation of "inferior" peoples by colonial powers.

Europeans considered fenced and cultivated gardens as the most appealing and idyllic landscapes during the nineteenth century, a kind of colonization of nature. The landscape legacy of this colonization is found in the national parks of the world: from Kenya to Ghana to Yosemite, protected landscapes became necessary to preserve at least some semblance of the wilderness and its wildlife that was nearly lost to the nineteenth- and early-twentieth-century rampages of imperialism. Colonial officers and other Europeans collected plants and animals from around the world to create botanical gardens and zoological parks.

Deforestation   From Thailand to the Amazon to equatorial Africa to the Pacific Northwest of the United States and Canada, the exploitation of forests changed global landscapes dramatically and impinged on centuries-long patterns of land and resource use. The global trend toward deforestation was not so much a response to the pressure of growing population as it was a consequence of world market forces, generated by European demand for commodities and raw materials. In particular, the markets of industrialized nations have demanded timber for construction, newsprint, and other paper products. A product of the collaboration between wealthy and less-developed nations, deforestation made many rural populations more dependent on international market needs and external control. The irony is that in many parts of the world, as scientific information about the forest systems was increasing, the forests themselves, increasingly exploited, disappeared.

Deforestation is but one aspect of the global attack on environmental balance. Growing demands for electric power created by the needs of expanding technology and population have resulted in massive alterations in the landscape and the environment. The Aswan High Dam along the southern Nile was built in the 1960s at a cost of $1 billion to provide hydroelectric power. Supported in part by Soviet aid, the dam created a 300-mile-long lake, named Lake Nasser after Egypt's president, and inundated many villages along the Nile as well as some historical monuments. In the 1990s China planned the enormous Three Gorges Dam along the upper reaches of the Yangzi River at a projected cost of $25 billion. If completed, this dam will inundate farmland and villages to create a 400-mile-long reservoir, forcing the evacuation of an estimated 1 million people from their homes. Criticism by environmental groups sensitive to its impact on landscape and people has delayed international financing for the project, which was to come largely from American, Canadian, and European banks.

Tropical Rainforests   The best current illustration of a global environmental problem is the fate of tropical rainforests. Rainforests girdle the globe in a 3200-mile belt near the equator, between the southern tropic of Capricorn and the northern tropic of Cancer. They make up 7 percent of the world's land surface but contain half of the globe's approximately 5 million plant and animal species. Only 2.5 billion of the original 4 billion acres of rainforest remain; a conservative deforestation rate (fifty acres a minute) means that the rainforests will be entirely gone in 100 years.

Plant and animal species that have adapted to the virtually fire-resistant rainforests cannot adapt to land that technology has allowed humans to ravage, and as many as 20 percent of all species on earth may be extinct within twenty years. Tropical plants vital to industry, medicine, agriculture, and horticulture will accordingly disappear. In addition to plants and animals, numerous human cultures that have thrived for centuries in the rainforests without harming their environment will disappear.

The plight of rainforests is specifically related to global warming. Their loss is cited as the second leading cause of the increased concentration of carbon dioxide in the atmosphere, just behind the burning of fossil fuels by internal combustion engines such as the automobile. Plants absorb carbon dioxide for growth and give off oxygen and thus help control the greenhouse effect. The massive destruction of forest areas severely lessens that control. The irony of the destruction of forest resources in many parts of the world is that its recognition has come at a time when scientific information indicates how essential forests are to the global environment and the survival of species. The need to balance forest ecology with the needs of expanding populations and the demands of international market forces is one of the major global issues at the end of the twentieth century.

ECOLOGY AND TECHNOLOGY

The soaring of human numbers continues to have a direct impact on the environment today. Two factors decide how much damage each person does to the environment: (1) consumption patterns, and (2) technological style (the kind of technology used and the waste and pollution it creates). While industrialized countries, the "top billion" have lower birth rates, they are responsible for the largest share of resources used, waste created, damage to the ozone layer, acidification, and roughly two-thirds of global warming. The combination of poverty and population growth among the "bottom billion" is, of course, also damaging the environment through deforestation and land degradation. Resultant climate change is a major threat to human life. The projected rise in temperature in the next half century is 2.8 degrees Celsius, a climate shift unmatched in human history.

Much of the responsibility for the world's ecological crisis lies in the kind of technology developed since World War II. Contemporary technology is potentially cleaner than the coal-produced iron technology of the eighteenth-century industrial revolution, but most technical developments in the last half century have been more harmful than earlier ones. The main difference is the development of synthetic products to replace natural, organic ones.

Since the end of World War II, synthetic fibers have replaced natural ones (cotton products have declined by 36 percent, wool by 42 percent, while synthetic fibers have increased by nearly 6000 percent), and lumber (down 1 percent) has given way to plastic (up nearly 2000 percent). In agriculture, land has been abused by emphasis on synthetic (nitrogen) fertilizers, herbicides, and synthetic pesticides, which have replaced the traditional use of animal fertilizers and methods of pest control. In transportation rail freight has given way to truck freight, and low-powered automobile engines to high-powered ones.

ENVIRONMENTAL POLLUTION

Technological transformations have not produced a conspicuous rise in the quality of life since World War II, and their ecological impact has reached crisis proportions. In the United States alone, pollution levels have risen between 200 and 2000 percent since 1946. This situation is not the result of population growth or affluence alone, but to the unqualified uses of late-twentieth-century technology. New technologies—and the profits made from them—account for as much as 95 percent of the added environmental pollution of the last quarter century.

The Minamata Sickness In the 1970s industrial pollution became a serious national issue in Japan and revealed the most negative aspects of Japan's rapid economic growth over the last century. Mercury poisoning was suspected in the town of Minamata on the southern-most island of Kyûshû, but authorities refused to recognize the obvious source of pollution, a chemical company that was pouring wastes into the bay where most of the residents caught fish for food.

Although the link between effluents discharged into Minamata Bay by the company and the cases of mercury poisoning began to be made as early as 1953, twenty years passed before formal legal action was taken and before any compensation was awarded to the victims of "Minamata disease." Reluctant to jeopardize its relations with business and to threaten productivity, the government hesitated to pursue the claims of victims until it could no longer ignore the evidence.

Cars and Trucks The greatest source of urban pollution is the automobile, and the bigger the automobile, the greater the pollution. But the bigger the automobile, the larger the profit. Detroit makes less than a 10 percent profit on compact cars and more than a 10 percent profit on larger, more expensive models. As Henry Ford II remarked, "Minicars made mini-profits." A similar situation exists in the use of trucks in preference to trains to transport goods. Trucks require six times the amount of fuel as trains; that is, trucks emit six times the environmental pollution for the same haulage compared to trains. In addition, the amount of cement and steel needed for a four-lane highway takes about four times the energy required for a similar mileage of railroad. Nonetheless, the profits from trucking are 8.84 percent, while those from railroads are 2.61 percent, which goes far toward explaining the expansion of freight hauled by trucks and the relative decline of rail haulage.

There are countless other examples of the union of technology and profit at the expense of the environment. Obviously, the problem is not technology alone. Modern technology does exactly what is asked of it. It is asked to overlook long-term global needs in the interests of immediate and individual profit. The goal of technology has been separated from the total context in which it functions. The modern technological flaw is the tubular vision that commands it.

Technology so construed cannot cope with the whole ecological system into which pesticides and synthetic fertilizers, automobiles and trucks, not to mention the atomic bomb, intrude; accordingly disastrous ecological "surprises," such as water pollution, smog, and global radioactive fallout, cannot be avoided. The twentieth-century technological explosion has created the first worldwide culture, a technological culture. It has resulted in fundamental environmental problems that, as the century draws to an end, are truly global concerns and the ultimate concerns of our time.

MEDICINE AND TECHNOLOGY

Industrial pollution brought about by the union of modern technology with exploitation of the environment in the service of economic growth has created health problems such as the Minamata mercury poisoning. Similarly, radiation sickness was produced by the discovery of nuclear power and weaponry. Such illnesses presented new challenges to medical research and practice against the background of nineteenth- and twentieth-century advances in the understanding and treatment of disease.

As early as 1839 scientists had demonstrated that the tiny creatures observed with microscopes consisted of cells, and by 1860 further improvements in the microscope enabled the French scientist Louis Pasteur (1822–1895) to prove that these minute living organisms, or bacteria, caused diseases in plants and animals. Pasteur further showed that many dangerous disease-causing bacteria could be killed simply by raising the temperature of their environment (pasteurization) and that others could be combated by inoculation or immunization. Pasteur's research led to methods of sterilization and asepsis, processes that kill disease-producing microorganisms and have wide application in medicine, surgery, and bacteriology.

 DAILY LIVES

OPERATION CROSSROADS

One of the most impressive manifestations of the power of technology in the modern world and its human and environmental impact is the horrifying blast of an atomic bomb. Witnesses to the development and use of nuclear weapons during World War II range from the scientists of the Manhattan Project and Los Alamos, New Mexico, laboratories working in secret to the victims of the Hiroshima and Nagasaki bombings by the U.S. warplane, the Enola Gay. None of the witnesses was immune from the feelings of distress and fear at the horrific nature of the atomic bomb.

One witness, the scientist Otto Frisch, described the scene of the first nuclear detonation, called the Trinity Test, on July 16, 1945, in the desert of New Mexico:

> And then without a sound, the sun was shining; or so it looked. The sand hills at the edge of the desert were shimmering in a very bright light, almost colourless and shapeless. This light did not seem to change for a couple of seconds and then began to dim. I turned round, but that object on the horizon which looked like a small sun was still too bright to look at. It was an awesome spectacle.

The atomic scientist Robert Oppenheimer, who later opposed nuclear weapons and became an outspoken critic of U.S. nuclear energy policy, also was a witness that day:

> A few people laughed, a few people cried, most people were silent. There floated through my mind a line from the *Bhagavad-Gita* in which Krishna is trying to persuade the Prince that he should do his duty: "I am become death, the shatterer of worlds."[1]

The multiple worlds of human history had been once and for all united in a single destiny. No part of the world was too isolated not to realize that there was "no place to hide." By the following year in the Pacific coral island of Bikini, in the Kwajalein Atoll, an experiment aptly called "Operation Crossroads" was underway. The targets of experimental bombings there were obsolete naval carriers like the ship *Independence* that would be sacrificed to nuclear blasts. Dr. David Bradley was a civilian medical doctor on board an observer ship, whose task it was to measure the fallout of radioactivity. There was the blast itself and what followed over seconds, hours, and days:

> "Ten seconds . . . three . . . two . . . one."
>
> What his last word was I have no idea, nor can I tell what the color of that flash was. A gigantic flash—then it was gone. And where it had been now stood a white chimney of water reaching up and up. Then a huge hemispheric mushroom of vapor appeared like a parachute suddenly opening up.

Dr. Bradley describes the process of scientifically measuring the impact of the blast:

> The pattern was one of radiation coming up from the ships and from the water. Starting down a leg we would get just the usual irregular click—click, click—click of "background" over our Geiger earphones. Then suddenly there would be a burst of clicks, a crescendo, merging into the high-toned screaming of increasing radioactivity.

Bradley's description of the growing recognition of the blast's impact on observer ships remains eerie and chilling:

> The gangways swarm with the monitors of the Radiological Safety Section heavily laden with gear, sweating and irate; the laboratories are filled with queer stenches and flickering lights; stacks of secret and dangerous information pile up in the corridors. We appear to have struck it rich. This is still Operation Crossroads, only now the crossroads has a large psychological sign placed across it: DETOUR. DANGER AHEAD!"[2]

[1]Peter Goodchild, *J. Robert Oppenheimer: Shatterer of Worlds* (Boston: Houghton Mifflin Company, 1981), pp. 161–2.
[2]David Bradley, *No Place to Hide* (Boston: Little, Brown and Company, 1948), pp. 92, 95, 99, and 121.

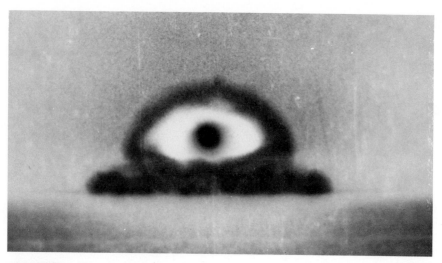

FIGURE 20.6A   The Trinity Sequence: The First Four Seconds of First Nuclear Explosion
at Los Alamos, New Mexico, 1945

SOURCE: Los Alamos National Laboratory.

Physicians such as the Prussian Robert Koch (1843–1910) rapidly carried Pasteur's work forward, and within a decade (1884–1894) bacteria that caused such great scourges and plagues as typhoid, cholera, diphtheria, tuberculosis, and others were identified and immunizations against them discovered. The work of the English doctor Joseph Lister (1827–1912)

FIGURE 20.6B   The Trinity Sequence: The First Four Seconds of First Nuclear
Explosion at Los Alamos, New Mexico, 1945

SOURCE: Los Alamos National Laboratory.

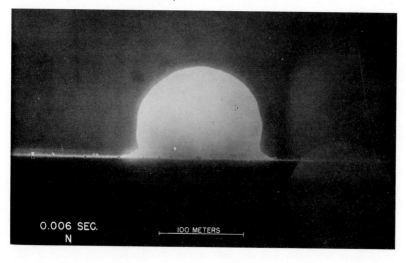

FIGURE 20.6C The Trinity Sequence: The First Four Seconds of First Nuclear Explosion at Los Alamos, New Mexico, 1945

SOURCE: Los Alamos National Laboratory.

made significant contributions to surgery. Lister's practice of aseptic surgery (1867) established safeguards against infection and made surgical operations less risky. Operations were made less painful by the use of anaesthesia, first introduced in 1842, and their success was improved by the development of X-ray technology (1895), which aided diagnosis and surgical accuracy.

With the aid of improved tools, such as the electron microscope (1931), new medications and vaccines essential to combating disease have proliferated, among them insulin (1922), used to treat diabetes, and penicillin (discovered in 1921 but put into practical medical use only in 1941), used widely to combat infectious diseases. The development of the iron lung (1928) improved treatment of the crippling and often fatal disease polio, and eradication of that disease came within the realm of possibility as a result of the Salk and Sabin vaccines (1953, 1955). Surgery has developed in ease and accuracy since the introduction of laser technology in 1958. In 1967 South African Christian Barnard performed the first heart transplant surgery, an operation that has since become increasingly common, as has the transplant of other organs. In 1982 the first permanent artificial heart was implanted in a human.

FIGURE 20.6D The Trinity Sequence: The First Four Seconds of First Nuclear Explosion at Los Alamos, New Mexico, 1945

SOURCE: Los Alamos National Laboratory.

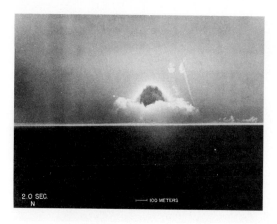

FIGURE 20.6E The Trinity Sequence: The First Four Seconds of First Nuclear Explosion at Los Alamos, New Mexico, 1945

SOURCE: Los Alamos National Laboratory.

By the 1960s polio and other dreaded infectious diseases had been conquered, and human catastrophes such as the influenza pandemic of 1918, which killed 20 million people worldwide (matching the casualties of World War I), had been consigned to the past. In the place of these infectious diseases, chronic, constitutional disorders such as heart disease and cancer became the focus of medical research and public health awareness by mid-century.

New infectious diseases have appeared in the last quarter of the twentieth century. Some are antibiotic-resistant strains of well-known diseases such as tuberculosis, but others are new diseases, such as the Ebola virus identified in Central Africa, that so far have puzzled epidemiologists and defied cures. There is great likelihood that new strains of flu could bring about an epidemic that would affect large numbers of people, even with the resources of modern medicine available.

HIV/AIDS

The first case of acquired immunodeficiency syndrome (AIDS) was diagnosed in New York in 1979, and the virus that causes it, human immunodeficiency virus (HIV), was identified by medical researchers in France and the United States in the mid-1980s. Social responses to the most deadly and rapidly spreading virus of the twentieth century have been likened to the re-

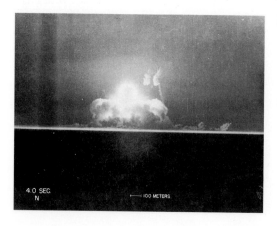

FIGURE 20.6F The Trinity Sequence: The First Four Seconds of First Nuclear Explosion at Los Alamos, New Mexico, 1945

SOURCE: Los Alamos National Laboratory.

sponses of fear and panic that followed the historic plagues and infectious diseases, such as the Black Death (bubonic plague) and cholera. The development of tests for AIDS has enabled researchers to trace the transmission of the virus and to study its origins and progress through a population. The virus that causes AIDS is transmitted by blood, through intimate sexual contact, through infected mothers passing it on to their babies, and through infected needles in intravenous drug use.

Often regarded as the plague of the twentieth century, AIDS raises many ethical, legal, social, and cultural issues. Victims of AIDS have been subject to discrimination in housing, employment, and education, often because of ignorance about the means of transmission of the disease. AIDS has been identified in the United States in particular as a disease that disproportionately affects homosexuals, regarded as a population that engages in indiscriminate sex with multiple partners and thereby increases the possibility of contracting AIDS and passing it on. In recent years it has become evident that the potential for an AIDS epidemic lies in unsafe heterosexual sex as well. An estimated 70 percent of reported cases are attributed to heterosexual transmission.

Attempts by the United Nations to monitor the disease in Asia and Africa have produced alarming statistics that suggest that AIDS is spreading fast among populations that are least prepared to respond to the need for treatment and prevention. Around the world an estimated 21 million adults are infected with the HIV virus, 42 percent of whom are women, who can infect their unborn children. More than a million people worldwide were expected to die of AIDS-related disease in 1996 alone.

While the disease is still raging in parts of Africa, the Caribbean, and the United States, where it first appeared in the early 1980s, the largest increases now are expected in China and Vietnam, as well as India and southern Africa. In South Africa 10 percent of the adult population is believed to be infected with HIV, and there are even higher rates in nearby Zambia and Zimbabwe, where 17 percent of adults have HIV. In contrast, only 0.5 percent of adults in North America carry the HIV virus and 0.2 percent in Europe. This discrepancy between HIV infection rates in the Euro-American world and much of Asia and Africa can be seen as an extension of the underdevelopment created by colonialism. India probably has the largest number of cases in the world, and HIV is rapidly spreading in Pakistan, where Islam discourages or even forbids discussion of sexuality, let alone the transmission of HIV through sexual contact.

Parts of the population in South and Southeast Asia most at risk for infection with HIV are also among the poorest and the least politically powerful, such as prostitutes whose clients are long-distance truck drivers who spread the disease back to their families and among the prostitutes they patronize. AIDS is also spread through sexual activity between foreign businessmen in Southeast Asian cities and young women from the countryside seeking work to support their families, a situation that reflects the residue of imperialism and colonialism in Asia and Africa. The most dramatic and frightening trend is that the number of young women infected is growing in nearly every region of the world, raising the possibility of their infecting infants.

Yet AIDS research funds projects based in developed countries, while developing countries lack anything near the comparable investments in basic health care. Governments that have been reluctant to provide AIDS education and to pursue prevention are gradually becoming aware that they face devastating consequences if the spread of the HIV virus is not controlled. With AIDS, modern medical technology faces its most difficult challenge.

■

FAMILY AT THE CROSSROADS OF IDENTITY

Innovations in medical technology were a major cause of the growth in population in the nineteenth and twentieth centuries while the concentration of population through urbanization and the migration of peoples created new conditions conducive to the spread of disease. Expanding populations, the processes of migration from rural areas to urban centers, and technological changes—especially medical technology that made it possible to control births or extend life—have had a profound impact on the composition and structure of families and the nature of family life.

One of the most powerful influences that shapes individual identity is the family. At the same time differences in family values, life, and structure reflect profound cultural differences. At the beginning of the twentieth century, family forms varied widely. In Western Europe, the two-generational or nuclear family was the norm at least since the seventeenth century. The family was patriarchical and authoritarian. Complex, extended families comprising three generations in a household were common in Russia and Eastern Europe. In peasant societies families were closely linked with the land, but many rural inhabitants engaged in rural industries such as textile production formed families without taking land into consideration. In urban communities family size was not the same consideration as it was in the countryside where labor was demanded in the fields. Demographic historians believe that the French were deliberately practicing birth control from the beginning of the nineteenth century, perhaps related to the Napoleonic code that required an equal division of property. In practice, the strength of paternal authority in both rural and urban families varied. Where the heritage of slavery had left its mark, as it did in the United States and in the circum-Caribbean region, both rural and urban families often tended to be matriarchical in form, for slavery had broken up nuclear family life and laws accorded children the status of their mother while allowing their father neither authority nor responsibility.

Under the impact of urbanization and industrialization, the two-generational nuclear family tended everywhere to replace the extended rural family. The urban model, in turn, was affected by changing economic conditions, the changing status of women, changing attitudes toward children, and the progress of democratization and individualization. Urban families as a result were reduced in size, modified in function, democratized in structure, and became increasingly unstable as a social group.

FAMILY PLANNING

As advances in medical technology improved life expectancy for much of the world's population (in the United States it was forty-seven years in 1900 and seventy years in 1960) and therefore contributed to population expansion, other innovations made it possible to control the birth rate, both altering family size and changing the status of women by providing artificial means to plan births. Following the development of special material heating techniques (1839), a flexible rubber was commonly used for contraceptive devices such as the condom. Oral contraceptives were introduced in 1954, followed 25 years later by Norplant, a set of small tubes implanted under a woman's skin to release a hormone that can prevent contraception for a period of five years.

The trend in Euro-American urban society has been toward a decrease in family size. Under twentieth-century urban conditions, children became economic liabilities rather than assets, because child labor laws and compulsory education postponed their economic contribution and lengthened their period of dependency. The idea that the size of the family could be a matter of conscious planning and control emerged during the last quarter of the nineteenth century and spread rapidly in the twentieth. The work of nineteenth-century pioneers in family planning and birth control, such as the Dutch physician, Dr. Aletta Jacobs, or Mrs. Annie Besant in England, was forwarded in the twentieth century by the efforts of Dr. Marie Stopes in Britain and Margaret Sanger (1883–1966), a public health nurse who was imprisoned during her fight for birth control in the United States. The general downward spiral of the birthrate during the early twentieth century was attributed to the legalization of contraception and its widespread acceptance by the female population. According to Sanger:

> Today, however, woman is rising in fundamental revolt . . . Millions of women are asserting their right to voluntary motherhood. They are determined to decide for themselves whether they shall become mothers, under what conditions and when. This is the fundamental revolt referred to. It is for woman the key to the temple of liberty.

Family reformers wanted to limit the family to the number of children it was able to support. Some were motivated by the belief that women should have reproductive choice and should not be subject to continuous or undesired childbearing. As the twentieth century progressed, emphasis shifted from the prevention of unwanted pregnancies to comprehensive family planning. The Birth Control League (founded in 1914) was replaced by Planned Parenthood, whose objective went beyond birth control to helping families have the number of healthy children they felt they could take care of. Clinics offered help in overcoming sterility as well as in using effective means of contraception. By the second half of the century, making choices about family size had become a common practice in industrially developed countries.

A decline in family size has been most noticeable in larger cities and among the more educated and affluent elements of the population. By World War II the number of urban inhabitants had fallen below the level at which cities could maintain their populations through natural increase, and the continued urban growth around the world has occurred as a result of migration into cities from rural areas. This trend is less marked in certain parts of the globe, such as Latin America, where the pattern of large families has persisted in urban as well as rural areas.

FAMILIES AS UNITS OF CULTURAL AND ECONOMIC IDENTITY

Developments in the twentieth century have stripped the urban family in the West of many traditional functions. Factory production under capitalist industrialism replaced the family as a unit of production with individual employment. Whereas the family has retained few of its traditional economic features as a unit of production, the urban family remains an economic unit for purposes of consumption. The educational role of the family has been diminished as the task of education was assumed by the state through public education; urban society has made it necessary for children to acquire a rapidly expanding body of scientific, technical, and literary knowledge that schools were better able to provide than families. While family connections might contribute to advancement, opportunity, or marriage, they tend to play a supplementary and diminishing role in economic, educational, and status-giving functions.

In non-European parts of the world, the joint or extended family, in which two family groups and multiple generations are recognized as have been joined together through marriage and residence patterns, has been the central social institution for centuries. Twentieth-century developments have altered, and in many cases broke up that structure. Factors responsible for such modification vary from area to area, but social changes have undeniably weakened the traditional family group. European influences resulting from both economic and political imperialism played a large role. European legal systems and practices recognized individual—as opposed to family or group—ownership, individual contractual relationships, and individual obligations. Employment was on an individual basis in factories, businesses, or the civil service, and commerce and industry brought income and property to individuals, not always to family groups. These economic and legal factors did not automatically destroy the traditional joint or extended family, but they did alter it.

One factor tending to alter the family in the twentieth century was the changing position of women. In the joint family women generally had no rights of inheritance or independence of action. Movements for equal rights of women have sought to establish their equality with men before the law, to grant them their rights of inheritance as well as provide them with opportunities for education and the right to vote. Revolutionary changes occurring in the second half of the twentieth century dealt the traditional joint family direct blows. For example, the constitution and laws of modern India have accelerated the break up of the extended family by taxation, inheritance laws, and laws according rights to women.

The Chinese Family In China the traditional family and its institutions came under attack during the early part of the twentieth century and became a major target following the establishment of a Communist regime in 1949. Chinese women, Mao had written in 1927, were dominated by four thick ropes: those of political, clan, religious, and male domination. In the People's Republic of China, customary family practices such as arranged marriages, concubinage, and the selling of daughters have been replaced by emphasis on marriage as a matter of personal choice and responsibility and by government efforts to regulate and control family size. Confucian emphasis on respect for elders and family as the foundation of society were initially rejected by the regime as obstacles to Communist ideals of an egalitarian society, and collective ownership of land and enterprises replaced family ownership. Mao had accurately recognized that women's participation in labor would be a devastating blow to the feudal-patriarchal ideology.

The radical collectivization of the mid-1950s emphasized suprafamily units, such as the work team, production brigade, or large-scale agricultural collectives known as communes. More recently, especially in urban areas, the policy of limiting couples to having one child has produced a new phenomenon: the "little emperor" or "little empress," a term coined to describe an only child whose parents spare no cost to feed, dress, and educate their precious single offspring. In China, as in many other Asian societies, male children are preferred and fetal scanning, abortion, and female infanticide are practices that provide testimony to the persistence of sex-based discrimination despite major social and economic gains made by women.

The Muslim Family In Islamic countries the Muslim family became a focal point of conflict relating to social reform, especially in the second half of the twentieth century. Except in the most conservative Islamic countries, those known as Islamic republics, there has been some effort to establish monogamy, to liberate the women—one-tenth of the world's population—from restrictive practices of dress and custom, such as whether they should go covered or uncovered by veils, and to allow children increasing independence. This transformation of tradition is especially true in urban areas of countries such as Egypt or Turkey, in which there has been the greatest interaction with the West. But even more conservative countries, such as Saudi Arabia or Afghanistan, have experienced some weakening of the traditional family system, at least in cities and before the rise of Islamic fundamentalist movements.

Reformist Islamic scholars as early as the turn of the century began to debate the issues of women and family in the modern urban world. The Indian Muslim scholar Mawlana Ashraf Ali Thanawi (1864–1943) argued that women should be expected to have all the Islamic knowledge that would enable them to establish Islamic rule inside their households. The struggle between secular state power and religious authority has made Muslim women's destinies the object of conflict. Although seen by some as the symbol of oppression, the veil also has become for other women the symbol of cultural authenticity that has permitted a new generation's movement into the changing public space of modernity, institutions of higher education, for example.

The African Family The disruption of the African family as a result of European contact and urban industrial development brought about perhaps the most drastic change in traditional family structures in the twentieth century. Family and kinship systems, which provided the essential structure of individual and social relationships, have been radically undermined where European influences have been strongest. Traditional family structures varied with different ethnic groups, but each form was strongly sanctioned by custom. In most communities the family or kinship group was a self-contained economic unit in which all shared for purposes of production and consumption. It was also a unit for childrearing. The authority of elders extended to all, so that immediate parents did not have full or unsupported responsibility for the young.

Whatever its form, the African family largely determined the status of the individuals in it. Each member had a defined role while ultimate responsibility for individual members was generally borne by the head of household. Families contributed to social and political structures through a system of chieftancies, councils, or other institutions of authority based on lineage and kinship. The family also played a religious role, and the responsibilities of heads of families were no less spiritual than material.

In the course of the twentieth century, family structures in many parts of Africa have been altered and reduced as a source of identity in cities and weakened in many parts of the countryside. Rural areas have been especially affected by Christian missionary teaching and activity that, for example, attacked such practices as polygamy. Muslim influence has been less disruptive in that sense, since the Qur'an permits polygamy and religious leaders have not sought to stop it. Colonial administrators generally left customary family institutions intact unless they affected measures designed to deal with commerce and administration. Such measures did, however, contribute to undermining the family forms that held communities together.

The principal disruption of African family structures came from industrialization and urbanization. Men who went away to work left the family group impaired. A major breakdown occurred when women accompanied men to urban areas and established urban family units in

African cities such as Johannesburg, Nairobi, Dakar, Lagos, Accra, Mombasa, and Kinshasa. From one end of Africa to the other, the ever growing number of urban African families represents a break with virtually every element of traditional African family structure, even though close ties are maintained with rural relatives.

Traditional familial economic self-sufficiency based on the contribution and shared consumption by all has virtually disappeared. The structure of authority has been undermined: elders no longer are able to reinforce parental authority over children, having been undermined by the forces of the state and Western education, yet parents are often inexperienced in carrying out their responsibilities alone. Urban African families have been forced to reconstruct themselves almost from the ground up; and coming from a society in which family structures ensured that no one should experience uncertainty as to who they are or what was expected of them, many urban Africans have found themselves in a society in which these certainties have been swept away.

GENDER AT THE CROSSROADS OF IDENTITY

Gender as a category of identity is a cultural construct: the meaning of being female or male is shaped and transformed according to cultural and historical context, not simply biological destiny. Gender played a key role in the anticolonialist, nationalist struggles for independence in Asia and Africa, where women's emancipation was often connected to the liberation of the nations from imperialism and colonialism. Nearly everywhere, though, beginning as early as the American and French revolutions, women's rights became subordinated to the patriarchal authority of the new nation state.

Nationalisms, for example, were always gendered, even in the obvious, if superficial, claims of loyalty to the "fatherland" or "motherland." Gandhi, more than other nationalist leaders, elevated the feminine through his strategy of passive resistance, known as *satyagraha* ("truth force"). *Satyagraha* embraced the female strengths of passive resistance honed by necessity as a way of life for women who were constantly subjected to oppression within the household as well as in society. Gandhi himself engaged in spinning, identifying himself with this humble domestic female occupation, both to demonstrate the power of the feminine and to mobilize women and men for his strategy of nonviolent resistance to the Raj.

Gandhi idealized the female role in the household and in society, as well as in history and religious myth, holding up the images of female Hindu deities as representations of the power of women. Gandhi's legacy to the emancipation of women was a contradictory one: he confirmed the patriarchal authority structures of the Indian family and society, while exhorting men to adopt feminine ways of being and acting in order to carry out the nationalist struggle through passive resistance.

Women in the Modern Chinese Nation — Women's rights and the emancipation of women from the traditional patriarchal authority structures of family and society were a prominent feature of the revolutionary ideas of the May 4th Movement in early twentieth-century China. Though women's issues—liberation from family authority, freedom to marry, the right to be educated and to exercise political rights—were part of the May 4th Movement, they quickly were subordinated to the dual struggle to win control of China from warlords and to expel foreign dominance as the basis for consolidating the new nation. Neither the Nationalists nor the Communists maintained as a priority the emancipation of women, though particularly the Communists continued to pay lip service to it and many Chinese women struggled to achieve it.

Japan: Good Wives, Wise Mothers   The position of women in the construction of the modern Japanese nation state shows how the roles of women were redefined to serve the goals of the patriarchal authority of the new nation state. In the nineteenth century Meiji leaders created the doctrine of the "good wife, wise mother" as the paradigm for women's service to the nation. Women were exhorted to be frugal in household management (thus to serve the financial needs of the industrializing state by savings that could be invested in development) and to educate their children so that they could be recruited to the service of the nation.

Sons would go to schools where they would be instructed in such subjects as history, mathematics, science, and economics, and daughters would learn at home from their mothers how to become "good wives, wise mothers." Schools for girls were largely for the privileged daughters of the new political aristocracy, such as Baroness Ishimoto, whose memoirs reveal much about the social changes of the late nineteenth and early twentieth centuries.

Education and Gender in Latin America   Latin America is an example of a world region that comprises many complex, multiracial and multicultural societies under numerous umbrellas of national identity. In turn, the forces of capitalism and social changes have produced powerful, if sometimes competing, identities crosscut by complex class and gender issues.

The Brazilian educator Paolo Friere (1921–1997) warned about the need for a society to remain open to change. Respect for diversity of cultures and opinions allows for full participation by all. According to Friere:

> In the revolutionary process, the leaders cannot use the banking method [of education—i.e., in which the teacher makes a "deposit" and tells people what they should know, followed by the student "account" returning the same, perhaps with interest] as an interim measure, justified on grounds of expediency, with the intention of *later* behaving in a genuinely revolutionary fashion. They must be revolutionary—that is to say, dialogical [engaging in dialogue]—from the outset.

Education has served as a major catalyst for change, and since colonial times educated women were important agents of this change. For example, in Peru, where universities were closed to women until 1908, public cultural events called *veladas literarias* (literary evenings) were alternative venues for the generation of women, who had been educated at home. In 1888 Mercedes Cabello de Carbonera wrote about her colleague Manuela Villaran de Plascencia, another woman writer, and expressed the frustration of many modern intellectuals:

> If you could only see me writing, my friend, you would feel sorry for me: I write surrounded by four or six children—while one takes away my pen, the other takes my eraser, this one screams at me because he thinks I haven't heard what he's asking for, and in the middle of all that racket and confusion, I finish off my composition and go on with my other occupations.

While the confusing and competing interests of modernity were not unique to late-nineteenth-century Latin America, they were confounded there by the deep divisions and contradictions of racial, cultural, and class interests.

Women, Islam, and The emancipation of women was part of the building of the new Turkish
the Turkish Nation nation under Ataturk and was tied to the secular nature of the new na-
▬▬▬▬▬▬▬▬▬ tion he declared (see Chapter 18). Ataturk's policy of emancipation was
part of his attempts to completely eradicate tradition, to sever the ties between past and present in the creation of a modern secular nation state, on the model of European nation states.
But Islamic influences persisted in Turkish society, and Islamic ideals of women's role in the
family and society continued to shape the lives of women in modern Turkey. Islamic tradi-
tionalists strongly resist all forms of secularization, including the liberation of women, as the
case of Turkey's first woman prime minister Tansu Ciller makes clear. Ciller's regime, elected
in 1993, became the first secular Turkish government to lose power to an Islamic fundamentalist party, the Islamic Welfare Party, in 1996.

THE CULTURAL CROSSROADS OF FEMINISM

The 1949 publication of the feminist manifesto *The Second Sex* by the French intellectual
Simone de Beauvoir marks the formal beginning of postwar feminism, the awareness of women
that they belong to a subordinate group that is culturally and societally determined. Emerging in the context of changing women's roles, feminism questioned the biologically determined construction of gender. The successful political struggle for female suffrage in European and American societies, largely between 1900 and 1920, had increased women's
dissatisfaction with their subservient status and economic dependency. The reproductive freedoms afforded by technological and medical research in the postwar era also contributed to
feminist demands for a woman's identity to be perceived independent of her reproductive
role.

Yet even as feminist scholarship began to be applied to many disciplines, it became apparent to many that women *were* different. Carol Gilligan's controversial study *In a Different
Voice* (1982) developed the thesis that women both viewed and experienced the world in ways
that were different from those previously described in the literature of psychology and human
development. Gilligan's research suggested that women and men assigned essentially different meanings to their experiences. For example, women were more likely to make moral
judgments based on the concept of relationships, rather than solely on external concepts of
justice. Furthermore, at each stage of development they put a high value on human connectedness, consequences, cohesiveness, and cooperation. The continuing debate about difference
reflects the deep divisions based on gender and its intersection with other categories of class,
race, and culture.

Recent research on the brain has confirmed that male and female brains are wired differently: although men and women have the capacity to reach the same conclusions, the human
female brain processes sensory information in a more comprehensive way than by human male
brains. This study, of course, presents an apparent contradiction, since feminists have repeatedly pointed out that gender is a social and cultural construct, rather than a biological given.

International Feminism Whereas feminism began in the context of Euro-American cultural
▬▬▬▬▬▬▬▬▬ and political change, it has not remained culturally limited in its
application to Euro-American experience. Probably the most visible twentieth-century expressions of an international feminist movement have been the three United Nations Conferences on Women, the first in Mexico City, in 1969, the second in Nairobi, Kenya, in 1984,

and the third in Beijing, a decade later, at which women from nations around the world demanded in solidarity global recognition for their struggle to make women's causes tantamount to human rights issues. An organization founded in 1984, Sisterhood is Global, grew out of the international women's movement and is dedicated to recognizing cultural difference as a factor in achieving women's rights around the globe.

The movement for Islamic women's rights is one of the most interesting results from the 1995 Beijing conference. In recent years Muslim women from throughout the Islamic world have begun to organize to advocate for their rights to education, both secular and religious, economic freedoms, and reform in family laws. These women are laying claim to their right as Muslims to retain their religious beliefs but also to exercise their rights as human beings equal to men. They want to argue for these rights from within Islam as well as from a secular and international viewpoint. This difficult and complicated undertaking reflects the complexities of international feminism crossing cultural boundaries, breaking down barriers, but also validating cultural difference.

Feminism and Pacifism The historical link between feminism and pacifism (Chapter 18) can be seen in the movement called "Peace People" organized by two women, Mairead Corrigan and Betty Williams, in Northern Ireland to oppose the violence of the struggle to free Northern Ireland from British rule. These two women were awarded the Nobel Peace Prize in 1976. Women also organize to protest political oppression. A group of mothers in Argentina demonstrated for *los desaparecidos* (the ones who disappeared) in the Plaza de Mayo at the center of Buenos Aires against the brutality and terror of the military government's assault on all political opposition and activism.

■

RACE, ETHNICITY, AND IDENTITY

Since the 1850s race has been a powerful historical construct built on erroneous claims about human identity and difference. Scientific research eventually demonstrated that biologically distinct "races" do not exist. The human species is singular and no significant features, physical typologies (head size or skin color), or biological difference (such as blood type) can be demonstrated as being linked with identifying human groups as racial groups. Simply speaking, there is no such thing as biological race. Nonetheless, the erroneous concept has been used and is still widely used in the construction of identity. The consciousness of difference can be a powerful ingredient in individual and group identity whether or not it rests on supportable scientific facts. In the words of the African American scholar Cornel West, "race matters."

Racial consciousness and racism have been key determinants in an individual's sense of belonging to a group and in a person's and group's exclusion from social and economic opportunities. Yet when peoples compete as individuals, racial boundaries dissolve. This was apparent in the history of South Africa, perhaps the most blatant example of a racially divided nation state of the twentieth century. After the initial discovery of diamonds and gold (1867, 1884), individual whites found themselves ill-equipped to compete with Africans in a rapidly industrialized economy. Racial boundaries between groups were constructed to protect whites from competition from African workers. The racialized society intensified after the apartheid election of 1948. Yet by the 1980s the economic success of some of the African majority was beginning to blur, if not dissolve, the distinctiveness of the artificially constructed racial boundaries. The 1994 South African constitution was drafted to guarantee the rights of all—including the white minority oppressors—in a multiracial society.

Hidden in this history of hegemony is another history, that of miscegenation, or mixing of peoples and their identities. Under the impact of imperialism and colonialism in particular, societies increasingly experienced racial mixing through forced sexual and cultural encounters (rape is a frequent allegory for imperialism) and through intermarriage, whether by choice or expediency. How societies deal with the fact of miscegenation has varied across time and space. Between 1913 and 1949, 80 percent of the Asian Indian (Punjabi) men in California married Hispanic women, despite state laws prohibiting interracial marriage. In fact, three-quarters of African Americans, virtually all Latino Americans, a large majority of American Indians, and millions of whites today are multiracial or have multiracial roots. Other ethnically complex societies are also in the making in South Africa, in Britain, in the Caribbean, in Australia, in France, in Hong Kong, and elsewhere. Historical forces propelling the mixing of peoples in the twentieth century are likely to undermine the notion of race as a source of identity.

The pseudoscientific foundations of racism in the nineteenth century, however, were linked to the primacy of scientific method and to the notion that the world could be understood with certainty through the rational application of scientific principles. In the twentieth century the underpinnings of this view of the world have come under increasing attack, and a new paradigm has emerged in which irrationality, uncertainty, and chaos play the key roles, in contrast to reason, certainty, and order.

■

RELIGION AND THE CONSTRUCTION OF IDENTITY

Since ancient times human societies have used language and art to describe and understand their world. While many living in post-1800 societies used the tools and language of science for these purposes, the role of faith and belief in a supernatural dimension did not disappear. For the first time in world history, many late nineteenth-century people began to identify themselves with no connection to world religions: as atheists (nonbelievers in a god or supernatural power) or agnostics (doubting the existence of god). For most people of the world, however, religious convictions have provided both personal solace in the age of uncertainty and a source of community in a world of rapid social, economic, and political change.

RELIGIOUS DIVERSITY

Of the twentieth-century's religions, about 70 percent are rooted in belief systems that have roots extending across 1000 or more years. According to the World Development Forum statistics, if our world today were a village of 1000 people, there would be 300 Christians (183 Catholics, 84 Protestants, 33 Orthodox), 175 Muslims, 128 Hindus, 55 Buddhists, 47 Animists, 85 from other religious groups, and 201 atheists. Not surprisingly, these religious ideologies have shaped individual and community identities and directed the course of social and political change at many historical crossroads.

Islam and Christianity In a world of constant change, belief systems offer many people a stability and certainty that is both universal and individual. Sometimes,
however, religious movements have disguised or hidden change by appealing to a return to
ancient basic religious tenets. Both Islam and Christianity have used such appeals around the
globe to support political and social agendas identified with religious ideas that would drastically change modern secular society.

An early spokesperson for Muslims was the British-educated lawyer and founder of the
Muslim League, Mohammed Ali Jinnah (1876–1948). He led the Muslim community in demanding a separate identity in the wake of the movement for Indian national independence.
He believed that the differences between Hindu and Muslim religious philosophies were too
great to sustain the national identity of a single state. In a 1940 speech, Jinnah urged the
division of India into two separate, autonomous states. The Egyptian leader Hasan al-Banna
(1906–1949) rejected Western culture and secular law altogether. Seeking to create a society
based on the traditional tenets of Islam, he established the Muslim Brotherhood, a worldwide
organization that still works for the creation of states based on Islamic law and principles.

Secular Nationalism In many parts of the world, the secular nationalism of the nineteenth
century was followed in the twentieth century by a desire to establish
the moral grounds of political life, by the rise of religious leadership, or both. In the 1990s
Michael Lerner, a Jewish rabbi with doctoral degrees in both philosophy and psychology and
editor of the Jewish journal *Tikkun,* wrote a tract entitled "The Politics of Meaning," which
addressed what Lerner perceived to be a crisis of meaning in the lives of many Americans.

FIGURE 20.7 Thousands of Pilgrims gather at El
Haran, The Great Mosque at Mecca,
1975

The pilgrimage of devout Muslims brings believers
from all parts of the world together to share in the ancient traditions.

SOURCE: Corbis-Bettmann.

Lerner's political and social activism in the 1960s in the interest of liberal causes was transformed by the 1990s into a "politics of meaning," which argued for reasserting values into political discussion and attacked ideologues of both the left and the right, arguing that people cannot rest on old assumptions about either conservative or liberal politics. Although its earliest settlers sought religious freedom and tolerance, the United States is a secular nation with Judaeo-Christian tradition and beliefs deeply ingrained therein. During the administration of President Dwight Eisenhower (in office 1953–1961), the phrase "under God" was added to the words "one nation, indivisible" that formed part of the Pledge of Allegiance phrase commonly recited by American schoolchildren in the first half of the century, "one nation, under God, indivisible". The tensions between church and state, and the protection of individual rights within an ideological climate shaped in part by Christian fundamentalist tenets about marriage, family, sexual practices, abortion, and so on have been at the heart of an ongoing debate within the United States.

Religion and Violence The U.S. Constitution guarantees freedom from religious persecution; American lawmakers, however, continuously legislate morality from the historical basis of religious tradition. In contrast, the North African nation of Tunisia is 98.5 percent Muslim yet has banned religion from any political role. This stance was a clear response to the historical experience of religious persecution during the French colonial period and the contemporary experience of being surrounded by Islamic extremists.

"Extremism of belief" is, of course, a highly subjective term; it suggests an ideological stance not held by the majority of believers. In the twentieth century the "extremist" label has been given to many proponents of religions whose political stance is in opposition to the powers that be. Some Jews, Palestinians, and Arabs, for example, have been labeled extremist because their actions were grounded in religious conviction.

Religious divisions have been consistent factors in the political conflicts of the nineteenth and twentieth centuries. The violence that has characterized South Asia since the partitioning of India and Pakistan in 1948 included setting on fire or dowsing with vitriol or sulphuric acid unsuspecting Hindu, Sikh, and Muslim families. Religious identification motivated and inspired the conflict between parties, and religious and political tensions have continued in India and elsewhere to the end of the century. In Northern Ireland divisions and conflict are similarly described in religious terms: Protestant Unionists wishing to remain part of Protestant Great Britain, against Catholic Republicans, who want to be part of a separate Republic of Ireland.

The containment of religious difference has challenged imperialist and nationalist goals throughout the nineteenth and twentieth centuries. In the Ottoman Empire the "millet" system made religious leaders of minority communities responsible for their groups. A similar system survives in modern Israel. The disintegration of many national identities in independent Africa (for example, Rwanda) or postwar Europe (Bosnia) has occurred in the context of the politics of cultural subnationalism. Cultural (including religious) differences that had been submerged under the artificial and often alien construct of the nation state have emerged as powerful, competing organizing principles in the face of failing state systems.

The global migrations of the nineteenth and twentieth centuries contributed to the movement of ideas from the homeplace of their original expression to quite different social, cultural, and economic settings. The search for freedom from religious persecution not only led to movements of refugees but also contributed to religious change, as peoples and ideas were transformed by new cultural and physical environments. Both the Jewish diaspora and its counterpart, a Palestinian liberation movement, represent struggling political identities based on ethnicity and religion that emerged from the displacement of territorial control over a homeland. The persecution of European Jews by Nazi Germany also led to a mass exodus of intellectuals to the territory that would become the nation state of Israel and also to Britain and the United States during the 1920s through the 1940s.

Borrowed Religious Identity Although religion can divide people and cause conflict, it can also bring about the integration of cultural differences. Western interest in Asian religion began to rise in the 1960s and shows little sign of abating. Many Americans and Europeans sought new kinds of spiritual understanding from such sources as Zen Buddhism from East Asia, or from India, as represented by the Beatles' adoption of the Indian spiritual leader Mahareshi Mahesh Yogi as their spiritual mentor. In turn, Christianity made inroads in parts of Asia, such as South Korea where an estimated 40 percent of the population are Christians. Though Christianity has still not had great impact in Japan, "new religions" have proliferated there since the mid-nineteenth century, in a context of social dislocation. These new religions are drawn from Buddhism, Shinto, and sometimes other beliefs, creating syncretic doctrines and practices that mirror the social anxieties of the adherents.

RELIGIOUS CHANGE, CULTURAL IDENTITY, AND EMPOWERMENT

Even at the height of European political hegemony in the late nineteenth century, most conquered and colonized societies were never really transformed into European ones. Religious beliefs were sometimes outlawed and often submerged, but seldom did they entirely disappear without a trace. The survival of the belief systems of native North Americans is an example of the persistence of religious values in the face of systematic efforts to undermine them. Despite oppressive treatment by educational systems, Native American belief systems retained ritual, language, and outlook that helped protect territorial and environmental rights.

Australian aborigines have managed to retain their concepts of history as Dreamtime, a spirit-filled, time-free realm, in the face of dislocation from a cosmology once rooted in territorial identity. Other contradictions abound in the global history of migrations. For example, the creation of the African diaspora, while originating from slavery and conditions of extreme oppression, nonetheless is also synonymous with the creation of vibrant, syncretic belief systems in the Atlantic world. These religions blended the disparate Kongolese, Yoruba, Catholic, and Masonic beliefs into coherent forms of Caribbean spirituality which promoted resistance by preserving historical memory.

African-Caribbean Empowerment The African Atlantic world was a spiritually empowered and interactive universe of living persons, spirits, and ancestors who functioned as critical links to the past, that is, to human memory of the past. Slaves carried their empowerment objects and beliefs from the West African regions of the Guinea Coast, the Slave Coast, and the Bight of Benin to the New World and used them to alter and even subvert the condition of enslavement. Empowerment arts, like performance arts, allow unseen processes to unfold outside the parameters of political or physical control, creating spiritual sites of freedom and transcendence over slavery. Today these forces are applied to modern technology. For example, Ogun (the Yoruba god of iron) is the protector of taxis and airplanes; his imagery appears across the Atlantic world and even in unlikely extensions of Yoruba culture, as far from West Africa and the Caribbean as Brooklyn and East Los Angeles.

The Cargo Cult Another example of the emergence of religious syncretism from traumatic ▬▬▬▬▬▬▬ historical experience comes from the Pacific Islands, where contact with twentieth-century Western industrial technology was abrupt and disturbing. The "cargo cult," as the religion came to be called, emerged as a consequence of the delivery of wartime cargo via airplane, an unfamiliar form of technology that the islanders interpreted in traditional cosmological terms. The planes that came from the heavens were believed to have been sent by the supreme god, who sent material goods because of the islanders' adherence to rituals. This cult incorporated the novel technology of human flight and the other cultural changes that accompanied air travel and made sense of it all in accordance with traditional beliefs. The syncretism of traditional beliefs with modern technology provided meaning that enabled people to explain a rapidly changing world.

Spiritual Capital While secular ideologies such as capitalism have decided to shift beliefs ▬▬▬▬▬▬▬ away from religion in the twentieth century, new hybrid religious ideas and practices have emerged in some parts of the world. In contemporary Vietnam, which is emerging as a fast-growing economy of small entrepreneurs and is shedding socialism's planned economic development, the new freedoms of religion and capitalism intersect in worship at a temple to the "Goddess of the Treasury" near Hanoi, where a twelfth-century goddess, an obscure local deity, has become the center of a cult. Worshipers converge at the temple to seek spiritual "loans" from the goddess in the hope of economic success, combining traditional religion with the demands and desires of capitalism and consumer society.

■

THE CULTURAL CROSSROADS OF GLOBAL COMMUNITY

Cultural identities shaped by such things as religion, gender, and ethnicity are also products of interactions across cultures. These are sometimes forced interactions, as under colonialism; but they are often actively undertaken in the search for cultural revitalization. Dialogues across cultures and the construction of global community through cross-cultural encounters can be expressed in many ways, including art, music, and literature.

GLOBAL MUSICAL ENCOUNTERS

By the end of the nineteenth century, ethnomusicology, the study of the music of ethnic groups, was on a secure international and scientific basis. Technical innovations greatly enhanced such study and broadened its influence. The gramophone was invented in 1877, and the earliest ethnographic recordings made in the field date from 1890. Transcriptions of such recordings greatly facilitated ethnomusicological field work by both musicians and anthropologists until around 1950, when a newer technology, the tape recorder, made the work even easier. Archives of recorded sound and international support from such groups as the Organization of American States and the United Nations Educational, Scientific, and Cultural Organization have made the massive exploration of the musics of humanity universally available.

African Highlife One form of syncretic music is worldbeat, a musical category forged from global connections between cultures, that includes global popular music like hiphop, funk, reggae, and highlife. The West African musical form called "Highlife" originated in the coastal interaction of Africans and Europeans. Along the Fanti coast of southwestern Ghana, traditional African rhythms and melodies were fused with European instruments, such as the sixteenth-century guitar of the Portuguese and the harmonies of the eighteenth- and nineteenth-century regimental fife and brass military bands of Europe and the West Indies, the sea shanties and folk songs sung by sailors in African seaports, and the piano music and hymns favored by missionaries during colonial times. At the heart of Highlife is the experience of many cultural as well as musical encounters.

By the 1920s three types of early African ensembles were playing Highlife and related music: (1) the prestigious dance orchestras of the big city—with brass sections, woodwinds, strings, guitars and drums. Groups such as the Excelsior Orchestra and the Jazz Kings played fox-trots, quicksteps, rumbas, waltzes, and ragtimes, in addition to Highlifes; (2) the provincial brass bands provided another style of the same Highlife music; and finally (3) the even earlier guitar bands using accordions, harmonicas, and local drums played the rural Konkomba music, a kind of poor man's Highlife, with choral components.

Some of the early influences on Highlife styles like ragtime, imported from the United States, were introduced through coastal vaudeville acts. Contact with European musicians and Western acting styles led to the addition of a performance stage that separated the audience from and the performers. Some musical influences came to West Africa through recordings or in the form of written piano music. Dance musical styles were even introduced through silent films.

World War II brought to Ghana the music of army bands, many playing swing music and using jazz techniques. An increasing number of Ghanaians traveled abroad, and the ports of Ghana were filled with soldiers from America and the British Commonwealth. The era marked the beginning of smaller dance bands and racially mixed bands in Ghana. The cities teemed with nightlife: the California Club was one popular nightclub in Accra. During the war years many of the British and American soldiers who were stationed in Accra showered Ghanaian women with affectionate terms. "Kiss Me" was one of a number of Highlife songs written in English and built around these popular expressions.

In 1957 the colonial era came to an end with the independence of Ghana. After self-government many big bands were formed—and there was a subtle leaning toward the influence of American music. The combination of Glenn Miller, Count Basie, black American jazz, Caribbean calypso, and the harmonies of the traditional music of Ghana began to create some new Highlife sounds. Kwame Nkrumah, Ghana's first president after independence formed political bands. These bands, the Brigade Band and Farmer's Band, played Highlife, but they also performed songs for the government—songs such as "Africa," "Kwame Nkrumah Never Dies," and "Kwame Nkrumah Showboy" were played in more correct Highlife rhythms. Other bands were becoming more and more Westernized. The Highlife "Africa" celebrates the spirit of the newly won African independence and the spirit of solidarity of Pan-Africanism among the nations: "Africa must be free/Africa unite" was sung at the time of political independence.

The songs and musical traditions of a people are more than entertainment. They constitute historical records and uniquely reflect the human responses and attitudes towards historical change. The people of Ghana are no exception to the rule that societies under the influence of new ideas and materials will attempt to maintain an identity while integrating and adapting to what is consonant with their own world view. As a result of trade, European musical instruments, performance styles, and ideas were reworked into the distinctively African fabric of Highlife. The fusion of African and European music illustrated by African Highlife also occurred in the Caribbean, where calypso evolved.

Global Influences on European Music   The admixture of non-European and European musics has not, of course, been in one direction. As early as the end of the seventeenth century, Turkish music was influencing that of Europe, a by-product of the continued efforts made by Europeans to expel the Turks from Europe. Turkish army bands were greatly admired and were imitated by Europeans, rather in the manner that European regimental fife and brass bands influenced West Africans. Indeed, Austrian military bands were referred to as "Turkish bands" until World War I. It was the quality of sound made by the percussion and winds of the bands, as well as the distinctive musical language of the Turks, that appealed to Western Europeans. It made its way from army bands into nonmilitary court music, and prominent European court composers, such as Franz Joseph Haydn (1732–1809), Wolfgang Amadeus Mozart (1756–1791), and Ludwig van Beethoven (1770–1827), adapted instrumentation and tempos that were designated *alla turca,* in the Turkish manner, in a number of their works.

Recent composers such as Carlos Chavez (1899–1978) in Mexico, Hector Villa-Lobos (1887–1959) in Brazil, and Alberto Ginastero (1916–1983) in Argentina were successful in creating recognizably indigenous sounds to portray events or a sense of place representative of their countries. Chavez was interested in native (non-European) Mexican music and legends and incorporated these in his works, for which he often used native instruments along with traditional European ones. Villa-Lobos, in his series of *Bachianas brasilieros,* produced a classic example of the appropriation of European musical forms in new national settings. By adapting the models of J. S. Bach to Brazilian purposes and materials, Villa-Lobos created a music that would startle the German master but that Brazilians would recognize and admire.

Examples abound of the contemporary integration of European and non-European musics that suggest the achievement of a global musical culture. Perhaps the most convincing illustration of this promise is the fusion achieved by the American composer Philip Glass (b. 1937) in his opera *Satyagraha* (1980). Though he had conventional Western musical beginnings, Glass discovered Indian music on a chance encounter while studying in Paris. To earn money, he undertook to transcribe into Western notation some of the Indian Ravi Shankar's *ragas* (the arrangement of notes on which a melody is based). Glass knew little about Indian music at the time, and his work for Shankar constituted a crash course in Indian rhythms and scales. He learned how to notate the intricate Indian *ragas* and thus found out how to make Indian music work. *Satyagraha* is the mature result of such a beginning.

Glass states that it never occurred to him to create a standard (that is, traditional Western) orchestral sound for *Satyagraha,* and his orchestra uses what he calls "international" instruments, instruments that can be found in both India and America in one form or another. He uses them to produce sounds that are entirely suitable to the subject of his opera, a subject that is quintessentially Indian. *Satyagraha,* which is sung in Sanskrit, is about the period Gandhi spent in South Africa (1893–1914) where, in fighting the restrictive Black Act, he developed his concept of truth force, *satyagraha.* Both in the metamorphic repetitive character of the music and the recurrent, recycling unfolding of the opera on stage, Glass pays homage to Hindu philosophic concepts, yet in a language that is undeniably a contemporary expression. *Satyagraha* is philosophically, musically, and aesthetically remarkable, perhaps the most advanced example of a genuinely global musical to date.

GLOBAL LITERATURE

If music has the potential to be a universal language of humanity, grounded in particular cultural idioms that are capable of fusion and interaction, literature likewise has the capacity to address universal themes, even when originating in distinct languages and cultural idioms. Translation is an imperfect art, but one that enables cross-cultural communication and synthesis. Literature is not merely a reflection of broad political, cultural, and social patterns. Writers articulate visions of society and culture that help to shape the world around them and can play key roles in transforming the world they inherit from the past.

The interchange and interaction of global literatures has probably never been greater than in the second half of the twentieth century. This cross-fertilization has to do, of course, with the ease of publication, including translation, with the internationalization of the publishing business (most great publishing houses are now international corporations), and with the expansion of literacy in non-Western as well as in Western societies. Translated books provide a useful way to understand other peoples and their cultures and as such make a major contribution toward global understanding. At the same time literature can be the site of political conflicts and highlight tensions and ambiguities present at the crossroads of global culture.

Few would claim that the Nobel Prize for Literature, the most prestigious achievement award given to a writer, is a criterion for a great work of literature, but the selection of Nobel laureates from Africa, Asia, and Latin America during the last quarter of a century indicates recognition of the international character of modern literature. As early as 1913, the Nobel Prize was awarded to a Bengali writer, Rabindranath Tagore (1864–1941), who was known for his attempts to deepen mutual understanding between East and West. Two years later Tagore was knighted by the British monarch, but he was also an ardent Indian nationalist and renounced his knighthood after the Amritsar massacre in 1919.

The career of the British writer Salman Rushdie (b. 1947) exemplifies the internationalization of literature as well as the political impact that literature can have. Born in Bombay, Rushdie was educated at Cambridge University, and in 1981 his novel *Midnight's Children* won the prestigious Booker Prize in Britain. Rushdie's international fame, however, came with the publication in 1988 of *The Satanic Verses,* a satirical work that was denounced as an attack on the Qur'an and the Islamic faith. India, Pakistan, South Africa, Egypt, and Saudi Arabia banned the book, and in 1989 the Iranian leader Ayatollah Khomeini issued a death warrant for Rushdie and all those involved in the publication of the book. Rushdie went into hiding, and even though he apologized and made a formal statement of his own adherence to Islam, he remains a fugitive from Islamic fundamentalists who continue to demand his death.

FILM, TELEVISION, AND TWENTIETH-CENTURY GLOBAL CULTURE

It has often been said that film is the quintessential art form of the twentieth century. Modern technology, from televisions to computers, has made visual expression and communication paramount in people's lives. The invention of still photography in the nineteenth century was followed almost immediately by a consideration of the potential of stringing together photographic images to create a moving picture. By the late twentieth century, virtually every region of the world had begun to participate in the creation of visual culture through film and television. Satellite technology and the distribution of television and film (and, most recently, print media) rights by multinational corporations have an impact on what gets seen and read and by whom. By the end of the twentieth century, global audiences had come together electronically as a single media community.

World Cinema One of the earliest film directors to receive international attention was ▬▬▬▬▬▬ Swedish director and producer Ingmar Bergman (b. 1918), who achieved recognition for his wide range of films made from the 1950s through the 1980s. The content of Bergman's films varied from comedy, such as *Smiles of a Summer Night* (1955), to powerful allegories, such as *The Seventh Seal* (1956), a meditation on death infused with Christian symbolism. Bergman explores human psychology in *Persona* (1966), a film that uses the techniques of dreams and flashbacks and shows the influence of existentialism. Although film has a rich background in various European countries, such as France, Italy, Germany, as well as Sweden, some of the most distinctive, impressive, and powerful examples of this new art form have been produced in non-European countries. Film has created the possibility for multidimensional expression of complex cultural and social questions. It has also provided a means of communication across cultures that is not limited to the translation of verbal expression, either written or oral/aural.

Japan's position in the late twentieth century as a major economic force is reflected in the richness of its cinema, although the greatest Japanese directors were making some of their finest films in the 1950s, not long after Japan's cataclysmic defeat in World War II. Ozu Yasujirô (1903–1963) chronicled the inner life of the Japanese family, the core of Japanese society, in films such as *Tokyo Story* (1953). The technical aesthetics of Ozu's filmmaking are classically Japanese: spare, restrained, and subtle, with great emotional appeal. Naruse Mikio, established as a director already in prewar Japan, sympathetically documented the dramatic changes in women's lives in the postwar period in many of his films, such as *When a Woman Ascends the Stairs* (1960).

Each director had his own personal style and thematic focus, but a broad and persistent concern in the work of virtually all serious Japanese filmmakers is the ongoing dilemma of modernity in conflict with tradition. Japan's rapid development as a modern nation in the late nineteenth century, on the surface a great success in contrast with most other non-European developing nations, took a heavy psychological toll. A society accustomed to order and stability and a rigid social hierarchy determined by birth changed literally overnight into a society where individual destiny was no longer dependent on birth.

Perhaps the greatest Japanese director, and certainly the best known outside Japan, is Kurosawa Akira (b. 1910), whose films show Western influence and have a universal appeal that transcends the distinctive concerns of modern Japanese society. *Rashômon* (1950), based on a story written in 1915 by the modern Japanese writer, Akutagawa Ryûnosuke (1892–1927), recounts an incident from the viewpoint of four people who were involved or witnessed it. Each interpretation differs, suggesting the modern notion that truth is relative. Two of Kurosawa's films were explicitly based on Shakespearean plays, *Throne of Blood* (*Macbeth*) and *Ran* (*King Lear*).

A director of stature comparable to that of Kurosawa is Satyajit Ray who stands alone as an Indian filmmaker with an international reputation. Ray frequently uses stories from the work of Rabindranath Tagore, the Bengali Nobel laureate, a poet, writer, playwright, painter, composer, reformer, and philosopher, the greatest figure in modern Indian literature. Like Japanese filmmakers, Ray deals with the conflicts between old and new mentalities in a changing society, in this case India. Unlike Japan, which was never colonized by any foreign power, India was a part of the British Empire, and thus modern India is a product not only of Indian history and tradition in conflict with modernity but also of conflicts related specifically to its colonial past.

In one of his more recent films, *The Home and the World* (1984), Ray echoes themes developed in earlier films. The particular history detailed is that of the *swadeshi* ("of our own country") movement against foreign commodities, such as cloth manufactured in England from Indian cotton, that symbolized India's colonial exploitation by the British. The film plays on many themes suggested by the title: home and world, love and politics, woman and man, tradition and modernism. A love triangle achieves only a momentary resolution before disaster overtakes the hero, and a strong sense of fatalism lurks beneath the forceful declarations of free will and choice.

Film, Colonialism, and Imperialism
The importance of film as an artistic medium is reflected in its translation to television and video technologies and its prominent role in the sale and dissemination of the products of both culture and commerce. As a medium of communication, film surpasses all other inventions to date in its potential for creating propaganda. Not surprisingly, some of the earliest records of colonial history are films made in the colonies.

Beginning in 1913 German and British filmmakers used their access to different parts of the globe as a canvas on which they could stage action and tell a story. Fiction and documentary were forms not always distinguishable, as in the case of the work of documentary filmmaker Hans Schomburgk. Schomburgk also made films such as the *White Goddess of the Wangora,* which was filmed in colonial West Africa, with its fictional script supported by documentation of local customs and industries.

For much of the twentieth century, the world center of the filmmaking industry was in Hollywood, California, where megacorporations organized the resources and capital to develop the product to its fullest extent and also directly controlled the content of world cinema. From the 1920s, Hollywood helped to export stereotypical images of many parts of the world, including Africa as a "dark continent" and Asians as servants. In turn, the film images of Americans and the United States fueled stereotypes around the globe, including those of cowboys and gangsters and interpretations of historical events, such as the westward expansion in North America and the experiences of the two world wars.

Film as Political Propaganda
The shallowness and stereotypical nature of non-European peoples as projected by Hollywood conformed to the racist ways in which African Americans were also portrayed. Some of these stereotypes were intentionally produced, and many were unconsciously perpetuated as part and parcel of accepted majority culture. In 1935 the British established the Bantu Educational Cinema Experiment, based in part on the idea that Africans and other colonized peoples, rather than being allowed to view films from the West, should see films that would educate adults to their roles in the colony

and world. Films like *Mister English at Home* and *An African in London* were propaganda films designated for this colonized audience. Other national film industries have been called upon to serve political, especially nationalist, goals. An example of such powerful filmmaking in the service of governments are the films of Leni Riefenstahl in Nazi Germany or Sergei Eisenstein in Soviet Russia (see Chapter 18).

Film and Cultural Continuity While the control over film production and distribution by ▨▨▨▨▨▨▨▨▨▨▨▨▨ multinational corporations since the 1950s has generally impeded independent filmmaking, some filmmakers have successfully used film and video to promote countercultural ideas, validating the early observation that film is "truth twenty-four times a second." For example, the Senegalese filmmaker Ousmane Sembene found ways to connect the traditional role of West African griot, an oral historian/storyteller, with the medium of film. A pioneer of African film, Sembene sees the modern filmmaker as replacing the griot, as "the historian, the reconteur, the living memory and the conscience of his people." His films (*Emitai* [1971] and *Ceddo* [1976], for example) were drawn from historical events. Sembene also has used the possibilities of the medium of film to portray the nonlinear nature of time and the magical/spiritual beliefs of his African culture. Unlike many filmmakers from developing countries, Sembene has successfully made films in African languages.

Film as Cultural Critique Filmmakers in the People's Republic of China began to experiment ▨▨▨▨▨▨▨▨▨▨▨▨▨ in the late 1970s and 1980s with previously forbidden topics, such as sexual relationships, the oppression of women, and the many flaws and failures of life in the new society. By far the most powerful and controversial film to be produced in this period was a six-part television documentary, "*He shang*" (River Elegy). The 1988 production uses the Yellow River as a metaphor for China. The central theme is that of cultural continuity and cultural renewal, familiar to the experiences of all non-Western "modernizing" societies.

The question of cultural continuity in the face of profound change seems particularly acute in the case of China. Its history is portrayed in the rapid juxtaposition of various images with historical narration, and contrasts between images provide dramatic statements about the complexities of culture change. The Yellow River historically was known as "China's Sorrow" because of its periodic flooding of the north China plain and the devastation it wrought. It has been a ubiquitous source of sustenance as well as tragedy for as long as human memory. The filmmakers seem to be suggesting that China's culture, too, is both a source of strength and a heavy burden that modern Chinese have yet to reconcile with the demands of recent history and the model of the West.

■

NEW DIRECTIONS AT THE CROSSROADS: THE SHAPE OF HISTORY

Postmodern cultural critics, like their physicist cohorts, have argued that reality is always shifting and truth is an illusion, since it is always shaped by the relationship of the observer to what is observed, of researcher to respondent, and of text to reader. The historiographical debate about what legitimizes and defines "real" history has intensified in the twentieth-century age of uncertainty.

CHANGING TECHNOLOGY AND CULTURE

Changes in technology since the nineteenth century have brought about significant changes in the stuff of history: photographs, telephones, tape recorders, televisions, radiocarbon dating, and electronic mail have changed the nature of what constitutes historical documents. Other kinds of changes, in the practice of history and in its values, have fundamentally altered the kinds of historical questions that interest students and researchers and the modes of inquiry used to address those questions. Oral histories of the world wars exist on audiotape, and video cameras accompany field researchers who reconstruct community history, whether conducted in Africa or Los Angeles.

World History In the 1930s a former textile mill worker in the United States, Harold Rugg, ▬▬▬▬▬▬▬ created a series of popular world history books. In less than a decade businesspeople and military organizations attacked Rugg's books as unpatriotic because they portrayed a complex story of the past from the perspective of people without power. Some communities blacklisted and burned them. To paraphrase Cornel West, it seems that "history matters." Historical roots confer status and privilege and help establish identity. Historical recognition is validated in the politics of identity, in which belonging to a group has as much to do with the past as the present. Historical scholarship stands at the center of these identity struggles. For example, a great debate has raged around the arguments presented in the historian Martin Bernal's *Black Athena,* which suggests the African origins of many aspects of Greek civilization, a notion that is profoundly disturbing to some. History now includes the

FIGURE 20.8 White Men Broadcasting from an *Mbari* (ritual) House, Ibo, Nigeria

African artists borrowed images of the tools of the European empire, capturing their power for purposes of resistance.

SOURCE: Photo courtesy of Herbert Cole.

pasts of the world beyond Europe, challenging the discipline's content and methods (see volume I).

The concept of "subaltern" studies emerged from South Asian studies and has been defined by one practitioner, Ranajit Guha, as history written from the perspective of "persons of inferior rank," understood in South Asian society as a matter of gender, class, caste, age, office, or any other category that establishes subordinate status. The purpose of subaltern studies was to rewrite history from the perspective of the subalterns, the people whose story had remained untold in the history dominated by two different elites: the British Raj and Indian nationalist elites, such as those represented by Nehru. This approach has applications and implications far beyond the realm of South Asian studies and is an important example of alternatives to traditional history, which uses the nation state as the primary focus of historical narrative.

The concept of the nation state and of national identity as a defining criterion of historical study has been effectively challenged—though not eradicated—by historians who emphasize the recent evolution of this identity as a composite of many different categories: ethnic, religious, kinship, place, and gender. Other kinds of community, such as lineage or family, preceded the nation state and have provided individuals with a sense of belonging. The nation state is not the definitive form of modern identity. Similarly, shifting gender identities in the latter part of the twentieth century are complex and culturally constructed. Women's history offers a fundamentally different perspective on power, place, and historical experience from that of traditional political histories from which most women were excluded. The most powerful source of identity at the end of the twentieth century is global history, and it is one induced not only by the common environmental and other crises human beings share but also by the potential enrichment of individuals through participating in new global cultures.

Finally, no history is separate from its context: historians live in a specific time and breathe a specific air. The debates over Afrocentrism, erased Watergate tapes, historical invisibility, and stolen histories demonstrate that "history matters." Like their physicist counterparts, historians have become global citizens in an age of uncertainty, which constantly debates not whether or not there is a single historical truth, but which competing past should be unleashed on history's virtual screen. Today world historians honor both the story of nameless illiterate peasant farmers in Brazil or Papua New Guinea and the story of media-hounded U.S. presidents' wives by giving them voice and making them as visible as the threads they weave together in a single world history. In the balance are the complex, multiple stories *and* the single fabric of the past.

SUMMARY

This chapter returned to some of the continuing themes of this global textbook: the relationship of human beings to each other and to the communities in which they live. Since our earliest consideration, these relationships have varied but perhaps only in degree: humans persist in the hierarchical and gender relationships that have always placed some in dominant and others in subordinate positions; they are as mobile as they have always been, if not always because they want to be; but, above all, there are more of them than there used to be. Population growth greatly complicated human and environmental relationships. Increased numbers, however, are not the only cause of serious ecological problems. The self-generating demands of technologies that humans thoughtlessly use to control and exploit environments make their own contributions.

The human failure to resolve issues of difference and inequality of individual relations remains: slavery, in the form of human bondage, may have disappeared in most parts of the world, but forms of servitude reflecting the realities of the modern world persist. Inmates of Auschwitz, of Soviet gulags, of Asian or African refugee camps, or of Japanese detention camps in the United States were in political servitude. Social servitude is a common feature of the market place: consumerism and "wage slavery" underlie much social unrest; technological servitude, being bound to factory routines or to computers, is widely being recognized as one of the major human problems of the late twentieth century. Gender relationships provide an uninterrupted continuum of servitude.

Human beings have also remained mobile creatures. The mobility of the earliest humans was one of their most astounding achievements, as they covered vast areas without benefit of horsepower or the wheel, much less of jet-propelled, air-conditioned comfort and speed. Throughout their history, people have continued to move about. Migration, variously occurring from no fixed locales, was the product of many things: the need for food and occupation; the need for protection; and because of population pressures or the sense of adventure. The peopling of the globe was the result, but by no means the end, of demographic movement.

In the late twentieth century, with its comfortable and rapid means of transportation, the movement of peoples (even in virtual space) continues unabated. New kinds of human interaction are taking place on the Internet. Forces propelling contemporary migrations are political (flight from war or oppression), economic, and environmental. Ecological destruction in the twenty-first century may make nomads of us all while reducing alternative possibilities of habitation.

According to the wisdom of many peoples around the globe, "some things never change," or as the French say "plus ça change, plus c'est le même chose": the more things change, the more they are the same. The saying contains the essence of truths. A quick rehearsal of the themes we have pursued over the long span of human history from "Emergence" to "Order" to "Transformation" to "Balance," tends to bear out the wisdom of this adage.

As we pursued our examination of peoples in the various places they inhabit, from their origins until today, we tried to focus on a number of common themes: on mobility and interrelationship of peoples; on their connection with their environments; on the kinds of involvements people have with each other—the patterns of dominance and submission involved in the ways they organize themselves politically, economically, and socially; how they expressed themselves in thought and art; and how their technologies affected and reflected their societies. These were some of the earliest human concerns about the interrelated dimensions of individual, knowledge, and community; they remain pressing concerns at the end of the twentieth century.

ENGAGING THE PAST

The fundamental issues that this book addresses have remained remarkably constant factors in human history, issues worthy of examination across space and time. Changes that have occurred are changes of scope not kind and are recurring variations on common human themes.

What does this observation have to say about another of the concerns of this book—that is, historiography—the act of observing and conveying what is known of the past? Our emphasis on continuity and recurrence, the implication that many things seem to repeat, that human concerns of the first century are much the same as those in the twentieth century, might suggest a cyclical view of history. Since many peoples, notably the Hindus, held to a cyclical view of history, it would indeed be shortsighted in a global history text to reject such a view of the human story. It would be equally imprudent, if not impossible, for authors trained in the Western tradition to abandon completely the linear approach to historiography. What may legitimately be questioned, however, is unequivocal acceptance of the linear understanding of history and the progress that it implies.

Evidence examined in this book suggests that the ongoing unfolding of human events has been as repetitive and circular a process (however erratic and irregular) as it has been linear. Such a process is continuous as well as various and has the quality of impermanence that indicates the lack of any one solution to the problems humanity faces and the absence of any one preferred, preeminent, or superior form of human achievement. The vision of the past as viewed from world history suggests that history is neither exclusively linear nor cyclical; it follows no singular pattern of development and transformation. This conclusion does not deny progressive change, though the seemingly endless recurrence of the same concerns does question the validity of a doctrine of progress. If there is progress, it lies in the ultimate recognition of the mutual affinity in all human experience and the realization that all peoples equally have something to contribute to our common humanity. This is the lesson of global history; this is the hope for a shared future; this has been the purpose of this book.

The furthest extension of complex technology, seen in the presence of humans on the moon, viewing the earth through space as a globe in the distance, thus turns us back toward ourselves, and again begins the age-old process of redefinition and identity seeking, refocusing and rebalancing the forces of continuity and change. World historians of the next century are certain to face a new set of historical documents, as video and audio tapes and e-mail printouts replace the oral traditions and written records of earlier generations. It seems just as likely that the historical processes they will seek to understand will remain as global and daunting as those encountered by the balancing acts of their twentieth-century ancestors.

SUGGESTIONS FOR FURTHER READING

John Collins, *West African Pop Roots* (Philadelphia: Temple University Press, 1992). A lively overview of one strand of worldbeat music.

Johannes Fabian, *Remembering the Present: Painting and Popular History in Zaire* (Berkeley: University of California Press, 1996). Provides the example of one African artist's struggle to paint the past in a contemporary context of oppression and silencing: raises critical questions about what historians do to represent the past and reproduce the power relationships of the present.

Peter Goodchild, *J. Robert Oppenheimer: Shatterer of Worlds* (Boston: Houghton Mifflin, 1981). A history of the complex life of a key and controversial nuclear scientist.

Mel Gurtov, ed., *Global Politics in the Human Interest,* 3rd ed. (Boulder: Lynne Rienner, 1994). Sweeping overview of global issues in the politics of the twentieth century.

Paul Kennedy, *Preparing for the Twenty-First Century* (Toronto: Harper Collins, 1993). A challenging review of transnational themes that will shape the future of the globe.

David Robinson, *The History of World Cinema* (New York: Stein and Day, 1974). Overview of the first century of film in its social and historical context.

Francis Robinson, *Cambridge Illustrated History of the Islamic World* (Cambridge: Cambridge University Press, 1996). Comprehensive coverage of the Islamic world.

Credits

■ LITERARY CREDITS

PART I

Chapter 1 *P. 4:* Donald Johanson and Maitland Edey, *Lucy: The Beginnings of Humankind* (New York: Simon & Schuster, 1981), p. 155.

P. 14: William Theodore de Bary, ed., *Sources of Indian Tradition* (New York: Columbia University Press, 1958), pp. 13–15.

P. 14: A. L. Basham, *The Wonder That Was India* (New York: Hawthorn Books, 1963), 249–50.

P. 15: *The Holy Bible* (King James Version), Genesis I:1–31.

P. 15: W. T. de Bary, Wing-tsit Chan, and Burton Watson, eds. and trans., *Sources of Chinese Tradition,* vol. 1 (New York: Columbia University Press, 1960, p. 193.

P. 15: James B. Pritchard, ed., *Ancient Near Eastern Texts Relating to the Old Testament* (Princeton, N.J.: Princeton University Press, 1969), p. 60.

P. 16: Donald L. Philippi, trans., *Kojiki* (Tokyo: University of Tokyo Press, 1983), p. 37.

P. 18: Arthur Waley, trans., *The Book of Songs* (New York: Grove Press, 1978 [1937], pp. 241–43).

P. 38: Clae Waltham, ed. and trans., *Shu Ching: Book of History* (Chicago: Henry Regnery Company, 1971), pp. 42, 52–3.

Chapter 2 *P. 42:* Pliny the Younger, "The Eruption of Vesuvius, 24 August, AD 79," in John Carey, ed., *Eyewitness to History* (New York: Avon Books, 1987), pp. 19–20.

P. 57: Francesca Bray, "Swords into Plowshares: A Study of Agricultural Technology and Society in Early China," *Technology and Culture,* 19 (1978): 3.

P. 64: Eduardo Galeano, *Memory of Fire: Genesis* (New York: Pantheon Books, 1985), p. 28.

P. 65: Richard Erdoes and Alfonso Ortiz, eds., *American Indian Myths and Legends* (New York: Pantheon Books, ca. 1984), pp. 11–12.

P. 68: C. H. Oldfather, *Diodorus of Sicily,* bk. 3, vol. 2 (Cambridge, Mass.: Harvard University Press 1933), pp. 115–118.

P. 73: Quoted in Theodore A. Wertime, "The Pyrotechnologic Background," in Theodore A. Wertime and James D. Muhly, *The Coming of the Age of Iron* (New Haven, Conn.: Yale University Press, 1980), p. 1.

P. 74: Xunzi, quoted in Joseph Needham, "The Evolution of Iron and Steel Technology in East and Southeast Asia," Theodore A. Wertime and James D. Muhly, *The Coming of The Age of Iron* (New Haven, Conn.: Yale University Press, 1980), p. 518.

Chapter 3 *P. 80:* A. L. Basham, *The Wonder That Was India* (New York: Grove Press, 1954), pp. 203–204.

PART II

Chapter 4 *P. 124:* Camara Laye, *The Dark Child: The Autobiography of an African Boy* (New York: Farrar, Straus and Giroux, 1954), p. 93.

P. 124: Linda Schele and David Friedel, *A Forest of Kings: The Untold Story of the Ancient Maya* (New York: William Morrow, 1990), pp. 99–103. *Ahau* means "living god," and *ahauob* means "divine destiny."

P. 125: Schele and Friedel, (New York: William Morrow and Company, 1990 pp. 98–103.

P. 142: Homer, *The Iliad,* E. V. Rieu, ed. (Harmondsworth, England: Penguin, 1966); quoted in Warren Hollister, ed., *Landmarks of the Western Heritage,* vol. 1 (New York: Wiley, 1973), pp. 41–42.

P. 155: Patricia B. Ebrey, ed., *Chinese Civilization: A Sourcebook* (New York: Macmillan Free Press, 1993), p. 22.

P. 156: Ibid., p. 29.

P. 157: Ibid., p. 24.

P. 162: *The Republic of Plato,* trans. Francis M. Cornford (New York: Oxford University Press, 1945), p. 199.

Chapter 5 *P. 176:* W. T. de Bary, Wing-tsit Chan, and Burton Watson, eds. and trans., *Sources of Chinese Tradition,* vol. 1 (New York: Columbia University Press, 1960), p. 282.

P. 176: Arthur F. Wright, *Buddhism in Chinese History* (Stanford, Calif.: Stanford University Press, 1971), p. 67.

P. 176–77: De Bary et al., *Sources of Chinese Tradition,* p. 373.

Chapter 6 *P. 214:* Bernard Groslier and Jacques Arthaud, *Angkor Art and Civilization* (New York: Praeger, 1966), p. 97.

P. 214: Ross E. Dunn, *The Adventures of Ibn Battuta: A Muslim Traveler of the 14th Century* (Los Angeles: University of California Press, 1989), p. 302.

P. 214: Ibid., pp. 296–297.

P. 214: Ibid., p. 297.

P. 244: Thomas T. Allsen, *Mongol Imperialism* (Berkeley, Calif.: University of California Press, 1987), p. 7.

P. 254: Cyprian, *De Mortalitate* (Mary Louise Hannon, trans.), quoted in William H. McNeill, *Plagues and Peoples* (Garden City, N.Y.: Anchor Books, 1976), pp. 108–109.

Chapter 7 *P. 256:* Ibn Khaldun, *Muqaddimah,* quoted in Yves Lacoste, *Ibn Khaldun: The Birth of History and the Past of the Third World* (London: Verso, 1984), p. 105.

P. 264: Patricia B. Ebrey, *Chinese Civilization: A Sourcebook* (New York: Free Press, 1993), p. 55.

P. 266: Peter Jackson and David Morgan, eds., *The Mission of Friar William of Rubruck: His Journey to the Court of the Great Khan Möngke, 1253–1255* (Peter Jackson, trans.) (London: Hakluyt Society, 1990), 72–74, 90–91.

P. 273: N. Levtzion and J. F. P. Hopkins (eds.), *Corpus of Early Arabic Sources for West African History* (Cambridge, England: Cambridge University Press, 1981), pp. 296–297.

P. 285: Marjorie Rowling, *Life in Medieval Times* (New York: Perigee Books, 1979), pp. 31–32.

P. 285: Quoted in Marjorie Rowling, *Life in Medieval Times* (New York: Perigee Books, 1979), p. 41.

Chapter 8 *P. 298:* Christoforo Fioravanti, "Norwegian Fisherfolk, 1432," in John Carey, ed., *Eyewitness to History* (New York: Avon Books, 1987), pp. 77–78.

P. 305: Cited in Mark Anthony Meyer, *Landmarks of Western Civilization* (Guilford, Conn.: The Dushkin Publishing Group, 1994), p. 28, citing C. H. W. Johns, ed., *Babylonian and Assyrian Laws, Contracts, and Letters,* Library of Ancient Inscriptions (New York: Charles Scribner's Sons, 1904).

P. 309: Sakhawi quoted in Francis Robinson, ed., *The Cambridge Illustrated History of the Islamic World* (Cambridge, England: Cambridge University Press, 1996), p. 194.

P. 312: Translated by Jonathan Chaves in Wu-chi Liu and Irving Yucheng Lo, eds., *Sunflower Splendor: Three Thousand Years of Chinese Poetry* (Garden City, New York: Anchor Doubleday, 1975), p. 315.

P. 314: Cited in Liu and Lo 1975, p. 384 (trans. James J. Y. Liu).

P. 314: Liu and Lo (trans. Michael R. Workman), p. 356.

P. 316: Patricia B. Ebrey, *Chinese Civilization: A Sourcebook* (New York: Free Press, 1993), pp. 166–168.

P. 320: Cited in Thomas J. Barfield, *The Perilous Frontier: Nomadic Empires and China* (Cambridge, Mass.: Basil Blackwell, 1989): p. 26, citing Francis Cleaves, trans., *The Secret History of the Mongols* (Cambridge: Harvard University Press, 1982): 16, 48, citing Antoine Mostaert, *Sur quelques passages de l'Histoire Secrète des Mongols* (Cambridge, Mass.: Harvard University Press, 1953), p. 10.

P. 320: Berthold Spuler, *History of the Mongols: Based on Eastern and Western Accounts of the Thirteenth and Four-teenth Centuries* (Berkeley, California: University of California Press, 1972): pp. 80–81.

P. 322–23: Laws of Manu, Book 5, law 148; cited in Sarah Shaver Hughes and Brady Hughes, ed., *Women in World History,* vol. 1 (Armonk, New York: M. E. Sharpe, 1995), p. 49.

P. 328: Sarah B. Pomeroy, *Goddesses, Whores, Wives, and Slaves* (New York: Schocken Books, 1975).

P. 341: Priscus, "Dinner with Attila the Hun," in John Carey, ed., *Eyewitness to History* (New York: Avon Books, 1987), pp. 23–24.

Chapter 9 *P. 351:* Niane, *The Epic of Sundiata*

P. 3360: Ibn Khaldun quoted in Francis Robinson, ed., *The Cambridge Illustrated History of the Islamic World* (Cambridge, England: Cambridge University Press, 1996), p. 223.

P. 366: Liu and Lo 1975, p. 23.

P. 367: Liu and Lo 1975, pp. 141–142.

P. 370: Donald Keene, ed., *Anthology of Japanese Literature* (New York: Grove Press, 1955), pp. 137–138, citing the *Pillow Book* (Makura soshi) of Sei Shonagon.

P. 400: Quoted in Viviano Domenici and Davide Domenici, "Talking Knots of the Inka," *Archaeology* (November–December 1996): 50–51.

Chapter 10 *P. 406:* Maxamed Good, "Shimbir," in Katheryn Loughran et al., eds., *Somalia in Word and Image* (Washington, D.C. and Bloomington: Foundation for Cross Cultural Understanding and Indiana University Press, 1986), p. 42.

P. 406: Axmed Ismaaciil Diiriye, quoted in Katheryn Loughran et al., eds., *Somalia in Word and Image* (Washington, D.C. and Bloomington: Foundation for Cross Cultural Understanding and Indiana University Press, 1986), p. 63.

P. 416: Edwin O. Reischauer, trans., *Ennin's Travels in T'ang China* (New York: Ronald Press, 1955), pp. 150–151.

P. 429: Henry Knighton, "The Black Death, 1348," in John Carey, ed., *Eyewitness to History* (New York: Avon Books, 1987), pp. 47–48.

PART III

Chapter 11 *P. 443:* Denis Twitchett, "Merchant, Trade, and Government in Late Tang," *Asia Major,* 14(1) (September 1968): 81–81.

P. 443: Denis Twitchett, "The Tang Merchant System," *Asia Major,* 12 (1966): 230–231.

P. 468: S. D. Goitein, *A Mediterranean Society: The Jewish Communities of the Arab World as Portrayed in the Documents of the Cairo Geniza,* vol. 3 (Berkeley: University of California Press, 1978), pp. 193–194.

P. 478: Lisa Jardine, *Worldly Goods: A New History of the Renaissance* (New York: Nan A. Talese/Doubleday, 1996), p. 00.

Chapter 12 *P. 482:* Peter Hulme and Neil L. Whitehead, eds., *Wild Majesty: Encounters with Caribs from*

Columbus to the Present Day, An Anthology (Oxford: Clarendon Press, 1992), p. 21.

P. 490: From T. C. Mendenhall, B. D. Henning, and A. S. Foord, Ideas and Institutions in European History, 800–1715, (New York, Henry Holt, 1948), p. 266.

P. 495: Roger D. Abrahams and John F. Szwed, eds., *After Africa* (New Haven: Yale University Press, 1983), p. 329.

P. 499: L. Jadin and M. Dicorato, eds., *Correspondence de Dom Afonso, roi de Congo, 1506–1543* (Brussels, 1974), pp. 167, 156.

P. 506: Peter Hulme and Neil L. Whitehead, eds., *Wild Majesty: Encounters with Caribs from Columbus to the Present Day, An Anthology* (Oxford: Clarendon Press, 1992), p. 26.

P. 512: Donald F. Lach and Carol Flaumenhaft, eds., *Asia on the Eve of Europe's Expansion* (Englewood Cliffs, N.J.: Prentice-Hall, 1965), pp. 19–20.

Chapter 13 *P. 526:* Donald F. Lach and Carol Flaumenhaft, eds., *Asia on the Eve of Europe's Expansion* (Englewood Cliffs, N.J.: Prentice-Hall, 1965), p. 68.

P. 534: John Hale, *The Civilization of Europe in the Renaissance* (New York: Atheneum, 1994), p. 587.

P. 538: Ibid., p. 156.

P. 554: Olaudah Equiano, *The Interesting Narrative of Olaudah Equiano,* Robert J. Allison, ed. (Boston: Bedford Books, 1995).

P. 567: Cited in Robert Bellah, *Tokugawa Religion* (Glencoe, Illinois: The Free Press, 1957): 157; from Ishida Baigan, *Seikaron* (Essay on Household Management) in *Shingaki Sosho* (The Shingaku Library), Tokyo, 1904), vol. I: 158.

P. 573: Anthony Reid, *Southeast Asia in the Age of Commerce, 1450–1680: The Lands below the Winds* (New Haven: Yale University Press, 1988), p. 143.

P. 574: Ibid., p. 92.

P. 574: Ibid., p. 216.

Chapter 14 *P. 578:* James Lockhart, *Nahuas and Spaniards: Postconquest Central Mexican History and Philology* (Stanford and Los Angeles: Stanford University Press/UCLA Latin American Center Publications, 1991), pp. 70–74.

P. 583: Pauline Turner Strong, "Captivity in White and Red: Convergent Practice and Colonial Representation on the British-Amerindian Frontier, 1606–1736," in Daniel Segal, ed., *Crossing Cultures: Essays in the Displacement of Western Civilization* (Tucson: University of Arizona Press, 1992), pp. 35–36.

P. 601: Joanna Waley-Cohen, *Exile in Mid-Qing China* (Cambridge, Mass.: Harvard University Press, 1991), pp. 105, 152–154.

P. 611: Lady Maria Nugent, *Lady Nugent's Journal, of Her Residence in Jamaica from 1801 to 1805* (Kingston, Jamaica: Institute of Jamaica, 1966 [1907]), p. 219.

P. 614: Alexander Mackenzie, *Journal of the Voyage to the Pacific,* Walter Sharpe, ed. (New York: Dover, 1995), pp. 115–117.

Chapter 15 *P. 618:* James Cahill, *Parting at the Shore: Chinese Painting of the Early and Middle Ming Dynasty, 1368–1580* (New York:, 1978), p. 90.

P. 633: Stephanie Golden, *The Women Outside: Meanings and Myths of Homelessness* (Berkeley: University of California Press, 1992), p. 109.

P. 639: H. Ling Roth, *Great Benin: Its Customs, Art and Horrors* (London: Routledge, 1968), p. 160.

P. 633: Lisa Jardine, *Worldly Goods: A New History of the Renaissance* (New York: Nan A. Talese/Doubleday, 1996), pp. 333–334.

P. 639: Sophie D. Coe, *America's First Cuisines* (Austin: University of Texas Press, 1994), p. 105.

PART IV

Chapter 16 *P. 668:* Ronald H. Fritze, James S. Olson, and Randy W. Roberts, eds. and compilers, *Reflections on World Civilization.* vol. 2: 1600 to the Present (New York: Harper Collins, 1993), p. 3.

P. 685: Alfred J. Andrea and James H. Overfield, *The Human Record: Sources of Global History* (Boston: Houghton Mifflin, 1994), p. 187.

P. 696: Herbert H. Rowen, ed., *Absolutism to Revolution, 1648–1848* (2nd ed.) (Englewood Cliffs, NJ Prentice-Hall, 1969), p. 277.

P. 710: Bonnie S. Anderson and Judith P. Zinsser, *A History of Their Own,* vol. 2 (New York: Harper and Row, 1988), p. 234.

P. 713: Anderson and Zinsser, vol. 2, p. 377.

Chapter 17 *P. 769:* E. Bradford Burns, *Latin America: Conflict and Creation, A Historical Reader* (Englewood Cliffs, NJ: Prentice Hall, 1993), p. 110.

P. 724: Aime Cesaire, *Discourse on Colonialism,* trans. Joan Pinkham (New York: Monthly Review Press, 1972, pp. 10–12.

P. 750: Arthur Cotterell, *East Asia* (Oxford: Oxford University Press, 1993), p. 157.

P. 743: Basil Davidson, *African Civilization Revisited from Antiquity to Modern Times* (Trenton, NJ: Africa World Press, 1991), pp. 417–418.

P. 738: Joseph W. Esherick, *The Origins of the Boxer Uprising* (Berkeley, CA: University of California Press, 1987), p. 75.

P. 737: Patricia Grimshaw, *Paths of Duty: American Missionary Wives in Nineteenth-Century Hawaii* (Honolulu: University of Hawaii Press, 1989), p. 16.

P. 777: John Mack, *Emile Torday and the Art of the Congo, 1900–1909* (Seattle: University of Washington Press, n.d.), p. 11.

P. 726: G. Palmer Patterson, *The Canadian Indian: Indian Peoples of Canada* quoted in J. M. Bumsted, *The Peoples of Canada,* vol. 1 (Toronto: Oxford University Press, 1992), p. 188.

P. 770: Francis Paul Prucha, *The Great Father: The United States Government and the American Indians,* vol. 2

(Lincoln, Nebraska: University of Nebraska Russ, 1984) p. 19.

P. 770: Norman K. Risjord, *America: A History of the United States,* vol. 2 (Englewood Cliffs, NJ: Prentice Hall, 1988), p. 79.

Chapter 18 *P. 805:* Gordon Rohlehr, "Images of Men and Women in the 1930s Calypsoes: The Sociology of Food Acquisition in a Context of Survivalism," in Patricia Mohammed and Catherine Shepherd, ed. *Gender in Caribbean Development* (Kingston, Jamaica: University of the West Indies, Women and Development Studies Project, reprinted by Institute of Social and Economic Research, 1988), pp. 235–309.

P. 822: John W. Dower, *Japan in War and Peace: Selected Essays* (New York: New Press, 1993). pp. 124–125; 128.

P. 829: Ruth Milkman, "Gender at Work: The Sexual Division of Labor During World War II," in Linda K. Kerber and Jane Sherron De Hart, *Women's America: Refocusing the Past* (New York: Oxford University Press, 1995), p. 449.

P. 804: Lynn H. Nelson and Steven K. Drummond, eds., *The Human Perspective: Readings in World Civilization,* vol. 2 (Fort Worth, TX: Harcourt Brace, 1997 pp. 352–353.

P. 789: Alfred J. Andrea and James H. Overfield, *The Human Record: Sources of Global History,* volume II: Since 1500 (Boston, MA: Houghton Mifflin, 1994)

P. 790: Andrea and Overfield, vol. II: 384; from Erich Maria Remarque, *All Quiet on the Western Front,* trans. by A. W. Wheen (New York: Fawcett Crest, 1984).

P. 790: Andrea and Overfield, vol. II, p. 380.

P. 785: Gordon Rohlehr, "Images of Men and Women in the 1930s Calypsoes: The Sociology of Food Acquisition in a Context of Survivalism," in Patricia Mohammed and Catherine Shepherd, ed. *Gender in Caribbean Development* (Kingston, Jamaica: University of the West Indies, Women and Development Studies Project, reprinted by Institute of Social and Economic Research, 1988), pp. 235–309.

P. 784: Robert W. Rydell, "A Cultural Frankenstein? The Chicago World's Columbian Exposition of 1893,"

in Neil Harris, Wim de Wit, James Gilbert, and Robert W. Rydell, eds. *Grand Illusions: Chicago's World's Fair of 1893* (Chicago: Chicago Historical Society, 1993), pp. 163–164.

P. 784: Rydell, p. 146.

Chapter 19 *P. 840:* B. Marley and P. Tosh, "Get Up Stand Up" (Island Records, 1973) on the compact disc *Legend: The Best of Bob Marley and the Wailers* (New York: Tuff Gong, 1984). [distributed by Island Records, 14 East 4th Street, NYC, NY 10012]

P. 840: Op. cit., B. Marley and N. G. Williams, "Buffalo Soldier" (Island Records, 1983).

P. 844: James P. Harrison, *The Long March to Power: A History of the Chinese Communist Party, 1921–1972* (New York: Praeger, 1974), p. 84.

P. 880: Barbara Browning, *Samba: Resistance in Motion* (Bloomington: Indiana University Press, 1995), p. 114.

P. 880: Browning, p. 167.

P. 883: Shirley C. Gordon, *Caribbean Generations* (New York: Longman Caribbean, 1983), pp. 239–240.
Martin Luther King Jr., *Letter from the Birmingham Jail* (San Francisco: Harper, 1994), pp. 21–22.

Chapter 20 *P. 894:* Robert Farris Thompson, *Black Gods and Kings: Yoruba Art at UCLA* (Bloomington, IN: Indian University Press 1976), p. ch4/4.

P. 923: Margaret Sanger, *Woman and the New Race* (New York: Brentano's, 1920) p.5 ; quoted in Helga H. Harrinan, *Woman in the Western Heritage* (Guilford, CT: Dushkin, 1995), p. 308.

P. 927: Maritza Villavicencio, "Women's Movement in Peru: The Early Years," in Askia Wieringa, editor, *Subversive Women: Women's Movements in Africa, Asia, Latin America and the Caribbean* (London and Atlantic Highlands, NJ: Zed Books, 1995), p. 51.

P. 927: Paolo Friere, *Pedagogy of the Oppressed,* trans. Myra Bergman Ramos, in Mel Gurtov, Global Politics in the Human Interest. 3rd d. (Boulder, CO: Lynne Rienner, 1994), p. 58.

P. 940: Françoise Pfaff *The Cinema of Ousmane Sembene, A Pioneer of African Film* (Westport, CT and London: Greenwood Press, 1984), p. 40.

Index